2012 Conference of the North American Chapter of the Association for Computational Linguistics: Human Language Technologies

(NAACL HLT 2012)

Montreal, Quebec, Canada
3-8 June 2012

ISBN: 978-1-62276-172-2

Printed from e-media with permission by:

Curran Associates, Inc.
57 Morehouse Lane
Red Hook, NY 12571

Some format issues inherent in the e-media version may also appear in this print version.

Printed by Curran Associates, Inc. (2012)

For permission requests, please contact the Association for Computational Linguistics
at the address below.

Association for Computational Linguistics
209 N. Eighth Street
Stroudsburg, Pennsylvania 18360

Phone: 1-570-476-8006
Fax: 1-570-476-0860

acl@aclweb.org

Additional copies of this publication are available from:

Curran Associates, Inc.
57 Morehouse Lane
Red Hook, NY 12571 USA
Phone: 845-758-0400
Fax: 845-758-2634
Email: curran@proceedings.com
Web: www.proceedings.com

TABLE OF CONTENTS

Preface: General Chair

It is my pleasure and honor to welcome you to the 2012 NAACL Human Language Technologies Conference in beautiful Montreal, Canada (in our Canadian spirit, let me add, bienvenue!). The organizing committee has put in a great deal of effort on the programs in the upcoming week. I hope you will enjoy what the conference has to offer!

The core of the conference is the 3-day main technical program consisting of oral and poster presentations of papers, keynote addresses, and a novel "NLP Idol" session. I am very fortunate to have this key piece of the conference in the hands of Eric Fosler-Lussier, Ellen Riloff, and Srinivas Bangalore, three extremely dedicated and capable program co-chairs. Eric, Ellen, and Srini managed the whole process so well that I realized early on in the conference-planning process that I could leave this important part of the conference entirely in their hands. The main technical program that you will see here is the fruit of their labor, with the assistance of 22 area chairs and hundreds of people who reviewed or submitted papers, or both. Thank you all!

To be held in conjunction with the main conference poster session is the Demonstrations program. I would like to thank Aria Haghighi and Yaser Al-Onaizan for selecting a dozen interesting system demos as part of this program. Another component of the poster session is presentations from the Student Research Workshop. I am grateful to co-chairs Rivka Levitan and Myle Ott as well as faculty advisors Roger Levy and Ani Nenkova for identifying our rising stars, and for organizing a roundtable discussion on peer review standards and practices for all participants.

For the Tutorials program, I thank Jacob Eisenstein and Radu Florian for managing the submission and reviewing process to identify 8 diverse and interesting half-day tutorials for presentation. Continuing a new tradition, the Workshops program is coordinated among the EACL, NAACL, and ACL conferences, with a joint submission and review process. I am indebted to the NAACL Workshop co-chairs Colin Cherry and Mona Diab who worked as part of the *ACL workshop committee to select a strong suite of 16 workshops for NAACL and put in significant effort working with the workshop organizers to bring the whole program together. Thank you also to the organizers of the *SEM conference, Eneko Agirre, Johan Bos, and Mona Diab, for choosing to collocate their first conference with NAACL HLT.

The USB key that contains the entire proceedings of this conference is the production of Publications co-chairs Nizar Habash and William Schuler. Special thanks go to them for their efforts in assembling all the materials and working to keep everyone on schedule for the production of the proceedings.

I would like to thank Publicity chair Smaranda Muresan for her efforts in helping to attract submissions and attendees from various communities, and Exhibits chair Joel Tetreault for helping to arrange show-and-tell space for our sponsors and other exhibitors. The website that you undoubtedly consulted countless times before getting to Montreal has been designed and maintained by Dirk Hovy. A heartfelt thank you to Dirk for taking on this task, and to Lucy Roark for designing the NAACL HLT 2012 logo.

For the financial aspects of the conference, I would like to thank our corporate, academic, and government sponsors for their contributions, and our North American sponsorship co-chairs Michael Gamon and Patrick Pantel for the role they played.

The NAACL executive board has been very supportive and helpful during the planning of this conference. I am very grateful for the guidance and suggestions the board members, especially the two chairs Rebecca Hwa and Chris Callison-Burch, have provided.

Finally, the conference would not be happening without the expertise and dedication of Priscilla Rasmussen, ACL's business manager and this conference's Local Arrangements Chair. Working with local advisory committee members Sabine Bergler and Guy Lapalme, Priscilla is taking on local arrangements responsibilities usually split among multiple faculty members and doing a fabulous job. With her vast array of experience in every aspect of organizing a *ACL conference, Priscilla has been my go-to person and life-saver for the last 9 months. I just want to say, thank you Priscilla, it's been great working with you!

For those of you who made it this far, here's a conference-appropriate pun for your amusement.

Q: What do linguists call Santa's elves?
A: Subordinated Clauses.

Enjoy the conference!

Jennifer Chu-Carroll
IBM T.J. Watson Research Center
NAACL HLT 2012 General Chair

Preface: Program Chairs

Welcome to NAACL HLT 2012! This year's conference brings to Montreal an exciting array of work ranging across the human language technology disciplines. The main conference features both oral and poster sessions for full and short papers; the main conference is preceded by eight tutorials and followed by sixteen separate workshops as well as the First Joint Conference on Lexical and Computational Semantics (*SEM).

Within the main program, we are pleased to announce several special events. We have two excellent invited speakers starting off two days of our program. On Monday morning, we will hear from Eduard Hovy, Director of the Human Language Technology Group, Information Sciences Institute of the University of Southern California, who will speak about "A New Semantics: Merging Propositional and Distributional Information." Wednesday morning's invited speaker is James W. Pennebaker, Centennial Liberal Arts Professor and Chair of Psychology at the University of Texas at Austin; his talk is entitled "A, is, I, and, the: How our smallest words reveal the most about who we are."

Two special discussion-oriented events are also planned — on Monday during the lunch hour, the Student Research Workshop will be hosting a panel discussion on "Reviewing Practices," which is open to all conference participants. We will also have a special fun event Tuesday afternoon called "NLP Idol," where senior researchers will try to convince a panel of judges (and the audience!) that we should be paying attention to a forgotten line of research from the past by presenting papers "plucked from obscurity."

This year, 196 full papers were submitted to the conference, with 61 papers being accepted (a 31% acceptance rate); 105 short papers were submitted, with 36 acceptances (34% acceptance). The breakdown of papers by area of submission (based on author designation) and acceptances (in parentheses) were as follows:

Author-assigned Paper Category	**# Full Papers**	**# Short Papers**
Discourse, Dialogue, and Pragmatics	14 (7)	8 (3)
Document Categorization / Topic Clustering	13 (1)	7 (2)
End-to-end Language Processing Systems	4 (3)	4 (3)
Information Extraction	17 (4)	6 (0)
Information Retrieval and Question Answering	7 (3)	5 (0)
Language Resources, Novel Evaluation Methods	8 (5)	8 (3)
Machine Learning for Language Processing	21 (11)	8 (2)
Machine Translation	26 (8)	18 (5)
Phonology and Morphology, Word Segmentation	7 (1)	5 (3)
Semantics	25 (5)	7 (3)
Sentiment Analysis and Opinion Mining	12 (1)	8 (3)
Social Media Analysis and Processing	7 (2)	3 (1)
Spoken Language Processing	8 (2)	4 (2)
Summarization and Generation	8 (1)	5 (3)
Syntactic Tagging and Chunking	3 (1)	1 (0)
Syntax and Parsing	16 (6)	8 (3)

(As part of the review and assignment process, some of the papers were recategorized by the program chairs, so the acceptance numbers based on author categorization do not necessarily match the assignment of papers in the program.)

The oral and poster slots were allocated based on the suggestions of reviewers and area chairs for appropriate presentation style; both presentation types carry the same status. Fourteen full and seven short papers will be presented during an evening poster session, with buffet dinner, in conjunction with the Demo session and the Student Research Workshop posters. Preceding the poster session will be a reprise of the one-minute madness session introduced at NAACL HLT 2010, in which attendees can see an overview of the poster presentations.

Oral sessions will be held in three parallel sessions on Monday and Wednesday, with four parallel sessions on Tuesday. We have expanded presentation times to 30-minute slots for full papers, and 20-minute slots for short papers, to facilitate more discussion of papers. We are excited that the conference is able to present such a dynamic array of papers, and would like to thank the authors for their fine work.

The review process for the conference was double-blind, and included an author response period for clarifying reviewers' questions. We were very pleased to have the assistance of 476 reviewers in deciding the program. We are especially thankful for the reviewers who spent time reading the author responses and engaging other reviewers in the discussion board. Constructing the program would not have been possible without 22 excellent area chairs forming the Senior Program Committee: Roberto Basili, Guiseppe Carenini, Yejin Choi, Christine Doran, Jason Eisner, George Foster, Roxana Girju, Heng Ji, Sadao Kurohashi, Matt Lease, Diane Litman, Deepak Ravichandran, Giuseppe Riccardi, Richard Rose, Giorgio Satta, Fei Sha, Suzanne Stevenson, David Traum, Scott Yih, Luke Zettlemoyer, Bowen Zhou, and Jerry Zhu. Area chairs were responsible for recruiting reviewers, managing paper assignments, collating reviewer responses, handling papers for other area chairs or program chairs who had conflicts of interest, making recommendations for paper acceptance or rejection, and nominating best papers from their areas. We are very grateful for the time and energy that they have put into the program.

The Best Paper Award session starts off Tuesday morning; this year we are pleased to present three awards — for best full paper, best short paper, and best student paper. This year's winners are:

- Best Full Paper Award: **Vine Pruning for Efficient Multi-Pass Dependency Parsing,** Alexander Rush and Slav Petrov
- Best Short Paper Award: **Trait-Based Hypothesis Selection For Machine Translation,** Jacob Devlin and Spyros Matsoukas
- IBM Best Student Paper Award: **Cross-lingual Word Clusters for Direct Transfer of Linguistic Structure,** Oscar Täckström, Ryan McDonald, Jakob Uszkoreit

We would like to thank reviewers and area chairs for nominating the best paper candidates. A subset of area chairs with expertise in the areas of the nominated papers were invaluable in helping the program chairs in the decision process. In particular, we would like to thank Christine Doran, Jason Eisner, George Foster, Diane Litman, Giorgio Satta, Luke Zettlemoyer, and Bowen Zhou for their assistance in the decision process. We would like to note that the Best Full Paper and IBM Best Student Paper awardees both have students as first authors. The authors will be presented with a certificate and cash prize at the opening of Tuesday's session. We gratefully acknowledge IBM's support for the Student Best Paper Award.

There are a number of other people that we interacted with who deserve a hearty thanks for the success of the program. Rich Gerber and the START team at Softconf have been invaluable for helping us with the mechanics of the reviewing process. Nizar Habash and William Schuler, as publications co-chairs, have been very helpful in assembling the final program and coordinating the publications of the workshop proceedings. There are several crucial parts of the overall program that were the responsibility of various contributors, including Rivka Levitan, Myle Ott, Roger Levy, and Ani Nenkova (Student Research Workshop); Jacob Eisenstein and Radu Florian (Tutorial Chairs); Colin Cherry and Mona Diab (Workshop Chairs); and Aria Haghighi and Yaser Al-Onaizan (Demo Chairs). We would also like to thank Chris Callison-Burch, Rebecca Hwa, and the NAACL Executive Board for guidance during the process. Dirk Hovy was also a valuable team member in helping us disseminate information as Webmaster.

Deserving special mention is the ever-unflappable Priscilla Rasmussen, who is doing double duty this conference as local arrangements chair and general business manager. Priscilla makes everything she is involved with go more smoothly, and we have relied on her advice greatly during the run-up to the conference.

Finally, we would like to thank our General Chair, Jennifer Chu-Carroll, for entrusting us with this job, for walking us through some of the more sticky moments, and for being a great sounding board for different ideas. In particular, her guidance was crucial in developing the concept for the NLP Idol session.

We hope that you enjoy the conference!

Eric Fosler-Lussier, The Ohio State University
Ellen Riloff, University of Utah
Srinivas Bangalore, AT&T Research

General Chair:

Jennifer Chu-Carroll, IBM T.J. Watson Research Center

Program Co-Chairs:

Eric Fosler-Lussier, The Ohio State University
Ellen Riloff, University of Utah
Srinivas Bangalore, AT&T

Area Chairs:

Roberto Basili, University of Rome: Semantics
Guiseppe Carenini, University of British Columbia: Summarization and Generation
Yejin Choi, Stony Brook University: Sentiment Analysis and Opinion Mining
Christy Doran, MITRE: Language Resources Novel Evaluation Methods
Jason Eisner, Johns Hopkins University: Phonology and Morphology Word Segmentation
George Foster, National Research Council Canada: Machine Translation
Roxana Girju University of Illinois Urbana-Champaign: Social Media Analysis and Processing
Heng Ji, City University of New York: Information Extraction
Sadao Kurohashi, Kyoto University: Syntactic Tagging and Chunking
Matt Lease, University of Texas Austin: Information Retrieval and Question Answering
Diane Litman, University of Pittsburgh: Discourse Dialogue and Pragmatics
Deepak Ravichandran, Google: Information Extraction
Guiseppe Ricardi, University of Trento: Spoken Language Processing
Richard Rose, McGill University: Spoken Language Processing
Giorgio Satta, University of Padova: Syntax and Parsing
Fei Sha, University of Southern California: Machine Learning for Language Processing
Suzanne Stevenson, University of Toronto: Semantics
David Traum, University of Southern California: End-to-end Language Processing Systems
Scott Yih, Microsoft: Machine Learning for Language Processing
Luke Zettlemoyer, University of Washington: Syntax and Parsing
Bowen Zhou, IBM: Machine Translation
Jerry Zhu, University of Wisconsin: Document Categorization/Topic Clustering

Local Arrangements:

Chair:

Priscilla Rasmussen, ACL Business Office, acl-AT-aclweb.org

Advisory committee:

Sabine Bergler, Concordia University
Guy Lapalme, Université de Montréal

Workshops Co-Chairs:

Colin Cherry, National Research Council of Canada
Mona Diab, Columbia University

Tutorials Co-Chairs:

Jacob Eisenstein, CMU
Radu Florian, IBM T.J. Watson Research Center

Demos Co-Chairs:

Aria Haghighi, Prismatic
Yaser Al-Onaizan, IBM T.J. Watson Research Center

Student Workshop:

Co-chairs:

Rivka Levitan, Columbia University
Myle Ott, Cornell University

Faculty Advisors:

Roger Levy, UCSD
Ani Nenkova, University of Pennsylvania

Publications:

Nizar Habash, Columbia University
William Schuler, OSU

Publicity:

Smaranda Muresan, Rutgers University

Exhibits:

Joel Tetreault, Education Testing Services

Webmaster:

Dirk Hovy, USC/ISI

Americas Sponsorship Co-chairs:

Michael Gamon, Microsoft Research
Patrick Pantel, Microsoft Research

Program Committee Members:

Hua Ai
Gregory Aist
Cem Akkaya
Afra Alishahi
Cecilia O. Alm
Giambattista Amati
Ion Androutsopoulos
David Andrzejewski
Mark Arehart
Victoria Arranz
Javier Artiles
Ron Artstein
Abhishek Arun
Javed Aslam
Giuseppe Attardi
Necip Fazil Ayan
Michiel Bacchiani
Timothy Baldwin
Krisztian Balog
Eva Banik
Michele Banko
Ken Barker
Roberto Bayardo
Nick Belkin
Anja Belz
Emily Bender
Michael Bendersky
Paul Bennett
Edward Benson
Sabine Bergler
Shane Bergsma
Raffaella Bernardi
Steven Bethard
Rahul Bhagat
Alan W. Black
Roi Blanco
John Blitzer
Branimir Boguraev
Dan Bohus
Johan Bos
Alexandre Bouchard-Cote
Gosse Bouma
Jordan Boyd-Graber
Kristy Boyer
Thorsten Brants
Ulf Brefeld
Fabio Brugnara
Sabine Buchholz
Bill Byrne
Aoife Cahill
Clarie Cardie
Andrew Carlson
Marine Carpuat
John Carroll
Francisco Casacuberta
Diamantino Caseiro
Tommaso Caselli
Mauro Cettolo
Joyce Chai
Yllias Chali
Ming-Wei Chang
Pi-Chuan Chang
Eugene Charniak
Ciprian Chelba
Boxing Chen
John Chen
Zheng Chen
Wenliang Chen
Colin Cherry
David Chiang
Yejin Choi
Christos Christodoulopoulos
Wei Chu
Philipp Cimiano
Stephen Clark
Alex Clark
Martin Cmejrek
Shay Cohen
Ronan Collobert
Sherri Condon
Gao Cong
Michael Connor
Paul Cook
Mark Core
Stephen Cox
Mark Craven
Danilo Croce
Aron Culotta
Walter Daelemans
Geraldine Damnati
Hoa Trang Dang
Dipanjan Das
Sajib Dasgupta
Hal Daume III
Adria de Gispert
Renato De Mori
Rodolfo Delmonte
Dina Demner-Fushman
Steve DeNeefe
John DeNero
Hongbo Deng
Nicholas Diakopoulos
Laura Dietz
Chrysanne DiMarco
Xiaowen Ding
Denise DiPersio
Doug Downey
Markus Dreyer
Kevin Duh
Chris Dyer
Marc Dymetman
Myroslava Dzikovska
Jens Edlund
Koji Eguchi
Jacob Eisenstein
Charles Elkan
Jonathan Elsas
Micha Elsner
Ahmad Emami
Hakan Erdogan
Hui Fang
Faisal Farooq
Afsaneh Fazly
Anna Feldman
Donghui Feng
Elena Filatova

Katja Filippova
Tim Finin
Jenny Finkel
Dan Flickinger
Radu Florian
Kate Forbes-Riley
Jennifer Foster
Francesca Frontini
Michel Galley
Kuzman Ganchev
Kavita Ganesan
Jianfeng Gao
Qin Gao
Albert Gatt
Niyu Ge
Dmitriy Genzel
Kallirroi Georgila
Panayiotis Georgiou
Matthew Gerber
Shalini Ghosh
Arnab Ghoshal
Daniel Gildea
Kevin Gimpel
Roxana Girju
Alfio Gliozzo
Amir Globerson
Vibhav Gogate
Yoav Goldberg
Sharon Goldwater
Carlos Gomez Rodriguez
Julio Gonzalo
Joao Graca
Agustin Gravano
Nancy Green
Gregory Grefenstette
Ralph Grishman
Markus Guhe
Iryna Gurevych
Nizar Habash
Gholamreza Haffari
Dilek Hakkani-Tur
Keith Hall
David Hall
Olivier Hamon
Sandra Harabagin
Lisa Harper
Helen Hastie
Timothy J. Hazen
Xiaodong He
Marti Hearst
Jeffrey Heinz
Aurelie Herbelot
Sanjika Hewavitharana
Silja Hildebrand
Graeme Hirst
Barbora Hladka
Hieu Hoang
Julia Hockenmaier
Minlie Huang
Zhongqiang Huang
Jimmy Huang
Yang Hui
Nancy Ide
Amy Isard
Abraham Ittycheriah
Emily Jamison
Jing Jiang
Richard Johansson
Howard Johnson
Mark Johnson
Kristiina Jokinen
Doug Jones
Pamela Jordan
Shafiq Joty
Nobuhiro Kaji
Hiroshi Kanayama
Daisuke Kawahara
Anna Kazantseva
Alistair Kennedy
Joseph Keshet
Tracy King
Brian Kingsbury
Katrin Kirchhoff
Dietrich Klakow
Alexandre Klementiev
Philipp Koehn
Rob Koeling
Stanley Kok
Alexander Koller
Grzegorz Kondrak
Terry Koo
Zornitsa Kozareva
Taku Kudoh
Sandra Kuebler
Marco Kuhlmann
Roland Kuhn
Seth Kulick
Shankar Kumar
Oren Kurland
Philippe Langlais
Guy Lapalme
Mirella Lapata
Alon Lavie
Matt Lease
John Lehmann
Alessandro Lenci
James Lester
Gregor Leusch
Anton Leuski
Haibo Li
Shoushan Li
Hang Li
Zhifei Li
Fangtao Li
Mu Li
Fennie Liang
Percy Liang
Elizabeth Liddy
Ding Liu
Zhiyuan Liu
Qun Liu
Yang Liu
Yan Liu
Eduardo Lleida Solano
Oier Lopez de Lacalle
Annie Louis
Pengfei Lu
Bin Lu
Yue Lu
Klaus Macherey
Wolfgang Macherey
Nitin Madnani
Andreas Maletti
Arindam Mandal
Gideon Mann
Christopher Manning
Daniel Marcu
James Martin

Andre Martins
Yuval Marton
Sameer Maskey
Spyros Matsoukas
Takuya Matsuzaki
Mike Maxwell
Jon May
James Mayfield
Diana Maynard
Diana McCarthy
Ryan McDonald
Paul McNamee
Dan Melamed
Chris Mellish
Arul Menezes
Donald Metzler
Haitao Mi
Rada Mihalcea
Keith J. Miller
Andriy Mnih
Saif Mohammad
Bob Moore
Alessandro Moschitti
Dragos Munteanu
Smaranda Muresan
Gabriel Murray
Meenakshi Nagarajan
Tetsuji Nakagawa
Roberto Navigli
Mark-Jan Nederhof
Ani Nenkova
Alena Neviarouskaya
Hwee Tou Ng
Alexandru Niculescu-Mizil
Jian-Yun Nie
Joakim Nivre
Stephan Oepen
Constantin Orasan
Beatrice Oshika
Christopher Pal
Sinno Jialin Pan
Bo Pang
Soo-Min Pantel
Cecile Paris
Chris Parisien
S Parthasarathy
Marius Pasca
Siddharth Patwardhan
Michael Paul
Adam Pauls
Anselmo Penas
Marco Pennacchiotti
Slav Petrov
Fabio Pianesi
Emily Pitler
Paul Piwek
Thierry Poibeau
Joe Polifroni
Hoifung Poon
Martin Popel
Adrian Popescu
Maja Popovic
Matt Post
Sameer Pradhan
John Prager
Mark Przybocki
Stephen Pulman
Matthew Purver
Yanjun Qi
Silvia Quarteroni
Chris Quirk
Dragomir Radev
Piyush Rai
Owen Rambow
Delip Rao
Ari Rappoport
Lev-Arie Ratinov
Sujith Ravi
Sravana Reddy
Ines Rehbein
Ehud Reiter
Jason Riggle
Laura Rimell
Alan Ritter
Antonio Roque
Carolyn Rose
Andrew Rosenberg
Afshin Rostamizadeh
Dan Roth
Marta Ruiz
Josef Ruppenhofer
Irene Russo
Kenji Sagae
Alicia Sagae
Horacio Saggion
Murat Saraclar
Anoop Sarkar
Manabu Sassano
Hassan Sawaf
Frank Schilder
David Schlangen
Sabine Schulte im Walde
Holger Schwenk
Donia Scott
Frédérique Segond
Satoshi Sekine
Hendra Setiawan
Burr Settles
Wade Shen
Shuming Shi
Michel Simard
Vikas Sindhwani
Kevin Small
David Smith
Ronnie Smith
Benjamin Snyder
Morgan Sonderegger
Lucia Specia
Caroline Sporleder
Matthew Stone
Veselin Stoyanov
Carlo Strapparava
Stephanie Strassel
Kristina Striegnitz
Michael Strube
Jian Su
L Venkata Subramaniam
Amarnag Subramanya
Richard Sutcliffe
Charles Sutton
Hiroya Takamura
Partha Talukdar
Joerg Tiedemann
Christoph Tillmann
Ivan Titov
Noriko Tomuro
Sara Tonelli
Audrey Tong

Cigdem Toprak
Kristina Toutanova
Vivian Tsang
Oren Tsur
Yoshimasa Tsuruoka
Gokhan Tur
Joseph Turian
Oscar Täckström
Jacob Uszkoreit
Lonneke van der Plas
Ielka van der Sluis
Gertjan van Noord
Lucy Vanderwende
Ashish Venugopal
Guido Vetere
David Vilar
Aline Villavicencio
Ellen Voorhees
Xiaojun Wan
Stephen Wan
Lidan Wang
Chong Wang
Haifeng Wang
Nigel Ward
Taro Watanabe
Bonnie Webber
Fuliang Weng
Michael White
Richard Wicentowski
Jason Williams
Theresa Wilson
Guillaume Wisniewski
Kamfai Wong
Frank Wood
Dekai Wu
Yunqing Xia
Bing Xiang
Deyi Xiong
Peng Xu
Nianwen Xue
Fan Yang
Muyun Yang
Tianbao Yang
Roman Yangarber
Alex Yates
Ainur Yessenalina
Yisong Yue
Murawaki Yugo
François Yvon
Fabio Massimo Zanzotto
Beñat Zapirain
Richard Zens
Zhongwu Zhai
Chengxiang Zhai
Hao Zhang
Ying Zhang
Min Zhang
Lei Zhang
Yi Zhang
Tiejun Zhao
Bing Zhao
Jing Zheng
Zhi-Hua Zhou
Dengyong Zhou
Guodong Zhou
Ming Zhou
Jerry Zhu
Xiaodan Zhu
Imed Zitouni
Chengqing Zong
Geoffrey Zweig
Diarmuid Ó Séaghdha
Lilja Øvrelid

Production and Manufacturing by
Omnipress, Inc.
2600 Anderson Street
Madison, WI 53707
USA

PLATINUM SPONSORS:

NUANCE

GOLD SPONSORS:

Google

SILVER SPONSORS:

Microsoft Research

BRONZE SPONSORS:

at&t

Appen ButlerHill

ETS

Listening. Learning. Leading.®

Rakuten

W
UNIVERSITY *of* WASHINGTON

SUPPORTERS:

BAOBAB

SDL Your Content Their Language

IBM Research

Multiple Narrative Disentanglement: Unraveling *Infinite Jest*

Byron C. Wallace
Tufts University and Tufts Medical Center
Boston, MA
byron.wallace@gmail.com

Abstract

Many works (of both fiction and non-fiction) span multiple, intersecting narratives, each of which constitutes a story in its own right. In this work I introduce the task of *multiple narrative disentanglement* (MND), in which the aim is to tease these narratives apart by assigning *passages* from a text to the sub-narratives to which they belong. The motivating example I use is David Foster Wallace's fictional text *Infinite Jest*. I selected this book because it contains multiple, interweaving narratives within its sprawling 1,000-plus pages. I propose and evaluate a novel unsupervised approach to MND that is motivated by the theory of *narratology*. This method achieves strong empirical results, successfully disentangling the threads in *Infinite Jest* and significantly outperforming baseline strategies in doing so.

1 Introduction

Both fictional and non-fictional texts often comprise multiple, intersecting and inter-related narrative arcs. This work considers the task of identifying the (sub-)narratives latent within a narrative text and the set of passages that comprise them. As a motivating example, I consider David Foster Wallace's opus *Infinite Jest* (Wallace, 1996),[1] which contains several disparate sub-narratives interleaved throughout its voluminous (meta-)story. By sub-narrative I mean, loosely, that these threads constitute their own independent stories, coherent on their own (i.e., without the broader context of the overarching narrative). I refer to the task of identifying these independent threads and untangling them from one another as *multiple narrative disentanglement* (MND).

The task is of theoretical interest because disentanglement is a necessary pre-requisite to making sense of narrative texts, an interesting direction in NLP that has received an increasing amount of attention (Elson et al., 2010; Elson and McKeown, 2010; Celikyilmaz et al., 2010; Chambers and Jurafsky, 2008; Chambers and Jurafsky, 2009). Recognizing the (main) narrative threads comprising a work provides a context for interpreting the text. Disentanglement may thus be viewed as the first step in a literary processing 'pipeline'. Identifying threads and assigning them to passages may help in automatic plot summarization, social network construction and other literary analysis tasks. Computational approaches to literature look to make narrative sense of unstructured text, i.e., construct models that relate characters and events chronologically: disentanglement is at the heart of this re-construction.

But MND is also potentially of more pragmatic import: disentanglement may be useful for identifying and extracting disparate threads in, e.g., a newsmagazine article that covers multiple (related) stories.[2] Consider an article covering a political race. It would likely contain multiple sub-narratives (the story of one candidate's rise and fall, a scandal in a political party, etc.) that may be of interest independently of the particular race at hand. Narrative dis-

[1]No relation.

[2]While *narrative* colloquially tends to refer to fictional texts, the narrative voice is also frequently used in non-fictional contexts (Bal, 1997).

entanglement thus has applications outside of computational methods for fiction.

In this work, I treat MND as an unsupervised learning task. Given a block of narrative text, the aim is to identify the top k sub-narratives therein, and then to extract the passages comprising them. The proposed task is similar in spirit to the problem of *chat disentanglement* (Elsner and Charniak, 2010), in which the aim is to assign each utterance in a chat transcription to an associated conversational thread. Indeed, the main objective is the same: disentangle fragments of a monolithic text into chronologically ordered, independently coherent 'threads'. Despite their similarities, however, narrative disentanglement is a qualitatively different task than chat disentanglement, as I highlight in Section 3.

I take inspiration from the literary community, which has studied the theoretical underpinnings of the narrative form at length (Prince, 1982; Prince, 2003; Abbott, 2008). I rely especially on the seminal work of Bal (1997), *Narratology*, which provides a comprehensive theoretical framework for treating narratives. This narratological theory motivates my strategy of *narrative modeling*, in which I first extract the entities in each passage of a text. I then uncover the latent narrative compositions of these passages by performing latent Dirichlet allocation (LDA) (Blei et al., 2003) over the extracted entities.

The main contributions of this work are as follows. First, I introduce the task of multiple narrative disentanglement (MND). Second, motivated by the theory of narratology (Section 2) I propose a novel, unsupervised method for this task (Section 5) and demonstrate its superiority over baseline strategies empirically (Section 6). Finally, I make available a corpus for this task: the text of *Infinite Jest* manually annotated with narrative tags (Section 4).

2 Narratology

I now introduce some useful definitions and concepts (Table 1) central to the theory of narratology (Bal, 1997). These constructs motivate my approach to the task of disentanglement.

These definitions imply that the observed narrative text has been generated with respect to some number of latent *fabulas*. A story is a particular telling of an underlying fabula, i.e., a sequence of events involving actors. Figure 1 schematizes the relationships between the above constructs. The dotted line between author and fabula implies that authors *sometimes* generate the fabula, sometimes not. In particular, an author may re-tell a widely known fabula (e.g., *Hamlet*); perhaps from a different perspective. Consider, for example, the play *Rosencrantz and Guildenstern are Dead* (Stoppard, 1967), a narrative that re-tells the fabula of *Hamlet* from the perspective of the titular characters (both of whom play a minor part in *Hamlet* itself). From a narratological view, this story is an instantiation of the *Hamlet* fabula imbued with novel *aspects* (e.g., the focalizers in this telling are Rosencrantz and Guildenstern, rather than Hamlet). In non-fictional works the fabula corresponds to the actual event sequence as it happened, and thus is not invented by the author (save for cases of outright fabrication).

Actor	an agent that performs actions. Actors are not necessarily persons.
Fabula	a series of logically and chronologically related events that are caused or experienced by actors.
Story	an instantiation of a fabula, told in a particular style (a story *tells* a fabula). Stories are not necessarily told in chronological order.
Focalizer	a special actor from whose point of view the story is told.

Table 1: A small glossary of narratology.

Fabulas are essentially actor-driven. Further, actors tend to occupy particular places, and indeed Bal (1997) highlights locations as one of the defining elements of fabulas. Given these observations, it thus seems fruitful to attempt to identify the agents and locations (or *entities*) in each passage of a text as a first step toward disentanglement. I will return to this intuition when I present the *narrative modeling* method in Section 5. First, I place the present work in context by relating it to existing work on mining literature and chat disentanglement.

3 Relationship to Existing Work

Most similar to MND is the task of *chat disentanglement* (Shen et al., 2006; Elsner and Charniak, 2010; Elsner and Charniak, 2011), wherein utterances (perhaps overheard at a cocktail party) are to

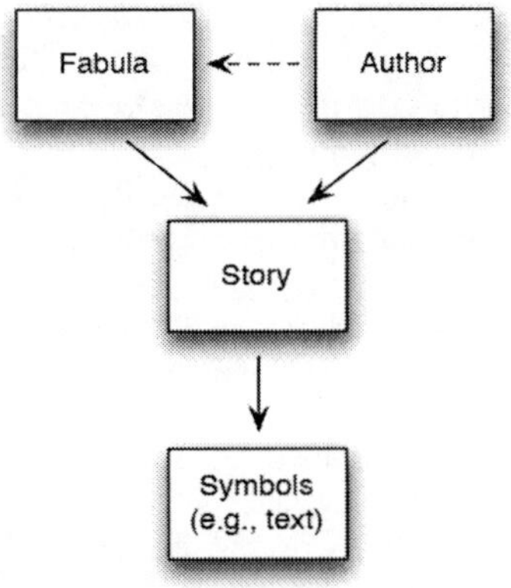

Figure 1: A schematic of the narratology theory. The dotted line between author and fabula implies that when generating a narrative text, an author may invent a fabula, or may draw upon an existing one. Together, the author and fabula jointly give rise to the story, which is communicated via the text.

be assigned to conversational threads. There are, however, important differences between these two tasks. Notably, utterances in a chat belong to a single discussion thread, motivating 'hard' assignments of utterances to threads, e.g., using graph-partitioning (Elsner and Charniak, 2010) or k-means like approaches (Shen et al., 2006). Narratives, however, often intersect: a single passage may belong to multiple narrative threads. This motivates soft, probabilistic assignments of passages to threads. Moreover, narratives are inherently hierarchical. The latter two observations suggest that probabilistic generative models are appropriate for MND.

There has also been recent interesting related work in the unsupervised induction of *narrative schemas* (Chambers and Jurafsky, 2008; Chambers and Jurafsky, 2009). In this work, the authors proposed the task of (automatically) discovering the events comprising a narrative chain. Here *narrative event chains* were defined by Chambers and Jurafsky (2008) as partially ordered sets of events involving the same protagonist. While similar in that these works attempt to make sense of narrative texts, the task at hand is quite different.

In particular, narrative schema induction presupposes a single narrative thread. Indeed, the authors explicitly make the assumption that a single protagonist participates in all of the events forming a narrative chain. Thus the discovered chains describe actions experienced by the protagonist localized within a particular narrative structure. By contrast, in this work I treat narrative texts as instantiations of fabulas, in line with Bal (1997). Fabulas can be viewed as distributions over characters, events and other entities; this conceptualization of what constitutes a narrative is broader than Chambers and Jurafsky (2008). inducing narrative schemas (Chambers and Jurafsky, 2009) may be viewed as a possible next step in a narrative induction pipeline, *subsequent* to disentangling the text comprising individual narrative threads. Indeed, the latter task might be viewed as attempting to automatically re-construct the fabula latent in a specific narrative thread.

Elsewhere, Elson et al. (2010) proposed a method for extracting social networks from literary texts. Their method relies on dialogue detection. This is used to construct a graph representing social interactions, in which an edge connecting two characters implies that they have interacted at least once; the weight of the edge encodes the frequency of their interactions. Their method is a pipelined process comprising three steps: character identification, speech attribution and, finally, graph construction. Their results from the application of this method to a large collection of novels called into question a long-held literary hypothesis: namely that there is an inverse correlation between the number of characters in a novel and the amount of dialogue it contains (Moretti, 2005) (it seems there is not). By answering a literary question empirically, their work demonstrates the power of computational methods for literature analysis.

4 Corpus (*Infinite Jest*)

I introduce a new corpus for the task of multiple narrative disentanglement (MND): David Foster Wallace's novel *Infinite Jest* (Wallace, 1996) that I have manually annotated with narrative tags.[3] *Infinite Jest* is an instructive example for experimenting with MND, as the story moves frequently between a few mostly independent – though ultimately connected and occasionally intersecting – narrative threads.

[3]Available at http://github.com/bwallace/computationaljest. I also note that the text comprises ~100 pages of footnotes, but I did not annotate these.

Annotation, i.e., manually assigning text to one or more narratives, is tricky due primarily to having to make decisions about new thread designation and label granularity.[4] Start with the first. There is an inherent subjectivity in deciding what constitutes a narrative thread. In this work, I was liberal in making this designation, in total assigning 49 unique narrative labels. Most of these tell the story of particular (minor) characters, who are themselves actors in a 'higher-level' narrative – as previously mentioned, narrative structures are inherently hierarchical. This motivates my liberal introduction of narratives: lesser threads are subsumed by their parent narratives, and can thus simply be ignored during analysis if one is uninterested in them. Indeed, this work focuses only on the three main narratives in the text (see below).

Granularity poses another challenge. At what level ought the text be annotated? Should each *sentence* be tagged with associated threads? Each *paragraph*? I let context guide this decision: in some cases tags span a single sentence; more often they span paragraphs. As an example, consider the following example of annotated text, wherein the AFR briefly narrative intersects the story of the ETA (see Table 2).

> <**AFR**>Marathe was charged with this operation's details ... <**ETA**>A direct assault upon the Academy of Tennis itself was impossible. A.F.R.s fear nothing in this hemisphere except tall and steep hillsides. ... </**ETA**></**AFR**>

Here the ellipses spans several paragraphs. Precision probably matters less than context in MND: identifying only sentences that involve a particular sub-narrative, sans context, would probably not be useful. Because the appropriate level of granularity depends on the corpus at hand, the task of segmenting the text into useful chunks is a sub-task of MND. I refer to the segmented pieces of text as *passages* and say that a passage belongs to all of the narrative threads that appear anywhere within it. Hence in the above example, the passage containing this excerpt would be designated as belonging to both the **ETA** and **AFR** threads.

[4]These complexities seem to be inherent to disentanglement tasks in general: Elsner and Charniak (2010) describe analogues issues in the case of chat.

AFR	This is the tale of the *wheelchair assassins*, a Quèbècois terrorist group, and their attempts to seize an original copy of a dangerous film. *Focalizer*: Marathe.
EHDRH	The Ennet House Drug Recovery House (sic). This narrative concerns the going-ons at a drug recovery house. *Focalizer*: Don Gately.
ETA	This narrative follows the students and faculty at the Enfield Tennis Academy. *Focalizer*: Hal.

Table 2: Brief summaries of the main narratives comprising *Infinite Jest*.

narrative	# of passages	prevalence
AFR	30	16%
EHDRH	42	23%
ETA	69	38%

Table 3: Summary statistics for the three main narratives.

Infinite Jest is naturally segmented by breaks, i.e., blank lines in the text which typically indicate some sort of context-shift (functionally, these are like mini-chapters). There are 182 such breaks in the book, demarcating 183 passages. Each of these comprises about 16,000 words and contains an average of 4.6 (out of 49) narratives, according to my annotations.

There are three main narrative threads in *Infinite Jest*, summarized briefly in Table 2.[5] I am not alone in designating these as the central plot-lines in the book.[6] Nearly all of the other threads in the text are subsumed by these (together the three cover 72% of the passages in the book). These three main threads are ideal for evaluating an MND system, for a few reasons. First, they are largely independent of one another, i.e., overlap only occasionally (though they do overlap). Second, they are relatively unambiguous: it is mostly clear when a passage tells a piece of one of these story-lines, and when it does not. These narratives are thus well-defined, providing a minimal-noise dataset for the task of MND. That I am the single annotator of the corpus (and hence inter-annotator agreement cannot be assessed) is unfortunate; the difficulty of finding someone both qualified and willing to annotate the 1000+ page book precluded this possibility. I hope to address

[5]I include these only for interested readers: the descriptions are not technically important for the work here, and one may equivalently substitute 'narrative 1', 'narrative 2', etc.

[6]e.g., http://www.sampottsinc.com/ij/file/IJ_Diagram.pdf.

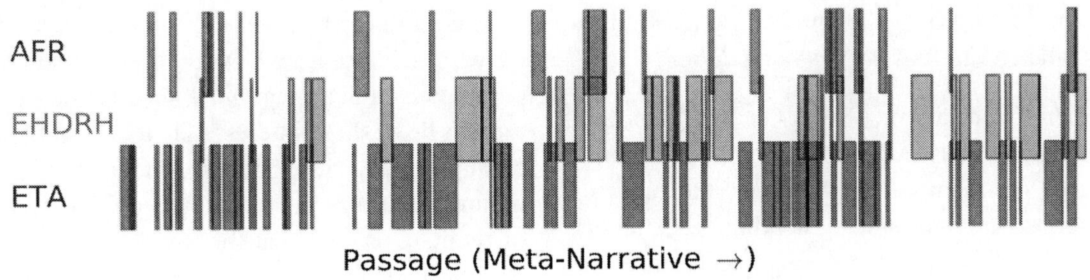

Figure 2: The three main narratives in *Infinite Jest*. A colored box implies that the corresponding narrative is present in the passage at that location in the text; these are scaled relative to the passage length.

this shortcoming in future work.

Figure 2 depicts the location and duration of these sub-narratives within the text. Passages run along the bottom axis. A colored box indicates that the corresponding narrative is present in the passage found at that location in the book. Passages are normalized by their length: a wide box implies a long passage. The aim of MND, then, is to automatically infer this structure from the narrative text.

5 Narrative Modeling for Multiple Narrative Disentanglement

The proposed method is motivated by the theory of narratology (Bal, 1997), reviewed in Section 2. Specifically I assume that passages are mixtures of different narratives with associated underlying fabulas. Fabulas, in turn, are viewed as distributions over *entities*. Entities are typically actors, but may also be locations, etc.; they are what fabulas are *about*. The idea is to infer from the observed passages the probable latent fabulas.

This is a generative view of narrative texts, which lends itself naturally to a topic-modeling approach (Steyvers and Griffiths, 2007). Further, this generative vantage allows one to exploit the machinery of latent Dirichelet allocation (LDA) (Blei et al., 2003). LDA is a generative model for texts (and discrete data, in general) in which it is assumed that each document in a corpus reflects a mixture of (latent) topics. The words in the text are thus assumed to be generated by these topics: topics are multinomials over words. Graphically, this model is depicted by Figure 3. All of the parameters in this model must be estimated; only the words in documents are observed. To uncover the topic mixtures latent in documents, standard inference procedures can be used for parameter estimation (Jordan et al., 1999).

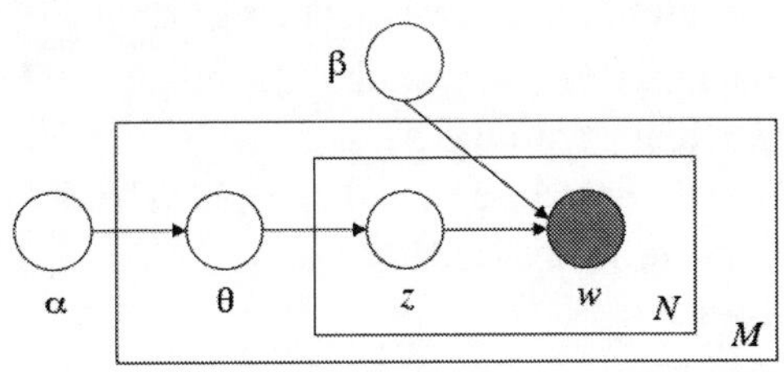

Figure 3: The graphical model of latent Dirichlet allocation (LDA; Figure from Blei et al. (2003)). Θ parameterizes the multinomial governing topics, i.e., zs. The observed words w are then assumed to be drawn from a multinomial conditioned on z. Here the plates denote that there are N (observed) words and M topics.

I propose the following approach for MND, which I will refer to as *narrative modeling*. (This pipeline is also described by Figure 4).

1. Segment the raw text into *passages*. It is at the level of this unit that narratives will be assigned: if a given narrative tag is anywhere in a passage, that passage is deemed as being a part of said narrative.[7] In many cases (including the present one) this step will be relatively trivial; e.g., segmenting the text into chapters or paragraphs.

2. (Automatically) extract from each of these segments *named entities*. The idea is that these include the primary players in the respective narratives, i.e., important actors and locations.

3. Perform latent Dirichelet analysis (LDA) over the entities extracted in (2). When this topic mod-

[7]This is analogous to a multi-label scenario.

eling is performed over the entities, rather than the text, I shall refer to it as *narrative modeling*.

As mentioned above, Step (1) will be task-specific: what constitutes a passage is inherently subjective. In many cases, however, the text will lend itself to a 'natural' segmenting, e.g., at the chapter-level. Standard statistical techniques for named entity recognition (NER) can be used for Step (2) (McCallum and Li, 2003).

Algorithm 1 The story of LDA over extracted entities for multiple narrative disentanglement.

Draw a mixture of narrative threads $\theta \sim Dir(\alpha)$
for each entity in the passage e_i **do**
  Draw a narrative thread $t_i \sim Multinomial(\theta)$
  Draw e_i from $p(e_i|t_i)$
end for

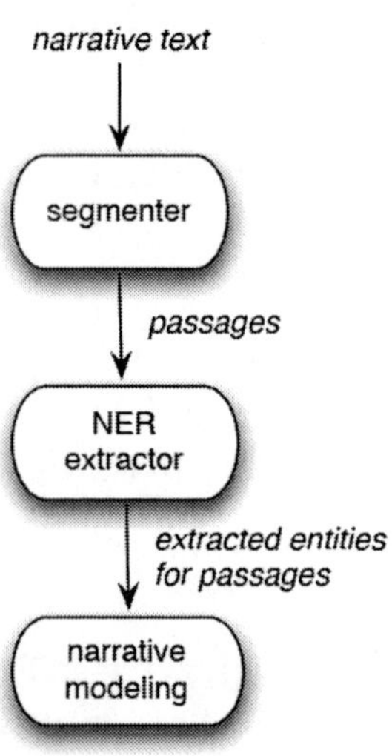

Figure 4: The MND pipeline.

For the narrative modeling Step (3), I use LDA (Blei et al., 2003); the generative story for narrative modeling is told by Algorithm 1.[8] This squares with the narratological view: entities are observed in the text with probability proportional to their likelihood of being drawn from the corresponding latent fabulas (which we are attempting to recover). Focusing on these entities, rather than the raw text, is crucial if one is to be compatible with the narratological view. The text is merely a particular telling of the underlying fabula, made noisy by story specific aspects; extracting entities from the passages effectively removes this noise, allowing the model to operate over a space more closely tied to the fabulas. In the following section, I demonstrate that this shift to the entity-space substantially boosts MND performance.

[8]Liu and Liu (2008) have also proposed topic models over NEs, though in a very different context.

The aim is to uncover the top k most salient narrative threads in a text, where k is a user-provided parameter. Indeed one *must* specify the number of threads he or she is interested in identifying (and disentangling), because because, due to the hierarchical nature of narratives, there is no single 'right number' of them. Consider that the input block of text constitutes a perfectly legitimate (meta-)narrative on its own, for example. A related issue that must be addressed is that of deciding when to assign a passage to multiple threads. That is, given the (estimated) narrative mixtures for each passage as an input, to which (if any) narrative threads ought this passage be assigned?

My approach to this is two-fold. First, I set a threshold probability α such that a passage p_i cannot be assigned to a narrative thread t if the estimated mixture component is $\leq \alpha$. I use $\alpha = 1/k$, as this value implies that the passage is dominated by other threads (in the case that all k threads contribute equally to a passage, the corresponding mixture elements would all be $1/k$). Second, I enforce a constraint that in order to be assigned to the narrative t, a passage must contain at least one of the top l entities involved in t (according to the narrative model). This constraint encodes the intuition that the main actors (and locations) that constitute a given fabula are (extremely) likely to be present in any given passage in which it is latent. I set $l = 100$, reflecting intuition. These were the first values I used for both of these parameters; I did not tune them to the corpus at hand. I did, however, experiment with other values after the primary analysis to assess sensitivity. The proposed algorithm is not terribly sensitive to either parameter, though both exert influence in the expected directions: increasing α decreases recall, as passages are less likely to be assigned to narratives. Decreasing l has a similar effect, but does not substantially impact performance unless extreme values are used.[9]

5.1 Focalizer Detection

Recall that the focalizer of a narrative is the agent responsible for perception: it is from their point of view that the story is told (Bal, 1997). One can easily exploit the narrative modeling method above to

[9]Fewer than 10 or more than 500, for example.

automatically identify the (main) focalizer of the uncovered narratives.[10] To this end, I simply identify the highest ranking entity from each narrative that has also been labeled as a 'person' (as opposed, e.g., to an 'organization').

6 Empirical Results

I now present experimental results over the *Infinite Jest* corpus, described in Section 4. The task here is to uncover the three main narratives in the text, depicted in Figure 2. To implement the proposed narrative modeling method (Section 5), I first chunked the text into passages, delineated in *Jest* by breaks in the text. I performed entity extraction over these passages using the NLTK toolkit (Bird et al., 2009). I then performed LDA via Mallet (McCallum, 2002) to estimate the narrative mixture components of each passage.

$$recall = TP/(TP+FN) \quad (1)$$

$$precision = TP/(TP+FP) \quad (2)$$

$$F = 2 \cdot \frac{precision \cdot recall}{precision + recall} \quad (3)$$

I compare the narrative modeling approach presented in the preceding section to three baselines. The simplest of these, **round-robin** and **all-same** are similar to the baselines used for chat disentanglement (Elsner and Charniak, 2010). Respectively, these strategies designate each passage as: belonging to the next narrative in a given sequence ('narrative 1', 'narrative 2', 'narrative 3'), and, belonging to the majority narrative. In both cases I show the best result attainable using the method: thus in the case of the former, I report the best scoring results from all 3! possible thread sequences (with respect to macro-averaged F-score) and in the latter case I use the true majority narrative.

I also evaluate a simple topic-modeling baseline, which is the same as narrative modeling, except that: 1) LDA is performed over the full-text (rather than the extracted entities) and, 2) there is no constraint enforcing that passages reference an entity associated with the assigned narrative. I evaluate results with respect to per-narrative recall, precision and F-score (Equations 1-3) (where TP=true positive, FN=false negative, etc.). I also consider micro- and macro-averages of these.

To calculate the micro-average, one considers each passage at a time by counting up the TPs, FPs, TNs and FNs therein for each narrative under consideration (w.r.t. the model being evaluated). The micro-average is then calculated using these tallied counts. Note that in this case certain narratives may contribute more to the overall result than others, e.g. those that are common. By contrast, to calculate the macro-average, one considers each narrative in turn and calculates the average of the metrics of interest (recall, precision) w.r.t. this narrative over all passages. An average is then taken over these mean performances. This captures the average performance of a model over all of the narratives, irrespective of their prevalence; in this case, each thread contributes equally to the overall result. Finally, note that none of the methods explicitly labels the narratives they uncover: this assignment can be made by simply matching the returned narratives to the thread labels (e.g., **ETA**) that maximize performance. This labeling is strictly aesthetic; the aim is to recover the latent narrative threads in text, not to label them.

Table 4 presents the main empirical results. Neither of the simple baseline methods (**round-robin** and **all-same**) performed very well. Both cases, for example, completely failed to identify the EHDRH thread (though this is hardly surprisingly in the **all-same** case, which identifies only one thread by definition). The macro-averaged precisions and F-measures are thus undefined in these cases (these give rise to a denominator of 0). With respect to micro-averaged performance, **all-same** achieves a substantially higher F-score than **round-robin** here, though in general this will be contingent on how dominated the text is by the majority thread.

Next consider the two more sophisticated strategies, including the proposed narrative modeling method. Start with the performance of **full-text TM**, i.e., performing standard topic-modeling over the full-text. This method improves considerably on the baselines, achieving a macro-averaged F-score of .545.[11] But the narrative modeling method (Section 5) performs substantially better, boosting the

[10] Technically, there may be multiple focalizers in a narrative, but more often there is only one.

[11] In the full-text case, I evaluated the performance of every possible assignment of topics to threads, and report the best scoring result.

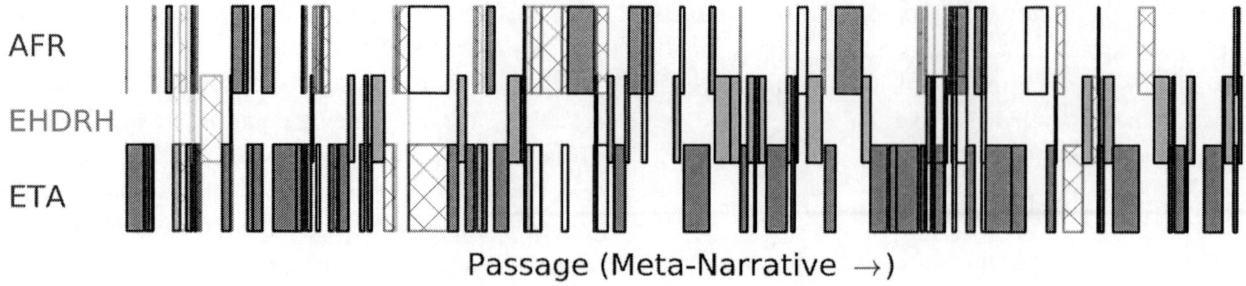

Figure 5: The unsupervised re-construction of the three main narratives using the narrative modeling approach. Hatched boxes denote false-positives (designating a passage as belonging to a narrative when it does not); empty boxes false negatives (failing to assign a passage to narrative to which it belongs).

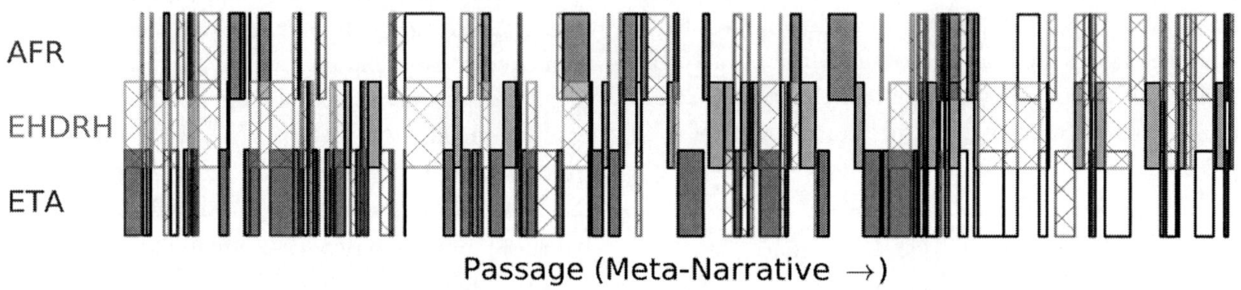

Figure 6: Results using full-text topic modeling (see above caption).

macro-averaged F-score by over 15 points (a percent gain of nearly 30%).

Figures 5 and 6 depict the unsupervised re-construction of the narrative threads using narrative modeling and the full-text topic modeling approach, respectively. Recall that the aim is to re-construct the narratives depicted in Figure 2. In these plots, an empty box represents a false negative (i.e., implies that this passage contained the corresponding narrative but this was not inferred by the model), and a hatched box denotes a false positive (the model assigned the passage to the corresponding narrative, but the passage did not belong to it). One can see that the narrative modeling method (Figure 5) re-constructs the hidden threads much better than does the full-text topic modeling approach (Figure 6). Once can see that the latter method has particular trouble with the EHDRH thread.

I also experimented with the focalizer detection method proposed in Section 5.1. This simple strategy achieved 100% accuracy on the three main narratives, correctly identifying by name each of the corresponding focalizers (see Table 2).

6.1 A More Entangled Thread

The preceding results are positive, insofar as the proposed method substantially improves on baselines and is able to disentangle threads with relatively high fidelity. These results considered the three main narratives that comprise the novel (Figure 2). This is the sort of structure I believe will be most common in narrative disentanglement, as it is likely that one will mostly be interested in extracting coherent threads that are largely independent of one another.

That said, I will next consider a more entangled thread to see if the method handles these well. More specifically, I introduce the narrative **INC**, which relates the story of the Incandenza family. This family is (arguably) the focus of the novel. The story of the Incandenza's overlaps extremely frequently with the three main, mostly independent narratives considered thus far (see Figure 6). This thread is thus difficult from an MND perspective.

I apply the same methods as above to this task, requesting four (rather than three) sub-narratives, i.e., $k = 4$. Results are summarized in Table 5.[12] We ob-

[12] I omit the two baseline strategies due to space constraints;

	round-robin			all-same			full-text TM			narrative modeling		
narrative	recall	prec.	F	recall	prec.	F	recall	prec.	F	recall	prec.	F
AFR	0.433	0.210	0.283	0.000	*undef.*	*undef.*	0.900	0.300	0.450	0.933	0.359	0.519
EHDRH	0.000	*undef.*	*undef.*	0.000	*undef.*	*undef.*	0.786	0.402	0.532	0.929	0.736	0.821
ETA	0.369	0.348	0.393	1.000	0.375	0.545	0.667	0.639	0.653	0.855	0.694	0.766
macro-avg.	0.260	*undef.*	*undef.*	0.333	*undef.*	*undef.*	0.752	0.447	0.545	0.906	0.596	0.702
micro-avg.	0.262	0.300	0.280	0.489	0.375	0.425	0.752	0.434	0.551	0.894	0.583	0.706

Table 4: Empirical results using different strategies for MND. The top three rows correspond to performance for individual narratives; the bottom two provide micro- and macro-averages, which are taken over the individual passages and the narrative-level results, respectively.

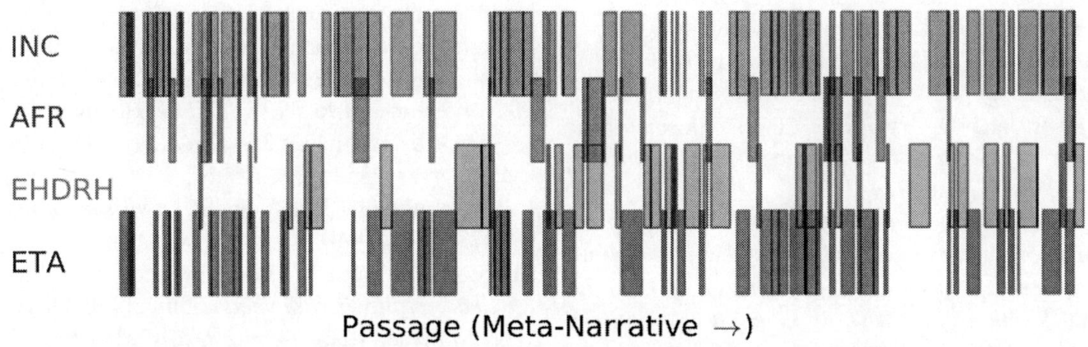

Figure 7: The INC narrative thread (green, top). This narrative is substantially more entangled than the others, i.e., more frequently intersects with the other narratives.

	full-text TM			narrative modeling		
narrative	recall	prec.	F	recall	prec.	F
AFR	0.60	0.30	0.40	0.83	0.50	0.63
EHDRH	0.83	0.57	0.67	0.79	0.75	0.77
ETA	0.67	0.69	0.68	0.67	0.89	0.76
INC	0.57	0.46	0.51	0.43	0.75	0.54
macro-avg.	0.67	0.50	0.56	0.68	0.72	0.67
micro-avg.	0.65	0.50	0.57	0.62	0.72	0.67

Table 5: Results when the fourth narrative, more entangled narrative (INC) is added.

serve that the narrative modeling strategy again bests the baseline strategies, achieving a macro-averaged F-score of about 10 points greater than that achieved using the full-text TM method (a ~20% gain).

Focalizer identification is tricky in this case because there are multiple focalizers. However I note that using the proposed strategy, four members of the Incandenza clan rank in the top five entities associated with this narrative, an encouraging result.[13]

7 Conclusions

I have introduced the task of multiple narrative disentanglement (MND), and provided a new annotated corpus for this task. I proposed a novel method (narrative modeling) for MND that is motivated by the theory of narratology. I demonstrated that this method is able to disentangle the narrative threads comprising *Infinite Jest* and that it substantially outperforms baselines in terms of doing so. I also extended the method to automatically identify narrative focalizers, and showed that it is possible to do so with near-perfect accuracy.

Interesting future directions include exploring *supervised* narrative disentanglement, combining MND with narrative induction (Chambers and Jurafsky, 2009) and applying MND to non-fictional texts.

Acknowledgments

Thanks to Kevin Small and Carla Brodley for suggesting improvements to this work, and to all of the members of the Inman Square Existentialist Book Club for insightful discussions about *Jest*.

both performed worse than the displayed methods.

[13]The fifth top-ranking entity is Joelle, a girl who plays an important part in the family saga.

References

H.P. Abbott. 2008. *The Cambridge introduction to narrative*. Cambridge Univ Pr.

M Bal. 1997. *Narratology: Introduction to the theory of narrative, 3rd ed.* University of Toronto Press.

S. Bird, E. Klein, and E. Loper. 2009. *Natural language processing with Python*. O'Reilly Media.

D.M. Blei, A.Y. Ng, and M.I. Jordan. 2003. Latent dirichlet allocation. *The Journal of Machine Learning Research*, 3:993–1022.

A. Celikyilmaz, D. Hakkani-Tur, H. He, G. Kondrak, and D. Barbosa. 2010. The actortopic model for extracting social networks in literary narrative. In *NIPS Workshop: Machine Learning for Social Computing*.

N. Chambers and D. Jurafsky. 2008. Unsupervised learning of narrative event chains. *Proceedings of ACL-08: HLT*, pages 789–797.

N. Chambers and D. Jurafsky. 2009. Unsupervised learning of narrative schemas and their participants. In *Proceedings of the Joint Conference of the 47th Annual Meeting of the ACL and the 4th International Joint Conference on Natural Language Processing of the AFNLP*, pages 602–610. Association for Computational Linguistics.

M. Elsner and E. Charniak. 2010. Disentangling chat. *Computational Linguistics*, 36(3):389–409.

M. Elsner and E. Charniak. 2011. Disentangling chat with local coherence models. In *Proceedings of the 49th Annual Meeting of the Association for Computational Linguistics: Human Language Technologies*, volume 1, pages 1179–1189. Association for Computational Linguistics.

D.K. Elson and K.R. McKeown. 2010. Automatic attribution of quoted speech in literary narrative. In *Proceedings of AAAI*.

D.K. Elson, N. Dames, and K.R. McKeown. 2010. Extracting social networks from literary fiction. In *Proceedings of the 48th Annual Meeting of the Association for Computational Linguistics*, pages 138–147. Association for Computational Linguistics.

M.I. Jordan, Z. Ghahramani, T.S. Jaakkola, and L.K. Saul. 1999. An introduction to variational methods for graphical models. *Machine learning*, 37(2):183–233.

Y. Liu and F. Liu. 2008. Unsupervised language model adaptation via topic modeling based on named entity hypotheses. In *Acoustics, Speech and Signal Processing, 2008. ICASSP 2008. IEEE International Conference on*, pages 4921–4924. IEEE.

A. McCallum and W. Li. 2003. Early results for named entity recognition with conditional random fields, feature induction and web-enhanced lexicons. In *Proceedings of the seventh conference on Natural language learning at HLT-NAACL 2003-Volume 4*, pages 188–191. Association for Computational Linguistics.

Andrew Kachites McCallum. 2002. Mallet: A machine learning for language toolkit. http://mallet.cs.umass.edu.

F. Moretti. 2005. *Graphs, Maps, Trees: Abstract models for a literary history*. Verso Books.

G. Prince. 1982. *Narratology: The form and functioning of narrative*. Mouton Berlin.

G. Prince. 2003. *A dictionary of narratology*. University of Nebraska Press.

D. Shen, Q. Yang, J.T. Sun, and Z. Chen. 2006. Thread detection in dynamic text message streams. In *Proceedings of the 29th annual international ACM SIGIR conference on Research and development in information retrieval*, pages 35–42. ACM.

M. Steyvers and T. Griffiths. 2007. Probabilistic topic models. *Handbook of latent semantic analysis*, 427(7):424–440.

T. Stoppard. 1967. *Rosencrantz & Guildenstern are dead: a play in three acts*. Samuel French Trade.

D.F. Wallace. 1996. *Infinite Jest*. Little Brown & Co.

Acoustic-Prosodic Entrainment and Social Behavior

Rivka Levitan[1], Agustín Gravano[2], Laura Willson[1],
Štefan Beňuš[3], Julia Hirschberg[1], Ani Nenkova[4]

[1] Dept. of Computer Science, Columbia University, New York, NY 10027, USA
[2] Departamento de Computación (FCEyN), Universidad de Buenos Aires, Argentina
[3] Constantine the Philosopher University & Institute of Informatics, Slovak Academy of Sciences, Slovakia
[4] Dept. of Computer and Information Science, University of Pennsylvania, Philadelphia, PA 19104, USA

rlevitan@cs.columbia.edu, gravano@dc.uba.ar, law2142@barnard.edu,
sbenus@ukf.sk, julia@cs.columbia.edu, nenkova@seas.upenn.edu

Abstract

In conversation, speakers have been shown to entrain, or become more similar to each other, in various ways. We measure entrainment on eight acoustic features extracted from the speech of subjects playing a cooperative computer game and associate the degree of entrainment with a number of manually-labeled social variables acquired using Amazon Mechanical Turk, as well as objective measures of dialogue success. We find that male-female pairs entrain on all features, while male-male pairs entrain only on particular acoustic features (intensity mean, intensity maximum and syllables per second). We further determine that entrainment is more important to the perception of female-male social behavior than it is for same-gender pairs, and it is more important to the smoothness and flow of male-male dialogue than it is for female-female or mixed-gender pairs. Finally, we find that entrainment is more pronounced when intensity or speaking rate is especially high or low.

1 Introduction

Entrainment, also termed *alignment*, *adaptation*, *priming* or *coordination*, is the phenomenon of conversational partners becoming more similar to each other in what they say, how they say it, and other behavioral phenomena. Entrainment has been shown to occur for numerous aspects of spoken language, including speakers' choice of referring expressions (Brennan & Clark, 1996); linguistic style (Niederhoffer & Pennebaker, 2002; Danescu-Niculescu-Mizil et al., 2011); syntactic structure (Reitter et al., 2006); speaking rate (Levitan & Hirschberg, 2011); acoustic/prosodic features such as fundamental frequency, intensity, voice quality (Levitan & Hirschberg, 2011); and phonetics (Pardo, 2006).

Entrainment in many of these dimensions has also been associated with different measures of dialogue success. For example, Chartrand and Bargh (1999) demonstrated that mimicry of posture and behavior led to increased liking between the dialogue participants as well as a smoother interaction. They also found that naturally empathetic individuals exhibited a greater degree of mimicry than did others. Nenkova et al. (2008) found that entrainment on high-frequency words was correlated with naturalness, task success, and coordinated turn-taking behavior. Natale (1975) showed that an individual's social desirability, or "propensity to act in a social manner," can predict the degree to which that individual will match her partner's vocal intensity. Levitan et al. (2011) showed that entrainment on backchannel-preceding cues is correlated with shorter latency between turns, fewer interruptions, and a higher degree of task success. In a study of married couples discussing problems in their relationships, Lee et al. (2010) found that entrainment measures derived from pitch features were significantly higher in positive interactions than in negative interactions and were predictive of the polarity of the participants' attitudes.

These studies have been motivated by theoretical models such as Giles' Communication Accommodation Theory (Giles & Coupland, 1991), which proposes that speakers promote social approval or efficient communication by adapting to their interlocutors' communicative behavior. Another theory informing the association of entrainment and dialogue success is the coordination-rapport hypothesis (Tickle-Degnen & Rosenthal, 1990), which posits that the degree of liking between conversational partners should be correlated with the degree of nonverbal coordination between them.

Motivated by such theoretical proposals and empirical findings, we hypothesized that entrainment on acoustic/prosodic dimensions such as pitch, intensity, voice quality and speaking rate might also be correlated with positive aspects of perceived social behaviors as well as other perceived characteristics of efficient, well-coordinated conversations. In this paper we describe a series of experiments investigating the relationship between objective acoustic/prosodic dimensions of entrainment and manually-annotated perception of a set of social variables designed to capture important aspects of conversational partners' social behaviors. Since prior research on other dimensions of entrainment has sometimes observed differences in degree of entrainment between female-female, male-male and mixed gender groups (Bilous & Krauss, 1988; Pardo, 2006; Namy et al., 2002), we also examined our data for variation by gender pair, considering female-female, male-male, and female-male pairs of speakers separately. If previous findings extend to acoustic/prosodic entrainment, we would expect female-female pairs to entrain to a greater degree than male-male pairs and female partners in mixed gender pairs to entrain more than their male counterparts. Since prior findings posit that entrainment leads to smoother and more natural conversations, we would also expect degree of entrainment to correlate with perception of other characteristics descriptive of such conversations.

Below we describe the corpus and annotations used in this study and how our social annotations were obtained in Sections 2 and 3. We next discuss our method and results for the prevalence of entrainment among different gender groups (Section 4). In Sections 5 and 6, we present the results of correlating acoustic entrainment with social variables and objective success measures, respectively. Finally, in Section 7, we explore entrainment in cases of outlier feature values.

2 The Columbia Games Corpus

The Columbia Games Corpus (Gravano & Hirschberg, 2011) consists of approximately nine hours of spontaneous dialogue between pairs of subjects playing a series of computer games. Six females and seven males participated in the collection of the corpus; eleven of the subjects returned on a different day for another session with a new partner.

During the course of each session, a pair of speakers played three Cards games and one Objects game. The work described here was carried out on the Objects games. This section of each session took 7m 12s on average. We have a total of 4h 19m of Objects game speech in the corpus.

For each task in an Objects game, the players saw identical collections of objects on their screens. However, one player (the Describer) had an additional target object positioned among the other objects, while the other (the Follower) had the same object at the bottom of her screen. The Describer was instructed to describe the position of the target object so that the Follower could place it in exactly the same location on her screen. Points (up to 100) were awarded based on how well the Follower's target location matched the describers. Each pair of partners completed 14 such tasks, alternating roles with each task. The partners were separated by a curtain to ensure that all communication was oral.

The entire corpus has been orthographically transcribed and words aligned with the speech source. It has also been ToBI-labeled (Silverman et al., 1992) for prosodic events, as well as labeled for turn-taking behaviors.

3 Annotation of Social Variables

In order to study how entrainment in various dimensions correlated with perceived social behaviors of our subjects, we asked Amazon Mechanical Turk[1] annotators to label the 168 Objects games in our corpus for an array of social behaviors perceived for each of the speakers, which we term here "social variables."

Each Human Intelligence Task (HIT) presented to the AMT workers for annotation consisted of a single Objects game task. To be eligible for our HITs,

[1] http://www.mturk.com

annotators had to have a 95% success rate on previous AMT HITs and to be located in the United States. They also had to complete a survey establishing that they were native English speakers with no hearing impairments. The annotators were paid $0.30 for each HIT they completed. Over half of the annotators completed fewer than five hits, and only four completed more than twenty.

The annotators listened to an audio clip of the task, which was accompanied by an animation that displayed a blue square or a green circle depending on which speaker was currently talking. They were then asked to answer a series of questions about each speaker: *Does Person A/B believe s/he is better than his/her partner? Make it difficult for his/her partner to speak? Seem engaged in the game? Seem to dislike his/her partner? Is s/he bored with the game? Directing the conversation? Frustrated with his/her partner? Encouraging his/her partner? Making him/herself clear? Planning what s/he is going to say? Polite? Trying to be liked? Trying to dominate the conversation?* They were also asked questions about the dialogue as a whole: *Does it flow naturally? Are the participants having trouble understanding each other? Which person do you like more? Who would you rather have as a partner?*

A series of check questions with objectively determinable answers (e.g. "Which speaker is the Describer?") were included among the target questions to ensure that the annotators were completing the task with integrity. HITs for which the annotator failed to answer the check questions correctly were disqualified.

Each task was rated by five unique annotators who answered "yes" or "no" to each question, yielding a score ranging from 0 to 5 for each social variable, representing the number of annotators who answered "yes." A fuller description of the annotation for social variables can be found in (Gravano et al., 2011).

In this study, we focus our analysis on annotations of four social variables:

- Is the speaker trying to be liked?
- Is the speaker trying to dominate the conversation?
- Is the speaker giving encouragement to his/her partner?
- Is the conversation awkward?

We correlated annotations of these variables with an array of acoustic/prosodic features.

4 Acoustic entrainment

We examined entrainment in this study in eight acoustic/prosodic features:

- Intensity mean
- Intensity max
- Pitch mean
- Pitch max
- Jitter
- Shimmer
- Noise-to-harmonics ratio (NHR)
- Syllables per second

Intensity is an acoustic measure correlated with perceived loudness. Jitter, shimmer, and noise-to-harmonics ratios are three measures of voice quality. Jitter describes varying pitch in the voice, which is perceived as a rough sound. Shimmer describes fluctuation of loudness in the voice. Noise-to-harmonics ratio is associated with perceived hoarseness. All features were speaker-normalized using z-scores.

For each task, we define entrainment between partners on each feature f as

$$ENT_p = -|\text{speaker1}_f - \text{speaker2}_f|$$

where speaker[1,2]$_f$ represents the corresponding speaker's mean for that feature over the task.

We say that the corpus shows evidence of entrainment on feature f if ENT_p, the similarities between partners, are significantly greater than ENT_x, the similarities between non-partners:

$$ENT_x = -\frac{\sum_i |\text{speaker1}_f - \text{X}_{i,f}|}{|\text{X}|}$$

where X is the set of speakers of same gender and role as the speaker's partner who are not paired with the speaker in any session. We restrict the comparisons to speakers of the same gender and role as the speaker's partner to control for the fact that differences may simply be due to differences in gender or role. The results of a series of paired t-tests comparing ENT_p and ENT_x for each feature are summarized in Table 1.

Feature	FF	MM	FM
Intensity mean	✓	✓	✓
Intensity max	✓	✓	✓
Pitch mean			✓
Pitch max			✓
Jitter	✓		✓
Shimmer	✓		✓
NHR			✓
Syllables per sec	✓	✓	✓

Table 1: Evidence of entrainment for gender pairs. A tick indicates that the data shows evidence of entrainment on that row's feature for that column's gender pair.

We find that **female-female** pairs in our corpus entrain on, in descending order of significance, jitter, intensity max, intensity mean, syllables per second and shimmer. They do not entrain on pitch mean or max or NHR. **Male-male** pairs show the least evidence of entrainment, entraining only on intensity mean, intensity max, and syllables per second, supporting the hypothesis that entrainment is less prevalent among males. **Female-male** pairs entrain on, again in descending order of significance, intensity mean, intensity max, jitter, syllables per second, pitch mean, NHR, shimmer, and pitch max – in fact, on every feature we examine, with significance values in each case of p<0.01.

To look more closely at the entrainment behavior of males and females in mixed-gender pairs, we define $ENT2_p$ as follows:

$$ENT2_p = -\frac{\sum_i |\mathrm{P}_{i,f} - \mathrm{T}_{i,f}|}{|\mathrm{T}|}$$

where T is the set of the pause-free chunks of speech that begin a speaker's turns, and P is the corresponding set of pause-free chunks that end the interlocutor's preceding turns. Unlike ENT_p, this measure is asymmetric, allowing us to consider each member of a pair separately.

We compare $ENT2_p$ for each feature for males and females of mixed gender pairs. Contrary to our hypothesis that females in mixed-gender pairs would entrain more, we found no significant differences in partner gender. Females in mixed-gender pairs do not match their interlocutor's previous turn any more than do males. This may be due to the fact that, as shown in Table 1, the overall differences between partners in mixed-gender pairs are quite low, and so neither partner may be doing much turn-by-turn matching.

Feature	FM	MM	F	p
Intensity mean	↑	↓	3.83	0.02
Intensity max	↑	↓	4.01	0.02
Syllables per sec	↓	↓	2.56	0.08

Table 2: Effects of gender pair on entrainment. An arrow pointing up indicates that the group's normalized entrainment for that feature is greater than that of female-female pairs; an arrow pointing down indicates that it is smaller.

However, as we expected, entrainment is least prevalent among male-male pairs. Although we expected female-female pairs to exhibit the highest prevalence of entrainment, they do not show evidence of entrainment on pitch mean, pitch max or NHR, while female-male pairs entrain on every feature. In fact, although ENT_p for these features is not significantly smaller between female-female pairs than between female-male pairs, ENT_x, the overall similarity among non-partners for these features, is significantly larger between females than between females and males. The degree of similarity between female-female partners is therefore attributable to the overall similarity between females rather than the effect of entrainment.

All three types of pairs exhibit entrainment on intensity mean, intensity max, and syllables per second. We look more closely into the gender-based differences in entrainment behavior with an ANOVA with the ratio of ENT_p to ENT_x as the dependent variable and gender pair as the independent variable. Normalizing ENT_p by ENT_x allows us to compare the degree of entrainment across gender pairs. Results are shown in Table 2. Male-male pairs have lower entrainment than female-female pairs for every feature; female-male pairs have higher entrainment than female-female pairs for intensity mean and max and lower for syllables per second ($p < 0.1$). These results are consistent with the general finding that male-male pairs entrain the least and female-male pairs entrain the most.

5 Entrainment and social behavior

We next correlate each of the social variables described in Section 3 with ENT_p for our eight acoustic features. Based on Communication Accommodation Theory, we would expect *gives encouragement*, a variable representing a desirable social characteristic, to be positively correlated with entrainment. Conversely, *conversation awkward* should be negatively correlated with entrainment. We note that *Trying to be liked* is negatively correlated with the *like more* variable in our data – that is, annotators were less likely to prefer speakers whom they perceived as trying to be liked. This reflects the intuition that someone overly eager to be liked may be perceived as annoying and socially inept. However, similarity-attraction theory states that similarity promotes attraction, and someone might therefore entrain in order to obtain his partner's social approval. This idea is supported by Natale's finding that the need for social approval is predictive of the degree of a speaker's convergence on intensity (Natale, 1975). We can therefore expect *trying to be liked* to positively correlate with entrainment. Speakers who are perceived as *trying to dominate* may be *overly* entraining to their interlocutors in what is sometimes called "dependency overaccommodation." Dependency overaccommodation causes the interlocutor to appear dependent on the speaker and gives the impression that the speaker is controlling the conversation (West & Turner, 2009).

The results of our correlations of social variables with acoustic/prosodic entrainment are generally consonant with these intuitions. Although it is not straightforward to compare correlation coefficients of groups for which we have varying amounts of data, for purposes of assessing trends, we will consider a correlation strong if it is significant at the $p < 0.00001$ level, moderate at the $p < 0.01$ level, and weak at the $p < 0.05$ level. The results are summarized in Table 3; we present only the significant results for space considerations.

For **female-female pairs**, *giving encouragement* is weakly correlated with entrainment on intensity max and shimmer. *Conversation awkward* is weakly correlated with entrainment on jitter. For **male-male pairs**, *trying to be liked* is moderately correlated with entrainment on intensity mean and weakly correlated with entrainment on jitter and NHR. *Giving encouragement* is moderately correlated with entrainment on intensity mean, intensity max, and NHR. For **female-male pairs**, *trying to be liked* is moderately correlated with entrainment on pitch mean. *Giving encouragement* is strongly correlated with entrainment on intensity mean and max and moderately correlated with entrainment on pitch mean and shimmer. However, it is *negatively* correlated with entrainment on jitter, although the correlation is weak. *Conversation awkward* is weakly correlated with entrainment on jitter.

As we expected, *giving encouragement* is correlated with entrainment for all three gender groups, and *trying to be liked* is correlated with entrainment for male-male and female-male groups. However, *trying to dominate* is not correlated with entrainment on any feature, and *conversation awkward* is actually positively correlated with entrainment on jitter.

Entrainment on jitter is a clear outlier here, with all of its correlations contrary to our hypotheses. In addition to being positively correlated with *conversation awkward*, it is the only feature to be negatively correlated with *giving encouragement*.

Entrainment is correlated with the most social variables for female-male pairs; these correlations are also the strongest. We therefore conclude that acoustic entrainment is not only most prevalent for mixed-gender pairs, it is also more important to the perception of female-male social behavior than it is for same-gender pairs.

6 Entrainment and objective measures of dialogue success

We now examine acoustic/prosodic entrainment in our corpus according to four objective measures of dialogue success: the mean latency between turns, the percentage of turns that are interruptions, the percentage of turns that are overlaps, and the number of turns in a task.

High latency between turns can be considered a sign of an unsuccessful conversation, with poor turn-taking behavior indicating a possible lack of rapport and difficulty in communication between the partners. A high percentage of interruptions, another example of poor turn-taking behavior, may be a symptom of or a reason for hostility or awkwardness be-

Social	Acoustic	df	r	p
Female-Female				
Giving enc.	Int. max		-0.24	0.03
	Shimmer		-0.24	0.03
Conv. awkward	Jitter		-0.23	0.03
Male-Male				
Trying to be liked	Int. mean		-0.30	0.006
	Jitter		-0.27	0.01
	NHR		-0.23	0.03
Giving enc.	Int. mean		-0.39	0.0003
	Int. max		-0.31	0.005
	NHR		-0.30	0.005
Female-Male				
Trying to be liked	Pitch mean		-0.26	0.001
Giving enc.	Int. mean		-0.36	2.8e-06
	Int. max		-0.31	7.7e-05
	Pitch mean		-0.23	0.003
	Jitter		0.19	0.02
	Shimmer		-0.16	0.04
Conv. awkward	Jitter		-0.17	0.04

Table 3: Correlations between entrainment and social variables.

tween partners. We expect these measures to be negatively correlated with entrainment. Conversely, a high percentage of overlaps may be a symptom of a well-coordinated conversation that is flowing easily. In the guidelines for the turn-taking annotation of the Games Corpus (Gravano, 2009), overlaps are defined as cases in which Speaker 2 takes the floor, overlapping with the completion of Speaker 1's utterance. Overlaps require the successful reading of turn-taking cues and by definition preclude awkward pauses. We expect a high percentage of overlaps to correlate positively with entrainment.

The number of turns in a task can be interpreted either positively or negatively. A high number is negative in that it is the sign of an inefficient dialogue, one which takes many turn exchanges to accomplish the objective. However, it may also be the sign of easy, flowing dialogue between the partners. In our domain, it may also be a sign of a high-achieving pair who are placing the object meticu-

Objective	Acoustic	df	r	p
Female-Female				
Latency	Int. mean		0.22	0.04
	Int. max		0.31	0.005
	Pitch mean		0.24	0.02
	Jitter		0.29	0.007
	Shimmer		0.33	0.002
	Syllables/sec		0.39	0.0002
# Turns	Int. max		-0.30	0.006
	Shimmer		-0.34	0.002
	NHR		-0.24	0.03
	Syllables/sec		-0.28	0.01
% Overlaps	Int. max		-0.23	0.04
	Shimmer		-0.30	0.005
% Interruptions	Shimmer		-0.33	0.005
Male-Male				
Latency	Int. mean		0.57	8.8e-08
	Int. max		0.43	0.0001
	Pitch mean		0.52	2.4e-06
	Pitch max		0.61	5.7e-09
	Jitter		0.65	4.5e-10
	NHR		0.40	0.0004
# Turns	Int. mean		-0.29	0.0002
	Pitch mean		-0.32	0.003
	Pitch max		-0.29	0.007
	NHR		-0.47	7.9e-06
	Syllables/sec		-0.25	0.02
% Overlaps	Int. mean		-0.39	0.0002
	Int. max		-0.39	0.0002
% Interruptions	NHR		-0.33	0.002
Female-Male				
# Turns	Int. mean		-0.24	0.003
	Int. max		-0.19	0.02
	Shimmer		-0.16	0.04
% Overlaps	Shimmer		-0.26	0.001

Table 4: Correlations between entrainment and objective variables.

lously in order to secure every single point. We therefore expect the number of turns to be positively correlated with entrainment. As before, we consider a correlation strong if it is significant at the $p < 0.00001$ level, moderate at the $p < 0.01$ level, and weak at the $p < 0.05$ level. The significant correlations are presented in Table 4.

For **female-female pairs**, mean latency between

turns is *negatively* correlated with entrainment on all variables except pitch max and NHR. The correlations are weak for intensity mean and pitch mean and moderate for intensity max, jitter, shimmer, and syllables per second. The number of turns is moderately correlated with entrainment on intensity max and shimmer and weakly correlated with entrainment on syllables per second. Contrary to our expectations, the percentage of interruptions is *positively* (though moderately) correlated with entrainment on shimmer; the percentage of overlaps is moderately correlated with entrainment on shimmer and weakly correlated with entrainment on intensity max.

Male-male pairs show the most correlations between entrainment and objective measures of dialogue success. The latency between turns is *negatively* correlated with entrainment on all variables except shimmer and syllables per second; the correlations are moderate for intensity max and NHR and strong for the rest. The number of turns in a task is *positively* correlated with entrainment on every variable except intensity mean, jitter and shimmer: strongly for NHR; moderately for intensity mean, pitch mean, and pitch max; and weakly for syllables per second.. The percentage of overlaps is moderately correlated with entrainment on intensity mean and max. The percentage of interruptions is moderately correlated with entrainment on NHR.

For **female-male pairs**, the number of turns is moderately correlated with entrainment on intensity mean and weakly correlated with entrainment on intensity max and shimmer. The percentage of overlaps is moderately correlated with entrainment on shimmer.

For the most part, the directions of the correlations we have found are in accordance with our hypotheses. Latency is negatively correlated with entrainment and overlaps and the number of turns are positively correlated. A puzzling exception is the percentage of interruptions, which is positively correlated with entrainment on shimmer (for female-female pairs) and NHR (for male-male pairs).

While the strongest correlations were for mixed-gender pairs for the social variables, we find that the strongest correlations for objective variables are for male-male pairs, which also have the greatest number of correlations. It therefore seems that while entrainment is more important to the perception of social behavior for mixed-gender pairs than it is for same-gender pairs, it is more important to the smoothness and flow of dialogue for male-male pairs than it is for female-female or female-male pairs.

7 Entrainment in outliers

Since acoustic entrainment is generally considered an unconscious phenomenon, it is interesting to consider tasks in which a particular feature of a person's speech is particularly salient. This will occur when a feature differs significantly from the norm – for example, when a person's voice is unusually loud or soft. Chartrand and Bargh (1999) suggest that the psychological mechanism behind the entrainment is the perception-behavior link, the finding that the act of observing another's behavior increases the likelihood of the observer's engaging in that behavior. Based on this finding, we hypothesize that a partner pair containing one "outlier" speaker will exhibit more entrainment on the salient feature, since that feature is more likely to be observed and therefore imitated.

We consider values in the 10th or 90th percentile for a feature "outliers." We can consider ENT_x, the similarity between a speaker and the speakers of her partner's role and gender with whom she is never paired, the "baseline" value for the similarity between a speaker and her interlocutor when no entrainment occurs. $ENT_p - ENT_x$, the difference between the similarity existing between partners and the baseline similarity, is then a measure of how much entrainment exists relative to baseline.

We compare $ENT_p - ENT_x$ for "normal" versus "outlier" speakers. ENT_p should be smaller for outlier speakers, since their interlocutors are not likely to be similarly unusual. However, ENT_x should also be lower for outlier speakers, since by definition they diverge from the norm, while the normal speakers by definition represent the norm. It is therefore reasonable to expect $ENT_p - ENT_x$ to be the same for outlier speakers and normal speakers.

If $ENT_p - ENT_x$ is *higher* for outlier speakers, that means that ENT_p is higher than we expect, and entrainment is *greater* relative to baseline for pairs containing an outlier speaker. If $ENT_p - ENT_x$ is *lower* for outlier speakers, that means that ENT_p is

Acoustic	t	df	p
Intensity mean	5.66	94.26	1.7e-07
Intensity max	8.29	152.05	5.5e-14
Pitch mean	-1.20	76.82	N.S.
Pitch max	-0.84	76.76	N.S.
Jitter	0.36	70.23	N.S.
Shimmer	2.64	102.23	0.02
NHR	-0.92	137.34	N.S.
Syllables per sec	2.41	72.60	0.02

Table 5: *T*-tests for relative entrainment for outlier vs. normal speakers.

lower than we expect, and pairs containing an outlier speaker entrain *less* than do pairs of normal speakers, even allowing for the fact that their usual values should be further apart to begin with.

The results for *t*-tests comparing $ENT_p - ENT_x$ for "normal" versus "outlier" speakers are shown in Table 5. Outlier pairs have *higher* relative entrainment than do normal pairs for intensity mean and max, shimmer, and syllables per second. This means that speakers confronted with an interlocutor who diverges widely from the norm for those four features make a *larger* adjustment to their speech in order to converge to that interlocutor.

An ANOVA shows that relative entrainment on intensity max is higher in outlier cases for male-male pairs than for female-female pairs and even higher for female-male pairs (F=11.33, p=5.3e-05). Relative entrainment on NHR in these cases is *lower* for male-male pairs than for female-female pairs and higher for female-male pairs (F=11.41, p=6.5e-05). Relative entrainment on syllables per second is lower for male-male pairs and higher for female-male pairs (F=5.73, p=0.005). These results differ slightly from the results in Table 2 for differences in entrainment in the general case among gender pairs, reinforcing the idea that cases in which feature values diverge widely from the norm are unique in terms of entrainment behavior.

8 Conclusion

Our study of entrainment on acoustic/prosodic variables yields new findings about entrainment behavior for female-female, male-male, and mixed-gender dyads, as well as the association of entrainment with perceived social characteristics and objective measures of dialogue smoothness and efficiency. We find that entrainment is the most prevalent for mixed-gender pairs, followed by female-female pairs, with male-male pairs entraining the least. Entrainment is the most important to the perception of social behavior of mixed-gender pairs, and it is the most important to the efficiency and flow of male-male dialogues.

For the most part, the directions of the correlations of entrainment with success variables accord with hypotheses motivated by the relevant literature. Giving encouragement and trying to be liked are positively correlated with entrainment, as are percentage of overlaps and number of turns. Mean latency, a symptom of a poorly-run conversation, is negatively associated with entrainment. However, several exceptions suggest that the associations are not straightforward and further research must be done to fully understand the relationship between entrainment, social characteristics and dialogue success. In particular, the explanation behind the associations of entrainment on certain variables with certain social and objective measures is an interesting direction for future work.

Finally, we find that in "outlier" cases where a particular speaker diverges widely from the norm for intensity mean, intensity max, or syllables per second, entrainment is more pronounced. This supports the theory that the perception-behavior link is the mechanism behind entrainment and provides a possible direction for research into why speakers entrain on certain features and not others. In future work we will explore this direction and go more thoroughly into individual differences in entrainment behavior.

Acknowledgments

This material is based upon work supported in part by NSF IIS-0307905, NSF IIS-0803148, UBACYT 20020090300087, ANPCYT PICT-2009-0026, CONICET, VEGA No. 2/0202/11; and the EUSF (ITMS 26240220060).

References

Amazon Mechanical Turk, *http://www.mturk.com.*

Frances R. Bilous and Robert M. Krauss 1988. Dominance and accommodation in the conversational behaviours of same- and mixed-gender dyads. *Language and Communication*, 8(3/4):183–194.

Susan E. Brennan and Herbert H. Clark. 1996. Conceptual Pacts and Lexical Choice in Conversation. *Journal of Experimental Psychology: Learning, Memory and Cognition*, 22(6):1482–1493.

Tanya L. Chartrand and John A. Bargh. 1999. The Chameleon Effect: The Perception-Behavior Link and Social Interaction. *Journal of Personality and Social Psychology*, 76(6):893–910.

Cristian Danescu-Niculescu-Mizil, Michael Gamon, and Susan Dumais. 2011. Mark My Words! Linguistic Style Accommodation in Social Media. *Proceedings of WWW 2011.*

H. Giles and N. Coupland. 1991. *Language: Contexts and Consequences.* Pacific Grove, CA: Brooks/Cole.

Agustín Gravano. 2009. *Turn-Taking and Affirmative Cue Words in Task-Oriented Dialogue.* Ph.D. thesis, Columbia University, New York.

Agustín Gravano and Julia Hirschberg. 2011. Turn-taking cues in task-oriented dialogue. *Computer Speech and Language*, 25(3):601–634.

Agustín Gravano, Rivka Levitan, Laura Willson, Štefan Beňuš, Julia Hirschberg, Ani Nenkova. 2011. Acoustic and Prosodic Correlates of Social Behavior. *Interspeech 2011.*

Chi-Chun Lee, Matthew Black, Athanasios Katsamanis, Adam Lammert, Brian Baucom, Andrew Christensen, Panayiotis G. Georgiou, Shrikanth Narayanan. 2010. Quantification of Prosodic Entrainment in Affective Spontaneous Spoken Interactions of Married Couples. *Eleventh Annual Conference of the International Speech Communication Association.*

Rivka Levitan, Agustín Gravano, and Julia Hirschberg. 2011. Entrainment in Speech Preceding Backchannels. *Proceedings of ACL/HLT 2011.*

Rivka Levitan and Julia Hirschberg. 2011. Measuring acoustic-prosodic entrainment with respect to multiple levels and dimensions. *Proceedings of Interspeech 2011.*

Laura L. Namy, Lynne C. Nygaard, Denise Sauerteig. 2002. Gender differences in vocal accommodation: the role of perception. *Journal of Language and Social Psychology*, 21(4):422–432.

Michael Natale. 1975. Convergence of Mean Vocal Intensity in Dyadic Communication as a Function of Social Desirability. *Journal of Personality and Social Psychology*, 32(5):790–804.

Ani Nenkova, Agustín Gravano, and Julia Hirschberg. 2008. High-frequency word entrainment in spoken dialogue. *Proceedings of ACL/HLT 2008.*

Kate G. Niederhoffer and James W. Pennebaker. 2002. Linguistic style matching in social interaction. *Journal of Language and Social Psychology*, 21(4):337–360.

Jennifer S. Pardo. 2006. On phonetic convergence during conversational interaction. *Journal of the Acoustical Society of America*, 119(4):2382–2393.

David Reitter, Johanna D. Moore, and Frank Keller. 1996. Priming of Syntactic Rules in Task-Oriented Dialogue and Spontaneous Conversation. *Proceedings of the 28th Annual Conference of the Cognitive Science Society.*

Kim Silverman, Mary Beckman, John Pitrelli, Mori Ostendorf, Colin Wightman, Patti Price, Janet Pierrehumbert, Julia Hirschberg. 1992. TOBI: A Standard for Labeling English Prosody. *ICSLP-1992*, 867-870.

Linda Tickle-Degnen and Robert Rosenthal. 1990. The Nature of Rapport and its Nonverbal Correlates. *Psychological Inquiry*, 1(4):285–293.

Richard West & Lynn Turner. 2009. *Introducing Communication Theory: Analysis and Application.* McGraw-Hill Humanities/Social Sciences/Languages, 4th edition.

Identifying High-Level Organizational Elements in Argumentative Discourse

Nitin Madnani Michael Heilman Joel Tetreault
Educational Testing Service
Princeton, NJ, USA
{nmadnani,mheilman,jtetreault}@ets.org

Martin Chodorow
Hunter College of CUNY
New York, NY, USA
martin.chodorow@hunter.cuny.edu

Abstract

Argumentative discourse contains not only language expressing claims and evidence, but also language used to organize these claims and pieces of evidence. Differentiating between the two may be useful for many applications, such as those that focus on the content (e.g., relation extraction) of arguments and those that focus on the structure of arguments (e.g., automated essay scoring). We propose an automated approach to detecting high-level organizational elements in argumentative discourse that combines a rule-based system and a probabilistic sequence model in a principled manner. We present quantitative results on a dataset of human-annotated persuasive essays, and qualitative analyses of performance on essays and on political debates.

1 Introduction

When presenting an argument, a writer or speaker usually cannot simply state a list of claims and pieces of evidence. Instead, the arguer must explicitly structure those claims and pieces of evidence, as well as explain how they relate to an opponent's argument. Consider example 1 below, adapted from an essay rebutting an opponent's argument that grizzly bears lived in a specific region of Canada.

> **The argument states that** based on the result of the recent research, there probably were grizzly bears in Labrador. **It may seem reasonable at first glance, but actually, there are some logical mistakes in it.** ... **There is a possibility that** they were a third kind of bear apart from black and grizzly bears. Also, the explorer accounts were recorded in the nineteenth century, which was more than 100 years ago. ... **In sum, the conclusion of this argument is not reasonable since the account and the research are not convincing enough.** ...

The argument begins by explicitly restating the opponent's claim, prefacing the claim with the phrase "The argument states that." Then, the second sentence explicitly marks the opponent's argument as flawed. Later on, the phrase "There is a possibility that" indicates the subsequent clause introduces evidence contrary to the opponent's claim. Finally, the sentence "In sum, ..." sums up the arguer's stance in relation to the opponent's claim.[1]

As illustrated in the above example, argumentative discourse can be viewed as consisting of language used to express claims and evidence, and language used to organize them. We believe that differentiating organizational elements from content would be useful for analyzing persuasive discourse.

[1]The word *Also* signals that additional evidence is about to be presented and should also be marked as shell. However, it was not marked in this specific case by our human annotator (§3.2).

We refer to such organizational elements as **shell**, indicating that they differ from the specific claims and evidence, or "meat," of an argument. In this work, we develop techniques for detecting shell in texts. We envision potential applications in political science (e.g., to better understand political debates), information extraction or retrieval (e.g., to help a system focus on content rather than organization), and automated essay scoring (e.g., to analyze the quality of a test-taker's argument), though additional work is needed to determine exactly how to integrate our approach into such applications.

Detecting organizational elements could also be a first step in parsing an argument to infer its structure. We focus on this initial step, leaving the other steps of categorization of spans (as to whether they evaluate the opponent's claims, connect one's own claims, etc.), and the inference of argumentation structure to future work.

Before describing our approach to identifying shell, we begin by defining it. Shell refers to sequences of words used to refer to claims and evidence in persuasive writing or speaking, providing an organizational framework for an argument. It may be used by the writer or the speaker in the following ways:

- to declare one's own claims (e.g., "There is the possibility that")
- to restate an opponent's claims (e.g., "The argument states that")
- to evaluate an opponent's claims (e.g., "It may seem reasonable at first glance, but actually, there are some logical mistakes in it")
- to present evidence and relate it to specific claims (e.g., "To illustrate my point, I will now give the example of")

There are many ways of analyzing discourse. The most relevant is perhaps rhetorical structure theory (RST) (Mann and Thompson, 1988). To our knowledge, the RST parser from Marcu (2000) is the only RST parser readily available for experimentation. The parser is trained to model the RST corpus (Carlson et al., 2001), which treats complete clauses (i.e., clauses with their obligatory complements) as the elementary units of analysis. Thus, the parser treats the first sentence in example 1 as a single unit and does not differentiate between the main and subordinate clauses. In contrast, our approach distinguishes the sequence "The argument states that . . . " as shell (which is used here to restate the external claim). Furthermore, we identify the entire second sentence as shell (here, used to evaluate the external claim), whereas the RST parser splits the sentence into two clauses, "It may seem . . . " and "but actually . . . ", linked by a "contrast" relationship.[2] Finally, our approach focuses on explicit markers of organizational structure in arguments, whereas RST covers a broader range of discourse connections (e.g., elaboration, background information, etc.), including implicit ones. (Note that additional related work is described in §6.)

This work makes the following contributions:

- We describe a principled approach to the task of detecting high-level organizational elements in argumentative discourse, combining rules and a probabilistic sequence model (§2).
- We conduct experiments to validate the approach on an annotated sample of essays (§3, §4).
- We qualitatively explore how the approach performs in a new domain: political debate (§5).

2 Detection Methods

In this section, we describe three approaches to the problem of shell detection: a rule-based system (§2.1), a supervised probabilistic sequence model (§2.2), and a simple lexical baseline (§2.3).

2.1 Rule-based system

We begin by describing a knowledge-based approach to detecting organizational elements in argumentative discourse. This approach uses a set of 25 hand-written regular expression patterns.[3]

In order to develop these patterns, we created a sample of 170 annotated essays across 57 distinct prompts.[4] The essays were written by test-takers of a standardized test for graduate admissions. This sample of essays was similar in nature to but did not overlap with those discussed in other sections

[2] We used the RST parser of Marcu (2000) to analyze the original essay from which the example was adapted.

[3] We use the PyParsing toolkit to parse sentences with the grammar for the rule system.

[4] Prompts are short texts that present an argument or issue and ask test takers to respond to it, either by analyzing the given argument or taking a stance on the given issue.

MODAL $\rightarrow$ do | don't | can | cannot | will | would | ...

ADVERB $\rightarrow$ strongly | totally | fundamentally | vehemently | ...

AGREEVERB $\rightarrow$ disagree | agree | concur | ...

AUTHORNOUN $\rightarrow$ writer | author | speaker | ...

SHELL $\rightarrow$ I [MODAL] [ADVERB] AGREEVERB with the AUTHORNOUN

Figure 1: An example pattern that recognizes shell language describing the author's position with respect to an opponent's, e.g., *I totally agree with the author* or *I will strongly disagree with the speaker.*

of the paper (§2.2, §3.2). The annotations were carried out by individuals experienced in scoring persuasive writing. No formal annotation guidelines were provided. Besides shell language, there were other annotations relevant to essay scoring. However, we ignored them for this study because they are not directly relevant to the task of shell language detection.

From this sample, we computed lists of n-grams ($n = 1, 2, \ldots, 9$) that occurred more than once in essays from at least half of the 57 distinct essay prompts. We then wrote rules to recognize the shell language present in the n-gram lists. Additional rules were added to cover instances of shell that we observed in the annotated essays but that were not frequent enough to appear in the n-gram analysis.

We use "Rules" to refer to this method.

2.2 Supervised Sequence Model

The next approach we describe is a supervised, probabilistic sequence model based on conditional random fields (CRFs) (Lafferty et al., 2001), using a small number of general features based on lexical frequencies. We assume access to a labeled dataset of N examples $(\mathbf{w}, \mathbf{y})$ indexed by i, containing sequences of words $w^{(i)}$ and sequences of labels $y^{(i)}$, with individual words and labels indexed by j (§3 describes our development and testing sets). $y^{(i)}$ is a sequence of binary values, indicating whether each word $w_j^{(i)}$ in the sequence is shell ($y_j^{(i)} = 1$) or not ($y_j^{(i)} = 0$). Following Lafferty et al. (2001), we find a parameter vector θ that maximizes the following log-likelihood objective function:

$$\begin{aligned} L(\theta|\mathbf{w},\mathbf{y}) &= \sum_{i=1}^{N} \log p\left(y^{(i)} \mid w^{(i)}, \theta\right) \qquad (1) \\ &= \sum_{i=1}^{N} \left(\theta^{\top}\mathbf{f}(w^{(i)}, y^{(i)}) - \log Z^{(i)}\right) \end{aligned}$$

The normalization constant Z_i is a sum over all possible label sequences for the ith example, and $\mathbf{f}$ is a feature function that takes pairs of word and label sequences and returns a vector of feature values, equal in dimensions to the number of parameters in θ.[5]

The feature values for the jth word and label pair are as follows (these are summed over all elements to compute the values of $\mathbf{f}$ for the entire sequence):

- The relative frequency of $w_j^{(i)}$ in the British National Corpus.
- The relative frequency of $w_j^{(i)}$ in a set of 100,000 essays (see below).
- Eight binary features for whether the above frequencies meet or exceed the following thresholds: $10^{\{-6,-5,-4,-3\}}$.
- The proportion of prompts for which $w_j^{(i)}$ appeared in at least one essay about that prompt in the set of 100,000.
- Three binary features for whether the above proportion of prompts meets or exceeds the following thresholds: $\{0.25, 0.50, 0.75\}$.
- A binary feature with value 1 if $w_j^{(i)}$ consists only of letters a-z, and 0 otherwise. This feature distinguishes punctuation and numbers from other tokens.

[5]We used CRFsuite 0.12 (Okazaki, 2007) to implement the CRF model.

- A binary feature with value 1 if the rule-based system predicts that $w_j^{(i)}$ is shell, and 0 otherwise.
- A binary feature with value 1 if the rule-based system predicts that $w_{j-1}^{(i)}$ is shell, and 0 otherwise.
- Two binary features for whether or not the current token was the first or last in the sentence, respectively.
- Four binary features for the possible transitions between previous and current labels ($y_j^{(i)}$ and $y_{j-1}^{(i)}$, respectively).

To define the features related to essay prompts and lexical frequencies in essays, we created a set of 100,000 essays from a larger set of essays written by test-takers of a standardized test for graduate admissions (the same domain as in §2.1). The essays were written in response to 228 different prompts that asked students to analyze various issues or arguments. We use additional essays sampled from this source later to acquire annotated training and test data (§3.2).

We developed the above feature set using cross-validation on our development set (§3). The intuition behind developing the word frequency features is that shell language generally consists of chunks of words that occur frequently in persuasive language (e.g., "claims," "conclude") but not necessarily as frequently in general text (e.g., the BNC). The sequence model can also learn to disprefer changes of state, such that multi-word subsequences are labeled as shell even though some of the individual words in the subsequence are stop words, punctuation, etc.

Note there are a relatively small number of parameters in the model,[6] which allows us to estimate parameters on a relatively small set of labeled data. We briefly experimented with adding an ℓ_2 penalty on the magnitude of θ in Equation 2, but this did not seem to improve performance.

When making predictions $\hat{y}^{(i)}$ about the label sequence for a new sentence, the most common approach is to find the most likely sequence of labels y given the words $w^{(i)}$, found with Viterbi decoding:

$$\hat{y}^{(i)} = \underset{y}{\operatorname{argmax}}\, p_\theta(y \mid w^{(i)}) \quad (2)$$

We use "CRF$_v$" to refer to this approach. We use the suffix "+R" to denote models that include the two rule-based system prediction features, and we use "-R" to denote models that exclude these two features.

In development, we observed that this decoding approach seemed to very strongly prefer labeling an entire sentence as shell or not, which is often not desirable since shell often appears at just the beginnings of sentences (e.g., "The argument states that").

We therefore test an alternative prediction rule that works at the word-level, rather than sequence-level. This approach labels each word as shell if the sum of the probabilities of all paths in which the word was labeled as shell—that is, the marginal probability—exceeds some threshold λ. Words are labeled as non-shell otherwise. Specifically, an individual word $w_j^{(i)}$ is labeled as shell (i.e., $\hat{y}_j^{(i)} = 1$) according to the following equation, where $1(q)$ is an indicator function that returns 1 if its argument q is true, and 0 otherwise.

$$\hat{y}_j^{(i)} = 1\left(\left(\sum_y p_\theta(y \mid w^{(i)})\, y_j\right) \geq \lambda\right) \quad (3)$$

We tune λ using the development set, as discussed in §3.

We use "CRF$_m$" to refer to this approach.

2.3 Lexical Baseline

As a simple baseline, we also evaluated a method that labels words as shell if they appear frequently in persuasive writing—specifically, in the set of 100,000 unannotated essays described in §2.2. In this approach, word tokens are marked as shell if they belonged to the set of k most frequent words from the essays. Using the development set discussed in §3.2, we tested values of k in $\{100, 200, \ldots, 1000\}$. Setting $k = 700$ led to the highest F_1.

We use "TopWords" to refer to this method.

[6] There were 42 parameters in our implementation of the full CRF model. Excluding the four transition features, each of the 19 features had two parameters, one for the positive class and one for the negative class. Having two parameters for each is unnecessary, but we are not aware of how to have the crfsuite toolkit avoid these extra features.

3 Experiments

In this section, we discuss the design of our experimental evaluation and present results on our development set, which we used to select the final methods to evaluate on the held-out test set.

3.1 Metrics

In our experiments, we evaluated the performance of the shell detection methods by comparing token-level system predictions to human labels. Shell language typically occurs as fairly long sequences of words, but identifying the exact span of a sequence of shell seems less important than in related tagging tasks, such as named entity recognition. Therefore, rather than evaluating based on spans (either with exact or a partial credit system), we measured performance at the word token-level using standard metrics: precision, recall, and the F_1 measure. For example, for precision, we computed the proportion of tokens predicted as shell by a system that were also labeled as shell in our human-annotated datasets.

3.2 Annotated Data

To evaluate the methods described in §2, we gathered annotations for 200 essays that were not in the larger, unannotated set discussed in §2.2. We split this set of essays into a development set of 150 essays (68,601 word tokens) and a held-out test set of 50 essays (21,277 word tokens). An individual with extensive experience at scoring persuasive writing and familiarity with shell language annotated all tokens in the essays with judgments of whether they were shell or not (in contrast to §2.1, this annotation only involved labeling shell language).

From the first annotator's judgments on the development set, we created a set of annotation guidelines and trained a second annotator. The second annotator marked the held-out test set so that we could measure human agreement. Comparing the two annotators' test set annotations, we observed agreement of $F_1 = 0.736$ and Cohen's $\kappa = 0.699$ (we do not use κ in our experiments but report it here since it is a common measure of human agreement). Except for measuring agreement, we did not use the second annotator's judgments in our experiments.[7]

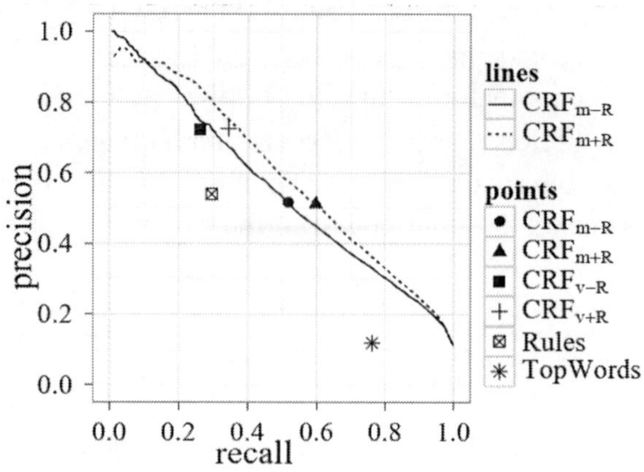

Figure 2: Precision and recall of the detection methods at various thresholds, computed through cross-validation on the development set. Points indicate performance for the rule-based and baseline system as well as points where F_1 is highest.

3.3 Cross-validation Results

To develop the CRF's feature set, to tune hyperparameters, and to select the most promising systems to evaluate on the test set, we randomly split the sentences from the development set into two halves and conducted tests with two-fold cross-validation.

We tested thresholds for the CRF at $\lambda = \{0.01, 0.02, \ldots, 1.00\}$.

Figure 2 shows the results on the development set. For the rule-based system, which did not require labeled data, performance is computed on the entire development set. For the CRF approaches, the precision and recall were computed after concatenating predictions on each of the cross-validation folds.

The TopWords baseline performed quite poorly, with $F_1 = 0.205$. The rule-based system performed much better, with $F_1 = 0.382$, but still not as well as the CRF systems. The CRF systems that predict maximum sequences had $F_1 = 0.382$ without the rule-based system features (CRF$_{v-R}$), and $F_1 = 0.467$ with the rule-based features (CRF$_{v+R}$). The CRF systems that made predictions from marginal scores performed best, with $F_1 = 0.516$ without the rule-based features, and $F_1 = 0.551$ with the rule-based features. Thus, both the rule-based sys-

[7]In the version of this paper submitted for review, we measured test set agreement with judgments from a third individual, who was informally trained by the first, without the formal guidelines. Agreement was somewhat lower: $F_1 = 0.668$ and $\kappa = 0.613$.

Method	P	R	F_1	Len
TopWords	0.125	0.759	0.214 $*$	2.80
Rules	0.561	0.360	0.439 $*$	4.99
CRF_{v-R}	0.729	0.268	0.392 $*$	15.67
CRF_{v+R}	0.763	0.369	0.498 $*$	13.30
CRF_{m-R}	0.586	0.574	0.580	9.00
CRF_{m+R}	0.556	0.670	0.607	9.96
Human	0.685	0.796	0.736 $*$	7.91

Table 1: Performance on the held-out test set, in terms of precision (P), recall (R), F_1 measure, and average length in tokens of sequences of one or more words labeled as shell (Len). $*$ indicates F_1 scores that are statistically reliably different from CRF_{m+R} at the $p < 0.01$ level.

tem features and the marginal prediction approach led to gains in performance.

From an examination of the predictions from the CRF_{m+R} and CRF_{m-R} systems, it appears that a major contribution of the features derived from the rule-based system is to help the hybrid CRF_{m+R} system avoid tagging entire sentences as shell when only parts of them are actually shell. For example, consider the sentence "According to this statement, the speaker asserts that technology can not only influence but also determine social customs and ethics" (typographical errors included). CRF_{m-R} tags everything up to "determine" as shell, whereas the rule-based system and CRF_{m+R} correctly stop after "asserts that."

4 Test Set Results

Next, we present results on the held-out test set. For the CRF_m systems, we used the thresholds that led to the highest F_1 scores on the development set ($\lambda = 0.26$ for CRF_{m+R} and $\lambda = 0.32$ for CRF_{m-R}). Table 1 presents the results for all systems, along with results comparing the second annotator's labels ("Human") to the gold standard labels from the first annotator.

The same pattern emerged as on the development set, with CRF_{m+R} performing the best. The F_1 score of 0.607 for the CRF_{m+R} system was relatively close to the F_1 score of 0.736 for agreement between human annotators. To test whether CRF_{m+R}'s relatively high performance was due to chance, we computed 99% confidence intervals for the differences in F_1 score between CRF_{m+R} and each of the other methods. We used the bias-corrected and accelerated (BC_a) Bootstrap (Efron and Tibshirani, 1993) with 10,000 rounds of resampling at the sentence level for each comparison. A difference is statistically reliable at the α level (i.e., $p < \alpha$) if the $(1 - \alpha)\%$ confidence interval for the difference does not contain zero, which corresponds to the null hypothesis. Statistically reliable differences are indicated in Table 1. The only system that did not have a reliably lower F_1 score than CRF_{m+R} was CRF_{m-R}, though due to the relatively small size of our test set, we do not take this as strong evidence against using the rule-based system features in the CRF.

We note that while the CRF_{m+R} system had lower precision (0.556) than the CRF_{v+R} system (0.763), its threshold λ could be tuned to prefer high precision rather than the best development set F_1. Such tuning could be very important depending on the relative costs of false positives and false negatives for a particular application.

We also computed the mean length of sequences of one or more contiguous words labeled as shell. Here also, we observed that the CRF_{m+R} approach provided a close match to human performance. The mean lengths of shell for the first and second annotators were 8.49 and 7.91 tokens, respectively. For the CRF_{m+R} approach, the mean length was slightly higher at 9.96 tokens, but this was much closer to the means of the human annotators than the mean for the CRF_{v+R} system, which was 13.30 tokens. For the rule-based system, the mean length was 4.99 tokens, indicating that it captures short sequences such as "In addition," more often than the other systems.

5 Observations about a New Domain

In this section, we apply our system to a corpus of transcripts of political debates[8] in order to understand whether the system can generalize to a new domain with a somewhat different style of argumentation. Our analyses are primarily qualitative in nature due to the lack of gold-standard annotations. We chose two historically well-known debates

[8]The Lincoln–Douglas debates were downloaded from `http://www.bartleby.com/251/`. The other debates were downloaded from `http://debates.org/`.

(Lincoln–Douglas from 1858 and Kennedy–Nixon from 1960) and two debates that occurred more recently (Gore–Bush from 2000 and Obama–McCain from 2008). These debates range in length from 38,000 word tokens to 65,000 word tokens.

Political debates are similar to the persuasive essays we used above in that debate participants state their own claims and evidence as well as evaluate their opponents' claims. They are different from essays in that they are spoken rather than written—meaning that they contain more disfluencies, colloquial language, etc.—and that they cover different social and economic issues. Also, the debates are in some sense a dialogue between two people.

We tagged all the debates using the CRF_{m+R} system, using the same parameters as for the test set experiments (§4).

First, we observed that a smaller percentage of tokens were tagged as shell in the debates than in the essays. For the annotated essay test set (§3.2), the percentage of tokens tagged as shell was 14.0% (11.6% were labeled as shell by the first annotator). In contrast, the percentage of tokens tagged as shell was 4.2% for Lincoln–Douglas, 5.4% for Kennedy–Nixon, 4.6% for Gore–Bush, and 4.8% for Obama–McCain. It is not completely clear whether the smaller percentages tagged as shell are due to a lack of coverage by the shell detector or more substantial differences in the domain.

However, it seems that these debates genuinely include less shell. One potential reason is that many of the essay prompts asked test-takers to respond to a particular argument, leading to responses containing many phrases such as "The speaker claims that" and "However, the argument lacks specificity ...".

We analyzed the system's predictions and extracted a set of examples, some of which appear in Table 2, showing true positives, where most of the tokens appear to be labeled correctly as shell; false positives, where tokens were incorrectly labeled as shell; and false negatives, where the system missed tokens that should have been marked.

Table 2 also provides some examples from our development set, for comparison.

We observed many instances of correctly marked shell, including many that appeared very different in style than the language used in essays. For example, Lincoln demonstrates an aggressive style in the following: "Now, I say that there is no charitable way to look at that statement, except to conclude that he is actually crazy." Also, Bush employs a somewhat atypical sentence structure here: "It's not what I think and its not my intentions and not my plan."

However, the system also incorrectly tagged sequences as shell, particularly in short sentences (e.g., "Are we as strong as we should be?"). It also missed shell, partially or entirely, such as in the following example: "But let's get back to the core issue here."

These results suggest that although there is potential for improvement in adapting to new domains, our approach to shell detection at least partially generalizes beyond our initial domain of persuasive essay writing.

6 Related Work

There has been much previous work on analyzing discourse. In this section, we describe similarities and differences between that work and ours.

Rhetorical structure theory (Mann and Thompson, 1988) is perhaps the most relevant area of work. See §1 for a discussion.

In research on intentional structure, Grosz and Sidner (1986) propose that any discourse is composed of three interacting components: the linguistic structure defined by the actual utterances, the intentional structure defined by the purposes underlying the discourse, and an attentional structure defined by the discourse participants' focus of attention. Detecting shell may also be seen as trying to identify explicit cues of intentional structure in a discourse. Additionally, the categorization of shell spans as to whether they evaluate the opponents claims, connect ones own claims, etc., may be seen as determining what Grosz and Sidener call "discourse segment purposes" (i.e., the intentions underlying the segments containing the shell spans).

We can also view shell detection as the task of identifying phrases that indicate certain types of speech acts (Searle, 1975). In particular, we aim to identify markers of assertive speech acts, which declare that the speaker believes a certain proposition, and expressive speech acts, which express attitudes toward propositions.

Shell also overlaps with the concept of discourse markers (Hutchinson, 2004), such as "however" or

LINCOLN (L) — DOUGLAS (D) DEBATES	
TP	**L:** **Now, I say that there is no charitable way to look at that statement, except to conclude that he is actually crazy.** **L:** **The first thing I see fit to notice is the fact that** …
FP	**D:** He became noted as the author of the scheme to … **D:** … such amendments were to be made to it as would render it useless and inefficient …
FN	**D:** **I wish to impress it upon you,** that every man who voted for those resolutions … **L:** **That statement he makes, too, in the teeth of the knowledge that I had made the stipulation to come down here** …
KENNEDY (K) — NIXON (N) DEBATES	
TP	**N:** **I favor that because I believe that's the best way to** aid our schools … **N:** **And in our case, I do believe that** our programs will stimulate the creative energies of …
FP	**N:** We are for programs, in addition, which will see that our medical care for the aged … **K:** Are we as strong as we should be?
FN	**K:** **I should make it clear that I do not think** we're doing enough … **N:** **Why did Senator Kennedy take that position then? Why do I take it now?**
BUSH (B) — GORE (G) DEBATES	
TP	**B:** **It's not what I think and its not my intentions and not my plan.** **G:** And FEMA has been a major flagship project of our reinventing government efforts. **And I agree, it works extremely well** now.
FP	**B:** **First of all,** most of this is at the state level. **G:** And it focuses not only on increasing the supply, **which I agree we have to do,** but also on …
FN	**B:** **My opponent thinks** the government—the surplus is the government's money. **That's not what I think** **G:** **I strongly support** local control, **so does Governor Bush.**
OBAMA (O) — MCCAIN (M) DEBATES	
TP	**M:** **But the point is—the point is,** we have finally seen Republicans and Democrats sitting down and negotiating together … **O:** **And one of the things I think we have to do is make** sure that college is affordable …
FP	**O:** … but in the short term there's an outlay and we may not see that money for a while. **O:** We have to do that now, because it will actually make our businesses and our families better off.
FN	**O:** **So I think the lesson to be drawn is that** we should never hesitate to use military force … to keep the American people safe. **O:** **But let's get back to the core issue here.**
PERSUASIVE ESSAYS (DEVELOPMENT SET, SPELLING ERRORS INCLUDED)	
TP	**However, the argument lacks specificity and relies on too many questionable assumptions to make a strong case for** adopting an expensive and logistically complicated program. **I believe that both of these claims have been made in hase and other factors need to be considered.**
FP	Since they are all far from now, **the prove is not strong enough to support the conclusion.** As we know that one mind can not think as the other does.
FN	**History has proven that** … **The given issue which states that** in any field of inquiry … **is a controversional one.**

Table 2: Examples of CRF_{m+R} performance. Underlining marks tokens predicted to be shell, and bold font indicates shell according to human judgments (our judgments for the debate transcripts, and the annotator's judgments for the development set). Examples include true positives (**TP**), false positives (**FP**), and false negatives (**FN**). Note that some **FP** and **FN** examples include partially accurate predictions.

"therefore." Discourse markers, however, are typically only single words or short phrases that express a limited number of relationships. On the other hand, shell can capture longer sequences that express more complex relationships between the components of an argumentative discourse (e.g., "But let's get back to the core issue here" signals that the following point is more important than the previous one).

There are also various other approaches to analyzing arguments. Notably, much recent theoretical research on argumentation has focused on argumentation schemes (Walton et al., 2008), which are high-level strategies for constructing arguments (e.g., argument from consequences). Recently, Feng and Hirst (2011) developed automated methods for classifying texts by argumentation scheme. In similar work, Anand et al. (2011) use argumentation schemes to identify tactics in blog posts (e.g., moral appeal, social generalization, appeals to external authorities etc.). Although shell language can certainly be found in persuasive writing, it is used to organize the persuader's tactics and claims rather than to express them. For example, consider the following sentence: "**It must be the case that** this diet works **since** it was recommended by someone who lost 20 pounds on it." In shell detection, we focus on the lexico-syntactic level, aiming to identify the bold words as shell. In contrast, work on argumentation schemes focuses at a higher level of abstraction, aiming to classify the sentence as an attempt to persuade by appealing to an external authority.

7 Conclusions

In this paper, we described our approach to detecting language used to explicitly structure an arguer's claims and pieces of evidence as well as explain how they relate to an opponent's argument. We implemented a rule-based system, a supervised probabilistic sequence model, and a principled hybrid version of the two. We presented evaluations of these systems using human-annotated essays, and we observed that the hybrid sequence model system performed the best. We also applied our system to political debates and found evidence of the potential to generalize to new domains.

Acknowledgments

We would like to thank the annotators for helping us create the essay data sets. We would also like to thank James Carlson, Paul Deane, Yoko Futagi, Beata Beigman Klebanov, Melissa Lopez, and the anonymous reviewers for their useful comments on the paper and annotation scheme.

References

P. Anand, J. King, J. Boyd-Graber, E. Wagner, C. Martell, D. Oard, and P. Resnik. 2011. Believe me–we can do this! annotating persuasive acts in blog text. In *Proc. of AAAI Workshop on Computational Models of Natural Argument*.

L. Carlson, D. Marcu, and M. E. Okurowski. 2001. Building a discourse-tagged corpus in the framework of rhetorical structure theory. In *Proc. of the Second SIGdial Workshop on Discourse and Dialogue*.

B. Efron and R. Tibshirani. 1993. *An Introduction to the Bootstrap*. Chapman and Hall/CRC.

V. W. Feng and G. Hirst. 2011. Classifying arguments by scheme. In *Proc. of ACL*.

Barbara J. Grosz and Candace L. Sidner. 1986. Attention, Intentions, and the Structure of Discourse. *Comput. Linguist.*, 12(3):175–204.

B. Hutchinson. 2004. Acquiring the meaning of discourse markers. In *Proc. of ACL*.

J. Lafferty, A. McCallum, and F. Pereira. 2001. Conditional random fields: Probabilistic models for segmenting and labeling sequence data. In *Proc. of ICML*.

W. C. Mann and S. A. Thompson. 1988. Rhetorical structure theory: Toward a functional theory of text organization. *Text*, 8(3).

D. Marcu. 2000. *The Theory and Practice of Discourse Parsing and Summarization*. MIT Press.

N. Okazaki. 2007. CRFsuite: a fast implementation of conditional random fields (CRFs).

J. R. Searle. 1975. A classification of illocutionary acts. *Language in Society*, 5(1).

D. Walton, C. Reed, and F. Macagno. 2008. *Argumentation Schemes*. Cambridge University Press.

Fast Inference in Phrase Extraction Models with Belief Propagation

David Burkett and **Dan Klein**
Computer Science Division
University of California, Berkeley
{dburkett,klein}@cs.berkeley.edu

Abstract

Modeling overlapping phrases in an alignment model can improve alignment quality but comes with a high inference cost. For example, the model of DeNero and Klein (2010) uses an ITG constraint and beam-based Viterbi decoding for tractability, but is still slow. We first show that their model can be approximated using structured belief propagation, with a gain in alignment quality stemming from the use of marginals in decoding. We then consider a more flexible, non-ITG matching constraint which is less efficient for exact inference but *more* efficient for BP. With this new constraint, we achieve a relative error reduction of 40% in F_5 and a 5.5x speed-up.

1 Introduction

Modern statistical machine translation (MT) systems most commonly infer their transfer rules from word-level alignments (Koehn et al., 2007; Li and Khudanpur, 2008; Galley et al., 2004), typically using a deterministic heuristic to convert these to phrase alignments (Koehn et al., 2003). There have been many attempts over the last decade to develop model-based approaches to the phrase alignment problem (Marcu and Wong, 2002; Birch et al., 2006; DeNero et al., 2008; Blunsom et al., 2009). However, most of these have met with limited success compared to the simpler heuristic method. One key problem with typical models of phrase alignment is that they choose a single (latent) segmentation, giving rise to undesirable modeling biases (DeNero et al., 2006) and reducing coverage, which in turn reduces translation quality (DeNeefe et al., 2007; DeNero et al., 2008). On the other hand, the extraction heuristic identifies many overlapping options, and achieves high coverage.

In response to these effects, the recent phrase alignment work of DeNero and Klein (2010) models *extraction sets*: collections of overlapping phrase pairs that are consistent with an underlying word alignment. Their extraction set model is empirically very accurate. However, the ability to model overlapping – and therefore non-local – features comes at a high computational cost. DeNero and Klein (2010) handle this in part by imposing a structural ITG constraint (Wu, 1997) on the underlying word alignments. This permits a polynomial-time algorithm, but it is still $O(n^6)$, with a large constant factor once the state space is appropriately enriched to capture overlap. Therefore, they use a heavily beamed Viterbi search procedure to find a reasonable alignment within an acceptable time frame. In this paper, we show how to use belief propagation (BP) to improve on the model's ITG-based structural formulation, resulting in a new model that is simultaneously faster and more accurate.

First, given the model of DeNero and Klein (2010), we decompose it into factors that admit an efficient BP approximation. BP is an inference technique that can be used to efficiently approximate posterior marginals on variables in a graphical model; here the marginals of interest are the phrase pair posteriors. BP has only recently come into use in the NLP community, but it has been shown to be effective in other complex structured classification tasks, such as dependency parsing (Smith and Eisner, 2008). There has also been some prior success in using BP for both discriminative (Niehues and Vogel, 2008) and generative (Cromières and Kurohashi, 2009) word alignment models.

By aligning all phrase pairs whose posterior under BP exceeds some fixed threshold, our BP approximation of the model of DeNero and Klein (2010) can achieve a comparable phrase pair F_1. Furthermore, because we have posterior marginals rather than a single Viterbi derivation, we can explicitly force the aligner to choose denser extraction sets simply by lowering the marginal threshold. Therefore, we also show substantial improvements over DeNero and Klein (2010) in recall-heavy objectives, such as F_5.

More importantly, we also show how the BP factorization allows us to relax the ITG constraint, replacing it with a new set of constraints that permit a wider family of alignments. Compared to ITG, the resulting model is *less* efficient for exact inference (where it is exponential), but *more* efficient for our BP approximation (where it is only quadratic). Our new model performs even better than the ITG-constrained model on phrase alignment metrics while being faster by a factor of 5.5x.

2 Extraction Set Models

Figure 1 shows part of an aligned sentence pair, including the word-to-word alignments, and the extracted phrase pairs licensed by those alignments. Formally, given a sentence pair $(\mathbf{e}, \mathbf{f})$, a word-level alignment a is a collection of links between target words e_i and source words f_j. Following past work, we further divide word links into two categories: sure and possible, shown in Figure 1 as solid and hatched grey squares, respectively. We represent a as a grid of ternary word link variables a_{ij}, each of which can take the value *sure* to represent a sure link between e_i and f_j, *poss* to represent a possible link, or *off* to represent no link.

An extraction set π is a set of aligned phrase pairs to be extracted from $(\mathbf{e}, \mathbf{f})$, shown in Figure 1 as green rounded rectangles. We represent π as a set of boolean variables $\pi_{ghk\ell}$, which each have the value *true* when the target span $[g, h]$ is phrase-aligned to the source span $[k, \ell]$. Following previous work on phrase extraction, we limit the size of π by imposing a phrase length limit d: π only contains a variable $\pi_{ghk\ell}$ if $h - g < d$ and $\ell - k < d$.

There is a deterministic mapping $\pi(a)$ from a word alignment to the extraction set licensed by that word alignment. We will briefly describe it here, and then present our factorized model.

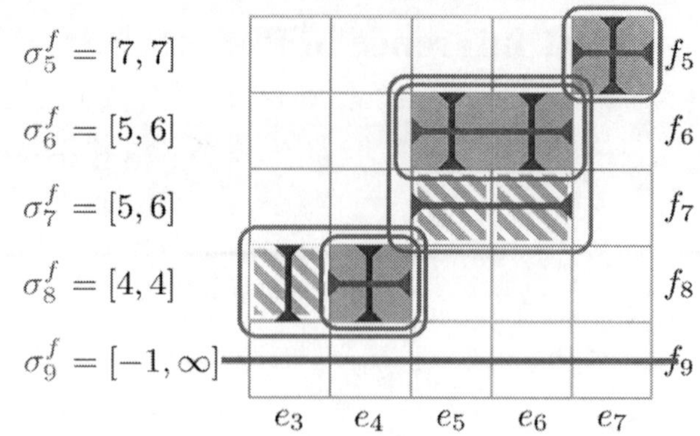

Figure 1: A schematic representation of part of a sentence pair. Solid grey squares indicate sure links (e.g. $a_{48} = \textit{sure}$), and hatched squares possible links (e.g. $a_{67} = \textit{poss}$). Rounded green rectangles are extracted phrase pairs (e.g. $\pi_{5667} = \textit{true}$). Target spans are shown as blue vertical lines and source spans as red horizontal lines. Because there is a sure link at a_{48}, $\sigma_8^f = [4,4]$ does not include the possible link at a_{38}. However, f_7 only has possible links, so $\sigma_7^f = [5,6]$ is the span containing those. f_9 is null-aligned, so $\sigma_9^f = [-1,\infty]$, which blocks all phrase pairs containing f_9 from being extracted.

2.1 Extraction Sets from Word Alignments

The mapping from a word alignment to the set of licensed phrase pairs $\pi(a)$ is based on the standard rule extraction procedures used in most modern statistical systems (Koehn et al., 2003; Galley et al., 2006; Chiang, 2007), but extended to handle possible links (DeNero and Klein, 2010). We start by using a to find a projection from each target word e_i onto a source *span*, represented as blue vertical lines in Figure 1. Similarly, source words project onto target spans (red horizontal lines in Figure 1). $\pi(a)$ contains a phrase pair iff every word in the target span projects within the source span and vice versa. Figure 1 contains an example for $d = 2$.

Formally, the mapping introduces a set of spans σ. We represent the spans as variables whose values are intervals, where $\sigma_i^e = [k, \ell]$ means that the target word e_i projects to the source span $[k, \ell]$. The set of legal values for σ_i^e includes any interval with $0 \le k \le \ell < |\mathbf{f}|$ and $\ell - k < d$, plus the special interval $[-1, \infty]$ that indicates e_i is null-aligned. The span variables for source words σ_j^f have target spans $[g, h]$ as values and are defined analogously.

For a set I of positions, we define the *range* function:

$$range(I) = \begin{cases} [-1, \infty] & I = \emptyset \\ [\min_{i \in I} i, \max_{i \in I} i] & \text{else} \end{cases} \quad (1)$$

For a fixed word alignment a we set the target span variable σ_i^e:

$$\sigma_{i,s}^e = range(\{j : a_{ij} = sure\}) \quad (2)$$

$$\sigma_{i,p}^e = range(\{j : a_{ij} \neq off\}) \quad (3)$$

$$\sigma_i^e = \sigma_{i,s}^e \cap \sigma_{i,p}^e \quad (4)$$

As illustrated in Figure 1, this sets σ_i^e to the minimal span containing all the source words with a *sure* link to e_i if there are any. Otherwise, because of the special case for *range(I)* when I is empty, $\sigma_{i,s}^e = [-1, \infty]$, so σ_i^e is the minimal span containing all *poss*-aligned words. If all word links to e_i are *off*, indicating that e_i is null-aligned, then σ_i^e is $[-1, \infty]$, preventing the alignment of any phrase pairs containing e_i.

Finally, we specify which phrase pairs should be included in the extraction set π. Given the spans σ based on a, $\pi(a)$ sets $\pi_{ghk\ell} = true$ iff every word in each phrasal span projects within the other:

$$\begin{aligned} \sigma_i^e &\subseteq [k, \ell] & \forall i \in [g, h] \\ \sigma_j^f &\subseteq [g, h] & \forall j \in [k, \ell] \end{aligned} \quad (5)$$

2.2 Formulation as a Graphical Model

We score triples (a, π, σ) as the dot product of a weight vector w that parameterizes our model and a feature vector $\phi(a, \pi, \sigma)$. The feature vector decomposes into word alignment features ϕ_a, phrase pair features ϕ_π and target and source null word features $\phi_\emptyset^e$ and $\phi_\emptyset^f$:[1]

$$\phi(a, \pi, \sigma) = \sum_{i,j} \phi_a(a_{ij}) + \sum_{g,h,k,\ell} \phi_\pi(\pi_{ghk\ell}) + \sum_i \phi_\emptyset^e(\sigma_i^e) + \sum_j \phi_\emptyset^f(\sigma_j^f) \quad (6)$$

This feature function is exactly the same as that used by DeNero and Klein (2010).[2] However, while they formulated their inference problem as a search for the highest scoring triple (a, π, σ) for an observed sentence pair $(\mathbf{e}, \mathbf{f})$, we wish to derive a conditional probability distribution $p(a, \pi, \sigma | \mathbf{e}, \mathbf{f})$. We do this with the standard transformation for linear models: $p(a, \pi, \sigma | \mathbf{e}, \mathbf{f}) \propto \exp(w \cdot \phi(a, \pi, \sigma))$. Due to the factorization in Eq. (6), this exponentiated form becomes a product of local multiplicative factors, and hence our model forms an undirected graphical model, or Markov random field.

In addition to the scoring function, our model also includes constraints on which triples (a, π, σ) have nonzero probability. DeNero and Klein (2010) implicitly included these constraints in their representation: instead of sets of variables, they used a structured representation that *only* encodes triples (a, π, σ) satisfying both the mapping $\pi = \pi(a)$ and the structural constraint that a can be generated by a block ITG grammar. However, our inference procedure, BP, requires that we represent (a, π, σ) as an assignment of values to a set of variables. Therefore, we must explicitly encode all constraints into the multiplicative factors that define the model. To accomplish this, in addition to the soft scoring factors we have already mentioned, our model also includes a set of hard constraint factors. Hard constraint factors enforce the relationships between the variables of the model by taking a value of 0 when the constraints they encode are violated and a value of 1 when they are satisfied. The full factor graph representation of our model, including both soft scoring factors and hard constraint factors, is drawn schematically in Figure 2.

2.2.1 Soft Scoring Factors

The scoring factors all take the form $\exp(w \cdot \phi)$, and so can be described in terms of their respective local feature vectors, ϕ. Depending on the values of the variables each factor depends on, the factor can be active or inactive. Features are only extracted for active factors; otherwise ϕ is empty and the factor produces a value of 1.

SURELINK. Each word alignment variable a_{ij} has a corresponding SURELINK factor L_{ij} to incorporate scores from the features $\phi_a(a_{ij})$. L_{ij} is active whenever $a_{ij} = sure$. $\phi_a(a_{ij})$ includes posteriors from unsupervised jointly trained HMM word alignment models (Liang et al., 2006), dictionary

[1] In addition to the arguments we write out explicitly, all feature functions have access to the observed sentence pair $(\mathbf{e}, \mathbf{f})$.

[2] Although the null word features are not described in DeNero and Klein (2010), all of their reported results include these features (DeNero, 2010).

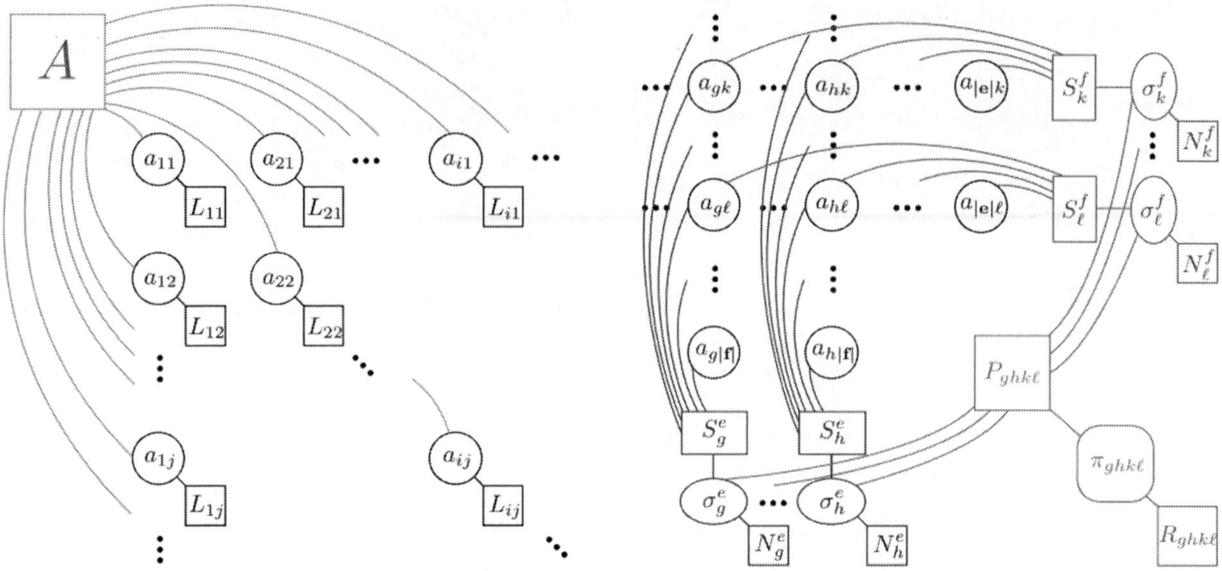

(a) ITG factor

(b) SPAN and EXTRACT factors

Figure 2: A factor graph representation of the ITG-based extraction set model. For visual clarity, we draw the graph separated into two components: one containing the factors that only neighbor word link variables, and one containing the remaining factors.

and identical word features, a position distortion feature, and features for numbers and punctuation.

PHRASEPAIR. For each phrase pair variable $\pi_{ghk\ell}$, scores from $\phi_\pi(\pi_{ghk\ell})$ come from the factor $R_{ghk\ell}$, which is active if $\pi_{ghk\ell} = \textit{true}$. Most of the model's features are on these factors, and include relative frequency statistics, lexical template indicator features, and indicators for numbers of words and Chinese characters. See DeNero and Klein (2010) for a more comprehensive list.

NULLWORD. We can determine if a word is null-aligned by looking at its corresponding span variable. Thus, we include features from $\phi^e_\emptyset(\sigma^e_i)$ in a factor N^e_i that is active if $\sigma^e_i = [-1, \infty]$. The features are mostly indicators for common words. There are also factors N^f_j for source words, which are defined analogously.

2.2.2 Hard Constraint Factors

We encode the hard constraints on relationships between variables in our model using three families of factors, shown graphically in Figure 2. The SPAN and EXTRACT factors together ensure that $\pi = \pi(a)$. The ITG factor encodes the structural constraint on a.

SPAN. First, for each target word e_i we include a factor S^e_i to ensure that the span variable σ^e_i has a value that agrees with the projection of the word alignment a. As shown in Figure 2b, S^e_i depends on σ^e_i and all the word alignment variables a_{ij} in column i of the word alignment grid. S^e_i has value 1 iff the equality in Eq. (4) holds. Our model also includes a factor S^f_j to enforce the analogous relationship between each σ^f_j and corresponding row j of a.

EXTRACT. For each phrase pair variable $\pi_{ghk\ell}$ we have a factor $P_{ghk\ell}$ to ensure that $\pi_{ghk\ell} = \textit{true}$ iff it is licensed by the span projections σ. As shown in Figure 2b, in addition to $\pi_{ghk\ell}$, $P_{ghk\ell}$ depends on the range of span variables σ^e_i for $i \in [g, h]$ and σ^f_j for $j \in [k, \ell]$. $P_{ghk\ell}$ is satisfied when $\pi_{ghk\ell} = \textit{true}$ and the relations in Eq. (5) all hold, *or* when $\pi_{ghk\ell} = \textit{false}$ and at least one of those relations does *not* hold.

ITG. Finally, to enforce the structural constraint on a, we include a single global factor A that depends on *all* the word link variables in a (see Figure 2a). A is satisfied iff a is in the family of block inverse transduction grammar (ITG) alignments. The block ITG family permits multiple links to be on ($a_{ij} \neq \textit{off}$) for a particular word e_i via terminal block productions, but ensures that every word is in at most one such terminal production, and that the full set of terminal block productions is consistent with ITG reordering patterns (Zhang et al., 2008).

3 Relaxing the ITG Constraint

The ITG factor can be viewed as imposing two different types of constraints on allowable word alignments a. First, it requires that each word is aligned to at most one relatively short subspan of the other sentence. This is a linguistically plausible constraint, as it is rarely the case that a single word will translate to an extremely long phrase, or to multiple widely separated phrases.[3]

The other constraint imposed by the ITG factor is the ITG reordering constraint. This constraint is imposed primarily for reasons of computational tractability: the standard dynamic program for bitext parsing depends on ITG reordering (Wu, 1997). While this constraint is not dramatically restrictive (Haghighi et al., 2009), it is plausible that removing it would permit the model to produce better alignments. We tested this hypothesis by developing a new model that enforces *only* the constraint that each word align to one limited-length subspan, which can be viewed as a generalization of the at-most-one-to-one constraint frequently considered in the word-alignment literature (Taskar et al., 2005; Cromières and Kurohashi, 2009).

Our new model has almost exactly the same form as the previous one. The only difference is that A is replaced with a new family of simpler factors:

ONESPAN. For each target word e_i (and each source word f_j) we include a hard constraint factor U_i^e (respectively U_j^f). U_i^e is satisfied iff $|\sigma_{i,\mathrm{p}}^e| < d$ (length limit) and either $\sigma_{i,\mathrm{p}}^e = [-1, \infty]$ or $\forall j \in \sigma_{i,\mathrm{p}}^e, a_{ij} \neq$ *off* (no gaps), with $\sigma_{i,\mathrm{p}}^e$ as in Eq. (3). Figure 3 shows the portion of the factor graph from Figure 2a redrawn with the ONESPAN factors replacing the ITG factor. As Figure 3 shows, there is no longer a global factor; each U_i^e depends only on the word link variables from column i.

[3]Short gaps can be accomodated within block ITG (and in our model are represented as possible links) as long as the total aligned span does not exceed the block size.

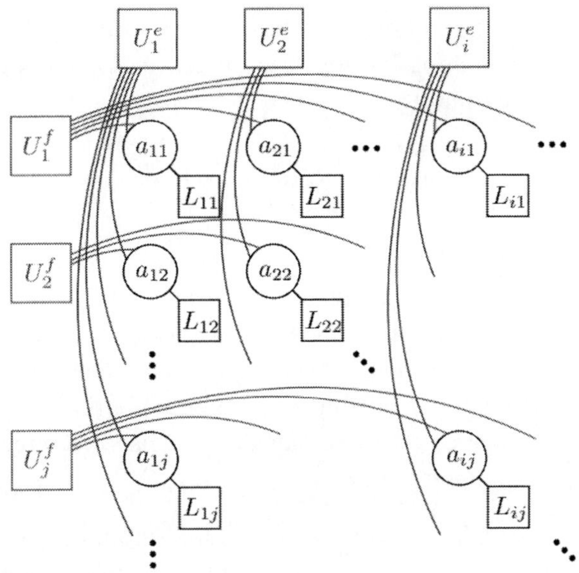

Figure 3: ONESPAN factors

4 Belief Propagation

Belief propagation is a generalization of the well known sum-product algorithm for undirected graphical models. We will provide only a procedural sketch here, but a good introduction to BP for inference in structured NLP models can be found in Smith and Eisner (2008), and Chapters 16 and 23 of MacKay (2003) contain a general introduction to BP in the more general context of message-passing algorithms.

At a high level, each variable maintains a local distribution over its possible values. These local distribution are updated via *messages* passed between variables and factors. For a variable V, $\mathcal{N}(V)$ denotes the set of factors neighboring V in the factor graph. Similarly, $\mathcal{N}(F)$ is the set of variables neighboring the factor F. During each round of BP, messages are sent from each variable to each of its neighboring factors:

$$q_{V \to F}^{(k+1)}(v) \propto \prod_{G \in \mathcal{N}(V), G \neq F} r_{G \to V}^{(k)}(v) \qquad (7)$$

and from each factor to each of its neighboring variables:

$$r_{F \to V}^{(k+1)}(v) \propto \sum_{\mathcal{X}_F, \mathcal{X}_F[V]=v} F(\mathcal{X}_F) \prod_{U \in \mathcal{N}(F), U \neq V} q_{U \to F}^{(k)}(v) \qquad (8)$$

where $\mathcal{X}_F$ is a partial assignment of values to just the variables in $\mathcal{N}(F)$.

Marginal beliefs at time k can be computed by simply multiplying together all received messages and normalizing:

$$b_V^{(k)}(v) \propto \prod_{G \in \mathcal{N}(V)} r_{G \to V}^{(k)}(v) \quad (9)$$

Although messages can be updated according to any schedule, generally one iteration of BP updates each message once. The process iterates until some stopping criterion has been met: either a fixed number of iterations or some convergence metric.

For our models, we say that BP has converged whenever $\sum_{V,v}\left(b_V^{(k)}(v) - b_V^{(k-1)}(v)\right)^2 < \delta$ for some small $\delta > 0$.[4] While we have no theoretical convergence guarantees, it usually converges within 10 iterations in practice.

5 Efficient BP for Extraction Set Models

In general, the efficiency of BP depends directly on the arity of the factors in the model. Performed naïvely, the sum in Eq. (8) will take time that grows exponentially with the size of $\mathcal{N}(F)$. For the soft-scoring factors, which each depend only on a single variable, this isn't a problem. However, our model also includes factors whose arity grows with the input size: for example, explicitly enumerating all assignments to the word link variables that the ITG factor depends on would take $O(3^{n^2})$ time.[5]

To run BP in a reasonable time frame, we need efficient factor-specific propagators that can exploit the structure of the factor functions to compute outgoing messages in polynomial time (Duchi et al., 2007; Smith and Eisner, 2008). Fortunately, all of our hard constraints permit dynamic programs that accomplish this propagation. Space does not permit a full description of these dynamic programs, but we will briefly sketch the intuitions behind them.

SPAN and ONESPAN. Marginal beliefs for S_i^e or U_i^e can be computed in $O(nd^2)$ time. The key observation is that for any legal value $\sigma_i^e = [k, \ell]$, S_i^e and U_i^e require that $a_{ij} = off$ for all $j \notin [k, \ell]$.[6] Thus, we start by computing the product of all the off beliefs: $\bar{b} = \prod_j q_{a_{ij}}(\mathit{off})$. Then, for each of the $O(nd)$ legal source spans $[k, \ell]$ we can efficiently find a joint belief by summing over consistent assignments to the $O(d)$ link variables in that span.

EXTRACT. Marginal beliefs for $P_{ghk\ell}$ can be computed in $O(d^3)$ time. For each of the $O(d)$ target words, we can find the total incoming belief that σ_i^e is within $[k, \ell]$ by summing over the $O(d^2)$ values $[k', \ell']$ where $[k', \ell'] \subseteq [k, \ell]$. Likewise for source words. Multiplying together these per-word beliefs and the belief that $\pi_{ghk\ell} = \mathit{true}$ yields the joint belief of a consistent assignment with $\pi_{ghk\ell} = \mathit{true}$, which can be used to efficiently compute outgoing messages.

ITG. To build outgoing messages, the ITG factor A needs to compute marginal beliefs for *all* of the word link variables a_{ij}. These can all be computed in $O(n^6)$ time by using a standard bitext parser to run the inside-outside algorithm. By using a normal form grammar for block ITG with nulls (Haghighi et al., 2009), we ensure that there is a 1-1 correspondence between the ITG derivations the parser sums over and word alignments a that satisfy A.

Factor	Runtime	Count	Total
SURELINK	$O(1)$	$O(n^2)$	$O(n^2)$
PHRASEPAIR	$O(1)$	$O(n^2d^2)$	$O(n^2d^2)$
NULLWORD	$O(nd)$	$O(n)$	$O(n^2d)$
SPAN	$O(nd^2)$	$O(n)$	$O(n^2d^2)$
EXTRACT	$O(d^3)$	$O(n^2d^2)$	$O(n^2d^5)$
ITG	$O(n^6)$	1	$O(n^6)$
ONESPAN	$O(nd^2)$	$O(n)$	$O(n^2d^2)$

Table 1: Asymptotic complexity for all factors.

The asymptotic complexity for all the factors is shown in Table 1. The total complexity for inference in each model is simply the sum of the complexities of its factors, so the complexity of the ITG model is $O(n^2d^5 + n^6)$, while the complexity of the relaxed model is just $O(n^2d^5)$. The complexity of exact inference, on the other hand, is exponential in d for the ITG model and exponential in both d and n for the relaxed model.

[4] We set $\delta = 0.001$.

[5] For all asymptotic analysis, we define $n = \max(|\mathbf{e}|, |\mathbf{f}|)$.

[6] For ease of exposition, we assume that all alignments are either *sure* or *off*; the modifications to account for the general case are straightforward.

6 Training and Decoding

We use BP to compute marginal posteriors, which we use at training time to get expected feature counts and at test time for posterior decoding. For each sentence pair, we continue to pass messages until either the posteriors converge, or some maximum number of iterations has been reached.[7] After running BP, the marginals we are interested in can all be computed with Eq. (9).

6.1 Training

We train the model to maximize the log likelihood of manually word-aligned gold training sentence pairs (with L_2 regularization). Because π and σ are determined when a is observed, the model has no latent variables. Therefore, the gradient takes the standard form for loglinear models:

$$\nabla LL = \phi(a, \pi, \sigma) - \sum_{a', \pi', \sigma'} p(a', \pi', \sigma' | \mathbf{e}, \mathbf{f}) \phi(a', \pi', \sigma') - \lambda w \quad (10)$$

The feature vector ϕ contains features on sure word links, extracted phrase pairs, and null-aligned words. Approximate expectations of these features can be efficiently computed using the marginal beliefs $b_{a_{ij}}(\textit{sure})$, $b_{\pi_{ghk\ell}}(\textit{true})$, and $b_{\sigma_i^e}([-1, \infty])$ and $b_{\sigma_j^f}([-1, \infty])$, respectively. We learned our final weight vector w using AdaGrad (Duchi et al., 2010), an adaptive subgradient version of standard stochastic gradient ascent.

6.2 Testing

We evaluate our model by measuring precision and recall on extracted phrase pairs. Thus, the decoding problem takes a sentence pair $(\mathbf{e}, \mathbf{f})$ as input, and must produce an extraction set π as output. Our approach, posterior thresholding, is extremely simple: we set $\pi_{ghk\ell} = \textit{true}$ iff $b_{\pi_{ghk\ell}}(\textit{true}) \geq \tau$ for some fixed threshold τ. Note that this decoding method does not require that there be any underlying word alignment a licensing the resulting extraction set π,[8] but the structure of the model is such that two conflicting phrase pairs are unlikely to simultaneously have high posterior probability.

Most publicly available translation systems expect word-level alignments as input. These can also be generated by applying posterior thresholding, aligning target word i to source word j whenever $b_{a_{ij}}(\textit{sure}) \geq t$.[9]

7 Experiments

Our experiments are performed on Chinese-to-English alignment. We trained and evaluated all models on the NIST MT02 test set, which consists of 150 training and 191 test sentences and has been used previously in alignment experiments (Ayan and Dorr, 2006; Haghighi et al., 2009; DeNero and Klein, 2010). The unsupervised HMM word aligner used to generate features for the model was trained on 11.3 million words of FBIS newswire data. We test three models: the Viterbi ITG model of DeNero and Klein (2010), our BP ITG model that uses the ITG factor, and our BP Relaxed model that replaces the ITG factor with the ONESPAN factors. In all of our experiments, the phrase length d was set to 3.[10]

7.1 Phrase Alignment

We tested the models by computing precision and recall on extracted phrase pairs, relative to the gold phrase pairs of up to length 3 induced by the gold word alignments. For the BP models, we trade off precision and recall by adjusting the decoding threshold τ. The Viterbi ITG model was trained to optimize F_5, a recall-biased measure, so in addition to F_1, we also report the recall-biased F_2 and F_5 measures. The maximum number of BP iterations was set to 5 for the BP ITG model and to 10 for the BP Relaxed model.

The phrase alignment results are shown in Figure 4. The BP ITG model performs comparably to the Viterbi ITG model. However, because posterior decoding permits explicit tradeoffs between precision and recall, it can do much better in the recall-biased measures, even though the Viterbi ITG model was explicitly trained to maximize F_5 (DeNero and

[7] See Section 7.2 for an empirical investigation of this maximum.

[8] This would be true even if we computed posteriors exactly, but is especially true with approximate marginals from BP, which are not necessarily consistent.

[9] For our experiments, we set $t = 0.2$.

[10] Because the runtime of the Viterbi ITG model grows exponentially with d, it was not feasible to perform comparisons for higher phrase lengths.

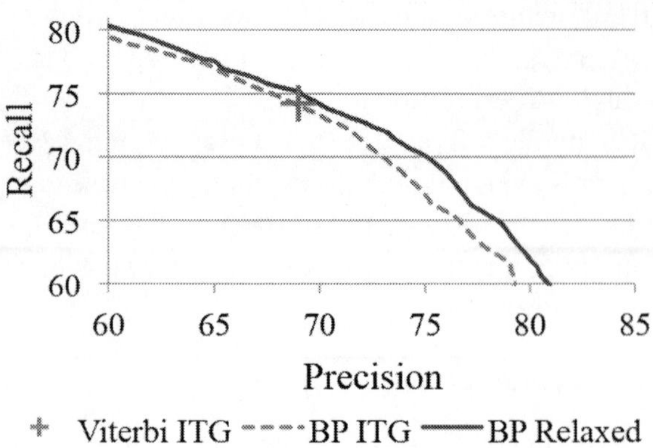

Model	Best Scores			Sentences per Second
	F_1	F_2	F_5	
Viterbi ITG	71.6	73.1	74.0	0.21
BP ITG	71.8	74.8	83.5	0.11
BP Relaxed	**72.6**	**75.2**	**84.5**	**1.15**

Figure 4: Phrase alignment results. A portion of the Precision/Recall curve is plotted for the BP models, with the result from the Viterbi ITG model provided for reference.

Klein, 2010). The BP Relaxed model performs the best of all, consistently achieving higher recall for fixed precision than either of the other models. Because of its lower asymptotic runtime, it is also much faster: over 5 times as fast as the Viterbi ITG model and over 10 times as fast as the BP ITG model.[11]

7.2 Timing

BP approximates marginal posteriors by iteratively updating beliefs for each variable based on current beliefs about other variables. The iterative nature of the algorithm permits us to make an explicit speed/accuracy tradeoff by limiting the number of iterations. We tested this tradeoff by limiting both of the BP models to run for 2, 3, 5, 10, and 20 iterations. The results are shown in Figure 5. Neither model benefits from running more iterations than used to obtain the results in Figure 4, but each can be sped up by a factor of almost 1.5x in exchange for a modest (< 1 F_1) drop in accuracy.

[11]The speed advantage of Viterbi ITG over BP ITG comes from Viterbi ITG's aggressive beaming.

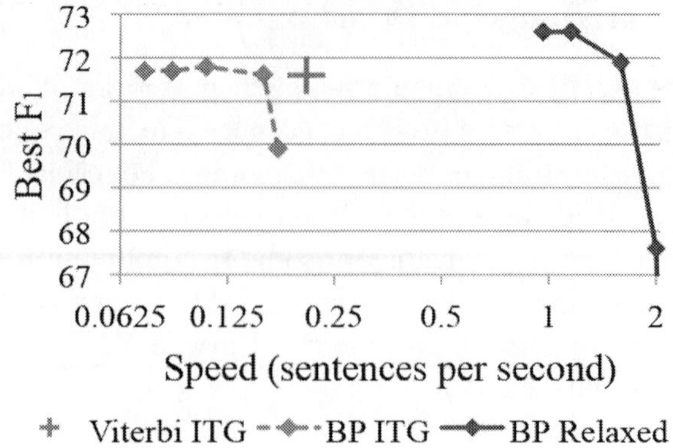

Figure 5: Speed/accuracy tradeoff. The speed axis is on a logarithmic scale. From fastest to slowest, data points correspond to maximums of 2, 5, 10, and 20 BP iterations. F_1 for the BP Relaxed model was very low when limited to 2 iterations, so that data point is outside the visible area of the graph.

Model	BLEU	Relative Improve.	Hours to Train/Align
Baseline	32.8	+0.0	5
Viterbi ITG	33.5	+0.7	831
BP Relaxed	33.6	+0.8	39

Table 2: Machine translation results.

7.3 Translation

We ran translation experiments using Moses (Koehn et al., 2007), which we trained on a 22.1 million word parallel corpus from the GALE program. We compared alignments generated by the baseline HMM model, the Viterbi ITG model and the Relaxed BP model.[12] The systems were tuned and evaluated on sentences up to length 40 from the NIST MT04 and MT05 test sets. The results, shown in Table 2, show that the BP Relaxed model achives a 0.8 BLEU improvement over the HMM baseline, comparable to that of the Viterbi ITG model, but taking a fraction of the time,[13] making the BP Relaxed model a practical alternative for real translation applications.

[12]Following a simplified version of the procedure described by DeNero and Klein (2010), we added rule counts from the HMM alignments to the extraction set aligners' counts.

[13]Some of the speed difference between the BP Relaxed and Viterbi ITG models comes from better parallelizability due to drastically reduced memory overhead of the BP Relaxed model.

8 Conclusion

For performing inference in a state-of-the-art, but inefficient, alignment model, belief propagation is a viable alternative to greedy search methods, such as beaming. BP also results in models that are much more scalable, by reducing the asymptotic complexity of inference. Perhaps most importantly, BP permits the relaxation of artificial constraints that are generally taken for granted as being necessary for efficient inference. In particular, a relatively modest relaxation of the ITG constraint can directly be applied to any model that uses ITG-based inference (e.g. Zhang and Gildea, 2005; Cherry and Lin, 2007; Haghighi et al., 2009).

Acknowledgements

This project is funded by an NSF graduate research fellowship to the first author and by BBN under DARPA contract HR0011-06-C-0022.

References

Necip Fazil Ayan and Bonnie J. Dorr. 2006. Going beyond AER: An extensive analysis of word alignments and their impact on MT. In *ACL*.

Alexandra Birch, Chris Callison-Burch, and Miles Osborne. 2006. Constraining the phrase-based, joint probability statistical translation model. In *AMTA*.

Phil Blunsom, Trevor Cohn, Chris Dyer, and Miles Osborne. 2009. A gibbs sampler for phrasal synchronous grammar induction. In *ACL-IJCNLP*.

Colin Cherry and Dekang Lin. 2007. Inversion transduction grammar for joint phrasal translation modeling. In *NAACL Workshop on Syntax and Structure in Statistical Translation*.

David Chiang. 2007. Hierarchical phrase-based translation. *Computational Linguistics*, 33(2):201–228.

Fabien Cromières and Sadao Kurohashi. 2009. An alignment algorithm using belief propagation and a structure-based distortion model. In *EACL*.

Steve DeNeefe, Kevin Knight, Wei Wang, and Daniel Marcu. 2007. What can syntax-based MT learn from phrase-based MT? In *EMNLP-CoNLL*.

John DeNero and Dan Klein. 2010. Discriminative modeling of extraction sets for machine translation. In *ACL*.

John DeNero, Dan Gillick, James Zhang, and Dan Klein. 2006. Why generative phrase models underperform surface heuristics. In *NAACL Workshop on Statistical Machine Translation*.

John DeNero, Alexandre Bouchard-Côté, and Dan Klein. 2008. Sampling alignment structure under a Bayesian translation model. In *EMNLP*.

John DeNero. 2010. Personal Communication.

John Duchi, Danny Tarlow, Gal Elidan, and Daphne Koller. 2007. Using combinatorial optimization within max-product belief propagation. In *NIPS 2006*.

John Duchi, Elad Hazan, and Yoram Singer. 2010. Adaptive subgradient methods for online learning and stochastic optimization. In *COLT*.

Michel Galley, Mark Hopkins, Kevin Knight, and Daniel Marcu. 2004. What's in a translation rule? In *HLT-NAACL*.

Michel Galley, Jonathan Graehl, Kevin Knight, Daniel Marcu, Steve DeNeefe, Wei Wang, and Ignacio Thayer. 2006. Scalable inference and training of context-rich syntactic translation models. In *COLING-ACL*.

Aria Haghighi, John Blitzer, John DeNero, and Dan Klein. 2009. Better word alignments with supervised ITG models. In *ACL-IJCNLP*.

Philipp Koehn, Franz Josef Och, and Daniel Marcu. 2003. Statistical phrase-based translation. In *ACL*.

Philipp Koehn, Hieu Hoang, Alexandra Birch, Chris Callison-Burch, Marcello Federico, Nicola Bertoldi, Brooke Cowan, Wade Shen, Christine Moran, Richard Zens, Chris Dyer, Ondrej Bojar, Alexandra Constantin, and Evan Herbst. 2007. Moses: Open source toolkit for statistical machine translation. In *ACL*.

Zhifei Li and Sanjeev Khudanpur. 2008. A scalable decoder for parsing-based machine translation with equivalent language model state maintenance. In *ACL SSST*.

Percy Liang, Ben Taskar, and Dan Klein. 2006. Alignment by agreement. In *HLT-NAACL*.

David J.C. MacKay. 2003. *Information theory, inference, and learning algorithms*. Cambridge Univ Press.

Daniel Marcu and Daniel Wong. 2002. A phrase-based, joint probability model for statistical machine translation. In *EMNLP*.

Jan Niehues and Stephan Vogel. 2008. Discriminative word alignment via alignment matrix modeling. In *ACL Workshop on Statistical Machine Translation*.

David A. Smith and Jason Eisner. 2008. Dependency parsing by belief propagation. In *EMNLP*.

Ben Taskar, Simon Lacoste-Julien, and Dan Klein. 2005. A discriminative matching approach to word alignment. In *EMNLP*.

Dekai Wu. 1997. Stochastic inversion transduction grammars and bilingual parsing of parallel corpora. *Computational Linguistics*, 23(3):377–404.

Hao Zhang and Daniel Gildea. 2005. Stochastic lexicalized inversion transduction grammar for alignment. In *ACL*.

Hao Zhang, Chris Quirk, Robert C. Moore, and Daniel Gildea. 2008. Bayesian learning of non-compositional phrases with synchronous parsing. In *ACL:HLT*.

Continuous Space Translation Models with Neural Networks

Le Hai Son and **Alexandre Allauzen** and **François Yvon**
Univ. Paris-Sud, France and LIMSI/CNRS
rue John von Neumann, 91403 Orsay cedex, France
Firstname.Lastname@limsi.fr

Abstract

The use of conventional maximum likelihood estimates hinders the performance of existing phrase-based translation models. For lack of sufficient training data, most models only consider a small amount of context. As a partial remedy, we explore here several continuous space translation models, where translation probabilities are estimated using a continuous representation of translation units in lieu of standard discrete representations. In order to handle a large set of translation units, these representations and the associated estimates are jointly computed using a multi-layer neural network with a SOUL architecture. In small scale and large scale English to French experiments, we show that the resulting models can effectively be trained and used on top of a n-gram translation system, delivering significant improvements in performance.

1 Introduction

The phrase-based approach to statistical machine translation (SMT) is based on the following inference rule, which, given a source sentence $\mathbf{s}$, selects the target sentence $\mathbf{t}$ and the underlying alignment $\mathbf{a}$ maximizing the following term:

$$P(\mathbf{t}, \mathbf{a}|\mathbf{s}) = \frac{1}{Z(\mathbf{s})} \exp\Big(\sum_{k=1}^{K} \lambda_k f_k(\mathbf{s}, \mathbf{t}, \mathbf{a})\Big), \quad (1)$$

where K feature functions (f_k) are weighted by a set of coefficients (λ_k), and Z is a normalizing factor. The phrase-based approach differs from other approaches by the hidden variables of the translation process: the segmentation of a parallel sentence pair into phrase pairs and the associated phrase alignments.

This formulation was introduced in (Zens et al., 2002) as an extension of the word based models (Brown et al., 1993), then later motivated within a discriminative framework (Och and Ney, 2004). One motivation for integrating more feature functions was to improve the estimation of the translation model $P(\mathbf{t}|\mathbf{s})$, which was initially based on relative frequencies, thus yielding poor estimates.

This is because the units of phrase-based models are *phrase pairs*, made of a source and a target phrase; such units are viewed as the events of discrete random variables. The resulting representations of phrases (or words) thus entirely ignore the morphological, syntactic and semantic relationships that exist among those units in both languages. This lack of structure hinders the generalization power of the model and reduces its ability to adapt to other domains. Another consequence is that phrase-based models usually consider a very restricted context[1].

This is a general issue in statistical Natural Language Processing (NLP) and many possible remedies have been proposed in the literature, such as, for instance, using smoothing techniques (Chen and Goodman, 1996), or working with linguistically enriched, or more abstract, representations. In statistical language modeling, another line of research considers numerical representations, trained automatically through the use of neural network (see eg.

[1] typically a small number of preceding phrase pairs for the n-gram based approach (Crego and Mariño, 2006), or no context at all, for the standard approach of (Koehn et al., 2007).

(Collobert et al., 2011)). An influential proposal, in this respect, is the work of (Bengio et al., 2003) on *continuous space language models*. In this approach, n-gram probabilities are estimated using a continuous representation of words in lieu of standard discrete representations. Experimental results, reported for instance in (Schwenk, 2007) show significant improvements in speech recognition applications. Recently, this model has been extended in several promising ways (Mikolov et al., 2011; Kuo et al., 2010; Liu et al., 2011). In the context of SMT, Schwenk et al. (2007) is the first attempt to estimate translation probabilities in a continuous space. However, because of the proposed neural architecture, the authors only consider a very restricted set of translation units, and therefore report only a slight impact on translation performance. The recent proposal of (Le et al., 2011a) seems especially relevant, as it is able, through the use of class-based models, to handle arbitrarily large vocabularies and opens the way to enhanced neural translation models.

In this paper, we explore various neural architectures for translation models and consider three different ways to factor the joint probability $P(\mathbf{s}, \mathbf{t})$ differing by the units (respectively phrase pairs, phrases or words) that are projected in continuous spaces. While these decompositions are theoretically straightforward, they were not considered in the past because of data sparsity issues and of the resulting weaknesses of conventional *maximum likelihood* estimates. Our main contribution is then to show that such joint distributions can be efficiently computed by neural networks, even for very large context sizes; and that their use yields significant performance improvements. These models are evaluated in a n-best rescoring step using the framework of n-gram based systems, within which they integrate easily. Note, however that they could be used with any phrase-based system.

The rest of this paper is organized as follows. We first recollect, in Section 2, the n-gram based approach, and discuss various implementations of this framework. We then describe, in Section 3, the neural architecture developed and explain how it can be made to handle large vocabulary tasks as well as language models over bilingual units. We finally report, in Section 4, experimental results obtained on a large-scale English to French translation task.

2 Variations on the n-gram approach

Even though n-gram translation models can be integrated within standard phrase-based systems (Niehues et al., 2011), the n-gram based framework provides a more convenient way to introduce our work and has also been used to build the baseline systems used in our experiments. In the n-gram based approach (Casacuberta and Vidal, 2004; Mariño et al., 2006; Crego and Mariño, 2006), translation is divided in two steps: a source reordering step and a translation step. Source reordering is based on a set of learned rewrite rules that non-deterministically reorder the input words so as to match the target order thereby generating a lattice of possible reorderings. Translation then amounts to finding the most likely path in this lattice using a n-gram translation model [2] of *bilingual units*.

2.1 The standard n-gram translation model

n-gram translation models (TMs) rely on a specific decomposition of the joint probability $P(\mathbf{s}, \mathbf{t})$, where $\mathbf{s}$ is a sequence of I reordered source words $(s_1, ..., s_I)$ and $\mathbf{t}$ contains J target words $(t_1, ..., t_J)$. This sentence pair is further assumed to be decomposed into a sequence of L bilingual units called *tuples* defining a joint segmentation: $(\mathbf{s}, \mathbf{t}) = u_1, ..., u_L$. In the approach of (Mariño et al., 2006), this segmentation is a by-product of source reordering, and ultimately derives from initial word and phrase alignments. In this framework, the basic translation units are *tuples*, which are the analogous of phrase pairs, and represent a matching $u = (\overline{s}, \overline{t})$ between a source $\overline{s}$ and a target $\overline{t}$ phrase (see Figure 1). Using the n-gram assumption, the joint probability of a segmented sentence pair decomposes as:

$$P(\mathbf{s}, \mathbf{t}) = \prod_{i=1}^{L} P(u_i | u_{i-1}, ..., u_{i-n+1}) \quad (2)$$

A first issue with this model is that the elementary units are bilingual pairs, which means that the underlying vocabulary, hence the number of parameters, can be quite large, even for small translation tasks. Due to data sparsity issues, such models are bound

[2] Like in the standard phrase-based approach, the translation process also involves additional feature functions that are presented below.

to face severe estimation problems. Another problem with (2) is that the source and target sides play symmetric roles, whereas the source side is known, and the target side must be predicted.

2.2 A factored n-gram translation model

To overcome some of these issues, the n-gram probability in equation (2) can be factored by decomposing tuples in two (source and target) parts :

$$\begin{aligned} P(u_i|u_{i-1},...,u_{i-n+1}) = \\ P(\bar{t}_i|\bar{s}_i, \bar{s}_{i-1}, \bar{t}_{i-1}, ..., \bar{s}_{i-n+1}, \bar{t}_{i-n+1}) \\ \times P(\bar{s}_i|\bar{s}_{i-1}, \bar{t}_{i-1} ..., \bar{s}_{i-n+1}, \bar{t}_{i-n+1}) \end{aligned} \quad (3)$$

Decomposition (3) involves two models: the first term represents a TM, the second term is best viewed as a reordering model. In this formulation, the TM only predicts the target phrase, given its source and target contexts.

Another benefit of this formulation is that the elementary events now correspond either to source or to target phrases, but never to pairs of such phrases. The underlying vocabulary is thus obtained as the union, rather than the cross product, of phrase inventories. Finally note that the n-gram probability $P(u_i|u_{i-1},...,u_{i-n+1})$ could also factor as:

$$\begin{aligned} P(\bar{s}_i|\bar{t}_i, \bar{s}_{i-1}, \bar{t}_{i-1}, ..., \bar{s}_{i-n+1}, \bar{t}_{i-n+1}) \\ \times P(\bar{t}_i|\bar{s}_{i-1}, \bar{t}_{i-1}, ..., \bar{s}_{i-n+1}, \bar{t}_{i-n+1}) \end{aligned} \quad (4)$$

2.3 A word factored translation model

A more radical way to address the data sparsity issues is to take (source and target) words as the basic units of the n-gram TM. This may seem to be a step backwards, since the transition from word (Brown et al., 1993) to phrase-based models (Zens et al., 2002) is considered as one of the main recent improvement in MT. One important motivation for considering phrases rather than words was to capture local context in translation and reordering. It should then be stressed that the decomposition of phrases in words is only re-introduced here as a way to mitigate the parameter estimation problems. Translation units are still pairs of *phrases*, derived from a bilingual segmentation in tuples synchronizing the source and target n-gram streams, as defined by equation (3). In fact, the estimation policy described in section 3 will actually allow us to design n-gram models with *longer contexts* than is typically possible in the conventional n-gram approach.

Let s_i^k denote the kth word of source tuple $\bar{s}_i$. Considering again the example of Figure 1, s_{11}^1 is to the source word *nobel*, s_{11}^4 is to the source word *paix*, and similarly t_{11}^2 is the target word *peace*. We finally denote $h^{n-1}(t_i^k)$ the sequence made of the $n-1$ words preceding t_i^k in the target sentence: in Figure 1, $h^3(t_{11}^2)$ thus refers to the three word context *receive the nobel* associated with the target word *peace*. Using these notations, equation (3) is rewritten as:

$$\begin{aligned} P(\mathbf{s}, \mathbf{t}) = \prod_{i=1}^{L} \Big[\prod_{k=1}^{|\bar{t}_i|} P(t_i^k | h^{n-1}(t_i^k), h^{n-1}(s_{i+1}^1)) \\ \times \prod_{k=1}^{|\bar{s}_i|} P(s_i^k | h^{n-1}(t_i^1), h^{n-1}(s_i^k)) \Big] \end{aligned} \quad (5)$$

This decomposition relies on the n-gram assumption, this time at the word level. Therefore, this model estimates the joint probability of a sentence pair using two sliding windows of length n, one for each language; however, the moves of these windows remain synchronized by the tuple segmentation. Moreover, the context is not limited to the current phrase, and continues to include words in adjacent phrases. Using the example of Figure 1, the contribution of the target phrase $\bar{t}_{11}$ = *nobel, peace* to $P(\mathbf{s}, \mathbf{t})$ using a 3- gram model is

$$\begin{aligned} P(\text{nobel}|[\text{receive, the}], [\text{la, paix}]) \\ \times P(\text{peace}|[\text{the, nobel}], [\text{la, paix}]). \end{aligned}$$

Likewise, the contribution of the source phrase $\bar{s}_{11}$ =*nobel, de, la, paix* is:

$$\begin{aligned} P(\text{nobel}|[\text{receive, the}], [\text{recevoir,le}]) \\ \times P(\text{de}|[\text{receive, the}], [\text{le,nobel}]) \\ \times P(\text{la}|[\text{receive, the}], [\text{nobel, de}]) \\ \times P(\text{paix}|[\text{receive, the}], [\text{de,la}]). \end{aligned}$$

A benefit of this new formulation is that the involved vocabularies only contain words, and are thus much smaller. These models are thus less bound to be affected by data sparsity issues. While the TM defined by equation (5) derives from equation (3), a variation can be equivalently derived from equation (4).

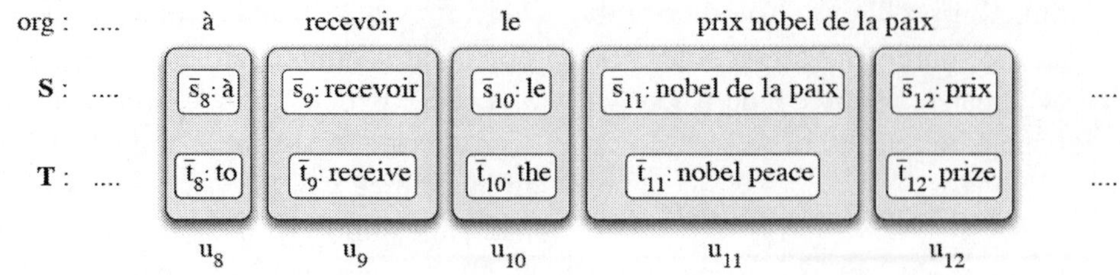

Figure 1: Extract of a French-English sentence pair segmented in bilingual units. The original (*org*) French sentence appears at the top of the figure, just above the reordered source $\mathbf{s}$ and target $\mathbf{t}$. The pair $(\mathbf{s}, \mathbf{t})$ decomposes into a sequence of L bilingual units (*tuples*) $u_1, ..., u_L$. Each tuple u_i contains a source and a target phrase: $\overline{s}_i$ and $\overline{t}_i$.

3 The SOUL model

In the previous section, we defined three different n-gram translation models, based respectively on equations (2), (3) and (5). As discussed above, a major issue with such models is to reliably estimate their parameters, the numbers of which grow exponentially with the order of the model. This problem is aggravated in natural language processing, due to well known data sparsity issues. In this work, we take advantage of the recent proposal of (Le et al., 2011a): using a specific neural network architecture (the *Structured OUtput Layer* model), it becomes possible to handle large vocabulary language modeling tasks, a solution that we adapt here to MT.

3.1 Language modeling in a continuous space

Let $\mathcal{V}$ be a finite vocabulary, n-gram language models (LMs) define distributions over finite sequences of tokens (typically words) w_1^L in $\mathcal{V}^+$ as follows:

$$P(w_1^L) = \prod_{i=1}^{L} P(w_i | w_{i-n+1}^{i-1}) \tag{6}$$

Modeling the joint distribution of several discrete random variables (such as words in a sentence) is difficult, especially in NLP applications where $\mathcal{V}$ typically contains dozens of thousands words.

In spite of the simplifying n-gram assumption, maximum likelihood estimation remains unreliable and tends to underestimate the probability of very rare n-grams. Smoothing techniques, such as Kneser-Ney and Witten-Bell back-off schemes (see (Chen and Goodman, 1996) for an empirical overview, and (Teh, 2006) for a Bayesian interpretation), perform back-off to lower order distributions, thus providing an estimate for the probability of these unseen events.

One of the most successful alternative to date is to use *distributed word representations* (Bengio et al., 2003), where distributionally similar words are represented as neighbors in a continuous space. This turns n-grams distributions into smooth functions of the word representations. These representations and the associated estimates are jointly computed in a multi-layer neural network architecture. Figure 2 provides a partial representation of this kind of model and helps figuring out their principles. To compute the probability $P(w_i | w_{i-n+1}^{i-1})$, the $n-1$ context words are projected in the same continuous space using a shared matrix R; these continuous word representations are then concatenated to build a single vector that represents the context; after a non-linear transformation, the probability distribution is computed using a softmax layer.

The major difficulty with the neural network approach remains the complexity of inference and training, which largely depends on the size of the output vocabulary (i.e. the number of words that have to be predicted). One practical solution is to restrict the output vocabulary to a short-list composed of the most frequent words (Schwenk, 2007). However, the usual size of the short-list is under 20k, which does not seem sufficient to faithfully represent the translation models of section 2.

3.2 Principles of SOUL

To circumvent this problem, Structured Output Layer (SOUL) LMs are introduced in (Le et al., 2011a). Following Mnih and Hinton (2008), the SOUL model combines the neural network approach with a class-based LM (Brown et al., 1992). Structuring the output layer and using word class information makes the estimation of distributions over the entire vocabulary computationally feasible.

To meet this goal, the output vocabulary is structured as a clustering tree, where each word belongs to only one class and its associated sub-classes. If w_i denotes the ith word in a sentence, the sequence $c_{1:D}(w_i) = c_1, \ldots, c_D$ encodes the path for word w_i in the clustering tree, with D being the depth of the tree, $c_d(w_i)$ a class or sub-class assigned to w_i, and $c_D(w_i)$ being the leaf associated with w_i (the word itself). The probability of w_i given its history h can then be computed as:

$$P(w_i|h) = P(c_1(w_i)|h) \times \prod_{d=2}^{D} P(c_d(w_i)|h, c_{1:d-1}). \quad (7)$$

There is a softmax function at each level of the tree and each word ends up forming its own class (a leaf).

The SOUL model, represented on Figure 2, is thus the same as for the standard model up to the output layer. The main difference lies in the output structure which involves several layers with a softmax activation function. The first *(class layer)* estimates the class probability $P(c_1(w_i)|h)$, while other output *sub-class layers* estimate the sub-class probabilities $P(c_d(w_i)|h, c_{1:d-1})$. Finally, the *word layers* estimate the word probabilities $P(c_D(w_i)|h, c_{1:D-1})$. Words in the short-list remain special, since each of them represents a (final) class.

Training a SOUL model can be achieved by maximizing the log-likelihood of the parameters on some training corpus. Following (Bengio et al., 2003), this optimization is performed by stochastic back-propagation. Details of the training procedure can be found in (Le et al., 2011b).

Neural network architectures are also interesting as they can easily handle larger contexts than typical n-gram models. In the SOUL architecture, enlarging the context mainly consists in increasing the size of the projection layer, which corresponds to a simple look-up operation. Increasing the context length at the input layer thus only causes a linear growth in complexity in the worst case (Schwenk, 2007).

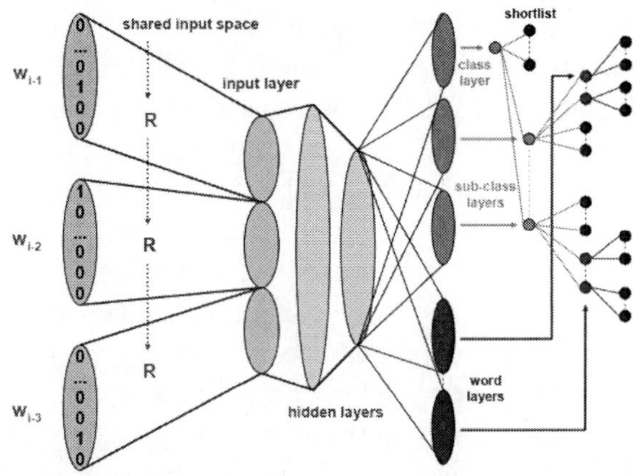

Figure 2: *The architecture of a SOUL Neural Network language model in the case of a 4-gram model.*

3.3 Translation modeling with SOUL

The SOUL architecture was used successfully to deliver (monolingual) LMs probabilities for speech recognition (Le et al., 2011a) and machine translation (Allauzen et al., 2011) applications. In fact, using this architecture, it is possible to estimate n-gram distributions for any kind of discrete random variables, such as a phrase or a tuple. The SOUL architecture can thus be readily used as a replacement for the standard n-gram TM described in section 2.1. This is because all the random variables are events over the same set of tuples.

Adopting this architecture for the other n-gram TM respectively described by equations (3) and (5) is more tricky, as they involve two different languages and thus two different vocabularies: the predicted unit is a target phrase (resp. word), whereas the context is made of both source and target phrases (resp. words). A subsequent modification of the SOUL architecture was thus performed to make up for "mixed" contexts: rather than projecting all the context words or phrases into the same continuous space (using the matrix R, see Figure 2), we used two different projection matrices, one for each language. The input layer is thus composed of two vectors in two different spaces; these two representations are then combined through the hidden layer, the other layers remaining unchanged.

4 Experimental Results

We now turn to an experimental comparison of the models introduced in Section 2. We first describe the tasks and data that were used, before presenting our n-gram based system and baseline set-up. Our results are finally presented and discussed.

Let us first emphasize that the design and integration of a SOUL model for large SMT tasks is far from easy, given the computational cost of computing n-gram probabilities, a task that is performed repeatedly during the search of the best translation. Our solution was to resort to a two pass approach: the first pass uses a conventional back-off n-gram model to produce a k-best list (the k most likely translations); in the second pass, the probability of a m-gram SOUL model is computed for each hypothesis, added as a new feature and the k-best list is accordingly reordered[3]. In all the following experiments, we used a fixed context size for SOUL of $m = 10$, and used $k = 300$.

4.1 Tasks and corpora

The two tasks considered in our experiments are adapted from the text translation track of IWSLT 2011 from English to French (the "TED" talk task): a *small data* scenario where the only training data is a small in-domain corpus; and a large scale condition using all the available training data. In this article, we only provide a short overview of the task; all the necessary details regarding this evaluation campaign are on the official website[4].

The in-domain training data consists of $107,058$ sentence pairs, whereas for the large scale task, all the data available for the WMT 2011 evaluation[5] are added. For the latter task, the available parallel data includes a large Web corpus, referred to as the GigaWord parallel corpus. This corpus is very noisy and is accordingly filtered using a simple perplexity criterion as explained in (Allauzen et al., 2011). The total amount of training data is approximately 11.5 million sentence pairs for the bilingual part, and about 2.5 billion of words for the monolingual part. As the provided development data was quite small, development and test set were inverted, and we finally used a development set of 1,664 sentences, and a test set of 934 sentences. The table 1 provides the sizes of the different vocabularies. The n-gram TMs are estimated over a training corpus composed of tuple sequences. Tuples are extracted from the word-aligned parallel data (using MGIZA++[6] with default settings) in such a way that a unique segmentation of the bilingual corpus is achieved, allowing to directly estimate bilingual n-gram models (see (Crego and Mariño, 2006) for details).

Model	**Vocabulary size**			
	Small task		*Large task*	
	src	*trg*	*src*	*trg*
Standard	$317k$		$8847k$	
Phrase factored	$96k$	$131k$	$4262k$	$3972k$
Word factored	$45k$	$53k$	$505k$	$492k$

Table 1: Vocabulary sizes for the English to French tasks obtained with various SOUL translation (TM) models. For the factored models, sizes are indicated for both source (*src*) and target (*trg*) sides.

4.2 n-gram based translation system

The n-gram based system used here is based on an open source implementation described in (Crego et al., 2011). In a nutshell, the TM is implemented as a stochastic finite-state transducer trained using a n-gram model of (source, target) pairs as described in section 2.1. Training this model requires to reorder source sentences so as to match the target word order. This is performed by a non-deterministic finite-state reordering model, which uses part-of-speech information generated by the TreeTagger to generalize reordering patterns beyond lexical regularities.

In addition to the TM, fourteen feature functions are included: a *target-language model*; four *lexicon models*; six *lexicalized reordering models* (Tillmann, 2004; Crego et al., 2011); a distance-based *distortion model*; and finally a *word-bonus model* and a *tuple-bonus model*. The four *lexicon models* are similar to the ones used in standard phrase-based systems: two scores correspond to the relative frequencies of the tuples and two lexical weights are estimated from the automatically generated word

[3] The probability estimated with the SOUL model is added as a new feature to the score of an hypothesis given by Equation 1. The coefficients are retuned before the reranking step.

[4] iwslt2011.org

[5] www.statmt.org/wmt11/

[6] geek.kyloo.net/software

alignments. The weights associated to feature functions are optimally combined using the Minimum Error Rate Training (MERT) (Och, 2003). All the results in BLEU are obtained as an average of 4 optimization runs[7].

For the small task, the target LM is a standard 4-gram model estimated with the Kneser-Ney discounting scheme interpolated with lower order models (Kneser and Ney, 1995; Chen and Goodman, 1996), while for the large task, the target LM is obtained by linear interpolation of several 4-gram models (see (Lavergne et al., 2011) for details). As for the TM, all the available parallel corpora were simply pooled together to train a 3-gram model. Results obtained with this large-scale system were found to be comparable to some of the best official submissions.

4.3 Small task evaluation

Table 2 summarizes the results obtained with the baseline and different SOUL models, TMs and a target LM. The first comparison concerns the standard n-gram TM, defined by equation (2), when estimated conventionally or as a SOUL model. Adding the latter model yields a slight BLEU improvement of 0.5 point over the baseline. When the SOUL TM is phrased factored as defined in equation (3) the gain is of 0.9 BLEU point instead. This difference can be explained by the smaller vocabularies used in the latter model, and its improved robustness to data sparsity issues. Additional gains are obtained with the word factored TM defined by equation (5): a BLEU improvement of 0.8 point over the phrase factored TM and of 1.7 point over the baseline are respectively achieved. We assume that the observed improvements can be explained by the joint effect of a better smoothing and a longer context.

The comparison with the condition where we only use a SOUL target LM is interesting as well. Here, the use of the word factored TM still yields to a 0.6 BLEU improvement. This result shows that there is an actual benefit in smoothing the TM estimates, rather than only focus on the LM estimates.

Table 3 reports a comparison among the different components and variations of the word factored TM. In the upper part of the table, the model defined by equation (5) is evaluated component by component: first the translation term $P\big(t_i^k|h^{n-1}(t_i^k), h^{n-1}(s_{i+1}^1)\big)$, then its distortion counterpart $P\big(s_i^k|h^{n-1}(t_i^1), h^{n-1}(s_i^k)\big)$ and finally their combination, which yields the joint probability of the sentence pair. Here, we observe that the best improvement is obtained with the translation term, which is 0.7 BLEU point better than the latter term. Moreover, the use of just a translation term only yields a BLEU score equal to the one obtained with the SOUL target LM, and its combination with the distortion term is decisive to attain the additional gain of 0.6 BLEU point. The lower part of the table provides the same comparison, but for the variation of the word factored TM. Besides a similar trend, we observe that this variation delivers slightly lower results. This can be explained by the restricted context used by the translation term which no longer includes the current source phrase or word.

[7]The standard deviations are below 0.1 and thus omitted in the reported results.

Model	**BLEU**	
	dev	*test*
Baseline	31.4	25.8
Adding a SOUL model		
Standard TM	32.0	26.3
Phrase factored TM	32.7	26.7
Word factored TM	33.6	**27.5**
Target LM	32.6	26.9

Table 2: Results for the small English to French task obtained with the baseline system and with various SOUL translation (TM) or target language (LM) models.

Model	**BLEU**	
	dev	*test*
Adding a SOUL model		
+ $P\big(t_i^k|h^{n-1}(t_i^k), h^{n-1}(s_{i+1}^1)\big)$	32.6	**26.9**
+ $P\big(s_i^k|h^{n-1}(t_i^1), h^{n-1}(s_i^k)\big)$	32.1	26.2
+ the combination of both	33.2	27.5
+ $P\big(s_i^k|h^{n-1}(s_i^k), h^{n-1}(t_{i+1}^1)\big)$	31.7	26.1
+ $P\big(t_i^k|h^{n-1}(s_i^1), h^{n-1}(t_i^k)\big)$	32.7	**26.8**
+ the combination of both	33.4	27.2

Table 3: Comparison of the different components and variations of the word factored translation model.

Model	BLEU	
	dev	*test*
Baseline	33.7	28.2
Adding a word factored SOUL TM		
+ in-domain TM	35.2	29.4
+ out-of-domain TM	34.8	29.1
+ out-of-domain adapted TM	35.5	**29.8**
Adding a SOUL LM		
+ out-of-domain adapted LM	35.0	29.2

Table 4: Results for the large English to French translation task obtained by adding various SOUL translation and language models (see text for details).

4.4 Large task evaluation

For the large-scale setting, the training material increases drastically with the use of the additional out-of-domain data for the baseline models. Results are summarized in Table 4. The first observation is the large increase of BLEU (+2.4 points) for the baseline system over the small-scale baseline. For this task, only the word factored TM is evaluated since it significantly outperforms the others on the small task (see section 4.3).

In a first scenario, we use a word factored TM, trained only on the small in-domain corpus. Even though the training corpus of the baseline TM is one hundred times larger than this small in-domain data, adding the SOUL TM still yields a BLEU increase of 1.2 point[8]. In a second scenario, we increase the training corpus for the SOUL, and include parts of the out-of-domain data (the WMT part). The resulting BLEU score is here slightly worse than the one obtained with just the in-domain TM, yet delivering improved results with the respect to the baseline.

In a last attempt, we amended the training regime of the neural network. In a fist step, we trained conventionally a SOUL model using the same out-of-domain parallel data as before. We then *adapted* this model by running five additional epochs of the back-propagation algorithm using the in-domain data. Using this adapted model yielded our best results to date with a BLEU improvement of 1.6 points over the baseline results. Moreover, the gains obtained using this simple domain adaptation strategy are respectively of +0.4 and +0.8 BLEU, as compared with the small in-domain model and the large out-of-domain model. These results show that the SOUL TM can scale efficiently and that its structure is well suited for domain adaptation.

[8]Note that the in-domain data was already included in the training corpus of the baseline TM.

5 Related work

To the best of our knowledge, the first work on machine translation in continuous spaces is (Schwenk et al., 2007), where the authors introduced the model referred here to as the the standard n-gram translation model in Section 2.1. This model is an extension of the continuous space language model of (Bengio et al., 2003), the basic unit is the tuple (or equivalently the phrase pair). The resulting vocabulary being too large to be handled by neural networks without a structured output layer, the authors had thus to restrict the set of the predicted units to a 8k short-list . Moreover, in (Zamora-Martinez et al., 2010), the authors propose a tighter integration of a continuous space model with a n-gram approach but only for the target LM.

A different approach, described in (Sarikaya et al., 2008), divides the problem in two parts: first the continuous representation is obtained by an adaptation of the Latent Semantic Analysis; then a Gaussian mixture model is learned using this continuous representation and included in a hidden Markov model. One problem with this approach is the separation between the training of the continuous representation on the one hand, and the training of the translation model on the other hand. In comparison, in our approach, the representation and the prediction are learned in a joined fashion.

Other ways to address the data sparsity issues faced by translation model were also proposed in the literature. Smoothing is obviously one possibility (Foster et al., 2006). Another is to use *factored language models*, introduced in (Bilmes and Kirchhoff, 2003), then adapted for translation models in (Koehn and Hoang, 2007; Crego and Yvon, 2010). Such approaches require to use external linguistic analysis tools which are error prone; moreover, they did not seem to bring clear improvements, even when translating into morphologically rich languages.

6 Conclusion

In this paper, we have presented possible ways to use a neural network architecture as a translation model. A first contribution was to produce the first large-scale neural translation model, implemented here in the framework of the n-gram based models, taking advantage of a specific hierarchical architecture (SOUL). By considering several decompositions of the joint probability of a sentence pair, several bilingual translation models were presented and discussed. As it turned out, using a factorization which clearly distinguishes the source and target sides, and only involves word probabilities, proved an effective remedy to data sparsity issues and provided significant improvements over the baseline. Moreover, this approach was also experimented within the systems we submitted to the shared translation task of the seventh workshop on statistical machine translation (WMT 2012). These experimentations in a large scale setup and for different language pair corroborate the improvements reported in this article.

We also investigated various training regimes for these models in a cross domain adaptation setting. Our results show that adapting an out-of-domain SOUL TM is both an effective and very fast way to perform bilingual model adaptation. Adding up all these novelties finally brought us a 1.6 BLEU point improvement over the baseline. Even though our experiments were carried out only within the framework of n-gram based MT systems, using such models in other systems is straightforward. Future work will thus aim at introducing them into conventional phrase-based systems, such as Moses (Koehn et al., 2007). Given that Moses only implicitly uses n-gram based information, adding SOUL translation models is expected to be even more helpful.

Acknowledgments

This work was partially funded by the French State agency for innovation (OSEO), in the Quaero Programme.

References

Alexandre Allauzen, Gilles Adda, Hélène Bonneau-Maynard, Josep M. Crego, Hai-Son Le, Aurélien Max, Adrien Lardilleux, Thomas Lavergne, Artem Sokolov, Guillaume Wisniewski, and François Yvon. 2011. LIMSI @ WMT11. In *Proceedings of the Sixth Workshop on Statistical Machine Translation*, pages 309–315, Edinburgh, Scotland.

Yoshua Bengio, Réjean Ducharme, Pascal Vincent, and Christian Janvin. 2003. A neural probabilistic language model. *JMLR*, 3:1137–1155.

Jeff A. Bilmes and Katrin Kirchhoff. 2003. Factored language models and generalized parallel backoff. In *NAACL '03: Proceedings of the 2003 Conference of the North American Chapter of the Association for Computational Linguistics on Human Language Technology*, pages 4–6.

Peter F. Brown, Peter V. deSouza, Robert L. Mercer, Vincent J. Della Pietra, and Jenifer C. Lai. 1992. Class-based n-gram models of natural language. *Computational Linguistics*, 18(4):467–479.

Peter F. Brown, Vincent J. Della Pietra, Stephen A. Della Pietra, and Robert L. Mercer. 1993. The mathematics of statistical machine translation: parameter estimation. *Computational Linguistics*, 19(2):263–311.

Francesco Casacuberta and Enrique Vidal. 2004. Machine translation with inferred stochastic finite-state transducers. *Computational Linguistics*, 30(3):205–225.

Stanley F. Chen and Joshua Goodman. 1996. An empirical study of smoothing techniques for language modeling. In *Proc. ACL'96*, pages 310–318, San Francisco.

Ronan Collobert, Jason Weston, Léon Bottou, Michael Karlen, Koray Kavukcuoglu, and Pavel Kuksa. 2011. Natural language processing (almost) from scratch. *Journal of Machine Learning Research*, 12:2493–2537.

Josep M. Crego and José B. Mariño. 2006. Improving statistical MT by coupling reordering and decoding. *Machine Translation*, 20(3):199–215.

Josep M. Crego and François Yvon. 2010. Factored bilingual n-gram language models for statistical machine translation. *Machine Translation*, pages 1–17.

Josep M. Crego, François Yvon, and José B. Mariño. 2011. N-code: an open-source Bilingual N-gram SMT Toolkit. *Prague Bulletin of Mathematical Linguistics*, 96:49–58.

George Foster, Roland Kuhn, and Howard Johnson. 2006. Phrase-table smoothing for statistical machine translation. In *Proceedings of the 2006 Conference on Empirical Methods in Natural Language Processing*, pages 53–61, Sydney, Australia.

Reinhard Kneser and Hermann Ney. 1995. Improved backing-off for m-gram language modeling. In *Proceedings of the IEEE International Conference on Acoustics, Speech and Signal Processing*, volume I, pages 181–184, Detroit, Michigan.

Philipp Koehn and Hieu Hoang. 2007. Factored translation models. In *Proceedings of the 2007 Joint Conference on Empirical Methods in Natural Language Processing and Computational Natural Language Learning (EMNLP-CoNLL)*, pages 868–876.

Philipp Koehn, Hieu Hoang, Alexandra Birch, Chris Callison-Burch, Marcello Federico, Nicola Bertoldi, Brooke Cowan, Wade Shen, Christine Moran, Richard Zens, Chris Dyer, Ondrej Bojar, Alexandra Constantin, and Evan Herbst. 2007. Moses: Open source toolkit for statistical machine translation. In *Proc. ACL'07*, pages 177–180, Prague, Czech Republic.

Hong-Kwang Kuo, Lidia Mangu, Ahmad Emami, and Imed Zitouni. 2010. Morphological and syntactic features for Arabic speech recognition. In *Proc. ICASSP 2010*.

Thomas Lavergne, Alexandre Allauzen, Hai-Son Le, and François Yvon. 2011. LIMSI's experiments in domain adaptation for IWSLT11. In *Proceedings of the eight International Workshop on Spoken Language Translation (IWSLT), San Francisco, CA*.

Hai-Son Le, Ilya Oparin, Alexandre Allauzen, Jean-Luc Gauvain, and François Yvon. 2011a. Structured output layer neural network language model. In *Proceedings of ICASSP'11*, pages 5524–5527.

Hai-Son Le, Ilya Oparin, Abdel Messaoudi, Alexandre Allauzen, Jean-Luc Gauvain, and François Yvon. 2011b. Large vocabulary SOUL neural network language models. In *Proceedings of InterSpeech 2011*.

Xunying Liu, Mark J. F. Gales, and Philip C. Woodland. 2011. Improving lvcsr system combination using neural network language model cross adaptation. In *INTERSPEECH*, pages 2857–2860.

José B. Mariño, Rafael E. Banchs, Josep M. Crego, Adrià de Gispert, Patrick Lambert, José A.R. Fonollosa, and Marta R. Costa-Jussà. 2006. N-gram-based machine translation. *Computational Linguistics*, 32(4):527–549.

Tomas Mikolov, Stefan Kombrink, Lukas Burget, Jan Cernocký, and Sanjeev Khudanpur. 2011. Extensions of recurrent neural network language model. In *Proc. of ICASSP'11*, pages 5528–5531.

Andriy Mnih and Geoffrey E Hinton. 2008. A scalable hierarchical distributed language model. In D. Koller, D. Schuurmans, Y. Bengio, and L. Bottou, editors, *Advances in Neural Information Processing Systems 21*, volume 21, pages 1081–1088.

Jan Niehues, Teresa Herrmann, Stephan Vogel, and Alex Waibel. 2011. Wider context by using bilingual language models in machine translation. In *Proceedings of the Sixth Workshop on Statistical Machine Translation*, pages 198–206, Edinburgh, Scotland. Association for Computational Linguistics.

Franz Josef Och and Hermann Ney. 2004. The alignment template approach to statistical machine translation. *Computational Linguistics*, 30:417–449, December.

Franz Josef Och. 2003. Minimum error rate training in statistical machine translation. In *ACL '03: Proc. of the 41st Annual Meeting on Association for Computational Linguistics*, pages 160–167.

Ruhi Sarikaya, Yonggang Deng, Mohamed Afify, Brian Kingsbury, and Yuqing Gao. 2008. Machine translation in continuous space. In *Proceedings of Interspeech*, pages 2350–2353, Brisbane, Australia.

Holger Schwenk, Marta R. Costa-Jussà, and José A.R. Fonollosa. 2007. Smooth bilingual n-gram translation. In *Proceedings of the 2007 Joint Conference on Empirical Methods in Natural Language Processing and Computational Natural Language Learning (EMNLP-CoNLL)*, pages 430–438, Prague, Czech Republic.

Holger Schwenk. 2007. Continuous space language models. *Computer Speech and Language*, 21(3):492–518.

Yeh W. Teh. 2006. A hierarchical Bayesian language model based on Pitman-Yor processes. In *Proc. of ACL'06*, pages 985–992, Sidney, Australia.

Christoph Tillmann. 2004. A unigram orientation model for statistical machine translation. In *Proceedings of HLT-NAACL 2004*, pages 101–104.

Francisco Zamora-Martinez, Maria José Castro-Bleda, and Holger Schwenk. 2010. N-gram-based Machine Translation enhanced with Neural Networks for the French-English BTEC-IWSLT'10 task. In *Proceedings of the seventh International Workshop on Spoken Language Translation (IWSLT)*, pages 45–52.

Richard Zens, Franz Josef Och, and Hermann Ney. 2002. Phrase-based statistical machine translation. In *KI '02: Proceedings of the 25th Annual German Conference on AI*, pages 18–32, London, UK. Springer-Verlag.

Machine Translation of Arabic Dialects

Rabih Zbib, Erika Malchiodi, Jacob Devlin, David Stallard, Spyros Matsoukas, Richard Schwartz, John Makhoul, Omar F. Zaidan†, Chris Callison-Burch‡
Raytheon BBN Technologies, Cambridge MA
†Microsoft Research, Redmond WA
‡Johns Hopkins University, Baltimore MD

Abstract

Arabic Dialects present many challenges for machine translation, not least of which is the lack of data resources. We use crowdsourcing to cheaply and quickly build Levantine-English and Egyptian-English parallel corpora, consisting of 1.1M words and 380k words, respectively. The dialectal sentences are selected from a large corpus of Arabic web text, and translated using Amazon's Mechanical Turk. We use this data to build Dialectal Arabic MT systems, and find that small amounts of dialectal data have a dramatic impact on translation quality. When translating Egyptian and Levantine test sets, our Dialectal Arabic MT system performs 6.3 and 7.0 BLEU points higher than a Modern Standard Arabic MT system trained on a 150M-word Arabic-English parallel corpus.

1 Introduction

The Arabic language is a well-known example of *diglossia* (Ferguson, 1959), where the formal variety of the language, which is taught in schools and used in written communication and formal speech (religion, politics, etc.) differs significantly in its grammatical properties from the informal varieties that are acquired natively, which are used mostly for verbal communication. The spoken varieties of the Arabic language (which we refer to collectively as *Dialectal Arabic*) differ widely among themselves, depending on the geographic distribution and the socio-economic conditions of the speakers, and they diverge from the formal variety known as Modern Standard Arabic (MSA) (Embarki and Ennaji, 2011). Significant differences in the phonology, morphology, lexicon and even syntax render some of these varieties mutually incomprehensible.

The use of Dialectal Arabic has traditionally been confined to informal personal speech, while writing has been done almost exclusively using MSA (or its ancestor *Classical Arabic*). This situation is quickly changing, however, with the rapid proliferation of social media in the Arabic-speaking part of the world, where much of the communication is composed in dialect. The focus of the Arabic NLP research community, which has been mostly on MSA, is turning towards dealing with informal communication, with the introduction of the DARPA BOLT program. This new focus presents new challenges, the most obvious of which is the lack of dialectal linguistic resources. Dialectal text, which is usually user-generated, is also noisy, and the lack of standardized orthography means that users often improvise spelling. Dialectal data also includes a wider range of topics than formal data genres, such as newswire, due to its informal nature. These challenges require innovative solutions if NLP applications are to deal with Dialectal Arabic effectively.

In this paper:

- We describe a process for cheaply and quickly developing parallel corpora for Levantine-English and Egyptian-English using Amazon's Mechanical Turk crowdsourcing service (§3).
- We use the data to perform a variety of machine translation experiments showing the impact of morphological analysis, the limited value of adding MSA parallel data, the usefulness of cross-dialect training, and the effects of translating from dialect to MSA to English (§4).

We find that collecting dialect translations has a low cost ($0.03/word) and that relatively small amounts of data has a dramatic impact on translation quality. When trained on 1.5M words of dialectal data, our system performs 6.3 to 7.0 BLEU points higher than when it is trained on 100 times more MSA data from a mismatching domain.

2 Previous Work

Existing work on natural language processing of Dialectal Arabic text, including machine translation, is somewhat limited. Previous research on Dialectal Arabic MT has focused on normalizing dialectal input words into MSA equivalents before translating to English, and they deal with inputs that contain a limited fraction of dialectal words. Sawaf (2010) normalized the dialectal words in a hybrid (rule-based and statistical) MT system, by performing a combination of character- and morpheme-level mappings. They then translated the normalized source to English using a hybrid MT or alternatively a Statistical MT system. They tested their method on proprietary test sets, observing about 1 BLEU point (Papineni et al., 2002) increase on broadcast news/conversation and about 2 points on web text. Salloum and Habash (2011) reduced the proportion of dialectal out-of-vocabulary (OOV) words also by mapping their affixed morphemes to MSA equivalents (but did not perform lexical mapping on the word stems). They allowed for multiple morphological analyses, passing them on to the MT system in the form of a lattice. They tested on a subset of broadcast news and broadcast conversation data sets consisting of sentences that contain at least one region marked as non-MSA, with an initial OOV rate against an MSA training corpus of 1.51%. They obtained a 0.62 BLEU point gain. Abo Bakr et al. (2008) suggested another hybrid system to map Egyptian Arabic to MSA, using morphological analysis on the input and an Egyptian-MSA lexicon.

Other work that has focused on tasks besides MT includes that of Chiang et al. (2006), who built a parser for spoken Levantine Arabic (LA) transcripts using an MSA treebank. They used an LA-MSA lexicon in addition to morphological and syntactic rules to map the LA sentences to MSA. Riesa and Yarowsky (2006) built a statistical morphological segmenter for Iraqi and Levantine speech transcripts, and showed that they outperformed rule-based segmentation with small amounts of training. Some tools exist for preprocessing and tokenizing Arabic text with a focus on Dialectal Arabic. For example, MAGEAD (Habash and Rambow, 2006) is a morphological analyzer and generator that can analyze the surface form of MSA and dialect words into their root/pattern and affixed morphemes, or generate the surface form in the opposite direction.

Amazon's Mechanical Turk (MTurk) is becoming an essential tool for creating annotated resources for computational linguistics. Callison-Burch and Dredze (2010) provide an overview of various tasks for which MTurk has been used, and offer a set of best practices for ensuring high-quality data.

Zaidan and Callison-Burch (2011a) studied the quality of crowdsourced translations, by quantifying the quality of non-professional English translations of 2,000 Urdu sentences that were originally translated by the LDC. They demonstrated a variety of mechanisms that increase the translation quality of crowdsourced translations to near professional levels, with a total cost that is less than one tenth the cost of professional translation.

Zaidan and Callison-Burch (2011b) created the Arabic Online Commentary (AOC) dataset, a 52M-word monolingual dataset rich in dialectal content. Over 100k sentences from the AOC were annotated by native Arabic speakers on MTurk to identify the dialect level (and dialect itself) in each, and the collected labels were used to train automatic dialect identification systems. Although a large number of dialectal sentences were identified (41% of sentences), none were passed on to a translation phase.

3 Data Collection and Annotation

Following Zaidan and Callison-Burch (2011a,b), we use MTurk to identify Dialectal Arabic data and to create a parallel corpus by hiring non-professional translators to translate the sentences that were labeled as being dialectal. We had Turkers perform three steps for us: dialect classification, sentence segmentation, and translation.

Since Dialectal Arabic is much less common in written form than in spoken form, the first challenge is to simply find instances of written Dialectal Arabic. We draw from a large corpus of monolingual Arabic text (approximately 350M words) that was harvested from the web by the LDC, largely from weblog and online user groups.[1] Before presenting our data to annotators, we filter it to identify

[1]Corpora: LDC2006E32, LDC2006E77, LDC2006E90, LDC2007E04, LDC2007E44, LDC2007E102, LDC2008E41, LDC2008E54, LDC2009E14, LDC2009E93.

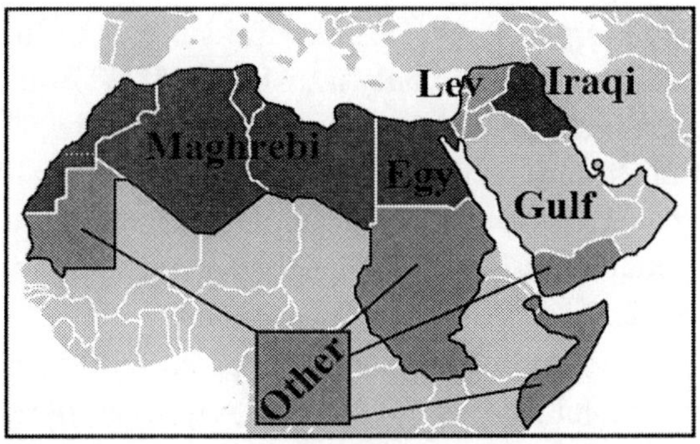

Figure 1: One possible breakdown of spoken Arabic into dialect groups: Maghrebi, Egyptian, Levantine, Gulf and Iraqi. Habash (2010) gives a breakdown along mostly the same lines. We used this map as an illustration for annotators in our dialect classification task (Section 3.1), with Arabic names for the dialects instead of English.

segments most likely to be dialectal (unlike Zaidan and Callison-Burch (2011b), who did no such pre-filtering). We eliminate documents with a large percentage of non-Arabic or MSA words. We then retain documents that contain some number of dialectal words, using a set of manually selected dialectal words that was assembled by culling through the transcripts of the Levantine Fisher and Egyptian CallHome speech corpora. After filtering, the dataset contained around 4M words, which we used as a starting point for creating our Dialectal Arabic-English parallel corpus.

3.1 Dialect Classification

To refine the document set beyond our keyword filtering heuristic and to label which dialect each document is written in, we hire Arabic annotators on MTurk to perform classification similar to Zaidan and Callison-Burch (2011b). Annotators were asked to classify the filtered documents for being in MSA or in one of four regional dialects: *Egyptian, Levantine, Gulf/Iraqi* or *Maghrebi*, and were shown the map in Figure 1 to explain what regions each of the dialect labels corresponded to. We allowed an additional "General" dialect option for ambiguous documents. Unlike Zaidan and Callison-Burch, our classification was applied to whole documents (corresponding to a user online posting) instead of individual sentences. To perform quality control, we used a set of documents for which correct labels were known. We presented these 20% of the time, and

Dialect Classification HIT	$10,064
Sentence Segmentation HIT	$1,940
Translation HIT	$32,061
Total cost	$44,065
Num words translated	1,516,856
Cost per word	2.9 cents/word

Table 1: The total costs for the three MTurk subtasks involved with the creation of our Dialectal Arabic-English parallel corpus.

eliminated workers who did not correctly classify them (2% of labels).

Identifying the dialect of a text snippet can be challenging in the absence of phonetic cues. We therefore required 3 classifications from different workers for every document, and accepted a dialect label if at least two of them agreed. The dialect distribution of the final output was: 43% Gulf/Iraqi, 28% Levantine, 11% Egyptian, and 16% could not be classified. MSA and the other labels accounted for 2%. We decided to translate only the Levantine and Egyptian documents, since the pool of MTurk workers contained virtually no workers from Iraq or the Gulf region.

3.2 Sentence Segmentation

Since the data we annotated was mostly user-generated informal web content, the existing punctuation was often insufficient to determine sentence boundaries. Since sentence boundaries are important for correct translation, we segmented passages into individual sentences using MTurk. We only required sentences longer than 15 words to be segmented, and allowed Turkers to split and rejoin at any point between the tokens. The instructions were simply to "divide the Arabic text into individual sentences, where you believe it would be appropriate to insert a period." We also used a set of correctly segmented passages for quality control, and scored Turkers using a metric based on the precision and recall of correct segmentation points. The rejection rate was 1.2%.

3.3 Translation to English

Following Zaidan and Callison-Burch (2011a), we hired non-professional translators on MTurk to translate the Levantine and Egyptian sentences into

Data Set	Sentence Pairs	Arabic Tokens	English Tokens
MSA-150MW	8.0M	151.4M	204.4M
Dialect-1500KW	180k	1,545,053	2,257,041
MSA-1300KW	71k	1,292,384	1,752,724
MSA-Web-Tune	6,163	145,260	184,185
MSA-Web-Test	5,454	136,396	172,357
Lev-Web-Tune	2,600	20,940	27,399
Lev-Web-Test	2,600	21,092	27,793
Egy-Web-Test	2,600	23,671	33,565
E-Facebook-Tune	3,351	25,130	34,753
E-Facebook-Test	3,188	25,011	34,244

Table 2: Statistics about the training/tuning/test datasets used in our experiments. The token counts are calculated before MADA segmentation.

English. Among several quality control measures, we rendered the Arabic sentences as images to prevent Turkers from simply copying the Arabic text into translation software. We still spot checked the translations against the output of Google Translate and Bing Translator. We also rejected gobbledygook garbage translations that have a high percentage of words not found in an English lexicon.

We quantified the quality of an individual Turker's translations in two ways: first by asking native Arabic speaker judges to score a sample of the Turker's translations, and second by inserting control sentences for which we have good reference translations and measuring the Turker's METEOR (Banerjee and Lavie, 2005) and BLEU-1 scores (Papineni et al., 2002).[2] The rejection rate of translation assignments was 5%. We promoted good translators to a restricted access "preferred worker queue". They were paid at a higher rate, and were required to translate control passages only 10% of the time as opposed to 20% for general Turkers, thus providing us with a higher translation yield for unseen data.

Worker turnout was initially slow, but increased quickly as our reputation for being reliable payers was established; workers started translating larger volumes and referring their acquaintances. We had 121 workers who each completed 20 or more translation assignments. We eventually reached and sustained a rate of 200k words of acceptable quality translated per week. Unlike Zaidan and Callison-Burch (2011a), who only translated 2,000 Urdu sentences, we translated sufficient volumes of Dialectal Arabic to train machine translation systems. In total, we had 1.1M words of Levantine and 380k words of Egyptian translated into English, corresponding to about 2.3M words on the English side.

Table 1 outlines the costs involved with creating our parallel corpus. The total cost was $44k, or $0.03/word – an order of magnitude cheaper than professional translation.

4 Experiments in Dialectal Arabic-English Machine Translation

We performed a set of experiments to contrast systems trained using our dialectal parallel corpus with systems trained on a (much larger) MSA-English parallel corpus. All experiments use the same methods for training, decoding and parameter tuning, and we only varied the corpora used for training, tuning and testing. The MT system we used is based on a phrase-based hierarchical model similar to that of Shen et al. (2008). We used GIZA++ (Och and Ney, 2003) to align sentences and extract hierarchical rules. The decoder used a log-linear model that combines the scores of multiple feature scores, including translation probabilities, smoothed lexical probabilities, a dependency tree language model, in addition to a trigram English language model. Additionally, we used 50,000 sparse, binary-valued source and target features based on Chiang et al. (2009). The English language model was trained on 7 billion words from the Gigaword and from a web crawl. The feature weights were tuned to maximize the BLEU score on a tuning set using the Expected-BLEU optimization procedure (Devlin, 2009).

The Dialectal Arabic side of our corpus consisted of 1.5M words (1.1M Levantine and 380k Egyptian). Table 2 gives statistics about the various train/tune/test splits we used in our experiments. Since the Egyptian set was so small, we split it only to training/test sets, opting not to have a tuning set. The MSA training data we used consisted of Arabic-English corpora totaling 150M tokens (Arabic side). The MSA train/tune/test sets were constructed for the DARPA GALE program.

We report translation quality in terms of BLEU

[2]BLEU-1 provided a more reliable correlation with human judgment in this case that the regular BLEU score (which uses n-gram orders $1, \ldots, 4$), given the limited size of the sample measured.

Training	Tuning	Simple Segment BLEU	Simple Segment OOV	MADA Segment BLEU	MADA Segment OOV	ΔBLEU	ΔOOV
				MSA-Web-Test			
MSA-150MW	**MSA-Web**	26.21	1.69%	27.85	0.48%	+1.64	-1.21%
MSA-1300KW		21.24	7.20%	25.23	1.95%	+3.99	-5.25%
				Egyptian-Web-Test			
Dialect-1500KW	**Levantine-Web**	18.55	6.31%	20.66	2.85%	+2.11	-3.46%
				Levantine-Web-Test			
Dialect-1500KW	**Levantine-Web**	17.00	6.22%	19.29	2.96%	+2.29	-3.26%

Table 3: Comparison of the effect of morphological segmentation when translating MSA web text and Dialectal Arabic web text. The morphological segmentation uniformly improves translation quality, but the improvements are more dramatic for MSA than for Dialectal Arabic when comparing similarly-sized training corpora.

Training	Tuning	BLEU	OOV	BLEU	OOV	BLEU	OOV
		Egyptian-Web-Test		Levantine-Web-Test		MSA-Web-Test	
MSA-150MW	**MSA-Web**	14.76	4.42%	11.83	5.53%	**27.85**	0.48%
MSA-150MW	**Lev-Web**	14.34	4.42%	12.29	5.53%	24.63	0.48%
MSA-150MW+Dial-1500KW		20.09	**2.04%**	19.11	**2.27%**	24.30	**0.45%**
Dialect-1500KW		**20.66**	2.85%	**19.29**	2.96%	15.53	3.70%
Egyptian-360KW		19.04	4.62%	11.21	9.00%	-	-
Levantine-360KW		14.05	7.11%	16.36	5.24%	-	-
Levantine-1100KW		17.79	4.83%	**19.29**	3.31%	-	-

Table 4: A comparison of translation quality of Egyptian, Levantine, and MSA web text, using various training corpora. The highest BLEU scores are achieved using the full set of dialectal data (which combines Levantine and Egyptian), since the Egyptian alone is sparse. For Levantine, adding Egyptian has no effect. In both cases, adding MSA to the dialectal data results in marginally worse translations.

score.[3] In addition, we also report the OOV rate of the test set relative to the training corpus in each experimental setups.

4.1 Morphological Decomposition

Arabic has a complex morphology compared to English. Preprocessing the Arabic source by morphological segmentation has been shown to improve the performance of Arabic MT (Lee, 2004; Habash and Sadat, 2006) by decreasing the size of the source vocabulary, and improving the quality of word alignments. The morphological analyzers that underlie most segmenters were developed for MSA, but the different dialects of Arabic share many of the morphological affixes of MSA, and it is therefore not unreasonable to expect MSA segmentation to also improve Dialect Arabic to English MT. To test this, we ran experiments using the MADA morphological analyzer (Habash and Rambow, 2005). Table 3 shows the effect of applying segmentation to the text, for both MSA and Dialectal Arabic. The BLEU score improves uniformly, although the improvements are most dramatic for smaller datasets, which is consistent with previous work (Habash and Sadat, 2006). Morphological segmentation gives a smaller gain on dialectal input, which could be due to two factors: the segmentation accuracy likely decreases since we are using an unmodified MSA segmenter, and there is higher variability in the written form of dialect compared to MSA. Given the significant, albeit smaller gain on dialectal input, we use MADA segmentation in all our experiments.

4.2 Effect of Dialectal Training Data Size

We next examine how the size of the dialectal training data affects MT performance, and whether it is useful to combine it with MSA training data. We

[3]We also computed TER (Snover et al., 2006) and METEOR scores, but omit them because they demonstrated similar trends.

Arabic	TL	Count	English Equivalent
عنجد	*Enjd*	31	really/for real – Levantine.
كتيير	*ktyyyr*	17	a looot (corruption of MSA *kvyrA*).
النعوم	*AlnEwm*	16	The last name (Al-Na'oom) of a forum admin.
وحشتيني	*wH$tyny*	14	I miss you (spoken to a female) – Egyptian.
يازمن	*yAzmn*	11	oh time (space omitted). Appeared within a poem.
بكتير	*bktyr*	11	by much (corruption of MSA *bkvyr*).
متلك	*mtlk*	10	like you (corruption of MSA *mvlk*).

Table 5: The most frequent OOV's (with counts $\geq$ 10) of the dialectal test sets against the MSA training data.

Source (*EGY*): انت بتعمل له اعلان ولا ايه؟!!
Transliteration: *Ant btEml lh AElAn wlA Ayh?!!*
MSA-Sys. Output: You are working for a declaration and not?
Dial-Sys. Output: You are making the advertisement for him or what?
Reference: Are you promoting it or what?!!

Source (*EGY*): نفسي اطمئن عليه بعد ما شاف الصوره دي
Transliteration: *nfsY Atm}n Elyh bEd mA $Af AlSwrh dy*
MSA-Sys. Output: Myself feel to see this image.
Dial-Sys. Output: I wish to check on him after he saw this picture.
Reference: I wish to be sure that he is fine after he saw this images

Source (*LEV*): لهيك الجو كتيير كووول
Transliteration: *lhyk Aljw ktyyyr kwwwl*
MSA-Sys. Output: God you the atmosphere.
Dial-Sys. Output: this is why the weather is so cool
Reference: This is why the weather is so cool

Source (*LEV*): طول بالك عم نمزح
Transliteration: *Twl bAlk Em nmzH*
MSA-Sys. Output: Do you think about a joke long.
Dial-Sys. Output: Calm down we are kidding
Reference: calm down, we are kidding

Figure 2: Examples of improvement in MT output when training on our Dialectal Arabic-English parallel corpus instead of an MSA-English parallel corpus.

Source (*EGY*): قالتلة **طب** تعالى نعد ،
Transliteration: *qAltlp **Tb** tEAlY nEd ,*
MSA-Sys. Output: **Medicine** almighty promise.
Dial-Sys. Output: She said, **OK**, come and then
Reference: She told him, **OK**, lets count them ,

Source (*LEV*): فبقرا وأحيانا بقضيها **عم** أتسلى مع رفقاتي
Transliteration: *fbqrA w>HyAnA bqDyhA **Em** >tslY mE rfqAty*
MSA-Sys. Output: I read and sometimes with go with my **uncle**.
Dial-Sys. Output: So I read, and sometimes I spend try**ing** to make my self comfort with my friends
Reference: So i study and sometimes I spend the time hav**ing** fun with my friends

Source (*LEV*): الله يسامحكن هلق كل واحد طالب قرب بيكون **بدو** عروس
Transliteration: *Allh ysAmHkn hlq kl wAHd TAlb qrb bykwn **bdw** Erws*
MSA-Sys. Output: God now each student near the **Bedouin** bride.
Dial-Sys. Output: God forgive you, each one is a close student would **want** the bride
Reference: God forgive you. Is every one asking to be close, **want** a bride!

Figure 3: Examples of ambiguous words that are translated incorrectly by the MSA-English system, but correctly by the Dialectal Arabic-English system.

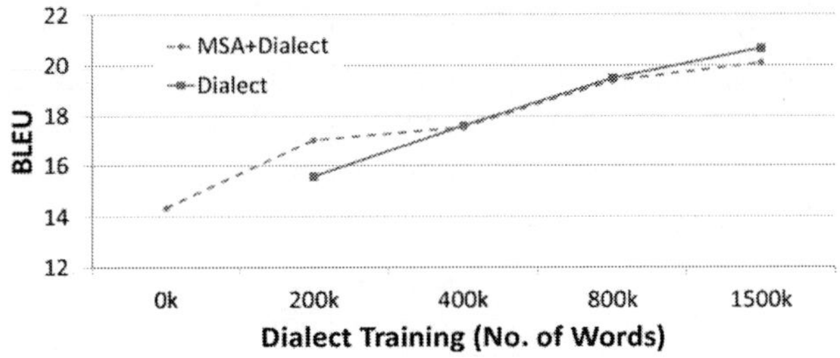

Egyptian web test

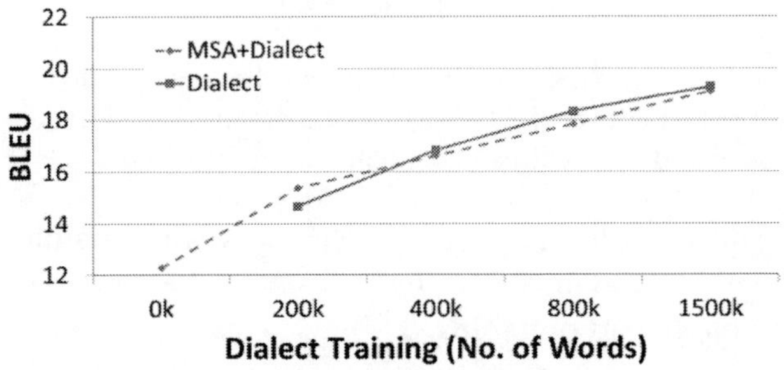

Levantine web test

Figure 4: Learning curves showing the effects of increasing the size of dialectal training data, when combined with the 150M-word MSA parallel corpus, and when used alone. Adding the MSA training data is only useful when the dialectal data is scarce (200k words).

started with a baseline system trained on the 150M-word MSA parallel corpus, and added various sized portions of the dialect parallel corpus to it. Figure 4 shows the resulting learning curve, and compares it to the learning curve for a system trained solely on the dialectal parallel corpus. When only 200k words of dialectal data are available, combining it with the 150M-word MSA corpus results in improved BLEU scores, adding 0.8–1.5 BLEU points. When 400k words or more of dialectal data are available, the MSA training data ceases to provide any gain, and in fact starts to hurt the performance.

The performance of a system trained on the 1.5M-word dialectal data is dramatically superior to a system that uses only the 150M-word MSA data: +6.32 BLEU points on the Egyptian test set, or 44% relative gain, and +7.00 BLEU points on the Levantine test set, or 57% relative gain (fourth line vs. second line of Table 4). In Section 4.4, we show that those gains are not an artifact of the similarity between test and training datasets, or of using the same translator pool to translate both sets.

Inspecting the difference in the outputs of the Dialectal vs. MSA systems, we see that the improvement in score is a reflection of a significant improvement in the quality of translations. Figure 2 shows a few examples of sentences whose translations improve significantly using the Dialectal system. Figure 3 shows a particularly interesting category of examples. Many words are homographs, with different meanings (and usually different pronunciations) in MSA vs. one or more dialects. The bolded tokens in the sentences in Figure 3 are examples of such words. They are translated incorrectly by the MSA system, while the dialect system translates them correctly.[4] If we examine the most frequent OOV words against the MSA training data (Table 5), we find a number of corrupted MSA words and names, but that a majority of OOVs are dialect words.

4.3 Cross-Dialect Training

Since MSA training data appeared to have little effect when translating dialectal input, we next investigated the effect of training data from one dialect on translating the input of another dialect. We trained a system with the 360k-word Egyptian training subset of our dialectal parallel corpus, and another system with a similar amount of Levantine training data. We used each system to translate the test set of the other dialect. As expected, a system performs better when it translates a test set in the same dialect that it was trained on (Table 4).

That said, since the Egyptian training set is so small, *adding* the (full) Levantine training data improves performance (on the Egyptian test set) by 1.62 BLEU points, compared to using only Egyptian training data. In fact, using the Levantine training data by itself outperforms the MSA-trained system on the Egyptian test set by more than 3 BLEU points. (For the Levantine test set, adding the Egyptian training data has no affect, possibly due to the small amount of Egyptian data.) This may suggest that the mismatch between dialects is less severe than the mismatch between MSA and dialects. Alternatively, the differences may be due to the changes in genre from the MSA parallel corpus (which is mainly formal newswire) to the newsgroups and weblogs that mainly comprise the dialectal corpus.

[4]The word *nfsY* of Figure 2 (first word of second example) is also a homograph, as it means *myself* in MSA and *I wish* in Dialectal Arabic.

Training	Tuning	BLEU	OOV
MSA-150MW	**Levantine-Web**	13.80	4.16%
MSA-150MW+Dialect-1500KW		**16.71**	**2.43%**
Dialect-1500KW		15.75	3.79%
MSA-150MW	**Egyptian-Facebook**	15.80	4.16%
MSA-150MW+Dialect-1500KW		**18.50**	**2.43%**
Dialect-1500KW		17.90	3.79%
Dialect-1000KW (random selection)	**Egyptian-Facebook**	17.09	4.64%
Dialect-1000KW (no Turker overlap)		17.10	4.60%

Table 6: Results on a truly independent test set, consisting of data harvested from Egyptian Facebook pages that are entirely distinct from the our dialectal training set. The improvements over the MSA baseline are still considerable: +2.9 BLEU points when no Facebook data is available for tuning and +2.7 with a Facebook tuning set.

4.4 Validation on Independent Test Data

To eliminate the possibility that the gains are solely due to similarity between the test/training sets in the dialectal data, we ran experiments using the same dialectal training data, but using truly independent test/tuning data sets selected at random from a larger set of monolingual data that we collected from public Egyptian Facebook pages. This data consists of a set of original user postings and the subsequent comments on each, giving the data a more conversational style than our other test sets. The postings deal with current Egyptian political affairs, sports and other topics. The test set we selected consisted of 25,011 words (3,188 comments and 427 postings from 86 pages), and the tuning set contained 25,130 words (3,351 comments and 415 conversations from 58 pages). We obtained reference translations for those using MTurk as well.

Table 6 shows that using the 1.5M-word dialect parallel corpus for training yields a 2 point BLEU improvement over using the 150M-word MSA corpus. Adding the MSA training data does yield an improvement, though of less than a single BLEU point. It remains true that training on 1.5M words of dialectal data is better than training on 100 times more MSA parallel data. The system performance is sensitive to the tuning set choice, and improves when it matches the test set in genre and origin.

To eliminate another potential source of artificial bias, we also performed an experiment where we removed any training translation contributed by a Turker who translated any sentence in the Egyptian Facebook set, to eliminate translator bias. For this, we were left with 1M words of dialect training data. This gave the same BLEU score as when training with a randomly selected subset of the same size (bottom part of Table 6).

4.5 Mapping from Dialectal Arabic to MSA Before Translating to English

Given the large amount of linguistic resources that have been developed for MSA over the past years, and the extensive research that was conducted on machine translation from MSA to English and other languages, an obvious research question is whether Dialectal Arabic is best translated to English by first pivoting through MSA, rather than directly. The proximity of Dialectal Arabic to MSA makes the mapping in principle easier than general machine translation, and a number of researchers have explored this direction (Salloum and Habash, 2011). In this scenario, the dialectal source would first be automatically transformed to MSA, using either a rule-based or statistical mapping module.

The Dialectal Arabic-English parallel corpus we created presents a unique opportunity to compare the MSA-pivoting approach against direct translation. First, we collected equivalent MSA data for the Levantine Web test and tuning sets, by asking Turkers to transform dialectal passages to valid and fluent MSA. Turkers were shown example transformations, and we encouraged fewer changes where applicable (e.g. morphological rather than lexical mapping), but allowed any editing operation in general (deletion, substitution, reordering). Sample submissions were independently shown to native Arabic speaking judges, who confirmed they were valid MSA. A low OOV rate also indicated the correctness of the mappings. By manually transforming the test

Training	BLEU	OOV	BLEU	OOV	ΔBLEU	ΔOOV
	Direct dialect trans		Map to MSA then trans			
MSA-150MW	12.29	5.53%	14.59	1.53%	+2.30	-4.00%
MSA-150MW+Dialect-200KW	15.37	3.59%	15.53	1.22%	+0.16	-2.37%
MSA-150MW+Dialect-400KW	16.62	3.06%	16.25	1.13%	-0.37	-1.93%
MSA-150MW+Dialect-800KW	17.83	2.63%	16.69	1.04%	-1.14	-1.59%
MSA-150MW+Dialect-1500KW	19.11	2.27%	17.20	0.98%	-1.91	-1.29%

Table 7: A comparison of the effectiveness of performing Levantine-to-MSA mapping before translating into English, versus translating directly from Levantine into English. The mapping from Levantine to MSA was done manually, so it is an optimistic estimate of what might be done automatically. Although initially helpful to the MSA baseline system, the usefulness of pivoting through MSA drops as more dialectal data is added, eventually hurting performance.

dialectal sentence into MSA, we establish an optimistic estimate of what could be done automatically.

Table 7 compares direct translation versus pivoting to MSA before translating, using the baseline MSA-English MT system.[5] The performance of the system improves by 2.3 BLEU points with dialect-to-MSA pivoting, compared to attempting to translate the untransformed dialectal input directly. As we add more dialectal training data, the BLEU score when translating the untransformed dialect test set improves rapidly (as seen previously in the MSA+Dialect learning curve in Figure 4), while the improvement is less rapid when the text is first transformed to MSA. Direct translation becomes a better option than mapping to MSA once 400k words of dialectal data are added, despite the significantly lower OOV rate with MSA-mapping. This indicates that simple vocabulary coverage is not sufficient, and data domain mismatch, quantified by more complex matching patterns, is more important.

5 Conclusion

We have described a process for building a Dialectal Arabic-English parallel corpus, by selecting passages with a relatively high percentage of non-MSA words from a monolingual Arabic web text corpus, then using crowdsourcing to classify them by dialect, segment them into individual sentences and translate them to English. The process was successfully scaled to the point of reaching and sustaining a rate of 200k translated words per week, at 1/10 the cost of professional translation. Our parallel corpus, consisting of 1.5M words, was produced at a total cost of $40k, or roughly $0.03/word.

We used the parallel corpus we constructed to analyze the behavior of a Dialectal Arabic-English MT system as a function of the size of the dialectal training corpus. We showed that relatively small amounts of training data render larger MSA corpora from different data genres largely ineffective for this test data. In practice, a system trained on the combined Dialectal-MSA data is likely to give the best performance, since informal Arabic data is usually a mixture of Dialectal Arabic and MSA. An area of future research is using the output of a dialect classifier, or other features to bias the translation model towards the Dialectal or the MSA parts of the data.

We also validated the models built from the dialectal corpus by using them to translate an independent data set collected from Egyptian Facebook public pages. We finally investigated using MSA as a "pivot language" for Dialectal Arabic-English translation, by simulating automatic dialect-to-MSA mapping using MTurk. We obtained limited gains from mapping the input to MSA, even when the mapping is of good quality, and only at lower training set sizes. This suggests that the mismatch between training and test data is an important aspect of the problem, beyond simple vocabulary coverage.

The aim of this paper is to contribute to setting the direction of future research on Dialectal Arabic MT. The gains we observed from using MSA morphological segmentation can be further increased with dialect-specific segmenters. Input preprocessing can also be used to decrease the noise of the user-generated data. Topic adaptation is another important problem to tackle if the large MSA linguistic resources already developed are to be leveraged for Dialectal Arabic-English MT.

[5]The systems in each column of the table are tuned consistently, using their corresponding tuning sets.

Acknowledgments

This work was supported in part by DARPA/IPTO Contract No. HR0011-12-C-0014 under the BOLT Program, and in part by the EuroMatrixPlus project funded by the European Commission (7th Framework Programme). The views expressed are those of the authors and do not reflect the official policy or position of the Department of Defense or the U.S. Government. Distribution Statement A (Approved for Public Release, Distribution Unlimited).

References

Hitham M. Abo Bakr, Khaled Shaalan, and Ibrahim Ziedan. 2008. A hybrid approach for converting written Egyptian colloquial dialect into diacritized Arabic. In *The 6th International Conference on Informatics and Systems, INFOS2008*, Cairo, Egypt.

Satanjeev Banerjee and Alon Lavie. 2005. Meteor: An automatic metric for MT evaluation with improved correlation with human judgments. In *In Proc. of ACL 2005 Workshop on Intrinsic and Extrinsic Evaluation Measures for MT and/or Summarization*, Ann Arbor, Michigan.

Chris Callison-Burch and Mark Dredze. 2010. Creating speech and language data with Amazon's Mechanical Turk. In *Proceedings of the NAACL HLT 2010 Workshop on Creating Speech and Language Data with Amazon's Mechanical Turk*, pages 1–12, Los Angeles, June.

David Chiang, Mona Diab, Nizar Habash, Owen Rambow, and Safiullah Shareef. 2006. Parsing Arabic dialects. In *Proceedings of the Conference of the European Chapter of the Association for Computational Linguistics*, Trento, Italy.

David Chiang, Kevin Knight, and Wei Wang. 2009. 11,001 new features for statistical machine translation. In *NAACL '09: Proceedings of the 2009 Human Language Technology Conference of the North American Chapter of the Association for Computational Linguistics*, Boulder, Colorado.

Jacob Devlin. 2009. Lexical features for statistical machine translation. Master's thesis, University of Maryland, December.

Mohamed Embarki and Moha Ennaji, editors. 2011. *Modern Trends in Arabic Dialectology*. The Red Sea Press.

Charles A. Ferguson. 1959. Diglossia. *Word*, 15:325–340.

Nizar Habash and Owen Rambow. 2005. Arabic tokenization, part-of-speech tagging and morphological disambiguation in one fell swoop. In *Proceedings of the 43th Annual Meeting of the Association for Computational Linguistics (ACL)*, Ann Arbor, Michigan.

Nizar Habash and Owen Rambow. 2006. MAGEAD: A morphological analyzer and generator for the Arabic dialects. In *Proceedings of the 44th Annual Meeting of the Association for Computational Linguistics (ACL)*, Sydney, Australia.

Nizar Habash and Fatiha Sadat. 2006. Arabic preprocessing schemes for statistical machine translation. In *Proceedings of the 2006 Human Language Technology Conference of the North American Chapter of the Association for Computational Linguistics*, New York, New York.

Nizar Y. Habash. 2010. *Introduction to Arabic Natural Language Processing*. Morgan & Claypool.

Young-Suk Lee. 2004. Morphological analysis for statistical machine translation. In *HLT-NAACL '04: Proceedings of HLT-NAACL 2004*, Boston, Massachusetts.

Franz Josef Och and Hermann Ney. 2003. A systematic comparison of various statistical alignment models. *Computational Linguistics*, 29(1):19–51.

Kishore Papineni, Salim Roukos, Todd Ward, and Wei-Jing Zhu. 2002. Bleu: a method for automatic evaluation of machine translation. In *Proceedings of the 40th Annual Meeting of the Association for Computational Linguistics (ACL)*, Philadelphia, PA.

Jason Riesa and David Yarowsky. 2006. Minimally supervised morphological segmentation with applications to machine translation. In *Proceedings of the 7th Conf. of the Association for Machine Translation in the Americas (AMTA 2006)*, Cambridge, MA.

Wael Salloum and Nizar Habash. 2011. Dialectal to standard Arabic paraphrasing to improve Arabic-English statistical machine translation. In *Proceedings of the 2011 Conference of Empirical Methods in Natural Language Processing*, Edinburgh, Scotland, UK.

Hassan Sawaf. 2010. Arabic dialect handling in hybrid machine translation. In *Proceedings of the 9th Conf. of the Association for Machine Translation in the Americas (AMTA 2010)*, Denver, Colorado.

Libin Shen, Jinxi Xu, and Ralph Weischedel. 2008. A new string-to-dependency machine translation algorithm with a target dependency language model. In *Proceedings of the 46th Annual Meeting of the Association for Computational Linguistics (ACL)*, pages 577–585, Columbus, Ohio.

Matthew Snover, Bonnie Dorr, Richard Schwartz, Linnea Micciulla, and Ralph Weischedel. 2006. A study of translation error rate with targeted human annotation. In *Proceedings of the 7th Conf. of the Association for Machine Translation in the Americas (AMTA 2006)*, pages 223–231, Cambridge, MA.

Omar F. Zaidan and Chris Callison-Burch. 2011a. The Arabic online commentary dataset: an annotated dataset of informal Arabic with high dialectal content. In *Proceedings of the 49th Annual Meeting of the Association for Computational Linguistics: Human Language Technologies*, pages 37–41, Portland, Oregon, June.

Omar F. Zaidan and Chris Callison-Burch. 2011b. Crowdsourcing translation: Professional quality from non-professionals. In *Proceedings of the 49th Annual Meeting of the Association for Computational Linguistics: Human Language Technologies*, pages 1220–1229, Portland, Oregon, June.

Entity Clustering Across Languages

Spence Green[*], **Nicholas Andrews**[†], **Matthew R. Gormley**[†],
Mark Dredze[†], **and Christopher D. Manning**[*]

[*]Computer Science Department, Stanford University
{spenceg,manning}@stanford.edu

[†]Human Language Technology Center of Excellence, Johns Hopkins University
{noa,mrg,mdredze}@cs.jhu.edu

Abstract

Standard entity clustering systems commonly rely on mention (string) matching, syntactic features, and linguistic resources like English WordNet. When co-referent text mentions appear in different languages, these techniques cannot be easily applied. Consequently, we develop new methods for clustering text mentions across documents and languages simultaneously, producing cross-lingual entity clusters. Our approach extends standard clustering algorithms with cross-lingual mention and context similarity measures. Crucially, we do not assume a pre-existing entity list (knowledge base), so entity characteristics are unknown. On an Arabic-English corpus that contains seven different text genres, our best model yields a 24.3% F1 gain over the baseline.

1 Introduction

This paper introduces techniques for clustering co-referent text mentions across documents and languages. On the web today, a breaking news item may instantly result in mentions to a real-world entity in multiple text formats: news articles, blog posts, tweets, etc. Much NLP work has focused on model adaptation to these diverse text genres. However, the *diversity of languages* in which the mentions appear is a more significant challenge. This was particularly evident during the 2011 popular uprisings in the Arab world, in which electronic media played a prominent role. A key issue for the outside world was the aggregation of information that appeared simultaneously in English, French, and various Arabic dialects.

To our knowledge, we are the first to consider clustering entity mentions across languages without *a priori* knowledge of the quantity or types of real-world entities (a knowledge base). The cross-lingual setting introduces several challenges. First, we cannot assume a prototypical name format. For example, the Anglo-centric first/middle/last prototype used in previous name modeling work (*cf.* (Charniak, 2001)) does not apply to Arabic names like *Abdullah ibn Abd Al-Aziz Al-Saud* or Chinese names like *Hu Jintao* (referred to as *Mr. Hu*, not *Mr. Jintao*). Second, organization names often require both transliteration and translation. For example, the Arabic شركة جنرال موتورز 'General Motors Corp' contains transliterations of جنرال موتورز 'General Motors', but a translation of شركة 'Corporation'.

Our models are organized as a pipeline. First, for each document, we perform standard mention detection and coreference resolution. Then, we use pairwise cross-lingual similarity models to measure both mention and context similarity. Finally, we cluster the mentions based on similarity.

Our work makes the following contributions: (1) introduction of the task, (2) novel models for cross-lingual entity clustering of person and organization entities, (3) cross-lingual annotation of the NIST Automatic Content Extraction (ACE) 2008 Arabic-English evaluation set, and (4) experimental results using both gold and automatic within-document processing. We will release our software and annotations to support future research.

1.1 Task Description via a Simple Example

Consider the toy corpus in Fig. 1. The English documents contain mentions of two people: Steven Paul Jobs and Mark Elliot Zuckerberg. Of course, the surface realization of Mr. Jobs' last name in English is also an ordinary nominal, hence the ambiguous mention string (absent context) in the second document. The Arabic document introduces an organization entity (Apple Inc.) along with proper and pronominal references to Mr. Jobs. Finally, the French document refers to Mr. Jobs by the honorific 'Monsieur,' and to

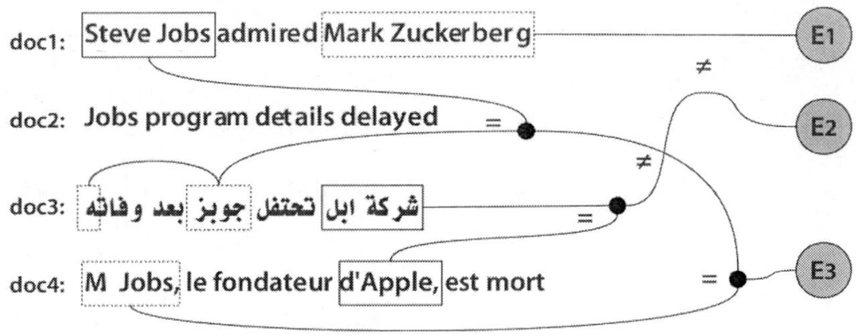

Figure 1: Clustering entity mentions across languages and documents. The toy corpus contains English (doc1 and doc2), Arabic (doc3), and French (doc4). Together, the documents make reference to three real-world entities, the identification of which is the primary objective of this work. We use a separately-trained system for within-document mention detection and coreference (indicated by the text boxes and intra-document links, respectively). Our experimental results are for Arabic-English only.

Apple without its corporate designation.

Our goal is to automatically produce the cross-lingual entity clusters E_1 (*Mark Elliot Zuckerberg*), E_2 (*Apple Inc.*), and E_3 (*Steven Paul Jobs*). Both the true number and characteristics of these entities are unobserved. Our models require two pre-processing steps: mention detection and within-document coreference/anaphora resolution, shown in Fig. 1 by the text boxes and intra-document links, respectively. For example, in doc3, a within-document coreference system would pre-link جوبز *joobz* 'Jobs' with the masculine pronoun ه *h* 'his'. In addition, the mention detector determines that the surface form "Jobs" in doc2 is not an entity reference. For this within-document pre-processing we use Serif (Ramshaw et al., 2011).[1]

Our models measure cross-lingual similarity of the coreference chains to make clustering decisions (• in Fig. 1). The similarity models (indicated by the $=$ and $\neq$ operators in Fig. 1) consider both mention string and context similarity (§2). We use the mention similarities as hard constraints, and the context similarities as soft constraints. In this work, we investigate two standard constrained clustering algorithms (§3). Our methods can be used to extend existing systems for mono-lingual entity clustering (also known as "cross-document coreference resolution") to the cross-lingual setting.

[1]Serif is a commercial system that assumes each document contains only one language. Currently, there are no publicly available within-document coreference systems for Arabic and many other languages. To remedy this problem, the CoNNL-2012 shared task aims to develop multilingual coreference systems.

2 Mention and Context Similarity

Our goal is to create cross-lingual sets of co-referent mentions to real-world entities (people, places, organizations, etc.). In this paper, we adopt the following notation. Let M be a set of distinct text mentions in a collection of documents; C is a partitioning of M into document-level sets of co-referent mentions (called *coreference chains*); E is a partitioning of C into sets of co-referent chains (called *entities*). Let i, j be non-negative integers less than or equal to $|M|$ and a, b be non-negative integers less than or equal to $|C|$. Our experiments use a separate within-document coreference system to create C, which is fixed. We will learn E, which has size no greater than $|C|$ since the set of mono-lingual chains is the largest valid partitioning.

We define accessor functions to access properties of mentions and chains. For any mention m_i, define the following functions: $lang(m_i)$ is the language; $doc(m_i)$ is the document containing m_i; $type(m_i)$ is the semantic type, which is assigned by the within-document coreference system. We also extract a set of mention contexts S, which are the sentences containing each mention (i.e., $|S| = |M|$).

We learn the partition E by considering mention and context similarity, which are measured with separate component models.

2.1 Mention Similarity

We use separate methods for within- and cross-language mention similarity. The pairwise similarity

Arabic Rules			
ب → b	ت → t	ث → th	ج → j
ح → h	خ → kh	د → d	ذ → th
ر → r	ز → z	س → s	ش → sh
ص → s	ض → d	ط → t	ظ → th
ع → a	غ → g	ف → f	ق → q
ك → k	ل → l	م → m	ن → n
ه → h	ا → a	و → w	ى → a
ة → ah	ي → ∅	ء → ∅	
English Rules			
k → c	**p** → b	**x** → ks	**e,i,o,u** → ∅

Table 1: English-Arabic mapping rules to a common orthographic representation. "∅" indicates a null mapping. For English, we also lowercase and remove determiners and punctuation. For Arabic, we remove the determiner ال *Al* 'the' and the elongation character *tatwil* 'ـ'.

OVERLAP	Active for each bigram in $cbigrams(m_{i,u}) \bigcup cbigrams(m_{j,v})$
BIGRAM-DIFF-m_i	Active for each bigram in $cbigrams(m_i) - cbigrams(m_j)$
BIGRAM-DIFF-m_j	Active for each bigram in $cbigrams(m_j) - cbigrams(m_i)$
BIGRAM-LEN-DIFF	Value of abs($size(cbigrams(m_i) - cbigrams(m_j))$)
BIG-EDIT-DIST	Count of token pairs with $Lev(m_{i,u}, m_{j,v}) > 3.0$
TOTAL-EDIT-DIST	Sum of aligned token edit distances
LENGTH	Active for one of: $len(m_i) > len(m_j)$ or $len(m_i) < len(m_j)$ or $len(m_i) = len(m_j)$
LENGTH-DIFF	abs($len(m_i) - len(m_j)$)
SINGLETON	Active if $len(m_i) = 1$
SINGLETON-PAIR	Active if $len(m_i) = len(m_j) = 1$

Table 2: Cross-language Maxent feature templates for a *whitespace-tokenized* mention pair $\langle m_i, m_j \rangle$ with alignment A_{m_i,m_j}. Let $(u, v) \in A_{m_i,m_j}$ indicate aligned token indices. Define the following functions for strings: $cbigrams(\cdot)$ returns the set of character bigrams; $len(\cdot)$ is the token length; $Lev(\cdot,\cdot)$ is the Levenshtein edit distance between two strings. Prior to feature extraction, we add unique start and end symbols to the mention strings.

of any two mentions m_i and m_j is:

$$sim(m_i, m_j) = \begin{cases} jaro\text{-}winkler(m_i, m_j) & \text{if } lang(m_i) = lang(m_j) \\ maxent(m_i, m_j) & \text{otherwise} \end{cases}$$

Jaro-Winkler Distance (within-language) If $lang(m_i) = lang(m_j)$, we use the Jaro-Winkler edit distance (Porter and Winkler, 1997). Jaro-Winkler rewards matching prefixes, the empirical justification being that less variation typically occurs at the beginning of names.[2] The metric produces a score in the range [0,1], where 0 indicates equality.

Maxent model (cross-language) When $lang(m_i) \neq lang(m_j)$, then the two mentions might be in different writing systems. Edit distance calculations no longer apply directly. One solution would be full-blown transliteration (Knight and Graehl, 1998), followed by application of Jaro-Winkler. However, transliteration systems are complex and require significant training resources. We find that a simpler, low-resource approach works well in practice.

First, we deterministically map both languages to a common phonetic representation (Tbl. 1).[3] Next, we align the mention pairs with the Hungarian algorithm, which produces a word-to-word alignment A_{m_i,m_j}.[4] Finally, we build a simple binary Maxent classifier $p(y|m_i, m_j; \lambda)$ that extracts features from the aligned mentions (Tbl. 2). We learn the parameters λ using a quasi-Newton procedure with L_1 (lasso) regularization (Andrew and Gao, 2007).

2.2 Context Mapping and Similarity

Mention strings alone are not always sufficient for disambiguation. Consider again the simple example in Fig. 1. Both doc3 and doc4 reference "Steve Jobs" and "Apple" in the same contexts. Context cooccurence and/or similarity can thus disambiguate these two entities from other entities with similar references (e.g., "Steve Jones" or "Apple Corps"). As with the mention strings, the contexts may originate in different writing systems. We consider both high- and low-resource approaches for mapping contexts to a common representation.

[2]For multi-token names, we sort the tokens prior to computing the score, as suggested by Christen (2006).

[3]This idea is reminiscent of Soundex, which Freeman et al. (2006) used for cross-lingual name matching.

[4]The Hungarian algorithm finds an optimal minimum-cost alignment. For pairwise costs between tokens, we used the Levenshtein edit distance

Machine Translation (MT) For the high-resource setting, if $lang(m_i) \neq$ English, then we translate both m_i and its context s_i to English with an MT system. We use Phrasal (Cer et al., 2010), a phrase-based system which, like most public MT systems, lacks a transliteration module. We believe that this approach yields the most accurate context mapping for high-resource language pairs (like English-Arabic).

Polylingual Topic Model (PLTM) The polylingual topic model (PLTM) (Mimno et al., 2009) is a generative process in which document tuples—groups of topically-similar documents—share a topic distribution. The tuples need not be sentence-aligned, so training data is easier to obtain. For example, one document tuple might be the set of Wikipedia articles (in all languages) for Steve Jobs.

Let D be a set of document tuples, where there is one document in each tuple for each of L languages. Each language has vocabulary V_l and each document d_t^l has N_t^l tokens. We specify a fixed-size set of topics K. The PLTM generates the document tuples as follows:

POLYLINGUAL TOPIC MODEL

$\theta_t \sim \text{Dir}(\alpha^K)$ [cross-lingual tuple-topic prior]
$\phi_k^l \sim \text{Dir}(\beta^{V_l})$ [word-topic prior]
for each token $w_{t,n}^l$ with $n = \{1, \ldots, N_t^l\}$:
  $z_{t,n} \sim \text{Mult}(\theta_t)$
  $w_{t,n}^l \sim \text{Mult}(\phi_{z_{t,n}}^l)$

For cross-lingual context mapping, we infer the 1-best topic assignments for each token in all S mention contexts. This technique reduces $V_l = k$ for all l. Moreover, all languages have a common vocabulary: the set of K topic indices. Since the PLTM is not a contribution of this paper, we refer the interested reader to (Mimno et al., 2009) for more details.

After mapping each mention context to a common representation, we measure context similarity based on the choice of clustering algorithm.

3 Clustering Algorithms

We incorporate the mention and context similarity measures into a clustering framework. We consider two algorithms. The first is hierarchical agglomerative clustering (HAC), with which we assume basic familiarity (Manning et al., 2008). A shortcoming of HAC is that a stop threshold must be tuned. To avoid this requirement, we also consider non-parametric probabilistic clustering in the form of a Dirichlet process mixture model (DPMM) (Antoniak, 1974) .

Both clustering algorithms can be modified to accommodate pairwise constraints. We have observed better results by encoding mention similarity as a hard constraint. Context similarity is thus the cluster distance measure.[5]

To turn the Jaro-Winkler distance into a hard boolean constraint, we tuned a threshold η on held-out data, i.e., $\textit{jaro-winkler}(m_i, m_j) \leq \eta \Rightarrow m_i = m_j$. Likewise, the Maxent model is a binary classifier, so $p(y = 1|m_i, m_j; \lambda) > 0.5 \Rightarrow m_i = m_j$.

In both clustering algorithms, any two chains C_a and C_b cannot share the same cluster assignment if:

1. **Document origin**: $doc(C_a) = doc(C_b)$
2. **Semantic type**: $type(C_a) \neq type(C_b)$
3. **Mention Match**: $sim(m_i, m_j) = false$, where $m_i = repr(C_a)$ and $m_j = repr(C_b)$.

The deterministic accessor function $repr(C_a)$ returns the *representative mention* of a chain. The heuristic we used was "first mention": the function returns the earliest mention that appears in the associated document. In many languages, the first mention is typically more complete than later mentions. This heuristic also makes our system less sensitive to within-document coreference errors.[6] The representative mention only has special status for mention similarity: context similarity considers *all* mention contexts.

3.1 Constrained Hierarchical Clustering

HAC iteratively merges the "nearest" clusters according to context similarity. In our system, each cluster context is a bag of words W formed from the contexts of all coreference chains in that cluster. For each word in W we estimate a unigram Entity Language Model (ELM) (Raghavan et al., 2004):

$$P(w) = \frac{count_W(w) + \rho P_V(w)}{\sum_{w'} count_W(w') + \rho}$$

$P_V(w)$ is the unigram probability in *all* contexts in the corpus[7] and ρ is a smoothing parameter. For any

[5]Specification of a combined similarity measure is an interesting direction for future work.

[6]These constraints are similar to the *pair-filters* of Mayfield et al. (2009).

[7]Recall that after context mapping, all languages have a common vocabulary V.

two entity clusters E_a and E_b, the distance between P_{E_a} and P_{E_b} is given by a metric based on the Jensen-Shannon Divergence (JSD) (Endres and Schindelin, 2003):

$$\begin{aligned} dist(P_{E_a}, P_{E_b}) &= \sqrt{2 \cdot JSD(P_{E_a}||P_{E_b})} \\ &= \sqrt{KL(P_{E_a}||M) + KL(M||P_{E_b})} \end{aligned}$$

where $KL(P_{E_a}||M)$ is the Kullback-Leibler divergence and $M = \frac{1}{2}(P_{E_a} + P_{E_b})$.

We initialize HAC to $E = C$, i.e., the initial clustering solution is just the set of all coreference chains. Then we remove all links in the HAC proximity matrix that violate pairwise cannot-link constraints. During clustering, we do not merge E_a and E_b if *any* pair of chains violates a cannot-link constraint. This procedure propagates the cannot-link constraints (Klein et al., 2002). To output E, we stop clustering when the minimum JSD exceeds a stop threshold γ, which is tuned on a development set.

3.2 Constrained Dirichlet Process Mixture Model (DPMM)

Instead of tuning a parameter like γ, it would be preferable to let the data dictate the number of entity clusters. We thus consider a non-parametric Bayesian mixture model where the mixtures are multinomial distributions over the entity contexts S. Specifically, we consider a DPMM, which automatically infers the number of mixtures. Each C_a has an associated mixture θ_a:

$$\begin{aligned} C_a|\theta_a &\sim \text{Mult}(\theta_a) \\ \theta_a|G &\sim \text{G} \\ G|\alpha, G_0 &\sim \text{DP}(\alpha, G_0) \\ \alpha &\sim \text{Gamma}(1, 1) \end{aligned}$$

where α is the concentration parameter of the DP prior and G_0 is the base distribution with support V. For our experiments, we set $G_0 = \text{Dir}(\pi_1, \ldots, \pi_V)$, where $\pi_i = P_V(w_i)$.

For inference, we use the Gibbs sampler of Vlachos et al. (2009), which can incorporate pairwise constraints. The sampler is identical to a standard collapsed, token-based sampler, except the conditional probability $p(E_a = E|E_{-a}, C_a) = 0$ if C_a cannot be merged with the chains in cluster E. This property makes the model non-exchangeable, but in practice non-exchangeable models are sometimes useful (Blei and Frazier, 2010). During sampling, we also learn α using the auxiliary variable procedure of West (1995), so the only fixed parameters are those of the vague Gamma prior. However, we found that these hyper-parameters were not sensitive.

4 Training Data and Procedures

We trained our system for Arabic-English cross-lingual entity clustering.[8]

Maxent Mention Similarity The Maxent mention similarity model requires a parallel name list for training. Name pair lists can be obtained from the LDC (e.g., LDC2005T34 contains nearly 450,000 parallel Chinese-English names) or Wikipedia (Irvine et al., 2010). We extracted 12,860 name pairs from the parallel Arabic-English translation treebanks,[9] although our experiments show that the model achieves high accuracy with significantly fewer training examples. We generated a uniform distribution of training examples by running a Bernoulli trial for each aligned name pair in the corpus. If the coin was heads, we replaced the English name with another English name chosen randomly from the corpus.

MT Context Mapping For the MT context mapping method, we trained Phrasal with all data permitted under the NIST OpenMT Ar-En 2009 constrained track evaluation. We built a 5-gram language model from the Xinhua and AFP sections of the Gigaword corpus (LDC2007T07), in addition to all of the target side training data. In addition to the baseline Phrasal feature set, we used the lexicalized re-ordering model of Galley and Manning (2008).

PLTM Context Mapping For PLTM training, we formed a corpus of 19,139 English-Arabic topically-aligned Wikipedia articles. Cross-lingual links in Wikipedia are abundant: as of February 2010, there were 77.07M cross-lingual links among Wikipedia's 272 language editions (de Melo and Weikum, 2010). To increase vocabulary coverage for our ACE2008 evaluation corpus, we added 20,000 document singletons from the ACE2008 training corpus. The

[8] We tokenized all English documents with packages from the Stanford parser (Klein and Manning, 2003). For Arabic documents, we used Mada (Habash and Rambow, 2005) for orthographic normalization and clitic segmentation.

[9] LDC Catalog numbers LDC2009E82 and LDC2009E88.

topically-aligned tuples served as "glue" to share topics between languages, while the ACE documents distribute those topics over in-domain vocabulary.[10]

We used the PLTM implementation in Mallet (McCallum, 2002). We ran the sampler for 10,000 iterations and set the number of topics $K = 512$.

5 Task Evaluation Framework

Our experimental design is a cross-lingual extension of the standard cross-document coreference resolution task, which appeared in ACE2008 (Strassel et al., 2008; NIST, 2008). We evaluate name (NAM) mentions for cross-lingual person (PER) and organization (ORG) entities. Neither the number nor the attributes of the entities are known (i.e., the task does not include a knowledge base). We report results for both gold and automatic within-document mention detection and coreference resolution.

Evaluation Metrics We use *entity-level* evaluation metrics, i.e., we evaluate the E entity clusters rather than the mentions. For the gold setting, we report:

- B^3 (Bagga and Baldwin, 1998a): Precision and recall are computed from the intersection of the hypothesis and reference clusters.
- CEAF (Luo, 2005): Precision and recall are computed from a maximum bipartite matching between hypothesis and reference clusters.
- NVI (Reichart and Rappoport, 2009): Information-theoretic measure that utilizes the entropy of the clusters and their mutual information. Unlike the commonly-used Variation of Information (VI) metric, normalized VI (NVI) is not sensitive to the size of the data set.

For the automatic setting, we must apply a different metric since the number of system chains may differ from the reference. We use B^3_{sys} (Cai and Strube, 2010), a variant of B^3 that was shown to penalize both twinless reference chains and spurious system chains more fairly.

Evaluation Corpus The automatic evaluation of cross-lingual coreference systems requires annotated multilingual corpora. Cross-document annotation is expensive (Strassel et al., 2008), so we chose the ACE2008 Arabic-English evaluation corpus as a starting point for cross-lingual annotation. The corpus consists of seven genres sampled from independent sources over the course of a decade (Tbl. 3). The corpus provides gold mono-lingual cross-document coreference annotations for both PER and ORG entities. Using these annotations as a starting point, we found and annotated 216 cross-lingual entities.[11]

	Docs	Tokens	Entities	Chains	Mentions
ARABIC	412	178,269	2,594	4,216	9,222
ENGLISH	414	246,309	2,278	3,950	9,140

Table 3: ACE2008 evaluation corpus PER and ORG entity statistics. Singleton chains account for 51.4% of the Arabic data and 46.2% of the English data. Just 216 entities appear in both languages.

Because a similar corpus did not exist for development, we split the evaluation corpus into development and test sections. However, the usual method of splitting by document would not confine all mentions of each entity to one side of the split. We thus split the corpus by *global entity id*. We assigned one-third of the entities to development, and the remaining two-thirds to test.

6 Comparison to Related Tasks and Work

Our modeling techniques and task formulation can be viewed as cross-lingual extensions to cross-document coreference resolution. The classic work on this task was by Bagga and Baldwin (1998b), who adapted the Vector Space Model (VSM) (Salton et al., 1975). Gooi and Allan (2004) found effective algorithmic extensions like agglomerative clustering. Successful feature extensions to the VSM for cross-document coreference have included biographical information (Mann and Yarowsky, 2003) and syntactic context (Chen and Martin, 2007). However, neither of these feature sets generalize easily to the cross-lingual setting with multiple entity types. Fleischman and Hovy (2004) added a discriminative pairwise mention classifier to a VSM-like model, much as we do. More

[10] Mimno et al. (2009) showed that so long as the proportion of topically-aligned to non-aligned documents exceeded 0.25, the topic distributions (as measured by mean Jensen-Shannon Divergence between distributions) did not degrade significantly.

[11] The annotators were the first author and another fluent speaker of Arabic. The annotations, corrections, and corpus split are available at http://www.spencegreen.com/research/.

recent work has considered new models for web-scale corpora (Rao et al., 2010; Singh et al., 2011).

Cross-document work on languages other than English is scarce. Wang (2005) used a combination of the VSM and heuristic feature selection strategies to cluster transliterated Chinese personal names. For Arabic, Magdy et al. (2007) started with the output of the mention detection and within-document coreference system of Florian et al. (2004). They clustered the entities incrementally using a binary classifier. Baron and Freedman (2008) used complete-link agglomerative clustering, where merging decisions were based on a variety of features such as document topic and name uniqueness. Finally, Sayeed et al. (2009) translated Arabic name mentions to English and then formed clusters greedily using pairwise matching.

To our knowledge, the cross-lingual entity clustering task is novel. However, there is significant prior work on similar tasks:

- **Multilingual coreference resolution**: Adapt English within-document coreference models to other languages (Harabagiu and Maiorano, 2000; Florian et al., 2004; Luo and Zitouni, 2005).
- **Named entity translation**: For a non-English document, produce an inventory of entities in English. An ACE2007 pilot task (Song and Strassel, 2008).
- **Named entity clustering**: Assign semantic types to text mentions (Collins and Singer, 1999; Elsner et al., 2009).
- **Cross-language name search / entity linking**: Match a *single* query name against a list of known multilingual names (knowledge base). A track in the 2011 NIST Text Analysis Conference (TAC-KBP) evaluation (Aktolga et al., 2008; McCarley, 2009; Udupa and Khapra, 2010; McNamee et al., 2011).

Our work incorporates elements of the first three tasks. Most importantly, we avoid the key element of entity linking: a knowledge base.

7 Experiments

We performed intrinsic evaluations for both mention and context similarity. For context similarity, we analyzed mono-lingual entity clustering, which also facilitated comparison to prior work on the ACE2008 evaluation set. Our main results are for the new task: cross-lingual entity clustering.

Genre	#Train	#Test	Accuracy(%)
wb	125	16	87.5
bn	2,720	340	95.6
nw	7,443	930	96.6
all	10,288	1,286	97.1 (+7.55)

Table 4: Cross-lingual mention matching accuracy [%]. The training data contains names from three genres: broadcast news (bn), newswire (nw), and weblog (wb). We used the full training corpus (all) for the cross-lingual clustering experiments, but the model achieved high accuracy with significantly fewer training examples (e.g., bn).

	CEAF↑	NVI↓	B^3 ↑			
			#hyp	P	R	F1
Mono-lingual Arabic (#gold=1,721)						
HAC	87.2	0.052	1,669	89.8	89.8	89.8
Mono-lingual English (#gold=1,529)						
HAC	88.5	0.042	1,536	93.7	89.0	91.4

Table 5: Mono-lingual entity clustering evaluation (test set, *gold* within-document processing). Higher scores (↑) are better for CEAF and B^3, whereas lower (↓) is better for NVI. #gold indicates the number of reference entities, whereas #hyp is the size of E.

7.1 Intrinsic Evaluations

Cross-lingual Mention Matching We created a random 80/10/10 (train, development, test) split of the Maxent training corpus and evaluated binary classification accuracy (Tbl. 4). Of the mis-classified examples, we observed three major error types. First, the model learns that high edit distance is predictive of a mismatch. However, singleton strings that do not match often have a lower edit distance than longer strings that do match. As a result, singletons often cause false positives. Second, names that originate in a third language tend to violate the phonemic correspondences. For example, the model gives a false negative for a German football team: اف سي كيزرسلوترن (phonetic mapping: *af s kazrslawtrn*) versus "FC Kaiserslautern." Finally, names that require translation are problematic. For example, the classifier produces a false negative for ⟨God, *gd*⟩ $\stackrel{?}{=}$ ⟨ألّله, *allh*⟩.

#gold = 3,057	CEAF↑	NVI↓	B^3 ↑				B^3_{target} ↑ (#gold = 146)			
			#hyp	P	R	F1	#hyp	P	R	F1
SINGLETON	64.9	0.165	5,453	**100.0**	56.1	71.8	1,587	**100.0**	9.20	16.9
NO-CONTEXT	57.4	0.136	2,216	65.6	75.2	70.1	517	78.3	41.8	54.5
HAC+MT	**79.8**	**0.070**	2,783	84.4	**86.4**	**85.4**	310	91.7	**69.1**	**78.8**
DPMM+MT	74.3	0.122	3,649	89.3	64.1	74.6	634	93.3	24.3	38.6
HAC+PLTM	72.1	0.110	2,746	76.9	77.6	77.3	506	84.4	44.6	58.4
DPMM+PLTM	57.2	0.180	2,609	64.0	62.8	63.4	715	73.9	22.2	34.1

Table 6: Cross-lingual entity clustering (test set, *gold* within-document processing). B^3_{target} is the standard B^3 metric applied to the subset of target cross-lingual entities in the test set. For CEAF and B^3, SINGLETON is the stronger baseline due to the high proportion of singleton entities in the corpus. Of course, cross-lingual entities have at least two chains, so NO-CONTEXT is a better baseline for cross-lingual clustering.

Mono-lingual Entity Clustering For comparison, we also evaluated our system on a standard mono-lingual cross-document coreference task (Arabic and English) (Tbl. 5). We configured the system with HAC clustering and Jaro-Winkler (within-language) mention similarity. We built mono-lingual ELMs for context similarity.

We used two baselines:

- SINGLETON: $E = C$, i.e., the cross-lingual clustering solution is just the set of mono-lingual coreference chains. This is a common baseline for mono-lingual entity clustering (Baron and Freedman, 2008).
- NO-CONTEXT: We run HAC with $\rho = \infty$. Therefore, E is the set of fully-connected components in C subject to the pairwise constraints.

For HAC, we manually tuned the stop threshold γ, the Jaro-Winkler threshold η, and the ELM smoothing parameter ρ on the development set. For the DPMM, no development tuning was necessary, and we evaluated a single sample of E taken after 3,000 iterations.

To our knowledge, Baron and Freedman (2008) reported the only previous results on the ACE2008 data set. However, they only gave gold results for English, and clustered the entire evaluation corpus (test+development). To control for the effect of within-document errors, we considered their gold input (mention detection and within-document coreference resolution) results. They reported B^3 for the two entity types separately: ORG (91.5% F1) and PER (94.3% F1). The different experimental designs preclude a precise comparison, but the accuracy of the two systems are at least in the same range.

#gold = 3,057	B^3_{sys} ↑			
	#hyp	P	R	F1
SINGLETON	7,655	**100.0**	57.1	72.7
NO-CONTEXT	2,918	63.3	71.1	67.0
HAC+MT	3,804	75.6	**77.8**	**76.7**
DPMM+MT	4,491	77.1	62.5	69.0
HAC+PLTM	6,353	94.1	62.8	75.3
DPMM+PLTM	3,522	64.6	62.0	63.3

Table 7: Cross-lingual entity clustering (test set, *automatic* (Serif) within-document processing). For HAC, we used the same parameters as the gold setting.

7.2 Cross-lingual Entity Clustering

We evaluated four system configurations on the new task: HAC+MT, HAC+PLTM, DPMM+MT, and DPMM+PLTM. First, we established an upper bound by assuming gold within-document mention detection and coreference resolution (Tbl. 6). This setting isolated the new cross-lingual clustering methods from within-document processing errors. Then we evaluated with Serif (automatic) within-document processing (Tbl. 7). This second experiment replicated an application setting. We used the same baselines and tuning procedures as in the mono-lingual clustering experiment.

Results In the gold setting, HAC+MT produces the best results, as expected. The dimensionality reduction of the vocabulary imposed by PLTM significantly reduces accuracy, but HAC+PLTM still exceeds the baseline. We tried increasing the number of PLTM topics k, but did not observe an improvement in task accuracy. For both context-mapping methods, the DPMM suffers from low-recall. Upon inspection, the clustering solution of DPMM+MT contains a high proportion of singleton hypotheses, suggesting that the model finds lower similarity in the presence of a larger vocabulary. When the context vocabulary consists of PLTM topics, larger clusters are discovered (DPMM+PLTM).

The effect of dimensionality reduction is also apparent in the clustering solutions of the PLTM models. For example, for the Serif output, DPMM+PLTM produces a cluster consisting of "White House", "Senate", "House of Representatives", and "Parliament". Arabic mentions of the latter three entities pass the pairwise mention similarity constraints due to the word مجلس 'council', which appears in text mentions for all three legislative bodies. A cross-language matching error resulted in the linking of "White House", and the reduced granularity of the contexts precluded further disambiguation. Of course, these entities probably appear in similar contexts.

The caveat with the Serif results in Tbl. 7 is that 3,251 of the 7,655 automatic coreference chains are *not* in the reference. Consequently, the evaluation is dominated by the penalty for spurious system coreference chains. Nonetheless, all models except for DPMM+PLTM exceed the baselines, and the relationships between models depicted in the gold experiments hold for the this setting.

8 Conclusion

Cross-lingual entity clustering is a natural step toward more robust natural language understanding. We proposed pipeline models that make clustering decisions based on cross-lingual similarity. We investigated two methods for mapping documents in different languages to a common representation: MT and the PLTM. Although MT may achieve more accurate results for some language pairs, the PLTM training resources (e.g., Wikipedia) are readily available for many languages. As for the clustering algorithms, HAC appears to perform better than the DPMM on our dataset, but this may be due to the small corpus size. The instance-level constraints represent tendencies that could be learned from larger amounts of data. With more data, we might be able to relax the constraints and use an exchangeable DPMM, which might be more effective. Finally, we have shown that significant quantities of within-document errors cascade into the cross-lingual clustering phase. As a result, we plan a model that clusters the mentions directly, thus removing the dependence on within-document coreference resolution.

In this paper, we have set baselines and proposed models that significantly exceeded those baselines. The best model improved upon the cross-lingual entity baseline by 24.3% F1. This result was achieved without a knowledge base, which is required by previous approaches to cross-lingual entity linking. More importantly, our techniques can be used to extend existing cross-document entity clustering systems for the increasingly multilingual web.

Acknowledgments We thank Jason Eisner, David Mimno, Scott Miller, Jim Mayfield, and Paul McNamee for helpful discussions. This work was started during the SCALE 2010 summer workshop at Johns Hopkins. The first author is supported by a National Science Foundation Graduate Fellowship.

References

E. Aktolga, M. Cartright, and J. Allan. 2008. Cross-document cross-lingual coreference retrieval. In *CIKM*.

G. Andrew and J. Gao. 2007. Scalable training of L1-regularized log-linear models. In *ICML*.

C. E. Antoniak. 1974. Mixtures of Dirichlet processes with applications to Bayesian nonparametric problems. *The Annals of Statistics*, 2(6):1152–1174.

A. Bagga and B. Baldwin. 1998a. Algorithms for scoring coreference chains. In *LREC*.

A. Bagga and B. Baldwin. 1998b. Entity-based cross-document coreferencing using the vector space model. In *COLING-ACL*.

A. Baron and M. Freedman. 2008. Who is Who and What is What: Experiments in cross-document co-reference. In *EMNLP*.

D. Blei and P. Frazier. 2010. Distance dependent Chinese restaurant processes. In *ICML*.

J. Cai and M. Strube. 2010. Evaluation metrics for end-to-end coreference resolution systems. In *Proceedings of the SIGDIAL 2010 Conference*.

D. Cer, M. Galley, D. Jurafsky, and C. D. Manning. 2010. Phrasal: A statistical machine translation toolkit for exploring new model features. In *HLT-NAACL, Demonstration Session*.

E. Charniak. 2001. Unsupervised learning of name structure from coreference data. In *NAACL*.

Y. Chen and J. Martin. 2007. Towards robust unsupervised personal name disambiguation. In *EMNLP-CoNLL*.

P. Christen. 2006. A comparison of personal name matching: Techniques and practical issues. Technical Report TR-CS-06-02, Australian National University.

M. Collins and Y. Singer. 1999. Unsupervised models for named entity classification. In *EMNLP*.

G. de Melo and G. Weikum. 2010. Untangling the cross-lingual link structure of Wikipedia. In *ACL*.

M. Elsner, E. Charniak, and M. Johnson. 2009. Structured generative models for unsupervised named-entity clustering. In *HLT-NAACL*.

D. M. Endres and J. E. Schindelin. 2003. A new metric for probability distributions. *IEEE Transactions on Information Theory*, 49(7):1858 – 1860.

M. Fleischman and E. Hovy. 2004. Multi-document person name resolution. In *ACL Workshop on Reference Resolution and its Applications*.

R. Florian, H. Hassan, A. Ittycheriah, H. Jing, N. Kambhatla, et al. 2004. A statistical model for multilingual entity detection and tracking. In *HLT-NAACL*.

A. T. Freeman, S. L. Condon, and C. M. Ackerman. 2006. Cross linguistic name matching in English and Arabic: a one to many mapping extension of the Levenshtein edit distance algorithm. In *HLT-NAACL*.

M. Galley and C. D. Manning. 2008. A simple and effective hierarchical phrase reordering model. In *EMNLP*.

C. H. Gooi and J. Allan. 2004. Cross-document coreference on a large scale corpus. In *HLT-NAACL*.

N. Habash and O. Rambow. 2005. Arabic tokenization, part-of-speech tagging and morphological disambiguation in one fell swoop. In *ACL*.

S. M. Harabagiu and S. J. Maiorano. 2000. Multilingual coreference resolution. In *ANLP*.

A. Irvine, C. Callison-Burch, and A. Klementiev. 2010. Transliterating from all languages. In *AMTA*.

D. Klein and C. D. Manning. 2003. Accurate unlexicalized parsing. In *ACL*.

D. Klein, S. D. Kamvar, and C. D. Manning. 2002. From instance-level constraints to space-level constraints: Making the most of prior knowledge in data clustering. In *ICML*.

K. Knight and J. Graehl. 1998. Machine transliteration. *Computational Linguistics*, 24:599–612.

X. Luo and I. Zitouni. 2005. Multi-lingual coreference resolution with syntactic features. In *HLT-EMNLP*.

X. Luo. 2005. On coreference resolution performance metrics. In *HLT-EMNLP*.

W. Magdy, K. Darwish, O. Emam, and H. Hassan. 2007. Arabic cross-document person name normalization. In *Workshop on Computational Approaches to Semitic Languages*.

G. S. Mann and D. Yarowsky. 2003. Unsupervised personal name disambiguation. In *NAACL*.

C. D. Manning, P. Raghavan, and H. Schütze. 2008. *Introduction to Information Retrieval*. Cambridge University Press.

J. Mayfield, D. Alexander, B. Dorr, J. Eisner, T. Elsayed, et al. 2009. Cross-document coreference resolution: A key technology for learning by reading. In *AAAI Spring Symposium on Learning by Reading and Learning to Read*.

A. K. McCallum. 2002. MALLET: A machine learning for language toolkit. http://mallet.cs.umass.edu.

J. S. McCarley. 2009. Cross language name matching. In *SIGIR*.

P. McNamee, J. Mayfield, D. Lawrie, D.W. Oard, and D. Doermann. 2011. Cross-language entity linking. In *IJCNLP*.

D. Mimno, H. M. Wallach, J. Naradowsky, D. A. Smith, and A. McCallum. 2009. Polylingual topic models. In *EMNLP*.

NIST. 2008. Automatic Content Extraction 2008 evaluation plan (ACE2008): Assessment of detection and recognition of entities and relations within and across documents. Technical Report rev. 1.2d, National Institute of Standards and Technology (NIST), 8 August.

E. H. Porter and W. E. Winkler, 1997. *Approximate String Comparison and its Effect on an Advanced Record Linkage System*, chapter 6, pages 190–199. U.S. Bureau of the Census.

H. Raghavan, J. Allan, and A. McCallum. 2004. An exploration of entity models, collective classification and relation description. In *KDD Workshop on Link Analysis and Group Detection*.

L. Ramshaw, E. Boschee, M. Freedman, J. MacBride, R. Weischedel, and A. Zamanian. 2011. SERIF language processing—effective trainable language understanding. In J. Olive et al., editors, *Handbook of Natural Language Processing and Machine Translation: DARPA Global Autonomous Language Exploitation*, pages 636–644. Springer.

D. Rao, P. McNamee, and M. Dredze. 2010. Streaming cross document entity coreference resolution. In *COLING*.

R. Reichart and A. Rappoport. 2009. The NVI clustering evaluation measure. In *CoNLL*.

G. Salton, A. Wong, and C. S. Yang. 1975. A vector space model for automatic indexing. *CACM*, 18:613–620, November.

A. Sayeed, T. Elsayed, N. Garera, D. Alexander, T. Xu, et al. 2009. Arabic cross-document coreference detection. In *ACL-IJCNLP, Short Papers*.

S. Singh, A. Subramanya, F. Pereira, and A. McCallum. 2011. Large-scale cross-document coreference using distributed inference and hierarchical models. In *ACL*.

Z. Song and S. Strassel. 2008. Entity translation and alignment in the ACE-07 ET task. In *LREC*.

S. Strassel, M. Przybocki, K. Peterson, Z. Song, and K. Maeda. 2008. Linguistic resources and evaluation techniques for evaluation of cross-document automatic content extraction. In *LREC*.

R. Udupa and M. M. Khapra. 2010. Improving the multilingual user experience of Wikipedia using cross-language name search. In *HLT-NAACL*.

A. Vlachos, A. Korhonen, and Z. Ghahramani. 2009. Unsupervised and constrained Dirichlet process mixture models for verb clustering. In *Proc. of the Workshop on Geometrical Models of Natural Language Semantics*.

H. Wang. 2005. Cross-document transliterated personal name coreference resolution. In L. Wang and Y. Jin, editors, *Fuzzy Systems and Knowledge Discovery*, volume 3614 of *Lecture Notes in Computer Science*, pages 11–20. Springer.

M. West. 1995. Hyperparameter estimation in Dirichlet process mixture models. Technical report, Duke University.

Multi Event Extraction Guided by Global Constraints

Roi Reichart **Regina Barzilay**
Computer Science and Artificial Intelligence Laboratory
Massachusetts Institute of Technology
{roiri, regina}@csail.mit.edu

Abstract

This paper addresses the extraction of event records from documents that describe multiple events. Specifically, we aim to identify the fields of information contained in a document and aggregate together those fields that describe the same event. To exploit the inherent connections between field extraction and event identification, we propose to model them jointly. Our model is novel in that it integrates information from separate sequential models, using global potentials that encourage the extracted event records to have desired properties. While the model contains high-order potentials, efficient approximate inference can be performed with dual-decomposition. We experiment with two data sets that consist of newspaper articles describing multiple terrorism events, and show that our model substantially outperforms traditional pipeline models.

1 Introduction

Today, most efforts in information extraction have focused on the field extraction task, commonly formulated as a sequence tagging problem. When a document describes a single event, the list of extracted fields provides a useful abstraction of the input document. In practice, however, a typical newspaper document describes multiple events, and a flat list of field values may not contain the sufficient structure required for many NLP applications. Our goal is therefore to extract event templates which aggregate field values for individual events.

Consider, for instance, the New York Times article excerpt in Figure 1 that describes three related terrorist events. As this example illustrates, in order to populate the corresponding event templates, the model needs to identify segments that describe individual events. Such segmentation is challenging, as event boundaries are not explicitly demarcated in the text. Moreover, descriptions of different events are often intermingled, as in the above example, further complicating boundary recovery.

In this paper, we consider a model that jointly performs event segmentation and field extraction. This model capitalizes on the inherent connection between the two tasks in order to reduce the ambiguity of template-based extraction. For example, the distribution of field values in the text provides strong clues about event segmentation, such as the presence of multiple new fields strongly signaling a segment boundary. Likewise, knowledge of the boundaries enables the model to rule out mutually inconsistent predictions, such as extracting two distinct locations for the same event.

We formulate our approach as a joint model that marks each word with field and event labels simultaneously. At the sentence level, segmentation and field extraction taggers are implemented using separate sequence models operating over local features. At the document level, the model encourages global consistency via potentials that link the extracted event records and their fields. Some of these potentials are limited to fields of an individual event such as the "single city per event" constraint. Others encode discourse-level properties of the whole document and thus involve records of multiple events,

A powerful **car bomb exploded** today in **Baghdad** inside the holiest **Shiite shrine** . As many as **95 people** were killed in the event, according to sources in Washington. The **blast** came only two days after another **car bomb exploded** in a crowded **street** in **Mosul** in the northern part of **Iraq**, killing **13 pedestrians**, in an attack carried out by **Al Qaeda**. Together with the previous attack by **Al Qaeda**, the **shooting** in **Najaf** three weeks ago that killed **15 American soldiers**, violence seemed to spike to its highest level. The **bombing** today, happened around 9am, when the roads are crowded with people. ...

	Organization	Tactic	Target	Weapon	Fatalities	City	Country
Event 1	—	bombing	Shiite shrine	car bomb	95 people	Baghdad	—
Event 2	Al Qaeda	bombing	—	car bomb	13 pedestrians	Mosul	Iraq
Event 3	Al Qaeda	shooting	—	—	15 American Soldiers	Najaf	—

Figure 1: A New York times article describing three terrorist events and a table demonstrating the corresponding event records.

such as the tendency in newspaper reporting to feature the main event at the beginning and repeatedly throughout the document.

While these high-order potentials encode important linguistic properties of valid assignments, they greatly complicate learning and inference. Therefore, our method estimates the parameters of the local sequence models and the global potentials separately. Then, at inference time, it finds variable assignments that are most consistent with both the local models and the global potentials. Inference is implemented via dual-decomposition, an efficient algorithm shown to be effective for complex joint inference problems.

We evaluate our approach for event extraction on two data sets, one is a new collection of long newspaper articles and the other is a subset of the MUC-4 documents. Both data sets consist of articles that describe multiple terrorist events (40.3 and 12.4 sentences and 4.4 and 3.1 events per article for each data set on average). We demonstrate the benefits of the joint model for event extraction; it outperforms a traditional pipeline model by a significant margin. For instance, it yields an absolute gain of 8.5% for our new corpus when measured using document-level F-score. Our results show the effectiveness of global constraints in the context of template extraction and motivate their exploration in other IE tasks.

2 Previous Work

Event-Template Extraction Event template extraction has been previously explored in the MUC-4 scenario template task. Work on this task has focused on pipeline models which decouple the task into the sub-tasks of field extraction and event-based text segmentation. For example, rule-based methods (Rau et al., 1992; Chinchor et al., 1993) identify generalizations both for single field fillers and for relations between fields and use them to fill event templates. Likewise, classifier-based algorithms (Chieu et al., 2003; Xiao et al., 2004; Maslennikov and Chua, 2007; Patwardhan and Riloff, 2009) generally train individual classifiers for each type of field and aggregate candidate fillers based on a sentential event classifier. Finally, unsupervised techniques (Chambers and Jurafsky, 2011) have combined clustering, semantic roles, and syntactic relations in order to both construct and fill event templates.

In our work, we also address the sub-tasks of field extraction and event segmentation individually; however, we link them through soft global constraints and encourage consistency through joint inference. To facilitate the joint inference, we use a linear-chain CRF for each sub-task.

Global Constraints Previous work demonstrated the benefits of applying declarative constraints in information extraction (Finkel et al., 2005; Roth and tau Yih, 2004; Chang et al., 2007; Druck and McCallum, 2010). Constraints have been explored both at sentence and document level. For example, Finkel et al. (2005) employ document-level constraints to encourage global consistency of named entity assignments. Likewise, Chang et al. (2007) use constraints at multiple levels, such as sentence-level constraints to specify field boundaries and global constraints to ensure relation-level consistency. In our work we focus on document-level constraints. We utilize both discourse and record-coherence constraints to encourage consistency between local sequence models.

There has also been unsupervised work that demonstrates the benefit of domain-specific constraints (Chen et al., 2011). In our work we show that domain-specific constraints based on the common structure of newspaper articles are also useful to guide a supervised model.

3 Model

Problem Formulation Given a document, our goal is to extract field values and aggregate them into event records. The training data consists of event annotations where each word in the document is tagged with a field and with an event id. If a word is not a filler for a field, it is annotated with a default NULL field value. At test time, the number of events is not given and has to be inferred from the data.

Model Structure Our model is built around the connection between local extraction decisions and global constraints on event structure. Based on local cues, the model can identify candidate field fillers. However, connecting them to events requires a broader document context. To effectively capture this context, the model needs to group together portions of the document that describe the same event. Global constraints are instrumental in this process, as they drive the aggregation of contiguous segments computed by a local segmentation model. In addition, global constraints coordinate local decisions and thereby enable us to express important discourse dependencies between various assignments.

To implement these ideas in a computational framework, we define an undirected graphical model with a vertex set $V = X \cup Y \cup Z$. X is a set of observed nodes; x_i represents the $i$the word in a document. Y and Z are sets of unobserved nodes corresponding to the field and event assignments respectively of the ith word. The number of input words in a document is denoted by n.

We define three types of potentials:

- *Field-labeling Potentials* associate words in a document with field labels based on their local sentential context.
- *Event-labeling Potentials* associate words in a document with event boundaries based on the local surroundings of a candidate boundary.
- *Global Consistency Potentials* link the extracted event records and their fields to encourage global consistency. These potentials are defined over the entire set of variables related to a document.

The resulting maximum aposteriori problem is:

$$MAP(\theta) = \sum_{f \in F} \theta_f(r_f)$$

where θ_f are the potential functions and $\{r_f | f \subseteq \{1, \ldots, n\}, f \in F\}$ is the set of their variables.

3.1 Modeling Local Dependencies

Field Labeling The first step of the model is tagging the words in the input document with fields. Following traditional approaches, we employ a linear-chain CRF (Lafferty et al., 2001) that operates over standard lexical, POS-based and syntactic features (Finkel et al., 2005; Finkel and Manning, 2009; Bellare and McCallum, 2009; Yao et al., 2010).

Event Segmentation At the local level, event analysis involves identification of event boundaries which we model as linear segmentation. To this end, we employ a binary CRF that predicts whether a given word starts a description of a new event or continues the description of the current event, based on lexical and POS-based features. In addition, we add features obtained from the output of the field extraction CRF. These features capture the intuition that boundary sentences often contain multiple fields.

The potential functions of these components are given by the likelihoods of the corresponding CRFs.

3.2 Modeling Global Dependencies

The main function of the global constraints is to link extracted fields to the corresponding events. In addition, the model can use global constraints to resolve potentially inconsistent decisions of the local models by encouraging them to agree with global, document-level properties. We consider two types of global consistency potentials: *discourse potentials* that involve interactions between multiple records, and *record coherence potentials* that capture patterns at the level of individual records.

The general form of a global potential p is:

$$\theta_f(x_{f-p}, y_{f-p}, z_{f-p}) = \begin{cases} \alpha_p & \text{if potential-property holds} \\ 0 & \text{otherwise} \end{cases}$$

Where $f - p$ is the index set of variables over which the potential is defined. Table 1 gives a formal description of all the potentials. Below we describe the linguistic intuition behind these potentials.

Discourse Potentials To populate event records with extracted information, the model needs to

Discourse	
MAIN EVENT	*Two consecutive sentences without fields indicate a transition to the main event:* $(\exists S_i, S_{i+1} \text{ s.t. } (\forall k \in S_i, y_k = NULL) \wedge (\forall k \in S_{i+1}, y_k = NULL)) \rightarrow$ $(\forall l \geq i \text{ s.t. } (\forall u, u \geq i, u < l, 1_{f_{ME}(S_u)=1}), \forall p \in S_l, z_p = CENTRAL)$
SEGMENT BOUNDARY	*Event changes should take place in multi-field sentences:* $\forall i, j \in I, ((i = j + 1) \wedge (z_i != z_j)) \rightarrow$ $(\exists i_1 \dots i_t \in I \text{ s.t. } 1_{[f_{s-SB}(i, i_1, \dots i_t)=1]} \wedge 1_{[f_{f-SB}(i_1, \dots i_t)=1]})$
EVENT REDUNDANCY	*Events should not significantly overlap:* $\forall i, j \in \{1, \dots, \lvert Z \rvert\}, \exists k, l \in I \text{ s.t.}$ $((y_k = y_l) \wedge (y_k != NULL) \wedge (z_k = i) \wedge (z_l = j) \wedge (x_k != x_l))$
Record Coherence	
FIELD SPARSITY	*Some fields take a single unique value per record:* $\forall K, L \subset I, C \in \xi, ((Y_K = C) \wedge (Y_L = C) \wedge (Z_K = Z_L)) \rightarrow (X_K = X_L)$
RECORD DENSITY	*Words associated with a field should fill the field if it is otherwise empty:* $\forall i \in \zeta, C \in \xi, (\exists k \in I \text{ s.t. } (1_{[C_{ind}(x_k)=1]}) \wedge (z_k = i)) \rightarrow (\exists l \in I \text{ s.t. } (y_l = C) \wedge (z_l = i))$

Table 1: Logical formulations of the properties encouraged by the global potentials. S_i is the set of indexes corresponding the the ith sentence. $f_{ME}(S_u) = 1$ *iff* there is no event change in sentence S_u. $f_{s-SB}(i_1, \dots, i_t) = 1$ *iff* the corresponding words appear in the same sentence. $f_{f-SB}(i_1, \dots, i_t) = 1$ *iff* the corresponding words have different, non-NULL, field values. $C_{ind}(x_k) = 1$ *iff* x_k is assigned to C in a training event record. $CENTRAL$ is the central event of the document, defined to be its first event. $I = \{1, \dots, n\}, \xi = \{1, \dots \lvert Y \rvert\}, \zeta = \{1, \dots, \lvert Z \rvert\}$.

group together sentences that describe the same event. The local boundary model can only predict contiguous blocks of event descriptions, but it cannot link together blocks that appear in different parts of the document. Our approach towards this task is informed by regularity in the discourse organization of news articles. A typical news story is devoted to a single event, mixed with short descriptions of other events. Therefore, we prefer event assignments where long segments with no field values – e.g., background descriptions – are associated with the main event. This intuition is formalized in the *Main Event Potential* shown in Table 1.

The second discourse constraint concerns detection of event boundaries. We prefer assignments in which the boundary sentence contains a large number of fields. This preference is expressed in the *Segment Boundary Potential* shown in Table 1.

The final discourse constraint favors assignments that reduce redundancy in generated records. It is unlikely that a document describes several events with significant factual overlap. This constraint is implemented in the *Event Redundancy Potential* shown in Table 1.

Record Coherence Potentials These potentials capture properties of valid field assignments in the context of a given event record. The first potential in this group — *Field Sparsity Potential* — is applied to fields, such as City, that tend to take a single unique value per event record.[1] This potential discourages assignments that link this field with multiple values within the same event. Similar constraints have been effectively used in information extraction in the past (Finkel et al., 2005). In our work, we apply this constraint at the event level, rather than at the document level, thereby enabling multiple variable values for multi-event documents.

The second record coherence potential — *Record Density Potential* — aims to reduce empty fields in the event record. This potential turns on when a local extractor fails to identify a filler for a field when processing a given event segment. If this segment contains words that are labeled as potential fillers in the context of other events in the training data, we prefer assignments that associate them with the field that otherwise would have been empty. This potential is inspired by the *one sense per discourse* constraint (Gale et al., 1992) that associates all the occurrences of the word in a document with the same semantic meaning.

[1] The potential is defined for the following fields: Terrorist Organization, Weapon, City, and Country.

4 Inference

Dual Decomposition The global potentials encode important document level information that links together the extracted event records and their fields. Introducing these potentials, however, greatly complicates inference. Consider the MAP equation of Section 3. If the intersection between each pair of subsets, $f_i, f_j \in F$, had been empty, we could have found the MAP assignment by solving each potential separately. However, since many subset pairs do overlap, we must enforce agreement among the assignments which results in an NP-hard problem.

In order to avoid this computational bottleneck we turn to dual-decomposition (Rush et al., 2010; Koo et al., 2010), an inference technique that enables efficient computation of a tight upper bound on the MAP objective, while preserving the original dependencies of the model. Dual decomposition has been recently applied to a joint model for biomedical entity and event extraction by Riedel and McCallum (2011). In their work, however, events are defined in the sentence level. Here we show how this technique can be applied to a model which involves document-level potentials.

We first re-write the MAP equation, such that it contains a local potential for each of the unobserved variables, as required by the inference algorithm:

$$MAP(\theta) = \max_{y,z} \sum_{j \in J} \theta_j(r_j) + \sum_{f \in F} \theta_f(r_f)$$

where we denote the set of indexes of all unobserved variables with J and refer to each of them with r_j. We then define the dual problem:

$$\min_{\delta} L(\delta),\ L(\delta) = \sum_{j \in J} \max_{r_j}[\theta_j(r_j) + \sum_{f:j \in f} \delta_{fj}(r_j)] + \sum_{f \in F} \max_{r_f}[\theta_f(r_f) - \sum_{j \in f} \delta_{fj}(r_j)]$$

where for every $f \in F$ and $j \in f$, δ_{fj} is a vector of Lagrange multipliers with an entry for each possible assignment of r_j. We add the notation δ_f for the matrix of Lagrange multipliers for all the variables in f, and for an assignment M of the variables in f we define $\delta_f(M)$ to be the corresponding vector of Lagrange multipliers. The multipliers can be viewed as messages transferred between the potentials to encourage agreement between their assignments.

The dual objective, $L(\delta)$, forms an upper bound on the MAP objective. Our inference algorithm therefore searches for its minimum, i.e. the tightest upper bound of the original MAP objective. $L(\delta)$ is convex and non-differentiable and can therefore be minimized by the subgradient descent algorithm in Figure 2 (a).

Set $g^0_{fj} \leftarrow 0$ for all $j \in J, f \in F$
for $k = 1$ to K **do**
  for $j \in J$ **do**
    $rl^k_j = \arg\max_{r_j}[\theta_j(r_j) + \sum_{f:j \in f} \delta_{fj}(r_j)]$
  $end \leftarrow TRUE$
  for $f \in F$ **do**
    $rp^k_f = \arg\max_{r_f}[\theta_f(r_f) - \sum_{j \in f} \delta_{fj}(r_j)]$
    for $j \in f$ **do**
      if $rl^k_j \neq rp^k_{fj}$ **then**
        $g^k_{fj}(rl^k_j)\ += 1$
        $g^k_{fj}(rp^k_{fj})\ -= 1$
        $end \leftarrow FALSE$
      $\delta^{k+1}_{fj} = \delta^k_{fj} - \beta_k \cdot g^k_{fj}$
  if end **then**
    return R^k
  $\beta_k \leftarrow 1/k$
return (R^K)

(a)

rl^k_j: Sort $[\theta_j(r_j) + \sum_{f:j \in f} \delta_{fj}(r_j)]$. Return the minimizing r_j.

rp^k_f:
$MMA^k_f \leftarrow$: Minimum-Message assignment
$PRA^k_f \leftarrow$: Property-Respecting assignment
if $(\alpha_p - sum(\delta_f(PRA)) > (-1) * sum(\delta_f(MMA))$ **then**
  $rp^k_f = PRA^k_f$
else
  $rp^k_f = MMA^k_f$

(b)

Figure 2: The inference algorithm. (a): The dual-decomposition algorithm. (b): Algorithms for the arg max operations of the dual-decomposition algorithm.

Individual Potentials Maximization The inference algorithm requires efficient solvers for its arg max problems. For the field labeling and event segmentation potentials, the messages are encoded into the feature space of the CRF, and exact maximization is achieved through standard CRF decoding. For the local potentials, (rl^k_j), the maximizing assignments are computed by sorting the messages for each unobserved variable (Figure 2 (b)).

The global potentials are more challenging. Ideally, we could find the optimal assignment, rp^*_f, that agrees with the assignments of the other potentials ($rp^*_f = argmin \sum_{j \in f} \delta_{fj}(rp_j)$) and at the same time respects the property encouraged by its own potential ($\theta_p(rp^*_f) > 0$). In practice, however, there may be no such assignment, in which case the assignment conflict needs to be resolved.

We first compute the *minimum-message assignment (MMA)*, the assignment that minimizes the message sum. If this assignment respects the potential property then it is the optimal assignment. Otherwise, we compute the *property-respecting assignment (PRA)*, the assignment with the (approximate) lowest message sum under the condition that the potential property holds. From these two assignments we select the one with the higher score.

Finding the MMA is simple, as it is the minimum-message assignment of each unobserved variable separately. However, finding the global optimal PRA is computationally demanding, as it requires searching over a very large assignment space. We therefore trade accuracy for efficiency and restrict each potential to modify the MMA assignment for only one type of variables: Y (fields) or Z (events). The discourse potentials and the FIELD SPARSITY potential are restricted to changes of the event variables, while the RECORD DENSITY potential is restricted to changes of the field variables.

For the MAIN EVENT potential, consecutive sentences with no fields trigger a return to the main event. For the SEGMENT BOUNDARY potential, event changes that take place in sentences with a small number of fields are removed. For our work, this threshold is set to three. For the EVENT REDUNDANCY potential, redundant events are integrated with the largest event in which they are contained. For the RECORD DENSITY potential, words seen in both training records and event text are used to fill empty fields. For each empty field in each event, words labeled with event are scanned for candidate fillers, and those with the minimal impact on the message sum are assigned to that field.

Finally, for the FIELD SPARSITY potential, if a field contains more than one word or phrase per event, the event assignments of these words or phrases are recomputed. This computation is implemented as a minimum matching problem in a bipartite graph. One side of the graph consists of a vertex for every word or phrase assigned to the addressed field, and the other side consists of one vertex for each event in the document. If the number of phrases assigned to the field is larger than the number of events in the document, some of the event vertices will be assigned to new events. The edge weights are the sum of message changes corresponding to relabeling the word or phrase with the new event. We solve this problem efficiently ($O(n^3)$) using the Kuhn-Munkres algorithm (Kuhn, 1955).

5 Experiments

Data This work focuses on multi-event extraction. While some of the articles in the MUC test corpus do have multiple events, the majority contain only one (77.5%) or two (12%). We therefore created two corpora for our experiments. The first is a new corpus of 70 articles from New York Times (NYT) LDC corpus, each describing one or more terrorist events from various parts of the world. The second, also of 70 articles, consists of a subset of the MUC articles that describe more than one event. We stripped this corpus from the MUC annotation and annotated it according to our scheme.

Annotations were provided by two annotators with graduate school educations. Every word was tagged with a field and an event id. The 8 fields we use are: Terrorist Organization, Target, Tactic, Weapon, Fatalities, Injuries, Country and City.

We compared the agreement between annotators on 10 articles by computing the percentage of words for which the annotators gave the same labeling. The inter-annotator agreement was 90.9% (kappa = 0.9) when fields and events are evaluated together (i.e., the annotators are considered to agree only when they assign the same field and event id to the word), 97.8% (kappa = 0.97) for events only, and 92% (kappa = 0.91) for fields only.

The two corpora differ from each other with respect to several important properties. The New-York Times articles are longer (40.3 compared to 12.4 sentences per article) and describe a larger number of events (4.4 compared to 3.1 events per article on average). In addition, while our hypothesis about the predominance of the main (first) event coverage holds for both corpora, it better characterizes the New-York Times corpus, as is demonstrated by the following two statistics.

First, in the NYT corpus the average number of sentences containing field fillers for the main event is 14.7, while for any other event the average number is 3.2. In the MUC corpus the corresponding numbers are 5.3 and 2.0. Second, in the NYT corpus the number of times an article goes back to a previously described event is 182 (average of 2.6 times per article), of which 154 (84.6%) are transitions to the main event. In the MUC corpus the number of times an article goes back to a previously described event is only 38 (average of 0.54 times per article), but, similarly to the NYT, in as much as 32 (84.2%) of these cases the transitions are to the main event.

Experimental Setup For both corpora, we used 30 articles for training (1218 sentences in NYT, 423 in MUC), 7 articles for development (358 sentences in NYT, 79 in MUC) and 33 articles for test (1244 sentences in NYT, 367 in MUC). The sentences were POS tagged with the MXPOST tagger (Ratnaparkhi, 1996) and parsed with the Charniak parser (Charniak and Johnson, 2005).

We trained our model with a two steps procedure. First, the local CRFs were separately trained on the training articles. Then, we trained the parameters of the global potentials using the structured perceptron algorithm (Collins, 2002) on the development data.

We perform joint inference over the local CRFs as well as the global potentials with dual decomposition. This algorithm is guaranteed to give the MAP assignment if it converges to a solution in which all the potentials agree on the label assignment for the variables in their scope. To deal with disagreements, we ran the algorithm for 200 iterations past the point of fluctuations around the dual minimum. The final label assignment is determined by a majority vote between the potentials in the 10 iterations with the highest total inter potential agreement (Sontag et al., 2010).

Baselines We compare our algorithm to two baseline models. The first baseline is related to previous techniques that decompose the task into field extraction and event segmentation sub-tasks (Jean-Louis et al., 2011; Patwardhan and Riloff, 2007; Patwardhan and Riloff, 2009). For this PIPELINE baseline, we run the CRF models described in Section 3.1, first the field CRF and then the event CRF. The field-based features of the event CRF are extracted from the output of the field CRF.

Our model incorporates global dependencies into a document level model. An alternative approach is to encode this information as local features that reflect global dependencies (Liang et al., 2008). We therefore constructed a second baseline, the bidirectional pipeline model (BI-PIPELINE), that considers global features which encode similar properties to those encouraged by our global potentials. We implement this by incorporating event-based features into the feature set of the field labeling CRF, while kipping the event segmentation CRF fixed. [2] As in the pipeline model, each CRF is trained separately on the training data. The BI-PIPELINE model, however, emulates our joint inference procedure by iteratively running a field labeling and an event segmentation CRFs. The number of iterations for this model was estimated on development data.

Evaluation Measures We follow the MUC-4 scoring guidelines (Chinchor, 1992). To compare between a learned and a gold standard event, we compute the word-level F-score between each of their fields and average the results. If a field is empty in both event records, it is not counted in the mutual event score, while if it is empty in only one of the event records, its F-score is 0.

Ideally, the measure should be able to capture paraphrases. For example, if the *Tactic* field in a gold event record contains the words "bombing" and "blast", the measure is expected to give a perfect score to a learned record that contains one of these words. Therefore, as in the MUC-4 guidelines, we count pre-specified synonyms and morphological derivations of the same word only once.

For every document, we then map the learned events to the gold events in a greedy 1-1 manner using the Kuhn-Munkres algorithm (Kuhn, 1955). Once we have an event mapping, we can report an average recall, precision and F-score across the test set for all fields, events and documents (where the document F-score is the average F-score of its events). We use the sign test to measure the statistical significance for our results. Since the number of events described in a document is not given to the models as input, we also report the average ratio between the number of induced and gold events.

[2] Example additional features are: (1) whether a word with the same most frequent field (MFF) as the encoded word previously appeared in its event; (2) whether a new event is started in the sentence of the encoded word; and (3) whether the event of the encoded word contains at least one word annotated with the MFF of the encoded word.

NYT	Documents			Events			Fields			Event Number
	R	P	F	R	P	F	R	P	F	Ratio
Joint Model	**38.7**	**42.4**	**38.5**	**36.2**	**40.8**	**36.4**	**43.6**	**49.1**	**43.8**	0.95
Bi-pipeline Model	33.3	30.8	30.2	31.9	30.1	29.4	38.8	36.6	35.7	1.14
Pipeline Model	28.3	27.0	26.2	27.1	26.8	25.5	35.4	34.8	33.2	1.5

MUC	Documents			Events			Fields			Event Number
	R	P	F	R	P	F	R	P	F	Ratio
Joint Model	**49.8**	**43.2**	**43.5**	**48.7**	**43.0**	**42.7**	**53.6**	**45.9**	**46.2**	0.88
Bi-pipeline Model	38.1	38.6	36.3	34.3	33.9	32.2	41.5	40.5	38.6	0.92
Pipeline Model	30.8	32.8	29.7	29.9	32.0	28.9	37.9	40.1	36.6	0.89

Table 2: Performance of the joint model and the pipeline models on the event record extraction task. Top table is for the New-York Times data. Bottom table is for the MUC data. All results are statistically significant with $p < 0.05$.

NYT	TO	TAR	TAC	WEAP	INJ	FAT	CO	CITY
Joint Model	**21.9**	**23.4**	**49.0**	**39.6**	**40.8**	**49.1**	**43.1**	46.6
Bi-pipeline Model	8.4	19.7	47.5	20.9	25.9	18.3	38.8	38.1
Pipeline Model	7.1	18.1	41.9	36.9	19.1	16.5	38.0	**46.1**

MUC	TO	TAR	TAC	WEAP	INJ	FAT	CO	CITY
Joint Model	**49.0**	**25.2**	**63.6**	**62.0**	**43.3**	21.1	19.7	**38.3**
Bi-pipeline Model	28.0	24.7	38.2	55.8	42.7	**25.6**	**37.5**	37.2
Pipeline Model	34.9	23.4	50.3	56.5	10.4	12.4	30.0	32.0

Table 3: Comparison between the joint model and the pipeline models for the different fields. When the joint model is superior results are statistically significance with $p < 0.05$.

(a)

NYT	Fields			Events	
	R	P	F	GF	LF
Joint model	**47.3**	51.3	**49.2**	**54.8**	**61.3**
Bi-Pipeline	31.0	43.8	36.3	48.8	56.2
Pipeline Model	39.2	**55.4**	45.9	51.3	52.9

(b)

MUC	Fields			Events	
	R	P	F	GF	LF
Joint model	47.3	**51.3**	**49.2**	62.8	70.0
Bi-Pipeline	**49.5**	36.1	41.8	62.2	62.0
Pipeline Model	31.0	43.8	36.3	**65.5**	**70.3**

Table 4: Performance of the joint and the pipeline models on the labeling tasks of assigning words to fields (left) and to events (right). Field values are computed for words tagged with the non-NULL field. Events values are computed for words that are assigned to a non-NULL field by the gold standard (GF) or by the model (LF). When the joint model is superior, results for fields are statistically significant with $p < 0.01$ and for events with $p < 0.05$.

6 Results

Event-Records Results for event record extraction, the main task addressed in this paper, are presented in Table 2. For all measures, the model outperforms the pipeline baselines, with an F-score difference of up to 13.8%.

The rightmost column of the table demonstrates the tendency of our model to under-segment. For both corpora our model extracts a smaller number of events than the gold standard on average (5% for NYT, 12% for MUC). The pipeline baselines extract more events than our model on average. For NYT they over-segment (14% for bi-pipeline, 53% for the pipeline) while for MUC they under-segment (8% and 11% respectively). These differences are expected as the baselines cannot combine different text segments that describe the same event.

Table 3 presents per-field F-score performance. The joint model outperforms the pipeline baselines for 7 out of the 8 fields in the NYT experiments, and for 6 out of 8 fields in the MUC experiments.

Model Components Table 6 presents the performance of variants of the joint model created by excluding each potential type. The results demonstrate the significance of both discourse and record coherence potentials for the performance of the full model.

Sub-tasks Performance A model for our task

(a)

NYT	Gold Fields				Gold Events		
	Doc.	Events	Fields	Ratio	Doc.	Events	Fields
Joint Model	**69.1**	**62.5**	**64.4**	1.05	**45.7**	**46.5**	**50.0**
Bi-Pipeline	—	—	—	—	41.7	40.8	46.1
Pipeline	47.9	43.9	51.3	1.56	40.8	40.4	43.9

(b)

MUC	Gold Fields				Gold Events		
	Doc.	Events	Fields	Ratio	Doc.	Events	Fields
Joint model	**78.5**	**75.0**	**74.5**	0.76	**50.8**	**47.9**	**51.4**
Bi-Pipeline	—	—	—	—	37.0	34.3	39.9
Pipeline	76.1	71.1	72.0	0.78	32.6	31.2	36.0

Table 5: Performance of the joint model and the pipeline models when the gold standard for one of the labeling tasks is given at test time. Results are statistically significant with $p < 0.05$.

	NYT			
Excluded Component	Documents	Events	Fields	Event Rat.
Record Coherence	32.1	31.0	37.7	1.04
Discourse	26.7	26.3	34.3	1.5
	MUC			
Record Coherence	37.4	33.6	39.6	0.88
Discourse	37.7	36.6	42.7	0.89

Table 6: The effect of the record coherence potentials and of the discourse potentials on the performance of the joint model. Results are presented for F-scores, each line is for the full model when potentials of one type are excluded.

should determine both when a word is a good field filler and to which event the field belongs. Since our main evaluation collapses the effect of these decisions together, we performed two additional sets of experiments to analyze the model's accuracy on each sub-task separately.

Figure 4 presents the performance of the different models on the labeling tasks of assigning words to fields and to events. The number of words associated with a field differs between the gold standard and the models' output. For fields, we therefore report word level recall, precision and F-score between the set of words assigned a non-NULL field by a model and the corresponding gold standard set. For events, we compute the fraction of words assigned the correct event among the words assigned to a non-NULL field in either the gold standard or the output of the model.

Figure 5 presents the document F-score when the gold-standard fields (left) or events (right) of the test set are known at test time. Note that when the gold standard fields are known, the BI-PIPELINE model is not applicable anymore since it is designed to improve field assignment using event-informed features. The results demonstrate that encoding field information to the models is more valuable than encoding information about events. This provides us with an important direction for future improvement of our model.

Accuracy and Efficiency When we ran our algorithm on the joint task of the NYT data-set it converged after 89 iterations. For the MUC joint task and the ablation analysis experiments we ran the algorithm for 200 iterations past the point of fluctuations around the dual minimum.

On a 2GHz CPU, 2GB RAM machine, it took our dual-decomposition algorithm 15 minutes and 10 seconds to complete its run on the entire NYT test set. For the MUC joint task experiment, in the 10 iterations considered for the majority vote, there is full agreement between the potentials for 97.77% of the unobserved variables. That is, the voting scheme affects the assignment of only 2.23% of the unobserved variables.

7 Conclusions

In this paper we presented a joint model for identifying fields of information and aggregating them into event records. We experimented with two data sets of newspaper articles containing multiple event descriptions. Our results demonstrate the importance and effectiveness of global constraints for event record extraction.

Acknowledgements

The authors gratefully acknowledge the support of the DARPA Machine Reading Program under AFRL prime contract no. FA8750-09-C0172. Any opinions, findings and conclusions expressed in the material are those of the author(s) and do not necessarily reflect the views of DARPA, AFRL or the US government. Thanks also to the members of the MIT NLP group and to Amir Globerson for their suggestions and comments.

References

Kedar Bellare and Andrew McCallum. 2009. Generalized expectation criteria for bootstrapping extractors using record-text alignment. In *EMNLP*.

Nathanael Chambers and Dan Jurafsky. 2011. Template-based information extraction without the templates. In *ACL*.

Ming-Wei Chang, Lev Ratinov, and Dan Roth. 2007. Guiding semi-supervision with constraint driven learning. In *ACL*.

Eugene Charniak and Mark Johnson. 2005. Coarse-to-fine n-best parsing and maxent discriminative reranking. In *ACL*.

Harr Chen, Edward Benson, Tahira Naseem, and Regina Barzilay. 2011. In-domain relation discovery with meta-constraints via posterior regularization. In *ACL*.

Hai Leong Chieu, Hwee Tou Ng, and Yoong Keok Lee. 2003. Closing the gap: Learning-based information extraction rivaling knowledge-engineering methods. In *ACL*.

Nancy Chinchor, David Lewis, and Lynette Hirschman. 1993. Evaluating message understanding systems: an analysis of the third message understanding conference. *Computational Linguistics*, 19(3):409–449.

Nancy Chinchor. 1992. Muc-4 evaluation metrics. In *Fourth Message Understanding Conference (MUC-4)*.

Michael Collins. 2002. Discriminative training methods for hidden markov models: Theory and experiments with perceptron algorithms. In *EMNLP*.

Gregory Druck and Andrew McCallum. 2010. High-performance semi-supervised learning using discriminatively constrained generative models. In *ICML*.

Jenny Rose Finkel and Christopher D. Manning. 2009. Joint parsing and named entity recognition. In *NAACL*.

Jenny Rose Finkel, Trond Grenager, and Christopher D. Manning. 2005. Incorporating non-local information into information extraction systems by gibbs sampling. In *ACL*.

William Gale, Kenneth Church, and David Yarowsky. 1992. One sense per discourse. In *Proceedings of the 4th DARPA Speech and Natural Language Workshop*.

Ludovic Jean-Louis, Romaric Besancon, and Olivier Ferret. 2011. Text segmentation and graph-based methods for template filling in information extraction. In *IJCNLP*.

Terry Koo, Alexander M. Rush, Michael Collins, Tommi Jaakkola, and David Sontag. 2010. Dual decomposition for parsing with non-projective head automata. In *EMNLP*.

Harold W. Kuhn. 1955. The hungarian method for the assignment problem. *Naval Research Logistics Quarterly*, 2:83–97.

John Lafferty, Andrew McCallum, and Fernando Pereira. 2001. Conditional random fields: Probabilistic models for segmenting and labeling sequence data. In *ICML*.

Percy Liang, Hal Daume, and Dan Klein. 2008. Structure compilation: trading structure for features. In *ICML*.

Mstislav Maslennikov and Tat-Seng Chua. 2007. A multi-resolution framework for information extraction from free text. In *ACL*.

Siddharth Patwardhan and Ellen Riloff. 2007. Effective ie with semantic affinity patterns and relevant regions. In *EMNLP*.

Siddharth Patwardhan and Ellen Riloff. 2009. A unified model of phrasal and sentential evidence for information extraction. In *EMNLP*.

Adwait Ratnaparkhi. 1996. A maximum entropy part-of-speech tagger. In *WVLC*.

Lisa Rau, George Krupka, Paul Jacobs, Ira Sider, and Lois Childs. 1992. Muc-4 test results and analysis. In *Fourth Message Understanding Conference (MUC-4)*.

Sebastian Riedel and Andrew McCallum. 2011. Fast and robust joint models for biomedical event extraction. In *EMNLP*.

Dan Roth and Wen tau Yih. 2004. A linear programming formulation for global inference in natural language tasks. In *CoNLL*.

Alexander M. Rush, David Sontag, Michael Collins, and Tommi Jaakkola. 2010. On dual decomposition and linear programming relaxations for natural language processing. In *EMNLP*.

David Sontag, Amir Globerson, and Tommi Jaakkola. 2010. Introduction to dual decomposition for inference. In *Optimization for Machine Learning, editors S. Sra, S. Nowozin, and S. J. Wright: MIT Press*.

Jing Xiao, Tat-Seng Chua, and Hang Cui. 2004. Cascading use of soft and hard matching pattern rules for weakly supervised information extraction. In *COLING*.

Limin Yao, Sebastian Riedel, and Andrew McCallum. 2010. Collective cross-document relation extraction-without labelled data. In *EMNLP*.

Reference Scope Identification in Citing Sentences

Amjad Abu-Jbara
EECS Department
University of Michigan
Ann Arbor, MI, USA
amjbara@umich.edu

Dragomir Radev
EECS Department
University of Michigan
Ann Arbor, MI, USA
radev@umich.edu

Abstract

A citing sentence is one that appears in a scientific article and cites previous work. Citing sentences have been studied and used in many applications. For example, they have been used in scientific paper summarization, automatic survey generation, paraphrase identification, and citation function classification. Citing sentences that cite multiple papers are common in scientific writing. This observation should be taken into consideration when using citing sentences in applications. For instance, when a citing sentence is used in a summary of a scientific paper, only the fragments of the sentence that are relevant to the summarized paper should be included in the summary. In this paper, we present and compare three different approaches for identifying the fragments of a citing sentence that are related to a given target reference. Our methods are: word classification, sequence labeling, and segment classification. Our experiments show that segment classification achieves the best results.

1 Introduction

Citation plays an important role in science. It makes the accumulation of knowledge possible. When a reference appears in a scientific article, it is usually accompanied by a span of text that highlights the important contributions of the cited article. We call a sentence that contains an explicit reference to previous work a *citation sentence*. For example, sentence (1) below is a citing sentence that cites a paper by Philip Resnik and describes the problem Resnik addressed in his paper.

*(1) **Resnik (1999)** addressed the issue of language identification for finding Web pages in the languages of interest.*

Previous work has studied and used citation sentences in various applications such as: scientific paper summarization (Elkiss et al., 2008; Qazvinian and Radev, 2008; Mei and Zhai, 2008; Qazvinian et al., 2010; Qazvinian and Radev, 2010; Abu-Jbara and Radev, 2011), automatic survey generation (Nanba et al., 2000; Mohammad et al., 2009), citation function classification (Nanba et al., 2000; Teufel et al., 2006; Siddharthan and Teufel, 2007; Teufel, 2007), and paraphrase recognition (Nakov et al., 2004; Schwartz et al., 2007).

Sentence (1) above contains one reference, and the whole sentence is talking about that reference. This is not always the case in scientific writing. Sentences that contain references to multiple papers are very common. For example, sentence (2) below contains three references.

*(2) Grefenstette and Nioche (2000) and Jones and Ghani (2000) use the web to generate corpora for languages where electronic resources are scarce, while **Resnik (1999)** describes a method for mining the web for bilingual texts.*

The first fragment describes the contribution of Grefenstette and Nioche (2000) and Jones and Ghani (2000). The second fragment describes the contribution of Resnik (1999).

This observation should be taken into consideration when using citing sentences in the aforementioned applications. For example, in citation-based summarization of scientific papers, a subset of citing sentences that cite a given target paper is selected and used to form a summary of that paper. It is very likely that one or more of the selected sentences cite multiple papers besides the target. This means that some of the text included in the summary might be irrelevant to the summarized paper. Including irrelevant text in the summary introduces several problems. First, the summarization task aims at summarizing the contributions of the target paper using minimal text. Extraneous text takes space in the summary while being irrelevant and less important. Second, including irrelevant text in the summary breaks the context and confuses the reader. Therefore, if sentence (2) above is to be added to a citation-based summary of Resnikś (1999) paper, only the underlined fragment should be added to the summary and the rest of the sentence should be excluded.

For another example, consider the task of citation function classification. The goal of this task is to determine the reason for citing paper B by paper A based on linguistic and structural features extracted from citing sentences that appear in A and cite B. If a citing sentence in A cites multiple papers besides B, classification features should be extracted only from the fragments of the sentence that are relevant to B. Sentence (3) below shows an examples of this case.

(3) Cohn and Lapata (2008) used the GHKM extraction method (Galley et al., 2004), which is limited to constituent phrases and thus produces a reasonably small set of syntactic rules.

If the target reference is Cohn and Lapata (2008), only the underlined segment should be used for feature extraction. The limitation stated in the second segment of sentence is referring to Galley et al., (2004).

In this paper, we address the problem of identifying the fragments of a citing sentence that are related to a given target reference. Henceforth, we use the term *Reference Scope* to refer to those fragments. We present and compare three different approaches to this problem.

In the first approach, we define the problem as a word classification task. We classify each word in the sentence as *inside* or *outside* the scope of the target reference.

In the second approach, we define the problem as a sequence labeling problem. This is different from the first approach in that the label assigned to each word is dependent on the labels of nearby words. In the third approach, instead of classifying individual words, we split the sentence into segments and classify each segment as *inside* or *outside* the scope of the target reference.

Applying any of the three approaches is preceded by a preprocessing stage. In this stage, citing sentences are analyzed to tag references, identify groups of references, and distinguish between syntactic and non-syntactic references.

The rest of this paper is organized as follows. Section 2 examines the related work. We define the problem in Section3. Section 4 presents our approaches. Experiments, results and analysis are presented in Section 5. We conclude and provide directions to future work in Section 6

2 Related Work

Our work is related to a large body of research on citations (Hodges, 1972; Garfield et al., 1984). The interest in studying citations stems from the fact that bibliometric measures are commonly used to estimate the impact of a researcher's work (Borgman and Furner, 2002; Luukkonen, 1992). White (2004) provides a good recent survey of the different research lines that use citations. In this section we review the research lines that are relevant to our work and show how our work is different.

One line of research that is related to our work has to do with identifying what Nanba and Okumura (1999) call the *citing area* They define the citing area as the succession of sentences that appear around the location of a given reference in a scientific paper and have connection to it. Their algorithm starts by adding the sentence that contains the target reference as the first member sentence in the citing area. Then, they use a set of cue words and hand-crafted rules to determine whether the surrounding sentences should be added to the citing area or not. In (Nanba et al., 2000) they use their citing area identification algorithm to improve citation type classification and automatic survey generation.

Qazvinian and Radev (2010) addressed a similar problem. They proposed a method based on probabilistic inference to extract non-explicit citing sentences; i.e., sentences that appear around the sentence that contains the target reference and are related to it. They showed experimentally that citation-based survey generation produces better results when using both explicit and non-explicit citing sentences rather than using the explicit ones alone.

Although this work shares the same general goal with ours (i.e identifying the pieces of text that are relevant to a given target reference), our work is different in two ways. First, previous work mostly ignored the fact that the citing sentence itself might be citing multiple references. Second, it defined the *citing area* (Nanba and Okumura, 1999) or the *citation context* (Qazvinian and Radev, 2010) as a set of whole contiguous sentences. In our work, we address the case where one citing sentence cites multiple papers, and define what we call the *reference scope* to be the fragments (not necessarily contiguous) of the citing sentence that are related to the target reference.

In a recent work on citation-based summarization by Abu-Jbara and Radev (2011), the authors noticed the issue of having multiple references in one sentence. They raised this issue when they discussed the factors that impede the coherence and the readability of citation-based summaries. They suggested that removing the fragments of a citing sentence that are not relevant to the summarized paper will significantly improve the quality of the produced summaries. In their work, they defined the scope of a given reference as the shortest fragment of the citing sentence that contains the reference and could form a grammatical sentence if the rest of the sentence was removed. They identify the scope by generating the syntactic parse tree of the sentence and then finding the text that corresponds to the smallest subtree rooted at an S node and contains the target reference node as one of its leaf nodes. They admitted that their method was very basic and works only when the scope forms one grammatical fragment, which is not true in many cases.

Athar (2011) noticed the same issue with citing sentences that cite multiple references, but this time in the context of sentiment analysis in citations. He showed experimentally that identifying what he termed the *scope of citation influence* improves sentiment classification accuracy. He adapted the same basic method proposed by Abu-Jbara and Radev (2011). We use this method as a baseline in our evaluation below.

In addition to this related work, there is a large body of research that used citing sentences in different applications. For example, citing sentences have been used to summarize the contributions of a scientific paper (Qazvinian and Radev, 2008; Qazvinian et al., 2010; Qazvinian and Radev, 2010; Abu-Jbara and Radev, 2011). They have been also used to generate surveys of scientific paradigms (Nanba and Okumura, 1999; Mohammad et al., 2009). Several other papers analyzed citing sentences to recognize the citation function; i.e., the author's reason for citing a given paper (Nanba et al., 2000; Teufel et al., 2006; Teufel, 2007). Schwartz et al. (2007) proposed a method for aligning the words within citing sentences that cite the same paper. The goal of his work was to aid named entity recognition and paraphrase identification in scientific papers.

We believe that all the these applications will benefit from the output of our work.

3 Problem Definition

The problem that we are trying to solve is to identify which fragments of a given citing sentence that cites multiple references are semantically related to a given target reference. As stated above, we call these fragments the *reference scope*. Formally, given a citing sentence $S = \{w1, w2, ..., w_n\}$ where $w1, w2, ..., w_n$ are the tokens of the sentence and given that S contains a set of two or more references R, we want to assign the label 1 to the word w_i if it falls in the scope of a given target reference $r \in R$, and 0 otherwise.

For example, sentences (4) and (5) below are labeled for the target references Tetreault and Chodorow (2008), and Cutting et al.(1992) respectively. The underlined words are labeled 1 (i.e., inside the target reference scope), while all others are labeled 0.

(4) *For example, **Tetreault and Chodorow (2008)** use a maximum entropy classifier to build a model of correct preposition usage, with 7 million instances in their training set, and Lee and Knutsson (2008) use memory-based learning, with 10 million sentences in their training set.*

(5) *There are many POS taggers developed using different techniques for many major languages such as transformation-based error-driven learning (Brill, 1995), decision trees (Black et al., 1992), Markov model (**Cutting et al., 1992**), maximum entropy methods (Ratnaparkhi, 1996) etc for English.*

4 Approach

In this section, we present our approach for addressing the problem defined in the previous section. Our approach involves two stages: 1) preprocessing and 2) reference scope identification. We present three alternative methods for the second stage. The following two subsections describe the two stages.

4.1 Stage 1: Preprocessing

The goal of the preprocessing stage is to clean and prepare the citing sentence for the next processing steps. The second stage involves higher level text processing such as part-of-speech tagging, syntactic parsing, and dependency parsing. The available tools for these tasks are not trained on citing sentences which contain references written in a special format. For example, it is very common in scientific writing to have references (usually written between parentheses) that are not a syntactic part of the sentence. It is also common to cite a group of references who share the same contribution by listing them between parentheses separated by a comma or a semi-colon. We address these issues to improve the accuracy of the processing done in the second stage. The preprocessing stage involves three tasks:

4.1.1 Reference Tagging

The first preprocessing task is to find and tag all the references that appear in the citing sentence. Authors of scientific articles use standard patterns to include references in text. We apply a regular expression to find all the references that appear in a sentence. We replace each reference with a placeholder. The target reference is replaced by TREF. Each other reference is replaced by REF. We keep track of the original text of each replaced reference. Sentence (6) below shows an example of a citing sentence with the references replaced.

(6) *These constraints can be lexicalized (REF.1; REF.2), unlexicalized (REF.3; **TREF.4**) or automatically learned (REF.5; REF.6).*

4.1.2 Reference Grouping

It is common in scientific writing to attribute one contribution to a group of references. Sentence (6) above contains three groups of references. Each group constitutes one entity. Therefore, we replace each group with a placeholder. We use GTREF to replace a group of references that contains the target reference, and GREF to replace a group of references that does *not* contain the target reference.

Sentence (7) below is the same as sentence (6) but with the three groups of references replaced.

(7) These constraints can be lexicalized (GREF.1), unlexicalized (GTREF.2) or automatically learned (GREF.3).

4.1.3 Non-syntactic Reference Removal

A reference (REF or TREF) or a group of references (GREF or GTREF) could either be a syntactic constituent and has a semantic role in the sentence (e.g. GTREF.1 in sentence (8) below) or not (e.g. REF.2 in sentence (8)).

(8) (GTREF.1) apply fuzzy techniques for integrating source syntax into hierarchical phrase-based systems (REF.2).

The task in this step is to determine whether a reference is a syntactic component in the sentence or not. If yes, we keep it as is. If not, we remove it from the sentence and keep track of its position. Accordingly, after this step, REF.2 in sentence (8) will be removed. We use a rule-based algorithm to determine whether a reference should be removed from the sentence or kept. Our algorithm (Algorithm 1) uses stylistic and linguistic features such as the style of the reference, the position of the reference, and the surrounding words to make the decision.

When a reference is removed, we pick a word from the sentence to represent it. This is needed for feature extraction in the next stage. We use as a representative the head of the closest noun phrase (NP) that comes before the position of the removed reference. For example, in sentence (8) above, the closest NP before REF.2 is *hierarchical phrase-based systems* and the head is the noun *systems*.

4.2 Stage 2: Reference Scope Identification

In this section we present three different methods for identifying the scope of a given reference within a citing sentence. We compare the performance of these methods in Section 5. The following three subsections describe the methods.

Algorithm 1 Remove Non-syntactic References

```
Require: A citing sentence S
for all Reference R (REF, TREF, GREF, or GTREF) in S do
    if R style matches "Authors (year)" then
        Keep R // syntactic
    else if R is the first word in the sentence or in a clause then
        Keep R // syntactic
    else if R is preceded by a preposition (in, of, by, etc.) then
        Keep R // syntactic
    else
        Remove R // non-syntactic
    end if
end for
```

4.2.1 Word Classification

In this method we define reference scope identification as a classification task of the individual words of the citing sentence. Each word is classified as *inside* or *outside* the scope of a given target reference. We use a number of linguistic and structural features to train a classification model on a set of labeled sentences. The trained model is then used to label new sentences. The features that we use to train the model are listed in Table 1. We use the Stanford parser (Klein and Manning, 2003) for syntactic and dependency parsing. We experiment with two classification algorithms: Support Vector Machines (SVM) and logistic regression.

4.2.2 Sequence Labeling

In the method described in Section 4.2.1 above, we classify each word independently from the labels of the nearby words. The nature of our task, however, suggests that the accuracy of word classification can be improved by considering the labels of the words surrounding the word being classified. It is very likely that the word takes the same label as the word before and after it if they all belong to the same clause in the sentence. In this method we define the problem as a sequence labeling task. Now, instead of looking for the best label for each word individually, we look for the globally best sequence

Feature	Description
Distance	The distance (in words) between the word and the target reference.
Position	This feature takes the value 1 if the word comes before the target reference, and 0 otherwise.
Segment	After splitting the sentence into segments by punctuation and coordination conjunctions, this feature takes the value 1 if the word occurs in the same segment with the target reference, and 0 otherwise.
Part of speech tag	The part of speech tag of the word, the word before, and the word after.
Dependency Distance	Length of the shortest dependency path (in the dependency parse tree) that connects the word to the target reference or its representative. It has been shown in previous work on relation extraction that the shortest path between any two entities captures the information required to assert a relationship between them (Bunescu and Mooney, 2005)
Dependency Relations	This item includes a set of features. Each features corresponds to a dependency relation type. If the relation appears in the dependency path that connects the word to the target reference or its representative, its corresponding feature takes the value 1, and 0 otherwise.
Common Ancestor Node	The type of the node in the syntactic parse tree that is the least common ancestor of the word and the target reference.
Syntactic Distance	The number of edges in the shortest path that connects the word and the target reference in the syntactic parse tree.

Table 1: The features used for word classification and sequence labeling

of labels for all the words in the sentence at once.

We use Conditional Random Fields (CRF) as our sequence labeling algorithm. In particular, we use first-order chain-structured CRF. The chain consists of two sets of nodes: a set of hidden nodes **Y** which represent the scope labels (0 or 1) in our case, and a set of observed nodes **X** which represent the observed features. The task is to estimate the probability of a sequence of labels Y given the sequence of observed features X: $P(\mathbf{Y}|\mathbf{X})$

Lafferty et al. (2001) define this probability to be a normalized product of potential functions ψ:

$$P(\mathbf{y}|\mathbf{x}) = \prod_t \psi_k(y_t, y_{t-1}, \mathbf{x}) \quad (1)$$

Where $\psi_k(y_t, y_{t-1}, \mathbf{x})$ is defined as

$$\psi_k(y_t, y_{t-1}, \mathbf{x}) = exp(\sum_k \lambda_k f(y_t, y_{t-1}, \mathbf{x})) \quad (2)$$

where $f(y_t, y_{t-1}, \mathbf{x})$ is a transition feature function of the label at positions $i-1$ and i and the observation sequence **x**; and λ_j is parameter to be estimated from training data. We use, as the observations at each position, the same features that we used in Section 4.2.1 above (Table 1).

4.2.3 Segment Classification

We noticed that the scope of a given reference often consists of units of higher granularity than words. Therefore, in this method, we split the sentence into segments of contiguous words and, instead of labeling individual words, we label the whole segment as *inside* or *outside* the scope of the target reference. We experimented with two different segmentation methods. In the first method (method-1), we segment the sentence at punctuation marks, coordination conjunctions, and a set of special expressions such as "for example", "for instance", "including", "includes", "such as", "like", etc. Sentence (8) below shows an example of this segmentation method (Segments are enclosed in square brackets).

(8) [Rerankers have been successfully applied to numerous NLP tasks such as] [parse selection (GTREF)], [parse reranking (GREF)], [question-answering (REF)].

In the second segmentation method (method-2), we split the sentence into segments of finer granularity. We use a chunking tool to identify noun groups, verb groups, preposition groups, adjective groups, and adverb groups. Each such group (or chunk) forms a segment. If a word does not belong to any chunk, it forms a singleton segment by itself. Sentence (9) below shows an example of this segmentation method (Segments are enclosed in square brackets).

(9) [To] [score] [the output] [of] [the coreference models], [we] [employ] [the commonly-used MUC scoring program (REF)] [and] [the recently-developed CEAF scoring program (TREF)].

We assign a label to each segment in two steps. In the first step, we use the sequence labeling method described in Section 4.2.2 to assign labels to all the individual words in the sentence. In the second step, we aggregate the labels of all the words contained in a segment to assign a label to the whole segment. We experimented with three different label aggregation rules: 1) rule-1: assign to the segment the majority label of the words it contains, and 2) rule-2: assign to the segment the label 1 (i.e., *inside*) if at least one of the words contained in the segment is labeled 1, and assign the label 0 to the segment otherwise, and 3) rule-3: assign the label 0 to the segment if at least of the words it contains is labeled 0, and assign 1 otherwise.

5 Evaluation

5.1 Data

We use the ACL Anthology Network corpus (AAN) (Radev et al., 2009) in our evaluation. AAN is a publicly available collection of more than 19,000 NLP papers. AAN provides a manually curated citation network of its papers and the citing sentence(s) associated with each edge. The current release of AAN contains about 76,000 unique citing sentences 56% of which contain 2 or more references and 44% contain 1 reference only. From this set, we randomly selected 3500 citing sentences, each containing at least two references (3.75 references on average with a standard deviation of 2.5). The total number of references in this set of sentences is 19,591.

We split the data set into two random subsets: a development set (200 sentences) and a training/testing set (3300 sentences). We used the development set to study the data and develop our strategies of addressing the problem. The second set was used to train and test the system in a cross-validation mode.

5.2 Annotation

We asked graduate students with good background in NLP (the area of the annotated sentences) to provide three annotations for each sentence in the data set described above. First, we asked them to determine whether each of the references in the sentence was correctly tagged or not. Second, we asked them to determine for each reference whether it is a syntactic constituent in the sentence or not. Third, we asked them to determine and label the scope of one reference in each sentence which was marked as a target reference (TREF). We designed a user-friendly tool to collect the annotations from the students.

To estimate the inter-annotator agreement, we picked 500 random sentences from our data set and assigned them to two different annotators. The inter-annotator agreement was perfect on both the reference tagging annotation and the reference syntacticality annotation. This is expected since both are objective, clear, and easy tasks. To measure the inter-annotator agreement on the scope annotation task, we deal with it as a word classification task. This allows us to use the popular classification agreement measure, the Kappa coefficient (Cohen, 1968). The Kappa coefficient is defined as follows:

$$K = \frac{P(A) - P(E)}{1 - P(E)} \tag{3}$$

where P(A) is the relative observed agreement among raters and P(E) is the hypothetical probability of chance agreement. The agreement between the two annotators on the scope identification task was $K = 0.61$. On Landis and Kochs (Landis and Koch, 1977) scale, this value indicates substantial agreement.

5.3 Experimental Setup

We use the Edinburgh Language Technology Text Tokenization Toolkit (LT-TTT) (Grover et al., 2000) for text tokenization, part-of-speech tagging, chunking, and noun phrase head identification. We use the Stanford parser (Klein and Manning, 2003) for syntactic and dependency parsing. We use LibSVM (Chang and Lin, 2011) for Support Vector Machines (SVM) classification. Our SVM model uses a linear kernel. We use Weka (Hall et al., 2009) for logistic regression classification. We use the Machine Learning for Language Toolkit (MALLET) (McCallum, 2002) for CRF-based sequence labeling. In all the scope identification experiments and results below, we use 10-fold cross validation for training/testing.

5.4 Preprocessing Component Evaluation

We ran our three rule-based preprocessing modules on the testing data set and compared the output to the human annotations. The test set was not used in the tuning of the system but was done using the development data set as described above. We report the results for each of the preprocessing modules. Our reference tagging module achieved 98.3% precision and 93.1% recall. Most of the errors were due to issues with text extraction from PDF or due to bad references practices by some authors (i.e., not following scientific referencing standards). Our reference grouping module achieved perfect accuracy for all the correctly tagged references. This was expected since this is a straightforward task. The non-syntactic reference removal module achieved 90.08% precision and 90.1% recall. Again, most of the errors were the result of bad referencing practices by the authors.

5.5 Reference Scope Identification Experiments

We conducted several experiments to compare the methods proposed in Section 4 and their variants. We ran all the experiments on the training/testing set (the 3300 sentences) described in Section 5.1.

Method	Accuracy	Precision	Recall	F-measure
AR-2011	54.0%	63.3%	33.1%	41.5%
WC-SVM	74.9%	74.5%	93.4%	82.9%
WC-LR	74.3%	76.8%	88.0%	82.0%
SL-CRF	78.2%	80.1%	94.2%	86.6%
SC-S1-R1	73.7%	72.1%	97.8%	83.0%
SC-S1-R2	69.3%	68.4%	**98.9%**	80.8%
SC-S1-R3	60.0%	61.8%	73.3%	60.9%
SC-S2-R1	**81.8%**	**81.2%**	93.8%	**87.0%**
SC-S2-R2	78.2%	77.3%	94.9%	85.2%
SC-S2-R3	66.1%	67.1%	71.2%	69.1%

Table 3: Results of scope identification using the different algorithms described in the paper

The experiments that we ran are as follows: 1) word classification using a SVM classifier (WC-SVM); 2) word classification using a logistic regression classifier(WC-LR); 3) CRF-based sequence labeling (SL-CRF); 4) segment classification using segmentation method-1 and label aggregation rule-1 (SC-S1-R1); 5,6,7,8,9) same as (4) but using different combinations of segmentation methods 1 and 2, and label aggregation rules 1,2 and 3: SC-S1-R2, SC-S1-R3, SC-S2-R1, SC-S2-R2, SC-S2-R3 (where Sx refers to segmentation method x and Ry refers to label aggregation rule y all as explained in Section 4.2.3). Finally, 10) we compare our methods to the baseline method proposed by Abu-Jbara and Radev (2011) which was described in Section 4 (AR-2011).

To better understand which of the features listed in Table 1 are more important for the task, we use Guyon et al.'s (2002) method for feature selection using SVM to rank the features based on their importance. The results of the experiments and the feature analysis are presented and discussed in the following subsection.

5.6 Results and Discussion

5.6.1 Experimental Results

We ran the experiments described in the previous subsection on the testing data described in Sec-

	Method	Output
Example 1	Word Classification (WC-SVM)	A wide range of contextual information, such as surrounding words (GREF), dependency or case structure (GTREF), and dependency path (GREF), has been utilized for similarity calculation, and achieved considerable success.
	Sequence Labeling (SL-CRF)	A wide range of contextual information, such as surrounding words (GREF), dependency or case structure (GTREF), and dependency path (GREF), has been utilized for similarity calculation, and achieved considerable success.
	Segment Classification (SC-S2-R1)	A wide range of contextual information, such as surrounding words (GREF), dependency or case structure (GTREF), and dependency path (GREF), has been utilized for similarity calculation, and achieved considerable success.
Example 2	Word Classification (WC-SVM)	Some approaches have used WordNet for the generalization step (GTREF), others EM-based clustering (REF).
	Sequence Labeling (SL-CRF)	Some approaches have used WordNet for the generalization step (GTREF), others EM-based clustering (REF).
	Segment Classification (SC-S2-R1)	Some approaches have used WordNet for the generalization step (GTREF), others EM-based clustering (REF).

Table 2: Two example outputs produced by the three methods

tion 5.1. Table 3 compares the precision, recall, F1, and accuracy for the three methods described in Section 4 and their variations. All the metrics were computed at the word level. The results show that all our methods outperform the baseline method AR-2011 that was proposed by Abu-Jbara and Radev (2011). In the word classification method, we notice no significant difference between the performance of the SVM vs Logistic Regression classifier. We also notice that the CRF-based sequence labeling method performs significantly better than the word classification method. This result corroborates our intuition that the labels of neighboring words are dependent. The results also show that segment labeling generally performs better than word labeling. More specifically, the results indicate that segmentation based on chunking and the label aggregation based on plurality when used together (i.e., SC-S2-R1) achieve higher precision, accuracy, and F-measure than the punctuation-based segmentation and the other label aggregation rules.

Table 2 shows the output of the three methods on two example sentences. The underlined words are labeled by the system as scope words.

5.6.2 Feature Analysis

We performed an analysis of our classification features using Guyon et al. (2002) method. The analysis revealed that both structural and syntactic features are important. Among the syntactic features, the dependency path is the most important. Among the structural features, the *segment* feature (as described in Table 1) is the most important.

6 Conclusions

We presented and compared three different methods for reference scope identification: word classification, sequence labeling, and segment classification. Our results indicate that segment classification achieves the best performance. The next direction in this research is to extract the scope of a given reference as a standalone grammatical sentence. In many cases, the scope identified by our method can form a grammatical sentence with no or minimal postprocessing. In other cases, more advanced *text regeneration* techniques are needed for scope extraction.

References

Amjad Abu-Jbara and Dragomir Radev. 2011. Coherent citation-based summarization of scientific papers. In *Proceedings of the 49th Annual Meeting of the Association for Computational Linguistics: Human Lan-*

guage Technologies, pages 500–509, Portland, Oregon, USA, June. Association for Computational Linguistics.

Awais Athar. 2011. Sentiment analysis of citations using sentence structure-based features. In *Proceedings of the ACL 2011 Student Session*, pages 81–87, Portland, OR, USA, June. Association for Computational Linguistics.

Christine L. Borgman and Jonathan Furner. 2002. Scholarly communication and bibliometrics. *ANNUAL REVIEW OF INFORMATION SCIENCE AND TECHNOLOGY*, 36(1):2–72.

Razvan Bunescu and Raymond Mooney. 2005. A shortest path dependency kernel for relation extraction. In *Proceedings of Human Language Technology Conference and Conference on Empirical Methods in Natural Language Processing*, pages 724–731, Vancouver, British Columbia, Canada, October. Association for Computational Linguistics.

Chih-Chung Chang and Chih-Jen Lin. 2011. LIBSVM: A library for support vector machines. *ACM Transactions on Intelligent Systems and Technology*, 2:27:1–27:27.

J. Cohen. 1968. Weighted kappa: Nominal scale agreement with provision for scaled disagreement or partial credit. *Psychological Bulletin*, 70:213–220.

Aaron Elkiss, Siwei Shen, Anthony Fader, Güneş Erkan, David States, and Dragomir Radev. 2008. Blind men and elephants: What do citation summaries tell us about a research article? *J. Am. Soc. Inf. Sci. Technol.*, 59(1):51–62.

E. Garfield, Irving H. Sher, and R. J. Torpie. 1984. *The Use of Citation Data in Writing the History of Science*. Institute for Scientific Information Inc., Philadelphia, Pennsylvania, USA.

Claire Grover, Colin Matheson, Andrei Mikheev, and Marc Moens. 2000. Lt ttt - a flexible tokenisation tool. In *In Proceedings of Second International Conference on Language Resources and Evaluation*, pages 1147–1154.

Isabelle Guyon, Jason Weston, Stephen Barnhill, and Vladimir Vapnik. 2002. Gene selection for cancer classification using support vector machines. *Mach. Learn.*, 46:389–422, March.

Mark Hall, Eibe Frank, Geoffrey Holmes, Bernhard Pfahringer, Peter Reutemann, and Ian H. Witten. 2009. The weka data mining software: an update. *SIGKDD Explor. Newsl.*, 11(1):10 18.

T. L. Hodges. 1972. Citation indexing-its theory and application in science, technology, and humanities. *Ph.D. thesis, University of California at Berkeley.Ph.D. thesis, University of California at Berkeley.*

Dan Klein and Christopher D. Manning. 2003. Accurate unlexicalized parsing. In *IN PROCEEDINGS OF THE 41ST ANNUAL MEETING OF THE ASSOCIATION FOR COMPUTATIONAL LINGUISTICS*, pages 423–430.

John D. Lafferty, Andrew McCallum, and Fernando C. N. Pereira. 2001. Conditional random fields: Probabilistic models for segmenting and labeling sequence data. In *Proceedings of the Eighteenth International Conference on Machine Learning*, ICML '01, pages 282–289, San Francisco, CA, USA. Morgan Kaufmann Publishers Inc.

J. Richard Landis and Gary G. Koch. 1977. The Measurement of Observer Agreement for Categorical Data. *Biometrics*, 33(1):159–174, March.

Terttu Luukkonen. 1992. Is scientists' publishing behaviour rewardseeking? *Scientometrics*, 24:297–319. 10.1007/BF02017913.

Andrew Kachites McCallum. 2002. Mallet: A machine learning for language toolkit. http://mallet.cs.umass.edu.

Qiaozhu Mei and ChengXiang Zhai. 2008. Generating impact-based summaries for scientific literature. In *Proceedings of ACL-08: HLT*, pages 816–824, Columbus, Ohio, June. Association for Computational Linguistics.

Saif Mohammad, Bonnie Dorr, Melissa Egan, Ahmed Hassan, Pradeep Muthukrishan, Vahed Qazvinian, Dragomir Radev, and David Zajic. 2009. Using citations to generate surveys of scientific paradigms. In *Proceedings of Human Language Technologies: The 2009 Annual Conference of the North American Chapter of the Association for Computational Linguistics*, pages 584–592, Boulder, Colorado, June. Association for Computational Linguistics.

Preslav I. Nakov, Ariel S. Schwartz, and Marti A. Hearst. 2004. Citances: Citation sentences for semantic analysis of bioscience text. In *In Proceedings of the SIGIR04 workshop on Search and Discovery in Bioinformatics*.

Hidetsugu Nanba and Manabu Okumura. 1999. Towards multi-paper summarization using reference information. In *IJCAI '99: Proceedings of the Sixteenth International Joint Conference on Artificial Intelligence*, pages 926–931, San Francisco, CA, USA. Morgan Kaufmann Publishers Inc.

Hidetsugu Nanba, Noriko Kando, Manabu Okumura, and Of Information Science. 2000. Classification of research papers using citation links and citation types: Towards automatic review article generation.

Vahed Qazvinian and Dragomir R. Radev. 2008. Scientific paper summarization using citation summary networks. In *Proceedings of the 22nd International Conference on Computational Linguistics (Coling 2008)*, pages 689–696, Manchester, UK, August. Coling 2008 Organizing Committee.

Vahed Qazvinian and Dragomir R. Radev. 2010. Identifying non-explicit citing sentences for citation-based summarization. In *Proceedings of the 48th Annual Meeting of the Association for Computational Linguistics*, pages 555–564, Uppsala, Sweden, July. Association for Computational Linguistics.

Vahed Qazvinian, Dragomir R. Radev, and Arzucan Ozgur. 2010. Citation summarization through keyphrase extraction. In *Proceedings of the 23rd International Conference on Computational Linguistics (Coling 2010)*, pages 895–903, Beijing, China, August. Coling 2010 Organizing Committee.

Dragomir R. Radev, Pradeep Muthukrishnan, and Vahed Qazvinian. 2009. The acl anthology network corpus. In *NLPIR4DL '09: Proceedings of the 2009 Workshop on Text and Citation Analysis for Scholarly Digital Libraries*, pages 54–61, Morristown, NJ, USA. Association for Computational Linguistics.

Ariel Schwartz, Anna Divoli, and Marti Hearst. 2007. Multiple alignment of citation sentences with conditional random fields and posterior decoding. In *Proceedings of the 2007 Joint Conference on Empirical Methods in Natural Language Processing and Computational Natural Language Learning (EMNLP-CoNLL)*, pages 847–857.

Advaith Siddharthan and Simone Teufel. 2007. Whose idea was this, and why does it matter? attributing scientific work to citations. In *In Proceedings of NAACL/HLT-07*.

Simone Teufel, Advaith Siddharthan, and Dan Tidhar. 2006. Automatic classification of citation function. In *In Proc. of EMNLP-06*.

Simone Teufel. 2007. Argumentative zoning for improved citation indexing. computing attitude and affect in text. In *Theory and Applications, pages 159170*.

Howard D. White. 2004. Citation analysis and discourse analysis revisited. *Applied Linguistics*, 25(1):89–116.

Intrinsic and Extrinsic Evaluation of an Automatic User Disengagement Detector for an Uncertainty-Adaptive Spoken Dialogue System

Kate Forbes-Riley and **Diane Litman** and **Heather Friedberg** and **Joanna Drummond***
University of Pittsburgh
Pittsburgh, PA 15260, USA
forbesk@pitt.edu, litman@pitt.edu, haf13@pitt.edu

Abstract

We present a model for detecting user disengagement during spoken dialogue interactions. Intrinsic evaluation of our model (i.e., with respect to a gold standard) yields results on par with prior work. However, since our goal is immediate implementation in a system that already detects and adapts to user uncertainty, we go further than prior work and present an extrinsic evaluation of our model (i.e., with respect to the real-world task). Correlation analyses show crucially that our automatic disengagement labels correlate with system performance in the same way as the gold standard (manual) labels, while regression analyses show that detecting user disengagement adds value over and above detecting only user uncertainty when modeling performance. Our results suggest that automatically detecting and adapting to user disengagement has the potential to significantly improve performance even in the presence of noise, when compared with only adapting to one affective state or ignoring affect entirely.

1 Introduction

Spoken dialogue systems that can detect and adapt to user affect[1] are fast becoming reality (Schuller et al., 2009b; Batliner et al., 2008; Prendinger and Ishizuka, 2005; Vidrascu and Devillers, 2005; Lee and Narayanan, 2005; Shafran et al., 2003). The benefits are clear: affect-adaptive systems have been shown to increase task success (Forbes-Riley and Litman, 2011a; D'Mello et al., 2010; Wang et al., 2008) or improve other system performance metrics such as user satisfaction (Liu and Picard, 2005; Klein et al., 2002). However, to date most affective systems researchers have focused either only on affect detection, or only on detecting and adapting to a single affective state. The next step is thus to develop and evaluate spoken dialogue systems that detect and respond to multiple affective states.

We previously showed that detecting and responding to user *uncertainty* during spoken dialogue computer tutoring significantly improves task success (Forbes-Riley and Litman, 2011a). We are now taking the next step: incorporating automatic detection and adaptation to user *disengagement* as well, with the goal of further improving task success. We targeted user uncertainty and disengagement because manual annotation showed them to be the two most common user affective states in our system and both are negatively correlated with task success (Litman and Forbes-Riley, 2009; Forbes-Riley and Litman, 2011b). Thus, we hypothesize that providing appropriate responses to these states would reduce their frequency, consequently improving task success. Although we address these user states in the tutoring domain, spoken dialogue researchers across domains and applications have investigated the automatic detection of both user uncertainty (e.g. (Drummond and Litman, 2011; Pon-Barry and Shieber, 2011; Paek and Ju, 2008; Alwan et al., 2007)) and user disengagement (e.g., (Schuller

*Now at Univ. Toronto: jdrummond@cs.toronto.edu

[1]We use *affect* for emotions and attitudes that affect how users communicate. Other speech researchers also combine concepts of emotion, arousal, and attitudes where emotion is not full-blown (Cowie and Cornelius, 2003).

et al., 2010; Wang and Hirschberg, 2011; Schuller et al., 2009a)), to improve system performance. The detection of user disengagement in particular has received substantial attention in recent years, due to growing awareness of its potential for negatively impacting commercial applications (Wang and Hirschberg, 2011; Schuller et al., 2009a).

In this paper we present a model for automatically detecting user disengagement during spoken dialogue interactions. Intrinsic evaluation of our model yields results on par with those of prior work. However, we argue that while intrinsic evaluations are necessary, they aren't sufficient when immediate implementation is the goal, because there is no a priori way to know when the model's performance is acceptable to use in a working system. This problem is particularly relevant to affect detection because it is such a difficult task, where no one achieves near-perfect results. We argue that for such tasks some extrinsic evaluation is also necessary, to show that the automatic labels are useful and/or are a reasonable substitute for a gold standard *before* undertaking a labor-intensive and time-consuming evaluation with real users. Here we use correlational analyses to show that our automatic disengagement labels are related to system performance in the same way as the gold standard (manual) labels. We further show through regression analyses that detecting user disengagement adds value over and above detecting only user uncertainty when modeling performance. These results provide strong evidence that enhancing a spoken dialogue system to detect and adapt to multiple affective states (specifically, user disengagement and uncertainty) has the potential to significantly improve performance even in the presence of noise due to automatic detection, when compared with only adapting to one affective state or ignoring affect entirely.

2 Related Work

Our focus in this paper is on first using machine learning to develop a detector of user disengagement for spoken dialogue systems, and then evaluating its usefulness as fully as possible prior to its implementation and deployment with real users.

Disengaged users are highly undesirable in human-computer interaction because they increase the potential for user dissatisfaction and task failure; thus over the past decade there has already been substantial prior work focused on detecting user disengagement and the closely related states of boredom, motivation and lack of interest (e.g., (Schuller et al., 2010; Wang and Hirschberg, 2011; Jeon et al., 2010; Schuller et al., 2009a; Bohus and Horvitz, 2009; Martalo et al., 2008; Porayska-Pomsta et al., 2008; Kapoor and Picard, 2005; Sidner and Lee, 2003; Forbes-Riley and Litman, 2011b)).

Within this work, specific affect definitions vary slightly with the intention of being coherent within the application and domain and being relevant to the specific adaptation goal (Martalo et al., 2008). However, affective systems researchers generally agree that disengaged users show little involvement in the interaction, and often display facial, gestural and linguistic signals such as gaze avoidance, finger tapping, humming, sarcasm, et cetera.

The features used to detect disengagement also vary depending on system domain and application. For example, Sidner & Lee (2003) are interested in modeling more natural and collaborative human-robot interactions during basic conversations. They define an algorithm for the engagement process that involves appropriate eye gaze and turn-taking. Martalo et al. (2008) study how user engagement influences dialogue patterns during interactions with an embodied agent that gives advice about healthy dieting. They model engagement using manually coded dialogue acts based on the SWBDL-DAMSL scheme (Stolcke et al., 2000). Bohus and Horvitz (2009) study systems that attract and engage users for dynamic, multi-party dialogues in open-world settings. They model user intentions to engage the system with cues from facial sensors and the dialogue. Within recent spoken dialogue research, acoustic-prosodic, lexical and contextual features have been found to be effective detectors of disengagement (Schuller et al., 2010; Wang and Hirschberg, 2011; Jeon et al., 2010); we will briefly compare our own results with these in Section 5.

While all of the above-mentioned research has presented intrinsic evaluations of their disengagement modeling efforts that indicate a reasonable degree of accuracy as compared to a gold standard (e.g., manual coding), only a few have yet demonstrated that the model's detected values are useful in practice and/or are a reasonable substitute for the gold standard with respect to some practical objective (e.g., a relationship to performance). In particular, two studies (Bohus and Horvitz, 2009; Schuller et al., 2009a) have gone directly from intrinsic evaluation of (dis)engagement models to performing user studies with the implemented model, thereby bypassing other less expensive and less labor-intensive means of extrinsic evaluation to quantify their model's usefulness–and potentially indicate its need to be further improved–before deployment with real users. Neither study reports statistically significant improvements in system performance as a result of detecting user (dis)engagement.

Finally, while substantial spoken dialogue and affective systems research has shown that users display a range of affective states while interacting with a system (e.g. (Schuller et al., 2009b; Conati and Maclaren, 2009; Batliner et al., 2008; Devillers and Vidrascu, 2006; Lee and Narayanan, 2005; Shafran et al., 2003; Ang et al., 2002)), to date only a few affective systems have been built that detect and adapt to multiple user affective states (e.g., (D'Mello et al., 2010; Aist et al., 2002; Tsukahara and Ward, 2001)), and most of these have been deployed with crucial natural language processing components "wizarded" by a hidden human agent (e.g., who performs speech recognition or affect annotation on the user turns); moreover, none have yet shown significant improvements in system performance as a result of adapting to multiple user affective states.

3 ITSPOKE: Spoken Dialogue Tutor

We develop and evaluate our disengagement detector using a corpus of spoken dialogues from a 2008 controlled experiment evaluating our uncertainty-adaptive spoken dialogue tutoring system, ITSPOKE (**I**ntelligent **T**utoring **SPOKE**n dialog system) (Forbes-Riley and Litman, 2011a).[2]

ITSPOKE tutors 5 Newtonian physics problems (one per dialogue), using a Tutor Question - Student Answer - Tutor Response format. After each tutor question, the student speech is digitized from head-mounted microphone input and sent to the Sphinx2 recognizer, which yields an automatic transcript (Huang et al., 1993). This answer's (in)correctness is then automatically classified based on this transcript, using the TuTalk semantic analyzer (Jordan et al., 2007), and the answer's (un)certainty is automatically classified by inputting features of the speech signal, the automatic transcript, and the dialogue context into a logistic regression model. We will discuss these features further in Section 5. All natural language processing components were trained using prior ITSPOKE corpora. The appropriate tutor response is determined based on the answer's automatically labeled (in)correctness and (un)certainty and then sent to the Cepstral text-to-speech system[3], whose audio output is played through the student headphones and is also displayed on a web-based interface.

The experimental procedure was as follows: college students with no college-level physics (1) read a short physics text, (2) took a pretest, (3) worked 5 "training" problems with ITSPOKE, where each user received a varying level of uncertainty adaptation based on condition, (4) took a user satisfaction survey, (5) took a posttest isomorphic to the pretest, and (6) worked a "test" problem with ITSPOKE that was isomorphic to the 5th training problem, where no user received any uncertainty adaptation.

The resulting corpus contains 432 dialogues (6 per student) and 7216 turns from 72 students, 47 female and 25 male. All turns are used in the disengagement detection experiments described next. However, only the *training* problem dialogues (360, 5 per student, 6044 student turns) are used for the performance analyses in Sections 6-7, because the final *test* problem was given after the instruments measuring performance (survey and posttest).

Our survey and tests are the same as those used in multiple prior ITSPOKE experiments (c.f., (Forbes-Riley and Litman, 2011a)). The pretest and posttest each contain 26 multiple choice questions querying knowledge of the topics covered in the dialogues. Average pretest and posttest scores in the corpus were 51.0% and 73.1% (out of 100%) with standard deviations of 14.5% and 13.8%, respectively. The user satisfaction survey contains 16 statements rated on a 5-point Likert scale. Average total sur-

[2]ITSPOKE is a speech-enhanced and otherwise modified version of the Why2-Atlas text-based qualitative physics tutor (VanLehn et al., 2002).

[3]an outgrowth of Festival (Black and Taylor, 1997).

vey score was 60.9 (out of 80), with a standard deviation of 8.5. While the statements themselves are listed elsewhere (Forbes-Riley and Litman, 2009), 9 statements concern the tutoring domain (e.g., The tutor was effective/precise/useful), 7 of which were taken from (Baylor et al., 2003) and 2 of which were created for our system. 3 statements concern user uncertainty levels and were created for our system. 4 statements concern the spoken dialogue interaction (e.g., It was easy to understand the tutor's speech) and were taken from (Walker et al., 2002). Our survey has also been incorporated into other recent work exploring user satisfaction in spoken dialogue computer tutors (Dzikovska et al., 2011). In Section 6 we discuss how user scores on these instruments are used to measure system performance. See (Forbes-Riley and Litman, 2011a) for further details of ITSPOKE and the 2008 experiment.

Following the experiment, the entire corpus was manually labeled for (in)correctness (correct, incorrect), (un)certainty (CER, UNC) and (dis)engagement (ENG, DISE) by one trained annotator. Table 1 shows the distribution of the labeled turns in the 2008 ITSPOKE corpus. In prior ITSPOKE corpora, our annotator displayed interannotator agreement of 0.85 and 0.62 Kappa on correctness and uncertainty, respectively (Forbes-Riley and Litman, 2011a). For the disengagement label, a reliability analysis was performed over several annotation rounds on subsets of the 2008 ITSPOKE corpus by this and a second trained annotator, yielding 0.55 Kappa (this analysis is described in detail elsewhere (Forbes-Riley et al., 2011)). Our Kappas indicate that user uncertainty and disengagement can both be annotated with moderate reliability in our dataset, on par with prior emotion annotation work (c.f., (Pon-Barry and Shieber, 2011)). Note however that the best way to label users' internal affective state(s) is still an open question. Many system researchers (including ourselves) rely on trained labelers (e.g., (Pon-Barry et al., 2006; Porayska-Pomsta et al., 2008)) while others use self-reports (e.g., (Conati and Maclaren, 2009; Gratch et al., 2009; McQuiggan et al., 2008)). Both methods are problematic; for example both can be rendered inaccurate when users mask their true feelings. Two studies that have compared self-reports, peer labelers, trained labelers, and combinations of labelers (Afzal and Robinson, 2011; D'Mello et al., 2008) both illustrate the common finding that human annotators display low to moderate interannotator reliability for affect annotation, and both studies show that trained labelers yield the highest reliability on this task. Despite the lack of high interannotator reliability, responding to affect detected by trained human labels has still been shown to improve system performance (see Section 1).

Table 1: 2008 ITSPOKE Corpus Description (N=7216)

Turn Label	Total	Percent
Disengaged	1170	16.21%
Correct	5330	73.86%
Uncertain	1483	20.55%
Uncertain+Disengaged	373	5.17%

4 Automatically Detecting User Disengagement (DISE) in ITSPOKE

As noted in Section 1, we have developed a user disengagement detector to incorporate into our existing uncertainty-adaptive spoken dialogue system. The result will be a state of the art system that adapts to multiple affective states during the dialogue.

4.1 Binary DISE Label

Our disengagement annotation scheme (Forbes-Riley et al., 2011) was derived from empirical observations in our data but draws on prior work, including work mentioned in Section 2, appraisal theory-based emotion models (e.g., Conati and Maclaren (2009))[4], and prior approaches to annotating disengagement or related states in tutoring (Lehman et al., 2008; Porayska-Pomsta et al., 2008).

Briefly, our **overall Disengagement label (DISE)** is used for turns expressing moderate to strong disengagement towards the interaction, i.e., responses given without much effort or without caring about appropriateness. Responses might also be accompanied by signs of inattention, boredom, or irritation. Clear examples include answers spoken quickly in leaden monotone, with sarcastic or playful tones, or with off-task sounds such as rhythmic tapping or

[4]Appraisal theorists distinguish emotional behaviors from their underlying causes, arguing that emotions result from an evaluation of a context.

electronics usage.[5] Note that our DISE label is defined independently of the tutoring domain and thus should generalize across spoken dialogue systems.

Figure 1 illustrates the DISE, (in)correctness, and (un)certainty labels across 3 tutor/student turn pairs. $\mathbf{U}_1$ is labeled DISE and UNC because the student gave up immediately and with irritation when too much prior knowledge was required. $\mathbf{U}_2$ is labeled DISE and UNC because the student avoided giving a specific numerical value, offering instead a vague (and obviously incorrect) answer. $\mathbf{U}_3$ is labeled DISE and CER because the student sang the correct answer, indicating a lack of interest in the larger purpose of the material being discussed.[6]

$\mathbf{T}_1$: What is the definition of Newton's Second Law?

$\mathbf{U}_1$: I have no idea <*sigh*>. **(DISE, *incorrect*, UNC)**

...

$\mathbf{T}_2$: What's the numerical value of the man's acceleration? Please specify the units too.

$\mathbf{U}_2$: The speed of the elevator. Meters per second. **(DISE, *incorrect*, UNC)**

...

$\mathbf{T}_3$: What are the forces acting on the keys after the man releases them?

$\mathbf{U}_3$: graaa-vi-tyyyyy <*sings the answer*> **(DISE, *correct*, CER)**

Figure 1: Corpus Example Illustrating the User Turn Labels ((Dis)Engagement, (In)Correctness, (Un)Certainty)

4.2 DISE Detection Method

Machine learning classification was done at the turn level using WEKA software[7] and 10-fold cross validation. A J48 decision tree was chosen because of its easily read output and the fact that previous experiments with our data showed little variance between different machine learning algorithms (Drummond and Litman, 2011). We also use a cost matrix, which heavily penalizes classifying a true DISE instance as false, because our class distributions are highly skewed (16.21% DISE turns) and the cost matrix successfully mitigated the skew's effect in our prior work, where the uncertainty distribution is also skewed (20.55% UNC turns) (Drummond and Litman, 2011).

To train our DISE model, we first extracted the set of speech and dialogue features shown in Figure 2 from the user turns in our corpus. As shown, the acoustic-prosodic features represent duration, pausing, pitch, and energy, and were normalized by the first user turn, as well as totaled and averaged over each dialogue. The lexical and dialogue features consist of the current dialogue name (i.e., one of the six physics problems) and turn number, the current ITSPOKE question's name (e.g.,T_3 in Figure 1 has a unique identifier) and depth in the discourse structure (e.g., an ITSPOKE remediation question after an incorrect user answer would be at one greater depth than the prior question), a word occurrence vector for the automatically recognized text of the user turn, an automatic (in)correctness label, and lastly, the number of user turns since the last correct turn ("incorrect runs"). We also included two user-based features, gender and pretest score.

- **Acoustic-Prosodic Features**

  temporal features: turn duration, prior pause duration, turn-internal silence

  fundamental frequency (f0) and energy (RMS) features: maximum, minimum, mean, std. deviation

  running totals and averages for all features

- **Lexical and Dialogue Features**

  dialogue name and turn number

  question name and question depth

  ITSPOKE-recognized lexical items in turn

  ITSPOKE-labeled turn (in)correctness

  incorrect runs

- **User Identifier Features**:

  gender and pretest score

Figure 2: Features Used to Detect Disengagement (DISE) for each User Turn

[5] Affective systems research has found total disengagement rare in laboratory settings (Lehman et al., 2008; Martalo et al., 2008). As in that research, we equate the DISE label with no or low engagement. Since total disengagement is common in real-world unobserved human-computer interactions (deleting unsatisfactory software being an extreme example) it remains an open question as to how well laboratory findings generalize.

[6] Our original scheme distinguished six DISE subtypes that trained annotators distinguished with a reliability of .43 Kappa (Forbes-Riley et al., 2011). However, pilot experiments indicated that our models cannot accurately distinguish them, thus our DISE detector focuses on the DISE label.

[7] http://www.cs.waikato.ac.nz/ml/weka/

Table 2: Results of 10-fold Cross-Validation Experiment with J48 Decision Tree Algorithm Detecting the Binary DISE Label in the 2008 ITSPOKE Corpus (N=7216 user turns)

Algorithm	Accuracy	UA Precision	UA Recall	UA Fmeasure	CC	MLE
Decision Tree	83.1%	68.9%	68.7%	68.8%	0.52	0.25
Majority Label	83.8%	41.9%	50.0%	45.6%	–	0.27

Note that although our feature set was drawn primarily from our prior uncertainty detection experiments (Forbes-Riley and Litman, 2011a; Drummond and Litman, 2011), we have also experimented with other features, including state-of-the-art acoustic-prosodic features used in the last Interspeech Challenges (Schuller et al., 2010; Schuller et al., 2009b) and made freely available in the openSMILE Toolkit (Florian et al., 2010). To date, however, these features have only decreased the cross-validation performance of our models.[8] While some of our features are tutoring-specific, these have similar counterparts in other applications (i.e., answer (in)correctness corresponds to a more general notion of "response appropriateness" in other domains, while pretest score corresponds to the general notion of domain expertise). Moreover, all of our features are fully automatic and available in real-time, so that the model can be directly implemented and deployed. To that end, we now describe the results of our intrinsic and extrinsic evaluations of our DISE model, aimed at determining whether it is ready to be evaluated with real users.

5 Intrinsic Evaluation: Cross-Validation

Table 2 shows the averaged results of the cross-validation with the J48 decision tree algorithm. In addition to accuracy, we use Unweighted Average (UA) Precision[9], Recall, and F-measure because they are the standard measures used to evaluate current affect recognition technology, particularly for unbalanced two-class problems (Schuller et al., 2009b). In addition, we use the cross correlation (CC) measure and mean linear error (MLE) because these metrics were used in recent work for evaluating disengagement (level of interest) detectors for the Interspeech 2010 challenge (Schuller et al., 2010; Wang and Hirschberg, 2011; Jeon et al., 2010)).[10] Note however that the Interspeech 2010 task differs from ours not only in the corpus and features, but also in the learning task: they used regression to detect a continuous level of interest ranging from 0 to 1, while we detect a binary class. Thus comparison between our results and those are only suggestive rather than conclusive.

As shown in Table 2, we also compare our results with those of majority class (ENG) labeling of the same turns. Since (7216-1170)/7216 user turns in the corpus are engaged (recall Table 1), always selecting the majority class (ENG) label for these turns thus yields 83.8% accuracy (with 0% precision and recall for DISE, and 83.8% precision and 100% recall for ENG). While our DISE model does not outperform majority class labeling with respect to accuracy, this is not surprising given the steep skew in class distribution, and our learned model significantly outperforms the baseline with respect to all the other measures ($p<.001$).[11]

Our CC and MLE results are on par with the best results from the state-of-the-art systems competing in the 2010 Interspeech Challenge, where the task was to detect level of interest. In particular, the winner obtained a CC of 0.428 (higher numbers are better) and an MLE of 0.146 (lower numbers are better) (Jeon et al., 2010), while a subsequent study yielded a CC of 0.480 and an MLE of 0.131 on the same corpus (Wang and Hirschberg, 2011). Our results are also on par with the best results of the other prior research on detecting disengagement discussed in Section 2 that detects a small number of disengagement classes and reports accuracy and/or recall and precision. For example, (Martalo et al., 2008) report average precision of 75% and recall

[8] We also tried using our automatic UNC label as a feature in our DISE model, but our results weren't significantly improved.

[9] simply ((Precision(DISE) + Precision(ENG))/2)

[10] Pearson product-moment correlation coefficient (CC) is a measure of the linear dependence that is widely used in regression settings. MLE is a regression performance measure for the mean absolute error between an estimator and the true value.

[11] CC is undefined for majority class labeling.

of 74% (detecting three levels of disengagement), while (Kapoor and Picard, 2005) report an accuracy of 86% for detecting binary (dis)interest.

Our final DISE model was produced by running the J48 algorithm over our entire corpus. The resulting decision tree contains 141 nodes and 75 leaves. Inspection of the tree reveals that all of the feature types in Figure 2 (acoustic-prosodic, lexical/dialogue, user identifier) are used as decision nodes in the tree, although not all variations on these types were used. The upper-level nodes of the tree are usually considered to be more informative features as compared to lower-level nodes, since they are queried for more leaves. The upper level of the DISE model consists entirely of temporal, lexical, pitch and energy features as well as question name and depth and incorrect runs, while features such as gender, turn number, and dialogue name appear only near the leaves, and pretest score and turn (in)correctness don't appear at all. The amount of pausing prior to the start of the user turn is the most important feature for determining disengagement, with pauses shorter than a quarter second being labeled DISE, suggesting that fast answers are a strong signal of disengagement in our system. Users who answer quickly may do so without taking the time to think it through; the more engaged user, in contrast, takes more time to prepare an answer.

Three lexical items from the student turns, "friction", "light", and "greater", are the next most important features in the tree, suggesting that particular concepts and question types can be typically associated with user disengagement in a system. For example, open-ended system questions may lead users to disengage due to frustration from not knowing when their answer is complete. One common case in ITSPOKE involves asking users to name all the forces on an object; some users don't know how many to list, so they start listing random forces, such as "friction." On the other hand, multiple choice questions can also lead users to disengage; they begin with a reasonable chance of being correct and thus don't take the time to think through their answer. One common case in ITSPOKE involves asking users to determine which of two objects has the greater or lesser force, acceleration, and velocity.

While our feature set is highly generalizable to other domains, it is an empirical question as to whether the feature values we found maximally effective for predicting disengagement also generalize to other domains. Intuition is often unreliable, and it has been widely shown in affect prediction that the answer can depend on domain, dataset, and learning algorithm employed. Moreover, there are many types of spoken dialogue systems with different styles and no single type can represent the entire field. That said, it is also important to note that there are lessons to be learned from the features selected for one particular domain, in terms of the take-home message for other domains. For example, the fact that "prior pause" is selected as a strong signal of disengagement in ITSPOKE dialogues may indicate that the feature itself (regardless of its selected value) could be transferred to different domains, alone or in the demonstrated combinations with the other selected features.

6 Extrinsic Evaluation: Correlation

Next we use extrinsic evaluation to confirm that our final DISE model is both useful and a reasonable substitute for our gold standard manual DISE labels. With respect to showing the utility of detecting DISE, we use a correlational analysis to show that the gold standard (manual) DISE values are significantly predictive of two different measures of system performance.[12] With respect to showing the adequacy of our current level of detection performance for the learned DISE model, we demonstrate that after replacing the manual DISE labels with the automatic DISE labels when running our correlations, the automatic labels are related to performance in the same way as the gold standard labels.

Thus for both our automatically detected DISE labels (auto) and our gold standard DISE labels (manual), we first computed the total number of occurrences for each student, and then computed a bivariate Pearson's correlation between this total and two different metrics of performance: learning gain (LG) and user satisfaction (US). In the tutoring domain, learning is the primary performance metric and as is common in this domain we compute it as normalized learning gain ((posttest score-pretest score)/(1-

[12]Spoken dialogue research has shown that redesigning a system in light of such correlational analysis can indeed yield performance improvements (Rotaru and Litman, 2009).

Table 3: Correlations between Disengagement and both Satisfaction and Learning in ITSPOKE Corpus (N=72 users)

Measure	Mean (SD)	User Satisfaction		Learning Gain	
		R	p	R	p
Total Manual DISE	12.3 (7.3)	-0.25	0.031	-0.35	0.002
Total Automatic DISE	12.6 (7.4)	-0.26	0.029	-0.31	0.009

pretest score)). In spoken dialogue systems, user satisfaction is the primary performance metric and as is common in this domain we compute it by totaling over the user satisfaction survey scores.[13]

Table 3 shows first the mean and standard deviation for the DISE label over all students, the Pearson's Correlation coefficient (R) and its significance (p). As shown, both our manual and automatic DISE labels are significantly related to performance, regardless of whether we measure it as user satisfaction or learning gain.[14] Moreover, in both cases the correlations are nearly identical between the manual and automatic labels. These results indicate that the detected DISE values are a useful substitute for the gold standard, and suggest that redesigning ITSPOKE to recognize and respond to DISE can significantly improve system performance.

7 Extrinsic Evaluation: Affective State Multiple Regression

Because we are adding our disengagement detector to a spoken dialogue system that already detects and adapts to user uncertainty, we argue that it is also necessary to evaluate whether greater performance benefits are likely to be obtained by adapting to a second state. In other words, given how difficult it is to effectively detect and adapt to one user affective state, is performance likely to improve by detecting and adapting to multiple affective states?

To answer this question, we performed a multiple linear regression analysis aimed at quantifying the relative usefulness of the automatically detected disengagement and uncertainty labels when predicting our system performance metrics. We ran four stepwise linear regressions. The first regression predicted learning gain, and gave the model two possible inputs: the total number of automatic DISE labels and UNC labels per user. We then ran the same regression again, this time predicting user satisfaction. For comparison, we ran the same two regressions using the manual DISE and UNC labels.

As the trained regression models in Figure 3 show, when predicting learning gain, selecting both automatically detected affective state metrics as inputs significantly increases the model's predictive power as compared to only selecting one.[15] The (standardized) feature weights indicate relative predictive power in accounting for the variance in learning gain. As shown, both automatic affect metrics have the same weight in the final model. This result suggests that adapting to our automatically detected disengagement and uncertainty labels can further improve learning over and above adapting to uncertainty alone. Although the final model's predictive power is low (R^2=0.15), our interest here is only in investigating whether the two affective states are more useful in combination than in isolation for predicting performance. In similar types of stepwise regressions on prior ITSPOKE corpora, we've shown that more complete models of system performance incorporating many predictors of learning (i.e. affective states in conjunction with other dialogue features) can yield R^2 values of over .5 (Forbes-Riley et al., 2008).[16]

[13]Identical results were obtained by using an average instead of a total, and only slightly weaker results were obtained when normalizing the DISE totals as the percentages of total turns.

[14]We previously found a related correlation between different DISE and learning measures, during the analysis of our DISE annotation scheme (Forbes-Riley and Litman, 2011b). In particular, we showed a significant partial correlation between the percentage of manual DISE labels and posttest controlled for pretest score.

[15]Using the stepwise method, Automatic DISE was the first feature selected, and Automatic UNC the second. However, note that a model consisting of only the Automatic UNC metric also yields significantly worse predictive power than selecting both affective state metrics. Further note that almost identical models were produced using percentages rather than totals.

[16]R^2 is the standard reported metric for linear regressions. However, for consistency with Table 3, note that the two models in Figure 3 yield R values of -.31 and -.38, respectively.

Learning Gain = -.31 * `Total Automatic DISE` *(R^2=.09, p=.009)*
Learning Gain = -.24 * `Total Automatic DISE` - .24 * `Total Automatic UNC` *(R^2=.15, p=.004)*

Figure 3: Performance Model's Predictive Power Increases Significantly with Multiple Affective Features

Interestingly, for the regression models of learning gain that used manual affect metrics, only the DISE metric was selected as an input. This indicates that the automatic affective state labels are useful in combination for predicting performance in a way that is not reflected in their gold standard counterparts. Detecting multiple affective states might thus be one way to compensate for the noise that is introduced in a fully-automated affective spoken dialogue system.

Similarly, only the DISE metric was selected for inclusion in the regression model of user satisfaction, regardless of whether manual or automatic labels were used. A separate correlation analysis showed that user uncertainty is not significantly correlated with user satisfaction in our system, though we previously found that multiple uncertainty-related metrics do significantly correlate with learning (Litman and Forbes-Riley, 2009).

8 Summary and Current Directions

In this paper we used extrinsic evaluations to provide evidence for the utility of a new system design involving the complex task of user affect detection, prior to undertaking an expensive and time-consuming evaluation of an affect-adaptive system with real users. In particular, we first presented a novel model for automatically detecting user disengagement in spoken dialogue systems. We showed through intrinsic evaluations (i.e., cross-validation experiments using gold-standard labels) that the model yields results on par with prior work. We then showed crucially through novel extrinsic evaluation that the resulting automatically detected disengagement labels correlate with two primary performance metrics (user satisfaction and learning) in the same way as gold standard (manual) labels. This suggests that adapting to the automatic disengagement labels has the potential to significantly improve performance even in the presence of noise from the automatic labeling. Finally, further extrinsic analyses using multiple regression suggest that adapting to our automatic disengagement labels can improve learning (though not user satisfaction) over and above the improvement achieved by only adapting to automatically detected user uncertainty.

We have already developed and implemented an adaptation for user disengagement in ITSPOKE. The disengagement adaptation draws on empirical analyses of our data and effective responses to user disengagement presented in prior work (c.f., (Forbes-Riley and Litman, 2011b)), We are currently evaluating our disengagement adaptation in the "ideal" environment of a Wizard of Oz experiment, where user disengagement, uncertainty, and correctness are labeled by a hidden human during user interactions with ITSPOKE.

Based on the evaluations here, we believe our disengagement model is ready for implementation in ITSPOKE. We will then evaluate the resulting spoken dialogue system for detecting and adapting to multiple affective states in an upcoming controlled experiment with real users.

Acknowledgments

This work is funded by NSF award 0914615. We thank Scott Silliman for systems support.

References

S. Afzal and P. Robinson. 2011. Natural affect data: Collection and annotation. In Sidney D'Mello and Rafael Calvo, editors, *Affect and Learning Technologies*. Springer.

G. Aist, B. Kort, R. Reilly, J. Mostow, and R. Picard. 2002. Experimentally augmenting an intelligent tutoring system with human-supplied capabilities: Adding human-provided emotional scaffolding to an automated reading tutor that listens. In *Proc. Intelligent Tutoring Systems Conference (ITS) Workshop on Empirical Methods for Tutorial Dialogue Systems*, pages 16–28, San Sebastian, Spain.

A. Alwan, Y. Bai, M. Black, L. Caseyz, M. Gerosa, M. Heritagez, M. Iseliy, M. Jonesz, A. Kazemzadeh, S. Lee, S. Narayanan, P. Pricex, J. Tepperman, and

S. Wangy. 2007. A system for technology based assessment of language and literacy in young children: the role of multiple information sources. In *Proceedings of the 9th IEEE International Workshop on Multimedia Signal Processing (MMSP)*, pages 26–30, Chania, Greece, October.

J. Ang, R. Dhillon, A. Krupski, E.Shriberg, and A. Stolcke. 2002. Prosody-based automatic detection of annoyance and frustration in human-computer dialog. In J. H. L. Hansen and B. Pellom, editors, *Proceedings of the International Conference on Spoken Language Processing (ICSLP)*, pages 2037–2039, Denver, USA.

A. Batliner, S. Steidl, C. Hacker, and E. Noth. 2008. Private emotions vs. social interaction - a data-driven approach towards analysing emotion in speech. *User Modeling and User-Adapted Interaction: The Journal of Personalization Research*, 18:175–206.

A. L. Baylor, J. Ryu, and E. Shen. 2003. The effect of pedagogical agent voice and animation on learning, motivation, and perceived persona. In *Proceedings of the ED-MEDIA Conference*, Honolulu, Hawaii, June.

A. Black and P. Taylor. 1997. Festival speech synthesis system: system documentation (1.1.1). The Centre for Speech Technology Research, University of Edinburgh, http://www.cstr.ed.ac.uk/projects/festival/.

D. Bohus and E. Horvitz. 2009. Models for multiparty engagement in open-world dialog. In *Proceedings of SIGdial*, London, UK.

C. Conati and H. Maclaren. 2009. Empirically building and evaluating a probabilistic model of user affect. *User Modeling and User-Adapted Interaction*, 19(3):267–303.

R. Cowie and R. R. Cornelius. 2003. Describing the emotional states that are expressed in speech. *Speech Communication*, 40(1-2):5–32.

L. Devillers and L. Vidrascu. 2006. Real-life emotions detection with lexical and paralinguistic cues on human-human call center dialogs. In *Ninth International Conference on Spoken Language Processing (ICSLP*, pages 801–804, Pittsburgh, PA, September.

S. D'Mello, S. Craig, A. Witherspoon, B. McDaniel, and A. Graesser. 2008. Automatic detection of learner's affect from conversational cues. *User Modeling and User-Adapted Interaction: The Journal of Personalization Research*, 18:45–80.

S. D'Mello, B. Lehman, J. Sullins, R. Daigle, R. Combs, K. Vogt, L. Perkins, and A. Graesser. 2010. A time for emoting: When affect-sensitivity is and isn't effective at promoting deep learning. In *Intelligent Tutoring Systems Conference*, pages 245–254, Pittsburgh, PA, USA, June.

J. Drummond and D. Litman. 2011. Examining the impacts of dialogue content and system automation on affect models in a spoken tutorial dialogue system. In *Proc. 12th Annual Meeting of the Special Interest Group on Discourse and Dialogue (SIGDIAL)*, pages 312–318, Portland, Oregon, June.

M. Dzikovska, J. Moore, N. Steinhauser, and G. Campbell. 2011. Exploring user satisfaction in a tutorial dialogue system. In *Proc. 12th Annual Meeting of the Special Interest Group on Discourse and Dialogue (SIGDIAL)*, pages 162–172, Portland, Oregon, June.

E. Florian, M. Wollmer, and B. Schuller. 2010. The Munich versatile and fast open-source audio feature extractor. In *Proc. ACM Multimedia (MM)*, pages 1459–1462, Florence, Italy.

K. Forbes-Riley and D. Litman. 2009. A user modeling-based performance analysis of a wizarded uncertainty-adaptive dialogue system corpus. In *Proc. Interspeech*, Brighton, UK, September.

K. Forbes-Riley and D. Litman. 2011a. Benefits and challenges of real-time uncertainty detection and adaptation in a spoken dialogue computer tutor. *Speech Communication*, 53(9–10):1115–1136.

K. Forbes-Riley and D. Litman. 2011b. When does disengagement correlate with learning in spoken dialog computer tutoring? In *Proceedings 15th International Conference on Artificial Intelligence in Education (AIED)*, Auckland, NZ, June.

K. Forbes-Riley, M. Rotaru, and D. Litman. 2008. The relative impact of student affect on performance models in a spoken dialogue tutoring system. *User Modeling and User-Adapted Interaction*, 18(1-2):11–43.

K. Forbes-Riley, D. Litman, and H. Friedberg. 2011. Annotating disengagement for spoken dialogue computer tutoring. In Sidney D'Mello and Rafael Calvo, editors, *Affect and Learning Technologies*. Springer.

Jonathan Gratch, Stacy Marsella, Ning Wang, and Brooke Stankovic. 2009. Assessing the validity of appraisal-based models of emotion. In *Proceedings of ACII*, Amsterdam, Netherlands.

X. D. Huang, F. Alleva, H. W. Hon, M. Y. Hwang, K. F. Lee, and R. Rosenfeld. 1993. The SphinxII speech recognition system: An Overview. *Computer, Speech and Language*.

J. H. Jeon, R. Xia, and Y. Liu. 2010. Level of interest sensing in spoken dialog using multi-level fusion of acoustic and lexical evidence. In *INTERSPEECH'10*, pages 2802–2805.

P. Jordan, B. Hall, M. Ringenberg, Y. Cui, and C.P. Rose. 2007. Tools for authoring a dialogue agent that participates in learning studies. In *Proc. Artificial Intelligence in Education (AIED)*, pages 43–50.

A. Kapoor and R. W. Picard. 2005. Multimodal affect recognition in learning environments. In *13th Annual ACM International Conference on Multimedia*, pages 677–682, Singapore.

J. Klein, Y. Moon, and R. Picard. 2002. This computer responds to user frustration: Theory, design, and results. *Interacting with Computers*, 14:119–140.

C. M. Lee and S. Narayanan. 2005. Towards detecting emotions in spoken dialogs. *IEEE Transactions on Speech and Audio Processing*, 13(2), March.

B. Lehman, M. Matthews, S. D'Mello, and N. Person. 2008. What are you feeling? Investigating student affective states during expert human tutoring sessions. In *Intelligent Tutoring Systems Conference (ITS)*, pages 50–59, Montreal, Canada, June.

D. Litman and K. Forbes-Riley. 2009. Spoken tutorial dialogue and the feeling of another's knowing. In *Proceedings 10th Annual Meeting of the Special Interest Group on Discourse and Dialogue (SIGDIAL)*, London, UK, September.

K. Liu and R. W. Picard. 2005. Embedded empathy in continuous, interactive health assessment. In *CHI Workshop on HCI Challenges in Health Assessment*.

A. Martalo, N. Novielli, and F. de Rosis. 2008. Attitude display in dialogue patterns. In *Proc. AISB 2008 Symposium on Affective Language in Human and Machine*, pages 1–8, Aberdeen, Scotland, April.

S. McQuiggan, B. Mott, and J. Lester. 2008. Modeling self-efficacy in intelligent tutoring systems: An inductive approach. *User Modeling and User-Adapted Interaction (UMUAI)*, 18(1-2):81–123, February.

T. Paek and Y.-C. Ju. 2008. Accommodating explicit user expressions of uncertainty in voice search or something like that. In *Proceedings of the 9th Annual Conference of the International Speech Communication Association (INTERSPEECH 08)*, pages 1165–1168, Brisbane, Australia, September.

H. Pon-Barry and S. Shieber. 2011. Recognizing uncertainty in speech. *EURASIP Journal on Advances in Signal Processing*.

H. Pon-Barry, K. Schultz, E. Owen Bratt, B. Clark, and S. Peters. 2006. Responding to student uncertainty in spoken tutorial dialogue systems. *International Journal of Artificial Intelligence in Education*, 16:171–194.

K. Porayska-Pomsta, M. Mavrikis, and H. Pain. 2008. Diagnosing and acting on student affect: the tutor's perspective. *User Modeling and User-Adapted Interaction: The Journal of Personalization Research*, 18:125–173.

H. Prendinger and M. Ishizuka. 2005. The Empathetic Companion: A character-based interface that addresses users' affective states. *International Journal of Applied Artificial Intelligence*, 19(3):267–285.

M. Rotaru and D. Litman. 2009. Discourse structure and performance analysis: Beyond the correlation. In *Proceedings 10th Annual Meeting of the Special Interest Group on Discourse and Dialogue (SIGDIAL)*, London, UK.

B. Schuller, R. Muller, F. Eyben, J. Gast, B. Hrnler, M. Wollmer, G. Rigoll, A. Hthker, and H. Konosu. 2009a. Being bored? recognising natural interest by extensive audiovisual integration for real-life application. *Image and Vision Computing Journal, Special Issue on Visual and Multimodal Analysis of Human Spontaneous Behavior*, 27:1760–1774.

B. Schuller, S. Steidl, and A. Batliner. 2009b. The Interspeech 2009 Emotion Challenge. In *Proceedings of the 10th Annual Conference of the International Speech Communication Association (Interspeech)*, ISCA, Brighton, UK, September.

B. Schuller, S. Steidl, A. Batliner, F. Burkhardt, L. Devillers, C. Muller, and S. Narayanan. 2010. The Interspeech 2010 Paralinguistic Challenge. In *Proceedings of the 11th Annual Conference of the International Speech Communication Assocation (Interspeech)*, pages 2794–2797, Chiba, Japan, September.

I. Shafran, M. Riley, and M. Mohri. 2003. Voice signatures. In *Proceedings of the IEEE Automatic Speech Recognition and Understanding Workshop (ASRU)*, pages 31–36, St. Thomas, US Virgin Islands.

C. Sidner and C. Lee. 2003. An architecture for engagement in collaborative conversations between a robot and a human. Technical Report TR2003-12, MERL.

A. Stolcke, N. Coccaro, R. Bates, P. Taylor, C. Van Ess-Dykema, K. Ries, E. Shriberg, D. Jurafsky, R. Martin, and M. Meteer. 2000. Dialogue act modeling for automatic tagging and recognition of conversational speech. *Computational Linguistics*, 26(3).

W. Tsukahara and N. Ward. 2001. Responding to subtle, fleeting changes in the user's internal state. In *Proceedings of the SIG-CHI on Human factors in computing systems*, pages 77–84, Seattle, WA. ACM.

K. VanLehn, P. W. Jordan, C. Rosé, D. Bhembe, M. Böttner, A. Gaydos, M. Makatchev, U. Pappuswamy, M. Ringenberg, A. Roque, S. Siler, R. Srivastava, and R. Wilson. 2002. The architecture of Why2-Atlas: A coach for qualitative physics essay writing. In *Proc. Intl. Conf. on Intelligent Tutoring Systems*.

L. Vidrascu and L. Devillers. 2005. Detection of real-life emotions in dialogs recorded in a call center. In *Proceedings of INTERSPEECH*, Lisbon, Portugal.

M. Walker, A. Rudnicky, R. Prasad, J. Aberdeen, E. Bratt, J. Garofolo, H. Hastie, A. Le, B. Pellom, A. Potamianos, R. Passonneau, S. Roukos, G. Sanders, S. Seneff, and D. Stallard. 2002. DARPA communicator: Cross-system results for the 2001 evaluation. In *Proc. ICSLP*.

W. Wang and J. Hirschberg. 2011. Detecting levels of interest from spoken dialog with multistream prediction feedback and similarity based hierarchical fusion learning. In *Proc. 12th Annual Meeting of the Special Interest Group on Discourse and Dialogue (SIGDIAL)*, pages 152–161, Portland, Oregon, June.

N. Wang, W.L. Johnson, R. E. Mayer, P. Rizzo, E. Shaw, and H. Collins. 2008. The politeness effect: Pedagogical agents and learning outcomes. *International Journal of Human-Computer Studies*, 66(2):98–112.

Exploring Content Features for Automated Speech Scoring

Shasha Xie, Keelan Evanini, Klaus Zechner
Educational Testing Service (ETS)
Princeton, NJ 08541, USA
{sxie,kevanini,kzechner}@ets.org

Abstract

Most previous research on automated speech scoring has focused on restricted, predictable speech. For automated scoring of unrestricted spontaneous speech, speech proficiency has been evaluated primarily on aspects of pronunciation, fluency, vocabulary and language usage but not on aspects of content and topicality. In this paper, we explore features representing the accuracy of the content of a spoken response. Content features are generated using three similarity measures, including a lexical matching method (Vector Space Model) and two semantic similarity measures (Latent Semantic Analysis and Pointwise Mutual Information). All of the features exhibit moderately high correlations with human proficiency scores on human speech transcriptions. The correlations decrease somewhat due to recognition errors when evaluated on the output of an automatic speech recognition system; however, the additional use of word confidence scores can achieve correlations at a similar level as for human transcriptions.

1 Introduction

Automated assessment of a non-native speaker's proficiency in a given language is an attractive application of automatic speech recognition (ASR) and natural language processing (NLP) technology; the technology can be used by language learners for individual practice and by assessment providers to reduce the cost of human scoring. While much research has been done about the scoring of restricted speech, such as reading aloud or repeating sentences verbatim (Cucchiarini et al., 1997; Bernstein et al., 2000; Cucchiarini et al., 2000; Witt and Young, 2000; Franco et al., 2000; Bernstein et al., 2010b), much less has been done about the scoring of spontaneous speech. For automated scoring of unrestricted, spontaneous speech, most automated systems have estimated the non-native speakers' speaking proficiency primarily based on low-level speaking-related features, such as pronunciation, intonation, rhythm, rate of speech, and fluency (Cucchiarini et al., 2002; Zechner et al., 2007; Chen et al., 2009; Chen and Zechner, 2011a), although a few recent studies have explored features based on vocabulary and grammatical complexity (Zechner et al., 2007; Bernstein et al., 2010a; Bernstein et al., 2010b; Chen and Zechner, 2011b).

To date, little work has been conducted on automatically assessing the relatively higher-level aspects of spontaneous speech, such as the content and topicality, the structure, and the discourse information. Automated assessment of these aspects of a non-native speaker's speech is very challenging for a number of reasons, such as the short length of typical responses (approximately 100 words for a typical 1 minute response, compared to over 300 words in a typical essay/written response), the spontaneous nature of the speech, and the presence of disfluencies and possible grammatical errors. Moreover, the assessment system needs text transcripts of the speech to evaluate the high level aspects, and these are normally obtained from ASR systems. The recognition accuracy of state-of-the-art ASR systems on non-native spontaneous speech is still relatively low, which will sequentially impact the reliability and accuracy of automatic scoring systems using these noisy transcripts. However, despite these difficulties, it is necessary for an automated assessment system to address the high level information of a spoken response in order to fully cover all aspects that are considered by human raters. Thus, in this paper we focus on exploring features to represent the high-level aspect of speech mainly on the accuracy of the content.

As a starting point, we consider approaches that have been used for the automated assessment of content in essays. However, due to the qualitative differences between written essays and spontaneous speech, the techniques developed for written texts may not perform as well on spoken responses. Still, as a baseline, we will evaluate the content features used for essay scoring on spontaneous speech. In addition to a straightforward lexical Vector Space Model (VSM), we investigate approaches using two other similarity measures, Latent Semantic Analysis (LSA) and Pointwise Mutual Information (PMI), in order to represent the semantic-level proficiency of a speaker. All of the content features are analyzed using both human transcripts and speech recognizer output, so we can have a better understanding of the impact of ASR errors on the performance of the features. As expected, the results show that the performance on ASR output is lower than when human transcripts are used. Therefore, we propose improved content features that take into account ASR confidence scores to emphasize responses whose estimated word accuracy is comparatively higher than others. These improved features can obtain similar performance when compared to the results using human transcripts.

This paper is organized as follows. In the next section we introduce previous research on automated assessment of content in essays and spoken responses. The content features we generated and the model we used to build the final speaking scores are described in Sections 3 and Section 4, respectively. In Section 5 we show the performance of all our proposed features. Finally, we conclude our work and discuss potential future work in Section 6.

2 Related Work

Most previous research on assessment of non-native speech has focused on restricted, predictable speech; see, for example, the collection of articles in (Eskenazi et al., 2009). When assessing spontaneous speech, due to relatively high word error rates of current state-of-the-art ASR systems, predominantly features related to low-level information have been used, such as features related to fluency, pronunciation or prosody (Zechner et al., 2009).

For scoring of written language (automated essay scoring), on the other hand, several features related to the high level aspects have been used previously, such as the content and the discourse information. In one approach, the lexical content of an essay was evaluated by using a VSM to compare the words contained in each essay to the words found in a sample of essays from each score category (Attali and Burstein, 2006). In addition, this system also used an organization feature measuring the difference between the ideal structure of an essay and the actual discourse elements found in the essay. The features designed for measuring the overall organization of an essay assumed a writing strategy that included an introductory paragraph, at least a three-paragraph body with each paragraph in the body consisting of a pair of main point, supporting idea elements, and a concluding paragraph. In another approach, the content of written essays were evaluated using LSA by comparing the test essays with essays of known quality in regard of their degree of conceptual relevance and the amount of relevant content (Foltz et al., 1999).

There has been less work measuring spoken responses in terms of the higher level aspects. In (Zechner and Xi, 2008), the authors used a content feature together with other features related to vocabulary, pronunciation and fluency to build an automated scoring system for spontaneous high-entropy responses. This content feature was the cosine word vector product between a test response and the training responses which have the highest human score. The experimental results showed that this feature did not provide any further contribution above a baseline of only using non-content features, and for some tasks the system performance was even slightly worse after including this feature. However, we think the observations about the content features used in this paper were not reliable for the following two reasons: the number of training responses was limited (1000 responses), and the ASR system had a relatively high Word Error Rate (39%).

In this paper, we provide further analysis on the performance of several types of content features. Additionally, we used a larger amount of training data and a better ASR system in an attempt to extract more meaningful and accurate content features.

3 Automatic Content Scoring

In automatic essay scoring systems, the content of an essay is typically evaluated by comparing the words it contains to the words found in a sample of essays from each score category (1-4 in our experiments), where the scores are assigned by trained human raters. The basic idea is that good essays will resemble each other in their word choice, as will poor essays. We follow this basic idea when extracting content features for spoken responses.

3.1 Scoring Features

For each test spoken response, we calculate its similarity scores to the sample responses from each score category. These scores indicate the degree of similarity between the words used in the test response and the words used in responses from different score points. Using these similarity scores, 3 content features are generated in this paper:

- Sim_{max}: the score point which has the highest similarity score between test response and score vector
- Sim_4: the similarity score to the responses with the highest score category (4 in our experiments).
- Sim_{cmb}: the linear combination of the similarity scores to each score category.

$$\sum_{i=1}^{4} w_i * Sim_i \quad (1)$$

where w_i is scaled to [-1, 1] to imply its positive or negative impact.

3.2 Similarity Measures

There are many ways to calculate the similarity between responses. A simple and commonly used method is the Vector Space Model, which is also used in automated essay scoring systems. Under this approach, all the responses are converted to vectors, whose elements are weighted using TF*IDF (term frequency, inverse document frequency). Then, the cosine similarity score between vectors can be used to estimate the similarity between the responses the vectors originally represent.

Other than this lexical matching method, we also try two additional similarity measures to better capture the semantic level information: Latent Semantic Analysis (Landauer et al., 1998) and a corpus-based semantic similarity measure based on pointwise mutual information (Mihalcea et al., 2006). LSA has been widely used for computing document similarity and other information retrieval tasks. Under this approach, Singular Value Decomposition (SVD) is used to analyze the statistical relationship between a set of documents and the words they contain. A $m*n$ word-document matrix X is first built, in which each element X_{ij} represents the weighted term frequency of word i in document j. The matrix is decomposed into a product of three matrices as follows:

$$X = U\Sigma V^T \quad (2)$$

where U is an $m \times m$ matrix of left-singular vectors, Σ is an $m \times n$ diagonal matrix of singular values, and V is the $n \times n$ matrix of right-singular vectors.

The top ranked k singular values in Σ are kept, and the left is set to be 0. So Σ is reformulated as Σ_k. The original matrix X is recalculated accordingly,

$$X_k = U\Sigma_k V^T \quad (3)$$

This new matrix X_k can be considered as a smoothed or compressed version of the original matrix. LSA measures the similarity of two documents by calculating the cosine between the corresponding compressed column vectors.

PMI was introduced to calculate the semantic similarity between words in (Turney, 2001). It is based on the word co-occurrence on a large corpus. Given two words, their PMI is computed using:

$$PMI(w_1, w_2) = log_2 \frac{p(w_1 \& w_2)}{p(w_1) * p(w_2)} \quad (4)$$

This indicates the statistical dependency between w_1 and w_2, and can be used as a measure of the semantic similarity of two words.

Given the word-to-word similarity, we can calculate the similarity between two documents using the following function,

$$sim(D_1, D_2) = \frac{1}{2}\left(\frac{\sum_{w\in\{D_1\}}(maxSim(w, D_2) * idf(w))}{\sum_{w\in\{D_1\}} idf(w)} + \frac{\sum_{w\in\{D_2\}}(maxSim(w, D_1) * idf(w)}{\sum_{w\in\{D_2\}} idf(w))}\right) \quad (5)$$

$$maxSim(w, D_i) = max_{w_j\in\{D_i\}}PMI(w, w_j) \quad (6)$$

For each word w in document D_1, we find the word in document D_2 which has the highest similarity to w. Similarly, for each word in D_2, we identify the most similar words in D_1. The similarity score between two documents is then calculated by combining the similarity of the words they contain, weighted by their word specificity (i.e., IDF values).

In this paper, we use these three similarity measures to calculate the similarity between the test response and the training responses for each score category. Using the VSM method, we convert all the training responses in one score category into one big vector, and for a given test response we calculate its cosine similarity to this vector as its similarity to that corresponding score point vector. For the other similarity measures, we calculate the test response's similarity to each of the training responses in one score category, and report the average score as its similarity to this score point. We also tried using this average similarity score for the VSM method, but our experimental results showed that this average score obtained lower performance than using one big vector generated from all the training samples due to data sparsity. After the similarity scores to each of the four score categories are computed, the content features introduced in Section 3.1 are then extracted and are used to evaluate the speaking proficiency of the speaker.

4 System Architecture

This section describes the architecture of our automated content scoring system, which is shown in Figure 1. First, the test taker's voice is recorded, and sent to the automatic speech recognition system. Second, the feature computation module takes the output hypotheses from the speech recognizer and generates the content features. The last component considers all the scoring features, and produces the final score for each spoken response.

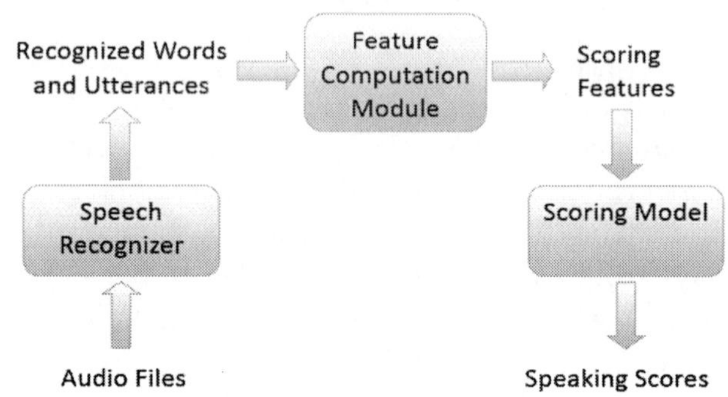

Figure 1: Architecture of the automated content scoring system.

While we are using human transcripts of spoken responses as a baseline in this paper, we want to note that in an operational system as depicted in this figure, the scoring features are computed and extracted using the hypotheses from the ASR system, which exhibits a relatively high word error rate. These recognition errors will sequentially impact the process of calculating the similarity and computing the content scores, and decrease the performance of the final speaking scores. In order to improve the system performance in this ASR condition, we explore the use of word confidence scores from the ASR system during feature generation. In particular, the similarity scores between the test response and each score category are weighted using the recognition confidence score of the response, so that the scores can also contain information related to its acoustic accuracy. The confidence score for one response is the average value of all the confidence scores for each word contained in the response. In Section 5, we will evaluate the performance of our proposed content features using both human transcripts and ASR outputs, as well as the enhanced content features using ASR confidence scores.

5 Experimental Results

5.1 Data

The data we use for our experiments are from the Test of English as a Foreign Language® internet-based test (TOEFL iBT) in which test takers respond to several stimuli using spontaneous speech. This data set contains 24 topics, of which 8 are opinion-based tasks, and 16 are contextual-based tasks. The opinion-based tasks ask the test takers to provide information or opinions on familiar topics based on their personal experience or background knowledge. The purpose of these tasks is to measure the speaking ability of examinees independent of their ability to read or listen to English language. The contextual-based tasks engage reading, listening and speaking skills in combination to mimic the kinds of communication expected of students in campus-based situations and in academic courses. Test takers read and/or listen to some stimulus materials and then respond to a question based on them. For each of the tasks, after task stimulus materials and/or test questions are delivered, the examinees are allowed a short time to consider their response and then provide their responses in a spontaneous manner within either 45 seconds (for the opinion-based tasks) or 60 seconds (for the contextual-based tasks).

For each topic, we randomly select 1800 responses for training, and 200 responses as development set for parameter tuning. Our evaluation data contains 1500 responses from the same English proficiency test, which contain the same 24 topics. All of these data are scored on a 0-4 scale by expert human raters. In our automated scoring system, we use a filtering model to identify responses which should have a score of 0, such as responses with a technical difficulty (e.g., equipment problems, high ambient noise), responses containing uncooperative behavior from the speakers (e.g., non-English speech, whispered speech). So in this paper we only focused on the responses with scores of 1-4. Statistics for this data set are shown in Table 1. As the table shows, the score distributions are similar across the training, development, and evaluation data sets.

5.2 Speech recognizer

We use an ASR system containing a cross-word triphone acoustic model trained on approximately 800 hours of spoken responses from the same English proficiency test mentioned above and a language model trained on the corresponding transcripts, which contain a total of over 5 million words. The Word Error Rate (WER) of this system on the evaluation data set is 33%.

5.3 Evaluation metric

To measure the quality of the developed features, we employ a widely used metric, the Pearson correlation coefficient (r). In our experiments, we use the value of the Pearson correlation between the feature values and the human proficiency scores for each spoken response.

5.4 Feature performance on transcripts

In Section 3.1, we introduced three features derived from the similarity between the test responses and the training responses for each score point. We first build the training samples for each topic, and then compare the test responses with their corresponding models. Three similarity measures are used for calculating the similarity scores, VSM, LSA, and the PMI-based method. In order to avoid the impact of recognition errors, we first evaluate these similarity methods and content features using the human transcripts. The Pearson correlation coefficients on the evaluation data set for this experiment are shown in Table 2. The parameters used during model building, such as the weights for each score category in the feature Sim_{cmb} and the number of topics k in LSA, are all tuned on the development set, and applied directly on the evaluation set.

The correlations show that even the simple vector space model can obtain a good correlation of 0.48 with the human rater scores. The feature Sim_{cmb} performs the best across almost all the test setups, since it combines the information from all score categories. The PMI-based features outperform the other two similarity methods when evaluated both on all responses or only on the contextual-based topics. We also observe that the correlations on *contextual-based* tasks are much higher than on *opinion-based* tasks. The reason for this is that

Table 1: Summary statistics of training, development and evaluation data set.

Data sets	*Responses*	*Speakers*	*score_avg*	*score_sd*	*Score distribution (percentage %)*			
					1	2	3	4
Train	43200	8000	2.63	0.79	1750 (4.1)	15128 (35.0)	20828 (48.2)	4837 (11.2)
Dev	4800	3760	2.61	0.79	215 (4.5)	1719 (35.8)	2295 (47.8)	499 (10.4)
Eval	1500	250	2.57	0.81	95 (6.3)	549 (36.6)	685 (45.7)	152 (10.1)

Table 2: Pearson correlations of the content features using human transcripts.

	VSM			*LSA*			*PMI*		
	Sim_{max}	Sim_4	Sim_{cmb}	Sim_{max}	Sim_4	Sim_{cmb}	Sim_{max}	Sim_4	Sim_{cmb}
ALL	0.46	0.32	**0.48**	0.32	0.38	**0.45**	0.18	0.51	**0.53**
Contextual	0.50	0.51	**0.58**	0.36	0.55	**0.57**	0.21	0.57	**0.62**
Opinion	**0.37**	0.03	0.25	**0.29**	0.14	0.22	0.06	0.42	**0.51**

the contextual-based tasks are more constrained to the materials provided with the test item, whereas the opinion-based tasks are relatively open-ended. Therefore, it is easier for the similarity measures to track the content, the topics, or the vocabulary usage of the contextual-based topics. Overall, the best correlations are obtained using the feature combining the similarity scores to each score category and the PMI-based methods to calculate the similarity. Here, the Pearson correlations are 0.53 for all responses, and 0.62 for the contextual-based tasks only.

We also investigated whether additional performance gains could be achieved by combining information from the three different content features to build a single overall content score, since the three features may measure disparate aspects of the response. The combination model we use is multiple regression, in which the score assigned to a test response is estimated as a weighted linear combination of a selected set of features. The features are the similarity values to each score category ($Sim_i, i \in \{1, 2, 3, 4\}$), calcuated using the three similairty measures. In total we have 12 content features. The regression model is also built on the development set, and tested on the evaluation set. The correlation for the final model is 0.60 on all responses, which is significantly better than the individual models (0.48 for VSM, 0.45 for LSA, and 0.53 for PMI). Compared to results reported in previous work on similar speech scoring tasks but measuring other aspects of speech, our correlation results are very competitive (Zechner and Xi, 2008; Zechner et al., 2009).

5.5 Feature Performance on ASR output

The results shown in the previous section were obtained using human transcripts of test responses, and were reported in order to demonstrate the meaningfulness of the proposed features. However, in practical automated speech scoring systems, the only available text is the output of the ASR system, which may contain a large number of recognition errors. Therefore, in this section we show the performance of the content features extracted using ASR hypotheses. Note that we still use the human transcripts of the training samples to train the models, the parameter values and the regression weights; however, we only use ASR output of the evaluation data for testing the feature performance. These correlations are shown in Table 3.

Compared to the results in Table 2, we find that the VSM and LSA methods are very robust to recognition errors, and we only observe slight correlation decreases on these features. However, the decrease for the PMI-based method is quite large. A possible reason for this is that this method is based on word-to-word similarity computed on the training data, so the mismatch between training and evaluation set likely has a great impact on the computation of the similarity scores, since we train on human transcripts, but test using ASR hypotheses. Likely for the same reason, the regression model combining all the features does not provide any further contribution to the correlation result (0.44 when evaluated

Table 3: Pearson correlations of the content features using ASR output.

	VSM			LSA			PMI		
	Sim_{max}	Sim_4	Sim_{cmb}	Sim_{max}	Sim_4	Sim_{cmb}	Sim_{max}	Sim_4	Sim_{cmb}
ALL	0.43	0.34	**0.48**	0.30	0.37	**0.43**	0.11	0.24	**0.42**
Contextual	0.49	0.53	**0.58**	0.34	0.54	**0.57**	0.16	0.31	**0.53**
Opinion	**0.30**	0.05	0.07	**0.25**	0.12	0.15	0.05	0.17	**0.27**

Table 4: Pearson correlations of the content features using ASR output with confidence scores.

	VSM			LSA			PMI		
	Sim_{max}	Sim_4	Sim_{cmb}	Sim_{max}	Sim_4	Sim_{cmb}	Sim_{max}	Sim_4	Sim_{cmb}
ALL	0.43	0.36	**0.48**	0.30	0.40	**0.45**	0.11	0.39	**0.51**
Contextual	0.49	0.55	**0.58**	0.34	0.57	**0.59**	0.16	0.46	**0.59**
Opinion	**0.30**	0.24	0.25	**0.25**	0.18	0.20	0.05	0.32	**0.40**

on all responses).

In Section 4, we proposed using ASR confidence scores during feature extraction to introduce acoustic level information and, thus, penalize responses for which the ASR output is less likely to be correct. Under this approach, all similarity scores are multiplied by the average word confidence score contained in the test response. The performance of these enhanced features is provided in Table 4. Compared to the scores in Table 3, the enhanced features perform better than the basic features that do not take the confidence scores into consideration. Using this approach, we can improve the correlation scores for most of the features, especially for the PMI-based features. These features had lower correlations because of the recognition errors, but with the confidence scores, they outperform the other features when evaluated both on all responses or only on contextual-based responses. Note that the correlations for feature Sim_{max} remains the same because the same average confidence scores for each test response is multiplied by the similarity scores to each of the score points, so the score point obtaining the highest similarity score is the same whether the confidence scores are considered or not. The correlation of the regression model also improves from 0.44 to 0.51 when the confidence scores are included. Overall, the best correlations for the individual similarity features with the confidence scores are very close to those obtained using human transcripts, as shown in Tables 2 and 4: the difference is 0.53 vs. 0.51 for all responses, and 0.62 vs. 0.59 for contextual-based tasks only.

Because all models and parameter values are trained on human transcripts, this experimental setup might not be optimal for using ASR outputs. For instance, the regression model does not outperform the results of individual features using ASR outputs, although the confidence scores help improve the overall correlation scores. We expect that we can obtain better performance by using a regression model trained on ASR transcripts, which can better model the impact of noisy data on the features. In our future work, we will build sample responses for each score category, tune the parameter values, and train the regression model all on ASR hypotheses. We hope this can solve the mismatch problem during training and evaluation, and can provide us even better correlation results.

6 Conclusion and Future Work

Most previous work on automated scoring of spontaneous speech used features mainly related to low-level information, such as fluency, pronunciation, prosody, as well as a few features measuring aspects such as vocabulary diversity and grammatical accuracy. In this paper, we focused on extracting content features to measure the speech proficiency in relatively higher-level aspect of spontaneous speech. Three features were computed to measure the similarity between a test response and a set of sample responses representing different levels of speaking proficiency. The similarity was calculated using different methods, including the lexical matching method VSM, and two corpus-based semantic similarity measures, LSA and PMI. Our experimental results showed that all the features obtained good correlations with human proficiency scores if there are no recognition errors in the text transcripts, with the PMI-based method performing the best over three similarity measures. However, if we used ASR transcripts, we observed a marked performance drop for the PMI-based method. Although we found that VSM and LSA were very robust to ASR errors, the overall correlations for the ASR condition were not as good as using human transcripts. To solve this problem, we proposed to use ASR confidence scores to improve the feature performance, and achieved similar results as when using human transcripts.

As we discussed in Section 5, all models were trained using human transcripts, which might decrease the performance when these models are applied directly to the ASR outputs. In our future work, we will compare models trained on human transcripts and on ASR outputs, and investigate whether we should use matching data for training and evaluation, or whether we should not introduce noise during training in order to maintain the validity of the models. We will also investigate whether the content features can provide additional information for automated speech scoring, and help build better scoring systems when they are combined with other non-content features, such as the features representing fluency, pronunciation, prosody, vocabulary diversity information. We will also explore generating other features measuring the higher-level aspects of the spoken responses. For example, we can extract features assessing the responses' relatedness to the stimulus of an opinion-based task. For contextual-based tasks, the test takers are asked to read or listen to some stimulus material, and answer a question based on this information. We can build models using these materials to check the correctness and relatedness of the spoken responses.

References

Yigal Attali and Jill Burstein. 2006. Automated essay scoring with e-rater® v.2. *The Journal of Technology, Learning, and Assessment*, 4(3):3–30.

Jared Bernstein, John De Jong, David Pisoni, and Brent Townshend. 2000. Two experiments on automatic scoring of spoken language proficiency. In *Proceedings of Integrating Speech Tech. in Learning (InSTIL)*.

Jared Bernstein, Jian Cheng, and Masanori Suzuki. 2010a. Fluency and structural complexity as predictors of L2 oral proficiency. In *Proceedings of Interspeech*.

Jared Bernstein, Alistair Van Moere, and Jian Cheng. 2010b. Validating automated speaking tests. *Language Testing*, 27(3):355–377.

Lei Chen and Klaus Zechner. 2011a. Applying rhythm features to automatically assess non-native speech. In *Proceedings of Interspeech*.

Miao Chen and Klaus Zechner. 2011b. Computing and evaluating syntactic complexity features for automated scoring of spontaneous non-native speech. In *Proceedings of ACL-HLT*.

Lei Chen, Klaus Zechner, and Xiaoming Xi. 2009. Improved pronunciation features for construct-driven assessment of non-native spontaneous speech. In *Proceedings of NAACL-HLT*.

Catia Cucchiarini, Helmer Strik, and Lou Boves. 1997. Automatic evaluation of Dutch pronunciation by using speech recognition technology. In *IEEE Workshop on Auotmatic Speech Recognition and Understanding*.

Catia Cucchiarini, Helmer Strik, and Lou Boves. 2000. Quantitative assessment of second language learners' fluency by means of automatic speech recognition technology. *Journal of the Acoustical Society of America*, 107:989–999.

Catia Cucchiarini, Helmer Strik, and Lou Boves. 2002. Quantitative assessment of second language learners' fluency: comparisons between read and spontaneous speech. *Journal of the Acoustical Society of America*, 111(6):2862–2873.

Maxine Eskenazi, Abeer Alwan, and Helmer Strik. 2009. Spoken language technology for education. *Speech Communication*, 51(10):831–1038.

Peter W. Foltz, Darrell Laham, and Thomas K. Landauer. 1999. The Intelligent Essay Assessor: Applications to educational technology. *Interactive multimedia Electronic Journal of Computer-Enhanced Learning*, 1(2).

Horacio Franco, Leonardo Neumeyer, Vassilios Digalakis, and Orith Ronen. 2000. Combination of machine scores for automatic grading of pronunciation quality. *Speech Communication*, 30(1-2):121–130.

Thomas K Landauer, Peter W. Foltz, and Darrell Laham. 1998. Introduction to Latent Semantic Analysis. *Discourse Processes*, 25:259–284.

Rada Mihalcea, Courtney Corley, and Carlo Strapparava. 2006. Corpus-based and knowledge-based measures of text semantic similarity. In *Proceedings of the American Association for Artificial Intelligence*, September.

Peter D. Turney. 2001. Mining the web for synonyms: PMI-IR versus LSA on TOEFL. In *Proceedings of ECML.*

Silke M. Witt and Steve J. Young. 2000. Phone-level pronunciation scoring and assessment for interactive language learning. *Speech Communication*, 30(1-2):95–108.

Klaus Zechner and Xiaoming Xi. 2008. Towards automatic scoring of a test of spoken language with heterogeneous task types. In *Proceedings of the Third Workshop on Innovative Use of NLP for Building Educational Applications.*

Klaus Zechner, Derrick Higgins, and Xiaoming Xi. 2007. Speechrater^{TM}: A construct-driven approach to score spontaneous non-native speech. In *Proceedings of the 2007 Workshop of the International Speech Communication Association (ISCA) Special Interest Group on Speech and Language Technology in Education (SLaTE).*

Klaus Zechner, Derrick Higgins, Xiaoming Xi, and David M. Williamson. 2009. Automatic scoring of non-native spontaneous speech in tests of spoken English. *Speech Communication*, 51(10):883–895.

Hello, Who is Calling?: Can Words Reveal the Social Nature of Conversations?

Anthony Stark, Izhak Shafran and Jeffrey Kaye
Center for Spoken Language Understanding, OHSU, Portland USA.
{starkan, shafrani, kaye}@ohsu.edu

Abstract

This study aims to infer the social nature of conversations from their content automatically. To place this work in context, our motivation stems from the need to understand how social disengagement affects cognitive decline or depression among older adults. For this purpose, we collected a comprehensive and naturalistic corpus comprising of all the incoming and outgoing telephone calls from 10 subjects over the duration of a year. As a first step, we learned a binary classifier to filter out business related conversation, achieving an accuracy of about 85%. This classification task provides a convenient tool to probe the nature of telephone conversations. We evaluated the utility of openings and closing in differentiating personal calls, and find that empirical results on a large corpus do not support the hypotheses by Schegloff and Sacks that personal conversations are marked by unique closing structures. For classifying different types of social relationships such as family vs other, we investigated features related to language use (entropy), hand-crafted dictionary (LIWC) and topics learned using unsupervised latent Dirichlet models (LDA). Our results show that the posteriors over topics from LDA provide consistently higher accuracy (60-81%) compared to LIWC or language use features in distinguishing different types of conversations.

1 Introduction

In recent years, there has been a growing interest in analyzing text in informal interactions such as in Internet chat, newsgroups and twitter. The emphasis of most such research has been in estimating network structure (Kwak et al., 2010) and detecting trending topics (Ritter et al., 2010), sentiments (Pak and Paroubek, 2010) and first stories (Petrović et al., 2010). The focus has been on aggregating information from large number of users to analyze population level statistics.

The study reported in this paper, in contrast, focuses on understanding the social interactions of an individual over long periods of time. Our motivation stems from the need to understand the factors of social engagement that ameliorate the rate of cognitive decline and depression in older adults. Since the early work of Glass (1997) and colleagues, several studies on large cohorts over extended duration have confirmed that older adults with few social relationships are at an increased risk of suffering depression and dementia. The limited information available in currently used coarse measures, often based on self-reports, have hindered epidemiologists from probing the nature of this association further.

While social engagement is typically multi-faceted, older adults, who are often less mobile, rely on telephone conversations to maintain their social relationships. This is reflected in a recent survey by Pew Research Center which reported that among adults 65 years and older, nine in ten talk with family or friends every day and more than 95% use land-line telephones for all or most of their calls (Taylor et al., June 29 2009). Conveniently for us, telephone conversations present several advantages for analysis. Unlike many other forms of communication, the interaction is restricted solely to an audio channel, without recourse to gestures or facial expressions. While we do not discount the importance of multi-modal communication, having a communication channel restricted to a unimodal format does significantly simplify both collection and analysis. Furthermore, the use of a handset affords the opportunity to capture naturalistic speech samples at relatively high signal-to-noise ratio. Lastly, automatic speech recognition (ASR) systems can now transcribe telephone conversations with sufficient accuracy for useful automated analysis.

Given the above premise, we focus our attention on studying social interactions of older adults over land-line telephones. To facilitate such a study, we collected telephone conversations from several older adults for approximately one year. Note that our corpus is unlike the publicly available Switchboard and Fisher corpora, which contain conversations between unfamiliar speakers discussing a topic from a pre-determined list such as music, crime, air pollution (Godfrey et al., 1992). In contrast, the conversations in our corpus are completely natural, covering a wide range of topics, conversational partners and types of interactions. Our corpus is also comprehensive in that it includes all the outgoing/incoming calls from subjects' homes during the observation period.

As a step toward understanding social networks and associated relationships, our first task was to classify social and non-social (business) conversations. While reverse listing was useful to a certain extent, we were unable to find listing on up to 50% of the calls in our corpus due to lack of caller ID information on many calls as well as unlisted numbers. Moreover, we cannot preclude the possibility that a social conversation may occur on a business number (e.g., a friend or a relative working in a business establishment) and vice versa. Using the subset of calls for which we have reliable listing, we learned a supervised classifier and then employed the classifier to label the remaining calls for further analysis.

The focus of this study was not so much on learning a binary classifier, but using the resulting classifier as a tool to probe the nature of telephone conversations as well as to test whether the scores obtained from it can serve as a proxy for degree of social familiarity. The classifier also affords us an opportunity to re-examine hypotheses proposed by Schegloff and Sacks (1974; 1968; 1973) about the structure of openings and closing in business and personal conversations. Within social conversation, we investigated the accuracy of identifying conversations with close friends and relatives from others.

The rest of this paper is arranged as follows. After describing the corpus and ASR system in Sections 2 and 3, we probe the nature of telephone conversations in Section 4. We present direct binary classification experiments in Section 5 and lastly, we close with a few remarks in Section 6.

2 Corpus: Everyday Telephone Conversations Spanning a Year

Our corpus consists of 12,067 digitized land-line telephone conversations. Recordings were taken from 10 volunteers, 79 years or older, over a period of approximately 12 months. Subjects were all native English speakers recruited from the USA. In addition to the conversations, our corpus includes a rich set of meta-data, such as call direction (incoming vs outgoing), time of call, duration and DTMF/caller ID when available. At the end of the data collection, for each subject, twenty telephone numbers were identified corresponding to top ten most frequent calls and top ten longest calls. Subjects were asked to identify their relationship with the speakers at these numbers as immediate family, near relatives, close friends, casual friends, strangers and business.

For this initial study, we discard conversations with less than 30 automatically transcribed words. This was done primarily to get rid of spurious and/or noisy recordings related to device failure as well as incorrectly dialed telephone numbers. Moreover, short conversations are less likely to provide enough social context to be useful.

Of the 8,558 available conversations, 2,728 were identified as residential conversations and 1,095 were identified as business conversations using reverse listings from multiple sources; e.g. phone directory lookup, exit interviews, internet lookup. This left 4,395 unlabeled records, for which the reverse listing was either inconclusive or for which the phone number information was missing and/or improperly recorded.

3 Automatic Speech Recognition

Conversations in our corpus were automatically transcribed using an ASR system. Our ASR system is structured after IBM's conversation telephony system which gave the top performance in the most recent evaluation of speech recognition technology for telephony by National Institute of Standards and Technology (Soltau et al., 2005). The acoustic models were trained on about 2000 hours of telephone speech from Switchboard and Fisher corpora (Godfrey et al., 1992). The system has a vocabulary of 47K and uses a trigram language model with about 10M n-grams, estimated from a mix of transcripts and web-harvested data. Decoding is performed in three stages using speaker-independent models, vocal-tract normalized models and speaker-adapted models. The three sets of models are similar in complexity with 4000 clustered pentaphone states and 150K Gaussians with diagonal covariances. Our system does not include discriminative training and performs at a word error rate of about 24% on NIST RT Dev04 which is comparable to state of the art performance for such systems. The privacy requirements in place for our corpus prohibit human listening – precluding the transcriptions needed reporting recognition accuracy. However, while our corpus differs from Switchboard, we expect the performance of the 2000 hour recognizer to be relatively close to results on NIST benchmark.

4 Nature of Telephone Conversations

4.1 Classification Experiments

As mentioned earlier, we first learned a baseline binary classifier to filter out business calls from residential calls. Apart from using this as a tool to probe the characteristics of social calls, it also helps us to classify unlabeled calls and thus avoid discard half the corpus from subsequent analysis of social network and relationships. Recall, the labels for the calls were obtained using reverse lookup from multiple sources. We assume that the majority of our training set reflect the true nature of the conversations and expect to employ the classifier subsequently for correcting the errors arising when personal conversations occur on business lines and vice versa.

We learned a baseline SVM classifier using a balanced training set. From the labeled records we created a balanced verification set containing 164,115 words over 328 conversations. The remainder was used to create a balanced training set consisting of 866,696 words over 1,862 conversations. The SVM was trained on 20-fold cross validation and evaluated on the verification set. After experimenting with different kernels, we found an RBF kernel to be most effective, achieving an accuracy of 87.50% on the verification data.

4.2 Can the Scores of the Binary Classifier Differentiate Types of Social Relationship?

Since the SVM score has utility in measuring a conversation on the social-business axis, we now examine its usefulness in differentiating social ties. To test this, we computed SVM score statistics for all conversations with family and friends. For comparison, we also computed the statistics for all conversations automatically tagged as residential as well as all conversations in the data. Table 1 shows the average family score is unambiguously higher than the average residential conversation (independent sample t-test, $p < 0.001$). This is an interesting result since distinction of family conversations (from general social calls) never factored into the SVM. Rather, it appears to arise naturally as an extrapolation from the more general residential/business discriminator. The friend sub-population exhibited statistics much closer to the general residential population and its differences were not significant to any degree. The overlap between scores for conversations with family and friends overlap significantly. Notably, the conversations with family have a significantly higher mean and a tighter variance than with other social ties.

Table 1: SVM scores for phone number sub-categories.

Category	# Calls	Mean score	STD
Family	1162	1.12	0.50
Friends	532	0.95	0.51
Residential	2728	0.93	0.63
Business	1095	-1.16	0.70
Global	8558	0.46	0.96

4.3 How Informative are Openings and Closings in Differentiating Telephone Conversations?

Schegloff and Sacks assert openings (beginnings) and closings (ends) of telephone conversations have certain identifiable structures (Sacks et al., 1974). For example, the structure of openings facilitate establishing identity of the conversants and the purpose of their call (Schegloff, 1968). Closings in personal conversations are likely to include a preclosing signal that allows either party to mention any unmentioned mentionables before conversation ends (Schegloff and Sacks, 1973).

Given the above assertions, we expect openings and closings to be informative about the type of conversations. Using our classifier, we compare the accuracy of predicting the type from openings, closings and random segments of the conversations. For different lengths of the three types of segments, the observed performance of the classifier is plotted in Figure 1. The results for the random segment were computed by averaging over 100 trials. Several important results are immediately apparent. Openings possess much higher utility than closings. This is consistent with general intuition that the opening exchange is expected to clarify the nature and topic of the call. Closings were found to be only as informative as random segments from the conversations. This is contrary to what one might expect from Schegloff and Sack's assertion that pre closing differ significantly in personal telephone calls (Schegloff and Sacks, 1973). Less intuitive is the fact that increasing the length of the opening segment does not improve performance. Surprisingly, a 30-word segment from the opening appears to be sufficient to achieve high classification accuracy (87.20%).

4.4 Data Sparsity or Inherent Ambiguity: Why are Short Conversations difficult to Classify?

Sparsity often has a deleterious effect on classification performance. In our experiments, we noticed that shorter conversations suffer from poor classification. However, the results from the above section appear to contradict this assertion, as a 30-word window can give very good performance. This seems to suggest short conversations suffer poor recognition

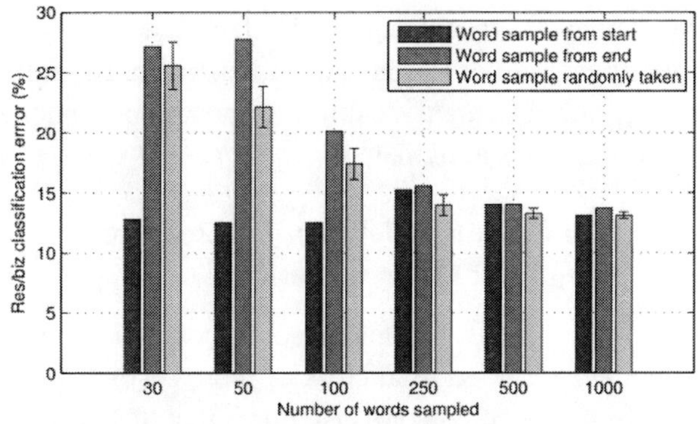

Figure 1: Comparison of classification accuracy in predicting the type of conversation from openings, closings and random segments. Error bars are one standard deviation.

due to properties beyond the obvious sparsity effect. To test this, we investigated the differences in short and long conversations in greater detail. We separate calls into quintile groups based on word counts. However, we now calculate all features from a 30-word opening – eliminating effects directly related to size. The results in Table 2 show that the ability to predict the type of conversation does not degrade when long conversations are truncated. Meanwhile, the accuracy of classification drops for (originally) short conversations. There is a surprisingly small performance loss due to the artificial truncation. These observations suggest that the long and short conversations are inherently different in nature, at least in their openings.

Table 2: Accuracy in predicting the type of conversation when they are truncated to 30-words of openings based on conversation length quintiles. The column, Res / Biz, split gives the label distributions for the quintiles.

Orig. Word Counts		Split	Accuracy
Quintile	#Words	Res. / Biz.	
0-20	30-87	62.12 / 37.88	78.6
20-40	88-167	48.48 / 51.52	82.8
40-60	168-295	39.39 / 60.61	91.4
60-80	296-740	40.91 / 59.09	87.8
80-100	741+	59.38 / 40.62	93.4

We should point out that spurious recordings in our corpus are concentrated in the low word count group – undoubtedly dropping their accuracies. However, the trend of improving accuracy persists well into the high word count ranges where spurious records are rare. Given this fact, it appears that individuals in our corpus are more careful in enunciating the reasons for calling if an extended phone conversation is anticipated.

4.5 Can Openings Help Predict Relative Lengths of Conversations?

From the results presented so far, we know that openings are good predictors of the type of conversations yet to unfold. We also know that there are inherent language differences between short and long conversations. So, it is natural to ask whether openings can predict relative lengths of conversations. To test this hypothesis, we bin conversations into 5 groups or ranks based on their percentile lengths (word counts) – very short, short, moderate, long and very long durations, as in Table 2. Using independent features from the 30-word opening, we attempt to predict the relative rank of two conversations by learning a rank SVM (Joachims, 2006). We found the ranker to give 27% error rate, significantly lower (independent sample t-test, d.f. $\approx$ 1M, p<0.01) than the random chance of 40%. Chance baseline was determined using Monte Carlo simulation (1M random rankings) in conjunction with the rank SVM evaluation (Joachims, 2006).

Features from very short conversations may contain both openings and closings, i.e., both a *hello* and a *goodbye*, making them easier to rank. To avoid this confounding factor, we also compute performance after discarding the shortest grouping of conversations ($<$ 88 words) to ensure closings are avoided in the 30-word window. The resulting classifier over *short, medium, long, very long* conversations ranked 30% of the pairs erroneously, somewhat better than chance at 37%. Though the performance gain over the random ranker has shrunk considerably, there is still some utility in using the opening of a conversation to determine its ultimate duration. However, it is clear predicting duration via conversation opening is a much more difficult task overall.

5 Supervised Classification of Types of Social Relationships

While the scores of the binary classifier provided statistically significant differences between calls to different types of social relationships, they are not particularly useful in classifying the calls with high accuracy. In this section, we investigate the performance of classifiers to differentiate the following binary classes.

- *Residential vs business*
- *Family vs all other*
- *Family vs other residential*
- *Familiar vs non-familiar*

Familiar denotes calls to those numbers with whom subject has conversed more than 5 times. Recall that the numbers corresponding to family members were identified by the subjects in a post-collection interview. We learned binary classifier for the four cases, a few of which were reported in our early work (Stark et al., 2011). We investigated a variety of features in these tasks. A breakdown of the corpus is give in Table 3. Not all categories are mutually exclusive. For example the majority of *family* conversations also fall into the *familiar* and *residential* categories.

Table 3: Number of conversations per category.

Category	Instances
Biz.	1095
Residential	2728
Family	1111
Res. non-family	1462
Familiar	3010
All	8558

5.1 Lexical Statistics

Speakers who share close social ties are likely to engage in conversations on a wide variety of topics and this is likely to reflect in the entropy of their language use. We capture this aspect of language use by computing language entropy over the unigram word distribution for each conversation, i.e; $H(d) = -\sum_w p(w|d) \log p(w|d)$, where $p(w|d)$ is the probability of word w given conversation d. We also included two other lexical statistics namely the speaking rate and the word count (in log domain). Table 4 lists the utility of these language properties for differentiating the four binary classes mentioned earlier, where the p-value is computed using two tailed independent sample t-test.

Table 4: T-statistics for different context groups. Labels: a) Log-word count, b) speaking rate, c) language entropy. Asterisk denotes significance at $p<0.0001$. Sample sizes (n) may be found in Table 3.

Task	d.f.	a)	b)	c)
Res. v. biz.	7646	1.9	10.1*	-1.9
Family v. other	8556	16.3*	9.0*	13.4*
Family v. other res.	2571	12.9*	5.1*	11.3*
Familiar v. other	8556	10.4*	6.4*	9.3*

For the most part, the significance tests conform with preconceived ideas of language use over the telephone. It is shown that people talk longer, more rapidly and have wider range of language use when conversing with a familiar contact and/or family member. Surprisingly, only the speaking rate showed significant differences among the residential/business categories, with business conversations being conducted at a slower pace at least for the elderly demographic in our corpus.

5.2 Linguistic inquiry and Word Count

We investigated a hand-crafted dictionary of salient words, called *Linguistic Inquiry and Word Count* (LIWC), employed in social psychology studies (Pennebaker et al., 2003). This dictionary group words into 64 categories such as pronouns, activity words, positive emotion and health. The categories have significant overlap and a given word can map to zero or more categories. The clear benefit of LIWC is that the word categories have very clear and pre-labeled meanings. They suffer from the obvious drawback that the words are labeled in isolation without taking their context into account. The tags are not chosen under any mathematical criteria and so there are no guarantees the resultant feature will be useful or optimal for classifying utterances.

Table 5 lists the LIWC categories significant ($p< 0.001$) to the different classes. The listed terms are sorted according to their t-statistic, with early and later terms more indicative of first and second class labels respectively.

5.3 Latent Dirichlet allocation

Unsupervised clustering and feature selection can make use of data for which we have no labels. For example, in the case of business and residential labels, unlabeled data amounts to about 50% of our corpus. Motivated by this consideration, we examined unsupervised clustering using Latent Dirichlet Allocation (LDA) (Blei et al., 2003).

LDA models a conversation as a bag of words. The model generates a conversation by: (a) sampling a topic distribution θ for the conversation using a per-conversation Dirichlet topic distribution with a hyper-parameter α, (b) sampling a topic z for each word in the conversation using a multinomial distribution using the topic mixture θ, and (c) sampling the word from a per-topic multinomial word distribution with a hyper-parameter β (Blei et al., 2003). The number of topics are assumed to be given. The per-conversation topic distribution and the per-topic word distribution can be automatically estimated to maximize the likelihood of training data. The sparsity of these two distributions can be controlled by tweaking α and β; lower values increase sparsity.

For our experiments, we estimated a maximum likelihood 30-topic LDA model from the corpus. Experimentally, we found best cross-validation results were obtained when α and β were set to 0.01 and 0.1 respectively.

When peering into the topics learned by the LDA method, it did appear that topics were approximately separated into contextual categories. Most interesting, when the number of clusters are reduced to two, the LDA model managed to segment residential and business conversations with relatively high accuracy (80%). This suggests the LDA model was able to approximately learn these classes in an unsupervised manner.

Table 6 lists words strongly associated with the two topics and clearly the unsupervised clustering appears to have automatically differentiated the business-oriented calls from the rest. On closer examination, we found that most of the probability was distributed in a limited number of words in the business-oriented topic. On the contrary, the probability was more widely distributed among words in the other cluster, reflecting the diversity of content in personal calls.

5.4 Classifying Types of Social Relationships

Though t-tests are useful for ruling out insignificant relationships, they are insufficient for quantifying the degree of separability – and thus, ultimately their

Table 5: LIWC categories found to be significant in classifying relationships, ranked according to their t-statistic.

Relationship	Categories
Res. v. biz.	I, Past, Self, Motion, Other, Insight, Eating, Pronoun, Down, Physcal, Excl, Space, Cogmech, Home, Sleep, Tentat, Assent, / Article, Optim, Fillers, Senses, Hear, We, Feel, Inhib, Incl, You, School, Money, Occup, Job, Number
Family v. all	Other, Past, Assent, Sleep, Insight, I, Pronoun, Cogmech, Tentat, Motion, Self / Affect, Optim, Certain, Future, School, Comm, Job, We, Preps, Incl, Occup, You, Number
Family v. res.	Other, Past, Sleep, Pronoun, Tentat, Cogmech, Insight, Humans / Comm, We, Incl, You, Preps, Number
Familiar v. other	Other, Assent, Past, I, Leisure, Self, Insight / Fillers, Certain, Social, Posemo, We, Future, Affect, Incl, Comm, Achieve, School, You, Optim, Job, Occup

Table 6: Per-topic word distribution learned using unsupervised clustering with LDA. Words are sorted according to their posterior topic distribution. Words with identical distributions are sorted alphabetically.

Topic 1	Topic 2
Invalid, helpline, eligibility, transactions, promotional, representative, mastercard, touchtone, activation, nominating, receiver, voicemail, digit, representatives, Chrysler, ballots, staggering, refills, resented, classics, metro, represented, administer, transfers, reselling, recommendations, explanation, floral, exclusive, submit.	Adorable, aeroplanes, Arlene, Astoria, baked, biscuits, bitches, blisters, bluegrass, bracelet, brains, bushes, calorie, casinos, Charlene, cheeses, chit, Chris, clam, clientele, cock, cookie, copying, crab, Davenport, debating, dementia, dictionary, dime, Disneyland, eek, Eileen, fascinated, follies, fry, gained.

utility in discrimination. To directly test discrimination performance, we use support vector machine classifiers. Before performing classification, we produce balanced datasets that have equal numbers of conversations for each category. Our primary motivation for artificially balancing the label distribution in each experiment is to provide a consistent baseline over which each classifier may be compared. We learn SVM classifiers with an RBF kernel using 85% of data for development. SVM parameters are tuned with 20-fold cross-validation on the devset. The accuracies of the classifiers, measured on a held out set, are reported in Table 7.

We tested four feature vectors: 1) unigram frequencies, 2) surface language features (log word count, speaking rate, entropy), 3) the 64 dimension LIWC frequency vector and 4) a 30-dimension vector of LDA topic posterior log-probabilities.

Table 7: SVM performance for the language features. Labels: a) unigram vector, b) lexical statistics, c) LIWC and d) LDA topic posterior log-probabilities

Task	1-grams	L.Stats	LIWC	LDA
Res. v. biz.	84.95	67.61	78.70	81.03
Family v. all	78.03	61.16	72.77	74.75
Family v. res.	76.13	62.92	71.06	72.37
Familiarity	69.17	60.92	64.20	69.56

Overall, the plain unigram frequency vector provided the best discrimination performance. However, this comes at significant training costs as the unigram feature vector has a dimensionality of approximately 20,000. While the surface features did possess a degree of classification utility, there are clearly outclassed by the content-based features. Furthermore, their integration into the content-features yielded only insignificant improvements to accuracy. Finally, it is of interest to note that the 30-topic LDA feature trained with ML criterion outperformed the 64-topic LIWC vector in all cases.

6 Conclusions

This paper studies a unique corpus of conversational telephone speech, a comprehensive and naturalistic sample of all the incoming and outgoing telephone calls from 10 older adults over the duration of one year. Through empirical experiments we show that the business calls can be separated from social calls with accuracies as high as 85% using standard techniques. Subgroups such as family can also be differentiated automatically with accuracies above 74%. When compared to language use (entropy) and hand-crafted dictionaries (LIWC), posteriors over topics computed using a latent Dirichlet model provide superior performance.

For the elderly demographic, openings of conversations were found to be more informative in classifying conversation than closings or random segments, when using automated transcripts. The high accuracy in classifying business from personal conversations suggests potential applications in designing context user interface for smartphones to offer icons related to work email, work calendar or Facebook apps. In future work, we plan to examine subject specific language use, turn taking and affect to further improve the classification of social calls (Shafran et al., 2003).

7 Acknowledgements

This research was supported in part by NIH Grants 5K25AG033723-02 and P30 AG024978-05 and NSF Awards 1027834, 0958585 and 0905095. Any opinions, findings, conclusions or recommendations expressed in this publication are those of the authors and do not reflect the views of the NIH or NSF. We thank Brian Kingsbury and IBM for making their ASR software tools available to us. We are also grateful to Nicole Larimer, Maider Lehr and Katherine Wild for their contributions to data collection.

References

David M. Blei, Andrew Y. Ng, and Michael I. Jordan. 2003. Latent dirichlet allocation. *J. Mach. Learn. Res.*, 3:993–1022, March.

T A Glass, C F Mendes de Leon, T E Seeman, and L F Berkman. 1997. Beyond single indicators of social networks: a lisrel analysis of social ties among the elderly. *Soc Sci Med*, 44(10):1503–1517.

J. Godfrey, E. Holliman, and J. McDaniel. 1992. SWITCHBOARD: Telephone speech corpus for research and development. In *IEEE International Conference on Acoustics, Speech, and Signal Processing*, pages 517–520.

T. Joachims. 2006. Training linear svms in linear time. In *ACM Conference on Knowledge Discovery and Data Mining*.

Haewoon Kwak, Changhyun Lee, Hosung Park, and Sue Moon. 2010. What is twitter, a social network or a news media? In *Proceedings of the 19th international conference on World wide web*, WWW '10, pages 591–600, New York, NY, USA. ACM.

Alexander Pak and Patrick Paroubek. 2010. Twitter as a corpus for sentiment analysis and opinion mining. In Nicoletta Calzolari (Conference Chair), Khalid Choukri, Bente Maegaard, Joseph Mariani, Jan Odijk, Stelios Piperidis, Mike Rosner, and Daniel Tapias, editors, *Proceedings of the Seventh International Conference on Language Resources and Evaluation (LREC'10)*, Valletta, Malta, may. European Language Resources Association (ELRA).

J. W. Pennebaker, M. R. Mehl, and K. G. Niederhoffer. 2003. Psychological aspects of natural language use: Our words, our selves. *Annual Review of Psychology*, 54(1):547–577.

Saša Petrović, Miles Osborne, and Victor Lavrenko. 2010. Streaming first story detection with application to twitter. In *Human Language Technologies: The 2010 Annual Conference of the North American Chapter of the Association for Computational Linguistics*, HLT '10, pages 181–189, Stroudsburg, PA, USA. Association for Computational Linguistics.

Alan Ritter, Colin Cherry, and Bill Dolan. 2010. Unsupervised modeling of twitter conversations. In *Human Language Technologies: The 2010 Annual Conference of the North American Chapter of the Association for Computational Linguistics*, HLT '10, pages 172–180, Stroudsburg, PA, USA. Association for Computational Linguistics.

Harvey Sacks, Emanuel A. Schegloff, and Gail Jefferson. 1974. A simplest systematics for the organization of turn-taking for conversation language. *Language*, 50(4(1)):696–735.

Emanuel A. Schegloff and Harvey Sacks. 1973. Opening up closings. *Semiotica*, 8:289–327.

Emanuel A. Schegloff. 1968. Sequencing in conversational openings. *American Anthropologist*, 70(6):1075–1095.

Izhak Shafran, Michael Riley, and Mehryar Mohri. 2003. Voice signatures. In *Proc. IEEE Automatic Speech Recognition and Understanding Workshop*.

H. Soltau, B. Kingsbury, L. Mangu, D. Povey, G. Saon, and G. Zweig. 2005. The IBM 2004 conversational telephony system for rich transcription. In *IEEE International Conference on Acoustics, Speech, and Signal Processing*, volume 1, pages 205–208.

Anthony Stark, Izhak Shafran, and Jeffrey Kaye. 2011. Supervised and unsupervised feature selection for inferring social nature of telephone conversations from their content. In *Proc. IEEE Automatic Speech Recognition and Understanding Workshop*.

Paul Taylor, Rich Morin, Kim Parker, D'Vera Cohn, and Wendy Wang. June 29, 2009. Growing old in America: Expectations vs. reality. http://pewsocialtrends.org/files/2010/10/Getting-Old-in-America.pdf.

Minimum-Risk Training of Approximate CRF-Based NLP Systems

Veselin Stoyanov and **Jason Eisner**
HLTCOE and Center for Language and Speech Processing
Johns Hopkins University
Baltimore, MD 21218
{ves, jason}@cs.jhu.edu

Abstract

Conditional Random Fields (CRFs) are a popular formalism for structured prediction in NLP. It is well known how to train CRFs with certain topologies that admit exact inference, such as linear-chain CRFs. Some NLP phenomena, however, suggest CRFs with more complex topologies. Should such models be used, considering that they make exact inference intractable? Stoyanov et al. (2011) recently argued for training parameters to minimize the task-specific loss of whatever *approximate* inference and decoding methods will be used at test time. We apply their method to three NLP problems, showing that (i) using more complex CRFs leads to improved performance, and that (ii) minimum-risk training learns more accurate models.

1 Introduction

Conditional Random Fields (CRFs) (Lafferty et al., 2001) are often used to model dependencies among linguistic variables. CRF-based models have improved the state of the art in a number of natural language processing (NLP) tasks ranging from part-of-speech tagging to information extraction and sentiment analysis (Lafferty et al., 2001; Peng and McCallum, 2006; Choi et al., 2005).

Robust and theoretically sound training procedures have been developed for CRFs when the model can be used with exact inference and decoding.[1] However, some NLP problems seem to call for higher-treewidth graphical models in which exact inference is expensive or intractable. These "loopy" CRFs have cyclic connections among the output and/or latent variables. Alas, standard learning procedures assume exact inference: they do not compensate for approximations that will be used at test time, and can go surprisingly awry if approximate inference is used at training time (Kulesza and Pereira, 2008).

While NLP research has been consistently evolving toward more richly structured models, one may hesitate to add dependencies to a graphical model if there is a danger that this will end up *hurting* performance through approximations. In this paper we illustrate how to address this problem, even for extremely interconnected models in which every pair of output variables is connected.

Wainwright (2006) showed that if approximate inference will be used at test time, it may be beneficial to use a learning procedure that does not converge to the true model but to one that performs well *under the approximations*. Stoyanov et al. (2011) argue for minimizing a certain non-convex training objective, namely the empirical risk of the entire system comprising the CRF *together* with whatever approximate inference and decoding procedures will be used at test time. They regard this entire system as simply a complex decision rule, analogous to a neural network, and show how to use back-propagation to tune its parameters to locally minimize the empirical risk (i.e., the average task-specific loss on training data). Stoyanov et al. (2011) show that on certain *synthetic-data* problems, this frequentist training regimen significantly reduced test-data loss

[1] "Inference" typically refers to computing posterior marginal or max-marginal probability distributions of output random variables, given some evidence. "Decoding" derives a single structured output from the results of inference.

compared to approximate maximum likelihood estimation (MLE). However, this method has not been evaluated on *real-world* problems until now.

We will refer to the Stoyanov et al. (2011) approach as "ERMA"—Empirical Risk Minimization under Approximations. ERMA is attractive for NLP because the freedom to use arbitrarily structured graphical models makes it possible to include latent linguistic variables, predict complex structures such as parses (Smith and Eisner, 2008), and do collective prediction in relational domains (Ji and Grishman, 2011; Benson et al., 2011; Dreyer and Eisner, 2009). In training, ERMA considers not only the approximation method but also the task-specific loss function. This means that ERMA is careful to use the additional variables and dependencies only in ways that help training set performance. (Overfitting on the enlarged parameter set should be avoided through regularization.)

We have developed a simple syntax for specifying CRFs with complex structures, and a software package (available from `http://www.clsp.jhu.edu/~ves/software.html`) that allows ERMA training of these CRFs for several popular loss functions (e.g., accuracy, mean-squared error, F-measure). In this paper, we use these tools to revisit three previously studied NLP applications that can be modeled naturally with approximate CRFs (we will use **approximate CRFs** to refer to CRF-based systems that are used with approximations in inference or decoding). We show that (i) natural language can be modeled more effectively with CRFs that are not restricted to a linear structure and (ii) that ERMA training represents an improvement over previous learning methods.

The first application, predicting congressional votes, has not been previously modeled with CRFs. By using a more principled probabilistic approach, we are able to improve the state-of-the-art accuracy from 71.2% to 78.2% when training to maximize the approximate log-likelihood of the training data. By switching to ERMA training, we improve this result further to 85.1%.

The second application, information extraction from seminar announcements, has been modeled previously with skip-chain CRFs (Sutton and McCallum, 2005; Finkel et al., 2005). The skip-chain CRF introduces loops and requires approximate inference, which motivates minimum risk training. Our results show that ERMA training improves F-measures from 89.5 to 90.9 (compared to 87.1 for the model without skip-chains).

Finally, for our third application, we perform collective multi-label text classification. We follow previous work (Ghamrawi and McCallum, 2005; Finley and Joachims, 2008) and use a fully connected CRF to model all pairwise dependencies between labels. We observe similar trends for this task: switching from a maximum entropy model that does not model label dependencies to a loopy CRF leads to an improvement in F-measure from 81.6 to 84.0, and using ERMA leads to additional improvement (84.7).

2 Preliminaries

2.1 Conditional Random Fields

A **conditional random field** (CRF) is an undirected graphical model defined by a tuple $(\mathcal{X}, \mathcal{Y}, \mathcal{F}, f, \theta)$. $\mathcal{X} = (X_1, X_2, \ldots)$ is a set of random variables and $\mathcal{Y} = (Y_1, Y_2, \ldots)$ is a set of output random variables.[2] We use $\mathbf{x} = (x_1, x_2, \ldots)$, to denote a possible assignment of values to $\mathcal{X}$, and similarly for $\mathbf{y}$, with $\mathbf{xy}$ denoting the joint assignment. Each $\alpha \in \mathcal{F}$ is a subset of the random variables, $\alpha \subseteq \mathcal{X} \cup \mathcal{Y}$, and we write $\mathbf{xy}_\alpha$ to denote the restriction of $\mathbf{xy}$ to α. Finally, for each $\alpha \in \mathcal{F}$, the CRF specifies a function $\vec{f}_\alpha$ that extracts a feature vector $\in \mathbb{R}^d$ from the restricted assignment $\mathbf{xy}_\alpha$. We define the overall feature vector $\vec{f}(\mathbf{x}, \mathbf{y}) = \sum_{\alpha \in \mathcal{F}} \vec{f}_\alpha(\mathbf{xy}_\alpha) \in \mathbb{R}^d$. The model defines conditional probabilities

$$p_\theta(\mathbf{y}|\mathbf{x}) = \frac{\exp \vec{\theta} \cdot \vec{f}(\mathbf{x}, \mathbf{y})}{\sum_{\mathbf{y}'} \exp \vec{\theta} \cdot \vec{f}(\mathbf{x}, \mathbf{y}')} \tag{1}$$

where $\vec{\theta} \in \mathbb{R}^d$ is a global weight vector (to be learned). This is a log-linear model; the denominator (traditionally denoted $Z_\mathbf{x}$) sums over all possible output assignments to normalize the distribution.

Provided that all probabilities needed at training or test time are conditioned on an observation of the form $\mathcal{X} = \mathbf{x}$, CRFs can include arbitrary overlapping features of the input without having to explicitly model input feature dependencies.

[2] Stoyanov et al. (2011) distinguished some of the $\mathcal{Y}$ variables as latent (i.e., unsupervised and ignored by the loss function). We omit this possibility, to simplify the notation.

2.2 Inference in CRFs

Inference in general CRFs is intractable (Koller and Friedman, 2009). Nevertheless, there exist several approximate algorithms that have theoretical motivation and tend to exhibit good performance in practice. Those include variational methods such as loopy belief propagation (BP) (Murphy et al., 1999) and mean-field, as well as Markov Chain Monte Carlo methods.

ERMA training is applicable to any approximation that corresponds to a differentiable function, even if the function has no simple closed form but is computed by an iterative update algorithm. In this paper we select BP, which is exact when the factor graph is a tree, such as a linear-chain CRF, but whose results can be somewhat distorted by loops in the factor graph, as in our settings. BP computes beliefs about the marginal distribution of each random variable using iterative updates. We standardly approximate the *posterior* CRF marginals given the input observations by running BP over a CRF that enforces those observations.

2.3 Decoding

Conditional random fields are models of probability. A **decoder** is a procedure for converting these probabilities into system outputs. Given $\mathbf{x}$, the decoder would ideally choose $\mathbf{y}$ to minimize the loss $\ell(\mathbf{y}, \mathbf{y}^*)$, where ℓ compares a candidate assignment $\mathbf{y}$ to the true assignment $\mathbf{y}^*$. But of course we do not know the truth at test time. Instead we can average over *possible* values $\mathbf{y}'$ of the truth:

$$\operatorname*{argmin}_{\mathbf{y}} \sum_{\mathbf{y}'} p(\mathbf{y}' \mid \mathbf{x}) \cdot \ell(\mathbf{y}, \mathbf{y}') \tag{2}$$

This is the **minimum Bayes risk (MBR)** principle from statistical decision theory: choose $\mathbf{y}$ to minimize the *expected* loss (i.e., the risk) according to the CRF's posterior beliefs given $\mathbf{x}$.

In the NLP literature, CRFs are often decoded by choosing $\mathbf{y}$ to be the maximum posterior probability assignment (e.g., Sha and Pereira (2003), Sutton et al. (2007)). This is the MBR procedure for the 0-1 loss function that simply tests whether $\mathbf{y} = \mathbf{y}^*$. For other loss functions, however, the corresponding MBR procedure is preferable. For some loss functions it is tractable given the posterior marginals of p, while in other cases approximations are needed.

In our experiments we use MBR decoding (or a tractable approximation) but substitute the *approximate* posterior marginals of p as computed by BP. For example, if the loss of y is the number of incorrectly recovered output variables, MBR says to separately pick the most probable value for each output variable, according to its (approximate) marginal.

3 Minimum-Risk CRF Training

This section briefly describes the ERMA training algorithm from Stoyanov et al. (2011) and compares it to related structured learning methods. We assume a standard ML setting, with a set of training inputs $\mathbf{x}^i$ and corresponding correct outputs $\mathbf{y}^{i*}$. All the methods below are regularized in practice, but we omit mention of regularizers for simplicity.

3.1 Related Structured Learning Methods

When inference and decoding can be performed exactly, the CRF parameters $\vec{\theta}$ are often trained by maximum likelihood estimation (MLE):

$$\operatorname*{argmax}_{\theta} \sum_{i} \log p_\theta(\mathbf{y}^{i*} \mid \mathbf{x}^i) \tag{3}$$

The gradient of each summand $\log p_\theta(\mathbf{y}^{i*} \mid \mathbf{x}^i)$ can be computed by performing inference in two settings, one with $\mathbf{x}^i, \mathbf{y}^{i*}$ observed and one with only the conditioning events $\mathbf{x}^i$ observed. The gradient emerges as the difference between the feature expectations in the two cases. If exact inference is intractable, one can compute approximate feature expectations by loopy BP. Computing the approximate gradient in this way, and training the CRF with some gradient-based optimization method, has been shown to work relatively well in practice (Vishwanathan et al., 2006; Sutton and McCallum, 2005).

The above method takes into account neither the loss function that will be used for evaluation, nor the approximate algorithms that have been selected for inference and decoding at test time. Other structure learning methods do consider loss, though it is not obvious how to make them consider approximations. Those include maximum margin (Taskar et al., 2003; Finley and Joachims, 2008) and softmax-margin (Gimpel and Smith, 2010). The idea of margin-based methods is to choose weights $\vec{\theta}$ so that the correct alternative $\mathbf{y}^{i*}$ always gets a better score than each possible alternative $\mathbf{y}^i \in \mathcal{Y}$. The loss is incorporated in these methods by requiring the margin $(\vec{\theta} \cdot \vec{f}(\mathbf{x}^i, \mathbf{y}^{i*}) - \vec{\theta} \cdot \vec{f}(\mathbf{x}^i, \mathbf{y}^i)) \geq \ell(\mathbf{y}^i, \mathbf{y}^{i*})$, with penalized slack in these constraints. The softmax-margin method uses a different criterion—it resembles MLE but modifies the denominator of (1) to $Z_\mathbf{x} = \sum_{\mathbf{y}' \in \mathcal{Y}} \exp(\vec{\theta} \cdot \vec{f}(\mathbf{x}, \mathbf{y}') + \ell(\mathbf{y}', \mathbf{y}^*))$.

In our experiments we compare against MLE training (which is common) and softmax-margin, which incorporates loss and which Gimpel and Smith (2010) show is either better or competitive when compared to other margin methods on an NLP task. We adapt these methods to the loopy case in the obvious way, by replacing exact inference with loopy BP and keeping everything else the same.

3.2 Minimum-Risk Training

We wish to consider the approximate inference and decoding algorithms and the loss function that will be used during testing. Thus, we want θ to minimize the expected loss under the true data distribution P:

$$\underset{\theta}{\operatorname{argmin}}\, \mathbb{E}_{\mathbf{xy} \sim P}[\ell(\delta_\theta(\mathbf{x}), \mathbf{y})] \tag{4}$$

where δ_θ is the decision rule (parameterized by θ), which decodes the results of inference under p_θ.

In practice, we do not know the true data distribution, but we can do **empirical risk minimization** (ERM), instead averaging the loss over our sample of $(\mathbf{x}^i, \mathbf{y}^i)$ pairs. ERM for structured prediction was first introduced in the speech community (Bahl et al., 1988) and later used in NLP (Och, 2003; Kakade et al., 2002; Suzuki et al., 2006; Li and Eisner, 2009, etc.). Previous applications of risk minimization assume *exact* inference, having defined the hypothesis space by a precomputed n-best list, lattice, or packed forest over which exact inference is possible.

The ERMA approach (Stoyanov et al., 2011) works with approximate inference and computes exact gradients of the output loss (or a differentiable surrogate) in the context of the approximate inference and decoding algorithms. To determine the gradient of $\ell(\delta_\theta(\mathbf{x}^i), \mathbf{y}^i)$ with respect to θ, the method relies on automatic differentiation in the reverse mode (Griewank and Corliss, 1991), a general technique for sensitivity analysis in computations. The intuition behind automatic differentiation is that the entire computation is a sequence of elementary differentiable operations. For each elementary operation, given that we know the input and result values, and the partial derivative of the loss with respect to the result, we can compute the partial derivative of the loss with respect to the inputs to the step. Differentiating the whole complicated computation can be carried out in backward pass in this step-by-step manner as long as we record intermediate results during the computation of the function (the forward pass). At the end, we accumulate the partials of the loss with respect to each parameter θ_i.

ERMA is similar to back-propagation used in recurrent neural networks, which involve cyclic updates like those in belief propagation (Williams and Zipser, 1989). It considers an "unrolled" version of the forward pass, in which "snapshots" of a variable at times t and $t+1$ are treated as distinct variables, with one perhaps influencing the other. The forward pass computes $\ell(\delta_\theta(\mathbf{x}^i), \mathbf{y}^i)$ by performing approximate inference, then decoding, then evaluation. These steps convert $(\mathbf{x}^i, \theta) \rightarrow$ marginals $\rightarrow$ decision $\rightarrow$ loss. The backward pass rewinds the entire computation, differentiating each phase in term. The total time required by this algorithm is roughly twice the time of the forward pass, so its complexity is comparable to approximate inference.

In this paper, we do not advocate any particular test-time inference or decoding procedures. It is reasonable to experiment with several choices that may produce faster or more accurate systems. We simply recommend doing ERMA training to match each selected test-time condition. Stoyanov et al. (2011) specifically showed how to train a system that will use *sum-product* BP for inference at test time (unlike margin-based methods). This may be advantageous for some tasks because it marginalizes over latent variables. However, it is popular and sometimes faster to do 1-best decoding, so we also include experiments where the test-time system returns a 1-best value of $\mathbf{y}$ (or an approximation to this if the CRF is loopy), based on *max-product* BP inference. Although 1-best systems are not differentiable functions, we can approach their behavior during ERM training by annealing the training objective (Smith and Eisner, 2006). In the annealed case we evaluate (4) and its gradient under sum-product BP, except that we perform inference under $p_{(\theta/T)}$ instead of p_θ.

We gradually reduce the temperature $T \in \mathbb{R}$ from 1 to 0 as training proceeds, which turns sum-product inference into max-product by moving all the probability mass toward the highest-scoring assignment.

4 Modeling Natural Language with CRFs

This section describes three NLP problems that can be naturally modeled with approximate CRFs. The first problem, modeling congressional votes, has not been previously modeled with a CRF. We show that by switching to the principled CRF framework we can learn models that are much more accurate when evaluated on test data, though using the same (or less expressive) features as previous work. The other two problems, information extraction from semi-structured text and collective multi-label classification, have been modeled with loopy CRFs before. For all three models, we show that ERMA training results in better test set performance.[3]

4.1 Modeling Congressional Votes

The Congressional Vote (ConVote) corpus was created by Thomas et al. (2006) to study whether votes of U.S. congressional representatives can be predicted from the speeches they gave when debating a bill. The corpus consists of transcripts of congressional floor debates split into speech segments. Each speech segment is labeled with the representative who is speaking and the recorded vote of that representative on the bill. We aim to predict a high percentage of the recorded votes correctly.

Speakers often reference one another (e.g., "I thank the gentleman from Utah"), to indicate agreement or disagreement. The ConVote corpus manually annotates each phrase such as "the gentleman from Utah" with the representative that it denotes.

Thomas et al. (2006) show that classification using the agreement/disagreement information in the local context of such references, *together with* the rest of the language in the speeches, can lead to significant improvement over using either of these two sources of information in isolation. The original approach of Thomas et al. (2006) is based on training two Support Vector Machine (SVM) classifiers—one for classifying speeches as supporting/opposing the legislation and another for classifying references as agreement/disagreement. Both classifiers rely on bag-of-word (unigram) features of the document and the context surrounding the link respectively. The scores produced by the two SVMs are used to weight a global graph whose vertices are the representatives; then the min-cut algorithm is applied to partition the vertices into "yea" and "nay" voters.

While the approach of Thomas et al. (2006) leads to significant improvement over using the first SVM alone, it does not admit a probabilistic interpretation and the two classifiers are not trained jointly. We also remark that the min-cut technique would not generalize beyond binary random variables (yea/nay).

We observe that congressional votes together with references between speakers can be naturally modeled with a CRF. Figure 1 depicts the CRF constructed for one of the debates in the development part of the ConVote corpus. It contains a random variable for each representative's vote. In addition, each speech is an observed input random variable: it is connected by a factor to its speaker's vote and encourages it to be "yea" or "nay" according to features of the text of the speech. Finally, each reference in each speech is an observed input random variable connected by a factor to two votes—those of the speaker and the referent—which it encourages to agree or disagree according to features of the text surrounding the reference. Just as in (Thomas et al., 2006), the score of a global assignment to all votes is defined by considering both kinds of factors. However, unlike min-cut, CRF inference finds a probability distribution over assignments, not just a single best assignment. This fact allows us to train the two kinds of factors jointly (on the set of training debates where the votes are known) to predict the correct votes accurately (as defined by accuracy).

As Figure 1 shows, the reference factors introduce arbitrary loops, making exact inference intractable and thus motivating ERMA. Our experiments described in section 5.2 show that switching to a CRF model (keeping the same features) leads to a sizable improvement over the previous state of the art—

[3] We also experimented with a fourth application, joint POS tagging and shallow parsing (Sutton et al., 2007) and observed the same overall trend (i.e., minimum risk training improved performance significantly). We do not include those experiments, however, because we were unable to make our baseline results replicate (Sutton et al., 2007).

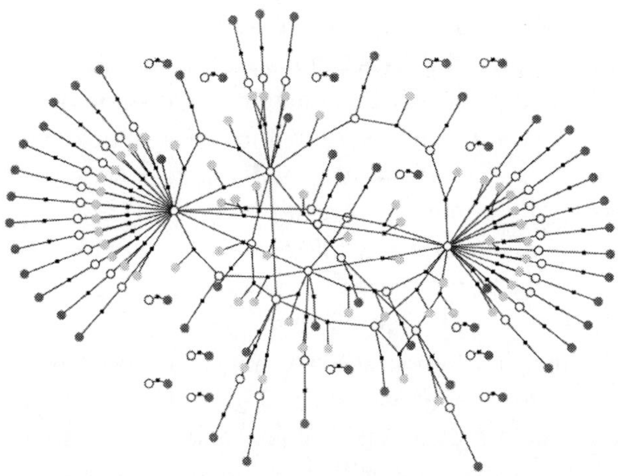

Figure 1: An example of a debate structure from the ConVote corpus. Each black square node represents a factor and is connected to the variables in that factor, shown as round nodes. Unshaded variables correspond to the representatives' votes and depict the output variables that we learn to jointly predict. Shaded variables correspond to the observed input data— the text of all speeches of a representative (in dark gray) or all local contexts of references between two representatives (in light gray).

and that ERMA further significantly improves performance, particularly when it properly trains with the same inference algorithm (max-product vs. sum-product) to be used at test time.

Baseline. As an exact baseline, we compare against the results of Thomas et al. (2006). Their test-time Min-Cut algorithm is exact in this case: binary variables and a two-way classification.

4.2 Information Extraction from Semi-Structured Text

We utilize the CMU seminar announcement corpus of Freitag (2000) consisting of emails with seminar announcements. The task is to extract four fields that describe each seminar: *speaker, location, start time* and *end time*. The corpus annotates the document with all mentions of these four fields.

Sequential CRFs have been used successfully for semi-structured information extraction (Sutton and McCallum, 2005; Finkel et al., 2005). However, they cannot model non-local dependencies in the data. For example, in the seminar announcements corpus, if "Sutner" is mentioned once in an email in a context that identifies him as a speaker, it is likely that other occurrences of "Sutner" in the same email should be marked as *speaker*. Hence Finkel et al. (2005) and Sutton and McCallum (2005) propose adding non-local edges to a sequential CRF to represent soft consistency constraints. The model, called a "skip-chain CRF" and shown in Figure 2, contains a factor linking each pair of capitalized words with the same lexical form. The skip-chain CRF model exhibits better empirical performance than its sequential counterpart (Sutton and McCallum, 2005; Finkel et al., 2005).

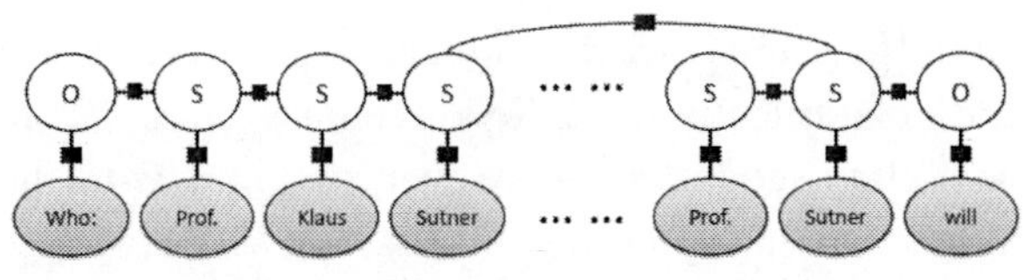

Figure 2: Skip-chain CRF for semi-structured information extraction.

The non-local skip links make exact inference intractable. To train the full model, Finkel et al. (2005) estimate the parameters of a sequential CRF and then manually select values for the weights of the non-local edges. At test time, they use Gibbs sampling to perform inference. Sutton and McCallum (2005) use max-product loopy belief propagation for test-time inference, and compare a training procedure that uses a piecewise approximation of the partition function against using sum-product loopy belief propagation to compute output variable marginals. They find that the two training regimens perform similarly on the overall task. All of these training procedures try to approximately maximize conditional likelihood, whereas we will aim to minimize the empirical loss of the approximate inference and decoding procedures.

Baseline. As an exact (non-loopy) baseline, we train a model without the skip chains. We give two baseline numbers in Table 1—for training the exact CRF with MLE and with ERM. The ERM setting resulted in a statistically significant improvement even in the exact case, thanks to the use of the loss function at training time.

4.3 Multi-Label Classification

Multi-label classification is the problem of assigning multiple labels to a document. For example, a news article can be about both "Libya" and "civil war." The most straightforward approach to multi-label classification employs a binary classifier for each class separately. However, previous work has shown that incorporating information about label dependencies can lead to improvement in performance (Elisseeff and Weston, 2001; Ghamrawi and McCallum, 2005; Finley and Joachims, 2008).

For this task we follow Ghamrawi and McCallum (2005) and Finley and Joachims (2008) and model the label interactions by constructing a fully connected CRF between the output labels. That is, for every document, we construct a CRF that contains a binary random variable for each label (indicating that the corresponding label is on/off for the document) and one binary edge for *every* unique pair of labels. This architecture can represent dependencies between labels, but leads to a setting in which the output variables form one massive clique. The resulting intractability of inference (and decoding) motivates the use of ERMA training.

Baseline. We train a model without any of the pairwise edges (i.e., a separate logistic regression model for each class). We report the single best baseline number, since MLE and ERM training resulted in statistically indistinguishable results.

5 Experiments

5.1 Learning Methodology

For all experiments we split the data into train/development/test sets using the standard splits when available. We tune optimization algorithm parameters (initial learning rate, batch size and meta-parameters λ and μ for stochastic meta descent) on the training set based on training objective convergence rates. We tune the regularization parameter β (below) on development data when available, otherwise we use a default value of 0.1—performance was generally robust for small changes in the value of β. All statistical significance testing is performed using paired permutation tests (Good, 2000).

Gradient-based Optimization. Gradient information from the back-propagation procedure can be used in a local optimization method to minimize empirical loss. In this paper we use stochastic meta descent (SMD) (Schraudolph, 1999). SMD is a second-order method that requires vector-Hessian products. For computing those, we do not need to maintain the full Hessian matrix. Instead, we apply more automatic differentiation magic—this time in the forward mode. Computing the vector-Hessian product and utilizing it in SMD does not add to the asymptotic runtime, it requires about twice as many arithmetic operations, and leads to much faster convergence of the learner in our experience. See Stoyanov et al. (2011) for details.

Since the empirical risk objective could overfit the training data, we add an L_2 regularizer $\beta \sum_j \theta_j^2$ that prefers parameter values close to 0. This improves generalization, like the margin constraints in margin-based methods.

Training Procedure Stoyanov et al. (2011) observed that the minimum-risk objective tends to be highly non-convex in practice. The usual approximate log likelihood training objective appeared to be smoother over the parameter space, but exhibited global maxima at parameter values that were relatively good, but sub-optimal for other loss functions. Mean-squared error (MSE) also gave a smoother objective than other loss functions. These observations motivated Stoyanov et al. (2011) to use a continuation method. They optimized approximate log-likelihood for a few iterations to get to a good part of the parameter space, then switched to using the hybrid loss function $\lambda\ell(y, y') + (1-\lambda)\ell_{\text{MSE}}(y, y')$. The coefficient λ changed gradually from 0 to 1 during training, which morphs from optimizing a smoother loss to optimizing the desired bumpy test loss. We follow the same procedure.

Experiments in this paper use two evaluation metrics: percentage accuracy and F-measure. For both of these losses we decode by selecting the most probable value under the marginal distribution of each random variable. This is an exact MBR decode for accuracy but an approximate one for the F-measure; our ERMA training will try to compensate for this approximate decoder. This decoding procedure is not differentiable due to the use of the argmax function. To make the decoder differentiable, we replace argmax with a stochastic (softmax) version during training, averaging loss over all possible values v in proportion to their exponentiated probability $p(y_i = v \mid \mathbf{x})^{1/T_{\text{decode}}}$. This decoder loses smoothness and approaches an argmax

Problem	Congressional Vote		Semi-structured IE		Multi-label class.	
Loss function	*Accuracy*		*Token-wise F-score*		*F-score*	
Non-loopy Baseline	71.2		86.2 (87.1)		81.6	
Loopy CRF models	INFERENCE:					
TRAINING:	maxprod	sumprod	maxprod	sumprod	maxprod	sumprod
MLE	78.2	78.2	89.0	89.5	84.2	84.0
Softmax-margin	79.0	79.0	90.1	90.2	84.3	83.8
Min-risk (maxprod)	**85.1**	80.1	**90.9**	**90.7**	**84.5**	**84.4**
Min-risk (sumprod)	83.6	**84.5**	90.3	**90.9**	**84.7**	**84.6**

Table 1: Results. The top of the table lists the loss function used for each problem and the score for the best exact baseline. The bottom lists results for the full models used with loopy BP. Models are tested with either sum-product BP (*sumprod*) or max-product BP (*maxprod*) and trained with MLE or the minimum risk criterion. Min-risk training runs are either annealed (*maxprod*), which matches max-product test, or not (*sumprod*), which matches sum-product test; grey cells in the table indicate matched training and test settings. In each column, we boldface the best result as well as all results that are not significantly worse (paired permutation test, $p < 0.05$).

decoder as T_{decode} decreases toward 0. For simplicity, our experiments just use a single fixed value of 0.1 for T_{decode}. Annealing the decoder slowly did not lead to significant differences in early experiments on development data.

5.2 Results

Table 1 lists results of our evaluation. For all three of our problems, using approximate CRFs results in statistically significant improvement over the exact baselines, for any of the training procedures. But among the training procedures for approximate CRFs, our ERMA procedure—minimizing empirical risk with the training setting matched to the test setting—improves over the two baselines, namely MLE and softmax-margin. MLE and softmax-margin training were statistically indistinguishable in our experiments with the exception of semi-structured IE. ERMA's improvements over them are statistically significant at the $p < .05$ level for the Congressional Vote and Semi-Structured IE problems and at the $p < .1$ level for the Multi-label classification problem (comparing each matched min-risk setting shown in a gray cell in Table 1 vs. MLE).

When minimizing risk, we also observe that matching training and test-time procedures can result in improved performance in one of the three problems, Congressional Vote. For this problem, the matched training condition performs better than the alternatives (accuracy of 85.1 vs. 83.6 for the annealed max-product testing and 84.5 vs 80.1 for the sum-product setting), significant at $p < .01$). We observe the same effect for semi-structured IE when testing using max-product inference. For the other remaining three problem setting training with either minimal risk training regiment.

Finally, we hypothesized that sum-product inference may produce more accurate results in certain cases as it allows more information about different parts of the model to be exchanged. However, our results show that for these three problems, sum-product and max-product inference yield statistically indistinguishable results. This may be because the particular CRFs we used included no latent variables (in constrast to the synthetic CRFs in Stoyanov et al. (2011)). As expected, we found that max-product BP converges in fewer iterations—sum-product BP required as many as twice the number of iterations for some of the runs.

Results in this paper represent a new state-of-the-art for the first two of the problems, Congressional Vote and Semi-structured IE. For Multi-Label classification, comparing against the SVM-based method of Finley and Joachims (2008) goes beyond the scope of this paper.

6 Related Work

Minimum-risk training has been used in speech recognition (Bahl et al., 1988), machine translation (Och, 2003), and energy-based models generally (LeCun et al., 2006). In graphical models, methods have been proposed to directly minimize loss in tree-shaped or linear chain MRFs and CRFs (Kakade et al., 2002; Suzuki et al., 2006; Gross et al., 2007).

All of the above focus on exact inference. Our approach can be seen as generalizing these methods to arbitrary graph structures, arbitrary loss functions and approximate inference.

Lacoste-Julien et al. (2011) also consider the effects of approximate inference on loss. However, they assume the parameters are given, and modify the approximate inference algorithm at test time to consider the loss function.

Using empirical risk minimization to *train* graphical models was independently proposed by Domke (2010; 2011). Just as in our own paper (Stoyanov et al., 2011), Domke took a decision-theoretic stance and proposed ERM as a way of calibrating the graphical model for use with approximate inference, or for use with data that do not quite match the modeling assumptions.[4]

In particular, (Domke, 2011) is similar to (Stoyanov et al., 2011) in using ERMA to train model parameters to be used with "truncated" inference that will be run for only a fixed number of iterations. For a common pixel-labeling benchmark in computer vision, Domke (2011) shows that this procedure improves training time by orders of magnitude, and slightly improves accuracy if the same number of message-passing iterations is used at test time.

Stoyanov and Eisner (2011) extend the ERMA objective function by adding an explicit runtime term. This allows them to tune model parameters and stopping criteria to learn models that obtain a given speed-accuracy tradeoff. Their approach improves this hybrid objective over a range of coefficients when compared to the traditional way of inducing sparse structures through L_1 regularization. Eisner and Daumé III (2011) propose the same linear combination of speed and accuracy as a reinforcement learning objective. In general, our proposed ERMA setting resembles the reinforcement learning problem of trying to directly learn a policy that minimizes loss or maximizes reward.

We have been concerned with the fact that ERMA training objectives may suffer from local optima and non-differentiability. Stoyanov et al. (2011) studied several such settings, graphed the difficult objective, and identified some practical workarounds that are used in the present paper. Although these methods have enabled us to get strong results by reducing the empirical risk, we suspect that ERMA training objectives will benefit from more sophisticated optimization methods. This is true even when the approximate inference itself is restricted to be something as simple as a convex minimization. While that simplified setting can make it slightly more convenient to *compute* the gradient of the inference result with respect to the parameters (Domke, 2008; Domke, 2012), there is still no guarantee that *following* that gradient will minimize the empirical risk. Convex inference does not imply convex training.

[4]However, he is less focused than we are on matching training conditions to test conditions (by including the decoder and task loss in the ERMA objective).

7 Conclusions

Motivated by the recently proposed method of Stoyanov et al. (2011) for minimum-risk training of CRF-based systems, we revisited three NLP domains that can naturally be modeled with approximate CRF-based systems. These include applications that have not been modeled with CRFs before (the ConVote corpus), as well as applications that have been modeled with loopy CRFs trained to minimize the approximate log-likelihood (semi-structured information extraction and collective multi-label classification). We show that (i) the NLP models are improved by moving to richer CRFs that require approximate inference, and (ii) empirical performance is always significantly improved by training to reduce the loss that would be achieved by approximate inference, even compared to another state-of-the-art training method (softmax-margin) that also considers loss and uses approximate inference. The general software package that implements the algorithms in this paper is available at `http://www.clsp.jhu.edu/~ves/software.html`.

Acknowledgments

This material is based upon work supported by the National Science Foundation under Grant #0937060 to the Computing Research Association for the CIFellows Project.

References

L. Bahl, P. Brown, P. de Souza, and R. Mercer. 1988. A new algorithm for the estimation of hidden Markov model parameters. In *Proceedings of ICASSP*, pages 493–496.

E. Benson, A. Haghighi, and R. Barzilay. 2011. Event discovery in social media feeds. In *Proceedings of ACL-HLT*, pages 389–398.

Y. Choi, C. Cardie, E. Riloff, and S. Patwardhan. 2005. Identifying sources of opinions with conditional random fields and extraction patterns. In *Proceedings of HLT/EMNLP*, pages 355–362.

J. Domke. 2008. Learning convex inference of marginals. In *Proceedings of UAI*.

J. Domke. 2010. Implicit differentiation by perturbation. In *Advances in Neural Information Processing Systems*, pages 523–531.

J. Domke. 2011. Parameter learning with truncated message-passing. In *Proceedings of the IEEE Conference on Computer Vision and Pattern Recognition (CVPR)*.

J. Domke. 2012. Generic methods for optimization-based modeling. In *Proceedings of AISTATS*.

M. Dreyer and J. Eisner. 2009. Graphical models over multiple strings. In *Proceedings of EMNLP*, pages 101–110.

J. Eisner and Hal Daumé III. 2011. Learning speed-accuracy tradeoffs in nondeterministic inference algorithms. In *COST: NIPS 2011 Workshop on Computational Trade-offs in Statistical Learning*, Sierra Nevada, Spain, December.

A. Elisseeff and J. Weston. 2001. Kernel methods for multi-labelled classification and categorical regression problems. In *Advances in Neural Information Processing Systems*, pages 681–687.

J.R. Finkel, T. Grenager, and C. Manning. 2005. Incorporating non-local information into information extraction systems by Gibbs sampling. In *Proceedings of ACL*, pages 363–370.

T. Finley and T. Joachims. 2008. Training structural SVMs when exact inference is intractable. In *Proceedings of ICML*, pages 304–311.

D. Freitag. 2000. Machine learning for information extraction in informal domains. *Machine learning*, 39(2).

N. Ghamrawi and A. McCallum. 2005. Collective multi-label classification. In *Proceedings of CIKM*, pages 195–200.

K. Gimpel and N.A. Smith. 2010. Softmax-margin CRFs: Training log-linear models with cost functions. In *Proceedings of ACL*, pages 733–736.

P. I. Good. 2000. *Permutation Tests*. Springer.

A. Griewank and G. Corliss, editors. 1991. *Automatic Differentiation of Algorithms*. SIAM, Philadelphia.

S. Gross, O. Russakovsky, C. Do, and S. Batzoglou. 2007. Training conditional random fields for maximum labelwise accuracy. *Advances in Neural Information Processing Systems*, 19:529.

H. Ji and R. Grishman. 2011. Knowledge base population: Successful approaches and challenges. In *Proceedings of ACL-HLT*, pages 1148–1158.

S. Kakade, Y.W. Teh, and S. Roweis. 2002. An alternate objective function for Markovian fields. In *Proceedings of ICML*, pages 275–282.

D. Koller and N. Friedman. 2009. *Probabilistic Graphical Models: Principles and Techniques*. The MIT Press.

A. Kulesza and F. Pereira. 2008. Structured learning with approximate inference. In *Advances in Neural Information Processing Systems*, pages 785–792.

S. Lacoste-Julien, F. Huszr, and Z. Ghahramani. 2011. Approximate inference for the loss-calibrated Bayesian. In *Proceedings of AISTATS*.

J. Lafferty, A. McCallum, and F. Pereira. 2001. Conditional random fields: Probabilistic models for segmenting and labeling sequence data. In *Proceedings of ICML*, pages 282–289.

Y. LeCun, S. Chopra, R. Hadsell, M.A. Ranzato, and F.-J. Huang. 2006. A tutorial on energy-based learning. In G. Bakir, T. Hofman, B. Schlkopf, A. Smola, and B. Taskar, editors, *Predicting Structured Data*. MIT Press.

Z. Li and J. Eisner. 2009. First- and second-order expectation semirings with applications to minimum-risk training on translation forests. In *Proceedings of EMNLP*, pages 40–51.

K. P. Murphy, Y. Weiss, and M. I. Jordan. 1999. Loopy belief propagation for approximate inference: An empirical study. In *Proceedings of UAI*.

F. Och. 2003. Minimum error rate training in statistical machine translation. In *Proceedings of ACL*, pages 160–167.

F. Peng and A. McCallum. 2006. Information extraction from research papers using conditional random fields. *Information Processing & Management*, 42(4):963–979.

N.N. Schraudolph. 1999. Local gain adaptation in stochastic gradient descent. In *Proceedings of ANN*, pages 569–574.

F. Sha and F. Pereira. 2003. Shallow parsing with conditional random fields. In *Proceedings of ACL/HLT*, pages 134–141.

D.A. Smith and J. Eisner. 2006. Minimum risk annealing for training log-linear models. In *Proceedings of the COLING/ACL*, pages 787–794.

D. Smith and J. Eisner. 2008. Dependency parsing by belief propagation. In *Proceedings of EMNLP*, pages 145–156.

V. Stoyanov and J. Eisner. 2011. Learning cost-aware, loss-aware approximate inference policies for probabilistic graphical models. In *COST: NIPS 2011 Workshop on Computational Trade-offs in Statistical Learning*, Sierra Nevada, Spain, December.

V. Stoyanov, A. Ropson, and J. Eisner. 2011. Empirical risk minimization of graphical model parameters given approximate inference, decoding, and model structure. In *Proceedings of AISTATS*.

C. Sutton and A. McCallum. 2005. Piecewise training of undirected models. In *Proceedings of UAI*, pages 568–575.

C. Sutton, A. McCallum, and K. Rohanimanesh. 2007. Dynamic conditional random fields: Factorized probabilistic models for labeling and segmenting sequence data. *The Journal of Machine Learning Research*, 8:693–723.

J. Suzuki, E. McDermott, and H. Isozaki. 2006. Training conditional random fields with multivariate evaluation measures. In *Proceedings of COLING/ACL*, pages 217–224.

B. Taskar, C. Guestrin, and D. Koller. 2003. Max-margin Markov networks. *Proceedings of NIPS*, pages 25–32.

M. Thomas, B. Pang, and L. Lee. 2006. Get out the vote: Determining support or opposition from congressional floor-debate transcripts. In *Proceedings of EMNLP*, pages 327–335.

S. Vishwanathan, N. Schraudolph, M. Schmidt, and K. Murphy. 2006. Accelerated training of conditional random fields with stochastic gradient methods. In *Proceedings of ICML*, pages 969–976.

M. Wainwright. 2006. Estimating the "wrong" graphical model: Benefits in the computation-limited setting. *Journal of Machine Learning Research*, 7:1829–1859, September.

R.J. Williams and D. Zipser. 1989. A learning algorithm for continually running fully recurrent neural networks. *Neural Computation*, 1(2):270–280.

Unsupervised Learning on an Approximate Corpus*

Jason Smith and **Jason Eisner**
Center for Language and Speech Processing
Johns Hopkins University
3400 N. Charles St., Baltimore, MD 21218, USA
{jsmith, jason}@cs.jhu.edu

Unsupervised learning techniques can take advantage of large amounts of unannotated text, but the largest text corpus (the Web) is not easy to use in its full form. Instead, we have statistics about this corpus in the form of n-gram counts (Brants and Franz, 2006). While n-gram counts do not directly provide sentences, a distribution over sentences can be estimated from them in the same way that n-gram language models are estimated. We treat this distribution over sentences as an *approximate corpus* and show how unsupervised learning can be performed on such a corpus using variational inference. We compare hidden Markov model (HMM) training on exact and approximate corpora of various sizes, measuring speed and accuracy on unsupervised part-of-speech tagging.

1 Introduction

We consider the problem of training generative models on very large datasets in sublinear time. It is well known how to train an HMM to maximize the likelihood of a corpus of sentences. Here we show how to train faster on a distribution over sentences that compactly approximates the corpus. The distribution is given by an 5-gram backoff language model that has been estimated from statistics of the corpus.

In this paper, we demonstrate our approach on a traditional testbed for new structured-prediction learning algorithms, namely HMMs. We focus on unsupervised learning. This serves to elucidate the structure of our variational training approach, which stitches overlapping n-grams together rather than treating them in isolation. It also confirms that at least in this case, accuracy is not harmed by the key approximations made by our method. In future, we hope to scale up to the Google n-gram corpus (Brants and Franz, 2006) and learn a more detailed, explanatory joint model of tags, syntactic dependencies, and topics. Our intuition here is that web-scale data may be needed to learn the large number of lexically and contextually specific parameters.

*Work was supported in part by NSF grant No. 0347822.

1.1 Formulation

Let $\boldsymbol{w}$ ("words") denote an observation sequence, and let $\boldsymbol{t}$ ("tags") denote a hidden HMM state sequence that may explain $\boldsymbol{w}$. This terminology is taken from the literature on inducing part-of-speech (POS) taggers using a first-order HMM (Merialdo, 1994), which we use as our experimental setting.

Maximum a posteriori (MAP) training of an HMM p_θ seeks parameters θ to maximize

$$N \cdot \sum_{\boldsymbol{w}} c(\boldsymbol{w}) \log \sum_{\boldsymbol{t}} p_\theta(\boldsymbol{w}, \boldsymbol{t}) + \log \Pr_{\text{prior}}(\theta) \quad (1)$$

where c is an empirical distribution that assigns probability $1/N$ to each of the N sentences in a training corpus. Our technical challenge is to **generalize this MAP criterion** to other, structured distributions c that compactly approximate the corpus.

Specifically, we address the case where c is given by any **probabilistic FSA**, such as a **backoff language model**—that is, a variable-order Markov model estimated from corpus statistics. Similar sentences $\boldsymbol{w}$ share subpaths in the FSA and cannot easily be disentangled. The support of c is typically infinite (for a cyclic FSA) or at least exponential. Hence it is no longer practical to compute the tagging distribution $p(\boldsymbol{t} \mid \boldsymbol{w})$ for each sentence $\boldsymbol{w}$ separately, as in traditional MAP-EM or gradient ascent approaches. We will maximize our exact objective, or a cheaper variational approximation to it, in a way that crucially allows us to retain the structure-sharing.

1.2 Motivations

Why train from a distribution rather than a corpus? First, the foundation of statistical NLP is distributions over strings that are specified by weighted automata and grammars. We regard parameter estimation from such a distribution c (rather than from a sample) as a **natural question**. Previous work on modeling c with a distribution from another family was motivated by *approximating a grammar or* *model* rather than *generalizing from a dataset*, and hence removed latent variables while adding parameters (Nederhof, 2000; Mohri and Nederhof, 2001; Liang et al., 2008), whereas we do the reverse.

Second, in practice, one may want to incorporate massive amounts of (possibly out-of-domain) data in order to get **better coverage** of phenomena. Massive datasets usually require a simple model (given a time budget). We propose that it may be possible to use a lot of data *and* a good model by reducing the accuracy of the data representation instead. While training will become more complicated, it can still result in an overall speedup, because a frequent 5-gram collapses into a single parameter of the estimated distribution that only needs to be processed once per training iteration. By pruning low-count n-grams or reducing the maximum n below 5, one can further increase data volume for the fixed time budget at the expense of approximation quality.

Third, one may not have **access** to the original corpus. If one lacks the resources to harvest the web, the Google n-gram corpus was derived from over a trillion words of English web text. Privacy or copyright issues may prevent access, but one may still be able to work with n-gram statistics: Michel et al. (2010) used such statistics from 5 million scanned books. Several systems use n-gram counts (Bergsma et al., 2009; Lin et al., 2009) or other web statistics (Lapata and Keller, 2005) as features within a classifier. A large language model from n-gram counts yields an effective prior over hypotheses in tasks like machine translation (Brants et al., 2007). We similarly construct an n-gram model, but treat it as the primary *training* data whose structure is to be explained by the generative HMM. Thus our criterion does not explain the n-grams in isolation, but rather tries to explain the likely full sentences $\boldsymbol{w}$ that the model reconstructed from overlapping n-grams. This is something like shotgun sequencing, in which likely DNA strings are reconstructed from overlapping short reads (Staden, 1979); however, we train an HMM on the resulting distribution rather than merely trying to find its mode.

Finally, unsupervised HMM training discovers latent structure by approximating an empirical distribution c (the corpus) with a latent-variable distribution p (the trained HMM) that has fewer parameters. We show how to do the same where the distribution c is not a corpus but a finite-state distribution. In general, this finite-state c could represent some sophisticated estimate of the ***population* distribution**, using shrinkage, word classes, neural-net predictors, etc. to generalize in some way beyond the training sample *before* fitting p. For the sake of speed and clear comparison, however, our present experiments take c to be a compact approximation to the *sample* distribution, requiring only n-grams.

Spectral learning of HMMs (Hsu et al., 2009) also learns from a collection of n-grams. It has the striking advantage of converging globally to the true HMM parameters (under a certain reparameterization), with enough data and under certain assumptions. However, it does not exploit context beyond a trigram (it will not maximize, even locally, the likelihood of a finite sample of sentences), and cannot exploit priors or structure—e.g., that the emissions are consistent with a tag dictionary or that the transitions encode a higher-order or factorial HMM. Our more general technique extends to other latent-variable models, although it suffers from variational EM's usual local optima and approximation errors.

2 A variational lower bound

Our starting point is the variational EM algorithm (Jordan et al., 1999). Recall that this maximizes a lower bound on the MAP criterion of equation 1, by bounding the log-likelihood subterm as follows:

$$\log \textstyle\sum_{\boldsymbol{t}} p_\theta(\boldsymbol{w}, \boldsymbol{t}) \quad (2)$$
$$= \log \textstyle\sum_{\boldsymbol{t}} q(\boldsymbol{t})(p_\theta(\boldsymbol{w}, \boldsymbol{t})/q(\boldsymbol{t}))$$
$$\geq \textstyle\sum_{\boldsymbol{t}} q(\boldsymbol{t}) \log(p_\theta(\boldsymbol{w}, \boldsymbol{t})/q(\boldsymbol{t}))$$
$$= \mathbb{E}_{q(\boldsymbol{t})}[\log p_\theta(\boldsymbol{w}, \boldsymbol{t}) - \log q(\boldsymbol{t})] \quad (3)$$

This use of Jensen's inequality is valid for any distribution q. As Neal and Hinton (1998) show, the EM algorithm (Dempster et al., 1977) can be regarded as locally maximizing the resulting lower bound by alternating optimization, where q is a free parameter. The E-step optimizes q for fixed θ, and the M-step optimizes θ for fixed q. These computations are tractable for HMMs, since the distribution $q(\boldsymbol{t}) = p_\theta(\boldsymbol{t} \mid \boldsymbol{w})$ that is optimal at the E-step (which makes the inequality tight) can be represented as a lattice (a certain kind of weighted DFA), and this makes the M-step tractable via the forward-backward algorithm. However, there are many extensions such as factorial HMMs and Bayesian HMMs in which an expectation under $p_\theta(\boldsymbol{t} \mid \boldsymbol{w})$ involves an intractable sum. In this setting, one may use variational EM, in which q is restricted to some parametric family q_ϕ that will permit a tractable M-step. In this case the E-step chooses the optimal values of the *variational parameters* ϕ; the inequality is no longer tight.

There are two equivalent views of how this procedure is applied to a training *corpus*. One view is that the corpus log-likelihood is just as in (2), where $\boldsymbol{w}$ is taken to be the concatenation of all training sentences. The other view is that the corpus log-likelihood is a sum over many terms of the form (2), one for each training sentence $\boldsymbol{w}$, and we bound each summand individually using a different q_ϕ.

However, neither view leads to a practical implementation in our setting. We can neither concatenate all the relevant $\boldsymbol{w}$ nor loop over them, since we want the expectation of (2) under some distribution $c(\boldsymbol{w})$ such that $\{\boldsymbol{w} : c(\boldsymbol{w}) > 0\}$ is very large or infinite. Our move is to make q be a *conditional* distribution $q(\boldsymbol{t} \mid \boldsymbol{w})$ that applies to all $\boldsymbol{w}$ at once. The following holds by applying Jensen's inequality separately to each $\boldsymbol{w}$ in the expectation (this is valid since for each $\boldsymbol{w}$, $q(\boldsymbol{t} \mid \boldsymbol{w})$ is a distribution):

$$\mathbb{E}_{c(\boldsymbol{w})} \log \textstyle\sum_{\boldsymbol{t}} p_\theta(\boldsymbol{w}, \boldsymbol{t}) \tag{4}$$
$$= \mathbb{E}_{c(\boldsymbol{w})} \log \textstyle\sum_{\boldsymbol{t}} q(\boldsymbol{t} \mid \boldsymbol{w})(p_\theta(\boldsymbol{w}, \boldsymbol{t})/q(\boldsymbol{t} \mid \boldsymbol{w}))$$
$$\geq \mathbb{E}_{c(\boldsymbol{w})} \textstyle\sum_{\boldsymbol{t}} q(\boldsymbol{t} \mid \boldsymbol{w}) \log(p_\theta(\boldsymbol{w}, \boldsymbol{t})/q(\boldsymbol{t} \mid \boldsymbol{w}))$$
$$= \mathbb{E}_{cq(\boldsymbol{w},\boldsymbol{t})}[\log p_\theta(\boldsymbol{w}, \boldsymbol{t}) - \log q(\boldsymbol{t} \mid \boldsymbol{w})] \tag{5}$$

where we use $cq(\boldsymbol{w}, \boldsymbol{t})$ to denote the joint distribution $c(\boldsymbol{w}) \cdot q(\boldsymbol{t} \mid \boldsymbol{w})$. Thus, just as c is our approximate corpus, cq is our approximate *tagged* corpus. Our variational parameters ϕ will be used to parameterize cq directly. To ensure that cq_ϕ can indeed be expressed as $c(\boldsymbol{w}) \cdot q(\boldsymbol{t} \mid \boldsymbol{w})$, making the above bound valid, it suffices to guarantee that our variational family preserves the marginals:

$$(\forall \boldsymbol{w}) \textstyle\sum_{\boldsymbol{t}} cq_\phi(\boldsymbol{w}, \boldsymbol{t}) = c(\boldsymbol{w})$$

3 Finite-state encodings and algorithms

In the following, we will show how to maximize (5) for particular families of p, c, and cq that can be expressed using finite-state machines (FSMs)—that is, finite-state acceptors (FSAs) and transducers (FSTs). This general presentation of our method enables variations using other FSMs.

A path in an FSA accepts a string. In an FST, each arc is labeled with a "word : tag" pair, so that a path accepts a string *pair* $(\boldsymbol{w}, \boldsymbol{t})$ obtained by respectively concatenating the words and the tags encountered along the path. Our FSMs are weighted in the $(+, \times)$ semiring: the weight of any path is the product $(\times)$ of its arc weights, while the weight assigned to a string or string pair is the total weight $(+)$ of all its accepting paths. An FSM is *unambiguous* if each string or string pair has at most one accepting path.

Figure 1 reviews how to represent an HMM POS tagger as an FST (b), and how composing this with an FSA that accepts a single sentence gives us the familiar HMM tagging lattice as an FST (c). The forward-backward algorithm sums over paths in the lattice via dynamic programming (Rabiner, 1989).

In section 3.1, we replace the straight-line FSA of Figure 1a with an FSA that defines a more general distribution $c(\boldsymbol{w})$ over many sentences. Note that we cannot simply use this as a drop-in replacement in the construction of Figure 1. That would correspond to running EM on a single but uncertain sentence (distributed as $c(\boldsymbol{w})$) rather than a collection of observed sentences. For example, in the case of an ordinary training corpus of N sentences, the new FSA would be a parallel *union* (sum) of N straight-line paths—rather than a serial *concatenation* (product) of those paths as in ordinary EM (see above). Running the forward algorithm on the resulting lattice would compute $\mathbb{E}_{c(\boldsymbol{w})} \sum_{\boldsymbol{t}} p(\boldsymbol{w}, \boldsymbol{t})$, whose log is $\log \mathbb{E}_{c(\boldsymbol{w})} \sum_{\boldsymbol{t}} p(\boldsymbol{w}, \boldsymbol{t})$ rather than our desired $\mathbb{E}_{c(\boldsymbol{w})} \log \sum_{\boldsymbol{t}} p(\boldsymbol{w}, \boldsymbol{t})$. Instead, we use c in section 3.2 to construct a variational family cq_ϕ. We then show in sections 3.3–3.5 how to compute and locally maximize the variational lower bound (5).

3.1 Modeling a corpus with n-gram counts

n-gram backoff language models have been used for decades in automatic speech recognition and statistical machine translation. We follow the usual FSA construction (Allauzen et al., 2003). The state of a 5-gram FSA model $c(\boldsymbol{w})$ must remember the previous 4-gram. For example, it would include an arc from state defg (the previous 4-gram) to state efgh with label h and weight $c(\mathsf{h} \mid \mathsf{defg})$. Then, with appropriate handling of boundary conditions, a sentence $\boldsymbol{w} = \ldots\mathsf{defghi}\ldots$ is accepted along a single path of weight $c(\boldsymbol{w}) = \cdots c(\mathsf{h} \mid \mathsf{defg}) \cdot c(\mathsf{i} \mid \mathsf{efgh}) \cdots$. Arcs

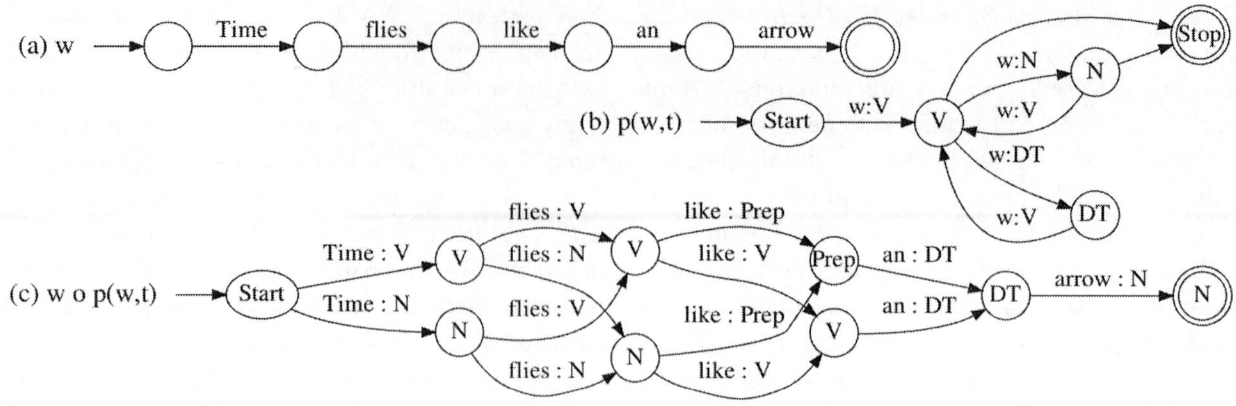

Figure 1: Ordinary HMM tagging with finite-state machines. An arc's label may have up to three components: "word:tag / weight." (Weights are suppressed for space. State labels are not part of the machine but suggest the history recorded by each state.) (a) $\boldsymbol{w}$ is an FSA that generates the sentence "Time flies like an arrow"; all arcs have probability 1. (b) $p(\boldsymbol{w}, \boldsymbol{t})$ is an FST representing an HMM (many arcs are not shown and words are abbreviated as "w"). Each arc $w : t$ is weighted by the product of transition and emission probabilities, $p(t \mid \text{previous } t) \cdot p(w \mid t)$. Composing (a) with (b) yields (c), an FST that encodes the joint probabilities $p(\boldsymbol{w}, \boldsymbol{t})$ of all possible taggings of the sentence $\boldsymbol{w}$.

of weight 0 can be omitted from the FSA.[1]

To estimate a conditional probability like $c(\mathsf{h} \mid \mathsf{defg})$ above, we simply take an unsmoothed ratio of two n-gram counts. This ML estimation means that c will approximate as closely as possible the training sample from which the counts were drawn. That gives a fair comparison with ordinary EM, which trains directly on that sample. (See discussion at the end of section 1.2 for alternatives.)

Yet we decline to construct a full 5-gram model, which would not be as compact as desired. A collection of all web 5-grams would be nearly as large as the web itself (by Zipf's Law). We may not have such a collection. For example, the Google n-gram corpus version 2 contains counts only for 1-grams that appear at least 40 times and 2-, 3-, 4-, and 5-grams that appear at least 10 times (Lin et al., 2009).

Instead, we construct a *backoff* language model. This FSA has one arc for each n-gram *in the collection*. Our algorithm's runtime (per iteration) will be linear in the number of arcs. If the 5-gram defgh is not in our collection, then there can be no h arc leaving defg. When encountering h in state defg, the automaton will instead take a *failure arc* (Allauzen et al., 2003) to the "backoff state" efg. It may be able to consume the h from that state, on an arc with weight $c(\mathsf{h} \mid \mathsf{efg})$; or it may have to back off further to fg. Each state's failure arc is weighted such that the state's outgoing arcs sum to 1. It is labeled with the special symbol Φ, which does not contribute to the word string accepted along a path.

We take care never to allow backoff to the empty state ϵ,[2] since we find that $c(\boldsymbol{w})$ is otherwise too coarse an approximation to English: sampled sentences tend to be disjointed, with some words generated in complete ignorance of their left context.

3.2 The variational distribution $cq(\boldsymbol{w}, \boldsymbol{t})$

The "variational gap" between (4) and (5) is $\mathbb{E}_{c(\boldsymbol{w})}\mathrm{KL}(q(\boldsymbol{t} \mid \boldsymbol{w}) \mid\mid p_\theta(\boldsymbol{t} \mid \boldsymbol{w}))$. That is, the bound is good if q does a good job of approximating p_θ's tagging distribution on a randomly drawn sentence.

Note that $n-1$ is the order of our n-gram Markov

[1] The FSA's initial state is the unigram history #, and its final states (which have no outgoing arcs) are the other states whose n-gram labels end in #. Here # is a boundary symbol that falls between sentences. To compute the weighted transitions, sentence boundaries must be manually or automatically annotated, either on the training corpus as in our present experiments, or directly on the training n-grams if we have only those.

To automatically find boundaries in an n-gram collection, one could apply a local classifier to each n-gram. But in principle, one could exploit more context and get a globally consistent annotation by stitching the n-grams together and applying the methods of this paper—replacing p_θ with an existing CRF sentence boundary detector, replacing c with a document-level (not sentence-level) language model, and optimizing cq_ϕ to be a version of c that is probabilistically annotated with sentence boundaries, which yields our desired distribution over sentences.

[2] To prevent such backoff, it suffices to include all 2-grams with count > 0. But where the full collection of 2-grams is unavailable or too large, one can remove the empty state (and recursively remove all states that transition only to removed states), and then renormalize the model locally or globally.

model $c(\boldsymbol{w})$ (i.e., each word is chosen given the previous $n-1$ words). Let $n_p - 1$ be the order of the HMM $p_\theta(\boldsymbol{w}, \boldsymbol{t})$ that we are training: i.e., each tag is chosen given the previous $n_p - 1$ tags. Our experiments take $n_p = 2$ (a bigram HMM) as in Figure 1.

We will take $q_\phi(\boldsymbol{t} \mid \boldsymbol{w})$ to be a *conditional Markov model* of order $n_q - 1$.[3] It will predict the tag at position i using a multinomial conditioned on the preceding $n_q - 1$ tags and on the word n-gram ending at position i (where n is as large as possible such that this n-gram is in our training collection). ϕ is the collection of all multinomial parameters.

If $n_q = n_p$, then our variational gap can be made 0 as in ordinary non-variational EM (see section 3.5). In our experiments, however, we save memory by choosing $n_q = 1$. Thus, our variational gap is tight to the extent that a word's POS tag under the model p_θ is conditionally independent of previous tags and the rest of the sentence, *given an n-word window*.[4] This is the assumption made by local classification models (Punyakanok et al., 2005; Toutanova and Johnson, 2007). Note that it is milder than the "one tagging per n-gram" hypothesis (Dawborn and Curran, 2009; Lin et al., 2009), which claims that each 5-gram (and therefore each sentence!) is unambiguous as to its full tagging. In contrast, we allow that a tag may be ambiguous even given an n-word window; we merely suppose that there is no *further* disambiguating information accessible to p_θ.[5]

We can encode the resulting $cq(\boldsymbol{w}, \boldsymbol{t})$ as an FST. With $n_q = 1$, the *states* of cq are isomorphic to the states of c. However, an *arc* in c from defg with label h and weight 0.2 is replaced in cq by several arcs—one per tag t—with label h : t and weight $0.2 \cdot q_\phi(t \mid \text{defgh})$.[6] We remark that an encoding of $q(\boldsymbol{t} \mid \boldsymbol{w})$ as an FST would be identical except for dropping the c factor (e.g., 0.2) from each weight. Composing $c \circ q$ would then recover cq.

This construction associates one variational parameter in ϕ with each arc in cq—that is, with each pair (arc in c, tag t), if $n_q = 1$. There would be little point in sharing these parameters across arcs of cq, as that would reduce the expressiveness of the variational distribution without reducing runtime.[7]

Notice that maximizing equation (5) jointly learns not only a compact slow HMM tagger p_θ, but also a large fast tagger q_ϕ that simply memorizes the likely tags in each n-gram context. This is reminiscent of structure compilation (Liang et al., 2008).

3.3 Computing the variational objective

The expectation in equation (5) can now be computed efficiently and elegantly by dynamic programming over the FSMs, for a given θ and ϕ.

We exploit our representation of cq_ϕ as an FSM over the $(+, \times)$ semiring. The path weights represent a probability distribution over the paths. In general, it is efficient to compute the expected **value** of a random FSM path, for any definition of value that decomposes additively over the path's arcs. The approach is to apply the forward algorithm to a version of cq_ϕ where we now regard each arc as weighted by an *ordered pair* of real numbers. The $(+, \times)$ operations for combining weights (section 3) are replaced with the operations of an "expectation semiring" whose elements are such pairs (Eisner, 2002).

Suppose we want to find $\mathbb{E}_{cq_\phi(\boldsymbol{w},\boldsymbol{t})} \log q_\phi(\boldsymbol{t} \mid \boldsymbol{w})$. To reduce this to an expected value problem, we must assign a *value* to each arc of cq_ϕ such that the

[3]A conditional Markov model is a simple case of a maximum-entropy Markov model (McCallum et al., 2000).

[4]At present, the word being tagged is the *last* word in the window. We do have an efficient modification in which the window is *centered* on the word, by using an FST cq that delays the emission of a tag until up to 2 subsequent words have been seen.

[5]With difficulty, one can construct English examples that violate our assumption. (1) "Some monitor lizards from Africa ..." versus "Some monitor lizards from a distance ...": there are words far away from "monitor" that help disambiguate whether "monitor" is a noun or a verb. ("Monitor lizards" are a species, but some people like to monitor lizards.) (2) "Time flies": "flies" is more likely to be a noun if "time" is a verb.

[6]In the case $n_q > 1$, the states of c would need to be split in order to remember $n_q - 1$ tags of history. For example, if c is Figure 1a, splitting its states with $n_q = 2$ would yield a cq with a topology like Figure 1c, but with each arc having an independent variational parameter.

[7]One could increase the number of arcs and hence variational parameters by splitting the states of cq to remember more history. In particular, one could increase the width n_q of the tag window, or one could increase the width of the word window by splitting states of c (without changing the distribution $c(\boldsymbol{w})$).

Conversely, one could reduce the number of variational parameters by further restricting the variational family. For example, requiring $q(\boldsymbol{t} \mid \boldsymbol{w})$ to have entropy 0 (analogous to "hard EM" or "Viterbi EM") would associate a single deterministic tag with each arc of c. This is fast, makes cq as compact as c, and is still milder than "one tagging per n-gram." More generously, one could allow up to 2 tags per arc of c, or use a low-dimensional representation of the arc's distribution over tags.

total value of a path accepting $(\boldsymbol{w}, \boldsymbol{t})$ is $\log q_\phi(\boldsymbol{t} \mid \boldsymbol{w})$. Thus, let the value of each arc in cq_ϕ be the log of its weight in the isomorphic FST $q_\phi(\boldsymbol{t} \mid \boldsymbol{w})$.[8]

We introduce some notation to make this precise. A state of cq_ϕ is a pair of the form $[h_c, h_q]$, where h_c is a state of c (e.g., an $(n-1)$-word history) and h_q is an $(n_q - 1)$-tag history. We saw in the previous section that an arc a leaving this state, and labeled with $w : t$ where w is a word and t is a tag, will have a weight of the form $k_a \stackrel{\text{def}}{=} c(w \mid h_c)\phi_a$ where $\phi_a \stackrel{\text{def}}{=} q_\phi(t \mid h_c w, h_q)$. We now let the value $v_a \stackrel{\text{def}}{=} \log \phi_a$.[9] Then, just as the weight of a path accepting $(\boldsymbol{w}, \boldsymbol{t})$ is $\prod_a k_a = cq_\phi(\boldsymbol{w}, \boldsymbol{t})$, the value of that path is $\sum_a v_a = \log q_\phi(\boldsymbol{t} \mid \boldsymbol{w})$, as desired.

To compute the *expected* value $\bar{r}$ over all paths, we follow a generalized forward-backward recipe (Li and Eisner, 2009, section 4.2). First, run the forward and backward algorithms over cq_ϕ.[10] Now the expected value is a sum over all arcs of cq_ϕ, namely $\bar{r} = \sum_a \alpha_a k_a v_a \beta_a$, where α_a denotes the forward probability of arc a's *source* state and β_a denotes the backward probability of arc a's *target* state.

Now, in fact, the expectation we need to compute is not $\mathbb{E}_{cq_\phi(\boldsymbol{w},\boldsymbol{t})} \log q_\phi(\boldsymbol{t} \mid \boldsymbol{w})$ but rather equation (5). So the value v_a of arc a should not actually be $\log \phi_a$ but rather $\log \theta_a - \log \phi_a$ where $\theta_a \stackrel{\text{def}}{=} p_\theta(t \mid h_p) \cdot p_\theta(w \mid t)$. This is a minor change—except that v_a now depends on h_p, which is the history of $n_p - 1$ previous tags. If $n_p > n_q$, then a's start state does not store such a long history. Thus, the value of a actually depends on how one reaches a! It is properly written as $v_{\boldsymbol{z}a}$, where $\boldsymbol{z}a$ is a path ending with a and $\boldsymbol{z}$ is sufficiently long to determine h_p.[11]

Formally, let $\mathcal{Z}_a$ be a "partitioning" set of paths to a, such that any path in cq_ϕ from an initial state to the start state of a must have *exactly one* $\boldsymbol{z} \in \mathcal{Z}_a$ as a suffix, and each $\boldsymbol{z} \in \mathcal{Z}_a$ is sufficiently long so that $v_{\boldsymbol{z}a}$ is well-defined. We can now find the expected value as $\bar{r} = \sum_a \sum_{\boldsymbol{z} \in \mathcal{Z}_a} \alpha_{\boldsymbol{z}} \left(\prod_{z \in \boldsymbol{z}} k_z\right) k_a v_{\boldsymbol{z}a} \beta_a$.

The above method permits p_θ to score the tag sequences of length n_p that are hypothesized by cq_ϕ. One can regard it as *implicitly* running the generalized forward-backward algorithm over a larger FST that marries the structure of cq_ϕ with the n_p-gram HMM structure,[12] so that each value is again local to a single arc $\overline{\boldsymbol{z}a}$. However, it saves space by working directly on cq_ϕ (which has manageable size because we deliberately kept n_q small), rather than materializing the larger FST (as bad as increasing n_q to n_p).

The $\mathcal{Z}_a$ trick uses $O(CT^{n_q})$ rather than $O(CT^{n_p})$ space to store the FST, where C is the number of arcs in c (= number of training n-grams) and T is the number of tag types. With or without the trick, runtime is $O(CT^{n_p} + BCT^{n_q})$, where B is the num-

[8]The total value is then the sum of the logs, i.e., the log of the product. This works because q_ϕ is unambiguous, i.e., it computes $q_\phi(\boldsymbol{t} \mid \boldsymbol{w})$ as a product along a single accepting path, rather than summing over multiple paths.

[9]The special case of a failure arc a goes from $[h_c, h_q]$ to $[h'_c, h_q]$, where h'_c is a backed-off version of h_c. It is labeled with $\Phi : \epsilon$, which does not contribute to the word string or tag string accepted along a path. Its weight k_a is the weight $c(\Phi \mid h_c)$ of the corresponding failure arc in c from h_c to h'_c. We define $v_a \stackrel{\text{def}}{=} 0$, so it does not contribute to the total value.

[10]Recall that the forward probability of each state is defined recursively from the forward probabilities of the states that have arcs leading to it. As our FST is cyclic, it is not possible to visit the states in topologically sorted order. We instead solve these simultaneous equations by a relaxation algorithm (Eisner, 2002, section 5): repeatedly sweep through all states, updating their forward probability, until the total forward probability of all final states is close to the correct total of $1 = \sum_{\boldsymbol{w},\boldsymbol{t}} cq_\phi(\boldsymbol{w}, \boldsymbol{t})$ (showing that we have covered all high-prob paths). A corresponding backward relaxation is actually not needed yet (we do need it for $\hat{\beta}$ in section 3.4): backward probabilities are just 1, since cq_ϕ is constructed with locally normalized probabilities.

When we rerun the forward-backward algorithm after a parameter update, we use the previous solution as a starting point for the relaxation algorithm. This greatly speeds convergence.

[11]By concatenating $\boldsymbol{z}$'s start state's h_q with the tags along $\boldsymbol{z}$. Typically $\boldsymbol{z}$ has length $n_p - n_q$ (and $\mathcal{Z}_a$ consists of the paths of that length to a's start state). However, $\boldsymbol{z}$ may be longer if it contains Φ arcs, or shorter if it begins with an initial state.

[12]Constructed by lazy finite-state intersection of cq_ϕ and p_θ (Mohri et al., 2000). These do not have to be n-gram taggers, but must be same-length FSTs (these are closed under intersection) and unambiguous. Define arc *values* in both FSTs such that for any $(\boldsymbol{w}, \boldsymbol{t})$, cq_ϕ and p_θ accept $(\boldsymbol{w}, \boldsymbol{t})$ along unique paths of total values $v = -\log q_\phi(\boldsymbol{t} \mid \boldsymbol{w})$ and $v' = \log p_\theta(\boldsymbol{w}, \boldsymbol{t})$, respectively. We now lift the weights into the expectation semiring (Eisner, 2002) as follows. In cq_ϕ, replace arc a's weight k_a with the semiring weight $\langle k_a, k_a v_a \rangle$. In p_θ, replace arc a''s weight with $\langle 1, v'_{a'} \rangle$. Then if $k = cq_\phi(\boldsymbol{w}, \boldsymbol{t})$, the intersected FST accepts $(\boldsymbol{w}, \boldsymbol{t})$ with weight $\langle k, k(v + v') \rangle$. The expectation of $v + v'$ over all paths is then a sum $\sum_{\overline{\boldsymbol{z}a}} \alpha_{\overline{\boldsymbol{z}a}} r_{\overline{\boldsymbol{z}a}} \beta_{\overline{\boldsymbol{z}a}}$ over arcs $\overline{\boldsymbol{z}a}$ of the intersected FST—we are using $\overline{\boldsymbol{z}a}$ to denote the arc in the intersected FST that corresponds to "a in cq_ϕ when reached via path $\boldsymbol{z}$," and $r_{\overline{\boldsymbol{z}a}}$ to denote the second component of its semiring weight. Here $\alpha_{\overline{\boldsymbol{z}a}}$ and $\beta_{\overline{\boldsymbol{z}a}}$ denote the forward and backward probabilities in the intersected FST, defined from the first components of the semiring weights. We can get them more efficiently from the results of running forward-backward on the smaller cq_ϕ: $\alpha_{\overline{\boldsymbol{z}a}} = \alpha_{\boldsymbol{z}} \prod_{z \in \boldsymbol{z}} k_z$ and $\beta_{\overline{\boldsymbol{z}a}} = \beta_a = 1$.

ber of forward-backward sweeps (footnote 10). The ordinary forward algorithm requires $n_q = n_p$ and takes $O(CT^{n_p})$ time *and* space on a length-C string.

3.4 Computing the gradient as well

To maximize our objective (5), we compute its gradient with respect to θ and ϕ. We follow an efficient recipe from Li and Eisner (2009, section 5, case 3). The runtime and space match those of section 3.3, except that the runtime rises to $O(BCT^{n_p})$.[13]

First suppose that each v_a is local to a single arc. We replace each weight k_a with $\hat{k}_a = \langle k_a, k_a v_a \rangle$ in the so-called expectation semiring, whose sum and product operations can be found in Li and Eisner (2009, Table 1). Using these in the forward-backward algorithm yields quantities $\hat{\alpha}_a$ and $\hat{\beta}_a$ that also fall in the expectation semiring.[14] (Their first components are the old α_a and β_a.) The desired gradient[15] $\langle \nabla \bar{k}, \nabla \bar{r} \rangle$ is $\sum_a \hat{\alpha}_a (\nabla \hat{k}_a) \hat{\beta}_a$,[16] where $\nabla \hat{k}_a = (\nabla k_a, \nabla (k_a v_a)) = (\nabla k_a, (\nabla k_a) v_a + k_a (\nabla v_a))$. Here ∇ gives the vector of partial derivatives with respect to *all* ϕ and θ parameters. Yet each $\nabla \hat{k}_a$ is sparse, with only 3 nonzero components, because $\hat{k}_a$ depends on only one ϕ parameter (ϕ_a) and two θ parameters (via θ_a as defined in section 3.3).

When $n_p > n_q$, we sum not over arcs a of cq_ϕ but over arcs $\overline{za}$ of the larger FST (footnote 12). Again we can do this *implicitly*, by using the short path za in cq_ϕ in place of the arc $\overline{za}$. Each state of cq_ϕ must then store $\hat{\alpha}$ and $\hat{\beta}$ values for *each* of the $T^{n_p - n_q}$ states of the larger FST that it corresponds to. (In the case $n_p - n_q = 1$, as in our experiments, this fortunately does not increase the total asymptotic space, since each state of cq_ϕ already has to store T arcs.)

With more cleverness, one can eliminate this extra storage while preserving asymptotic runtime (still using sparse vectors). Find $\langle \nabla \bar{k}, (\nabla \bar{r})^{(1)} \rangle = \sum_a \hat{\alpha}_a \langle \nabla k_a, 0 \rangle \hat{\beta}_a$. Also find $\langle \bar{r}, (\nabla \bar{r})^{(2)} \rangle = \sum_a \sum_{z \in \mathcal{Z}_a} \alpha_z \left(\prod_{z \in z} \langle k_z, \nabla k_z \rangle\right) \langle k_a v_{za}, \nabla(k_a v_{za}) \rangle\, \beta_a$. Now our desired gradient $\nabla \bar{r}$ emerges as $(\nabla \bar{r})^{(1)} + (\nabla \bar{r})^{(2)}$. The computation of $(\nabla \bar{r})^{(1)}$ uses *modified* definitions of $\hat{\alpha}_a$ and $\hat{\beta}_a$ that depend only on (respectively) the source and target states of a—not $\overline{za}$.[17] To compute them, initialize $\hat{\alpha}$ (respectively $\hat{\beta}$) at each state to $\langle 1, 0 \rangle$ or $\langle 0, 0 \rangle$ according to whether the state is initial (respectively final). Now iterate repeatedly (footnote 10) over all arcs a: Add $\hat{\alpha}_a \langle k_a, 0 \rangle + \sum_{z \in \mathcal{Z}_a} \alpha_z \left(\prod_{z \in z} k_z\right) \langle 0, k_a v_{za} \rangle$ to the $\hat{\alpha}$ at a's *target* state. Conversely, add $\langle k_a, 0 \rangle \hat{\beta}_a$ to the $\hat{\beta}$ at a's *source* state, and for each $z \in \mathcal{Z}_a$, add $\left(\prod_{z \in z} k_z\right) \langle 0, k_a v_{za} \rangle \beta_a$ to the $\hat{\beta}$ at z's source state.

3.5 Locally optimizing the objective

Recall that cq_ϕ associates with each $[h_c, h_q, w]$ a block of ϕ parameters that must be ≥ 0 and sum to 1. Our optimization method must enforce these constraints. A standard approach is to use a projected gradient method, where after each gradient step on ϕ, the parameters are projected back onto the probability simplex. We implemented another standard approach: reexpress each block of parameters $\{\phi_a : a \in \mathcal{A}\}$ as $\phi_a \stackrel{\text{def}}{=} \exp \eta_a / \sum_{b \in \mathcal{A}} \exp \eta_b$, as is possible iff the ϕ_a parameters satisfy the constraints. We then follow the gradient of $\bar{r}$ with respect to the new η parameters, given by $\partial \bar{r} / \partial \eta_a = \phi_a (\partial \bar{r} / \partial \phi_a - E_{\mathcal{A}})$ where $E_{\mathcal{A}} = \sum_b \phi_b (\partial \bar{r} / \partial \phi_b)$.

Another common approach is block coordinate ascent on θ and ϕ—this is "variational EM." **M-step:** Given ϕ, we can easily find optimal estimates of the emission and transition probabilities θ. They are respectively proportional to the posterior expected counts of arcs a and paths za under cq_ϕ, namely $N \cdot \alpha_a k_a \beta_a$ and $N \cdot \alpha_z \left(\prod_{z \in z} k_z\right) k_a \beta_a$. **E-step:** Given θ, we cannot easily find the optimal ϕ (even if $n_q = n_p$).[18] This was the rea-

[13] An alternative would be to apply back-propagation (reverse-mode automatic differentiation) to section 3.3's computation of the objective. This would achieve the same runtime as in section 3.3, but would need as much space as time.

[14] This also computes our objective $\bar{r}$: summing the $\hat{\alpha}$'s of the final states of cq_ϕ gives $\langle \bar{k}, \bar{r} \rangle$ where $\bar{k} = 1$ is the total probability of all paths. This alternative computation of the expectation $\bar{r}$, using the forward algorithm (instead of forward-backward) but over the expectation semiring, was given by Eisner (2002).

[15] We are interested in $\nabla \bar{r}$. $\nabla \bar{k}$ is just a byproduct. We remark that $\nabla \bar{k} \neq 0$, even though $\bar{k} = 1$ for any valid parameter vector ϕ (footnote 14), as increasing ϕ *invalidly* can increase $\bar{k}$.

[16] By a product of pairs we always mean $\langle k, r \rangle \langle s, t \rangle \stackrel{\text{def}}{=} \langle ks, kt + rs \rangle$, just as in the expectation semiring, even though the pair $\nabla \hat{k}_a$ is not in that semiring (its components are vectors rather than scalars). See (Li and Eisner, 2009, section 4.3). We also define scalar-by-pair products as $k \langle s, t \rangle \stackrel{\text{def}}{=} \langle ks, kt \rangle$.

[17] First components α_a and β_a remain as in cq_ϕ. $\hat{\alpha}_a$ sums paths to a. $\langle \nabla k_a, 0 \rangle \hat{\beta}_a$ can't quite sum over paths starting with a (their early weights depend on z), but $(\nabla \bar{r})^{(2)}$ corrects this.

[18] Recall that cq_ϕ must have locally normalized probabilities (to ensure that its marginal is c). If $n_q = n_p$, the optimal ϕ is as follows: we can reduce the variational gap to 0 by setting

son for gradient ascent. However, for any *single* sum-to-1 block of parameters $\{\phi_a : a \in \mathcal{A}\}$, it is easy to find the optimal values if the others are held fixed. We maximize $L_\mathcal{A} \stackrel{\text{def}}{=} \bar{r} + \lambda_\mathcal{A} \sum_{a \in \mathcal{A}} \phi_a$, where $\lambda_\mathcal{A}$ is a Lagrange multiplier chosen so that the sum is 1. The partial derivative $\partial \bar{r} / \partial \phi_a$ can be found using methods of section 3.4, restricting the sums to za for the given a. For example, following paragraphs 2–3 of section 3.4, let $\langle \alpha_a, r_a \rangle \stackrel{\text{def}}{=} \sum_{z \in \mathcal{Z}_a} \langle \alpha_{\overline{za}}, r_{\overline{za}} \rangle$ where $\langle \alpha_{\overline{za}}, r_{\overline{za}} \rangle \stackrel{\text{def}}{=} \hat{\alpha}_{\overline{za}} \hat{\beta}_{\overline{za}}$.[19] Setting $\partial L_\mathcal{A} / \partial \phi_a = 0$ implies that ϕ_a is proportional to $\exp((r_a + \sum_{z \in \mathcal{Z}_a} \alpha_{\overline{za}} \log \theta_{\overline{za}}) / \alpha_a)$.[20]

Rather than doing block coordinate ascent by updating one ϕ block at a time (and then recomputing r_a values for all blocks, which is slow), one can take an approximate step by updating all blocks in parallel. We find that replacing the E-step with a single parallel step still tends to improve the objective, and that this approximate variational EM is faster than gradient ascent with comparable results.[21]

4 Experiments

4.1 Constrained unsupervised HMM learning

We follow the unsupervised POS tagging setup of Merialdo (1994) and many others (Smith and Eisner, 2005; Haghighi and Klein, 2006; Toutanova and Johnson, 2007; Goldwater and Griffiths, 2007; Johnson, 2007). Given a corpus of sentences, one seeks the maximum-likelihood or MAP parameters of a bigram HMM ($n_p = 2$). The observed sentences, for us, are replaced by the faux sentences extrapolated from observed n-grams via the language model c.

The states of the HMM correspond to POS tags as in Figure 1. All transitions are allowed, but not all emissions. If a word is listed in a provided "dictionary" with its possible tags, then other tags are given 0 probability of emitting that word. The EM algorithm uses the corpus to learn transition and emission probabilities that explain the data under this constraint. The constraint ensures that the learned states have something to do with true POS tags.

Merialdo (1994) spawned a long line of work on this task. Ideas have included Bayesian learning methods (MacKay, 1997; Goldwater and Griffiths, 2007; Johnson, 2007), better initial parameters (Goldberg et al., 2008), and learning how to constrain the possible parts of speech for a word (Ravi and Knight, 2008), as well as non-HMM sequence models (Smith and Eisner, 2005; Haghighi and Klein, 2006; Toutanova and Johnson, 2007).

Most of this work has used the Penn Treebank (Marcus et al., 1993) as a dataset. While this million-word *Wall Street Journal* (WSJ) corpus is one of the largest that is *manually* annotated with parts of speech, unsupervised learning methods could take advantage of vast amounts of unannotated text. In practice, runtime concerns have sometimes led researchers to use small subsets of the Penn Treebank (Goldwater and Griffiths, 2007; Smith and Eisner, 2005; Haghighi and Klein, 2006). Our goal is to point the way to using even larger datasets.

The reason for all this past research is that (Merialdo, 1994) was a *negative* result: while EM is guaranteed to improve the model's likelihood, it degrades the match between the latent states and true parts of speech (if the starting point is a good one obtained with some supervision). Thus, for the task of POS induction, there must be something wrong with the HMM model, the likelihood objective, or the search procedure. It is clear that the model is far too weak: there are many latent variables in natural language, so the HMM may be picking up on something other than POS tags. Ultimately, fixing this will require richer models with many more parameters. But learning these (lexically specific) parameters will require large training datasets—hence our present methodological exploration on whether it is possible to scale up the original setting.

$q_\phi(t \mid h_c w, h_q)$ to the probability that $\boldsymbol{t}$ begins with t if we randomly draw a suffix $\boldsymbol{w} \sim c(\cdot \mid h_c w)$ and randomly tag $w\boldsymbol{w}$ with $\boldsymbol{t} \sim p_\theta(\cdot \mid w\boldsymbol{w}, h_q)$. This is equivalent to using p_θ with the backward algorithm to conditionally tag *each* possible suffix.

[19]The first component of $\hat{\alpha}_{\overline{za}} \hat{\beta}_{\overline{za}}$ is $\alpha_{\overline{za}} \beta_{\overline{za}} = \alpha_{\overline{za}} \cdot 1$.

[20]If a is an arc of cq_ϕ then $\partial \bar{r} / \partial \phi_a$ is the second component of $\sum_{z \in \mathcal{Z}_a} \hat{\alpha}_{\overline{za}} (\partial \hat{k}_{\overline{za}} / \partial \phi_a) \hat{\beta}_{\overline{za}}$. Then $\partial L_\mathcal{A} / \partial \phi_a$ works out to $\sum_{z \in \mathcal{Z}_a} c_a (r_{\overline{za}} + \alpha_{\overline{za}} (\log \theta_{\overline{za}} - \log \phi_a - 1)) + \lambda_\mathcal{A}$. Set to 0 and solve for ϕ_a, noting that $c_a, \alpha_a, \lambda_\mathcal{A}$ are constant over $a \in \mathcal{A}$.

[21]In retrospect, an even faster strategy might be to do a *series* of block ϕ and $\hat{\beta}$ updates, updating $\hat{\beta}$ at a state (footnote 10) immediately after updating ϕ on the arcs leading from that state, which allows a better block update at predecessor states. On an *acyclic* machine, a single *backward* pass of this sort will reduce the variational gap to 0 if $n_q = n_p$ (footnote 18). This is because, thanks to the up-to-date $\hat{\beta}$, each block of arcs gets new ϕ weights in proportion to relative suffix path probabilities *under the new* θ. After this backward pass, a single *forward* pass can update the α values and collect expected counts for the M-step that will update θ. Standard EM is a special case of this strategy.

4.2 Setup

We investigate how much performance degrades when we approximate the corpus *and* train approximately with $n_q = 1$. We examine two measures: likelihood on a held-out corpus and accuracy in POS tagging. We train on corpora of three different sizes:

- WSJ-big (910k words $\rightarrow$ 441k n-grams @ cutoff 3),
- Giga-20 (20M words $\rightarrow$ 2.9M n-grams @ cutoff 10),
- Giga-200 (200M wds $\rightarrow$ 14.4M n-grams @ cutoff 20).

These were drawn from the Penn Treebank (sections 2–23) and the English Gigaword corpus (Parker et al., 2009). For held-out evaluation, we use WSJ-small (Penn Treebank section 0) or WSJ-big.

We estimate backoff language models for these corpora based on collections of n-grams with $n \leq 5$. In this work, we select the n-grams by simple count cutoffs as shown above,[22] taking care to keep all 2-grams as mentioned in footnote 2.

Similar to Merialdo (1994), we use a tag dictionary which limits the possible tags of a word to those it was observed with in the WSJ, provided that the word was observed at least 5 times in the WSJ. We used the reduced tagset of Smith and Eisner (2005), which collapses the original 45 fine-grained part-of-speech tags into just 17 coarser tags.

4.3 Results

In all experiments, our method achieves similar accuracy though slightly worse likelihood. Although this method is meant to be a fast approximation of EM, standard EM is faster on the smallest dataset (WSJ-big). This is because this corpus is not much bigger than the 5-gram language model built from it (at our current pruning level), and so the overhead of the more complex n-gram EM method is a net disadvantage. However, when moving to larger corpora, the iterations of n-gram EM become as fast as standard EM and then faster. We expect this trend to continue as one moves to much larger datasets, as the compression ratio of the pruned language model relative to the original corpus will only improve. The Google n-gram corpus is based on 50× more data than our largest but could be handled in RAM.

[22] Entropy-based pruning (Stolcke, 2000) may be a better selection method when one is in a position to choose. However, count cutoffs were already used in the creation of the Google n-gram corpus, and more complex methods of pruning may not be practical for very large datasets.

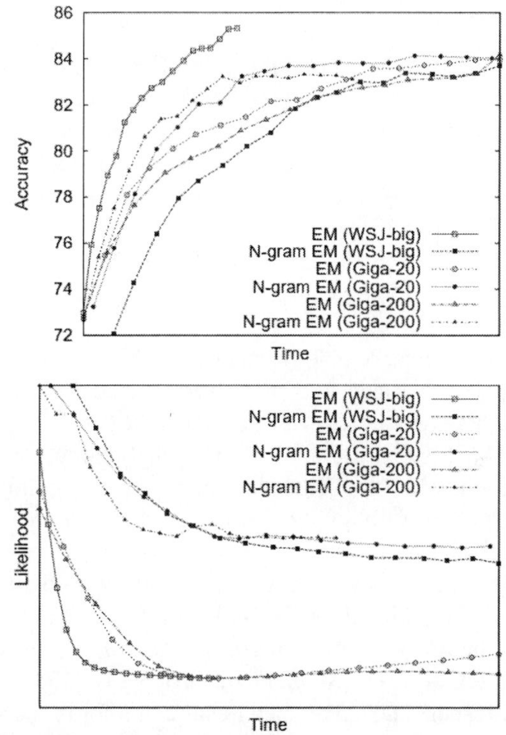

Figure 2: POS-tagging accuracy and log-likelihood after each iteration, measured on WSJ-big when training on the Gigaword datasets, else on WSJ-small. Runtime and log-likelihood are scaled differently for each dataset. Replacing EM with our method changes runtime per iteration from 1.4s → 3.5s, 48s → 47s, and 506s → 321s.

5 Conclusions

We presented a general approach to training generative models on a *distribution* rather than on a training sample. We gave several motivations for this novel problem. We formulated an objective function similar to MAP, and presented a variational lower bound.

Algorithmically, we gave nontrivial general methods for computing and optimizing our variational lower bound for *arbitrary* finite-state data distributions c, generative models p, and variational families q, provided that p and q are unambiguous same-length FSTs. We also gave details for specific useful families for c, p, and q.

As proof of principle, we used a traditional HMM POS tagging task to demonstrate that we can train a model from n-grams almost as accurately as from full sentences, and do so faster to the extent that the n-gram dataset is smaller. More generally, we offer our approach as an intriguing new tool to help semi-supervised learning benefit from very large datasets.

References

Cyril Allauzen, Mehryar Mohri, and Brian Roark. 2003. Generalized algorithms for constructing statistical language models. In *Proc. of ACL*, pages 40–47.

Shane Bergsma, Dekang Lin, and Randy Goebel. 2009. Web-scale n-gram models for lexical disambiguation. In *Proc. of IJCAI*.

Thorsten Brants and Alex Franz. 2006. Web 1T 5-gram version 1. Linguistic Data Consortium, Philadelphia. LDC2006T13.

Thorsten Brants, Ashok C. Popat, Peng Xu, Franz J. Och, and Jeffrey Dean. 2007. Large language models in machine translation. In *Proc. of EMNLP*.

Tim Dawborn and James R. Curran. 2009. CCG parsing with one syntactic structure per n-gram. In *Australasian Language Technology Association Workshop*, pages 71–79.

Arthur P. Dempster, Nan M. Laird, and Donald B. Rubin. 1977. Maximum likelihood from incomplete data via the EM algorithm. *Journal of the Royal Statistical Society. Series B (Methodological)*, 39(1):1–38.

Jason Eisner. 2002. Parameter estimation for probabilistic finite-state transducers. In *Proc. of ACL*, pages 1–8.

Yoav Goldberg, Meni Adler, and Michael Elhadad. 2008. EM can find pretty good HMM POS-taggers (when given a good start). In *Proc. of ACL*, pages 746–754.

Sharon Goldwater and Thomas Griffiths. 2007. A fully Bayesian approach to unsupervised part-of-speech tagging. In *Proc. of ACL*, pages 744–751.

Aria Haghighi and Dan Klein. 2006. Prototype-driven learning for sequence models. In *Proc. of NAACL*, pages 320–327.

Daniel Hsu, Sham M. Kakade, and Tong Zhang. 2009. A spectral algorithm for learning hidden Markov models. In *Proc. of COLT*.

Mark Johnson. 2007. Why doesn't EM find good HMM POS-taggers? In *Proc. of EMNLP-CoNLL*, pages 296–305.

M. I. Jordan, Z. Ghahramani, T. S. Jaakkola, and L. K. Saul. 1999. An introduction to variational methods for graphical models. In M. I. Jordan, editor, *Learning in Graphical Models*. Kluwer.

Mirella Lapata and Frank Keller. 2005. Web-based models for natural language processing. *ACM Transactions on Speech and Language Processing*.

Zhifei Li and Jason Eisner. 2009. First- and second-order expectation semirings with applications to minimum-risk training on translation forests. In *Proc. of EMNLP*, pages 40–51.

Percy Liang, Hal Daumé III, and Dan Klein. 2008. Structure compilation: Trading structure for features. In *International Conference on Machine Learning (ICML)*, Helsinki, Finland.

D. Lin, K. Church, H. Ji, S. Sekine, D. Yarowsky, S. Bergsma, K. Patil, E. Pitler, R. Lathbury, V. Rao, K. Dalwani, and S. Narsale. 2009. Unsupervised acquisition of lexical knowledge from n-grams. Summer workshop technical report, Center for Language and Speech Processing, Johns Hopkins University.

David J. C. MacKay. 1997. Ensemble learning for hidden Markov models. `http://www.inference.phy.cam.ac.uk/mackay/abstracts/ensemblePaper.html`.

Mitchell P. Marcus, Mary Ann Marcinkiewicz, and Beatrice Santorini. 1993. Building a large annotated corpus of English: The Penn Treebank. *Computational Linguistics*.

Andrew McCallum, Dayne Freitag, and Fernando Pereira. 2000. Maximum entropy Markov models for information extraction and segmentation. In *Proc. of ICML*, pages 591–598.

B. Merialdo. 1994. Tagging English text with a probabilistic model. *Computational Linguistics*, 20(2):155–171.

J.-B. Michel, Y. K. Shen, A. P. Aiden, A. Veres, M. K. Gray, W. Brockman, The Google Books Team, J. P. Pickett, D. Hoiberg, D. Clancy, P. Norvig, J. Orwant, S. Pinker, M. A. Nowak, and E. L. Aiden. 2010. Quantitative analysis of culture using millions of digitized books. *Science*, 331(6014):176–182.

Mehryar Mohri and Mark-Jan Nederhof. 2001. Regular approximation of context-free grammars through transformation. In Jean-Claude Junqua and Gertjan van Noord, editors, *Robustness in Language and Speech Technology*, chapter 9, pages 153–163. Kluwer Academic Publishers, The Netherlands, February.

Mehryar Mohri, Fernando Pereira, and Michael Riley. 2000. The design principles of a weighted finite-state transducer library. *Theoretical Computer Science*, 231(1):17–32, January.

Radford M. Neal and Geoffrey E. Hinton. 1998. A view of the EM algorithm that justifies incremental, sparse, and other variants. In M.I. Jordan, editor, *Learning in Graphical Models*, pages 355–368. Kluwer.

Mark-Jan Nederhof. 2000. Practical experiments with regular approximation of context-free languages. *Computational Linguistics*, 26(1).

Robert Parker, David Graff, Junbo Kong, Ke Chen, and Kazuaki Maeda. 2009. English Gigaword fourth edition. Linguistic Data Consortium, Philadelphia. LDC2009T13.

V. Punyakanok, D. Roth, W. Yih, and D. Zimak. 2005. Learning and inference over constrained output. In *Proc. of IJCAI*, pages 1124–1129.

Lawrence R. Rabiner. 1989. A tutorial on hidden Markov models and selected applications in speech recognition. *Proc. of the IEEE*, 77(2):257–286, February.

Sujith Ravi and Kevin Knight. 2008. Minimized models for unsupervised part-of-speech tagging. In *Proc. of ACL*, pages 504–512.

Noah A. Smith and Jason Eisner. 2005. Contrastive estimation: Training log-linear models on unlabeled data. In *Proc. of ACL*, pages 354–362.

R. Staden. 1979. A strategy of DNA sequencing employing computer programs. *Nucleic Acids Research*, 6(7):2601–2610, June.

Andreas Stolcke. 2000. Entropy-based pruning of backoff language models. In *DARPA Broadcast News Transcription and Understanding Workshop*, pages 270–274.

Kristina Toutanova and Mark Johnson. 2007. A Bayesian LDA-based model for semi-supervised part-of-speech tagging. In *Proc. of NIPS*, volume 20.

Structured Perceptron with Inexact Search

Liang Huang
Information Sciences Institute
University of Southern California
liang.huang.sh@gmail.com

Suphan Fayong
Dept. of Computer Science
University of Southern California
suphan.ying@gmail.com

Yang Guo
Bloomberg L.P.
New York, NY
yangg86@gmail.com

Abstract

Most existing theory of structured prediction assumes exact inference, which is often intractable in many practical problems. This leads to the routine use of approximate inference such as beam search but there is not much theory behind it. Based on the structured perceptron, we propose a general framework of "violation-fixing" perceptrons for inexact search with a theoretical guarantee for convergence under new separability conditions. This framework subsumes and justifies the popular heuristic "early-update" for perceptron with beam search (Collins and Roark, 2004). We also propose several new update methods within this framework, among which the "max-violation" method dramatically reduces training time (by 3 fold as compared to early-update) on state-of-the-art part-of-speech tagging and incremental parsing systems.

1 Introduction

Discriminative structured prediction algorithms such as conditional random fields (Lafferty et al., 2001), structured perceptron (Collins, 2002), max-margin markov networks (Taskar et al., 2003), and structural SVMs (Tsochantaridis et al., 2005) lead to state-of-the-art performance on many structured prediction problems such as part-of-speech tagging, sequence labeling, and parsing. But despite their success, there remains a major problem: these learning algorithms all assume exact inference (over an exponentially-large search space), which is needed to ensure their theoretical properties such as convergence. This exactness assumption, however, rarely holds in practice since exact inference is often intractable in many important problems such as machine translation (Liang et al., 2006), incremental parsing (Collins and Roark, 2004; Huang and Sagae, 2010), and bottom-up parsing (McDonald and Pereira, 2006; Huang, 2008). This leads to routine use of approximate inference such as beam search as evidenced in the above-cited papers, but the inexactness unfortunately abandons existing theoretical guarantees of the learning algorithms, and besides notable exceptions discussed below and in Section 7, little is known for *theoretical properties* of structured prediction under inexact search.

Among these notable exceptions, many examine how and which approximations break theoretical guarantees of existing learning algorithms (Kulesza and Pereira, 2007; Finley and Joachims, 2008), but we ask a deeper and practically more useful question: can we *modify* existing learning algorithms to *accommodate* the inexactness in inference, so that the theoretical properties are still maintained?

For the structured perceptron, Collins and Roark (2004) provides a partial answer: they suggest variant called "early update" for beam search, which updates on partial hypotheses when the correct solution falls out of the beam. This method works significantly better than standard perceptron, and is followed by later incremental parsers, for instance in (Zhang and Clark, 2008; Huang and Sagae, 2010). However, two problems remain: first, up till now there has been no theoretical justification for early update; and secondly, it makes learning extremely slow as witnessed by the above-cited papers because it only learns on partial examples and often requires 15–40 iterations to converge while normal perceptron converges in 5–10 iterations (Collins, 2002).

We develop a theoretical framework of "violation-fixing" perceptron that addresses these challenges. In particular, we make the following contributions:

- We show that, somewhat surprisingly, exact

search is **not** required by perceptron convergence. All we need is that each update involves a "violation", i.e., the 1-best sequence has a higher model score than the correct sequence. Such an update is considered a "valid update", and any perceptron variant that maintains this is bound to converge. We call these variants "violation-fixing perceptrons" (Section 3.1).

- This theory explains why standard perceptron update may fail to work with inexact search, because violation is no longer guaranteed: the correct structure might indeed be preferred by the model, but was pruned during the search process (Sec. 3.2). Such an update is thus considered invalid, and experiments show that invalid updates lead to bad learning (Sec. 6.2).

- We show that the early update is always valid and is thus a special case in our framework; this is the first theoretical justification for early update (Section 4). We also show that (a variant of) LaSO (Daumé and Marcu, 2005) is another special case (Section 7).

- We then propose several other update methods within this framework (Section 5). Experiments in Section 6 confirm that among them, the max-violation method can learn equal or better models with dramatically reduced learning times (by 3 fold as compared to early update) on state-of-the-art part-of-speech tagging (Collins, 2002)[1] and incremental parsing (Huang and Sagae, 2010) systems. We also found strong correlation between search error and invalid updates, suggesting that the advantage of valid update methods is more pronounced with harder inference problems.

Our techniques are widely applicable to other structured prediction problems which require inexact search like machine translation and protein folding.

2 Structured Perceptron

We review the convergence properties of the standard structured perceptron (Collins, 2002) in our own notations that will be reused in later sections for non-exact search. We first define a new concept:

[1]Incidentally, we achieve the best POS tagging accuracy to date (97.35%) on English Treebank by early update (Sec. 6.1).

Algorithm 1 Structured Perceptron (Collins, 2002).

Input: data $D = \{(x^{(t)}, y^{(t)})\}_{t=1}^{n}$ and feature map $\mathbf{\Phi}$
Output: weight vector $\mathbf{w}$
Let: $\textsc{Exact}(x, \mathbf{w}) \stackrel{\Delta}{=} \mathbf{argmax}_{s \in \mathcal{Y}(x)}\, \mathbf{w} \cdot \mathbf{\Phi}(x, s)$
Let: $\Delta\mathbf{\Phi}(x, y, z) \stackrel{\Delta}{=} \mathbf{\Phi}(x, y) - \mathbf{\Phi}(x, z)$
1: **repeat**
2:   **for each** example (x, y) **in** D **do**
3:     $z \leftarrow \textsc{Exact}(x, \mathbf{w})$
4:     **if** $z \neq y$ **then**
5:       $\mathbf{w} \leftarrow \mathbf{w} + \Delta\mathbf{\Phi}(x, y, z)$
6: **until** converged

Definition 1. The **standard confusion set** $C_s(D)$ for training data $D = \{(x^{(t)}, y^{(t)})\}_{t=1}^{n}$ is the set of triples (x, y, z) where z is a wrong label for input x:

$$C_s(D) \stackrel{\Delta}{=} \{(x, y, z) \mid (x, y) \in D, z \in \mathcal{Y}(x) - \{y\}\}.$$

The rest of the theory, including separation and violation, all builds upon this concept. We call such a triple $S = \langle D, \mathbf{\Phi}, C \rangle$ a **training scenario**, and in the remainder of this section, we assume $C = C_s(D)$, though later we will define other confusion sets to accommodate other update methods.

Definition 2. The training scenario $S = \langle D, \mathbf{\Phi}, C \rangle$ is said to be **linearly separable** (i.e., dataset D is linearly separable in C by representation $\mathbf{\Phi}$) with **margin** $\delta > 0$ if there exists an *oracle vector* $\mathbf{u}$ with $\|\mathbf{u}\| = 1$ such that it can correctly classify all examples in D (with a gap of at least δ), i.e., $\forall (x, y, z) \in C, \mathbf{u} \cdot \Delta\mathbf{\Phi}(x, y, z) \geq \delta$. We define the *maximal margin* $\delta(S)$ to be the maximal such margin over all unit oracle vectors:

$$\delta(S) \stackrel{\Delta}{=} \max_{\|\mathbf{u}\|=1} \min_{(x,y,z) \in C} \mathbf{u} \cdot \Delta\mathbf{\Phi}(x, y, z).$$

Definition 3. A triple (x, y, z) is said to be a **violation** in training scenario $S = \langle D, \mathbf{\Phi}, C \rangle$ with respect to weight vector $\mathbf{w}$ if $(x, y, z) \in C$ **and** $\mathbf{w} \cdot \Delta\mathbf{\Phi}(x, y, z) \leq 0$.

Intuitively, this means model $\mathbf{w}$ is possible to mislabel example x (though not necessarily to z) since y is not its single highest scoring label under $\mathbf{w}$.

Lemma 1. *Each update triple (x, y, z) in Algorithm 1 (line 5) is a violation in $S = \langle D, \mathbf{\Phi}, C_s(D) \rangle$.*

Proof. $z = \textsc{Exact}(x, \mathbf{w})$, thus for all $z' \in \mathcal{Y}(x)$, $\mathbf{w} \cdot \mathbf{\Phi}(x, z) \geq \mathbf{w} \cdot \mathbf{\Phi}(x, z')$, i.e., $\mathbf{w} \cdot \Delta\mathbf{\Phi}(x, y, z) \leq 0$. On the other hand, $z \in \mathcal{Y}(x)$ and $z \neq y$, so $(x, y, z) \in C_s(D)$. □

This lemma basically says exact search guarantees violation in each update, but as we will see in the convergence proof, violation itself is more fundamental than search exactness.

Definition 4. The **diameter** $R(S)$ for scenario $S = \langle D, \mathbf{\Phi}, C \rangle$ is $\max_{(x,y,z) \in C} \|\Delta\mathbf{\Phi}(x, y, z)\|$.

Theorem 1 (convergence, Collins). *For a separable training scenario $S = \langle D, \mathbf{\Phi}, C_s(D) \rangle$ with $\delta(S) > 0$, the perceptron algorithm in Algorithm 1 will make finite number of updates (before convergence):*

$$err(S) \leq R^2(S)/\delta^2(S).$$

Proof. Let $\mathbf{w}^{(k)}$ be the weight vector **before** the kth update; $\mathbf{w}^{(0)} = \mathbf{0}$. Suppose the kth update happens on the triple (x, y, z). We will bound $\|\mathbf{w}^{(k+1)}\|$ from two directions:

1. $\mathbf{w}^{(k+1)} = \mathbf{w}^{(k)} + \Delta\mathbf{\Phi}(x, y, z)$. Since scenario S is separable with max margin $\delta(S)$, there exists a unit oracle vector $\mathbf{u}$ that achieves this margin. Dot product both sides with $\mathbf{u}$, we have

$$\begin{aligned} \mathbf{u} \cdot \mathbf{w}^{(k+1)} &= \mathbf{u} \cdot \mathbf{w}^{(k)} + \mathbf{u} \cdot \Delta\mathbf{\Phi}(x, y, z) \\ &\geq \mathbf{u} \cdot \mathbf{w}^{(k)} + \delta(S) \end{aligned}$$

   by Lemma 1 that $(x, y, z) \in C_s(D)$ and by the definition of margin. By induction, we have $\mathbf{u} \cdot \mathbf{w}^{(k+1)} \geq k\delta(S)$. Since for any two vectors $\mathbf{a}$ and $\mathbf{b}$ we have $\|\mathbf{a}\|\|\mathbf{b}\| \geq \mathbf{a} \cdot \mathbf{b}$, thus $\|\mathbf{u}\|\|\mathbf{w}^{(k+1)}\| \geq \mathbf{u} \cdot \mathbf{w}^{(k+1)} \geq k\delta(S)$. As $\mathbf{u}$ is a unit vector, we have $\|\mathbf{w}^{(k+1)}\| \geq k\delta(S)$.

2. On the other hand, since $\|\mathbf{a} + \mathbf{b}\|^2 = \|\mathbf{a}\|^2 + \|\mathbf{b}\|^2 + 2\,\mathbf{a} \cdot \mathbf{b}$ for any vectors $\mathbf{a}$ and $\mathbf{b}$,we have

$$\begin{aligned} \|\mathbf{w}^{(k+1)}\|^2 &= \|\mathbf{w}^{(k)} + \Delta\mathbf{\Phi}(x, y, z)\|^2 \\ &= \|\mathbf{w}^{(k)}\|^2 + \|\Delta\mathbf{\Phi}(x, y, z)\|^2 \\ &\quad + \underline{2\,\mathbf{w}^{(k)} \cdot \Delta\mathbf{\Phi}(x, y, z)} \\ &\leq \|\mathbf{w}^{(k)}\|^2 + R^2(S) + \underline{0}. \end{aligned}$$

   By Lemma 1, the update triple is a violation so that $\mathbf{w}^{(k)} \cdot \Delta\mathbf{\Phi}(x, y, z) \leq 0$, and that $(x, y, z) \in C_s(D)$ thus $\|\Delta\mathbf{\Phi}(x, y, z)\|^2 \leq R^2(S)$ by the definition of diameter. By induction, we have $\|\mathbf{w}^{(k+1)}\|^2 \leq kR^2(S)$.

Algorithm 2 Local Violation-Fixing Perceptron.

Input: training scenario $S = \langle D, \mathbf{\Phi}, C \rangle$

repeat
  for each example (x, y) **in** D **do**
    $(x, y', z) = \textsc{FindViolation}(x, y, \mathbf{w})$
    if $z \neq y$ **then** ▷ (x, y', z) is a violation
      $\mathbf{w} \leftarrow \mathbf{w} + \Delta\mathbf{\Phi}(x, y', z)$
until converged

Combining the two bounds, we have $k^2\delta^2(S) \leq \|\mathbf{w}^{(k+1)}\|^2 \leq kR^2(S)$, thus $k \leq R^2(S)/\delta^2(S)$. □

3 Violation is All We Need

We now draw the central observation of this work from part 2 of the above proof: note that exact search (**argmax**) is **not** required in the proof, instead, it just needs a *violation*, which is a much weaker condition.[2] Exact search is simply used to ensure violation. In other words, if we can guarantee violation in each update (which we call **"valid update"**), it does not matter whether or how exact the search is.

3.1 Violation-Fixing Perceptron

This observation leads us to two generalized variants of perceptron which we call "violation-fixing perceptrons". The local version, Algorithm 2 still works on one example at a time, and searches for one violation (if any) in that example to update with. The global version, Algorithm 3, can update on any violation in the dataset at any time. We state the following generalized theorem:

Theorem 2. *For a separable training scenario S the perceptrons in Algorithms 2 and 3 both converge with the same update bounds of $R^2(S)/\delta^2(S)$ as long as the* FindViolation *and* FindViolationInData *functions always return violation triples if there are any.*

Proof. Same as the proof to Theorem 1, except for replacing Lemma 1 in part 2 by the fact that the update triples are guaranteed to be violations. (Note a violation triple is by definition in the confusion set, thus we can still use separation and diameter). □

These generic violation-fixing perceptron algorithms can been seen as "interfaces" (or APIs),

[2] Crammer and Singer (2003) further demonstrates that a convex combination of violations can also be used for update.

Algorithm 3 Global Violation-Fixing Perceptron.

Input: training scenario $S = \langle D, \mathbf{\Phi}, C \rangle$

repeat
  $(x, y, z) \leftarrow$ FINDVIOLATIONINDATA$(C, \mathbf{w})$
  if $x = \epsilon$ **then break** ▷ no more violation?
  $\mathbf{w} \leftarrow \mathbf{w} + \Delta\mathbf{\Phi}(x, y, z)$
until converged

data $D = \{(x, y)\}$:

x	fruit	flies	fly	.
y	N	N	V	.

search space: $\mathcal{Y}(x) = \{\text{N}\} \times \{\text{N}, \text{V}\} \times \{\text{N}, \text{V}\} \times \{.\}$.

feature map: $\mathbf{\Phi}(x, y) = (\#_{\text{N}\to\text{N}}(y),\ \#_{\text{V}\to.}(y))$.

iter	label z	$\Delta\mathbf{\Phi}(x, y, z)$	$\mathbf{w} \cdot \Delta\mathbf{\Phi}$		new $\mathbf{w}$
0					$(0, 0)$
1	N N N .	$(-1, +1)$	0	✓	$(-1, 1)$
2	N V N .	$(+1, +1)$	0	✓	$(0, 2)$
3	N N N .	$(-1, +1)$	2	×	$(-1, 3)$
4	N V N .	$(+1, +1)$	2	×	$(0, 4)$

... infinite loop ...

Figure 1: Example that standard perceptron does not converge with greedy search on a *separable* scenario (e.g. $\mathbf{u} = (1, 2)$ can separate D with exact search).

where later sections will supply different implementations of the FINDVIOLATION and FINDVIOLATIONINDATA subroutines, thus establishing alternative update methods for inexact search as special cases in this general framework.

3.2 Non-Convergence with Inexact Search

What if we can not guarantee valid updates? Well, the convergence proof in Theorems 1 and 2 would break in part 2. This is exactly why standard structured perceptron may not work well with inexact search: with search errors it is no longer possible to guarantee violation in each update. For example, an inexact search method explores a (proper) subset of the search space $\mathcal{Y}'_{\mathbf{w}}(x) \subsetneq \mathcal{Y}(x)$, and finds a label

$$z = \operatorname*{\mathbf{argmax}}_{s \in \mathcal{Y}'_{\mathbf{w}}(x)} \mathbf{w} \cdot \mathbf{\Phi}(x, s).$$

It is possible that the correct label y is outside of the explored subspace, and yet has a higher score: $\Delta\mathbf{\Phi}(x, y, z) > 0$ but $y \notin \mathcal{Y}'_{\mathbf{w}}(x)$. In this case, (x, y, z) is *not* a violation, which breaks the proof. We show below that this situation actually exists.

Algorithm 4 Greedy Search.

Let: NEXT$(x, z) \triangleq \{z \circ a \mid a \in \mathcal{Y}_{|z|+1}(x)\}$ ▷ set of possible one-step extensions (successors)

BEST$(x, z, \mathbf{w}) \triangleq \mathbf{argmax}_{z' \in \text{NEXT}(x,z)}\ \mathbf{w} \cdot \mathbf{\Phi}(x, z')$
▷ best one-step extension based on history

function GREEDYSEARCH$(x, \mathbf{w})$
  $z \leftarrow \epsilon$ ▷ empty sequence
  for $i \in 1 \ldots |x|$ **do**
    $z \leftarrow$ BEST$(x, z, \mathbf{w})$
  return z

Theorem 3. *For a separable training scenario* $S = \langle D, \mathbf{\Phi}, C_s(D) \rangle$, *if the* **argmax** *in Algorithm 1 is not exact, the perceptron might not converge.*

Proof. See the example in Figure 1. □

This situation happens very often in NLP: often the search space $\mathcal{Y}(x)$ is too big either because it does not factor locally, or because it is still too big after factorization, which requires some approximate search. In either case, updating the model $\mathbf{w}$ on a non-violation (i.e., "invalid") triple (x, y, z) does not make sense: it is **not** the model's problem: $\mathbf{w}$ does score the correct label y higher than the incorrect z; rather, it is a problem of the search, or its interaction with the model that prunes away the correct (sub)sequence during the search.

What shall we do in this case? Collins and Roark (2004) suggest that instead of the standard full update, we should only update on the prefix $(x, y_{[1:i]}, z_{[1:i]})$ up to the point i where the correct sequence falls off the beam. This intuitively makes a lot of sense, since up to i we can still guarantee violation, but after i we may not. The next section formalizes this intuition.

4 Early Update is Violation-Fixing

We now proceed to show that early update is always valid and it is thus a special case of the violation-fixing perceptron framework. First, let us study the simplest special case, greedy search (beam=1).

4.1 Greedy Search and Early Update

Greedy search is the simplest form of inexact search. Shown in Algorithm 4, at each position, we commit to the single best action (e.g., tag for the current word) given the previous actions and continue to the

√	√	···	√	×	
⟵	update		⟶	skip ⟶	

Figure 2: Early update at the first error in greedy search.

Algorithm 5 Early update for greedy search adapted from Collins and Roark (2004).

Input: training scenario $S = \langle D, \mathbf{\Phi}, C_{\mathrm{g}}(D)\rangle$

repeat
  for each example (x, y) **in** D **do**
    $z \leftarrow \epsilon$ ▷ empty sequence
    for $i \in 1 \ldots |x|$ **do**
      $z \leftarrow \textsc{Best}(x, z, \mathbf{w})$
      if $z_i \neq y_i$ **then** ▷ first wrong action
        $\mathbf{w} \leftarrow \mathbf{w} + \Delta\mathbf{\Phi}(x, y_{[1:i]}, z)$ ▷ early update
        break ▷ skip the rest of this example
until converged

next position. The notation $\mathcal{Y}_i(x)$ denotes the set of possible actions at position i for example x (for instance, the set of possible tags for a word).

The early update heuristic, originally proposed for beam search (Collins and Roark, 2004), now simplifies into "update at the first wrong action", since this is exactly the place where the correct sequence falls off the singleton beam (see Algorithm 5 for pseudocode and Fig. 2). Informally, it is easy to show (below) that this kind of update is always a valid violation, but we need to redefine confusion set.

Definition 5. The **greedy confusion set** $C_{\mathrm{g}}(D)$ for training data $D = \{(x^{(t)}, y^{(t)})\}_{t=1}^{n}$ is the set of triples $(x, y_{[1:i]}, z_{[1:i]})$ where $y_{[1:i]}$ is a i-prefix of the correct label y, and $z_{[1:i]}$ is an incorrect i-prefix that agrees with the correct prefix on all decisions except the last one:

$$C_{\mathrm{g}}(D) \triangleq \{(x, y_{[1:i]}, z_{[1:i]}) \mid (x, y, z) \in C_{\mathrm{s}}(D), \\ 1 \leq i \leq |y|, z_{[1:i-1]} = y_{[1:i-1]}, z_i \neq y_i\}.$$

We can see intuitively that this new defintion is specially tailored to the early updates in greedy search. The concepts of separation/margin, violation, and diameter all change accordingly with this new confusion set. In particular, we say that a dataset D is **greedily separable** in representation $\mathbf{\Phi}$ if and only if $\langle D, \mathbf{\Phi}, C_{\mathrm{g}}(D)\rangle$ is linearly separable, and we say (x, y', z') is a **greedy violation** if $(x, y', z') \in C_{\mathrm{g}}(D)$ and $\mathbf{w} \cdot \Delta\mathbf{\Phi}(x, y', z') \leq 0$.

Algorithm 6 Alternative presentation of Alg. 5 as a Local Violation-Fixing Perceptron (Alg. 2).

1: **function** $\textsc{FindViolation}(x, y, \mathbf{w})$
2:   $z \leftarrow \epsilon$ ▷ empty sequence
3:   **for** $i \in 1 \ldots |x|$ **do**
4:     $z \leftarrow \textsc{Best}(x, z, \mathbf{w})$
5:     **if** $z_i \neq y_i$ **then** ▷ first wrong action
6:       **return** $(x, y_{[1:i]}, z)$ ▷ return for early update
7:   **return** (x, y, y) ▷ success ($z = y$), no violation

We now express early update for greedy search (Algorithm 5) in terms of violation-fixing perceptron. Algorithm 6 implements the FINDVIOLATION function for the generic Local Violation-Fixing Perceptron in Algorithm 2. Thus Algorithm 5 is equivalent to Algorithm 6 plugged into Algorithm 2.

Lemma 2. *Each triple $(x, y_{[1:i]}, z)$ returned at line 6 in Algorithm 6 is a greedy violation.*

Proof. Let $y' = y_{[1:i]}$. Clearly at line 6, $|y'| = i = |z|$ and $y'_i \neq z_i$. But $y'_j = z_j$ for all $j < i$ otherwise it would have returned before position i, so $(x, y', z) \in C_{\mathrm{g}}(D)$. Also $z = \textsc{Best}(x, z, \mathbf{w})$, so $\mathbf{w} \cdot \mathbf{\Phi}(x, z) \geq \mathbf{w} \cdot \mathbf{\Phi}(x, y')$, thus $\mathbf{w} \cdot \Delta\mathbf{\Phi}(x, y', z) \leq 0$. □

Theorem 4 (convergence of greedy search with early update)**.** *For a separable training scenario $S = \langle D, \mathbf{\Phi}, C_{\mathrm{g}}(D)\rangle$, the early update perceptron by plugging Algorithm 6 into Algorithm 2 will make finite number of updates (before convergence):*

$$err(S) < R^2(S)/\delta^2(S).$$

Proof. By Lemma 2 and Theorem 2. □

4.2 Beam Search and Early Update

To formalize beam search, we need some notations:

Definition 6 (k-best)**.** We denote $\mathbf{argtop}^{k}_{z \in \mathcal{Z}} f(z)$ to return (a sorted list of) the top k **unique** z in terms of $f(z)$, i.e., it returns a list $\mathcal{B} = [z^{(1)}, z^{(2)}, \ldots, z^{(k)}]$ where $z^{(i)} \in \mathcal{Z}$ and $f(z^{(1)}) \geq f(z^{(2)}) \geq \ldots \geq f(z^{(k)}) \geq f(z')$ for all $z' \in \mathcal{Z} - \mathcal{B}$.

By unique we mean that no two elements are equivalent with respect to some equivalence relation, i.e., $z^{(i)} \equiv z^{(j)} \Rightarrow i = j$. This equivalence relation is useful for dynamic programming (when used with beam search). For example, in trigram tagging, two tag sequences are equivalent if they are of the

Algorithm 7 Beam-Search.

$\textsc{Best}_k(x, \mathcal{B}, \mathbf{w}) \triangleq \mathbf{argtop}^k_{z' \in \cup_{z \in \mathcal{B}} \textsc{Next}(z)} \mathbf{w} \cdot \mathbf{\Phi}(x, z')$
  ▷ top k (unique) extensions from the beam

1: **function** $\textsc{BeamSearch}(x, \mathbf{w}, k)$ ▷ k is beam width
2:   $\mathcal{B}_0 \leftarrow [\epsilon]$ ▷ initial beam
3:   **for** $i \in 1 \ldots |x|$ **do**
4:     $\mathcal{B}_i \leftarrow \textsc{Best}_k(x, \mathcal{B}_{i-1}, \mathbf{w})$
5:   **return** $\mathcal{B}_{|x|}[0]$ ▷ best sequence in the final beam

Algorithm 8 Early update for beam search (Collins and Roark 04) as Local Violation-Fixing Perceptron.

1: **function** $\textsc{FindViolation}(x, y, \mathbf{w})$
2:   $\mathcal{B}_0 \leftarrow [\epsilon]$
3:   **for** $i \in 1 \ldots |x|$ **do**
4:     $\mathcal{B}_i \leftarrow \textsc{Best}_k(x, \mathcal{B}_{i-1}, \mathbf{w})$
5:     **if** $y_{[1:i]} \notin \mathcal{B}_i$ **then** ▷ correct seq. falls off beam
6:       **return** $(x, y_{[1:i]}, \mathcal{B}_i[0])$ ▷ update on prefix
7:   **return** $(x, y, \mathcal{B}_{|x|}[0])$ ▷ full update if wrong final

same length and if they agree on the last two tags, i.e. $z \equiv z'$ iff. $|z| = |z'|$ and $z_{|z|-1:|z|} = z'_{|z|-1:|z|}$. In incremental parsing this equivalence relation could be relevant bits of information on the last few trees on the stack (depending on feature templates), as suggested in (Huang and Sagae, 2010). [3]

Algorithm 7 shows the pseudocode for beam search. It is trivial to verify that greedy search is a special case of beam search with $k = 1$. However, the definition of confusion set changes considerably:

Definition 7. The **beam confusion set** $C_b(D)$ for training data $D = \{(x^{(t)}, y^{(t)})\}_{t=1}^n$ is the set of triples $(x, y_{[1:i]}, z_{[1:i]})$ where $y_{[1:i]}$ is a i-prefix of the correct label y, and $z_{[1:i]}$ is an incorrect i-prefix that differs from the correct prefix (in at least one place):

$$C_b(D) \triangleq \{(x, y_{[1:i]}, z_{[1:i]}) \mid (x, y, z) \in C_s(D), \\ 1 \le i \le |y|, z_{[1:i]} \neq y_{[1:i]}\}.$$

Similarly, we say that a dataset D is **beam separable** in representation $\mathbf{\Phi}$ if and only if

[3]Note that when checking whether the correct sequence falls off the beam (line 5), we could either store the whole (sub)sequence for each candidate in the beam (which is what we do for non-DP anyway), or check if the equivalence class of the correct sequence is in the beam, i.e. $[\![y_{[1:i]}]\!]_\equiv \in \mathcal{B}_i$, and if its backpointer points to $[\![y_{[1:i-1]}]\!]_\equiv$. For example, in trigram tagging, we just check if $\langle y_{i-1}, y_i \rangle \in \mathcal{B}_i$ and if its backpointer points to $\langle y_{i-2}, y_{i-1} \rangle$.

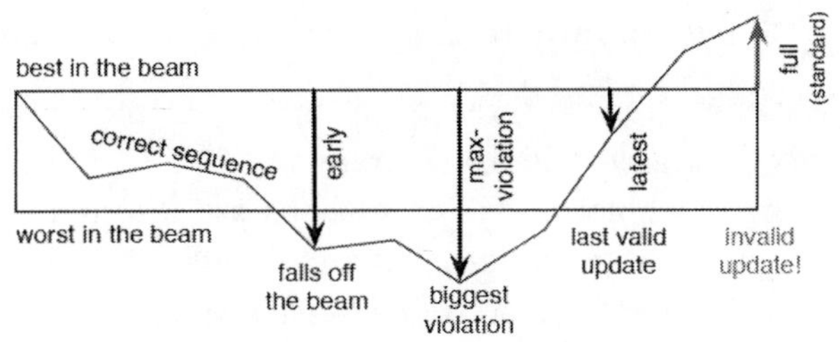

Figure 3: Illustration of various update methods: early, max-violation, latest, and standard (full) update, in the case when standard update is invalid (shown in red). The rectangle denotes the beam and the blue line segments denote the trajectory of the correct sequence.

$\langle D, \mathbf{\Phi}, C_b(D) \rangle$ is linearly separable, and we say (x, y', z') is a **beam violation** if $(x, y', z') \in C_b(D)$ and $\mathbf{w} \cdot \Delta\mathbf{\Phi}(x, y', z') \le 0$.

It is easy to verify that beam confusion set is superset of both greedy and standard confusion sets: for all dataset D, $C_g(D) \subsetneq C_b(D)$, and $C_s(D) \subsetneq C_b(D)$. This means that beam separability is the strongest condition among the three separabilities:

Theorem 5. *If a dataset D is beam separable, then it is also greedily and (standard) linear separable.*

We now present early update for beam search as a Local Violation Fixing Perceptron in Algorithm 8. See Figure 3 for an illustration.

Lemma 3. *Each update (lines 6 or 7 in Algorithm 8) involves a beam violation.*

Proof. Case 1: early update (line 6): Let $z' = \mathcal{B}_i[0]$ and $y' = y_{[1:i]}$. Case 2: full update (line 8): Let $z' = \mathcal{B}_{|x|}[0]$ and $y' = y$. In both cases we have $z' \neq y'$ and $|z'| = |y'|$, thus $(x, y', z') \in C_b(D)$. Also we have $\mathbf{w} \cdot \mathbf{\Phi}(x, z') \ge \mathbf{w} \cdot \mathbf{\Phi}(x, y')$ by defintion of **argtop**, so $\mathbf{w} \cdot \Delta\mathbf{\Phi}(x, y', z') \le 0$. □

Theorem 6 (convergence of beam search with early update). *For a separable training scenario $S = \langle D, \mathbf{\Phi}, C_b(D) \rangle$, the early update perceptron by plugging Algorithm 8 into Algorithm 2 will make finite number of updates (before convergence):*

$$err(S) < R^2(S)/\delta^2(S).$$

Proof. By Lemma 3 and Theorem 2. □

5 New Update Methods for Inexact Search

We now propose three novel update methods for inexact search within the framework of violation-fixing perceptron. These methods are inspired by early update but addresses its very limitation of slow learning. See Figure 3 for an illustration.

1. **"hybrid" update.** When the standard update is valid (i.e., a violation), we perform it, otherwise we perform the early update.

2. **"max-violation" update.** While there are more than one possible violations on one example x, we choose the triple that is most violated:

$$(x, y^*, z^*) = \underset{(x,y',z') \in C, z' \in \cup_i \{B_i[0]\}}{\mathbf{argmin}} \mathbf{w} \cdot \Delta\Phi(x, y', z').$$

3. **"latest" update.** Contrary to early update, we can also choose the latest point where the update is still a violation:

$$(x, y^*, z^*) = \underset{(x,y',z') \in C, z' \in \cup_i \{B_i[0]\}, \mathbf{w} \cdot \Delta\Phi(x,y',z') > 0}{\mathbf{argmax}} |z'|.$$

All these three methods go beyond early update but can be represented in the Local Violation Fixing Perceptron (Algorithm 2), and are thus all guaranteed to converge. As we will see in the experiments, these new methods are motivated to address the major limitation of early update, that is, it learns too slowly since it only updates on prefixes and neglect the rest of the examples. Hybrid update is trying to do as much standard ("full") updates as possible, and latest update further addresses the case when standard update is invalid: instead of backing-off to early update, it uses the longest possible update.

6 Experiments

We conduct experiments on two typical structured learning tasks: part-of-speech tagging with a trigram model where exact search is possible, and incremental dependency parsing with arbitrary non-local features where exact search is intractable. We run both experiments on state-of-the-art implementations.

6.1 Part-of-Speech Tagging

Following the standard split for part-of-speech tagging introduced by Collins (2002), we use sections 00–18 of the Penn Treebank (Marcus et al., 1993) for training, sections 19–21 as a held-out development set, and sections 22–24 for testing. Our baseline system is a faithful implementation of the perceptron tagger in Collins (2002), i.e., a trigram model with spelling features from Ratnaparkhi (1996), except that we replace one-count words as <unk>. With standard perceptron and exact search, our baseline system performs slightly better than Collins (2002) with a beam of 20 (M. Collins, p.c.).

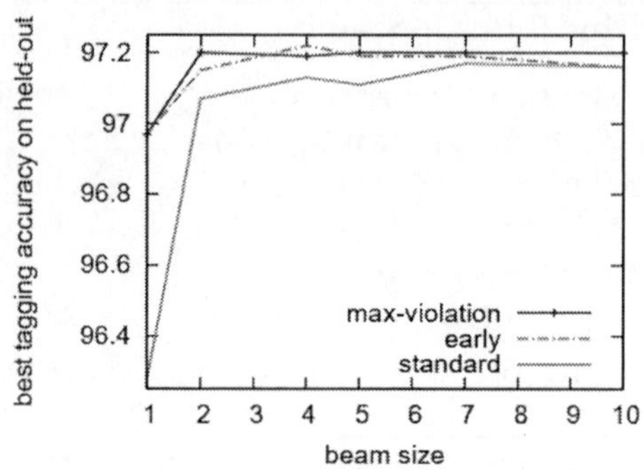

Figure 4: POS tagging using beam search with various update methods (hybrid/latest similar to early; omitted).

	$b=1$		$b=2$		$b=7$	
method	it	dev	it	dev	it	dev
standard	12	96.27	6	97.07	**4**	97.17
early	13	**96.97**	6	97.15	7	97.19
max-viol.	**7**	**96.97**	**3**	**97.20**	**4**	**97.20**

Table 1: Convergence rate of part-of-speech tagging. In general, max-violation converges faster and better than early and standard updates, esp. in smallest beams.

We then implemented beam search on top of dynamic programming and experimented with standard, early, hybrid, and max-violation update methods with various beam settings ($b = 1, 2, 4, 7, 10$). Figure 4(a) summarizes these experiments. We observe that, first of all, the standard update performs poorly with the smallest beams, esp. at $b = 1$ (greedy search), when search error is the most severe causing lots of invalid updates (see Figure 5). Secondly,max-violation is almost consistently the best-performing method (except for $b = 4$). Table 1 shows convergence rates, where max-violation update also converges faster than early and standard methods. In particular, at $b = 1$, it achieves a 19% error reduction over standard update, while converg-

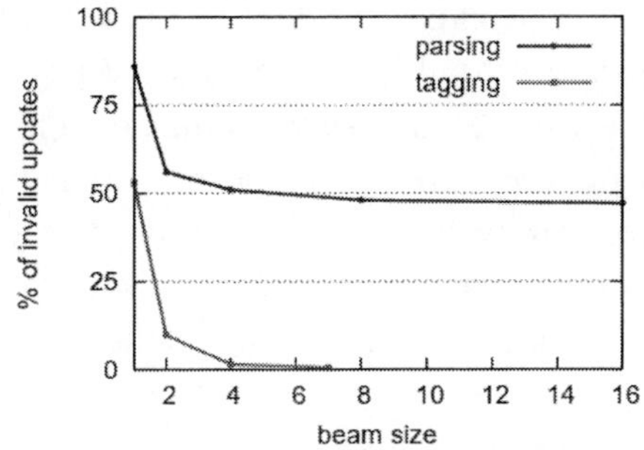

Figure 5: Percentages of invalid updates for standard update. In tagging it quickly drops to 0% while in parsing it converges to $\sim 50\%$. This means search-wise, parsing is much harder than tagging, which explains why standard update does OK in tagging but terribly in parsing. The harder the search is, the more needed valid updates are.

method	b	it	time	dev	test
standard*	∞	6	162 m	97.17	97.28
early	4	6	37 m	**97.22**	**97.35**
hybrid	5	5	30 m	97.18	97.19
latest	7	5	45 m	97.17	97.13
max-viol.	**2**	3	**26 m**	97.20	97.33
standard	20	Collins (2002)			97.11
guided	3	Shen et al. (2007)			97.33

Table 2: Final test results on POS tagging. *:baseline.

method	b	it	time	dev	test
early*		38	15.4 h	92.24	92.09
standard		1	0.4 h	*78.99*	*79.14*
hybrid	8	11	5.6 h	92.26	91.95
latest		9	4.5 h	92.06	91.96
max-viol.		12	5.5 h	**92.32**	**92.18**
early	8	Huang & Sagae 2010			92.1

Table 3: Final results on incremental parsing. *: baseline.

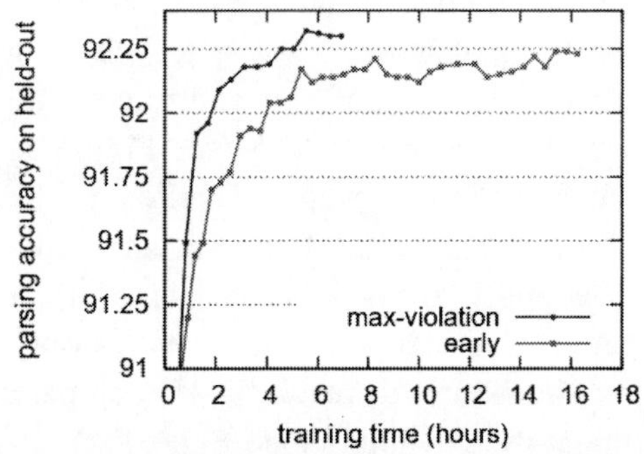

Figure 6: Training progress curves for incremental parsing ($b = 8$). Max-violation learns faster and better: it takes 4.6 hours (10 iterations) to reach 92.25 on held-out, compared with early update's 15.4 hours (38 iterations), even though the latter is faster in each iteration due to early stopping (esp. at the first few iterations).

ing twice as fast as early update.[4] This agrees with our intuition that by choosing the "most-violated" triple for update, the perceptron should learn faster.

Table 2 presents the final tagging results on the test set. For each of the five update methods, we choose the beam size at which it achieves the highest accuracy on the held-out. For standard update, its best held-out accuracy 97.17 is indeed achieved by exact search (i.e., $b = +\infty$) since it does not work well with beam search, but it costs 2.7 hours (162 minutes) to train. By contrast, the four valid update methods handle beam search better. The max-violation method achieves its highest held-out/test accuracies of 97.20 / 97.33 with a beam size of only 2, and only 26 minutes to train. Early update achieves the highest held-out/test accuracies of 97.22 / **97.35** across all update methods at the beam size of 4. This test accuracy is even better than Shen et al. (2007), the best tagging accuracy reported on the Penn Treebank to date.[5,6] To conclude, with valid update methods, we can learn a better tagging model with 5 times faster training than exact search.

6.2 Incremental Parsing

While part-of-speech tagging is mainly a proof of concept, incremental parsing is much harder since non-local features rules out exact inference.

We use the standard split for parsing: secs 02–21 for training, 22 as held-out, and 23 for testing. Our baseline system is a faithful reimplementation of the beam-search dynamic programming parser of Huang and Sagae (2010). Like most incremental parsers, it used early update as search error is severe.

[4]for tagging (but not parsing) the difference in per-iteration speed between early update and max-violation update is small.

[5]according to ACL Wiki: http://aclweb.org/aclwiki/.

[6]Note that Shen et al. (2007) employ contextual features up to 5-gram which go beyond our local trigram window. We suspect that adding *genuinely* non-local features would demonstrate even better the advantages of valid update methods with beam search, since exact inference will no longer be tractable.

We first confirm that, as reported by Huang and Sagae, early update learns very slowly, reaching 92.24 on held-out with 38 iterations (15.4 hours).

We then experimented with the other update methods: standard, hybrid, latest, and max-violation, with beam size $b = 1, 2, 4, 8$. We found that, first of all, the standard update performs horribly on this task: at $b = 1$ it only achieves 60.04% on held-out, while at $b = 8$ it improves to 78.99% but is still vastly below all other methods. This is because search error is much more severe in incremental parsing (than in part-of-speech tagging), thus standard update produces an enormous amount of invalid updates even at $b = 8$ (see Figure 5). This suggests that the advantage of valid update methods is more pronounced with tougher search problems. Secondly, max-violation learns much faster (and better) than early update: it takes only 10 iterations (4.6 hours) to reach 92.25, compared with early update's 15.4 hours (see Fig. 6). At its peak, max-violation achieves 92.18 on test which is better than (Huang and Sagae, 2010). To conclude, we can train a parser with only 1/3 of training time with max-violation update, and the harder the search is, the more needed the valid update methods are.

7 Related Work and Discussions

Besides the early update method of Collins and Roark (2004) which inspired us, this work is also related to the **LaSO** method of Daumé and Marcu (2005). LaSO is similar to early update, except that after each update, instead of skipping the rest of the example, LaSO *continues* on the same example with the correct hypothesis. For example, in the greedy case LaSO is just replacing the **break** statement in Algorithm 5 by

$$8': \quad z_i = y_i$$

and in beam search it is replacing it with

$$8': \quad \mathcal{B}_i = [y_{[1:i]}].$$

This is beyond our Local Violation-Fixing Perceptron since it makes more than one updates on one example, but can be easily represented as a Global Violation-Fixing Perceptron (Algorithm 3), since we can prove any further updates on this example is a violation (under the new weights). We thus establish LaSO as a special case within our framework.[7]

More interestingly, it is easy to verify that the greedy case of LaSO update is equivalent to training a local **unstructured** perceptron which **independently** classifies at each position based on history, which is related to SEARN (Daumé et al., 2009).

Kulesza and Pereira (2007) study perceptron learning with approximate inference that *overgenerates* instead of *undergenerates* as in our work, but the underlying idea is similar: by learning in a harder setting (LP-relaxed version in their case and prefix-augmented version in our case) we can learn the simpler original setting. Our "beam separability" can be viewed as an instance of their "algorithmic separability". Finley and Joachims (2008) study similar approximate inference for structural SVMs.

Our max-violation update is also related to other training methods for large-margin structured prediction, in particular the cutting-plane (Joachims et al., 2009) and subgradient (Ratliff et al., 2007) methods, but detailed exploration is left to future work.

8 Conclusions

We have presented a unifying framework of "violation-fixing" perceptron which guarantees convergence with inexact search. This theory satisfingly explained why standard perceptron might not work well with inexact search, and why the early update works. We also proposed some new variants within this framework, among which the max-violation method performs the best on state-of-the-art tagging and parsing systems, leading to better models with greatly reduced training times. Lastly, the advantage of valid update methods is more pronounced when search error is severe.

Acknowledgements

We are grateful to the four anonymous reviewers, especially the one who wrote the comprehensive review. We also thank David Chiang, Kevin Knight, Ben Taskar, Alex Kulesza, Joseph Keshet, David McAllester, Mike Collins, Sasha Rush, and Fei Sha for discussions. This work is supported in part by a Google Faculty Research Award to the first author.

[7] It turns out the original theorem in the LaSO paper (Daumé and Marcu, 2005) contains a bug; see (Xu et al., 2009) for corrections. Thanks to a reviewer for pointing it out.

References

Collins, Michael. 2002. Discriminative training methods for hidden markov models: Theory and experiments with perceptron algorithms. In *Proceedings of EMNLP*.

Collins, Michael and Brian Roark. 2004. Incremental parsing with the perceptron algorithm. In *Proceedings of ACL*.

Crammer, Koby and Yoram Singer. 2003. Ultraconservative online algorithms for multiclass problems. *Journal of Machine Learning Research (JMLR)*, 3:951–991.

Daumé, Hal, John Langford, and Daniel Marcu. 2009. Search-based structured prediction.

Daumé, Hal and Daniel Marcu. 2005. Learning as search optimization: Approximate large margin methods for structured prediction. In *Proceedings of ICML*.

Finley, Thomas and Thorsten Joachims. 2008. Training structural SVMs when exact inference is intractable. In *Proceedings of ICML*.

Huang, Liang. 2008. Forest reranking: Discriminative parsing with non-local features. In *Proceedings of the ACL: HLT*, Columbus, OH, June.

Huang, Liang and Kenji Sagae. 2010. Dynamic programming for linear-time incremental parsing. In *Proceedings of ACL 2010*.

Joachims, T., T. Finley, and Chun-Nam Yu. 2009. Cutting plane training of structural svms. *Machine Learning*, 77(1):27–59.

Kulesza, Alex and Fernando Pereira. 2007. Structured learning with approximate inference. In *NIPS*.

Lafferty, John, Andrew McCallum, and Fernando Pereira. 2001. Conditional random fields: Probabilistic models for segmenting and labeling sequence data. In *Proceedings of ICML*.

Liang, Percy, Alexandre Bouchard-Côté, Dan Klein, and Ben Taskar. 2006. An end-to-end discriminative approach to machine translation. In *Proceedings of COLING-ACL*, Sydney, Australia, July.

Marcus, Mitchell P., Beatrice Santorini, and Mary Ann Marcinkiewicz. 1993. Building a large annotated corpus of English: the Penn Treebank. *Computational Linguistics*, 19:313–330.

McDonald, Ryan and Fernando Pereira. 2006. Online learning of approximate dependency parsing algorithms. In *Proceedings of EACL*.

Ratliff, Nathan, J. Andrew Bagnell, and Martin Zinkevich. 2007. (online) subgradient methods for structured prediction. In *Proceedings of AIStats*.

Ratnaparkhi, Adwait. 1996. A maximum entropy model for part-of-speech tagging. In *Proceedings of EMNLP*.

Shen, Libin, Giorgio Satta, and Aravind Joshi. 2007. Guided learning for bidirectional sequence classification. In *Proceedings of ACL*.

Taskar, Ben, Carlos Guestrin, and Daphne Koller. 2003. Max-margin markov networks. In *Proceedings of NIPS*. MIT Press.

Tsochantaridis, I., T. Joachims, T. Hofmann, and Y. Altun. 2005. Large margin methods for structured and interdependent output variables. *Journal of Machine Learning Research*, 6:1453–1484.

Xu, Yuehua, Alan Fern, and Sungwook Yoon. 2009. Learning linear ranking functions for beam search with application to planning. *Journal of Machine Learning Research (JMLR)*, 10:1349–1388.

Zhang, Yue and Stephen Clark. 2008. A tale of two parsers: investigating and combining graph-based and transition-based dependency parsing using beam-search. In *Proceedings of EMNLP*.

Segmentation Similarity and Agreement

Chris Fournier
University of Ottawa
Ottawa, ON, Canada
cfour037@eecs.uottawa.ca

Diana Inkpen
University of Ottawa
Ottawa, ON, Canada
diana@eecs.uottawa.ca

Abstract

We propose a new segmentation evaluation metric, called *segmentation similarity* (S), that quantifies the similarity between two segmentations as the proportion of boundaries that are not transformed when comparing them using edit distance, essentially using edit distance as a penalty function and scaling penalties by segmentation size. We propose several adapted inter-annotator agreement coefficients which use S that are suitable for segmentation. We show that S is configurable enough to suit a wide variety of segmentation evaluations, and is an improvement upon the state of the art. We also propose using inter-annotator agreement coefficients to evaluate automatic segmenters in terms of human performance.

1 Introduction

Segmentation is the task of splitting up an item, such as a document, into a sequence of segments by placing boundaries within. The purpose of segmenting can vary greatly, but one common objective is to denote shifts in the topic of a text, where multiple boundary types can also be present (*e.g.*, major versus minor topic shifts). Human-competitive automatic segmentation methods can help a wide range of computational linguistic tasks which depend upon the identification of segment boundaries in text.

To evaluate automatic segmentation methods, a method of comparing an automatic segmenter's performance against the segmentations produced by human judges (coders) is required. Current methods of performing this comparison designate only one coder's segmentation as a reference to compare against. A single "true" reference segmentation from a coder should not be trusted, given that inter-annotator agreement is often reported to be rather poor (Hearst, 1997, p. 54). Additionally, to ensure that an automatic segmenter does not over-fit to the preference and bias of one particular coder, an automatic segmenter should be compared directly against multiple coders.

The state of the art segmentation evaluation metrics (P_k and WindowDiff) slide a window across a designated reference and hypothesis segmentation, and count the number of windows where the number of boundaries differ. Window-based methods suffer from a variety of problems, including: i) unequal penalization of error types; ii) an arbitrarily defined window size parameter (whose choice greatly affects outcomes); iii) lack of clear intuition; iv) inapplicability to multiply-coded corpora; and v) reliance upon a "true" reference segmentation.

In this paper, we propose a new method of comparing two segmentations, called *segmentation similarity* [1] (S), that: i) equally penalizes all error types (unless explicitly configured otherwise); ii) appropriately responds to scenarios tested; iii) defines no arbitrary parameters; iv) is intuitive; and v) is adapted for use in a variety of popular inter-annotator agreement coefficients to handle multiply-coded corpora; and vi) does not rely upon a "true" reference segmentation (it is symmetric). Capitalizing on the adapted inter-annotator agreement coefficients, the relative difficulty that human segmenters have with various segmentation tasks can now be quantified. We also propose that these coefficients can be used to evaluate and compare automatic segmentation methods in terms of human agreement.

This paper is organized as follows. In Section 2, we review segmentation evaluation and inter-annotator agreement. In Section 3, we present S and

[1] A software implementation of segmentation similarity (S) is available at http://nlp.chrisfournier.ca/

inter-annotator agreement coefficient adaptations. In Section 4, we evaluate S and WindowDiff in various scenarios and simulations, and upon a multiply-coded corpus.

2 Related Work

2.1 Segmentation Evaluation

Precision, recall, and their mean (F_β-measure) have been previously applied to segmentation evaluation. Precision is the proportion of boundaries chosen that agree with a reference segmentation, and recall is the proportion of boundaries chosen that agree with a reference segmentation out of all boundaries in the reference and hypothesis (Pevzner and Hearst, 2002, p. 3). For segmentation, these metrics are unsuitable because they penalize near-misses of boundaries as full-misses, causing them to drastically overestimate the error. Near-misses are prevalent in segmentation and can account for a large proportion of the errors produced by a coder, and as inter-annotator agreement often shows, they do not reflect coder error, but the difficulty of the task.

P_k (Beeferman and Berger, 1999, pp. 198–200)[2] is a window-based metric which attempts to solve the harsh near-miss penalization of precision, recall, and F_β-measure. In P_k, a window of size k, where k is defined as half of the mean reference segment size, is slid across the text to compute penalties. A penalty of 1 is assigned for each window whose boundaries are detected to be in different segments of the reference and hypothesis segmentations, and this count is normalized by the number of windows.

Pevzner and Hearst (2002, pp. 5–10) highlighted a number of issues with P_k, specifically that: i) False negatives (FNs) are penalized more than false positives (FPs); ii) It does not penalize FPs that fall within k units of a reference boundary; iii) Its sensitivity to variations in segment size can cause it to linearly decrease the penalty for FPs if the size of any segments fall below k; and iv) Near-miss errors are too harshly penalized.

To attempt to mitigate the shortcomings of P_k, Pevzner and Hearst (2002, p. 10) proposed a modified metric which changed how penalties were counted, named *WindowDiff* (WD). A window of size k is still slid across the text, but now penalties are attributed to windows where the number of boundaries in each segmentation differs (see Equation 1, where $\mathrm{b}(R_{ij})$ and $\mathrm{b}(H_{ij})$ represents the number of boundaries within the segments in a window of size k from position i to j, and N the number of sentences plus one), with the same normalization.

$$\mathrm{WD}(R,H) = \frac{1}{N-k} \sum_{i=1,j=i+k}^{N-k} \left(|\mathrm{b}(R_{ij}) - \mathrm{b}(H_{ij})| > 0\right) \quad (1)$$

WindowDiff is able to reduce, but not eliminate, sensitivity to segment size, gives more equal weights to both FPs and FNs (FNs are, in effect, penalized less[3]), and is able to catch mistakes in both small and large segments. It is not without issues though; Lamprier et al. (2007) demonstrated that WindowDiff penalizes errors less at the beginning and end of a segmentation (this is corrected by padding the segmentation at each end by size k). Additionally, variations in the window size k lead to difficulties in interpreting and comparing WindowDiff's values, and the intuition of the method remains vague.

Franz et al. (2007) proposed measuring performance in terms of the number of words that are FNs and FPs, normalized by the number of word positions present (see Equation 2).

$$R_{FN} = \frac{1}{N} \sum_w FN(w), \quad R_{FP} = \frac{1}{N} \sum_w FP(w) \quad (2)$$

R_{FN} and R_{FP} have the advantage that they take into account the severity of an error in terms of segment size, allowing them to reflect the effects of erroneously missing, or added, words in a segment better than window based metrics. Unfortunately, R_{FN} and R_{FP} suffer from the same flaw as precision, recall, and F_β-measure in that they do not account for near misses.

2.2 Inter-Annotator Agreement

The need to ascertain the agreement and reliability between coders for segmentation was recognized

[2] P_k is a modification of P_μ (Beeferman et al., 1997, p. 43). Other modifications such as TDT C_{seg} (Doddington, 1998, pp. 5–6) have been proposed, but P_k has seen greater usage.

[3] Georgescul et al. (2006, p. 48) note that both FPs and FNs are weighted by $^1/_{N-k}$, and although there are "equiprobable possibilities to have a [FP] in an interval of k units", "the total number of equiprobable possibilities to have a [FN] in an interval of k units is smaller than $(N-k)$", making the interpretation of a full miss as a FN less probable than as a FP.

by Passonneau and Litman (1993), who adapted the percentage agreement metric by Gale et al. (1992, p. 254) for usage in segmentation. This percentage agreement metric (Passonneau and Litman, 1993, p. 150) is the ratio of the total observed agreement of a coder with the majority opinion for each boundary over the total possible agreements. This measure failed to take into account chance agreement, or to less harshly penalize near-misses.

Hearst (1997) collected segmentations from 7 coders while developing the automatic segmenter TextTiling, and reported mean κ (Siegel and Castellan, 1988) values for coders and automatic segmenters (Hearst, 1997, p. 56). Pairwise mean κ scores were calculated by comparing a coder's segmentation against a reference segmentation formulated by the majority opinion strategy used in Passonneau and Litman (1993, p. 150) (Hearst, 1997, pp. 53–54). Although mean κ scores attempt to take into account chance agreement, near misses are still unaccounted for, and use of Siegel and Castellan's (1988) κ has declined in favour of other coefficients (Artstein and Poesio, 2008, pp. 555–556).

Artstein and Poesio (2008) briefly touch upon recommendations for coefficients for segmentation evaluation, and though they do not propose a measure, they do conjecture that a modification of a weighted form of α (Krippendorff, 1980; Krippendorff, 2004) using unification and WindowDiff may suffice (Artstein and Poesio, 2008, pp. 580–582).

3 Segmentation Similarity

For discussing segmentation, a segment's size (or mass) is measured in units, the error is quantified in potential boundaries (PBs), and we have adopted a modified form of the notation used by Artstein and Poesio (2008), where the set of:

- *Items* is $\{i|i \in I\}$ with cardinality **i**;
- *Categories* is $\{k|k \in K\}$ with cardinality **k**;
- *Coders* is $\{c|c \in C\}$ with cardinality **c**;
- *Segmentations* of an item i by a coder c is $\{s|s \in S\}$, where when s_{ic} is specified with only one subscript, it denotes s_c, for all relevant items (i); and
- *Types* of segmentation boundaries is $\{t|t \in T\}$ with cardinality **t**.

3.1 Sources of Dissimilarity

Linear segmentation has three main types of errors:

1. s_1 contains a boundary that is off by n PBs in s_2;
2. s_1 contains a boundary that s_2 does not; or
3. s_2 contains a boundary that s_1 does not.

These types of errors can be seen in Figure 1, and are conceptualized as a pairwise *transposition* of a boundary for error 1, and the insertion or deletion (depending upon your perspective) of a boundary for errors 2 and 3. Since we do not designate either segmentation as a reference or hypothesis, we refer to insertions and deletions both as *substitutions*.

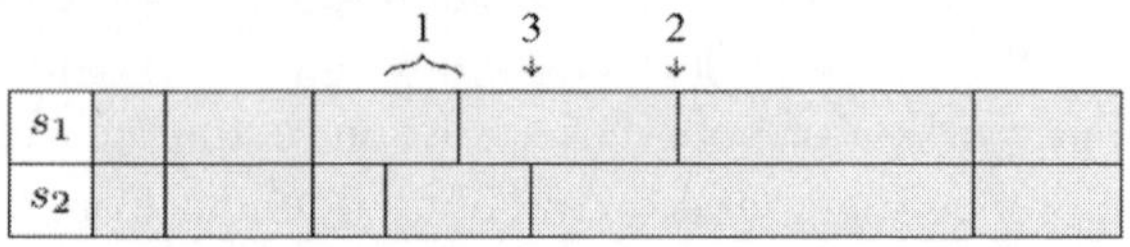

Figure 1: Types of segmentations errors

It is important to not penalize near misses as full misses in many segmentation tasks because coders often agree upon the existence of a boundary, but disagree upon its exact location. In the previous scenario, assigning a full miss would mean that even a boundary loosely agreed-upon, as in Figure 1, error 1, would be regarded as completely disagreed-upon.

3.2 Edit Distance

In S, concepts from Damereau-Levenshtein edit distance (Damereau, 1964; Levenshtein, 1966) are applied to model segmentation edit distance as two operations: substitutions and transpositions.[4] These two operations represent full misses and near misses, respectively. Using these two operations, a new globally-optimal minimum edit distance is applied to a pair of sequences of sets of boundaries to model the sources of dissimilarity identified earlier.[5]

Near misses that are remedied by transposition are penalized as b PBs of error (where b is the number of boundaries transposed), as opposed to the $2b$ PBs of errors by which they would be penalized if they were considered to be two separate substitution operations. Transpositions can also be considered over $n > 2$ PBs (n-wise transpositions). This is useful if, for a specific task, near misses of up to n PBs are not to be penalized as full misses (default $n = 2$).

The error represented by the two operations can also be scaled (*i.e.*, weighted) from 1 PB each to a

[4] Beeferman et al. (1997, p. 42) briefly mention using an edit distance without transpositions, but discard it in favour of P_μ.

[5] For multiple boundaries, an *add/del* operation is added, and transpositions are considered only within boundary types.

fraction. The distance over which an n-wise transposition occurred can also be used in conjunction with the scalar operation weighting so that a transposition is weighted using the function in Equation 3.

$$\text{te}(n, b) = b - \left({}^{1}/{}_{b}\right)^{n-2} \quad \text{where } n \geq 2 \text{ and } b > 0 \tag{3}$$

This transposition error function was chosen so that, in an n-wise transposition where $n = 2$ PBs and the number of boundaries transposed $b = 2$, the penalty would be 1 PB, and the maximum penalty as $\lim_{n\to\infty} \text{te}(n)$ would be b PBs, or in this case 2 PBs (demonstrated later in Figure 5b).

3.3 Method

In S, we conceptualize the entire segmentation, and individual segments, as having mass (*i.e.*, unit magnitude/length), and quantify similarity between two segmentations as the proportion of boundaries that are not transformed when comparing segmentations using edit distance, essentially using edit distance as a penalty function and scaling penalties by segmentation size. S is a symmetric function that quantifies the similarity between two segmentations as a percentage, and applies to any granularity or segmentation unit (*e.g.*, paragraphs, sentences, clauses, etc.).

Consider a somewhat contrived example containing–for simplicity and brevity–only one boundary type ($\mathbf{t} = 1$). First, a segmentation must be converted into a sequence of segment mass values (see Figure 2).

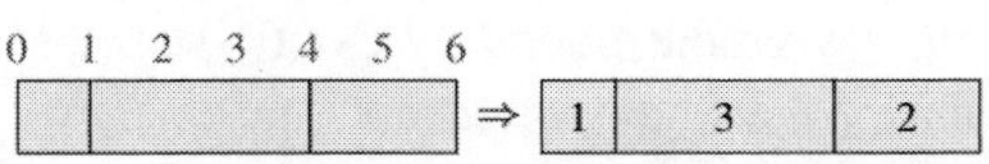

Figure 2: Annotation of segmentation mass

Then, a pair of segmentations are converted into parallel sequences of boundary sets, where each set contains the types of boundaries present at that potential boundary location (if there is no boundary present, then the set is empty), as in Figure 3.

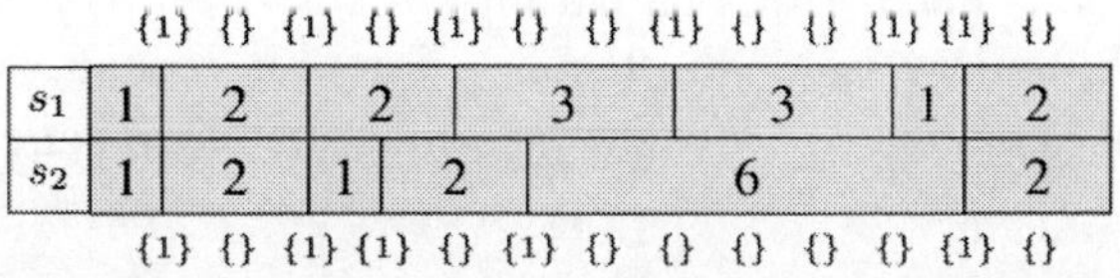

Figure 3: Segmentations annotated with mass and their corresponding boundary set sequences

The edit distance is calculated by first identifying all potential substitution operations that could occur (in this case 5). A search for all potential n-wise transpositions that can be made over n adjacent sets between the sequences is then performed, searching from the beginning of the sequence to the end, keeping only those transpositions which do not overlap and which result in transposing the most boundaries between the sequences (to minimize the edit distance). In this case, we have only one non-overlapping 2-wise transposition. We then subtract the number of boundaries involved in transpositions between the sequences (2 boundaries) from the number of substitutions, giving us an edit distance of 4 PBs: 1 transposition PB and 3 substitution PBs.

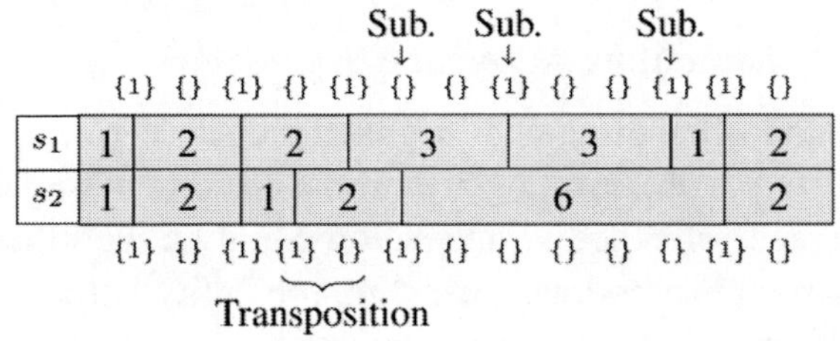

Figure 4: Edit operations performed on boundary sets

Edit distance, and especially the number of operations of each type performed, is useful in identifying the number of full and near misses that have occurred–which indicates whether one's choice of transposition window size n is either too generous or too harsh. Edit distance as a penalty does not incorporate information on the severity of an error with respect to the size of a segment, and is not an easily comparable value without some form of normalization. To account for these issues, we define S so that boundary edit distance is used to subtract penalties for each edit operation that occurs, from the number of potential boundaries in a segmentation, normalizing this value by the total number of potential boundaries in a segmentation.

$$\text{S}(s_{i1}, s_{i2}) = \frac{\mathbf{t} \cdot \text{mass}(i) - \mathbf{t} - \text{d}(s_{i1}, s_{i1}, T)}{\mathbf{t} \cdot \text{mass}(i) - \mathbf{t}} \tag{4}$$

S, as shown in Equation 4, scales the mass of the item by the cardinality of the set of boundary types ($\mathbf{t}$) because the edit distance function $\text{d}(s_{i1}, s_{i1}, T)$ will return a value of $[0, \mathbf{t} \cdot \text{mass}(i)]$ PBs, where $\mathbf{t} \in \mathbb{Z}^{+}$–while subtracting the edit distance and $\mathbf{t}$.[6]

[6]The number of potential boundaries in a segmentation s_i

The numerator is normalized by the total number of potential boundaries per boundary type. This results in a function with a range of $[0, 1]$. It returns 0 when one segmentation contains no boundaries, and the other contains the maximum number of possible boundaries. It returns 1 when both segmentations are identical.

Using the default configuration of this equation, $\text{S} = {}^{9}/_{13} = 0.6923$, a very low similarity, which WindowDiff also agrees upon ($1 - WD = 0.6154$). The edit-distance function $\text{d}(s_{i1}, s_{i1}, T)$ can also be assigned values of the range $[0, 1]$ as scalar weights (w_{sub}, w_{trp}) to reduce the penalty attributed to particular edit operations, and configured to use a transposition error function (Equation 3, used by default).

3.4 Evaluating Automatic Segmenters

Coders often disagree in segmentation tasks (Hearst, 1997, p. 56), making it improbable that a single, correct, reference segmentation could be identified from human codings. This improbability is the result of individual coders adopting slightly different segmentation strategies (*i.e.*, different granularity). In light of this, we propose that the best available evaluation strategy for automatic segmentation methods is to compare performance against multiple coders directly, so that performance can be quantified relative to human reliability and agreement.

To evaluate whether an automatic segmenter performs on par with human performance, inter-annotator agreement can be calculated with and without the inclusion of an automatic segmenter, where an observed drop in the coefficients would signify that the automatic segmenter does not perform as reliably as the group of human coders.[7] This can be performed independently for multiple automatic segmenters to compare them to each other–assuming that the coefficients model chance agreement appropriately–because agreement is calculated (and quantifies reliability) over all segmentations.

3.5 Inter-Annotator Agreement

Similarity alone is not a sufficiently insightful measure of reliability, or agreement, between coders. Chance agreement occurs in segmentation when coders operating at slightly different granularities agree due to their codings, and not their own innate segmentation heuristics. Inter-annotator agreement coefficients have been developed that assume a variety of prior distributions to characterize chance agreement, and to attempt to offer a way to identify whether agreement is primarily due to chance, or not, and to quantify reliability.

Artstein and Poesio (2008) note that most of a coder's judgements are non-boundaries. The class imbalance caused by segmentations often containing few boundaries, paired with no handling of near misses, causes most inter-annotator agreement coefficients to drastically underestimate agreement on segmentations. To allow for agreement coefficients to account for near misses, we have adapted S for use with Cohen's κ, Scott's π, Fleiss's multi-π (π^*), and Fleiss's multi-κ (κ^*), which are all coefficients that range from $[{}^{A_e}/_{1-A_e}, 1]$, where 0 indicates chance agreement, and 1 perfect agreement. All four coefficients have the general form:

$$\kappa, \pi, \kappa^*, \text{ and } \pi^* = \frac{\text{A}_a - \text{A}_e}{1 - \text{A}_e} \quad (5)$$

For each agreement coefficient, the set of categories is defined as solely the presence of a boundary ($K = \{\text{seg}_t | t \in T\}$), per boundary type ($t$). This category choice is similar to those chosen by Hearst (1997, p. 53), who computed chance agreement in terms of the probability that coders would say that a segment boundary exists (seg_t), and the probability that they would not (unseg_t). We have chosen to model chance agreement only in terms of the presence of a boundary, and not the absence, because coders have only two choices when segmenting: to place a boundary, or not. Coders do not place non-boundaries. If they do not make a choice, then the default choice is used: no boundary. This default option makes it impossible to determine whether a segmenter is making a choice by not placing a boundary, or whether they are not sure whether a boundary is to be placed.[8] For this reason, we only characterize chance agreement between coders in terms of one boundary presence category per type.

with **t** boundary types is $\mathbf{t} \cdot \text{mass}(i) - \mathbf{t}$.

[7] Similar to how human competitiveness is ascertained by Medelyan et al. (2009, pp. 1324–1325) and Medelyan (2009, pp. 143–145) by comparing drops in inter-indexer consistency.

[8] This could be modelled as another boundary type, which would be modelled in S by the set of boundary types T.

3.5.1 Scott's π

Proposed by Scott (1955), π assumes that chance agreement between coders can be characterized as the proportion of items that have been assigned to category k by both coders (Equation 7). We calculate agreement (A_a^π) as pairwise mean S (scaled by each item's size) to enable agreement to quantify near misses leniently, and chance agreement (A_e^π) can be calculated as in Artstein and Poesio (2008).

$$A_a^\pi = \frac{\sum_{i \in I} \text{mass}(i) \cdot S(s_{i1}, s_{i2})}{\sum_{i \in I} \text{mass}(i)} \tag{6}$$

$$A_e^\pi = \sum_{k \in K} \left(P_e^\pi(k)\right)^2 \tag{7}$$

We calculate chance agreement per category as the proportion of boundaries (seg_t) assigned by all coders over the total number of potential boundaries for segmentations, as shown in Equation 8.

$$P_e^\pi(\text{seg}_t) = \frac{\sum_{c \in C} \sum_{i \in I} |\text{boundaries}(t, s_{ic})|}{\mathbf{c} \cdot \sum_{i \in I} (\text{mass}(i) - 1)} \tag{8}$$

This adapted coefficient appropriately estimates chance agreement in situations where there no individual coder bias.

3.5.2 Cohen's κ

Proposed by Cohen (1960), κ characterizes chance agreement as individual distributions per coder, calculated as shown in Equations 9-10 using our definition of agreement (A_a^π) as shown earlier.

$$A_a^\kappa = A_a^\pi \tag{9}$$

$$A_e^\kappa = \sum_{k \in K} P_e^\kappa(k|c_1) \cdot P_e^\kappa(k|c_2) \tag{10}$$

We calculate category probabilities as in Scott's π, but per coder, as shown in Equation 11.

$$P_e^\kappa(\text{seg}_t|c) = \frac{\sum_{i \in I} |\text{boundaries}(t, s_{ic})|}{\sum_{i \in I} (\text{mass}(i) - 1)} \tag{11}$$

This adapted coefficient appropriately estimates chance agreement for segmentation evaluations where coder bias is present.

3.5.3 Fleiss's Multi-π

Proposed by Fleiss (1971), multi-π (π^*) adapts Scott's π for multiple annotators. We use Artstein and Poesio's (2008, p. 564) proposal for calculating actual and expected agreement, and because all coders rate all items, we express agreement as pairwise mean S between all coders as shown in Equations 12-13, adapting only Equation 12.

$$A_a^{\pi^*} = \frac{1}{\binom{\mathbf{c}}{2}} \sum_{m=1}^{\mathbf{c}-1} \sum_{n=m+1}^{\mathbf{c}} \frac{\sum_{i \in I} \text{mass}(i) \cdot S(s_{im}, s_{in})}{\sum_{i \in I} (\text{mass}(i) - 1)} \tag{12}$$

$$A_e^{\pi^*} = \sum_{k \in K} \left(P_e^\pi(k)\right)^2 \tag{13}$$

3.5.4 Fleiss's Multi-κ

Proposed by Davies and Fleiss (1982), multi-κ (κ^*) adapts Cohen's κ for multiple annotators. We use Artstein and Poesio's (2008, extended version) proposal for calculating agreement just as in π^*, but with separate distributions per coder as shown in Equations 14-15.

$$A_a^{\kappa^*} = A_a^{\pi^*} \tag{14}$$

$$A_e^{\kappa^*} = \sum_{k \in K} \left(\frac{1}{\binom{\mathbf{c}}{2}} \sum_{m=1}^{\mathbf{c}-1} \sum_{n=m+1}^{\mathbf{c}} P_e^\kappa(k|c_m) \cdot P_e^\kappa(k|c_n) \right) \tag{15}$$

3.6 Annotator Bias

To identify the degree of bias in a group of coders' segmentations, we can use a measure of variance proposed by Artstein and Poesio (2008, p. 572) that is quantified in terms of the difference between expected agreement when chance is assumed to vary between coders, and when it is assumed to not.

$$B = A_e^{\pi^*} - A_e^{\kappa^*} \tag{16}$$

4 Experiments

To demonstrate the advantages of using S, as opposed to WindowDiff (WD), we compare both metrics using a variety of contrived scenarios, and then compare our adapted agreement coefficients against pairwise mean WD[9] for the segmentations collected by Kazantseva and Szpakowicz (2012).

In this section, because WD is a penalty-based metric, it is reported as $1-WD$ so that it is easier to compare against S values. When reported in this way, $1-WD$ and S both range from $[0, 1]$, where 1 represents no errors and 0 represents maximal error.

[9] Permuted, and with window size recalculated for each pair.

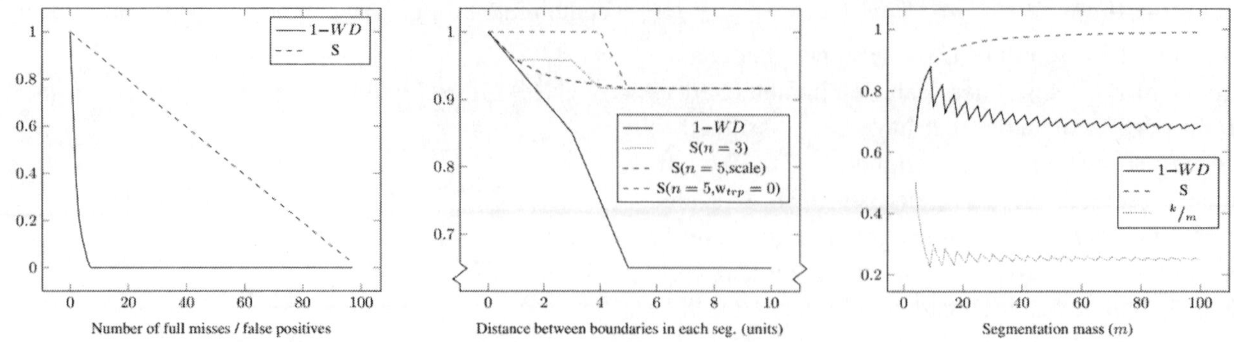

(a) Increasing the number of full misses, or FPs, where $k = 25$ for WD

(b) Increasing the distance between two boundaries considered to be a near miss until metrics consider them a full miss

(c) Increasing the mass m of segmentations configured as shown in Figure 10 showing the effect of k on $1-WD$

Figure 5: Responses of $1-WD$ and S to various segmentation scenarios

4.1 Segmentation Cases

Maximal versus minimal segmentation When proposing a new metric, its reactions to extrema must be illustrated, for example when a maximal segmentation is compared to a minimal segmentation, as shown in Figure 6. In this scenario, both $1-WD$ and S appropriately identify that this case represents maximal error, or 0. Though not shown here, both metrics also report a similarity of 1.0 when identical segmentations are compared.

s_1	14													
s_2	1	1	1	1	1	1	1	1	1	1	1	1	1	1

Figure 6: Maximal versus minimal seg. masses

Full misses For the most serious source of error, full misses (*i.e.*, FPs and FNs), both metrics appropriately report a reduction in similarity for cases such as Figure 7 that is very similar ($1-WD$ = 0.8462, S= 0.8461). Where the two metrics differ is when this type of error is increased.

s_1	1	2	2	2	4	2	1
s_2	1	2	8			2	1

Figure 7: Full misses in seg. masses

S reacts to increasing full misses linearly, whereas WindowDiff can prematurely report a maximal number of errors. Figure 5a demonstrates this effect, where for each iteration we have taken segmentations of 100 units of mass with one matching boundary at the first hypothesis boundary position, and uniformly increased the number of internal hypothesis segments, giving us 1 matching boundary, and $[0, 98]$ FPs. This premature report of maximal error (at 7 FP) by WD is caused by the window size ($k = 25$) being greater than all of the internal hypothesis segment sizes, making all windows penalized for containing errors.

Near misses When dealing with near misses, the values of both metrics drop ($1-WD = 0.8182$, S $= 0.9231$), but to greatly varying degrees. In comparison to full misses, WindowDiff penalizes a near miss, like that in Figure 8, far more than S. This difference is due to the distance between the two boundaries involved in a near miss; S shows, in this case, 1 PB of error until it is outside of the n-wise transposition window (where $n = 2$ PBs), at which point it is considered an error of not one transposition, but two substitutions (2 PBs).

s_1	6	8
s_2	7	7

Figure 8: Near misses in seg. masses

If we wanted to completely forgive near misses up to n PBs, we could set the weighting of transpositions in S to $w_{trp} = 0$. This is useful if a specific segmentation task accepts that near misses are very probable, and that there is little cost associated with a near miss in a window of n PBs. We can also set n to a high number, *i.e.*, 5 PBs, and use the scaled transposition error (te) function (Equation 3) to slowly increase the error from $b = 1$ PB to $b = 2$ PBs, as shown in Figure 5b, which shows how both

	Scenario 1: FN, $p = 0.5$		Scenario 2: FP, $p = 0.5$		Scenario 3: FP and FN, $p = 0.5$	
	(20,30)	(15,35)	(20,30)	(15,35)	(20,30)	(15,35)
WD	0.2340 ± 0.0113	0.2292 ± 0.0104	0.2265 ± 0.0114	0.2265 ± 0.0111	0.3635 ± 0.0126	0.3599 ± 0.0117
S	0.9801 ± 0.0006	0.9801 ± 0.0006	0.9800 ± 0.0006	0.9800 ± 0.0006	0.9605 ± 0.0009	0.9603 ± 0.0009
	(10,40)	(5,45)	(10,40)	(5,45)	(10,40)	(5,45)
WD	0.2297 ± 0.0105	0.2206 ± 0.0079	0.2256 ± 0.0102	0.2184 ± 0.0069	0.3516 ± 0.0110	0.3254 ± 0.0087
S	0.9799 ± 0.0007	0.9796 ± 0.0007	0.9800 ± 0.0006	0.9796 ± 0.0007	0.9606 ± 0.0010	0.9598 ± 0.0011

Table 1: Stability of mean (with standard deviation) values of WD and S in three different scenarios, each defining the: probability of a false positive (FP), false negative (FN), or both. Each scenario varies the range of internal segment sizes (*e.g.*, $(20, 30)$). Low standard deviation and similar within-scenario means demonstrates low sensitivity to variations in internal segment size.

metrics react to increases in the distance between a near miss in a segment of 25 units. These configurations are all preferable to the drop of $1-WD$.

4.2 Segmentation Mass Scale Effects

It is important for a segmentation evaluation metric to take into account the severity of an error in terms of segment size. An error in a 100 unit segment should be considered less severe than an error in a 2 unit segment, because an extra boundary placed within a 100 unit segment (*e.g.*, Figure 9 with $m = 100$) could probably indicate a weak boundary, whereas in a 4 unit segment the probability that an extra boundary exists right next to two agreed-upon boundaries should be small for most tasks, meaning that it is probable that the extra boundary is an error, and not a weak boundary.

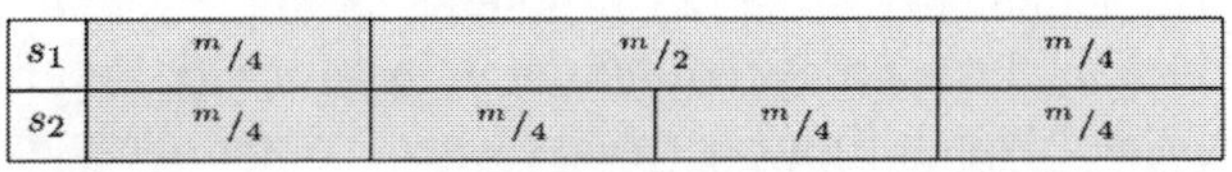

Figure 9: Two segmentations of mass m with a full miss

To demonstrate that S is sensitive to segment size, Figure 5c shows how S and $1-WD$ respond when comparing segmentations configured as shown in Figure 10 (containing one match and one full miss) with linearly increasing mass ($4 \leq m \leq 100$). $1-WD$ will eventually indicate 0.68, whereas S appropriately discounts the error as mass is increased, approaching 1 as $\lim_{m \to \infty}$. $1-WD$ behaves in this way because of how it calculates its window size parameter, k, which is plotted as k/m to show how its value influences $1-WD$.

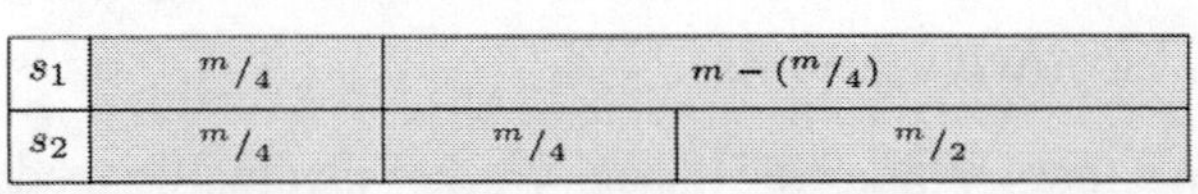

Figure 10: Two segmentations of mass m compared with increasing m in Figure 5c (s_1 as reference)

4.3 Variation in Segment Sizes

When Pevzner and Hearst (2002) proposed WD, they demonstrated that it was not as sensitive as P_k to variations in the size of segments inside a segmentation. To show this, they simulated how WD performs upon a segmentation comprised of 1000 segments with four different uniformly distributed ranges of internal segment sizes (keeping the mean at approximately 25 units) in comparison to a hypothesis segmentation with errors (false positives, false negatives, and both) uniformly distributed within segments (Pevzner and Hearst, 2002, pp. 11–12). 10 trials were performed for each segment size range and error probability, with 100 hypotheses generated per trial. Recreating this simulation, we compare the stability of S in comparison to WD, as shown in Table 1. We can see that WD values show substantial within-scenario variation for each segment size range, and larger standard deviations, than S.

4.4 Inter-Annotator Agreement Coefficients

Here, we demonstrate the adapted inter-annotator agreement coefficients upon topical paragraph-level segmentations produced by 27 coders of 20 chapters from the novel *The Moonstone* by Wilkie Collins collected by Kazantseva and Szpakowicz (2012). Figure 11 shows a heat map of each chapter where the percentage of coders who agreed upon each potential boundary is represented. Comparing this heat map to the inter-annotator agreement coefficients in Table 2 allows us to better understand why certain chapters have lower reliability.

Chapter 1 has the lowest π^*_S score in the table, and also the highest bias (B_S). One of the reasons for this low reliability can be attributed to the chapter's small mass (m) and few coders ($|c|$), which makes it more sensitive to chance agreement. Visually, the

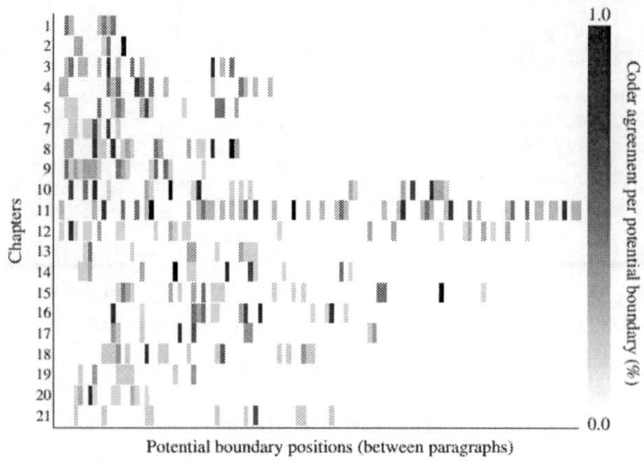

Figure 11: Heat maps for the segmentations of each chapter showing the percentage of coders who agree upon boundary positions (darker shows higher agreement)

Ch.	π^*_S	κ^*_S	B_S	$1-WD$	$\lvert c\rvert$	$\lvert b\rvert$	m
1	0.7452	0.7463	0.0039	0.6641 ± 0.1307	4	13	13
2	0.8839	0.8840	0.0009	0.7619 ± 0.1743	6	20	15
3	0.8338	0.8340	0.0013	0.6732 ± 0.1559	4	23	38
4	0.8414	0.8417	0.0019	0.6019 ± 0.2245	4	25	46
5	0.8773	0.8774	0.0003	0.6965 ± 0.1106	6	34	42
7	0.8132	0.8133	0.0002	0.6945 ± 0.1822	6	20	15
8	0.8495	0.8496	0.0006	0.7505 ± 0.0911	6	48	39
9	0.8104	0.8105	0.0009	0.6502 ± 0.1319	6	35	33
10	0.9077	0.9078	0.0002	0.7729 ± 0.0770	6	56	83
11	0.8130	0.8135	0.0022	0.6189 ± 0.1294	4	73	111
12	0.9178	0.9178	0.0001	0.6504 ± 0.1277	6	40	102
13	0.9354	0.9354	0.0002	0.5660 ± 0.2187	6	21	58
14	0.9367	0.9367	0.0001	0.7128 ± 0.1744	6	35	70
15	0.9344	0.9344	0.0001	0.7291 ± 0.0856	6	40	97
16	0.9356	0.9356	0.0000	0.8016 ± 0.0648	6	41	69
17	0.9447	0.9447	0.0002	0.6717 ± 0.2044	5	23	70
18	0.8921	0.8922	0.0005	0.5998 ± 0.1614	5	28	59
19	0.9021	0.9022	0.0009	0.4796 ± 0.2666	5	15	36
20	0.8590	0.8591	0.0003	0.6657 ± 0.1221	6	21	21
21	0.9286	0.9286	0.0004	0.6255 ± 0.2003	5	17	60

Table 2: S-based inter-annotator agreements and pairwise mean $1-WD$ and standard deviation with the number of coders, boundaries, and mass per chapter

predominance of grey indicates that, although there are probably two boundaries, their exact location is not very well agreed upon. In this case, $1-WD$ incorrectly indicates the opposite, that this chapter may have relatively moderate reliability, because it is not corrected for chance agreement.

$1-WD$ indicates that the lowest reliability is found in Chapter 19. π^*_S indicates that this is one of the higher agreement chapters, and looking at the heat map, we can see that it does not contain any strongly agreed upon boundaries. In this chapter, there is little opportunity to agree by chance due to the low number of boundaries ($|b|$) placed, and because the judgements are tightly clustered in a fair amount of mass, the S component of π^*_S appropriately takes into account the near misses observed and gives it a high reliability score.

Chapter 17 received the highest π^*_S in the table, which is another example of how tight clustering of boundary choices in a large mass leads π^*_S to appropriately indicate high reliability despite that there are not as many individual highly-agreed-upon boundaries, whereas $1-WD$ indicates that there is low reliability. $1-WD$ and π^*_S both agree, however, that chapter 16 has high reliability.

Despite WindowDiff's sensitivity to near misses, it is evident that its pairwise mean cannot be used to consistently judge inter-annotator agreement, or reliability. S demonstrates better versatility when accounting for near misses, and when used as part of inter-annotator agreement coefficients, it properly takes into account chance agreement. Following Artstein and Poesio's (2008, pp. 590–591) recommendation, and given the low bias (mean coder group $B_S = 0.0061 \pm 0.0035$), we propose reporting reliability using π^* for this corpus, where the mean coder group π^*_S for the corpus is 0.8904 ± 0.0392 (counting 1039 full and 212 near misses).

5 Conclusion and Future Work

We have proposed a segmentation evaluation metric which solves the key problems facing segmentation analysis today, including an inability to: appropriately quantify near misses when evaluating automatic segmenters and human performance; penalize errors equally (or, with configuration, in a manner that suits a specific segmentation task); compare an automatic segmenter directly against human performance; require a "true" reference; and handle multiple boundary types. Using S, task-specific evaluation of automatic and human segmenters can be performed using multiple human judgements unhindered by the quirks of window-based metrics.

In current and future work, we will show how S can be used to analyze hierarchical segmentations, and illustrate how to apply S to linear segmentations containing multiple boundary types.

Acknowledgments

We thank Anna Kazantseva for her invaluable feedback and corpora, and Stan Szpakowicz, Martin Scaiano, and James Cracknell for their feedback.

References

Ron Artstein and Massimo Poesio. 2008. Inter-coder agreement for computational linguistics. *Computational Linguistics*, 34(4):555–596. MIT Press, Cambridge, MA, USA.

Doug Beeferman, Adam Berger, and John Lafferty. 1997. Text Segmentation Using Exponential Models. *Proceedings of the Second Conference on Empirical Methods in Natural Language Processing*, 2:35–46. Association for Computational Linguistics, Stroudsburg, PA, USA.

Doug Beeferman and Adam Berger. 1999. Statistical models for text segmentation. *Machine learning*, 34(1–3):177–210. Springer Netherlands, NL.

Jacob Cohen. 1960. A Coefficient of Agreement for Nominal Scales. *Educational and Psychological Measurement*, 20(1):37–46. Sage, Beverly Hills, CA, USA.

Frederick J. Damerau. 1964. A technique for computer detection and correction of spelling errors. *Communications of the ACM*, 7(3):171–176. Association for Computing Machinery, Stroudsburg, PA, USA.

Mark Davies and Joseph L. Fleiss. 1982. Measuring agreement for multinomial data. *Biometrics*, 38(4):1047–1051. Blackwell Publishing Inc, Oxford, UK.

George R. Doddington. 1998. The topic detection and tracking phase 2 (TDT2) evaluation plan. *DARPA Broadcast News Transcription and Understanding Workshop*, pp. 223–229. Morgan Kaufmann, Waltham, MA, USA.

Joseph L. Fleiss. 1971. Measuring nominal scale agreement among many raters. *Psychological Bulletin*, 76(5):378–382. American Psychological Association, Washington, DC, USA.

Martin, Franz, J. Scott McCarley, and Jian-Ming Xu. 2007. User-oriented text segmentation evaluation measure. *Proceedings of the 30th annual international ACM SIGIR conference on Research and development in information retrieval*, pp. 701–702. Association for Computing Machinery, Stroudsburg, PA, USA.

William Gale, Kenneth Ward Church, and David Yarowsky. 1992. Estimating upper and lower bounds on the performance of word-sense disambiguation programs. *Proceedings of the 30th annual meeting of the Association for Computational Linguistics*, pp. 249–256. Association for Computational Linguistics, Stroudsburg, PA, USA.

Maria Georgescul, Alexander Clark, and Susan Armstrong. 2006. An analysis of quantitative aspects in the evaluation of thematic segmentation algorithms. *Proceedings of the 7th SIGdial Workshop on Discourse and Dialogue*, pp. 144–151. Association for Computational Linguistics, Stroudsburg, PA, USA.

Marti A. Hearst. 1997. TextTiling: Segmenting Text into Multi-paragraph Subtopic Passages. *Computational Linguistics*, 23(1):33–64. MIT Press, Cambridge, MA, USA.

Anna Kazantseva and Stan Szpakowicz. 2012. Topical Segmentation: a Study of Human Performance. *Proceedings of Human Language Technologies: The 2012 Annual Conference of the North American Chapter of the Association for Computational Linguistics*. Association for Computational Linguistics, Stroudsburg, PA, USA.

Klaus Krippendorff. 1980. *Content Analysis: An Introduction to Its Methodology*, Chapter 12. Sage, Beverly Hills, CA, USA.

Klaus Krippendorff. 2004. *Content Analysis: An Introduction to Its Methodology*, Chapter 11. Sage, Beverly Hills, CA, USA.

Sylvain Lamprier, Tassadit Amghar, Bernard Levrat, and Frederic Saubion 2007. On evaluation methodologies for text segmentation algorithms. *Proceedings of the 19th IEEE International Conference on Tools with Artificial Intelligence*, 2:19–26. IEEE Computer Society, Washington, DC, USA.

Vladimir I. Levenshtein. 1966. Binary codes capable of correcting deletions, insertions, and reversals. *Soviet Physics Doklady*, 10(8):707–710. American Institute of Physics, College Park, MD, USA.

Olena Medelyan. 2009. Human-competitive automatic topic indexing. PhD Thesis. University of Waikato, Waikato, NZ.

Olena Medelyan, Eibe Frank, and Ian H. Witten. 2009. Human-competitive tagging using automatic keyphrase extraction. *Proceedings of the 2009 Conference on Empirical Methods in Natural Language Processing*, pp. 1318–1327. Association for Computational Linguistics, Stroudsburg, PA, USA.

Rebecca J. Passonneau and Diane J. Litman. 1993. Intention-based segmentation: human reliability and correlation with linguistic cues. *Proceedings of the 31st annual meeting of the Association for Computational Linguistics*, pp. 148–155). Association for Computational Linguistics, Stroudsburg, PA, USA.

Lev Pevzner and Marti A. Hearst. 2002. A critique and improvement of an evaluation metric for text segmentation. *Computational Linguistics*, 28(1):19–36. MIT Press, Cambridge, MA, USA.

William A. Scott. 1955. Reliability of content analysis: The case of nominal scale coding. *Public Opinion Quarterly*, 19(3):321–325. American Association for Public Opinion Research, Deerfield, IL, USA.

Sidney Siegel and N. John Castellan, Jr. 1988. *Nonparametric Statistics for the Behavioral Sciences*. 2nd Edition, Chapter 9.8. McGraw-Hill, New York, USA.

HyTER: Meaning-Equivalent Semantics for Translation Evaluation

Markus Dreyer
SDL Language Weaver
6060 Center Drive, Suite 150
Los Angeles, CA 90045, USA
mdreyer@sdl.com

Daniel Marcu
SDL Language Weaver
6060 Center Drive, Suite 150
Los Angeles, CA 90045, USA
dmarcu@sdl.com

Abstract

It is common knowledge that translation is an ambiguous, 1-to-n mapping process, but to date, our community has produced no empirical estimates of this ambiguity. We have developed an annotation tool that enables us to create representations that compactly encode an exponential number of correct translations for a sentence. Our findings show that naturally occurring sentences have billions of translations. Having access to such large sets of meaning-equivalent translations enables us to develop a new metric, HyTER, for translation accuracy. We show that our metric provides better estimates of machine and human translation accuracy than alternative evaluation metrics.

1 Motivation

During the last decade, automatic evaluation metrics (Papineni et al., 2002; Snover et al., 2006; Lavie and Denkowski, 2009) have helped researchers accelerate the pace at which they improve machine translation (MT) systems. And human-assisted metrics (Snover et al., 2006) have enabled and supported large-scale U.S. government sponsored programs, such as DARPA GALE (Olive et al., 2011). However, these metrics have started to show signs of wear and tear.

Automatic metrics are often criticized for providing non-intuitive scores – few researchers can explain to casual users what a BLEU score of 27.9 means. And researchers have grown increasingly concerned that automatic metrics have a strong bias towards preferring statistical translation outputs; the NIST (2008, 2010), MATR (Gao et al., 2010) and WMT (Callison-Burch et al., 2011) evaluations held during the last five years have provided ample evidence that automatic metrics yield results that are inconsistent with human evaluations when comparing statistical, rule-based, and human outputs.

In contrast, human-informed metrics have other deficiencies: they have large variance across human judges (Bojar et al., 2011) and produce unstable results from one evaluation to another (Przybocki et al., 2011). Because evaluation scores are not computed automatically, systems developers cannot automatically tune to human-based metrics.

Table 1 summarizes the dimensions along which evaluation metrics should do well and the strengths and weaknesses of the automatic and human-informed metrics proposed to date. Our goal is to develop metrics that do well along all these dimensions. The fundamental insight on which our research relies is that the failures of current automatic metrics are not algorithmic: BLEU, Meteor, TER (Translation Edit Rate), and other metrics efficiently and correctly compute informative distance functions between a translation and one or more human references. We believe that these metrics fail simply because they have access to sets of human references that are too small. If we had access to the set of *all* correct translations of a given sentence, we could measure the minimum distance between a translation and the set. When a translation is perfect, it can be found in the set, so it requires no editing to produce a perfect translation. Therefore, its score should be zero. If the translation has errors, we can

Desiderata	Auto.	Manu.	HyTER
Metric is intuitive	N	Y	Y
Metric is computed automatically	Y	N	Y
Metric is stable and reproducible from one evaluation to another	Y	N	Y
Metric works equally well when comparing human and automatic outputs and when comparing rule-based, statistical-based, and hybrid engines	N	Y	Y
System developers can tune to the metric	Y	N	Y
Metric helps developers identify deficiencies of MT engines	N	N	Y

Table 1: Desiderata of evaluation metrics: Current automatic and human metrics, proposed metric.

efficiently compute the minimum number of edits (substitutions, deletions, insertions, moves) needed to rewrite the translation into the "closest" reference in the set. Current automatic evaluation metrics do not assign their best scores to most perfect translations because the set of references they use is too small; their scores can therefore be perceived as less intuitive.

Following these considerations, we developed an annotation tool that enables one to efficiently create an exponential number of correct translations for a given sentence, and present a new evaluation metric, HyTER, which efficiently exploits these massive reference networks. In the rest of the paper, we first describe our annotation environment, process, and meaning-equivalent representations that we create (Section 2). We then present the HyTER metric (Section 3). We show that this new metric provides better support than current metrics for machine translation evaluation (Section 4) and human translation proficiency assessment (Section 5).

2 Annotating sentences with exponential numbers of meaning equivalents

2.1 Annotation tool

We have developed a web-based annotation tool that can be used to create a representation encoding an exponential number of meaning equivalents for a given sentence. The meaning equivalents are constructed in a bottom-up fashion by typing translation equivalents for larger and larger phrases. For example, when building the meaning equivalents for the Spanish phrase "el primer ministro italiano Silvio Berlusconi", the annotator first types in the meaning equivalents for "primer ministro" – ⟨prime-minister; PM; prime minister; head of government; premier; etc.⟩; "italiano" – ⟨Italian⟩; and "Silvio Berlusconi" – ⟨Silvio Berlusconi; Berlusconi⟩. The tool creates a *card* that stores all the alternative meanings for a phrase as a determinized FSA and gives it a name in the target language that is representative of the underlying meaning-equivalent set: [PRIME-MINISTER], [ITALIAN], and [SILVIO-BERLUSCONI]. Each base card can be thought of expressing a semantic concept. A combination of existing cards and additional words can be subsequently used to create larger meaning equivalents that cover increasingly larger source sentence segments. For example, to create the meaning equivalents for "el primer ministro italiano" one can drag-and-drop existing cards or type in new words: ⟨the [ITALIAN] [PRIME-MINISTER]; the [PRIME-MINISTER] of Italy⟩; to create the meaning equivalents for "el primer ministro italiano Silvio Berlusconi", one can drag-and-drop and type: ⟨[SILVIO-BERLUSCONI] , [THE-ITALIAN-PRIME-MINISTER]; [THE-ITALIAN-PRIME-MINISTER] , [SILVIO-BERLUSCONI]; [THE-ITALIAN-PRIME-MINISTER] [SILVIO-BERLUSCONI] ⟩. All meaning equivalents associated with a given card are expanded and used when that card is re-used to create larger meaning-equivalent sets.

The annotation tool supports, but does not enforce, re-use of annotations created by other annotators. The resulting meaning equivalents are stored as recursive transition networks (RTNs), where each card is a subnetwork; if needed, these non-cyclic RTNs can be automatically expanded into finite-state acceptors (FSAs, see Section 3).

2.2 Data and Annotation Protocols

Using the annotation tool, we have created meaning-equivalent annotations for 102 Arabic and 102 Chinese sentences – a subset of the "progress set" used in the 2010 Open MT NIST evaluation (the average sentence length was 24 words). For each sentence, we had access to four human reference translations produced by LDC and five MT system outputs, which were selected by NIST to cover a variety of system architectures (statistical, rule-based, hybrid) and performances. For each MT output, we also had access to sentence-level HTER scores (Snover et al., 2006), which were produced by experienced LDC annotators.

We have experimented with three annotation protocols:

- Ara-A2E and Chi-C2E: Foreign language natives built English networks starting from foreign language sentences.
- Eng-A2E and Eng-C2E: English natives built English networks starting from "the best translation" of a foreign language sentence, as identified by NIST.
- Eng*-A2E and Eng*-C2E: English natives built English networks starting from "the best translation", but had access to three additional, independently produced human translations to boost their creativity.

Each protocol was implemented independently by at least three annotators. In general, annotators need to be fluent in the target language, familiar with the annotation tool we provide and careful not to generate incorrect paths, but they do not need to be linguists.

2.3 Exploiting multiple annotations

For each sentence, we combine all networks that were created by the different annotators. We evaluate two different combination methods, each of which combines networks N_1 and N_2 of two annotators (see an example in Figure 1):

(a) Standard union U(N_1, N_2): The standard finite-state union operation combines N_1 and N_2 on the whole-network level. When traversing U(N_1, N_2), one can follow a path that comes from either N_1 or N_2.

(b) Source-phrase-level union SPU(N_1, N_2): As an alternative, we introduce SPU, a more fine-grained union which operates on sub-sentence segments. Here we exploit the fact that each annotator explicitly aligned each of her various subnetworks for a given sentence to a source span of that sentence. Now for each pair of subnetworks (S_1, S_2) from N_1 and N_2, we build their union if they are *compatible*; two subnetworks S_1, S_2 are defined to be compatible if they are aligned to the same source span and have at least one path in common.

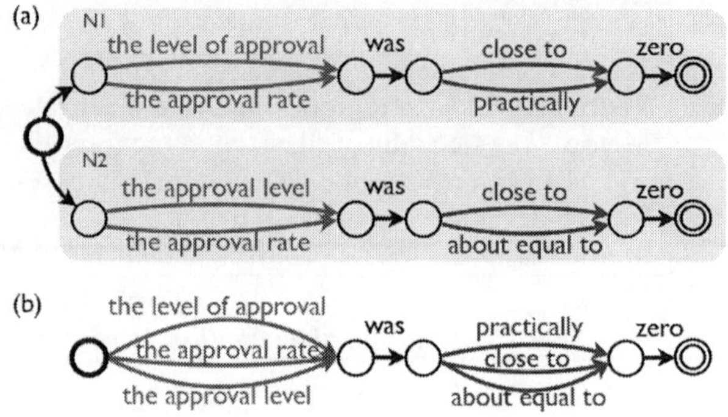

Figure 1: (a) Finite-state union versus (b) source-phrase-level union (SPU). The former does not contain the path "the approval level was practically zero".

The purpose of SPU is to create new paths by mixing paths from N_1 and N_2. In Figure 1, for example, the path "the approval level was practically zero" is contained in the SPU, but not in the standard union. We build SPUs using a dynamic programming algorithm that builds subnetworks bottom-up, building unions of intermediate results. Two larger subnetworks can be compatible only if their recursive smaller subnetworks are compatible. Each SPU contains at least all paths from the standard union.

2.4 Empirical findings

Now that we have described how we created particular networks for a given dataset, we describe some empirical findings that characterize our annotation process and the created networks.

Meaning-equivalent productivity. When we compare the productivity of the three annotation protocols in terms of the number of reference translations that they enable, we observe that target language natives that have access to multiple human references produce the largest networks. The median number of paths produced by one annotator under the three protocols varies from 7.7×10^5 paths for Ara-A2E, to 1.4×10^8 paths for Eng-A2E, to 5.9×10^8 paths for Eng*-A2E; in Chinese, the medians vary from 1.0×10^5 for Chi-C2E, to 1.7×10^8 for Eng-C2E, to 7.8×10^9 for Eng*-C2E.

Protocol productivity. When we compare the annotator time required by the three protocols, we find that foreign language natives work faster – they need about 2 hours per sentence – while target language natives need 2.5 hours per sentence. Given that target language natives build significantly larger networks and that bilingual speakers are in shorter supply than monolingual ones, we conclude that using target language annotators is more cost-effective overall.

Exploiting multiple annotations. Overall, the median number of paths produced by a single annotator for A2E is 1.5×10^6, two annotators (randomly picked per sentence) produce a median number of 4.7×10^7 (Union), for all annotators together it is 2.1×10^{10} (Union) and 2.1×10^{11} (SPU). For C2E, these numbers are 5.2×10^6 (one), 1.1×10^8 (two), and 2.6×10^{10} (all, Union) and 8.5×10^{11} (all, SPU).

Number of annotators and annotation time. We compute the minimum number of edits and length-normalized distance scores required to rewrite machine and human translations into translations found in the networks produced by one, two, and three annotators. We find that the length-normalized distances do not vary by more than 1% when adding the meaning equivalents produced by a third annotator. We conclude that 2-3 annotators per sentence produce a sufficiently large set of alternative meaning equivalents, which takes 4-7.5 hours. We are currently investigating alternative ways to create networks more efficiently.

Grammaticality. For each of the four human translation references and each of the five machine translation outputs (see Section 2.2), we algorithmically find the closest path in the annotated networks of meaning equivalents (see Section 3). We presented the resulting 1836 closest paths extracted from the networks (2 language pairs $\times 102$ sentences $\times 9$ human/machine translations) to three independent English speakers. We asked each English path to be labeled as grammatical, grammatical-but-slightly-odd, or non-grammatical. The metric is harsh: paths such as "he said that withdrawing *US force* without promoting security would be cataclysmic" are judged as non-grammatical by all three judges although a simple rewrite of "force" into "forces" would make this path grammatical. We found that 90% of the paths are judged as grammatical and 96% as grammatical or grammatical-but-slightly-odd, by at least one annotator. We interpret these results as positive: the annotation process leads to some ungrammatical paths being created, but most of the closest paths to human and machine outputs, those that matter from an evaluation perspective, are judged as correct by at least one judge.

Coverage. We found it somewhat disappointing that networks that encode billions of meaning-equivalent translations for a given sentence do not contain every independently produced human reference translation. The average length-normalized edit distance (computed as described in Section 3) between an independently produced human reference and the corresponding network is 19% for Arabic-English and 34% for Chinese-English across the entire corpus. Our analysis shows that about half of the edits are explained by several non-content words ("the", "of", "for", "their", ",") being optional in certain contexts; several "obvious" equivalents not being part of the networks ("that"–"this"; "so"–"accordingly"); and spelling alternatives/errors ("rockstrom"–"rockstroem"). We hypothesize that most of these ommissions/edits can be detected automatically and dealt with in an appropriate fashion. The rest of the edits would require more sophisticated machinery, to figure out, for example, that in a particular context pairs like "with"–"and" or "that"–"therefore" are interchangeable.

Given that Chinese is significantly more underspecified compared to Arabic and English, it is consistent with our intuition to see that the average minimal distance is higher between Chinese-English references and their respective networks (34%) than between Arabic-English references and their respective networks (19%).

3 Measuring translation quality with large networks of meaning equivalents

In this section, we present HyTER (Hybrid Translation Edit Rate), a novel metric that makes use of large reference networks.

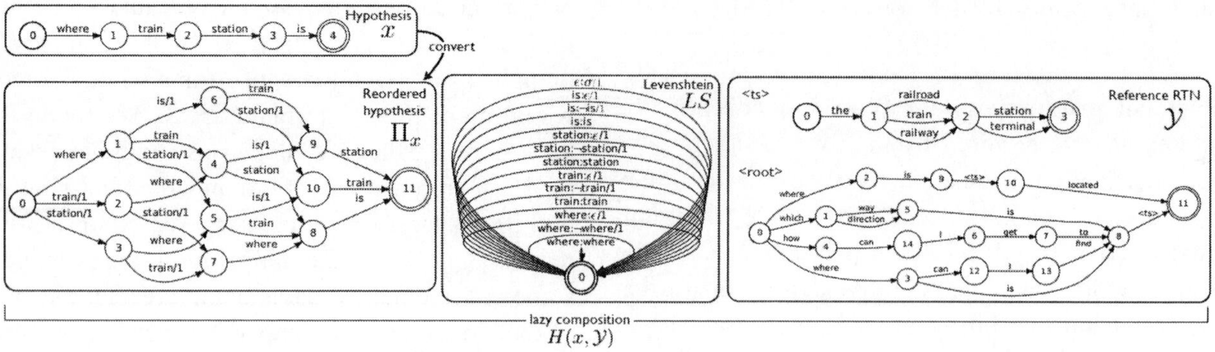

Figure 2: Defining the search space $H(x, \mathcal{Y})$ through (lazy) composition. x is a translation hypothesis *"where train station is"*, $\mathcal{Y}$ contains all correct translations. Π_x may be defined in various ways, here local reordering ($k = 3$) is used.

HyTER is an automatically computed version of HTER (Snover et al., 2006); HyTER computes the minimum number of edits between a translation x and an exponentially sized reference set $\mathcal{Y}$, which is encoded as a Recursive Transition Network (RTN). Perfect translations have a HyTER score of 0.

General Setup. The unnormalized HyTER score is defined as in equation (1) where Π_x is a set of permutations of the hypothesis x, $d(x, x')$ is the distance between x and a permutation x'—typically measured as the number of reordering moves between the two—and $\mathrm{LS}(x', y)$ is the standard Levenshtein distance (Levenshtein, 1966) between x' and y, defined as the minimum number of insertions, deletion, and substitutions. We normalize uhyter by the number of words in the found closest path.

$$\mathrm{uhyter}(x, \mathcal{Y}) \stackrel{\text{def}}{=} \min_{\substack{x' \in \Pi_x, \\ y \in \mathcal{Y}}} d(x, x') + \mathrm{LS}(x', y) \quad (1)$$

We treat this minimization problem as graph-based search. The search space over which we minimize is implicitly represented as the Recursive Transition Network H (see equation (2)), where Π_x is encoded as a weighted FSA that represents the set of permutations of x with their associated distance costs, and LS is the one-state Levenshtein transducer whose output weight for a string pair (x,y) is the Levenshtein distance between x, and y, and the symbol $\circ$ denotes composition. The model is depicted in Figure 2.

$$H(x, \mathcal{Y}) \stackrel{\text{def}}{=} \Pi_x \circ LS \circ \mathcal{Y} \quad (2)$$

Permutations. We define an FSA Π_x that allows permutations according to certain constraints. Allowing *all* permutations of the hypothesis x would increase the search space to factorial size and make inference NP-complete (Cormode and Muthukrishnan, 2007). We use local-window constraints (see, e.g., Kanthak et al. (2005)), where words may move within a fixed window of size k; these constraints are of size $O(n)$ with a constant factor k, where n is the length of the translation hypothesis x.

Lazy Evaluation. For efficiency, we use lazy evaluation when defining the search space $H(x, \mathcal{Y})$. This means we never explicitly compose Π_x, LS, and $\mathcal{Y}$. Parts of the composition that our inference algorithm does not explore are not constructed, saving computation time and memory. Permutation paths in Π_x are constructed on demand. Similarly, the reference set $\mathcal{Y}$ is expanded on demand, and large parts may remain unexpanded.[1]

Exact Inference. To compute $\mathrm{uhyter}(x, \mathcal{Y})$, we define the composition $H(x, \mathcal{Y})$ and can apply any shortest-path search algorithm (Mohri, 2002). We found that using the A* algorithm (Hart et al., 1972) was the most efficient; we devised an A* heuristic similar to Karakos et al. (2008).

Runtime. Computing the HyTER score takes 30 ms per sentence on networks by single annotators (combined all-annotator networks: 285 ms) if no

[1]These on-demand operations are supported by the OpenFst library (Allauzen et al., 2007); specifically, to expand the RTNs into FSAs we use the `Replace` operation.

	Arabic-English			Chinese-English		
Metric	Human mean	Machine mean	m/h	Human mean	Machine mean	m/h
[100-0]-BLEU, 1 ref	59.90	69.14	1.15	71.86	84.34	1.17
[100-0]-BLEU, 3 refs	41.49	57.44	1.38	54.25	75.22	1.39
[100-0]-Meteor, 1 ref	60.13	65.70	1.09	66.81	73.66	1.10
[100-0]-Meteor, 3 refs	55.98	62.91	1.12	62.95	70.68	1.12
[100-0]-TERp, 1 ref	35.87	46.48	1.30	53.58	71.70	1.34
[100-0]-TERp, 3 refs	27.08	39.52	1.46	41.79	60.61	1.45
HyTER U	18.42	34.94	1.90	27.98	52.08	1.86
HyTER SPU	17.85	34.39	1.93	27.57	51.73	1.88
[100-0]-Likert	5.26	50.37	9.57	4.35	48.37	11.12

Table 2: Scores assigned to human versus machine translations, under various metrics. Each score is normalized to range from 100 (worst) to 0 (perfect translation).

reordering is used. These numbers increase to 143 ms (1.5 secs) for local reordering with window size 3, and 533 ms (8 secs) for window size 5. Many speedups for computing the score with reorderings are possible, but we will see below that using reordering does not give consistent improvements (Table 3).

Output. As a by-product of computing the HyTER score, one can obtain the closest path itself, for error analysis. It can be useful to separately count the numbers of insertions, deletions, etc., and inspect the types of error. For example, one may find that a particular system output tends to be missing the finite verb of the sentence or that certain word choices were incorrect.

4 Using meaning-equivalent networks for machine translation evaluation

We now present experiments designed to measure how well HyTER performs, compared to other evaluation metrics. For these experiments, we sample 82 of the 102 available sentences; 20 sentences are held out for future use in optimizing our metric.

4.1 Differentiating human from machine translation outputs

We score the set of human translations and machine translations separately, using several popular metrics, with the goal of determining which metric performs better at separating machine translations from human translations. To ease comparisons across different metrics, we normalize all scores to a number between 0 (best) and 100 (worst). Table 2 shows the normalized mean scores for the machine translations and human translations under multiple automatic and one human evaluation metric (Likert). The quotient of interest, m/h, is the mean score for machine translations divided by the mean score for the human translations: the higher this number, the better a metric separates machine from human produced outputs.

Under HyTER, m/h is about 1.9, which shows that the HyTER scores for machine translations are, on average, almost twice as high as for human translations. Under Likert – a score assigned by human annotators who compare pairs of sentences at a time–, the quotient is higher, suggesting that human raters make stronger distinctions between human and machine translations. The quotient is lower under the automatic metrics Meteor (Version 1.3, (Denkowski and Lavie, 2011)), BLEU and TERp (Snover et al., 2009). These results show that HyTER separates machine from human translations better than alternative metrics.

4.2 Ranking MT systems by quality

We rank the five machine translation systems according to several widely used metrics (see Figure 3). Our results show that BLEU, Meteor and TERp do not rank the systems in the same way as HTER and humans do, while the HyTER metric yields the correct ranking. Also, separation between the quality of the five systems is higher under HyTER, HTER, and Likert than under alternative metrics.

4.3 Correlations with HTER

We know that current metrics (e.g., BLEU, Meteor, TER) correlate well with HTER and human judg-

Size	Likert	Meteor 1	Meteor 4	BLEU 1	BLEU 4	TERp 1	TERp 4	HyTER U (r5)	HyTER SPU (r5)
Arabic-English									
1	.653	.529	.541	.512	.675	.452	.547	.643 (.661)	.647 (.655)
2	.645	.614	.636	.544	.706	.599	.649	.733 (.741)	.735 (.732)
4	.739	.782	.804	.710	.803	.782	.803	.827 (.840)	.831 (.838)
8	.741	.809	.822	.757	.818	.796	.833	.827 (.828)	.830 (.825)
16	.868	.840	.885	.815	.887	.824	.862	.888 (.890)	.893 (.894)
32	.938	.945	.957	.920	.948	.930	.947	.938 (.935)	.940 (.936)
64	.970	.973	.979	.964	.973	.966	.968	.964 (.960)	.966 (.961)
Chinese-English									
Size	Likert	Meteor 1	Meteor 4	BLEU 1	BLEU 4	TERp 1	TERp 4	HyTER U (r5)	HyTER SPU (r5)
1	.713	.495	.557	.464	.608	.569	.594	.708 (.721)	.668 (.681)
2	.706	.623	.673	.569	.655	.639	.651	.713 (.716)	.702 (.701)
4	.800	.628	.750	.593	.734	.651	.726	.822 (.825)	.820 (.814)
8	.810	.745	.778	.783	.808	.754	.754	.852 (.856)	.854 (.845)
16	.881	.821	.887	.811	.884	.826	.844	.912 (.914)	.914 (.908)
32	.915	.873	.918	.911	.930	.851	.911	.943 (.942)	.941 (.937)
64	.950	.971	.976	.979	.973	.952	.970	.962 (.958)	.958 (.957)

Table 3: Document-level correlations of various scores to HTER. Meteor, BLEU and TERp are shown with 1 and 4 references each, HyTER is shown with the two combination methods (U and SPU), and with reordering (r5).

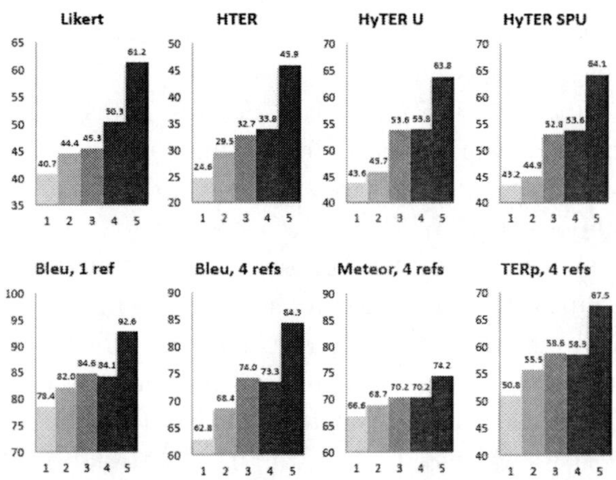

Figure 3: Five MT systems (Chinese-English), scored by 8 different metrics. The x-axis shows the five systems, the y-axis shows the [100-0] normalized scores, with 0 corresponding to a perfect translation. (Note that the scale is similar in all eight graphs.) HTER and HyTER show a similar pattern and similar ranking of the systems.

ments on large test corpora (Papineni et al., 2002; Snover et al., 2006; Lavie and Denkowski, 2009). We believe, however, that the field of MT will be better served if researchers have access to metrics that provide high correlation at the sentence level as well. To this end, we estimate how well various metrics correlate with the Human TER (HTER) metric for corpora of increasingly larger sizes.

Table 3 shows Pearson correlations between HTER and various metrics for scoring documents of size s =1, 2, 4, …, and 64 sentences. To get more reliable results, we create 50 documents per size s, where each document is created by selecting s sentences at random from the available 82 sentences. For each document, there are 5 translations from different systems, so we have 250 translated documents per size. For each language and size, we score the 250 documents under HTER and the other metrics and report the Pearson correlation. Our results show that for large documents, all metrics correlate well with HTER. However, as the sizes of the documents decrease, and especially at the sentence level, HyTER provides especially high correlation with HTER as compared to the other metrics. As a side note, we can see that using reordering when computing the HyTER score does not give consistently better results – see the (r5) numbers, which searched over hypothesis permutations within a local window of size 5; this shows that most reorderings are already captured in the networks. In all experiments, we use BLEU with plus-one smoothing (Lin and Och, 2004).

5 Using meaning-equivalent networks for human translation evaluation

In this section, we present a use case for the HyTER metric outside of machine translation.

5.1 Setup and problem

Language Testing units assess the translation proficiency of thousands of applicants interested in performing language translation work for the US Government. Job candidates typically take a written test in which they are asked to translate four passages (i.e., paragraphs) of increasing difficulty into English. The passages are at difficulty levels 2, 2+, 3, and 4 on the Interagency Language Roundable (ILR) scale.[2] The translations produced by each candidate are manually reviewed to identify mistranslation, word choice, omission, addition, spelling, grammar, register/tone, and meaning distortion errors. Each passage is then assigned one of five labels: Successfully Matches the definition of a successful translation (SM); Mostly Matches the definition (MM); Intermittently Matches (IM); Hardly Matches (HM); Not Translated (NT) for anything where less than 50% of a passage is translated.

We have access to a set of more than 100 rules that agencies practically use to assign each candidate an ILR translation proficiency level: 0, 0+, 1, 1+, 2, 2+, 3, and 3+. For example, a candidate who produces passages labeled as SM, SM, MM, IM for difficulty levels 2, 2+, 3, and 4, respectively, is assigned an ILR level of 2+.

We investigate whether the assessment process described above can be automated. To this end, we obtained the exam results of 195 candidates, where each exam result consists of three passages translated into English by a candidate, as well as the manual rating for each passage translation (i.e., the gold labels SM, MM, IM, HM, or NT). 49 exam results are from a Chinese exam, 71 from a Russian exam and 75 from a Spanish exam. The three passages in each exam are of difficulty levels 2, 2+, and 3; level 4 is not available in our data set. In each exam result, the translations produced by each candidate are sentence-aligned to their respective foreign sentences. We applied the passage-to-ILR mapping rules described above to automatically create a gold overall ILR assessment for each exam submission. Since the languages used here have only 3 passages each, some rules map to several different ILR ratings. Table 4 shows the label distribution at the ILR assessment level across all languages.

Lang.	0	0+	1	1+	2	2+	3	3+
Chi.	0.0	8.2	40.8	65.3	59.2	10.2	4.1	0.0
Rus.	0.0	2.8	12.7	42.3	60.6	46.5	25.4	5.6
Spa.	0.0	1.3	33.3	66.7	88.0	24.0	4.0	0.0
All	0.0	3.6	27.7	57.4	70.8	28.7	11.8	2.1

Table 4: Percentage of exams with ILR levels 0, 0+, ..., 3+ as gold labels. Multiple levels per exam possible.

5.2 Experiments

We automatically assess the proficiency of candidates who take a translation exam. We treat this as a classification task where, for each translation of the three passages, we predict the three passage assessment labels as well as one overall ILR rating.

In support of our goal, we asked annotators to create an English HyTER network for each foreign sentence in the exams. These HyTER networks then serve as English references for the candidate translations. The median number of paths in these HyTER networks is 1.6×10^6 paths/network.

In training, we observe a set of submitted exam translations, each of which is annotated with three passage-level ratings and one overall ILR rating. We develop features (Section 5.3) that describe each passage translation in its relation to the HyTER networks for the passage. We then train a classifier to predict passage-level ratings given the passage-level features that describe the candidate translation. As classifier, we use a multi-class support-vector machine (SVM, Krammer and Singer (2001)). In decoding, we observe a set of exams without their ratings, derive the features and use the trained SVM to predict ratings of the passage translations. We then derive an overall ILR rating based on the predicted passage-level ratings. Since our dataset is small we run 10-fold cross-validation.

5.3 Features

We define features describing a candidate's translation with respect to the corresponding HyTER reference networks. Each of the feature values is computed based on a passage translation as a whole, rather than sentence-by-sentence. As features, we use the HyTER score, as well as the number of insertions, deletions, substitutions, and insertions-or-deletions. We use these numbers normalized by the

[2]See `http://www.govtilr.org/skills/AdoptedILRTranslationGuidelines.htm`.

Level	Measure	Baseline	HyTER-enabled
All	Accuracy	72.31	90.77
2 or better	Precision	85.62	82.11
	Recall	84.93	98.63
	F_1	85.27	89.62

Table 5: Predicting final ILR ratings for candidate exams.

length of the passage, as well as unnormalized. We also use n-gram precisions (for n=1,...,20) as features.

5.4 Results

We report the accuracy on predicting the overall ILR rating of the 195 exams (Table 5). The results in *2 or better* show how well we predict a performance level of 2, 2+, 3 or 3+. It is important to retrieve such relatively good exams with high recall, so that a manual review QA process can confirm the choices while avoid discarding qualified candidates. The results show that high recall is reached while preserving good precision. Since we have several possible gold labels per exam, precision and recall are computed similar to precision and recall in the NLP task of word alignment. $F_1(P,R) = \frac{2PR}{P+R}$ is the harmonic mean of precision and recall. The row *All* shows the accuracy in predicting ILR performance labels overall. As a baseline method we assign the most frequent label per language; these are 1+ for Chinese, and 2 for Russian and Spanish. The results in Table 5 strongly suggest that the process of assigning a proficiency level to human translators can be automated.

6 Discussion

We have introduced an annotation tool and process that can be used to create meaning-equivalent networks that encode an exponential number of translations for a given sentence. We have shown that these networks can be used as foundation for developing improved machine translation evaluation metrics and automating the evaluation of human translation proficiency. We plan to release the OpenMT HyTER networks to the community after the 2012 NIST Open MT evaluation. We believe that our meaning-equivalent networks can be used to support interesting research programs in semantics, paraphrase generation, natural language understanding, generation, and machine translation.

Acknowledgments

We thank our colleagues and the anonymous reviewers for their valuable feedback. This work was partially sponsored by DARPA contract HR0011-11-C-0150 and TSWG contract N41756-08-C-3020 to Language Weaver Inc.

References

C. Allauzen, M. Riley, J. Schalkwyk, W. Skut, and M. Mohri. 2007. OpenFst: a general and efficient weighted finite-state transducer library. In *Proceedings of the 12th international conference on Implementation and application of automata*, page 1123.

O. Bojar, M. Ercegovčević, M. Popel, and O. Zaidan. 2011. A grain of salt for the wmt manual evaluation. In *Proceedings of the Sixth Workshop on Statistical Machine Translation*, pages 1–11, Edinburgh, Scotland, July. Association for Computational Linguistics.

C. Callison-Burch, Ph. Koehn, Ch. Monz, and O. Zaidan. 2011. Findings of the 2011 workshop on statistical machine translation. In *Proceedings of the Sixth Workshop on Statistical Machine Translation*, pages 22–64, Edinburgh, Scotland, July. Association for Computational Linguistics.

G. Cormode and S. Muthukrishnan. 2007. The string edit distance matching problem with moves. *ACM Transactions on Algorithms (TALG)*, 3(1):1–19.

M. Denkowski and A. Lavie. 2011. Meteor 1.3: Automatic Metric for Reliable Optimization and Evaluation of Machine Translation Systems. In *Proceedings of the EMNLP 2011 Workshop on Statistical Machine Translation*.

Q. Gao, N. Bach, S. Vogel, B. Chen, G. Foster, R. Kuhn, C. Callison-Burch, P. Koehn, C. Monz, K. Peterson, et al., 2010. *Proceedings of the Joint Fifth Workshop on Statistical Machine Translation and Metrics (MATR)*, pages 121–126.

P.E. Hart, N.J. Nilsson, and B. Raphael. 1972. Correction to "A formal basis for the heuristic determination of minimum cost paths". *ACM SIGART Bulletin*, pages 28–29, December. ACM ID: 1056779.

S. Kanthak, D. Vilar, E. Matusov, R. Zens, and H. Ney. 2005. Novel reordering approaches in phrase-based statistical machine translation. In *Proceedings of the ACL Workshop on Building and Using Parallel Texts*, pages 167–174.

D. Karakos, J. Eisner, S. Khudanpur, and M. Dreyer. 2008. Machine translation system combination using

ITG-based alignments. *Proc. ACL-08: HLT, Short Papers (Companion Volume)*, page 8184.

K. Krammer and Y. Singer. 2001. On the algorithmic implementation of multi-class SVMs. In *Proc. of JMLR*.

A. Lavie and M. Denkowski. 2009. The meteor metric for automatic evaluation of machine translation. *Machine Translation*, 23(2-3):105–115.

L. I. Levenshtein. 1966. Binary codes capable of correcting deletions, insertions and reversals. *Soviet Physics Doklady*, 10:707–710.

C.Y. Lin and F.J. Och. 2004. Orange: a method for evaluating automatic evaluation metrics for machine translation. In *Proceedings of the 20th international conference on Computational Linguistics*, page 501. Association for Computational Linguistics.

M. Mohri. 2002. Semiring frameworks and algorithms for shortest-distance problems. *Journal of Automata, Languages and Combinatorics*, 7(3):321–350.

J. Olive, C. Christianson, and J. McCary, editors. 2011. *Handbook of Natural Language Processing and Machine Translation*. DARPA Global Autonomous Language Exploitation. Springer.

K. Papineni, S. Roukos, T. Ward, and W.-J. Zhu. 2002. BLEU: a method for automatic evaluation of machine translation. In *Proceedings of 40th Annual Meeting of the Association for Computational Linguistics*, pages 311–318, Philadelphia, Pennsylvania, USA, July. Association for Computational Linguistics.

M. Przybocki, A. Le, G. Sanders, S. Bronsart, S. Strassel, and M. Glenn, 2011. *GALE Machine Translation Metrology: Definition, Implementation, and Calculation*, chapter 5.4, pages 583–811. Springer.

M. Snover, B. Dorr, R. Schwartz, L. Micciulla, and J. Makhoul. 2006. A study of translation edit rate with targeted human annotation. In *Proceedings of the Association for Machine Translation in the Americas*, pages 223–231.

M. Snover, N. Madnani, B. Dorr, and R. Schwartz. 2009. Fluency, adequacy, or HTER? Exploring different human judgments with a tunable MT metric. In *Proceedings of the Fourth Workshop on Statistical Machine Translation at the 12th Meeting of the EACL*.

Apples to Oranges: Evaluating Image Annotations from Natural Language Processing Systems

Rebecca Mason and **Eugene Charniak**
Brown Laboratory for Linguistic Information Processing (BLLIP)
Brown University, Providence, RI 02912
{rebecca,ec}@cs.brown.edu

Abstract

We examine evaluation methods for systems that automatically annotate images using co-occurring text. We compare previous datasets for this task using a series of baseline measures inspired by those used in information retrieval, computer vision, and extractive summarization. Some of our baselines match or exceed the best published scores for those datasets. These results illuminate incorrect assumptions and improper practices regarding preprocessing, evaluation metrics, and the collection of gold image annotations. We conclude with a list of recommended practices for future research combining language and vision processing techniques.

1 Introduction

Automatic image annotation is an important area with many applications such as tagging, generating captions, and indexing and retrieval on the web. Given an input image, the goal is to generate relevant descriptive keywords that describe the visual content of the image. The Computer Vision (CV) literature contains countless approaches to this task, using a wide range of learning techniques and visual features to identify aspects such as objects, people, scenes, and events.

Text processing is computationally less expensive than image processing and easily provides information that is difficult to learn visually. For this reason, most commerical image search websites identify the semantic content of images using co-occurring text exclusively. But co-occurring text is also a noisy source for candidate annotations, since not all of the text is visually relevant. Techniques from Natural Language Processing help align descriptive words and images. Some examples of previous research use named-entity recognition to identify people in images (Deschacht and Moens, 2007); term association to estimate the "visualness" of candidate annotations (Boiy et al., 2008; Leong et al., 2010); and topic models to annotate images given both visual and textual features (Feng and Lapata, 2010b).

Image annotation using NLP is still an emerging area with many different tasks, datasets, and evaluation methods, making it impossible to compare many recent systems to each other. Although there is some effort being made towards establishing shared tasks[1], it is not yet clear which kinds of tasks and datasets will provide interesting research questions and practical applications in the long term. Until then, establishing general "best practices" for NLP image annotation will help advance and legitimize this work. In this paper, we propose some good practices and demonstrate why they are important.

2 Image Annotation Evaluation in CV and NLP

In this section, we first review related work in image annotation evaluation in computer vision, specific challenges, and proposed solutions. We then relate these challenges to the NLP image annotation task and some of the specific problems we propose to address.

[1] http://imageclef.org/

2.1 Related Work in Computer Vision

The work of Müller et al. (2002) is one of the first to address the issue of evaluation for image annotation systems. While using the exact same annotation system, dataset, and evaluation metric, they dramatically improve the apparent performance of their system by using dataset pruning heuristics.

Others have criticized commonly-used CV datasets for being too "easy" — images with the same keywords are extremely similar in low-level features such as orientation, lighting, and color; while differences between images with different keywords are very clear (Westerveld and de Vries, 2003; Ponce et al., 2006; Hervé and Boujemaa, 2007; Tang and Lewis, 2007). These features are unwittingly exploited by certain algorithms and obscure the benefits of using more complex techniques (Ponce et al., 2006). The problem is further exacerbated by evaluation metrics which essentially prefer precision over recall and are biased towards certain keywords. Annotations in test data might not include all of the "correct" keywords, and evaluation metrics need to account for the fact that frequent keywords in the corpus are safer guesses than keywords that appear less frequently (Monay and Gatica-Perez, 2003).

New baseline techniques, evaluation metrics, and datasets for image annotation have been developed in response to these problems. Makadia et al. (2008; 2010) define a basic set of low-level features, and propose new baselines for more complex systems to evaluate against. Barnard et al. (2003) present a normalized loss function to address the preference towards precision in evaluation metrics. New datasets are larger and provide more diverse images, and it is now easy to obtain multiple human-annotations per image thanks to distributed services such as Amazon's Mechanical Turk, and the ESP game (von Ahn and Dabbish, 2004). Hanbury (2008) provides an overview of popular CV annotation datasets and methods used for building them.

2.2 Image Annotation using Natural Language Processing

Many of the problems from CV image annotation are also applicable to NLP image annotation, and bringing NLP to the task brings new challenges as well. One of these challenges is whether to allow infrequent words to be pruned. In CV annotation it is typical to remove infrequent terms from both the keyword vocabulary and the evaluation data because CV algorithms typically need a large number of examples to train on. However, using NLP systems and baselines one can correctly annotate using keywords that did not appear in the training set. Removing "unlearnable" keywords from evaluation data, as done in (Boiy et al., 2008; Feng and Lapata, 2010b), artificially inflates performance against simple baselines such as term frequency.

Nearly all NLP annotation datasets use naturally-occurring sources of images and text. A particularly popular source is news images alongside captions or articles, which are collected online from sources such as Yahoo! News (Berg et al., 2004; Deschacht and Moens, 2007). There are also domain-specific databases with images and descriptions such as the art, antiques, and flowers corpora used in Boiy et al. (2008). Wikipedia has also been used as a source of images and associated text (Tsikrika et al., 2011). These sources typically offer well-written and cleanly formatted text but introduce the problem of converting text into annotations, and the annotations may not meet the requirements of the new task (as shown in Section 3.1). Obtaining data via image search engines is a common practice in CV (Fei-Fei et al., 2004; Berg and Forsyth, 2006) and can also be used to provide more challenging and diverse instances of images and co-occurring text. The additional challenge for NLP is that text content on many websites is written to improve their rank in search engines, using techniques such as listing dozens of popular keywords. Co-occurring text for retrieved images on popular queries may not be representative of the task to be performed.

3 Datasets

In this paper, we examine two established image annotation datasets: the BBC News Dataset of Feng and Lapata (2008) (henceforth referred to as *BBC*), and the general web dataset of Leong et al. (2010) (henceforth referred to as *UNT*). These datasets were both built to evaluate image annotation systems that use longer co-occurring text such as a news article or a webpage, but they use data from differ-

Dataset	BBC	UNT
data instances	article, image, and caption from a news story	image and text from a webpage
source of data	scraped from BBC News website	Google Image Search results
candidate keywords or collocations for annotation	descriptive unigram words from training data	$n \leq 7$-grams extracted from co-occurring text; collocations must appear as article names on Wikipedia
gold annotations	descriptive words from held-out image captions	multiple human-authored annotations for each image
evaluation metric	precision and recall against gold annotations	metrics adapted from evaluation of lexical substitutions (SemEval)
number of train instances	3121 instances of related news article, image, and caption	none (train using cross-validation)
number of test instances	240 instances of news article and related image	300 instances of webpage with text and image
preprocessing procedure	lemmatize tokens, remove from dataset all words that are not descriptive or that appear fewer than five times in training articles	stem all tokens
average number of text tokens after preprocessing	169 word tokens per article, 4.5 per caption	278 word tokens per webpage
average document title length	4 word tokens	6 word tokens
total vocabulary after preprocessing	10479 word types	8409 word types

Table 1: Comparison of the BBC and UNT image annotation datasets.

ent domains, different sources of gold image annotations, different preprocessing procedures, and different evaluation measures.

Table 1 provides an overview of the datasets; while this section covers the source of the datsets and their gold annotations in more detail.

3.1 BBC

The BBC Dataset (Feng and Lapata, 2008)[2] contains news articles, image captions, and images taken from the BBC News website. Training instances consist of a news article, image, and image caption from the same news story. Test instances are just the image and the article, and hold-out the caption as a source of gold image annotations.

Using news image captions as annotations has the disadvantage that captions often describe background information or relate the photo to the story, rather than listing important entities in the image. It also fails to capture variation in how humans describe images, since it is limited to one caption per image.[3] However, captions are a cheap source of data; BBC has ten times as many images as UNT.

To address the problem of converting natural language into annotations, a large amount of preprocessing is performed. The established preprocessing procedure for this dataset is to lemmatize and POS-tag using TreeTagger (Schmid, 1994) then remove all but the "descriptive" words (defined as nouns, adjectives, and certain classes of verbs). This leaves a total text vocabulary of about 32K words, which

[2]Downloaded from `http://homepages.inuf.ed.ac.uk/s0677528/data.html`

[3]The Pascal Sentences dataset (`vision.cs.uiuc.edu/pascal-sentences`) provides multiple captions per image, but they are not naturally-occurring.

is further reduced by removing words that appear fewer than five times in the training set articles. Table 1 shows the number of word tokens and types after performing these steps.[4]

3.2 UNT

The UNT Dataset (Leong et al., 2010)[5] consists of images and co-occurring text from webpages. The webpages are found by querying Google Image Search with frequent English words, and randomly selecting from the results.

Each image in UNT is annotated by five people via Mechanical Turk. In order to make human and system results comparable, human annotators are required to only select words and collocations that are directly extracted from the text, and the gold annotations are the count of how many times each keyword or collocation is selected. The human annotators write keywords into a text box; while the collocations are presented as a list of candidates and annotators mark which ones are relevant. Human annotators tend to select subsets of collocations in addition to the entire collocation. For example, the gold annotation for one image has "university of texas", "university of texas at dallas", "the university of texas", and "the university of texas at dallas", each selected by at least four of the five annotators. Additionally, annotators can select multiple forms of the same word (such as "tank" and "tanks"). Gold annotations are stemmed after they are collected, and keywords with the same stem have their counts merged. For this reason, many keywords have a higher count than the number of annotators.

[4] We are unable to reproduce work from Feng & Lapata (2008; 2010a; 2010b) and Feng (2011). Specifically, our vocabulary counts after preprocessing (as in Table 1) are much higher than reported counts, although the number of tokens per article/caption they report is higher than ours. We have contacted the authors, who confirmed that they took additional steps to reduce the size of the vocabulary, but were unable to tell us exactly what those steps are. Therefore, all system and baseline scores presented on their dataset are of our own implementation, and do not match those reported in previous publications.

[5] Downloaded from `http://lit.csci.unt.edu/index.php?P=research/downloads`

4 Baselines

We run several baselines on the datasets. Term frequency, tf*idf, and corpus frequency are features that are often used in annotation systems, so it is important to test them on their own. Document Title and tf*idf are both baselines that were used in the original papers where these datasets came from.

Sentence extraction is a new baseline that we propose specifically for the BBC dataset, in order see if we can exploit certain properties of the gold annotations, which are also derived from sentences.

4.1 Term Frequency

Term frequency has been shown to be a powerful feature in summarization (Nenkova and Vanderwende, 2005). Words that appear frequently are considered more meaningful than infrequent words. Term frequency is the number of times a term (excluding function words) appears in a document, divided by the total number of terms in that document. On the UNT dataset we use the stopword list included with the MALLET[6] toolkit, while the BBC dataset doesn't matter because the function words have already been removed.

4.2 tf*idf

While term frequency baseline requires the use of an *ad hoc* function word list, tf*idf adjusts the weights of different words depending on how important they are in the corpus. It is a standard baseline used for information retrieval tasks, based on the intuition that a word that appears in a smaller number of documents is more likely to be meaningful than a word that appears in many documents.

tf*idf is the product of term frequency and inverse document frequency – $idf(t_i) = \log \frac{N}{n_i}$ where N is the number of documents in the corpus, and n_i is the number of documents that contain the term t_i. For the BBC Dataset, we base the idf weights on the document frequency of the training articles. For UNT, we use the reported tf*idf score which uses the British National Corpus to calculate the idf scores.[7]

[6] `mallet.cs.umass.edu`

[7] We also ran tf*idf where for each document we recalculate idf using the other 299, but it didn't make any meaningful difference.

4.3 Corpus Frequency

Image annotations in both NLP and CV tend to be distributed with a relatively small number of frequently occuring keywords, and a long tail of keywords that only appear a few times. For UNT, we use the total keyword frequency of all the gold annotations, except for the one document that we are currently scoring. For BBC, we only measure the frequency of keywords in the training set captions, since we are specifically interested in the frequency of terms in captions.

4.4 Document Title

For BBC, the news article headline, and for UNT, the title of the webpage.

4.5 Sentence Extraction

Our baseline extracts the most central sentence from the co-occurring text and uses descriptive words from that sentence as the image annotation. Unlike sentence extraction techniques from Feng and Lapata (2010a), we determine which sentence to extract using the term frequency distribution directly. We extract the sentence with the minimum KL-divergence to the entire document.[8]

5 BBC Dataset Experiments

5.1 System Comparison

In addition to the baselines, we compare against the Mix LDA system from Feng and Lapata (2010b). In Mix LDA, each instance is represented as a bag of textual features (unigrams) and visual features (SIFT features quantized to discrete "image words" using k-means). A Latent Dirichlet Allocation topic model is trained on articles, images, and captions from the training set. Keywords are generated for an unseen image and article pair by estimating the distribution of topics that generates the test instance, then multiplying them with the word distributions in each topic to find the probability of textual keywords for the image. Text LDA is is the same model but only using words and not image features.

[8]One could also think of this as a version of the KLSum summarization system (Haghighi and Vanderwende, 2009) that stops after one sentence.

5.2 Evaluation

The evaluation metric and the source of gold annotations is described in Table 1. For the baselines 4.1, 4.2, 4.3 and the Mix LDA system, the generated annotation for each test image is its ten most likely keywords. We also run all baselines and the Mix LDA system on an unpruned version of the dataset, where infrequent terms are not removed from training data, test data, or the gold annotations. The purpose of this evaluation is to see if candidate keywords deemd "unlearnable" by the Mix LDA system can be learned by the baselines.

5.3 Results

The evaluation results for the BBC Dataset are shown in Table 2. Clearly, term frequency is a stronger baseline than tf*idf by a large margin. The reason for this is simple: since nearly all of BBC's function words are removed during preprocessing, the only words downweighted by the idf score are common – but meaningful – words such as *police* or *government*. This is worth pointing out because, in many cases, the choice of using a term frequency or tf*idf baseline is made based on what was used in previous work. As we show here and in Section 6.3, the choice of frequency baseline should be based on the data and processing techniques being used.

We use the corpus frequency baseline to illustrate the difference between *standard* and *include-infrequent* evaluations. Since including infrequent words doesn't change which are most frequent in the dataset, precision for corpus frequency doesn't change. But since infrequent words are now included in the evaluation data, we see a 0.5% drop in recall (since corpus frequency won't capture infrequent words). Compared to the other baselines, this is not a large difference. Other baselines see a larger drop in recall because they have both more gold keywords to estimate and more candidate keywords to consider. tf*idf is the most affected by this, because idf overly favors very infrequent keywords, despite their low term frequency. In comparison, the term frequency baseline is not as negatively affected and even improves in precision because there are some cases where a word is very important to an article in the test set but just didn't appear very often in the training set (see Table 3 for examples). But the base-

	Standard			Include-infrequent		
	Precision	**Recall**	**F1**	**Precision**	**Recall**	**F1**
Term Frequency	13.13	27.84	17.84	13.62	25.71	17.81
tf * idf	9.21	19.97	12.61	7.25	13.52	9.44
Doc Title	17.23	13.70	15.26	15.91	11.86	13.59
Corpus Frequency	3.17	6.52	4.26	3.17	6.02	4.15
Sentence Extraction	16.67	15.61	16.13	18.62	16.83	17.68
Mix LDA	7.30	16.16	10.06	7.50	13.98	9.76
Text LDA	8.38	17.46	11.32	7.79	14.52	10.14

Table 2: Image annotation results for previous systems and our proposed baselines on the BBC Dataset.

	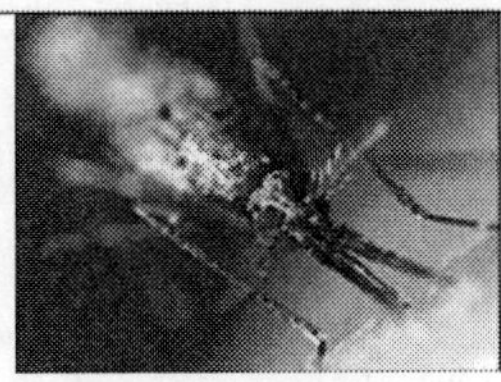
Cadbury increase **contamination testing level**	malaria parasite **spread** mosquito

Table 3: Examples of gold annotations from the test section of the BBC Dataset. The bolded words are the ones that appear five or more times in the training set; the unbolded words appear fewer than five times and would be removed from both the candidate and gold keywords in the standard BBC evaluation.

lines with the best precision are the Doc Title and Sentence Extraction baselines, which do not need to generate ten keywords for every image.

While sentence extraction has a lower recall than term frequency, it is the only baseline or system that has improved recall when including infrequent words. This is unexpected because our baseline selects a sentence based on the term frequency of the document, and the recall for term frequency fell. One possible explanation is that extraction implicitly uses correlations between keywords. Probabilities of objects appearing together in an image are not independent; and the accuracy of annotations can be improved by generating annotation keywords as a set (Moran and Lavrenko, 2011). Recent works in image captioning also use these correlations: explicitly, using graphical models (Kulkarni et al., 2011; Yang et al., 2011); and implicitly, using language models (Feng and Lapata, 2010a). In comparison, sentence extraction is very implicit.

Unsurprisingly, the Text LDA and Mix LDA systems do worse on the include-infrequent evaluation than they do on the standard, because words that do not appear in the training set will not have high probability in the trained topic models. We were unable to reproduce the reported scores for Mix LDA from Feng and Lapata (2010b) where Mix LDA's scores were double the scores of Text LDA (see Footnote 4). We were also unable to reproduce reported scores for tf*idf and Doc Title (Feng and Lapata, 2008). However, we have three reasons why we believe our results are correct. First, BBC has more keywords, and fewer images, than typically seen in CV datasets. The BBC dataset is simply not suited for learning from visual data. Second, a single SIFT descriptor describes which way edges are oriented at a certain point in an image (Lowe, 1999). While certain types of edges may correlate to visual objects also described in the text, we do not expect SIFT features to be as informative as textual features for this task. Third, we refer to the best system scores reported by Leong et al. (2010), who evaluate their text mining system (see section 6.1) on the standard BBC dataset.[9] While their f1 score is slightly worse than our term frequency baseline, they do 4.86% better than tf*idf. But, using the baselines reported in Feng and Lapata (2008), their improvement over tf*idf is 12.06%. Next, we compare their system against frequency baselines using the 10 keyword generation task on the UNT dataset (the *oot normal* scores in table 5). Their best system performs 4.45% better

[9]Combined model; precision: 13.38, recall: 25.17, f1: 17.47. Crucially, they do not reimplement previous systems or baselines, but use scores reported from Feng and Lapata (2008).

than term frequency, and 0.55% worse than tf*idf.[10] Although it is difficult to compare different datasets and evaluation metrics, our baselines for BBC seem more reasonable than the reported baselines, given their relative performance to Leong et al's system.

6 UNT Dataset Experiments

6.1 System Comparison

We evaluate against the text mining system from (Leong et al., 2010). Their system generates image keywords by extracting text from the co-occurring text of an image. It uses three features for selecting keywords. *Flickr Picturability* queries the Flickr API with words from the text in order to find related image tags. Retrieved tags that appear as surface forms in the text are rewarded proportional to their frequency in the text. *Wikipedia Salience* assigns scores to words based on a graph-based measure of importance that considers each term's document frequency in Wikipedia. *Pachinko Allocation Model* is a topic model that captures correlations between topics (Li and McCallum, 2006). PAM infers subtopics and supertopics for the text, then retrieves top words from the top topics as annotations. There is also a combined model of these features using an SVM with 10-fold cross-validation.

6.2 Evaluation

Evaluation on UNT uses a framework originally developed for the SemEval lexical substitution task (McCarthy and Navigli, 2007). This framework accounts for disagreement between annotators by weighting each generated keyword by the number of human annotators who also selected that keyword. The scoring framework consists of four evaluation measures: *best normal*, *best mode*, *oot* (out-of-ten) *normal*, and *oot mode*.[11]

The two *best* evaluations find the accuracy of a single "best" keyword generated by the system[12].

[10]And as we stated earlier, the relative performance of term frequency vs tf*idf is different from dataset to dataset.

[11]Both the original framework and its adaptation by Leong et al. (2010) give precision and recall for each of the evaluation measures. However, precision and recall are identical for all baselines and systems, and only slightly different on the upper bound (human) scores. To preserve space, we only present the metric and scores for precision.

[12]In contrast to the original SemEval task, where systems can make from zero to many "best" guesses, penalized by the total number of guesses made.

Best normal measures the accuracy for each system annotation a_j as the number of times a_j appears in the R_j, the multi-set union of human tags, and averages over all the test images.

$$Bestnormal = \frac{\sum_{i_j \in I} \frac{|a_j \in R_j|}{|R_j|}}{|I|}$$

In *oot normal*, up to ten unordered guesses can be made without penalty.

$$ootnormal = \frac{\sum_{i_j \in I} \frac{\sum_{a_j \in A_j} |a_j \in R_j|}{|R_j|}}{|I|}$$

where A_j is the set of ten system annotations for image i_j.

The *best mode* and *oot mode* metrics are the same as the *normal* metrics except they only evaluate system annotations for images where R_j contains a single most frequent tag. We use the scoring software provided by SemEval[13] with the gold annotation file provided in the UNT Dataset.

6.3 Results

The results of the lexical substitution evaluation on the UNT Dataset are shown in Table 5. The results from the *normal* show support for our earlier idea that the relative performance of term frequency vs tf*idf depends on the dataset. Although the term frequency baseline uses a stopword list, there are other words that appear frequently enough to suggest they are not meaningful to the document – such as copyright disclaimers.

Recall that the *mode* evaluation is only measured on data instances where the gold annotations have a single most frequent keyword. While running the evaluation script on the gold annotation file that came with the UNT dataset, we discover that SemEval only identifies 28 of the 300 instances as having a single mode annotation, and that for 21 of those 28 instances, the mode keyword is "cartoon". Those 21/28 images correspond to the 75% *best mode* score obtained by Corpus Frequency baseline. Given the small number of instances that actually

[13]`http://nlp.cs.swarthmore.edu/semeval/tasks/task10/data.shtml`

		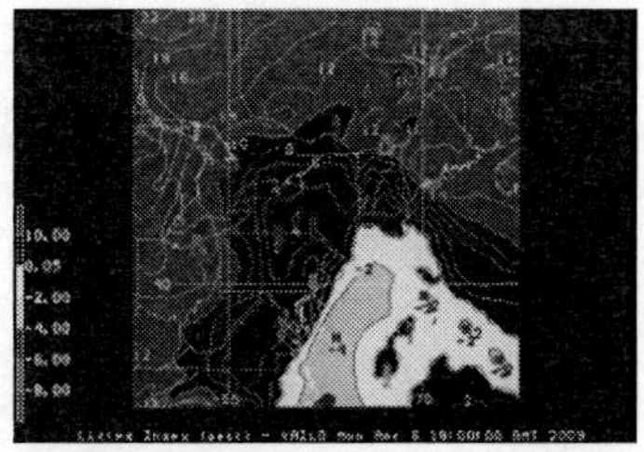
cartoon(6), market(5), market share(5), declin(3), imag(3), share(3), pictur(1), illustr(1), cartoonstock(1), origin(1), artist(1), meet(1), jfa0417(1), meeting-copyright(1)	cartoon(6), bill gate(5), gate(4), monopoli(4), pearli gate(4), bill(3), imag(3), caricatur(2), pictur(2), illustr(1), copyright(1), artist(1), own(1), pearli(1)	lift index(5), gener(3), index(3), condit(2), comput(2), comput gener(2), unstabl(2), zone(2), area(1), field(1), between(1), stabl(1), encyclopedia(1), thunderstorm(1), lift(1), free encyclopedia(1), wikipedia(1)

Table 4: Examples of gold annotations from the UNT Dataset.

	Best		Out-of-ten (oot)	
	Normal	**Mode**	**Normal**	**Mode**
Term Frequency	5.67	14.29	33.40	89.29
tf * idf	5.94	14.29	38.40	78.57
Doc Title	6.40	7.14	35.19	92.86
Corpus Frequency	2.54	75.00	8.22	82.14
Flickr Picturability	6.32	78.57	35.61	92.86
Wikipedia Salience	6.40	7.14	35.19	92.86
Topic Model (PAM)	5.99	42.86	37.13	85.71
Combined (SVM)	6.87	67.49	37.85	100.00

Table 5: Image annotation results for our proposed baselines, the text mining systems from (Leong et al., 2010)

count towards these metrics, we conclude that *mode* evaluation is not a meaningful way to compare image annotation systems on the UNT dataset.

That said, the number of cartoons in the dataset does seem to be strikingly high. Looking at the source of the images, we find that 45 of the 300 images were collected from a single online cartoon library. Predictably, we find that the co-occurring text to these images contains a long list of keywords, and little other text that is relevant to the image. We looked at a small sample of the rest of the dataset and found that many of the other text documents in UNT also have keyword lists.

Including this types of text in a general web corpus is not necessarily a problem, but it's difficult to measure the benefits of using complex techniques like topic modeling and graph similarily to find and extract annotations when in so many cases the annotations have already been found and extracted. This is shown in the *normal* evaluation results, where the combined system is only slightly better at selecting the single best keyword, and no better than tf*idf for the *out-of-ten* measure.

7 Conclusion

The intent of this paper is not to teach researchers how to inflate their own results, but to encourage better practices. With that purpose in mind, we make the following suggestions regarding future work in this area:

Get to know your data. The ability to quickly and cheaply collect very large – but very noisy – collections of data from the internet is a great advance for both NLP and CV research. However, there still needs to be an appopriate match betwen the task being performed, the system being proposed, and the dataset being used; and large noisy datasets can hide unintended features or incorrect assumptions about the data.

Use relevant gold annotations. Do not convert other sources of data into annotations. When collecting human annotations, avoid postprocessing steps such as merging or deleting keywords that change the annotators' original intent. Keep an open dialogue with annotators about issues that they find confusing, since that is a sign of an ill-formed task.

Preprocessing should be simple and reproducable. The use of different preprocessing procedures affects the apparent performance of systems and sometimes has unintended consequences.

Use strong baselines and compare to other work only when appropriate. Systems developed for different tasks or datasets can make for misleading comparisons if they don't use all features available. Strong baselines explicitly exploit low-level features that are implicitly exploited by proposed systems, as well as low-level features of the dataset.

Don't remove keywords from gold annotations. Just because keywords are impossible for one system to learn, does not mean they are impossible for all systems to learn. Removing evaluation data artificially inflates system scores and limits comparison to related work.

If a proposed system is to learn associations between visual and textual features, then it is necessary to **use larger datasets**. In general, global annotations, such as scenes, is easiest; identifying specific objects is more difficult; and identification of events, activities, and other abstract qualities has a very low success rate (Fluhr et al., 2006). Alternately, **use simpler image features** that are known to have a high sucess rate. For example, Deschacht and Moens (2007) used a face detector to determine the number of faces in an image, and then used NLP to determine the names of those people from associated text.

References

K. Barnard, P. Duygulu, D. Forsyth, N. De Freitas, D.M. Blei, and M.I. Jordan. 2003. Matching words and pictures. *The Journal of Machine Learning Research*, 3:1107–1135.

Tamara L. Berg and David A. Forsyth. 2006. Animals on the web. In *Proceedings of the 2006 IEEE Computer Society Conference on Computer Vision and Pattern Recognition - Volume 2*, CVPR '06, pages 1463–1470, Washington, DC, USA. IEEE Computer Society.

T.L. Berg, A.C. Berg, J. Edwards, M. Maire, R. White, Yee-Whye Teh, E. Learned-Miller, and D.A. Forsyth. 2004. Names and faces in the news. In *Computer Vision and Pattern Recognition, 2004. CVPR 2004. Proceedings of the 2004 IEEE Computer Society Conference on*, volume 2, pages II–848 – II–854 Vol.2, june-2 july.

E. Boiy, K. Deschacht, and M.-F. Moens. 2008. Learning visual entities and their visual attributes from text corpora. In *Database and Expert Systems Application, 2008. DEXA '08. 19th International Workshop on*, pages 48 –53, sept.

Koen Deschacht and Marie-Francine Moens. 2007. Text analysis for automatic image annotation. In *ACL*, volume 45, page 1000.

Li Fei-Fei, Rob Fergus, and Pietro Perona. 2004. Learning generative visual models from few training examples: An incremental bayesian approach tested on 101 object categories. In *Proceedings of the 2004 Conference on Computer Vision and Pattern Recognition Workshop (CVPRW'04) Volume 12 - Volume 12*, CVPRW '04, pages 178–, Washington, DC, USA. IEEE Computer Society.

Yansong Feng and Mirella Lapata. 2008. Automatic image annotation using auxiliary text information. *Proceedings of ACL-08: HLT*, pages 272–280.

Yansong Feng and Mirella Lapata. 2010a. How many words is a picture worth? automatic caption generation for news images. In *Proceedings of the 48th Annual Meeting of the Association for Computational Linguistics*, ACL '10, pages 1239–1249, Stroudsburg, PA, USA. Association for Computational Linguistics.

Yansong Feng and Mirella Lapata. 2010b. Topic models for image annotation and text illustration. In *HLT-NAACL*, pages 831–839.

Yansong Feng. 2011. *Automatic caption generation for news images*. Ph.D. thesis, University of Edinburgh.

Christian Fluhr, Pierre-Alain Mollic, and Patrick Hde. 2006. Usage-oriented multimedia information retrieval technological evaluation. In James Ze Wang, Nozha Boujemaa, and Yixin Chen, editors, *Multimedia Information Retrieval*, pages 301–306. ACM.

Aria Haghighi and Lucy Vanderwende. 2009. Exploring content models for multi-document summarization. In *Proceedings of Human Language Technologies: The 2009 Annual Conference of the North American Chapter of the Association for Computational Linguistics*, pages 362–370, Boulder, Colorado, June. Association for Computational Linguistics.

Allan Hanbury. 2008. A survey of methods for image annotation. *J. Vis. Lang. Comput.*, 19:617–627, October.

Nicolas Hervé and Nozha Boujemaa. 2007. Image annotation: which approach for realistic databases? In *Proceedings of the 6th ACM international conference on Image and video retrieval*, CIVR '07, pages 170–177, New York, NY, USA. ACM.

Girish Kulkarni, Visruth Premraj, Sagnik Dhar, Siming Li, Yejin Choi, Alexander C. Berg, and Tamara L. Berg. 2011. Baby talk: Understanding and generating simple image descriptions. In *CVPR*, pages 1601–1608.

Chee Wee Leong, Rada Mihalcea, and Samer Hassan. 2010. Text mining for automatic image tagging. In *COLING*, pages 647–655.

Wei Li and Andrew McCallum. 2006. Pachinko allocation: Dag-structured mixture models of topic correlations. In *Proceedings of the 23rd international conference on Machine learning*, ICML '06, pages 577–584, New York, NY, USA. ACM.

D.G. Lowe. 1999. Object recognition from local scale-invariant features. In *Computer Vision, 1999. The Proceedings of the Seventh IEEE International Conference on*, volume 2, pages 1150 –1157 vol.2.

Ameesh Makadia, Vladimir Pavlovic, and Sanjiv Kumar. 2008. A new baseline for image annotation. In *Proceedings of the 10th European Conference on Computer Vision: Part III*, ECCV '08, pages 316–329, Berlin, Heidelberg. Springer-Verlag.

A. Makadia, V. Pavlovic, and S. Kumar. 2010. Baselines for image annotation. *International Journal of Computer Vision*, 90(1):88–105.

D. McCarthy and R. Navigli. 2007. Semeval-2007 task 10: English lexical substitution task. In *Proceedings of the 4th International Workshop on Semantic Evaluations (SemEval-2007)*, pages 48–53.

Florent Monay and Daniel Gatica-Perez. 2003. On image auto-annotation with latent space models. In *Proceedings of the eleventh ACM international conference on Multimedia*, Multimedia '03, pages 275–278, New York, NY, USA. ACM.

S. Moran and V. Lavrenko. 2011. Optimal tag sets for automatic image.

Henning Müller, Stéphane Marchand-Maillet, and Thierry Pun. 2002. The truth about corel - evaluation in image retrieval. In *Proceedings of the International Conference on Image and Video Retrieval*, CIVR '02, pages 38–49, London, UK, UK. Springer-Verlag.

Ani Nenkova and Lucy Vanderwende. 2005. The impact of frequency on summarization. Technical report, Microsoft Research.

J. Ponce, T. Berg, M. Everingham, D. Forsyth, M. Hebert, S. Lazebnik, M. Marszalek, C. Schmid, B. Russell, A. Torralba, C. Williams, J. Zhang, and A. Zisserman. 2006. Dataset issues in object recognition. In Jean Ponce, Martial Hebert, Cordelia Schmid, and Andrew Zisserman, editors, *Toward Category-Level Object Recognition*, volume 4170 of *Lecture Notes in Computer Science*, pages 29–48. Springer Berlin / Heidelberg. 10.1007/11957959_2.

H. Schmid. 1994. Probabilistic part-of-speech tagging using decision trees. In *Proceedings of international conference on new methods in language processing*, volume 12, pages 44–49. Manchester, UK.

Jiayu Tang and Paul Lewis. 2007. A study of quality issues for image auto-annotation with the corel dataset. *IEEE Transactions on Circuits and Systems for Video Technology*, Vol. 1(NO. 3):384–389, March.

T. Tsikrika, A. Popescu, and J. Kludas. 2011. Overview of the wikipedia image retrieval task at imageclef 2011. In *CLEF (Notebook Papers/LABs/Workshops): CLEF*.

Luis von Ahn and Laura Dabbish. 2004. Labeling images with a computer game. In *Proceedings of the SIGCHI conference on Human factors in computing systems*, CHI '04, pages 319–326, New York, NY, USA. ACM.

Thijs Westerveld and Arjen P. de Vries. 2003. Experimental evaluation of a generative probabilistic image retrieval model on 'easy' data. In *In Proceedings of the SIGIR Multimedia Information Retrieval Workshop 2003, Aug*.

Yezhou Yang, Ching Lik Teo, Hal Daumé III, and Yiannis Aloimonos. 2011. Corpus-guided sentence generation of natural images. In *Empirical Methods in Natural Language Processing (EMNLP)*, Edinburgh, Scotland.

Re-examining Machine Translation Metrics for Paraphrase Identification

Nitin Madnani **Joel Tetreault**
Educational Testing Service
Princeton, NJ, USA
{nmadnani, jtetreault}@ets.org

Martin Chodorow
Hunter College of CUNY
New York, NY, USA
martin.chodorow@hunter.cuny.edu

Abstract

We propose to re-examine the hypothesis that automated metrics developed for MT evaluation can prove useful for paraphrase identification in light of the significant work on the development of new MT metrics over the last 4 years. We show that a meta-classifier trained using nothing but recent MT metrics outperforms all previous paraphrase identification approaches on the Microsoft Research Paraphrase corpus. In addition, we apply our system to a second corpus developed for the task of plagiarism detection and obtain extremely positive results. Finally, we conduct extensive error analysis and uncover the top systematic sources of error for a paraphrase identification approach relying solely on MT metrics. We release both the new dataset and the error analysis annotations for use by the community.

1 Introduction

One of the most important reasons for the recent advances made in Statistical Machine Translation (SMT) has been the development of automated metrics for evaluation of translation quality. The goal of any such metric is to assess whether the translation hypothesis produced by a system is semantically equivalent to the source sentence that was translated. However, cross-lingual semantic equivalence is even harder to assess than monolingual, therefore, most MT metrics instead try to measure whether the hypothesis is semantically equivalent to a human-authored reference translation of the same source sentence. Using such automated metrics as proxies for human judgments can provide a quick assessment of system performance and allow for short feature and system development cycles, which are important for evaluating research ideas.

In the last 5 years, several shared tasks and competitions have led to the development of increasingly sophisticated metrics that go beyond the computation of n-gram overlaps (BLEU, NIST) or edit distances (TER, WER, PER etc.). Note that the task of an MT metric is essentially one of identifying whether the translation produced by a system is a paraphrase of the reference translation. Although the notion of using MT metrics for the task of paraphrase identification is not novel (Finch et al., 2005; Wan et al., 2006), it merits a re-examination in the light of the development of these novel MT metrics for which we can ask "How much better, if at all, do these newer metrics perform for the task of paraphrase identification?"

This paper describes such a re-examination. We employ 8 different MT metrics for identifying paraphrases across two different datasets - the well-known Microsoft Research paraphrase corpus (MSRP) (Dolan et al., 2004) and the plagiarism detection corpus (PAN) from the 2010 Uncovering Plagiarism, Authorship and Social Software Misuse shared task (Potthast et al., 2010). We include both MSRP and PAN in our study because they represent two very different sources of paraphrased text. The creation of MSRP relied on the massive redundancy of news articles on the web and extracted sentential paraphrases from different stories written about the same topic. In the case of PAN, humans consciously paraphrased existing text to generate new, plagiarized text.

In the next section, we discuss previous work on paraphrase identification. In §3, we describe our approach to paraphrase identification using MT metrics as features. Our approach yields impressive results – the current state of the art for MSRP and extremely positive for PAN. In the same section, we examine whether each metric's purported strength is demonstrated in our datasets. Next, in §4 we conduct an analysis of our system's misclassifications for both datasets and outline a taxonomy of errors that our system makes. We also look at annotation errors in the datasets themselves. We discuss the findings of the error analysis in §5 and conclude in §6.

2 Related Work & Our Contributions

Our goal in this paper is to examine the utility of a paraphrase identification approach that relies solely on MT evaluation metrics and no other evidence of semantic equivalence. Given this setup, the most relevant previous work is by Finch et al. (2005) which uses BLEU, NIST, WER and PER as features for a supervised classification approach using SVMs. In addition, they also incorporate part-of-speech information as well as the Jiang-Conrath WordNet-based lexical relatedness measure (Jiang and Conrath, 1997) into their edit distance calculations. In the first part of our paper, we present classification experiments with newer MT metrics not available in 2005, a worthwhile exercise in itself. However, we go much further in our study:

- We apply our approach to two different paraphrase datasets (MSRP and PAN) that were created via different processes.
- We attempt to find evidence of each metric's purported strength in both datasets.
- We conduct an extensive error analysis to find types of errors that a system based solely on MT metrics is likely to make. In addition, we also discover interesting paraphrase pairs in the datasets.
- We release our sentence-level PAN dataset (see §3.3.2) which contains more realistic examples of paraphrase and can prove useful to the community for future evaluations of paraphrase identification.

BLEU-based features were also employed by Wan et al. (2006) who use them in combination with several other features based on dependency relations and tree edit-distance inside an SVM.

There are several other supervised approaches to paraphrase identification that do not use any features based on MT metrics. Mihalcea et al. (2006) combine pointwise mutual information, latent semantic analysis and WordNet-based measures of word semantic similarity into an arbitrary text-to-text similarity metric. Qiu et al. (2006) build a framework that detects dissimilarities between sentences and makes its paraphrase judgment based on the significance of such dissimilarities. Kozareva and Montoyo (2006) use features based on LCS, skip n-grams and WordNet with a meta-classifier composed of SVM, k-nearest neighbor and maximum entropy classifiers. Islam and Inkpen (2007) measure semantic similarity using a corpus-based measure and a modified version of the Longest Common Subsequence (LCS) algorithm. Rus et al. (2008) take a graph-based approach originally developed for recognizing textual entailment and adapt it for paraphrase identification. Fernando and Stevenson (2008) construct a matrix of word similarities between all pairs of words in both sentences instead of relying only on the maximal similarities. Das and Smith (2009) use an explicit model of alignment between the corresponding parts of two paraphrastic sentences and combine it with a logistic regression classifier built from n-gram overlap features. Most recently, Socher et al. (2011) employ a joint model that incorporates the similarities between both single word features as well as multi-word phrases extracted from the parse trees of the two sentences.

We compare our results to those from all the approaches described in this section later in §3.4.

3 Classifying with MT Metrics

In this section, we first describe our overall approach to paraphrase identification that utilizes only MT metrics. We then discuss the actual MT metrics we used. Finally, we describe the datasets on which we evaluated our approach and present our results.

MSRP	They had published an advertisement on the Internet on June 10, offering the cargo for sale, he added.
	On June 10, the ship's owners had published an advertisement on the Internet, offering the explosives for sale.
	Security lights have also been installed and police have swept the grounds for booby traps.
	Security lights have also been installed on a barn near the front gate.
PAN	Dense fogs wrapped the mountains that shut in the little hamlet, but overhead the stars were shining in the near heaven.
	The hamlet is surrounded by mountains which is wrapped with dense fogs, though above it, near heaven, the stars were shining.
	In still other places, the strong winds carry soil over long distances to be mixed with other soils.
	In other places, where strong winds blow with frequent regularity, sharp soil grains are picked up by the air and hurled against the rocks, which, under this action, are carved into fantastic forms.

Table 1: Examples of paraphrases and non-paraphrases (in italics) from the MSRP and PAN corpora.

3.1 Classifier

Our best system utilized a classifier combination approach. We used a simple meta-classifier that uses the average of the unweighted probability estimates from the constituent classifiers to make its final decision. We used three constituent classifiers: Logistic regression, the SMO implementation of a support vector machine (Platt, 1999; Keerthi et al., 2001) and a lazy, instance-based classifier that extends the nearest neighbor algorithm (Aha et al., 1991). We used the WEKA machine learning toolkit to perform our experiments (Hall et al., 2009). [1]

3.2 MT metrics used

1. **BLEU** (Papineni et al., 2002) is the most commonly used metric for MT evaluation. It is computed as the amount of n-gram overlap—for different values of n—between the system output and the reference translation, tempered by a penalty for translations that might be too short. BLEU relies on exact matching and has no concept of synonymy or paraphrasing. We use BLEU1 through BLEU4 as 4 different features for our classifier (hereafter BLEU(1-4)).

2. **NIST** (Doddington, 2002) is a variant of BLEU that uses the arithmetic mean of n-gram overlaps, rather than the geometric mean. It also weights each n-gram according to its informativeness as indicated by its frequency. We use NIST1 through NIST5 as 5 different features for our classifier (hereafter NIST(1-5)).

3. **TER** (Snover et al., 2006) is defined as the number of edits needed to "fix" the translation output so that it matches the reference. TER differs from WER in that it includes a heuristic algorithm to deal with shifts in addition to insertions, deletions and substitutions.

4. **TERp** (TER-Plus) (Snover et al., 2009) builds upon the core TER algorithm by providing additional edit operations based on stemming, synonymy and paraphrase.

5. **METEOR** (Denkowski and Lavie, 2010) uses a combination of both precision and recall unlike BLEU which focuses on precision. Furthermore, it incorporates stemming, synonymy (via WordNet) and paraphrase (via a lookup table).

6. **SEPIA** (Habash and El Kholy, 2008) is a syntactically-aware metric designed to focus on

[1]These constituent classifiers were chosen since they were the top 3 performers in 5-fold cross-validation experiments conducted on both MSRP and PAN training sets. The meta-classifier was chosen similarly once the constituent classifiers had been chosen.

structural n-grams with long surface spans that cannot be captured efficiently with surface n-gram metrics. Like BLEU, it is a precision-based metric and requires a length penalty to minimize the effects of length.

7. **BADGER** (Parker, 2008) is a language independent metric based on compression and information theory. It computes a compression distance between the two sentences that utilizes the Burrows Wheeler Transformation (BWT). The BWT enables taking into account common sentence contexts with no limit on the size of these contexts.

8. **MAXSIM** (Chan and Ng, 2008) treats the problem as one of bipartite graph matching and maps each word in one sentence to at most one word in the other sentence. It allows the use of arbitrary similarity functions between words.[2]

Our choice of metrics was based on their popularity in the MT community, their performance in open competitions such as the NIST MetricsMATR challenge (NIST, 2008) and the WMT shared evaluation task (Callison-Burch et al., 2010), their availability, and their relative complementarity.

3.3 Datasets

In this section, we describe the two datasets that we used to evaluate our approach.

3.3.1 Microsoft Research Paraphrase Corpus

The MSRP corpus was created by mining news articles on the web for topically similar articles and then extracting potential sentential paraphrases using a set of heuristics. Extracted pairs were then shown to two human judges with disagreements handled by a third adjudicator. The kappa was reported as 0.62, which indicates moderate to high agreement. We used the pre-stipulated train-test splits (4,076 sentence pairs in training and 1,725 in test) to train and test our classifier.

[2]We also experimented with TESLA—a variant of MAXSIM that performs better for MT evaluation—in our preliminary experiments However, both MAXSIM and TESLA performed almost identically in our cross-validation experiments. Therefore, we only retained MAXSIM in our final experiment since it was significantly faster to run than the version of TESLA we had.

3.3.2 Plagiarism Detection Corpus (PAN)

We wanted to evaluate our approach on a set of paraphrases where the semantic similarity was not simply an accidental by-product of topical similarity but rather consciously generated. We used the test collection from the PAN 2010 plagiarism detection competition. This dataset consists of 41,233 text documents from Project Gutenberg in which 94,202 cases of plagiarism have been inserted. The plagiarism was created either by using an algorithm or by explicitly asking Turkers to paraphrase passages from the original text. We focus only on the human-created plagiarism instances.

Note also that although the original PAN dataset has been used in plagiarism detection shared tasks, those tasks are generally formulated differently in that the goal is to find all potentially plagiarized passages in a given set of documents along with the corresponding source passages from other documents. In this paper, we wanted to focus on the task of identifying whether two given *sentences* can be considered paraphrases.

To generate a sentence-level PAN dataset, we wrote a heuristic alignment algorithm to find corresponding pairs of sentences within a passage pair linked by the plagiarism relationship. The alignment algorithm utilized only bag-of-words overlap and length ratios and no MT metrics. For our negative evidence, we sampled sentences from the same document and extracted sentence pairs that have at least 4 content words in common. We then sampled randomly from both the positive and negative evidence files to create a training set of 10,000 sentence pairs and a test set of 3,000 sentence pairs.

Table 1 shows examples of paraphrastic and non-paraphrastic sentence pairs from both the MSRP and PAN datasets.

3.4 Results

Before presenting the results of experiments that used multiple metrics as features, we wanted to determine how well each metric performs on its own when used for paraphrase identification. Table 2 shows the classification results on both the MSRP and PAN datasets using each metric as the only feature. Although previously explored metrics such as BLEU and NIST perform reasonably well, they are

	MSRP		PAN	
Metric	Acc.	F1	Acc.	F1
MAXSIM	67.2	79.4	84.7	83.4
BADGER	67.6	79.9	88.5	87.9
SEPIA	68.1	79.8	87.7	86.8
TER	69.9	80.9	85.7	83.8
BLEU(1-4)	72.3	80.9	87.9	87.1
NIST(1-5)	72.8	81.2	88.2	87.3
METEOR	73.1	81.0	89.5	88.9
TERp	74.3	81.8	91.2	90.9

Table 2: Classification results for MSRP and PAN with individual metrics as features. Entries are sorted by accuracies on MSRP.

clearly outperformed by some of the more robust metrics such as TERp and METEOR.

Table 3 shows the results of our experiments employing multiple metrics as features, for both MSRP and PAN. The final row in the table shows the results of our best system. The remaining rows of this table show the top performing metrics for both datasets; we treat BLEU, NIST and TER as our baseline metrics since they are not new and are not the primary focus of our investigation. In terms of novel metrics, we find that the top 3 metrics for both datasets were TERp, METEOR and BADGER respectively as shown. Combining all 8 metrics led to the best performance for MSRP but showed no performance increase for PAN.

	MSRP		PAN	
Features	Acc.	F1	Acc.	F1
Base Metrics	74.1	81.5	88.6	87.8
+ TERp	75.6	82.5	91.5	91.2
+ METEOR	76.6	83.2	92.0	91.8
+ BADGER	77.0	83.7	**92.3**	**92.1**
+ Others	**77.4**	**84.1**	**92.3**	**92.1**

Table 3: The top 3 performing MT metrics for both MSRP and PAN datasets as identified by ablation studies. BLEU(1-4), NIST(1-5) and TER were used as the 10 base features in the classifiers.

Our results for the PAN dataset are much better than those for MSRP since:

(a) It is likely that our negative evidence is too easy for most MT metrics.

(b) Many plagiarized pairs are linked simply via lexical synonymy which can be easily captured by metrics like METEOR and TERp, e.g., the sentence "*Young's main contention is that in literature genius must make rules for itself, and that imitation is suicidal*" is simply plagiarized as "*Young's major argument is that in literature intellect must make rules for itself, and that replication is dangerous.*" However, the PAN corpus does contains some very challenging and interesting examples of paraphrases—even more so than MSRP—which we describe in §4.

Finally, Table 4 shows that the results from our best system are the best ever reported on the MSRP test set when compared to all previously published work. Furthermore, the single best performing metric (TERp)—also shown in the table—outperforms, by itself, many previous approaches utilizing multiple, complex features.

Model	Acc.	F1
All Paraphrase Baseline	66.5	79.9
(Mihalcea et al., 2006)	70.3	81.3
(Rus et al., 2008)	70.6	80.5
(Qiu et al., 2006)	72.0	81.6
(Islam and Inkpen, 2007)	72.6	81.3
(Fernando and Stevenson, 2008)	74.1	82.4
TERp	74.3	81.8
(Finch et al., 2005)	75.0	82.7
(Wan et al., 2006)	75.6	83.0
(Das and Smith, 2009)	76.1	82.7
(Kozareva and Montoyo, 2006)	76.6	79.6
(Socher et al., 2011)	76.8	83.6
Best MT Metrics	**77.4**	**84.1**

Table 4: Comparing the accuracy and F-score for the single best performing MT metric TERp (in gray) as well as the best metric combination system (in gray and bold) with previously reported results on the MSRP test set ($N = 1,752$). Entries are sorted by accuracy.

3.5 Metric Contributions

In addition to quantitative results, we also wanted to highlight specific examples from our datasets that can demonstrate the strength of the new metrics over simple n-gram overlap and edit-distance based metrics. Below we present examples for the 4 best metrics across both datasets:

- **TERp** uses stemming and phrasal paraphrase recognition to accurately classify the sentence pair "*For the weekend, the top 12 movies grossed $157.1 million, up 52 percent from the same weekend a year earlier.*" and "*The overall box office soared, with the top 12 movies grossing $157.1 million, up 52 percent from a year ago.*" from MSRP as paraphrases.

- **METEOR** uses synonymy and stemming to accurately classify the sentence pair "*Her letters at this time exhibited the two extremes of feeling in a marked degree.*" and "*Her letters at this time showed two extremes of feelings.*" from PAN as plagiarized.

- **BADGER** uses unsupervised contextual similarity detection to accurately classify the sentence pair "*Otherwise they were false or mistaken reactions*" and "*Otherwise, were false or wrong responses*" from PAN as plagiarized.

- **SEPIA** uses structural n-grams via dependency trees to accurately classify the sentence pair "*At his sentencing, Avants had tubes in his nose and a portable oxygen tank beside him.*" and "*Avants, wearing a light brown jumpsuit, had tubes in his nose and a portable oxygen tank beside him.*" from MSRP as paraphrases.

4 Error Analysis

In this section, we conduct an analysis of the misclassifications that our system makes on both datasets. Our analyses consisted of finding the sentences pairs from the test set for each dataset which *none* of our systems (not just the best one) ever classified correctly and inspecting a random sample of 100 of these. This inspection yields not only the top sources of error for an approach that relies solely on MT metrics but also uncovers sources of annotation errors in both datasets themselves.

4.1 MSRP

In their paper describing the creation of the MSRP corpus, Dolan et al. (2004) clearly state that "the degree of mismatch allowed before the pair was judged non-equivalent was left to the discretion of the individual rater" and that "many of the 33% of sentence pairs judged to be not equivalent still overlap significantly in information content and even wording". We found evidence that the raters were not always consistent in applying the annotation guidelines. For example, in some cases the lack of attribution for a quotation led the raters to label a pair as paraphrastic whereas in other cases it did not. For example, the pair "*These are real crimes that hurt a lot of people.*" and "*'These are real crimes that disrupt the lives of real people,' Smith said.*" was not marked as paraphrastic. Furthermore, even though the guidelines instruct the raters to "treat anaphors and their full forms as equivalent, regardless of how great the disparity in length or lexical content between the two sentences", we found pairs of sentences marked as non-paraphrastic which only differed in anaphora. However, the primary goal of this analysis is to find sources of errors in an MT-metric driven approach and below we present the top 5 such sources:

1. **Misleading Lexical Overlap.** Non-paraphrastic pairs where there is large lexical overlap of secondary material between the two sentences but the primary semantic content is different. For example, "*Gyorgy Heizler, head of the local disaster unit, said the coach had been carrying 38 passengers.*" and "*The head of the local disaster unit, Gyorgy Heizler, said the coach driver had failed to heed red stop lights.*".

2. **Lack of World Knowledge.** Paraphrastic pairs that require world knowledge. For example, "*Security experts are warning that a new mass-mailing worm is spreading widely across the Internet, sometimes posing as e-mail from the Microsoft founder.*" and "*A new worm has been spreading rapidly across the Internet, sometimes pretending to be an e-mail from Microsoft Chairman Bill Gates, antivirus vendors said Monday.*".

3. **Tricky Phrasal Paraphrases.** Paraphras-

tic pairs that contain domain-dependent semantic alternations. For example, "*The leading actress nod went to energetic newcomer Marissa Jaret Winokur as Edna's daughter Tracy.*" and "*Marissa Jaret Winokur, as Tracy, won for best actress in a musical.*".

4. **Date, Time and Currency Differences**. Paraphrastic pairs that contain different temporal or currency references. These references were normalized to generic tokens (e.g., `$NUMBER`) before being shown to MSRP raters but are retained in the released dataset. For example, "*Expenses are expected to be approximately $2.3 billion, at the high end of the previous expectation of $2.2-to-$2.3 billion.*" and "*Spending on research and development is expected to be $4.4 billion for the year, compared with the previous expectation of $4.3 billion.*".

5. **Anaphoric References**. Paraphrastic pairs wherein one member of the pair contains anaphora and the other doesn't (these are considered paraphrases according to MSRP guidelines). For example, "*They certainly reveal a very close relationship between Boeing and senior Washington officials.*" and "*The e-mails reveal the close relationship between Boeing and the Air Force.*".

Note that most misclassified sentence pairs can be categorized into more than one of the above categories.

4.2 PAN

For the PAN corpus, the only real source of error in the dataset itself was the sentence alignment algorithm. There were many sentence pairs that were erroneously linked as paraphrases. Leaving aside such pairs, the 3 largest sources of error for our MT-metric based approach were:

1. **Complex Sentential Paraphrases**. By far, most of the misclassified pairs were paraphrastic pairs that could be categorized as real world plagiarism, i.e., where the plagiarizer copies the idea from the source but makes several complex transformations, e.g., sentence splitting, structural paraphrasing etc. so as to render an MT-metric based approach powerless. For example, consider the pair "*The school bears the honored name of one who, in the long years of the anti-slavery agitation, was known as an uncompromising friend of human freedom.*" and "*The school is named after a man who defended the right of all men and women to be free, all through the years when people campaigned against slavery.*" Another interesting example is the pair "*The most unpromising weakly-looking creatures sometimes live to ninety while strong robust men are carried off in their prime.*" and "*Sometimes the strong personalities live shorter than those who are unexpected.*".

2. **Misleading Lexical Overlap**. Similar to MSRP. For example, "*Here was the second period of Hebraic influence, an influence wholly moral and religious.*" and "*This was the second period of Hellenic influence, an influence wholly intellectual and artistic.*".

3. **Typographical and Spelling Errors**. Paraphrastic pairs where the Turkers creating the plagiarism also introduced other typos and spelling errors. For example, "*The boat then had on board over 1,000 souls in all*" and "*1000 people where on board at that tim*".

5 Discussion

The misses due to "Date, Time, and Currency Differences" are really just the result of an artifact in the testing. It is possible that an MT metrics based approach could accurately predict these cases if the references to dates etc. were replaced with generic tokens as was done for the human raters. In a similar vein, some of the misses that are due to a lack of world knowledge might become hits if a named entity recognizer could discover that "*Microsoft founder*" is the same as "*Microsoft Chairman*". Similarly, some of the cases of anaphoric reference might be recognized with an anaphora resolution system. And the problem of misspelling in PAN could be remedied with automatic spelling correction. Therefore, it is possible to improve the MT metrics based approach further by utilizing certain NLP systems as pre-processing modules for the text.

The only error category in MSRP and PAN

that caused false positives was "Misleading Lexical Overlap". Here, the take-away message is that not every part of a sentence is equally important for recognizing semantic equivalence or non-equivalence. In a sentence that describes what someone communicated, the content of what was said is crucial. For example, despite lexical matches everywhere else, the mismatch of "*the coach had been carrying 38 passengers*" and "*the driver had failed to heed the red stop lights*" disqualifies the respective sentences from being paraphrases. Along the same line, differences in proper names and their variants should receive more weight than other words. A sentence about "*Hebraic influence*" on a period in history is not the same as a sentence which matches in every other way but is instead about "*Hellenic influence*". These sentences represent a bigger challenge for an approach based solely on MT metrics. Given enough pairs of "near-miss" non-paraphrases, our system might be able to figure this out, but this would require a large amount of annotated data.

6 Conclusions

In this paper, we re-examined the idea that automatic metrics used for evaluating translation quality can perform well explicitly for the task of paraphrase recognition. The goal of our paper was to determine whether approaches developed for the related but different task of MT evaluation can be as competitive as approaches developed specifically for the task of paraphrase identification. While we do treat the metrics as black boxes to an extent, we explicitly chose metrics that were high performing but also complementary in nature.

Specifically, our re-examination focused on the more sophisticated MT metrics of the last few years that claim to go beyond simple n-gram overlap and edit distance. We found that a meta-classifier trained using only MT metrics outperforms all previous approaches for the MSRP corpus. Unlike previous studies, we also applied our approach to a new plagiarism dataset and obtained extremely positive results. We examined both datasets not only to find pairs that demonstrated the strength of each metric but also to conduct an error analysis to discover the top sources of errors that an MT metric based approach is susceptible to. Finally, we discovered that using the TERp metric by itself provides fairly good performance and can outperform many other supervised classification approaches utilizing multiple, complex features.

We also have two specific suggestions that we believe can benefit the community. First, we believe that binary indicators of semantic equivalence are not ideal and a continuous value between 0 and 1 indicating the degree to which two pairs are paraphrastic is more suitable for most approaches. However, rather than asking annotators to rate pairs on a scale, a better idea might be to show the sentence pairs to a large number of Turkers (≥ 20) on Amazon Mechanical Turk and ask them to classify it as either a paraphrase or a non-paraphrase. A simple estimate of the degree of semantic equivalence of the pair is simply the proportion of the Turkers who classified the pair as paraphrastic. An example of such an approach, as applied to the task of grammatical error detection, can be found in (Madnani et al., 2011).[3] Second, we believe that the PAN corpus—with Turker simulated plagiarism—contains much more realistic examples of paraphrase and should be incorporated into future evaluations of paraphrase identification. In order to encourage this, we are releasing our PAN dataset containing 13,000 sentence pairs.

We are also releasing our error analysis data (100 pairs for MSRP and 100 pairs for PAN) since they might prove useful to other researchers as well. Note that the annotations for this analysis were produced by the authors themselves and, although, they attempted to accurately identify all error categories for most sentence pairs, it is possible that the errors in some sentence pairs were not comprehensively identified.[4]

Acknowledgments

We would like to thank Aoife Cahill, Michael Heilman and the three anonymous reviewers for their useful comments and suggestions.

[3]A good approximation is to use an ordinal scale for the human judgments as in the Semantic Textual Similarity task of SemEval 2012. See `http://www.cs.york.ac.uk/semeval-2012/task6/` for more details.

[4]The data is available at `http://bit.ly/mt-para`.

References

D. W. Aha, D. Kibler, and M. K. Albert. 1991. Instance-based learning algorithms. *Mach. Learn.*, 6:37–66.

C. Callison-Burch, P. Koehn, C. Monz, K. Peterson, and O. Zaidan, editors. 2010. *Proceedings of the Joint Fifth Workshop on Statistical Machine Translation and MetricsMATR.*

Y. S. Chan and H. T. Ng. 2008. MAXSIM: A maximum similarity metric for machine translation evaluation. In *Proceedings of ACL-HLT*, pages 55–62.

D. Das and N.A. Smith. 2009. Paraphrase Identification as Probabilistic Quasi-synchronous Recognition. In *Proceedings of ACL-IJCNLP*, pages 468–476.

M. Denkowski and M. Lavie. 2010. Extending the METEOR Machine Translation Metric to the Phrase Level. In *Proceedings of NAACL.*

G. Doddington. 2002. Automatic Evaluation of Machine Translation Quality using N-gram Co-occurrence Statistics. In *Proceedings of HLT*, pages 138–145.

B. Dolan, C. Quirk, and C. Brockett. 2004. Unsupervised Construction of Large Paraphrase Corpora: Exploiting Massively Parallel News Sources. In *Proceedings of COLING*, pages 350–356, Geneva, Switzerland.

S. Fernando and M. Stevenson. 2008. A Semantic Similarity Approach to Paraphrase Detection. In *Proceedings of the Computational Linguistics UK (CLUK) 11th Annual Research Colloquium.*

A. Finch, Y.S. Hwang, and E. Sumita. 2005. Using Machine Translation Evaluation Techniques to Determine Sentence-level Semantic Equivalence. In *Proceedings of the Third International Workshop on Paraphrasing*, pages 17–24.

N. Habash and A. El Kholy. 2008. SEPIA: Surface Span Extension to Syntactic Dependency Precision-based MT Evaluation. In *Proceedings of the Workshop on Metrics for Machine Translation at AMTA.*

M. Hall, E. Frank, Geoffrey Holmes, Bernhard Pfahringer, Peter Reutemann, and Ian H. Witten. 2009. The WEKA Data Mining Software: An Update. *SIGKDD Explorations*, 11.

A. Islam and D. Inkpen. 2007. Semantic Similarity of Short Texts. In *Proceedings of RANLP*, pages 291–297.

J. J. Jiang and D. W. Conrath. 1997. Semantic Similarity Based on Corpus Statistics and Lexical Taxonomy. *CoRR*, cmp-lg/9709008.

S. S. Keerthi, S. K. Shevade, C. Bhattacharyya, and K. R. K. Murthy. 2001. Improvements to Platt's SMO Algorithm for SVM Classifier Design. *Neural Comput.*, 13(3):637–649.

Z. Kozareva and A. Montoyo. 2006. Paraphrase Identification on the Basis of Supervised Machine Learning Techniques. In *Proceedings of FinTAL*, pages 524–233.

N. Madnani, J. Tetreault, M. Chodorow, and A. Rozovskaya. 2011. They Can Help: Using Crowdsourcing to Improve the Evaluation of Grammatical Error Detection Systems. In *Proceedings of ACL (Short Papers).*

R. Mihalcea, C. Corley, and C. Strapparava. 2006. Corpus-based and Knowledge-based Measures Of Text Semantic Similarity. In *Proceedings of AAAI*, pages 775–780.

NIST. 2008. NIST MetricsMATR Challenge. Information Access Division. `http://www.itl.nist.gov/iad/mig/tests/metricsmatr/.`

K. Papineni, S. Roukos, T. Ward, and W. J. Zhu. 2002. BLEU: A Method for Automatic Evaluation of Machine Translation. In *Proceedings of ACL.*

S. Parker. 2008. BADGER: A New Machine Translation Metric. In *Proceedings of the Workshop on Metrics for Machine Translation at AMTA.*

John C. Platt. 1999. Advances in kernel methods. chapter Fast Training of Support Vector Machines using Sequential Minimal Optimization, pages 185–208. MIT Press.

M. Potthast, B. Stein, A. Barrón-Cedeño, and P. Rosso. 2010. An Evaluation Framework for Plagiarism Detection. In *Proceedings of COLING*, pages 997–1005.

L. Qiu, M. Y. Kan, and T. S. Chua. 2006. Paraphrase Recognition via Dissimilarity Significance Classification. In *Proceedings of the EMNLP*, pages 18–26.

V. Rus, P.M. McCarthy, M.C. Lintean, D.S. McNamara, and A.C. Graesser. 2008. Paraphrase Identification with Lexico-Syntactic Graph Subsumption. In *Proceedings of FLAIRS*, pages 201–206.

M. Snover, B. Dorr, R. Schwartz, L. Micciulla, and J. Makhoul. 2006. A Study of Translation Edit Rate with Targeted Human Annotation. In *Proceedings of AMTA.*

M. Snover, N. Madnani, B. Dorr, and R. Schwartz. 2009. TER-Plus: Paraphrase, Semantic, and Alignment Enhancements to Translation Edit Rate. *Machine Translation*, 23(2–3):117–127.

R. Socher, E.H. Huang, J. Pennington, A.Y. Ng, and C.D. Manning. 2011. Dynamic Pooling and Unfolding Recursive Autoencoders for Paraphrase Detection. In *Advances in Neural Information Processing Systems 24 (NIPS).*

S. Wan, R. Dras, M. Dale, and C. Paris. 2006. Using Dependency-based Features to Take the "para-farce" Out of Paraphrase. In *Proceedings of the Australasian Language Technology Workshop (ALTW)*, pages 131–138.

A Dependency Treebank of Classical Chinese Poems

John Lee and Yin Hei Kong
The Halliday Centre for Intelligent Applications of Language Studies
Department of Chinese, Translation and Linguistics
City University of Hong Kong
{jsylee,yhkong}@cityu.edu.hk

Abstract

As interest grows in the use of linguistically annotated corpora in research and teaching of foreign languages and literature, treebanks of various historical texts have been developed. We introduce the first large-scale dependency treebank for Classical Chinese literature. Derived from the Stanford dependency types, it consists of over 32K characters drawn from a collection of poems written in the 8th century CE. We report on the design of new dependency relations, discuss aspects of the annotation process and evaluation, and illustrate its use in a study of parallelism in Classical Chinese poetry.

1 Introduction

Recent efforts in creating linguistically annotated text corpora have overwhelmingly focused on modern languages. Among the earliest and most well-known are the part-of-speech (POS) tagged Brown Corpus (Francis & Kučera, 1982), and the syntactically analyzed Penn Treebank (Marcus et al., 1993). However, the first digital corpus, which emerged soon after the invention of computers, had as its subject matter a collection of 13th-century texts --- in 1949, Roberto Busa initiated the POS tagging of the complete works of Thomas Aquinas, written in Latin.

In the past decade, Humanities scholars have begun to use digital corpora for the study of ancient languages and historical texts. They come in a variety of languages and genres, from Old English (Taylor et al., 2003) to Early New High German (Demske et al., 2004) and Medieval Portuguese (Rocio et al. 2000); and from poetry (Pintzuk & Leendert, 2001) to religious texts such as the New Testament (Haug & Jøhndal, 2008) and the Quran (Dukes & Buckwalter, 2010). They are increasingly being leveraged in teaching (Crane et al., 2009) and in research (Lancaster, 2010).

This paper describes the first large-scale dependency treebank for Classical Chinese. The treebank consists of poems from the Tang Dynasty (618 – 907 CE), considered one of the crowning achievements in traditional Chinese literature. The first half of the paper reviews related work (section 2), then describes the design of the treebank (section 3), its text and evaluation (section 4). The second half shows the research potentials of this treebank with a study on parallelism in (section 5).

2 Previous Work

Existing linguistic resources for Chinese is predominantly for the modern language. This section first describes the major Modern Chinese treebanks on which we based our work (section 2.1), then summarizes previous research in word segmentation and POS tagging, two pre-requisites for building a Classical Chinese treebank (section 2.2).

2.1 Modern Chinese

Most treebanks have been annotated under one of two grammatical theories, the phrase structure grammar, which is adopted by the Penn Treebank (Marcus et al., 1993), or dependency grammar, adopted by the Prague Dependency Treebank

(Hajic, 1998). The most widely used treebank for Modern Chinese, the Penn Chinese Treebank (Xue et al., 2005), belongs to the former kind.

Rather than encoding constituency information, dependency grammars give information about grammatical relations between words. Modern Chinese has been analyzed in this framework, for example at Stanford University (Chang et al., 2009). The dependency relations follow the design principles of those initially applied to English (de Marneffe and Manning, 2008), with a few added relations to accommodate Chinese-specific features, such as the "ba"-construction. Their POS tagset is borrowed from that of the Penn Chinese Treebank.

2.2 Classical Chinese

Like its modern counterpart, two pre-requisites for constructing a Classical Chinese treebank are word segmentation and part-of-speech tagging. In this section, we first summarize existing POS tagging frameworks, then describe the only current treebank of Classical Chinese.

Word boundaries and parts-of-speech tags have been added to the Academia Sinica Ancient Chinese Corpus (Wei et al., 1997) and the Sheffield Corpus of Chinese (Hu et al., 2005). Since there is not yet a scholarly consensus on word segmentation in Chinese (Feng 1998), it is not surprising that there are wide-ranging levels of granularity of the POS tagsets. They range from 21 tags in (Huang et al., 2002), 26 in the Peking University corpus (Yu et al., 2002), 46 in the Academia Sinica Balanced Corpus (Chen et al., 1996), to 111 in the Sheffield Corpus of Chinese (Hu et al., 2005). This treebank uses a system of nested POS tags (Lee, 2012), which accommodates different policies for word segmentation and maximize interoperability between corpora.

The only previous syntactic treebank for Classical Chinese is a constituent-based one (Huang et al., 2002), composed of 1000 sentences from pre-Tsin Classical Chinese. No word segmentation was performed for this treebank.

3 Treebank design

Although Classical Chinese is not mutually intelligible with Modern Chinese, the two share considerable similarities in vocabulary and grammar. Given the seminal work already achieved for Modern Chinese, our principle is to borrow from existing annotation framework as much as possible. For example, our POS tagset is based on that of the Penn Chinese Treebank, after a slight revision of its 33 tags (Lee, 2012). This approach not only gives users a familiar point of reference, and also makes the treebank interoperable with existing Modern Chinese resources. Interoperability allows the potential of bootstrapping with Modern Chinese data, as well as contrastive studies for the two languages.

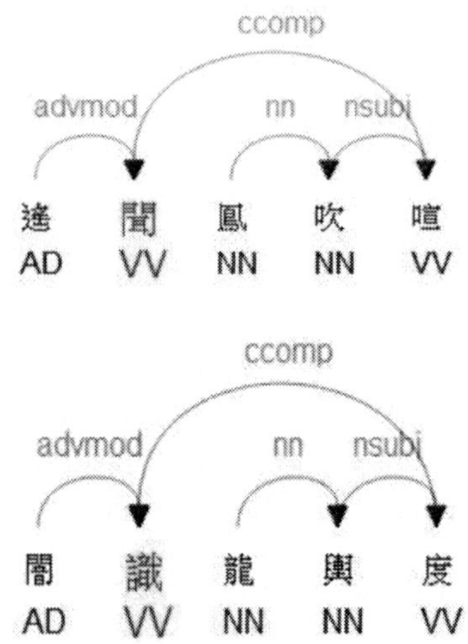

遙	聞	鳳	吹	喧
'far'	'hear'	'phoenix'	'call'	'make noise'
[I] hear from afar the call of the phoenix making noise.				
闇	識	龍	輿	度
'faint'	'sense'	'dragon'	'carriage'	'come'
[I] faintly sense the dragon-decorated carriage coming.				

Figure 1. Dependency trees of two adjacent 5-character lines (forming a parallel *couplet*)[1]. The POS tags are based on (Xue et al., 2005); the dependency relations on (Chang et al., 2009). The two lines are perfectly parallel both in terms of POS and dependencies.

A dependency framework is chosen for two reasons. First, words in Classical Chinese poems, our target text (section 4), tend to have relatively free word order. Dependency grammars can handle this phenomenon well. Second, our treebank is expected to be used pedagogically, and we expect explicit grammatical relations between words to be helpful to students. These relations also encode

[1] From Wang Wei 《奉和聖制御春明樓臨右相園亭賦樂賢詩應制》

semantic information, which lend themselves to meaning extraction applications.

Our set of dependency relations is based on those developed at Stanford University for Modern Chinese (see section 2.2). Our approach is to map their 44 dependency relations, as much as possible, to Classical Chinese. Modern Chinese, a non-inflectional language, does not mark many linguistic features, including person, gender, and number, etc. It uses a small number of function words to encode other features, such as tense, voice, and case. Many of these function words do not exist in Classical Chinese. In particular, prepositions are rare[2]; instead, nouns expressing time, locations, instruments, indirect recipients, etc., modify the verb directly. This phenomenon prompted the introduction of two new relations "locative modifiers" (section 3.1) and "oblique objects" (section 3.2); and the re-instatement of two relations, "noun phrases as adverbial modifiers" (section 3.3) and "indirect objects", from the Stanford dependencies (de Marneffe and Manning, 2008) that are excluded from the Modern Chinese variant (Chang et al., 2009) . An overview is provided in Table 1.

Dependency	Stanford English	Stanford Modern Chinese	This paper
Direct object (`dobj`)	√	√	√
Indirect object (`iobj`)	√		√
Locative modifier (`lmod`)			√
Noun phrase as adverbial modifier (`npadvmod`)	√		√
Oblique objects (`obl`)			√
Concessive, temporal, conditional, and causal modifier (`conc`, `temp`, `cond`, `caus`)			√

Table 1. Comparison of our set of dependency relations with the Stanford dependencies for English (de Marneffe and Manning, 2008) and for Modern Chinese (Chang et al., 2009). All other relations from Stanford Modern Chinese are retained and are not listed here.

3.1 Locative modifiers

To indicate time, English usually requires a preposition (e.g., '*on* Monday'), but sometimes does not (e.g., 'today'). For the latter case, the bare noun phrase is considered a "temporal modifier" in a `tmod` relation with the verb in (de Marneffe and Manning, 2008).

Similarly, to indicate locations, a preposition is normally required in English (e.g., '*on* the hill'). However, in Classical Chinese, the preposition is frequently omitted, with the bare locative noun phrase modifying the verb directly. To mark these nouns, we created the "locative modifier" relation (`lmod`). Consider sentence (1) in Table 2. Although the word "hill" occupies the position normally reserved for the subject, it actually indicates a location, and is therefore assigned the `lmod` relation. In sentence (2), the locative noun 'alley' is placed after the verb.

3.2 Oblique objects

Oblique objects are a well-known category in the analysis of ancient Indo-European languages, for example Latin and ancient Greek. In the PROIEL treebank (Haug and Jøhndal, 2008), for example, the "oblique" (`obl`) relation marks arguments of the verb which are not subjects or non-accusative 'objects'. These are most commonly nouns in the dative or ablative case, as well as prepositional phrases. It is believed that oblique objects exist in Classical Chinese, but have been replaced by prepositional phrases in Modern Chinese (Li and Li, 1986).

The `obl` relation is imported to our treebank to mark nouns that directly modify a verb to express means, instrument, and respect, similar to the functions of datives and ablatives. They typically come after the verb. In sentence (6) in Table 2, the noun 'cup' is used in an instrumental sense to modify 'drunk' in an `obl` relation.

3.3 Noun phrase as adverbial modifier

A temporal modifier such as "today" is an example where a noun phrase serves as an adverbial modifier in English. This usage is more general and extends to other categories such as floating reflexives (e.g., it is *itself* adequate), and other PP-like NPs (e.g., two *times* a day). These noun phrases are marked with the relation `npadvmod` in (de Marneffe and Manning, 2008).

[2] Classical Chinese has a category of verbs called "coverbs" which function like prepositions, but are less frequently used. (Pulleyblank, 1995).

<table>
<tr><td colspan="5">Locative modifier</td></tr>
<tr><td>千</td><td>山</td><td>響</td><td colspan="2">杜鵑</td></tr>
<tr><td>'thousand'</td><td>'hill'</td><td>'make sound'</td><td colspan="2">'bird'</td></tr>
<tr><td colspan="5">(1) Birds are singing on a thousand hills.
lmod('make sound', 'hill')</td></tr>
<tr><td>五</td><td>馬</td><td>驚</td><td>窮</td><td>巷</td></tr>
<tr><td>'five'</td><td>'horse'</td><td>'scare'</td><td>'end'</td><td>'alley'</td></tr>
<tr><td colspan="5">(2) Five horses are scared at the end of the alley.</td></tr>
<tr><td colspan="5">lmod('scare', 'alley')</td></tr>
<tr><td colspan="5">Indirect Objects</td></tr>
<tr><td>寄</td><td>語</td><td>邊</td><td>塞</td><td>人</td></tr>
<tr><td>'send'</td><td>'word'</td><td>'edge'</td><td>'region'</td><td>'person'</td></tr>
<tr><td colspan="5">(3) [I] send a word to the person at the frontier.</td></tr>
<tr><td colspan="5">iobj('send', 'person')</td></tr>
<tr><td colspan="5">Noun phrase as adverbial modifier</td></tr>
<tr><td>風</td><td>物</td><td>自</td><td colspan="2">瀟灑</td></tr>
<tr><td>'scene'</td><td>'thing'</td><td>'self'</td><td colspan="2">'natural, unrestrained'</td></tr>
<tr><td colspan="5">(4) The scenes are being natural and unrestrained in themselves.</td></tr>
<tr><td colspan="5">npadvmod('natural', 'self')</td></tr>
<tr><td>年</td><td>年</td><td>梁</td><td>甫</td><td>吟</td></tr>
<tr><td>'year'</td><td>'year'</td><td>'Liang'</td><td>'Fu'</td><td>'song'</td></tr>
<tr><td colspan="5">(5) [He sings] the Liangfu Song year after year.</td></tr>
<tr><td colspan="5">npadvmod('song', 'year')</td></tr>
<tr><td colspan="5">Oblique objects</td></tr>
<tr><td>同</td><td>醉</td><td>菊</td><td>花</td><td>杯</td></tr>
<tr><td>'together'</td><td>'drunk'</td><td>'chrysan-themus'</td><td>'flower'</td><td>'cup'</td></tr>
<tr><td colspan="5">(6) [We] get drunk together with the chrysanthemus cup.</td></tr>
<tr><td colspan="5">obl('drunk', 'cup')</td></tr>
</table>

Table 2. Example sentences illustrating the use of the dependency relations `lmod` (locative modifier), `iobj` (indirect object), `npadvmod` (noun phrase as adverbial modifier), and `obl` (oblique object)[3].

In Modern Chinese, this usage is less frequent[4], perhaps leading to its exclusion in (Chang et al., 2009). In contrast, in Classical Chinese, nouns function much more frequently in this capacity, expressing metaphoric meaning, reasons, moods, repetitions, etc., and typically preceding the verb (Li and Li, 1986). Sentences (4) and (5) in Table 2 provide examples of this kind, with the noun 'self' as a reflexive, and the noun 'year' indicating repetition.

3.4 Indirect objects

The double object construction contains two objects in a verb phrase. The direct object is the thing or person that is being transferred or moved (e.g., "he gave me a *book*"); the indirect object is the recipient ("he gave *me* a book"). In inflected languages, the noun representing the indirect object may be marked by case. Since Classical Chinese does not have this linguistic device, the indirect object is unmarked; we distinguish it with the "indirect object" label (`iobj`).

The `iobj` label exists in Stanford English dependencies (de Marneffe and Manning, 2008), but was not included in the Modern Chinese version (Chang et al., 2009), likely due to its infrequent appearance in Modern Chinese. It is re-instated in our Classical Chinese treebank. Sentence (3) in Table 2 provides an example, with 'word' as the direct object and 'person' as the indirect.

3.5 Absence of copular verbs

In a copular construction such as "A is B", A is considered the "topic" (`top`) of the copular verb "is" (Chang et al., 2009). The copular, however, is rarely used in Classical Chinese (Pulleyblank, 1995). In some cases, it is replaced by an adverb that functions as a copular verb. If so, that adverb is POS-tagged as such (`VC`) in our treebank, and the dependency tree structure is otherwise normal. In other cases, the copular is absent altogether. Rather than inserting implicit nodes as in (Haug and Jøhndal, 2008), we expand the usage of the `top` relation. It usually connects the subject ("A") to the copular, but would in this case connect it with the noun predicate ("B") instead. In the example sentence below, the relation `top`('capable', 'general') would be assigned.

將軍	武	庫	才
'general'	'weapon'	'warehouse'	'capable'

The general [is] a capable manager of the arsenal[5].

[3] The verses are from Wang Wei 《送梓州李使君》,《鄭果州相過》; Meng Haoran 《同張明府清鏡歌》,《宴包二融宅》,《與白明府游江》,《和賈主簿弁九日登峴山》.

[4] Mostly restricted to temporal and location modifiers.

3.6 Discourse relations

Two clauses may be connected by a discourse relation, such as causal or temporal. In English, these relations may be explicitly realized, most commonly by discourse connectives, such as 'because' or 'when'. Even in the absence of these connectives, however, two adjacent clauses can still hold an implicit discourse relation. A detailed study, which resulted in the Penn Discourse Treebank (Prasad et al., 2008), found that explicit relations outnumber implicit ones in English, but the latter is nonetheless quite common and can be annotated with high inter-annotator agreement.

Temporal relation				
為	童	憶	聚	沙
'be'	'child'	'remember'	'gather'	'sand'
(1) [When I] was a child, [I] remember [playing] a game with sand.				
`dep-temp`('remember', 'be')				
Causal relation				
不	才	明	主	棄
'not'	'capable'	'good'	'ruler'	'forsake'
(2) The good ruler does not appoint me [as an official], [because] I am not capable.				
`dep-caus`('forsake', 'capable')				
Concessive relation				
國	破	山	河	在
'country'	'broken'	'mountain'	'river'	'exist'
(3) [Although] the country is broken, the mountains and the rivers still stay.				
`dep-conc`('exist', 'broken')				

Table 3. Example sentences illustrating the use of discourse labels for discourse relations[6].

In many ancient languages, explicit realization of discourse relations is less frequent. In Latin and Ancient Greek, for instance, these connectives are often replaced by a participial clause. The participle is marked only by the genitive or ablative case, leaving the reader to decide from context how it relates to the main clause. As a non-inflectional language, Classical Chinese cannot use this device, and instead typically constructs a complex sentence with a series of verbs without any marking (Pulleyblank, 1995). For example, sentence (2) in Table 3 literally says 'not capable, good ruler forsake'; the onus is put on the reader to interpret the first two characters to form a clause that provides the reason for the rest of the line.

This condensed style of expression often erects a barrier for understanding. Although the focus of the treebank is on syntax rather than discourse, we decided to annotate these relations. Implicit connectives are more difficult to achieve inter-annotator agreement (Prasad et al., 2008); since they are mostly implicit in Classical Chinese, we adopted a coarse-grained classification system, rather than the hierarchical system of sense tags in the Penn Discourse Treebank. More precisely, it contains only the four categories posited by (Wang, 2003) --- causal, concessive, temporal, and conditional. Table 3 gives some examples.

When it is impossible to determine the discourse relation between two lines, the default "dependent" (`dep`) label is assigned. This label is originally used when "the system is unable to determine a more precise dependency relation between two words" (de Marneffe and Manning, 2008).

4 Data

Among the various literary genres, poetry enjoys perhaps the most elevated status in the Classical Chinese tradition. The Tang Dynasty is considered the golden age of *shi*, one of the five subgenres of Chinese poetry[7]. The *Complete Shi Poetry of the Tang* (Peng, 1960), originally compiled in 1705, consists of nearly 50,000 poems by more than two thousand poets. This book is treasured by scholars and the public alike. Even today, Chinese people informally compose couplets (see section 5), in the style of *shi* poetry, to celebrate special occasions such as birthdays. Indeed, NLP techniques have been applied to generate them automatically (Jiang and Zhou, 2008).

4.1 Material

This treebank contains the complete works, a total of over 32,000 characters in 521 poems, by two Chinese poets in the 8th century CE, Wang Wei and Meng Haoran. Wang, also known as the Poet-Buddha (*shifo* 詩佛), is considered one of the three most prominent Tang poets. Meng is often asso-

[5] From Meng Haoran 《與張折衝遊耆闍寺》

[6] From top to bottom, Meng Haoran 《登龍興寺閣》,《歲暮歸南山》, and Du Fu 杜甫《八陣圖》

[7] The other four genres are *ci*, *fu*, *qu*, and *sao*.

ciated with Wang due to the similarity of his poems in style and content.

Aside from the dependency relations, word boundaries and POS tags, the treebank contains a number of metadata. For each character, the tone is noted as either level (*ping* 平) or oblique (*ze* 仄). Each poem is also recorded for its title, author, and genre, which may be 'recent-style' (*jintishi* 近體詩) or 'ancient-style' (*gutishi* 古體詩).

This choice of our text stems from three motivations. Classical Chinese is typically written in a compressed style, especially so with poetry, where the word order is relatively flexible, and grammatical exceptions are frequent. These characteristics pose a formidable challenge for students of Classical Chinese, for whom Tang poetry often forms part of the introductory material. It is hoped that this treebank will serve a pedagogical purpose. Second, this challenging text makes it more likely that the resulting dependency framework can successfully handle other Classical Chinese texts. Third, Tang poetry is an active area of research in Chinese philology, and we aspire to contribute to their endeavor.

4.2 Inter-annotator agreement

Two annotators, both university graduates with a degree in Chinese, created this treebank. To measure inter-annotator agreement, we set apart a subset of about 1050 characters, on which both of them independently perform three tasks: POS tagging, head selection, and dependency labeling.

Their agreement rate is 95.1%, 92.3%, and 91.2% for the three respective tasks. For POS tagging, the three main error categories are the confusion between adverbs (AD) and verbs with an adverbial force, between measure words (M) and nouns (NN), and between adjectives (JJ) and nouns. The interested reader is referred to (Lee, 2012) for a detailed analysis.

These differences in POS tags trickle down to head selection and dependency labeling. In fact, all words which received different POS tags also received different dependency relations. To illustrate with a disagreement between adverb and verb, consider the following sentence. The word 恐 *kong* 'afraid' may be considered as an adverb, expressing the psychological state for the verb 'attract'; or, alternatively, as a verb in its own right. Depending on the decision, it bears either the relation `advmod` or `root`.

恐	招	負	時	累
'afraid'	'attract'	'burden'	'fame'	'affect'

[I am] afraid [I] will attract and be burdened by fame[8].

Some differences are genuine alternative annotations, resulting from a mixture of polysemy and flexible word order. Consider the sentence 簞食伊何 *dan shi yi he*, consisting of four characters meaning, in order, 'bowl / blanket', 'food', a copular or a particle, and 'what'. If the meaning 'bowl' and copular is taken, it means 'What food is contained in that bowl?' In this case, the relation `clf` is required for 簞 *dan*, and 伊 *yi* is the root word. Alternatively, if the meaning 'blanket' and particle is taken, it is interpreted as 'What food is placed on the blanket?' Here, *dan* takes on the relation `nn`, and the root word would be 何 *he* instead.

5 Application: Parallel Couplets

We now demonstrate one use of this treebank by analyzing a well-known but understudied feature of Classical Chinese poetry: the parallel couplets.

5.1 Introduction

Parallelism in poetry refers to the correspondence of one line with another; the two lines may bear similar or opposite meaning, and have comparable grammatical constructions. This phenomenon is perhaps most well known in classical Hebrew poetry, but it is also one of the defining features of Chinese poetry; "it pervades their poetry universally, forms its chief characteristic feature, and is the source of a great deal of its artificial beauty", observed Sir John Francis Davis, author of one of the earliest commentaries on Chinese poetry published in the West (Davis 1969).

The lines in a Chinese poem almost always contain the same number of characters, most commonly either five or seven characters. This exact equality of the number of characters makes it especially suited for expressing parallelism, which became a common feature ever since 'recent-style' poetry (section 4.1) was developed during the Tang

[8] From Wang Wei 《贈從弟司庫員外絿弟》

Dynasty. Unlike those in 'ancient-style', poems of this style are tonally regulated and assume a high degree of parallelism within a couplet, i.e., two adjacent lines. See Figure 1 for an example.

5.2 Methodology

The couplet in Figure 1 is undisputedly symmetric, both in terms of POS tags and dependency labels. The definition for parallelism is, however, quite loose; in general, the corresponding characters must 'agree' in part-of-speech and have related meaning. These are unavoidably subjective notions.

While a vast amount of Tang poems have been digitized, they have not been POS-tagged or syntactically analyzed in any significant amount. It is not surprising, therefore, that no large-scale, empirical study on how, and how often, the characters 'agree'. There have been a study on 1,000 couplets (Cao, 1998), and another on a small subset of the poems of Du Mu (Huang, 2006), but neither clarify the criteria for parallelism. We undertake a descriptive, rather than prescriptive, approach, using only the treebank data as the basis.

Character-level parallelism. Even given the POS tags, this study is not straightforward. The naive metric of requiring exactly matched POS tags yields a parallel rate of only 74% in the corpus as a whole. This figure can be misleading, because it would vary according to the granularity of the POS tagset: the more fine-grained it is, the less agreement there would be. As a metric for parallelism, it has high precision but lower recall, and would only be appropriate for certain applications such as couplet generation (Jiang and Zhou, 2008).

Equivalence	POS tags and dependency links
Noun modifier	`CD`, `OD`, `JJ`, `DT`
Verbs	`BA`, `<verb>`, and `P` (head of `pobj` or `plmod`)
Adverbials	`AD`, `CS`, `<verb>` (head of `mmod`), <noun> (head of `npadvmod`)
Adjectival	`<noun>` (head of `nn` or `assmod`), `<verb>` (head of `vmod`), `JJ` (head of `amod`)
Nouns	`<noun>`, `<verb>` (head of `csubj` or `csubjpass`), `M` (except `clf`)

Table 4. Equivalence sets of POS tags for the purpose of parallelism detection. `<noun>` includes `NN`, `NT`, `NR`, `PN`; `<verb>` includes `VA`, `VC`, `VE`, `VV`.

By examining portions of the regulated verse where parallelism is expected, we derived five 'equivalence sets' of POS tags, shown in Table 4. Two tags in the same set are considered parallel, even though they do not match. In many sets, a tag needs to be qualified with its dependency relations, since it is considered parallel to other members in the set only when it plays certain syntactic roles. When applying these equivalence sets as well as exact matching, the parallel rate increases to 87%.

The algorithm is of course not perfect[9]. It cannot detect, for example, parallelism involving the use of a polysemous character with a 'out-of-context' meaning (*jieyi* 借義). For instance, the character 者 *zhe*, the fourth character in the second line in the couplet[10] "欲就終焉志，恭聞智者名," means 'person'. On the surface, it does not match its counterpart, 焉 *yan*, the fourth character in the first line, since *yan* is a sentence particle and *zhe* is a noun. However, the poet apparently viewed them as parallel, because *zhe* can also function as a sentence particle in other contexts.

Phrase-level parallelism. The character-level metric, however, still rejects some couplets that would be deemed parallel by scholars. Most of these couplets are parallel not at the character level, but at the phrase level.

A line in a 'recent-style' poem is almost always segmented into two syntactic units (Cai, 1998). A pentasyllabic (5-character) line is composed of a disyllabic unit (the first two characters) followed by a trisyllabic unit (the last three characters)[11]. Consider two corresponding disyllabic units, 抱琴 *bao qin* 'hold' 'violin', and 垂釣 *sui diao* 'look down' 'fish'. They are tagged as *bao*/VV *qin*/NN and *sui*/AD *diao*/VV, respectively. There is a complete mismatch at the character level: *bao* is a verb but *sui* is an adverb; *qin* is a noun but *diao* is a verb. Taken as a whole, however, both units are verb phrases describing an activity ('to hold a violin' and 'to fish while looking down'), and so the poet likely considered them to be parallel at the unit, or phrase, level.

[9] The quality of these equivalence sets were evaluated on 548 characters. The human expert agrees with the decision of the algorithm 96.4% of the time at the character level, and 94% of the time at the phrase level.

[10] From Meng Haoran 《陪張丞相祠紫蓋山，途經玉泉寺》

[11] Equivalently, the seven characters in the heptasyllabic regulated verse are segmented in a 4+3 fashion.

The dependencies provide a convenient way to gauge the level of parallelism at the phrase level. One can extract the head word in the corresponding units in the couplet (*bao*/VV and *diao*/VV in the example above), then compare their POS tags, using the algorithm for character-level parallelism describe above.

5.3 Results

The results are shown in Table 5. All couplets from an 'ancient-style' poem are considered "parallelism optional". A couplet from a 'recent-style' poem with eight or more lines[12] is either "parallelism not expected", if it is the first or last couplet in the poem; or "parallelism expected", if it is in the middle of the poem. We first determine whether a character is parallel to its counterpart in the couplet at the character level; if not, then we back off to the phrase level.

In the "parallelism expected" category, the couplets of Wang are highly parallel, at both the character (91%) and phrase levels (95%). This is hardly surprising, given that his poems are highly regarded. It is notable, however, that the proportion is still relatively high (57% at the character level) even among those couplets for which parallelism is not expected, suggesting that the poet placed a high view on parallelism. He also employed much parallelism (64% at the character level) in 'ancient-style' poems, perhaps to aim at a higher artistic effect.

Among the couplets of Wang which are not parallel at the phrase level, the most frequent combination is a verb phrase matching a noun phrase. The verb, as the second character, is modified by an adverb; the noun, also as the second character, is modified by an adjective. This implies that the "AD VV" vs. "JJ NN" combination may be considered to be parallel by poets at the time.

The trends for Meng are similar, with a significantly higher score for couplets expected to be parallel than those that are not (82% vs. 53% at the character level). Compared to Wang, however, both percentages are lower. One wonders if this has any correlation with Meng being commonly considered a less accomplished poet. Since the 'rules' for parallelism have never been codified, Meng may also have simply espoused a more coarse-grained view of parts-of-speech. This hypothesis would be consistent with the fact that, at the phrase level, the proportion of parallelism for Meng is much closer to that for Wang. This suggests that Meng was content with parallelism at the phrase level and emphasized less on matching character to character.

Couplet type	Metric	Wang	Meng
Parallelism expected	Char-level only	91%	82%
	+ Phrase-level	95%	91%
Parallelism not expected	Char-level only	57%	53%
	+ Phrase-level	71%	71%
Parallelism optional	Char-level only	64%	65%
	+ Phrase-level	78%	81%

Table 5. The proportion of characters that are parallel to their counterparts in the couplet (see section 5.2). The couplets are classified into three types, depending on the genre of poetry and their position in the poem (see section 5.3).

6 Conclusion

We have presented the first large-scale dependency treebank of Classical Chinese literature, which encodes works by two poets in the Tang Dynasty. We have described how the dependency grammar framework has been derived from existing treebanks for Modern Chinese, and shown a high level of inter-annotator agreement. Finally, we have illustrated the utility of the treebank with a study on parallelism in Classical Chinese poetry.

Future work will focus on parsing Classical Chinese poems of other poets, and on enriching the corpus with semantic information, which would facilitate not only deeper study of parallelism but also other topics such as imagery and metaphorical coherence (Zhu and Cui, 2010).

Acknowledgments

We thank Tin Ho Chan and Cheuk Ho Wan for their assistance in annotating this treebank. This work was supported by a Strategic Research Grant (#7002549) from City University of Hong Kong.

[12] These are known as the 'regulated verse' (*lushi* 律詩) and are subject to definite patterns of parallelism. Those with fewer lines are left out, since their patterns are less regular.

References

Zong-Qi Cai. 2008. *How to Read Chinese Poetry*. Columbia University Press, New York.

Fengfu Cao 曹逢甫. 1998. *A Linguistic Study of the Parallel Couplets in Tang Poetry*. Technical Report, Linguistics Graduate Institute, National Tsing Hua University, Taiwan.

Pi-Chuan Chang, Huihsin Tseng, Dan Jurafsky, and Christopher Manning. 2009. Discriminative Reordering with Chinese Grammatical Relations Features. *Proc. 3rd Workshop on Syntax and Structure in Statistical Translation.Psychological Association*.

Gregory Crane, Brent Seales, and Melissa Terras. 2009. Cyberinfrastructure for Classical Philology. *Digital Humanities Quarterly* 3(1).

John F. Davis. 1969. *The Poetry of the Chinese*. Paragon Book, New York.

Ulrike Demske, Nicola Frank, Stefanie Laufer and Hendrik Stiemer, 2004. Syntactic Interpretation of an Early New High German Corpus. *Proc. Workshop on Treebanks and Linguistic Theories (TLT)*.

Kais Dukes and Tim Buckwalter, 2010. A Dependency Treebank of the Quran using Traditional Arabic Grammar. *Proc. 7th International Conference on Informatics and Systems (INFOS)*, Cairo, Egypt.

Shengli Feng. 1998. Prosodic Structure and Compound Words in Classical Chinese. In *New Approaches to Chinese Word Formation*, Jerome Packard (ed.), Mouton de Gruyter.

W. Nelson Francis and Henry Kučera. 1982. *Frequency Analysis of English Usage: Lexicon and Grammar*. Houghton Mifflin.

J. Hajic. 1998. Building a syntactically annotated corpus: The Prague Dependency Treebank. Issues of Valency and Meaning, Charles University Press.

Dag Haug and Marius Jøhndal. 2008. Creating a Parallel Treebank of the Old Indo-European Bible Translations. *Proc. Language Resources and Evaluation Conference (LREC)*.

X. Hu, N. Williamson, and J. McLaughlin. 2005. Sheffield Corpus of Chinese for Diachronic Linguistic Study. *Literary and Linguistic Computing* 20(3).

Li-min Huang. 2006. *The Study of Classical Poems of Tu-mu*. Master's Thesis, National Sun Yat-sen University, Taiwan.

Liang Huang, Yinan Peng, Huan Wang, and Zhengyu Wu. 2002. PCFG Parsing for Restricted Classical Chinese Texts. *Proc. 1st SIGHAN Workshop on Chinese Language Processing*.

Long Jiang and Ming Zhou. 2008. Generating Chinese Couplets using a Statistical MT Approach. *Proc. COLING*.

Lewis Lancaster. 2010. Pattern Recognition and Analysis in the Chinese Buddhist Canon: A Study of "Original Enlightenment". *Pacific World* 3(60).

Zuonan Li 李作南 and Renhou Li 李仁厚. 1986. A comparison of Classical Chinese and Modern Chinese 古今漢語語法比較 (in Chinese). Nei Menggu Renmin Chubanshe, China.

Marie-Catherine de Marneffe and Christopher D. Manning. 2008. *Stanford typed dependencies manual*. California: Stanford University.

Dingqiu Peng. 1960. Quan Tang Shi 全唐詩. Zhonghua Shuju, Beijing.

Susan Pintzuk and Plug Leendert. 2001. York-Helsinki Parsed Corpus of Old English Poetry. http://www-users.york.ac.uk/~lang18/pcorpus.html

Rashmi Prasad, Nikhil Dinesh, Alan Lee, Eleni Miltsakaki, Livio Robaldo, Aravind Joshi, and Bonnie Webber. 2008. The Penn Discourse Treebank 2.0. *Proc. LREC*.

Edwin Pulleyblank. 1995. *Outline of Classical Chinese Grammar*. UBC Press, Vancouver, Canada.

Vitor Rocio, Mário Amado Alves, J. Gabriel Lopes, Maria Francisca Xavier, and Graça Vicente. 2000. Automated Creation of a Medieval Portuguese Partial Treebank. In Anne Abeillé (ed.), *Treebanks: Building and Using Parsed Corpora* (Dordrecht: Kluwer Academic Publishers), pp. 211-227.

Ann Taylor, Anthony Warner, Susan Pintzuk and Frank Beths. 2003. *York-Toronto-Helsinki Parsed Corpus of Old English Prose*. University of York.

Pei-chuan Wei, P. M. Thompson, Cheng hui Liu, Chu-Ren Huang, and Chaofen Sun. 1997. Historical Corpora for Synchronic and Diachronic Linguistics Studies. *Computational Linguistics and Chinese Language Processing* 2(1):131—145.

Li Wang 王力. 2004. A sketch of the history of Chinese language 漢語史稿 (in Chinese). Zhonghua Shuju, Beijing.

Jiaolu Xu. 許嘉璐. 1992. *Classical Chinese 古代漢語* (in Chinese). Higher Education Press, Beijing.

Nianwen Xue, Fei Xia, Fu-Dong Chiou, and Martha Palmer, 2005. The Penn Chinese TreeBank: Phrase Structure Annotation of a Large Corpus. *Natural Language Engineering* 11:pp.207—238.

John Lee. 2012. A Classical Chinese Corpus with Nested Part-of-Speech Tags. *Proc. EACL Workshop on Language Technology for Cultural Heritage, Social Sciences, and Humanities (LaTeCH)*.

Chunshen Zhu and Ying Cui, 2010. Imagery Focalization and the Evocation of a Poetic World. *Chinese Translators Journal*.

Towards Effective Tutorial Feedback for Explanation Questions: A Dataset and Baselines

Myroslava O. Dzikovska* and **Rodney D. Nielsen†** and **Chris Brew‡**
*School of Informatics, University of Edinburgh, Edinburgh, EH8 9AB, UK
†Computational Language & Education Research Center
University of Colorado at Boulder, Boulder, CO 80309-0594, USA
‡Educational Testing Service, Princeton, NJ 08451, USA
m.dzikovska@ed.ac.uk, rodney.nielsen@colorado.edu, cbrew@ets.org

Abstract

We propose a new shared task on grading student answers with the goal of enabling well-targeted and flexible feedback in a tutorial dialogue setting. We provide an annotated corpus designed for the purpose, a precise specification for a prediction task and an associated evaluation methodology. The task is feasible but non-trivial, which is demonstrated by creating and comparing three alternative baseline systems. We believe that this corpus will be of interest to the researchers working in textual entailment and will stimulate new developments both in natural language processing in tutorial dialogue systems and textual entailment, contradiction detection and other techniques of interest for a variety of computational linguistics tasks.

1 Introduction

In human-human tutoring, it is an effective strategy to ask students to explain instructional material in their own words. Self-explanation (Chi et al., 1994) and contentful talk focused on the domain are correlated with better learning outcomes (Litman et al., 2009; Chi et al., 1994). There has therefore been much interest in developing automated tutorial dialogue systems that ask students open-ended explanation questions (Graesser et al., 1999; Aleven et al., 2001; Jordan et al., 2006; VanLehn et al., 2007; Nielsen et al., 2009; Dzikovska et al., 2010a). In order to do this well, it is not enough to simply ask the initiating question, because students need the experience of engaging in meaningful dialogue about the instructional content. Thus, systems must respond appropriately to student explanations, and must provide detailed, flexible and appropriate feedback (Aleven et al., 2002; Jordan et al., 2004).

In simple domains, we can adopt a knowledge engineering approach and build a domain model and a diagnoser, together with a natural language parser to produce detailed semantic representations of student input (Glass, 2000; Aleven et al., 2002; Pon-Barry et al., 2004; Callaway et al., 2006; Dzikovska et al., 2010a). The advantage of this approach is that it allows for flexible adaptation of feedback to a variety of factors such as student performance. For example, it is easy for the system to know if the student made the same error before, and adjust its feedback to reflect it. Moreover, this approach allows for easy addition of new exercises : as long as an exercise relies on the concepts covered by the domain model, the system can apply standard instructional strategies to each new question automatically. However, this approach is significantly limited by the requirement that the domain be small enough to allow comprehensive knowledge engineering, and it is very labor-intensive even for small domains.

Alternatively, we can adopt a data-driven approach, asking human tutors to anticipate in advance a range of possible correct and incorrect answers, and associating each answer with an appropriate remediation (Graesser et al., 1999; Jordan et al., 2004; VanLehn et al., 2007). The advantage of this approach is that it allows more complex and interesting domains and provides a good framework for eliciting the necessary information from the human experts. A weakness of this approach, which also arises in content-scoring applications such as ETS's c-rater (Leacock and Chodorow, 2003), is that human experts find it extremely difficult to predict with any certainty what the full range of student responses will be. This leads to a lack of adaptivity and generality – if the system designers have failed to predict the full range of possibilities, students will often receive the default feedback. It is frustrating and confusing for students to repeatedly receive the same feedback, regardless of their past performance or dialogue context (Jordan, 2004).

Our goal is to address the weaknesses of the data-driven approach by creating a framework for supporting more flexible and systematic feedback. Our approach identifies general classes of error, such as omissions, incorrect statements and off-topic statements, then aims to develop general remediation strategies for each error type. This has the potential to free system designers from the need to pre-author separate remediations for each individual question. A precondition for the success of this approach is that the system be able to identify error types based on the student response and the model answers.

A contribution of this paper is to provide a new dataset that will enable researchers to develop classifiers specifically for this purpose. The hope is that with an appropriate dataset the data-driven approach will be flexible and responsive enough to maintain student engagement. We provide a corpus that is labeled for a set of five student response types, develop a precise definition of the corresponding supervised classification task, and report results for a variety of simple baseline classifiers. This will provide a basis for the development, comparison and evaluation of alternative approaches to the error classification task. We believe that the natural language capabilities needed for this task will be directly applicable to a far wider range of tasks in educational assessment, information extraction and computational semantics. This dataset is publicly available and will be used in a community-wide shared task.

2 Corpus

The data set we developed draws on two established sources – a data set collected and annotated during an evaluation of the BEETLE II tutorial dialogue system (Dzikovska et al., 2010a) (henceforth, BEETLE corpus) and a set of student answers to questions from 16 science modules in the Assessing Science Knowledge (ASK) assessment inventory (Lawrence Hall of Science, 2006) (henceforth, the Science Entailments Bank or SCIENTSBANK).

In both corpora, each question was associated with one or more reference answers provided by the experts. Student answers were evaluated against these reference answers and, using corpus-specific annotation schemes, assigned labels for correctness. In order to reconcile the two different schemes and to cast the task in terms of standard supervised machine classification at the sentence level, we derived a new set of annotations, using the annotation scheme shown in Figure 1.

Our label set has some similarity to the RTE5 3-way task (Bentivogli et al., 2009), which used "entailment", "contradiction" and "unknown" labels. The additional distinctions in our labels reflect typical distinctions made by tutorial dialogue systems. They match our human tutors' intuitions about the general error types observed in student answers and corresponding teaching tactics. For example, a likely response to "partially_correct_incomplete" would be to tell the student that what they said so far was correct but it had some gaps, and to encourage them to fill in those gaps. In contrast, the response to "contradictory" would emphasize that there is a mistake and the student needs to change their answer rather than just expand it. Finally, the response to "irrelevant" may encourage the student to address relevant concepts. The "non_domain" content could be an indicator that the student is frustrated or confused, and may require special attention.

The annotations in the source corpora make some more fine-grained distinctions based on the needs of the corresponding systems. In principle, it is possible to have answers that have both correct and contradictory parts, and acknowledge correct parts before pointing out mistakes. There are also distinct classes of "non_domain" utterances, e.g., social and metacognitive statements, to which an ITS may want to react differently (described in Section 2.1). However, these situations were rare in our corpora, and we decided to use a single class for all contradictory answers and a single non-domain class. This may be expanded in the future as more data becomes available for new versions of this challenge task.

Label	Definition
non_domain	does not contain domain content, e.g., a help request or "I don't know"
correct	the student answer is correct
partially_correct_incomplete	the answer does not contradict the reference answer and includes some correct nuggets, but parts are missing
contradictory	an answer that contradicts some part of the reference answer
irrelevant	contains domain content, but does not answer the question

Figure 1: The set of answer labels used in our task

We further discuss the relationship with the task of recognizing textual entailment in Section 5. In the rest of this section, we describe our corpora and discuss how we obtained these labels from the raw data available in our datasets.

2.1 BEETLE II data

The BEETLE corpus consists of the interactions between students and the BEETLE II tutorial dialogue system (Dzikovska et al., 2010b). The BEETLE II system is an intelligent tutoring system that teaches students with no knowledge of high-school physics concepts in basic electricity and electronics. In the first system evaluation, students spend 3-5 hours going through prepared reading material, building and observing circuits in the simulator and interacting with a dialogue-based tutor. The interaction was by keyboard, with the computer tutor asking questions, receiving replies and providing feedback via a text-based chat interface. The data from 73 undergraduate volunteer participants at southeastern US university were recorded and annotated to form the BEETLE human-computer dialogue corpus.

The BEETLE II lesson material contains two types of questions. Factual questions require them to name a set of objects or a simple property, e.g., "Which components in circuit 1 are in a closed path?" or "Are bulbs A and B wired in series or in parallel". Explanation and definition questions require longer answers that consist of 1-2 sentences, e.g., "Why was bulb A on when switch Z was open?" (expected answer "Because it was still in a closed path with the battery") or "What is voltage?" (expected answer "Voltage is the difference in states between two terminals"). From the full BEETLE evaluation corpus, we automatically extracted only the students' answers to explanation and definition questions, since reacting to them appropriately requires processing more complex input than factual questions.

The extracted answers were filtered to remove duplicates. In the BEETLE II lesson material there are a number of similar questions and the tutor effectively had a template answer such as "Terminal X is connected to the negative/positive battery terminal". A number of students picked up on this and used the same pattern in their responses (Steinhauser et al., 2011). This resulted in a number of answers to certain questions that came from different speakers but which were exact copies of each other. We removed such answers from the data set, since they were likely to be in both the training and test set, thus inflating our results. Note that only exact matches were removed: for example, answers that were nearly identical but contained spelling errors were retained, since they would need to be handled in a practical system.

Student utterances were manually labeled using a simplified version of the DEMAND coding scheme (Campbell et al., 2009) shown in Figure 2. The utterances were first classified as related to domain content, student's metacognitive state, or social interaction. Utterances addressing domain content were further classified with respect to their correctness as described in the table. The Kappa value for this annotation effort was $\kappa = 0.69$.

This annotation maps straightforwardly into our set of labels. The social and metacognitive statements are mapped to the "non_domain" label; "pc_some_error", "pc" and "incorrect" are mapped to the "contradictory" label; and the other classes have a one-to-one correspondence with our task labels.

2.2 SCIENTSBANK data

The SCIENTSBANK corpus (Nielsen et al., 2008) consists of student responses to science assessment

Category	Subcategory	Description
Metacognitive	positive negative	content-free expressions describing student knowledge, e.g., "I don't know"
Social	positive negative neutral	expressions describing student's attitudes towards themselves and the computer (mostly negative in this data, e.g., "You are stupid")
Content		the utterance addresses domain content.
	correct	the student answer is fully correct
	pc_some_missing	the student said something correct, but incomplete
	incorrect	the student's answer is completely incorrect
	pc_some_error	the student's answer contains correct parts, but some errors as well
	pc	the answer contains a mixture of correct, incorrect and missing parts
	irrelevant	the answer may be correct or incorrect, but it is not answering the question.

Figure 2: Annotation scheme used in the BEETLE corpus

questions. Specifically, around 16k answers were collected spanning 16 distinct science subject areas within physical sciences, life sciences, earth sciences, space sciences, scientific reasoning and technology. The tests were part of the Berkeley Lawrence Hall of Science Assessing Science Knowledge (ASK) standardized assessments covering material from their Full Option Science System (FOSS) (Lawrence Hall of Science, 2011). The answers came from students in grades 3-6 in schools across North America.

The tests included a variety of questions including "fill in the blank" and multiple choice, but the SCIENTSBANK corpus only used a subset that required students to explain their beliefs about topics, typically in one to two sentences. We reviewed the questions and a sample of the responses and decided to filter the following types of questions from the corpus, because they did not mesh with our goals. First, we removed questions whose expected answer was more than two full sentences (typically multi-step procedures), which were beyond the scope of our task. Second, we removed questions where the expected answer was ill-defined or very open-ended. Finally, the most frequent reason for removing questions was an extreme imbalance in the answer classifications (e.g., for many questions, almost all of the answers were labeled "partially_correct_incomplete"). Specifically, we removed questions where more than 80% of the answers had the same label and questions with fewer than three correct answers, since these questions were unlikely to be useful in differentiating between the quality of assessment systems.

The SCIENTSBANK corpus was developed for the purpose of assessing student responses at a very fine-grained level. The reference answers were broken down into several facets, which consisted roughly of two key terms and the relation connecting them. Nielsen et al. annotated student responses to indicate for each reference answer facet whether the response 1) implied the student understood the facet, 2) implied they held a contradictory belief, 3) included a related, non-contradicting facet, or 4) left the facet unaddressed. Reported agreement was 86.2% with a kappa statistic (Cohen, 1960) of 0.728, which is in the range of substantial agreement.[1]

Because our task focuses on answer classification rather than facet classification, we developed a set of rules indicating which combinations of facets constituted a correct answer. We were then able to compute an answer label from the gold-standard facet annotations, as follows. First, if any facet was annotated as contradictory, the answer was also labeled "contradictory". Second, if all of the expected facets for any valid answer were annotated as being understood, the answer was labeled "cor-

[1] These statistics were actually based on five labels, but we chose to combine the fifth, a self-contradiction, with other contradictions for the purposes of our task.

rect". Third, the remaining answers that included some but not all of the expected facets were labeled "partially_correct_incomplete". Fourth, if an answer matched none of the expected facets, and had not been previously labeled as "contradictory" it was given the label "irrelevant". Finally, all "irrelevant" answers were reviewed manually to determine whether they should be relabeled as "non_domain". However, since Nielsen et al. had already removed most of the responses that originally fell into this category, we only found 24 "non_domain" answers.

3 Baselines

We established three baselines for our data set – a straightforward majority class baseline, an existing system baseline (BEETLE II system performance, which we report only for the BEETLE portion of the dataset), and the performance of a simple classifier based on lexical similarity, which we report in order to offer a substantial example of applying the same classifier to both portions of the dataset.

3.1 BEETLE II system baseline

The interpretation component of the BEETLE II system uses a syntactic parser and a set of hand-authored rules to extract the domain-specific semantic representations of student utterances from the text. These representations were then matched against the semantic representations of expected correct answers supplied by tutors. The resulting system output was automatically mapped into our target labels as discussed in (Dzikovska et al., 2012).

3.2 Lexical similarity baseline

To provide a higher baseline that is comparable across both subsets of the data, we built a simple decision tree classifier using the Weka 3.6.2 implementation of C4.5 pruned decision trees (weka.classifiers.trees.J48 class), with default parameters. As features, we used lexical similarity scores computed by the `Text::Similarity` package with default parameters[2]. The code computes four similarity metrics – the raw number of overlapping words, F1 score, Lesk score and cosine score. We compared the learner response to the expected answer(s) and the question, resulting in eight total features (the four values indicated above for the comparison with the question and the highest of each value from the comparisons with each possible expected answer).

This baseline is based on the lexical overlap baseline used in RTE tasks (Bentivogli et al., 2009). However, we measured overlap with the question text in addition to the overlap with the expected answers. Students often repeat parts of the question in their answer and this needs to be taken into account to differentiate, for example, "partially_correct_incomplete" and "correct" answers.

4 Results

4.1 Experimental Setup

We held back part of the data set for use as standard test data in the future challenge tasks. For BEETLE, this consisted of all student answers to 9 out of 56 explanation questions asked by the system, plus approximately 15% of the student answers to the remaining 47 questions, sampling so that the distribution of labels in test data was similar to the training data. For SCIENTSBANK, we used a previous train-test split (Nielsen et al., 2009). For both data sets, the data was split so that in the future we can test how well the different systems generalize: i.e., how well they perform on answers to questions for which they have some sample student answers vs. how well they perform on answers to questions that were not in the training data (e.g., newly created questions in a deployed system). We discuss this in more detail in Section 5.

In this paper, we report baseline performance on the training set to demonstrate that the task is sufficiently challenging to be interesting and that systems can be compared using our evaluation metrics. We preserve the true test data for use in the planned large-scale system comparisons in a community shared task.

For the lexical similarity baseline, we use 10-fold cross-validation.[3] For the BEETLE II system baseline, the language understanding module was de-

[2] http://search.cpan.org/dist/Text-Similarity/

[3] We did not take the student id into account explicitly during cross-validation. While there is some risk that the classifiers will learn features specific to the student, we concluded (based on our understanding of data collection specifics for both data sets) that there is little enough overlap in cross-validation on the training data that this should not have a big effect on the results.

veloped based on eight transcripts, each taken from the interaction of a different student with an earlier version of the system. These sessions were completed prior to the beginning of the experiment during which the BEETLE corpus was collected, and are not included in the corpus presented here. Thus, the dataset used in the paper constitutes unseen data for the BEETLE II system.

We process the two corpora separately because the additional system baseline is available for beetle, and because the corpora may be different enough that it will be helpful for shared task participants to devise processing strategies that are sensitive to the provenance of the data.

4.2 Evaluation Metrics

Table 1 shows the distribution of codes in the annotated data. The distribution is unbalanced, and therefore in our evaluation results we report per-class precision, recall and F_1 scores, plus the averaged scores using two different ways to average over per-class evaluation scores, micro- and macro- averaging.

For a set of classes C, each represented with N_c instances in the test set, the macro-averaged recall is defined as

$$R_{macro} = \frac{1}{|C|} \sum_{c \epsilon C} R(c)$$

and the micro-averaged recall as

$$R_{micro} = \sum_{c \epsilon C} \frac{1}{N_c} R(c)$$

Micro- and macro-averaged precision and F_1 are defined similarly.

Micro-averaging takes class sizes into account, so a system that performs well on the most common classes will have a high micro-average score. This is the most commonly used classifier evaluation metric. Note that, in particular, overall classification accuracy (defined as the number of correctly classified instances out of all instances) is mathematically equivalent to micro-averaged recall (Abudawood and Flach, 2011). However, macro-averaging better reflects performance on small classes, and is commonly used for unbalanced classification problems (see, e.g., (Lewis, 1991)). We report both values in our results.

	BEETLE		SCIENTSBANK	
Label	Count	Freq.	Count	Freq.
correct	1157	0.42	2095	0.40
partially_correct_incomplete	626	0.23	1431	0.27
contradictory	656	0.24	526	0.10
irrelevant	86	0.03	1175	0.22
non_domain	204	0.07	24	0.005
total	2729		5251	

Table 1: Distribution of annotated labels in the data

In addition, we report the system scores on the binary decision of whether or not the corrective feedback should be issued (denoted "corrective feedback" in the results table). It assumes that a tutoring system using a classifier will give corrective feedback if the classifiers returns any label other than "correct". Thus, every instance classified as "partially_correct_incomplete", "contradictory", "irrelevant" or "non_domain" is counted as true positive if the hand-annotated label also belongs to this set (even if the classifier disagrees with the annotation); and as false positive if the hand-annotated label is "correct". This reflects the idea that students are likely to be frustrated if the system gives corrective feedback when their answer is in fact a fully accurate paraphrase of a correct answer.

4.3 BEETLE baseline performance

The detailed evaluation results for all baselines are presented in Table 2.

The majority class baseline is to assign "correct" to every test instance. It achieves 42% overall accuracy. However, this is obviously at the expense of serious errors; for example, such a system would tell the students that they are correct if they are saying something contradictory. This is reflected in a much lower macro-averaged F_1 score.

The BEETLE II system performs only slightly better than the baseline on the overall accuracy (0.44 vs. 0.42 micro-averaged recall). However, the macro-averaged F_1 score of the BEETLE II system is substantially higher (0.46 vs. 0.12). The micro-averaged results show a similar pattern, although the majority-class baseline performs slightly better than in the macro-averaged case, as expected.

Comparing the BEETLE II parser to our lexical

similarity baseline, BEETLE II has lower overall accuracy, but performs similarly on micro- and macro-averaged scores. BEETLE II precision is higher than that of the classifier in all cases except for the binary decision as to whether corrective feedback should be issued. This is not unexpected given how the system was designed – since misunderstandings caused dialogue breakdown in pilot tests, the parser was built to prefer rejecting utterances as uninterpretable rather than assigning them an incorrect class, leading to a considerably lower recall. Around 31% of utterances could not be interpreted.

Our recent analysis shows that both incorrect interpretations (in particular, confusions between "partially_correct_incomplete" and "contradictory") and rejections have significant negative effects on learning gain (Dzikovska et al., 2012). Classifiers can be tuned to reject examples where classification confidence falls below a given threshold, resulting in precision-recall trade-offs. Our baseline classifier classified all answer instances; exploring the possibilities for rejecting some low-confidence answers is planned for future work.

4.4 SCIENTSBANK baseline performance

The accuracy of the majority class baseline (which assumes all answers are "correct") is 40% for SCIENTSBANK, about the same as it was for BEETLE. The evaluation results, based on 10-fold cross-validation, for our simple lexical similarity classifier are presented in Table 3. The lexical similarity based classifier outperforms the majority class baseline by 0.18 and 3% on the macro-averaged F_1-measure and accuracy, respectively. The F_1-measure for the two-way classification detecting answers which need corrective feedback is 0.66.

The scores on SCIENTSBANK are noticeably lower than those for BEETLE. The SCIENTSBANK includes questions from 12 distinct science subject areas, rather than a single area as in BEETLE. This decision tree classifier learns a function from the eight text similarity features to the desired answer label. Because the features do not mention particular words, the model can be applied to items other than the ones on which it was trained, and even to items from different subject areas. However, the correct weighting of the textual similarity features depends on the extent and nature of the expected textual overlap, which does vary from subject-area to subject-area. We suspect that the differences between subject areas made it hard for the decision-tree classifier to find a single, globally appropriate strategy. Nielsen (2009) reported the best results for classifying facets when training separate question-specific or even facet-specific classifiers. Although separate training for each item reduces the amount of relevant training data for each classifier, it allows each classifier to learn the specifics of how that item works. A comparison using this style of training would be a reasonable next step,

Predictn	correct	pc_inc	contra	irrlvnt	nondom
correct	1213	553	209	392	2
pc_inc	432	497	128	241	2
contra	115	109	58	74	3
irrlvnt	335	272	131	468	17
nondom	0	0	0	0	0

Figure 4: Confusion matrix for lexical classifier on SCIENTSBANK. Predictions in rows, gold labels in columns

5 Discussion and Future Work

The results presented satisfy two critical requirements for a challenge task. First, we have shown that it is feasible to develop a system that performs significantly better than the majority class baseline. On the macro-averaged F_1-measure, our lexical classifier outperformed the majority-class baseline by 0.33 (on BEETLE) and 0.18 (on SCIENTSBANK) and by 13% and 3% on accuracy. Second, we have also shown, as is desired for a challenge task, that the task is not trivial. With a system specifically designed to parse the BEETLE corpus answers, the macro-averaged F_1-measure was just 0.46 and on the binary decision regarding whether the response needed corrective feedback, it achieved just 0.63.

One contribution of this work was to define a general classification scheme for student responses that allows more specific learner feedback. Another key contribution was to unify two, previously incompatible, large student response corpora under this common annotation scheme. The resultant corpus will enable researchers to train learning algorithms to classify student responses. These classifications can then be used by a dialogue manager to generate targeted learner feedback. The corpus is available

Classifier:	majority			lexical similarity			BEETLE II		
Predicted label	prec.	recall	F1	prec.	recall	F1	prec.	recall	F1
correct	0.42	1.00	0.60	0.68	0.75	0.72	0.93	0.53	0.68
partially_correct_incomplete	0.00	0.00	0.00	0.41	0.38	0.39	0.43	0.53	0.47
contradictory	0.00	0.00	0.00	0.39	0.34	0.36	0.58	0.23	0.33
irrelevant	0.00	0.00	0.00	0.05	0.02	0.03	0.23	0.17	0.20
non_domain	0.00	0.00	0.00	0.66	0.82	0.73	0.92	0.46	0.61
macroaverage	0.09	0.20	0.12	0.44	0.46	0.45	0.62	0.39	0.46
microaverage	0.18	0.42	0.25	0.53	0.55	0.54	0.71	0.44	0.53
corrective feedback	0.00	0.00	0.00	0.80	0.74	0.77	0.73	0.56	0.63

Table 2: Evaluation results for BEETLE corpus

Classifier:	lexical similarity					BEETLE II				
Predicted label	corrct	pc_inc	contra	irrlvnt	nondom	corrct	pc_inc	contra	irrlvnt	nondom
correct	870	187	199	20	2	617	20	23	0	3
part_corr_incmp	138	239	178	24	11	249	332	146	29	20
contradictory	139	153	221	33	22	68	38	149	3	0
irrelevant	3	20	12	2	1	4	22	23	15	1
non_domain	7	27	46	7	168	3	3	1	1	94
uninterpretable	n/a	n/a	n/a	n/a	n/a	216	211	314	38	86

Figure 3: Confusion matrix for BEETLE corpus. Predictions in rows, gold labels in columns

Classifier:	baseline			lexical similarity		
Predicted label	prec.	recall	F1	prec.	recall	F1
correct	0.40	1.00	0.57	0.51	0.58	0.54
partially_correct_incomplete	0.00	0.00	0.00	0.38	0.35	0.36
contradictory	0.00	0.00	0.00	0.16	0.11	0.13
irrelevant	0.00	0.00	0.00	0.38	0.40	0.39
non_domain	0.00	0.00	0.00	0.00	0.00	0.00
macroaverage	0.08	0.20	0.11	0.29	0.29	0.29
microaverage	0.16	0.40	0.23	0.41	0.43	0.42
corrective feedback	0.00	0.00	0.00	0.69	0.63	0.66

Table 3: Evaluation results for SCIENTSBANK baselines

for general research purposes and forms the basis of SEMEVAL-2013 shared task "Textual entailment and paraphrasing for student input assessment".[4]

A third contribution of this work was to provide basic evaluation benchmark metrics and the corresponding evaluation scripts (downloadable from the site above) for other researchers, including shared task participants. This will facilitate the comparison and, hence, the progress, of research.

The work reported here is based on approximately 8000 student responses to questions covering 12 distinct science subjects and coming from a wide range of student ages. These responses comprise the training data for our task. The vast majority of prior work, including BEETLE II, which was included as a benchmark here, has been designed to provide ITS feedback for relatively small, well-defined domains. The corpus presented in this paper is intended to encourage research into more generalizable, domain-independent techniques. Following Nielsen (2009), from whom the SCIENTSBANK corpus was adapted, our shared task evaluation corpus will be composed of three types of data: additional student responses for all of the questions in the training data (Unseen Answers), student responses to questions that were not seen in the training data, but that are from the same subject areas (Unseen Questions), and responses to questions from three entirely different subject areas (Unseen Domains), though in this case the questions are still from the same general domain – science. Unseen Answers is the typical scenario for the vast majority of prior work – training and testing on responses to the same questions. Unseen Questions and Unseen Domains allow researchers to evaluate how well their systems generalize to near and far domains, respectively.

The primary target application for this work is intelligent tutoring systems, where the classification of responses is intended to facilitate specific pedagogic feedback. Beneath the surface, the baseline systems reported here are more similar to grading systems that use the approach of (Leacock and Chodorow, 2003), which uses classifier technology to detect expressions of facet-like concepts, then converts the result to a numerical score, than to grading systems like (Mohler et al., 2011), which directly produces a numerical score, using support vector regression and similar techniques. Either approach is reasonable, but we think that feedback is the more challenging test of a system's ultimate abilities, and therefore a better candidate for the shared task. The corpora from those systems, alongside with new corpora currently being collected in BEETLE and SCIENTSBANK domains, can serve as sources of data for future tasks extensions.

Future systems developed for this task can benefit from the large amount of existing work on recognizing textual entailment (Giampiccolo et al., 2007; Giampiccolo et al., 2008; Bentivogli et al., 2009) and on detecting contradiction (Ritter et al., 2008; De Marneffe et al., 2008). However, there are substantial challenges in applying the RTE tools directly to this data set. Our set of labels is more fine-grained than RTE labels to reflect the needs of intelligent tutoring systems (see Section 2). In addition, the top-performing systems in RTE5 3-way task, as well as contradiction detection methods, rely on NLP tools such as dependency parsers and semantic role labelers; these do not perform well on specialized terminology and language constructs coming from (typed) dialogue context. We chose to use lexical similarity as a baseline specifically because a similar measure was used as a standard baseline in RTE tasks, and we expect that adapting the more complex RTE approaches for purposes of this task will result in both improved results on our data set and new developments in computational linguistics algorithms used for RTE and related tasks.

Acknowledgments

We thank Natalie Steinhauser, Gwendolyn Campbell, Charlie Scott, Simon Caine, Leanne Taylor, Katherine Harrison and Jonathan Kilgour for help with data collection and preparation. The research reported here was supported by the US ONR award N000141010085 and by the Institute of Education Sciences, U.S. Department of Education, through Grant R305A110811 to Boulder Language Technologies Inc. The opinions expressed are those of the authors and do not represent views of the Institute or the U.S. Department of Education.

[4]See http://www.cs.york.ac.uk/semeval-2013/task4/

References

Tarek Abudawood and Peter Flach. 2011. Learning multi-class theories in ilp. In *The 20th International Conference on Inductive Logic Programming (ILP'10)*. Springer, June.

V. Aleven, O. Popescu, and K. R. Koedinger. 2001. Towards tutorial dialog to support self-explanation: Adding natural language understanding to a cognitive tutor. In *Proceedings of the 10th International Conference on Artificial Intelligence in Education (AIED '01)"*.

Vincent Aleven, Octav Popescu, and Koedinger Koedinger. 2002. Pilot-testing a tutorial dialogue system that supports self-explanation. *Lecture Notes in Computer Science*, 2363:344–354.

Luisa Bentivogli, Ido Dagan, Hoa Trang Dang, Danilo Giampiccolo, and Bernando Magnini. 2009. The fifth PASCAL recognizing textual entailment challenge. In *Notebook papers and results, Text Analysis Conference (TAC)*.

Charles Callaway, Myroslava Dzikovska, Colin Matheson, Johanna Moore, and Claus Zinn. 2006. Using dialogue to learn math in the LeActiveMath project. In *Proceedings of the ECAI Workshop on Language-Enhanced Educational Technology*, pages 1–8, August.

Gwendolyn C. Campbell, Natalie B. Steinhauser, Myroslava O. Dzikovska, Johanna D. Moore, Charles B. Callaway, and Elaine Farrow. 2009. The DeMAND coding scheme: A "common language" for representing and analyzing student discourse. In *Proceedings of 14th International Conference on Artificial Intelligence in Education (AIED), poster session*, Brighton, UK, July.

Michelene T. H. Chi, Nicholas de Leeuw, Mei-Hung Chiu, and Christian LaVancher. 1994. Eliciting self-explanations improves understanding. *Cognitive Science*, 18(3):439–477.

Jacob Cohen. 1960. A coefficient of agreement for nominal scales. *Educational and Psychological Measurement*, 20(1):3746.

M.C. De Marneffe, A.N. Rafferty, and C.D. Manning. 2008. Finding contradictions in text. *Proceedings of ACL-08: HLT*, pages 1039–1047.

Myroslava Dzikovska, Diana Bental, Johanna D. Moore, Natalie B. Steinhauser, Gwendolyn E. Campbell, Elaine Farrow, and Charles B. Callaway. 2010a. Intelligent tutoring with natural language support in the Beetle II system. In *Sustaining TEL: From Innovation to Learning and Practice - 5th European Conference on Technology Enhanced Learning, (EC-TEL 2010)*, Barcelona, Spain, October.

Myroslava O. Dzikovska, Johanna D. Moore, Natalie Steinhauser, Gwendolyn Campbell, Elaine Farrow, and Charles B. Callaway. 2010b. Beetle II: a system for tutoring and computational linguistics experimentation. In *Proceedings of the 48th Annual Meeting of the Association for Computational Linguistics (ACL-2010) demo session*, Uppsala, Sweden, July.

Myroslava O. Dzikovska, Peter Bell, Amy Isard, and Johanna D. Moore. 2012. Evaluating language understanding accuracy with respect to objective outcomes in a dialogue system. In *Proceedings of the 13th Conference of the European Chapter of the Association for computational Linguistics*, Avignon, France, April.

Danilo Giampiccolo, Bernardo Magnini, Ido Dagan, and Bill Dolan. 2007. The third PASCAL recognizing textual entailment challenge. In *Proceedings of the ACL-PASCAL Workshop on Textual Entailment and Paraphrasing*, pages 1–9, Prague, June.

Danilo Giampiccolo, Hoa Trang Dang, Bernardo Magnini, Ido Dagan, Elena Cabrio, and Bill Dolan. 2008. The fourth PASCAL recognizing textual entailment challenge. In *Proceedings of Text Analysis Conference (TAC) 2008*, Gaithersburg, MD, November.

Michael Glass. 2000. Processing language input in the CIRCSIM-Tutor intelligent tutoring system. In *Proceedings of the AAAI Fall Symposium on Building Dialogue Systems for Tutorial Applications*.

A. C. Graesser, P. Wiemer-Hastings, K. Wiemer-Hastings, and R. Kreuz. 1999. Autotutor: A simulation of a human tutor. *Cognitive Systems Research*, 1:35–51.

Pamela W. Jordan, Maxim Makatchev, and Kurt VanLehn. 2004. Combining competing language understanding approaches in an intelligent tutoring system. In James C. Lester, Rosa Maria Vicari, and Fábio Paraguaçu, editors, *Intelligent Tutoring Systems*, volume 3220 of *Lecture Notes in Computer Science*, pages 346–357. Springer.

Pamela Jordan, Maxim Makatchev, Umarani Pappuswamy, Kurt VanLehn, and Patricia Albacete. 2006. A natural language tutorial dialogue system for physics. In *Proceedings of the 19th International FLAIRS conference*.

Pamela W. Jordan. 2004. Using student explanations as models for adapting tutorial dialogue. In Valerie Barr and Zdravko Markov, editors, *FLAIRS Conference*. AAAI Press.

Lawrence Hall of Science. 2006. Assessing Science Knowledge (ask). University of California at Berkeley, NSF-0242510.

Lawrence Hall of Science. 2011. Full option science system.

Claudia Leacock and Martin Chodorow. 2003. C-rater: Automated scoring of short-answer questions. *Computers and the Humanities*, 37(4):389–405.

David D. Lewis. 1991. Evaluating text categorization. In *Proceedings of the workshop on Speech and Natural Language*, HLT '91, pages 312–318, Stroudsburg, PA, USA.

Diane Litman, Johanna Moore, Myroslava Dzikovska, and Elaine Farrow. 2009. Using natural language processing to analyze tutorial dialogue corpora across domains and modalities. In *Proceedings of 14th International Conference on Artificial Intelligence in Education (AIED)*, Brighton, UK, July.

Michael Mohler, Razvan Bunescu, and Rada Mihalcea. 2011. Learning to grade short answer questions using semantic similarity measures and dependency graph alignments. In *Proceedings of the 49th Annual Meeting of the Association for Computational Linguistics: Human Language Technologies*, pages 752–762, Portland, Oregon, USA, June. Association for Computational Linguistics.

Rodney D. Nielsen, Wayne Ward, James H. Martin, and Martha Palmer. 2008. Annotating students' understanding of science concepts. In *Proceedings of the Sixth International Language Resources and Evaluation Conference, (LREC08)*, Marrakech, Morocco.

Rodney D. Nielsen, Wayne Ward, and James H. Martin. 2009. Recognizing entailment in intelligent tutoring systems. *The Journal of Natural Language Engineering*, 15:479–501.

Heather Pon-Barry, Brady Clark, Karl Schultz, Elizabeth Owen Bratt, and Stanley Peters. 2004. Advantages of spoken language interaction in dialogue-based intelligent tutoring systems. In *Proceedings of ITS-2004*, pages 390–400.

A. Ritter, D. Downey, S. Soderland, and O. Etzioni. 2008. It's a contradiction—no, it's not: a case study using functional relations. In *Proceedings of the Conference on Empirical Methods in Natural Language Processing*, pages 11–20.

Natalie B. Steinhauser, Gwendolyn E. Campbell, Leanne S. Taylor, Simon Caine, Charlie Scott, Myroslava O. Dzikovska, and Johanna D. Moore. 2011. Talk like an electrician: Student dialogue mimicking behavior in an intelligent tutoring system. In *Proceedings of the 15th International Conference on Artificial Intelligence in Education (AIED-2011)*.

Kurt VanLehn, Pamela Jordan, and Diane Litman. 2007. Developing pedagogically effective tutorial dialogue tactics: Experiments and a testbed. In *Proceedings of SLaTE Workshop on Speech and Language Technology in Education*, Farmington, PA, October.

Topical Segmentation: a Study of Human Performance and a New Measure of Quality

Anna Kazantseva
School of Electrical Engineering
and Computer Science,
University of Ottawa
ankazant@eecs.uottawa.ca

Stan Szpakowicz
School of Electrical Engineering
and Computer Science,
University of Ottawa &
Institute of Computer Science,
Polish Academy of Sciences
szpak@eecs.uottawa.ca

Abstract

In a large-scale study of how people find topical shifts in written text, 27 annotators were asked to mark topically continuous segments in 20 chapters of a novel. We analyze the resulting corpus for inter-annotator agreement and examine disagreement patterns. The results suggest that, while the overall agreement is relatively low, the annotators show high agreement on a subset of topical breaks – places where most prominent topic shifts occur. We recommend taking into account the prominence of topical shifts when evaluating topical segmentation, effectively penalizing more severely the errors on more important breaks. We propose to account for this in a simple modification of the *windowDiff* metric. We discuss the experimental results of evaluating several topical segmenters with and without considering the importance of the individual breaks, and emphasize the more insightful nature of the latter analysis.

1 Introduction

Topical segmentation is a useful intermediate step in many high-level NLP applications such as information retrieval, automatic summarization and question answering. It is often necessary to split a long document into topically continuous segments. Segmentation may be particularly beneficial when working with documents without overt structure: speech transcripts (Malioutov and Barzilay, 2006), newswire (Misra et al., 2011) or novels (Kazantseva and Szpakowicz, 2011). The customary approach is to cast text segmentation as a binary problem: is there a shift of topic between any two adjacent textual units (e.g., sentences or paragraphs)? While necessary, this simplification is quite crude. Topic in discourse usually changes continually; some shifts are subtle, others – more prominent.

The evaluation of text segmentation remains an open research problem. It is a tradition to compile a gold-standard segmentation reference using one or more annotations created by humans. If an automatic segmenter agrees with the reference, it is rewarded, otherwise it is penalized (see Section 4 for details). The nature of the task, however, is such that creating and applying a reference segmentation is far from trivial. The identification of topical shifts requires discretization of a continuous concept – how much the topic changes between two adjacent units. That is why annotators often operate at different levels of granularity. Some people mark only the most prominent topic fluctuations, while others also include finer changes. The task is also necessarily under-defined. In addition to topic changes *per se*, annotators effectively must classify some rhetorical and pragmatic phenomena – exactly how much it is depends on the document genre. For simplicity we do not directly address the latter problem here; we concentrate on the former.

To study how people identify topical shifts in written text, we asked 27 annotators to segment into *episodes* 20 chapters of the novel *The Moonstone* by Wilkie Collins. Each chapter was annotated by 4-6 people. An episode roughly corresponds to a topically continuous segment – the term is defined in Section 3. The analysis of the resulting corpus reveals that while the overall inter-annotator agreement is quite low and is not uniform throughout each chapter. Some topical shifts are marked by most or all annotators, others – by one or by a minority. In fact, only about 50% of all annotated topical shifts are supported by at least 50% of annotators (including near-hits), while the other half is only marked by a minority. In this work we take the agreement about a certain topical shift as a measure of its prominence, and show how this measure can be simply utilized for the purpose of evaluation.

The main claim of this paper is perhaps the following: when evaluating the performance of automatic segmenters, it is important to consider not only the overall similarity between human and machine segmentations, but also to examine the regions of disagreement. When a program misses or misplaces a prominent topic shift – a segment boundary marked by all annotators – it should be penalized more than if it was mistaken about a boundary marked by one person. Similarly, a false positive in the region where none of the annotators found a change in topic is worse than a boundary inserted in a place where at least one person perceived a topic change. We suggest that it is important to use all available reference segmentations instead of compiling them into a single gold standard. We show how a small modification to the popular *windowDiff* (Pevzner and Hearst, 2002) metric can allow considering multiple annotations at once.

To demonstrate the increased interpretive power of such evaluation we run and evaluate several state-of-the art segmenters on the corpus described in this work. We evaluate their performance first in a conventional manner – by combining all available references into one – and then by using the proposed modification. Comparing the results suggests that the information provided by this method differs from what existing methods provide.

Section 2 gives a brief background on text segmentation. Section 3 describes the corpus and how it was collected. Section 4 contain quantitative and qualitative analysis of the corpus and its interpretations. Section 5 proposes a modified version of *windowDiff* and motivates it. Section 6 compares evaluation of three segmenters in several different ways. Section 7 contains the conclusions and outlines directions for future work.

2 Background and Related Work

The goal of topical text segmentation is to identify segments within which the topic under discussion remains relatively constant. A flip-side of this definition is identifying topic shifts – places where the topic shifts significantly or abruptly. In the context of this paper we allow ourselves to use these two definitions interchangeably, sometimes talking about identifying topic shifts, at other times – about identifying topically continuous segments. While the theoretical correctness of such usage remains questionable, it is sufficient for the purpose of our discussion, and it is in line with the literature on the topic.

There is a number of corpora annotated for the presence of topical shifts by one or more annotators. Passonneau and Litman (1997) describe an experiment where seven untrained annotators were asked to find discourse segments in a corpus of transcribed narratives about a movie. While the authors show that the agreement is significant, they also note that people include segment boundaries at different rates.

Gruenstein, Niekrasz, and Purver (2005) describe the process of annotating parts of two corpora of meeting transcripts: ICSI (Janin et al., 2003) and ISL (Burger, MacLaren, and Yu, 2002). Two people annotated the texts at two levels: major and minor, corresponding to the more and less important topic shifts. Topical shifts were to be annotated so as to allow an outsider to glance at the transcript and get the gist of what she missed. Not unlike our work, the authors report rather low overall inter-annotator agreement. Galley et al. (2003) also compiled a layer of annotation for topical shifts for part of the ICSI corpus, using a somewhat different procedure with three annotators. Malioutov and Barzilay (2006) created a corpus of course lectures segmented by four annotators, noting that the annotators operated at different levels of granularity. In these three projects, manual annotations were compiled into a single gold standard reference for use in evaluating and fine-tuning automatic segmenters.

The work described in this paper is different in several ways. To the best of our knowledge, this is the first attempt to annotate literary texts for topical shifts. Because we collected relatively many annotations for each chapter (four to six), we can make some generalizations as to the nature of the process. In addition to compiling and describing the corpus, we analyze disagreement patterns between annotators. We claim that even though the annotators may not agree on granularity, they do agree at some level, at least with respect to most prominent breaks. We propose that instead of compiling a single reference from multiple annotations it may be more useful to evaluate automatic segmenters against several annotations at once. We will show how to do that.

3 The Overview of the Corpus

Our current work on text segmentation is part of a larger project on automatic summarization of fiction, which is why we chose a XIX century novel, *The Moonstone* by Wilkie Collins, as the text to be annotated. We used two chapters for a pilot study and then another 20 for the large-scale experiment. The annotators worked with individual chapters and were required to align segment boundaries with paragraph breaks.

Objectives. The main question behind this study was this: "How do people identify topical shifts in literature?" This vague question can be mapped to several more specific objectives. First, we sought to verify that topical segmentation of literature was a sensible task from the viewpoint of an untrained annotator. Next, it was important to examine inter-annotator agreement to make sure that the annotators in fact worked on the same phenomena and that the resulting corpus is a reasonable approximation of how people segment literature in general. Third, in addition to analyzing the overall agreement we also took a close look at the type of common disagreements, in search of patterns and insights to evaluate automatic segmenters.

Subjects. The participants were undergraduate students of an English department at the University of Ottawa, recruited by email. They received $50 each for their participation. Everyone had to annotate four chapters from *The Moonstone*, not necessarily consecutive ones. The chapters were divided so as to ensure an approximately equal workload.

We had planned six independent annotations for each chapter of the novel.[1] The annotators were divided into five groups, each group asked to read and annotate four distinct chapters. In the end we had three groups with six people, one group with five and one group with four.

Procedure. The experiment was conducted remotely. The students received email packages with detailed instructions and an example of a segmented chapter from a different novel. They had two weeks to annotate the first two chapters and then two more weeks to annotate another two chapters.

The annotators were instructed to read each chapter and split it into episodes – topically continuous spans of text demarcated by the most perceptible shifts of topic in the chapter. We asked the annotators to provide a brief one-sentence description of each episode, effectively creating a chapter outline. The students were also asked to record places they found challenging and to note the time it takes to complete the task.

Because even short chapters of most traditional novels are rather lengthy, we chose to use paragraphs as the basic unit of annotation (sentences are more common in text segmentation literature).

4 Corpus Analysis

Time. On average, an annotator required 137.9 minutes to complete both tasks. The standard deviation was $\sigma = 98.32$ minutes appropriately reflecting the fact that some students are very fast readers and besides have already read the novel in one of their classes, while others are quite slow.

The average chapter has 53.85 paragraphs ($\sigma = 29.31$), the average segment length across all annotators is 9.25 paragraphs ($\sigma = 9.77$). On average the annotators identified 5.80 episodes ($\sigma = 2.45$) per chapter. Figure 1 shows the distribution of the number of segments identified in each chapter. An individual box plot is compiled using all available annotations for that chapter – six for most, four or five for several. The data are plotted for individual chapters, so the only source of variance is the disagreement between annotators as to what is the appropriate level of detail for the task. Figure 1 confirms

[1] We hired 30 students. Three did not complete the task.

Figure 1: Distribution of segment counts across chapters.

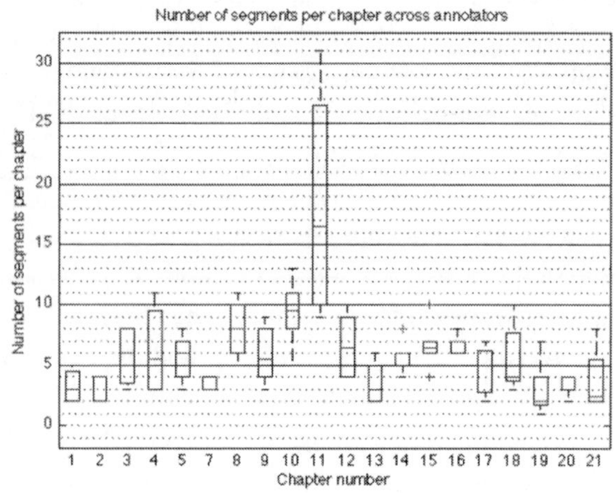

other researchers' findings: people find topical shifts at different levels of granularity (Malioutov and Barzilay, 2006; Gruenstein, Niekrasz, and Purver, 2005). We take this investigation further and explore whether there are patterns to this disagreement and how they can be interpreted and leveraged.

4.1 Inter-annotator Agreement

In order to make sure that our guidelines are sufficiently clear and the annotators in fact annotate the same phenomenon, it is important to measure inter-annotator agreement (Artstein and Poesio, 2008). This is particularly important given the fact that the resulting corpus is intended as a benchmark dataset for evaluation of automatic segmenters.

When looking at inter-annotator agreement independently of the domain, the most commonly used metrics are coefficients of agreement – α (Krippendorff, 2004), κ (Cohen, 1960; Shrout and Fleiss, 1979), π (Scott, 1955) and several others. In this work we use a multi-annotator version of π, also known in the CL community as Fleiss's κ (Shrout and Fleiss, 1979; Siegel and Castellan, 1988) .

Fleiss's κ is computed as follows:

$$\kappa = \frac{Agreement_{observed} - Agreement_{expected}}{1 - Agreement_{expected}} \quad (1)$$

$$Agreement_{observed} = \frac{1}{ic(c-1)} \sum_{i \in I} \sum_{k \in K} n_{ik}(n_{ik} - 1) \quad (2)$$

$$Agreement_{expected} = \frac{1}{(ic)^2} \sum_{k \in K} n_k^2 \quad (3)$$

where i is the number of items to be classified in set I, k is the number of available categories in set K, c is the number of annotators, n_{ik} is the number of annotators who assign item i to category k, n_k is the total number of items assigned to category k by all annotators (Artstein and Poesio, 2008, pp. 562-563). Effectively κ measures how much the annotators agree above what can be expected by chance. The value of κ is 0 where there is no agreement above chance and 1 where the annotators agree completely.

While we report κ values for our dataset, it is important to note that κ is ill-suited to measuring agreement in segmentation. The main problem is its insensitivity to near-hits. When asked to segment a document, the annotators often disagree about the exact placement of the boundary but agree that there is a boundary somewhere in the region (e.g., consider paragraphs 9-11 in segmentations in Figure 2). It is desirable to give partial credit to such near-hits instead of dismissing them as utter disagreement. This cannot be achieved with κ. The second problem is the independence assumption: the label for each item must be independent from the labels of all other items. In our case, this would amount to claiming, highly unrealistically, that the probability of a topical shift between two sentences is independent of the topical landscape of the rest of the document.

Two other commonly used agreement metrics are *Pk* (Beeferman, Berger, and Lafferty, 1999) and *windowDiff* (Pevzner and Hearst, 2002), both designed to compare a hypothetical segmentation to a reference, not to measure agreement *per se*. A common feature of both metrics is that they award partial credit to near-hits by sliding a fixed-length window through the sequence and comparing the reference segmentation and hypothetical segmentation at each window position. The window size is generally set at half the average segment length.

Pk (Equation 4) measures the probability that two units randomly drawn from a document are correctly classified as belonging to the same topical segment. *Pk* has been criticized for penalizing false negatives less than false positives and for being altogether insensitive to certain types of error; see (Pevzner and

Hearst, 2002, pp. 22-26) for details. Despite its shortcomings, *Pk* is widely used. We report it for comparison with other corpora.

$$Pk(ref, hyp) = \sum_{1 \le i \le j \le n} D(i,j)(\delta_{ref}(i,j)\ XNOR\ \delta_{hyp}(i,j)) \quad (4)$$

Functions δ_{hyp} and δ_{ref} indicate whether the two segment endpoints *i* and *j* belong to the same segment in the hypothetical segmentation and reference segmentation respectively.

windowDiff was designed to remedy some of *Pk*'s shortcomings. It counts erroneous windows in the hypothetical sequence normalized by the total number of windows. A window is judged erroneous if the boundary counts in the reference segmentation and hypothetical segmentation differ; that is (|ref - hyp| $\neq$ 0) in Equation 5).

$$winDiff = \frac{1}{N-k}\sum_{i=1}^{N-k}(|ref - hyp| \neq 0) \quad (5)$$

Both *Pk* and *windowDiff* produce penalty scores between 0 and 1, with 1 corresponding to all windows being in error, and 0 – to a perfect segmentation.

Table 1 reports *Pk*, *windowDiff* and κ values for our corpus. *Pk* and *windowDiff* are computed pairwise for all annotators within one group and then averaged. We set the window size to half the average segment length as measured across all annotators who worked on a given chapter. The values are computed for each group separately; Table 1 shows the averages across five groups.

Even by most relaxed standards, e.g., (Landis and Koch, 1977), the κ value of 0.38 corresponds to low agreement. This is not surprising, since it only includes the cases when the annotators agree exactly where the boundary should be. For the purpose of our task, such a definition is too strict.

The values of *windowDiff* and *Pk* are more reasonable; *windowDiff* = 0.34 means that on average a pair of annotators disagrees on 34% of windows. *windowDiff* was originally designed to compare only two segmentations. Our strategy of computing its values pairwise is perhaps not optimal but in the absence of another metric allowing to account for near-hits we are practically forced to use it as a primary means of inter-annotator agreement.

Table 1: Overview of inter-annotator agreement.

	Mean	Std. dev.
κ	0.29	0.15
Pk	0.33	0.17
windowDiff	0.38	0.09

Figure 2: Example segmentation for Chapter 1.

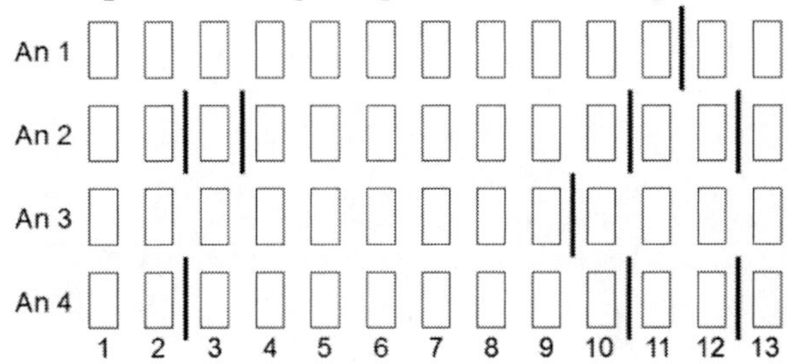

4.2 Patterns of Disagreement

Figure 2 shows the segmentation of the shortest chapter in the dataset. The overall agreement is quite low (*windowDiff*=0.38, κ = 0.28). This is not surprising, since annotators 1 and 3 found two segments, annotator 3 – five segments, and annotator 4 – four. Yet all annotators agree on certain things: everyone found that there was a significant change of topic between paragraphs 9 and 11 (though they disagree on its exact placement). It is therefore likely that the topical shift between paragraphs 9 and 11 is quite prominent. Annotators 2 and 4 chose to place a segment boundary after paragraph 2, while annotators 1 and 3 did not place one there. It is likely that the topical shift occurring there is less prominent, although perceptible. According to these annotations, the least perceptible topic shifts in the chapter occur after paragraph 4 (marked only by annotator 2) and possibly after paragraph 11 (marked only by annotator 1). Overall, glancing at these segmentations suggests that there is a prominent topical shift between paragraphs 9-11, three significant ones (after 2, 10 and 12) and several minor fluctuations (after 3 and possibly after 10 and 11).

Looking at the segmentations in Figure 2 it seems likely that the disagreements between annotators 2 and 4 are due to granularity, while the annotators 1 and three disagree more fundamentally on where the topic changes. When measuring agreement, we would like to be able to distinguish between dis-

Figure 3: Quality of segment boundaries.

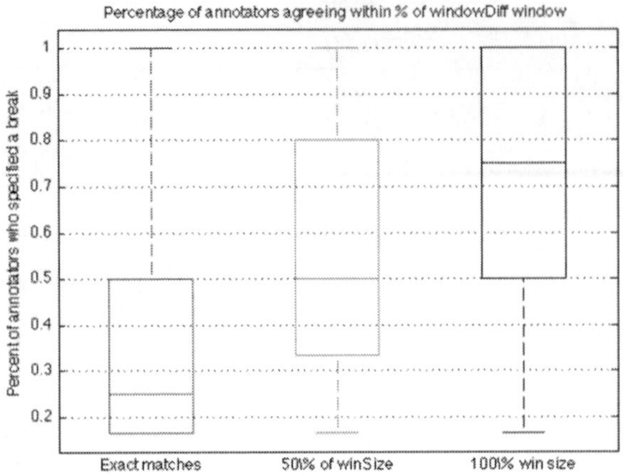

agreements due to granularity and disagreements due to true lack of agreement (annotator 1 and 3). We would also like to leverage this information for the evaluation of automatic segmenters.

Distinguishing between true disagreement and different granularity while taking into account near-hits is not trivial, especially since we are working with multiple annotations simultaneously and there is no *one* correct segmentation.

In order to estimate the quality of individual boundaries and look inside the segmented sequence, we approximate the quality of each suggested segment boundary by the percentage of annotators who marked it. Since the annotators may disagree on the exact placement of the boundaries, our measurement must be relaxed to allow for near-hits.

Figure 3 shows the distribution of segment boundaries using three different standards of quality. We consider all segment boundaries introduced by at least one annotator. Then, for each suggested boundary we compute how much support there is from peer annotators: what percentage of annotators included this boundary in their segmentation. The leftmost box plot in Figure 3 corresponds to the most strict standard. When computing support we only consider perfect matches: segment boundaries specified in exactly the same location (window size = 0). The middle box plot is more relaxed: we consider boundaries found within half of a *windowDiff* window size of the boundary under inspection. The rightmost box plot corresponds to the inclusion of boundaries found within a full *windowDiff* window size of the boundary under inspection.

Looking at exact matches (the leftmost box plot), we observe that at least a half of segment boundaries were specified by less than 25% of annotators (which corresponds to one person). It explains why κ values in Table 1 are so low: this is the only sort of agreement κ captures. Also one can notice that at most 25% of the boundaries have the support of more than 50% of the annotators.

The picture changes if we consider all boundaries within a tight window around the candidate boundary (the middle box plot). This standard is twice as strict as the regular *windowDiff* evaluation. Here 50% of all boundaries are marked by at least 35% at and most 80% of annotators. Only 25% of boundaries are marked by less than 30% of the annotators.

The rightmost plot looks even better. If we consider the support found within a window size of any candidate boundary, then 50% of all boundaries are supported by over 70% of annotators. However, we find this way of measuring support too optimistic. The reason is, again, the difference in the granularity of segmentations. The window size used for these measurements is based on the average segment length across all annotations. For example, the average segment length for segmentation shown in Figure 2 is 4, making the window size 2. This size is too relaxed for annotators 2 and 3, who were very detailed. Due to the excessively large window there will almost always be a boundary where fine-grained annotations are concerned, but those boundaries will not correspond to the same phenomena. That is why we think that a stricter standard is generally more appropriate. This is especially the case since we work with paragraphs, not sentences. A distance of 2-3 sentences is quite tolerable, but a distance of 2-3 paragraphs is considerable, and it is far more likely that a stricter notion of near-hits must be considered.

5 Proposed Modification to *windowDiff*

WindowDiff compares two segmentations by taking into account near-hits – penalizing them proportionally to how far a hypothetical segment boundary is from a reference boundary. Section 4.2 argued that some boundaries are more prominent. We aim to modify *windowDiff* so the prominence of the boundaries matters in evaluating automatic segmenters.

Recall that to compute *windowDiff* we slide a window through the reference and the hypothetical segmentation and check whether the number of boundaries is equal at each window position. The number of erroneous windows is then normalized:

$$winDiff = \frac{1}{N-k} \sum_{i=1}^{N-k} (|ref_i - hyp_i| \neq 0) \quad (6)$$

ref_i and $hypo_i$ are the counts of boundaries in a given window in the reference and the hypothetical sequence, N is the length of the complete sequence, k is the window size (so there are N - k windows).

The prominence of a boundary can be approximated by how many annotators specified it in their segmentations. One simple way to take prominence into account is to slide a window through all available segmentations, not just one. A straighforward modification to equation (6) achieves that:

$$winDiff' = \frac{1}{h(N-m)} \sum_{a=1}^{h} \sum_{i=1}^{N-m} (|ref_{ai} - hyp_i| \neq 0) \quad (7)$$

A is the set of all available annotations and h is their total number. Effectively, for each position of the window the hypothetical output is penalized as many times as there are reference annotations with which it disagrees. Note that the window size m is different from that used for pair-wise comparisons. Following the convention, we recommend setting it to half of the size of an average segment length (averaged over all available references). The size of the window effectively specifies a tolerance threshold for what is an acceptable near-hit (as opposed to a plain miss), and can be modified accordingly.

windowDiff and *Pk* range from 0 to 1, with 0 corresponding to an ideal segmentation. The upper and lower bounds for Equation 7 are different and depend on how much the reference segmentations agree between themselves.[2]

Let us refer to the most popular opinion for a given position of the window as the *majority opinion*. Then, for each window, the smallest possible penalty is assigned if the hypothetical segmentation correctly "guesses" the majority opinion (the window then receives a penalty equal to the number of annotators disagreeing with the majority opinion):

$$best\_case = \frac{1}{N-m} \sum_{i=1}^{N-m} (h - majority\_support) \quad (8)$$

Here $majority\_support$ is the number of annotators who support the most frequent opinion.

Conversely, to merit the highest penalty, a hypothetical segmentation must "guess" the least popular opinion (possibly an opinion not supported by any annotators) at each window position. In Equation 9, $unpopular\_support$ is the number of annotators who agree with the least popular opinion.

$$worst\_case = \frac{1}{N-m} \sum_{i=1}^{N-m} (h - unpopular\_support) \quad (9)$$

In order to have a multi-annotator version of *windowDiff* interpretable within the familiar $[0, 1]$ interval, we normalize Equation 7:

$$multWinDiff = \frac{(\sum_{a=1}^{h} \sum_{i=1}^{N-m} (|ref_a - hyp| \neq 0)) - best\_case}{h(N-m)(worst\_case - best\_case)} \quad (10)$$

The best and the worst-case bounds serve as indicators of how much agreement there can be between reference segmentations and so as indicators of how difficult to segment a given document is.

The *multWinDiff* metric in Equation 10 has the same desirable properties as the original metric, namely it takes into account near hits and penalizes according to how far the reference and hypothetical boundaries are. Additionally, for each window position it takes into account how much a hypothetical segmentation is similar to all available annotations, thus penalizing mistakes according to the prominence of boundaries (or to the certainty that there are no boundaries).[3]

---

[2] We find that the upper bound corresponds to the worst-case, and the lower bound to the best-case scenario. To avoid confusion, we talk of the *best-case bound* and the *worst-case bound*.

[3] Java code to compute *multWinDiff* is available as a part of the APS segmenter. The corpus and the software can be downloaded at ⟨`www.eecs.uottawa.ca/~ankazant`⟩.

6 Experiments

In order to illustrate why using a single gold-standard reference segmentation can be problematic, we evaluate three publicly available segmenters, MinCutSeg (Malioutov and Barzilay, 2006), BayesSeg (Eisenstein and Barzilay, 2008) and APS (Kazantseva and Szpakowicz, 2011), using several different gold standards and then using all available annotations. The corpus used for evaluation is *The Moonstone* corpus described in Sections 3-4. We withheld the first four chapters for development and used the remaining 16 for testing. We also compared the segmenters to a random baseline which consisted of randomly selecting a number of boundaries equal to the average number of segments across all available annotations.

None of the segmenters requires training in the conventional sense, but APS and MinCutSeg segmeters come with scripts allowing to fine-tune several parameters. We selected the best parameters for these two segmenters using the first four chapters of the corpus. BayesSeg segmeter, a probabilistic segmenter, does not require setting any parameters.

Table 2 sums up the results. Each row corresponds to one reference segmentation and metric – regular *windowDiff* in the first six rows. We compiled several flavours of consensus reference segmentations: 1) all boundaries marked by $\geq$ 50% of the annotators (*windowDiff* $\geq$ 50%), 2) all boundaries marked by $\geq$ 30% of the annotators (*windowDiff* $\geq$ 30%), 3) all boundaries marked by at least one annotator (*windowDiff* union). To illustrate why comparing against a single annotation is unreliable, we report comparisons against three single-person annotations (*windowDiff* annotator 1, 4, 2). *multWinDiff* is the proposed multi-annotator version from Equation 10. The best-case bound for *multWinDiff* is 0.21 and the worst-case bound is 1.0.

Each segmenter produced just one segmentation, so the numbers in the Table 2 differ only depending on the mode of evaluation. The cells are coloured. The lightest shade correspond to the best performance, darker shades – to poorer performance. The actual values for the first six rows are rather low, but what is more bothersome is the lack of consistency in the ranking of segmenters. Only the random baseline remains the worst in most cases. The APS and BayesSeg segmenters tend to appear better than the MinCutSeg but it is not always the case and the rankings among the three are not consistent.

	APS	Bayes	MinCut	Rand.
windowDiff $\geq$50%	0.60.	0.66	0.73	0.73
windowDiff $\geq$30%	0.61	0.52	0.69	0.61
windowDiff union	0.6	0.53	0.63	0.65
windowDiff annotator 1	0.66	0.57	0.74	0.76
windowDiff annotator 4	0.62	0.7	0.69	0.74
windowDiff annotator 2	0.61	0.6	0.66	0.69
multWinDiff	0.23	0.28	0.31	0.41

Table 2: The three segmenters and a random baseline compared using different references for computing *windowDiff*. *windowDiff* $\geq$50%: the gold standard consists of all boundaries specified by at least 50% of the annotators; *windowDiff* $\geq$30%: all boundaries specified by at least 30% of the annotators; *windowDiff* union: all boundaries specified by at least one person; *windowDiff* annotator a: comparisons against individual annotators. *multWinDiff* is multi-annotator *windowDiff* from equation (10).

The last row reports multi-annotator *windowDiff* which takes into account all available references and also the best-case and the worst-case bounds. In principle, there is no way to prove that the metric is better than using *windowDiff* and a single reference annotation. It does, however, take into account all available information and provides a different, if not unambiguously more true, picture of the comparative performance of automatic segmenters.

7 Conclusions and Future Work

We have described a new corpus which can be used in research on topical segmentation. The corpus is compiled for fiction, a genre for which no such corpus exists. It contains a reasonable number of annotations per chapter to allow an in-depth analysis of topical segmentation as performed by humans.

Our analysis of the corpus confirms the hypothesis that when asked to find topical segments, people operate at different levels of granularity. We show that only a small percentage of segment boundaries is agreed upon by all or almost all annotators. If, however, near-hits are considered, suggested segment boundaries can be ranked by their prominence using the information about how many people include each boundary in their annotation.

We propose a simple modification to *windowDiff* which allows for taking into account more than one reference segmentation, and thus rewards or penalizes the output of automatic segmenters by considering the severity of their mistakes. The proposed metric is not trouble-free. It is a window-based metric so its value depends on the choice of the window size. While it has become a convention to set the window size to half of the average segment length in the reference segmentation, it is not obvious that the same logic applies in case of multi-annotator *windowDiff*. The metric also hides whether false positives or false negatives are the main source of error.

All these shortcomings notwithstanding, the metric offers an advantage of allowing the evaluation of hypothetical segmentations with more subtlety than those using a single gold standard reference. When using regular *windowDiff* and a single reference segmentation, one is restricted to an evaluation based on binary comparisons: whether a given hypothetical boundary is similar to the gold standard segmentation (e.g., the majority opinion). Divergent segmentations are penalized even if they are similar to minority opinions (and thus feasible, though maybe less likely) or if they are completely different from anything created by humans (and thus probably genuinely erroneous). Our version of *windowDiff*, however, takes into account multiple annotations and gives partial reward to segmentations based on how similar there are to any human segmentation, not just the majority opinion (while giving preference to high agreement with the majority opinion).

To evaluate the output of topical segmenters is hard. There is disagreement between the annotators about the appropriate level of granularity and about the exact placement of segment boundaries. The task itself is also a little vague. Just as it is the case in automatic text summarization, generation and other advanced NLP tasks, there is no single correct answer and the goal of a good evaluation metric is to reward plausible hypotheses and to penalize improbable ones. It is quite possible that a better metric than the one proposed here can be devised; see, for example, (Fournier and Inkpen, 2012)(Scaiano and Inkpen, 2012). We feel, however, that any reliable metric for evaluating segmentations must – in one manner or another – take into account more than one annotation and the prominence of segment breaks.

Acknowledgments

We thank William Klement and Chris Fournier for commenting on an early draft of this paper. The first author also thanks Chris Fournier and Martin Scaiano for insightful discussions about the evaluation of topical segmenters. This work is partially funded by the National Sciences and Engineering Research Council of Canada and by the Ontario Graduate Scholarship program.

References

Artstein, Ron and Massimo Poesio. 2008. Inter-Coder Agreement for Computational Linguistics. *Computational Linguistics*, 34(4):555–596.

Beeferman, Doug, Adam Berger, and John Lafferty. 1999. Statistical Models for Text Segmentation. *Machine Learning*, 34:177 210, February.

Burger, Susanne, Victoria MacLaren, and Hua Yu. 2002. The ISL meeting corpus: the impact of meeting type on speech style. In *INTERSPEECH'02*.

Cohen, Jacob. 1960. A coefficient of agreement for nominal scales . *Educational and Psychological Measurement*, 20:37–46.

Eisenstein, Jacob and Regina Barzilay. 2008. Bayesian unsupervised topic segmentation. In *Proceedings of the 2008 Conference on Empirical Methods in Natural Language Processing*, pages 334–343, Honolulu, Hawaii, October.

Fournier, Chris and Diana Inkpen. 2012. Segmentation similarity and agreement. In *Proceedings of NAACL HLT 2012 (this volume)*, Montréal, Canada, June.

Galley, Michel, Kathleen McKeown, Eric Fosler-Lussier, and Hongyan Jing. 2003. Discourse segmentation of multi-party conversation. In *Proceedings of the 41st Annual Meeting on Association for Computational Linguistics - Volume 1*, ACL '03, pages 562–

569, Stroudsburg, PA, USA. Association for Computational Linguistics.

Gruenstein, Alexander, John Niekrasz, and Matthew Purver. 2005. Meeting Structure Annotation: Data and Tools. In *In Proceedings of the SIGdial Workshop on Discourse and Dialogue*, pages 117–127.

Janin, Adam, Don Baron, Jane Edwards, D. Ellis, David Gelbart, Nelson Morgan, Barbara Peskin, Thilo Pfau, Elizabeth Shriberg, A.ndreas Stolcke, and Chuck Wooters. 2003. The ICSI Meeting Corpus. In *Proceedings of the IEEE International Conference on Acoustics, Speech, and Signal Processing (ICASSP-03)*, volume 1, pages 364–367, April.

Kazantseva, Anna and Stan Szpakowicz. 2011. Linear Text Segmentation Using Affinity Propagation. In *Proceedings of the 2011 Conference on Empirical Methods in Natural Language Processing*, pages 284–293, Edinburgh, Scotland, UK., July. Association for Computational Linguistics.

Krippendorff, Klaus. 2004. *Content Analysis. An Introduction to Its Methodology.* Sage Publications.

Landis, J. Richards and Garry G. Koch. 1977. The Measurement of Observer Agreement for Categorical Data. *Biometrics*, 33(1):159–174.

Malioutov, Igor and Regina Barzilay. 2006. Minimum Cut Model for Spoken Lecture Segmentation. In *Proceedings of the 21st International Conference on Computational Linguistics and 44th Annual Meeting of the Association for Computational Linguistics*, pages 25–32, Sydney, Australia, July.

Misra, Hemant, François Yvon, Olivier Cappé, and Joemon M. Jose. 2011. Text segmentation: A topic modeling perspective. *Information Processing and Management*, 47(4):528–544.

Passonneau, Rebecca J. and Diane J. Litman. 1997. Discourse segmentation by human and automated means. *Computational Linguistics*, 23(1):103–139, March.

Pevzner, Lev and Marti A. Hearst. 2002. A Critique and Improvement of an Evaluation Metric for Text Segmentation. *Computational Linguistics*, 28(1):19–36.

Scaiano, Martin and Diana Inkpen. 2012. Getting more from segmentation evaluation. In *Proceedings of NAACL-HLT 2012 (this volume)*, Montréal, Canada, June.

Scott, William. 1955. Reliability of content analysis: The case of nominal scale coding. *Public Opinion Quaterly*, 19(3):321–325.

Shrout, Patrick E. and Joseph L. Fleiss. 1979. Intraclass correlations: uses in assessing rater reliability. *Psychological Bulletin*, 86(2):420–428.

Siegel, Sidney and John. N. Jr. Castellan. 1988. *Nonparametric statistics for the behavioral sciences.* McGraw Hill, Boston, MA.

Structured Ramp Loss Minimization for Machine Translation

Kevin Gimpel and **Noah A. Smith**
Language Technologies Institute
Carnegie Mellon University
Pittsburgh, PA 15213, USA
{kgimpel,nasmith}@cs.cmu.edu

Abstract

This paper seeks to close the gap between training algorithms used in statistical machine translation and machine learning, specifically the framework of empirical risk minimization. We review well-known algorithms, arguing that they do not optimize the loss functions they are assumed to optimize when applied to machine translation. Instead, most have implicit connections to particular forms of **ramp loss**. We propose to minimize ramp loss directly and present a training algorithm that is easy to implement and that performs comparably to others. Most notably, our structured ramp loss minimization algorithm, RAMPION, is less sensitive to initialization and random seeds than standard approaches.

1 Introduction

Every statistical MT system relies on a training algorithm to fit the parameters of a scoring function to examples from parallel text. Well-known examples include MERT (Och, 2003), MIRA (Chiang et al., 2008), and PRO (Hopkins and May, 2011). While such procedures can be analyzed as machine learning algorithms—e.g., in the general framework of **empirical risk minimization** (Vapnik, 1998)—their *procedural* specifications have made this difficult. From a practical perspective, such algorithms are often complex, difficult to replicate, and sensitive to initialization, random seeds, and other hyperparameters.

In this paper, we consider training algorithms that are first specified *declaratively*, as **loss functions** to be minimized. We relate well-known training algorithms for MT to particular loss functions. We show that a family of **structured ramp** loss functions (Do et al., 2008) is useful for this analysis. For example, McAllester and Keshet (2011) recently suggested that, while Chiang et al. (2008, 2009) described their algorithm as "MIRA" (Crammer et al., 2006), in fact it targets a kind of ramp loss. We note here other examples: Liang et al. (2006) described their algorithm as a variant of the perceptron (Collins, 2002), which has a unique loss function, but the loss actually optimized is closer to a particular ramp loss (that differs from the one targeted by Chiang et al.). Och and Ney (2002) sought to optimize log loss (likelihood in a probabilistic model; Lafferty et al., 2001) but actually optimized a version of the *soft* ramp loss.

Why isn't the application of ML to MT more straightforward? We note two key reasons: (i) ML generally assumes that the correct output can always be scored by a model, but in MT the reference translation is often unreachable, due to a model's limited expressive power or search error, requiring the use of "surrogate" references; (ii) MT models nearly always include latent derivation variables, leading to non-convex losses that have generally received little attention in ML. In this paper, we discuss how these two have caused a disconnect between the loss function minimized by an algorithm in ML and the loss minimized when it is adapted for MT.

From a practical perspective, our framework leads to a simple training algorithm for structured ramp loss based on general optimization techniques. Our algorithm is simple to implement and, being a *batch* algorithm like MERT and PRO, can easily be integrated with any decoder. Our experiments show that our algorithm, which we call RAMPION, performs comparably to MERT and PRO, is less sensitive to randomization and initialization conditions, and is robust in large-feature scenarios.

2 Notation and Background

Let $\mathcal{X}$ denote the set of all strings in a source language and, for a particular $\boldsymbol{x} \in \mathcal{X}$, let $\mathcal{Y}(\boldsymbol{x})$ denote the set of its possible translations (correct and incorrect) in the target language. In typical models for machine translation, a **hidden variable** is assumed to be constructed during the translation process.[1] Regardless of its specific form, we will refer to it as a **derivation** and denote it $\boldsymbol{h} \in \mathcal{H}(\boldsymbol{x})$, where $\mathcal{H}(\boldsymbol{x})$ is the set of possible values of $\boldsymbol{h}$ for the input $\boldsymbol{x}$. Derivations will always be coupled with translations and therefore we define the set $\mathcal{T}(\boldsymbol{x}) \subseteq \mathcal{Y}(\boldsymbol{x}) \times \mathcal{H}(\boldsymbol{x})$ of valid **output pairs** $\langle \boldsymbol{y}, \boldsymbol{h} \rangle$ for $\boldsymbol{x}$.

To model translation, we use a linear model parameterized by a parameter vector $\boldsymbol{\theta} \in \boldsymbol{\Theta}$. Given a vector $\boldsymbol{f}(\boldsymbol{x}, \boldsymbol{y}, \boldsymbol{h})$ of feature functions on $\boldsymbol{x}$, $\boldsymbol{y}$, and $\boldsymbol{h}$, and assuming $\boldsymbol{\theta}$ contains a component for each feature function, output pairs $\langle \boldsymbol{y}, \boldsymbol{h} \rangle$ for a given input $\boldsymbol{x}$ are selected using a simple argmax decision rule: $\langle \boldsymbol{y}^*, \boldsymbol{h}^* \rangle = \operatorname*{argmax}_{\langle \boldsymbol{y},\boldsymbol{h}\rangle \in \mathcal{T}(\boldsymbol{x})} \underbrace{\boldsymbol{\theta}^\top \boldsymbol{f}(\boldsymbol{x}, \boldsymbol{y}, \boldsymbol{h})}_{\text{score}(\boldsymbol{x},\boldsymbol{y},\boldsymbol{h};\boldsymbol{\theta})}$.

The training problem for machine translation corresponds to choosing $\boldsymbol{\theta}$. There are many ways to do this, and we will describe each in terms of a particular **loss function** $\text{loss} : \mathcal{X}^N \times \mathcal{Y}^N \times \boldsymbol{\Theta} \rightarrow \mathbb{R}$ that maps an input corpus, its reference translations, and the model parameters to a real value indicating the quality of the parameters. **Risk minimization** corresponds to choosing

$$\text{argmin}_{\boldsymbol{\theta} \in \boldsymbol{\Theta}} \; \mathbb{E}_{p(\boldsymbol{X},\boldsymbol{Y})} \left[\text{loss}\left(\boldsymbol{X}, \boldsymbol{Y}, \boldsymbol{\theta}\right)\right] \quad (1)$$

where $p(\boldsymbol{X}, \boldsymbol{Y})$ is the (unknown) true joint distribution over corpora. We note that the loss function depends on the entire corpus, while the decoder operates independently on one sentence at a time. This is done to fit the standard assumptions in MT systems: the evaluation metric (e.g., BLEU) depends on the entire corpus and does not decompose linearly, while the model score does. Since in practice we do not know $p(\boldsymbol{X}, \boldsymbol{Y})$, but we do have access to an actual corpus pair $\langle \tilde{\boldsymbol{X}}, \tilde{\boldsymbol{Y}} \rangle$, where $\tilde{\boldsymbol{X}} = \{\boldsymbol{x}^{(i)}\}_{i=1}^N$ and $\tilde{\boldsymbol{Y}} = \{\boldsymbol{y}^{(i)}\}_{i=1}^N$, we instead consider **regularized empirical risk minimization**:

$$\text{argmin}_{\boldsymbol{\theta} \in \boldsymbol{\Theta}} \; \text{loss}(\tilde{\boldsymbol{X}}, \tilde{\boldsymbol{Y}}, \boldsymbol{\theta}) + R(\boldsymbol{\theta}) \quad (2)$$

where $R(\boldsymbol{\theta})$ is the **regularization function** used to mitigate overfitting. The regularization function is frequently a squared norm of the parameter vector, such as the ℓ_1 or ℓ_2 norm, but many other choices are possible. In this paper, we use ℓ_2.

Models are evaluated using a task-specific notion of error, here encoded as a **cost function**, $\text{cost} : \mathcal{Y}^N \times \mathcal{Y}^N \rightarrow \mathbb{R}_{\geq 0}$, such that the worse a translation is, the higher its cost. The cost function will typically make use of an automatic evaluation metric for machine translation; e.g., cost might be 1 minus the BLEU score (Papineni et al., 2001).[2]

We note that our analysis in this paper is applicable for understanding the loss function being optimized *given a fixed set of k-best lists*.[3] However, most training procedures periodically invoke the decoder to generate new k-best lists, which are then typically merged with those from previous training iterations. It is an open question how this practice affects the loss function being optimized by the procedure as a whole.

Example 1: MERT. The most commonly-used training algorithm for machine translation is **minimum error rate training**, which seeks to directly minimize the cost of the predictions on the training data. This idea has been used in the pattern recognition and speech recognition communities (Duda and Hart, 1973; Juang et al., 1997); its first application to MT was by Och (2003). The loss function takes the following form: $\text{loss}_{\text{cost}}\left(\tilde{\boldsymbol{X}}, \tilde{\boldsymbol{Y}}, \boldsymbol{\theta}\right) =$

$$\text{cost}\left(\tilde{\boldsymbol{Y}}, \left\{ \operatorname*{argmax}_{\langle \boldsymbol{y},\boldsymbol{h}\rangle \in \mathcal{T}(\boldsymbol{x}^{(i)})} \text{score}(\boldsymbol{x}^{(i)}, \boldsymbol{y}, \boldsymbol{h}; \boldsymbol{\theta}) \right\}_{i=1}^{N} \right) \quad (3)$$

[1]For phrase-based MT, a segmentation of the source and target sentences into phrases and an alignment between them (Koehn et al., 2003). For hierarchical phrase-based MT, a derivation under a synchronous CFG (Chiang, 2005).

[2]We will abuse notation and allow cost to operate on both sets of sentences as well as individual sentences. For notational convenience we also let cost accept hidden variables but assume that the hidden variables do not affect the value; i.e., $\text{cost}(\langle \boldsymbol{y}, \boldsymbol{h} \rangle, \langle \boldsymbol{y}', \boldsymbol{h}' \rangle) = \text{cost}(\boldsymbol{y}, \langle \boldsymbol{y}', \boldsymbol{h}' \rangle) = \text{cost}(\boldsymbol{y}, \boldsymbol{y}')$.

[3]Cherry and Foster (2012) have concurrently performed a similar analysis.

MERT directly minimizes the corpus-level cost function of the best outputs from the decoder without any regularization (i.e., $R(\boldsymbol{\theta}) = 0$).[4] The loss is non-convex and not differentiable for cost functions like BLEU, so Och (2003) developed a coordinate ascent procedure with a specialized line search.

MERT avoids the need to compute feature vectors for the references (§1(i)) and allows corpus-level metrics like BLEU to be easily incorporated. However, the complexity of the loss and the difficulty of the search lead to instabilities during learning. Remedies have been suggested, typically involving additional search directions and experiment replicates (Cer et al., 2008; Moore and Quirk, 2008; Foster and Kuhn, 2009; Clark et al., 2011). But despite these improvements, MERT is ineffectual for training weights for large numbers of features; in addition to anecdotal evidence from the MT community, Hopkins and May (2011) illustrated with synthetic data experiments that MERT struggles increasingly to find the optimal solution as the number of parameters grows.

Example 2: Probabilistic Models. By exponentiating and normalizing $\text{score}(\boldsymbol{x}, \boldsymbol{y}, \boldsymbol{h}; \boldsymbol{\theta})$, we obtain a conditional log-linear model, which is useful for training criteria with probabilistic interpretations:

$$p_{\boldsymbol{\theta}}(\boldsymbol{y}, \boldsymbol{h} | \boldsymbol{x}) = \frac{1}{Z(\boldsymbol{x}, \boldsymbol{\theta})} \exp\{\text{score}(\boldsymbol{x}, \boldsymbol{y}, \boldsymbol{h}; \boldsymbol{\theta})\} \quad (4)$$

The **log loss** then defines $\text{loss}_{\text{log}}(\tilde{\boldsymbol{X}}, \tilde{\boldsymbol{Y}}, \boldsymbol{\theta}) = -\sum_{i=1}^{N} \log p_{\boldsymbol{\theta}}(\boldsymbol{y}^{(i)} \mid \boldsymbol{x}^{(i)})$.

Example 3: Bayes Risk. The term "risk" as used above should not be confused with the **Bayes risk** framework, which uses a probability distribution (Eq. 4) and a cost function to define a loss:

$$\text{loss}_{\text{B\_risk}} = \sum_{i=1}^{N} \mathbb{E}_{p_{\boldsymbol{\theta}}(\boldsymbol{y}, \boldsymbol{h} | \boldsymbol{x}^{(i)})}[\text{cost}(\boldsymbol{y}^{(i)}, \boldsymbol{y})] \quad (5)$$

The use of this loss is often simply called "risk minimization" in the speech and MT communities. Bayes risk is non-convex, whether or not latent variables are present. Like MERT, it naturally avoids the need to compute features for $\boldsymbol{y}^{(i)}$ and uses a cost function, making it appealing for MT. Bayes risk minimization first appeared in the speech recognition community (Kaiser et al., 2000; Povey and Woodland, 2002) and more recently has been applied to MT (Smith and Eisner, 2006; Zens et al., 2007; Li and Eisner, 2009).

[4]However, Cer et al. (2008) and Macherey et al. (2008) achieved a sort of regularization by altering MERT's line search.

3 Training Methods for MT

In this section we consider other ML-inspired approaches to MT training, situating each in the framework from §2: ramp, perceptron, hinge, and "soft" losses. Each of the first three kinds of losses can be understood as a way of selecting, for each $\boldsymbol{x}^{(i)}$, two candidate translation/derivation pairs: $\langle \boldsymbol{y}^{\uparrow}, \boldsymbol{h}^{\uparrow} \rangle$ and $\langle \boldsymbol{y}^{\downarrow}, \boldsymbol{h}^{\downarrow} \rangle$. During training, the loss function can be improved by increasing the score of the former and decreasing the score of the latter, through manipulation of the parameters $\boldsymbol{\theta}$. Figure 1 gives a general visualization of some of the key output pairs that are considered for these roles. Learning alters the score function, or, in the figure, moves points *horizontally* so that scores approximate negated costs.

3.1 Structured Ramp Loss Minimization

The **structured ramp loss** (Do et al., 2008) is a non-convex loss function with certain attractive theoretical properties. It is an upper bound on $\text{loss}_{\text{cost}}$ (Eq. 3) and is a tighter bound than other loss functions (Collobert et al., 2006). Ramp loss has been shown to be **statistically consistent** in the sense that, in the limit of infinite training data, minimizing structured ramp loss reaches the minimum value of $\text{loss}_{\text{cost}}$ that is achievable with a linear model (McAllester and Keshet, 2011). This is true whether or not latent variables are present.

Consistency in this sense is not a common property of loss functions; commonly-used convex loss functions such as the perceptron, hinge, and log losses (discussed below) are *not* consistent, because they are all sensitive to outliers or otherwise noisy training examples. Ramp loss is better at dealing with outliers in the training data (Collobert et al., 2006).

There are three forms of latent structured ramp loss: Eq. 6–8 (Fig. 2). Ramp losses are appealing for MT because they do not require computing the feature vector of $\boldsymbol{y}^{(i)}$ (§1(i)). The first form, Eq. 6, sets $\langle \boldsymbol{y}^{\uparrow}, \boldsymbol{h}^{\uparrow} \rangle$ to be the current model prediction ($\langle \hat{\boldsymbol{y}}, \hat{\boldsymbol{h}} \rangle$ in Fig. 1) and $\langle \boldsymbol{y}^{\downarrow}, \boldsymbol{h}^{\downarrow} \rangle$ to be an output that is both favored by the model *and* has high cost. Such an

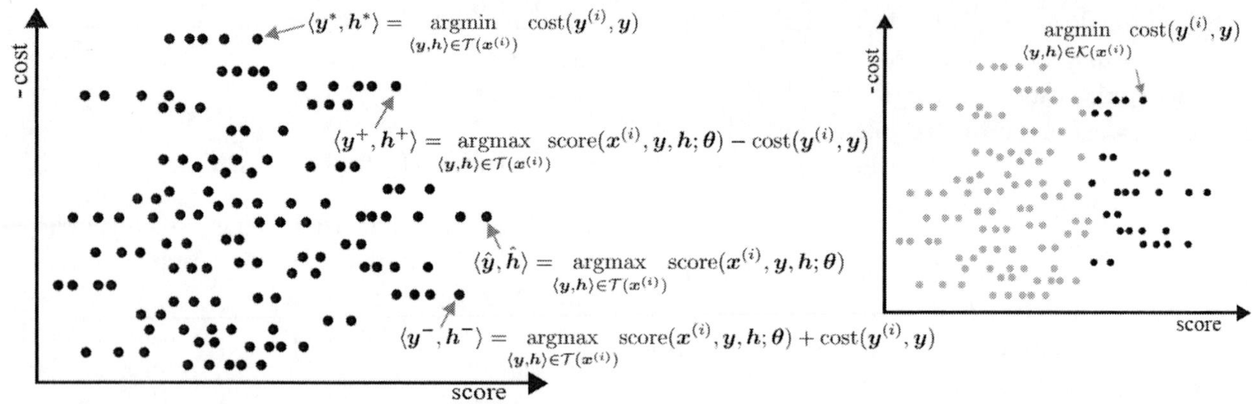

Figure 1: Hypothetical output space of a translation model for an input sentence $x^{(i)}$. Each point corresponds to a single translation/derivation output pair. Horizontal "bands" are caused by output pairs with the same translation (and hence the same cost) but different derivations. The left plot shows the entire output space and the right plot highlights outputs in the k-best list. Choosing the output with the lowest cost in the k-best list is similar to finding $\langle y^+, h^+ \rangle$.

output is shown as $\langle y^-, h^- \rangle$ in Fig. 1; finding $y^\downarrow$ is often called **cost-augmented decoding**, which is also used to define hinge loss (§3.3).

The second form, Eq. 7, *penalizes* the model prediction ($\langle y^\downarrow, h^\downarrow \rangle = \langle \hat{y}, \hat{h} \rangle$) and favors an output pair that has both high model score and low cost; this is the converse of cost-augmented decoding and therefore we call it **cost-*diminished* decoding**; $\langle y^\uparrow, h^\uparrow \rangle = \langle y^+, h^+ \rangle$ in Fig. 1. The third form, Eq. 8, sets $\langle y^\uparrow, h^\uparrow \rangle = \langle y^+, h^+ \rangle$ and $\langle y^\downarrow, h^\downarrow \rangle = \langle y^-, h^- \rangle$. This loss underlies RAMPION. It is similar to the loss optimized by the MIRA-inspired algorithm used by Chiang et al. (2008, 2009).

Optimization The ramp losses are continuous but non-convex and non-differentiable, so gradient-based optimization methods are not available.[5] Fortunately, Eq. 8 can be optimized by using a concave-convex procedure (CCCP; Yuille and Rangarajan, 2002). CCCP is a batch optimization algorithm for any function that is the the sum of a concave and a convex function. The idea is to approximate the sum as the convex term plus a tangent line to the concave function at the current parameter values; the resulting sum is convex and can be optimized with (sub)gradient methods.

With our loss functions, CCCP first imputes the outputs in the concave terms in each loss (i.e., solves the negated max expressions) for the entire training set and then uses an optimization procedure to optimize the loss with the imputed values fixed. Any convex optimization procedure can be used once the negated max terms are solved; we use stochastic subgradient descent (SSD) but MIRA could be easily used instead.

The CCCP algorithm we use for optimizing $\text{loss}_{\text{ramp 3}}$, which we call RAMPION, is shown as Alg. 1. Similar algorithms can easily be derived for the other ramp losses. The first step done on each iteration is to generate k-best lists for the full tuning set (line 3). We then run CCCP on the k-best lists for T' iterations (lines 4–15). This involves first finding the translation to update towards for all sentences in the tuning set (lines 5–7), then making parameter updates in an online fashion with T'' epochs of stochastic subgradient descent (lines 8–14). The subgradient update for the ℓ_2 regularization term is done in line 11 and then for the loss in line 12.[6]

Unlike prior work that targeted similar loss functions (Watanabe et al., 2007; Chiang et al., 2008; Chiang et al., 2009), we do not use a fully online algorithm such as MIRA in an outer loop because we are not aware of an online learning algorithm with theoretical guarantees for non-differentiable, non-convex loss functions like the ramp losses. CCCP

[5]For non-differentiable, continuous, *convex* functions, **subgradient**-based methods are available, such as stochastic subgradient descent (SSD), and it is tempting to apply them here. However, non-convex functions are not everywhere subdifferentiable and so a straightforward application of SSD may encounter problems in practice.

[6]ℓ_2 regularization done here regularizes toward θ_0, not $\mathbf{0}$.

$$\text{loss}_{\text{ramp 1}} = \sum_{i=1}^{N} - \max_{\langle \boldsymbol{y}, \boldsymbol{h} \rangle \in \mathcal{T}_i} (\text{score}_i(\boldsymbol{y}, \boldsymbol{h}; \boldsymbol{\theta})) + \max_{\langle \boldsymbol{y}, \boldsymbol{h} \rangle \in \mathcal{T}_i} (\text{score}_i(\boldsymbol{y}, \boldsymbol{h}; \boldsymbol{\theta}) + \text{cost}_i(\boldsymbol{y})) \tag{6}$$

$$\text{loss}_{\text{ramp 2}} = \sum_{i=1}^{N} - \max_{\langle \boldsymbol{y}, \boldsymbol{h} \rangle \in \mathcal{T}_i} (\text{score}_i(\boldsymbol{y}, \boldsymbol{h}; \boldsymbol{\theta}) - \text{cost}_i(\boldsymbol{y})) + \max_{\langle \boldsymbol{y}, \boldsymbol{h} \rangle \in \mathcal{T}_i} (\text{score}_i(\boldsymbol{y}, \boldsymbol{h}; \boldsymbol{\theta})) \tag{7}$$

$$\text{loss}_{\text{ramp 3}} = \sum_{i=1}^{N} - \max_{\langle \boldsymbol{y}, \boldsymbol{h} \rangle \in \mathcal{T}_i} (\text{score}_i(\boldsymbol{y}, \boldsymbol{h}; \boldsymbol{\theta}) - \text{cost}_i(\boldsymbol{y})) + \max_{\langle \boldsymbol{y}, \boldsymbol{h} \rangle \in \mathcal{T}_i} (\text{score}_i(\boldsymbol{y}, \boldsymbol{h}; \boldsymbol{\theta}) + \text{cost}_i(\boldsymbol{y})) \tag{8}$$

$$\text{loss}_{\text{perc}} = \sum_{i=1}^{N} - \max_{\boldsymbol{h}: \langle \boldsymbol{y}^{(i)}, \boldsymbol{h} \rangle \in \mathcal{T}_i} \text{score}_i(\boldsymbol{y}^{(i)}, \boldsymbol{h}; \boldsymbol{\theta}) + \max_{\langle \boldsymbol{y}, \boldsymbol{h} \rangle \in \mathcal{T}_i} \text{score}_i(\boldsymbol{y}, \boldsymbol{h}; \boldsymbol{\theta}) \tag{9}$$

$$\text{loss}_{\text{perc } k\text{best}} = \sum_{i=1}^{n} -\text{score}\left(\boldsymbol{x}^{(i)}, \operatorname*{argmin}_{\langle \boldsymbol{y}, \boldsymbol{h} \rangle \in \mathcal{K}_i} (\text{cost}_i(\boldsymbol{y})) ; \boldsymbol{\theta} \right) + \max_{\langle \boldsymbol{y}, \boldsymbol{h} \rangle \in \mathcal{T}_i} \text{score}_i(\boldsymbol{y}, \boldsymbol{h}; \boldsymbol{\theta}) \tag{10}$$

$$\approx \sum_{i=1}^{N} - \max_{\langle \boldsymbol{y}, \boldsymbol{h} \rangle \in \mathcal{T}_i} (\text{score}_i(\boldsymbol{y}, \boldsymbol{h}; \boldsymbol{\theta}) - \gamma_i \text{cost}_i(\boldsymbol{y})) + \max_{\langle \boldsymbol{y}, \boldsymbol{h} \rangle \in \mathcal{T}_i} \text{score}_i(\boldsymbol{y}, \boldsymbol{h}; \boldsymbol{\theta}) \tag{11}$$

Figure 2: Formulae mentioned in text for latent-variable loss functions. Each loss is actually a function $\text{loss}(\tilde{\boldsymbol{X}}, \tilde{\boldsymbol{Y}}, \boldsymbol{\theta})$; we suppress the arguments for clarity. "$\mathcal{T}_i$" is shorthand for "$\mathcal{T}(\boldsymbol{x}^{(i)})$." "$\mathcal{K}_i$" is shorthand for the k-best list for $\boldsymbol{x}^{(i)}$. "$\text{cost}_i(\cdot)$" is shorthand for "$\text{cost}(\boldsymbol{y}^{(i)}, \cdot)$." "$\text{score}_i(\cdot)$" is shorthand for "$\text{score}(\boldsymbol{x}^{(i)}, \cdot)$." As noted in §3.4, any operator of the form $\max_{s \in \mathcal{S}}$ can be replaced by $\log \sum_{s \in \mathcal{S}} \exp$, known as softmax, giving many additional loss functions.

is fundamentally a batch optimization algorithm and has been used for solving many non-convex learning problems, such as latent structured SVMs (Yu and Joachims, 2009).

3.2 Structured Perceptron

The stuctured perceptron algorithm (Collins, 2002) was considered by Liang et al. (2006) as an alternative to MERT. It requires only a decoder and comes with some attractive guarantees, at least for models without latent variables. Liang et al. modified the perceptron in several ways for use in MT. The first was to generalize it to handle latent variables. The second change relates to the need to compute the feature vector for the reference translation $\boldsymbol{y}^{(i)}$, which may be unreachable (§1(i)). To address this, researchers have proposed the use of surrogates that are both favored by the current model parameters and similar to the reference. Och and Ney (2002) were the first to do so, using the translation on a k-best list with the highest evaluation metric score as $\boldsymbol{y}^{\uparrow}$. This practice was followed by Liang et al. (2006) and others with success (Arun and Koehn, 2007; Watanabe et al., 2007).[7]

Perceptron Loss Though typically described and analyzed procedurally, it is straightforward to show that Collins' perceptron (without latent variables) equates to SSD with fixed step size 1 on loss:

$$\sum_{i=1}^{N} -\text{score}(\boldsymbol{x}^{(i)}, \boldsymbol{y}^{(i)}; \boldsymbol{\theta}) + \max_{\boldsymbol{y} \in \mathcal{Y}(\boldsymbol{x}^{(i)})} \text{score}(\boldsymbol{x}^{(i)}, \boldsymbol{y}; \boldsymbol{\theta}) \tag{12}$$

This loss is convex but ignores cost functions. In our notation, $\boldsymbol{y}^{\uparrow} = \boldsymbol{y}^{(i)}$ and $\boldsymbol{y}^{\downarrow} = \operatorname{argmax}_{\boldsymbol{y} \in \mathcal{Y}(\boldsymbol{x}^{(i)})} \text{score}(\boldsymbol{x}^{(i)}, \boldsymbol{y}; \boldsymbol{\theta})$.

Adaptation for MT We chart the transformations from Eq. 12 toward the loss Liang et al.'s algorithm actually optimized. First, generalize to latent variables; see Eq. 9 (Fig. 2), sacrificing convexity. Second, to cope with unreachable references, use a k-best surrogate as shown in Eq. 10 (Fig. 2), where $\mathcal{K}_i \in \mathcal{T}(\boldsymbol{x}^{(i)})^k$ is a set containing the k best output pairs for $\boldsymbol{x}^{(i)}$. Now the loss only depends on $\boldsymbol{y}^{(i)}$ through the cost function. (Even without hidden variables, this loss can only be convex when the k-best list is fixed, keeping $\boldsymbol{y}^{\uparrow}$ unchanged across iterations. Updating the k-best lists makes $\boldsymbol{y}^{\uparrow}$ depend on $\boldsymbol{\theta}$, resulting in a non-convex loss.)

It appears that Eq. 10 (Fig. 2) is the loss that Liang et al. (2006) *sought* to optimize, using SSD. In light of footnote 5 and the non-convexity of Eq. 10 (Fig. 2), we have no theoretical guarantee that such an algorithm will find a (local) optimum.

[7] Liang et al. (2006) also tried a variant that updated directly to the reference when it is reachable ("bold updating"), but they and others found that Och and Ney's strategy worked better.

Input: inputs $\{\boldsymbol{x}^{(i)}\}_{i=1}^N$, references $\{\boldsymbol{y}^{(i)}\}_{i=1}^N$, init. weights $\boldsymbol{\theta}_0$, k-best list size k, step size η, ℓ_2 reg. coeff. C, # iters T, # CCCP iters T', # SSD iters T''

Output: learned weights: $\boldsymbol{\theta}$

$\boldsymbol{\theta} \leftarrow \boldsymbol{\theta}_0$;
for $iter \leftarrow 1$ **to** T **do**
  $\{\mathcal{K}_i\}_{i=1}^N \leftarrow \texttt{Decode}(\{\boldsymbol{x}^{(i)}\}_{i=1}^N, \boldsymbol{\theta}, k)$;
  for $iter' \leftarrow 1$ **to** T' **do**
    for $i \leftarrow 1$ **to** N **do**
      $\langle \boldsymbol{y}_i^+, \boldsymbol{h}_i^+ \rangle \leftarrow \operatorname{argmax}_{\langle \boldsymbol{y}, \boldsymbol{h} \rangle \in \mathcal{K}_i} \text{score}_i(\boldsymbol{y}, \boldsymbol{h}; \boldsymbol{\theta}) - \text{cost}_i(\boldsymbol{y})$;
    end
    for $iter'' \leftarrow 1$ **to** T'' **do**
      for $i \leftarrow 1$ **to** N **do**
        $\langle \boldsymbol{y}^-, \boldsymbol{h}^- \rangle \leftarrow \operatorname{argmax}_{\langle \boldsymbol{y}, \boldsymbol{h} \rangle \in \mathcal{K}_i} \text{score}_i(\boldsymbol{y}, \boldsymbol{h}; \boldsymbol{\theta}) + \text{cost}_i(\boldsymbol{y})$;
        $\boldsymbol{\theta} \mathrel{-}= \eta C \left(\frac{\boldsymbol{\theta} - \boldsymbol{\theta}_0}{N}\right)$;
        $\boldsymbol{\theta} \mathrel{+}= \eta\big(\boldsymbol{f}(\boldsymbol{x}^{(i)}, \boldsymbol{y}_i^+, \boldsymbol{h}_i^+) - \boldsymbol{f}(\boldsymbol{x}^{(i)}, \boldsymbol{y}^-, \boldsymbol{h}^-)\big)$;
      end
    end
  end
end
return $\boldsymbol{\theta}$;

Algorithm 1: RAMPION.

We note that Eq. 10 is similar to Eq. 11 (Fig. 2), where each γ is used to trade off between model and cost. Fig. 1 illustrates the similarity by showing that the min-cost output on a k-best list resides in a similar region of the output space as $\langle \boldsymbol{y}^+, \boldsymbol{h}^+ \rangle$ computed from the full output space. While it is not the case that we can always choose γ_i so as to make the two losses equivalent, they are similar in that they update towards some $\boldsymbol{y}^\uparrow$ with high model score and low cost. Eq. 11 corresponds to Eq. 7 (Fig. 2), the second form of the latent structured ramp loss.

Thus, one way to understand Liang et al.'s algorithm is as a form of structured ramp loss. However, another interpretation is given by McAllester et al. (2010), who showed that procedures like that used by Liang et al. approach direct cost minimization in the limiting case.

3.3 Large-Margin Methods

A related family of approaches for training MT models involves the **margin-infused relaxed algorithm** (MIRA; Crammer et al., 2006), an online large-margin training algorithm. It has recently shown success for MT, particularly when training models with large feature sets (Watanabe et al., 2007; Chiang et al., 2008; Chiang et al., 2009). In order to apply it to MT, Watanabe et al. and Chiang et al. made modifications similar to those made by Liang et al. for perceptron training, namely the extension to latent variables and the use of a surrogate reference with high model score and low cost.

Hinge Loss It can be shown that 1-best MIRA corresponds to dual coordinate ascent for the **structured hinge loss** when using ℓ_2 regularization (Martins et al., 2010). The structured hinge is the loss underlying maximum-margin Markov networks (Taskar et al., 2003): setting $\boldsymbol{y}^\uparrow = \boldsymbol{y}^{(i)}$ and:

$$\boldsymbol{y}^\downarrow = \operatorname*{argmax}_{\boldsymbol{y} \in \mathcal{Y}(\boldsymbol{x}^{(i)})} \left(\text{score}(\boldsymbol{x}^{(i)}, \boldsymbol{y}; \boldsymbol{\theta}) + \text{cost}(\boldsymbol{y}^{(i)}, \boldsymbol{y})\right) \tag{13}$$

Unlike the perceptron losses, which penalize the highest-scoring outputs, hinge loss penalizes an output that is both favored by the model *and* has high cost. Such an output is shown as $\langle \boldsymbol{y}^-, \boldsymbol{h}^- \rangle$ in Fig. 1; the structured hinge loss focuses on pushing such outputs to the left. As mentioned in §3.1, finding $\boldsymbol{y}^\downarrow$ is often called **cost-augmented decoding**.

Structured hinge loss is convex, can incorporate a cost function, and can be optimized with several algorithms, including SSD (Ratliff et al., 2006).

Adaptation for MT While prior work has used MIRA-like algorithms for training machine translation systems, the proposed algorithms did not actually optimize the structured hinge loss, for similar reasons to those mentioned above for the perceptron: latent variables and surrogate references. Incorporating latent variables in the hinge loss results in the **latent structured hinge loss** (Yu and Joachims, 2009). Like the latent perceptron, this loss is nonconvex and inappropriate for MT because it requires computing the feature vector for $\boldsymbol{y}^{(i)}$. By using a surrogate instead of $\boldsymbol{y}^{(i)}$, the actual loss optimized becomes closer to Eq. 8 (Fig. 2), the third form of the latent structured ramp loss.

Watanabe et al. (2007) and Arun and Koehn (2007) used k-best oracles like Liang et al., but Chiang et al. (2008, 2009) used a different approach, explicitly defining the surrogate as $\langle \boldsymbol{y}^+, \boldsymbol{h}^+ \rangle$ in Fig. 1. While the method of Chiang et al. showed impressive performance improvements, its implementation is non-trivial, involving a complex cost function and a parallel architecture, and it has not yet been embraced by the MT community. Indeed, the complexity of Chiang et al's algorithm was one of the reasons cited for the development of PRO (Hopkins and May, 2011). In this paper, we have sought to isolate the loss functions used in prior work like that by Chiang et al. and identify simple, generic optimization procedures for optimizing them. We offer RAMPION as an alternative to Chiang et al's MIRA that is simpler to implement and achieves empirical success in experiments (§4).

3.4 Likelihood and Softened Losses

We can derive new loss functions from the above by converting any "max" operator to a "softmax" ($\log \sum \exp$, where the set of elements under the summation is the same as under the max). For example, the softmax version of the perceptron loss is the well-known **log loss** (§2, Ex. 2), the loss underlying the **conditional likelihood** training criterion which is frequently used when a probabilistic interpretation of the learned model is desired, as in conditional random fields (Lafferty et al., 2001).

Och and Ney (2002) popularized the use of log-linear models for MT and initially sought to optimize log loss, but by using the min-cost translation on a k-best list as their surrogate, we argue that their loss was closer to the **soft ramp loss** obtained by softening the second max in $\text{loss}_{\text{ramp }2}$ in Eq. 7 (Fig. 2). The same is true for others who aimed to optimize log loss for MT (Smith and Eisner, 2006; Zens et al., 2007; Cer, 2011).

The softmax version of the latent variable perceptron loss, Eq. 9 (Fig. 2), is the **latent log loss** inherent in latent-variable CRFs (Quattoni et al., 2004). Blunsom et al. (2008) and Blunsom and Osborne (2008) actually did optimize latent log loss for MT, discarding training examples for which $y^{(i)}$ was unreachable by the model.

Finally, we note that "softening" the ramp loss in Eq. 6 (Fig. 2) results in the **Jensen risk bound** from Gimpel and Smith (2010), which is a computationally-attractive upper bound on the Bayes risk.

4 Experiments

The goal of our experiments is to compare RAMPION (Alg. 1) to state-of-the-art methods for training MT systems. RAMPION minimizes $\text{loss}_{\text{ramp }3}$, which we found in preliminary experiments to work better than other loss functions tested.[8]

System and Datasets We use the Moses phrase-based MT system (Koehn et al., 2007) and consider Urdu→English (UR→EN), Chinese→English (ZH→EN) translation, and Arabic→English (AR→EN) translation.[9] We trained a Moses system using default settings and features, except for setting the distortion limit to 10. Word alignment was performed using GIZA++ (Och and Ney, 2003) in both directions, the `grow-diag-final-and` heuristic was used to symmetrize the alignments, and a max phrase length of 7 was used for phrase extraction. We estimated 5-gram language models using the SRI toolkit (Stolcke, 2002) with modified Kneser-Ney smoothing (Chen and Goodman, 1998). For each language pair, we used the English side of the parallel text and 600M words of randomly-selected sentences from the Gigaword v4 corpus (excluding NYT and LAT).

For UR→EN, we used parallel data from the NIST MT08 evaluation consisting of 1.2M Urdu words and 1.1M English words. We used half of the documents (882 sentences) from the MT08 test set for tuning. We used the remaining half for one test set ("MT08*") and MT09 as our other test set. For ZH→EN, we used 303k sentence pairs from the FBIS corpus (LDC2003E14). We segmented the Chinese data using the Stanford Chinese segmenter (Chang et al., 2008) in "CTB" mode, giving us 7.9M Chinese words and 9.4M English words. We used MT03 for tuning and used MT02 and MT05 for testing.

For AR→EN, we used data provided by the LDC

[8] We only present full results using $\text{loss}_{\text{ramp }3}$. We found that minimizing $\text{loss}_{\text{ramp }1}$ did poorly, resulting in single-digit BLEU scores, and that $\text{loss}_{\text{ramp }2}$ reached high BLEU scores on the tuning data but failed to generalize well. Softened versions of the ramp losses performed comparably to $\text{loss}_{\text{ramp }3}$ but were slightly worse on both tuning and held-out data.

[9] We found similar trends for other language pairs and systems, including Hiero (Chiang, 2005). A forthcoming report will present these results, as well as experiments with additional loss functions, in detail.

for the NIST evaluations, including 3.29M sentence pairs of UN data and 982k sentence pairs of non-UN data. The Arabic data was preprocessed using an HMM segmenter that splits off attached prepositional phrases, personal pronouns, and the future marker (Lee et al., 2003). The common stylistic sentence-initial *wa#* (*and ...*) was removed from the training and test data. The resulting corpus contained 130M Arabic tokens and 130M English tokens. We used MT06 for tuning and three test sets: MT05, the MT08 newswire test set ("MT08 NW"), and the MT08 weblog test set ("MT08 WB").

For all languages we evaluated translation output using case-insensitive IBM BLEU (Papineni et al., 2001).

Training Algorithms Our baselines are MERT and PRO as implemented in the Moses toolkit.[10] PRO uses the hyperparameter settings from Hopkins and May (2011), including k-best lists of size 1500 and 25 training iterations.[11] MERT uses k-best lists of size 100 and was run to convergence. For both MERT and PRO, previous iterations' k-best lists were merged in.

For RAMPION, we used $T = 20$, $T' = 10$, $T'' = 5$, $k = 500$, $\eta = 0.0001$, and $C = 1$. Our cost function is $\alpha(1 - \text{BLEU}_{+1}(\boldsymbol{y}, \boldsymbol{y}'))$ where $\text{BLEU}_{+1}(\boldsymbol{y}, \boldsymbol{y}')$ returns the BLEU_{+1} score (Lin and Och, 2004) for reference $\boldsymbol{y}$ and hypothesis $\boldsymbol{y}'$. We used $\alpha = 10$. We used these same hyperparameter values for all experiments reported here and found them to perform well across other language pairs and systems.[12]

4.1 Results

Table 1 shows our results. MERT and PRO were run 3 times with differing random seeds and averages and standard deviations are shown. The three algorithms perform very similarly on the whole, with certain algorithms performing better on certain languages. MERT shows larger variation across random seeds, as reported by many others in the community. On average across all language pairs and test sets, RAMPION leads to slightly higher BLEU scores.

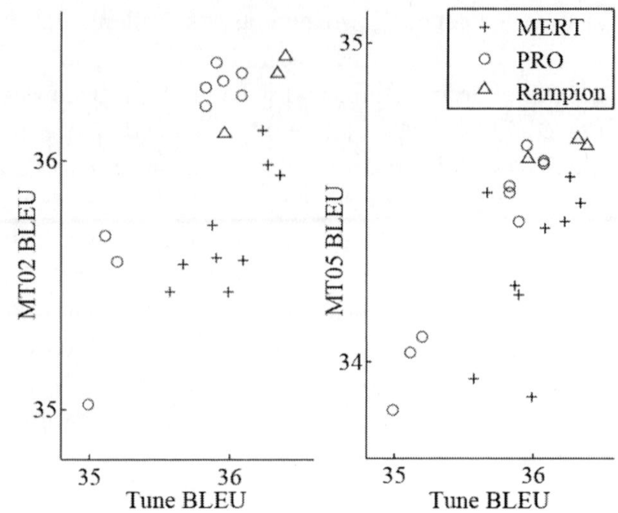

Figure 3: ZH→EN training runs. The cluster of PRO points to the left corresponds to one of the random initial models; MERT and RAMPION were able to recover while PRO was not.

4.2 Sensitivity Analysis

We now measure the sensitivity of these training methods to different initializers and to randomness in the algorithms. RAMPION is deterministic, but MERT uses random starting points and search directions and PRO uses random sampling to choose pairs for training its binary classifier.

For initial models, we used the default parameters in Moses as well as two randomly-generated models.[13] We ran RAMPION once with each of the three initial models, and MERT and PRO three times with each. This allows us to compare variance due to initializers as well as due to the nondeterminism in each algorithm. Fig. 3 plots the results. While PRO exhibits a small variance for a given initializer, as also reported by Hopkins and May (2011), it had

[10] The PRO algorithm samples pairs of translations from k-best lists on each iteration and trains a binary classifier to rank pairs according to the cost function. The loss function underlying PRO depends on the choice of binary classifier and also on the sampling strategy. We leave an analysis of PRO's loss function to future work.

[11] Hopkins and May used 30 iterations, but showed that training had converged by 25.

[12] We found performance to be better when using a smaller value of T'; we suspect that using small T' guards against overfitting to any particular set of k-best lists. We also found the value of α to affect performance, although $\alpha \in \{1, 5, 10\}$ all worked well. Performance was generally insensitive to C. We fixed $\eta = 0.0001$ early on and did little tuning to it.

[13] The default weights are 0.3 for reordering features, 0.2 for phrase table features, 0.5 for the language model, and -1 for the word penalty. We generated each random model by sampling each feature weight from a $\mathcal{N}(\mu, \sigma^2)$ with μ equal to the default weight for that feature and $\sigma = |\mu/2|$.

Method	UR→EN		ZH→EN		AR→EN			avg
	MT08*	MT09	MT02	MT05	MT05	MT08 NW	MT08 WB	
MERT	**24.5** (0.1)	**24.6** (0.0)	35.7 (0.3)	34.2 (0.2)	55.0 (0.7)	**49.8** (0.3)	**32.6** (0.2)	36.6
PRO	24.2 (0.1)	24.2 (0.1)	36.3 (0.1)	34.5 (0.0)	**55.6** (0.1)	49.6 (0.0)	31.7 (0.0)	36.6
RAMPION	**24.5**	**24.6**	**36.4**	**34.7**	55.5	**49.8**	32.1	**36.8**

Table 1: %BLEU on several test sets for UR→EN, ZH→EN, and AR→EN translation. Algorithms with randomization (MERT and PRO) were run three times with different random seeds and averages are shown in each cell followed by standard deviations in parentheses. All results in this table used a single initial model (the default Moses weights). The final column shows the average %BLEU across all individual test set scores, so 21 scores were used for MERT and PRO and 7 for RAMPION.

Method	UR→EN			ZH→EN		
	Tune	MT08*	MT09	Tune	MT02	MT05
PRO	**29.4**	22.3	23.0	**40.9**	35.7	33.6
RAMPION	27.8	**24.2**	**24.6**	38.8	**36.2**	**34.3**

Table 2: %BLEU with large feature sets.

trouble recovering from one of the random initializers. Therefore, while the within-initializer variance for PRO tended to be smaller than that of MERT, PRO's overall range was larger. RAMPION found very similar weights regardless of $\boldsymbol{\theta}_0$.

4.3 Adding Features

Finally, we compare RAMPION and PRO with an extended feature set; MERT is excluded as it fails in such settings (Hopkins and May, 2011).

We added count features for common monolingual and bilingual lexical patterns from the parallel corpus: the 1k most common bilingual word pairs from phrase extraction, 200 top unigrams, 1k top bigrams, 1k top trigrams, and 4k top trigger pairs extracted with the method of Rosenfeld (1996), ranked by mutual information. We integrated the features with our training procedure by using Moses to generate lattices instead of k-best lists. We used cube pruning (Chiang, 2007) to incorporate the additional (potentially non-local) features while extracting k-best lists from the lattices to pass to the training algorithms.[14]

Results are shown in Table 2. We find that PRO finds much higher BLEU scores on the tuning data but fails to generalize, leading to poor performance on the held-out test sets. We suspect that incorporating regularization into training the binary classifier within PRO may mitigate this overfitting. RAMPION is more stable by contrast. This is a challenging learning task, as lexical features are prone to overfitting with a small tuning set. Hopkins and May (2011) similarly found little gain on test data when using extended feature sets in phrase-based translation for these two language pairs.

Results for AR→EN translation were similar and are omitted for space; these and additional experiments will be included in a forthcoming report.

5 Conclusion

We have framed MT training as empirical risk minimization and clarified loss functions that were optimized by well-known procedures. We have proposed directly optimizing the structured ramp loss implicit in prior work with a novel algorithm—RAMPION—which performs comparably to state-of-the-art training algorithms and is empirically more stable. Our source code, which integrates easily with Moses, is available at `www.ark.cs.cmu.edu/MT`.

Acknowledgments

We thank Colin Cherry, Chris Dyer, Joseph Keshet, David McAllester, and members of the ARK research group for helpful comments that improved this paper. This research was supported in part by the NSF through CAREER grant IIS-1054319, the U. S. Army Research Laboratory and the U. S. Army Research Office under contract/grant number W911NF-10-1-0533, and Sandia National Laboratories (fellowship to K. Gimpel).

References

A. Arun and P. Koehn. 2007. Online learning methods for discriminative training of phrase based statistical machine translation. In *Proc. of MT Summit XI*.

P. Blunsom and M. Osborne. 2008. Probabilistic inference for machine translation. In *Proc. of EMNLP*.

P. Blunsom, T. Cohn, and M. Osborne. 2008. A discriminative latent variable model for statistical machine translation. In *Proc. of ACL*.

[14] In cube pruning, each node's local n-best list had $n = 100$.

D. Cer, D. Jurafsky, and C. Manning. 2008. Regularization and search for minimum error rate training. In *Proc. of ACL-2008 Workshop on Statistical Machine Translation*.

D. Cer. 2011. *Parameterizing Phrase Based Statistical Machine Translation Models: An Analytic Study*. Ph.D. thesis, Stanford University.

P. Chang, M. Galley, and C. Manning. 2008. Optimizing Chinese word segmentation for machine translation performance. In *Proc. of ACL-2008 Workshop on Statistical Machine Translation*.

S. Chen and J. Goodman. 1998. An empirical study of smoothing techniques for language modeling. Technical report 10-98, Harvard University.

C. Cherry and G. Foster. 2012. Batch tuning strategies for statistical machine translation. In *Proc. of NAACL*.

D. Chiang, Y. Marton, and P. Resnik. 2008. Online large-margin training of syntactic and structural translation features. In *Proc. of EMNLP*.

D. Chiang, W. Wang, and K. Knight. 2009. 11,001 new features for statistical machine translation. In *Proc. of NAACL-HLT*.

D. Chiang. 2005. A hierarchical phrase-based model for statistical machine translation. In *Proc. of ACL*.

D. Chiang. 2007. Hierarchical phrase-based translation. *Computational Linguistics*, 33(2):201–228.

J. H. Clark, C. Dyer, A. Lavie, and N. A. Smith. 2011. Better hypothesis testing for statistical machine translation: Controlling for optimizer instability. In *Proc. of ACL*.

M. Collins. 2002. Discriminative training methods for hidden Markov models: Theory and experiments with perceptron algorithms. In *Proc. of EMNLP*.

R. Collobert, F. Sinz, J. Weston, and L. Bottou. 2006. Trading convexity for scalability. In *ICML*.

K. Crammer, O. Dekel, J. Keshet, S. Shalev-Shwartz, and Y. Singer. 2006. Online passive-aggressive algorithms. *Journal of Machine Learning Research*, 7:551–585.

C. B. Do, Q. Le, C. H. Teo, O. Chapelle, and A. Smola. 2008. Tighter bounds for structured estimation. In *Proc. of NIPS*.

R. O. Duda and P. E. Hart. 1973. *Pattern classification and scene analysis*. John Wiley, New York.

G. Foster and R. Kuhn. 2009. Stabilizing minimum error rate training. In *Proc. of Fourth Workshop on Statistical Machine Translation*.

K. Gimpel and N. A. Smith. 2010. Softmax-margin CRFs: Training log-linear models with cost functions. In *Proc. of NAACL*.

M. Hopkins and J. May. 2011. Tuning as ranking. In *Proc. of EMNLP*.

B. H. Juang, W. Chou, and C. H. Lee. 1997. Minimum classification error rate methods for speech recognition. *Speech and Audio Processing, IEEE Transactions on*, 5(3):257–265, may.

J. Kaiser, B. Horvat, and Z. Kacic. 2000. A novel loss function for the overall risk criterion based discriminative training of hmm models. In *Proc. of ICSLP*.

P. Koehn, F. J. Och, and D. Marcu. 2003. Statistical phrase-based translation. In *Proc. of HLT-NAACL*.

P. Koehn, H. Hoang, A. Birch, C. Callison-Burch, M. Federico, N. Bertoldi, B. Cowan, W. Shen, C. Moran, R. Zens, C. Dyer, O. Bojar, A. Constantin, and E. Herbst. 2007. Moses: Open source toolkit for statistical machine translation. In *Proc. of ACL (demo session)*.

J. Lafferty, A. McCallum, and F. Pereira. 2001. Conditional random fields: Probabilistic models for segmenting and labeling sequence data. In *Proc. of ICML*.

Y. Lee, K. Papineni, S. Roukos, O. Emam, and H. Hassan. 2003. Language model based Arabic word segmentation. In *Proc. of ACL*.

Z. Li and J. Eisner. 2009. First- and second-order expectation semirings with applications to minimum-risk training on translation forests. In *Proc. of EMNLP*.

P. Liang, A. Bouchard-Côté, D. Klein, and B. Taskar. 2006. An end-to-end discriminative approach to machine translation. In *Proc. of COLING-ACL*.

Chin-Yew Lin and Franz Josef Och. 2004. Orange: a method for evaluating automatic evaluation metrics for machine translation. In *Proc. of Coling*.

W. Macherey, F. Och, I. Thayer, and J. Uszkoreit. 2008. Lattice-based minimum error rate training for statistical machine translation. In *EMNLP*.

A. F. T. Martins, K. Gimpel, N. A. Smith, E. P. Xing, P. M. Q. Aguiar, and M A. T. Figueiredo. 2010. Learning structured classifiers with dual coordinate descent. Technical report, Carnegie Mellon University.

D. McAllester and J. Keshet. 2011. Generalization bounds and consistency for latent structural probit and ramp loss. In *Proc. of NIPS*.

D. McAllester, T. Hazan, and J. Keshet. 2010. Direct loss minimization for structured prediction. In *Proc. of NIPS*.

R. C. Moore and C. Quirk. 2008. Random restarts in minimum error rate training for statistical machine translation. In *Proc. of Coling*.

F. J. Och and H. Ney. 2002. Discriminative training and maximum entropy models for statistical machine translation. In *Proc. of ACL*.

F. J. Och and H. Ney. 2003. A systematic comparison of various statistical alignment models. *Computational Linguistics*, 29(1).

F. J. Och. 2003. Minimum error rate training for statistical machine translation. In *Proc. of ACL*.

K. Papineni, S. Roukos, T. Ward, and W.J. Zhu. 2001. BLEU: a method for automatic evaluation of machine translation. In *Proc. of ACL*.

D. Povey and P. C. Woodland. 2002. Minimum phone error and I-smoothing for improved discrimative training. In *Proc. of ICASSP*.

A. Quattoni, M. Collins, and T. Darrell. 2004. Conditional random fields for object recognition. In *NIPS 17*.

N. Ratliff, J. A. Bagnell, and M. Zinkevich. 2006. Subgradient methods for maximum margin structured learning. In *ICML Workshop on Learning in Structured Output Spaces*.

R. Rosenfeld. 1996. A maximum entropy approach to adaptive statistical language modeling. *Computer, Speech and Language*, 10(3).

D. A. Smith and J. Eisner. 2006. Minimum risk annealing for training log-linear models. In *Proc. of COLING-ACL*.

A. Stolcke. 2002. SRILM—an extensible language modeling toolkit. In *Proc. of ICSLP*.

B. Taskar, C. Guestrin, and D. Koller. 2003. Max-margin Markov networks. In *Advances in NIPS 16*.

V. Vapnik. 1998. *Statistical learning theory*. Wiley.

T. Watanabe, J. Suzuki, H. Tsukada, and H. Isozaki. 2007. Online large-margin training for statistical machine translation. In *Proc. of EMNLP-CoNLL*.

C. J. Yu and T. Joachims. 2009. Learning structural SVMs with latent variables. In *Proc. of ICML*.

A. L. Yuille and Anand Rangarajan. 2002. The concave-convex procedure (CCCP). In *Proc. of NIPS*. MIT Press.

R. Zens, S. Hasan, and H. Ney. 2007. A systematic comparison of training criteria for statistical machine translation. In *Proc. of EMNLP*.

Implicitly Intersecting Weighted Automata using Dual Decomposition*

Michael J. Paul and **Jason Eisner**
Department of Computer Science / Johns Hopkins University
Baltimore, MD 21218, USA
{mpaul, jason}@cs.jhu.edu

Abstract

We propose an algorithm to find the best path through an intersection of arbitrarily many weighted automata, without actually performing the intersection. The algorithm is based on dual decomposition: the automata attempt to agree on a string by communicating about features of the string. We demonstrate the algorithm on the Steiner consensus string problem, both on synthetic data and on consensus decoding for speech recognition. This involves implicitly intersecting up to 100 automata.

1 Introduction

Many tasks in natural language processing involve functions that assign scores—such as log-probabilities—to candidate strings or sequences. Often such a function can be represented compactly as a weighted finite state automaton (WFSA). Finding the best-scoring string according to a WFSA is straightforward using standard best-path algorithms.

It is common to construct a scoring WFSA by combining two or more simpler WFSAs, taking advantage of the closure properties of WFSAs. For example, consider noisy channel approaches to speech recognition (Pereira and Riley, 1997) or machine translation (Knight and Al-Onaizan, 1998). Given an input f, the score of a possible English transcription or translation e is the sum of its language model score $\log p(e)$ and its channel model score $\log p(f \mid e)$. If each of these functions of e is represented as a WFSA, then their sum is represented as the intersection of those two WFSAs.

WFSA intersection corresponds to constraint conjunction, and hence is often a mathematically natural way to specify a solution to a problem involving multiple soft constraints on a desired string. Unfortunately, the intersection may be computationally inefficient in practice. The intersection of K WFSAs having $n_1, n_2, \ldots, n_K$ states may have $n_1 \cdot n_2 \cdots n_K$ states in the worst case.[1]

In this paper, we propose a more efficient method for finding the best path in an intersection without actually computing the full intersection. Our approach is based on *dual decomposition*, a combinatorial optimization technique that was recently introduced to the vision (Komodakis et al., 2007) and language processing communities (Rush et al., 2010; Koo et al., 2010). Our idea is to interrogate the several WFSAs separately, repeatedly visiting each WFSA to seek a high-scoring path in each WFSA that agrees with the current paths found in the other WSFAs. This iterative negotiation is reminiscent of message-passing algorithms (Sontag et al., 2008), while the queries to the WFSAs are reminiscent of loss-augmented inference (Taskar et al., 2005).

We remark that a general solution whose asymptotic worst-case runtime beat that of naive intersection would have important implications for complexity theory (Karakostas et al., 2003). Our approach is not such a solution. We have no worst-case bounds on how long dual decomposition will take to converge in our setting, and indeed it can fail to converge altogether.[2] However, when it does converge, we have a "certificate" that the solution is optimal.

Dual decomposition is usually regarded as a method for finding an optimal *vector* in $\mathbb{R}^d$, subject to several constraints. However, it is not obvious how best to represent strings as vectors—they

*The authors are grateful to Damianos Karakos for providing tools and data for the ASR experiments. This work was supported in part by an NSF Graduate Research Fellowship.

[1] Most regular expression operators combine WFSA sizes additively. It is primarily intersection and its close relative, composition, that do so multiplicatively, leading to inefficiency when two large WFSAs are combined, and to exponential blowup when many WFSAs are combined. Yet these operations are crucially important in practice.

[2] An example that oscillates can be constructed along lines similar to the one given by Rush et al. (2010).

have unbounded length, and furthermore the absolute position of a symbol is not usually significant in evaluating its contribution to the score.[3] One contribution of this work is that we propose a general, flexible scheme for converting strings to feature vectors on which the WFSAs must agree. In principle the number of features may be infinite, but the set of "active" features is expanded only as needed until the algorithm converges. Our experiments use a particular instantiation of our general scheme, based on n-gram features.

We apply our method to a particular task: finding the *Steiner consensus string* (Gusfield, 1997) that has low total edit distance to a number of given, unaligned strings. As an illustration, we are pleased to report that "`alia`" and "`aian`" are the consensus popular names for girls and boys born in the U.S. in 2010. We use this technique for consensus decoding from speech recognition lattices, and to reconstruct the common source of up to 100 strings corrupted by random noise. Explicit intersection would be *astronomically expensive* in these cases. We demonstrate that our approach tends to converge rather quickly, and that it finds good solutions quickly in any case.

2 Preliminaries

2.1 Weighted Finite State Automata

A weighted finite state automaton (WFSA) over the finite alphabet Σ is an FSA that has a cost or weight associated with each arc. We consider the case of real-valued weights in the tropical semiring. This is a fancy way of saying that the weight of a path is the sum of its arc weights, and that the weight of a string is the minimum weight of all its accepting paths (or ∞ if there are none).

When we intersect two WFSAs F and G, the effect is to add string weights: $(F \cap G)(x) = F(x) + G(x)$. Our problem is to find the x that *minimizes* this sum, but without constructing $F \cap G$ to run a shortest-path algorithm on it.

2.2 Dual Decomposition

The trick in dual decomposition is to decompose an intractable *global* problem into two or more tractable *subproblems* that can be solved independently. If we can somehow combine the solutions from the subproblems into a "valid" solution to the global problem, then we can avoid optimizing the joint problem directly. A valid solution is one in which the individual solutions of each subproblem all agree on the variables which are shared in the joint problem. For example, if we are combining a parser with a part-of-speech tagger, the tag assignments from both models must agree in the final solution (Rush et al., 2010); if we are intersecting a translation model with a language model, then it is the words that must agree (Rush and Collins, 2011).

More formally, suppose we want to find a global solution that is jointly optimized among K subproblems: $\text{argmin}_x \sum_{k=1}^{K} f_k(x)$. Suppose that x ranges over vectors. Introducing an auxiliary variable x_k for each subproblem f_k allows us to equivalently formulate this as the following constrained optimization problem:

$$\underset{\{x, x_1, \ldots, x_K\}}{\text{argmin}} \sum_{k=1}^{K} f_k(x_k) \quad \text{s.t.} \ (\forall k)\, x_k = x \tag{1}$$

For *any* set of vectors λ_k that sum to 0, $\sum_{k=1}^{K} \lambda_k = 0$, Komodakis et al. (2007) show that the following Lagrangian dual is a lower bound on (1):[4]

$$\min_{\{x_1, \ldots, x_K\}} \sum_{k=1}^{K} f_k(x_k) + \lambda_k \cdot x_k \tag{2}$$

where the Lagrange multiplier vectors λ_k can be used to penalize solutions that do not satisfy the agreement constraints $(\forall k)\, x_k = x$. Our goal is to maximize this lower bound and hope that the result does satisfy the constraints. The graphs in Fig. 2 illustrate how we increase the lower bound over time, using a subgradient algorithm to adjust the λ's. At each subgradient step, (2) can be computed by choosing each $x_k = \text{argmin}_{x_k} f_k(x_k) + \lambda_k \cdot x_k$ separately. In effect, each subproblem makes an independent prediction x_k influenced by λ_k, and if these outputs do not yet satisfy the agreement constraints, then the λ_k are adjusted to encourage the subproblems to agree on the next iteration. See Sontag et al. (2011) for a detailed tutorial on dual decomposition.

[3] Such difficulties are typical when trying to apply structured prediction or optimization techniques to predict linguistic objects such as strings or trees, rather than vectors.

[4] The objective in (2) can always be made as small as in (1) by choosing the vectors $(x_1, \ldots x_K)$ that minimize (1) (because then $\sum_k \lambda_k \cdot x_k = \sum_k \lambda_k \cdot x = 0 \cdot x = 0$). Hence (2) $\leq$ (1).

3 WFSAs and Dual Decomposition

Given K WFSAs, $F_1, \ldots, F_K$, we are interested in finding the string x which has the best score in the intersection $F_1 \cap \ldots \cap F_K$. The lowest-cost string in the intersection of all K machines is defined as:

$$\operatorname*{argmin}_x \sum_k F_k(x) \tag{3}$$

As explained above, the trick in dual decomposition is to recast (3) as independent problems of the form $\operatorname{argmin}_{x_k} F_k(x_k)$, subject to constraints that all x_k are the same. However, it is not so clear how to define agreement constraints on strings. Perhaps a natural formulation is that F_k should be urged to favor strings x_k that would be read by $F_{k'}$ along a similar path to that of $x_{k'}$. But F_k cannot keep track of the state of $F_{k'}$ for all k' without solving the full intersection—precisely what we are trying to avoid.

Instead of requiring the strings x_k to be equal as in (1), we will require their *features* to be equal:

$$(\forall k)\, \gamma(x_k) = \gamma(x) \tag{4}$$

Of course, we must define the features. We will use an infinite feature vector $\gamma(x)$ that completely characterizes x, so that agreement of the feature vectors implies agreement of the strings. At each subgradient step, however, we will only allow finitely many elements of λ_k to become nonzero, so only a finite portion of $\gamma(x_k)$ needs to be computed.[5]

We will define these "active" features of a string x by constructing some unweighted deterministic FSA, G (described in §4). The active features of x are determined by the collection of arcs on the accepting path of x in G. Thus, to satisfy the agreement constraint, x_i and x_j must be accepted using the same arcs of G (or more generally, arcs that have the same features).

We relax the constraints by introducing a collection $\lambda = \lambda_1, \ldots, \lambda_K$ of Lagrange multipliers, and defining $G_{\lambda_k}(x)$ such that the features of G are weighted by the vector λ_k (*all* of whose nonzero elements must correspond to features in G). As in (2), we assume $\lambda \in \Lambda$, where $\Lambda = \{\lambda : \sum_k \lambda_k = 0\}$. This gives the objective:

$$h(\lambda) = \min_{\{x_1,\ldots,x_K\}} \sum_k \left(F_k(x_k) + G_{\lambda_k}(x_k)\right) \tag{5}$$

This minimization fully decomposes into K subproblems that can be solved independently. The kth subproblem is to find $\operatorname{argmin}_{x_k} F_k(x_k) + G_{\lambda_k}(x_k)$, which is straightforward to solve with finite-state methods. It is the string on the lowest-cost path through $H_k = F_k \cap G_{\lambda_k}$, as found with standard path algorithms (Mohri, 2002).

The dual problem we wish to solve is $\max_{\lambda \in \Lambda} h(\lambda)$, where $h(\lambda)$ itself is a min over $\{x_1, \ldots, x_K\}$. We optimize λ via projected subgradient ascent (Komodakis et al., 2007). The update equation for λ_k at iteration t is then:

$$\lambda_k^{(t+1)} = \lambda_k^{(t)} + \eta_t \left(\gamma(x_k^{(t)}) - \frac{\sum_{k'} \gamma(x_{k'}^{(t)})}{K}\right) \tag{6}$$

where $\eta_t > 0$ is the step size at iteration t. This update is intuitive. It moves away from the current solution and toward the average solution (where they differ), by increasing the cost of the former's features and reducing the cost of the latter's features.

This update may be very dense, however, since $\gamma(x)$ is an infinite vector. So we usually only update the elements of λ_k that correspond to the small finite set of *active* features (the other elements are still "frozen" at 0), denoted Θ. This is still a valid subgradient step. This strategy is incorrect only if the updates for all active features are 0—in other words, only if we have achieved equality of the currently active features and yet still the $\{x_k\}$ do not agree. In that case, we must choose some inactive features that are still unequal and allow the subgradient step to update their λ coefficients to nonzero, making them active. At the next step of optimization, we must expand G to consider this enlarged set of active features.

4 The Agreement Machine

The agreement machine (or constraint machine) G can be thought of as a way of encoding features of

[5] The simplest scheme would define a binary feature for each string in Σ^*. Then the nonzero elements of λ_k would specify punishments and rewards for outputting various strings that had been encountered at earlier iterations: "Try subproblem k again, and try harder not to output `michael` this time, as it still didn't agree with other subproblems: try `jason` instead." This scheme would converge glacially if at all. We instead focus on featurizations that let subproblems negotiate about *substrings*: "Try again, avoiding `mi` if possible and favoring `ja` instead."

strings on which we enforce agreement. There are a number of different topologies for G that might be considered, with varying degrees of efficiency and utility. Constructing G essentially amounts to feature engineering; as such, it is unlikely that there is a universally optimal topology of G. Nevertheless, there are clearly *bad* ways to build G, as not all topologies are guaranteed to lead to an optimal solution. In this section, we lay out some abstract guidelines for appropriate G construction, before we describe specific topologies in the later subsections.

Most importantly, we should design G so that it accepts all strings in $F_1 \cap \ldots \cap F_K$. This is to ensure that it accepts the string that is the optimal solution to the joint problem. If G did not accept that string, then neither would $H_k = F_k \cap G$, and our algorithm would not be able to find it.

Even if H_k can accept the optimal string, it is possible that this string would never be the best path in this machine, regardless of λ. For example, suppose G is a single-state machine with self-loops accepting each symbol in the alphabet (i.e. a unigram machine). Suppose H_k outputs the string aaa in the current iteration, but we would like the machines to converge to aaaaa. We would lower the weight of $\lambda_{\mathtt{a}}$ to encourage H_k to output more of the symbol a. However, if H_k has a cyclic topology, then it could happen that a negative value of $\lambda_{\mathtt{a}}$ could create a negative-weight cycle, in which the lowest-cost path through H_k is infinitely long. It might be that adjusting $\lambda_{\mathtt{a}}$ can change the best string to either aaa or aaaaaaaaa... (depending on whether a cycle after the initial aaa has positive or negative weight), but never the optimal aaaaa. On the other hand, if G instead encoded 5-grams, this would not be a problem because a path through a 5-gram machine could accept aaaaa without traversing a cycle.

Finally, agreeing on (active) features does not necessarily mean that all x_k are the same string. For example, if we again use a unigram G (that is, $\Theta = \Sigma$, the set of unigrams), then $\gamma_\Theta(\mathtt{abc}) = \gamma_\Theta(\mathtt{cba})$, where γ_Θ returns a feature vector where all but the active features are zeroed out. In this instance, we satisfy the constraints imposed by G, even though we have not satisfied the constraint we truly care about: that the strings agree.

To summarize, we will aim to choose Θ such that G has the following characteristics:

1. The language $\mathcal{L}(F_k \cap G) = \mathcal{L}(F_k)$; i.e. G does not restrict the set of strings accepted by F_k.

2. When $\gamma_\Theta(x_i) = \gamma_\Theta(x_j)$, typically $x_i = x_j$.

3. $\exists \lambda \in \Lambda$ s.t. $\operatorname{argmin}_x F_k(x) + G_{\lambda_k}(x) = \operatorname{argmin}_x \sum_{k'} F_{k'}(x)$, i.e., the optimal string can be the best path in $F_k \cap G$.[6] This may not be the case if G is cyclic.

The first of these is required during every iteration of the algorithm in order to maintain optimality guarantees. However, even if we do not satisfy the latter two points, we may get lucky and the strings themselves will agree upon convergence, and no further work is required. Furthermore, the unigram machine G used in the above examples, despite breaking these requirements, has the advantage of being very efficient to intersect with F. This motivates our "active feature" strategy of using a simple G initially, and incrementally altering it as needed, for example if we satisfy the constraints but the strings do not yet match. We discuss this in §4.2.

4.1 N-Gram Construction of G

In principle, it is valid to use any G that satisfies the guidelines above, but in practice, some topologies will lead to faster convergence than others.

Perhaps the most obvious form is a simple vector encoding of strings, e.g. "a at position 1", "b at position 2", and so on. As a WFSA, this would simply have one state represent each position, with arcs for each symbol going from position i to $i + 1$. This is essentially a unigram machine where the loops have been "unrolled" to also keep track of position.

However, early experiments showed that with this topology for G, our algorithm converged very slowly, if at all. What goes wrong? The problem stems from the fact that the strings are unaligned and of varying length, and it is difficult to get the strings to agree quickly at specific positions. For example, if two subproblems have b at positions 6 and 8 in the current iteration, they might agree at position 7—but our features don't encourage this. The Lagrangian update would discourage accepting b at 6 and encourage b at 8 (and vice versa), without giving credit

[6] It is not always possible to construct a G to satisfy this property, as the Lagrangian dual may not be a tight bound to the original problem.

for meeting in the middle. Further, these features do not encourage the subproblems to preserve the relative order of neighboring symbols, and strings which are almost the same but slightly misaligned will be penalized essentially everywhere. This is an ineffective way for the subproblems to communicate.

In this paper, we focus on the feature set we found to work the best in our experiments: the strings should agree on their n-gram features, such as "number of occurrences of the bigram ab." Even if we don't yet know precisely where ab should appear in the string, we can still move toward convergence if we try to force the subproblems to agree on whether and how often ab appears at all.

To encode n-gram features in a WFSA, each state represents the $(n-1)$-gram history, and all arcs leaving the state represent the final symbol in the n-gram, weighted by the score of that n-gram. The machine will also contain start and end states, with appropriate transitions to/from the n-gram states. For example, if the trigram abc has weight λ_{abc}, then the trigram machine will encode this as an arc with the symbol c leaving the state representing ab, and this arc will have weight λ_{abc}. If our feature set also contains 1- and 2-grams, then the arc in this example would incorporate the weights of all of the corresponding features: $\lambda_{\text{abc}} + \lambda_{\text{bc}} + \lambda_{\text{c}}$.

A drawback is that these features give no information about *where* in the string the n-grams should occur. In a long string, we might want to encourage or discourage an n-gram in a certain "region" of the string. Our features can only encourage or discourage it *everywhere* in the string, which may lead to slow convergence. Nevertheless, in our particular experimental settings, we find that this works better than other topologies we have considered.

Sparse N-Gram Encoding A full n-gram language model requires $\approx |\Sigma|^n$ arcs to encode as a WFSA. This could be quite expensive. Fortunately, large n-gram models can be compacted by using failure arcs (ϕ-arcs) to encode *backoff* (Allauzen et al., 2003). These arcs act as ϵ-transitions that can be taken only when no other transition is available. They allow us to encode the sparse subset of n-grams that have nonzero Lagrangians. We encode G such that all features whose λ value is 0 will back off to the next largest n-gram having nonzero weight. This form of G still accepts Σ^* and has the same weights as a dense representation, but could require substantially fewer states.

4.2 Incrementally Expanding G

As mentioned above, we may need to alter G as we go along. Intuitively, we may want to start with features that are cheap to encode, to move the parameters λ to a good part of the solution space, then incrementally bring in more expensive features as needed. Shorter n-grams require a smaller G and will require a shorter runtime per iteration, but if they are too short to be informative, then they may require many more iterations to reach convergence. In an extreme case, we may reach a point where the subproblems all agree on n-grams currently in Θ, but the actual strings still do not match. Waiting until we hit such a point may be unnecessarily slow. We experimented with periodically increasing n (e.g. adding trigrams to the feature set if we haven't converged with bigrams after a fixed number of iterations), but this is expensive, and it is not clear how to define a schedule for increasing the order of n. We instead present a simple and effective heuristic for bringing in more features.

The idea is that if the subproblem solutions currently disagree on counts of the bigrams ab and bc, then an abc feature may be unnecessary, since the subproblems could still make progress with only these bigram constraints. However, once the subproblems agree on these two bigrams, but disagree on trigram abc, we bring this into the feature set Θ. More generally, we add an $(n+1)$-gram to the feature set if the current strings disagree on its counts despite agreeing on its n-gram prefix and n-gram suffix (which need not necessarily be Θ). This *selectively* brings in larger n-grams to target portions of the strings that may require longer context, while keeping the agreement machine small.

Algorithm 1 gives pseudocode for our complete algorithm when using n-gram features with this incremental strategy. To summarize, we solve for each x_k using the current λ_k, and if all the strings agree, we return them as the optimal solution. Otherwise, we update λ_k and repeat. At each iteration, we check for n-gram agreement, and bring in select $(n+1)$-grams to the feature set as appropriate.

Finally, there is another instance where we might

Algorithm 1 The dual decomposition algorithm with n-gram features.

```
Initialize Θ to some initial set of n-gram features.
for t = 1 to T do
  for k = 1 to K do
    Solve x_k = argmin_x (F_k ∩ G_{λ_k})(x) with a
    shortest-path algorithm
  end for
  if (∀i, j) x_i = x_j then
    return {x_1, ..., x_K}
  else
    Θ = Θ ∪ {z ∈ Σ* : all x_k agree on the features
    corresponding to the length-(|z| − 1) prefix and
    suffix of z, but not on z itself}
    for k = 1 to K do
      Update λ_k according to equation (6)
      Create G_{λ_k} to encode the features Θ
    end for
  end if
end for
```

need to expand G, which we omit from the pseudocode for conciseness. If both F_k and G are cyclic, then there is a chance that there will be a negative-weight cycle in $F_k \cap G_{\lambda_k}$. (If at least one of these machines is acyclic, then this is not a problem, because their intersection yields a finite set.) In the case of a negative-weight cycle, the best path is infinitely long, and so the algorithm will either return an error or fail to terminate. If this happens, then we need to backtrack, and either decrease the subgradient step size to avoid moving into this territory, or alter G to expand the cycles. This can be done by unrolling loops to keep track of more information—when encoding n-gram features with G, this amounts to expanding G to encode higher order n-grams. When using a sparse G with ϕ-arcs, it may also be necessary to increase the minimum n-gram history that is used for back-off. For example, instead of allowing bigrams to back off to unigrams, we might force G to encode the full set of bigrams (not just bigrams with nonzero λ) in order to avoid cycles in the lower order states. Our strategy for avoiding negative-weight cycles is detailed in §5.1.

5 Experiments with Consensus Decoding

To best highlight the utility of our approach, we consider applications that must (implicitly) intersect a large number of WFSAs. We will demonstrate that, in many cases, our algorithm converges to an exact solution on problems involving 10, 25, and even 100 machines, all of which would be hopeless to solve by taking the full intersection.

We focus on the problem of solving for the Steiner consensus string: given a set of K strings, find the string in Σ^* that has minimal total edit distance to all strings in the set. This is an NP-hard problem that can be solved as an intersection of K machines, as we will describe in §5.2. The consensus string also gives an implicit multiple sequence alignment, as we discuss in §6.

We begin with the application of minimum Bayes risk decoding of speech lattices, which we show can reduce to the consensus string problem. We then explore the consensus problem in depth by applying it to a variety of different inputs.

5.1 Experimental Details

We initialize Θ to include both unigrams and bigrams, as we find that unigrams alone are not productive features in these experiments. As we expand Θ, we allow it to include n-grams up to length five.

We run our algorithm for a maximum of 1000 iterations, using a subgradient step size of $\alpha/(t+500)$ at iteration t, which satisfies the general properties to guarantee asymptotic convergence (Spall, 2003). We initialize α to 1 and 10 in the two subsections, respectively. We halve α whenever we hit a negative-weight cycle and need to backtrack. If we still get negative-weight cycles after $\alpha \leq 10^{-4}$ then we reset α and increase the minimum order of n which is encoded in G. (If n is already at our maximum of five, then we simply end without converging.) In the case of non-convergence after 1000 iterations, we select the best string (according to the objective) from the set of strings that were solutions to any subproblem at any point during optimization.

Our implementation uses OpenFST 1.2.8 (Allauzen et al., 2007).

5.2 Minimum Bayes Risk Decoding for ASR

We first consider the task of automatic speech recognition (ASR). Suppose x^* is the true transcription (a string) of an spoken utterance, and $\pi(w)$ is an ASR system's probability distribution over possible transcriptions w. The *Bayes risk* of an output transcription x is defined as the expectation

$\sum_w \pi(w)\,\ell(x,w)$ for some loss function ℓ (Bickel and Doksum, 2006). Minimum Bayes risk decoding (Goel and Byrne, 2003) involves choosing the x that minimizes the Bayes risk, rather than simply choosing the x that maximizes $\pi(x)$ as in MAP decoding.

As a reasonable approximation, we will take the expectation over just the strings $w_1, \ldots, w_K$ that are most probable under π. A common loss function is the Levenshtein distance because this is generally used to measure the word error rate of ASR output. Thus, we seek a consensus transcription

$$\operatorname*{argmin}_x \sum_{k=1}^{K} \pi_k\, d(x, w_k) \tag{7}$$

that minimizes a weighted sum of edit distances to all of the top-K strings, where high edit distance to more probable strings is more strongly penalized. Here $d(x, w)$ is the unweighted Levenshtein distance between two strings, and $\pi_k = \pi(w_k)$. If each $\pi_k = 1/K$, then argmin_x is known as the *Steiner consensus string*, which is NP-hard to find (Sim and Park, 2003). Equation (7) is a weighted generalization of the Steiner problem.

Given an input string w_k, it is straightforward to define our WFSA F_k such that $F_k(x)$ computes $\pi_k\, d(x, w_k)$. A direct construction of F_k is as follows. First, create a "straight line" WFSA whose single path accepts (only) w_k; each each state corresponds to a position in w_k. These arcs all have cost 0. Now add various arcs with cost π_k that permit edit operations. For each arc labeled with a symbol $a \in \Sigma$, add competing "substitution" arcs labeled with the other symbols in Σ, and a competing "deletion" arc labeled with ϵ; these have the same source and target as the original arc. Also, at each state, add a self-loop labeled with each symbol in Σ; these are "insertion" arcs. Each arc that deviates from w_k has a cost of π_k, and thus the lowest-cost path through F_k accepting x has weight $\pi_k\, d(x, w_k)$.

The consensus objective in Equation (7) can be solved by finding the lowest-cost path in $F_1 \cap \ldots \cap F_K$, and we can solve this best-path problem using the dual decomposition algorithm described above.

5.2.1 Experiments

We ran our algorithm on Broadcast News data, using 226 lattices produced by the IBM Attila decoder

0	<s> I WANT TO BE TAKING A DEEP BREATH NOW </s>
	<s> WE WANT TO BE TAKING A DEEP BREATH NOW </s>
	<s> I DON'T WANT TO BE TAKING A DEEP BREATH NOW </s>
	<s> WELL I WANT TO BE TAKING A DEEP BREATH NOW </s>
	<s> THEY WANT TO BE TAKING A DEEP BREATH NOW </s>
300	<s> I WANT TO BE TAKING A DEEP BREATH NOW </s>
	<s> WE WANT TO BE TAKING A DEEP BREATH NOW </s>
	<s> I DON'T WANT TO BE TAKING A DEEP BREATH NOW </s>
	<s> WELL I WANT TO BE TAKING A DEEP BREATH NOW </s>
	<s> WELL WANT TO BE TAKING A DEEP BREATH NOW </s>
375	<s> I WANT TO BE TAKING A DEEP BREATH NOW </s>
	<s> I WANT TO BE TAKING A DEEP BREATH NOW </s>
	<s> I DON'T WANT TO BE TAKING A DEEP BREATH NOW </s>
	<s> I WANT TO BE TAKING A DEEP BREATH NOW </s>
	<s> I WANT TO BE TAKING A DEEP BREATH NOW </s>
472	<s> I WANT TO BE TAKING A DEEP BREATH NOW </s>
	<s> I WANT TO BE TAKING A DEEP BREATH NOW </s>
	<s> I WANT TO BE TAKING A DEEP BREATH NOW </s>
	<s> I WANT TO BE TAKING A DEEP BREATH NOW </s>
	<s> I WANT TO BE TAKING A DEEP BREATH NOW </s>

Figure 1: Example run of the consensus problem on $K = 25$ strings on a Broadcast News utterance, showing $x_1, \ldots, x_5$ at the 0th, 300th, 375th, and 472nd iterations.

(Chen et al., 2006; Soltau et al., 2010) on a subset of the NIST dev04f data, using models trained by Zweig et al. (2011). For each lattice, we found the consensus of the top $K = 25$ strings.

85% of the problems converged within 1000 iterations, with an average of 147.4 iterations. We found that the true consensus was often the most likely string under π, but not always—this was true 70% of the time. In the Bayes risk objective we are optimizing in equation (7)—the expected loss—our approach averaged a score of 1.59, while always taking the top string gives only a slightly worse average of 1.66. 8% of the problems encountered negative-weight cycles, which were all resolved either by decreasing the step size or encoding larger n-grams.

5.3 Investigating Consensus Performance with Synthetic Data

The above experiments demonstrate that we can exactly find the best path in the intersection of 25 machines—an intersection that could not feasibly be constructed in practice. However, these experiments do not exhaustively explore how dual decomposition behaves on the Steiner string problem in general.

Above, we experimented with only a fixed number of input strings, which were generally similar to one another. There are a variety of other inputs to the consensus problem which might lead to different behavior and convergence results, however. If we were to instead run this experiment on DNA sequences (for example, if we posit that the strings are all mutations of the same ancestor), the alphabet {A,T,C,G}

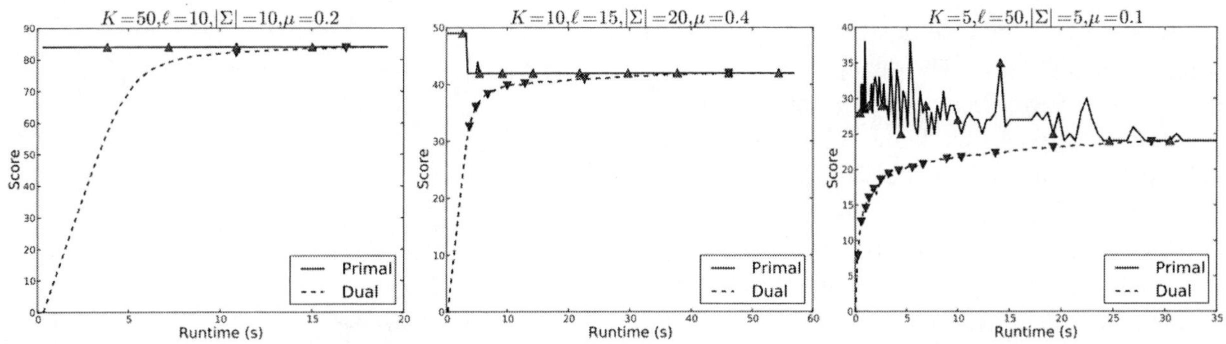

Figure 2: The algorithm's behavior on three specific consensus problems. The curves show the current values of the primal bound (based on the best string at the current iteration) and dual bound $h(\lambda)$. The horizontal axis shows runtime. Red upper triangles are placed every 10 iterations, while blue lower triangles are placed for every 10% increase in the size of the feature set Θ.

K	ℓ	$\|\Sigma\|$	μ	**Conv.**	**Iters.**	**Red.**
5	100	5	0.1	68%	257 (±110)	24%
5	100	5	0.2	0%	–	8%
5	50	5	0.1	80%	123 (± 65)	20%
5	50	5	0.2	10%	436 (±195)	18%
10	50	5	0.1	69%	228 (±164)	18%
10	50	5	0.2	0%	–	8%
10	50	5	0.4	0%	–	3%
10	30	10	0.1	100%	50 (± 69)	13%
10	30	10	0.2	93%	146 (±142)	20%
10	30	10	0.4	0%	–	16%
10	15	20	0.1	100%	26 (± 6)	1%
10	15	20	0.2	98%	43 (± 18)	10%
10	15	20	0.4	63%	289 (±217)	18%
10	15	20	0.8	0%	–	11%
25	15	20	0.1	98%	30 (± 5)	0%
25	15	20	0.2	92%	69 (±112)	6%
25	15	20	0.4	55%	257 (±149)	16%
25	15	20	0.8	0%	–	12%
50	10	10	0.2	68%	84 (±141)	0%
50	10	10	0.4	21%	173 (± 94)	9%
100	10	10	0.2	44%	147 (±220)	0%
100	10	10	0.4	13%	201 (±138)	6%

Table 1: A summary of results for various consensus problems, as described in §5.3.

is so small that n-grams are likely to be repeated in many parts of the strings, and the lack of position information in our features could make it hard to reach agreement. Another interesting case is when the input strings have little or nothing in common—can we still converge to an optimal consensus in a reasonable number of iterations?

We can investigate many different cases by creating synthetic data, where we tune the number of input strings K, the length of the strings, the size of the vocabulary $|\Sigma|$, as well as how similar the strings are. We do this by randomly generating a base string $x^* \in \Sigma^\ell$ of length ℓ. We then generate K random strings $w_1, \ldots, w_K$, each by passing x^* through a noisy edit channel, where each position has independent probability μ of making an edit. For each position in x^*, we uniformly sample once among the three types of edits (substitution, insertion, deletion), and in the case of the first two, we uniformly sample from the vocabulary (excluding the current symbol for substitution). The larger μ, the more mutated the strings will be. For small μ or large K, the optimal consensus of $w_1, \ldots, w_K$ will usually be x^*.

Table 1 shows results under various settings. Each line presents the percentage of 100 examples that converge within the iteration limit, the average number of iterations to convergence (± standard deviation) for those that converged, and the reduction in the objective value that is obtained over a simple baseline of choosing the best string in the input set, to show how much progress the algorithm makes between the 0th and final iteration.

As expected, a higher mutation probability slows convergence in all cases, as does having longer input strings. These results also confirm our hypothesis that a small alphabet would lead to slow convergence when using small n-gram features. For these types of strings, which might show up in biological data, one would likely need more informative constraints than position-agnostic n-grams.

Figure 2 shows example runs on problems generated at three different parameter settings. We plot the objective value as a function of runtime, showing both the primal objective (3) that we hope to minimize, which we measure as the quality of the best solution among the $\{x_k\}$ that are output at the current iteration, and the dual objective (5) that our algorithm is maximizing. The dual problem (which is concave in λ) lower bounds the primal. If the two functions ever touch, we know the solution to the dual problem is in the set of feasible solutions to the original primal problem we are attempting to solve, and indeed must be optimal. The figure shows that the dual function always has an initial value of 0, since we initialize each $\lambda_k = 0$, and then F_k will simply return the input w_k as its best solution (since w_k has zero distance to itself). As the algorithm begins to enforce the agreement constraints, the value of the relaxed dual problem gradually worsens, until it fully satisfies the constraints.

These plots indicate the number of iterations that have passed and the number of active features. We see that the time per iteration increases as the number of features increases, as expected, because more (and longer) n-grams are being encoded by G.

The three patterns shown are typical of almost all the trials we examined. When the solution is in the original input set (a likely occurrence for large K or small $\mu \cdot \ell$), the primal value will be optimal from the start, and our algorithm only has to *prove* its optimality. For more challenging problems, the primal solution may jump around in quality at each iteration before settling into a stable part of the space.

To investigate how different n-gram sizes affect convergence rates, we experiment with using the entire set of n-grams (for a fixed n) for the duration of the optimization procedure. Figure 3 shows convergence rates (based on both iterations and runtime) of different values of n for one set of parameters. While bigrams are very fast (average runtime of 14s among those that converged), this converged within 1000 iterations only 78% of the time, and the remaining 22% end up bringing down the average speed (with an overall average runtime over a minute). All larger n-grams converged every time; trigrams had an average runtime of 32s. Our algorithm, which begins with bigrams but brings in more features (up to 5-grams) as needed, had an average runtime of 19s (with 98% convergence).

6 Discussion and Future Work

An important (and motivating) property of Lagrangian relaxation methods is the certificate of optimality. Even in instances where approximate algorithms perform well, it could be useful to have a true optimality guarantee. For example, our algorithm can be used to produce reference solutions, which are important to have for research purposes.

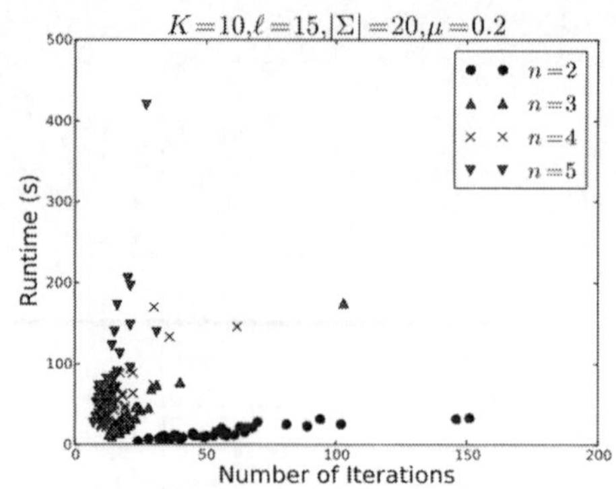

Figure 3: Convergence rates for a fixed set of n-grams.

Under a sum-of-pairs Levenshtein objective, the exact multi-sequence alignment can be directly obtained from the Steiner consensus string and vice versa (Gusfield, 1997). This implies that our exact algorithm could be also used to find exact multi-sequence alignments, an important problem in natural language processing (Barzilay and Lee, 2003) and computational biology (Durbin et al., 2006) that is almost always solved with approximate methods.

We have noted that some constraints are more useful than others. Position-specific information is hard to agree on and leads to slow convergence, while pure n-gram constraints do not work as well for long strings where the position may be important. One avenue we are investigating is the use of a non-deterministic G, which would allow us to encode latent variables (Dreyer et al., 2008), such as loosely defined "regions" within a string, and to allow for the encoding of alignments between the input strings. We would also like to extend these methods to other combinatorial optimization problems involving strings, such as inference in graphical models over strings (Dreyer and Eisner, 2009).

To conclude, we have presented a general framework for applying dual decomposition to implicit WFSA intersection. This could be applied to a number of NLP problems such as language model and lattice intersection. To demonstrate its utility on a large number of automata, we applied it to consensus decoding, determining the true optimum in a reasonable amount of time on a large majority of cases.

References

Cyril Allauzen, Mehryar Mohri, and Brian Roark. 2003. Generalized algorithms for constructing statistical language models. In *Proceedings of the 41st Annual Meeting of the Association for Computational Linguistics*, pages 40–47.

Cyril Allauzen, Michael Riley, Johan Schalkwyk, Wojciech Skut, and Mehryar Mohri. 2007. OpenFst: A general and efficient weighted finite-state transducer library. In *Proceedings of the 12th International Conference on Implementation and Application of Automata*, CIAA'07, pages 11–23.

Regina Barzilay and Lillian Lee. 2003. Learning to paraphrase: An unsupervised approach using multiple-sequence alignment. In *Proceedings of the 2003 Conference of the North American Chapter of the Association for Computational Linguistics on Human Language Technology - Volume 1*, NAACL '03, pages 16–23.

Peter J. Bickel and Kjell A. Doksum. 2006. *Mathematical Statistics: Basic Ideas and Selected Topics*, volume 1. Pearson Prentice Hall.

Stanley F. Chen, Brian Kingsbury, Lidia Mangu, Daniel Povey, George Saon, Hagen Soltau, and Geoffrey Zweig. 2006. Advances in speech transcription at IBM under the DARPA EARS program. *IEEE Transactions on Audio, Speech & Language Processing*, 14(5):1596–1608.

Markus Dreyer and Jason Eisner. 2009. Graphical models over multiple strings. In *Proceedings of the 2009 Conference on Empirical Methods in Natural Language Processing*, EMNLP '09, pages 101–110. Association for Computational Linguistics.

Markus Dreyer, Jason R. Smith, and Jason Eisner. 2008. Latent-variable modeling of string transductions with finite-state methods. In *Proceedings of the Conference on Empirical Methods in Natural Language Processing (EMNLP)*, pages 1080–1089, Honolulu, October.

R. Durbin, S. Eddy, A. Krogh, and G. Mitchison. 2006. *Biological Sequence Analysis*. Cambridge University Press.

Vaibhava Goel and William J. Byrne. 2003. Minimum Bayes risk methods in automatic speech recognition. In Wu Chou and Biing-Hwang Juan, editors, *Pattern Recognition in Speech and Language Processing*. CRC Press.

Dan Gusfield. 1997. *Algorithms on Strings, Trees, and Sequences: Computer Science and Computational Biology*. Cambridge University Press.

George Karakostas, Richard J Lipton, and Anastasios Viglas. 2003. On the complexity of intersecting finite state automata and NL versus NP. *Theoretical Computer Science*, pages 257–274.

Kevin Knight and Yaser Al-Onaizan. 1998. Translation with finite-state devices. In *AMTA'98*, pages 421–437.

N. Komodakis, N. Paragios, and G. Tziritas. 2007. MRF optimization via dual decomposition: Message-Passing revisited. In *Computer Vision, 2007. ICCV 2007. IEEE 11th International Conference on*, pages 1–8.

Terry Koo, Alexander M. Rush, Michael Collins, Tommi Jaakkola, and David Sontag. 2010. Dual decomposition for parsing with non-projective head automata. In *Proceedings of the 2010 Conference on Empirical Methods in Natural Language Processing*, EMNLP '10, pages 1288–1298.

Mehryar Mohri. 2002. Semiring frameworks and algorithms for shortest-distance problems. *J. Autom. Lang. Comb.*, 7:321–350, January.

Fernando C. N. Pereira and Michael Riley. 1997. Speech recognition by composition of weighted finite automata. *CoRR*.

Alexander M. Rush and Michael Collins. 2011. Exact decoding of syntactic translation models through Lagrangian relaxation. In *Proceedings of the 49th Annual Meeting of the Association for Computational Linguistics: Human Language Technologies - Volume 1*, HLT '11, pages 72–82.

Alexander M. Rush, David Sontag, Michael Collins, and Tommi Jaakkola. 2010. On dual decomposition and linear programming relaxations for natural language processing. In *Proceedings of the 2010 Conference on Empirical Methods in Natural Language Processing*, EMNLP '10, pages 1–11.

Jeong Seop Sim and Kunsoo Park. 2003. The consensus string problem for a metric is NP-complete. *J. of Discrete Algorithms*, 1:111–117, February.

H. Soltau, G. Saon, and B. Kingsbury. 2010. The IBM Attila speech recognition toolkit. In *Proc. IEEE Workshop on Spoken Language Technology*, pages 97–102.

David Sontag, Talya Meltzer, Amir Globerson, Yair Weiss, and Tommi Jaakkola. 2008. Tightening LP relaxations for MAP using message-passing. In *24th Conference in Uncertainty in Artificial Intelligence*, pages 503–510. AUAI Press.

David Sontag, Amir Globerson, and Tommi Jaakkola. 2011. Introduction to dual decomposition for inference. In Suvrit Sra, Sebastian Nowozin, and Stephen J. Wright, editors, *Optimization for Machine Learning*. MIT Press.

James C. Spall. 2003. *Introduction to Stochastic Search and Optimization*. John Wiley & Sons, Inc., New York, NY, USA, 1 edition.

Ben Taskar, Vassil Chatalbashev, Daphne Koller, and Carlos Guestrin. 2005. Learning structured prediction models: A large margin approach. In *Proceedings of the 22nd international conference on Machine learning*, ICML '05, pages 896–903.

Geoffrey Zweig, Patrick Nguyen, Dirk Van Compernolle, Kris Demuynck, Les E. Atlas, Pascal Clark, Gregory Sell, Meihong Wang, Fei Sha, Hynek Hermansky, Damianos Karakos, Aren Jansen, Samuel Thomas, Sivaram G. S. V. S., Sam Bowman, and Justine T. Kao. 2011. Speech recognition with segmental conditional random fields: A summary of the JHU CLSP 2010 Summer Workshop. In *ICASSP*.

Transliteration Mining Using Large Training and Test Sets

Ali El Kahki, Kareem Darwish, Ahmed Saad El Din
Qatar Computing Research Institute
Qatar Foundation, Doha, Qatar
ame2154@columbia.edu,
kdarwish@qf.org.qa, ataei@qf.org.qa

Mohamed Abd El-Wahab
Faculty of Computers and Information,
Cairo University, Cairo, Egypt
wahab@writeme.com

Abstract

Much previous work on Transliteration Mining (TM) was conducted on short parallel snippets using limited training data, and successful methods tended to favor recall. For such methods, increasing training data may impact precision and application on large comparable texts may impact precision and recall. We adapt a state-of-the-art TM technique with the best reported scores on the ACL 2010 NEWS workshop dataset, namely graph reinforcement, to work with large training sets. The method models observed character mappings between language pairs as a bipartite graph and unseen mappings are induced using random walks. Increasing training data yields more correct initial mappings but induced mappings become more error prone. We introduce parameterized exponential penalty to the formulation of graph reinforcement and we estimate the proper parameters for training sets of varying sizes. The new formulation led to sizable improvements in precision. Mining from large comparable texts leads to the presence of phonetically similar words in target and source texts that may not be transliterations or may adversely impact candidate ranking. To overcome this, we extracted related segments that have high translation overlap, and then we performed TM on them. Segment extraction produced significantly higher precision for three different TM methods.

1. Introduction

Transliteration Mining (TM) is the process of finding transliterations in parallel or comparable texts of different languages. For example, given the Arabic-English word sequence pairs: (الملك هالي سلاسي, Haile Selassie I of Ethiopia), successful TM would mine the transliterations: (هالي, Haile) and (سلاسي, Selassie). TM has been shown to be effective in several Information Retrieval (IR) and Natural Language Processing (NLP) applications. For example, in cross language IR, TM was used to handle out-of-vocabulary query words by mining transliterations between words in queries and top *n* retrieved documents and then using transliterations to expand queries (Udupa et al., 2009a). In Machine Translation (MT), TM can improve alignment at training time and help enrich phrase tables with named entities that may not appear in parallel training data. More broadly, TM is a character mapping problem. Having good character mapping models can be beneficial in a variety of applications such as learning stemming models, learning spelling transformations between similar languages, and finding variant spellings of names (Udupa and Kumar, 2010b).

TM has attracted interest in recent years with a dedicated evaluation in the ACL 2010 NEWS workshop. In that evaluation, TM was performed using limited training data, namely 1,000 parallel transliteration word-pairs, on short parallel text segments, namely cross-language Wikipedia titles which were typically a few words long. Since TM was performed on very short parallel segments, the chances that two phonetically similar words would appear within such a short text segment in one language were typically very low. Also, since TM training datasets were small, many valid mappings were not observed in training. For these two reasons, most of the successful techniques related to that evaluation have focused on improving recall, while hurting precision slightly. Some of these techniques involved the use of letter conflation based on a SOUNDEX like scheme (Darwish, 2010; Oh and Choi, 2006) and character n-gram similarity. The most successful technique on ACL-NEWS dataset, involved the use of graph reinforcement in which observed mappings between language pairs were modeled using a bipartite graph and unseen mappings were induced using random walks (El-Kahki et al., 2011).

In this paper, we focus on improving TM between Arabic and English in more realistic settings, compared to the NEWS workshop dataset. Specifically, we focus on the cases where:

1. Relatively large TM training sets, which are typical of production systems, are available. As we will show, using more training data in conjunction with recall-oriented techniques that perform well on small training sets can adversely hurt precision, leading to drops in F-measure. A more fundamental question is what constitutes "large" versus "small" training sets. Ideally, we want a unified solution for training sets of varying sizes.
2. TM is performed on large comparable texts which are ubiquitously available from different sources such as cross language news and Wikipedia articles. In this case, there are two phenomena that arise. First, there is an increased probability (compared to short texts) that words in the target and source texts may be phonetically similar, while not being transliterations of each other. One such example is the Arabic word "من", which means "in" and is pronounced as "min" and the English word "men". Such cases adversely affect precision. Second, given a source language word, there may be multiple target language words that are phonetically similar and TM may rank a wrong word higher than the correct one. For example, consider the Arabic word "جو", which is pronounced as "joe" but is in fact the rendition of the Chinese name "Zhou". If the English text has words such as "jaw", "joe", "jo", "joy", etc., one of them may rank higher than "Zhou". Since only the top choice is considered, this phenomenon would hurt precision and recall.

We address these two situations by making the following two contributions:

1. Modifying the TM technique with the best reported results on the ACL 2010 NEWS workshop, namely graph reinforcement (El-Kahki et al., 2011) to handle training sets of arbitrary sizes by introducing parameterized exponential penalty to the mapping induction process. We show that we can effectively learn the parameters that tune the penalty for two different training sets of varying sizes. In doing so, we achieve better results for graph reinforcement with larger training sets.
2. For large comparable texts, we use contextual clues, namely translations of neighboring words, to constrain TM and to preserve precision. Specifically, we initially extract text segments that are "related" based on cross lingual lexical overlap, and then we perform TM on these segments. Though there have been some papers on extracting sub-sentence alignments from comparable text (Hewavitharana and Vogel, 2011; Munteanu and Marcu, 2006), extracting related (as opposed to parallel) text segments may be preferable because: 1) transliterations may not occur in parallel contexts; 2) using simple lexical overlap is efficient; and as we will show 3) simultaneous use of phonetic and contextual evidences may be sufficient to produce high TM precision. Alternate solutions focused on performing TM on extracted named entities only (Udupa et al., 2009b). Some drawbacks of such an approach are: 1) named entity recognition (NER) may not be available for many languages; and 2) NER has inherently low recall for languages such as Arabic where no discriminating features such as capitalization exist.

The remainder of the paper is organized as follows: Section 2 provides background on TM; Section 3 describes the basic TM system that is used in the paper; Section 4 describes graph reinforcements, shows how it fairs in the presence of a large training set, and introduces modifications to graph reinforcement to improve its effectiveness with such data; Section 5 introduces the use of contextual clues to improve TM and reports on its effectiveness; and Section 6 concludes the paper.

2. Background

Much work has been done on TM for different language pairs such as English-Chinese (Kuo et al., 2006; Kuo et al., 2007; Kuo et al., 2008; Jin et al. 2008;), English-Tamil (Saravanan and Kumaran, 2008; Udupa and Khapra, 2010), English-Korean (Oh and Isahara, 2006; Oh and Choi, 2006), English-Japanese (Qu et al., 2000; Brill et al., 2001; Oh and Isahara, 2006), English-Hindi (Fei et al., 2003; Mahesh and Sinha, 2009), and English-Russian (Klementiev and Roth, 2006). TM typically involves finding character mappings between two languages and using these mappings to ascertain if two words are transliterations or not.

2.1 Finding Character Mappings

To find character sequence mappings between two languages, the most common approach entails using automatic letter alignment of transliteration pairs. Automatic alignment can be performed using different algorithms such as EM (Kuo et al., 2008; Lee and Chang, 2003) or HMM-based alignment (Udupa et al., 2009a; Udupa et al., 2009b). Another method uses automatic speech recognition confusion tables to extract phonetically equivalent character sequences to discover monolingual and cross-lingual pronunciation variations (Kuo and Yang, 2005). Alternatively, letters can be mapped into a common character set using a predefined transliteration scheme (Darwish, 2010; Oh and Choi, 2006).

2.2 Transliteration Mining

For the problem of ascertaining if two words can be transliterations of each other, a common approach involves using a generative model that attempts to generate all possible transliterations of a source word, given the character mappings between two languages, and restricting the output to words in the target language (Fei et al., 2003; Lee and Chang, 2003, Udupa et al., 2009a). This is similar to the baseline approach that we used in this paper. Noeman and Madkour (2010) implemented this technique using a finite state automaton by generating all possible transliterations along with weighted edit distance and then filtered them using appropriate thresholds and target language words. El-Kahki et al. (2011) combined a generative model with so-called graph reinforcement, which is described in greater detail in Section 4. They reported the best TM results on the ACL 2010 NEWS workshop dataset for 4 different languages. Alternatively back-transliteration can be used to determine if one sequence could have been generated by successively mapping character sequences from one language into another (Brill et al., 2001; Bilac and Tanaka, 2005; Oh and Isahara, 2006).

Udupa and Khapra (2010) proposed a method in which transliteration candidates are mapped into a "low-dimensional common representation space". Then, the similarity between the resultant feature vectors for both candidates can be computed. A similar approach uses context sensitive hashing (Udupa and Kumar, 2010).

Jiampojamarn et al. (2010) used classification to determine if source and target language words were valid transliterations. They used a variety of features including edit distance between an English token and the Romanized versions of the foreign token, forward and backward transliteration probabilities, and character n-gram similarity. Udupa et al. (2009b) used a similar classification-based approach.

3. Baseline Transliteration Mining

3.1 Description of the Baseline System

We used a generative TM model that was trained on a set of transliteration pairs. We automatically aligned these pairs at character level using an HMM-based aligner akin to that of He (2007). Alignment produced mappings between characters from both languages with associated probabilities. We restricted individual source language character sequences to be 3 characters at most. We always treated English as the target language and Arabic as the source language.

Briefly, we produced all possible segmentations of a source word along with their associated mappings into the target language. Valid target sequences were retained and sorted by the product of the constituent mapping probabilities. The candidate with the highest probability was generated given that the product of the mapping probabilities was higher than a certain threshold. Otherwise, no candidate was chosen.

The search for transliterated pairs was implemented as a variant of depth-first search (Pearl, 1984), where states represented valid mappings between source and target substrings. At each step, the mapping with the best score was selected and expanded using the mappings learnt from alignment. This process ran until mapping combinations produced target word(s) from a source word or until all possible states were explored. The pseudo code in Figure 1 describes the details of the algorithm. The implementation was optimized via incremental left to right processing of source words, the use of a radix tree to prune invalid paths, and the use of a sorted priority queue to insure that the highest weighing candidate was at the top of the queue.

```
Input: Mappings, set of mappings from source fragment to a list of target fragments and mapping Probability .
Input: SourceWord (F_i ∈ F_1^n), Source language word
Input: TargetWords, radix tree containing all target language words (E_1^m)
Data Structures: DFS, Priority queue to store candidate transliterations pair ordered by their transliteration score –
   Each candidate transliteration tuple = (SourceFragment, TargetTransliteration, TransliterationScore).
StartSymbol = ("", "", 1.0); DFS={StartSymbol}
While (DFS is not empty)
    SourceFragment= DFS.Top().SourceFragment
    TargetFragment= DFS.Top().TargetTransliteration
    FragmentScore =DFS.Top().TransliterationScore
    If (SourceWord == SourceFragment)
        If (FragmentScore > Threshold) Return (SourceWord, TargetTransliteration, FragmentScore)
        Else Return Null
    DFS.RemoveTop()
    For SubFragmentLength = 1 to 3
        SourceSubString = SubString( SourceWord, SourceFragment.Length , SubFragmentLength)
        Foreach mapping in Mappings[SourceSubString]
            If ((TargetFragment + mapping.TargetFragemnt) is a sub-string in TargetWords)
                DFS.Add(SourceFragment + SourceSubString, TargetFragment + mapping.TargetFragement,
                mapping.Score * FragmentScore)
    DFS.RemoveTop()
End While
Return Null
```

Figure 1: Pseudo code for transliteration mining

3.2 Thresholding

We used a threshold on the minimum acceptable transliteration score to filter out unreliable transliterations. Fixing a uniform threshold would have caused the model to filter out long transliterations. Thus, we tied the threshold to the length of transliterated words. We assumed a threshold d for single character mappings and the transliteration threshold for a target word of length l would be d^l. Since we did not have a validation set to estimate d, we created a synthetic validation set from the training set and then used cross-validation to estimate d as follows: we split the training data into 5 folds for cross validation; we modified each validation fold by adding 5 random words to each target word in the transliteration pair; then we performed TM with varying thresholds on the validation fold and computed F-measure; and we ascertained the threshold that led to the highest F-measure for each fold and then took the average threshold.

3.3 Linguistic Processing

For Arabic, we performed letter normalization of the different forms of alef, alef maqsoura and ya, and ta marbouta and ha. For English, we case-folded all letters and removed accents, umlaut, and similar diacritic like marks (ex. á, â, ä, à, ã, ā, ą).

4. Modifying Graph Reinforcement

4.1 Original Graph Reinforcement

To motivate graph reinforcement, consider the following example: if alignment produced the mappings (ط, ti), (ط, ta), (ت, ti), and (ت, t), then the mappings (ط, t) and (ت, ta) are likely valid – though not observed. These mappings can be induced by traversing the following paths: ط ➔ ti ➔ ت ➔ t and ت ➔ ti ➔ ط ➔ ta respectively.

In graph reinforcement, observed mappings were modeled as a bipartite graph with source (S) and target (T) character sequences and weighted with the learnt alignment probabilities (M). Thus the mapping between s ∈ S and t ∈ T was m(s,t).

Graph reinforcement was performed by traversing the graph from S ➔ T ➔ S ➔ T in order to deduce new mappings. Given a source sequence s'∈ S and a target sequence t' ∈ T, the deduced mapping weights were computed as follows:

$$m(t'|s') = 1 - \prod_{\forall s \in S, t \in T} \left(1 - m(t'|s)m(s|t)m(t|s')\right)$$

where the term $\left(m(t'|s)m(s|t)m(t|s')\right)$ is the score of the path between t' and s'. De Morgan's law was applied to aggregate different paths using an OR operator, which involved taking the negation of negations of all possible paths aggregated by an AND operator. Hence, the probability of an inferred mapping would be boosted if it was obtained from multiple paths.

Since some characters, mainly vowels, have a tendency to map to many other characters, link reweighting was applied after each iteration. Link reweighting had the effect of decreasing the weights of target character sequences that have many source character sequences mapping to them and hence reducing the effect of incorrectly inducing mappings. Link reweighting was performed as follows:

$$m'(s|t) = \frac{m(s|t)}{\sum_{s_i \in S} m(s_i|t)}$$

Where $s_i \in S$ is a source sequence that maps to t. This is akin to normalizing conditional probabilities.

4.2 Graph Reinforcement Results

We tested graph reinforcement using 10 iterations in 2 different settings, namely:

1. NEWS-1k: Using the ACL-NEWS workshop dataset. The dataset contained 1,000 parallel transliteration word pairs for training and 1,000 parallel Wikipedia titles for testing.
2. NEWS-10k: Using the test part of the ACL-NEWS dataset, while training with 10,000 manually curated parallel transliterations.

Table 1 reports on the results of the graph reinforcement results for the two setups. In the NEWS-1k setup, graph reinforcement generally had a positive effect on recall at the expense of precision. However, as we suspected, increasing the amount of training data (as in the NEWS-10k) led to more initial mappings from alignment, but with many erroneously induced mappings that adversely impacted precision. Though recall improved significantly, precision deteriorated significantly, leading to lower F-measure.

Table 1. Results for NEWS-1k and NEWS-10k

		Baseline	Reinforcement
NEWS-1k	P	0.988	0.977
	R	0.583	0.912
	F	0.733	0.943
NEWS-10k	P	0.917	0.689
	R	0.759	0.960
	F	0.787	0.802

4.3 Modifying Graph Reinforcement with Parameterized Exponential Penalty

To overcome the problem demonstrated in the NEWS-10k setup, we adjusted the graph reinforcement formula to give more confidence to mappings that were observed due to initial alignment and to successively penalize mappings that were induced in later graph reinforcement iterations. The adjustment was as follows:

$$m^i(t'|s') = 1 - \left(1 - m^{i-1}(t'|s')\right) \cdot \prod_{s \in S, t \in T} 1 - e^{-i\alpha} m^{i-1}(t'|s) m^{i-1}(s|t) m^{i-1}(t|s')$$

Where the parameter α adjusts how much we penalize induced mappings and i is the number of iterations. $m^i(t'|s')$ is the mapping score at iteration i. Basically, newly seen links at iteration i are penalized by $e^{-i\alpha}$. The equation is similar to the earlier reinforcement equation but with all paths except the original path $s' \to t'$ multiplied by exponential penalty $e^{-i\alpha}$. Since the ACL-NEWS dataset did not have a validation set to help us estimate α, we opted to use the approach we used earlier to estimate the proper thresholds, namely: we split the training data into 5 folds for cross validation; we modified each validation fold by adding 5 random words to each target word in the transliteration pair; and then we performed TM with varying values of α and with 10 graph reinforcement iterations on the validation fold and computed precision and recall. For the 10k training set, we opted to use a 90/10 training/validation split of the training data, where the validation part was modified in the same manner as the validation folds of the ACL-NEWS datasets. We varied the value of α between 0.0 and 1.0 with increments of 0.1 and with increments of 1 afterwards for values greater than 1. If two values of α yielded the same F-measure (up to 3 decimal places), we favored the larger α, favoring precision. Figures 2 and 3 plot the precision and recall respectively on the validation (-valid) and test (-test) sets for the 1,000 pair training set.

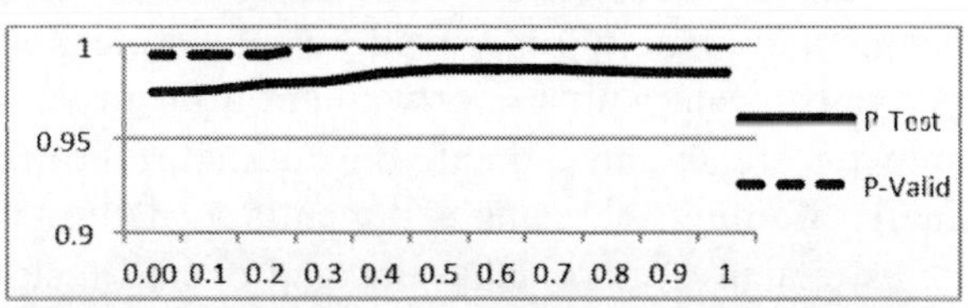

Figure 2. Precision (y-axis) on test and validation sets for varying values of a (x-axis) for the 1k set

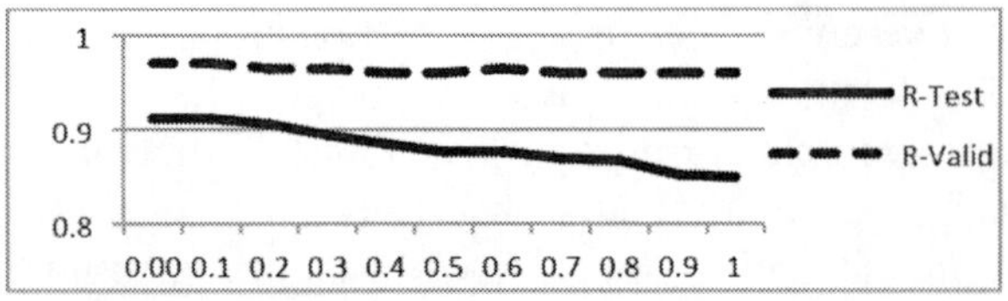

Figure 3. Recall (y-axis) on test and validation sets for varying values of α (x-axis) for the 1k set

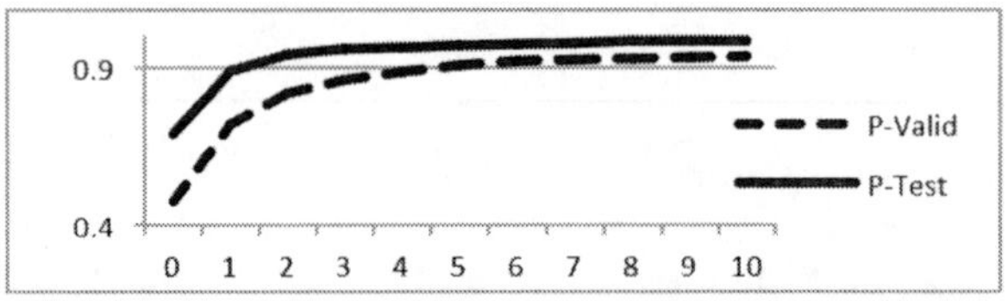

Figure 4. Precision (y-axis) on test and validation sets for varying values of α (x-axis) for the 10k set

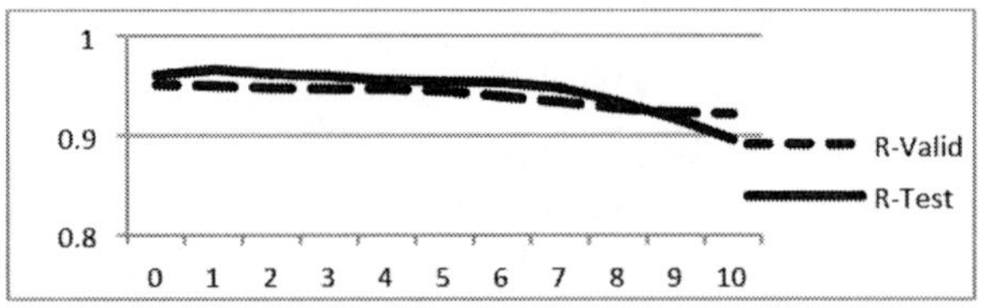

Figure 5. Recall (y-axis) on test and validation sets for varying values of α (x-axis) for the 10k set

Figures 4 and 5 plot the same for the 10k pair training set. The precision and recall values on the validation sets are indicative of their behavior on the test set. Due to the difference in training data sizes, the best values of α were significantly larger for the 10k dataset compared to the 1k dataset.

4.4 Modified Graph Reinforcement Results

We applied exponential penalty on graph reinforcement with the estimated value of α on the ACL-NEWS dataset as well as the 10k training set. Table 2 lists the estimated and optimal values of α for the different datasets on the training and test sets respectively along with the F-measure obtained for these values of α. Table 2 also compares the results to the results from baseline and graph reinforcement without exponential penalty. Tables 3 and 4 show precision, recall, and F-measure results for training using ACL-NEWS datasets and the larger training set respectively.

For the large dataset of 10k training words, using exponential penalty improved results noticeably, with a 16 basis points improvement in F-measure, and we were able to estimate the optimal α. For the smaller training set, using exponential penalty with the estimated α marginally changed overall results by (-0.006) compared to the optimal α. The change in overall F-measure was generally small, with most of the degradation in recall being offset by improvements in precision. The small error in estimating α for the ACL-NEWS dataset can be attributed to the small size of the validation set. Generally, smaller training sets require smaller values of α to allow reinforcement to deduce more unseen mappings, increasing recall. Larger training sets require larger values of α and exponential penalty becomes more important. The advantage of this formulation is that α can be learned to match training sets of varying sizes.

Table 2. F-measure for baseline, reinforcement, and exponential penalty at estimated and optimal α

	NEWS-1k	NEWS-10k
Baseline	0.757	0.787
Reinforcement (α=0)	0.941	0.802
Estimated α	0.3	6.0
@ Estimated α	0.935	0.963
Optimal α (on test)	0.1	6.0
@ optimal α	0.943	0.963

Table 3. Results for training using 1k training set

	P	R	F1
Baseline	0.975	0.619	0.757
Reinforcement (α=0)	0.975	0.912	0.941
@ estimated α	0.980	0.894	0.935

Table 4. Results for training using 10k training set

	P	R	F1
Baseline	0.917	0.759	0.787
Reinforcement (α=0)	0.689	0.960	0.802
@ estimated α	0.976	0.948	0.963

5. TM from Large Comparable Text

5.1 Baseline TM to Large Comparable Text

We tested TM using the 1,000 training pairs from the ACL-NEWS workshop on the longest 30 English Wikipedia articles with equivalent Arabic Wikipedia articles. The test articles had the following properties:

	Max. Len	Min. Len	Avg. Len
Arabic	10,165	1,837	3,614
English	10,710	3,133	4,896

The article pairs had 64.7 transliterations on average (with 1,942 in total).

To show the generality of using contextual clues, we tested TM using 3 different techniques, namely: the aforementioned baseline system, graph reinforcement, and using SOUNDEX-like letter conflation for English in the manner suggested by Darwish (2010). This letter conflation involved removing vowels, "H", and 'W"; and performing the following mappings:

B, F, P, V → 1 C, G, J, K, Q, S, X, Z → 2
D,T → 3 L → 4
M,N → 5 R → 6

Such letter conflation was shown to improve TM F-measure on the ACL-NEWS workshop from 0.73 to 0.85 (Darwish, 2010).

Table 5. Results for TM on full Wikipedia articles

	Baseline	SOUNDEX	Reinforcement
P	0.610	0.059	0.650
R	0.415	0.402	0.500
F	0.494	0.103	0.565

Table 5 reports the TM results on the Wikipedia articles. The increased size of the comparable text on which we were performing TM led to adverse effects on precision and recall for the baseline, graph reinforcement, and SOUNDEX setups – with 0.059 precision for SOUNDEX. Graph reinforcement performed slightly better than the baseline both in terms of precision and recall, but with such low precision values, TM may not be useful for many applications. As highlighted earlier, the reason behind the drop in precision was due to phonetically similar words that were in fact not transliterations. The reason behind the drop in recall was due to the following: when TM is performed, often the correct transliteration was found but not as the first candidate. Given that for evaluation we were considering the first candidate only, this hurt both precision and recall.

5.2 Using Context to Improve TM

To overcome the precision and recall problems, we used contextual information to improve TM for large comparable text. To do so, we filtered articles to extract potentially related fragments and then we applied TM on the extracted fragments. The filtering was performed based on lexical similarity between fragments. The idea was that words that do not share enough contexts were not likely to be transliterations. A byproduct of this approach was a significant reduction in TM running time since the search space was reduced. On the downside, this likely hurt recall as transliterations that do not share similar contexts could not be mined.

To extract fragments with similar context we used a phrase table from a phrase-based MT system, which was akin to Moses (Koehn et al., 2007), to detect similarity between fragments in articles. The MT system was trained using 14 million parallel Arabic-English sentence pairs. The extraction algorithm aimed to extract maximum length fragments that share contexts greater than a specific percentage of fragment lengths. The threshold that we used in our experimentation was 30%. When picking the threshold, our goal was to find transliterations that appear in similar and not necessarily identical contexts. The threshold was determined qualitatively on a validation set.

A brute force fragment extraction approach would extract all possible fragments in source and target articles, iterate on each word in each pair of fragments to find the mappings, and then include a fragment if the mappings count exceed the threshold. Such a brute force approach would have an order of N^3M^3, where N and M are the number of words in the source and target articles respectively. To improve the running time, we first removed stop words from the source list. Then, we created a list that contained the positions of each of the matching pairs in source and target articles sorted by source words' position. This operation had a complexity of O(N*log*M). Next, we iterated on source fragments of different size, which was $O(N^2)$, and added the positions of matches in the target article in a sorted list. This operation was O(K*log*K) where K is the number of matches. Then, we iterated on extracted matches to find target fragment that satisfied the condition:

$$\frac{\text{Fragment Length}}{\text{number of mappings}} \geq .3$$

The last step was O(K) in the worst case. The total complexity of this algorithm was $O(N^2K\log K)$ in the worst case, which had a much lower complexity than the brute force approach. In practice, the algorithm filtered 30 comparable pairs of articles with an average of 4.9k words for English and 3.6k for Arabic in less than 5 minutes. Details of the algorithm are shown in Figure 2.

5.3 Testing TM on Extracted Segments

Table 6 reports TM results on the extracted segments. As the results show, TM on extracted segments dramatically improved precision for all setups compared to TM on the full articles (as in Table 6). Except for the SOUNDEX setup, recall dropped by 9.3 and 8.3 basis points for the baseline and graph reinforcement setups respectively. Though F-measure dropped slightly for the baseline case and improved slightly for the reinforcement case, what is noteworthy is that

```
Input: Matches, a list of matches between word position in source article and its mapping in the target article sorted by
  source position
Input: Source, list of source words; Target, list of target words
Output: ParallelFragments : List of pairs of parallel fragments
  For startPosition=0 To Source.Lenght
      For endPosition = startPosition + MinimumFragmentLengh To Source.Lenght
          SortedList TargetMatches =[ ]
      ForEach match Between startPosistion And endPosition In Matches
          TargetMatches.Add(Matching[match].targetPosition)
      startItr=0; endItr=TargetMatches.Length - 1
      For i=0 to TargetMatches.Length
          If( (endItr-startItr+1)/ (TargetMatches [endItr]-TargetMatches[startItr]) >.3) Then
              ParallelFragments.Add(Source.GetRange(startPosition,
              endPosition),Target.GetRange(TargetMatches[startItr], TargetMatches[endItr]))
          Break
          Else
            If(TargetMatches[endItr]-TargetMatches[startItr+1]>TargetMatches[endItr-1]-
            TargetMatches[startItr]) Then startItr++
            Else endItr++
            End If
        End If
      End Loop
    End Loop
  End Loop
  Return ParallelFragments
```

Figure 2. Pseudo code for the fragment extraction algorithm

precision was high enough to make TM practically useful for a variety of applications. The major advantage of the proposed technique is the achievement of relatively high precision – comparable to precision on small text snippets. Though recall is relatively low, the ubiquity of comparable texts can help produce large mined transliterations of high quality.

Table 6. Results for TM on extracted segments

	Baseline	SOUNDEX	Reinforcement
P	0.962	0.524	0.946
R	0.322	0.418	0.417
F	0.482	0.465	0.579

6. Conclusion

In this paper, we explored the use of transliteration mining in the context of using large training and test sets. Since recent work was conducted on small parallel text segments that were just a few words long with limited training data, the state-of-the-art techniques generally favored recall by inducing mappings that were unseen in training. Since the parallel test segments were short, improvements in recall had a very small effect on precision. When we applied the best reported method in the literature using large training data or when performing TM on large comparable texts, drops in precision and recall were substantial.

We modified the formulation of graph reinforcement by introducing a parameterized exponential penalty to allow for the discovery of new letter mappings using graph walks while penalizing mappings that required more graph walk steps to be induced. We showed how to effectively estimate the exponential penalty parameter for training sets of different sizes. In the context of performing TM on short parallel segments using 10k training words, we improved TM precision from 0.689 to 0.976 at the expense of a small drop in recall from 0.960 to 0.948.

What we observed for graph reinforcement is symptomatic of algorithms that may fail when more data is present. Other such examples include stemming for MT and IR. Generally, with more MT parallel data or bigger IR collections, stemming may become less useful or harmful. It is advantageous to parameterize algorithms for tuning for dataset of different sizes.

When performing TM on large comparable texts, we initially filtered the text to produce short comparable text segments and then we performed TM on them. Though the approach is relatively simple, it led to pronounced improvement in TM precision from 0.650 to 0.946, with a drop in recall from 0.500 to 0.417. Given that comparable texts are ubiquitous, improvements in precision are likely more important than drops in recall.

For future work, we want to test the effect of improved TM in the context of different NLP applications such as MT and cross language IR.

Acknowledgements

Some of the experiments were conducted while the authors were at the Cairo Microsoft Innovation Center.

References

C. Bannard, C. Callison-Burch. 2005. Paraphrasing with Bilingual Parallel Corpora. ACL-2005, pp. 597—604.

S. Bilac, H. Tanaka. 2005. Extracting transliteration pairs from comparable corpora. NLP-2005.

E. Brill, G. Kacmarcik, C. Brockett. 2001. Automatically harvesting Katakana-English term pairs from search engine query logs. NLPRS 2001, pp. 393–399.

K. Darwish. 2010. Transliteration Mining with Phonetic Conflation and Iterative Training. ACL NEWS workshop 2010.

A. El Kahki, K. Darwish, A. Saad El Din, M. Abd El-Wahab, A Hefny, W. Ammar. Improved Transliteration Mining Using Graph Reinforcement. EMNLP-2011. pp. 1384—1393.

H. Fei, S. Vogel, A. Waibel. 2003. Extracting Named Entity Translingual Equivalence with Limited Resources. TALIP, 2(2):124–129.

X. He. 2007. Using Word-Dependent Transition Models in HMM based Word Alignment for Statistical Machine Translation. ACL-07 2nd SMT workshop.

S. Hewavitharana, S. Vogel. 2011. Extracting parallel phrases from comparable data. The 4th Workshop on Building and Using Comparable Corpora: Comparable Corpora and the Web, June 24-24, 2011, Portland, Oregon

S. Jiampojamarn, K. Dwyer, S. Bergsma, A. Bhargava, Q. Dou, M.Y. Kim and G. Kondrak. 2010. Transliteration Generation and Mining with Limited Training Resources. ACL NEWS workshop 2010.

C. Jin, D.I. Kim, S.H. Na, J.H. Lee. 2008. Automatic Extraction of English-Chinese Transliteration Pairs using Dynamic Window and Tokenizer. Sixth SIGHAN Workshop on Chinese Language Processing, 2008.

A. Klementiev, D. Roth. 2006. Named Entity Transliteration and Discovery from Multilingual Comparable Corpora. HLT Conf. of the North American Chapter of the ACL, pages 82–88.

P. Koehn, H. Hoang, A. Birch, C. Callison-Burch, M. Federico, N. Bertoldi, B. Cowan, W. Shen, C. Moran, R. Zens, C. Dyer, O. Bojar, A. Constantin, E. Herbst (2007). Moses: Open Source Toolkit for Statistical Machine Translation. ACL-2007, Demo Session.

S. Kok, C. Brockett. 2010. Hitting the Right Paraphrases in Good Time. Human Language Technologies: NAACL-2010.

A. Kumaran, M. Khapra, H. Li. 2010. Report of NEWS 2010 Transliteration Mining Shared Task. 2010 Named Entities Workshop, ACL 2010, pages 21–28.

J.S. Kuo, H. Li, Y.K. Yang. 2006. Learning Transliteration Lexicons from the Web. COLING-ACL-2006, 1129 – 1136.

J.S. Kuo, H. Li, Y.K. Yang. 2007. A phonetic similarity model for automatic extraction of transliteration pairs. TALIP, 2007

J.S. Kuo, H. Li, C.L. Lin. 2008. Mining Transliterations from Web Query Results: An Incremental Approach. Sixth SIGHAN Workshop on Chinese Language Processing, 2008.

J.S. Kuo, Y.K. Yang. 2005. Incorporating Pronunciation Variation into Extraction of Transliterated-term Pairs from Web Corpora. Journal of Chinese Language and Computing, 15 (1): (33-44).

C.J. Lee, J.S. Chang. 2003. Acquisition of English-Chinese transliterated word pairs from parallel-aligned texts using a statistical machine transliteration model. Workshop on Building and Using Parallel Texts, HLT-NAACL-2003, 2003.

D.S. Munteanu, D. Marcu. 2006. Extracting parallel sub-sentential fragments from non-parallel corpora. ACL-2006, p.81-88.

S. Noeman, A. Madkour. 2010. Language Independent Transliteration Mining System Using Finite State Automata Framework. ACL NEWS workshop 2010.

R. Mahesh, K. Sinha. 2009. Automated Mining Of Names Using Parallel Hindi-English Corpus. 7th Workshop on Asian Language Resources, ACL-IJCNLP 2009, pages 48–54, 2009.

J.H. Oh, K.S. Choi. 2006. Recognizing transliteration equivalents for enriching domain specific thesauri. 3rd Intl. WordNet Conf., pp. 231–237, 2006.

Jong-Hoon Oh, Hitoshi Isahara. 2006. Mining the Web for Transliteration Lexicons: Joint-Validation

Approach. pp.254-261, 2006 IEEE/WIC/ACM Intl. Conf. on Web Intelligence (WI'06), 2006.

Yan Qu, Gregory Grefenstette, David A. Evans. 2003. Automatic transliteration for Japanese-to-English text retrieval. SIGIR 2003:353-360

P. Resnik, N. Smith. 2003. The Web as a parallel corpus. Computational Linguistics - Special issue on web as corpus, Vol. 29 Issue 3, Sept. 2003

K Saravanan, A Kumaran. 2008. Some Experiments in Mining Named Entity Transliteration Pairs from Comparable Corpora. The 2nd Intl. Workshop on Cross Lingual Information Access: Addressing the Need of Multilingual Societies, 2008.

J. Smith, C. Quirk, K. Toutanova. 2010. Extracting parallel sentences from comparable corpora using document level alignment, Human Language Technologies: NAACL-2010, p.403-411.

R. Udupa, K. Saravanan, A. Bakalov, A. Bhole. 2009a. "They Are Out There, If You Know Where to Look": Mining Transliterations of OOV Query Terms for Cross-Language Information Retrieval. ECIR-2009.

R. Udupa, K. Saravanan, A. Kumaran, J. Jagarlamudi. 2009b. MINT: A Method for Effective and Scalable Mining of Named Entity Transliterations from Large Comparable Corpora. EACL 2009.

R. Udupa, M. Khapra. 2010a. Transliteration Equivalence using Canonical Correlation Analysis. ECIR-2010, 2010.

R. Udupa, S. Kumar. 2010b. Hashing-based Approaches to Spelling Correction of Personal Names. EMNLP 2010.

G.W. You, S.W. Hwang, Y.I. Song, L. Jiang, Z. Nie. 2010. Mining Name Translations from Entity Graph Mapping. EMNLP-2010, pp. 430–439.

S. Zhao, H. Wang, T. Liu, S. Li. 2008. Pivot Approach for Extracting Paraphrase Patterns from Bilingual Corpora. ACL-08: HLT, pp. 780–788.

Optimized Online Rank Learning for Machine Translation

Taro Watanabe
National Institute of Information and Communications Technology
3-5 Hikaridai, Seika-cho, Soraku-gun, Kyoto, 619-0289 JAPAN
{taro.watanabe}@nict.go.jp

Abstract

We present an online learning algorithm for statistical machine translation (SMT) based on stochastic gradient descent (SGD). Under the online setting of rank learning, a corpus-wise loss has to be approximated by a batch local loss when optimizing for evaluation measures that cannot be linearly decomposed into a sentence-wise loss, such as BLEU. We propose a variant of SGD with a larger batch size in which the parameter update in each iteration is further optimized by a passive-aggressive algorithm. Learning is efficiently parallelized and line search is performed in each round when merging parameters across parallel jobs. Experiments on the NIST Chinese-to-English Open MT task indicate significantly better translation results.

1 Introduction

The advancement of statistical machine translation (SMT) relies on efficient tuning of several or many parameters in a model. One of the standards for such tuning is minimum error rate training (MERT) (Och, 2003), which directly minimize the loss of translation evaluation measures, i.e. BLEU (Papineni et al., 2002). MERT has been successfully used in practical applications, although, it is known to be unstable (Clark et al., 2011). To overcome this instability, it requires multiple runs from random starting points and directions (Moore and Quirk, 2008), or a computationally expensive procedure by linear programming and combinatorial optimization (Galley and Quirk, 2011).

Many alternative methods have been proposed based on the algorithms in machine learning, such as averaged perceptron (Liang et al., 2006), maximum entropy (Och and Ney, 2002; Blunsom et al., 2008), Margin Infused Relaxed Algorithm (MIRA) (Watanabe et al., 2007; Chiang et al., 2008b), or pairwise rank optimization (PRO) (Hopkins and May, 2011). They primarily differ in the mode of training; online or MERT-like batch, and in their objectives; max-margin (Taskar et al., 2004), conditional log-likelihood (or softmax loss) (Berger et al., 1996), risk (Smith and Eisner, 2006; Li and Eisner, 2009), or ranking (Ilcrbrich ct al., 1999).

We present an online learning algorithm based on stochastic gradient descent (SGD) with a larger batch size (Shalev-Shwartz et al., 2007). Like Hopkins and May (2011), we optimize ranking in n-best lists, but learn parameters in an online fashion. As proposed by Haddow et al. (2011), BLEU is approximately computed in the local batch, since BLEU is not linearly decomposed into a sentence-wise score (Chiang et al., 2008a), and optimization for sentence-BLEU does not always achieve optimal parameters for corpus-BLEU. Setting the larger batch size implies the more accurate corpus-BLEU, but at the cost of slower convergence of SGD. Therefore, we propose an optimized update method inspired by the passive-aggressive algorithm (Crammer et al., 2006), in which each parameter update is further rescaled considering the tradeoff between the amount of updates to the parameters and the ranking loss. Learning is efficiently parallelized by splitting training data among *shards* and by merging parameters in each round (McDonald et al., 2010). Instead of simple averaging, we perform an additional line search step to find the optimal merging across parallel jobs.

Experiments were carried out on the NIST 2008 Chinese-to-English Open MT task. We found significant gains over traditional MERT and other tuning algorithms, such as MIRA and PRO.

2 Statistical Machine Translation

SMT can be formulated as a maximization problem of finding the most likely translation e given an input sentence f using a set of parameters θ (Brown et al., 1993)

$$\hat{e} = \arg\max_{e} p(e|f;\theta). \quad (1)$$

Under this maximization setting, we assume that $p(\cdot)$ is represented by a linear combination of feature functions $\mathbf{h}(f,e)$ which are scaled by a set of parameters $\mathbf{w}$ (Och and Ney, 2002)

$$\hat{e} = \arg\max_{e} \mathbf{w}^{\top}\mathbf{h}(f,e). \quad (2)$$

Each element of $\mathbf{h}(\cdot)$ is a feature function which captures different aspects of translations, for instance, log of n-gram language model probability, the number of translated words or log of phrasal probability.

In this paper, we concentrate on the problem of learning $\mathbf{w}$, which is referred to as *tuning*. One of the standard methods for parameter tuning is minimum error rate training (Och, 2003) (MERT) which directly minimizes the task loss $\ell(\cdot)$, i.e. negative BLEU (Papineni et al., 2002), given training data $D = \{(f^1, \mathbf{e}^1), ..., (f^N, \mathbf{e}^N)\}$, sets of paired source sentence f^i and its reference translations $\mathbf{e}^i$

$$\hat{\mathbf{w}} = \arg\min_{\mathbf{w}} \ell(\left\{\arg\max_{e} \mathbf{w}^{\top}\mathbf{h}(f^i,e)\right\}_{i=1}^{N}, \{\mathbf{e}^i\}_{i=1}^{N}). \quad (3)$$

The objective in Equation 3 is discontinuous and non-convex, and it requires decoding of all the training data given $\mathbf{w}$. Therefore, MERT relies on a derivative-free unconstrained optimization method, such as Powell's method, which repeatedly chooses one direction to optimize using a line search procedure as in Algorithm 1. Expensive decoding is approximated by an n-best merging technique in which decoding is carried out in each epoch of iterations t and the maximization in Eq. 3 is approximated by search over the n-bests merged across iterations. The merged n-bests are also used in the line search procedure to efficiently draw the error surface for efficient computation of the outer minimization of Eq. 3.

Algorithm 1 MERT

1: Initialize $\mathbf{w}^1$
2: **for** $t = 1, ..., T$ **do** ▷ Or, until convergence
3: Generate n-bests using $\mathbf{w}^t$
4: Learn new $\mathbf{w}^{t+1}$ by Powell's method
5: **end for**
6: **return** $\mathbf{w}^{T+1}$

3 Online Rank Learning

3.1 Rank Learning

Instead of the direct task loss minimization of Eq. 3, we would like to find $\mathbf{w}$ by solving the L_2-regularized constrained minimization problem

$$\arg\min_{\mathbf{w}} \frac{\lambda}{2}\|\mathbf{w}\|_2^2 + \ell(\mathbf{w}; D) \quad (4)$$

where $\lambda > 0$ is a hyperparameter controlling the fitness to the data. The loss function $\ell(\cdot)$ we consider here is inspired by a pairwise ranking method (Hopkins and May, 2011) in which pairs of correct translation and incorrect translation are sampled from n-bests and suffer a hinge loss

$$\frac{1}{M(\mathbf{w}; D)} \sum_{(f,\mathbf{e})\in D} \sum_{e^*,e'} \max\left\{0, 1 - \mathbf{w}^{\top}\Phi(f, e^*, e')\right\} \quad (5)$$

where

$$e' \in \textsc{NBest}(\mathbf{w}; f) \setminus \textsc{Oracle}(\mathbf{w}; f, \mathbf{e})$$
$$e^* \in \textsc{Oracle}(\mathbf{w}; f, \mathbf{e})$$
$$\Phi(f, e^*, e') = \mathbf{h}(f, e^*) - \mathbf{h}(f, e').$$

$\textsc{NBest}(\cdot)$ is the n-best translations of f generated with the parameter $\mathbf{w}$, and $\textsc{Oracle}(\cdot)$ is a set of oracle translations chosen among $\textsc{NBest}(\cdot)$. Note that each e' (and e^*) implicitly represents a derivation consisting of a tuple (e', ϕ), where ϕ is a latent structure, i.e. phrases in a phrase-based SMT, but we omit ϕ for brevity. $M(\cdot)$ is a normalization constant which is equal to the number of paired loss terms $\Phi(f, e^*, e')$ in Equation 5. Since it is impossible to enumerate all possible translations, we follow the convention of approximating the domain of translation by n-bests. Unlike Hopkins and May (2011), we do not randomly sample from all the pairs in the n-best translations, but extract pairs by selecting one oracle translation and one other translation in the n-bests other than those in ORACLE($\cdot$). Oracle translations are selected by minimizing the task loss,

$$\ell(\{e' \in \text{NBEST}(\mathbf{w}; f^i)\}_{i=1}^N, \{\mathbf{e}^i\}_{i=1}^N)$$

i.e. negative BLEU, with respect to a set of reference translations $\mathbf{e}$. In order to compute oracles with corpus-BLEU, we apply a greedy search strategy over n-bests (Venugopal, 2005). Equation 5 can be easily interpreted as a constant loss "1" for choosing a wrong translation under current parameters $\mathbf{w}$, which is in contrast with the direct task-loss used in max-margin approach to structured output learning (Taskar et al., 2004).

As an alternative, we would also consider a softmax loss (Collins and Koo, 2005) represented by

$$\frac{1}{N} \sum_{(f,\mathbf{e}) \in D} -\log \frac{Z_{\text{O}}(\mathbf{w}; f, \mathbf{e})}{Z_{\text{N}}(\mathbf{w}; f)} \tag{6}$$

where

$$Z_{\text{O}}(\mathbf{w}; f, \mathbf{e}) = \textstyle\sum_{e^* \in \text{ORACLE}(\mathbf{w}; f, \mathbf{e})} \exp(\mathbf{w}^\top \mathbf{f}(f, e^*))$$
$$Z_{\text{N}}(\mathbf{w}; f) = \textstyle\sum_{e' \in \text{NBEST}(\mathbf{w}; f)} \exp(\mathbf{w}^\top \mathbf{f}(f, e')).$$

Equation 6 is a log-linear model used in common NLP tasks such as tagging, chunking and named entity recognition, but differ slightly in that multiple correct translations are discriminated from the others (Charniak and Johnson, 2005).

3.2 Online Approximation

Hopkins and May (2011) applied a MERT-like procedure in Alg. 1 in which Equation 4 was solved to obtain new parameters in each iteration. Here, we employ stochastic gradient descent (SGD) methods as presented in Algorithm 2 motivated by Pegasos (Shalev-Shwartz et al., 2007). In each iteration, we randomly permute D and choose a set of batches $B^t = \{b_1^t, ..., b_K^t\}$ with each b_j^t consisting of N/K training data. For each batch b in B^t, we generate n-bests from the source sentences in b and compute oracle translations from the newly created n-bests

Algorithm 2 Stochastic Gradient Descent

1: $k = 1, \mathbf{w}_1 \leftarrow \mathbf{0}$
2: **for** $t = 1, ..., T$ **do**
3: Choose $B_t = \{b_1^t, ..., b_K^t\}$ from D
4: **for** $b \in B_t$ **do**
5: Compute n-bests and oracles of b
6: Set learning rate η_k
7: $\mathbf{w}_{k+\frac{1}{2}} \leftarrow \mathbf{w}_k - \eta_k \nabla(\mathbf{w}_k; b)$
$\triangleright$ Our proposed algorithm solve Eq. 12 or 16
8: $\mathbf{w}_{k+1} \leftarrow \min\left\{1, \frac{1/\sqrt{\lambda}}{\|\mathbf{w}_{k+\frac{1}{2}}\|_2}\right\} \mathbf{w}_{k+\frac{1}{2}}$
9: $k \leftarrow k + 1$
10: **end for**
11: **end for**
12: **return** $\mathbf{w}_k$

(line 5) using a batch local corpus-BLEU (Haddow et al., 2011). Then, we optimize an approximated objective function

$$\arg\min_{\mathbf{w}} \frac{\lambda}{2}\|\mathbf{w}\|_2^2 + \ell(\mathbf{w}; b) \tag{7}$$

by replacing D with b in the objective of Eq. 4. The parameters $\mathbf{w}_k$ are updated by the sub-gradient of Equation 7, $\nabla(\mathbf{w}_k; b)$, scaled by the learning rate η_k (line 7). We use an exponential decayed learning rate $\eta_k = \eta_0 \alpha^{k/K}$, which converges very fast in practice (Tsuruoka et al., 2009)[1]. The sub-gradient of Eq.7 with the hinge loss of Eq. 5 is

$$\lambda \mathbf{w}_k - \frac{1}{M(\mathbf{w}_k; b)} \sum_{(f,\mathbf{e}) \in b} \sum_{e^*, e'} \Phi(f, e^*, e') \tag{8}$$

such that

$$1 - \mathbf{w}_k^\top \Phi(f, e^*, e') > 0. \tag{9}$$

We found that the normalization term by $M(\cdot)$ was very slow in convergence, thus, instead, we used $M'(\mathbf{w}; b)$, which was the number of paired loss terms satisfied the constraints in Equation 9. In the case of the softmax loss objective of Eq. 6, the sub-gradient is

$$\lambda \mathbf{w}_k \quad - \quad \frac{1}{|b|} \sum_{(f,\mathbf{e}) \in b} \frac{\partial}{\partial \mathbf{w}} \mathcal{L}(\mathbf{w}; f, \mathbf{e})\Big|_{\mathbf{w}=\mathbf{w}_k} \tag{10}$$

[1] We set $\alpha = 0.85$ and $\eta_0 = 0.2$ which converged well in our preliminary experiments.

where $\mathcal{L}(\mathbf{w}; f, \mathbf{e}) = \log(Z_{\mathrm{O}}(\mathbf{w}; f, \mathbf{e})/Z_{\mathrm{N}}(\mathbf{w}; f))$. After the parameter update, $\mathbf{w}_{k+\frac{1}{2}}$ is projected within the L_2-norm ball (Shalev-Shwartz et al., 2007).

Setting smaller batch size implies frequent updates to the parameters and a faster convergence. However, as briefly mentioned in Haddow et al. (2011), setting batch size to a smaller value, such as $|b| = 1$, does not work well in practice, since BLEU is devised for a corpus based evaluation, not for an individual sentence-wise evaluation, and it is not linearly decomposed into a sentence-wise score (Chiang et al., 2008a). Thus, the smaller batch size may also imply less accurate batch-local corpus-BLEU and incorrect oracle translation selections, which may lead to incorrect sub-gradient estimations or slower convergence. In the next section we propose an optimized parameter update which works well when setting a smaller batch size is impractical due to its task loss setting.

4 Optimized Online Rank Learning

4.1 Optimized Parameter Update

In line 7 of Algorithm 2, parameters are updated by the sub-gradient of each training instance in a batch b. When the sub-gradient in Equation 8 is employed, the update procedure can be rearranged as

$$\mathbf{w}_{k+\frac{1}{2}} \leftarrow (1-\lambda\eta_k)\mathbf{w}_k + \sum_{(f,\mathbf{e})\in b, e^*, e'} \frac{\eta_k}{M(\mathbf{w}_k; b)} \Phi(f, e^*, e') \tag{11}$$

in which each individual loss term $\Phi(\cdot)$ is scaled uniformly by a constant $\eta_k/M(\cdot)$.

Instead of the uniform scaling, we propose to update the parameters in two steps: First, we suffer the sub-gradient from the L_2 regularization

$$\mathbf{w}_{k+\frac{1}{4}} \leftarrow (1 - \lambda\eta_k)\mathbf{w}_k.$$

Second, we solve the following problem

$$\arg\min_{\mathbf{w}} \frac{1}{2}\|\mathbf{w} - \mathbf{w}_{k+\frac{1}{4}}\|_2^2 + \eta_k \sum_{(f,\mathbf{e})\in b, e^*, e'} \xi_{f,e^*,e'} \tag{12}$$

such that

$$\mathbf{w}^\top \Phi(f, e^*, e') \geq 1 - \xi_{f,e^*,e'}$$
$$\xi_{f,e^*,e'} \geq 0.$$

The problem is inspired by the passive-aggressive algorithm (Crammer et al., 2006) in which new parameters are derived through the tradeoff between the amount of updates to the parameters and the margin-based loss. Note that the objective in MIRA is represented by

$$\arg\min_{\mathbf{w}} \frac{\lambda}{2}\|\mathbf{w} - \mathbf{w}_k\|_2^2 + \sum_{(f,\mathbf{e})\in b, e^*, e'} \xi_{f,e^*,e'} \tag{13}$$

If we treat $\mathbf{w}_{k+\frac{1}{4}}$ as our previous parameters and set $\lambda = 1/\eta_k$, they are very similar. Unlike MIRA, the learning rate η_k is directly used as a tradeoff parameter which decays as training proceeds, and the sub-gradient of the global L_2 regularization term is also combined in the problem through $\mathbf{w}_{k+\frac{1}{4}}$.

The Lagrangian dual of Equation 12 is

$$\arg\min_{\tau_{e^*,e'}} \frac{1}{2}\| \sum_{(f,\mathbf{e})\in b, e^*, e'} \tau_{e^*,e'}\Phi(f, e^*, e')\|_2^2 - \sum_{(f,\mathbf{e})\in b, e^*, e'} \tau_{e^*,e'} \left\{1 - \mathbf{w}_{k+\frac{1}{4}}^\top \Phi(f, e^*, e')\right\} \tag{14}$$

subject to

$$\sum_{(f,\mathbf{e})\in b, e^*, e'} \tau_{e^*,e'} \leq \eta_k.$$

We used a dual coordinate descent algorithm (Hsieh et al., 2008)[2] to efficiently solve the quadratic program (QP) in Equation 14, leading to an update

$$\mathbf{w}_{k+\frac{1}{2}} \leftarrow \mathbf{w}_{k+\frac{1}{4}} + \sum_{(f,\mathbf{e})\in b, e^*, e'} \tau_{e^*,e'}\Phi(f, e^*, e'). \tag{15}$$

When compared with Equation 11, the update procedure in Equation 15 rescales the contribution from each sub-gradient through the Lagrange multipliers $\tau_{e^*,e'}$. Note that if we set $\tau_{e^*,e'} = \eta_k/M(\cdot)$, we satisfy the constraints in Eq. 14, and recover the update in Eq. 11.

In the same manner as Eq. 12, we derive an optimized update procedure for the softmax loss, which replaces the update with Equation 10, by solving the

[2] Specifically, each parameter is bound constrained $0 \leq \tau \leq \eta_k$ but is not summation constrained $\sum \tau \leq \eta_k$. Thus, we renormalize τ after optimization.

following problem

$$\arg\min_{\mathbf{w}} \frac{1}{2}\|\mathbf{w} - \mathbf{w}_{k+\frac{1}{4}}\|_2^2 + \eta_k \sum_{(f,\mathbf{e})\in b} \xi_f \quad (16)$$

such that

$$\mathbf{w}^\top \Psi(\mathbf{w}_k; f, \mathbf{e}) \geq -\mathcal{L}(\mathbf{w}_k; f, \mathbf{e}) - \xi_f$$
$$\xi_f \geq 0$$

in which $\Psi(\mathbf{w}'; f, \mathbf{e}) = \frac{\partial}{\partial \mathbf{w}} \mathcal{L}(\mathbf{w}; f, \mathbf{e})\big|_{\mathbf{w}=\mathbf{w}'}$. Equation 16 can be interpreted as a cutting-plane approximation for the objective of Eq. 7, in which the original objective of Eq. 7 with the softmax loss in Eq. 6 is approximated by $|b|$ linear constraints derived from the sub-gradients at point $\mathbf{w}_k$ (Teo et al., 2010). Eq. 16 is efficiently solved by its Lagrange dual, leading to an update

$$\mathbf{w}_{k+\frac{1}{2}} \leftarrow \mathbf{w}_{k+\frac{1}{4}} + \sum_{(f,\mathbf{e})\in b} \tau_f \Psi(\mathbf{w}_k; f, \mathbf{e}) \quad (17)$$

subject to $\sum_{(f,\mathbf{e})\in b} \tau_f \leq \eta_k$. Similar to Eq. 15, the parameter update by $\Psi(\cdot)$ is rescaled by its Lagrange multipliers τ_f in place of the uniform scale of $1/|b|$ in the sub-gradient of Eq. 10.

4.2 Line Search for Parameter Mixing

For faster training, we employ an efficient parallel training strategy proposed by McDonald et al. (2010). The training data D is split into S disjoint *shards*, $\{D_1, ..., D_S\}$. Each shard learns its own parameters in each single epoch t and performs parameter mixing by averaging parameters across shards.

We propose an optimized parallel training in Algorithm 3 which performs better mixing with respect to the task loss, i.e. negative BLEU. In line 5, $\mathbf{w}^{t+\frac{1}{2}}$ is computed by averaging $\mathbf{w}^{t+1,s}$ from all the shards after local training using their own data D_s. Then, the new parameters $\mathbf{w}^{t+1}$ are obtained by linearly interpolating with the parameters from the previous epoch $\mathbf{w}^t$. The linear interpolation weight ρ is efficiently computed by a line search procedure which directly minimizes the negative corpus-BLEU. The procedure is exactly the same as the line search strategy employed in MERT using $\mathbf{w}^t$ as our starting point with the direction $\mathbf{w}^{t+\frac{1}{2}} - \mathbf{w}^t$. The idea of using the line search procedure is to find the optimum parameters under corpus-BLEU without a

Algorithm 3 Distributed training with line search

1: $\mathbf{w}^1 \leftarrow \mathbf{0}$
2: **for** $t = 1, ..., T$ **do**
3: $\quad \mathbf{w}^{t,s} \leftarrow \mathbf{w}^t$ ▷ Distribute parameters
4: $\quad$ Each shard learns $\mathbf{w}^{t+1,s}$ using D_s ▷ Line 3–10 in Alg. 2
5: $\quad \mathbf{w}^{t+\frac{1}{2}} \leftarrow 1/S \sum_s \mathbf{w}^{t+1,s}$ ▷ Mixing
6: $\quad \mathbf{w}^{t+1} \leftarrow (1-\rho)\mathbf{w}^t + \rho\mathbf{w}^{t+\frac{1}{2}}$ ▷ Line search
7: **end for**
8: **return** $\mathbf{w}^{T+1}$

batch-local approximation. Unlike MERT, however, we do not memorize nor merge all the n-bests generated across iterations, but keep only n-bests in each iteration for faster training and for memory saving. Thus, the optimum ρ obtained by the line search may be suboptimal in terms of the training objective, but potentially better than averaging for minimizing the final task loss.

5 Experiments

Experiments were carried out on the NIST 2008 Chinese-to-English Open MT task. The training data consists of nearly 5.6 million bilingual sentences and additional monolingual data, English Gigaword, for 5-gram language model estimation. MT02 and MT06 were used as our tuning and development testing, and MT08 as our final testing with all data consisting of four reference translations.

We use an in-house developed hypergraph-based toolkit for training and decoding with synchronous-CFGs (SCFG) for hierarchical phrase-bassed SMT (Chiang, 2007). The system employs 14 features, consisting of standard Hiero-style features (Chiang, 2007), and a set of indicator features, such as the number of synchronous-rules in a derivation. Two 5-gram language models are also included, one from the English-side of bitexts and the other from English Gigaword, with features counting the number of out-of-vocabulary words in each model (Dyer et al., 2011). For faster experiments, we precomputed translation forests inspired by Xiao et al. (2011). Instead of generating forests from bitexts in each iteration, we construct and save translation forests by intersecting the source side of SCFG with input sentences and by keeping the target side of the intersected rules. n-bests are generated from the precomputed forests on the fly using the forest rescoring framework (Huang and Chiang, 2007) with additional non-local features, such as 5-gram language models.

We compared four algorithms, MERT, PRO, MIRA and our proposed online settings, online rank optimization (ORO). Note that ORO without our optimization methods in Section 4 is essentially the same as Pegasos, but differs in that we employ the algorithm for ranking structured outputs with varied objectives, hinge loss or softmax loss[3]. MERT learns parameters from forests (Kumar et al., 2009) with 4 restarts and 8 random directions in each iteration. We experimented on a variant of PRO[4], in which the objective in Eq. 4 with the hinge loss of Eq. 5 was solved in each iteration in line 4 of Alg. 1 using an off-the-shelf solver[5]. Our MIRA solves the problem in Equation 13 in line 7 of Alg. 2. For a systematic comparison, we used our exhaustive oracle translation selection method in Section 3 for PRO, MIRA and ORO. For each learning algorithm, we ran 30 iterations and generated duplicate removed 1,000-best translations in each iteration. The hyperparameter λ for PRO and ORO was set to 10^{-5}, selected from among $\{10^{-3}, 10^{-4}, 10^{-5}\}$, and 10^2 for MIRA, chosen from $\{10, 10^2, 10^3\}$ by preliminary testing on MT06. Both decoding and learning are parallelized and run on 8 cores. Each online learning took roughly 12 hours, and PRO took one day. It took roughly 3 days for MERT with 20 iterations. Translation results are measured by case sensitive BLEU.

Table 1 presents our main results. Among the parameters from multiple iterations, we report the outputs that performed the best on MT06. With Moses (Koehn et al., 2007), we achieved 30.36 and 23.64 BLEU for MT06 and MT08, respectively. We denote the "O-" prefix for the optimized parameter updates discussed in Section 4.1, and the "-L" suffix

	MT06	MT08
MERT	31.45†	24.13†
PRO	31.76†	24.43†
MIRA-L	31.42†	24.15†
ORO-L_{hinge}	29.76	21.96
O-ORO-L_{hinge}	**32.06**	**24.95**
ORO-$L_{softmax}$	30.77	23.07
O-ORO-$L_{softmax}$	31.16†	23.20

Table 1: Translation results by BLEU. Results without significant differences from the MERT baseline are marked †. The numbers in boldface are significantly better than the MERT baseline (both measured by the bootstrap resampling (Koehn, 2004) with $p > 0.05$).

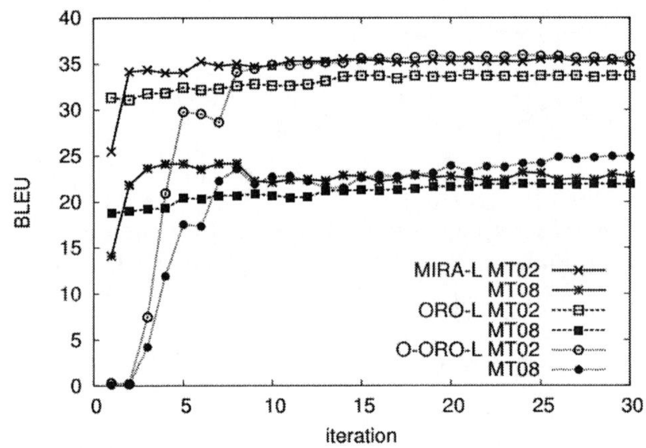

Figure 1: Learning curves for three algorithms, MIRA-L, ORO-L_{hinge} and O-ORO-L_{hinge}.

for parameter mixing by line search as described in Section 4.2. The batch size was set to 16 for MIRA and ORO. In general, our PRO and MIRA settings achieved the results very comparable to MERT. The hinge-loss and softmax objective OROs were lower than those of the three baselines. The softmax objective with the optimized update (O-ORO-$L_{softmax}$) performed better than the non-optimized version, but it was still lower than our baselines. In the case of the hinge-loss objective with the optimized update (O-ORO-L_{hinge}), the gain in MT08 was significant, and achieved the best BLEU.

Figure 1 presents the learning curves for three algorithms MIRA-L, ORO-L_{hinge} and O-ORO-L_{hinge}, in which the performance is measured by BLEU

[3]The other major difference is the use of a simpler learning rate, $\frac{1}{\lambda k}$, which was very slow in our preliminary studies.

[4]Hopkins and May (2011) minimized logistic loss sampled from the merged n-bests, and sentence-BLEU was used for determining ranks.

[5]We used liblinear (Fan et al., 2008) at `http://www.csie.ntu.edu.tw/~cjlin/liblinear` with the solver type of 3.

	MT06	MT08
MIRA	30.95	23.06
MIRA-L	31.42†	24.15†
$\text{ORO}_{\text{hinge}}$	29.09	21.93
$\text{ORO-L}_{\text{hinge}}$	29.76	21.96
$\text{ORO}_{\text{softmax}}$	30.80	23.06
$\text{ORO-L}_{\text{softmax}}$	30.77	23.07
$\text{O-ORO}_{\text{hinge}}$	31.15†	23.20
$\text{O-ORO-L}_{\text{hinge}}$	**32.06**	**24.95**
$\text{O-ORO}_{\text{softmax}}$	31.40†	23.93†
$\text{O-ORO-L}_{\text{softmax}}$	31.16†	23.20

Table 2: Parameter mixing by line search.

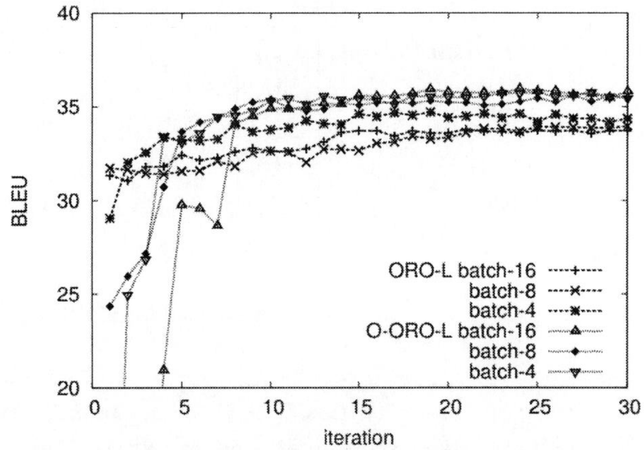

Figure 2: Learning curves on MT02 for $\text{ORO-L}_{\text{hinge}}$ and $\text{O-ORO-L}_{\text{hinge}}$ with different batch size.

on the training data (MT02) and on the test data (MT08). MIRA-L quickly converges and is slightly unstable in the test set, while $\text{ORO-L}_{\text{hinge}}$ is very stable and slow to converge, but with low performance on the training and test data. The stable learning curve in $\text{ORO-L}_{\text{hinge}}$ is probably influenced by our learning rate parameter $\eta_0 = 0.2$, which will be investigated in future work. $\text{O-ORO-L}_{\text{hinge}}$ is less stable in several iterations, but steadily improves its BLEU. The behavior is justified by our optimized update procedure, in which the learning rate η_k is used as a tradeoff parameter. Thus, it tries a very aggressive update at the early stage of training, but eventually becomes conservative in updating parameters.

Next, we compare the effect of line search for parameter mixing in Table 2. Line search was very effective for MIRA and $\text{O-ORO}_{\text{hinge}}$, but less effective for the others. Since the line search procedure directly minimizes a task loss, not objectives, this may hurt the performance for the softmax objective, where the margins between the correct and incorrect translations are softly penalized.

Finally, Table 3 shows the effect of batch size selected from $\{1, 4, 8, 16\}$. There seems to be no clear trends in MIRA, and we achieved BLEU score of 24.58 by setting the batch size to 8. Clearly, setting smaller batch size is better for ORO, but it is the reverse for the optimized variants of both the hinge and softmax objectives. Figure 2 compares $\text{ORO-L}_{\text{hinge}}$ and $\text{O-ORO-L}_{\text{hinge}}$ on MT02 with different batch size settings. $\text{ORO-L}_{\text{hinge}}$ converges faster when the batch size is smaller and fine tuning of the learning rate parameter will be required for a larger batch size. As discussed in Section 3, the smaller batch size means frequent updates to parameters and a faster convergence, but potentially leads to a poor performance since the corpus-BLEU is approximately computed in a local batch. Our optimized update algorithms address the problem by adjusting the tradeoff between the amount of update to parameters and the loss, and perform better for larger batch sizes with a more accurate corpus-BLEU.

6 Related Work

Our work is largely inspired by pairwise rank optimization (Hopkins and May, 2011), but runs in an online fashion similar to (Watanabe et al., 2007; Chiang et al., 2008b). Major differences come from the corpus-BLEU computation used to select oracle translations. Instead of the sentence-BLEU used by Hopkins and May (2011) or the corpus-BLEU statistics accumulated from previous translations generated by different parameters (Watanabe et al., 2007; Chiang et al., 2008b), we used a simple batch local corpus-BLEU (Haddow et al., 2011) in the same way as an online approximation to the objectives. An alternative is the use of a Taylor series approximation (Smith and Eisner, 2006; Rosti et al., 2011), which was not investigated in this paper.

Training is performed by SGD with a parameter projection method (Shalev-Shwartz et al., 2007). Slower training incurred by the larger batch size

	MT06				MT08			
batch size	1	4	8	16	1	4	8	16
MIRA-L	31.28†	31.53†	31.63†	31.42†	23.46	23.97†	**24.58**	24.15†
ORO-L_{hinge}	31.32†	30.69	29.61	29.76	23.63	23.12	22.07	21.96
O-ORO-L_{hinge}	31.44†	31.54†	31.35†	**32.06**	23.72	24.02†	24.28†	**24.95**
ORO-$L_{softmax}$	25.10	31.66†	31.31†	30.77	19.27	23.59	23.50	23.07
O-ORO-$L_{softmax}$	31.15†	31.17†	30.90	31.16†	23.62	23.31	23.03	23.20

Table 3: Translation results with varied batch size.

for more accurate corpus-BLEU is addressed by optimally scaling parameter updates in the spirit of a passive-aggressive algorithm (Crammer et al., 2006). The derived algorithm is very similar to MIRA, but differs in that the learning rate is employed as a hyperparameter for controlling the fitness to training data which decays when training proceeds. The non-uniform sub-gradient based update is also employed in an exponentiated gradient (EG) algorithm (Kivinen and Warmuth, 1997; Kivinen and Warmuth, 2001) in which parameter updates are maximum-likely estimated using an exponentially combined sub-gradients. In contrast, our approach relies on an ultraconservative update which tradeoff between the amount of updates performed to the parameters and the progress made for the objectives by solving a QP subproblem.

Unlike a complex parallelization by Chiang et al. (2008b), in which support vectors are asynchronously exchanged among parallel jobs, training is efficiently and easily carried out by distributing training data among shards and by mixing parameters in each iteration (McDonald et al., 2010). Rather than simple averaging, new parameters are derived by linearly interpolating with the previously mixed parameters, and its weight is determined by the line search algorithm employed in (Och, 2003).

7 Conclusion

We proposed a variant of an online learning algorithm inspired by a batch learning algorithm of (Hopkins and May, 2011). Training is performed by SGD with a parameter projection (Shalev-Shwartz et al., 2007) using a larger batch size for a more accurate batch local corpus-BLEU estimation. Parameter updates in each iteration is further optimized using an idea from a passive-aggressive algorithm (Crammer et al., 2006). Learning is efficiently parallelized (McDonald et al., 2010) and the locally learned parameters are mixed by an additional line search step. Experiments indicate that better performance was achieved by our optimized updates and by the more sophisticated parameter mixing.

In future work, we would like to investigate other objectives with a more direct task loss, such as max-margin (Taskar et al., 2004), risk (Smith and Eisner, 2006) or softmax-loss (Gimpel and Smith, 2010), and different regularizers, such as L_1-norm for a sparse solution. Instead of n-best approximations, we may directly employ forests for a better conditional log-likelihood estimation (Li and Eisner, 2009). We would also like to explore other mixing strategies for parallel training which can directly minimize the training objectives like those proposed for a cutting-plane algorithm (Franc and Sonnenburg, 2008).

Acknowledgments

We would like to thank anonymous reviewers and our colleagues for helpful comments and discussion.

References

Adam L. Berger, Vincent J. Della Pietra, and Stephen A. Della Pietra. 1996. A maximum entropy approach to natural language processing. *Computational Linguistics*, 22:39–71, March.

Phil Blunsom, Trevor Cohn, and Miles Osborne. 2008. A discriminative latent variable model for statistical machine translation. In *Proc. of ACL-08: HLT*, pages 200–208, Columbus, Ohio, June.

Peter F. Brown, Vincent J. Della Pietra, Stephen A. Della Pietra, and Robert L. Mercer. 1993. The mathematics of statistical machine translation: parameter estimation. *Computational Linguistics*, 19:263–311, June.

Eugene Charniak and Mark Johnson. 2005. Coarse-to-fine n-best parsing and maxent discriminative reranking. In *Proc. of ACL 2005*, pages 173–180, Ann Arbor, Michigan, June.

David Chiang, Steve DeNeefe, Yee Seng Chan, and Hwee Tou Ng. 2008a. Decomposability of translation metrics for improved evaluation and efficient algorithms. In *Proc. of EMNLP 2008*, pages 610–619, Honolulu, Hawaii, October.

David Chiang, Yuval Marton, and Philip Resnik. 2008b. Online large-margin training of syntactic and structural translation features. In *Proc. of EMNLP 2008*, pages 224–233, Honolulu, Hawaii, October.

David Chiang. 2007. Hierarchical phrase-based translation. *Computational Linguistics*, 33(2):201–228.

Jonathan H. Clark, Chris Dyer, Alon Lavie, and Noah A. Smith. 2011. Better hypothesis testing for statistical machine translation: Controlling for optimizer instability. In *Proc. of ACL 2011*, pages 176–181, Portland, Oregon, USA, June.

Michael Collins and Terry Koo. 2005. Discriminative reranking for natural language parsing. *Computational Linguistics*, 31:25–70, March.

Koby Crammer, Ofer Dekel, Joseph Keshet, Shai Shalev-Shwartz, and Yoram Singer. 2006. Online passive-aggressive algorithms. *Journal of Machine Learning Research*, 7:551–585, March.

Chris Dyer, Kevin Gimpel, Jonathan H. Clark, and Noah A. Smith. 2011. The cmu-ark german-english translation system. In *Proc. of SMT 2011*, pages 337–343, Edinburgh, Scotland, July.

Rong-En Fan, Kai-Wei Chang, Cho-Jui Hsieh, Xiang-Rui Wang, and Chih-Jen Lin. 2008. Liblinear: A library for large linear classification. *Journal of Machine Learning Research*, 9:1871–1874, June.

Vojtěch Franc and Soeren Sonnenburg. 2008. Optimized cutting plane algorithm for support vector machines. In *Proc. of ICML '08*, pages 320–327, Helsinki, Finland.

Michel Galley and Chris Quirk. 2011. Optimal search for minimum error rate training. In *Proc. of EMNLP 2011*, pages 38–49, Edinburgh, Scotland, UK., July.

Kevin Gimpel and Noah A. Smith. 2010. Softmax-margin crfs: Training log-linear models with cost functions. In *Proc. of NAACL-HLT 2010*, pages 733–736, Los Angeles, California, June.

Barry Haddow, Abhishek Arun, and Philipp Koehn. 2011. Samplerank training for phrase-based machine translation. In *Proc. of SMT 2011*, pages 261–271, Edinburgh, Scotland, July.

Ralf Herbrich, Thore Graepel, and Klaus Obermayer. 1999. Support vector learning for ordinal regression. In *In Proc. of International Conference on Artificial Neural Networks*, pages 97–102.

Mark Hopkins and Jonathan May. 2011. Tuning as ranking. In *Proc. of EMNLP 2011*, pages 1352–1362, Edinburgh, Scotland, UK., July.

Cho-Jui Hsieh, Kai-Wei Chang, Chih-Jen Lin, S. Sathiya Keerthi, and S. Sundararajan. 2008. A dual coordinate descent method for large-scale linear svm. In *Proc. of ICML '08*, pages 408–415, Helsinki, Finland.

Liang Huang and David Chiang. 2007. Forest rescoring: Faster decoding with integrated language models. In *Proc. of ACL 2007*, pages 144–151, Prague, Czech Republic, June.

Jyrki Kivinen and Manfred K. Warmuth. 1997. Exponentiated gradient versus gradient descent for linear predictors. *Information and Computation*, 132(1):1–63, January.

J. Kivinen and M. K. Warmuth. 2001. Relative loss bounds for multidimensional regression problems. *Machine Learning*, 45(3):301–329, December.

Philipp Koehn, Hieu Hoang, Alexandra Birch, Chris Callison-Burch, Marcello Federico, Nicola Bertoldi, Brooke Cowan, Wade Shen, Christine Moran, Richard Zens, Chris Dyer, Ondrej Bojar, Alexandra Constantin, and Evan Herbst. 2007. Moses: Open source toolkit for statistical machine translation. In *Procc of ACL 2007*, pages 177–180, Prague, Czech Republic, June.

Philipp Koehn. 2004. Statistical significance tests for machine translation evaluation. In *Proc. of EMNLP 2004*, pages 388–395, Barcelona, Spain, July.

Shankar Kumar, Wolfgang Macherey, Chris Dyer, and Franz Och. 2009. Efficient minimum error rate training and minimum bayes-risk decoding for translation hypergraphs and lattices. In *Proc. of ACL-IJCNLP 2009*, pages 163–171, Suntec, Singapore, August.

Zhifei Li and Jason Eisner. 2009. First- and second-order expectation semirings with applications to minimum-risk training on translation forests. In *Proc. of EMNLP 2009*, pages 40–51, Singapore, August.

Percy Liang, Alexandre Bouchard-Côté, Dan Klein, and Ben Taskar. 2006. An end-to-end discriminative approach to machine translation. In *Proc. of COLING/ACL 2006*, pages 761–768, Sydney, Australia, July.

Ryan McDonald, Keith Hall, and Gideon Mann. 2010. Distributed training strategies for the structured perceptron. In *Proc. of NAACL-HLT 2010*, pages 456–464, Los Angeles, California, June.

Robert C. Moore and Chris Quirk. 2008. Random restarts in minimum error rate training for statistical machine translation. In *Proc. of COLING 2008*, pages 585–592, Manchester, UK, August.

Franz Josef Och and Hermann Ney. 2002. Discriminative training and maximum entropy models for statistical machine translation. In *Proc. of ACL 2002*, pages 295–302, Philadelphia, July.

Franz Josef Och. 2003. Minimum error rate training in statistical machine translation. In *Proc. of ACL 2003*, pages 160–167, Sapporo, Japan, July.

Kishore Papineni, Salim Roukos, Todd Ward, and Wei-Jing Zhu. 2002. Bleu: a method for automatic evaluation of machine translation. In *Proc. of ACL 2002*, pages 311–318, Philadelphia, Pennsylvania, USA, July.

Antti-Veikko Rosti, Bing Zhang, Spyros Matsoukas, and Richard Schwartz. 2011. Expected bleu training for graphs: Bbn system description for wmt11 system combination task. In *Proc. of SMT 2011*, pages 159–165, Edinburgh, Scotland, July.

Shai Shalev-Shwartz, Yoram Singer, and Nathan Srebro. 2007. Pegasos: Primal estimated sub-gradient solver for svm. In *Proc. of ICML '07*, pages 807–814, Corvalis, Oregon.

David A. Smith and Jason Eisner. 2006. Minimum risk annealing for training log-linear models. In *Proc. of COLING/ACL 2006*, pages 787–794, Sydney, Australia, July.

Ben Taskar, Dan Klein, Mike Collins, Daphne Koller, and Christopher Manning. 2004. Max-margin parsing. In *Proc. of EMNLP 2004*, pages 1–8, Barcelona, Spain, July.

Choon Hui Teo, S.V.N. Vishwanthan, Alex J. Smola, and Quoc V. Le. 2010. Bundle methods for regularized risk minimization. *Journal of Machine Learning Research*, 11:311–365, March.

Yoshimasa Tsuruoka, Jun'ichi Tsujii, and Sophia Ananiadou. 2009. Stochastic gradient descent training for l1-regularized log-linear models with cumulative penalty. In *Proc. of ACL-IJCNLP 2009*, pages 477–485, Suntec, Singapore, August.

Ashish Venugopal. 2005. Considerations in maximum mutual information and minimum classification error training for statistical machine translation. In *Proc. of EAMT-05*, page 3031.

Taro Watanabe, Jun Suzuki, Hajime Tsukada, and Hideki Isozaki. 2007. Online large-margin training for statistical machine translation. In *Proc. of EMNLP-CoNLL 2007*, pages 764–773, Prague, Czech Republic, June.

Xinyan Xiao, Yang Liu, Qun Liu, and Shouxun Lin. 2011. Fast generation of translation forest for large-scale smt discriminative training. In *Proc. of EMNLP 2011*, pages 880–888, Edinburgh, Scotland, UK., July.

Every sensible extended top-down tree transducer is a multi bottom-up tree transducer

Andreas Maletti*
Institute for Natural Language Processing, Universität Stuttgart
Pfaffenwaldring 5b, 70569 Stuttgart, Germany
andreas.maletti@ims.uni-stuttgart.de

Abstract

A tree transformation is sensible if the size of each output tree is uniformly bounded by a linear function in the size of the corresponding input tree. Every sensible tree transformation computed by an arbitrary weighted extended top-down tree transducer can also be computed by a weighted multi bottom-up tree transducer. This further motivates weighted multi bottom-up tree transducers as suitable translation models for syntax-based machine translation.

1 Introduction

Several different translation models are used in syntax-based statistical machine translation. Koehn (2010) presents an introduction to statistical machine translation, and Knight (2007) presents an overview of syntax-based statistical machine translation. The oldest and best-studied tree transformation device is the top-down tree transducer of Rounds (1970) and Thatcher (1970). Gécseg and Steinby (1984) and Fülöp and Vogler (2009) present the existing results on the unweighted and weighted model, respectively. Knight (2007) promotes the use of weighted extended top-down tree transducers (XTOP), which have also been implemented in the toolkit TIBURON by May and Knight (2006) [more detail is reported by May (2010)]. In the context of bimorphisms, Arnold and Dauchet (1976) investigated XTOP, and Lilin (1978) and Arnold and Dauchet (1982) investigated multi bottom-up tree transducers (MBOT) [as k-morphisms]. Recently, weighted XTOP and MBOT, which are the central devices in this contribution, were investigated by Maletti (2011a) in the context of statistical machine translation.

Several tree transformation devices are used as translation models in statistical machine translation. Chiang (2007) uses synchronous context-free grammars, which force translations to be very similar as observed by Eisner (2003) and Shieber (2004). This deficiency is overcome by synchronous tree substitution grammars, which are state-less linear and nondeleting XTOP. Recently, Maletti (2010b) proposed MBOT, and Zhang et al. (2008b) and Sun et al. (2009) proposed the even more powerful synchronous tree-sequence substitution grammars. Those two models allow certain translation discontinuities, and the former device also offers computational benefits over linear and nondeleting XTOP as argued by Maletti (2010b).

The simplicity of XTOP makes them very appealing as translation models. In 2010 the ATANLP participants [workshop at ACL] identified 'copying' as the most exciting and promising feature of XTOP, but unrestricted copying can lead to an undesirable explosion of the size of the translation. According to Engelfriet and Maneth (2003) a tree transformation has linear size-increase if the size of each output tree is linearly bounded by the size of its corresponding input tree. The author believes that this is a very sensible restriction that intuitively makes sense and at the same time suitably limits the copying power of XTOP.

We show that every sensible tree transformation

*The author was supported by the German Research Foundation (DFG) grant MA 4959/1-1.

that can be computed by an XTOP can also be computed by an MBOT. For example, linear XTOP (i.e., no copying) compute only sensible tree transformations, and Maletti (2008) shows that for each linear XTOP there exists an equivalent MBOT. Here, we do not make any restrictions on the XTOP besides some sanity conditions (see Section 3). In particular, we consider copying XTOP. If we accept the restriction to linear size-increase tree transformation, then our main result further motivates MBOT as a suitable translation model for syntax-based machine translation because MBOT can implement each reasonable (even copying) XTOP. In addition, our result allows us to show that each reasonable XTOP preserves regularity under backward application. As demonstrated by May et al. (2010) backward application is the standard application of XTOP in the machine translation pipeline, and preservation of regularity is the essential property for several of the evaluation algorithms of May et al. (2010).

2 Notation

We start by introducing our notation for trees, whose nodes are labeled by elements of an alphabet Σ and a set V. However, only leaves can be labeled by elements of V. For every set T, we let

$$\Sigma(T) = \{\sigma(t_1, \dots, t_k) \mid \sigma \in \Sigma, t_1, \dots, t_k \in T\} ,$$

which contains all trees with a Σ-labeled root and direct successors in T. The set $T_\Sigma(V)$ of *Σ-trees with V-leaves* is the smallest set T such that $V \cup \Sigma(T) \subseteq T$. We use $X = \{x_1, x_2, \dots\}$ as a set of formal *variables*.

Each node of the tree $t \in T_\Sigma(V)$ is identified by a *position* $p \in \mathbb{N}_+$, which is a sequence of positive integers. The root is at position ε (the empty string), and the position ip with $i \in \mathbb{N}_+$ and $p \in \mathbb{N}_+^*$ is the position p in the i-th direct subtree. The set $\text{pos}(t)$ contains all positions of t, and the *size* of t is $|t| = |\text{pos}(t)|$. For each $p \in \text{pos}(t)$, the *label* of t at p is $t(p)$. Given a set $L \subseteq \Sigma \cup V$ of labels, we let $\text{pos}_L(t) = \{p \in \text{pos}(t) \mid t(p) \in L\}$ be the positions with L-labels. We write $\text{pos}_l(t)$ for $\text{pos}_{\{l\}}(t)$ for each $l \in L$. Finally, we write $t[u]_p$ for the tree obtained from t by replacing the subtree at position p by the tree $u \in T_\Sigma(V)$.

The following notions refer to the variables X. The tree $t \in T_\Sigma(V)$ [potentially $V \cap X = \emptyset$] is *linear* if every $x \in X$ occurs at most once in t (i.e., $|\text{pos}_x(t)| \leq 1$). Moreover,

$$\text{var}(t) = \{x \in X \mid \text{pos}_x(t) \neq \emptyset\}$$

contains the variables that occur in t. A *substitution* θ is a mapping $\theta \colon X \to T_\Sigma(V)$. When applied to t, it returns the tree $t\theta$, which is obtained from t by replacing all occurrences of $x \in X$ in t by $\theta(x)$. Our notions for trees are illustrated in Figure 1.

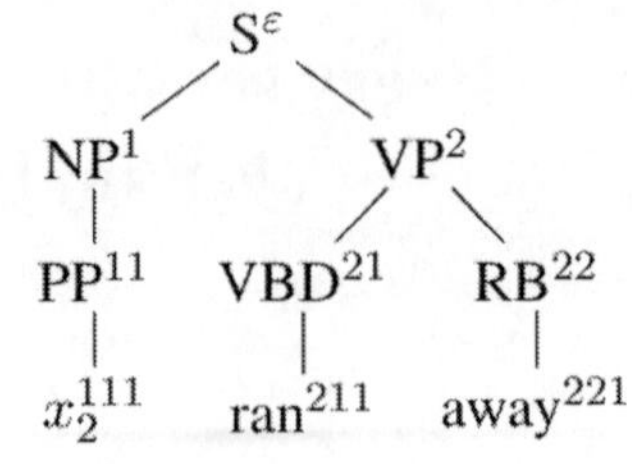

Figure 1: The tree t (with positions indicated as superscripts) is linear and $\text{var}(t) = \{x_2\}$. The tree $t[\text{He}]_{111}$ is the same tree with x_2 replaced by 'He'.

Finally, we present *weighted tree grammars* (WTG) as defined by Fülöp and Vogler (2009), who defined it for arbitrary semirings as weight structures. In contrast, our weights are always nonnegative reals, which form the semiring $(\mathbb{R}_+, +, \cdot, 0, 1)$ and are used in probabilistic grammars. For each weight assignment $f \colon T \to \mathbb{R}_+$, we let

$$\text{supp}(f) = \{t \in T \mid f(t) \neq 0\} .$$

WTG offer an efficient representation of weighted forests (i.e., set of weighted trees), which is even more efficient than the packed forests of Mi et al. (2008) because they can be minimized efficiently using an algorithm of Maletti and Quernheim (2011). In particular, WTG can share more than equivalent subtrees and can even represent infinite sets of trees. A WTG is a system $G = (Q, \Sigma, q_0, P, \text{wt})$ with

- a finite set Q of *states* (nonterminals),
- an alphabet Σ of *symbols*,
- a *starting state* $q_0 \in Q$,
- a finite set P of *productions* $q \to r$, where $q \in Q$ and $r \in T_\Sigma(Q) \setminus Q$, and
- a mapping $\text{wt} \colon P \to \mathbb{R}_+$ that assigns *production weights*.

Without loss of generality, we assume that we can distinguish states and symbols (i.e., $Q \cap \Sigma = \emptyset$). For all $\xi, \zeta \in T_\Sigma(Q)$ and a production $\rho = q \to r$,

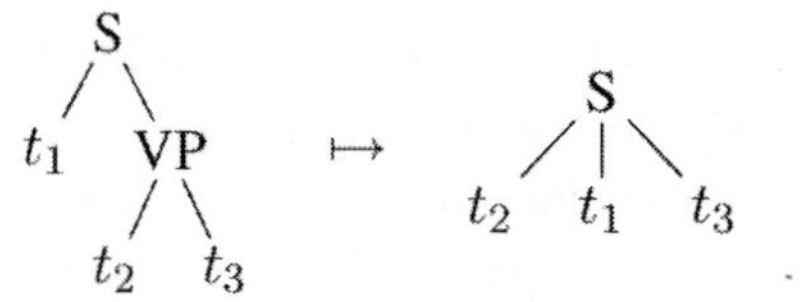

Figure 2: Example rotation. In principle, such rotations are required in the translation from English to Arabic.

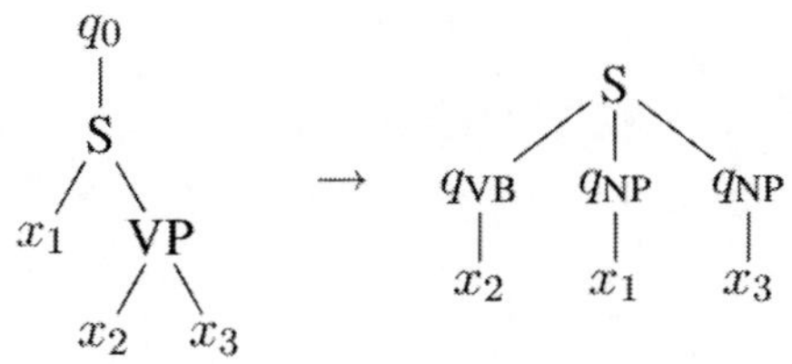

Figure 3: Example XTOP rule by Graehl et al. (2008).

we write $\xi \Rightarrow_G^{\rho} \zeta$ if $\xi = \xi[q]_p$ and $\zeta = \xi[r]_p$, where p is the lexicographically least element of $\mathrm{pos}_Q(\xi)$. The WTG G *generates* the weighted tree language $L_G \colon T_\Sigma \to \mathbb{R}_+$ such that

$$L_G(t) = \sum_{\substack{n\in\mathbb{N},\rho_1,\dots,\rho_n\in P\\ q_0\Rightarrow_G^{\rho_1}\cdots\Rightarrow_G^{\rho_n} t}} \mathrm{wt}(\rho_1)\cdot\ldots\cdot\mathrm{wt}(\rho_n)$$

for every $t \in T_\Sigma$. Each such language is *regular*, and $\mathrm{Reg}(\Sigma)$ contains all those languages over the alphabet Σ. A thorough introduction to tree languages is presented by Gécseg and Steinby (1984) and Gécseg and Steinby (1997) for the unweighted case and by Fülöp and Vogler (2009) for the weighted case.

3 Extended top-down tree transducers

We start by introducing the main model of this contribution. Extended top-down tree transducers (XTOP) are a generalization of the *top-down tree transducers* (TOP) of Rounds (1970) and Thatcher (1970). XTOP allow rules with several (non-state and non-variable) symbols in the left-hand side (as in the rule of Figure 3), whereas a TOP rule contains exactly one symbol in the left-hand side. Shieber (2004) and Knight (2007) identified that this extension is essential for many NLP applications because without it linear (i.e., non-copying) cannot compute rotations (see Figure 2). In the form of bimorphisms XTOP were investigated by Arnold and Dauchet (1976) and Arnold and Dauchet (1982) in the 1970s, and Knight (2007) invigorated research.

As demonstrated by Graehl et al. (2009) the most general XTOP model includes copying, deletion, and regular look-ahead in the spirit of Engelfriet (1977). More powerful models (such as synchronous tree-sequence substitution grammars and multi bottom-up tree transducers) can handle translation discontinuities naturally as evidenced by Zhang et al. (2008a) and Maletti (2011b), but XTOP need copying and deletion to handle them. Copying essentially allows an XTOP to translate certain parts of the input several times and was identified by the ATANLP 2010 participants as one of the most interesting and promising features of XTOP. Currently, the look-ahead feature is not used in machine translation, but we need it later on in the theoretical development.

Given an alphabet Q and a set T, we let

$$Q[T] = \{q(t) \mid q \in Q, t \in T\},$$

in which the root always has exactly one successor from T in contrast to $Q(T)$. We treat elements of $Q[T_\Sigma(V)]$ as special trees of $T_{\Sigma\cup Q}(V)$. Moreover, we let $\widetilde{1}_\Sigma(t) = 1$ for every $t \in T_\Sigma$. XTOP with regular look-ahead (XTOP^{R}) were also studied by Knight and Graehl (2005) and Graehl et al. (2008). Formally, an XTOP^{R} is a system

$$M = (Q, \Sigma, \Delta, q_0, R, c, \mathrm{wt})$$

with

- a finite set Q of *states*,
- alphabets Σ and Δ of *input* and *output symbols*,
- a *starting state* $q_0 \in Q$,
- a finite set R of *rules* of the form $\ell \to r$ with linear $\ell \in Q[T_\Sigma(X)]$ and $r \in T_\Delta(Q[\mathrm{var}(\ell)])$,
- $c \colon R \times X \to \mathrm{Reg}(\Sigma)$ assigns a regular *look-ahead* to each deleted variable of a rule [i.e., $c(\ell \to r, x) = \widetilde{1}_\Sigma$ for all $\ell \to r \in R$ and $x \in X \setminus (\mathrm{var}(\ell) \setminus \mathrm{var}(r))$], and
- $\mathrm{wt} \colon R \to \mathbb{R}_+$ assigns *rule weights*.

The XTOP^{R} M is *linear* [respectively, *nondeleting*] if r is linear [respectively, $\mathrm{var}(\ell) = \mathrm{var}(r)$] for every rule $\ell \to r \in R$. It has *no look-ahead* (XTOP) if $c(\rho, x) = \widetilde{1}_\Sigma$ for all $\rho \in R$ and $x \in X$. Figure 3 shows a rule of a linear and nondeleting XTOP.

The look-ahead can be used to restrict rule applications. It can inspect subtrees that are deleted by a

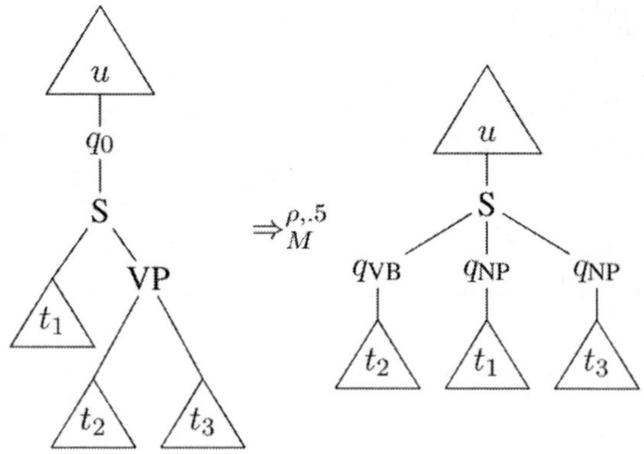

Figure 4: Rewrite step using rule ρ of Figure 3.

rule application, so for each rule $\rho = \ell \to r$, we let $\mathrm{del}(\rho) = \mathrm{var}(\ell) \setminus \mathrm{var}(r)$ be the set of deleted variables in ρ. If we suppose that a variable $x \in \mathrm{del}(\rho)$ matches to an input subtree t, then the weight of the look-ahead $c(\rho, x)(t)$, which we also write $c_{\rho,x}(t)$, is applied to the derivation. If it is 0, then this look-ahead essentially prohibits the application of ρ. It is important that the look-ahead is regular (i.e., there exists a WTG accepting it). The toolkit TIBURON by May and Knight (2006) implements XTOP together with a number of essential operations. Look-ahead is not implemented in TIBURON, but it can be simulated using a composition of two XTOP, in which the first XTOP performs the look-ahead and marks the results, so that the second XTOP can access the look-ahead information.

As for WTG the semantics for the XTOP^{R} $M = (Q, \Sigma, \Delta, I, R, c, \mathrm{wt})$ is presented using rewriting. Without loss of generality, we again suppose that $Q \cap (\Sigma \cup \Delta) = \emptyset$. Let $\xi, \zeta \in T_\Delta(Q[T_\Sigma])$, $w \in \mathbb{R}_+$, and $\rho = \ell \to r$ be a rule of R. We write $\xi \Rightarrow_M^{\rho,w} \zeta$ if there exists a substitution $\theta \colon X \to T_\Sigma$ such that

- $\xi = \xi[\ell\theta]_p$,
- $\zeta = \xi[r\theta]_p$, and
- $w = \mathrm{wt}(\rho) \cdot \prod_{x \in \mathrm{del}(\rho)} c_{\rho,x}(x\theta)$,

where $p \in \mathrm{pos}_Q(\xi)$ is the lexicographically least Q-labeled position in ξ. Figure 4 illustrates a derivation step.

The XTOP^{R} M computes a weighted tree transformation by applying rewrite steps to the tree $q_0(t)$, where $t \in T_\Sigma$ is the input tree, until an output tree $u \in T_\Delta$ has been produced. The weight of a particular derivation is obtained by multiplying the weights of the rewrite steps. The weight of the transformation from t to u is obtained by summing all weights of the derivations from $q_0(t)$ to u. Formally[1], the *weighted tree transformation computed by M in state $q \in Q$* is

$$\tau_M^q(t, u) = \sum_{\substack{n \in \mathbb{N}, \rho_1, \ldots, \rho_n \in R \\ q(t) \Rightarrow_M^{\rho_1, w_1} \cdots \Rightarrow_M^{\rho_n, w_n} u}} w_1 \cdot \ldots \cdot w_n \quad (1)$$

for every $t \in T_\Sigma$ and $u \in T_\Delta$. The XTOP^{R} M computes the weighted tree transformation $\tau_M^{q_0}$. Two XTOP^{R} M and N are equivalent, if $\tau_M = \tau_N$.

The sum (1) can be infinite, which we avoid by simply requiring that all our XTOP^{R} are *producing*, which means that $r \notin Q[X]$ for every rule $\ell \to r \in R$.[2] In a producing XTOP^{R} each rule application produces at least one output symbol, which limits the number n of rule applications to the size of the output tree u. A detailed exposition to XTOP^{R} is presented by Arnold and Dauchet (1982) and Graehl et al. (2009) for the unweighted case and by Fülöp and Vogler (2009) for the weighted case.

Example 1. Let $M_{\mathrm{ex}} = (Q, \Sigma, \Sigma, q, R, c, \mathrm{wt})$ be the nondeleting XTOP with

- $Q = \{q\}$,
- $\Sigma = \{\sigma, \gamma, \alpha\}$,
- the two rules

$$q(\alpha) \to \alpha \quad (\rho)$$

$$q(\gamma(x_1)) \to \sigma(q(x_1), q(x_1)) \quad (\rho')$$

- trivial look-ahead (i.e., $c(\rho, x) = \widetilde{1_\Sigma}$), and
- $\mathrm{wt}(\rho) = 2$ and $\mathrm{wt}(\rho') = 1$.

The XTOP^{R} M_{ex} computes the tree transformation that turns the input tree $\gamma^n(\alpha)$ into the fully balanced binary tree u of the same height with weight $2^{(2^n)}$. An example derivation is presented in Figure 5. □

Unrestricted copying (as in Example 1) yields very undesirable phenomena and is most likely not needed in the machine translation task. In fact, it is almost universally agreed that a translation model should be "linear-size increase", which means that

[1] There is an additional restriction that is discussed in the next paragraph.

[2] This is a convenience requirement. We can use other conditions on the XTOP^{R} or the used weight structures to guarantee a well-defined semantics.

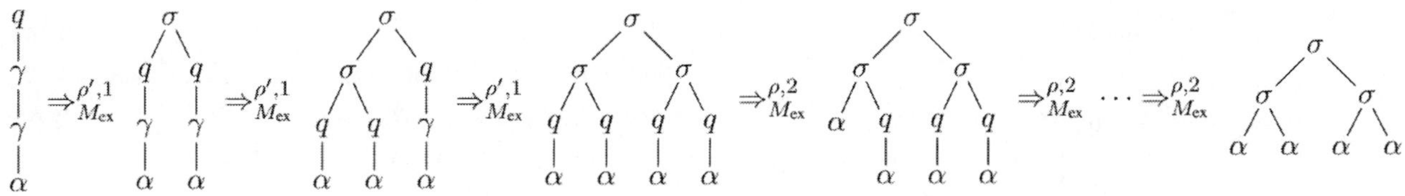

Figure 5: Example derivation using the XTOP M_{ex} with weight $1^3 \cdot 2^4 = 16$.

the size of each output tree should be linearly bounded in the size of the corresponding input tree according to Aho and Ullman (1971) and Engelfriet and Maneth (2003).

Definition 2. A mapping $\tau\colon T_\Sigma \times T_\Delta \to \mathbb{R}_+$ is *linear-size increase* if there exists an integer $n \in \mathbb{N}$ such that $|u| \leq n \cdot |t|$ for all $(t, u) \in \text{supp}(\tau)$. An XTOP^{R} M is *sensible* if τ_M is linear-size increase. □

'Sensible' is not a syntactic property of an XTOP^{R} as it does not depend on the actual rules, but only on its computed weighted tree transformation. The XTOP M_{ex} of Example 1 is not sensible because $|u| = 2^{|t|} - 1$ for every $(t, u) \in \tau_{M_{ex}}$. Intuitively, the number of times that M_{ex} can use the copying rule ρ' is not uniformly bounded.

We need an auxiliary result in the main part. Let $\tau\colon T_\Sigma \times T_\Delta \to \mathbb{R}_+$ be a weighted tree transformation. We need the weighted tree language $\tau^{-1}(u)\colon T_\Sigma \to \mathbb{R}_+$ of input trees weighted by their translation weight to a given output tree $u \in T_\Delta$. Formally, $(\tau^{-1}(u))(t) = \tau(t, u)$ for every $t \in T_\Sigma$.

Theorem 3. For every producing XTOP^{R} M and output tree $u' \in T_\Delta$, the weighted tree language $\tau_M^{-1}(u')$ is regular.

Proof sketch. We use some properties that are only defined in the next sections (for proof economy). It is recommended to skip this proof on the first reading and revisit it later. Maletti (2010a) shows that we can construct an XTOP^{R} M' such that

$$\tau_{M'}(t, u) = \begin{cases} \tau_M(t, u) & \text{if } u' = u \\ 0 & \text{otherwise} \end{cases}$$

for every $t \in T_\Sigma$ and $u \in T_\Delta$. This operation is called 'output product' by Maletti (2010a). The obtained XTOP^{R} M' is also producing, so we know that M' can take at most $|u'|$ rewrite steps to derive u'. Since M' can only produce the output tree u', this also limits the total number of rule applications in any successful derivation. Consequently, M' can only apply a copying rule at most $|u'|$ times, which shows that M' is finitely copying (see Definition 8). By Theorem 11 we can implement M' by an equivalent MBOT M'' (i.e., $\tau_{M''} = \tau_{M'}$; see Section 5), for which we know by Theorem 14 of Maletti (2011a) that $\tau_{M''}^{-1}(u) = \tau_{M'}^{-1}(u)$ is regular. □

Finally, let us illustrate the overall structure of our arguments to show that every sensible XTOP^{R} can be implemented by an equivalent MBOT. We first normalize the given XTOP^{R} such that the semantic property 'sensible' yields a syntactic property called 'finitely copying' (see Section 4). In a second step, we show that each finitely copying XTOP^{R} can be implemented by an equivalent MBOT (see Section 5). Figure 6 illustrates these steps towards our main result. In the final section, we derive some consequences from our main result (see Section 6).

4 From sensible to finite copying

First, we adjust a normal form of Engelfriet and Maneth (2003) to our needs. This section borrows heavily from Aho and Ullman (1971) and Engelfriet and Maneth (2003), where "sensible" (unweighted) deterministic macro tree transducers (MAC) [see Engelfriet and Vogler (1985)] are considered. Our setting is simpler on the one hand because XTOP^{R} do not have context parameters as MAC, but more difficult on the other hand because we consider nondeterministic and weighted transducers.

Intuitively, a sensible XTOP^{R} cannot copy a lot since the size of each output tree is linearly bounded in the size of the corresponding input tree. However, the actual presentation of the XTOP^{R} M might con-

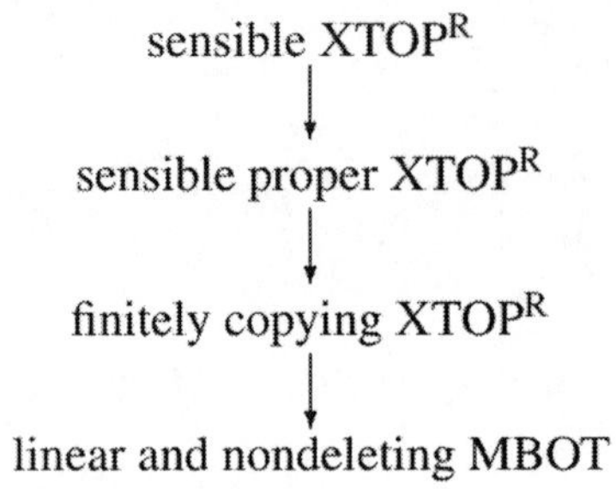

Figure 6: Overview of the proof steps.

tain rules that allow unbounded copying. This unbounded copying might not manifest due to the look-ahead restrictions or due to the fact that those rules cannot be used in a successful derivation. The purpose of the normal form is the elimination of those artifacts. To this end, we eliminate all states (except the initial state) that can only produce finitely many outputs. Such a state can simply be replaced by one of the output trees that it can produce and an additional look-ahead that checks whether the current input tree indeed allows that translation (and inserts the correct translation weight).

Normalized XTOP^R are called 'proper', and we define this property next. For the rest of this section, let $M = (Q, \Sigma, \Delta, q_0, R, c, \text{wt})$ be the considered sensible XTOP^R. Without loss of generality, we assume that the state q_0 does not occur in the right-hand sides of rules. Moreover, we write $\xi \Rightarrow_M^* \zeta$ if there exist nonzero weights $w_1, \dots, w_n \in \mathbb{R}_+ \setminus \{0\}$ and rules $\rho_1, \dots, \rho_n \in R$ with

$$\xi \Rightarrow_M^{\rho_1, w_1} \cdots \Rightarrow_M^{\rho_n, w_n} \zeta \ .$$

In essence, $\xi \Rightarrow_M^* \zeta$ means that M can transform ξ into ζ (in the unweighted setting).

Definition 4. A state $q \in Q$ is *proper* if there are infinitely many $u' \in T_\Delta$ such that there exists a derivation

$$q_0(t) \Rightarrow_M^* \xi[q(s)]_p \Rightarrow_M^* u[u']_p$$

where $s, t \in T_\Sigma$ are input trees, $\xi \in T_\Delta(Q[T_\Sigma])$, $p \in \text{pos}(\xi)$, and $u \in T_\Delta$ is an output tree. □

The derivation in Definition 4 is illustrated in Figure 7. In other words, a proper state is reachable from the initial state and can transform infinitely many input trees into infinitely many output trees. The latter is an immediate consequence of Definition 4 since each input tree can be transformed into only finitely many output trees due to sensibility. The restriction includes the look-ahead (because we require that the rewrite step weights are nonzero), which might further restrict the input trees.

Example 5. The state q of the XTOP M_{ex} is proper because we already demonstrated that it can transform infinitely many input trees into infinitely many output trees. □

The XTOP^R M is *proper* if all its states except the initial state q_0 are proper. Next, we show that each XTOP^R can be transformed into an equivalent proper XTOP^R using a simplified version of the construction of Lemma 5.4 by Engelfriet and Maneth (2003). Mind that we generally assume that all considered XTOP^R are producing.

Theorem 6. For every XTOP^R there exists an equivalent proper XTOP^R.

Proof sketch. The construction is iterative. Suppose that M is not yet proper. Then there exists a state $q \in Q$, which can produce only finitely many outputs U. It can be decided whether a state is proper using Theorem 4.5 of Drewes and Engelfriet (1998), and in case it is proper, the set U can also be computed effectively. The cited theorem applies to unweighted XTOP^R, but it can be applied also in our setting because $\Rightarrow_M^*$ in Definition 4 disregards weights. Now we consider each $u \in U$ individually. Clearly, $(\tau_M^q)^{-1}(u)$ is regular by Theorem 3. For each u and each occurrence of q in the right-hand side of a rule $\rho \in R$ of M, we create a copy ρ' of ρ, in which the selected occurrence of $q(x)$ is replaced by u and the new look-ahead is $c(\rho', x) = c(\rho, x) \cdot (\tau_M^q)^{-1}(u)$, which restricts the input tree appropriately and includes the adjustment of the weights. Since regular weighted tree languages are closed under HADAMARD products [see Fülöp and Vogler (2009)], the look-ahead $c(\rho, x) \cdot (\tau_M^q)^{-1}(u)$ is again regular.

Essentially, we precompute the action of q as much as possible, and immediately output one of the finitely many output trees, check that the input tree has the required shape using the look-ahead, and charge the weight for the precomputed transformation again using the look-ahead. This process is done for each occurrence, so if a rule contains two occurrences of q, then the process must be

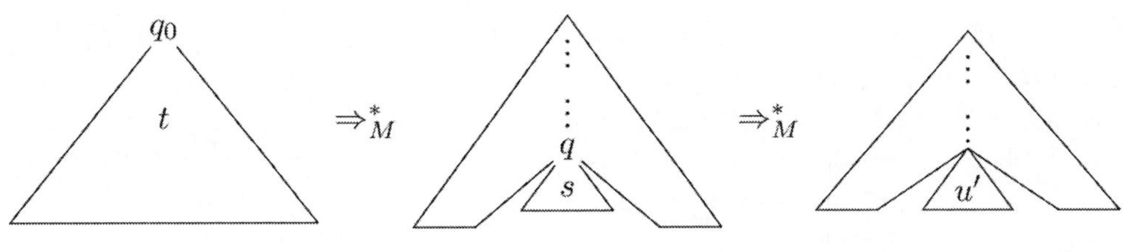

Figure 7: Illustration of the derivation in Definition 4.

done twice to this rule. In this way, we eventually purge all occurrences of q from the right-hand sides of rules of M without changing the computed transformation. Since $q \neq q_0$ and q is now unreachable, it is useless and can be deleted, which removes one non-proper state. This process is repeated until all states except the initial state q_0 are proper. □

Clearly, the construction of Theorem 6 applied to a sensible XTOP^{R} M yields a sensible proper XTOP^{R} M' since the property 'sensible' refers to the computed transformation and $\tau_M = \tau_{M'}$. Let us illustrate the construction on a small example.

Example 7. Let ρ be the rule displayed in Figure 3, and let us assume that the state q_{VB} is not proper. Moreover, suppose that q_{VB} can yield the output tree u and that we already computed the translation options that yield u. Let $t_1, \ldots, t_n \in T_\Sigma$ be those translation options. Then we create the copy ρ'

$$q_0(\text{S}(x_1, \text{VP}(x_2, x_3))) \to \text{S}(u, q_{\text{NP}}(x_1), q_{\text{NP}}(x_3))$$

of the rule ρ with look-ahead $c'(\rho', x)$ such that

$$c'_{\rho',x}(t) = \begin{cases} c_{\rho,x}(t) & \text{if } x \neq x_2 \\ \tau_M^{q_{\text{VB}}}(t, u) & \text{if } x = x_2 \ . \end{cases}$$
□

In general, there can be infinitely many input trees t_i that translate to a selected output tree u, so we cannot simply replace the variable in the left-hand side by all the options for the input tree. This is the reason why we use the look-ahead because the set $\tau_M^{-1}(u)$ is a regular weighted tree language.

From now on, we assume that the XTOP^{R} M is proper. Next, we want to invoke Theorem 7.1 of Engelfriet and Maneth (2003) to show that a proper sensible XTOP^{R} is finitely copying. Engelfriet and Maneth (2003) present a formal definition of finite copying, but we only present a high-level description of it.

Definition 8. The XTOP^{R} M is *finitely copying* if there is a copying bound $n \in \mathbb{N}$ such that no input subtree is copied more than n times in any derivation $q(t) \Rightarrow_M^* u$ with $q \in Q$, $t \in T_\Sigma$, and $u \in T_\Delta$. □

Example 9. The XTOP of Example 1 is not finitely copying as the input subtree α is copied 2^n times if the input tree is $\gamma^n(\alpha)$. Clearly, this shows that there is no uniform bound on the number of copies. □

It is worth noting that the properties 'sensible' and 'finitely copying' are essentially unweighted properties. They largely disregard the weights and a weighted XTOP^{R} does have one of those properties if and only if its associated unweighted XTOP^{R} has it. We now use this tight connection to lift Theorem 7.1 of Engelfriet and Maneth (2003) from the unweighted (and deterministic) case to the weighted (and nondeterministic) case.

Theorem 10. If a proper XTOP^{R} is sensible, then it is finitely copying.

Proof. Let M be the input XTOP^{R}. Since M is sensible, its associated unweighted XTOP^{R} N, which is obtained by setting all weights to 1 and computing in the BOOLEAN semiring, is sensible. Consequently, N is finitely copying by Theorem 7.1 of Engelfriet and Maneth (2003). Thus, also M is finitely copying, which concludes the proof. We remark that Theorem 7.1 of Engelfriet and Maneth (2003) only applies to deterministic XTOP^{R}, but the essential pumping argument, which is Lemma 6.2 of Engelfriet and Maneth (2003) also works for nondeterministic XTOP^{R}. Essentially, the pumping argument shows the contraposition. If M is not finitely copying, then M can copy a certain subtree an arbitrarily often. Due to the properness of M, all these copies have an impact on the output tree, which yields that its size grows beyond any uniform linear bound, which in turn demonstrates that M is not sensible. □

We showed that each sensible XTOP^{R} can be implemented by a finitely copying XTOP^{R} via the construction of the proper normal form. This approach actually yields a characterization because finitely copying XTOP^{R} are trivially sensible by Theorem 4.19 of Engelfriet and Maneth (2003).

5 From finite copying to an MBOT

We complete the argument by showing how to implement a finitely copying XTOP^{R} by a weighted multi bottom-up tree transducer (MBOT). First, we recall the MBOT, which was introduced by Arnold and Dauchet (1982) and Lilin (1978) in the unweighted case. Engelfriet et al. (2009) give an English presentation. We present the linear and nondeleting MBOT of Engelfriet et al. (2009).

A *weighted multi bottom-up tree transducer* is a system $M = (Q, \Sigma, \Delta, F, R, \mathrm{wt})$ with

- an alphabet Q of *states*,
- alphabets Σ and Δ of *input and output symbols*,
- a set $F \subseteq Q$ of *final states*,
- a finite set R of *rules* of the form $\ell \to r$ where $\ell \in T_\Sigma(Q(X))$ and $r \in Q(T_\Delta(X))$ are linear and $\mathrm{var}(\ell) = \mathrm{var}(r)$, and
- $\mathrm{wt}\colon R \to \mathbb{R}_+$ assigning *rule weights*.

We now use $T_\Sigma(Q(X))$ and $Q(T_\Delta(X))$ instead of $T_\Sigma(Q[X])$ and $Q[T_\Delta(X)]$, which highlights the difference between XTOP^{R} and MBOT. First, MBOT are a bottom-up device, which yields that Σ and Δ as well as ℓ and r exchange their place. More importantly, MBOT can use states with more than 1 successor (e.g, $Q(X)$ instead of $Q[X]$). An example rule is displayed in Figure 8.

Let $M = (Q, \Sigma, \Delta, F, R, \mathrm{wt})$ be an MBOT such that $Q \cap (\Sigma \cup \Delta) = \emptyset$.[3] We require that $r \notin Q(X)$ for each rule $\ell \to r \in R$ to guarantee finite derivations and thus a well-defined semantics.[4] As before, we present a rewrite semantics. Let $\xi, \zeta \in T_\Sigma(Q(T_\Delta))$, and let $\rho = \ell \to r$ be a rule. We write $\xi \Rightarrow^{\rho}_{M} \zeta$ if there exists a substitution $\theta\colon X \to T_\Delta$ such that $\xi = \xi[\ell\theta]_p$ and $\zeta = \xi[r\theta]_p$, where $p \in \mathrm{pos}(\xi)$ be is the lexicographically least reducible position in ξ. A rewrite step is illustrated in Figure 8.

[3]This restriction can always be achieved by renaming the states.

[4]Again this could have been achieved with the help of other conditions on the MBOT or the used weight structure.

The *weighted tree transformation computed by* M in state $q \in Q$ is

$$\tau^q_M(t, u_1 \cdots u_k) = \sum_{\substack{n \in \mathbb{N}, \rho_1, \ldots, \rho_n \in R \\ t \Rightarrow^{\rho_1}_M \cdots \Rightarrow^{\rho_n}_M q(u_1, \ldots, u_k)}} \mathrm{wt}(\rho_1) \cdot \ldots \cdot \mathrm{wt}(\rho_n)$$

for all $t \in T_\Sigma$ and $u_1, \ldots, u_k \in T_\Delta$. The semantics of M is $\tau_M(t, u) = \sum_{q \in F} \tau^q_M(t, u)$ for all $t \in T_\Sigma$ and $u \in T_\Delta$.

We move to the last step for our main result, in which we show how to implement each finitely copying XTOP^{R} by an MBOT using a weighted version of the construction in Lemma 15 of Maletti (2008). The computational benefits (binarization, composition, efficient parsing, etc.) of MBOT over XTOP^{R} are described by Maletti (2011a).

Theorem 11. Every finitely copying XTOP^{R} can be implemented by an MBOT.

Proof sketch. We plan to utilize Theorem 18 of Engelfriet et al. (2009), which proves the same statement in the unweighted and deterministic case. Again, the weights are not problematic, but we need to remove the nondeterminism before we can apply it. This is achieved by a decomposition into two XTOP^{R}. The first XTOP^{R} annotates the input tree with the rules that the second XTOP^{R} is supposed to use. Thus, the first XTOP^{R} remains nondeterministic, but the second XTOP^{R}, which simply executes the annotated rules, is now deterministic. This standard approach due to Engelfriet (1975) is used in many similar constructions.

Suppose that n is a copying bound for the input XTOP^{R} M, which means that no more than n rules are applied to each input symbol. The first XTOP^{R} is actually a nondeterministic linear and nondeleting XTOP that annotates each input tree symbol with exactly n rules of M that are consistent with the state behavior of M. Moreover, the annotation also prescribes with which of n rules the processing should continue at each subtree. Since we know all the rules that will potentially be applied for a certain symbol, we can make the assignment such that no annotated rule is used twice in the same derivation. The details for this construction can be found in Lemma 15 of Maletti (2008).

In this way, we obtain a weighted linear and nondeleting XTOP M_1, which includes the look-ahead,

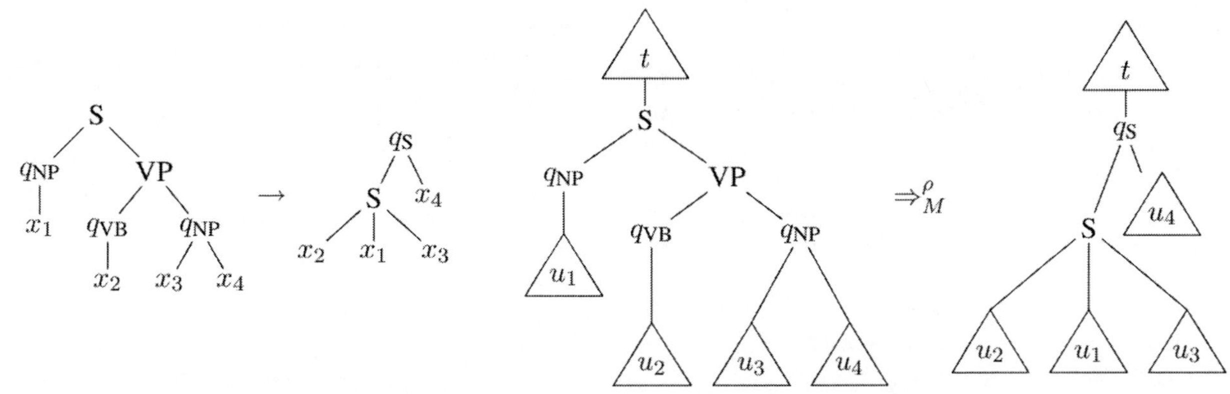

Figure 8: Example MBOT rule ρ [left] and its use in a rewrite step [right].

and an unweighted deterministic XTOP M_2. Only the weight and look-ahead of rules that are actually executed are applied (e.g., although we annotate n rules at the root symbol, we only execute the first rule and thus only apply its weight and look-ahead). The look-ahead of different rules is either resolved (i.e., pushed to the next rules) or multiplied using the HADAMARD product [see Fülöp and Vogler (2009)], which preserves regularity. This process is also used by Seemann et al. (2012). Now we can use Theorem 4 of Maletti (2011a) to obtain an MBOT N_1 that is equivalent to M_1. Similarly, we can use Theorem 18 of Engelfriet et al. (2009) to obtain an MBOT N_2 that is equivalent to M_2. Since MBOT are closed under composition by Theorem 23 of Engelfriet et al. (2009), we can compose N_1 and N_2 to obtain a single MBOT N that is equivalent to M. □

Corollary 12. For every sensible producing XTOP^{R} there exists an equivalent MBOT.

Proof. Theorem 6 shows that there exists an equivalent proper XTOP^{R}, which must be finitely copying by Theorem 10. This last fact allows us to construct an equivalent MBOT by Theorem 11. □

6 Preservation of regularity

Finally, we present an application of Corollary 12 to solve an open problem. The translation model is often used in a backwards manner in a machine translation system as demonstrated, for example, by May et al. (2010), which means that an output tree is supplied and the corresponding input trees are sought. This starting output tree is typically the best parse of the string that we want to translate. However, instead of a single tree, we want to use all parses of this sentence together with their parse scores. Those parses form a regular weighted tree language, and applying them backwards to the translation model yields another weighted tree language L of corresponding input trees. For an efficient representation and efficient modification algorithms (such a k-best extraction) we would like L to be regular. However, Fülöp et al. (2011) demonstrate that the backward application of a regular weighted tree language to an XTOP^{R} is not necessarily regular. The counterexample uses a variant of the XTOP of Example 1 and is thus not sensible. Theorem 14 of Maletti (2011a) shows that MBOT preserve regularity under backward application.

Corollary 13. Sensible XTOP^{R} preserve regularity under backward application.

Conclusion

We demonstrated that each sensible XTOP^{R} can be implemented by an MBOT. The latter formalism offers many computational advantages, so that the author believes that MBOT should be used instead of XTOP. We used real number weights, but the author believes that our results carry over to at least all zero-sum and zero-divisor free semirings [see Hebisch and Weinert (1998) and Golan (1999)], which are semirings such that (i) $a + b = 0$ implies $a = 0$ and (ii) $a \cdot b = 0$ implies $0 \in \{a, b\}$. Whether our results hold in other semirings (such as the semiring of all reals where $-1 + 1 = 0$) remains an open question.

References

Alfred V. Aho and Jeffrey D. Ullman. 1971. Translations on a context-free grammar. *Inform. and Control*, 19(5):439–475.

André Arnold and Max Dauchet. 1976. Bi-transductions de forêts. In *Proc. 3th Int. Coll. Automata, Languages and Programming*, pages 74–86. University of Edinburgh.

André Arnold and Max Dauchet. 1982. Morphismes et bimorphismes d'arbres. *Theoret. Comput. Sci.*, 20(1):33–93.

David Chiang. 2007. Hierarchical phrase-based translation. *Comput. Linguist.*, 33(2):201–228.

Frank Drewes and Joost Engelfriet. 1998. Decidability of the finiteness of ranges of tree transductions. *Inform. and Comput.*, 145(1):1–50.

Jason Eisner. 2003. Learning non-isomorphic tree mappings for machine translation. In *Proc. 41st Ann. Meeting Association for Computational Linguistics*, pages 205–208. Association for Computational Linguistics.

Joost Engelfriet and Sebastian Maneth. 2003. Macro tree translations of linear size increase are MSO definable. *SIAM J. Comput.*, 32(4):950–1006.

Joost Engelfriet and Heiko Vogler. 1985. Macro tree transducers. *J. Comput. System Sci.*, 31(1):71–146.

Joost Engelfriet, Eric Lilin, and Andreas Maletti. 2009. Extended multi bottom-up tree transducers — composition and decomposition. *Acta Inform.*, 46(8):561–590.

Joost Engelfriet. 1975. Bottom-up and top-down tree transformations — a comparison. *Math. Systems Theory*, 9(3):198–231.

Joost Engelfriet. 1977. Top-down tree transducers with regular look-ahead. *Math. Systems Theory*, 10(1):289–303.

Zoltán Fülöp and Heiko Vogler. 2009. Weighted tree automata and tree transducers. In Manfred Droste, Werner Kuich, and Heiko Vogler, editors, *Handbook of Weighted Automata*, EATCS Monographs on Theoret. Comput. Sci., chapter 9, pages 313–403. Springer.

Zoltán Fülöp, Andreas Maletti, and Heiko Vogler. 2011. Weighted extended tree transducers. *Fundam. Inform.*, 111(2):163–202.

Ferenc Gécseg and Magnus Steinby. 1984. *Tree Automata*. Akadémiai Kiadó, Budapest.

Ferenc Gécseg and Magnus Steinby. 1997. Tree languages. In Grzegorz Rozenberg and Arto Salomaa, editors, *Handbook of Formal Languages*, volume 3, chapter 1, pages 1–68. Springer.

Jonathan S. Golan. 1999. *Semirings and their Applications*. Kluwer Academic, Dordrecht.

Jonathan Graehl, Kevin Knight, and Jonathan May. 2008. Training tree transducers. *Comput. Linguist.*, 34(3):391–427.

Jonathan Graehl, Mark Hopkins, Kevin Knight, and Andreas Maletti. 2009. The power of extended top-down tree transducers. *SIAM J. Comput.*, 39(2):410–430.

Udo Hebisch and Hanns J. Weinert. 1998. *Semirings—Algebraic Theory and Applications in Computer Science*. World Scientific.

Kevin Knight and Jonathan Graehl. 2005. An overview of probabilistic tree transducers for natural language processing. In *Proc. 6th Int. Conf. Computational Linguistics and Intelligent Text Processing*, volume 3406 of LNCS, pages 1–24. Springer.

Kevin Knight. 2007. Capturing practical natural language transformations. *Machine Translation*, 21(2):121–133.

Philipp Koehn. 2010. *Statistical Machine Translation*. Cambridge University Press.

Eric Lilin. 1978. *Une généralisation des transducteurs d'états finis d'arbres: les S-transducteurs*. Thèse 3ème cycle, Université de Lille.

Andreas Maletti and Daniel Quernheim. 2011. Pushing for weighted tree automata. In *Proc. 36th Int. Symp. Mathematical Foundations of Computer Science*, volume 6907 of LNCS, pages 460–471. Springer.

Andreas Maletti. 2008. Compositions of extended top-down tree transducers. *Inform. and Comput.*, 206(9–10):1187–1196.

Andreas Maletti. 2010a. Input and output products for weighted extended top-down tree transducers. In *Proc. 14th Int. Conf. Developments in Language Theory*, volume 6224 of LNCS, pages 316–327. Springer.

Andreas Maletti. 2010b. Why synchronous tree substitution grammars? In *Proc. Human Language Technologies: Conf. North American Chapter of the ACL*, pages 876–884. Association for Computational Linguistics.

Andreas Maletti. 2011a. An alternative to synchronous tree substitution grammars. *J. Natur. Lang. Engrg.*, 17(2):221–242.

Andreas Maletti. 2011b. How to train your multi bottom-up tree transducer. In *Proc. 49th Ann. Meeting Association for Computational Linguistics: Human Language Technologies*, pages 825–834. Association for Computational Linguistics.

Jonathan May and Kevin Knight. 2006. Tiburon: A weighted tree automata toolkit. In *Proc. 11th Int. Conf. Implementation and Application of Automata*, volume 4094 of LNCS, pages 102–113. Springer.

Jonathan May, Kevin Knight, and Heiko Vogler. 2010. Efficient inference through cascades of weighted tree transducers. In *Proc. 48th Ann. Meeting Association for Computational Linguistics*, pages 1058–1066. Association for Computational Linguistics.

Jonathan May. 2010. *Weighted Tree Automata and Transducers for Syntactic Natural Language Processing*. Ph.D. thesis, University of Southern California, Los Angeles.

Haitao Mi, Liang Huang, and Qun Liu. 2008. Forest-based translation. In *Proc. 46th Ann. Meeting Association for Computational Linguistics*, pages 192–199. Association for Computational Linguistics.

William C. Rounds. 1970. Mappings and grammars on trees. *Math. Systems Theory*, 4(3):257–287.

Nina Seemann, Daniel Quernheim, Fabienne Braune, and Andreas Maletti. 2012. Preservation of recognizability for weighted linear extended top-down tree transducers. In *Proc. 2nd Workshop Applications of Tree Automata in Natural Language Processing*, pages 1–10. Association for Computational Linguistics.

Stuart M. Shieber. 2004. Synchronous grammars as tree transducers. In *Proc. 7th Int. Workshop Tree Adjoining Grammars and Related Formalisms*, pages 88–95.

Jun Sun, Min Zhang, and Chew Lim Tan. 2009. A non-contiguous tree sequence alignment-based model for statistical machine translation. In *Proc. 47th Ann. Meeting Association for Computational Linguistics*, pages 914–922. Association for Computational Linguistics.

James W. Thatcher. 1970. Generalized^2 sequential machine maps. *J. Comput. System Sci.*, 4(4):339–367.

Min Zhang, Hongfei Jiang, Aiti Aw, Haizhou Li, Chew Lim Tan, and Sheng Li. 2008a. A tree sequence alignment-based tree-to-tree translation model. In *Proc. 46th Ann. Meeting Association for Computational Linguistics*, pages 559–567. Association for Computational Linguistics.

Min Zhang, Hongfei Jiang, Haizhou Li, Aiti Aw, and Sheng Li. 2008b. Grammar comparison study for translational equivalence modeling and statistical machine translation. In *Proc. 22nd Int. Conf. Computational Linguistics*, pages 1097–1104. Association for Computational Linguistics.

NOMIT: Automatic Titling by Nominalizing

Cédric Lopez, Violaine Prince, and Mathieu Roche
LIRMM, CNRS, Univ. Montpellier 2
161, rue Ada
Montpellier, France
{lopez,prince,mroche}@lirmm.fr

Abstract

The important mass of textual documents is in perpetual growth and requires strong applications to automatically process information. Automatic titling is an essential task for several applications: 'No Subject' e-mails titling, text generation, summarization, and so forth. This study presents an original approach consisting in titling journalistic articles by nominalizing. In particular, morphological and semantic processing are employed to obtain a nominalized form which has to respect titles characteristics (in particular, relevance and catchiness). The evaluation of the approach, described in the paper, indicates that titles stemming from this method are informative and/or catchy.

1 Introduction

A title establishes a link between a reader and a text. It has two main functions. First of all, a title can be *informative* (it conveys relevant information about the text content and aim), and second, it can be *catchy* or incentive (Herrero Cecilia, 2007). A heading is said to be catchy when it succeeds in capturing the reader's attention on an aspect of the announced event, in a ingenious, metaphoric, enigmatic, or shocking way. From a syntactic point of view, a title can be a word, a phrase, an expression, a sentence, that designates a paper or one of its parts, by giving its subject.

Titles are used within applications such as automatic generation of contents, or summarization. So, it is interesting to automate the process that produces relevant titles by extracting them from texts, and supplying other applications with such data, while avoiding any human intervention: Direct applications (as automatic titling of "no object" e-mails) are thus possible.

The point is that several titles can be relevant for a same text: This constitutes the main difficulty of automatic titling. Some writers prefer informative titles, whereas others prefer catchy ones. Others juggle with both criteria according to the context and the type of the publication. So, evaluation of automatic titling is a complex step requiring a human intervention. Indeed, how can titles relevance be estimated ? How an automatic title can be compared to a human-written ("real") title, knowing that both can have a very different morphosyntactic structure?

Automatic titling is a full process, possessing its own functions. It has to be sharply differentiated from summarization and indexation tasks. Its purpose is to propose title(s) that have to be short, informative and/or catchy, and keep a coherent syntactic structure. NLP[1] methods will be exploited in order to abide by language morphosyntactic and semantic constraints in titling.

In this paper, we describe an approach of automatic titling relying on nominalization, i.e. rules transforming a verb phrase into a noun phrase (e.g. "the president left" is nominalized into " President's Departure"). This study raises two crucial questions: (1) Determining sentences and phrases containing relevant information (2) Nominalizing a chosen item and using it as a title. Example: From the following pair of sentences "The disappointing perfor-

[1] Natural Language Processing

mance, on Sunday October 9th, of Ségolène Royal, amazed the French citizens. For months, they defended their candidate on the Web.", containing the relevant information about an article in the French press in 2007, the idea is to built the following title: "Ségolène Royal: Surprise of the French citizens". In fact, other titles could apply such as "Ségolène Royal's Disappointing Performance" or "Surprising the French Citizens", but notice that both are less informative, since they drop a part of the information.

This article is organized as such: The following section briefly positions automatic titling in its research environment and describes previous work (section 2). The next one describes NOMIT, our approach of automatic titling by nominalization, which consists in three successive steps: Extracting candidate headings from the document (section 3.1), processing them linguistically (section 3.2), and last, selecting one among the produced headings, which will play the role of the system heading suggestion (section 3.3). Finally, the results of NOMIT evaluation are presented and discussed (section 4).

2 Previous Work

Automatic titling of textual documents is a subject often confused with summarization and indexation tasks. While a summary has to give an outline of the text contents, the title has to indicate the subject of the text without revealing all the contents. The process of summarization can use titles, as in (Blais et al., 2007) and (Amini et al., 2005), thus demonstrating their importance. Automatic summarization provides a set of relevant sentences extracted from the text: The total number of sentences is diminished, but sentences are not shortened by themselves. Ultimately reducing the number to one does not provide a title, since the latter is very rarely a sentence, but needs to be grammatically consistent. It is also necessary to differentiate automatic titling from text compression: Text compression might shorten sentences but keep the original number of sentences (Yousfi-Monod and Prince, 2008). Mixing both approaches appears as a very costly process to undertake, more adapted to a summarization task, when titling might be obtained by less expansive techniques.

Titling must also be differentiated from indexation because titles do not always contain the text key-words: Headings can present a partial or total reformulation of the text, not relevant for an index, which role is to facilitate the user's search and retrieval. Once again, the construction of an index can use titles appearing in the document. So, if determining relevant titles is a successful task, the quality of indexation will largely be improved.

An automatic titling approach, named POSTIT, extracts relevant noun phrases to be used as titles (Lopez et al., 2011b). One of its benefits is that long titles, syntactically correct, can be proposed. The main inconvenience is that it cannot provide original titles, using a funny form for example, unless this one already appears in the text (which can be rather scarce, even in newspapers articles). In the same environment, a variant of this approach, called CATIT, constructing short titles, has been developed by the same authors (Lopez et al., 2011a). It tries to built titles which are relevant to the texts. It evaluates their quality by browsing the Web (popular and recognized expressions), as well as including those titles dynamic context. Applied to a corpus of journalistic articles, CATIT was able to provide headings both informative and catchy. However, syntactical patterns used for titles building were short (two terms) and experience showed that longer titles were often preferred.

Another approach, presented by (Banko et al., 2000), consists in generating coherent summaries that are shorter than a single sentence. These summaries are called "headlines". The main difficulty is to adjust the threshold (i.e., the length of the headline), in order to obtain syntactically correct titles. This is the main difference with our method NOMIT, which ensures that its produced titles are always syntactically correct.

If a system were to produce informative, catchy, and variable-sized (in number of words) titles, the nominalization of constituents seems to be an interesting approach. *Nominalization* is a process transforming an adjective or a verb into a noun or noun phrase. In a nominalized constituent, the time of the event is not in touch with the time of the speech of the event (for example, "President's departure" does not infer that the president already left, contrary to "The president left"). In some languages such as German and French, nominalization answers an activity of conceptualization and conciseness. In a title, it allows to focus, according to the context of the author, on the dimension of the event considered the most relevant. (Moirand, 1975) already noticed that in French journalistic articles, numerous titles appear with a nominalized form. This observation was recently confirmed by (Herrero Cecilia, 2007). It is thus interesting to study automatic titling by nominalization of constituents when dealing with languages where it is often used. In English, the method stays the same, but the pattern changes: English headings patterns incline towards progressive present (e.g. "Tempest looming"), an infinitive form with a past participle (e.g. "Conference to be held"), and always with a deletion of articles. This paper focuses mostly on French because of its available data, but a shift in languages and patterns is contemplated in a further step.

3 NOMIT: Titling by Nominalizing

Since nominalization converts a sentence into a noun or a noun phrase, it can always be described by a transformation. Some transformations are easy-to-do, in particular, transforming verb participles into names or adjectives (such as defined by (Dubois and Dubois-Charlier, 1970)). For example, "arrivé(e)" (*arrived* is a French verbal participle which is equal to its nominalized shape "arrivée" (*arrival*). Others are more complex, for example the past participle "parti" (*gone*) which nominalized form is "départ" (*departure*). For these last ones, the use of a lexicon is necessary.

The nominalization process embedded in NOMIT develops three successive stages. The first one concerns the extraction of candidates according to a classical process in NLP: Data preparation, morphosyntactic labeling, selection of the data to be studied. The second phase consists in performing a linguistic process, including morphosyntactic and semantic aspects. Finally, the third phase focuses on selecting a relevant title. Figure 1 presents the global process, detailed in the following sub-sections.

We chose to focus our study on journalistic articles stemming from Le Monde (year 1994), a famous French daily paper, since their electronic form is available for scientific investigation. Note that the method presented in this paper is applicable to all types of texts (articles, news, blogs, and so forth).

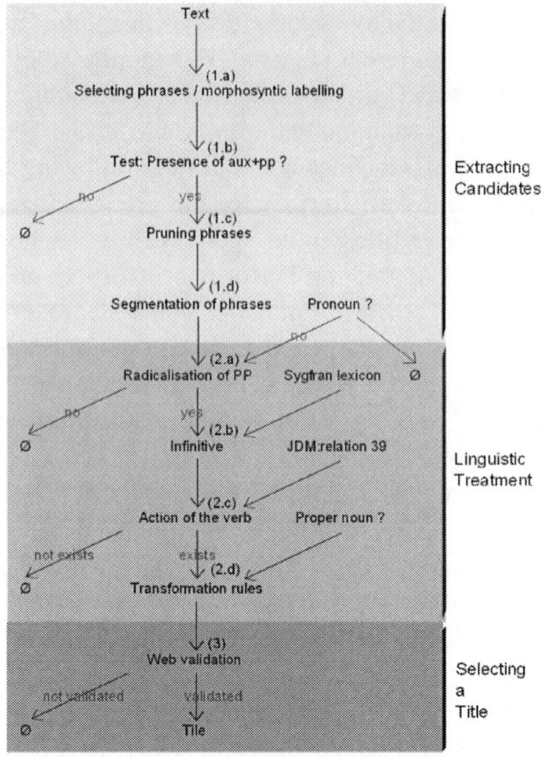

Figure 1: Global process of NOMIT

3.1 Extracting Candidates

This first phase consists in extracting the candidates (cf. section 3.2), which will be considered as potential titles after a linguistic treatment. It consists, in turn, of four steps. The first step determines the article relevant data (i.e. fragments or reformulations representing at best the main information emanating from the text).

The described approach relies on the assumption that good candidate phrases can be found in the first two sentences of the article. Actually the best covering rate of the words of real titles is obtained with these first sentences (see (Baxendale, 1958), (Vinet, 1993), (Jacques and Rebeyrolle, 2004), and (Lopez et al., 2011b) regarding the POSTIT approach), justifying this choice. So, here, the selection of relevant sentences (cf. Fig. 1, step 1.a) is limited to extracting the first two sentences of the text.

Step 1.b (cf. Fig. 1) consists in labeling these two sentences via SYGFRAN (Chauché and Prince,

2007), a morphosyntactic parser that tags words. Thus, the presence of a "auxiliary + past participle" form syntactic pattern is tested[2] (for example, "a augmenté" meaning *has increased*). If such a pattern is recognized in the sentence, then it is retained and goes into the following stages. Otherwise, the sentence is ignored. Then, sentences are pruned according to two heuristics.

(Knight and Marcu, 2002) have studied sentence compression by using a noisy-channel model which consists in making the following hypothesis: The sentence to be compressed was formerly short and the author has extended it with additional information (noise). Sentence compression, could, at a first glance, appear as a possible clue, however, our approach does not aim at reducing at most the treated sentence. Indeed, elements which can be pruned to obtain a good summary do not always need to be pruned to obtain a good title. So, the NOMIT sentence pruning step (cf. Fig. 1, step 1.c) does not only preserve the governors[3]. Here, the text is pruned according to three heuristics, inspired from (Yousfi-Monod and Prince, 2008), focusing on the function and position of constituents in the syntactic tree:

1. Elimination of dates (for example "The disappointing performance, on Sunday, October 9th, of Ségolène Royal" becomes "The disappointing performance of Ségolène Royal "),
2. Elimination of phrases directly juxtaposed to a past participle (for example "He chose, while he was still hesitating, to help him" becomes "He chose to help him"),
3. Elimination of the relative pronoun and the proposition introduced by it ("Its presence, which was not moreover wished, was noticed" becomes "Its presence was noticed ").

These three heuristics are crucial to obtain a coherent title. In this step, grammaticality[4] and concision[5] must be respected.

Finally, both sentences are segmented according to punctuation (points, commas, colons, brackets, interrogation marks, exclamation marks, and so forth[6]) and only segments containing a "auxiliary + past participle" pattern are preserved (cf. Fig. 1, step 1.d). Also, segments containing pronouns are not retained in the following steps to avoid problems related to referents [7].

In the following example, each step is indicated by a reference sending back to the global process presented in Figure 1:

Original text:

- Yet they truly believed in it. The disappointing performance, on Sunday, October 9th, of Ségolène Royal, amazed the French citizens. For months, they defended their candidate on the Web.

Treatments:

- (1.a) Yet they truly believed in it. The disappointing performance, on Sunday, October 9th, of Ségolène Royal, amazed the French citizens.
- (1.b) The disappointing performance, on Sunday, October 9th, of Ségolène Royal, amazed the French citizens.
- (1.c) The disappointing performance of Ségolène Royal, amazed the French citizens.
- (1.d) amazed the French citizens[8].

The following step enables to determine a relevant title from the result obtained at step 1.d.

3.2 Linguistic Treatment

The linguistic treatment of segments, present in those sentences retained in the previous section, is constituted by two stages aiming at nominalizing the

[2] the pattern features are tuned to French, but the same structure globally applies to English too.

[3] governors of constituents considered as indispensable to the grammatical and semantic coherence of the sentence

[4] The sentence must be well formed and must obey the language grammar.

[5] a pruned sentence has to contain the relevant information of the original sentence.

[6] Points marking an abbreviation are not obviously taken into account in this step.

[7] For example, the title "Disappointment of her partisans" would not be very informative because of the presence of "her" (unknown referent).

[8] We shall see in the section 3.2.2 how, in some cases, it is possible to take into account the subject, i.e. Ségolène Royal in this example.

"auxiliary + past participle" pattern. Here, the verbal basis is transformed into an action noun.

The first step consists in obtaining the infinitive of the verb to be nominalized from the past participle. Then, from the infinitive, possible nominalized forms are returned. Even if several linguistic studies propose classifications by families of suffixes, it is complex to process them automatically. The use of a lexicon is a good solution allowing to ensure a correct nominalized form.

3.2.1 Semantic Treatment

From past participle towards infinitive verb.

In step 1.b, segments of sentences containing the "auxiliary + past participle" syntactic pattern were extracted. For every past participle extracted, the endings of conjugation are eliminated, and only radicals are preserved (for example, "mangées" (*eaten*) becomes "mang" (*eat*) (cf. Fig. 1, step 2.a). Afterwards, every radical is associated with its infinitive verb using a lexicon[9] built for that purpose from the data established by the parser SYGFRAN (cf. Fig. 1, step 2.b).

From infinitive verb towards the verb action.

JeuxDeMots[10] is a French serious game enabling the construction of a lexical network via a recreational activity proposed on the Web. The prototype was created in 2008 (Lafourcade and Zampa, 2007). Today, more than 238,000 terms and more than 1,200,000 relations constitute the network. This popular, evolutionary, and good quality network, possesses a satisfactory knowledge coverage. All in all, more than 40 types of relations were recorded in the network. One of them interests us more particularly: The relation called "verb action". This "action" is very interesting for obtaining a nominalized form, in particular for verbs having their structure modified during their nominalization (addition of suffix or prefix in particular). For example, we obtain "départ" (*departure*) from the infinitive "partir" (to *leave*)(cf. Fig. 1, step 2.c).

Let us note that several action names can exist for the same verb. For example, "annonce" (*announcement*) and "annonciation" (*annunciation*) are two actions of the verb "annoncer" (*to announce*). At this stage, all action names are preserved and will be considered in the next phase, consisting in nominalizing the candidates determined in the step before.

3.2.2 Morphosyntactic Treatment

The morphosyntactic processing aims at establishing rules that automatically transform a constituent into its nominalized form. The purpose is not to establish an exhaustive list of transformation rules but to assure a correct transformation.

To transpose the agents of a verb into a nominalized constituent, the French language makes a proficient use of prepositions. So when nominalizing "auxiliary + past participle" in order to connect it with its complement, the preposition "de" ("of") is mandatory[11]. In English, although "X of Y" is an accepted pattern, the genitive form "Y('s) X" would be preferred. If the complement does not exist, the subject takes its place.

- **Rule 1**: Subject + Aux + PP + Complement => Verb action + (de) + Complement
  - **Original sentence:** Il a *annoncé* les gagnants (*He announced the winners*)
  - **Radicalisation** (2.a): *Annonc*
  - **Infinitive** (2.b): *Annoncer*
  - **Actions associated to the infinitive** (2.c): *Annonce* ; *annonciation*
  - **Nominalization** (2.d): *Annonce des gagnants* (*Announcement of the winners* or *Winners' announcement*) ; annonciation des gagnants (*Annunciation of the winners* or *Winners' annunciation*)
- **Rule 2**: Subject + Aux + PP => Action of the verb + (de) + Subject
  - **Original sentence**: Le président a *démissionné* (*The president resigned*)
  - **Radicalisation** (2.a): *Démission*
  - **Infinitive** (2.b): *Démissionner*
  - **Actions associated to the infinitive** (2.c): *Démission* (*Resignation*)
  - **Nominalization** (2.d): *Démission du président* (*Resignation of the president* or *President's resignation*)

[9] this lexicon contains 5,897 entries.

[10] `http://www.jeuxdemots.org`

[11] The preposition can be contracted if needed ("de le" = "du", "de les" = "des", and so forth.)

In section 3.1, relative subordinate pronoun and subordinate clauses are eliminated because the information they convey is too secondary to be emphasized in a title. For example, "My cousin, who lives in Paris, moved" becomes "My cousin moved". So, according to the second rule, the nominalized form will be "Moving of my cousin" and not "Moving of my cousin who lives in Paris".

The third rule leads to titles with a very popular form in French newspapers. It is about contextualizing the information via the use of a proper noun. So, if in the treated constituent a single proper noun appears (easily locatable by the presence of a capital letter), the common noun can be put in connection with the nominalized past participle (without concluding that this common noun is an agent of the nominalized verb). This new rule produces titles with the following form: "Proper noun: verb action + Prep + Complement". For example, "Ségolène returned to Strasburg" becomes "Ségolène: Strasburg comeback".

- **Rule 3**: Subject + Aux + PP => Proper Noun: Verb action + (de) + Complement (if it exists only one proper noun in the subject)
  - **Original sentence:** Bon nombre de par ticuliers se sont *précipités* (*rushed*)aux guichets des banques pour souscrire à des PEL (*Several individuals rushed to bank counters and subscribed to home-buying savings plans*)
  - **Radicalisation** (2.a): *Précipit*
  - **Infinitive** (2.b): *Précipiter*
  - **Action associated to the infinitive** (2.c): *Précipitation*
  - **Nominalization** (2.d): *PEL : précipitation aux guichets des banques* (*Home Buying Saving plans: Rush at Banks Counters*)

Section 3.2.1, pointed that several nominalized forms were possible for the same verb. So, the phase of linguistic treatment enables to determine a list of possible noun forms for every constituent. For example, if in step 1 we had "The restaurant Gazza, situated in a business area, announced a new price", rule 1 would transform this sentence into two candidates: "Gazza: New price announcement" and "Gazza: New price annunciation" (queer indeed!). The following phase consists in selecting the most relevant candidate.

3.3 Selecting a Title

The selection of the most relevant title relies on a Web validation (cf. Fig. 1, stage 3). A segment that frequently appears on the Web tends to be seen as: (1) popular, (2) structurally sound. Thus, the frequency of appearance of n-grams on the Web (via the Google search engine) appears as a good indicator of the n-gram popularity/soundness (Keller and Lapata, 2003) . In our case, a n-gram is a segment of the nominalized constituent, constituted by the nominalized past participle (NPP) and by the preposition followed by the short complement (i.e. reduced to the common noun).

The benefit of this validation is double. On one hand, it backs up the connection between the NPP and the complement (or subject according to the rule of used transformation). On the other hand, it helps eliminating semantically incorrect or unpopular constituents (for example, "Winners' annunciation") to prefer those which are more popular on the Web (for example, "Winners' announcement") [12].

3.4 Discussion

Our automatic titling approach (NOMIT) proposes titles for journalistic articles containing a "auxiliary + past participle" form in at least one of its first two sentences. The rationale for such a method is not only conciseness, but also presentation: How to generate a heading inciting the reader to go further on. Of course, transformation rules such as those presented here, can be numerous and various, and depend on language, genre, and purpose. The basic purpose of this work is to provide a sort of a "proof of concept", in which relevant titles might be automatically shaped.

[12] We do not here claim to select the most coherent constituents regarding the text. Since the main hypothesis underlying this study is that the first two sentences of the article contain the necessary and sufficient information to determine a relevant title, we consider implicitly obtaining nominalized constituents, that are relevant to the text

4 Evaluation

Evaluation of titles is a difficult and boring task. That is why we set up an online evaluation to share the amount of work. A call for participation was submitted in the French community of researchers (informatics, linguistics). Even if we do not know the information relative to every annotator (nationality, age, etc.), we think that a great majority of these annotators have a rather good level in French, to judge titles (this is confirmed by the well-writing of the collected definitions for "relevance" and "catchiness").

NOMIT has been evaluated according to two protocols. The first one consisted in a quantitative evaluation, stemming from an on-line user evaluation[13]. 103 people have participated to this evaluation. The second was an evaluation performed by 3 judges. This last one enables to compute the agreement inter-judges on the various criteria of the evaluation process. In both cases, the French daily paper Le Monde (1994) is used, thus avoiding any connection to the subjectivity of recent news personal analysis.

4.1 Quantitative Evaluation

4.1.1 Protocol Description

As previously seen, titles proposed by automatic methods cannot be automatically evaluated. So, an on-line evaluation was set up, opened to every person. The interest of such an evaluation is to compare the various methods of automatic titling (cf. section 2) according to several judgments. So, for every text proposed to the human judges, four titles were presented, each resulting from different methods of titling:

- NOMIT: Automatic Titling by Nominalizing.
- POSTIT: Based on the extraction of noun phrases to propose them as titles.
- CATIT: Based on the construction of short titles.
- Real Title (RT).

[13] http://www.lirmm.fr/~lopez/Titrage_general/evaluation_web2/

For every title, the user had to attribute one of the following labels: "relevant", "rather relevant", "irrelevant", "neutral". Also, the user had to estimate the catchiness, by choosing one of the following labels: "catchy", "not catchy", "neutral". Before beginning the evaluation, the user is asked about his/her own definition of a relevant title and of a catchy title (all in all, 314 definitions were collected). Globally, there is a popular consensus saying that a title is relevant if it is syntactically correct while reflecting the essential idea conveyed in the document. However, definitions of catchiness were less consensual. Here are some collected definitions:

1. A title is catchy if the words association is syntactically correct but semantically "surprising". However, a catchy title has to be close to the contents of the text.
2. A catchy title is a title which tempts the reader into going through the article.
3. A title which holds attention, a title which we remember, a funny title for example.
4. A title which is going to catch my attention because it corresponds to my expectations or my centers of personal interests.
5. A catchy title is a short and precise title.

The titled texts were distributed to the judges in a random way. Every title was estimated by a number of persons between 2 and 10. All in all, 103 persons participated in the evaluation of NOMIT.

Let $p1$ be the number of titles considered relevant, $p2$ the number of titles considered rather relevant, and let $p3$ be the number of titles considered irrelevant. Within the framework of this evaluation, it is considered that a title is relevant if $p1 \geq p3$, and rather relevant if $p2 \geq p3$.

A title is considered "catchy" if at least two judges considered it catchy.

4.1.2 Results

In spite of the weak number of titles estimated in this first evaluation, the significant number of judges helped obtaining representative results. In our experiments, 53 titles generated by the NOMIT approach were evaluated representing a total of 360 evaluations. These results were compared with the 200 titles generated with POSTIT, 200 with CATIT, and 200 RT (653 titles and 8354 evaluations). Results (cf. Table 1) show that 83% of the titles proposed by NOMIT were seen as relevant or rather relevant, against 70% for the titles stemming from the POSTIT approach, and 37% for the titles stemming from CATIT. Besides, NOMIT determines titles appreciably more catchy than both POSTIT and CATIT. Concerning the real titles (RT), 87.8% were judged relevant and 80.5% were catchy, meaning that humans still perform better than automated techniques, but only slightly for the relevance criterion, and anyway, are not judged as perfect (reference is far from absolute!).

en %	Relevant	Weak relevant	Irrelevant	Catchy	Not catchy
POSTIT	39.1	30.9	30	49.1	50.9
CATIT	15.7	21.3	63	47.2	52.8
NOMIT	**60.3**	**22.4**	**17.2**	**53.4**	**46.6**
RT	71.4	16.4	12.3	80.5	19.5

Table 1: Evaluation Results for POSTIT, CATIT, NOMIT, and RT (Real Titles).

4.2 Agreement Inter-judges

4.2.1 Protocol Description

This evaluation is similar to the previous one (same Web interface). The main difference is that we retained the first 100 articles appeared in Le Monde 1994 which enables our approach to return a title. Three judges estimated the real title as well as the NOMIT title for each of the texts, that is, a total of 600 evaluations.

4.2.2 Results

Kappa coefficient (noted K) is a measure defined by (Cohen, 1960) calculating the agreement between several annotators. It is based on the rate of **observed concordances (Po)** and on the rate of **random concordances (Pe)**. Here the Kappa coefficient estimates the agreement inter-judges about the relevance and of catchiness of NOMIT titles (cf. Tables 2 - 4). Considering the results and according to (Landis and Koch, 1977), judges seem to obtain an average concordance for the relevance of NOMIT titles. This can be justified by the fact that there is a consensus between the three judges about the definition of what is a relevant title (cf. Table 3). Approximately 71% of the titles were considered relevant by three judges (cf. Table 2).

On the other hand, the three judges obtain a bad concordance regarding catchiness; a catchy title for the one, could not be catchy for the other one. This is perfectly coherent with the definitions given by the three judges:

1. A title is catchy if the association of the words is syntactically correct but semantically "surprising".
2. A catchy title is a title which drives you to read the article.
3. A catchy title is a title which holds attention of the reader and tempts him/her to read the concerned text .

So, people have judged catchiness according to syntax, the relation between semantics of the title and semantic of the text, or have evaluated catchiness according to personal interests. The notion of catchiness is based on these three criteria. So, we could not expect a strong agreement between the assessors concerning the catchy character of a title (cf. Table 3).

in %	Relevant	Irrelevant	Neutral	Total
Relevant	70.7	10.3	0.7	81.7
Irrelevant	6.0	10.3	0.7	17.0
Neutral	1.0	0.3	0.0	1.3
Total	77.7	21.0	0.7	100.0

Table 2: Contingency Matrix for NOMIT (relevance).

in %	Catchy	Not Catchy	Neutral	Total
Catchy	13.3	7.7	0.0	21.0
Not catchy	34.7	41.0	1.3	77.0
Neutral	0.7	1.3	0.0	2.0
Total	48.7	50.0	1.3	100.0

Table 3: Contingency Matrix for NOMIT (catchiness).

As a rough guide, short journalistic articles[14] obtain better results than long articles (93% are relevant in that case and 69% are catchy). It thus seems

[14]We consider that an article is short when its number of words is less than 100.

	K avg.	Po avg.	Pe avg.
Relevance	0.42	0.81	0.67
Catchiness	0.10	0.54	0.49
Average	0.28	0.68	0.58

Table 4: Kappa average for relevance and catchiness of titles obtained with NOMIT.

that our approach of automatic titling by nominalization is more adapted to short texts. We are extremely prudent concerning this interpretation because it is based on only 29 articles.

5 Conclusion

Automatic titling is a complex task because titles must be at once informative, catchy, and syntactically correct. Based on linguistic and semantic treatments, our approach determines titles among which approximately 80% were evaluated as relevant and more than 60% were qualified as catchy. Experiment and results discussion have pointed at the following liability: The value of Kappa, the inter-judges agreement coefficient, is very difficult to evaluate, mostly when catchiness is at stake. The main cause is that it depends on personal interests. It is thus necessary to ask the following question: Do we have to consider that a title is definitely catchy when at least one person judges it so? Otherwise, how many people at least? This is still an open question and needs to be further investigated.

Also, some interesting extensions could be envisaged: The approach presented in this paper uses three rules of transformation based on the presence of an auxiliary followed by a past participle. The addition of new rules would enable a syntactic enrichment of the titles. So, it might be profitable to set up rules taking into account the presence of syntactical patterns (others than "auxiliary + past participle") to allow more texts to be titled by NOMIT.

Taking the punctuation of the end of sentences into account might also be a promising track. For example, "did it use an electric detonator?" would become "Use of an electric detonator?". It is an interesting point because the presence of a punctuation at the end of a title (in particular the exclamation or the interrogation) constitutes a catchy criterion.

Last, NOMIT is a method (easily reproducible in other languages, English in particular) that stepped out of preceding attempts in automatic headings generation (POSTIT, CATIT). Exploring syntactic patterns, as it does, means that increasing the amount of linguistic information in the process might lead to a reliable heading method. One of the perspectives can be to track the optimum point between the richness of involved information and processes, and the cost of the method. The incremental methodology followed from POSTIT to NOMIT tends to enhance the belief that parameters (i.e. length, shape, relevance, etc...) for an automatic heading procedure have to be studied and well defined, thus leading to a customized titling process.

References

Massih R. Amini, Nicolas Usunier, and Patrick Gallinari. 2005. Automatic text summarization based on word-clusters and ranking algorithms. *Advances in Information Retrieval*, pages 142–156.

Michele Banko, Vibhu O. Mittal, and Michael J. Witbrock. 2000. Headline generation based on statistical translation. In *Proceedings of the 38th Annual Meeting on Association for Computational Linguistics*, pages 318–325. Association for Computational Linguistics.

Phyllis B. Baxendale. 1958. Man-made index for technical literature - an experiment. *IBM Journal of Research and Development.*, pages 354–361.

Antoine Blais, Iana Atanassova, Jean-Pierre Desclés, Mimi Zhang, and Leila Zighem. 2007. Discourse automatic annotation of texts: an application to summarization. In *Proceedings of the Twentieth International Florida Artificial Intelligence Research Society Conference, May*, pages 7–9.

Jacques Chauché and Violaine Prince, Vp. 2007. Classifying texts through natural language parsing and semantic filtering. In *3rd International Language and Technology Conference*, pages 012–020, Poznan, Pologne, October.

Jacob Cohen. 1960. A coefficient of agreement for nominal scales. *Educational and psychological measurement*, 20(1):37–46.

Jean Dubois and Françoise Dubois-Charlier. 1970. *Eléments de linguistique française: syntaxe*. Larousse.

Juan Herrero Cecilia. 2007. Syntaxe, sémantique et pragmatique des titres des nouvelles de la presse française construits en forme de phrase nominale ou averbale: aspects cognitifs et communicatifs. In *Littérature, langages et arts: rencontres et création*, page 97. Servicio de Publicaciones.

Marie-Paule Jacques and Josette Rebeyrolle. 2004. Titres et structuration des documents. In *Actes International Symposium: Discourse and Document.*, pages 125–152.

Franck Keller and Mirella Lapata. 2003. Using the web to obtain frequencies for unseen bigrams. *Computational linguistics*, 29(3):459–484.

Kevin Knight and Daniel Marcu. 2002. Summarization beyond sentence extraction: A probabilistic approach to sentence compression. *Artificial Intelligence*, 139(1):91–107.

Mathieu Lafourcade and Virginie Zampa. 2007. Making people play for lexical acquisition. In *SNLP 2007, 7th Symposium on Natural Language Processing. Pattaya.*

J. Richard Landis and Garry G. Koch. 1977. The measurement of observer agreement for categorical data. *Biometrics*, 33(1):159.

Cédric Lopez, Violaine Prince, and Mathieu Roche. 2011a. Automatic generation of short titles. In *5th Language and Technology Conference, LTC'11*, pages 461–465.

Cédric Lopez, Violaine Prince, and Mathieu Roche. 2011b. Automatic titling of articles using position and statistical information. In *RANLP'11: Recent Advances in Natural Language Processing*, pages 727–732, Hissar, Bulgarie, September.

Sophie Moirand. 1975. Le rôle anaphorique de la nominalisation dans la presse écrite. *Langue française*, 28(1):60–78.

Marie-Thérèse Vinet. 1993. L'aspect et la copule vide dans la grammaire des titres. *Persee*, 100:83–101.

Mehdi Yousfi-Monod and Violaine Prince. 2008. Sentence compression as a step in summarization or an alternative path in text shortening. In *Coling'08: International Conference on Computational Linguistics, Manchester, UK.*, pages 139–142.

Correcting Comma Errors in Learner Essays, and Restoring Commas in Newswire Text

Ross Israel
Indiana University
Memorial Hall 322
Bloomington, IN 47405, USA
raisrael@indiana.edu

Joel Tetreault
Educational Testing Service
660 Rosedale Road
Princeton, NJ 08541, USA
jtetreault@ets.org

Martin Chodorow
Hunter College of CUNY
695 Park Avenue
New York, NY 10065, USA
mchodoro@hunter.cuny.edu

Abstract

While the field of grammatical error detection has progressed over the past few years, one area of particular difficulty for both native and non-native learners of English, *comma placement*, has been largely ignored. We present a system for comma error correction in English that achieves an average of 89% precision and 25% recall on two corpora of unedited student essays. This system also achieves state-of-the-art performance in the sister task of restoring commas in well-formed text. For both tasks, we show that the use of novel features which encode long-distance information improves upon the more lexically-driven features used in prior work.

1 Introduction

Automatically detecting and correcting grammatical errors in learner language is a growing sub-field of Natural Language Processing. As the field has progressed, we have seen research focusing on a range of grammatical phenomena including English articles and prepositions (c.f. Tetreault et al., 2010; De Felice and Pulman, 2008), particles in Korean and Japanese (c.f. Dickinson et al., 2011; Oyama, 2010), and broad approaches that aim to find multiple error types (c.f Rozovskaya et al., 2011; Gamon, 2011). However, to the best of our knowledge, there has not been any research published specifically on correcting erroneous comma usage in English (though there have been efforts such as the MS Word grammar checker, and products like Grammarly and White Smoke that include comma checking).

There are a variety of reasons that motivate our interest in attempting to correct comma errors. First of all, a review of error typologies in Leacock et al. (2010) reveals that comma usage errors are the fourth most common error type among non-native writers in the Cambridge Learner Corpus (Nicholls, 1999), which is composed of millions of words of text from essays written by learners of English. The problem of comma usage is not limited to non-native writers; six of the top twenty error types for native writers involve misuse of commas (Connors and Lunsford, 1988). Given these apparent deficits among both non-native and native speakers, developing a sound methodology for automatically identifying comma errors will prove useful in both learning and automatic assessment environments.

A quick examination of English learner essays reveals a variety of errors, with writers both overusing and underusing commas in certain contexts. Consider examples (1) and (2):

(1) **erroneous**: If you want to be a master you should know your subject well.
corrected: If you want to be a master , you should know your subject well.

(2) **erroneous**: I suppose , that it is better to specialize in one specific subject.
corrected: I suppose that it is better to specialize in one specific subject.

In example (1), an introductory conditional phrase begins the sentence, but the learner has not used the appropriate comma to separate the dependent clause from the independent clause. The comma in this case helps the reader to see where one clause ends and another begins. In example (2), the comma after *suppose* is unnecessary in American English, and although this error is related more to style than to readability, most native writers would omit the comma in this context, so it should be avoided by learners as well.

Another motivating factor for this work is the fact that sentence internal punctuation contributes to the overall readability of a sentence (Hill and Murray, 1998). Proper comma placement can lead to faster reading times and reduce the need to re-read entire sentences. Commas also help remove or reduce problems arising from difficult ambiguities; the garden path effect can be greatly reduced if commas are correctly inserted after introductory phrases and reduced relative clauses.

This paper makes the following contributions:

- We present the first published comma error correction system for English, evaluated on essays written by both native and non-native speakers of English.

- The same system also achieves state-of-the-art performance in the task of restoring commas in well-edited text.

- We describe a novel annotation scheme that allows for robust mark up of comma errors and use it to annotate two corpora of student essays.

- We show that distance and combination features can improve performance for both the error correction and restoration tasks.

The rest of this paper is organized as follows. In section 2, we review prior work. Section 3 details our typology of comma usage. We discuss our choice of classifier and selection of features in section 4. In section 5, we apply our system to the task of comma restoration. We describe our annotation scheme and error correction system and evaluation in sections 6 and 7. Finally, we summarize and outline plans for future research in section 8.

2 Previous Work

The only reported research that we are aware of which specifically deals with comma errors in learner writing is reported in Hardt (2001) and Alegria et al. (2006), two studies that deal with Danish and Basque, respectively. Hardt (2001) employs an error driven approach featuring the Brill tagger (Brill, 1993). The Brill tagger works as it would for the part-of-speech tagging task for which it was designed, i.e. it learns rules based on templates by iterating over a large corpus. This work is also evaluated on native text where all existing commas are considered correct, and additional "erroneous" commas are added randomly to a sub-corpus, so that the tagger can learn from the errors. The system is tested on a distinct subset for the task of correcting existing comma errors and achieves 91.4% precision and 76.9% recall.

Alegria et al. (2006) compare implementations of Naive Bayes, decision-tree, and support vector machine (SVM) classifiers and utilize a feature set based on word-forms, categories, and syntactic information about each decision point. While the system is designed as a possible means for correcting errors, it is only evaluated on the task of restoring commas in well-formed text produced by native writers. The system obtains good precision (96%) and recall (98.3%) for correctly *not* inserting commas, but performs less well at actually inserting commas (69.6% precision, 48.6% recall).

It is important to note that the results in both of the projects are based on constructed errors in an otherwise native corpus which is free of any other contextual errors that might be present in actual learner data. Moreover, as we will show in section 6, errors of omission (failing to use needed commas) are much more common than errors of commission (inserting commas inappropriately) in the English as a Foreign Language (EFL) data that we use. Crucially, our error correction efforts described in section 7 must be able to account for noise and be able to insert new commas as well as remove erroneous ones, as we do evaluate on a set of English learner essays.

Although we have not found any work published specifically on correcting comma errors in English, for language learners or otherwise, there is a fairly large amount of work that focuses on the task of comma restoration. Comma restoration refers to placing commas in a sentence which is presented with no sentence internal punctuation. This task is mostly attempted in the larger context of Automatic Speech Recognition (ASR), since there are no absolute cues of where commas should be placed in a stream of speech. Many of these systems use feature sets that include prosodic elements that are clearly not available for text based work (see e.g., Favre et al., 2009; Huang and Zweig, 2002; Moniz et al., 2009).

There are, however, a few punctuation restoration projects that have used well-formed text-only data. Shieber and Tao (2003) explore restoring commas to the Wall Street Journal (WSJ) section of the Penn Treebank (PTB). The authors augment a HMM trigram-based system with constituency parse information at each insertion point. Using fully correct parses directly from the PTB, the authors achieve an F-score of 74.8% and sentence accuracy of 57.9%[1]. However, a shortcoming of this methodology is that it dictates that all commas are missing, but these parses were generated with comma information present in the sentence and moreover hand-corrected by human annotators. Using parses automatically generated with commas removed from the data, they achieve an F-score of 70.1% and sentence accuracy of 54.9%.

More recently, Gravano et al. (2009), who work with newswire text, including WSJ, pursue the task of inserting all punctuation and correcting capitalization in a string of text in a single pass, rather than just comma restoration, but do provide results based solely on comma insertion. The authors employ an n-gram language model and experiment with n-grams from size $n = 3$ to $n = 6$, and with different training data sizes. The result relevant to our work is their comma F-score on WSJ test data, which is just over 60% when using 5-grams and 55 billion training tokens. Baldwin and Joseph (2009) also restore punctuation and capitalization to newswire texts, using machine based learning with retagging. Their results are difficult to compare with our work because they use a different data set and do not focus on commas in their evaluation.

Lu and Ng (2010) take an approach that inserts all punctuation symbols into text. They use transcribed English and Chinese speech data and do not provide specific evaluation for commas, however one important contribution of their research to our current task is the finding that Conditional Random Fields (CRFs) perform better at this task than Hidden Event Language Models, another algorithm that has been used for restoration. One reason for this could be CRFs' better handling of long range dependencies because they model the entire sequence, rather than making a singular decision based on information at each point in the sequence (Liu et al., 2005). CRFs also do not suffer from the label bias problem that affects Maximum Entropy classifiers (Lafferty et al., 2001).

3 Comma Usage

One of the challenges present in this research is the ambiguity as to what constitutes "correct" comma usage in American English. For one thing, not all commas contribute to grammaticality; some are more tied to stylistic rules and preferences. While there are certainly rule-based decision points for comma insertion (Doran, 1998), particularly in the case of commas that set off significant chunks or phrases within sentences, there are also some commas that appear to be more prescriptive, as they have less of an effect on sentence processing (such as in example (2) in the introduction), and opposing usage rules for the same contexts are attested in different style manuals. A common example of opposing rules is the notorious serial or Oxford comma that refers to the final comma found in a series, which is required by the Chicago Manual of Style (University of Chicago, 1993), but is considered incorrect by the New York Times Manual of Style (Siegal and Connolly, 1999).

As a starting point, we needed to know what kinds of commas are taught by English language teachers, as well as what style manuals recommend and/or require. However, creating a list of comma uses was a non-trivial part of the process. After consulting style manuals (University of Chicago, 1993; Siegal and Connolly, 1999; Strunk and White, 1999) and popular ESL websites, we compiled a list of over 30 rules for use of commas in English. We took the most commonly mentioned rules and created a final

[1] Sentence accuracy is a measure used by some in the field that counts sentences with 100% correct comma decisions as correct, and any sentence where a comma is missing or mistakenly placed as incorrect. It is motivated by the idea that all commas are essential to understanding a sentence.

Rule	Example
Elements in a List	*Paul put the kettle on, Don fetched the teapot, and I made tea.*
Initial Word/Phrase	*Hopefully, this car will last for a while.*
Dependent Clause	*After I brushed the cat, I lint-rollered my clothes.*
Independent Clause	*I have finished painting, but he is still sanding the doors.*
Parentheticals	*My father, a jaded and bitter man, ate the muffin.*
Quotations	*"Why," I asked, "do you always forget to do it?"*
Adjectives	*She is a strong, healthy woman.*
Conjunctive Adverbs	*I would be happy, however, to volunteer for the Red Cross.*
Contrasting Elements	*He was merely ignorant, not stupid.*
Numbers	*345,280,000*
Dates	*She met her husband on December 5, 2003.*
Geographical Names	*I lived in San Francisco, California, for 20 years.*
Titles	*Al Mooney, M.D., is a good doctor*
Introducing Words	*You may be required to bring many items, e.g., spoons, pans, and flashlights.*
Other	Catch-all rule for any other comma use

Table 1: Common Comma Uses

list of 15 usage rules (the 14 most common plus one miscellaneous category) for our annotation scheme, which is discussed in section 6. These rules are given in Table 1. The 16 rules that were removed from the list occurred in only one source or were similar enough to other rules to be conflated. It is worth noting here that while many of the comma uses in this table might be best served by some statistical methodology like the one we describe in section 4, one can envision fairly simple heuristic rules to insert commas and find errors in numbers, dates, geographical names, titles, and introducing words.

4 Classifier and Features

We use CRFs[2] as the basis for our system and treat the task of comma insertion as a sequence labeling task; each space between words is considered by the classifier, and a comma is either inserted or not. The feature set incorporates features that have proven useful in comma restoration and other error correction tasks, as well as a handful of new features devised for this specific task (combination and distance features). The full set of features used in our final system is given in Figure 1 along with examples of each feature for the sentence *If the teacher easily gets mad , then the child will always fear going to school and class.* The target insertion point is after the word *mad*.

[2]http://crfpp.sourceforge.net/

Feature	Example(s)
Lexical and Syntactic Features	
unigram	easily, gets, mad, then, the
bigram	easily gets, gets mad, mad then, ...
trigram	easily gets mad, gets mad then, ...
pos_uni	RB, VBZ, JJ, RB, DT
pos_bi	RB VBZ, VBZ JJ, JJ RB, ...
pos_tri	RB VBZ JJ, VBZ JJ RB, ...
combo	easily+RB, gets+VBZ,mad+JJ, ...
first_combo	If+RB
Distance Features	
bos_dist	5
eos_dist	10
prevCC_dist	-
nextCC_dist	9

Figure 1: CRF Features with examples for:
If the teacher easily gets mad , then the child will always fear going to school and class.

4.1 Lexical and Syntactic Features

The first six features in Figure 1 refer to simple unigrams, bigrams, and trigrams of the words and POS tags in a sliding 5 word window (target word, +/- 2 words). The lexical items help to encode any idiosyncratic relationships between words and commas that might not be exploited through the examination of more in-depth linguistic features. For example, *then* is a special case of an adverb (RB) that is often preceded by a comma, even if other adverbs are not, so POS tags might not capture this relationship. The lexical items also provide an approximation of a language model or hidden event language model approach, which has proven to be useful in comma restoration tasks (see e.g. Lu and Ng, 2010).

The POS features abstract away from the words and avoid the problem of data sparseness by allowing the classifier to focus on the categories of the words, rather than the lexical items themselves. The combination (combo) feature is a unigram of the word+pos for every word in the sliding window. It reinforces the relationship between the lexical items and their POS tags, further strengthening the evidence of entries like *then_RB*. All of these features have been used in previous grammatical error detection tasks which target particle, article, and preposition errors (c.f., Dickinson et al., 2011; Gamon, 2010; Tetreault and Chodorow, 2008).

The first_combo feature keeps track of the first combination feature of the sentence so that it can be referred to by the classifier throughout processing the entire sentence. This feature is helpful when an introductory phrase is longer than the classifier's five word window. Figure 1 provides a good example of the utility of this feature, as *If the teacher easily gets mad* is so long that by the time the window has moved to the target position of the space following *mad*, the first word and POS, *If_RB*, which can often indicate an introductory phrase, is beyond the scope of the sliding window.

4.2 Distance Features

Next, we encode four distance features. We keep track of the following distances: from the beginning of the sentence (bos_dist), to the end of the sentence (eos_dist), from the previous coordinating conjunction (prevCC_dist), and to the next coordinating conjunction (nextCC_dist). All of these distance features help the classifier by encoding measures for components of the sentence that can affect the decision to insert a comma. These features are especially helpful over long range dependencies, when the information encoded by the feature is far outside the scope of the 5-word window the CRF uses. The distance to the beginning of the sentence helps to encode introductory words and phrases, which make up the bulk of the commas used in essays by learners of English. The distance to the end of the sentence is less obviously useful, but it can let the classifier know the likelihood of a phrase beginning or ending at a certain point in the sentence. The distances to and from the nearest CC are useful because many commas are collocated with coordinating conjunctions. The distance features, as well as first_combo, were designed specifically for the task of comma error correction, and have not, as far as we know, been utilized in previous research.

5 Comma Restoration

Before applying our system to the task of error correction, we tested its utility in restoring commas in newswire texts. Specifically, we evaluate on section 23 of the WSJ, training on sections 02-22. Here, the task is straightforward: we remove all commas from the test data and performance is measured on the system's ability to put the commas back in the right places. After stripping all commas from our test data, the text is tokenized and POS tagged using a maximum entropy tagger (Ratnaparkhi, 1996) and every token is considered by the classifier as either requiring a following comma or not. Out of 53,640 tokens, 3062 should be followed by a comma. We provide accuracy, precision, recall, F_1-score, and sentence accuracy (S Acc.) for these tests, along with results from Gravano et al. (2009) and Shieber and Tao (2003) in Table 2. The first system (LexSyn) includes only the lexical and syntactic features from Figure 1; the second (LexSyn+Dist) includes all of the features.

System	Acc.	P	R	F	S Acc.
LexSyn	97.4	85.8	64.9	73.9	60.5
LexSyn+Dist	**97.5**	**85.8**	66.3	**74.8**	**61.4**
Shieber & Tao	97.0	79.7	62.6	70.1	54.9
Gravano et al.	N.A.	57	**67**	≈61	N.A.

Table 2: Comma Restoration System Results (%)

As can be seen in Table 2, the full system (LexSyn+Dist) performs significantly better than WSJ LexSyn ($p < .02$, two-tailed), achieving an F-score of 74.8 on WSJ. This F-score outperforms Shieber and Tao's system, which was also tested on section 23 of the WSJ, by about 4% and our sentence accuracy of 61.5% is about 7% higher than theirs. Our F-score is also about 13% higher than that of Gravano et al. (2009), however, they evaluate on the entire WSJ section of the Penn Treebank, so it is not totally fair to compare results.

6 Annotation

For the comma restoration task, we needed only to obtain well-formed text and remove the commas to produce a test set. However, this is not so in the case of error correction. In order to test a system that corrects errors in learner essays, we need an annotated test corpus that tells us where the errors are. Although there are a handful of corpora that include punctuation errors in their annotation scheme, such as NUCLE (Dahlmeier and Ng, 2011) and HOO (Dale and Kilgarriff, 2010), there are none to our knowledge that focus specifically on commas. Thus, we designed and implemented our own annotation scheme on a set of essays to allow us the freedom to identify the most important aspects of comma usage for our work.

Our annotation scheme allows the mark-up of a number of aspects of comma usage. First, each comma in a text is marked as rejected or accepted by the annotator. Additionally, any space between words can be treated as an insertion point for a missing comma. The annotators also marked all accepted and inserted commas as either required or optional. Finally, the annotation also includes the appropriate usage rule from the set in Table 1.[3] In contrast, the NUCLE and HOO data sets do not have this granularity of information (the annotation only indicates whether a comma should be inserted or removed) and are not exhaustively annotated.

After a one-hour training session on comma usage rules, three native English speakers were given a set of ten learner essays comprising 3,665 tokens to annotate for comma errors. To assess the difficulty of the annotation task, we calculated agreement and kappa. Agreement is a simple measure of how often the annotators agree, and kappa provides a more robust measure of agreement since it takes chance into account (Cohen, 1960). Table 3 provides the results of these measurements. As can be seen in the table, the agreement is quite high at either 97 or 98%, and kappa is a bit lower, ranging from 72 to 81%. The agreement is likely so high due to the great number of decision points where it is obvious to any native writer that no comma is needed. To account for this imbalance, we also provide an adjusted agreement in the final column of the table that excludes all decisions where both annotators agree that no comma is necessary.

Annotators	Agreement	Kappa	Adj. agr.
1 & 2	97	74	61
1 & 3	98	72	61
2 & 3	98	81	76

Table 3: Agreement over Annotation Training Set (%)

After completing the training phase, we assigned one annotator the task of annotating our development and test data from two different corpora: essays written by English as a foreign language learners (EFL) and essays written by native speakers of English (Native). For both data sets we selected 60 essays for development and 60 essays for test. The annotation was carried out using an annotation tool developed in-house that gives the annotator an easy to use interface and outputs standoff annotations in xml format. (3) is an example of an annotated sentence from an EFL essay, where "$_{-X}$" marks a span for annotation.

(3) The new millenium ,$_{-1}$ the 21st century $_{-2}$ has dawned upon us $_{-3}$ and this new century has brought many positive advancements in our daily lives .
1) Accept, required, parenthetical
2) Insert, required, parenthetical
3) Insert, required, independent clause

Table 4 provides the comma usage information for the essays in both sets used in development and testing. The table shows the total number of sentences, commas in the original text that were accepted by the annotator, and errors (rejected and missing commas) for the 60 essays in each set.

As can be seen in Table 4, the majority of existing commas (columns *Accept* plus *Rej*) in the texts were accepted by the annotator; about 84% in the EFL development set, 87% in the EFL test set, 85% in the Native development set, and 88% in the Native test set. The important fact uncovered by these numbers is that most of the commas that learners do

[3]The full annotation manual is available at `http://www.cs.rochester.edu/~tetreaul/comma-manual.pdf`

Data Set	Sent	Commas		
		Accept	Errors	
			Rej	Miss
EFL Dev	717	474	49	233
EFL Test	683	427	65	232
Native Dev	970	506	86	363
Native Test	839	377	50	314

Table 4: Comma Usage Statistics

use are correct. However, there are a great number of commas that the annotator inserted (over 80% of all errors are missing commas) meaning that these learners are more prone to underusing than overusing commas. Another interesting fact that can be gleaned from our annotation is that the top five comma uses, those listed in the first five rows of Table 1, account for more than 80% of all commas in these essays.

7 Error Correction

With a competitive comma restoration system in place, we turn to the primary task of correcting errors in learner essays. While the task remains similar to comma restoration, error correction in student writing brings a new set of challenges, especially when the writers are non-native. Newswire texts are most often well-formed, so the system should not experience interference from other contextual errors around the missing commas. Sentences taken from learner texts, though, often contain multiple errors that can make it difficult to focus on a single problem at a time. Spelling errors, for example, can exacerbate error correction efforts that use contextual lexical features because well-formed text that is often used for training data is usually free of such noise.

In these experiments, we use the annotated essays described in section 6 for evaluation and train on 40,000 sentences taken from essays written by both native and non-native high level college students. All of the essays are run through automatic spelling correction to reduce the noise in the test set before being tagged with the same tagger used in the comma restoration experiments.

Because we approach comma error correction as essentially a comma restoration task, we can we use largely the same system for error correction as we did for comma restoration. We still employ CRFs and label each space between words as requiring a comma or not, however, there is one significant change to our methodology for this task. Namely, we can leave the commas that were present in the text as provided by the writer as we pre-process the data for error correction, whereas they were removed in the comma restoration task. For error correction, the task is really comparing the system's answer to the annotator's and the learner's, as opposed to simply inserting commas into raw text. Leaving the learners' commas in the text does introduce some errors to the POS tagging phase. However, since over 85% of the existing commas in the development set were judged as acceptable by our annotator (cf. section 6) , the number of erroneous commas is not so great as to contaminate the system. Removing all of the commas would introduce unnecessary errors in the pre-processing phase.

We also augment the system with three post-processing filters that we tuned on the development set. One requires that the classifier be completely confident before a change is made to an existing comma; crf++ will give 100% confidence to a single class in some cases. This filter is based on the fact that 85% of the existing commas can be expected to be correct. A similar filter requires that the classifier be at least 90% confident in a decision to insert a new comma. The final filter, which overrides any other information provided by the system, does not allow commas to be inserted before the word *because*. These ensure high precision even though they may reduce recall.

Table 5 provides the accuracy, precision, recall, F-score, and number of errors in each set for tests on our 60 annotated EFL and Native essays, and the result for the combined corpus. The system performs quite well on the EFL test set, with scores of 94% precision, 31.7% recall, and 47.4% F-score for the LexSyn+Dist system. The results for the Native set are a bit lower, with 84.9% precision, 20% recall, and 32.4% F-score for the LexSyn+Dist system.

For both data sets, when the distance features are added to the model, precision increases by 1%, and in the EFL set, recall also increases. In keeping with practices established within the field of grammatical error correction, the system has been optimized for high precision even at the cost of recall, to ensure that feedback systems avoid confusing learners by

Data	System	Acc.	P	R	F	n
EFL	LexSyn	98.2	92.9	30.9	46.5	297
	LexSyn+Dist	98.3	**94.0**	**31.7**	**47.4**	297
Native	LexSyn	97.8	83.9	20.0	32.3	365
	LexSyn+Dist	97.8	84.9	20.0	32.4	365
Combined	LexSyn	98.1	88.7	24.9	38.9	662
	LexSyn+Dist	98.1	89.8	25.2	39.4	662

Table 5: Comma Error Correction Results (%)

marking correct comma usage as erroneous. Considering performance over all of the test data, the system achieves over 89% precision and 25% recall, results which are comparable to those in other error correction tasks. For example, the preposition error detection system described in Tetreault and Chodorow (2008) achieved 84% precision, 19% recall for prepositions.

It is worth noting that the results in Table 5 include commas that the annotator had marked as optional. For these, whatever decision the system makes is scored as correct. Since the grammaticality/readability of the sentence will not be affected by the presence or absence of a comma in these cases, we feel this is the fairest assessment of the system.

7.1 Error Analysis

In order to get a sense of what kinds of constructions are difficult for our system, we randomly extracted 50 sentences from the output that exhibited at least one wrong comma decision made by the system. The 50 sentences contained a combined total of 62 system errors. Among these cases, the most common context where the system makes the wrong decision is in introductory words and phrases, which is not surprising given the frequency with which commas occur in these environments in our development set (about 40% of all commas in the essays). In (4), for example, the first word, *Here*, should be followed by a comma. Since *Here* is not a common introductory word in this type of sentence structure in the training data, this is a difficult case for the system to correct.

(4) *Here we can get specific knowledge in the science that we like the most* .

The next most common misclassification involves comma splices, i.e. conjoining complete sentences with a comma rather than separating them with a full stop. In (5), for example, there should be a full stop between *college* and *I*, rather than a comma. This result is not surprising because the system is not yet equipped to deal with comma splices. Comma splices are a different type of phenomenon because correcting them requires removing the comma and inserting a full stop, essentially two separate steps rather than the single reject/accept step that the system currently handles.

(5) *I entered college, I could learn it and make an effort to achieve my goal.*

The next most common context for system errors was between clauses that are conjoined with a coordinating conjunction as in (6), where there should not be a comma. In (6), the second clause is actually a dependent clause, so no comma should precede the coordinating conjunction. There are a number of system errors dealing with commas between two independent clauses. For example in (7), our annotator recommended a comma between *things* and *but*, however the system did not make the insertion. The problem with these examples likely stems from the fact that the rule for comma usage in these contexts is not clearly stated, even in well-respected manuals, and therefore likely not clearly understood, even by high-level native writers. For example, the NYT style manual (Siegal and Connolly, 1999) states that "Commas should be used in compound sentences before conjunctions... When the clauses are exceptionally short, however, the comma may be omitted." Adding a feature that measures clause length might help, but even then the classifier must rely on training data that may have considerable variation as to what length of clauses requires an intervening comma.

(6) *They wants to see their portfolio, and what kind of skill do they have for company.*

(7) *I have many things but the best is my parents.*

Another facet of the data that consistently challenges the system is the existence of errors other than the commas in the sentences. Consider the sentence in (8), where **erroneous** is the original text from the essay and **corrected** is a well-formed interpretation.

(8) **erroneous:** *In the other hand , having just one specific subject , which represents a great downfall for many students*
corrected: *On the other hand, knowing only one subject is a downfall for many students.*

The comma after *subject* is unnecessary, but so is the word *which*. In fact, *which* would normally signify the beginning of a non-restrictive clause in this context, which should be set off with a comma. It is no surprise then, that the system has trouble removing commas in these types of contexts. At least 11 of the 62 system mistakes that we examined have grammatical errors in the immediate context of the comma in question, which makes the classification more difficult.

8 Summary and Conclusion

We presented a novel comma error correction system for English that achieves an average of 89% precision and 25% recall on essays written by learners of different levels and language backgrounds, including native English speakers. The system achieves state-of-the-art performance on the task of comma restoration, beating previous systems' F-score and sentence accuracy by 4% and 7%, respectively. We discovered that augmenting lexical features, which have been commonly used in previous work, with the combination and distance features can improve F-score by as much as 1% in both the error correction and comma restoration tasks. We also developed and implemented a novel comma error annotation scheme.

Additionally, we are interested in the effect of correct comma placement on other NLP processes. Jones (1994) and Briscoe and Carroll (1995) show that adding punctuation to grammars that utilize part-of-speech (POS) tags, rather than lexical items, adds more structure and reduces ambiguity as well as the number of parses for each sentence. Similarly, Doran (1998) and White and Rajkumar (2008) found that adding punctuation improved parsing results in tree-adjoining grammar (TAG) and combinatorial categorial grammar (CCG) parsing, respectively. These studies all highlight the importance of correctly inserted punctuation, especially commas, for parsing. Given these results, we believe that by enhancing the quality of the text, comma error correction will improve not only tagging and parsing, but also the ability of systems to correct many other forms of grammatical errors, such as those involving incorrect word order, number disagreement, and misuse of prepositions, articles, and collocations.

Acknowledgments

We would like to thank Melissa Lopez for help with annotating our corpora and Michael Flor for kindly developing an annotation tool for our purposes. We also thank Aoife Cahill, Robbie Kantor, Markus Dickinson, Michael Heilman, Nitin Madnani, and our anonymous reviewers for insightful comments and discussion.

References

Iñaki Alegria, Bertol Arrieta, Arantza Diaz de Ilarraza, Eli Izagirre, and Montse Maritxalar. 2006. Using machine learning techniques to build a comma checker for Basque. In *Proceedings of the COLING/ACL main conference poster sessions.*

Timothy Baldwin and Manuel Paul Anil Kumar Joseph. 2009. Restoring punctuation and casing in English text. In *Australasian Conference on Artificial Intelligence'09.*

E. Brill. 1993. *A Corpus-Based Approach to Language Learning*. Ph.D. thesis, The University of Pennsylvania, Philadelpha, PA.

Ted Briscoe and John Carroll. 1995. Developing and evaluating a probabilistic LR parser of part-of-speech and punctuation labels. In *Proceedings of the ACL/SIGPARSE 4th International Workshop on Parsing Technologies.*

Jacob Cohen. 1960. A coefficient of agreement for

nominal scales. *Educational and Psychological Measurement*, 20(1):37–46.

Robert J. Connors and Andrea A. Lunsford. 1988. Frequency of formal errors in current college writing, or Ma and Pa Kettle do research. *College Composition and Communication*, 39(4).

Daniel Dahlmeier and Hwee Tou Ng. 2011. Grammatical error correction with alternating structure optimization. In *Proceedings of the 49th Annual Meeting of the Association for Computational Linguistics: Human Language Technologies - Volume 1*. Association for Computational Linguistics.

Robert Dale and Adam Kilgarriff. 2010. Helping our own: Text massaging for computational linguistics as a new shared task. In *International Conference on Natural Language Generation*.

Rachele De Felice and Stephen Pulman. 2008. A classifier-based approach to preposition and determiner error correction in L2 English. In *Proceedings of COLING-08*. Manchester.

Markus Dickinson, Ross Israel, and Sun-Hee Lee. 2011. Developing methodology for Korean particle error detection. In *Proceedings of the 6th Workshop on Innovative Use of NLP for Building Educational Applications*. Portland, Oregon.

Christine Doran. 1998. *Incorporating Punctuation into the Sentence Grammar: A Lexicalized Tree-Adjoining Grammar Perspective*. Ph.D. thesis, University of Pennsylvania.

Benoit Favre, Dilek Hakkani-Tur, and Elizabeth Shriberg. 2009. Syntactically-informed models for comma prediction. In *Proceedings of the 2009 IEEE International Conference on Acoustics, Speech and Signal Processing*.

Michael Gamon. 2010. Using mostly native data to correct errors in learners' writing: A meta-classifier approach. In *Human Language Technologies: The 2010 Annual Conference of the North American Chapter of the Association for Computational Linguistics*.

Michael Gamon. 2011. High-order sequence modeling for language learner detection high-order sequence modeling for language learner error detection. In *Proceedings of the 6th Workshop on Innovative Use of NLP for Building Educational Applications*.

Agustin Gravano, Martin Jansche, and Michiel Bacchiani. 2009. Restoring punctuation and capitalization in transcribed speech. In *Proceedings of the 2009 IEEE International Conference on Acoustics, Speech and Signal Processing*.

Daniel Hardt. 2001. Comma Checking in Danish. In *Corpus Linguistics*.

Robin L. Hill and Wayne S. Murray. 1998. Commas and spaces: The point of punctuation. In *11th Annual CUNY Conference on Human Sentence Processing*.

Jing Huang and Geoffrey Zweig. 2002. Maximum entropy model for punctuation annotation from speech. In *Proceedings of ICSLP 2002*.

Bernard E. M. Jones. 1994. Exploring the role of punctuation in parsing natural text. In *Proceedings of the 15th conference on Computational linguistics - Volume 1*.

John D. Lafferty, Andrew McCallum, and Fernando C. N. Pereira. 2001. Conditional random fields: Probabilistic models for segmenting and labeling sequence data. In *Proceedings of the Eighteenth International Conference on Machine Learning*.

Claudia Leacock, Martin Chodorow, Michael Gamon, and Joel R. Tetreault. 2010. *Automated Grammatical Error Detection for Language Learners*. Synthesis Lectures on Human Language Technologies. Morgan & Claypool Publishers.

Yang Liu, Elizabeth Shriberg, Andreas Stolcke, and Mary Harper. 2005. Comparing hmm, maximum entropy, and conditional random fields for disfluency detection. In *In Proceeedings of the European Conference on Speech Communication and Technology*.

Wei Lu and Hwee T. Ng. 2010. Better punctuation prediction with dynamic conditional random fields. In *Proceedings of the 2010 Conference on Empirical Methods in Natural Language Processing*.

Helena Moniz, Fernando Batista, Hugo Meinedo, and Alberto Abad. 2009. Prosodically-based automatic segmentation and punctuation. In *Pro-*

ceedings of the 5th International Conference on Speech Prosody.

Diane Nicholls. 1999. The cambridge learner corpus - error coding and analysis for writing dictionaries and other books for english learners. In *Summer Workshop on Learner Corpora*. Showa Woman's University.

Hiromi Oyama. 2010. Automatic error detection method for japanese particles. *Polyglossia*, 18.

Adwait Ratnaparkhi. 1996. A Maximum Entropy Model for Part-Of-Speech Tagging. In Eric Brill and Kenneth Church, editors, *Proceedings of the Empirical Methods in Natural Language Processing*.

Alla Rozovskaya, Mark Sammons, Joshua Gioja, and Dan Roth. 2011. University of Illinois system in HOO text correction shared task. In *Proceedings of the Generation Challenges Session at the 13th European Workshop on Natural Language Generation*, pages 263–266. Association for Computational Linguistics, Nancy, France.

Stuart M. Shieber and Xiaopeng Tao. 2003. Comma restoration using constituency information. In *Proceedings of the 2003 Human Language Technology Conference and Conference of the North American Chapter of the Association for Computational Linguistics*.

Allan M. Siegal and William G. Connolly. 1999. *The New York Times Manual of Style and Usage : The Official Style Guide Used by the Writers and Editors of the World's Most Authoritative Newspaper*. Crown, rev sub edition.

William Strunk and E. B. White. 1999. *The Elements of Style, Fourth Edition*. Longman, fourth edition.

Joel Tetreault and Martin Chodorow. 2008. The ups and downs of preposition error detection in ESL writing. In *Proceedings of COLING-08*. Manchester.

Joel Tetreault, Jennifer Foster, and Martin Chodorow. 2010. Using parse features for preposition selection and error detection. In *Proceedings of the ACL 2010 Conference Short Papers*.

University of Chicago. 1993. *The Chicago Manual of Style*. University Of Chicago Press, Chicago, fourteenth edition.

Michael White and Rajakrishnan Rajkumar. 2008. A more precise analysis of punctuation for broad-coverage surface realization with CCG. In *Proceedings of the Workshop on Grammar Engineering Across Frameworks*.

The Challenges of Parsing Chinese with Combinatory Categorial Grammar

Daniel Tse and **James R. Curran**
School of Information Technologies
University of Sydney
Australia
{dtse6695,james}@it.usyd.edu.au

Abstract

We apply Combinatory Categorial Grammar to wide-coverage parsing in Chinese with the new Chinese CCGbank, bringing a formalism capable of transparently recovering non-local dependencies to a language in which they are particularly frequent.

We train two state-of-the-art English CCG parsers: the parser of Petrov and Klein (P&K), and the Clark and Curran (C&C) parser, uncovering a surprising performance gap between them not observed in English — 72.73 (P&K) and 67.09 (C&C) F-score on PCTB 6.

We explore the challenges of Chinese CCG parsing through three novel ideas: developing corpus variants rather than treating the corpus as fixed; controlling noun/verb and other POS ambiguities; and quantifying the impact of constructions like *pro*-drop.

1 Introduction

Automatic corpus conversions from the Penn Treebank (Marcus et al., 1994) have driven research in lexicalised grammar formalisms, such as LTAG (Xia, 1999), HPSG (Miyao et al., 2004) and CCG (Hockenmaier and Steedman, 2007), producing the lexical resources key to wide-coverage statistical parsing.

The Chinese Penn Treebank (PCTB; Xue et al., 2005) has filled a comparable niche, enabling the development of a Chinese LTAG (Xia et al., 2000), a wide-coverage HPSG parser (Yu et al., 2011), and recently Chinese CCGbank (Tse and Curran, 2010), a 750 000-word corpus of Combinatory Categorial Grammar (CCG; Steedman, 2000) derivations.

We train two CCG parsers, Clark and Curran (C&C; 2007), and the Petrov and Klein (P&K; 2007) PCFG parser, on Chinese CCGbank. We follow Fowler and Penn (2010), who treat the English CCGbank (Hockenmaier and Steedman, 2007) grammar as a CFG and train and evaluate the P&K parser directly on it.

We obtain the first Chinese CCG parsing results: F-scores of 72.73 (P&K) and 67.09 (C&C) on labelled dependencies computed over the PCTB 6 test set. While the state-of-the-art in Chinese syntactic parsing has always lagged behind English, this large gap is surprising, given that Fowler and Penn (2010) found only a small margin separated the two parsers on English CCGbank (86.0 versus 85.8).

Levy and Manning (2003) established that properties of Chinese such as noun/verb ambiguity contribute to the difficulty of Chinese parsing. We focus on two factors within our control: annotation decisions and parser architecture.

Existing research has varied parsers whilst keeping the corpus fixed. We vary the corpus whilst keeping the parsers fixed by exploring multiple design choices for particular constructions. By exploiting the fully automatic CCGbank extraction process, we can immediately implement these choices and assess their impact on parsing performance.

Secondly, we contrast the performance of C&C, with its tagging/parsing pipeline, with P&K, a parser which performs joint tagging and parsing, and establish that P&K is less sensitive to the greater lexical category ambiguity in Chinese CCGbank.

We demonstrate that Chinese CCG parsing is very difficult, and propose novel techniques for identifying where the challenges lie.

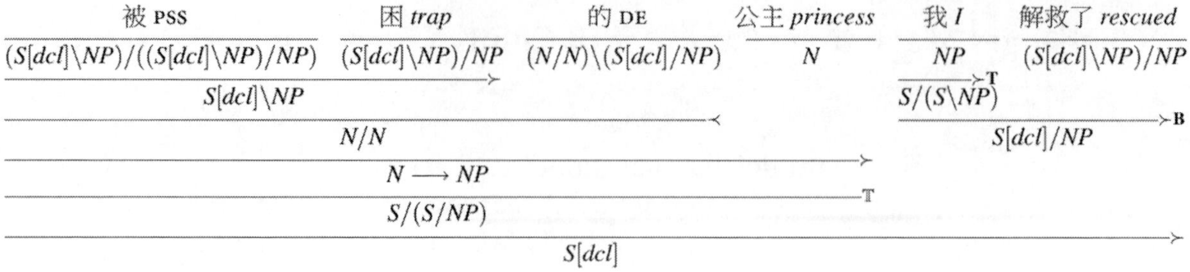

Figure 1: 3 types of non-local dependencies in 6 words: "*(As for) the trapped princess, I rescued (her).*"

2 Background

Bikel and Chiang (2000) developed the first PCTB parser, demonstrating that Chinese was similar enough to English for techniques such as a Collins-style head-driven parser or TAG to succeed. Later PCTB parsers used Tree Insertion Grammar (Chiang and Bikel, 2002), PCFGs (Levy and Manning, 2003), the Collins models (Bikel, 2004) and transition-based discriminative models (Wang et al., 2006; Zhang and Clark, 2009; Huang et al., 2009). These systems also established the relative difficulty of parsing Chinese and English; while PARSEVAL scores over 92% are possible for English (McClosky et al., 2006), systems for Chinese have achieved only 87% (Zhang and Clark, 2009) on the same metric.

Non-local dependencies (NLDs) are lexical dependencies which hold over unbounded distances. Guo et al. (2007) observed that despite the importance of NLDs for correct semantic interpretation, and the fact that Chinese syntax generates more NLDs than English, few parsers in Chinese are equipped to recover the traces which mark NLDs. For instance, extraction, a common NLD type, occurs more frequently in CPTB sentences (38%) compared to PTB (17%).

A more satisfying approach is to use a grammar formalism, such as CCG (Steedman, 2000), which generates them inherently, enabling a unified parsing model over local and non-local dependencies. This approach is taken in the C&C parser (Clark and Curran, 2007), which can directly and transparently recover NLDs in English (Rimell et al., 2009).

Chinese CCGbank (Tse and Curran, 2010) demonstrates that a parsimonious account of Chinese syntax with CCG is possible. Many familiar objects of Chinese syntax which generate NLDs, including the 把 *ba*/被 *bei* constructions, topicalisation and extraction receive natural CCG analyses in Chinese CCGbank. Figure 1 shows the CCGbank analysis of passivisation, topicalisation and extraction, creating NLDs between 公主 *princess* and each of 被 *PSS*, 困 *trap* and 解救 *rescue* respectively.

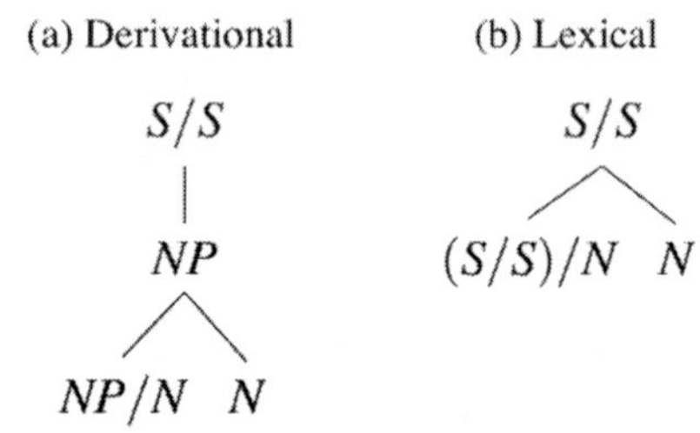

Figure 2: Two types of ambiguity

We take two state-of-the-art parsers and train them to establish the difficulty of parsing Chinese with CCG. The first is the Clark and Curran (C&C; 2007) parser, which uses *supertagging* (Clark and Curran, 2004), a local, linear-time tagging technique which drastically prunes the space of lexical categories which the polynomial-time parsing algorithm later considers. The second is the *coarse-to-fine* parser of Petrov and Klein (2007) which iteratively refines its grammar by splitting production rules to uncover latent distinctions. Fowler and Penn (2010) demonstrate that the English CCGbank grammar is strongly context-free, allowing them to treat it as a CFG and train the Petrov and Klein (2007) parser directly.

2.1 Derivational vs. lexical ambiguity

The designer of a CCGbank must frequently choose between derivational and lexical ambiguity (Hockenmaier, 2003; Tse and Curran, 2010). *Derivational ambiguity* analyses special constructions through arbitrary label-rewriting phrase structure rules, while *lexical ambiguity* assigns additional categories to lexical items for when they participate in special constructions.

Derivational and lexical ambiguity often arise in CCG because of the *form-function distinction* — when the syntactic *form* of a constituent does not coincide with its semantic *function* (Honnibal, 2010). For instance, in English, topicalisation causes an *NP* to appear in clause-initial position, fulfilling the *function* of a sentential pre-modifier while maintaining the *form* of an *NP*. Figure 2 shows two distinct CCG analyses which yield the same dependency edges.

Derivational ambiguity increases the parser search space, while lexical ambiguity enlarges the tag set, and hence the complexity of the supertagging task.

3 Three versions of Chinese CCGbank

We extract three versions of Chinese CCGbank to explore the trade-off between lexical and derivational ambiguity, training both parsers on each corpus to determine the impact of the annotation changes. Our hypothesis is that the scarcity of training data in Chinese means that derivational ambiguity results in better coverage and accuracy, at the cost of increasing time and space requirements of the resulting parser.

3.1 The lexical category *LC* (localiser)

In the following sentences, the words in bold have often been analysed as belonging to a lexical category *localiser* (Chao, 1968; Li and Thompson, 1989).

(1) a. 屋子 里面
house **inside**:LC
the inside of the house/inside the house

b. 大 树 旁边
big tree **beside**:LC
(the area) beside the big tree

Localisers, like English prepositions, identify a (temporal, spatial, etc.) extent of their complement. However, the combination *Noun + Localiser* is ambiguous between noun function (*the inside of the house*) and modifier function (*inside the house*).

We consider two possibilities to represent localisers in CCG, which trade derivational for lexical ambiguity. In (2-a), a direct CCG transfer of the PCTB analysis, the preposition 在 *at* expects arguments of type *LCP*. In (2-b), 在 *at* now expects only *NP* arguments, and the unary promotion *LCP* → *NP* allows *LCP*-form constituents to *function* as *NP*s.

(2) a. 在 at | 房子 room | 里 in:LC
PP/LCP | NP | $LCP\backslash NP$
LCP (<)
PP (>)

b. 在 at | 房子 room | 里 in:LC
PP/NP | NP | $LCP\backslash NP$
$LCP \rightarrow NP$ (<)
PP (>)

The analysis in (2-a) exhibits greater lexical ambiguity, with the lexical item 在 *at* carrying at least two categories, *PP/NP* and *PP/LCP*, while (2-b) trades off derivational for lexical ambiguity: the unary promotion *LCP* → *NP* becomes necessary, but 在 *at* no longer needs the category *PP/LCP*.

The base release of Chinese CCGbank, corpus **A**, like (2-a), makes the distinction between categories *LCP* and *NP*. However, in corpus **B**, we test the impact of applying (2-b), in which the unary promotion *LCP* → *NP* is available.

3.2 The bare/non-bare *NP* distinction

The most frequent unary rule in English CCGbank, occurring in over 91% of sentences, is the promotion from bare to non-bare nouns: *N* → *NP*. Hockenmaier (2003) explains that the rule accounts for the form-function distinction in determiner-less English nouns which nevertheless have definite reference, while preventing certain over-generations (e.g. *the the car). The *N-NP* distinction also separates adjectives and noun modifiers (category *N/N*), from predeterminers (category *NP/NP*) (Hockenmaier and Steedman, 2005), a distinction also made in Chinese.

While Chinese has strategies to mark definite or indefinite reference, they are not obligatory, and a bare noun is referentially ambiguous, calling into question whether the distinction is justified in CCG:

(3) a. 狗 很 聪明
dog very clever
Dogs are clever.

b. 我 看到 狗
1SG see dog
I saw a dog/dogs.

c. 狗 跑走 了
dog run-away ASP
The dog/dogs ran away.

The fact that the Chinese determiner is not necessarily a maximal projection of the noun – in other words, the determiner does not 'close off' a level of *NP* – also argues against importing the English analysis. In contrast, the English CCGbank determiner category *NP/N* reflects the fact that determiners 'close off' *NP* — further modification by noun modifiers is blocked after combining with a determiner.

(4) 共和党 这 举动
Republican Party this act
this action by the Republican Party

To test its impact on Chinese parsing, we create a version of Chinese CCGbank (corpus **C**) which neutralises the distinction. This eliminates the atomic category *N*, as well as the promotion rule $N \rightarrow NP$.

4 Experiments

While a standard split of PCTB 5 exists, as defined by Zhang and Clark (2008), we are not aware of a consistently used split for PCTB 6. We present a new split in Table 1 which adds data from the ACE broadcast section of PCTB 6, maintaining the same train/dev/test set proportions as the PCTB 5 split.

We train C&C using the *hybrid* model, the best-performing model for English, which extracts features from the dependency structure (Clark and Curran, 2007). We use $\beta = \langle 0.055, 0.01, 0.05, 0.1 \rangle$ during training with a Gaussian smoothing parameter $\alpha = 2.4$ (optimised on the corpus **A** dev set). We use $\beta = \langle 0.15, 0.075, 0.03, 0.01, 0.005, 0.001 \rangle$ during parsing, with the maximum number of supercats (chart entries) set to 5,000,000, reflecting the greater supertagging ambiguity of Chinese parsing.

The P&K parser is used "off-the-shelf" and trained with its default parameters, only varying the number of split-merge iterations and enabling the Chinese-specific lexicon features. The P&K parser involves no explicit POS tagging step, as the (super)tags correspond directly to non-terminals in a CFG.

Fowler and Penn (2010) use the C&C tool `generate` to convert P&K output to the C&C evaluation dependency format. `generate` critically does not depend on the C&C parsing model, permitting a fair comparison of the parsers' output.

	PCTB 5	+PCTB 6	#sents
Train	1–815, 1001–1136	2000–2980	22033
Test	816–885, 1137–1147	3030–3145	2758
Dev	900–931, 1148–1151	2981–3029	1101

Table 1: PCTB 5 and 6 dev/train/test splits

4.1 Evaluation

Carroll et al. (1998) argued against PARSEVAL in favour of a dependency-based evaluation. Rimell et al. (2009) focus on evaluating NLD recovery, proposing a dependency-based evaluation and a GR mapping procedure for inter-parser comparison.

Since the P&K parser plus `generate` produce dependencies in the same format as C&C, we can use the standard Clark and Curran (2007) dependency-based evaluation from the CCG literature: labelled F-score (LF) over dependency tuples, as used for CCG parser evaluation in English. Critically, this metric is also NLD-sensitive. We also report labelled sentence accuracy (Lsa), the proportion of sentences for which the parser returned all and only the gold standard dependencies. Supertagger accuracy compares leaf categories against the gold standard (*stag*).

For C&C, we report on two configurations: GOLD, evaluated using gold standard POS tags; and AUTO, with automatic POS tags provided by the C&C tagger (Curran and Clark, 2003). For P&K, we vary the number of split-merge iterations from one to six (following Fowler and Penn (2010), the k-iterations model is called *I-k*). Because the P&K parser does not use POS tags, the most appropriate comparison is against the AUTO configuration of C&C. For C&C, we use the average of the logarithm of the chart size ($\log C$) as a measure of ambiguity, that is, the number of alternative analyses the parser must choose between.

Following Fowler and Penn (2010), we perform two sets of experiments: one evaluated over all sentences in a section, and another evaluated only over sentences for which both parsers successfully parse and generate dependencies.

We define the *size* of a CCG grammar as the number of categories it contains. The size of a grammar affects the difficulty of the supertagging task (as the size of a grammar is the size of the supertag set). We also consider the number of categories of each *shape*, as defined in Table 2. Decomposing the category in-

Shape	Pattern
V (predicate-like)	$(S[dcl]\backslash NP)\$$
M (modifier)	$X\|X$
P (preposition-like)	$(X\|X)\|Y$
N (noun-like)	*N* or *NP*
O (all others)	

Table 2: Shapes of categories

	model	*LF*	*Lsa* %	stag	cov	log *C*
A	I-3	68.97	13.45	83.64	95.7	-
	I-6	**71.67**	15.70	85.00	96.4	-
	GOLD	75.45	16.70	89.43	99.4	14.55
	AUTO	66.32	12.81	83.88	98.6	14.69
B	I-3	69.75	14.15	84.07	96.0	-
	I-5	**71.40**	14.83	84.97	96.4	-
	GOLD	75.41	16.67	89.50	99.6	14.74
	AUTO	66.24	12.61	83.95	98.7	14.75
C	I-3	70.22	16.49	84.37	96.5	-
	I-5	**72.74**	18.59	85.61	96.5	-
	GOLD	76.73	20.56	89.66	99.5	13.58
	AUTO	66.95	14.62	83.90	99.2	13.86

Table 3: Dev set evaluation for P&K and C&C

ventory into shapes demonstrates how changes to the corpus annotation affect the distribution of types of category. Finally, we calculate the average number of tags per lexical item (*Avg. Tags/Word*), as a metric of the degree of lexical ambiguity in each corpus.

5 Results

Table 3 shows the performance of P&K and C&C on the three dev sets, and Table 4 only over sentences parsed by both parsers. (**A** is the base release, **B** includes the unary rule $LCP \rightarrow NP$, and **C** also collapses the *N-NP* distinction.) For P&K on corpus **A**, F-score and supertagger accuracy increase monotonically as further split-merge iterations refine the model. P&K on **B** and **C** overfits at 6 iterations, consistent with Fowler and Penn's findings for English.

The ~9% drop in F-score between the GOLD and AUTO figures shows that C&C is highly sensitive to POS tagging accuracy (92.56% on the dev set, compared to 96.82% on English). Considering Table 4, each best P&K model outperforms the corresponding AUTO model by 3-5%. However, while P&K is substantially better without gold-standard information, gold POS tags allow C&C to outperform P&K, again demonstrating the impact of incorrect POS tags.

	model	*LF*	*Lsa* %	stag	cov
A	I-6	71.74	15.87	85.29	100.0
	AUTO	67.50	15.36	84.52	100.0
B	I-5	71.40	14.97	85.26	100.0
	AUTO	67.72	14.97	84.68	100.0
C	I-5	72.84	18.69	86.04	100.0
	AUTO	68.43	16.17	84.57	100.0

Table 4: Dev set evaluation for P&K and C&C on PCTB 6 sentences parsed by *both* parsers

	model	*LF*	*Lsa* %	stag	cov	log *C*
C	I-5	72.73	20.28	85.43	97.1	-
	GOLD	76.89	22.90	89.63	99.1	14.53
	AUTO	67.09	15.28	83.95	98.7	14.89

Table 5: Test set evaluation for P&K and C&C

Supertagging and parsing accuracy are not entirely correlated between the parsers – in corpora **A** and **B**, AUTO supertagging is comparable or better than I-3, but F-score is substantially worse.

Comparing **A** and **B** in Table 3, C&C receives small increases in supertagger accuracy and coverage, but parsing performance remains largely unchanged; P&K performance degrades slightly. On both parsers, **C** yields the best results out of the three corpora, with *LF* gains of 1.07 (P&K), 1.28 (GOLD) and 0.63 (AUTO) over the base Chinese CCGbank. We select **C** for our remaining parser experiments.

Both C&C's GOLD and AUTO results show higher coverage than P&K (a combination of parse failures in P&K itself, and in `generate`). Since F-score is only computed over successful parses, it is possible that P&K is avoiding harder sentences. In Table 4, evaluated only over sentences parsed by *both* parsers shows that as expected, C&C gains more (1.15%) than P&K on the common sentences.

Table 5 shows that the behaviour of both parsers on the test section is consistent with the dev section.

corpus	Avg. tags/word	Grammar size all	Grammar size $f \geq 10$
A	1.84	1177	324
B	1.83	1084	303
C	1.79	964	274

Table 6: Corpus statistics

corpus	**V**	**P**	**M**	**N**	**O**	*Total*
A	791	158	56	2	170	1177
B	712	149	55	2	166	1084
C	670	119	41	1	133	964

Table 7: Grammar size, categorised by shape

Confusion	*LF*	ΔLF	stag	cov
Base (GOLD)	76.73		89.66	99.50
NR ⋈ NN	76.72	*-0.01*	89.64	99.37
JJ ⋈ NN	76.60	*-0.12*	89.57	99.37
DEC ⋈ DEG	75.10	*-1.50*	89.07	98.83
VV ⋈ NN	73.35	*-1.75*	87.68	98.74
All (AUTO)	66.95		83.90	99.20

Table 8: Corrupting C&C gold POS tags piecemeal on PCTB 6 dev set of corpus **C**. ΔLF is the change in LF when each additional confusion type is allowed.

5.1 Corpus ambiguity

To understand why corpus **C** is superior for parsing, we compare the ambiguity and sparsity characteristics of the three corpora. Examining $\log C$, the average log-chart size (Table 3) shows that the corpus **B** changes (the addition of the unary rule *LCP* → *NP*) increase ambiguity, while the additional corpus **C** changes (eliminating the *N-NP* distinction, resulting in the removal of the unary rule *N* → *NP*) have the net effect of reducing ambiguity.

Table 6 shows that the changes reduce the size of the lexicon, thus reducing the average number of tags each word can potentially receive, and therefore the difficulty of the supertagging task. This, in part, contributes to the reduced $\log C$ values in Table 3. While the size of the lexicon is reduced in **B**, the corresponding $\log C$ figure in Table 3 increases slightly, because of the additional unary rule.

Table 7 breaks down the size of each lexicon according to category shape. Introducing the rule *LCP* → *NP* reduces the number of **V**-shaped categories by 10%, while not substantially affecting the quantity of other category shapes, because the subcategorisation frames which previously referred to *LCP* are no longer necessary. Eliminating the *N-NP* distinction, however, reduces the number of **P** and **M**-shaped categories by over 20%, as the distinction is no longer made between attachment at *N* and *NP*.

6 Error analysis

The well-known noun/verb ambiguity in Chinese (where, e.g., 设计建设 *'design-build'* is both a verbal compound *'design and build'* and a noun compound *'design and construction'*) greatly affects parsing accuracy (Levy and Manning, 2003).

However, little work has quantified the impact of noun/verb ambiguity on parsing, and for that matter, the impact of other frequent confusion types. To quantify C&C's sensitivity to POS tagging errors, which we saw in Table 3, we perform an experiment where we corrupt the gold POS tags, by gradually reintroducing automatic POS errors on a cumulative basis, one confusion type at a time.

The notation X ⋈ Y indicates that the POS tags X and Y are frequently confused with each other by the POS tagger. For example, VV ⋈ NN represents the problematic noun/verb ambiguity, allowing the inclusion of noun/verb confusion errors.

Table 8 shows that while the confusion types NR ⋈ NN and JJ ⋈ NN have no impact on the evaluation, the confusions DEC ⋈ DEG and VV ⋈ NN, introduced one at a time, cause reductions in F-score of 1.50 and 1.75% respectively. This is expected; Chinese CCGbank does not distinguish between noun modifiers (NN) and adjectives (JJ). On the other hand, the critical noun/verb ambiguity, and the confusion between DEC/DEG (two senses of the particle 的 *de*) adversely impact F-score. We performed an experiment with C&C to merge DEC and DEG into a single tag, but found that this increased category ambiguity without improving accuracy.

The VV ⋈ NN confusion is particularly damaging to the CCG labelled dependency evaluation, because verbs generate a large number of dependencies. While Fowler and Penn (2010) report a gap of 6.31% between C&C's labelled and unlabelled F-score on the development set in English, we observe a gap of 10.35% for Chinese.

Table 10 breaks down the 8,414 false positives generated by C&C on the dev set, according to whether the head of each dependency was incorrectly POS-tagged and/or supertagged. The top-left cell shows that despite the correct POS and supertag, C&C makes a large number of pure attachment location errors. The vast majority of false positives, though, are

C&C AUTO		P&K I-5		category	NLD?	dependency function
LF	freq	LF	freq			
0.78	4204	0.78	3106	$NP/\mathbf{NP}$		*noun modifier attachment*
0.73	2173	0.81	1765	$(S[dcl]\backslash NP)/\mathbf{NP}$		*transitive object*
0.65	1717	0.72	1459	$(S[dcl]\backslash \mathbf{NP})/NP$		*transitive subject*
0.68	870	0.74	643	$(S[dcl]\backslash NP)/(\mathbf{S[dcl]}\backslash \mathbf{NP})$		*control/raising S complement*
0.70	862	0.67	697	$S[dcl]\backslash \mathbf{NP}$		*intransitive subject*
0.60	670	0.69	499	$(S[dcl]\backslash \mathbf{NP})/(S[dcl]\backslash NP)$	✓	*control/raising subject*
0.55	626	0.54	412	$(NP/NP)/(\mathbf{NP}/\mathbf{NP})$		*noun modifier modifier attachment*
0.57	370	0.68	321	$(NP/NP)\backslash(\mathbf{S[dcl]}\backslash \mathbf{NP})$		*subject extraction S complement*
0.59	343	0.70	314	$(NP/\mathbf{NP})\backslash(S[dcl]\backslash NP)$	✓	*subject extraction modifier attachment*
0.59	110	0.69	84	$(NP/NP)\backslash(\mathbf{S[dcl]}/\mathbf{NP})$		*object extraction S complement*
0.63	106	0.75	86	$(NP/\mathbf{NP})\backslash(S[dcl]/NP)$	✓	*object extraction modifier attachment*

Table 9: Accuracy per dependency, for selected dependency types

	correct POS	incorrect POS
correct stag	2307 (27.42%)	51 (0.61%)
incorrect stag	4493 (53.40%)	1563 (18.58%)

Table 10: Analysis of the 8,414 false positive dependencies from C&C on PCTB 6 dev set

caused by supertagging errors (the bottom row), but most of these are not a result of incorrect POS tags, demonstrating that supertagging and parsing are difficult even with correct POS tags.

The sensitivity of C&C to tagging errors, and the higher performance of the P&K parser, which does not directly use POS tags, calls into question whether POS tagging yields a net gain in a language where distinctions such as the noun/verb ambiguity are often difficult to resolve using local tagging approaches. The approach of Auli and Lopez (2011), which achieves superior results in English CCG parsing with a joint supertagging/parsing model, may be promising in light of the performance difference between P&K and C&C.

6.1 Non-local dependencies

Table 9 shows how well the best models of each parser recovered selected local and non-local dependencies. The slot represented by each row appears in boldface. While C&C and P&K perform similarly recovering *NP*-internal structure, the ability of P&K to recover verbal arguments, unbounded long-range dependencies such as subject and object extraction, and bounded long-range dependencies such as control/raising constructions, is superior.

The C&C AUTO parser appears to be biased towards generating far more of the frequent dependency types, yet does not typically have a higher recall for these dependency types than P&K.

6.2 Pro-drop and its impact on CCG parsing

One of the most common types of unary rules in Chinese CCGbank, occurring in 36% of Chinese CCGbank sentences, is the *subject pro-drop rule* $S[dcl]\backslash NP \rightarrow S[dcl]$, which accounts for the optional absence of the subject pronoun of a verb for pragmatic reasons where the referent can be recovered from the discourse (Li and Thompson, 1989).

The subject pro-drop rule is problematic in Chinese parsing because its left hand side, $S[dcl]\backslash NP$, is a very common category, and also because several syntactic distinctions in Chinese CCGbank hinge on the difference between $S[dcl]\backslash NP$ and $S[dcl]$.

The latter point is illustrated by two of the senses of 的 *de*, the Chinese subordinating particle. Two categories which 的 *de* receives in the grammar are $(NP/NP)\backslash(S[dcl]\backslash NP)$ (introducing a relative clause) and $(NP/NP)\backslash S[dcl]$ (in the construction *S de NP*). Because subject pro-drop promotes any unsaturated $S[dcl]\backslash NP$ to $S[dcl]$, whenever the supertagger returns both of the above categories for the lexical item 的 *de*, the parser must consider two alternative analyses which yield different dependencies:

(5) a. t_i 出来 的 问题$_i$
t_i come out DE question$_i$
the questions which arise

	English	Chinese
PTB/PCTB-based	92.1% (McClosky et al., 2006)	86.8% (Zhang and Clark, 2009)
CCGbank-based	86.0% (Fowler and Penn, 2010)	72.7% (this work)
	85.8% (Clark and Curran, 2007)	67.1% (this work)

Table 11: Summary of Chinese parsing approaches

	model	*LF*	*Lsa* %	stag	cov	log *C*
C	GOLD	74.99	7.42	89.36	98.6	18.35
		(76.73	*20.56*	*89.66*	*99.5*	*13.58)*
	AUTO	65.42	4.82	83.73	97.9	18.67
		(66.95	*14.62*	*83.90*	*99.2*	*13.86)*
	I-5	70.67	8.62	84.99	93.8	-
		(72.74	*18.59*	*85.61*	*96.5*	*-)*

Table 12: Dev set evaluation for C&C over *pro*-drop sentences only (and over full set in parentheses)

b. *pro* 出来 的 问题
pro come out DE question
the question of (him, her) coming out

38.1% of sentences in the development set contain at least one instance of *pro*-drop. The evaluation over only these sentences is given in Table 12. This restricted evaluation shows that while we cannot conclude that *pro*-drop is the causative factor, sentences with *pro*-drop are much more difficult for *both* parsers to analyse correctly, although the drops in *F*-score and supertagging accuracy are largest for P&K.

Critically, the fact that supertagging performance on these more difficult sentences is reasonably comparable with performance on the full set suggests that the bottleneck is in the parser rather than the supertagger. One measure of the complexity of *pro*-drop sentences is the substantial increase in the log C value of these sentences. This suggests that a key to bringing parser performance on Chinese in line with English lies in reining in the ambiguity caused by very productive unary rules such as *pro*-drop.

7 Conclusion

Using Chinese CCGbank (Tse and Curran, 2010), we have trained and evaluated the first CCG parsers for Chinese in the literature: the Clark and Curran (C&C; 2007) and Petrov and Klein (P&K; 2007) parsers. The P&K parser substantially outperformed (72.73) C&C with automatic POS tags (67.09).

Table 11 summarises the best performance of parsers on PTB and CCGbank, for English and Chinese. We observe a drop in performance between English and Chinese CCG parsers which is much larger than, but consistent with, PTB parsers. To close this gap, future research in Chinese parsing should be informed by quantifying the aspects of Chinese which account most for the deficit.

We start by using corpus conversion to compare different linguistic representation choices, rather than for generating a single immutable resource. This can also be exploited to develop syntactic corpora parameterised for particular applications. We found that collapsing categorial distinctions motivated by theory can yield less ambiguous corpora, and hence, more accurate parsers. We have also taken a novel approach to investigating the impact of noun/verb and other POS ambiguities on parsing.

The large gap between Chinese C&C and P&K is surprising, given that Fowler and Penn (2010) found only a small gap for English. We found that C&C is very sensitive to POS tagging performance, which leads to its inferior performance given automatically assigned POS tags. This suggests that joint supertagging/parsing approaches, as performed by P&K, are more suitable for Chinese. Finally, we have shown that *pro*-drop is correlated with poor performance on both parsers, suggesting an avenue to closing the Chinese-English parsing gap.

While developing the first wide-coverage Chinese CCG parsers, we have shed light on the nature of the Chinese-English parsing gap, and identified new and significant challenges for CCG parsing.

Acknowledgements

We thank our anonymous reviewers for their insightful and detailed feedback. James R. Curran was supported by Australian Research Council (ARC) Discovery grant DP1097291 and the Capital Markets Cooperative Research Centre.

References

Michael Auli and Adam Lopez. 2011. A comparison of loopy belief propagation and dual decomposition for integrated ccg supertagging and parsing. In *49th Annual Meeting of the Association for Computational Linguistics*, pages 470–480. Association for Computational Linguistics.

Daniel M. Bikel. 2004. *On the parameter space of generative lexicalized statistical parsing models*. Ph.D. thesis, Citeseer.

Daniel M. Bikel and David Chiang. 2000. Two statistical parsing models applied to the Chinese Treebank. In *Second workshop on Chinese language processing*, volume 12, pages 1–6. Morristown, NJ, USA.

John Carroll, Ted Briscoe, and Antonio Sanfilippo. 1998. Parser evaluation: a survey and a new proposal. In *Proceedings of the 1st International Conference on Language Resources and Evaluation*, pages 447–454.

Yuen-Ren Chao. 1968. *A grammar of spoken Chinese*. University of California Press.

David Chiang and Daniel M. Bikel. 2002. Recovering latent information in treebanks. In *Proceedings of the 19th international conference on Computational linguistics*, volume 1, pages 1–7. Association for Computational Linguistics.

Stephen Clark and James R. Curran. 2004. The importance of supertagging for wide-coverage CCG parsing. In *Proceedings of the 20th international conference on Computational Linguistics*. Association for Computational Linguistics.

Stephen Clark and James R. Curran. 2007. Wide-Coverage Efficient Statistical Parsing with CCG and Log-Linear Models. In *Computational Linguistics*, volume 33, pages 493–552.

James R. Curran and Stephen Clark. 2003. Investigating GIS and smoothing for maximum entropy taggers. In *Proceedings of the 10th Meeting of the EACL*, pages 91–98. Budapest, Hungary.

Timothy A.D. Fowler and Gerald Penn. 2010. Accurate context-free parsing with combinatory categorial grammar. *Proceedings of the 48th Annual Meeting of the Association for Computational Linguistics*, pages 335–344.

Yuqing Guo, Haifeng Wang, and Josef Van Genabith. 2007. Recovering non-local dependencies for Chinese. In *EMNLP/CoNLL*, pages 257–266.

Julia Hockenmaier. 2003. *Data and Models for Statistical Parsing with Combinatory Categorial Grammar*. Ph.D. thesis, University of Edinburgh.

Julia Hockenmaier and Mark Steedman. 2005. CCGbank: Users' manual. Technical report, MS-CIS-05-09, Computer and Information Science, University of Pennsylvania.

Julia Hockenmaier and Mark Steedman. 2007. CCGbank: A Corpus of CCG Derivations and Dependency Structures Extracted from the Penn Treebank. *Computational Linguistics*, 33(3):355–396.

Matthew Honnibal. 2010. *Hat Categories: Representing Form and Function Simultaneously in Combinatory Categorial Grammar*. Ph.D. thesis, University of Sydney.

Liang Huang, Wenbin Jiang, and Qun Liu. 2009. Bilingually-constrained (monolingual) shift-reduce parsing. In *Proceedings of the 2009 Conference on Empirical Methods in Natural Language Processing*, volume 3, pages 1222–1231. Association for Computational Linguistics.

Roger Levy and Christopher Manning. 2003. Is it harder to parse Chinese, or the Chinese Treebank? In *Annual Meeting of the Association for Computational Linguistics*, volume 1, pages 439–446. Morristown, NJ, USA.

Charles N. Li and Sandra A. Thompson. 1989. *Mandarin Chinese: A functional reference grammar*. University of California Press.

Mitchell P. Marcus, Beatrice Santorini, and Mary Ann Marcinkiewicz. 1994. Building a Large Annotated Corpus of English: The Penn Treebank. *Computational Linguistics*, 19(2):313–330.

David McClosky, Eugene Charniak, and Mark Johnson. 2006. Effective self-training for parsing. In *Proceedings of the main conference on Human Language Technology Conference of the North American Chapter of the Association of Computational Linguistics*, pages 152–159. Association for Computational Linguistics.

Yusuke Miyao, Takashi Ninomiya, and Jun'ichi Tsujii. 2004. Corpus-Oriented Grammar Development for Acquiring a Head-Driven Phrase Structure Grammar from the Penn Treebank. pages 684–693.

Slav Petrov and Dan Klein. 2007. Improved inference for unlexicalized parsing. In *Proceedings of NAACL HLT 2007*, pages 404–411.

Laura Rimell, Stephen Clark, and Mark Steedman. 2009. Unbounded dependency recovery for parser evaluation. In *Proceedings of the 2009 Conference on Empirical Methods in Natural Language Processing: Volume 2-Volume 2*, pages 813–821. Association for Computational Linguistics.

Mark Steedman. 2000. *The Syntactic Process*. MIT Press. Cambridge, MA, USA.

Daniel Tse and James R. Curran. 2010. Chinese CCG-bank: extracting CCG derivations from the Penn Chinese Treebank. *Proceedings of the 23rd International Conference on Computational Linguistics (COLING 2010)*, pages 1083–1091.

Mengqiu Wang, Kenji Sagae, and Teruko Mitamura. 2006. A fast, accurate deterministic parser for Chinese. In *Proceedings of the 21st International Conference on Computational Linguistics and the 44th annual meeting of the Association for Computational Linguistics*, pages 425–432. Association for Computational Linguistics.

Fei Xia. 1999. Extracting tree adjoining grammars from bracketed corpora. In *Proceedings of Natural Language Processing Pacific Rim Symposium '99*, pages 398–403.

Fei Xia, Chung-hye Han, Martha Palmer, and Aravind Joshi. 2000. Comparing lexicalized treebank grammars extracted from Chinese, Korean, and English corpora. In *Proceedings of the second workshop on Chinese language processing: held in conjunction with the 38th Annual Meeting of the Association for Computational Linguistics*, volume 12, pages 52–59. Association for Computational Linguistics.

Nianwen Xue, Fei Xia, Fu-Dong Chiou, and Martha Palmer. 2005. The Penn Chinese TreeBank: Phrase structure annotation of a large corpus. *Natural Language Engineering*, 11(02):207–238.

Kun Yu, Yusuke Miyao, Takuya Matsuzaki, Xiangli Wang, and Jun'ichi Tsujii. 2011. Analysis of the difficulties in chinese deep parsing. In *12th International Conference on Parsing Technologies*, page 48.

Yue Zhang and Stephen Clark. 2008. A tale of two parsers: investigating and combining graph-based and transition-based dependency parsing using beam-search. In *Proceedings of the Conference on Empirical Methods in Natural Language Processing*, pages 562–571. Association for Computational Linguistics.

Yue Zhang and Stephen Clark. 2009. Transition-based parsing of the Chinese treebank using a global discriminative model. In *Proceedings of the 11th International Conference on Parsing Technologies*, pages 162–171. Association for Computational Linguistics.

Using Supertags and Encoded Annotation Principles for Improved Dependency to Phrase Structure Conversion

Seth Kulick and **Ann Bies** and **Justin Mott**
Linguistic Data Consortium
University of Pennsylvania
Philadelphia, PA 19104
{skulick,bies,jmott}@ldc.upenn.edu

Abstract

We investigate the problem of automatically converting from a dependency representation to a phrase structure representation, a key aspect of understanding the relationship between these two representations for NLP work. We implement a new approach to this problem, based on a small number of supertags, along with an encoding of some of the underlying principles of the Penn Treebank guidelines. The resulting system significantly outperforms previous work in such automatic conversion. We also achieve comparable results to a system using a phrase-structure parser for the conversion. A comparison with our system using either the part-of-speech tags or the supertags provides some indication of what the parser is contributing.

1 Introduction and Motivation

Recent years have seen a significant increase in interest in dependency treebanks and dependency parsing. Since the standard training and test set for English parsing is a phrase structure (PS) treebank, the Penn Treebank (PTB) (Marcus et al., 1993; Marcus et al., 1994), the usual approach is to convert this to a dependency structure (DS) treebank, by means of various heuristics for identifying heads in a PS tree. The resulting DS representation is then used for training and parsing, with results reported on the DS representation.

Our goal in this paper is to go in the reverse direction, from the DS to PS representation, by finding a minimal DS representation from which we can use an approximate version of the principles of the PTB guidelines to reconstruct the PS. Work in this conversion direction is somewhat less studied (Xia et al., 2009; Xia and Palmer, 2001), but it is still an important topic for a number of reasons. First, because both DS and PS treebanks are of current interest, there is an increasing effort made to create multi-representational treebank resources with both DS and PS available from the beginning, without a loss of information in either direction (Xia et al., 2009). Second, it is sometimes the case that it is convenient to do annotation in a dependency representation (e.g., if the annotators are already familiar with such a representation), though the treebank will in final form be either phrase-structure or multi-representational (Xia et al., 2009).

However, our concern is somewhat different. We are specifically interested in experimenting with dependency parsing of Arabic as a step in the annotation of the Arabic Treebank, which is a phrase structure treebank (Maamouri et al., 2011). Although we currently use a phrase structure parser in this annotation pipeline, there are advantages to the flexibility of being able to experiment with advances in parsing technology for dependency parsing. We would like to parse with a dependency representation of the data, and then convert the parser output to a phrase structure representation so that it can feed into the annotation pipeline. Therefore, in order to make use of dependency parsers, we need a conversion from dependency to phrase structure with very high accuracy, which is the goal of this paper.

While one of our underlying concerns is DS to PS conversion for Arabic, we are first focusing on a conversion routine for the English PTB because it is so well-established and the results are easier to interpret. The intent is then to transfer this conversion algorithm work to the Arabic treebank as well. We expect this to be successful because the ATB has some fundamental similarities to the PTB in spite of the language difference (Maamouri and Bies, 2004).

As mentioned above, one goal in our DS to PS conversion work is to base it on a minimal DS representation. By "minimal", we mean that it does not include information that is redundant, together with our conversion code, with the implicit information in the dependency structure itself. As discussed more in Section 2.1, we aim to make our dependency representation simpler than "hybrid" representations such as Johansson and Nugues (2007). The reason for our interest in this minimal representation is parsing. We do not want to require the parser to recover such a complex dependency representations, when it is, in fact, unnecessary, as we believe our approach shows. The benefit of this approach can only be seen when this line of work is extended to experiments with parsing and Arabic conversion. The work described here is just the first step in this process.

A conversion scheme, such as ours, necessarily relies on some details of the annotation content in the DS and PS representations, and so our algorithm is not an algorithm designed to take as input any arbitrary DS representation. However, the fundamentals of our dependency representation are not radically different than others - e.g. we make an auxiliary verb the child of the main verb, instead of the other way, but such choices can be adjusted for in the conversion.

To evaluate the success of this conversion algorithm, we follow the same evaluation procedure as Xia et al. (2009) and Xia and Palmer (2001). We convert the PTB to a DS, and then use our algorithm to convert the DS back to a PS representation. The original PS and the converted-from-DS PS are then compared, in exactly the same way as parser output is compared with the original (gold) tree. We will show that our results in this area are a significant improvement above previous efforts.

A key aspect of this work is that our DS-to-PS conversion encodes many of the properties of the PTB annotation guidelines (Bies et al., 1995), both globally and for specific XP projections. The PTB guidelines are built upon broad decisions about PS representation that provide an overall framework and cohesion for the details of the PS trees. To implement these underlying principles of the guidelines, we defined a set of 30 "supertags" that indicate how a lexical item can project in the syntactic structure, allowing us to specify these principles. We describe these as supertags because of a conceptual similarity to the supertagging work in the Tree Adjoining Grammar (TAG) tradition (Bangalore and Joshi, 2010), although ours is far smaller than a typical supertag set, and indeed is actually smaller than the PTB POS tag set.

Our DS-to-PS code is based on this set of supertags, and can be run using either the supertags created from the gold POS tags, or using the POS tags, together with the dependency structure to first (imperfectly) derive the supertags, and then proceed with the conversion. This choice of starting point allows us to measure the impact of POS tag complexities on the DS-to-PS conversion, which provides an interesting insight on what a phrase structure parser contributes in addition to this sort of automated DS-to-PS conversion, as discussed in Section 4.

We have chosen this approach of encoding underlying principles of the PTB guidelines for two reasons. First, these principles are non-statistical, and thus we felt it would let us tease apart the contribution of the frequency information relating, e.g., heads, on the one hand, and the basic notions of phrase structure on the other. The second reason is that it was quite easy to implement these principles. We did not attempt a complete examination of every possible rule in Bies et al. (1995), but rather just selected the most obvious ones. As we will see in Section 4.2, our results indeed are sometimes hurt by such lack of thoroughness, although in future work we will make this more complete.

2 Overview and Example

Figures 1-4 provide a running example of the four steps in the process. Figure 1 is the original tree from the Penn Treebank. Figures 2 and 3 illustrate the two-step process of creating the dependency representation, and Figure 4 shows the conversion back to phrase structure.

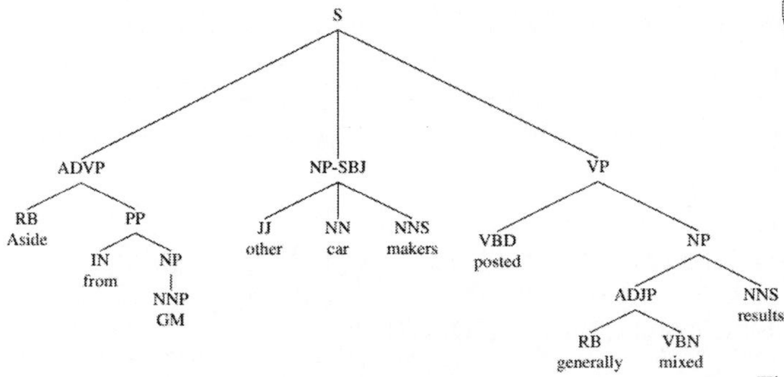

Figure 1: Penn Treebank tree

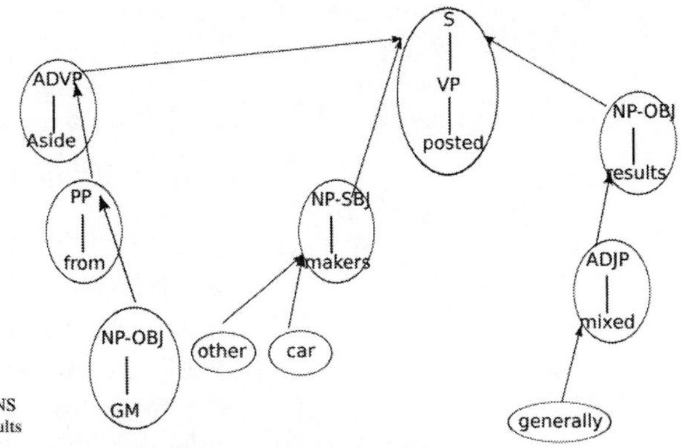

Figure 2: Tree Insertion Grammar decomposition of Figure 1

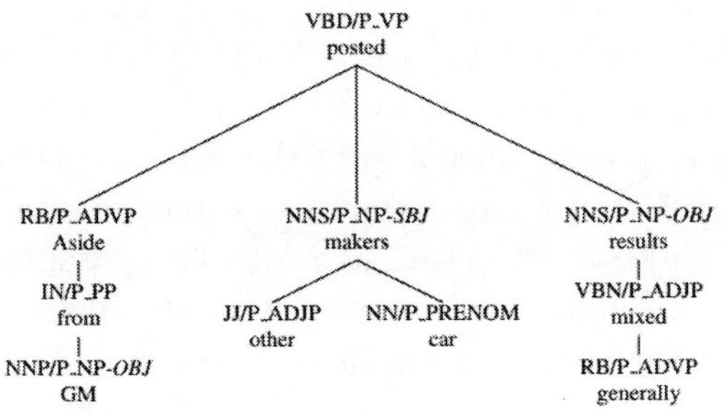

Figure 3: Dependency representation derived from TIG decomposition in Figure 2

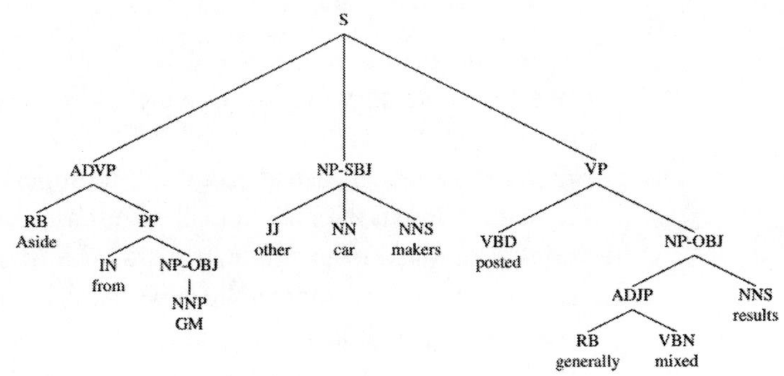

Figure 4: Conversion of dependency representation in Figure 3 back to phrase structure.

2.1 Creation of Dependency Representation

The creation of the dependency representation is similar in basic aspects to many other approaches, in that we utilize some basic assumptions about head relations to decompose the full tree into smaller units. However, we first decompose the original trees into a Tree Insertion Grammar representation (Chiang, 2003), utilizing tree substitution and sister adjunction. We refer the reader to Chiang (2003) for details of these operations, and instead focus on the fact that the TIG derivation tree in Figure 2 partitions the phrase structure representation in Figure 1 into smaller units, called elementary trees. We leave out the POS tags in Figure 2 to avoid clutter.

The creation of the dependency representation is structurally a simple rewrite of the TIG derivation, taking the word associated with each elementary tree and using it as a node in the dependency tree. In this way, the dependency representation in Figure 3 follows immediately from Figure 2.

However, in addition, we utilize the TIG derivation tree and the structures of the elementary trees to create a supertag (in the sense discussed in Section 1) for each word. For example, `aside` heads an elementary tree that projects to `ADVP`, so it is assigned the supertag P_ADVP in Figure 3, meaning that it projects to ADVP. We label each node in Figure 3 with both its POS tag and supertag, so in this case the node for `aside` has RB/P_ADVP.

There are two typical cases that are not so straightforward. The first concerns elementary trees with more than one level of projection, such as that for the verb, `posted`, which has two levels of projection, S and VP. In such cases we base the supertag only on the immediate parent of the word. For example, in this case the supertag for `posted` is P_VP, rather than P_S. As will be seen in Section 3.2, our perspective is that the local context of the dependency tree will provide the necessary disambiguation as to what node is above the VP.

Projection Type	Supertag
NP	P_NP
ADJP	P_ADJP
ADVP	P_ADVP
PP	P_PP, P_WHPP
S,SINV,SQ	P_VP
QP,NP,QP-NP,QP-ADJP	P_QP
WHNP	P_WHNP
default	P_WHADVP, P_INTJ, P_PRT, P_LST
none	P_AUX, P_PRENOM, P_DET, P_COMMA, P_PERIOD, P_CC, P_COMP, P_POS, P_PRP$, P_BACKDQUOTE, P_DQUOTE, P_COLON, P_DOLLAR, P_LRB, P_RB, P_PDT, P_SYM, P_FW, P_POUND

Table 1: 30 supertags handled by 14 projection types. The ambiguity in some, such as P_VP projecting as S, SINV, SQ is handled by an examination of the dependency structure.

The second non-straightforward case[1] is that of degenerate elementary trees, in which the "tree" is just the word itself, as for `other`, `car`, and `generally`. In such cases we default the supertag based on the original POS tag, and in some cases, the tree configuration. For example, a word with the JJ tag, such as `other`, would get the supertag P_ADJP, with the RB tag such as `generally` the supertag P_ADVP. We assign prenominal nouns such as `car` here the tag P_PRENOM.

Generating supertags in this way is a convenient way to correct some of the POS tag errors in the PTB (Manning, 2011). For example, if `that` has the (incorrect) tag DT in the complementizer position, it still receives the new POS tag `P_COMP`.

This procedure results in a set of 30 supertags, and Table 1 shows how they are partitioned into 14 projection types. These supertags and projection types are the basis of our DS-to-PS conversion, as discussed further in Section 2.2.

We note here a brief comparison with earlier work on "hybrid" representations, which encode a PS representation inside a DS one, in order to convert from the latter to the former. (Hall and Nivre, 2008; Johan Hall and Nilsson, 2007; Johansson and Nugues, 2007). Our goal is very different. Instead of encoding the phrase structure in the dependency tree via complex tags such as SBARQ in Johansson and Nugues (2007), we use a minimal representation and rely on our encoding of the general principles of PTB phrase structure to carry much of the weight. While supertags such as P_VP may appear to encode some of the structure, their primary role is as an intermediate link between the POS tags and the phrase structure conversion. The created supertags are not in fact necessary for this conversion. As we will see in the following sections, we convert from DS to PS using either just the original POS tags, or with our created supertags.

We also include five labels in the dependency representation: SBJ, OBJ, PRN, COORD_CONJ, APP. The example dependency tree in Figure 3 includes instances of the SBJ and OBJ labels, in italics on the node instead of the edges, for convenience. The SBJ label is of course already a function tag in the PTB. We process the PTB when creating the TIG decomposition to add an OBJ tag, as well basing the PRN label on the occurrence of the PRN node. We also use heuristics to identify cases of coordination and apposition, resulting in the COORD_CONJ and APP tags. The reasons for including these labels is that they prove useful in the conversion to phrase structure, as illustrated in some of the examples below.

Before moving on to the dependency-to-phrase-stucture conversion, we end this section with a comment on the role of function tags and empty categories. The PTB makes use of function tags to in-

[1]There are other details not discussed here. For example, we do not automatically assign a P_NP supertag to the head child of an NP, since such a head can legitimately be, e.g, a JJ, in which case we make the supertag P_ADJP, on the reasoning that it would be encoding "too much" to treat it as P_NP. Instead, we rely on the DS and such labels as SBJ or OBJ to determine when to project it as NP in the converted PS.

dicate certain syntactic and semantic information, and of empty categories (and co-indexing) for a more complete and accurate syntactic representation. There is some overlap between the five labels we use, as just described, and the PTB function tags, but in general we do not encode the full range of function tags in our representation, saving this for future work. More significantly, we also do not include empty categories and associated co-indexing, which has the consequence that the dependency trees are projective.

The reason we have not included these aspects in our representation and conversion yet is that we are focused here first on the evaluation for comparison with previous work, and the basis for this previous work is the usual evalb program (Sekine and Collins, 2008), which ignores function tags and empty categories. We return to this issue in the conclusion.

2.2 From Dependency to Phrase Structure

There are two key aspects to the conversion from dependency to phrase structure. (1) We encode general conventions about annotation that are used throughout the annotation guidelines for the PTB. A common example is that of the "single-word" rule, in which a constituent consisting of just a single word is reduced to just that word, without the constituent bracketing, in many cases. (2) We use the set of supertags as the basis for defining projection-specific rules for how to attach children on the left or right of the head, in many cases utilizing the supertag names that we include to determine the specific attachment.

For example, the leaf `GM` in Figure 3 has the supertag P_NP (with the label OBJ), so heading a NP projection, `(NP GM)`. Its parent node, `from`, has the supertag P_PP, indicating that it heads a PP projection, and so attaches the `(NP GM)` as a sister of `from`. It does not reduce it down as a single word, because the encoding of the PP projection specifies that it does not do so for children on its right.

A more substantial case is that of the NP `other car makers`. Here the head noun, `makers`, has the supertag P_NP, and so projects as an NP. Its first child, `other`, has the supertag P_ADJP, and so projects as an ADJP, resulting in `(ADJP other)`. The second child, `car`, has the supertag P_PRENOM (prenominal), and so does not project at all. When the NP projection for `makers` is assembled, it applies the "single-word" constraint to children on its left (as encoded in the definition of the NP projection), thus stripping the ADJP off of `other`, resulting in the desired flat NP `other car makers`. Likewise, the ADVP projection for `generally` is stripped off before it is attached as a left sister of the ADJP projection `mixed`. The encoding of a VP projection specifies that it must project above VP if it is the root of the tree, and so the VP projection for `posted` projects to S (by default).

In this way we can see that encoding some of the general characteristics of the annotation guidelines allows the particular details of the PTB phrase-structure representation to be created from the less-specific dependency representation.

3 Some Further Examples

3.1 QP Projection or Reduction

As mentioned in Section 2.2, the "single word" convention is implemented in the conversion to PS, as was the case with `other` in the previous section. The projection associated with P_QP has a slight twist to this principle, because of the nature of some of the financialspeak in the PTB. In particular, the dollar sign is treated as a displaced word and is therefore not counted, in a QP constituent, as a token for purposes of the "single token" rule.

For example, (1abc) in Figure 5 illustrates a case where the QP structure projects to an NP node as well. (1a) is the original PTB PS tree, and (1b) is the DS representation. Note that `billion` heads the `about $ 9 billion` subtree, with the supertag P_QP and the label OBJ.[2] Because it has more than one child in addition to the $, it is converted to phrase structure as a QP under an NP, implying the empty *U*, although we do not actually put it in.

In contrast, (2abc) is a case in which the QP node is not generated. 100 is the head of the phrase $ 100 *U* in the PTB PS (a), as shown in the dependency structure (b). However, because it only has one child in addition to the $, no additional QP node is created in the phrase structure representation in (c). We stress that the presence of the QP in (1a) and its ab-

[2]A good case can be made that in fact $ should be the daughter of `to` in the dependency tree, although we have not implemented this as such.

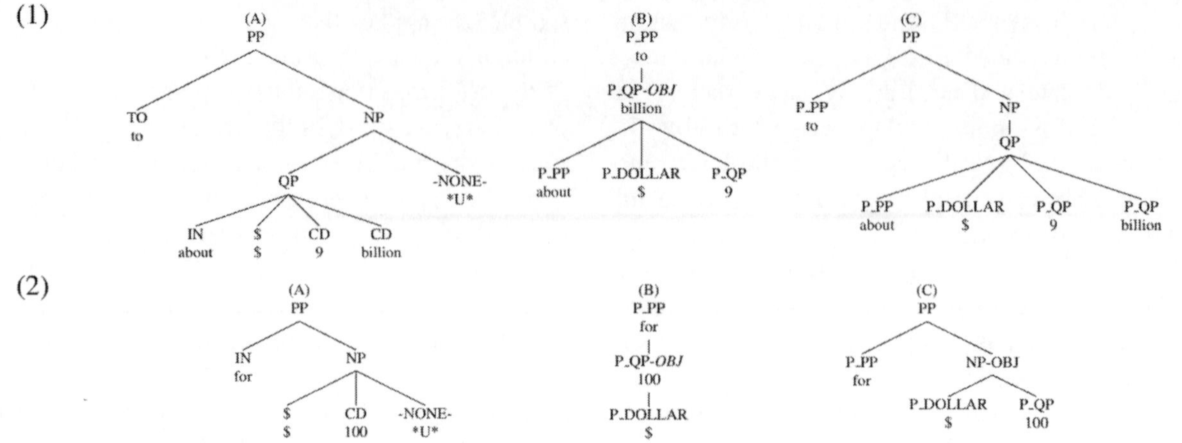

Figure 5: Examples of handling of QP in dependency to phrase-structure conversion.

sence in (2a) is correct annotation, consistent with the annotation guidelines.

3.2 Refinement of VP Projections

As mentioned above, instead of having separate supertags for S, SINV, SQ, SBAR, SBARQ, we use only the P_VP supertag and let the context determine the specifics of the projection. Sentences (3ab) in Figure 6 illustrate how the SBJ label is used to treat the P_VP supertag as indicating projection to SINV (or SQ) instead of S. The determination is based on the children of the P_VP node. For example, if there is a child with the P_AUX supertag which is before a child with the SBJ label, which in turn is before the P_VP node itself, then the latter is treated as projecting to either SINV or SQ, depending on the some additional factors, primarily whether there is a WH word among the children. In this example, there is no WH word, so it becomes a SINV.[3] We note here that we also include a simple listing of verbs that take complements of certain types - such as verbs of saying, etc., that take SBAR complements, so that a VP will project not just to S, but SBAR, even if the complement is missing.

3.3 Coordination

We represent coordination in the dependency in one of the standard ways, by making the following conjuncts be children of the head word of

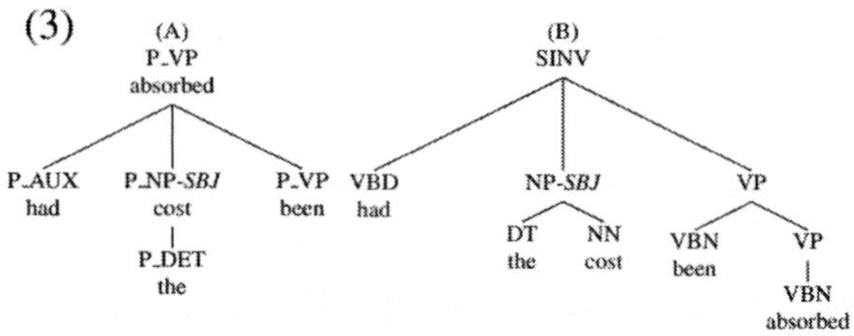

Figure 6: (3ab) shows that the local context of the P_VP supertag in the dependency tree results in a SINV structure in the converted phrase structure tree (3b).

the first conjunct. For example, a dependency representation of `...turn down the volume and close the curtains` is shown in (4a) in Figure 7. The conjunct `close the curtains` is converted as a VP projection projecting to S. However, when the projection for `turn` is assembled, the code checks if the conjuncts are missing subjects, and if so, reduces the configuration to standard VP coordination, as in (4b). The COORD label is used to identify such structures for examination.

4 Results of Dependency to Phrase Structure Conversion

To evaluate the correctness of conversion from dependency to phrase structure, we follow the same strategy as Xia and Palmer (2001) and Xia et al. (2009). We convert the phrase structure trees in the PTB to dependency structure and convert the dependency back to phrase structure. We then compare the original PTB trees with the newly-created phrase

[3]This is not a fully precise implementation of the conditions distinguishing SQ and SINV projections, in that it does not properly check for whether the clause is a question.

(4)

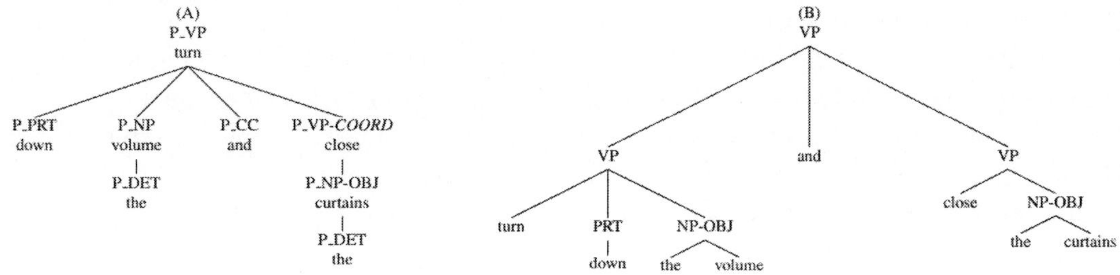

Figure 7: (4a) is the dependency representation of a coordination structure, and the resulting phrase structure (4b) shows that the conversion treated it as VP coordination, due to the absence of a subject.

Sec	System	rec	prec	f
00	Xia & Palmer '01	86.2	88.7	87.5
	Xia et al. '09	91.8	89.2	90.5
	USE-POS-UNLABEL	96.6	97.4	97.0
	USE-POS	94.6	95.4	95.0
	USE-SUPER	95.9	97.0	96.4
22	Xia et al. '09	90.7	88.1	89.4
	USE-POS	95.0	95.5	95.3
	USE-SUPER	96.4	97.1	96.7
23	Wang & Zong '10	95.9	96.3	96.1
	USE-POS	94.8	95.7	95.3
	USE-SUPER	96.2	97.3	96.7
24	USE-POS	94.0	94.7	94.4
	USE-SUPER	95.9	97.1	96.5

Table 2: Results of dependency to phrase structure conversion. For our system, the results are presented in two ways, using either the gold part-of-speech tags (USE-POS) or our gold supertags (USE-SUPER). For purposes of comparison with Xia and Palmer (2001) and Xia et al. (2009), we also present the results for Section 00 using part-of-speech tags, but with an unlabeled evaluation (USE-POS-UNLABEL).

structure trees, using the standard evalb scoring code (Sekine and Collins, 2008). Xia and Palmer (2001) defined three different algorithms for the conversion, utilizing different heuristics for how to build projection chains, and where to attach dependent subtrees. They reported results for their system for Section 00 of the PTB, and we include in Table 2 only their highest scoring algorithm. The system of Xia et al. (2009) uses conversion rules learned from Section 19, and then tested on Sections 00 and Section 22.

We developed the algorithm using Section 24, and we also report results for Sections 00, 22, and 23, for comparison with previous work. We ran our system in two ways. In one we use the "gold" supertags that were created as described in Section 2.1 (USE-SUPER), based on the TIG decomposition of the original tree. In the other (USE-POS) we use the gold POS tags, and not the supertags. Because our DS-to-PS algorithm is based on using the supertags to guide the conversion, the USE-POS runs work by using a few straightforward heuristics to guess the correct supertag from the POS tag and the dependency structure. For example, if a word x has the POS tag "TO" and the word y to its immediate right is its parent in the dependency tree and y has one of the verbal POS tags, then x receives the supertag P_AUX, and otherwise P_PP. Any word with the POS tag JJ, JJR, or JJS, receives the supertag P_ADJP, and so on. The results for Xia and Palmer (2001) and Xia et al. (2009) were reported using an unlabeled version of evalb, so to compare properly we also report our results for Section 00 using an unlabeled evaluation of the run using the POS tags (USE-POS-UNLABEL), while all the other results use a labeled evaluation.

We also compare our system with that of Wang and Zong (2010). Unlike the three other systems (including ours), this was not based on an automatic conversion from a gold dependency tree to phrase structure, but rather used the gold dependency tree as additional input for a phrase structure parser (the Berkeley parser).

4.1 Analysis

While our system was developed using Section 24, the f-measure results for USE-SUPER are virtually identical across all four sections (96.4, 96.7, 96.7, 96.5). Interestingly, there is more variation in the

USE-POS results (95.0, 95.3, 95.3, 94.4). We take this to be an indication of a difference in the sections as to the utility of the POS tags to "bootstrap" the syntactic structure. As just mentioned above, the USE-POS runs work by using heuristics to approximate the gold supertags from the POS tags.

The supertags, because they are partially derived from the phrase structure, can obscure a disconnect between a POS tag and the syntactic structure it projects. For example, the word `according` in the structure `(PP (VBG according) (PP (TO to) ...))` receives the gold supertag P_PP, a more explicit representation of the word's role in the structure than the ambiguous VBG. This is why the USE-POS score is lower than the USE-SUPER score, since the POS tag and dependency structure do not always, at least with our simple heuristics, lead to the gold supertag. For example, in the USE-POS run, `according` receives the incorrect supertag P_VP, leading to an incorrect structure, while in the USE-SUPER run, it is able to use P_PP, leading to the correct structure.

However, even with the lower performance of USE-POS, it is well above the results reported in Xia et al. (2009) for Section 22, and even more so with the unlabeled evaluation of Section 00 compared to Xia and Palmer (2001) and Xia et al. (2009). The comparison with Wang and Zong (2010) for Section 23 (they did not report results for any other section) shows something very different, however. Their result, using a gold dependency tree together with the Berkeley parser, is above our USE-POS version and below our USE-SUPER version.

Our interpretation of this is that it provides an indication of what the parser is providing on top of the gold dependency structure, which is roughly the same information that we have encoded in our DS to PS code. However, because the Wang and Zong (2010) system performs better than our USE-POS version, it is likely learning some of the non-straightforward cases of how USE-POS tags can bootstrap the syntactic structure that our USE-POS version is missing. However, any conclusions must be tentative since our dependency structures are not necessarily the same as theirs and so it is not an exact comparison.

Error type	count
problem with PTB annotation	8
ambiguous ADVP placement	3
incorrect use of "single token rule"	3
FRAG/X	2
multiple levels of recursion	2
other	5

Table 3: Analysis of errors in first 50 sentences of USE-SUPER run for Section 24

4.2 Errors from Dependency Structure with Supertags to Phrase Structure

We stressed in the introduction that we are interested in understanding better the relationship between the DS and PS representations. Identifying areas where the conversion from DS did not result in a perfect (evalb score) PS is therefore of particular interest.

For this analysis, we used our dev section, 24, with the run USE-SUPER. We use this run because we are interested in cases where, even with the gold supertags, there was still a problem with the conversion to the PS. We examined the first 50 sentences in the section, with a total of 23 errors. We recognize that this is a very small sample. An eyeball examination of other sentences does not reveal anything significantly different than what we present here as far as the sorts of errors, although we have only performed a rigorous analysis of these 23 errors, which is why we limit our discussion here to these cases.

Table 3 shows a breakdown of these 23 errors. Note that by "error" here we mean a difference between the reconstructed PS structure, and the PTB gold PS structure, causing the score for Section 24, USE-SUPER (last row) in Table 2 to be less than perfect.

The most common "error" is that in which the PTB annotation is itself in error, while our algorithm actually creates a correct phrase structure, in the sense that it is consistent with the PTB guidelines. Three of these eight annotation problems are of the same type, in which a NP is headed by a word with the RB tag. An example is shown in (5) in which (5a) shows (a fragment of) the original tree in the PTB, and (5b) is the resulting DS, with (5c) the reconstructed PS tree. The word `here` receives the supertag P_ADVP, thus resulting in a different reconstructed PS, with an ADVP. There is a mismatch between the POS tag and the node label in the original tree (5a), and in fact in this case the node label in the PTB tree should have been ADVP-LOC, instead of NP-LOC.

(5)

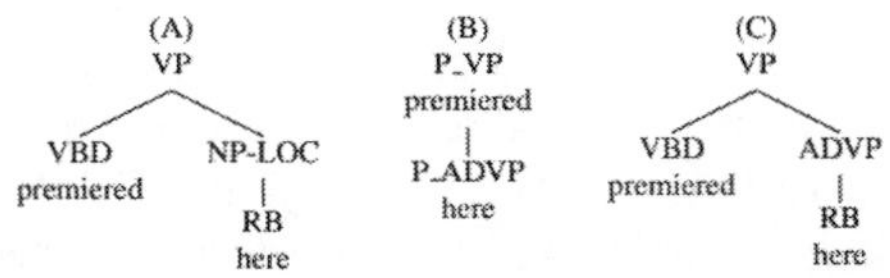

(6)

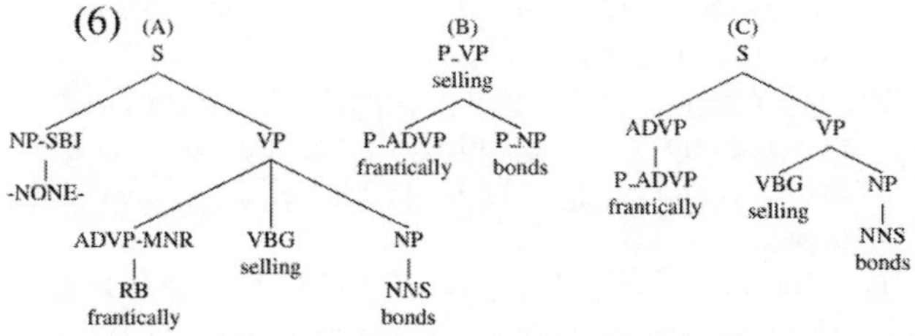

An example of the "ambiguous ADVP placement" error is shown in (6), in which the PTB tree has the adverb `frantically` inside the VP, information which is not available in the DS (6b). Our conversion code has to choose as to where to put such ADVPs, and it puts them outside the VP, as in (6c), which is sometimes correct, but not in this case.

5 Conclusion and Future Work

In this work we have described an approach to automatically converting DS to PS with significantly improved accuracy over previous efforts, and comparable results to that of using a phrase structure parser guided by the dependency structure.

Following the motivation discussed in Section 1, the next step is straightforward - to adapt the algorithm to work on conversion from a dependency representation of the Arabic Treebank to the phrase structure representation necessary for the annotation pipeline. Following this, we will then experiment with parsing the Arabic dependency representation, converting to phrase structure, and evaluating the resulting phrase structure representation as usual for parsing evaluation. We will also experiment with dependency parsing for the PTB dependency representation discussed in this paper. Habash and Roth (2009) discuss an already-existing dependency representation of parts of the ATB and it will be interesting to compare the conversion accuracy using the different dependency representations, although we expect that there will not be any major differences in the representations.

One other aspect of future work is to implement the algorithm in Wang and Zong (2010), using our own dependency representation, since this would allow a precise investigation of what the phrase structure parser is contributing as compared to our automatic conversion. We note that this work also experimented with dependency parsing, and then automatically converting the results to PS, a further basis of comparison.

Finally, we would like to stress that while we have used evalb for scoring the converting PS because it is the standard evaluation for PS work, it is a very insufficient standard for this work. As discussed at the end of Section 2, we have not included all the function tags or empty categories in our representation, a significant omission. We would like to expand our dependency representation to allow all the function tags and empty categories to be included in the converted PS. Our plan is to take our analogy to TAG more seriously (e.g., (Joshi and Rambow, 2003)) and use a label akin to adjunction to encode leftward (non-projective) movement in the tree, also using an appropriate dependency parser as well (Shen and Joshi, 2008).

Acknowledgements

This work was supported in part by the Defense Advanced Research Projects Agency, GALE Program Grant No. HR0011-06-1-0003. The views, opinions and/or findings contained in this article/presentation are those of the author/presenter and should not be interpreted as representing the official views or policies, either expressed or implied, of the Defense Advanced Research Projects Agency or the Department of Defense. We would also like to thank Mohamed Maamouri, Colin Warner, Aravind Joshi, and Mitch Marcus for valuable conversations and feedback.

References

Srinivas Bangalore and Aravind K. Joshi, editors. 2010. *Supertagging: Using Complex Lexical Descriptions in Natural Language Processing*. MIT Press.

Ann Bies, Mark Ferguson, Karen Katz, and Robert MacIntyre. 1995. Bracketing guidelines for Treebank II-style Penn Treebank project. Technical Report MS-CIS-95-06, University of Pennsylvania.

David Chiang. 2003. Statistical parsing with an automatically extracted Tree Adjoining Grammar. In *Data Oriented Parsing*. CSLI.

Nizar Habash and Ryan Roth. 2009. CATiB: The Columbia Arabic Treebank. In *Proceedings of the ACL-IJCNLP 2009 Conference Short Papers*, pages 221–224, Suntec, Singapore, August. Association for Computational Linguistics.

Johan Hall and Joakim Nivre. 2008. A dependency-driven parser for German dependency and constituency representations. In *Proceedings of the Workshop on Parsing German*, pages 47–54, Columbus, Ohio, June. Association for Computational Linguistics.

Joakim Nivre Johan Hall and Jens Nilsson. 2007. Hybrid constituency-dependency parser for Swedish. In *Proceedings of NODALIDA*, Tartu, Estonia.

Richard Johansson and Pierre Nugues. 2007. Extended constituent-to-dependency conversion for english. In *Proceedings of NODALIDA*, Tartu, Estonia.

Aravind Joshi and Owen Rambow. 2003. A formalism for dependency grammar based on Tree Adjoining Grammar. In *Proceedings of the Conference on Meaning-Text Theory*, Paris, France.

Mohamed Maamouri and Ann Bies. 2004. Developing an arabic treebank: Methods, guidelines, procedures, and tools. In Ali Farghaly and Karine Megerdoomian, editors, *COLING 2004 Computational Approaches to Arabic Script-based Languages*, pages 2–9, Geneva, Switzerland, August 28th. COLING.

Mohamed Maamouri, Ann Bies, and Seth Kulick. 2011. Upgrading and enhancing the Penn Arabic Treebank. In Joseph Olive, Caitlin Christianson, and John McCary, editors, *Handbook of Natural Language Processing and Machine Translation: DARPA Global Autonomous Language Exploitation*. Springer.

Christopher Manning. 2011. Part-of-speech tagging from 97% to 100%: Is it time for some linguistics? In Alexander Gelbukh, editor, *Computational Linguistics and Intelligent Text Processing, 12th International Conference, CICLing 2011, Proceedings, Part I. Lecture Notes in Computer Science 6608*.

Mitchell P. Marcus, Beatrice Santorini, and Mary Ann Marcinkiewicz. 1993. Building a large annotated corpus of English: The Penn Treebank. *Computational linguistics*, 19:313–330.

Mitchell Marcus, Grace Kim, Mary Ann Marcinkiewicz, Robert MacIntyre, Ann Bies, Mark Ferguson, Karen Katz, and Britta Schasberger. 1994. The Penn Treebank: Annotating predicate argument structure. In *Proceedings of HLT*.

Satoshi Sekine and Michael Collins. 2008. Evalb. http://nlp.cs.nyu.edu/evalb/.

Libin Shen and Aravind Joshi. 2008. LTAG dependency parsing with bidirectional incremental construction. In *Proceedings of the 2008 Conference on Empirical Methods in Natural Language Processing*, pages 495–504, Honolulu, Hawaii, October. Association for Computational Linguistics.

Zhiguo Wang and Chengqing Zong. 2010. Phrase structure parsing with dependency structure. In *COLING 2010: Posters*, pages 1292–1300, Beijing, China, August.

Fei Xia and Martha Palmer. 2001. Converting dependency structures to phrase structures. In *HLT-2001*.

Fei Xia, Owen Rambow, Rajesh Bhatt, Martha Palmer, and Dipti Misra Sharma. 2009. Towards a multi-representational treebank. In *Proceedings of the Workshop on Treebanks and Linguistic Theories*.

Getting More from Morphology in Multilingual Dependency Parsing

Matt Hohensee and Emily M. Bender
University of Washington
Department of Linguistics
Box 354340
Seattle WA 98195-4340, USA
{hohensee, ebender}@uw.edu

Abstract

We propose a linguistically motivated set of features to capture morphological agreement and add them to the MSTParser dependency parser. Compared to the built-in morphological feature set, ours is both much smaller and more accurate across a sample of 20 morphologically annotated treebanks. We find increases in accuracy of up to 5.3% absolute. While some of this results from the feature set capturing information unrelated to morphology, there is still significant improvement, up to 4.6% absolute, due to the agreement model.

1 Introduction

Most data-driven dependency parsers are meant to be language-independent. They do not use any information that is specific to the language being parsed, and they often rely heavily on n-grams, or sequences of words and POS tags, to make parsing decisions. However, designing a parser without incorporating any specific linguistic details does not guarantee its language-independence; even linguistically naïve systems can involve design decisions which in fact bias the system towards languages with certain properties (Bender, 2011).

It is often taken for granted that using linguistic information necessarily makes a system language-dependent. But it is possible to design a linguistically intelligent parser without tuning it to a specific language, by modeling at a high level phenomena which appear cross-linguistically. Such a system is still language-independent; it does not require any knowledge or modeling of specific languages, but it does use linguistic knowledge to make the most of the available data. We present modifications to an existing system, MSTParser (McDonald et al., 2006), to incorporate a very simple model of morphological agreement. These modifications improve parsing performance across a variety of languages by making better use of morphological annotations.

2 Background and related work

2.1 Morphological marking of agreement

Most languages show some morphological agreement via inflected noun, adjective, verb, and determiner forms, although the degree to which this happens varies. At one end of the spectrum are analytic, or "morphologically impoverished", languages. An extreme example is Chinese, which shows no inflection at all; words do not take different forms depending on features such as person or gender. English has some inflection, but is relatively morphologically poor.

At the other end are synthetic or "morphologically rich" languages such as Czech, which has, inter alia, four genders and seven cases. In synthetic languages, words which are syntactically related in certain ways must agree: e.g., subject-verb agreement for gender or determiner-noun agreement for case (Corbett, 2006). Words participating in agreement may be marked explicitly for the property in question (via affixing or other morphological changes), or may possess it inherently (with no specific affix encoding the property). Treebanks are often annotated to reflect some or all of these properties; the level of detail depends on the annotation guidelines.

zahraniční	investice	rostou
foreign	investment	grow
.F.PL.NOM	.F.3RD.PL.NOM	.3RD.PL.PRES
foreign	investments	grow
foreign	investment	grow
	.3RD.PL	.PL

Table 1: Sentence in Czech (Hajič, 1998) and English

A sample sentence in English and Czech (Table 1) demonstrates this contrast. In Czech, the adjective and noun agree for gender, number, and case, and the noun and verb agree for person and number. In the English version, only the noun and verb agree.

Agreement can be very useful for data-driven dependency parsing. A statistical parser can learn from training data that, for example, a third-person singular noun is a likely dependent of a verb marked as third-person singular. Similarly, it can learn that a determiner showing genitive case and a noun showing dative case are often not syntactically related.

It is often assumed that morphological complexity correlates with degree of variation in word order. This is because synthetic languages use inflection to mark the roles of constituents, while analytic languages generally assign these roles to specific phrase structural locations. Siewierska (1998) investigated this empirically and found that it holds to a certain extent: the absence of agreement and/or case marking predicts rigid word order, though their presence is not particularly predictive of flexible word order.

Many parsers rely on word order to establish dependencies, so they often perform best on languages with more rigid word order. Making use of morphological agreement could compensate for greater variation in word order and help to bring parsing performance on flexible-word-order languages up to par with that on rigid-word-order languages.

2.2 MSTParser

The CoNLL-X (Buchholz and Marsi, 2006) and CoNLL 2007 (Nivre et al., 2007) shared tasks focused on multilingual dependency parsing. Each system was trained on treebanks in a variety of languages and predicted dependency arcs and labels for POS-tagged data. The best performers in 2006 were MSTParser (McDonald et al., 2006), which we use here, and MaltParser (Nivre et al., 2006a).

MSTParser is a data-driven, graph-based parser which creates a model from training data by learning weights for arc-level features. The feature set includes combinations of the word and POS tag of the parent and child of each dependency arc; POS tags of words between the parent and child; and POS tags of the parent and child along with those of the preceding and following words. A similar feature set is conjoined with arc labels in order to perform labeling, and an optional set of "second-order" features includes analogous information about siblings.

Morphological features for an arc are generated by iterating over each pair in the cross product of the parent and child tokens' lists of attributes. For every such pair, thirteen groups of four features each are generated. The thirteen groups represent combinations of the head and child word forms/lemmas and attributes. Each group contains subgroups distinguished by whether they use word forms or lemmas and by whether or not they encode the direction and distance of the dependency. These features are summarized in Table 2. At run time, MSTParser finds the highest-scoring parse for each sentence according to the learned feature weights.

Decoding can be performed in projective or non-projective mode, depending on the type of trees desired. Projective trees are those in which every constituent (head plus all dependents) forms a complete subtree; non-projective parsing lacks this limitation.

2.3 Related work

The organizers of the CoNLL 2007 shared task noted that languages with free word order and high morphological complexity are the most difficult for dependency parsing (Nivre et al., 2007). Most of the participants took language-independent approaches toward leveraging this complexity into better performance: generating machine learning features based on each item in a token's list of morphological attributes (Nivre et al., 2006b; Carreras et al., 2006); using the entire list as an atomic feature (Chang et al., 2006; Titov and Henderson, 2007); or generating features based on each pair of attributes in the cross-product of the lists of a potential head and dependent (McDonald et al., 2006; Nakagawa, 2007).

Language-specific uses of morphological information have included using it to disambiguate function words (Bick, 2006) or to pick out finite verbs

```
<hdIdx>*<dpIdx>=<{hdForm|hdLemma}>(<dir+dist>)
<hdIdx>*<dpIdx>=<{dpForm|dpLemma}>(<dir+dist>)
<hdIdx>*<dpIdx>=<hdAtt>(<dir+dist>)
<hdIdx>*<dpIdx>=<dpAtt>(<dir+dist>)
<hdIdx>*<dpIdx>=<{hdForm|hdLemma}><{dpForm|dpLemma}>(<dir+dist>)
<hdIdx>*<dpIdx>=<{hdForm|hdLemma}><hdAtt>(<dir+dist>)
<hdIdx>*<dpIdx>=<{hdForm|hdLemma}><dpAtt>(<dir+dist>)
<hdIdx>*<dpIdx>=<{dpForm|dpLemma}><dpAtt>(<dir+dist>)
<hdIdx>*<dpIdx>=<{dpForm|dpLemma}><hdAtt>(<dir+dist>)
<hdIdx>*<dpIdx>=<hdAtt><dpAtt>(<dir+dist>)
<hdIdx>*<dpIdx>=<{hdForm|hdLemma}><hdAtt><dpAtt>(<dir+dist>)
<hdIdx>*<dpIdx>=<{dpForm|dpLemma}><hdAtt><dpAtt>(<dir+dist>)
<hdIdx>*<dpIdx>=<{hdForm|hdLemma}><{dpForm|dpLemma}><hdAtt><dpAtt>(<dir+dist>)
```

Table 2: Original MSTParser feature templates. `hdForm` and `dpForm` are the head and dependent word forms; `hdLemma` and `dpLemma` are the lemmas. `hdAtt` and `dpAtt` are the morphological attributes; `hdIdx` and `dpIdx` are their indices. `dir+dist` is a string encoding the direction and length of the arc. Each line represents one feature.

Unlabeled	`<attr>_agrees,head=<headPOS>,dep=<depPOS>`
	`<attr>_disagrees,head=<headPOS>,dep=<depPOS>`
	`head_<attr=value>,head=<headPOS>,dep=<depPOS>`
	`dep_<attr=value>,head=<headPOS>,dep=<depPOS>`
Labeled	`<attr>_agrees&label=<label>,head=<headPOS>,dep=<depPOS>`
	`<attr>_disagrees&label=<label>,head=<headPOS>,dep=<depPOS>`
	`head_<attr=value>&label=<label>,head=<headPOS>,dep=<depPOS>`
	`dep_<attr=value>&label=<label>,head=<headPOS>,dep=<depPOS>`

Table 3: Agreement feature templates. `headPOS` and `depPOS` are the head and dependent coarse POS tags.

(Carreras et al., 2006). Schiehlen and Spranger (2007) used language-specific rules to add detail to other features, such as fine-grained POS tags or lemmas. Attardi et al. (2007) modeled agreement explicitly, generating a morphological agreement feature whenever two tokens possess the same value for the same linguistic attribute. The authors note accuracy improvements of up to 0.5% for Italian and 0.8% for Catalan using a transition-based parser. A similar approach was used by Goldberg and Elhadad (2010), who improved the accuracy of their transition-based Hebrew parser by adding features for gender and number agreement in noun phrases.

The potential of morphological information to improve parsing performance has been documented in numerous experiments using MaltParser and with various morphological attributes as machine learning features, on several morphologically rich languages, including: Russian (Nivre et al., 2008); Swedish (Øvrelid and Nivre, 2007); Bangla, Telugu, and Hindi (Nivre, 2009); Turkish (Eryiğit et al., 2008); and Basque (Bengoetxea and Gojenola, 2010). These experiments, however, did not include any higher-level features such as agreement.

Goldberg and Elhadad (2009) found that using morphological features increased the accuracy of MSTParser on Hebrew only when the morphological annotations were gold-standard; automatic annotations decreased accuracy, although MaltParser showed improvement with both gold and automatic annotations. The accuracy of MaltParser on Arabic was improved by different types of morphological features depending on whether gold or automatic annotations were used (Marton et al., 2010).

As far as we can tell, no language-independent approaches to utilizing morphological data thus far have taken advantage of agreement specifically. We take a linguistically informed approach, maintaining language-independence, by explicitly modeling agreement between head and dependent morphology.

3 Methodology

3.1 Modifications to parser

Our approach builds on the observation that there are two kinds of information marked in morphology: symmetric, recorded on both head and depen-

ID	TOKEN	CPOS	MORPH	HEAD	REL	Gloss
1	Vznikají	VERB	num=PL|per=3	0	ROOT	arise.3RD.PL
2	zbytečné	ADJ	num=PL|gen=I|case=NOM	3	ATR	unnecessary.PL.INAN.NOM
3	konflikty	NOUN	num=PL|gen=I|case=NOM	1	SBJ	conflicts.PL.INAN.NOM

num_agrees,head=NOUN,dep=ADJ	num_agrees,head=VERB,dep=NOUN
num_agrees&label=ATR,head=NOUN,dep=ADJ	num_agrees&label=SBJ,head=VERB,dep=NOUN
gen_agrees,head=NOUN,dep=ADJ	head_per=3,head=VERB,dep=NOUN
gen_agrees&label=ATR,head=NOUN,dep=ADJ	head_per=3&label=SBJ,head=VERB,dep=NOUN
case_agrees,head=NOUN,dep=ADJ	dep_gen=I,head=VERB,dep=NOUN
case_agrees&label=ATR,head=NOUN,dep=ADJ	dep_gen=I&label=SBJ,head=VERB,dep=NOUN
	dep_case=NOM,head=VERB,dep=NOUN
	dep_case=NOM&label=SBJ,head=VERB,dep=NOUN

Table 4: Sample sentence (Hajič, 1998) and agreement features generated

dent, and asymmetric, marked on only one or the other. Symmetric information provides a natural, effectively non-lossy type of back-off that parsers can take advantage of; all that matters is whether the information on the head and dependent match.[1] Furthermore, we don't need to know ahead of time which types of morphological information are symmetric. This is extracted from the annotations.

In order to take advantage of this property of natural language, we devised a set of features which model agreement. These allow the learner to operate at a higher level, using agreement itself as a feature rather than having to discover agreement and forming generalizations about whether tokens which agree (or disagree) in various ways are related. Since agreement appears cross-linguistically, such features are applicable to a diverse set of languages.

Since MSTParser breaks down every parse into a set of arcs, our features are defined at the arc level. Each arc is a head and dependent pair, and each of those tokens has a list of morphological features in the normalized form `attribute=value`. We compare these lists and add, for every attribute which is present in both, either an agreement or a disagreement feature, depending on whether the head and dependent have the same value for that attribute. This feature encapsulates the attribute, but not the value, as well as the coarse POS tags of the head and the dependent. If an attribute is present in only one of the lists, we add a feature encapsulating whether the token is the head or the dependent, the single morphological feature (attribute and value), and the two coarse POS tags. We also generate both types of features conjoined with the arc label. Like the original feature set, we include only first-order morphological features. See Table 3 for a summary. A sample sentence in a simplified CoNLL format and the features it would trigger are shown in Table 4.[2]

We hypothesize that these agreement features will function as a type of back-off, allowing the parser to extract more information from the morphological marking. For instance, they can capture case agreement between a determiner and noun. We expect that this would lead to higher parsing accuracy, especially when training on smaller datasets, where morphological data might be sparse.

We made a slight modification to the parser so that underscores used in the treebanks to indicate the absence of morphological annotation for a token were not themselves treated as morphological information. This was necessary to ensure that all feature configurations performed identically on treebanks with no morphological information. Depending on the treebank, this increased or decreased the performance of the system slightly (by less than 0.5%).

3.2 Data collection and preparation

We gathered a range of dependency treebanks, representing as many language families as possible (Table 5). Many of these used the CoNLL shared task treebank format, so we adopted it as well, and con-

[1] If an attribute is marked on both head and dependent and the value matches, the specific value should not affect the probability or possibility of the dependency relationship. If the same attribute is marked on both elements but is independent (not a matter of agreement) we risk losing information, but we hypothesize that such information is unlikely to be very predictive.

[2] A more complete description of the system, as well as source code, can be found in (Hohensee, 2012).

Language	ISO	Treebank	Num. sents.	Ref. size	Avg. atts.	Reference
Hindi-Urdu	hin	HUTB	3,855	2,800	3.6	(Bhatt et al., 2009)
Hungarian	hun	Szeged DTB	92,176	9,000	3.3	(Vincze et al., 2010)
Czech	ces	PDT 1.0	73,068	9,000	2.8	(Hajič, 1998)
Tamil	tam	TamilTB v0.1	600	600	2.8	(Ramasamy and Žabokrtský, 2011)
Slovene	slv	SDT	1,998	1,500	2.6	(Džeroski et al., 2006)
Danish	dan	DDT	5,512	5,500	2.4	(Kromann, 2003)
Basque	eus	3LB*	3,175	2,800	2.4	(Aduriz et al., 2003)
Dutch	nld	Alpino	13,735	9,000	2.4	(Van der Beek et al., 2002)
Latin	lat	LDT	3,423	2,800	2.4	(Bamman and Crane, 2006)
Bulgarian	bul	BulTreeBank	13,221	9,000	2.1	(Simov et al., 2004)
Greek (ancient)	grc	AGDT	21,104	9,000	2.1	(Bamman et al., 2009)
Finnish	fin	Turku	4,307	2,800	2.0	(Haverinen et al., 2010)
German	deu	NEGRA	3,427	2,800	2.0	(Brants et al., 1999)
Turkish	tur	METU-Sabanci	5,620	5,500	1.6	(Oflazer et al., 2003)
Catalan	cat	CESS-ECE*	3,512	2,800	1.5	(Martı et al., 2007)
Arabic	ara	PADT 1.0	2,367	2,300	1.2	(Hajic et al., 2004)
Italian	ita	TUT	2,858	2,800	1.1	(Bosco et al., 2000)
Portuguese	por	Floresta	9,359	9,000	1.0	(Afonso et al., 2002)
Hebrew (modern)	heb	DepTB	6,214	5,500	0.9	(Goldberg, 2011)
English	eng	Penn*	49,208	9,000	0.4	(Marcus et al., 1993)
Chinese	cmn	Penn Chinese	28,035	9,000	0.0	(Xue et al., 2005)

*Acquired as part of NLTK (Bird et al., 2009)

Table 5: Language, ISO 639-2 code, treebank name, total number of sentences, reference size, average number of morphological attributes per token, and reference for each treebank used, ordered by average number of attributes.

verted the other treebanks to the same. It includes for each token: position in the sentence; the token itself; a lemma (not present in all datasets); a coarse POS tag; a fine POS tag; a list of morphological features; the token's head; and the label for the dependency relation to that head.[3] We retained all punctuation and other tokens in the treebanks.

The POS tagsets used in the treebanks varied widely. We normalized the coarse tags to the universal twelve-tag set suggested by Petrov et al. (2011), in order to ensure that every treebank had coarse tags for use in the agreement features, and to make the features easier to interpret. It is unlikely that information was lost in this process: for treebanks with one set of tags, information was added, and for those with two, the universal tags aligned closely with the coarse tags already in the data.

Two of the treebanks we used included no morphological information. We included the Penn Chinese Treebank as a representative of analytic languages.[4] We also included part of the (English) Penn Treebank, converted to dependency trees. For this data we generated morphological annotations based on fine POS tags, consisting of person and number information for nouns and verbs, and person, number, and case information for pronouns. The German NEGRA corpus includes detailed morphological annotations for about 3,400 sentences (of 20,600), and we used only that portion.

Note that the amount of morphological information present in any given treebank is a function of the morphological properties of the language as well as the annotation guidelines: annotations do not necessarily encode all of the morphological information which is actually marked in a language. Furthermore, the presence of a morphological feature does not imply that it participates in an agreement relationship; it merely encodes some piece of morphological information about the token. Finally, annotation guidelines vary as to whether they provide for the explicit marking of morphological properties which are inherent to a lemma (e.g., gender on nouns) and not marked by separate affixes.

[3]The original format also included two more fields, projective head and label; neither is used by MSTParser.

[4]Dependency trees were generated from the Penn Chinese Treebank using the Penn2Malt converter: `http://w3.msi.vxu.se/~nivre/research/Penn2Malt.html`.

We normalized all morphological annotations to the form `attribute=value` (e.g., `case=NOM`). For treebanks that provided values only, this involved adding attribute names, obtained from the annotation guidelines. The attributes person, number, gender, and case appeared often; also included in some data were verb tense, adjective degree, and pronoun type (e.g., personal, possessive, or reflexive). We normalized all features in the data, regardless of whether they participate in any agreement relations.

Many of the treebanks include data from multiple domains; to minimize the effects of this, we randomized the order of sentences in each treebank.

3.3 Experimental setup

All experiments were performed using 5-fold cross-validation. Reported accuracies, run times, and feature counts are averages over all five folds. We ran experiments on multiple cross-validation dataset sizes in order to assess the performance of our model when trained on different amounts of data. For each treebank, we report results on a "reference size": 9,000 sentences or the largest size available (for treebanks of less than 9,000 sentences).

For evaluation, we used the module built into MSTParser. We focused on the unlabeled accuracy score (percentage of tokens with correctly assigned heads, ignoring labels). We also looked at labeled accuracies, but found they displayed trends very similar, if not identical, to the unlabeled scores.

4 Results

We ran the system on each treebank at all dataset sizes in projective and non-projective modes, using no morphological features. For each language, subsequent tests used the algorithm which performed better (or non-projective in the case of a tie).

4.1 Overall results

We ran the parser on each treebank with each of four feature configurations: one with no morphological features (`no-morph`); one with the original morphological features (`orig`; Table 2); one using the agreement features (`agr`; Table 3); and one using both feature sets (`agr+orig`).

Table 6 displays the unlabeled accuracy, run time, and feature counts when parsing each treebank using each feature configuration at the reference size, with the highest accuracy highlighted. Excluding Chinese, `agr` generated the best performance in all but two cases, outperforming `orig` by margins ranging from 0.8% (Arabic) to 5.3% (Latin) absolute. In the other cases, `agr+orig` outperformed `agr` slightly. In all cases, the total number of machine learning features was approximately the same for `no-morph` and `agr`, and for `orig` and `agr+orig`, because the number of morphological features generated by `orig` is very large compared to the number generated by `agr`. Performance was noticeably faster for the two smaller feature configurations.

Figure 1 shows the error reduction of `orig`, `agr`, and `agr+orig` relative to `no-morph`, at the reference size. Despite its relative lack of morphological inflection, English shows a fairly high error reduction, because parsing performance on English was already high. Similarly, error reduction on some of the morphologically rich languages is lower because baseline performance was low. Calculating the correlation coefficient (Pearson's r) between average morphological attributes per token and error reduction gives $r = 0.608$ for `orig`, $r = 0.560$ for `agr`, and $r = 0.428$ for `agr+orig`, with $p < 0.01$ for the first two and $p < 0.10$ for the last, indicating moderate correlations for all feature sets.

The strength of these correlations depends on several factors. Languages differ in what information is marked morphologically, and in number of agreement relationships. Annotation schemes vary in what morphological information they encode, and in how relevant that information is to agreement. Some morphologically complex languages have rigid word order, leading to better performance with no morphological features at all, and limiting the amount of improvement that is possible. Finally, it is possible that a stronger correlation is obscured by other effects due to feature set design, as we will find later.

4.2 Performance vs. dataset size

Figures 2 presents unlabeled accuracy when parsing Czech with the `orig` and `agr` configurations. Improvement with `agr` is roughly uniform across all dataset sizes; this was the general trend for all treebanks. This is somewhat unexpected; we had predicted that the agreement features would be more helpful at smaller dataset sizes.

	no-morph			orig			agr			agr+orig		
Lang.	UAC	time	feats	UAC	Δtime	Δfeats	UAC	Δtime	Δfeats	UAC	Δtime	Δfeats
hin	90.0	1.4k	1.6m	92.0	116%	893%	**93.8**	50%	1%	93.0	144%	893%
hun	87.9	4.6k	5.3m	88.7	201%	687%	**90.3**	10%	0%	89.9	159%	687%
ces	80.9	3.3k	4.8m	81.6	71%	454%	**85.5**	27%	0%	84.5	114%	454%
tam	79.0	0.1k	0.5m	79.7	237%	329%	**82.1**	64%	1%	81.1	279%	330%
slv	80.8	0.8k	1.0m	80.4	103%	352%	**81.9**	21%	1%	80.8	129%	353%
dan	87.7	2.0k	1.6m	88.4	71%	256%	**89.3**	24%	0%	**89.3**	86%	256%
lat	61.7	1.8k	1.6m	65.0	54%	306%	**70.3**	91%	0%	68.6	119%	306%
nld	88.2	2.0k	3.6m	89.0	83%	270%	**90.5**	16%	0%	90.3	98%	270%
eus	78.7	0.7k	1.7m	80.2	80%	229%	**82.3**	10%	0%	82.3	78%	230%
bul	89.9	1.7k	2.6m	90.1	60%	221%	**93.0**	14%	0%	92.5	54%	222%
grc	74.9	8.6k	3.8m	76.9	36%	314%	**80.7**	45%	0%	79.5	70%	314%
deu	90.0	0.9k	1.3m	90.8	33%	189%	**92.0**	1%	0%	91.7	50%	186%
fin	73.3	0.7k	2.4m	76.3	74%	244%	**79.1**	23%	1%	78.7	84%	245%
tur	80.2	1.2k	2.1m	81.5	13%	178%	81.6	−2%	0%	**81.7**	29%	178%
cat	81.8	3.0k	2.5m	81.9	2%	142%	**84.9**	-9%	0%	84.0	−2%	143%
ara	78.0	3.2k	2.0m	78.1	65%	94%	**78.9**	23%	0%	78.7	20%	94%
ita	88.3	4.2k	1.8m	88.9	−3%	59%	90.2	9%	0%	**90.3**	6%	59%
por	88.1	6.4k	5.0m	88.1	18%	46%	**89.0**	−3%	0%	88.9	27%	46%
heb	87.4	4.3k	3.1m	87.4	−18%	31%	**89.2**	−16%	0%	89.1	−5%	31%
eng	88.1	5.2k	3.1m	88.0	5%	7%	**90.6**	3%	0%	**90.6**	−9%	8%
cmn	**82.4**	7.5k	6.0m	**82.4**	37%	0%	**82.4**	16%	0%	**82.4**	23%	0%

Table 6: Unlabeled accuracy, run time in seconds, and number of features for all treebanks and feature configurations. Run time and number of features for `orig`, `agr`, and `agr+orig` are given as percent change relative to `no-morph`

4.3 Gold vs. automatic tags

The Hebrew treebank includes both automatically generated and gold standard POS and morphological annotations. In order to test how sensitive the agreement features are to automatically predicted morphological information, tests were run on both versions at the reference size. These results are not directly comparable to those of Goldberg and Elhadad (2009), because of the parser modifications, POS tag normalization, and cross-validation described earlier. Comparing results qualitatively, we find less sensitivity to the automatic tags overall, and that the `orig` features improve accuracy even when using automatic tags.

Results appear in Table 7. Using the automatic data affects all feature sets negatively by 2.1% to 2.9%. Since the `no-morph` parser was affected the most, it appears that this decrease is due largely to errors in the POS tags, rather than the morphological annotations. The `orig` features compensate for this slightly (0.2%), and the `agr` features more (0.8%); this indicates that including even automatic morphological information can compensate for incorrect POS tags, and that the `agr` feature configuration is the most robust when given predicted tags.

Feature configuration	Acc. on gold data	Acc. on auto data	Difference
no-morph	87.4	84.5	−2.9
orig	87.4	84.7	−2.7
agr	89.3	87.2	−2.1
agr+orig	89.1	86.9	−2.2

Table 7: Unlabeled accuracy on Hebrew dataset, with gold and automatic POS and morphological annotations

4.4 PPL feature

Examining the feature weights from the first cross-validation fold when running the `agr` feature configuration on the Czech dataset indicated that 323 of the 1,000 highest-weighted features are agreement features. Of these, 79 are symmetric ("agrees" or "disagrees") `agr` features, and 244 asymmetric. This was unexpected, as the symmetric features would seem to be more useful, and it suggested that the labeled asymmetric `agr` features might be important for reasons other than their modeling of morphological information. Careful analysis of the MSTParser feature set revealed that it does not include a feature which incorporates head POS, dependent POS, and dependency label. We hypothesized that the labeled asymmetric `agr` features were highly ranked

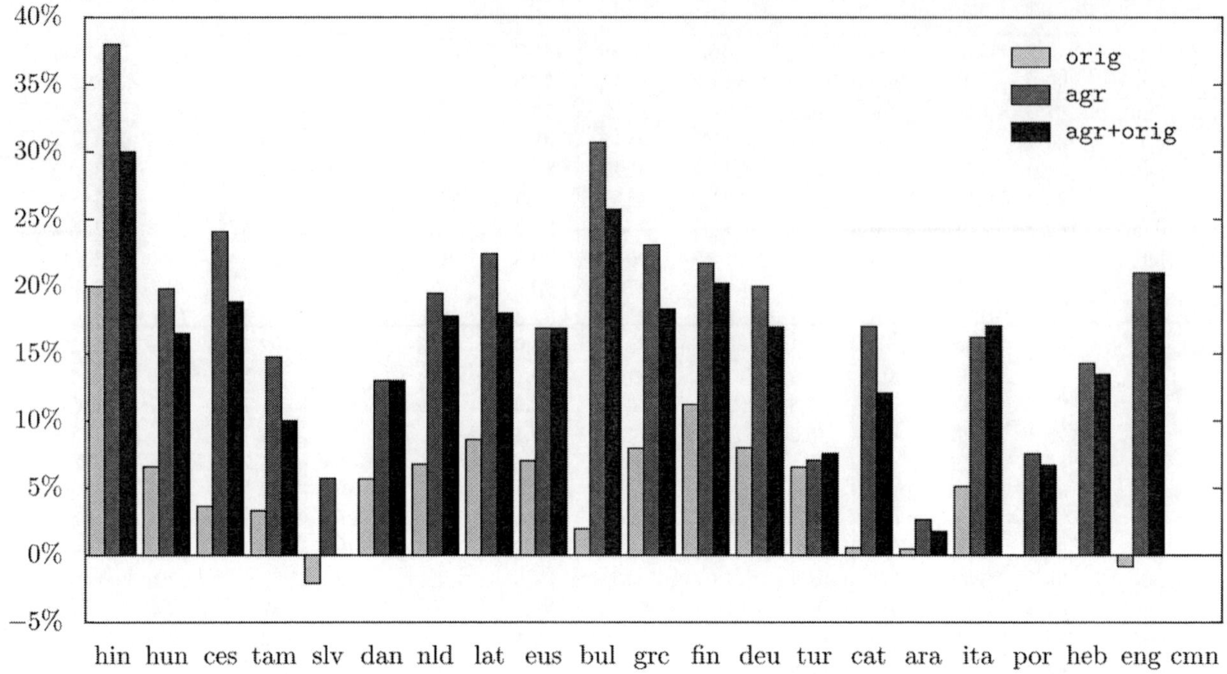

Figure 1: Error reduction relative to no-morph vs. language

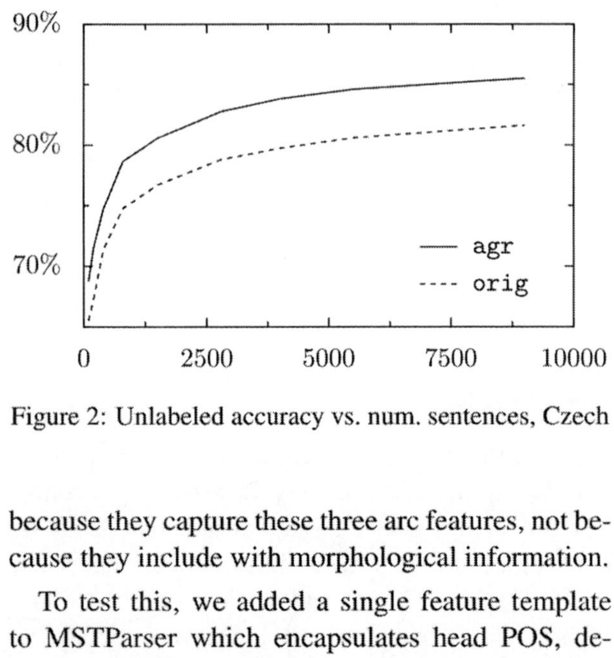

Figure 2: Unlabeled accuracy vs. num. sentences, Czech

because they capture these three arc features, not because they include with morphological information.

To test this, we added a single feature template to MSTParser which encapsulates head POS, dependent POS, and dependency label (the POS-POS-label, or PPL, feature). Running a subsequent experiment on the Czech data and looking at feature weights from the same cross-validation fold, 278 of the 1,000 highest-weighted features were PPL features, and 187 were asymmetric agr features. This indicated that the improvement seen with agr features was indeed due partly to their inclusion of features combining label and head and dependent POS.

All feature configurations were run on all treebanks with the PPL feature included; results appear in Table 8. Performance increases from orig to agr are generally smaller, with a maximum of 4.6% absolute. This is seen especially on languages with less morphological information, such as English and Hebrew; this indicates that for those languages, most of the previous improvement was due not to agreement modeling, but to the PPL effect.

Calculating Pearson's r between morphological features per token and the new error reduction data gives a stronger correlation coefficient of 0.748 for agr, with $p < 0.01$, demonstrating that improvement due solely to agreement modeling correlates strongly with quantity of morphological information. The earlier error reduction data were likely polluted by improvement due to capturing the PPL information. Correlation for the other feature configurations is still moderate (0.506 with $p < 0.02$ for orig and 0.621 with $p < 0.01$ for agr+orig).

5 Future work

In future work, we plan to experiment with more careful normalization of treebanks. For instance, if an adjective can agree with either a masculine or a feminine noun, annotating it with both gen=M

	no-morph			orig			agr			agr+orig		
Lang.	UAC	time	feats	UAC	Δtime	Δfeats	UAC	Δtime	Δfeats	UAC	Δtime	Δfeats
hin	90.0	1.4k	1.6	92.0	116%	893%	**93.8**	50%	1%	93.0	144%	893%
hun	87.9	4.6k	5.3	88.7	201%	687%	**90.3**	10%	0%	89.9	159%	687%
ces	80.9	3.3k	4.8	81.6	71%	454%	**85.5**	27%	0%	84.5	114%	454%
tam	79.0	0.1k	0.5	79.7	237%	329%	**82.1**	64%	1%	81.1	279%	330%
slv	80.8	0.8k	1.0	80.4	102%	352%	**81.8**	21%	0%	80.8	129%	353%
dan	87.8	2.0k	1.6	88.4	71%	256%	**89.3**	24%	0%	**89.3**	86%	256%
lat	61.7	1.8k	1.6	65.0	54%	306%	**70.3**	91%	0%	68.6	119%	306%
nld	88.2	2.0k	3.6	89.0	83%	270%	**90.5**	16%	0%	90.3	98%	270%
eus	78.7	0.7k	1.7	80.2	80%	229%	**82.3**	10%	0%	**82.3**	78%	230%
bul	89.9	1.7k	2.6	90.2	60%	221%	**93.0**	14%	0%	92.5	54%	222%
grc	74.9	8.6k	3.8	77.0	36%	314%	**80.7**	45%	0%	79.5	70%	314%
deu	90.0	0.9k	1.3	90.8	33%	189%	**92.0**	1%	0%	91.7	50%	186%
fin	73.3	0.7k	2.4	76.3	74%	244%	**79.1**	23%	0%	78.7	84%	245%
tur	80.2	1.2k	2.1	81.5	13%	178%	81.6	-2%	0%	**81.7**	29%	178%
cat	81.8	3.0k	2.5	81.9	1%	142%	**84.9**	-9%	0%	84.0	-2%	143%
ara	77.6	5.4k	1.8	77.7	20%	100%	**78.2**	-8%	0%	78.0	4%	100%
ita	88.4	4.2k	1.8	88.9	-2%	59%	90.2	9%	0%	**90.3**	6%	59%
por	88.1	6.4k	5.0	88.2	18%	46%	**89.0**	-3%	0%	88.9	27%	46%
heb	87.4	4.3k	3.1	87.4	-18%	31%	**89.2**	-16%	0%	89.1	-5%	31%
eng	88.1	5.2k	3.1	88.0	5%	7%	**90.6**	3%	0%	**90.6**	-9%	7%
cmn	**82.4**	7.5k	6.0	**82.4**	37%	0%	**82.4**	16%	0%	**82.4**	23%	0%

Table 8: Unlabeled accuracy, run time in seconds, and number of features with PPL feature included. Run time and number of features for `orig`, `agr`, and `agr+orig` are given as percent change relative to `no-morph`.

and `gen=F` (rather than `gen=X`) would ensure that agreement with a noun of either gender would be captured by our features. Furthermore, we may experiment with filtering morphological information based on part-of-speech, on attribute, or on whether the attribute participates in any agreement relationships. We also intend to perform feature selection on the original feature set, and investigate the importance of labeled morphological features, which are included in `agr` but not in `orig`. Finally, we plan to develop metrics to measure the degree of word order flexibility in a treebank, in order to explore the extent to which it correlates with the degree of improvement achieved by our system.

6 Conclusions

We developed a simple, language-independent model of agreement to better leverage morphological data in dependency parsing. Testing on treebanks containing varying amounts of morphological information resulted in substantial improvements in parsing accuracy while reducing feature counts and run times significantly. Although originally intended to compensate for lower accuracy on morphologically rich languages, the model improved performance on all treebanks with any morphological information.

We acknowledge that because our model was tested on treebanks which differ widely in annotation guidelines, variables such as the amount of morphological information included and the treatment of non-projective parses and coordination could affect parsing performance. We did not delve into these factors. However, we believe this is part of the strength of the approach: we were able to achieve performance gains without any detailed knowledge of the languages and treebanks used.

We hope these results will encourage similarly linguistically motivated design in future systems. This case study provides strong evidence that incorporating linguistic knowledge into NLP systems does not preclude language independence, and indeed may enhance it, by leveling performance across typologically differing languages.

Acknowledgments

We would like to thank everyone who assisted us in gathering treebanks, particularly Maite Oronoz and her colleagues at the University of the Basque Country and Yoav Goldberg, as well as three anonymous reviewers for their comments.

References

I. Aduriz, M.J. Aranzabe, J.M. Arriola, A. Atutxa, A.D. de Ilarraza, A. Garmendia, and M. Oronoz. 2003. Construction of a Basque dependency treebank. In *Proc. of the Second Workshop on Treebanks and Linguistic Theories (TLT 2003)*, pages 201–204.

S. Afonso, E. Bick, R. Haber, and D. Santos. 2002. Floresta Sintá(c)tica: A treebank for Portuguese. In *Proc. of the Third International Conference on Language Resources and Evaluation (LREC 2002)*, page 1698.

G. Attardi, F. DellOrletta, M. Simi, A. Chanev, and M. Ciaramita. 2007. Multilingual dependency parsing and domain adaptation using DeSR. In *Proc. of the 2007 Joint Conference on Empirical Methods in Natural Language Processing and Computational Natural Language Learning (EMNLP-CoNLL 2007)*, pages 1112–1118.

D. Bamman and G. Crane. 2006. The design and use of a Latin dependency treebank. In *Proc. of the Fifth International Workshop on Treebanks and Linguistic Theories (TLT 2006)*, pages 67–78.

D. Bamman, F. Mambrini, and G. Crane. 2009. An ownership model of annotation: The Ancient Greek Dependency Treebank. In *Proc. of the Eighth International Workshop on Treebanks and Linguistic Theories (TLT8)*, pages 5–15.

E.M. Bender. 2011. On achieving and evaluating language-independence in NLP. *Linguistic Issues in Language Technology: Special Issue on Interaction of Linguistics and Computational Linguistics*, 6(3):1–26.

K. Bengoetxea and K. Gojenola. 2010. Application of different techniques to dependency parsing of Basque. In *Proc. of the First Workshop on Statistical Parsing of Morphologically Rich Languages (SPMRL 2010)*, pages 31–39. Association for Computational Linguistics.

R. Bhatt, B. Narasimhan, M. Palmer, O. Rambow, D.M. Sharma, and F. Xia. 2009. A multi-representational and multi-layered treebank for Hindi/Urdu. In *Proc. of the Third Linguistic Annotation Workshop (LAW III)*, pages 186–189. Association for Computational Linguistics.

E. Bick. 2006. LingPars, a linguistically inspired, language-independent machine learner for dependency treebanks. In *Proc. of the Tenth Conference on Computational Natural Language Learning (CoNLL-X)*, pages 171–175. Association for Computational Linguistics.

S. Bird, E. Klein, and E. Loper. 2009. *Natural Language Processing with Python*. O'Reilly Media.

C. Bosco, V. Lombardo, D. Vassallo, and L. Lesmo. 2000. Building a treebank for Italian: a data-driven annotation schema. In *Proc. of the Second International Conference on Language Resources and Evaluation (LREC 2000)*, pages 99–106.

T. Brants, W. Skut, and H. Uszkoreit. 1999. Syntactic annotation of a German newspaper corpus. *Treebanks: Building and using parsed corpora*, 20:73.

S. Buchholz and E. Marsi. 2006. CoNLL-X shared task on multilingual dependency parsing. In *Proc. of the Tenth Conference on Computational Natural Language Learning (CoNLL-X)*, pages 149–164. Association for Computational Linguistics.

X. Carreras, M. Surdeanu, and L. Marquez. 2006. Projective dependency parsing with perceptron. In *Proc. of the Tenth Conference on Computational Natural Language Learning (CoNLL-X)*, pages 181–185. Association for Computational Linguistics.

M.W. Chang, Q. Do, and D. Roth. 2006. A pipeline model for bottom-up dependency parsing. In *Proc. of the Tenth Conference on Computational Natural Language Learning (CoNLL-X)*, pages 186–190. Association for Computational Linguistics.

G.G. Corbett. 2006. *Agreement*. Cambridge University Press.

S. Džeroski, T. Erjavec, N. Ledinek, P. Pajas, Z. Žabokrtsky, and A. Žele. 2006. Towards a Slovene dependency treebank. In *Proc. of the Fifth International Conference on Language Resources and Evaluation (LREC 2006)*.

G. Eryiğit, J. Nivre, and K. Oflazer. 2008. Dependency parsing of Turkish. *Computational Linguistics*, 34(3):357–389.

Y. Goldberg and M. Elhadad. 2009. Hebrew dependency parsing: Initial results. In *Proc. of the 11th International Conference on Parsing Technologies (IWPT'09)*, pages 129–133. Association for Computational Linguistics.

Y. Goldberg and M. Elhadad. 2010. Easy-first dependency parsing of Modern Hebrew. In *Proc. of the First Workshop on Statistical Parsing of Morphologically Rich Languages (SPMRL 2010)*, pages 103–107. Association for Computational Linguistics.

Yoav Goldberg. 2011. *Automatic Syntactic Processing of Modern Hebrew*. Ph.D. thesis, Ben Gurion University.

J. Hajic, O. Smrz, P. Zemánek, J. Šnaidauf, and E. Beška. 2004. Prague Arabic dependency treebank: Development in data and tools. In *Proc. of the NEMLAR International Conference on Arabic Language Resources and Tools*, pages 110–117.

Jan Hajič. 1998. Building a syntactically annotated corpus: The Prague Dependency Treebank. In Eva Hajičová, editor, *Issues of Valency and Meaning: Studies in Honor of Jarmila Panevová*, pages 12–19. Prague Karolinum, Charles University Press.

Katri Haverinen, Timo Viljanen, Veronika Laippala, Samuel Kohonen, Filip Ginter, and Tapio Salakoski. 2010. Treebanking Finnish. In *Proc. of the Ninth International Workshop on Treebanks and Linguistic Theories (TLT9*, volume 9, pages 79–90.

M. Hohensee. 2012. It's only morpho-logical: Modeling agreement in cross-linguistic dependency parsing. Master's thesis, University of Washington.

M.T. Kromann. 2003. The Danish Dependency Treebank and the DTAG treebank tool. In *Proc. of the Second Workshop on Treebanks and Linguistic Theories (TLT 2003)*, pages 217–220.

M.P. Marcus, M.A. Marcinkiewicz, and B. Santorini. 1993. Building a large annotated corpus of English: The Penn Treebank. *Computational Linguistics*, 19(2):313–330.

M.A. Martı, M. Taulé, L. Márquez, and M. Bertran. 2007. *CESS-ECE: A multilingual and multilevel annotated corpus.*

Y. Marton, N. Habash, and O. Rambow. 2010. Improving Arabic dependency parsing with lexical and inflectional morphological features. In *Proc. of the First Workshop on Statistical Parsing of Morphologically Rich Languages (SPMRL 2010)*, pages 13–21. Association for Computational Linguistics.

R. McDonald, K. Lerman, and F. Pereira. 2006. Multilingual dependency analysis with a two-stage discriminative parser. In *Proc. of the Tenth Conference on Computational Natural Language Learning (CoNLL-X)*, pages 216–220. Association for Computational Linguistics.

T. Nakagawa. 2007. Multilingual dependency parsing using global features. In *Proc. of the 2007 Joint Conference on Empirical Methods in Natural Language Processing and Computational Natural Language Learning (EMNLP-CoNLL 2007)*, pages 952–956.

J. Nivre, J. Hall, and J. Nilsson. 2006a. Maltparser: A data-driven parser-generator for dependency parsing. In *Proc. of the Fifth International Conference on Language Resources and Evaluation (LREC 2006)*, volume 6, pages 2216–2219.

J. Nivre, J. Hall, J. Nilsson, G. Eryiğit, and S. Marinov. 2006b. Labeled pseudo-projective dependency parsing with support vector machines. In *Proc. of the Tenth Conference on Computational Natural Language Learning (CoNLL-X)*, pages 221–225. Association for Computational Linguistics.

J. Nivre, J. Hall, S. Kübler, R. McDonald, J. Nilsson, S. Riedel, and D. Yuret. 2007. CoNLL 2007 shared task on dependency parsing. In *Proc. of the 2007 Joint Conference on Empirical Methods in Natural Language Processing and Computational Natural Language Learning (EMNLP-CoNLL 2007)*. Association for Computational Linguistics.

J. Nivre, I.M. Boguslavsky, and L.L. Iomdin. 2008. Parsing the SynTagRus treebank of Russian. In *Proc. of the 22nd International Conference on Computational Linguistics (COLING 2008)*, volume 1, pages 641–648. Association for Computational Linguistics.

J. Nivre. 2009. Parsing Indian languages with MaltParser. In *Proc. of the Seventh International Conference on Natural Language Processing (ICON 2009) NLP Tools Contest*, pages 12–18.

K. Oflazer, B. Say, D.Z. Hakkani-Tür, and G. Tür. 2003. Building a Turkish treebank. *Text, Speech, and Language Technology*, pages 261–277.

L. Øvrelid and J. Nivre. 2007. When word order and part-of-speech tags are not enough–Swedish dependency parsing with rich linguistic features. In *Proc. of the International Conference on Recent Advances in Natural Language Processing (RANLP)*, pages 447–451.

S. Petrov, D. Das, and R. McDonald. 2011. A universal part-of-speech tagset. *Arxiv preprint ArXiv:1104.2086*.

Loganathan Ramasamy and Zdeněk Žabokrtský. 2011. Tamil dependency parsing: Results using rule based and corpus based approaches. In *Proc. of the 12th International Conference on Intelligent Text Processing and Computational Linguistics (CICLING 2011)*, volume 1, pages 82–95, Berlin, Heidelberg. Springer-Verlag.

M. Schiehlen and K. Spranger. 2007. Global learning of labelled dependency trees. In *Proc. of the 2007 Joint Conference on Empirical Methods in Natural Language Processing and Computational Natural Language Learning (EMNLP-CoNLL 2007)*, pages 1156–1160.

Anna Siewierska. 1998. Variation in major constituent order: A global and a European perspective. In Anna Siewierska, editor, *Constituent Order in the Languages of Europe*, pages 475–551. Mouton De Gruyter.

K. Simov, P. Osenova, A. Simov, and M. Kouylekov. 2004. Design and implementation of the Bulgarian HPSG-based treebank. *Research on Language & Computation*, 2(4):495–522.

I. Titov and J. Henderson. 2007. Fast and robust multilingual dependency parsing with a generative latent variable model. In *Proc. of the 2007 Joint Conference on Empirical Methods in Natural Language Processing and Computational Natural Language Learning (EMNLP-CoNLL 2007)*, pages 947–951.

L. Van der Beek, G. Bouma, R. Malouf, and G. Van Noord. 2002. The Alpino dependency treebank. *Language and Computers*, 45(1):8–22.

V. Vincze, D. Szauter, A. Almási, G. Móra, Z. Alexin, and J. Csirik. 2010. Hungarian dependency treebank. In *Proc. of the Seventh Conference on Language Resources and Evaluation (LREC 2010)*.

N. Xue, F. Xia, F.D. Chiou, and M. Palmer. 2005. The Penn Chinese Treebank: Phrase structure annotation of a large corpus. *Natural Language Engineering*, 11(2):207–238.

Stylometric Analysis of Scientific Articles

Shane Bergsma, Matt Post, David Yarowsky
Department of Computer Science and Human Language Technology Center of Excellence
Johns Hopkins University
Baltimore, MD 21218, USA
sbergsma@jhu.edu, post@cs.jhu.edu, yarowsky@cs.jhu.edu

Abstract

We present an approach to automatically recover hidden attributes of scientific articles, such as whether the author is a native English speaker, whether the author is a male or a female, and whether the paper was published in a conference or workshop proceedings. We train classifiers to predict these attributes in computational linguistics papers. The classifiers perform well in this challenging domain, identifying non-native writing with 95% accuracy (over a baseline of 67%). We show the benefits of using *syntactic features* in stylometry; syntax leads to significant improvements over bag-of-words models on all three tasks, achieving 10% to 25% relative error reduction. We give a detailed analysis of which words and syntax most predict a particular attribute, and we show a strong correlation between our predictions and a paper's number of citations.

1 Introduction

Stylometry aims to recover useful attributes of documents from the style of the writing. In some domains, statistical techniques have successfully deduced author identity (Mosteller and Wallace, 1984), gender (Koppel et al., 2003), native language (Koppel et al., 2005), and even whether an author has dementia (Le et al., 2011). Stylometric analysis is important to marketers, analysts and social scientists because it provides demographic data directly from raw text. There has been growing interest in applying stylometry to the content generated by users of Internet applications, e.g., detecting author ethnicity in social media (Eisenstein et al., 2011; Rao et al., 2011), or whether someone is writing deceptive online reviews (Ott et al., 2011).

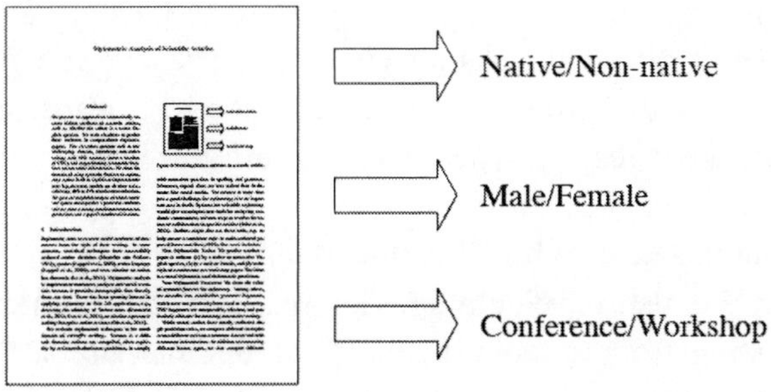

Figure 1: Predicting hidden attributes in scientific articles

We evaluate stylometric techniques in the novel domain of *scientific writing*. Science is a difficult domain; authors are encouraged, often explicitly by reviewers/submission-guidelines, to comply with normative practices in style, spelling and grammar. Moreover, topical clues are less salient than in domains like social media. Success in this challenging domain can bring us closer to correctly analyzing the huge volumes of online text that are currently unmarked for useful author attributes such as gender and native-language.

Yet science is more than just a good steppingstone for stylometry; it is an important area in itself. Systems for scientific stylometry would give sociologists new tools for analyzing academic communities, and new ways to resolve the nature of collaboration in specific articles (Johri et al., 2011). Authors might also use these tools, e.g., to help ensure a consistent style in multi-authored papers (Glover and Hirst, 1995), or to determine sections of a paper needing revision.

The contributions of our paper include:

New Stylometric Tasks: We predict whether a paper is written: (1) by a native or non-native speaker, (2) by a male or female, and (3) in the style of a conference or workshop paper. The latter is a fully novel stylometric and bibliometric prediction.

New Stylometric Features: We show the value of *syntactic features* for stylometry. Among others, we describe *tree substitution grammar* fragments, which have not previously been used in stylometry. TSG fragments are interpretable, efficient, and particularly effective for detecting non-native writing.

While recent studies have mostly evaluated single prediction tasks, we compare different strategies across different tasks on a common dataset and with a common infrastructure. In addition to contrasting different feature types, we compare different *training strategies*, exploring ways to make use of training instances with label uncertainty.

We also provide a detailed *analysis* that is interesting from a sociolinguistic standpoint. Precisely what words distinguish non-native writing? How does the syntax of female authors differ from males? What are the hallmarks of top-tier papers? Finally, we identify some strong correlations between our predictions and a paper's citation count, even when controlling for paper venue and origin.

2 Related Work

Bibliometrics is the empirical analysis of scholarly literature; *citation analysis* is a well-known bibliometric approach for ranking authors and papers (Borgman and Furner, 2001). Bibliometry and stylometry can share goals but differ in techniques. For example, in a work questioning the blindness of double-blind reviewing, Hill and Provost (2003) predict author identities. They ignore the article body and instead consider (a) potential self-citations and (b) similarity between the article's citation list and the citation lists of known papers. Radev et al. (2009a) perform a bibliometric analysis of computational linguistics. Teufel and Moens (2002) and Qazvinian and Radev (2008) summarize scientific articles, the latter by automatically finding and filtering sentences in other papers that cite the target article.

Our system does not consider citations; it is most similar to work that uses raw article text. Hall et al. (2008) build per-year topic models over scientific literature to track the evolution of scientific ideas. Gerrish and Blei (2010) assess the influence of individual articles by modeling their impact on the content of future papers. Yogatama et al. (2011) predict whether a paper will be cited based on both its content and its meta-data such as author names and publication venues. Johri et al. (2011) use per-author topic models to assess the nature of collaboration in a particular article (e.g., *apprenticeship* or *synergy*). One of the tasks in Sarawgi et al. (2011) concerned predicting gender in scientific writing, but they use a corpus of only ten "highly established" authors and make the prediction using twenty papers for each. Finally, Dale and Kilgarriff (2010) initiated a shared task on automatic editing of scientific papers written by non-native speakers, with the objective of developing "tools which can help non-native speakers of English (NNSs) (and maybe some native ones) write academic English prose of the kind that helps a paper get accepted."

Lexical and pragmatic choices in academic writing have also been analyzed within the applied linguistics community (Myers, 1989; Vassileva, 1998).

3 ACL Dataset and Preprocessing

We use papers from the ACL Anthology Network (Radev et al., 2009b, Release 2011) and exploit its manually-curated meta-data such as normalized author names, affiliations (including country, available up to 2009), and citation counts. We convert each PDF to text[1] but remove text before the *Abstract* (to anonymize) and after the *Acknowledgments/References* headings. We split the text into sentences[2] and filter any documents with fewer than 100 (this removes some short/demo papers, malconverted PDFs, etc. – about 23% of the 13K papers with affiliation information). In case the text was garbled, we then filtered the first 3 lines from every file and any line with an '@' symbol (which might be part of an affiliation). We remove footers like *Proceedings of ...*, table/figure captions, and any lines with non-ASCII characters (e.g. math equations). Papers are then parsed via the Berke-

[1]Via the open-source utility `pdftotext`

[2]Splitter from `cogcomp.cs.illinois.edu/page/tools`

Task	Training Set: *Strict*	*Lenient*	Dev Set	Test Set
NativeL	2127	3963	450	477
Venue	2484	3991	400	421
Gender	2125	3497	400	409

Table 1: Number of documents for each task

ley parser (Petrov et al., 2006), and part-of-speech (PoS) tagged using CRFTagger (Phan, 2006).

Training sets always comprise papers from 2001-2007, while test sets are created by randomly shuffling the 2008-2009 portion and then dividing it into development/test sets. We also use papers from 1990-2000 for experiments in §7.3 and §7.4.

4 Stylometric Tasks

Each task has both a *Strict* training set, using only the data for which we are most confident in the labels (as described below), and a *Lenient* set, which forcibly assigns every paper in the training period to some class (Table 1). All test papers are annotated using a *Strict* rule. While our approaches for automatically-assigning labels can be coarse, they allow us to scale our analysis to a realistic cross-section of academic papers, letting us discover some interesting trends.

4.1 *NativeL*: Native vs. Non-Native English

We introduce the task of predicting whether a scientific paper is written by a native English speaker (NES) or non-native speaker (NNS). Prior work has mostly made this prediction in learner corpora (Koppel et al., 2005; Tsur and Rappoport, 2007; Wong and Dras, 2011), although there have been attempts in elicited speech transcripts (Tomokiyo and Jones, 2001) and e-mail (Estival et al., 2007). There has also been a large body of work on *correcting* errors in non-native writing, with a specific focus on difficulties in preposition and article usage (Han et al., 2006; Chodorow et al., 2007; Felice and Pulman, 2007; Tetreault and Chodorow, 2008; Gamon, 2010).

We annotate papers using two pieces of associated meta-data: (1) author first names and (2) countries of affiliation. We manually marked each country for whether English is predominantly spoken there. We then built a list of common first names of English speakers via the top 150 male and female names from the U.S. census.[3] If the *first* author of a paper has an English first name *and* English-speaking-country affiliation, we mark as NES.[4] If *none* of the authors have an English first name *nor* an English-speaking-country affiliation, we mark as NNS. We use this rule to label our development and test data, as well as our *Strict* training set. For *Lenient* training, we decide based solely on whether the first author is from an English-speaking country.

4.2 *Venue*: Top-Tier vs. Workshop

This novel task aims to distinguish top-tier papers from those at workshops, based on style. We use the annual meeting of the ACL as our canonical top-tier venue. For evaluation and *Strict* training, we label all main-session ACL papers as *top-tier*, and all workshop papers as *workshop*. For *Lenient* training, we assign **all** conferences (LREC, Coling, EMNLP, etc.) to be *top-tier* except for their non-main-session papers, which we label as *workshop*.

4.3 *Gender*: Male vs. Female

Because we are classifying an international set of authors, U.S. census names (the usual source of gender ground-truth) provide incomplete information. We therefore use the data of Bergsma and Lin (2006).[5] This data has been widely used in coreference resolution but never in stylometry. Each line in the data lists how often a noun co-occurs with male, female, neutral and plural pronouns; this is commonly taken as an approximation of the true gender distribution. E.g., '*bill clinton*' is 98% male (in 8344 instances) while '*elsie wayne*' is 100% female (in 23). The data also has *aggregate counts* over all nouns with the same first token, e.g., '*elsie* ...' is 94% female (in 255 instances). For *Strict* training/evaluation, we label papers with the following rule based on the first author's first name:

[3] `www.census.gov/genealogy/names/names_files.html` We also manually added common nicknames for these, e.g. *Rob* for *Robert*, *Chris* for *Christopher*, *Dan* for *Daniel*, etc.

[4] Of course, assuming the first author writes each paper is imperfect. In fact, for some native/non-native collaborations, our system ultimately predicts the 2nd (non-native) author to be the main writer; in one case we confirmed the accuracy of this prediction by personal communication with the authors.

[5] `www.clsp.jhu.edu/~sbergsma/Gender/`

if the name has an aggregate count >30 and female probability >0.85, label as female; otherwise if the aggregate count is >30 and male probability >0.85, label male. This rule captures many of ACL's unambiguously-gendered names, both male (*Nathanael, Jens, Hiroyuki*) and female (*Widad, Yael, Sunita*). For *Lenient* training, we assign all papers based only on whether the male or female probability for the first author is higher. While potentially noisy, there is precedent for assigning a single gender to papers "co-authored by researchers of mixed gender" (Sarawgi et al., 2011).

5 Models and Training Strategies

Model: We take a discriminative approach to stylometry, representing articles as feature vectors (§6) and classifying them using a linear, L2-regularized SVM, trained via LIBLINEAR (Fan et al., 2008). SVMs are state-of-the-art and have been used previously in stylometry (Koppel et al., 2005).

Strategy: We test whether it's better to train with a smaller, more accurate *Strict* set, or a larger but noisier *Lenient* set. We also explore a third strategy, motivated by work in learning from noisy web images (Bergamo and Torresani, 2010), in which we fix the *Strict* labels, but also include the remaining examples as *unlabeled* instances. We then optimize a *Transductive* SVM, solving an optimization problem where we not only choose the feature weights, but also labels for unlabeled training points. Like a regular SVM, the goal is to maximize the margin between the positive and negative vectors, but now the vectors have both fixed and imputed labels. We optimize using Joachims (1999)'s software. While the classifier is trained using a transductive strategy, it is still tested *inductively*, i.e., on unseen data.

6 Stylometric Features

Koppel et al. (2003) describes a range of features that have been used in stylometry, ranging from early manual selection of potentially discriminative words, to approaches based on automated text categorization (Sebastiani, 2002). We use the following three feature classes; the particular features were chosen based on development experiments.

6.1 *Bow* Features

A variety of "discouraging results" in the text categorization literature have shown that simple bag-of-words (*Bow*) representations usually perform better than "more sophisticated" ones (e.g. using syntax) (Sebastiani, 2002). This was also observed in sentiment classification (Pang et al., 2002). One key aim of our research is to see whether this is true of scientific stylometry. Our *Bow* representation uses a feature for each unique lower-case word-type in an article. We also preprocess papers by making all digits '0'. Normalizing digits and filtering capitalized words helps ensure citations and named-entities are excluded from our features. The feature value is the log-count of how often the corresponding word occurs in the document.

6.2 *Style* Features

While text categorization relies on keywords, stylometry focuses on topic-independent measures like function word frequency (Mosteller and Wallace, 1984), sentence length (Yule, 1939), and PoS (Hirst and Feiguina, 2007). We define a *style-word* to be: (1) punctuation, (2) a stopword, or (3) a Latin abbreviation.[6] We create *Style* features for all unigrams and bigrams, replacing non-*style-words* separately with both PoS-tags and spelling signatures.[7] Each feature is an N-gram, the value is its log-count in the article. We also include stylistic *meta-features* such as mean-words-per-sentence and mean-word-length.

6.3 *Syntax* Features

Unlike recent work using generative PCFGs (Raghavan et al., 2010; Sarawgi et al., 2011), we use syntax directly as features in *discriminative* models, which can easily incorporate arbitrary and overlapping syntactic clues. For example, we will see that one indicator of native text is the use of certain determiners as stand-alone noun phrases (NPs), like *this* in Figure 2. This contrasts with a proposed non-native phrase, "this/DT growing/VBG area/NN," where *this* instead modifies a noun. The *Bow* features are clearly unhelpful: *this* occurs in both cases. The

[6]The stopword list is the standard set of 524 SMART-system stopwords (following Tomokiyo and Jones (2001)). Latin abbreviations are *i.e., e.g., etc., c.f., et* or *al.*

[7]E.g., signature '*LC-ing*' means lower-case, ending in *ing*. These are created via a script included with the Berkeley parser.

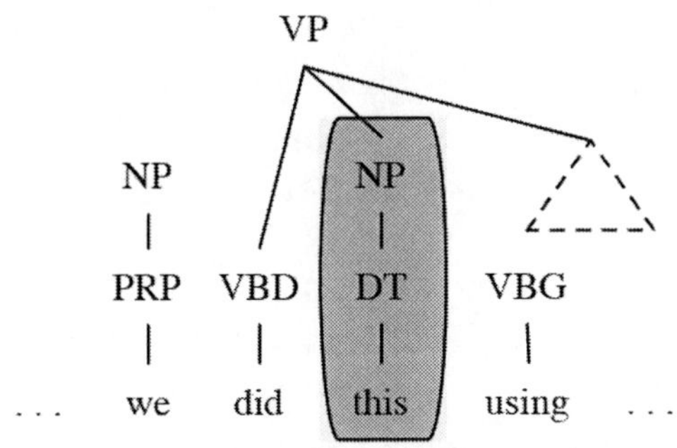

Figure 2: Motivating deeper syntactic features: The shaded TSG fragment indicates native English, but is not directly encoded in *Bow*, *Style*, nor standard CFG-rules.

Style features are likewise unhelpful; *this*-VBG also occurs in both cases. We need the deeper knowledge that a specific determiner is used as a complete NP.

We evaluate three feature types that aim to capture such knowledge. In each case, we aggregate the feature counts over all the parse trees constituting a document. The feature value is the log-count of how often each feature occurs. To remove *content* information from the features, we preprocess the parse tree terminals: all non-*style-word* terminals are replaced with their spelling signature (see §6.2).

CFG Rules: We include a feature for every unique, single-level context-free-grammar (CFG) rule application in a paper (following Baayen et al. (1996), Gamon (2004), Hirst and Feiguina (2007), Wong and Dras (2011)). The Figure 2 tree would have features: NP→PRP, NP→DT, DT→*this*, etc. Such features do capture that a determiner was used as an NP, but they do not jointly encode *which* determiner was used. This is an important omission; we'll see that other determiners acting as stand-alone NPs indicate *non-native* writing (e.g., the word *that*, see §7.2).

TSG Fragments: A tree-substitution grammar is a generalization of CFGs that allow rewriting to tree fragments rather than sequences of non-terminals (Joshi and Schabes, 1997). Figure 2 gives the example NP→(DT *this*). This fragment captures both the identity of the determiner and its syntactic function as an NP, as desired. Efficient Bayesian procedures have recently been developed that enable the training of large-scale probabilistic TSG grammars (Post and Gildea, 2009; Cohn et al., 2010).

While TSGs have not been used previously in stylometry, Post (2011) uses them to predict sentence *grammaticality* (i.e. detecting pseudo-sentences following Okanohara and Tsujii (2007) and Cherry and Quirk (2008)). We use Post's TSG training settings and his public code.[8] We parse with the TSG grammar and extract the fragments as features. We also follow Post by having features for aggregate TSG statistics, e.g., how many fragments are of a given size, tree-depth, etc. These syntactic meta-features are somewhat similar to the manually-defined stylometric features of Stamatatos et al. (2001).

C&J Reranking Features: We also extracted the reranking features of Charniak and Johnson (2005). These features were hand-crafted for reranking the output of a parser, but have recently been used for other NLP tasks (Post, 2011; Wong and Dras, 2011). They include lexicalized features for sub-trees and head-to-head dependencies, and aggregate features for conjunct parallelism and the degree of right-branching. We get the features using another script from Post.[9] While TSG fragments tile a parse tree into a few useful fragments, C&J features can produce thousands of features per sentence, and are thus much more computationally-demanding.

7 Experiments and Results

We take the *minority class* as the positive class: NES for *NativeL*, top-tier for *Venue* and female for *Gender*, and calculate the precision/recall of these classes. We tune three hyperparameters for F1-score on development data: (1) the SVM regularization parameter, (2) the threshold for classifying an instance as positive (using the signed hyperplane-distance as the score), and (3) for transductive training (§5), the fraction of unlabeled data to label as positive. Statistical significance on held-out test data is assessed with McNemar's test, $p<0.05$. For F1-score, we use the following reasonable *Baseline*: we label all instances with the label of the minority class (achieving 100% recall but low precision).

7.1 Selection of Syntax and Training Strategy

Development experiments showed that using all features, *Bow+Style+Syntax*, works best on all tasks, but there was no benefit in combining different

[8]http://github.com/mjpost/dptsg

[9]http://github.com/mjpost/extract-spfeatures.

Syntax	Strategy	*NativeL*	*Venue*	*Gender*
Baseline		50.5	45.0	28.7
CFG	*Strict*	93.5	59.9	**42.5**
CFG	*Lenient*	89.9	64.9	39.5
TSG	*Strict*	**93.6**	60.7	40.0
TSG	*Lenient*	90.9	64.4	39.1
C&J	*Strict*	90.5	62.3	37.1
C&J	*Lenient*	86.2	**65.2**	39.0

Table 2: F1 scores for *Bow+Style+Syntax* system on *development data*: The best training strategy and the best syntactic features depend on the task.

Features	*NativeL*	*Venue*	*Gender*
Baseline	49.8	45.5	33.1
Bow	88.8	60.7	42.5
Style	90.6	61.9	39.8
Syntax	88.7	64.6	41.2
Bow+Style	90.4	64.0	45.1
Bow+Syntax	90.3	65.8	42.9
Style+Syntax	89.4	65.5	43.3
Bow+Style+Syntax	**91.6**	**66.7**	**48.2**

Table 3: F1 scores with different features on *held-out test data*: Including style and syntactic features is superior to standard *Bow* features in all cases.

Syntax features. We also found no gain from transductive training, but greater cost, with more hyper-parameter tuning and a slower SVM solver. The best *Syntax* features depend on the task (Table 2). Whether *Strict* or *Lenient* training: TSG was best for *NativeL*, C&J was best for *Venue*, and CFG was best for *Gender*. These trends continue on test data, where TSG exceeds CFG (91.6% vs. 91.2%). For the training strategy, *Strict* was best on *NativeL* and *Gender*, while *Lenient* was best on *Venue* (Table 2). This latter result is interesting: recall that for *Venue*, *Lenient* training considers all conferences to be top-tier, but evaluation is just on detecting ACL papers. We suggest some reasons for this below, highlighting some general features of conference papers that extend beyond particular venues.

For the remainder of experiments on each task, we fix the syntactic features and training strategy to those that performed best on development data.

7.2 Test Results and Feature Analysis

Gender remains the most difficult task on *test* data, but our F1 still substantially outperforms the baseline (Table 3). Results on *NativeL* are particularly impressive; in terms of *accuracy*, we classify 94.6% of test articles correctly (the majority-class baseline is 66.9%). Regarding features, just using *Style+Syntax* always works better than using *Bow*. Combining all features always works better still. The gains of *Bow+Style+Syntax* over vanilla *Bow* are statistically significant in each case.

We also highlight important *individual features*:

NativeL: Table 4 gives *Bow* and *Style* features for *NativeL*. Some reflect differences in common native/non-native *topics*; e.g., '*probabilities*' predicts native while '*morphological*' predicts non-native. Several features, like '*obtained*', indicate L1 interference; i.e., many non-natives have a cognate for *obtain* in their native language and thus adopt the English word. As an example, the word *obtained* occurs 3.7 times per paper from Spanish-speaking areas (cognate *obtenir*) versus once per native paper and 0.8 times per German-authored paper.

Natives also prefer certain abbreviations (e.g. '*e.g.*') while non-natives prefer others ('*i.e.*', '*c.f.*', '*etc.*'). Exotic punctuation also suggests native text: the semi-colon, exclamation and question mark all predict NES. Note this also varies by region; semi-colons are most popular in NES countries but papers from Israel and Italy are close behind.

Table 5 gives highly-weighted TSG features for predicting *NativeL*. Note the determiner-as-NP usage described earlier (§ 6.3): *these*, *this* and *each* predict native when used as an NP; *that*-as-an-NP predicts non-native. Furthermore, while not all native speakers use a comma before a conjunction in a list, it's nevertheless a good flag for native writing ('NP→NP, NP, (CC *and*) NP'). In terms of non-native syntax, the passive voice is more common ('VP→(VBZ *is*) VP' and 'VP→VBN (PP (IN *as*) NP)'). We also looked for features involving determiners since correct determiner usage is a common difficulty for non-native speakers. We found cases where determiners were missing where natives might have used one ('NP→JJ JJ NN'), but also those where a determiner might be optional and skipped by a native speaker ('NP→(DT *the*) NN NNS'). Note that Table 5

Predicts native		Predicts non-native	
Bow feature	Wt.	*Bow* feature	Wt.
initial	2.25	obtained	-2.15
techniques	2.11	proposed	-2.06
probabilities	1.38	method	-2.06
additional	1.23	morphological	-1.96
fewer	1.02	languages	-1.23
Style feature	Wt.	*Style* feature	Wt.
used to	1.92	, i.e.	-2.60
JJR NN	1.90	have to	-1.65
has VBN	1.90	the *xxxx*-ing	-1.61
example ,	1.75	thus	-1.61
all of	1.73	usually	-1.24
's	1.69	mainly	-1.21
allow	1.47	, because	-1.12
has *xxxx*-ed	1.45	the VBN	-1.12
may be	1.35	JJ for	-1.11
; and	1.21	cf	-0.97
e.g.	1.10	etc.	-0.55
must VB	0.99	associated to	-0.23

Table 4: *NativeL*: Examples of highly-weighted style and content features in the *Bow+Style+Syntax* system.

TSG Fragment	Example
Predicts native English author:	
NP→NNP CD	(*Model*) (*1*)
NP→(DT *these*)	*six of* (*these*)
NP→(DT *that*) NN	*in* (*that*) (*language*)
NP→(DT *this*)	*we did* (*this*) *using ...*
VP→(VBN *used*) S	(*used*) (*to describe it*)
NP→NP, NP, (CC *and*) NP	(*X*), (*Y*), (*and*) (*Z*)
NP→(DT *each*)	(*each*) consists of ...
Predicts non-native English author:	
VP→(VBZ *is*) VP	*it* (*is*) (*shown below*)
VP→VBN (PP (IN *as*) NP)	(*considered*) (*as*) (*a term*)
NP→JJ JJ NN	*in* (*other*) (*large*) (*corpus*)
NP→DT JJ (CD *one*)	(*a*) (*correct*) (*one*)
NP→(DT *the*) NN NNS	*seen in* (*the*) (*test*) (*data*)
NP→(DT *that*)	*larger than* (*that*) *of ...*
QP→(IN *about*) CD	(*about*) (*200,000*) *words*

Table 5: *NativeL*: Highly-weighted syntactic features (descending order of absolute weight) and examples in the *Bow+Style+Syntax* system.

examples are based on actual usage in ACL papers. We also found that *complex* NPs were more associated with native text. Features such as 'NP→DT JJ NN NN NN', and 'NP→DT NN NN NNS' predict native writing.

Non-natives also rely more on boilerplate. For example, the exact phrase "The/This paper is organized as follows" occurs 3 times as often in non-native compared to native text (in 7.5% of all non-native papers). Sentence re-use is only indirectly captured by our features; it would be interesting to encode flags for it directly.

In general, we found very few highly-weighted features that pinpoint 'ungrammatical' non-native writing (the feature '*associated to*' in Table 4 is a rare example). Our classifiers largely detect non-native writing on a stylistic rather than grammatical basis.

Venue: Table 6 provides important *Bow* and *Style* features for the *Venue* task (syntactic features omitted due to space). While some features are topical (e.g. '*biomedical*'), the table gives a blueprint for writing a solid main-conference paper. That is, good papers often have an explicit probability model (or algorithm), experimental baselines, error analysis, and statistical significance checking. On the other hand, there might be a bias at main conferences for focused, incremental papers; features of workshop papers highlight the exploration of '*interesting*' new ideas/domains. Here, the objective might only be to show what is '*possible*' or what one is '*able to*' do. Main conference papers prefer work that improves '*performance*' by '*#%*' on established tasks.

Gender: The CFG features for *Gender* are given in Table 7. Several of the most highly-weighted female features include pronouns (e.g. PRP$). A higher frequency of pronouns in female writing has been attested previously (Argamon et al., 2003), but has not been traced to particular syntactic constructions. Likewise, we observe a higher frequency of not just negation (noted previously) but adverbs (RB) in general (e.g. 'VP→MD RB VP'). In terms of *Bow* features (not shown), the words *contrast* and *comparison* highly predict female, as do topical clues like *verb* and *resource*. The top-three male *Bow* features are (in order): *simply*, *perform*, *parsing*.

7.3 Author Rankings

While our objective is to predict attributes of *papers*, we also show how that we can identify *author* attributes using a larger body of work. We make *NativeL* and *Gender* predictions for all papers in the

Predicts ACL		Predicts Workshop	
Bow feature	Wt.	*Bow* feature	Wt.
model	2.64	semantic	-2.16
probability	1.66	analysis	-1.65
performance	1.40	verb	-1.35
baseline	1.36	lexical	-1.33
=	1.26	study	-0.92
algorithm	1.18	biomedical	-0.87
large	1.16	preliminary	-0.69
error	1.15	interesting	-0.69
outperforms	1.02	aim	-0.64
significant	0.96	manually	-0.62
statistically	0.75	appears	-0.54
Style feature	Wt.	*Style* feature	Wt.
by VBG	1.04	able to	-0.99
#%	0.82	*xxxx*-ed out	-0.77
NN over	0.79	further NN	-0.71
than the	0.79	NN should	-0.69
improvement	0.75	will be	-0.61
best	0.71	possible	-0.57
xxxx-s by	0.70	have not	-0.56
much JJR	0.67	currently	-0.56

Table 6: *Venue*: Examples of highly-weighted style content features in the *Bow+Style+Syntax* system.

CFG Rule	Example
Predicts female author:	
NP→PRP$ NN NN	(*our*) (*upper*) (*bound*)
QP→RB CD	(*roughly*) (*6000*)
NP→NP, CC NP	(*a new* NE *tag*), (*or*) (*no* NE *tag*)
NP→PRP$ JJ JJ NN	(*our*) (*first*) (*new*) (*approach*)
VP→MD RB VP	(*may*) (*not*) (*be useful*)
ADVP→RB RBR	(*significantly*) (*more*)
Predicts male author:	
ADVP→RB RB	(*only*) (*superficially*)
NP→NP, SBAR	*we use* (*XYZ*), (*which is ...*)
S→S: S.	(*Trust me*): (*I'm a doctor*)
S→S, NP VP	(*To do so*), (*it*) (*needs help*)
WHNP→WP NN	*depending on* (*what*) (*path*) *is ...*
PP→IN PRN	(*in*) ((*Jelinek, 1976*))

Table 7: *Gender*: Highly-weighted syntactic features (descending order of weight) and examples in the *Bow+Style+Syntax* system.

Highest NES Scores, non-English-country: *Gerald Penn,*[10] *Ezra W. Black, Nigel Collier, Jean-Luc Gauvain, Dan Cristea, Graham J. Russell, Kenneth R. Beesley, Dekai Wu, Christer Samuelsson, Raquel Martinez*
Highest NES Scores, English-country: *Eric V. Siegel, Lance A. Ramshaw, Stephanie Seneff, Victor W. Zue, Joshua Goodman, Patti J. Price, Stuart M. Shieber, Jean Carletta, Lynn Lambert, Gina-Anne Levow*

Table 8: Authors scoring highest on *NativeL*, in descending order, based exclusively on article text.

1990-2000 era using our *Bow+Style+Syntax* system. For each author+affiliation with $\geq$3 first-authored papers, we take the average classifier score on these papers.

Table 8 shows cases where our model strongly predicts native, showing top authors with foreign affiliations and top authors in English-speaking countries.[10] While not perfect, the predictions correctly identify some native authors that would be difficult to detect using only name and location data. For example, *Dekai Wu* (Hong Kong) speaks English natively; *Christer Samuelsson* lists near-native English on his C.V.; etc. Likewise, we have also been able to accurately identify a set of *non-native* speakers with common American names that were working at American universities.

Table 9 provides some of the extreme predictions of our system on *Gender*. The extreme male and female predictions are based on both style and content; females tend to work on summarization, discourse, etc., while many males focus on parsing. We also tried making these lists without *Bow* features, but the extreme examples still reflect topic to some extent. Topics themselves have their own style, which the style features capture; it is difficult to fully separate style from topic.

7.4 Correlation with Citations

We also test whether our systems' *stylometric* scores correlate with the most common *bibliometric* measure: citation count. To reduce the impact of *topic*, we only use *Style+Syntax* features. We plot results separately for *ACL*, *Coling* and *Workshop* papers (1990-2000 era). Papers at each venue are sorted by their classifier scores and binned into five score bins. Each point in the plot is the mean-score/mean-number-of-citations for papers in a bin (within-community citation data is via the AAN §3

[10]Note again that this is based on the affiliation of these authors during the 1990s; e.g. Gerald Penn published three papers while at the University of Tübingen.

Highest Model Scores (Male): *John Aberdeen, Chao-Huang Chang, Giorgio Satta, Stanley F. Chen, GuoDong Zhou, Carl Weir, Akira Ushioda, Hideki Tanaka, Koichi Takeda, Douglas B. Paul, Hideo Watanabe, Adam L. Berger, Kevin Knight, Jason M. Eisner*

Highest Model Scores (Female): *Julia B. Hirschberg, Johanna D. Moore, Judy L. Delin, Paola Merlo, Rebecca J. Passonneau, Bonnie Lynn Webber, Beth M. Sundheim, Jennifer Chu-Carroll, Ching-Long Yeh, Mary Ellen Okurowski, Erik-Jan Van Der Linden*

Table 9: Authors scoring highest (absolute values) on *Gender*, in descending order, based exclusively on article text.

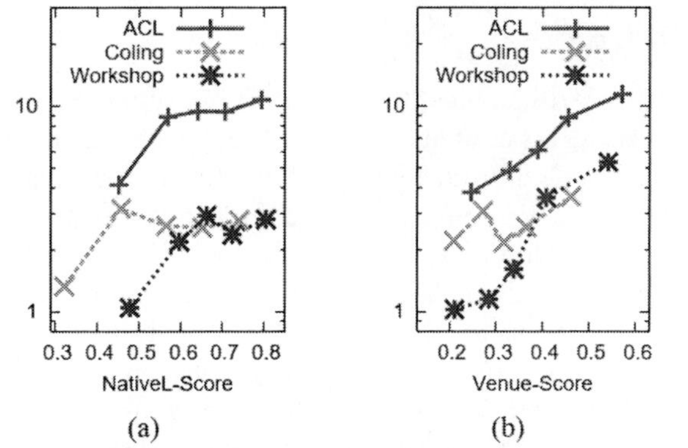

Figure 3: Correlation between predictions (x-axis) and mean number of citations (y-axis, *log-scale*).

and excludes self citations). We use a truncated mean for citation counts, leaving off the top/bottom five papers in each bin.

For *NativeL*, we only plot papers marked as **native** by our *Strict* rule (i.e. English name/country). Papers with the lowest *NativeL*-scores receive many fewer citations, but they soon level off (Figure 3(a)). Many *junior* researchers at English universities are non-native speakers; early-career non-natives might receive fewer citations than well-known peers. The correlation between citations and *Venue*-scores is even stronger (Figure 3(b)); the top-ranked workshop papers receive five times as many citations as the lowest ones, and are cited better than a good portion of ACL papers. These figures suggest that citation-predictors can get useful information beyond typical *Bow* features (Yogatama et al., 2011). Although we focused on a past era, stylistic/syntactic features should also be more robust to the evolution of scientific topics; we plan to next test whether we can better *forecast* future citations. It would also be interesting to see whether these trends transfer to other academic disciplines.

7.5 Further Experiments on *NativeL*

For *NativeL*, we also created a special test corpus of 273 papers written by first-time ACL authors (2008-2009 era). This set closely aligns with the system's potential use as a tool to help new authors compose papers. Two (native-speaking) annotators manually annotated each paper for whether it was primarily written by a native or non-native speaker (considering both content and author names/affiliations). The annotators agreed on 90% of decisions, with an inter-annotator kappa of 66%. We divided the papers into a test set and a development set. We applied our *Bow+Style+Syntax* system exactly as trained above, except we tuned its hyperparameters on the new development data. The system performed quite well on this set, reaching 68% F1 over a baseline of only 27%. Moreover, the system also reached 90% accuracy, matching the level of human agreement.

8 Conclusion

We have proposed, developed and successfully evaluated significant new tasks and methods in the stylometric analysis of scientific articles, including the novel resolution of publication venue based on paper style, and novel syntactic features based on tree substitution grammar fragments. In all cases, our syntactic and stylistic features significantly improve over a bag-of-words baseline, achieving 10% to 25% relative error reduction in all three major tasks. We have included a detailed and insightful analysis of discriminative stylometric features, and we showed a strong correlation between our predictions and a paper's number of citations. We observed evidence for L1-interference in non-native writing, for differences in topic between males and females, and for distinctive language usage which can successfully identify papers published in top-tier conferences versus wokrshop proceedings. We believe that this work can stimulate new research at the intersection of computational linguistics and bibliometrics.

References

Shlomo Argamon, Moshe Koppel, Jonathan Fine, and Anat Rachel Shimoni. 2003. Gender, genre, and writing style in formal written texts. *Text*, 23(3), August.

Harald Baayen, Fiona Tweedie, and Hans van Halteren. 1996. Outside the cave of shadows: Using syntactic annotation to enhance authorship attribution. *Literary and Linguistic Computing*, 11(3):121–132.

Alessandro Bergamo and Lorenzo Torresani. 2010. Exploiting weakly-labeled web images to improve object classification: a domain adaptation approach. In *Proc. NIPS*, pages 181–189.

Shane Bergsma and Dekang Lin. 2006. Bootstrapping path-based pronoun resolution. In *Proc. Coling-ACL*, pages 33–40.

Christine L. Borgman and Jonathan Furner. 2001. Scholarly communication and bibliometrics. *Annual Review of Information Science and Technology*, 36:3–72.

Eugene Charniak and Mark Johnson. 2005. Coarse-to-fine n-best parsing and MaxEnt discriminative reranking. In *Proc. ACL*, pages 173–180.

Colin Cherry and Chris Quirk. 2008. Discriminative, syntactic language modeling through latent SVMs. In *Proc. AMTA*.

Martin Chodorow, Joel R. Tetreault, and Na-Rae Han. 2007. Detection of grammatical errors involving prepositions. In *Proc. ACL-SIGSEM Workshop on Prepositions*, pages 25–30.

Trevor Cohn, Phil Blunsom, and Sharon Goldwater. 2010. Inducing tree-substitution grammars. *J. Mach. Learn. Res.*, 11:3053–3096.

Robert Dale and Adam Kilgarriff. 2010. Helping our own: Text massaging for computational linguistics as a new shared task. In *Proc. 6th International Natural Language Generation Conference*, pages 261–265.

Jacob Eisenstein, Noah A. Smith, and Eric P. Xing. 2011. Discovering sociolinguistic associations with structured sparsity. In *Proc. ACL*, pages 1365–1374.

Dominique Estival, Tanja Gaustad, Son-Bao Pham, Will Radford, and Ben Hutchinson. 2007. Author profiling for English emails. In *Proc. PACLING*, pages 263–272.

Rong-En Fan, Kai-Wei Chang, Cho-Jui Hsieh, Xiang-Rui Wang, and Chih-Jen Lin. 2008. LIBLINEAR: A library for large linear classification. *J. Mach. Learn. Res.*, 9:1871–1874.

Rachele De Felice and Stephen G. Pulman. 2007. Automatically acquiring models of preposition use. In *Proc. ACL-SIGSEM Workshop on Prepositions*, pages 45–50.

Michael Gamon. 2004. Linguistic correlates of style: authorship classification with deep linguistic analysis features. In *Proc. Coling*, pages 611–617.

Michael Gamon. 2010. Using mostly native data to correct errors in learners' writing: a meta-classifier approach. In *Proc. HLT-NAACL*, pages 163–171.

Sean Gerrish and David M. Blei. 2010. A language-based approach to measuring scholarly impact. In *Proc. ICML*, pages 375–382.

Angela Glover and Graeme Hirst. 1995. Detecting stylistic inconsistencies in collaborative writing. In *Writers at work: Professional writing in the computerized environment*, pages 147–168.

David Hall, Daniel Jurafsky, and Christopher D. Manning. 2008. Studying the history of ideas using topic models. In *Proc. EMNLP*, pages 363–371.

Na-Rae Han, Martin Chodorow, and Claudia Leacock. 2006. Detecting errors in English article usage by non-native speakers. *Nat. Lang. Eng.*, 12(2):115–129.

Shawndra Hill and Foster Provost. 2003. The myth of the double-blind review?: Author identification using only citations. *SIGKDD Explor. Newsl.*, 5:179–184.

Graeme Hirst and Ol'ga Feiguina. 2007. Bigrams of syntactic labels for authorship discrimination of short texts. *Literary and Linguistic Computing*, 22(4):405–417.

Thorsten Joachims. 1999. Transductive inference for text classification using support vector machines. In *Proc. ICML*, pages 200–209.

Nikhil Johri, Daniel Ramage, Daniel McFarland, and Daniel Jurafsky. 2011. A study of academic collaborations in computational linguistics using a latent mixture of authors model. In *Proc. 5th ACL-HLT Workshop on Language Technology for Cultural Heritage, Social Sciences, and Humanities*, pages 124–132.

Aravind K. Joshi and Yves Schabes. 1997. Tree-adjoining grammars. In G. Rozenberg and A. Salomaa, editors, *Handbook of Formal Languages: Beyond Words*, volume 3, pages 71–122.

Moshe Koppel, Shlomo Argamon, and Anat Rachel Shimoni. 2003. Automatically categorizing written texts by author gender. *Literary and Linguistic Computing*, 17(4):401–412.

Moshe Koppel, Jonathan Schler, and Kfir Zigdon. 2005. Determining an author's native language by mining a text for errors. In *Proc. KDD*, pages 624–628.

Xuan Le, Ian Lancashire, Graeme Hirst, and Regina Jokel. 2011. Longitudinal detection of dementia through lexical and syntactic changes in writing: A case study of three British novelists. *Literary and Linguistic Computing*, 26(4):435–461.

Frederick Mosteller and David L. Wallace. 1984. *Applied Bayesian and Classical Inference: The Case of the Federalist Papers*. Springer-Verlag.

Greg Myers. 1989. The pragmatics of politeness in scientific articles. *Applied Linguistics*, 10(1):1–35.

Daisuke Okanohara and Jun'ichi Tsujii. 2007. A discriminative language model with pseudo-negative samples. In *Proc. ACL*, pages 73–80.

Myle Ott, Yejin Choi, Claire Cardie, and Jeffrey T. Hancock. 2011. Finding deceptive opinion spam by any stretch of the imagination. In *Proc. ACL*, pages 309–319.

Bo Pang, Lillian Lee, and Shivakumar Vaithyanathan. 2002. Thumbs up?: Sentiment classification using machine learning techniques. In *Proc. EMNLP*, pages 79–86.

Slav Petrov, Leon Barrett, Romain Thibaux, and Dan Klein. 2006. Learning accurate, compact, and interpretable tree annotation. In *Proc. Coling-ACL*, pages 433–440.

Xuan-Hieu Phan. 2006. CRFTagger: CRF English POS Tagger. `crftagger.sourceforge.net`.

Matt Post and Daniel Gildea. 2009. Bayesian learning of a tree substitution grammar. In *Proc. ACL-IJCNLP*, pages 45–48.

Matt Post. 2011. Judging grammaticality with tree substitution grammar derivations. In *Proc. ACL*, pages 217–222.

Vahed Qazvinian and Dragomir R. Radev. 2008. Scientific paper summarization using citation summary networks. In *Proc. Coling*, pages 689–696.

Dragomir R. Radev, Mark Thomas Joseph, Bryan Gibson, and Pradeep Muthukrishnan. 2009a. A bibliometric and network analysis of the field of computational linguistics. *Journal of the American Society for Information Science and Technology*.

Dragomir R. Radev, Pradeep Muthukrishnan, and Vahed Qazvinian. 2009b. The ACL anthology network corpus. In *Proc. ACL Workshop on Natural Language Processing and Information Retrieval for Digital Libraries*, pages 54–61.

Sindhu Raghavan, Adriana Kovashka, and Raymond Mooney. 2010. Authorship attribution using probabilistic context-free grammars. In *Proc. ACL*, pages 38–42.

Delip Rao, Michael Paul, Clay Fink, David Yarowsky, Timothy Oates, and Glen Coppersmith. 2011. Hierarchical bayesian models for latent attribute detection in social media. In *Proc. ICWSM*, pages 598–601.

Ruchita Sarawgi, Kailash Gajulapalli, and Yejin Choi. 2011. Gender attribution: tracing stylometric evidence beyond topic and genre. In *Proc. CoNLL*, pages 78–86.

Fabrizio Sebastiani. 2002. Machine learning in automated text categorization. *ACM Comput. Surv.*, 34:1–47.

Efstathios Stamatatos, Nikos Fakotakis, and George Kokkinakis. 2001. Automatic text categorization in terms of genre and author. *Computational Linguistics*, 26(4):471–495.

Joel R. Tetreault and Martin Chodorow. 2008. The ups and downs of preposition error detection in ESL writing. In *Proc. Coling*, pages 865–872.

Simone Teufel and Marc Moens. 2002. Summarizing scientific articles - experiments with relevance and rhetorical status. *Computational Linguistics*, 28(4):409–445.

Laura Mayfield Tomokiyo and Rosie Jones. 2001. You're not from 'round here, are you? Naive Bayes detection of non-native utterances. In *Proc. NAACL*.

Oren Tsur and Ari Rappoport. 2007. Using classifier features for studying the effect of native language on the choice of written second language words. In *Proc. Workshop on Cognitive Aspects of Computational Language Acquisition*, pages 9–16.

Irena Vassileva. 1998. Who am I/who are we in academic writing? *International Journal of Applied Linguistics*, 8(2):163–185.

Sze-Meng Jojo Wong and Mark Dras. 2011. Exploiting parse structures for native language identification. In *Proc. EMNLP*, pages 1600–1610.

Dani Yogatama, Michael Heilman, Brendan O'Connor, Chris Dyer, Bryan R. Routledge, and Noah A. Smith. 2011. Predicting a scientific community's response to an article. In *Proc. EMNLP*, pages 594–604.

G. Udny Yule. 1939. On sentence-length as a statistical characteristic of style in prose: With application to two cases of disputed authorship. *Biometrika*, 30(3/4):363–390.

Using paraphrases for improving first story detection in news and Twitter

Saša Petrović
School of Informatics
University of Edinburgh
sasa.petrovic@ed.ac.uk

Miles Osborne
School of Informatics
University of Edinburgh
miles@inf.ed.ac.uk

Victor Lavrenko
School of Informatics
University of Edinburgh
vlavrenk@inf.ed.ac.uk

Abstract

First story detection (FSD) involves identifying first stories about events from a continuous stream of documents. A major problem in this task is the high degree of lexical variation in documents which makes it very difficult to detect stories that talk about the same event but expressed using different words. We suggest using paraphrases to alleviate this problem, making this the first work to use paraphrases for FSD. We show a novel way of integrating paraphrases with locality sensitive hashing (LSH) in order to obtain an efficient FSD system that can scale to very large datasets. Our system achieves state-of-the-art results on the first story detection task, beating both the best supervised and unsupervised systems. To test our approach on large data, we construct a corpus of events for Twitter, consisting of 50 million documents, and show that paraphrasing is also beneficial in this domain.

1 Introduction

First story detection (FSD), sometimes also called new event detection (NED), is the task of detecting the first story about a new event from a stream of documents. It began as one of the tasks in Topic Detection and Tracking (TDT) (Allan, 2002) where the overall goal of the project was to improve technologies related to event-based information organization tasks. Of the five TDT tasks, first story detection is considered the most difficult one (Allan et al., 2000a). A good FSD system would be very useful for business or intelligence analysts where timely discovery of events is crucial. With the significant increase in the amount of information being produced and consumed every day, a crucial requirement for a modern FSD system to be useful is efficiency. This means that the system should be able to work in a streaming setting where documents are constantly coming in at a high rate, while still producing good results. While previous work has addressed the efficiency (Petrović et al., 2010) aspect, there has been little work on improving FSD performance in the past few years. A major obstacle is the high degree of lexical variation in documents that cover the same event. Here we address this problem, while keeping in mind the efficiency constraints.

The problem of lexical variation plagues many IR and NLP tasks, and one way it has been addressed in the past is through the use of paraphrases. Paraphrases are alternative ways of expressing the same meaning in the same language. For example, the phrase *he got married* can be paraphrased as *he tied the knot*. Paraphrases were already shown to help in a number of tasks: for machine translation to translate unknown phrases by translating their paraphrases (Callison-Burch et al., 2006), for query expansion in information retrieval (Spärck Jones and Tait, 1984; Jones et al., 2006), or for improving question answering (Riezler et al., 2007). A much more detailed discussion on the use of paraphrases and ways to extract them is given in (Madnani and Dorr, 2010). Here, we present the first work to use paraphrases for improving first story detection. Using paraphrases, we are able to detect that some documents previously thought to be about new events are actually paraphrases of the documents already seen. Our approach is simple and we show a novel way of integrating paraphrases with locality sensitive hashing (LSH) (Indyk and Motwani, 1998). This way we obtain a very efficient FSD system with all the benefits of using paraphrases, while avoiding computationally expensive topic modeling approaches such as Ahmed et al. (2011).

First story detection was introduced as a task before the popularization of social media. Event detection in social media, especially Twitter is a very good fit: we cover a much larger set of events than would be possible by using newswire, and the stories are reported in real time, often much sooner than in news. Of course, social media carries additional problems not found in traditional media: we have to deal with huge amounts of data, the data is very noisy (both due to spam and due to spelling and grammar errors), and in the case of Twitter, documents are extremely short. There has been little effort in solving these problems for FSD. Arguably the main reason for this is the lack of a TDT-style corpus for Twitter that researchers could use to test their approaches. Here we build such a corpus and use it to measure the performance of TDT systems on Twitter.

Our main contributions are: i) we create a first corpus of events on Twitter, ii) we show how to use paraphrases in FSD, and how to combine it with LSH to handle high-volume streams, iii) our unsupervised system that uses paraphrases achieves the highest reported results on the TDT5 corpus, beating both the supervised and unsupervised state of the art, while still keeping a constant per-document time complexity, and iv) we show that paraphrases also help in Twitter, although less than in TDT.

2 Paraphrasing and FSD

2.1 Current approaches to efficient FSD

State-of-the-art FSD systems (Allan et al., 2000b) use a fairly simple approach. Documents are represented as TF-IDF weighted vectors, their distance is measured in terms of the cosine distance, and they use a k-nearest neighbors clustering algorithm, with k usually set to 1. The novelty score for a document is the cosine distance to the nearest neighbor:

$$score(d) = 1 - \max_{d' \in D_t} \cos(d, d'). \tag{1}$$

D_t is the set of all documents up to time t when document d arrived.

Because the $\max$ in equation (1) takes $O(|D_t|)$ time to compute in the worst case, Petrović et al. (2010) introduced a way of using locality sensitive hashing (LSH) to make this time $O(1)$, while retaining the same accuracy level. In particular, instead of computing the $\max$ over the entire set D_t, like in (1), they compute it over a smaller set S of potential nearest neighbors. The set S is the set of documents that collide with the current document under a certain type of hash function:

$$S(\mathbf{x}) = \{\mathbf{y} : h_{ij}(\mathbf{y}) = h_{ij}(\mathbf{x}), \exists i \in [1..L], \forall j \in [1..k]\}, \tag{2}$$

where the hash functions h_{ij} are defined as:

$$h_{ij}(\mathbf{x}) = \mathrm{sgn}(\mathbf{u}_{ij}^T \mathbf{x}), \tag{3}$$

with the random vectors $\mathbf{u}_{ij}$ being drawn independently for each i and j. The efficiency of this algorithm stems from the fact that it can be shown that the set S of potential nearest neighbors can be made constant in size, while still containing the nearest neighbor with high probability.

2.2 Paraphrases

There are several levels of paraphrasing – lexical paraphrases, where the relationship is restricted to individual lexical items, phrasal paraphrases, where longer phrases are considered, and sentential paraphrases, where entire sentences are in a paraphrastic relationship. Here we use the simplest form, lexical paraphrases, but our approach, described in section 2.3, is general and it would be trivial to use phrasal paraphrases in the same way – we leave this for future work.

We use three sources of paraphrases: Wordnet (Fellbaum, 1998), a carefully curated lexical database of English containing synonym sets, Microsoft Research paraphrase tables (Quirk et al., 2004), a set of paraphrase pairs automatically extracted from news texts, and syntactically-constrained paraphrases from Callison-Burch (2008) which are extracted from parallel text. We also considered using paraphrases from Cohn et al. (2008), but using them provided only minor improvement over the baseline model. This is likely due to the small size of that corpus (a total of 7 thousand pairs). We do not show results for this paraphrase corpus in our results section.

Wordnet paraphrases contained 150 thousand word pairs extracted from Wordnet's synsets, where all the pairs of words within one synset were considered to be paraphrases. MSR paraphrases were extracted from the phrase tables provided by MSR. Two words were considered paraphrases if they were aligned at least once in the most probable alignment, with the probability of both backward and forward alignment of at least 0.2. In our initial experiments we varied this threshold and found it has little effect on results. Using this method, we extracted 50 thousand paraphrase pairs. Finally, we use the method of Callison-Burch (2008) to extract syntactically constrained paraphrases from a parallel corpus. This method requires that phrases and their paraphrases be the same syntactic type, and has been shown to substantially improve the quality of extracted paraphrases (Callison-Burch, 2008). We extracted paraphrases for all the words that appeared in the MSR paraphrase corpus, and then kept all the pairs that had the paraphrase probability of at least 0.2. This way, we extracted 48 thousand pairs. All three resources we use are very different: they come from different domains (news text, legal text, general English), and they have very little overlap (less than 5% of pairs are shared by any two resources).

2.3 Efficient paraphrasing in FSD

In this section, we explain how to use paraphrases in a first story detection system. We account for paraphrases by changing how we compute the cosine in equation (1). Because the cosine measure depends on the underlying inner product, we change the way the inner product is computed. We model paraphrasing by using a binary word-to-word matrix of paraphrases $\mathbf{Q}$. An entry of 1 at row i and column j in the matrix indicates that words i and j are paraphrases of each other.[1] Note, however, that our approach is not limited to using single words – if the document representation includes n-grams with $n > 1$, the matrix $\mathbf{Q}$ can contain phrases, and thus we can capture non-compositional paraphrases like *he died* $\leftrightarrow$ *he kicked the bucket*. We use the matrix $\mathbf{Q}$ to define a new inner product space:[2]

$$\langle \mathbf{x}, \mathbf{y} \rangle_Q = \mathbf{y}^T \mathbf{Q} \mathbf{x}. \tag{4}$$

This way of using paraphrases basically achieves expansion of the terms in documents with their paraphrases. Thus, if two documents have no terms in common, but one has the term *explosion* and the other has the term *blast*, by knowing that the two terms are paraphrases, their similarity will be different from zero, which would have been the case if no paraphrasing was used. Alternatively, the new inner product in equation (4) can also be seen as introducing a linear kernel.

One problem with using $\mathbf{Q}$ as defined in (4) is that it is not very suitable for use in an online setting. In particular, if documents come in one at a time and we have to store each one, only for it to be retrieved at some later point, simply storing them and computing the inner product as in (4) would lead to frequent matrix-vector multiplications. Even though $\mathbf{Q}$ is sparse, these multiplications become expensive when done often, as is the case in first story detection. We thus have to store a modified document vector $\mathbf{x}$, call it $\mathbf{x}'$, such that when we compute $\langle \mathbf{x}', \mathbf{y}' \rangle$ we get $\langle \mathbf{x}, \mathbf{y} \rangle_Q$. Note that the inner product between $\mathbf{x}'$ and $\mathbf{y}'$ is computed in the original inner product space. It is clear that by using:

$$\mathbf{x}' = \mathbf{Q}^{1/2} \mathbf{x} \tag{5}$$

we have achieved our goal: $\langle \mathbf{x}', \mathbf{y}' \rangle = \mathbf{y}'^T \mathbf{x}' = (\mathbf{Q}^{1/2}\mathbf{y})^T (\mathbf{Q}^{1/2}\mathbf{x}) = (\mathbf{y}^T \mathbf{Q}^{1/2^T})(\mathbf{Q}^{1/2}\mathbf{x}) = \mathbf{y}^T \mathbf{Q} \mathbf{x} = \langle \mathbf{x}, \mathbf{y} \rangle_Q$. Again, if we view equation (4) as defining a kernel, we can think of equation (5) as performing an explicit mapping into the feature space defined by the kernel. Because ours is a linear kernel, performing this mapping is fairly efficient.

Unfortunately, the square root of the paraphrasing matrix $\mathbf{Q}$ is in general dense (and can even contain complex entries), which would make our approach infeasible in practice because we would have to expand every document with all (or a very large number of) the words in the vocabulary. Thus, we have to

[1] This is of course a simplification – in general, one might like the entries in the matrix to be real numbers corresponding to the probability that the two words are paraphrases. We leave this for future work.

[2] Equation (4) does not define a proper inner product in the strict technical sense because the positive definiteness property does not hold. However, because vectors $\mathbf{x}$ and $\mathbf{y}$ in practice always have positive entries, equation (4) behaves like a proper inner product for all practical purposes.

approximate $\mathbf{Q}^{1/2}$ with a sparse matrix, preferably one that is as sparse as the original $\mathbf{Q}$ matrix. To this end, we introduce the following approximation:

$$\tilde{\mathbf{Q}}_{ij}^{1/2} = \frac{\mathbf{Q}_{ij}}{\sqrt{\sum_k (\mathbf{Q}_{ik} + \mathbf{Q}_{kj})/2}} \tag{6}$$

To see how we arrive at this approximation, consider the paraphrase matrix $\mathbf{Q}$. If there was no polysemy in the language, $\mathbf{Q}$ would be a block matrix, where each non-zero submatrix would correspond to a single meaning. The square root of such a matrix would be given exactly by (6). While this approximation is somewhat simplistic, it has two major advantages over the exact $\mathbf{Q}^{1/2}$: i) it is very easy to compute and, with proper implementation, takes $O(n^2)$ time, as opposed to $O(n^3)$ for $\mathbf{Q}^{1/2}$, making it scalable to very large matrices, and ii) matrix $\tilde{\mathbf{Q}}^{1/2}$ is guaranteed to be as sparse as $\mathbf{Q}$, whereas $\mathbf{Q}^{1/2}$ will in most cases become dense, which would make it unusable in real applications.

2.4 Locality-sensitive hashing with paraphrasing

Here we explain how to integrate paraphrasing with efficient FSD, using LSH described in section 2.1. As we mentioned before, a single hash function h_{ij} in the original LSH scheme hashes the vector $\mathbf{x}$ to:

$$h(\mathbf{x}) = \text{sgn}(\mathbf{u}^T\mathbf{x}), \tag{7}$$

where $\mathbf{u}$ is a (dense) random vector. If we want to use paraphrases with LSH, we simply change the hash function to

$$h_1(\mathbf{x}) = \text{sgn}(\mathbf{u}^T(\tilde{\mathbf{Q}}^{1/2}\mathbf{x})). \tag{8}$$

It is not difficult to show that by doing this, the LSH bounds for probability of collision hold in the new inner product space defined by the matrix $\mathbf{Q}$. We omit this proof due to space constraints.

Space efficient LSH. While LSH can significantly reduce the running time, it is fairly expensive memory-wise. This memory overhead is due to the random vectors $\mathbf{u}$ being very large. To solve this problem, (Van Durme and Lall, 2010) used a *hashing trick* for space-efficient storing of these vectors. They showed that it is possible to project the vectors onto a much smaller random subspace, while still retaining good properties of LSH. They proposed the following hash function for a vector $\mathbf{x}$:

$$h_2(\mathbf{x}) = \text{sgn}(\mathbf{u}^T(\mathbf{A}\mathbf{x})), \tag{9}$$

where $\mathbf{A}$ is a random binary matrix with exactly one non-zero element in each column. This approach guarantees a constant space use which is bounded by the number of rows in the $\mathbf{A}$ matrix. Here we show that our paraphrasing approach can be easily used together with this space-saving approach by defining the following hash function for $\mathbf{x}$:

$$h_3(\mathbf{x}) = \text{sgn}(\mathbf{u}^T(\mathbf{A}\tilde{\mathbf{Q}}^{1/2}\mathbf{x})). \tag{10}$$

This way we get the benefits of the hashing trick (the constant space use), while also being able to use paraphrases. The hash function in (10) is the actual hash function we use in our system. Together with the heuristics from Petrović et al. (2010), it guarantees that our FSD system will use constant space and will take constant time to process each document.

3 Twitter Event Corpus

3.1 Event detection on Twitter

As we mentioned before, research on event detection in social media is hampered by the lack of a corpus that could be used to measure performance. The need for a standard corpus is evident from the related work on event detection in Twitter. For example, (Petrović et al., 2010) address the scaling problem in social media and present a system that runs in constant time per document, but the evaluation of their system on Twitter data was limited to very high-volume events. The only attempt in creating a corpus of events for Twitter that we are aware of was presented in Becker et al. (2011). Unfortunately, that corpus is not suitable for FSD evaluation for two main reasons: i) the events were picked from the highest-volume events identified by the system (similar to what was done in Petrović et al. (2010)), introducing not only a bias towards high-volume events, but also a bias toward the kinds of events that their system can detect, and ii) the authors only considered tweets by users who set their location to New York, which introduces a strong bias towards the type of events that can appear in the corpus. While these problems were not relevant to the work of (Becker et al., 2011) because the corpus was only used to compare different cluster representation techniques, they would certainly pose a serious problem if we wanted to use the corpus to compare FSD systems. In this paper we present a new corpus of tweets with labeled events by taking a very similar approach to that taken by NIST when creating the TDT corpora.

3.2 Annotating the Tweets

In this section we describe the annotation process for our event corpus. Note that due to Twitter's terms of service, we distribute the corpus as a set of tweet IDs and the corresponding annotations – users will have to crawl the tweets themselves, but this can be easily done using any one of the freely available crawlers for Twitter. This is the same method that the TREC microblog track[3] used to distribute their data. All our Twitter data was collected from the streaming API[4] and consists of tweets from beginning of July 2011 until mid-September 2011. After removing non-English tweets, our corpus consists of 50 million tweets.

In our annotation process, we have adopted the approach used by the National Institute of Standards and Technology (NIST) in labeling the data for TDT competitions. First, we defined a set of events that we want to find in the data, thus avoiding the bias of using events that are the output of any particular system. We choose the events from the set of important events for our time period according to Wikipedia.[5] Additionally, we used common knowledge of important events at that time to define more events. In total, we define 27 events, with an average of 112 on-topic tweets. This is comparable to the first TDT corpus which contained 25 events and average of 45 on-topic documents. However, in terms of the total number of documents, our corpus is three orders of magnitude larger than the first TDT corpus, and two orders of magnitude larger than the biggest TDT corpus (TDT5). Our corpus contains very different events, such as the death of Amy Winehouse, downgrading of US credit rating, increasing of US debt ceiling, earthquake in Virginia, London riots, terrorist attacks in Norway, Google announcing plans to buy Motorola Mobility, etc. The event with the most on-topic tweets had over 1,000 tweets (death of Amy Winehouse), and the smallest event had only 2 on-topic tweets (arrest of Goran Hadzic).

We faced the same problems as NIST when labeling the events – there were far too many stories to actually read each one and decide which (if any) events it corresponds to. In order to narrow down the set of candidates for each event, we use the same procedure as used by NIST. The annotator would first read a description of the event, and from that description compile a set of keywords to retrieve possibly relevant tweets. He would then read through this set, labeling each tweet as on- or off-topic, and also adding new keywords for retrieving a new batch of tweets. After labeling all the tweets in one batch, the newly added keywords were used to retrieve the next batch, and this procedure was repeated until no new keywords were added. Unlike in TDT, however, when retrieving tweets matching a keyword, we do not search through the whole corpus, as this would return far too many candidates than is feasible to label. Instead, we limit the search to a time window of one day around the time the event happened.

Finally, the annotator guidelines contained some Twitter-specific instructions. Links in tweets were not taken into account (the annotator would not click on links in the tweets), but retweets were (if the retweet was cut off because of the 140 character limit, the annotator would label the original tweet). Furthermore, hashtags were taken into account, so tweets like *#Amywinehouseisdead* were labeled as normal sentences. Also, to be labeled on-topic, the tweet would have to explicitly mention the event and the annotator should be able to infer what happened from the tweet alone, without any outside knowledge. This means that tweets like *Just heard about Lokomotiv, this is a terrible summer for hockey!* are off topic, even though they refer to the plane crash in which the Lokomotiv hockey team died.

In total, our corpus contains over 50 million tweets, of which 3035 tweets were labeled as being on-topic for one of the 27 events. While searching for first tweets (i.e., tweets that first mention an event), *fake* first tweets were sometimes discovered. For example, in the case of the death of Richard Bowes (victim of London riots), a Telegraph journalist posted a tweet informing of the man's death

[3]`http://trec.nist.gov/data/tweets/`

[4]`https://stream.twitter.com/`

[5]`http://en.wikipedia.org/wiki/2011`

more than 12 hours before he actually died. This tweet was later retracted by the journalist for being incorrect, but the man then died a few hours later. Cases like this were labeled off-topic.

4 Experiments

4.1 Evaluation

In the official TDT evaluation, each FSD system is required to assign a score between 0 and 1 to every document upon its arrival. Lower scores correspond to old stories, and vice versa. Evaluation is then carried out by first sorting all stories according to their scores and then performing a threshold sweep. For each value of the threshold, stories with a score above the threshold are considered new, and all others are considered old. Therefore, for each threshold value, one can compute the probability of a *false alarm*, i.e., probability of declaring a story new when it is actually not, and the *miss probability*, i.e., probability of declaring a new story old (missing a new story). Using the false alarm and the miss rate, the cost C_{det} is defined as follows:

$$C_{det} = C_{miss} * P_{miss} * P_{target} + C_{FA} * P_{FA} * P_{non-target},$$

where C_{miss} and C_{FA} are costs of miss and false alarm (0.02 and 0.98, respectively), P_{miss} and P_{FA} are the miss and false alarm rate, and P_{target} and $P_{non-target}$ are the prior target and non-target probabilities. Different FSD systems are compared on the minimal cost C_{min}, which is the minimal value of C_{det} over all threshold values. This means that in FSD evaluation, a *lower* value of C_{min} indicates a better system.

4.2 TDT results

For the TDT experiments, we use the English portion of TDT-5 dataset, consisting of 126 topics in 278,108 documents. Similar to (Petrović et al., 2010), we compare our approach to a state-of-the-art FSD system, namely the UMass system (Allan et al., 2000b). This system always scored high in the TDT competitions and is known to perform at least as well as other systems that also took part in the competition (Fiscus, 2001). Our system is based on the streaming FSD system of (Petrović et al., 2010) which has a constant per-document time complexity. We use stemming (Porter, 1980) and, the same as (Petrović et al., 2010), we use 13 bits per key and 70 hash tables for LSH. Additionally, we use the hashing trick described in section 2.4 with a pool of size 2^{18}. Paraphrasing is implemented in this system as described in section 2.4.

While the UMass system was among the best systems that took part in the TDT competitions, there has been research in event detection since the competitions stopped. Recent work on event detection includes a hybrid clustering and topic model with rich features such as entities, time, and topics (Ahmed et al., 2011). We do not compare our system to Ahmed et al. (2011) because in terms of the numerical $C_{\min}$ score, their approach does not outperform the UMass system. This is not surprising as the primary goal in Ahmed et al. (2011) was not to improve FSD performance, but rather to create storylines and support structured browsing.

We compare our approach to the best reported result in the literature on the TDT5 data. To the best of our knowledge, the highest reported results in FSD come from a supervised system described in Kumaran and Allan (2005). This system uses an SVM classifier with the features being FSD scores from unsupervised systems (the authors used scores computed in the same way as is done in the UMass system) computed using i) full text, ii) only named entities in the document, and iii) only topic terms. The classifier was trained on TDT3 and TDT4 corpora and tested on TDT5.

Table 1 shows the results for TDT5 data. UMass 1000 is the run that was submitted as the official run in the TDT competition.[6] We can see that using paraphrases improves the results over the unsupervised state of the art, regardless of which source of paraphrasing is used. However, it is clear that not all types of paraphrases are equally helpful. In particular, the automatically extracted paraphrases from Callison-Burch (2008) seem to be the most helpful, and by using them our unsupervised system is able to beat even the best known supervised FSD system. This is a very promising result because it indicates that we can use automatically extracted paraphrases and do not have to rely on hand-crafted resources like Wordnet as our source of paraphrases.

[6]Our experiments, and experiments in Allan et al. (2000b) showed that keeping full documents does not improve results, while increasing running time.

System	C_{min}
UMass 100	0.721
UMass 1000	0.706
Best supervised system	0.661
Wordnet	0.657
MSR Paraphrases	0.642
Syntactic paraphrases	**0.575**

Table 1: TDT FSD results for different systems, lower is better. The number next to UMass system indicates the number of features kept for each document (selected according to their TFIDF). All paraphrasing systems work with full documents. Results for the best supervised system were taken from Kumaran and Allan (2005).

Paraphrasing resource	$C_{\min}$
Precision 0.1	0.603
Precision 0.2	0.672
Precision 0.3	0.565
Precision 0.4	0.603
Precision 0.5	0.626
Recall 0.9	0.609
Recall 0.8	0.606
Recall 0.7	0.632
Recall 0.6	0.610
Recall 0.5	0.626

Table 2: Effect of paraphrase precision and recall on FSD performance. Numbers next to recall and precision indicate the sampling rate and the proportion of added random pairs, respectively.

The difference between our system and the UMass system is significant at $p = 0.05$ using a paired t-test over the individual topic costs. We were not able to test significance against the supervised state-of-the-art because we did not have access to this system. In terms of efficiency, our approach is still $O(1)$, like the approach in Petrović et al. (2010), but in practice it is somewhat slower because hashing the expanded documents takes more time. We measured the running time of our system, and it is 3.5 times slower than the basic approach of Petrović et al. (2010), but also 3.5 times faster than the UMass system, while outperforming both of these systems.

How does quality of paraphrases affect results? We have shown that using automatically obtained paraphrases to expand documents is beneficial in first story detection. Because there are different ways of extracting paraphrases, some of which are targeted more towards recall, and some towards precision, we want to know which techniques would be more suitable to extract paraphrases for use in FSD. Here, precision is the ratio between extracted word pairs that are actual paraphrases and all the word pairs extracted, and recall is the ratio between extracted word pairs that are actual paraphrases, and all the possible paraphrase pairs that could have been extracted. In this experiment we focus on the syntactic paraphrases which yielded the best results. To lower recall, we randomly remove paraphrase pairs from the corpus, and to lower precision, we add random paraphrase pairs to our table. All the results are shown in Table 2. Numbers next to precision and recall indicate the proportion of added random pairs and the proportion of removed pairs, respectively (e.g., recall 0.4 means that 40% of pairs were removed from the original resource). We can see that the results are much more stable with respect to recall – there is an initial drop in performance when we remove the first 10% of paraphrases, but after that removing more paraphrases does not affect performance very much. On the other hand, changing the precision has a bigger impact on the results. For example, we can see that our system using a paraphrase corpus with 30% of pairs added at random performs even better than the system that uses the original corpus. On the other hand, adding 20% of random pairs performs substantially worse than the original corpus. These results show that it is more important for the paraphrases to have good precision than to have good recall.

4.3 Twitter results

Because the Twitter event corpus that we use consists of over 50 million documents, we cannot use the UMass system here due to its linear per-document time complexity. Instead, our baseline system here is the FSD system of (Petrović et al., 2010), without any paraphrasing. This system uses the same approach as the UMass system, and (Petrović et al., 2010) showed that it achieves very similar results. This means that our baseline, although coming from a different system, is still state-of-the-art. We make some Twitter-specific modification to the baseline system that slightly improve the results. Specifically, the baseline uses no stemming, ignores links, @-mentions, and treats hashtags as normal words (i.e., removes the leading '#' character). While removing links and @-mentions was also done in (Petrović et al., 2010), our preliminary experiments showed that keeping hashtags, only without the hash sign improves the results. Additionally, we limit the number of documents in a bucket to at most 30% of the expected number of collisions for a single day (we assume one million documents per day).

Results for the different systems are shown in Table 3. First, we can see that not using stemming is much better than using it, which is the opposite from what is the case in TDT. Second, we can see that the improvements from using paraphrases that we had in TDT data are different here. Syntactic paraphrases and the MSR paraphrases do not help, whereas the paraphrases extracted from Wordnet did improve the results, although the gains are not as large as in TDT. A paired t-test revealed that none of the differences between the baseline system and the systems that use paraphrases were significant at $p = 0.05$.

To gain more insight into why the results are different here, we look at the proportion of words in the documents that are being paraphrased, i.e., the *coverage* of the paraphrasing resource. We can see from Table 4 that the situation in TDT and Twitter is very different. Coverage of MSR and syntactic paraphrases was lower in Twitter than in TDT, whereas Wordnet coverage was better on Twitter. While it seems that the benefits of using paraphrases in Twitter are not as clear as in news, our efficient approach enables us to answer questions like these, which could not be answered otherwise.

To illustrate how paraphrases help detect old tweets, consider the tweet *According to Russian aviation officials, two passengers survived the crash, but are in critical condition.* Before paraphrasing, the closest tweet returned by our system was *Shazaad Hussein has died in Birmingham after being run over, two others are in critical condition*, which is not very related. After applying paraphrasing, in particular knowing that *officials* is a paraphrase of *authorities*, the closest tweet returned was *Some Russian authorities are reporting one survivor, others are saying there are three. There were 37 total on board*, which is on the same event. There are also cases where paraphrases hurt. For example, before paraphrasing the tweet *Top News #debt #deal #ceiling #party* had the nearest neighbor *New debt ceiling deal explained*, whereas after paraphrasing, because the word *roof* is a paraphrase of *ceiling*, the nearest neighbor was *The roof the roof the roof is on fire!*. Cases like this could be fixed by looking at the context of the word, but we leave this for future work.

System	C_{min}
Baseline system (stemming)	0.756
Baseline system (no stemming)	0.694
Wordnet	**0.679**
MSR Paraphrases	0.739
Syntactic paraphrases	0.729

Table 3: Twitter FSD results for different systems, lower is better. The baseline system is that of (Petrović et al., 2010).

Paraphrases	Coverage TDT (%)	Coverage Twitter (%)
Wordnet	52.5	56.1
MSR	33.5	31.0
Syntactic	35.6	31.7

Table 4: Coverage of different resources.

5 Conclusion

We present a way of incorporating paraphrase information in a streaming first story detection system. To the best of our knowledge, this is the first work to use paraphrases in first story detection, and also the first work to combine paraphrases with locality-sensitive hashing to achieve fast retrieval of documents that are written with different words, but talk about the same thing. We compare different sources of paraphrases and show that our unsupervised FSD system that uses syntactically constrained paraphrases achieves state-of-the-art results, beating both the best supervised and unsupervised systems. To test our approach on very large data, we construct a corpus of events for Twitter. Our approach scales well on this data both in terms of time and memory, and we show that paraphrases again help, but this time the paraphrase sources yield different improvements from TDT data. We find that this difference can be explained by the different coverage of the paraphrasing resources.

Acknowledgments

The authors would like to thank Mirella Lapata for her help with paraphrasing resources. We also acknowledge financial support from EPSRC grant EP/J020664/1.

References

Amr Ahmed, Qirong Ho, Jacob Eisenstein, Eric Xing, Alex Smola, and Choon Hui Teo. 2011. Unified analysis of streaming news. In *Proceedings of WWW*, pages 267–276. ACM.

James Allan, Victor Lavrenko, and Hubert Jin. 2000a. First story detection in tdt is hard. In *Proceedings of the CIKM*, pages 374–381. ACM.

James Allan, Victor Lavrenko, Daniella Malin, and Russell Swan. 2000b. Detections, bounds, and timelines: Umass and tdt-3. In *Proceedings of Topic Detection and Tracking Workshop*, pages 167–174.

James Allan. 2002. *Topic detection and tracking: event-based information organization*. Kluwer Academic Publishers.

Hila Becker, Mor Naaman, and Luis Gravano. 2011. Selecting quality twitter content for events. In *Proceedings of ICWSM*.

Chris Callison-Burch, Philipp Koehn, and Miles Osborne. 2006. Improved statistical machine translation using paraphrases. In *Proceedings of NAACL*, pages 17–24. Association for Computational Linguistics.

Chris Callison-Burch. 2008. Syntactic constraints on paraphrases extracted from parallel corpora. In *Proceedings of the Conference on Empirical Methods in Natural Language Processing*, pages 196–205. Association for Computational Linguistics.

Trevor Cohn, Chris Callison-Burch, and Mirella Lapata. 2008. Constructing corpora for the development and evaluation of paraphrase systems. *Computational Linguistics*, 34(4):597–614.

Christiane Fellbaum. 1998. *WordNet: An electronic lexical database*. The MIT press.

Jonathan Fiscus. 2001. Overview of results (nist). In *Proceedings of the TDT 2001 Workshop*.

Piotr Indyk and Rajeev Motwani. 1998. Approximate nearest neighbors: towards removing the curse of dimensionality. In *STOC '98: Proceedings of the thirtieth annual ACM symposium on Theory of computing*, pages 604–613, New York, NY, USA. ACM.

Rosie Jones, Benjamin Rey, Omid Madani, and Wiley Greiner. 2006. Generating query substitutions. In *Proceedings of the 15th international conference on World Wide Web*, pages 387–396. ACM.

Giridhar Kumaran and James Allan. 2005. Using names and topics for new event detection. In *Proceedings of EMNLP*, pages 121–128. Association for Computational Linguistics.

Nitin Madnani and Bonnie Dorr. 2010. Generating phrasal and sentential paraphrases: A survey of data-driven methods. *Computational Linguistics*, 36(3):341–387.

Saša Petrović, Miles Osborne, and Victor Lavrenko. 2010. Streaming first story detection with application to twitter. In *Proceedings of the 11th annual conference of the North American Chapter of the ACL*, pages 181–189.

Martin F. Porter. 1980. An algorithm for suffix stripping. *Program*, 14(3):130–137.

Chris Quirk, Chris Brockett, and William Dolan. 2004. Monolingual machine translation for paraphrase generation. In *In proceedings of EMNLP*, pages 142–149.

Stefan Riezler, Alexander Vasserman, Ioannis Tsochantaridis, Vibhu Mittal, and Yi Liu. 2007. Statistical machine translation for query expansion in answer retrieval. In *Proceedings of ACL*, volume 45, page 464.

Karen Spärck Jones and John Tait. 1984. Automatic search term variant generation. *Journal of Documentation*, 40(1):50–66.

Benjamin Van Durme and Ashwin Lall. 2010. Online generation of locality sensitive hash signatures. In *Proceedings of the 48th Annual Meeting of the Association for Computational Linguistics*.

Jinxi Xu and W. Bruce Croft. 1996. Query expansion using local and global document analysis. In *In Proceedings of the 19th Annual International ACM SIGIR Conference on Research and Development in Information Retrieval*, pages 4–11.

Insertion and Deletion Models for Statistical Machine Translation

Matthias Huck and **Hermann Ney**
Human Language Technology and Pattern Recognition Group
Computer Science Department
RWTH Aachen University
D-52056 Aachen, Germany
{huck,ney}@cs.rwth-aachen.de

Abstract

We investigate insertion and deletion models for hierarchical phrase-based statistical machine translation. Insertion and deletion models are designed as a means to avoid the omission of content words in the hypotheses. In our case, they are implemented as phrase-level feature functions which count the number of inserted or deleted words. An English word is considered inserted or deleted based on lexical probabilities with the words on the foreign language side of the phrase. Related techniques have been employed before by Och et al. (2003) in an n-best reranking framework and by Mauser et al. (2006) and Zens (2008) in a standard phrase-based translation system. We propose novel thresholding methods in this work and study insertion and deletion features which are based on two different types of lexicon models. We give an extensive experimental evaluation of all these variants on the NIST Chinese→English translation task.

1 Insertion and Deletion Models

In hierarchical phrase-based translation (Chiang, 2005), we deal with rules $X \rightarrow \langle \alpha, \beta, \sim \rangle$ where $\langle \alpha, \beta \rangle$ is a bilingual phrase pair that may contain symbols from a non-terminal set, i.e. $\alpha \in (\mathcal{N} \cup V_F)^+$ and $\beta \in (\mathcal{N} \cup V_E)^+$, where V_F and V_E are the source and target vocabulary, respectively, and $\mathcal{N}$ is a non-terminal set which is shared by source and target. The left-hand side of the rule is a non-terminal symbol $X \in \mathcal{N}$, and the $\sim$ relation denotes a one-to-one correspondence between the non-terminals in α and in β. Let J_α denote the number of terminal symbols in α and I_β the number of terminal symbols in β. Indexing α with j, i.e. the symbol α_j, $1 \leq j \leq J_\alpha$, denotes the j-th terminal symbol on the source side of the phrase pair $\langle \alpha, \beta \rangle$, and analogous with β_i, $1 \leq i \leq I_\beta$, on the target side.

With these notational conventions, we now define our insertion and deletion models, each in both source-to-target and target-to-source direction. We give phrase-level scoring functions for the four features. In our implementation, the feature values are precomputed and written to the phrase table. The features are then incorporated directly into the log-linear model combination of the decoder.

Our insertion model in source-to-target direction $t_{\text{s2tIns}}(\cdot)$ counts the number of inserted words on the target side β of a hierarchical rule with respect to the source side α of the rule:

$$t_{\text{s2tIns}}(\alpha, \beta) = \sum_{i=1}^{I_\beta} \prod_{j=1}^{J_\alpha} \left[p(\beta_i | \alpha_j) < \tau_{\alpha_j} \right] \quad (1)$$

Here, $[\cdot]$ denotes a true or false statement: The result is 1 if the condition is true and 0 if the condition is false. The model considers an occurrence of a target word e an insertion iff no source word f exists within the phrase where the lexical translation probability $p(e|f)$ is greater than a corresponding threshold τ_f. We employ lexical translation probabilities from two different types of lexicon models, a model which is extracted from word-aligned training data and—given the word alignment matrix—relies on pure relative frequencies, and the IBM model 1 lexicon (cf. Section 2). For τ_f, previous authors have used a fixed heuristic value which was equal for all

$f \in V_f$. In Section 3, we describe how such a global threshold can be computed and set in a reasonable way based on the characteristics of the model. We also propose several novel thresholding techniques with distinct thresholds τ_f for each source word f.

In an analogous manner to the source-to-target direction, the insertion model in target-to-source direction $t_{\text{t2sIns}}(\cdot)$ counts the number of inserted words on the source side α of a hierarchical rule with respect to the target side β of the rule:

$$t_{\text{t2sIns}}(\alpha, \beta) = \sum_{j=1}^{J_\alpha} \prod_{i=1}^{I_\beta} [p(\alpha_j|\beta_i) < \tau_{\beta_i}] \quad (2)$$

Target-to-source lexical translation probabilities $p(f|e)$ are thresholded with values τ_e which may be distinct for each target word e. The model considers an occurrence of a source word f an insertion iff no target word e exists within the phrase with $p(f|e)$ greater than or equal to τ_e.

Our deletion model, compared to the insertion model, interchanges the connection of the direction of the lexical probabilities and the order of source and target in the sum and product of the term. The source-to-target deletion model thus differs from the target-to-source insertion model in that it employs a source-to-target word-based lexicon model.

The deletion model in source-to-target direction $t_{\text{s2tDel}}(\cdot)$ counts the number of deleted words on the source side α of a hierarchical rule with respect to the target side β of the rule:

$$t_{\text{s2tDel}}(\alpha, \beta) = \sum_{j=1}^{J_\alpha} \prod_{i=1}^{I_\beta} [p(\beta_i|\alpha_j) < \tau_{\alpha_j}] \quad (3)$$

It considers an occurrence of a source word f a deletion iff no target word e exists within the phrase with $p(e|f)$ greater than or equal to τ_f.

The target-to-source deletion model $t_{\text{t2sDel}}(\cdot)$ correspondingly considers an occurrence of a target word e a deletion iff no source word f exists within the phrase with $p(f|e)$ greater than or equal to τ_e:

$$t_{\text{t2sDel}}(\alpha, \beta) = \sum_{i=1}^{I_\beta} \prod_{j=1}^{J_\alpha} [p(\alpha_j|\beta_i) < \tau_{\beta_i}] \quad (4)$$

2 Lexicon Models

We restrict ourselves to the description of the source-to-target direction of the models.

2.1 Word Lexicon from Word-Aligned Data

Given a word-aligned parallel training corpus, we are able to estimate single-word based translation probabilities $p_{\text{RF}}(e|f)$ by relative frequency (Koehn et al., 2003). With $N(e, f)$ denoting counts of aligned cooccurrences of target word e and source word f, we can compute

$$p_{\text{RF}}(e|f) = \frac{N(e, f)}{\sum_{e'} N(e', f)} . \quad (5)$$

If an occurrence of e has multiple aligned source words, each of the alignment links contributes with a fractional count.

We denote this model as relative frequency (RF) word lexicon.

2.2 IBM Model 1

The IBM model 1 lexicon (IBM-1) is the first and most basic one in a sequence of probabilistic generative models (Brown et al., 1993). For IBM-1, several simplifying assumptions are made, so that the probability of a target sentence e_1^I given a source sentence f_0^J (with f_0 = NULL) can be modeled as

$$Pr(e_1^I|f_1^J) = \frac{1}{(J+1)^I} \prod_{i=1}^{I} \sum_{j=0}^{J} p_{\text{ibm1}}(e_i|f_j) . \quad (6)$$

The parameters of IBM-1 are estimated iteratively by means of the Expectation-Maximization algorithm with maximum likelihood as training criterion.

3 Thresholding Methods

We introduce thresholding methods for insertion and deletion models which set thresholds based on the characteristics of the lexicon model that is applied. For all the following thresholding methods, we disregard entries in the lexicon model with probabilities that are below a fixed floor value of 10^{-6}. Again, we restrict ourselves to the description of the source-to-target direction.

individual τ_f is a distinct value for each f, computed as the arithmetic average of all entries $p(e|f)$ of any e with the given f in the lexicon model.

NIST Chinese→English	MT06 (Dev) BLEU [%]	MT06 (Dev) TER [%]	MT08 (Test) BLEU [%]	MT08 (Test) TER [%]
Baseline (with s2t+t2s RF word lexicons)	32.6	61.2	25.2	66.6
+ s2t+t2s insertion model (RF, individual)	32.9	61.4	25.7	66.2
+ s2t+t2s insertion model (RF, global)	32.8	61.8	25.7	66.7
+ s2t+t2s insertion model (RF, histogram 10)	32.9	61.7	25.5	66.5
+ s2t+t2s insertion model (RF, all)	32.8	62.0	**26.1**	66.7
+ s2t+t2s insertion model (RF, median)	32.9	62.1	25.7	67.1
+ s2t+t2s deletion model (RF, individual)	32.7	61.4	25.6	66.5
+ s2t+t2s deletion model (RF, global)	33.0	61.3	25.8	66.1
+ s2t+t2s deletion model (RF, histogram 10)	32.9	61.4	**26.0**	66.1
+ s2t+t2s deletion model (RF, all)	33.0	61.4	25.9	66.4
+ s2t+t2s deletion model (RF, median)	32.9	61.5	25.8	66.7
+ s2t+t2s insertion model (IBM-1, individual)	33.0	61.4	**26.1**	66.4
+ s2t+t2s insertion model (IBM-1, global)	33.0	61.6	25.9	66.5
+ s2t+t2s insertion model (IBM-1, histogram 10)	**33.7**	61.3	**26.2**	66.5
+ s2t+t2s insertion model (IBM-1, median)	33.0	61.3	**26.0**	66.4
+ s2t+t2s deletion model (IBM-1, individual)	32.8	61.5	**26.0**	66.2
+ s2t+t2s deletion model (IBM-1, global)	32.9	61.3	25.9	66.1
+ s2t+t2s deletion model (IBM-1, histogram 10)	32.8	61.2	25.7	66.0
+ s2t+t2s deletion model (IBM-1, median)	32.8	61.6	25.6	66.7
+ s2t insertion + s2t deletion model (IBM-1, individual)	32.7	62.3	25.7	67.1
+ s2t insertion + t2s deletion model (IBM-1, individual)	32.7	62.2	25.9	66.8
+ t2s insertion + s2t deletion model (IBM-1, individual)	33.1	61.3	25.9	66.2
+ t2s insertion + t2s deletion model (IBM-1, individual)	33.0	61.3	**26.1**	66.0
+ source+target unaligned word count	32.3	61.8	25.6	66.7
+ phrase-level s2t+t2s IBM-1 word lexicons	**33.8**	**60.5**	**26.9**	**65.4**
+ source+target unaligned word count	**34.0**	**60.4**	**26.7**	**65.8**
+ s2t+t2s insertion model (IBM-1, histogram 10)	**34.0**	**60.3**	**26.8**	**65.2**
+ phrase-level s2t+t2s DWL + triplets + discrim. RO	**34.8**	**59.8**	**27.7**	**64.7**
+ s2t+t2s insertion model (RF, individual)	**35.0**	**59.5**	**27.8**	**64.4**

Table 1: Experimental results for the NIST Chinese→English translation task (truecase). *s2t* denotes source-to-target scoring, *t2s* target-to-source scoring. Bold font indicates results that are significantly better than the baseline ($p < .1$).

global The same value $\tau_f = \tau$ is used for all f. We compute this global threshold by averaging over the individual thresholds.[1]

histogram n τ_f is a distinct value for each f. τ_f is set to the value of the $n+1$-th largest probability $p(e|f)$ of any e with the given f.

all All entries with probabilities larger than the floor value are not thresholded. This variant may be considered as *histogram* ∞. We only apply it with RF lexicons.

median τ_f is a median-based distinct value for each f, i.e. it is set to the value that separates the higher half of the entries from the lower half of the entries $p(e|f)$ for the given f.

4 Experimental Evaluation

We present empirical results obtained with the different insertion and deletion model variants on the

[1] Concrete values from our experiments are: 0.395847 for the source-to-target RF lexicon, 0.48127 for the target-to-source RF lexicon. 0.0512856 for the source-to-target IBM-1, and 0.0453709 for the target-to-source IBM-1. Mauser et al. (2006) mention that they chose their heuristic thresholds for use with IBM-1 between 10^{-1} and 10^{-4}.

Chinese→English 2008 NIST task.[2]

4.1 Experimental Setup

To set up our systems, we employ the open source statistical machine translation toolkit Jane (Vilar et al., 2010; Vilar et al., 2012), which is freely available for non-commercial use. Jane provides efficient C++ implementations for hierarchical phrase extraction, optimization of log-linear feature weights, and parsing-based decoding algorithms. In our experiments, we use the cube pruning algorithm (Huang and Chiang, 2007) to carry out the search.

We work with a parallel training corpus of 3.0M Chinese-English sentence pairs (77.5M Chinese / 81.0M English running words). The counts for the RF lexicon models are computed from a symmetrized word alignment (Och and Ney, 2003), the IBM-1 models are produced with GIZA++. When extracting phrases, we apply several restrictions, in particular a maximum length of 10 on source and target side for lexical phrases, a length limit of five (including non-terminal symbols) for hierarchical phrases, and no more than two gaps per phrase. The models integrated into the baseline are: phrase translation probabilities and RF lexical translation probabilities on phrase level, each for both translation directions, length penalties on word and phrase level, binary features marking hierarchical phrases, glue rule, and rules with non-terminals at the boundaries, source-to-target and target-to-source phrase length ratios, four binary features marking phrases that have been seen more than one, two, three or five times, respectively, and an n-gram language model. The language model is a 4-gram with modified Kneser-Ney smoothing which was trained with the SRILM toolkit (Stolcke, 2002) on a large collection of English data including the target side of the parallel corpus and the LDC Gigaword v3.

Model weights are optimized against BLEU (Papineni et al., 2002) with standard Minimum Error Rate Training (Och, 2003), performance is measured with BLEU and TER (Snover et al., 2006). We employ MT06 as development set, MT08 is used as unseen test set. The empirical evaluation of all our setups is presented in Table 1.

[2] `http://www.itl.nist.gov/iad/mig/tests/mt/2008/`

4.2 Experimental Results

With the best model variant, we obtain a significant improvement (90% confidence) of +1.0 points BLEU over the baseline on MT08. A consistent trend towards one of the variants cannot be observed. The results on the test set with RF lexicons or IBM-1, insertion or deletion models, and (in most of the cases) with all of the thresholding methods are roughly at the same level. For comparison we also give a result with an unaligned word count model (+0.4 BLEU).

Huck et al. (2011) recently reported substantial improvements over typical hierarchical baseline setups by just including phrase-level IBM-1 scores. When we add the IBM-1 models directly, our baseline is outperformed by +1.7 BLEU. We tried to get improvements with insertion and deletion models over this setup again, but the positive effect was largely diminished. In one of our strongest setups, which includes discriminative word lexicon models (DWL), triplet lexicon models and a discriminative reordering model (discrim. RO) (Huck et al., 2012), insertion models still yield a minimal gain, though.

5 Conclusion

Our results with insertion and deletion models for Chinese→English hierarchical machine translation are twofold. On the one hand, we achieved significant improvements over a standard hierarchical baseline. We were also able to report a slight gain by adding the models to a very strong setup with discriminative word lexicons, triplet lexicon models and a discriminative reordering model. On the other hand, the positive impact of the models was mainly noticeable when we exclusively applied lexical smoothing with word lexicons which are simply extracted from word-aligned training data, which is however the standard technique in most state-of-the-art systems. If we included phrase-level lexical scores with IBM model 1 as well, the systems barely benefited from our insertion and deletion models. Compared to an unaligned word count model, insertion and deletion models perform well.

Acknowledgments

This work was achieved as part of the Quaero Programme, funded by OSEO, French State agency for innovation.

References

Peter F. Brown, Stephen A. Della Pietra, Vincent J. Della Pietra, and Robert L. Mercer. 1993. The Mathematics of Statistical Machine Translation: Parameter Estimation. *Computational Linguistics*, 19(2):263–311, June.

David Chiang. 2005. A Hierarchical Phrase-Based Model for Statistical Machine Translation. In *Proc. of the 43rd Annual Meeting of the Assoc. for Computational Linguistics (ACL)*, pages 263–270, Ann Arbor, MI, USA, June.

Liang Huang and David Chiang. 2007. Forest Rescoring: Faster Decoding with Integrated Language Models. In *Proc. of the Annual Meeting of the Assoc. for Computational Linguistics (ACL)*, pages 144–151, Prague, Czech Republic, June.

Matthias Huck, Saab Mansour, Simon Wiesler, and Hermann Ney. 2011. Lexicon Models for Hierarchical Phrase-Based Machine Translation. In *Proc. of the Int. Workshop on Spoken Language Translation (IWSLT)*, pages 191–198, San Francisco, CA, USA, December.

Matthias Huck, Stephan Peitz, Markus Freitag, and Hermann Ney. 2012. Discriminative Reordering Extensions for Hierarchical Phrase-Based Machine Translation. In *Proc. of the 16th Annual Conference of the European Association for Machine Translation (EAMT)*, Trento, Italy, May.

Philipp Koehn, Franz Joseph Och, and Daniel Marcu. 2003. Statistical Phrase-Based Translation. In *Proc. of the Human Language Technology Conf. / North American Chapter of the Assoc. for Computational Linguistics (HLT-NAACL)*, pages 127–133, Edmonton, Canada, May/June.

Arne Mauser, Richard Zens, Evgeny Matusov, Saša Hasan, and Hermann Ney. 2006. The RWTH Statistical Machine Translation System for the IWSLT 2006 Evaluation. In *Proc. of the Int. Workshop on Spoken Language Translation (IWSLT)*, pages 103–110, Kyoto, Japan, November.

Franz Josef Och and Hermann Ney. 2003. A Systematic Comparison of Various Statistical Alignment Models. *Computational Linguistics*, 29(1):19–51, March.

Franz Josef Och, Daniel Gildea, Sanjeev Khudanpur, Anoop Sarkar, Kenji Yamada, Alex Fraser, Shankar Kumar, Libin Shen, David Smith, Katherine Eng, Viren Jain, Zhen Jin, and Dragomir Radev. 2003. Syntax for Statistical Machine Translation. Technical report, Johns Hopkins University 2003 Summer Workshop on Language Engineering, Center for Language and Speech Processing, Baltimore, MD, USA, August.

Franz Josef Och. 2003. Minimum Error Rate Training for Statistical Machine Translation. In *Proc. of the Annual Meeting of the Assoc. for Computational Linguistics (ACL)*, pages 160–167, Sapporo, Japan, July.

Kishore Papineni, Salim Roukos, Todd Ward, and Wei-Jing Zhu. 2002. Bleu: a Method for Automatic Evaluation of Machine Translation. In *Proc. of the 40th Annual Meeting of the Assoc. for Computational Linguistics (ACL)*, pages 311–318, Philadelphia, PA, USA, July.

Matthew Snover, Bonnie Dorr, Richard Schwartz, Linnea Micciulla, and John Makhoul. 2006. A Study of Translation Edit Rate with Targeted Human Annotation. In *Conf. of the Assoc. for Machine Translation in the Americas (AMTA)*, pages 223–231, Cambridge, MA, USA, August.

Andreas Stolcke. 2002. SRILM – an Extensible Language Modeling Toolkit. In *Proc. of the Int. Conf. on Spoken Language Processing (ICSLP)*, volume 3, Denver, CO, USA, September.

David Vilar, Daniel Stein, Matthias Huck, and Hermann Ney. 2010. Jane: Open Source Hierarchical Translation, Extended with Reordering and Lexicon Models. In *ACL 2010 Joint Fifth Workshop on Statistical Machine Translation and Metrics MATR*, pages 262–270, Uppsala, Sweden, July.

David Vilar, Daniel Stein, Matthias Huck, and Hermann Ney. 2012. Jane: an advanced freely available hierarchical machine translation toolkit. *Machine Translation*, pages 1–20. http://dx.doi.org/10.1007/s10590-011-9120-y.

Richard Zens. 2008. *Phrase-based Statistical Machine Translation: Models, Search, Training*. Ph.D. thesis, RWTH Aachen University, Aachen, Germany, February.

TransAhead: A Computer-Assisted Translation and Writing Tool

[*]Chung-chi Huang [+]Ping-che Yang [**]Keh-jiann Chen [++]Jason S. Chang

[*]ISA, NTHU, HsinChu, Taiwan, R.O.C.
[+]III, Taipei, Taiwan, R.O.C.
[**]IIS, Academia Sinica, Taipei, Taiwan, R.O.C.
[++]CS, NTHU, HsinChu, Taiwan, R.O.C.

{[*]u901571,[+]maciaclark,[++]jason.jschang}@gmail.com; [**]kchen@iis.sinica.edu.tw

Abstract

We introduce a method for learning to predict text completion given a source text and partial translation. In our approach, predictions are offered aimed at alleviating users' burden on lexical and grammar choices, and improving productivity. The method involves learning syntax-based phraseology and translation equivalents. At run-time, the source and its translation prefix are sliced into ngrams to generate and rank completion candidates, which are then displayed to users. We present a prototype writing assistant, TransAhead, that applies the method to computer-assisted translation and language learning. The preliminary results show that the method has great potentials in CAT and CALL with significant improvement in translation quality across users.

1 Introduction

More and more language workers and learners use the MT systems on the Web for information gathering and language learning. However, web translation systems typically offer top-1 translations (which are usually far from perfect) and hardly interact with the user.

Text translation could be achieved more interactively and effectively if a system considered translation as a collaborative between the machine generating suggestions and the user accepting or overriding on those suggestions, with the system adapting to the user's action.

Consider the source sentence "我們在完成這筆交易上扮演重要角色" (We play an important role in closing this deal). The best man-machine interaction is probably not the one used by typical existing MT systems. A good working environment might be a translation assistant that offers suggestions and gives the user direct control over the target text.

We present a system, TransAhead[1], that learns to predict and suggest lexical translations (and their grammatical patterns) likely to follow the ongoing translation of a source text, and adapts to the user's choices. Example responses of TransAhead to the source sentence "我們在完成這筆交易上扮演重要角色" and two partial translations are shown in Figure 1. The responses include text and grammatical patterns (in all-cap labels representing parts-of-speech). TransAhead determines and displays the probable subsequent grammatical constructions and partial translations in the form of parts-of-speech and words (e.g., "IN[*in*] VBG[*close*,…]" for keywords "play role" where lexical items in square brackets are lemmas of potential translations) in a pop-up. TransAhead learns these constructs and translations during training.

At run-time, TransAhead starts with a source sentence, and iterates with the user, making predictions on the grammar patterns and lexical translations, while adapting to the user's translation choices to resolve ambiguities in the source sentence related to word segmentation and word sense. In our prototype, TransAhead mediates between users and suggestion modules to translation quality and productivity.

2 Related Work

Computer Assisted Translation (CAT) has been an area of active research. We focus on offering suggestions during the translation process with an

[1] http://140.114.214.80/theSite/TransAhead/ (Chrome only)

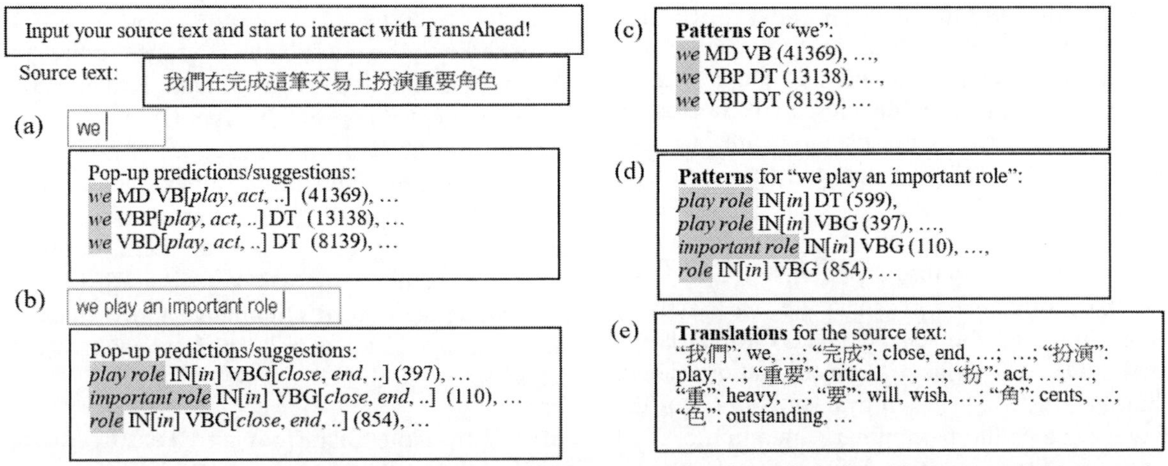

Figure 1. Example TransAhead responses to a source text under the translation (a) "we" and (b) "we play an important role". Note that the grammar/text predictions of (a) and (b) are not placed directly under the caret (current input focus) for space limit. (c) and (d) depict predominant grammar constructs which follow and (e) summarizes the confident translations of the source's character-based ngrams. The frequency of grammar pattern is shown in round brackets while the history (i.e., keyword) based on the user input is shown in shades.

emphasis on language learning. Specifically, our goal is to build a translation assistant to help translator (or learner-translator) with inline grammar help and translation. Unlike recent research focusing on professional (e.g., Brown and Nirenburg, 1990), we target on both professional and student translators.

More recently, interactive MT (IMT) systems have begun to shift the user's role from post-editing machine output to collaborating with the machine to produce the target text. Foster et al (2000) describe TransType, a pioneering system that supports next word predictions. Along the similar line, Koehn (2009) develops caitra which predicts and displays phrasal translation suggestions one phrase at a time. The main difference between their systems and TransAhead is that we also display grammar patterns to provide the general patterns of predicted translations so a student translator can learn and become more proficient.

Recent work has been done on using fully-fledged statistical MT systems to produce target hypotheses completing user-validated translation prefix in IMT paradigm. Barrachina et al. (2008) investigate the applicability of different MT kernels within IMT framework. Nepveu et al. (2004) and Ortiz-Martinez et al. (2011) further exploit user feedbacks for better IMT systems and user experience. Instead of triggered by user correction, our method is triggered by word delimiter and assists both translation and learning the target language.

In contrast to the previous CAT research, we present a writing assistant that suggests grammar constructs as well as lexical translations following users' partial translation, aiming to provide users with choice to ease mental burden and enhance performance.

3 The TransAhead System

3.1 Problem Statement

We focus on predicting a set of grammar patterns with lexical translations likely to follow the current partial target translation of a source text. The predictions will be examined by a human user directly. Not to overwhelm the user, our goal is to return a reasonable-sized set of predictions that contain suitable word choices and grammatical patterns to choose and learn from. Formally,

Problem Statement: We are given a target-language reference corpus C_t, a parallel corpus C_{st}, a source-language text S, and its translation prefix T_p. Our goal is to provide a set of predictions based on C_t and C_{st} likely to further translate S in terms of grammar and text. For this, we transform S and T_p into sets of ngrams such that the predominant grammar constructs with suitable translation options following T_p are likely to be acquired.

3.2 Learning to Find Pattern and Translation

In the training stage, we find and store syntax-based phraseological tendencies and translation pairs. These patterns and translations are intended to be used in a real-time system to respond to user input speedily.

First, we part of speech tag sentences in C_t. Using common phrase patterns (e.g., the **possessive noun** *one's* in "make up *one's* mind") seen in grammar books, we resort to parts-of-speech (POS) for syntactic generalization. Then, we build up inverted files of the words in C_t for the next stage (i.e., pattern grammar generation). Apart from sentence and position information, a word's lemma and POS are also recorded.

Subsequently, we use the procedure in Figure 2 to generate grammar patterns following any given sequence of words, either contiguous or skipped.

```
procedure PatternFinding(query,N,Ct)
(1) interInvList=findInvertedFile(w1 of query)
    for each word wi in query except for w1
(2)    InvList=findInvertedFile(wi)
(3a)   newInterInvList=φ ; i=1; j=1
(3b)   while i<=length(interInvList) and j<=lengh(InvList)
(3c)      if interInvList[i].SentNo==InvList[j].SentNo
(3d)         Insert(newInterInvList, interInvList[i],InvList[j])
          else
(3e)         Move i,j accordingly
(3f)   interInvList=newInterInvList
(4) Usage=φ
    for each element in interInvList
(5)    Usage+={PatternGrammarGeneration(element,Ct)}
(6) Sort patterns in Usage in descending order of frequency
(7) return the N patterns in Usage with highest frequency
```

Figure 2. Automatically generating pattern grammar.

The algorithm first identifies the sentences containing the given sequence of words, *query*. Iteratively, Step (3) performs an AND operation on the inverted file, *InvList*, of the current word w_i and *interInvList*, a previous intersected results.

After that, we analyze *query*'s syntax-based phraseology (Step (5)). For each *element* of the form ([wordPosi(w_1),..., wordPosi(w_n)], *sentence number*) denoting the positions of *query*'s words in the *sentence*, we generate grammar pattern involving replacing words in the sentence with POS tags and words in wordPosi(w_i) with lemmas, and extracting fixed-window [2] segments surrounding *query* from the transformed sentence. The result is a set of grammatical patterns (i.e., syntax-based phraseology) for the query. The procedure finally returns top *N* predominant syntactic patterns of the query. Such patterns characterizing the query's word usages in the spirit of pattern grammar in (Hunston and Francis, 2000) and are collected across the target language.

In the fourth and final stage, we exploit C_{st} for bilingual phrase acquisition, rather than a manual dictionary, to achieve better translation coverage and variety. We obtain phrase pairs through a number of steps, namely, leveraging IBM models for bidirectional word alignments, grow-diagonal-final heuristics to extract phrasal equivalences (Koehn et al., 2003).

3.3 Run-Time Grammar and Text Prediction

Once translation equivalents and phraseological tendencies are learned, they are stored for run-time reference. TransAhead then predicts/suggests the following grammar and text of a translation prefix given the source text using the procedure in Figure 3.

```
procedure MakePrediction(S,Tp)
(1) Assign sliceNgram(S) to {si}
(2) Assign sliceNgramWithPivot(Tp) to {tj}
(3) TransOptions=findTranslation({si},Tp)
(4) GramOptions=findPattern({tj})
(5) Evaluate translation options in TransOptions
        and incorporate them into GramOptions
(6) Return GramOptions
```

Figure 3. Predicting pattern grammar and translations at run-time.

We first slice the source text *S* into character-level ngrams, represented by $\{s_i\}$. We also find the word-level ngrams of the translation prefix T_p. But this time we concentrate on the ngrams, may skipped, ending with the last word of T_p (i.e., pivoted on the last word) since these ngrams are most related to the subsequent grammar patterns.

Step (3) and (4) retrieve translations and patterns learned from Section 3.2. Step (3) acquires the target-language active vocabulary that may be used to translate the source. To alleviate the word boundary issue in MT (Ma et al. (2007)), the word boundary in our system is loosely decided. Initially, TransAhead non-deterministically segments the source text using character ngrams for translations and proceeds with collaborations with the user to obtain the segmentation for MT and to complete the translation. Note that T_p may reflect some translated segments, reducing the size of the active vocabulary, and that a user vocabulary of preference (due to users' domain knowledge or

[2] Inspired by (Gamon and Leacock, 2010).

errors of the system) may be exploited for better system performance. In addition, Step (4) extracts patterns preceding with the history ngrams of $\{t_j\}$.

In Step (5), we first evaluate and rank the translation candidates using linear combination:

$$\lambda_1 \times (P_1(t \mid s_i) + P_1(s_i \mid t)) + \lambda_2 \times P_2(t \mid T_p)$$

where λ_i is combination weight, P_1 and P_2 are translation and language model respectively, and t is one of the translation candidates under S and T_p. Subsequently, we incorporate the lemmatized translation candidates according to their ranks into suitable grammar constituents in *GramOptions*. For example, we would include "close" in pattern "*play role* IN[*in*] VBG" as "*play role* IN[*in*] VBG[*close*]".

At last, the algorithm returns the representative grammar patterns with confident translations expected to follow the ongoing translation and further translate the source. This algorithm will be triggered by word delimiter to provide an interactive CAT and CALL environment. Figure 1 shows example responses of our working prototype.

4 Preliminary Results

In developing TransAhead, we used British National Corpus and Hong Kong Parallel Text as target-language reference corpus and parallel training corpus respectively, and deployed GENIA tagger for lemma and POS analyses.

To evaluate TransAhead in CAT and CALL, we introduced it to a class of 34 (Chinese) college freshmen learning English as foreign language. We designed TransAhead to be accessible and intuitive, so the user training tutorial took only one minute.

After the tutorial, the participants were asked to translate 15 Chinese texts from (Huang et al., 2011) (half with TransAhead assistance called experimental group, and the other without any system help whatsoever called control group). The evaluation results show that the experimental group achieved *much* better translation quality than the control group with an average BLEU score (Papineni et al., 2002) of **35.49** vs. 26.46. Admittedly, the MT system Google Translate produced translations with a higher BLEU score of 44.82.

Google Translate obviously has much more parallel training data and bilingual translation knowledge. No previous work in CAT uses Google Translate for comparison. Although there is a difference in average translation quality between the experimental TransAhead group and the Google Translate, it is not hard for us to notice the source sentences were better translated by language learners with the help of TransAhead. Take the sentence "我們在完成這筆交易上扮演重要角色" for example. A total of 90% of the participants in the experimental group produced more grammatical and fluent translations (see Figure 4) than that ("We conclude this transaction plays an important role") by Google Translate.

1. we play(ed) a critical role in closing this/the deal.
2. we play(ed) a critical role in sealing this/the deal.
3. we play(ed) an important role in ending this/the deal.
4. we play(ed) an important role in closing this/the deal.

Figure 4. Example translations with TransAhead assistance.

Post-experiment surveys indicate that (a) the participants found Google Translate lack human-computer interaction while TransAhead is intuitive to collaborate with in translation/writing; (b) the participants found TransAhead grammar and translation predictions useful for their immediate task and for learning; (c) interactivity made the translation and language learning a fun process (like image tagging game of (von Ahn and Dabbish, 2004)) and the participants found TransAhead very recommendable and would like to use it again in future translation tasks.

5 Summary

We have introduced a method for learning to offer grammar and text predictions expected to assist the user in translation and writing. We have implemented and evaluated the method. The preliminary results are encouragingly promising. As for the further work, we intend to evaluate and improve our system further in learner productivity in terms of output quality, typing speed, and the amount of using certain keys such as *delete* and *backspace*.

Acknowledgement

This study is conducted under the "Project Digital Convergence Service Open Platform" of the Institute for Information Industry which is subsidized by the Ministry of Economy Affairs of the Republic of China.

References

S. Barrachina, O. Bender, F. Casacuberta, J. Civera, E. Cubel, S. Khadivi, A. Lagarda, H. Ney, J. Tomas, E. Vidal, and J.-M. Vilar. 2008. Statistical approaches to computer-assisted translation. *Computational Linguistics*, 35(1): 3-28.

R. D. Brown and S. Nirenburg. 1990. Human-computer interaction for semantic disambiguation. In *Proceedings of COLING*, pages 42-47.

G. Foster, P. Langlais, E. Macklovitch, and G. Lapalme. 2002. TransType: text prediction for translators. In *Proceedings of ACL Demonstrations*, pages 93-94.

M. Gamon and C. Leacock. 2010. Search right and thou shalt find ... using web queries for learner error detection. In *Proceedings of the NAACL Workshop*.

C.-C. Huang, M.-H. Chen, S.-T. Huang, H.-C. Liou, and J. S. Chang. 2011. GRASP: grammar- and syntax-based pattern-finder in CALL. In *Proceedings of ACL Workshop*.

S. Hunston and G. Francis. 2000. *Pattern Grammar: A Corpus-Driven Approach to the Lexical Grammar of English*. Amsterdam: John Benjamins.

P. Koehn, F. J. Och, and D. Marcu. 2003. Statistical phrase-based translation. In *Proceedings of NAACL*.

P. Koehn. 2009. A web-based interactive computer aided translation tool. In *Proceedings of ACL*.

Y. Ma, N. Stroppa, and A. Way. 2007. Bootstrapping word alignment via word packing. In *Proceedings of ACL*.

L. Nepveu, G. Lapalme, P. Langlais, and G. Foster. 2004. Adaptive language and translation models for interactive machine translation. In *Proceedings of EMNLP*.

D. Ortiz-Martinez, L. A. Leiva, V. Alabau, I. Garcia-Varea, and F. Casacuberta. 2011. An interactive machine translation system with online learning. In *Proceedings of ACL System Demonstrations*, pages 68-73.

K. Papineni, S. Roukos, T. Ward, W.-J. Zhu. 2002. Bleu: a method for automatic evaluation of machine translation. In Proceedings of ACL, pages 311-318.

L. von Ahn and L. Dabbish. 2004. Labeling images with a computer game. In *Proceedings of CHI*.

Correction Detection and Error Type Selection as an ESL Educational Aid

Ben Swanson
Brown University
chonger@cs.brown.edu

Elif Yamangil
Harvard University
elif@eecs.harvard.edu

Abstract

We present a classifier that discriminates between types of corrections made by teachers of English in student essays. We define a set of linguistically motivated feature templates for a log-linear classification model, train this classifier on sentence pairs extracted from the Cambridge Learner Corpus, and achieve 89% accuracy improving upon a 33% baseline. Furthermore, we incorporate our classifier into a novel application that takes as input a set of corrected essays that have been sentence aligned with their originals and outputs the individual corrections classified by error type. We report the F-Score of our implementation on this task.

1 Introduction

In a typical foreign language education classroom setting, teachers are presented with student essays that are often fraught with errors. These errors can be grammatical, semantic, stylistic, simple spelling errors, etc. One task of the teacher is to isolate these errors and provide feedback to the student with corrections. In this body of work, we address the possibility of augmenting this process with NLP tools and techniques, in the spirit of Computer Assisted Language Learning (CALL).

We propose a step-wise approach in which a teacher first corrects an essay and then a computer program aligns their output with the original text and separates and classifies independent edits. With the program's analysis the teacher would be provided accurate information that could be used in effective lesson planning tailored to the students' strengths and weaknesses.

This suggests a novel NLP task with two components: The first isolates individual corrections made by the teacher, and the second classifies these corrections into error types that the teacher would find useful. A suitable corpus for developing this program is the Cambridge Learner Corpus (CLC) (Yannakoudakis et al., 2011). The CLC contains approximately 1200 essays with error corrections annotated in XML within sentences. Furthermore, these corrections are tagged with linguistically motivated error type codes.

To the best of our knowledge our proposed task is unexplored in previous work. However, there is a significant amount of related work in automated grammatical error correction (Fitzgerald et al., 2009; Gamon, 2011; West et al., 2011). The Helping Our Own (HOO) shared task (Dale and Kilgarriff, 2010) also explores this issue, with Rozovskaya et al. (2011) as the best performing system to date. While often addressing the problem of error type selection directly, previous work has dealt with the more obviously useful task of end to end error detection and correction. As such, their classification systems are crippled by poor recall of errors as well as the lack of information from the corrected sentence and yield very low accuracies for error detection and type selection, e.g. Gamon (2011).

Our task is fundamentally different as we assume the presence of both the original and corrected text. While the utility of such a system is not as obvious as full error correction, we note two possible applications of our technique. The first, mentioned above, is as an analytical tool for language teachers. The second is as a complementary tool for automated error correction systems themselves. Just as tools such as BLAST (Stymne, 2011) are useful in the development of machine translation systems, our system can produce accurate summaries of the corrections made by automated systems even if the systems themselves do not involve such fine grained error type analysis.

In the following, we describe our experimental methodology (Section 2) and then discuss the feature set we employ for classification (Section 3) and its performance. Next, we outline our application (Section 4), its heuristic correction detection strategy and empirical evaluation. We finish by discussing the implications for real world systems (Section 5) and avenues for improvement.

2 Methodology

Sentences in the CLC contain one or more error corrections, each of which is labeled with one of 75 error types (Nicholls, 2003). Error types include countability errors, verb tense errors, word order errors, etc. and are often predicated on the part of speech involved. For example, the category AG (agreement) is augmented to form AGN (agreement of a noun) to tag an error such as "here are some of my *opinion*". For ease of analysis and due to the high accuracy of state-of-the-art POS tagging, in addition to the full 75 class problem we also perform experiments using a compressed set of 15 classes. This compressed set removes the part of speech components of the error types as shown in Figure 1.

We create a dataset of corrections from the CLC by extracting sentence pairs (x, y) where x is the original (student's) sentence and y is its corrected form by the teacher. We create multiple instances out of sentence pairs that contain multiple corrections. For example, consider the sentence "With this letter I would ask you if you wuld change it". This consists of two errors: "ask" should be replaced with "like to ask" and "wuld" is misspelled. These are marked separately in the CLC, and imply the corrected sentence "With this letter I would *like to ask* you if you *would* change it". Here we extract two instances consisting of "With this letter I would *ask* you if you *would* change it" and "With this letter I would *like to ask* if you *wuld* change it", each paired with the fully corrected sentence. As each correction in the CLC is tagged with an error type t, we then form a dataset of triples (x, y, t). This yields 45080 such instances. We use these data in cross-validation experiments with the feature based MaxEnt classifier in the Mallet (McCallum, 2002) software package.

3 Feature Set

We use the minimum unweighted edit distance path between x and y as a source of features. The edit distance operations that compose the path are Delete, Insert, Substitute, and Equal. To illustrate, the operations we would get from the sentences above would be (Insert, "like"), (Insert, "to"), (Substitute, "wuld", "would"), and (Equal, w, w) for all other words w.

Our feature set consists of three main categories and a global category (See Figure 2). For each edit distance operation other than Equal we use an indicator feature, as well as word+operation indicators, for example "the word w was inserted" or "the word w_1 was substituted with w_2". The *POS Context* features encode the part of speech context of the edit, recording the parts of speech immediately preceding and following the edit in the corrected sentence. For all POS based features we use only tags from the corrected sentence y, as our tags are obtained automatically.

For a substitution of w_2 for w_1 we use several targeted features. Many of these are self explanatory and can be calculated easily without outside libraries. The *In Dictionary?* feature is indexed by two binary values corresponding to the presence of the words in the WordNet dictionary. For the *Same Stem?* feature we use the stemmer provided in the freely downloadable JWI (Java Wordnet Interface) library. If the two words have the same stem then we also trigger the *Suffixes* feature, which is indexed by the two suffix strings after the stem has been removed. For global features, we record the total number of non-Equal edits as well as a feature which fires if one sentence is a word-reordering of the other.

Description (Code)	Sample and Correction	Total #	% Accuracy
Unnecessary (U)	July is the *period of* time that suits me best July is the time that suits me best	5237	94.0
Incorrect verb tense (TV)	She gave me autographs and *talk* really nicely. She gave me autographs and *talked* really nicely.	2752	85.2
Countability error (C)	Please help them put away their *stuffs*. Please help them put away their *stuff*.	273	65.2
Incorrect word order (W)	I would like to know what kind of clothes *should I* bring. I would like to know what kind of clothes *I should* bring.	1410	76.0
Incorrect negative (X)	We recommend you *not to* go with your friends. We recommend you *don't* go with your friends.	124	18.5
Spelling error (S)	Our music lessons are *speccial*. Our music lessons are *special*.	4429	90.0
Wrong form used (F)	In spite of *think* I did well, I had to reapply. In spite of *thinking* I did well, I had to reapply.	2480	82.0
Agreement error (AG)	I would like to take some *picture* of beautiful scenery. I would like to take some *pictures* of beautiful scenery.	1743	77.9
Replace (R)	The idea *about* going to Maine is common. The idea *of* going to Maine is common.	14290	94.6
Missing (M)	Sometimes you surprised when you check the balance. Sometimes you *are* surprised when you check the balance.	9470	97.6
Incorrect argument structure (AS)	How much do I have to bring the money? How much money do I have to bring?	191	19.4
Wrong Derivation (D)	The *arrive* of every student is a new chance. The *arrival* of every student is a new chance.	1643	58.6
Wrong inflection (I)	I *enjoyded* it a lot. I *enjoyed* it a lot.	590	58.6
Inappropriate register (L)	The *girls'd* rather play table tennis or badminton. The *girls would* rather play table tennis or badminton.	135	23.0
Idiomatic error (ID)	The *level of life* in the USA is similar to the UK. The *cost of living* in the USA is similar to the UK.	313	15.7

Figure 1: Error types in the collapsed 15 class set.

3.1 Evaluation

We perform five-fold cross-validation and achieve a classification accuracy of 88.9% for the 15 class problem and 83.8% for the full 75 class problem. The accuracies of the most common class baselines are 33.3% and 7.8% respectively. The most common confusion in the 15 class case is between D (Derivation), R (Replacement) and S (Spelling). These are mainly due to context-sensitive spelling corrections falling into the Replace category or noise in the mark-up of derivation errors. For the 75 class case the most common confusion is between agreement of noun (AGN) and form of noun (FN). This is unsurprising as we do not incorporate long distance features which would encode agreement.

To check against over-fitting we performed an experiment where we take away the strongly lexicalized features (such as "word w is inserted") and observed a reduction from 88.9% to 82.4% for 15 class classification accuracy. The lack of a dramatic reduction demonstrates the generalization power of our feature templates.

4 An Educational Application

As mentioned earlier, we incorporate our classifier in an educational software tool. The input to this tool is a group of aligned sentence pairs from original and teacher edited versions of a set of essays. This tool has two components devoted to (1) isolation of individual corrections in a sentence pair, and (2) classification of these corrections. This software could be easily integrated in real world curriculum as it is natural for the teacher to produce corrected versions of student essays without stopping to label and analyze distribution of correction types.

We devise a family of heuristic strategies to separate independent corrections from one another. Heuristic h_i allows at most i consecutive Equal edit distance operations in a single correction. This implies that h_{n+1} would tend to merge more non-Equal edits than h_n. We experimented with $i \in \{0, 1, 2, 3, 4\}$. For comparison we also implemented

- Insert
  - Insert
  - Insert(w)
  - POS Context
- Delete
  - Delete
  - Delete(w)
  - POS Context
- Substitution
  - Substitution
  - Substitution(w_1,w_2)
  - Character Edit Distance
  - Common Prefix Length
  - In Dictionary?
  - Previous Word
  - POS of Substitution
  - Same Stem?
  - Suffixes
- Global
  - Same Words?
  - Number Of Edits

Figure 2: List of features used in our classifier.

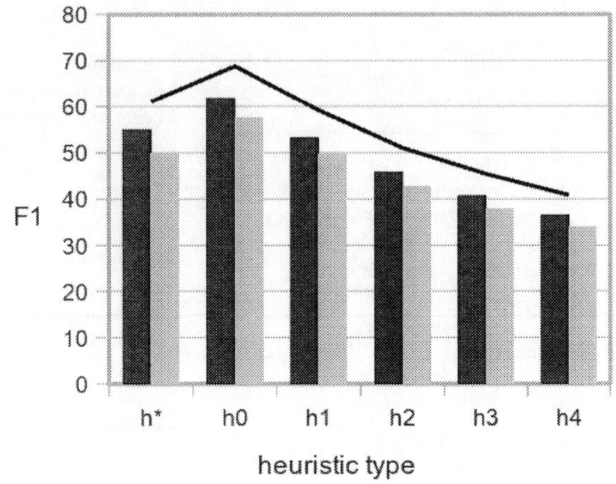

Figure 3: Application F-score against different correction detection strategies. The left and right bars show the 15 and 75 class cases respectively. The line shows the unlabeled F-score upper bound.

a heuristic h^* that treats every non-Equal edit as an individual correction. This is different than h_0, which would merge edits that do not have an intervening Equal operation. F-scores (using 5 fold cross-validation) obtained by different heuristics are reported in Figure 3 for the 15 and 75 class problems. For these F-scores we attempt to predict both the boundaries and the labels of the corrections. The unlabeled F-score (shown as a line) evaluates the heuristic itself and provides an upper bound for the labeled F-score of the overall application. We see that the best upper bound and F-scores are achieved with heuristic h_0 which merges consecutive non-Equal edits.

5 Future Work

There are several directions in which this work could be extended. The most obvious is to replace the correction detection heuristic with a more robust algorithm. Our log-linear classifier is perhaps better suited for this task than other discriminative classifiers as it can be extended in a larger framework which maximizes the joint probability of all corrections. Our work shows that h_0 will provide a strong baseline for such experiments.

While our classification accuracies are quite good, error analysis reveals that we lack the ability to capture long range lexical dependencies necessary to recognize many agreement errors. Incorporating such syntactic information through the use of synchronous grammars such as those used by Yamangil and Shieber (2010) would likely lead to improved performance. Furthermore, while in this work we focus on the ESL motivation, our system could also be used to aid development of automated correction systems, as was suggested by BLAST (Stymne, 2011) for machine translation.

Finally, there would be much to be gained by testing our application in real classroom settings. Every day, teachers of English correct essays and could possibly provide us with feedback. Our main concern from such testing would be the determination of a label set which is appropriate for the teachers' concerns. We expect that the 15 class case is too coarse and the 75 class case too fine grained to provide an effective analysis.

References

Robert Dale and Adam Kilgarriff. 2010. Helping our own: text massaging for computational linguistics as a new shared task. In *Proceedings of the 6th International Natural Language Generation Conference*,

INLG '10, pages 263–267, Stroudsburg, PA, USA. Association for Computational Linguistics.

Erin Fitzgerald, Frederick Jelinek, and Keith Hall. 2009. Integrating sentence- and word-level error identification for disfluency correction. In *Proceedings of the 2009 Conference on Empirical Methods in Natural Language Processing: Volume 2 - Volume 2*, EMNLP '09, pages 765–774, Stroudsburg, PA, USA. Association for Computational Linguistics.

Michael Gamon. 2011. High-order sequence modeling for language learner error detection. In *Proceedings of the 6th Workshop on Innovative Use of NLP for Building Educational Applications*, IUNLPBEA '11, pages 180–189, Stroudsburg, PA, USA. Association for Computational Linguistics.

Andrew Kachites McCallum. 2002. Mallet: A machine learning for language toolkit. http://www.cs.umass.edu/ mccallum/mallet.

D. Nicholls. 2003. The cambridge learner corpus: Error coding and analysis for lexicography and elt. In *Proceedings of the Corpus Linguistics 2003 conference*, pages 572–581.

A. Rozovskaya, M. Sammons, J. Gioja, and D. Roth. 2011. University of illinois system in hoo text correction shared task.

Sara Stymne. 2011. Blast: A tool for error analysis of machine translation output. In *ACL (System Demonstrations)*, pages 56–61.

Randy West, Y. Albert Park, and Roger Levy. 2011. Bilingual random walk models for automated grammar correction of esl author-produced text. In *Proceedings of the 6th Workshop on Innovative Use of NLP for Building Educational Applications*, IUNLPBEA '11, pages 170–179, Stroudsburg, PA, USA. Association for Computational Linguistics.

Elif Yamangil and Stuart M. Shieber. 2010. Bayesian synchronous tree-substitution grammar induction and its application to sentence compression. In *ACL*, pages 937–947.

Helen Yannakoudakis, Ted Briscoe, and Ben Medlock. 2011. A new dataset and method for automatically grading esol texts. In *Proceedings of the 49th Annual Meeting of the Association for Computational Linguistics: Human Language Technologies - Volume 1*, HLT '11, pages 180–189, Stroudsburg, PA, USA. Association for Computational Linguistics.

Getting More from Segmentation Evaluation

Martin Scaiano
University of Ottawa
Ottawa, ON, K1N 6N5, Canada
mscai056@uottawa.ca

Diana Inkpen
University of Ottawa
Ottawa, ON, K1N 6N5, Canada
diana@eecs.uottawa.com

Abstract

We introduce a new segmentation evaluation measure, WinPR, which resolves some of the limitations of WindowDiff. WinPR distinguishes between false positive and false negative errors; produces more intuitive measures, such as precision, recall, and F-measure; is insensitive to window size, which allows us to customize near miss sensitivity; and is based on counting errors not windows, but still provides partial reward for near misses.

1 Introduction

WindowDiff (Pevzner and Hearst, 2002) has become the most frequently used measure to evaluate segmentation. Segmentation is the task of dividing a stream of data (text or other media) into coherent units. These units may be motivated topically (Malioutov and Barzilay, 2006), structurally (Stokes, 2003) (Malioutov et al., 2007) (Jancsary et al., 2008), or visually (Chen et al., 2008), depending on the domain and task. Segmentation evaluation is difficult because exact comparison of boundaries is too strict; a partial reward is required for close boundaries.

2 WindowDiff

"The WindowDiff metric is a variant of the P_k measure, which penalizes false positives and near misses equally." (Malioutov et al., 2007). WindowDiff uses a sliding window over the segmentation; each window is evaluated as correct or incorrect. WindowDiff is effectively $1 - accuracy$ for all windows, but accuracy is sensitive to the balance of positive and negative data being evaluated. The positive and negative balance is determined by the window size. Small windows produce more negatives, thus WindowDiff recommends using a window size (k) of half the average segment length. This produces an almost equal number of positive windows (containing boundaries) and negative windows (without boundaries).

Equation 1 represents the window size (k), where N is the total number of sentences (or content units). Equation 2 is WindowDiff's traditional definition, where R is the number of reference boundaries in the window from i to i+k, and C is the number of computed boundaries in the same window. The comparison (> 0) is sometimes forgotten, which produces strange values not bound between 0 and 1; thus we prefer equation 3 to represent WindowDiff, as it emphasizes the comparison.

$$k = \frac{N}{2 * \textit{number of segments}} \quad (1)$$

$$\textit{WindowDiff} = \frac{1}{N-k}\sum_{i=0}^{N-k}(|R_{i,i+k} - C_{i,i+k}| > 0) \quad (2)$$

$$\textit{WindowDiff} = \frac{1}{N-k}\sum_{i=0}^{N-k}(R_{i,i+k} \neq C_{i,i+k}) \quad (3)$$

Figure 1 illustrates WindowDiff's sliding window evaluation. Each rectangle represents a sentence, while the shade indicates to which segment it truly belongs (reference segmentation). The vertical line represents a computed boundary. This example contains a near miss (misaligned boundary). In this example, we are using a window size of 5. The columns i, R, C, W represent the window position, the number of boundaries from the reference (true) segmentation in the window, the number of boundaries from the computed segmentation in the window, and whether the values agree, respectively. Only windows up to $i = 5$ are shown, but to process the entire segmentation 8 windows are required.

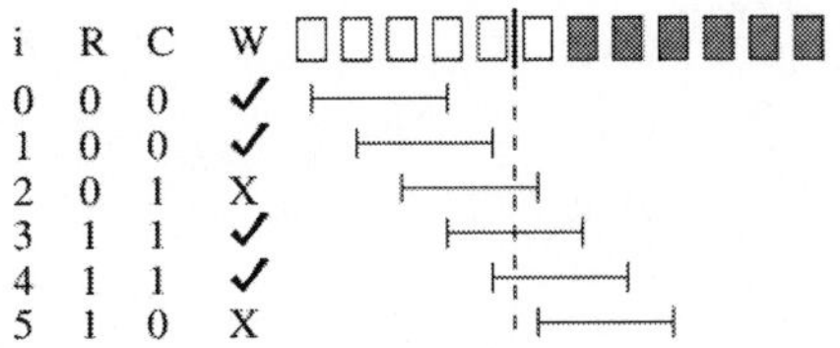

Figure 1: Illustration of counting boundaries in windows

Franz et al. (2007) note that WindowDiff does not allow different segmentation tasks to optimize different aspects, or tolerate different types of errors. Tasks requiring a uniform theme in a segment might tolerate false positives, while tasks requiring complete ideas or complete themes might accept false negatives.

Georgescul et al. (2009) note that while WindowDiff technically penalizes false positives and false negatives equally, false positives are in fact more likely; a false positive error occurs anywhere were there are more computed boundaries than boundaries in the reference, while a false negative error can only occur when a boundary is missed. Consider figure 1, only 3 of the 8 windows contain a boundary; only those 3 windows may have false negatives (a missed boundary), while all other windows may contain false positives (too many boundaries).

Lamprier et al. (2008) note that errors near the beginning and end of a segmentation are actually counted slightly less than other errors. Lamprier offers a simple correction for this problem, by adding $k-1$ phantom positions, which have no boundaries, at the beginning and at the end sequence. The addition of these phantom boundaries allows for windows extending outside the segmentation to be evaluated, and thus allowing for each position to be count k times. Example E in figure 4 in the next section will illustrate this point. Consider example D in figure 4; this error will only be accounted for in the first window, instead of the typical k windows.

Furthermore, tasks may want to adjust sensitivity or reward for near misses. Naturally, one would be inclined to adjust the window size, but changing the window size will change the balance of positive windows and negative windows. Changing this balance has a significant impact on how WindowDiff functions.

Some researchers have questioned what the WindowDiff value tells us; how do we interpret it?

3 WinPR

WinPR is derived from WindowDiff, but differs on one main point: WinPR evaluates boundary positions, while WindowDiff evaluates regions (or windows). WinPR is a set of equations (4-7) (Figure 2) producing a confusion matrix. The confusion matrix allows for the distinction between false positive and negative errors, and can be used with Precision, Recall, and F-measure. Furthermore, the window size may be changed to adjust near-miss sensitivity without affecting the the interpretation of the confusion matrix.

N is the number of content units and k represents the window size. WinPR includes the Lamprier (2008) correction, thus the sum is from $1-k$ to N instead of 1 to $N-k$ as with WindowDiff. min and max refer to the tradition computer science functions which select the minimal or maximal value from a set of two values. True negatives (5) start with a negative term, which removes the value of the phantom positions.

Each WinPR equation is a summation over all windows. To understand the intuition behind each equation, consider Figure 3. R and C represent the number of boundaries from the reference and computed segmentations, respectively, in the ith window, up to a maximum of k. The overlapping region represents the TPs. The difference is the error, while the sign of the difference indicates whether they are FPs or FNs. The WinPR equations select the difference using the max function, forcing negative values to 0. The remainder, up to k, represents the TNs.

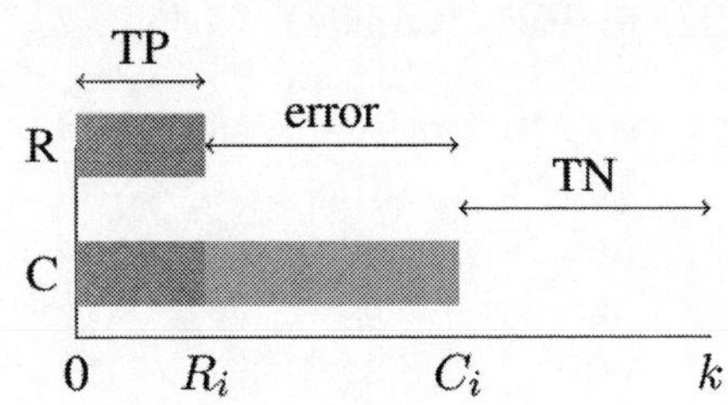

Figure 3: WinPR within Window Counting Demostration

Consider how WindowDiff and WinPR handle the examples in Figure 4. These examples use the same basic representation as Figure 1 in section 2. Each segment is 6 units long and the window size is

$$\text{\textit{True Positives}} = TP = \sum_{i=1-k}^{N} min(R_{i,i+k}, C_{i,i+k}) \tag{4}$$

$$\text{\textit{True Negatives}} = TN = -k(k-1) + \sum_{i=1-k}^{N} (k - max(R_{i,i+k}, C_{i,i+k})) \tag{5}$$

$$\text{\textit{False Positives}} = FP = \sum_{i=1-k}^{N} max(0, C_{i,i+k} - R_{i,i+k}) \tag{6}$$

$$\text{\textit{False Negatives}} = FN = \sum_{i=1-k}^{N} max(0, R_{i,i+k} - C_{i,i+k}) \tag{7}$$

Figure 2: Equations for the WinPR confusion matrix

$3 = (6/2)$. Each window contains 3 content units, thus we consider 4 potential boundary positions (the edges are inclusive).

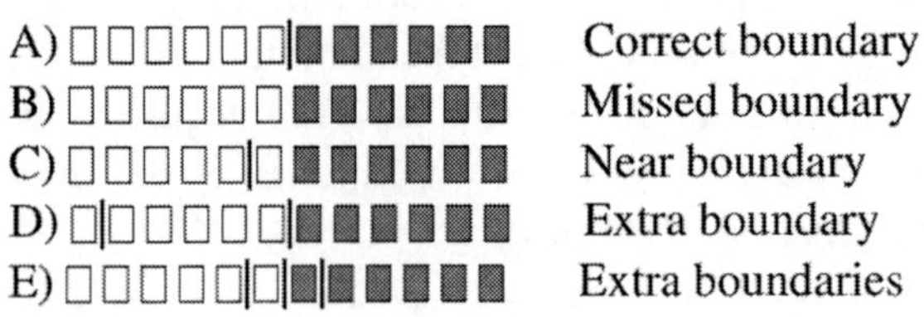

Figure 4: Example segmentations

Example A provides a baseline for comparison; B is a false negative (a missed boundary); C is a near miss; D is an extra boundary at the beginning of the sequence, providing an example of Lamprier's criticism. E includes two errors near each other. Notice how the additional errors in E have have a very small impact on the WindowDiff value. Table 1 lists the number of correct and incorrect windows, and the WindowDiff value for each example.

Example	Correct	Incorrect	WindowDiff
A	10	0	0
B	6	4	0.4
C	8	2	0.2
D	9	1	0.1
E	4	6	0.6

Table 1: WindowDiff values for examples A to E

WindowDiff should penalize an error k times, once for each window in which it appears, with the exception of near misses which have partial reward and penalization. D is only penalized in one window, because most of the other windows would be outside the sequence. E contains two errors, but they are not fully penalized because they appear in overlapping windows. Furthermore, using a single metric does not indicate if the errors are false positives or false negatives. This information is important to the development of a segmentation algorithm.

If we apply WinPR to examples A-E, we get the results in Table 2. We will calculate precision and recall using the WinPR confusion matrix, shown under WinP and WinR respectively. You will note that we can easily see whether an error is a false positive or a false negative. As we would expect, false positives affect precision, and false negatives affect recall. Near misses manifest as equal parts false positive and false negative. In example E, each error is counted, unlike WindowDiff.

Example	TP	TN	FP	FN	WinP	WinR
a	4	40	0	0	1	1.0
b	0	40	0	4	-	0
c	3	40	1	1	0.75	0.75
d	4	36	4	0	0.5	1.0
e	4	32	8	0	0.33	1.0

Table 2: WinPR values for examples A to E

In Table 2, note that each potential boundary position is considered k (the window size) times. Thus, each positive or negative boundary assignment is counted k times; near misses producing a blend of values: TP, FP, FN. We refer to the normalized confusion matrix (or normalized WinPR), as the confusion matrix divided by the window size. If near misses are not considered, this confusion matrix gives the exact count of boundary assignments.

What is not apparent in Table 2, is that WinPR is insensitive to window size, with the exception of near misses. Thus adjusting the window size can be used to adjust the tolerance or sensitivity to near misses. Large window sizes are more forgiving of near misses, smaller window size are more strict.

3.1 Near Misses and Window Size

WinPR does not provide any particular values indicating the number of near misses, their distance, or contribution to the evaluation. Because WinPR's window size only affects near miss sensitivity, and not the positive/negative balance like in WindowDiff, we can subtract two normalized confusion matrices using different window sizes. The difference between the confusion matrices gives the impact of near misses under different window sizes. Choosing a very strict window size ($k = 1$), and subtracting it from another window size would effectively provide the contribution of the near misses to the confusion matrix. In many circumstances, using several window sizes may be desirable.

3.2 Variations in Segment Size: Validation by Simulation

We ran numerous tests on artificial segmentation data composed of 40 segments, with a mean segment length of 40 content units, and standard deviations varying from 10 to 120. All tests showed that a false positive or a false negative error is always penalized k times, as expected.

3.3 WinPR Applied to a Complete Segmentation

Using a reference segmentation of 40 segments, we derived two flawed segments: we added 20 extra boundaries to one, and removed 18 boundaries from the other. Both produced WindowDiff values of 0.22, while WinPR provided WinP = 0.66 and WinR = 1.0 for the addition of boundaries and WinP = 1.00 and WinR = 0.54 for the removal of boundaries. WinPR highlights the differences in the nature of the two flawed segmentations, while WinDiff masks both the number and types of errors.

4 Conclusion

We presented a new evaluation method for segmentation, called WinPR because it produces a confusion matrix from which Precision and Recall can be derived. WinPR is easy to implement and provides more detail on the types of errors in a computed segmentation, as compared with the reference. Some of the major benefits of WinPR, as opposed to WindowDiff are presented below:

1. Distinct counting of false positives and false negatives, which helps in algorithm selection for downstream tasks and helps with analysis and optimization of an algorithm.
2. The confusion matrix is easier to interpret than a WindowDiff value.
3. WinPR counts errors from boundaries, not windows, thus close errors are not masked
4. Precision, and Recall are easier to understand than WindowDiff.
5. F-measure is effective when a single value is required for comparison.
6. WinPR incorporates Lamprier (2008) correction.
7. Adjusting the window size can customize an evaluation's tolerance of near misses
8. WinPR provides a method of detecting the impact of near misses on an evaluation

WinPR counts boundaries, not windows, which has analytical benefits, but WindowDiff's counting of windows provides an evaluation of segmentation by region. Thus WindowDiff is more appropriate when an evaluator is less interested in the types and the number of errors and more interested in the percentage of the sequence that is correct.

Acknowledgments

Thanks to Dr. Stan Szpakowicz for all his help refining the arguments and the presentation of this paper. Thanks to Anna Kazantseva for months of discussions about segmentation and the evaluation problems we each faced. Thanks to Natural Sciences and Engineering Research Council of Canada (NSERC) for funding our research.

References

L Chen, YC Lai, and H Liao. 2008. Movie scene segmentation using background information. *Pattern Recognition*, Jan.

M Franz, J McCarley, and J Xu. 2007. User-oriented text segmentation evaluation measure. *SIGIR '07 Proceedings of the 30th annual international ACM SIGIR conference on Research and development in information retrieval*, Jan.

M Georgescul, A Clark, and S Armstrong. 2009. An analysis of quantitative aspects in the evaluation of thematic segmentation algorithms. *SigDIAL '06 Proceedings of the 7th SIGdial Workshop on Discourse and Dialogue*, Jan.

J Jancsary, J Matiasek, and H Trost. 2008. Revealing the structure of medical dictations with conditional random fields. *EMNLP '08 Proceedings of the Conference on Empirical Methods in Natural Language Processing*, Jan.

S Lamprier, T Amghar, and B Levrat. 2008. On evaluation methodologies for text segmentation algorithms. *19th IEEE International Conference on Tools with Artificial Intelligence - Vol.2*, Jan.

I Malioutov and R Barzilay. 2006. Minimum cut model for spoken lecture segmentation. *ACL-44 Proceedings of the 21st International Conference on Computational Linguistics and the 44th annual meeting of the Association for Computational Linguistics*, Jan.

I Malioutov, A Park, R Barzilay, and R Glass. 2007. Making sense of sound: Unsupervised topic segmentation over acoustic input. *Proceeding of the Annual Meeting of the Association for Computation Linguistics 2007*, Jan.

L Pevzner and M Hearst. 2002. A critique and improvement of an evaluation metric for text segmentation. *Computational Linguistics*, Jan.

N Stokes. 2003. Spoken and written news story segmentation using lexical chains. *Proceedings of the 2003 Conference of the North American Chapter of the Association for Computational Linguistics on Human Language Technology: HLT-NAACL2003 Student Research Workshop*, Jan.

G2P Conversion of Proper Names Using Word Origin Information

Sonjia Waxmonsky and **Sravana Reddy**
Department of Computer Science
The University of Chicago
Chicago, IL 60637
{wax, sravana}@cs.uchicago.edu

Abstract

Motivated by the fact that the pronunciation of a name may be influenced by its language of origin, we present methods to improve pronunciation prediction of proper names using word origin information. We train grapheme-to-phoneme (G2P) models on language-specific data sets and interpolate the outputs. We perform experiments on US surnames, a data set where word origin variation occurs naturally. Our methods can be used with any G2P algorithm that outputs posterior probabilities of phoneme sequences for a given word.

1 Introduction

Speakers can often associate proper names with their language of origin, even when the words have not been seen before. For example, many English speakers will recognize that *Makowski* and *Masiello* are Polish and Italian respectively, without prior knowledge of either name. Such recognition is important for language processing tasks since the pronunciations of out-of-vocabulary (OOV) words may depend on the language of origin. For example, as noted by Llitjós (2001), 'sch' is likely to be pronounced as /sh/ for German-origin names (*Schoenenberg*) and /sk/ for Italian-origin words (*Schiavone*).

In this work, we apply word origin recognition to grapheme-to-phoneme (G2P) conversion, the task of predicting the phonemic representation of a word given its written form. We specifically study G2P conversion for personal surnames, a domain where OOVs are common and expected.

Our goal is to show how word origin information can be used to train language-specific G2P models, and how output from these models can be combined to improve prediction of the best pronunciation of a name. We deal with data sparsity in rare language classes by re-weighting the output of the language-specific and language-independent models.

2 Previous Work

Llitjós (2001) applies word origin information to pronunciation modeling for speech synthesis. Here, a CART decision tree system is presented for G2P conversion that maps letters to phonemes using local context. Experiments use a data set of US surnames that naturally draws from a diverse set of origin languages, and show that the inclusion of word origin features in the model improves pronunciation accuracy. We use similar data, as described in §4.1.

Some works on lexical modeling for speech recognition also make use of word origin. Here, the focus is on expanding the vocabulary of an ASR system rather than choosing a single best pronunciation. Maison et al. (2003) train language-specific G2P models for eight languages and output pronunciations to augment a baseline lexicon. This augmented lexicon outperforms a handcrafted lexicon in ASR experiments; error reduction is highest for foreign names spoken by native speakers of the origin language. Cremelie and ten Bosch (2001) carry out a similar lexicon augmentation, and make use of *penalty weighting*, with different penalties for pronunciations generated by the language-specific and language-independent G2P models.

The problem of machine transliteration is closely related to grapheme-to-phoneme conversion. Many transliteration systems (Khapra and Bhattacharyya, 2009; Bose and Sarkar, 2009; Bhargava and Kondrak, 2010) use word origin information. The method described by Hagiwara and Sekine (2011) is similar to our work, except that (a) we use a data set where multiple languages of origin occur naturally, rather than creating language-specific lists and merging them into a single set, and (b) we consider methods of smoothing against a language-independent model to overcome the problems of data sparsity and errors in word origin recognition.

3 Language-Aware G2P

Our methods are designed to be used with any statistical G2P system that produces the posterior probability $\Pr(\bar{\phi}|\bar{g})$ of a phoneme sequence $\bar{\phi}$ for a word (grapheme sequence) $\bar{g}$ (or a score that can be normalized to give a probability). The most likely pronunciation of a word is taken to be $\arg\max_{\bar{\phi}} \Pr(\bar{\phi}|\bar{g})$.

Our baseline is a single G2P model that is trained on all available training data. We train additional models on language-specific training subsets and incorporate the output of these models to re-estimate $\Pr(\bar{\phi}|\bar{g})$, which involves the following steps:

1. Train a supervised word origin classifier to predict $\Pr(l|w)$ for all $l \in L$, the set of languages in our hand-labeled word origin training set.
2. Train G2P models for each $l \in L$. Each model m_l is trained on words with $\Pr(l|w)$ greater than some threshold α. Here, we use $\alpha = 0.7$.
3. For each word w in the test set, generate candidate transcriptions from model m_l for each language with nonzero $\Pr(l|w)$. Re-estimate $\Pr(\bar{\phi}|\bar{g})$ by interpolating the outputs of the language-specific models. We may also use the output of the language-independent model.

We elaborate on our approaches to Steps 1 and 3.

3.1 Step 1: Word origin modeling

We apply a sequential conditional model to predict $\Pr(l|w)$, the probability of a language class given the word. A similar Maximum Entropy model is presented by Chen and Maison (2003), where features are the presence or absence of a given character n-gram in w. In our approach, feature functions are defined at character positions rather than over the entire word. Specifically, for word w_j composed of character sequence $c_1 \ldots c_m$ of length m (including start and end symbols), binary features test for the presence or absence of an n-gram *context* at each position m. A context is the presence of a character n-gram starting or ending at position m. Model features are represented as:

$$f_i(w, m, l_k) = \begin{cases} 1, & \text{if } lang(w) = l_k \text{ and context} \\ & i \text{ is present at position } m \\ 0, & \text{otherwise} \end{cases} \quad (1)$$

Then, for $w_j = c_i \ldots c_m$:

$$\Pr(l_k|w_j) = \frac{\exp \sum_m \sum_i \lambda_i f_i(c_m, l_k)}{\mathbf{Z}} \quad (2)$$

where $\mathbf{Z} = \sum_j \exp \sum_m \sum_i \lambda_i f_i(c_m, l_k)$ is a normalization factor. In practice, we can implement this model as a CRF, where a language label is applied at each character position rather than for the word.

While all the language labels in a sequence need not be the same, we find only a handful of words where a transition occurs from one language label to another within a word. For these cases, we take the label of the last character in the word as the language of origin. Experiments comparing this sequential Maximum Entropy method with other word origin classifiers are described by Waxmonsky (2011).

3.2 Step 3: Re-weighting of G2P output

We test two methods of re-weighting $\Pr(\bar{\phi}|\bar{g})$ using the word origin estimation and the output of language-specific G2P models.

Method A uses only language-specific models:

$$\tilde{\Pr}(\bar{\phi}|\bar{g}) = \sum_{l \in L} \Pr(\bar{\phi}|\bar{g}, l) \Pr(l|g) \quad (3)$$

where $\Pr(\bar{\phi}|\bar{g}, l)$ is estimated by model m_l.

Method B With the previous method, names from infrequent classes suffer from data sparsity. We therefore smooth with the output P_I of the baseline language-independent model.

$$\tilde{\Pr}(\bar{\phi}|\bar{g}) = \sigma \Pr_I(\bar{\phi}|\bar{g}) + (1-\sigma) \sum_{l \in L} \Pr(\bar{\phi}|\bar{g}, l) \Pr(l|g) \quad (4)$$

The factor σ is tuned on a development set.

Language Class	Train Count	Test Count	Base -line	(A)	(B)
British	16.1k	2111	71.8	73.1	**73.9**
German	8360	1109	75.8	74.2	**78.2**
Italian	3358	447	61.7	**66.2**	65.1
Slavic	1658	232	50.9	49.6	**51.7**
Spanish	1460	246	44.7	41.5	**48.0**
French	1143	177	42.9	42.4	**45.2**
Dutch	468	82	**70.7**	52.4	68.3
Scandin.	393	61	**77.1**	60.7	72.1
Japanese	116	23	73.9	52.2	**78.3**
Arabic	68	18	33.3	11.1	**38.9**
Portug.	34	4	25.0	25.0	**50.0**
Hungarian	28	3	**100.0**	66.7	**100.0**
Other	431	72	55.6	54.2	**59.7**
All			67.8	67.4	**70.0**

Table 1: G2P word accuracy for various weighting methods using a character-based word origin model.

4 Experiments

4.1 Data

We assemble a data set of surnames that occur frequently in the United States. Since surnames are often "Americanized" in their written and phonemic forms, our goal is to model how a name is most likely to be pronounced in standard US English rather than in its language of origin.

We consider the 50,000 most frequent surnames in the 1990 census[1], and extract those entries that also appear in the CMU Pronouncing Dictionary[2], giving us a set of 45,841 surnames with their phoneme representations transcribed in the Arpabet symbol set. We divide this data 80/10/10 into train, test, and development sets.

To build a word origin classification training set, we randomly select 3,000 surnames from the same census lists, and label by hand the *most likely* language of origin of each name when it occurs in the US. Labeling was done primarily using the *Dictionary of American Family Names* (Hanks, 2003) and Ellis Island immigration records.[3] We find that, in many cases, a surname cannot be attributed to a single language but can be assigned to a set of languages related by geography and language family. For example, we discovered several surnames that could be ambiguously labeled as English, Scottish, or Irish in origin. For languages that are frequently confusable, we create a single language group to be used as a class label. Here, we use groups for British Isles, Slavic, and Scandinavian languages. Names of undetermined origin are removed, leaving a final training set of 2,795 labeled surnames and 33 different language classes. We have made this annotated word origin data publicly available for future research.[4]

In these experiments, we use surnames from the 12 language classes that contain at least 10 hand-labeled words, and merge the remaining languages into an "Other" class. Table 1 shows the final language classes used. Unlike the training sets, we do not remove names with ambiguous or unknown origin from the test set, so our G2P system is also evaluated on the ambiguous names.

4.2 Results

The Sequitur G2P algorithm (Bisani and Ney, 2008) is used for all our experiments.

We use the CMU Dictionary as the gold standard, with the assumption that it contains the standard pronunciations in US English. While surnames may have multiple valid pronunciations, we make the simplifying assumption that a name has one best pronunciation. Evaluation is done on the test set of 4,585 names from the CMU Dictionary.

Table 1 shows G2P accuracy for the baseline system and Methods A and B. Test data is partitioned by the most likely language of origin.

We see that Method A, which uses only language-specific G2P models, has lower overall accuracy than the baseline. We attribute this to data sparsity introduced by dividing the training set by language. With the exception of British and German, language-specific training set sizes are less than 10% the size of the baseline training set of 37k names. Another cause of the lowered performance is likely due to errors made by our word origin model.

Examining results for individual language classes for Method A, we see that Italian and British are

[1] `http://www.census.gov/genealogy/names/`

[2] `http://www.speech.cs.cmu.edu/cgi-bin/cmudict`

[3] `http://www.ellisisland.org`

[4] The data may be downloaded from `http://people.cs.uchicago.edu/~wax/wordorigin/`.

Language	Surname	Baseline	Method B
Italian	Carcione	K AA R S IY OW N IY	K AA R CH OW N IY
	Cuttino	K AH T IY N OW	K UW T IY N OW
	Lubrano	L AH B R AA N OW	L UW B R AA N OW
	Pesola	P EH S AH L AH	P EH S OW L AH
Slavic	Kotula	K OW T UW L AH	K AH T UW L AH
	Jaworowski	JH AH W ER AO F S K IY	Y AH W ER AO F S K IY
	Lisak	L IY S AH K	L IH S AH K
	Wasik	W AA S IH K	V AA S IH K
Spanish	Bencivenga	B EH N S IH V IH N G AH	B EH N CH IY V EH NG G AH
	Vivona	V IH V OW N AH	V IY V OW N AH
	Zavadil	Z AA V AA D AH L	Z AA V AA D IY L

Table 2: Sample G2P output from the Baseline (language-independent) and Method B systems. Language labels shown here are the $\arg\max_l P(l|w)$ using the character-based word origin model. Phoneme symbols are from an Arpabet-based alphabet, as used in the CMU Pronouncing Dictionary.

the only language classes where accuracy improves. For Italian, we attribute this to two factors: high divergence in pronunciation from US English, and the availability of enough training data to build a successful language-specific model. In the case of British, a language-specific model removes foreign words but leaves enough training data to model the language sufficiently.

Method B shows accuracy gains of 2.2%, with gains for almost all language classes except Dutch and Scandinavian. This is probably because names in these two classes have almost standard US English pronunciations, and are already well-modeled by a language-independent model.

We next look at some sample outputs from our G2P systems. Table 2 shows names where Method B generated the gold standard pronunciation and the baseline system did not. For the Italian and Spanish sets, we see that the letter-to-phoneme mappings produced by Method B are indicative of the language of origin: (c → /CH/) in *Carcione*, (u → /UW/) in *Cuttino*, (o → /OW/) in *Pesola*, and (i → /IY/) in *Zavadil* and *Vivona*. Interestingly, the name *Bencivenga* is categorized as Spanish but appears with the letter-to-phoneme mapping (c → /CH/), which corresponds to Italian as the language of origin. We found other examples of the (c → /CH/) mappings, indicating that Italian-origin names have been folded into Spanish data. This is not surprising since Spanish and Italian names have high confusion with each other. Effectively, our word origin model produced a noisy Spanish G2P training set, but the re-weighted G2P system is robust to these errors.

We see examples in the Slavic set where the gold standard dictionary pronunciation is partially but not completely Americanized. In *Jaworowski*, we have the mappings (j → /Y/) and (w → /F/), both of which are derived from the original Polish pronunciation. But for the same name, we also have (w → /W/) rather than (w → /V/), although the latter is truer to the original Polish. This illustrates one of the goals of our project, which is is to capture these patterns of Americanization as they occur in the data.

5 Conclusion

We apply word origin modeling to grapheme-to-phoneme conversion, interpolating between language-independent and language-specific probabilistic grapheme-to-phoneme models. We find that our system outperforms the baseline in predicting Americanized surname pronunciations and captures several letter-to-phoneme features that are specific to the language of origin.

Our method operates as a wrapper around G2P output without modifying the underlying algorithm, and therefore can be applied to any state-of-the-art G2P system that outputs posterior probabilities of phoneme sequences for a word.

Future work will consider unsupervised or semi-supervised approaches to word origin recognition for this task, and methods to tune the smoothing weights σ at the language rather than the global level.

References

Aditya Bhargava and Grzegorz Kondrak. 2010. Language identification of names with SVMs. In *Proceedings of NAACL*.

Maximilian Bisani and Hermann Ney. 2008. Joint-sequence models for grapheme-to-phoneme conversion. *Speech Communication*.

Dipankar Bose and Sudeshna Sarkar. 2009. Learning multi character alignment rules and classification of training data for transliteration. In *Proceedings of the ACL Named Entities Workshop*.

Stanley F. Chen and Benoît Maison. 2003. Using place name data to train language identification models. In *Proceedings of Eurospeech*.

Nick Cremelie and Louis ten Bosch. 2001. Improving the recognition of foreign names and non-native speech by combining multiple grapheme-to-phoneme converters. In *Proceedings of ITRW on Adaptation Methods for Speech Recognition*.

Masato Hagiwara and Satoshi Sekine. 2011. Latent class transliteration based on source language origin. In *Proceedings of ACL*.

Patrick Hanks. 2003. Dictionary of American family names. *New York : Oxford University Press*.

Mitesh M. Khapra and Pushpak Bhattacharyya. 2009. Improving transliteration accuracy using word-origin detection and lexicon lookup. In *Proceedings of the ACL Named Entities Workshop*.

Ariadna Font Llitjós. 2001. Improving pronunciation accuracy of proper names with language origin classes. Master's thesis, Carnegie Mellon University.

Benoît Maison, Stanley F. Chen, and Paul S. Cohen. 2003. Pronunciation modeling for names of foreign origin. In *Proceedings of ASRU*.

Sonjia Waxmonsky. 2011. *Natural language processing for named entities with word-internal information*. Ph.D. thesis, University of Chicago.

Evaluating a Morphological Analyser of Inuktitut

Jeremy Nicholson†, Trevor Cohn‡ and Timothy Baldwin†
†Department of Computing and Information Systems, The University of Melbourne, Australia
‡Department of Computer Science, The University of Sheffield, UK
jeremymn@csse.unimelb.edu.au, tcohn@dcs.shef.ac.uk, tb@ldwin.net

Abstract

We evaluate the performance of an morphological analyser for Inuktitut across a medium-sized corpus, where it produces a useful analysis for two out of every three types. We then compare its segmentation to that of simpler approaches to morphology, and use these as a pre-processing step to a word alignment task. Our observations show that the richer approaches provide little as compared to simply finding the head, which is more in line with the particularities of the task.

1 Introduction

In this work, we evaluate a morphological analyser of Inuktitut, whose polysynthetic morphosyntax can cause particular problems for natural language processing; but our observations are also relevant to other languages with rich morphological systems. The existing NLP task for Inuktitut is that of word alignment (Martin et al., 2005), where Inuktitut tokens align to entire English clauses. While Langlais et al. (2005) theorises that a morphological analyser could aid in this task, we observed little to no improvement over a baseline model by making use of its segmentation. Nonetheless, morphological analysis does provide a great deal of information, but the task structure tends to disprefer its contribution.

2 Background

2.1 Inuktitut

Inuktitut is a macrolanguage of many more-or-less mutually intelligible dialects (Gordon, 2005). The morphosyntax of Inuktitut is particularly marked by a rich polysynthetic suffixing morphology, including incorporation of arguments into verbal tokens, as in *natsiviniqtulauqsimavilli* in (1). This phenomenon causes an individual token in Inuktitut to be approximately equivalent to an entire clause in English.

(1) *natsiq-* *-viniq-* *-tuq-* *-lauq-* *-sima-*
seal meat eat before ever
-vit *-li*
INT-2s but
"But have you ever eaten seal meat before?"

Lowe (1996) analyses the morphology as a four-place relationship: one head morpheme, zero or more lexical morphemes, one or more grammatical morphemes, and an optional enclitic. The morphotactics causes, amongst other phenomena, the final consonant of a morpheme to assimilate the manner of the initial consonant of the following morpheme (as in *-villi*), or to be dropped (as in *natsiviniq-*). Consequently, morphemes are not readily accessible from the realised surface form, thereby motivating the use of a morphological analyser.

2.2 Morphological analysis

For many languages with a less rich morphology than Inuktitut, an inflectional lexicon is often adequate for morphological analysis (for example, CELEX for English (Burnage, 1990), Le*fff* for French (Sagot et al., 2006) or Adolphs (2008) for German). Another typical approach is to perform morphological analysis at the same time as POS tagging (as in Hajič and Hladká (1998) for the fusional morphology in Czech), as it is often the case that determining the part-of-speech and choosing the appropriate inflectional paradigm are closely linked.

For highly inflecting languages more generally, morphological analysis is often treated as a segment-and-normalise problem, amenable to analysis by weighted finite state transducer (wFST), for example, Creutz and Lagus (2002) for Finnish.

3 Resources

3.1 A morphological analyser for Inuktitut

The main resource that we are evaluating in this work is a morphological analyser of Inuktitut called Uqa·Ila·Ut.[1] It is a rule-based system based on regular morphological variations of about 3200 head, 350 lexical, and 1500 grammatical morphemes, with heuristics for ranking the various readings. The head and lexical morphemes are collated with glosses in both English and French.

3.2 Word alignment

The training corpus we use in our experiments is a sentence-aligned segment of the Nunavut Hansards (Martin et al., 2003). The corpus consists of about 340K sentences, which comprise about 4.0M English tokens, and 2.2M Inuktitut. The challenge of the morphology becomes apparent when we contrast these figures with the types: about 416K for Inuktitut, but only 27K for English. On average, there are only 5 token instances per Inuktitut type; some 338K types (81%) are singletons.

Inuktitut formed part of one of the shared tasks in the ACL 2005 workshop on building and using parallel texts (Martin et al., 2005); for this, the above corpus was simplistically tokenised, and used as unsupervised training data. 100 sentences from this corpus were phrasally aligned by Inuit annotators. These were then extended into word alignments, where phrasal alignments of one token in both the source and target were (generally) called sure alignments, and one-to-many or many-to-many mappings were extended to their cartesian product, and called probable. The test set was composed of 75 of these sentences (about 2K English tokens, 800 Inuktitut tokens, 293 gold-standard sure alignments, and 1679 probable), which we use to evaluate word alignments.

Our treatment of the alignment problem is most similar to Schafer and Drábek (2005) who examine four systems: GIZA++ models (Och and Ney, 2000) for each source-target direction, another where the Inuktitut input has been syllabised, and a wFST model. They observe that aggregating these results through voting can create a very competitive system for Inuktitut word alignment.

4 Experimental approach

We used an out-of-the-box implementation of the Berkeley Aligner (DeNero and Klein, 2007), a competitive word alignment system, to construct an unsupervised alignment over the 75 test sentences, based on the larger training corpus. The default implementation of the system involves two jointly-trained HMMs (one for each source-target direction) over five iterations,[2] with so-called competitive thresholding in the decoding step; these are more fully described in DeNero and Klein (2007) and Liang et al. (2006).

Our approach examines morphological pre-processing of the Inuktitut training and test sets, with the idea of leveraging the morphological information into a corpus which is more amenable to alignment. The raw corpus appears to be under-segmented, where data sparseness from the many singletons would prevent reliable alignments. Segmentation might aid in this process by making sub-lexical units with semantic overlap transparent to the alignment system, so that types appear to have a greater frequency through the data. Through this, we attempt to examine the hypothesis that one-to-one alignments between English and Inuktitut would hold with the right segmentation. On the other hand, oversegmentation (for example, down to the character level) can leave the resulting sub-lexical items semantically meaningless and cause spurious matches.

We consider five different ways of tackling Inuktitut morphology:

1. **None**: simply treat each Inuktitut token as a monolithic entity. This is our baseline approach.

[1] `http://inuktitutcomputing.ca/Uqailaut/en/IMA.html`

[2] Better performance was observed with three iterations, but we preferred to maintain the default parameters of the system.

2. **Head**: attempt to separate the head morpheme from the non-head periphery. Our hypothesis is that we will be able to align the clausal head more reliably, as it tends to correspond to a single English token more reliably than the other morphemes, which may not be realised in the same manner in English. Head morphs in Inuktitut correspond to the first one or two syllables of a token; we treated them uniformly as two syllables, as other values caused a substantial degredation in performance.

3. **Syllabification**: treat the text as if Inuktitut had isolating morphology, and transform each token into a series of single-syllable pseudo-morphs. This effectively turns the task on its head, from a primarily one Inukitut-to-many English token problem to that of one English-to-many Inuktitut. Despite the overzealousness of this approach (as most Inuktitut morphemes are polysyllabic, and consequently there will be many plausible but spurious matches between tokens that share a syllable but no semantics), Schafer and Drábek (2005) observed it to be quite competitive.

4. **Morphs**: segment each word into morphs, thereby treating the morphology problem as pure segmentation. This uses the top output of the morphological analyser as the oracle segmentation of each Inuktitut token.

5. **Morphemes**: as previous, except include the normalisation of each morph to a morpheme, as provided by the morphological analyser, as a sort of "lemmatisation" step. The major advantage over the morph approach is due to the regular morphophonemic effects in Inuktitut, which cause equivalent morphemes to have different surface realisations.

5 Results

5.1 Analyser

In our analysis, the morphological analyser finds at least one reading for about 218K (= about 65%) of the Inuktitut types. Of the 120K types without readings, resource contraints account for about 11K. [3] Another 6K types caused difficulties due to punctuation, numerical characters or encoding issues, all of which could be handled through more sophisticated tokenisation.

A more interesting cause of gaps for the analyser was typographical errors (e.g. **kiinaujaqtaaruasirnirmut* for *kiinaujaqtaarusiarnirmut* "requests for proposals"). This was often due to consonant gemination, where it was either missing (e.g. *nunavummut* "in Nunavut" appeared in the corpus as **nunavumut*) or added (e.g. **tamakkununnga* instead of *tamakkununga* "at these ones here"). While one might expect these kinds of error to be rare, because Inuktitut has an orthography that closely reflects pronunciation, they instead are common, which means that the morphological analyser should probably accept incorrect gemination with a lower weighting.

More difficult to analyse directly is the impact of foreign words (particularly names) — these are typically subjectively transliterated based on Inuktitut morphophonology. Schafer and Drábek (2005) use these as motivation for an approach based on a wFST, but found few instances to analyse its accuracy. Finally, there are certainly missing roots, and possibly some missing affixes as well, for example *pirru-* "accident" (cf. *pirruaqi-* "to have an accident"). Finding these automatically remains as future work.

As for tokens, we briefly analysed the 768 tokens in the test set, of which 228 (30%) were not given a reading. Punctuation (typically commas and periods) account for 117 of these, and numbers another 7. Consonant gemination and foreign words cause gaps for at least 16 and 6 tokens, respectively (that we could readily identify).

5.2 Word Alignment

Following Och and Ney (2000), we assess using alignment error rate (AER) and define precision with respect to the probable set, and recall with respect to

[3] We only attempted to parse tokens of 30 characters or shorter; longer tokens tended to cause exceptions — this could presumably be improved with a more efficient analyser. While the number of analyses will continue to grow with the token length, which has implications in agglutinative languages, here there are only about 300 tokens of length greater than 40.

Approach	Prec	Rec	AER
None	0.783	0.863	0.195
Head	0.797	0.922	0.176
Syllabification	0.789	0.881	0.192
Morphs	0.777	0.860	0.207
Morphemes	0.777	0.863	0.206
S&D E-I	0.646	0.829	0.327
S&D Syll	0.849	0.826	0.156

Table 1: Precision, recall, and alignment error rate for various approaches to morphology, with Schafer and Drábek (2005) for comparison

the sure set.

We present word alignment results of the various methods — contrasted with Schafer and Drábek (2005) — in Table 1. The striking result is in terms of statistical significance: according to χ^2, most of the various approaches to morphology fail to give a significantly ($P < 0.05$) different result to the baseline system of using entire tokens. For comparison, whereas our baseline system is significantly better than the baseline system of Schafer and Drábek (2005) — which demonstrates the value that the Berkeley Aligner provides by training in both source-target directions — their syllablised model is significantly superior in precision ($P < 0.001$), while their recall is still worse than our model ($P < 0.05$). Intuitively, this seems to indicate that their model is making fewer judgments, but actually the opposite is true. It seems that their model achieves better performance than ours because it leverages many candidate probable alignments into high quality aggregates using a most-likely heuristic on the mapping of Inuktitut syllables to English words, whereas the Berkeley Aligner culls the candidate set in joint training.

Of the approaches toward morphology that we consider, only the recall of the head–based system improves upon the baseline ($P < 0.025$). This squares with our intuitions, where segmenting the root morpheme from the larger token allows for more effective alignment of the semantically straightforward sure alignments.

The three systems that involve a finer segmentation over the tokens are equivalent in performance to the baseline system. The oversegmentation seemed to caused the alignment system to abandon an implicit preference for monotonicity of the order of tokens between the source and target (which holds pretty well for the baseline system over the test data, thanks partly to the fidelity-focused structure of a Hansard corpus): presumably because the aligner perceives lexical similarity between disparate tokens due to them sharing a sublexical unit. This relaxing of monotonicity is most apparent for punctuation, where a comma with a correct alignment in the baseline becomes incorrectly aligned to a different comma in the sentence for the segmented system.

6 Conclusion

The only improvement toward the task that we observed using morphological approaches is that of head segmentation, where using two syllables as a head-surrogate allowed us to capture more of the sure (one-to-one) alignments in the test set. One possible extension would be to take the head morpheme as given the analyser, rather than the somewhat arbitrary syllabic approach. For other languages with rich morphology, it may be similarly valuable to target substantives for segmentation to improve alignment.

All in all, it appears that the lexical encoding of morphology of Inuktitut is so strikingly different than English, that the assumption of Inuktitut morphemes aligning to English words is untrue or at least unfindable within the current framework. Numerous common morphemes have no English equivalent, for example, *-liaq-* "to go to" which seems to act as a light verb, or *-niq-*, a (re-)nominaliser for abstract nominals. While the output of the morphological analyser could probably be used more effectively in other tasks, there are still important impacts in word alignment and machine translation, including leveraging a dictionary (which is based on morphemes, not tokens, and as such requires segmentation and normalisation) or considering grammatical forms for syntactic approaches.

References

Peter Adolphs. 2008. Acquiring a poor man's inflectional lexicon for German. In *Proc. of the 6th LREC*,

Marrakech, Morocco.

Gavin Burnage. 1990. CELEX: A guide for users. Technical report, University of Nijmegen.

Mathias Creutz and Krista Lagus. 2002. Unsupervised discovery of morphemes. In *Proc. of the 6th Workshop of ACL SIGPHON*, pages 21–30, Philadelphia, USA.

John DeNero and Dan Klein. 2007. Tailoring word alignments to syntactic machine translation. In *Proc. of the 45th Annual Meeting of the ACL*, pages 17–24, Prague, Czech Republic.

Raymund G. Gordon, Jr, editor. 2005. *Ethnologue: Languages of the World, Fifteenth Edition*. SIL International.

Jan Hajič and Barbora Hladká. 1998. Tagging inflective languages: Prediction of morphological categories for a rich, structured tagset. In *Proc. of the 36th Annual Meeting of the ACL and 17th International Conference on COLING*, pages 483–490, Montréal, Canada.

Philippe Langlais, Fabrizio Gotti, and Guihong Cao. 2005. NUKTI: English-Inuktitut word alignment system description. In *Proc. of the ACL Workshop on Building and Using Parallel Texts*, pages 75–78, Ann Arbor, USA.

Percy Liang, Ben Taskar, and Dan Klein. 2006. Alignment by agreement. In *Proc. of the HLT Conference of the NAACL*, pages 104–111, New York City, USA.

Ronald Lowe. 1996. Grammatical sketches: Inuktitut. In Jacques Maurais, editor, *Quebec's Aboriginal Languages: History, Planning and Development*, pages 204–232. Multilingual Matters.

Joel Martin, Howard Johnson, Benoit Farley, and Anna Maclachlan. 2003. Aligning and using an English-Inuktitut parallel corpus. In *Proc. of the HLT-NAACL 2003 Workshop on Building and Using Parallel Texts*, pages 115–118, Edmonton, Canada.

Joel Martin, Rada Mihalcea, and Ted Pedersen. 2005. Word alignment for languages with scarce resources. In *Proc. of the ACL Workshop on Building and Using Parallel Texts*, pages 65–74, Ann Arbor, USA.

Franz Josef Och and Hermann Ney. 2000. Improved statistical alignment models. In *Proc. of the 38th Annual Meeting of the ACL*, pages 440–447, Saarbrücken, Germany.

Benoît Sagot, Lionel Clément, Eric Villemonte de La Clergerie, and Pierre Boullier. 2006. The *Lefff* syntactic lexicon for French: Architecture, acquisition, use. In *Proc. of the 5th LREC*, pages 1348–1351, Genoa, Italy.

Charles Schafer and Elliott Drábek. 2005. Models for Inuktitut-English word alignment. In *Proc. of the ACL Workshop on Building and Using Parallel Texts*, pages 79–82, Ann Arbor, USA.

Intra-Speaker Topic Modeling for Improved Multi-Party Meeting Summarization with Integrated Random Walk

Yun-Nung Chen and Florian Metze
School of Computer Science, Carnegie Mellon University
5000 Forbes Avenue, Pittsburgh, PA 15213-3891, USA
{yvchen, fmetze}@cs.cmu.edu

Abstract

This paper proposes an improved approach to extractive summarization of spoken multi-party interaction, in which integrated random walk is performed on a graph constructed on topical/ lexical relations. Each utterance is represented as a node of the graph, and the edges' weights are computed from the topical similarity between the utterances, evaluated using probabilistic latent semantic analysis (PLSA), and from word overlap. We model intra-speaker topics by partially sharing the topics from the same speaker in the graph. In this paper, we perform experiments on automatically and manually generated transcripts. For automatic transcripts, our results show that intra speaker topic sharing and integrating topical/ lexical relations can help include the important utterances.

1 Introduction

Speech summarization is an active and important topic of research (Lee and Chen, 2005), because multimedia/ spoken documents are more difficult to browse than text or image content. While earlier work was focused primarily on broadcast news content, recent effort has been increasingly directed to new domains such as lectures (Glass et al., 2007; Chen et al., 2011) and multi-party interaction (Banerjee and Rudnicky, 2008; Liu and Liu, 2010). We describe experiments on multi-party interaction found in meeting recordings, performing extractive summarization (Liu et al., 2010) on transcripts generated by automatic speech recognition (ASR) and human annotators.

Graph-based methods for computing lexical centrality as importance to extract summaries (Erkan and Radev, 2004) have been investigated in the context of text summarization. Some works focus on maximizing coverage of summaries using the objective function (Gillick, 2011). Speech summarization carries intrinsic difficulties due to the presence of recognition errors, spontaneous speech effect, and lack of segmentation. A general approach has been found very successful (Furui et al., 2004), in which each utterance in the document d, $U = t_1 t_2 ... t_i ... t_n$, represented as a sequence of terms t_i, is given an importance score:

$$I(U,d) = \frac{1}{n}\sum_{i=1}^{n}[\lambda_1 s(t_i,d) + \lambda_2 l(t_i) + \lambda_3 c(t_i) + \lambda_4 g(t_i)] + \lambda_5 b(U), \quad (1)$$

where $s(t_i,d)$, $l(t_i)$, $c(t_i)$, $g(t_i)$ are respectively some statistical measure (such as TF-IDF), linguistic measure (e.g., different part-of-speech tags are given different weights), confidence score and N-gram score for the term t_i, and $b(U)$ is calculated from the grammatical structure of the utterance U, and $\lambda_1, \lambda_2, \lambda_3, \lambda_4$ and λ_5 are weighting parameters. For each document, the utterances to be used in the summary are then selected based on this score.

In recent work, Chen (2011) proposed a graphical structure to rescore $I(U,d)$, which can model the topical coherence between utterances using random walk within documents. Similarly, we now use a graph-based approach to consider the importance of terms and the similarity between utterances, where topical and lexical similarity are integrated in the graph, so that utterances topically or lexically similar to more important utterances are given higher scores. Using topical similarity can compensate the negative effects of recognition errors on similarity evaluated on word overlap to some extent. In addition, this paper proposes an approach of modeling intra-speaker topics in the graph to improve meeting summarization (Garg et al., 2009) using information from multi-party interaction, which is not available in lectures or broadcast news.

2 Proposed Approach

We apply word stemming and noise utterance filtering for utterances in all meetings. Then we construct a graph to compute the importance of all utterances.

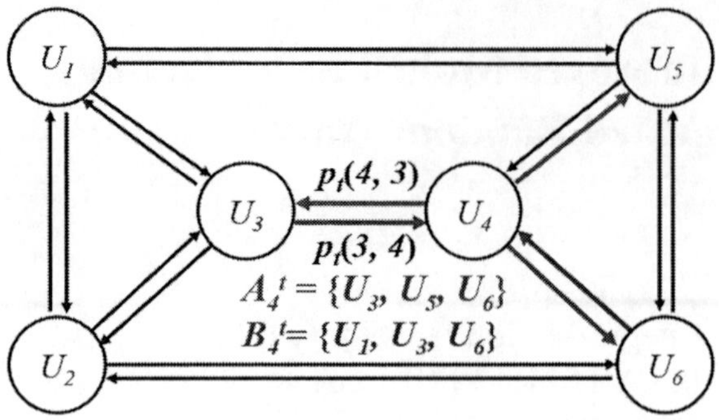

Figure 1: A simplified example of the graph considered.

We formulate the utterance selection problem as random walk on a directed graph, in which each utterance is a node and the edges between them are weighted by topical and lexical similarity. The basic idea is that an utterance similar to more important utterances should be more important (Chen et al., 2011). We formulate two types of directed edge, topical edges and lexical edges, which are weighted by topical and lexical similarity respectively. We then keep only the top N outgoing edges with the highest weights from each node, while consider incoming edges to each node for importance propagation in the graph. A simplified example for such a graph with topical edges is in Figure 1, in which A_i^t and B_i^t are the sets of neighbors of the node U_i connected respectively by outgoing and incoming topical edges.

2.1 Parameters from PLSA

Probabilistic latent semantic analysis (PLSA) (Hofmann, 1999) has been widely used to analyze the semantics of documents based on a set of latent topics. Given a set of documents $\{d_j, j = 1, 2, ..., J\}$ and all terms $\{t_i, i = 1, 2, ..., M\}$ they include, PLSA uses a set of latent topic variables, $\{T_k, k = 1, 2, ..., K\}$, to characterize the "term-document" co-occurrence relationships. The PLSA model can be optimized with EM algorithm by maximizing a likelihood function. We utilize two parameters from PLSA, latent topic significance (LTS) and latent topic entropy (LTE) (Kong and Lee, 2011) in the paper.

Latent Topic Significance (LTS) for a given term t_i with respect to a topic T_k can be defined as

$$\mathrm{LTS}_{t_i}(T_k) = \frac{\sum_{d_j \in D} n(t_i, d_j) P(T_k \mid d_j)}{\sum_{d_j \in D} n(t_i, d_j)[1 - P(T_k \mid d_j)]}, \quad (2)$$

where $n(t_i, d_j)$ is the occurrence count of term t_i in a document d_j. Thus, a higher $\mathrm{LTS}_{t_i}(T_k)$ indicates the term t_i is more significant for the latent topic T_k.

Latent Topic Entropy (LTE), for a given term t_i can be calculated from the topic distribution $P(T_k \mid t_i)$:

$$\mathrm{LTE}(t_i) = -\sum_{k=1}^{K} P(T_k \mid t_i) \log P(T_k \mid t_i), \quad (3)$$

where the topic distribution $P(T_k \mid t_i)$ can be estimated from PLSA. $\mathrm{LTE}(t_i)$ is a measure of how the term t_i is focused on a few topics, so a lower latent topic entropy implies the term carries more topical information.

2.2 Statistical Measures of a Term

The statistical measure of a term t_i, $s(t_i, d)$ in (1) can be defined in terms of $\mathrm{LTE}(t_i)$ in (3) as

$$s(t_i, d) = \frac{\gamma \cdot n(t_i, d)}{\mathrm{LTE}(t_i)}, \quad (4)$$

where γ is a scaling factor such that $0 \leq s(t_i, d) \leq 1$; the score $s(t_i, d)$ is inversely proportion to the latent topic entropy $\mathrm{LTE}(t_i)$. Some works (Kong and Lee, 2011) showed that the use in (1) of $s(t_i, d)$ as defined in (4) outperformed the very successful "significance score" (Furui et al., 2004) in speech summarization; then, we use it as the baseline.

2.3 Similarity between Utterances

Within a document d, we can first compute the probability that the topic T_k is addressed by an utterance U_i:

$$P(T_k \mid U_i) = \frac{\sum_{t \in U_i} n(t, U_i) P(T_k \mid t)}{\sum_{t \in U_i} n(t, U_i)}. \quad (5)$$

Then an asymmetric topical similarity $\mathrm{TopicSim}(U_i, U_j)$ for utterances U_i to U_j (with direction $U_i \rightarrow U_j$) can be defined by accumulating $\mathrm{LTS}_t(T_k)$ in (2) weighted by $P(T_k \mid U_i)$ for all terms t in U_j over all latent topics:

$$\mathrm{TopicSim}(U_i, U_j) = \sum_{t \in U_j} \sum_{k=1}^{K} \mathrm{LTS}_t(T_k) P(T_k \mid U_i), \quad (6)$$

where the idea is very similar to the generative probability in IR. We call it generative significance of U_i given U_j.

Within a document d, the lexical similarity is the measure of word overlap between the utterance U_i and U_j. We compute $\mathrm{LexSim}(U_i, U_j)$ as the cosine similarity between two TF-IDF vectors from U_i and U_j like well-known LexRank (Erkan and Radev, 2004). Note that $\mathrm{LexSim}(U_i, U_j) = \mathrm{LexSim}(U_j, U_i)$

2.4 Intra-Speaker Topic Modeling

We assume a single speaker usually focuses on similar topics, so if an utterance is important, the scores of the utterances from the same speaker should be increased. Then we increase the similarity between the utterances from the same speaker to share the topics:

$$\mathrm{TopicSim}'_k(U_i, U_j) = \begin{cases} \mathrm{TopicSim}(U_i, U_j)^{1+w} \\ \text{, if } U_i \in S_k \text{ and } U_j \in S_k \\ \mathrm{TopicSim}(U_i, U_j)^{1-w} \\ \text{, otherwise} \end{cases} \quad (7)$$

where S_k is the set including all utterances from speaker k, and w is a weighting parameter for modeling the speaker relation, which means the level of coherence of topics within a single speaker. Here the topics from the same speaker can partially shared.

2.5 Integrated Random Walk

We modify random walk (Hsu and Kennedy, 2007; Chen et al., 2011) to integrate two types of similarity over the graph obtained above. $v(i)$ is the new score for node U_i, which is the interpolation of three scores, the normalized initial importance $r(i)$ for node U_i and the score contributed by all neighboring nodes U_j of node U_i weighted by $p_t(j,i)$ and $p_l(j,i)$,

$$\begin{aligned} v(i) &= (1-\alpha-\beta)r(i) \quad (8)\\ &+ \alpha \sum_{U_j \in B_i^t} p_t(j,i)v(j) + \beta \sum_{U_j \in B_i^l} p_l(j,i)v(j), \end{aligned}$$

where α and β are the interpolation weights, B_i^t is the set of neighbors connected to node U_i via topical incoming edges, B_i^l is the set of neighbors connected to node U_i via lexical incoming edges, and

$$r(i) = \frac{I(U_i,d)}{\sum_{U_j} I(U_j,d)} \quad (9)$$

is normalized importance scores of utterance U_i, $I(U_i,d)$ in (1). We normalize topical similarity by the total similarity summed over the set of outgoing edges, to produce the weight $p_t(j,i)$ for the edge from U_j to U_i on the graph. Similarly, $p_l(j,i)$ is normalized in lexical edges.

(8) can be iteratively solved with the approach very similar to that for the PageRank problem (Page et al., 1998). Let $\mathbf{v} = [v(i), i = 1,2,...,L]^{\mathbf{T}}$ and $\mathbf{r} = [r(i), i = 1,2,...,L]^{\mathbf{T}}$ be the column vectors for $v(i)$ and $r(i)$ for all utterances in the document, where L is the total number of utterances in the document d and $\mathbf{T}$ represents transpose. (8) then has a vector form below,

$$\begin{aligned} \mathbf{v} &= (1-\alpha-\beta)\mathbf{r} + \alpha\mathbf{P_t}\mathbf{v} + \beta\mathbf{P_l}\mathbf{v} \quad (10)\\ &= \left((1-\alpha-\beta)\mathbf{r}\mathbf{e}^{\mathbf{T}} + \alpha\mathbf{P_t} + \beta\mathbf{P_l}\right)\mathbf{v} = \mathbf{P}'\mathbf{v}, \end{aligned}$$

where $\mathbf{P_t}$ and $\mathbf{P_l}$ are $L \times L$ matrices of $p_t(j,i)$ and $p_l(j,i)$ respectively, and $\mathbf{e} = [1,1,...,1]^{\mathbf{T}}$. It has been shown that the solution $\mathbf{v}$ of (10) is the dominant eigenvector of $\mathbf{P}'$ (Langville and Meyer, 2006), or the eigenvector corresponding to the largest absolute eigenvalue of $\mathbf{P}'$. The solution $v(i)$ can then be obtained.

3 Experiments

3.1 Corpus

The corpus used in this research consists of a sequence of naturally occuring meetings, which featured largely overlapping participant sets and topics of discussion. For each meeting, SmartNotes (Banerjee and Rudnicky, 2008) was used to record both the audio from each participant as well as his notes. The meetings were transcribed both manually and using a speech recognizer; the word error rate is around 44%. In this paper we use 10 meetings held from April to June of 2006. On average each meeting had about 28 minutes of speech. Across these 10 meetings there were 6 unique participants; each meeting featured between 2 and 4 of these participants (average: 3.7). The total number of utterances is 9837 across 10 meetings. In this paper, we separate dev set (2 meetings) and test set (8 meetings). Dev set is used to tune the parameters such as α, β, w.

The reference summaries are given by the set of "noteworthy utterances": two annotators manually labelled the degree (three levels) of "noteworthiness" for each utterance, and we extract the utterances with the top level of "noteworthiness" to form the summary of each meeting. In the following experiments, for each meeting, we extract the top 30% number of terms as the summary.

3.2 Evaluation Metrics

Automated evaluation utilizes the standard DUC evaluation metric ROUGE (Lin, 2004) which represents recall over various n-grams statistics from a system-generated summary against a set of human generated peer summaries. F-measures for ROUGE-1 (unigram) and ROUGE-L (longest common subsequence) can be evaluated in exactly the same way, which are used in the following results.

3.3 Results

Table 1 shows the performance achieved by all proposed approaches. In these experiments, the damping factor, $(1-\alpha-\beta)$ in (8), is empirically set to 0.1. Row (a) is the baseline, which use LTE-based statistical measure to compute the importance of utterances $I(U,d)$. Row (b) is the result only considering lexical similarity; row (c) only uses topical similarity. Row (d) are the results additionally including speaker information such as $\text{TopicSim}'(U_i,U_j)$. Row (e) is the result performed by integrated random walk (with $\alpha \neq 0$ and $\beta \neq 0$) using parameters that have been optimized on the dev set.

3.3.1 Graph-Based Approach

We can see the performance after graph-based recomputation, shown in rows (b) and (c), is significantly better than the baseline, shown in row (a), for both ASR and manual transcripts. For ASR transcripts, topical similarity and lexical similarity give similar results. For manual transcripts, topical similarity performs slightly worse than lexical similarity, because manual transcripts don't contain the recognition errors, and therefore word overlap can accurately measure the similarity between two utter-

F-measure		ASR Transcripts		Manual Transcripts	
		ROUGE-1	ROUGE-L	ROUGE-1	ROUGE-L
(a)	Baseline: LTE	46.816	46.256	44.987	44.162
(b)	LexSim ($\alpha = 0, \beta = 0.9$)	48.940	48.504	46.540	45.858
(c)	TopicSim ($\alpha = 0.9, \beta = 0$)	49.058	48.436	46.199	45.392
(d)	Intra-Speaker TopicSim	49.212	48.351	**47.104**	**46.299**
(e)	Integrated Random Walk	**49.792**	**49.156**	46.714	46.064
MAX RI		+6.357	+6.269	+4.706	+4.839

Table 1: Maximum relative improvement (RI) with respect to the baseline for all proposed approaches (%).

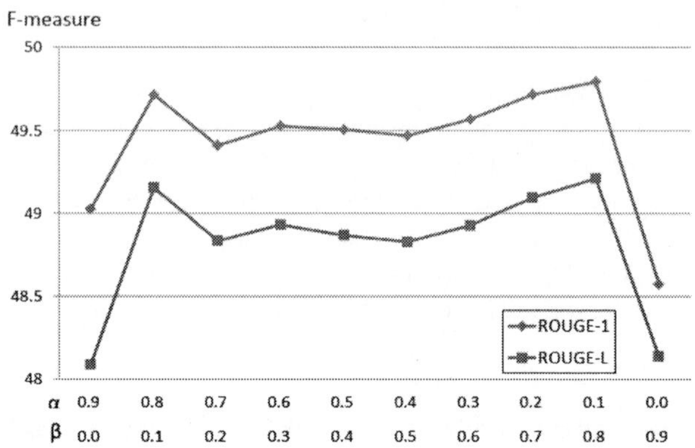

Figure 2: The performance from integrated random walk with different combination weights, α and β ($\alpha + \beta = 0.9$ in all cases) for ASR transcripts.

ances. However, for ASR transcripts, although topical similarity is not as accurate as lexical similarity, it can compensate for recognition errors, so that the approaches have similar performance. Thus, graph-based approaches can significantly improve the baseline results.

3.3.2 Effectiveness of Intra-Speaker Modeling

We find that modeling intra-speaker topics can improve the performance (row (c) and row (d)), which means speaker information is useful to model the topical similarity. The experiment shows intra-speaker modeling can help us include the important utterances for both ASR and manual transcripts.

3.3.3 Integration of Topical and Lexical Similarity

Row (e) shows the result of the proposed approach, which integrates topical and lexical similarity into a single graph, considering two types of relations together. For ASR transcripts, row (e) is better than row (b) and row (d), which means topical similarity and lexical similarity can model different types of relations, because of recognition errors. Figure 2 shows the sensitivity of the combination weights for integrated random walk. We can see topical similarity and lexical similarity are additive, i.e. they can compensate each other, improving the performance by integrating two types of edges in a single graph. Note that the exact values of α and β do not matter so much for the performance.

For manual transcripts, row (e) cannot perform better by combing two types of similarity, which means topical similarity can dominate lexical similarity, since without recognition errors topical similarity can model the relations accurately and additionally modeling intra-speaker topics can effectively improve the performance.

In addition, Banerjee and Rudnicky (2008) used supervised learning to detect noteworthy utterances on the same corpus, and achieved ROGURE-1 scores of around 43% for ASR, and 47% for manual transcriptions. Our unsupervised approach performs better, especially for ASR transcripts.

Note that the performance on ASR is better than on manual transcripts. Because a higher percentage of recognition errors occurs on "unimportant" words, these words tend to receive lower scores; we can then exclude the utterances with more errors, and achieve better summarization results. Other recent work has also demonstrated better performance for ASR than manual transcripts (Chen et al., 2011; Kong and Lee, 2011).

4 Conclusion and Future Work

Extensive experiments and evaluation with ROUGE metrics showed that intra-speaker topics can be modeled in topical similarity and that integrated random walk can combine the advantages from two types of edges for imperfect ASR transcripts, where we achieved more than 6% relative improvement. We plan to model inter-speaker topics in the graph-based approach in the future.

Acknowledgements

The first author was supported by the Institute of Education Science, U.S. Department of Education, through Grants R305A080628 to Carnegie Mellon University. Any opinions, findings, and conclusions or recommendations expressed in this publication are those of the authors and do not necessarily reflect the views or official policies, either expressed or implied of the Institute or the U.S. Department of Education.

References

Banerjee, S. and Rudnicky, A. I. 2008. An extractive-summarizaion baseline for the automatic detection of noteworthy utterances in multi-party human-human dialog. *Proc. of SLT.*

Chen, Y.-N., Huang, Y., Yeh, C.-F., and Lee, L.-S. 2011. Spoken lecture summarization by random walk over a graph constructed with automatically extracted key terms. *Proc. of InterSpeech.*

Erkan, G. and D. R. Radev., D. R. 2004. LexRank: Graph-based lexical centrality as salience in text summarization. *Journal of Artificial Intelligence Research*, Vol. 22.

Furui, S., Kikuchi, T., Shinnaka, Y., and Hori, C. 2004. Speech-to-text and speech-to-speech summarization of spontaneous speech. *IEEE Trans. on Speech and Audio Processing.*

Garg, N., Favre, B., Reidhammer, K., and Hakkani-Tür 2009. ClusterRank: A graph based method for meeting summarization. *Proc. of InterSpeech.*

Gillick, D. J. 2011. The elements of automatic summarization. *PhD thesis, EECS, UC Berkeley.*

Glass J., Hazen, T. J., Cyphers, S., Malioutov, I., Huynh, D., and Barzilay, R. 2007. Recent progress in the MIT spoken lecture processing project. *Proc. of InterSpeech.*

Hofmann, T. 1999. Probabilistic latent semantic indexing. *Proc. of SIGIR.*

Hsu, W. and Kennedy, L. 2007. Video search reranking through random walk over document-level context graph. *Proc. of MM.*

Kong, S.-Y. and Lee, L.-S. 2011. Semantic analysis and organization of spoken documents based on parameters derived from latent topics. *IEEE Trans. on Audio, Speech and Language Processing*, 19(7): 1875-1889.

Langville, A. and Meyer, C. 2005. A survey of eigenvector methods for web information retrieval. *SIAM Review.*

Lee, L.-S. and Chen, B. 2005. Spoken document understanding and organization. *IEEE Signal Processing Magazine.*

Lin, C. 2004. Rouge: A package for automatic evaluation of summaries. *Proc. of Workshop on Text Summarization Branches Out.*

Liu, F. and Liu, Y. 2010. Using spoken utterance compression for meeting summarization: A pilot study. *Proc. of SLT.*

Liu Y., Xie, S., and Liu, F. 2010. Using N-best recognition output for extractive summarization and keyword extraction in meeting speech. *Proc. of ICASSP.*

Page, L., Brin, S., Motwani, R., Winograd, T. 1998. The pagerank citation ranking: bringing order to the web. *Technical Report, Stanford Digital Library Technologies Project.*

Towards Using EEG to Improve ASR Accuracy

Yun-Nung Chen, Kai-Min Chang, and Jack Mostow
Project LISTEN (http://www.cs.cmu.edu/~listen)
School of Computer Science, Carnegie Mellon University
5000 Forbes Avenue, Pittsburgh, PA 15213-3891, USA
{yvchen,kkchang,mostow}@cs.cmu.edu

Abstract

We report on a pilot experiment to improve the performance of an automatic speech recognizer (ASR) by using a single-channel EEG signal to classify the speaker's mental state as reading easy or hard text. We use a previously published method (Mostow et al., 2011) to train the EEG classifier. We use its probabilistic output to control weighted interpolation of separate language models for easy and difficult reading. The EEG-adapted ASR achieves higher accuracy than two baselines. We analyze how its performance depends on EEG classification accuracy. This pilot result is a step towards improving ASR more generally by using EEG to distinguish mental states.

1 Introduction

Humans use speech to communicate what's on their mind. However, until now, automatic speech recognizers (ASR) and dialogue systems have had no direct way to take into account what is going on in a speaker's mind. Some work has attempted to infer cognitive states from volume and speaking rate to adapt language modeling (Ward and Vega, 2009) or from query click logs (Hakkani-Tür et al., 2011) to detect domains. A new way to address this limitation is to infer mental states from electroencephalogram (EEG) signals.

EEG is a voltage signal that can be measured on the surface of the scalp, arising from large areas of coordinated neural activity. This neural activity varies as a function of development, mental state, and cognitive activity, and EEG can measurably detect such variation.

Recently, a few companies have scaled back medical grade EEG technology to create portable EEG headsets that are commercially available and simple to use. The NeuroSky MindSet^{TM} (2009), for example, is an audio headset equipped with a single-channel EEG sensor. It measures the voltage between an electrode that rests on the forehead and electrodes in contact with the ear. Unlike the multi-channel electrode nets worn in labs, the sensor requires no gel or saline for recording, and requires no expertise to wear. Even with the limitations of recording from only a single sensor and working with untrained users, Furthermore, Mostow et al.(2011) used its output signal to distinguish easy from difficult reading, achieving above-chance accuracy. Here we build on that work by using the output of such classifiers to adapt language models for ASR and thereby improve recognition accuracy.

The most similar work is Jou and Schultz's (2008) use of electromyographic (EMG) signals generated by human articulatory muscles in producing speech. They showed that augmenting acoustic features with these EMG features can achieve rudimentary silent speech detection. Pasley et al. (2012) used electrocorticographic (ECoG) recordings from nonprimary auditory cortex in the human superior temporal gyrus to reconstruct acoustic information in speech sounds. Our work differs from these efforts in that we use a consumer-grade single-channel EEG sensor measuring frontal lobe activities, and that we use the detected mental state just to help improve ASR performance rather than to dictate or reconstruct speech, which are much harder tasks.

Section 2 describes how to use machine learning to distinguish mental states associated with easy and difficult readings. Section 3 describes how we use EEG classifier output to adapt ASR language models. Section 4 uses an oracle simulation to show how increasing EEG classifier accuracy will affect ASR accuracy. Section 5 concludes.

2 Mental State Classification Using EEG

We use training and testing data from Mostow et al.'s (2011) experiment, which presented text passages, one sentence at a time, to 10 adults and 11 nine- to ten-year-olds wearing a Neurosky Mindset^{TM} (2009). They read three easy and three difficult texts aloud, in alternating order. The "easy" passages were from texts classified by the Common Core Standards[1] at the K-1 level. The "difficult" passages were from practice materials for the Graduate Record Exam[2] and the ACE GED test[3]. Across the reading conditions, passages ranged from 62 to 83 words long. Although instructed to read the text aloud, the readers (especially children) did not always read correctly or follow the displayed sentences.

Following Mostow et al. (2011), we trained binary logistic regression classifiers to estimate the probability that an EEG signal is associated with reading an easy (or difficult) sentence. As features for logistic regression we used the streams of values logged by the MindSet:

1. The raw EEG signal, sampled at 512 Hz
2. A filtered version of the raw signal, also sampled at 512 Hz, which is raw signal smoothed over a window of 2 seconds
3. Proprietary "attention" and "meditation" measures, reported at 1 Hz
4. A power spectrum of 1Hz bands from 1-256 Hz, reported at 8 Hz
5. An indicator of signal quality, reported at 1 Hz

Head movement or system instability led to missing or poor-quality EEG data for some utterances, which we excluded in order to focus on utterances with clear acoustic and EEG signals. The features for each utterance consisted of measures 1-4, averaged over the utterance, excluding the 15% of observations where measure 5 reported poor signals. After filtering, the data includes 269 utterances from adults and 243 utterances from children, where 327 utterances are for the easy passages and 185 utterances are for the difficult passages. To balance the classes, we used the undersampling method for training.

We trained a reader-specific classifier on each reader's data from all but one text passage, tested it on each sentence in the held-out passage, performed this procedure for each passage, and averaged the results to cross-validate accuracy within readers. We computed classification accuracy as the percentage of utterances classified correctly. Classification accuracy for adults', children's, and total oral reading was 71.49%, 58.74%, and 65.45% respectively. A one-tailed t-test, with classification accuracy on an utterance as the random variable, showed that EEG classification was significantly better than chance.

3 Language Model Adaptation for ASR

Traditional ASR decodes a word sequence W^* from the acoustic model and language model as below:

$$\begin{aligned} W^* &= \text{argmax}_W\, P(W \mid A) \\ &= \text{argmax}_W \frac{P(A \mid W) \cdot P(W)}{P(A)} \end{aligned} \quad (1)$$

To incorporate EEG, we include mental state N as an additional observation in the decoding procedure:

$$\begin{aligned} W^* &= \text{argmax}_W\, P(W \mid A, N) \\ &= \text{argmax}_W \frac{P(A \mid W) \cdot P(W \mid N)}{P(A)} \end{aligned} \quad (2)$$

The six passages use a vocabulary of 430 distinct words. To evaluate the impact on ASR accuracy of using EEG to adapt language models, we needed acoustic models appropriate for the speakers. For adult speech, we used the US English HUB4 Acoustic Model from CMU Sphinx. For children's speech, we used Project LISTEN's acoustic models trained on children's oral reading.

We used separate trigram language models (with bigram and unigram backoff) for easy and difficult text – EasyLM, trained on the three easy passages, and DifficultLM, trained on the three difficult passages. Both language models used the same lexicon, consisting of the 430 words in all six target passages. All experiments used the same ASR parameter values.

As a gold standard, all utterances were manually transcribed by a native English speaker. To measure ASR performance, we computed Word Accuracy (WACC) as the number of words recognized correctly minus insertions divided by number of words in the reference transcripts for each reader, and averaged them.

Then we can adapt the language model to estimate $P(W \mid N)$ using mental state information. Using the EEG classifier described in Section 2, we adapted the language model separately for each utterance, using three types of language model adaptation: hard selection, soft selection, and combination with ASR output.

3.1 Hard Selection of Language Models

Given the probabilistic estimate that a given utterance was easy or difficult ($S_{\text{Easy}}(N)$ and $S_{\text{Difficult}}(N)$), hard selection simply picks EasyLM if the utterance was likelier to be easy, or DifficultLM otherwise:

$$\begin{aligned} P_{\text{Hard}}(W \mid N) &= I_C(N) \cdot P_{\text{Easy}}(W) \\ &+ (1 - I_C(N)) \cdot P_{\text{Diff}}(W). \end{aligned} \quad (3)$$

Here $I_C(N) = 1$ if $S_{\text{Easy}}(N) > S_{\text{Difficult}}(N)$, and $P_{\text{Easy}}(W)$ and $P_{\text{Diff}}(W)$ are the probability of word W in EasyLM and DifficultLM, respectively. For comparison, the Random Pick baseline randomly picks either EasyLM or DifficultLM:

[1] http://www.corestandards.org

[2] http://majortests.com/gre/reading_comprehension.php

[3] http://college.cengage.com:80/devenglish/resources/reading_ace/students

WACC		Adult			Child		
		Easy	Difficult	All	Easy	Difficult	All
(a)	Baseline 1: Random Pick	54.5	51.2	53.8	32.8	14.7	30.6
(b)	EEG-based: Hard Selection	**57.6**	49.4	52.7	**36.4**	**17.0**	**32.8**
(c)	Baseline 2: Equal Weight	63.2	59.9	56.5	37.3	19.5	33.4
(d)	EEG-based: Soft Selection w/o smoothing	57.2	48.8	52.4	35.8	17.2	32.5
(e)	EEG-based: Soft Selection w/ smoothing	**66.0**	**62.3**	**64.2**	**39.8**	**22.7**	**36.2**
(f)	Baseline 3: Weight from ASR ($\alpha = 0$)	63.8	60.6	61.5	39.2	20.0	35.0
(g)	Weight from ASR and EEG ($\alpha = 0.5$)	**64.5**	**63.4**	**63.5**	39.2	21.9	36.0

Table 1: ASR performance of proposed approaches using EEG-based classification of mental states.

$$P_{\text{Random}}(W) = I_R \cdot P_{\text{Easy}}(W) + (1 - I_{\text{Random}}) \cdot P_{\text{Diff}}(W). \quad (4)$$

Here I_R is randomly set to 0 or 1.

3.2 Soft Selection of Language Models

Mental state classification based on EEG is imperfect, and using only the corresponding language model (EasyLM or DifficultLM) to decode the target utterance is liable to perform worse when the classifier is wrong. Thus, we use the classifier's probabilistic estimate that the utterance is easy (or difficult) as interpolation weights to linearly combine EasyLM and DifficultLM:

$$P_{\text{Soft}}(W \mid N) = w_{\text{Easy}}(N) \cdot P_{\text{Easy}}(W) + w_{\text{Diff}}(N) \cdot P_{\text{Diff}}(W). \quad (5)$$

Here $w_{\text{Easy}}(N)$ and $w_{\text{Diff}}(N)$ are from classifier's output.

$$w_{\text{Easy}}(N) = S_{\text{Easy}}(N), w_{\text{Diff}}(N) = S_{\text{Diff}}(N) \quad (6)$$

Additionally, we can adjust the range of weights by smoothing the probability outputted by the EEG classifier:

$$w_{\text{Easy}}(N) = \frac{\delta + S_{\text{Easy}}(N)}{2\delta + 1}, \quad w_{\text{Diff}}(N) = \frac{\delta + S_{\text{Diff}}(N)}{2\delta + 1} \quad (7)$$

Here $S_{\text{Easy}}(N)$ (or $S_{\text{Diff}}(N)$) is the classifier's probabilistic estimate that the sentence is easy (or difficult) and δ is the smoothing weight, which we set to 0.5. After smoothing the probabilities, $w_{\text{Easy}}(N)$ and $w_{\text{Diff}}(N)$ each lie within the interval $[0.25, 0.75]$, and $w_{\text{Easy}}(N) + w_{\text{Diff}}(N) = 1$. That is, Soft Selection with smoothing interpolates the two language models, but assigns a weight of at least 0.25 to each one to reduce the impact of EEG classifier errors. Notice that $\delta = 0$ is equivalent to EEG Soft Selection without smoothing.

For comparison, the Equal Weight baseline interpolates EasyLM and DifficultLM with equal weights:

$$P_{\text{Equal}}(W) = 0.5 \cdot P_{\text{Easy}}(W) + 0.5 \cdot P_{\text{Diff}}(W) \quad (8)$$

3.3 Combination with ASR Output

Given the ASR results from the Equal Weight baseline, we can derive $S'_{\text{Easy}}(N)$ as:

$$S'_{\text{Easy}}(N) = \alpha \cdot S_{\text{Easy}}(N) + (1 - \alpha) \cdot \frac{P_{\text{Easy}}(W_0)}{P_{\text{Easy}}(W_0) + P_{\text{Diff}}(W_0)} \quad (9)$$

Here we can estimate $S'_{\text{Easy}}(N)$ based on the classifier's output and the probability of the recognized words W_0 in EasyLM. We can derive $S'_{\text{Diff}}(N)$ in the same way. Then we can use (5) and (7) to re-decode the utterances by using $S'_{\text{Easy}}(N)$ and $S'_{\text{Diff}}(N)$. Here α is a linear interpolation weight, where we set to 0.5 to give equal weights to ASR output and EEG. For comparison, the ASR baseline uses weights from only the ASR results, where $\alpha = 0$. Notice that the case of $\alpha = 1$ is equivalent to EEG Soft Selection with smoothing.

3.4 Results of Proposed Approaches

Table 1 shows the performance of our proposed approaches and the corresponding baselines as measured by WACC. According to one-tailed t-tests with word accuracy of an utterance as the random variable, the results in **boldface** are significantly better tgan their respective baselines ($p \leq 0.05$).

Hard Selection (row b) outperforms the Random Pick baseline (row a). Soft Selection without smoothing (row d) has similar performance as Hard Selection because the classifier often outputs probability estimates that are either 1 or 0. However, Soft Selection with smoothing (row e) outperforms the Equal Weight baseline (row c). The Weight from ASR baseline (row f) is better than the other baselines. Weight from ASR and EEG (row g) can further improve performance, but it's not better than Soft Selection with smoothing (row e) - evidence that EEG gives good estimation for choosing language models. In short, Table 1 shows that using EEG to choose between EasyLM and DifficultLM achieves higher ASR accuracy than the baselines that do not use EEG.

Comparing the first two baselines, the Equal Weight baseline (row c) outperforms the Random Pick baseline

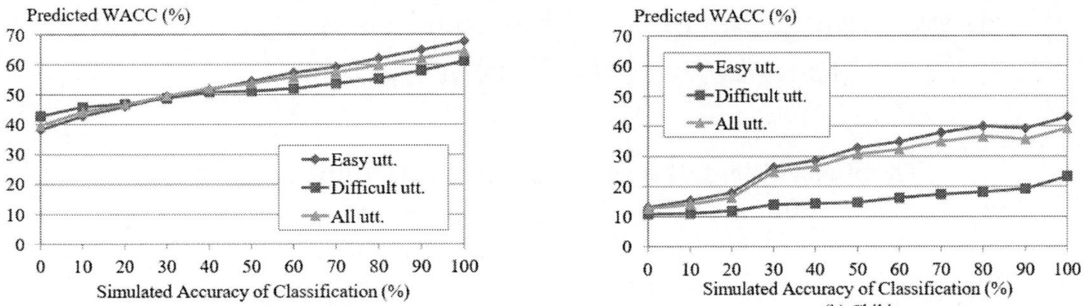

(a) Adult (b) Child

Figure 1: The simulated accuracy graphs plot the predicted ASR word accuracy against the level of EEG classification accuracy simulated by an oracle.

(row a) in every column, because the loss in ASR accuracy from picking the wrong language model outweighs the improvement from picking the right one. Similarly, EEG-based Soft Selection with smoothing (row e) outperforms EEG-based Hard Selection (row b) in every column because the interpolated language model is more robust to EEG classification error. The third base-line, Weight from ASR (row f) depends solely on ASR results to estimate weights; it performs better than other baselines, but not as well as EEG-based Soft Selection with smoothing (row e). That is, using EEG alone can weight the two language models better than ASR alone.

4 Oracle Simulation

To explore the relationship between EEG classifier accuracy and the effect of EEG-based adaptation on ASR accuracy, we simulate different classification accuracies and used Hard Selection to predict the resulting ASR accuracy by selecting between the ASR output from EasyLM and DifficultLM according to the simulated classifier accuracy. We use the resulting Word Accuracy to predict ASR performance at that level of EEG classifier accuracy.

Figure 1 plots predicted ASR WACC against simulated EEG classification accuracy. As expected, the predicted ASR accuracy increases as EEG classification accuracy increases, for both groups (adults and children) and both levels of difficulty (easy and difficult). However, Figure 1a and 1b shows that WACC was much lower for children than for adults, especially on difficult utterances, where even 100% simulated EEG classifier accuracy achieves barely 20% WACC. One explanation is that on difficult sentences, children produced reading mistakes and/ or off-task speech. In contrast, adults read better and stayed on task. Not only is predicted ASR accuracy higher on adults' reading, it improves substantially as simulated EEG classifier accuracy increases.

5 Conclusion

This paper shows that classifying EEG signals from an inexpensive single-channel device can help adapt language models to significantly improve ASR performance. An interpolated language model smoothed to compensate for classification errors yielded the best performance. ASR performance depended on the accuracy of mental state classification. Future work includes improving EEG classification accuracy, detecting other relevant mental states, such as emotion, and improving ASR by using word-level EEG classification. A neurologically-informed ASR may better capture what people intend to communicate, and augment acoustic input with non-verbal cues to ASR or dialogue systems.

Acknowledgements

This work was supported by the Institute of Education Sciences, U.S. Department of Education, through Grant R305A080628 to Carnegie Mellon University. Any opinions, findings, and conclusions or recommendations expressed in this publication are those of the authors and do not necessarily reflect the views or official policies, either expressed or implied of the Institute or the U.S. Department of Education. We thank the students, educators, and LISTENers who helped create our data, and the reviewers for their helpful comments.

References

Hakkani-Tür, D., Tur, G., Heck, L., and Shriberg, E. 2011. Bootstrapping domain detection using query click logs for new domains *Proceedings of InterSpeech*, 709-712.

Jou, S.-C. S. and Schultz, T.. 2008. Ears: Electromyograpical Automatic Recognition of Speech. *Proceedings of Biosignals*, 3-12.

Mostow, J., Chang, K.-M., and Nelson, J. 2011. Toward Exploiting EEG Input in a Reading Tutor. *Proceedings of the 15th International Conference on Artificial Intelligence in Education*, 230-237.

NeuroSky 2009. NeuroSky's Sense™ Meters and Detection of Mental State: Neurisky, Inc.

Pasley, B. N. and et al. 2012. Reconstructing speech from auditory cortex. *PLos Biology*, 10(1), 1-13.

Ward, N. G. and Vega, A. 2009. Towards the use of cognitive states in language modeling. *Proceedings of ASRU*, 323-326.

A Comparative Investigation of Morphological Language Modeling for the Languages of the European Union

Thomas Müller, Hinrich Schütze and Helmut Schmid
Institute for Natural Language Processing
University of Stuttgart, Germany
{muellets,schmid}@ims.uni-stuttgart.de

Abstract

We investigate a language model that combines morphological and shape features with a Kneser-Ney model and test it in a large crosslingual study of European languages. Even though the model is generic and we use the same architecture and features for all languages, the model achieves reductions in perplexity for all 21 languages represented in the Europarl corpus, ranging from 3% to 11%. We show that almost all of this perplexity reduction can be achieved by identifying suffixes by frequency.

1 Introduction

Language models are fundamental to many natural language processing applications. In the most common approach, language models estimate the probability of the next word based on one or more equivalence classes that the history of preceding words is a member of. The inherent productivity of natural language poses a problem in this regard because the history may be rare or unseen or have unusual properties that make assignment to a predictive equivalence class difficult.

In many languages, morphology is a key source of productivity that gives rise to rare and unseen histories. For example, even if a model can learn that words like "large", "dangerous" and "serious" are likely to occur after the relatively frequent history "potentially", this knowledge cannot be transferred to the rare history "hypothetically" without some generalization mechanism like morphological analysis.

Our primary goal in this paper is not to develop optimized language models for individual languages. Instead, we investigate whether a simple generic language model that uses shape and morphological features can be made to work well across a large number of languages. We find that this is the case: we achieve considerable perplexity reductions for all 21 languages in the Europarl corpus. We see this as evidence that morphological language modeling should be considered as a standard part of any language model, even for languages like English that are often not viewed as a good application of morphological modeling due to their morphological simplicity.

To understand which factors are important for good performance of the morphological component of a language model, we perform an extensive crosslingual analysis of our experimental results. We look at three parameters of the morphological model we propose: the frequency threshold θ that divides words subject to morphological clustering from those that are not; the number of suffixes used ϕ; and three different morphological segmentation algorithms. We also investigate the differential effect of morphological language modeling on different word shapes: alphabetical words, punctuation, numbers and other shapes.

Some prior work has used morphological models that require careful linguistic analysis and language-dependent adaptation. In this paper we show that simple frequency analysis performs only slightly worse than more sophisticated morphological analysis. This potentially removes a hurdle to using morphological models in cases where sufficient resources to do the extra work required for sophisticated morphological analysis are not available.

The motivation for using morphology in language modeling is similar to distributional clustering

(Brown et al., 1992). In both cases, we form equivalence classes of words with similar distributional behavior. In a preliminary experiment, we find that morphological equivalence classes reduce perplexity as much as traditional distributional classes – a surprising result we intend to investigate in future work.

The main contributions of this paper are as follows. We present a language model design and a set of morphological and shape features that achieve reductions in perplexity for all 21 languages represented in the Europarl corpus, ranging from 3% to 11%, compared to a Kneser-Ney model. We show that identifying suffixes by frequency is sufficient for getting almost all of this perplexity reduction. More sophisticated morphological segmentation methods do not further increase perplexity or just slightly. Finally, we show that there is one parameter that must be tuned for good performance for most languages: the frequency threshold θ above which a word is not subject to morphological generalization because it occurs frequently enough for standard word n-gram language models to use it effectively for prediction.

The paper is organized as follows. In Section 2 we discuss related work. In Section 3 we describe the morphological and shape features we use. Section 4 introduces language model and experimental setup. Section 5 discusses our results. Section 6 summarizes the contributions of this paper.

2 Related Work

Whittaker and Woodland (2000) apply language modeling to morpheme sequences and investigate data-driven segmentation methods. Creutz et al. (2007) propose a similar method that improves speech recognition for highly inflecting languages. They use Morfessor (Creutz and Lagus, 2007) to split words into morphemes. Both approaches are essentially a simple form of a factored language model (FLM) (Bilmes and Kirchhoff, 2003). In a general FLM a number of different back-off paths are combined by a back-off function to improve the prediction after rare or unseen histories. Vergyri et al. (2004) apply FLMs and morphological features to Arabic speech recognition.

These papers and other prior work on using morphology in language modeling have been language-specific and have paid less attention to the question as to how morphology can be useful across languages and what generic methods are appropriate for this goal. Previous work also has concentrated on traditional linguistic morphology whereas we compare linguistically motivated morphological segmentation with frequency-based segmentation and include shape features in our study.

Our initial plan for this paper was to use complex language modeling frameworks that allow experimenters to include arbitrary features (including morphological and shape features) in the model. In particular, we looked at publicly available implementations of maximum entropy models (Rosenfeld, 1996; Berger et al., 1996) and random forests (Xu and Jelinek, 2004). However, we found that these methods do not currently scale to running a large set of experiments on a multi-gigabyte parallel corpus of 21 languages. Similar considerations apply to other sophisticated language modeling techniques like Pitman-Yor processes (Teh, 2006), recurrent neural networks (Mikolov et al., 2010) and FLMs in their general, more powerful form. In addition, perplexity reductions of these complex models compared to simpler state-of-the-art models are generally not large.

We therefore decided to conduct our study in the framework of smoothed n-gram models, which currently are an order of magnitude faster and more scalable. More specifically, we adopt a class-based approach, where words are clustered based on morphological and shape features. This approach has the nice property that the number of features used to estimate the classes does not influence the time needed to train the class language model, once the classes have been found. This is an important consideration in the context of the questions asked in this paper as it allows us to use large numbers of features in our experiments.

3 Modeling of morphology and shape

Our basic approach is to define a number of morphological and shape features and then assign all words with identical feature values to one class. For the morphological features, we investigate three different automatic suffix identification algorithms: Res, e, d, ed, n, g, ng, ing, y, t, es, r, a, l, on, er, ion, ted, ly, tion, rs, al, o, ts, ns, le, i, ation, an, ers, m, nt, ting, h, c, te, sed, ated, en, ty, ic, k, ent, st, ss, ons, se, ity, ble, ne, ce, ess, ions, us, ry, re, ies, ve, p, ate, in, tions, ia, red, able, is, ive, ness, lly, ring, ment, led, ned, tes, as, ls, ding, ling, sing, ds, ded, ian, nce, ar, ating, sm, ally, nts, de, nd, ism, or, ge, ist, ses, ning, u, king, na, el

Figure 1: The 100 most frequent English suffixes in Europarl, ordered by frequency

ports (Keshava and Pitler, 2006), Morfessor (Creutz and Lagus, 2007) and Frequency, where Frequency simply selects the most frequent word-final letter sequences as suffixes. The 100 most frequent suffixes found by Frequency for English are given in Figure 1.

We use the ϕ most frequent suffixes for all three algorithms, where ϕ is a parameter. The focus of our work is to evaluate the utility of these algorithms for language modeling; we do not directly evaluate the quality of the suffixes.

A word is segmented by identifying the longest of the ϕ suffixes that it ends with. Thus, each word has one suffix feature if it ends with one of the ϕ suffixes and none otherwise.

In addition to suffix features, we define features that capture shape properties: capitalization, special characters and word length. If a word in the test set has a combination of feature values that does not occur in the training set, then it is assigned to the class whose features are most similar. We described the similarity measure and details of the shape features in prior work (Müller and Schütze, 2011). The shape features are listed in Table 1.

4 Experimental Setup

Experiments are performed using srilm (Stolcke, 2002), in particular the Kneser-Ney (KN) and generic class model implementations. Estimation of optimal interpolation parameters is based on (Bahl et al., 1991).

4.1 Baseline

Our baseline is a modified KN model (Chen and Goodman, 1999).

4.2 Morphological class language model

We use a variation of the model proposed by Brown et al. (1992) that we developed in prior work on English (Müller and Schütze, 2011). This model is a class-based language model that groups words into classes and replaces the word transition probability by a class transition probability and a word emission probability:

$$P_C(w_i|w_{i-N+1}^{i-1}) = P(g(w_i)|g(w_{i-N+1}^{i-1})) \cdot P(w_i|g(w_i))$$

where $g(w)$ is the class of word w and we write $g(w_i \dots w_j)$ for $g(w_i) \dots g(w_j)$.

Our approach targets rare and unseen histories. We therefore exclude all frequent words from clustering on the assumption that enough training data is available for them. Thus, clustering of words is restricted to those below a certain token frequency threshold θ. As described above, we simply group all words with identical feature values into one class. Words with a training set frequency above θ are added as singletons. The class transition probability $P(g(w_i)|g(w_{i-N+1}^{i-1}))$ is estimated using Witten-Bell smoothing.[1]

The word emission probability is defined as follows:

$$P(w|c) = \begin{cases} 1 & , \ N(w) > \theta \\ \frac{N(w)}{\sum_{w \in c} N(w)} - \frac{\epsilon(c)}{|c|-1}, & \theta \geq N(w) > 0 \\ \epsilon(c) & , \ N(w) = 0 \end{cases}$$

where $c = g(w)$ is w's class and $N(w)$ is the frequency of w in the training set. The class-dependent out-of-vocabulary (OOV) rate $\epsilon(c)$ is estimated on held-out data. Our final model P_M interpolates P_C with a modified KN model:

$$\begin{aligned} P_M(w_i|w_{i-1}^{i-N+1}) = \\ \lambda(g(w_{i-1})) \cdot P_{\text{C}}(w_i|w_{i-1}^{i-N+1}) \\ +(1 - \lambda(g(w_{i-1}))) \cdot P_{\text{KN}}(w_i|w_{i-1}^{i-N+1}) \end{aligned} \qquad (1)$$

This model can be viewed as a generalization of the simple interpolation $\alpha P_{\text{C}} + (1-\alpha)P_{\text{W}}$ used by Brown et al. (1992) (where P_{W} is a word n-gram

[1] Witten-Bell smoothing outperformed modified Kneser-Ney (KN) and Good-Turing (GT).

$is\_capital(w)$	first character of w is an uppercase letter
$is\_all\_capital(w)$	$\forall c \in w : c$ is an uppercase letter
$capital\_character(w)$	$\exists c \in w : c$ is an uppercase letter
$appears\_in\_lowercase(w)$	$\neg capital\_character(w) \vee w' \in \Sigma_T$
$special\_character(w)$	$\exists c \in w : c$ is not a letter or digit
$digit(w)$	$\exists c \in w : c$ is a digit
$is\_number(w)$	$w \in L([+ - \epsilon][0-9]\ (([.,][0-9])\|[0-9])*)$

Table 1: Shape features as defined by Müller and Schütze (2011). Σ_T is the vocabulary of the training corpus T, w' is obtained from w by changing all uppercase letters to lowercase and $L(expr)$ is the language generated by the regular expression $expr$.

model and P_C a class n-gram model). For the setting $\theta = \infty$ (clustering of all words), our model is essentially a simple interpolation of a word n-gram and a class n-gram model except that the interpolation parameters are optimized for each class instead of using the same interpolation parameter α for all classes. We have found that $\theta = \infty$ is never optimal; it is always beneficial to assign the most frequent words to their own singleton classes.

Following Yuret and Biçici (2009), we evaluate models on the task of predicting the next word from a vocabulary that consists of all words that occur more than once in the training corpus and the unknown word UNK. Performing this evaluation for KN is straightforward: we map all words with frequency one in the training set to UNK and then compute $P_{\text{KN}}(\text{UNK}\,|h)$ in testing.

In contrast, computing probability estimates for P_C is more complicated. We define the vocabulary of the morphological model as the set of all words found in the training corpus, including frequency-1 words, and one unknown word for each class. We do this because – as we argued above – morphological generalization is only expected to be useful for rare words, so we are likely to get optimal performance for P_C if we include all words in clustering and probability estimation, including hapax legomena. Since our testing setup only evaluates on words that occur more than once in the training set, we ideally would want to compute the following estimate when predicting the unknown word:

$$P_C(\text{UNK}_{\text{KN}}\,|h) = \sum_{\{w:N(w)=1\}} P_C(w|h) + \sum_c P_C(\text{UNK}_c\,|h) \quad (2)$$

where we distinguish the unknown words of the morphological classes from the unknown word used in evaluation and by the KN model by giving the latter the subscript KN.

However, Eq. 2 cannot be computed efficiently and we would not be able to compute it in practical applications that require fast language models. For this reason, we use the modified class model P'_C in Eq. 1 that is defined as follows:

$$P'_C(w|h) = \begin{cases} P_C(w|h) & , N(w) \geq 1 \\ P_C(\text{UNK}_{g(w)}\,|h), & N(w) = 0 \end{cases}$$

P'_C and – by extension – P_M are deficient. This means that the evaluation of P_M we present below is pessimistic in the sense that the perplexity reductions would probably be higher if we were willing to spend additional computational resources and compute Eq. 2 in its full form.

4.3 Distributional class language model

The most frequently used type of class-based language model is the distributional model introduced by Brown et al. (1992). To understand the differences between distributional and morphological class language models, we compare our morphological model P_M with a distributional model P_D that has exactly the same form as P_M; in particular, it is defined by Equations (1) and (2). The only difference is that the classes are morphological for P_M and distributional for P_D.

The exchange algorithm that was used by Brown et al. (1992) has very long running times for large corpora in standard implementations like srilm. It is difficult to conduct the large number of clusterings necessary for an extensive study like ours using standard implementations.

Language	T/T	ϵ	#Sentences
S bg Bulgarian	.0183	.0094	**181,415**
S cs Czech	.0185	.0097	369,881
S pl Polish	.0189	.0096	358,747
S sk Slovak	.0187	.0088	368,624
S sl Slovene	.0156	.0090	365,455
G da Danish	.0086	.0077	1,428,620
G de German	.0091	.0073	1,391,324
G en English	**.0028**	**.0023**	**1,460,062**
G nl Dutch	.0061	.0048	1,457,629
G sv Swedish	.0090	.0095	1,342,667
E el Greek	.0081	.0079	851,636
R es Spanish	.0040	.0031	1,429,276
R fr French	**.0029**	**.0024**	**1,460,062**
R it Italian	.0040	.0030	1,389,665
R pt Portuguese	.0042	.0032	1,426,750
R ro Romanian	.0142	.0079	**178,284**
U et Estonian	**.0329**	**.0198**	375,698
U fi Finnish	.0231	**.0183**	1,394,043
U hu Hungarian	**.0312**	.0163	364,216
B lt Lithuanian	.0265	.0147	365,437
B lv Latvian	.0182	.0086	363,104

Table 2: Statistics for the 21 languages. S = Slavic, G = Germanic, E = Greek, R = Romance, U = Uralic, B = Baltic. Type/token ratio (T/T) and # sentences for the training set and OOV rate ϵ for the validation set. The two smallest and largest values in each column are bold.

We therefore induce the distributional classes as clusters in a whole-context distributional vector space model (Schütze and Walsh, 2011), a model similar to the ones described by Schütze (1992) and Turney and Pantel (2010) except that dimension words are immediate left and right neighbors (as opposed to neighbors within a window or specific types of governors or dependents). Schütze and Walsh (2011) present experimental evidence that suggests that the resulting classes are competitive with Brown classes.

4.4 Corpus

Our experiments are performed on the Europarl corpus (Koehn, 2005), a parallel corpus of proceedings of the European Parliament in 21 languages. The languages are members of the following families: Baltic languages (Latvian, Lithuanian), Germanic languages (Danish, Dutch, English, German, Swedish), Romance languages (French, Italian, Portuguese, Romanian, Spanish), Slavic languages (Bulgarian, Czech, Polish, Slovak, Slovene), Uralic languages (Estonian, Finnish, Hungarian) and Greek. We only use the part of the corpus that can be aligned to English sentences. All 21 corpora are divided into training set (80%), validation set (10%) and test set (10%). The training set is used for morphological and distributional clustering and estimation of class and KN models. The validation set is used to estimate the OOV rates ϵ and the optimal parameters λ, θ and ϕ. Table 2 gives basic statistics about the corpus. The sizes of the corpora of languages whose countries have joined the European community more recently are smaller than for countries who have been members for several decades.

We see that English and French have the lowest type/token ratios and OOV rates; and the Uralic languages (Estonian, Finnish, Hungarian) and Lithuanian the highest. The Slavic languages have higher values than the Germanic languages, which in turn have higher values than the Romance languages except for Romanian. Type/token ratio and OOV rate are one indicator of how much improvement we would expect from a language model with a morphological component compared to a non-morphological language model.[2]

5 Results and Discussion

We performed all our experiments with an n-gram order of 4; this was the order for which the KN model performs best for all languages on the validation set.

5.1 Morphological model

Using grid search, we first determined on the validation set the optimal combination of three parameters: (i) $\theta \in \{100, 200, 500, 1000, 2000, 5000\}$, (ii) $\phi \in \{50, 100, 200, 500\}$ and (iii) segmentation method. Recall that we only cluster words whose frequency is below θ and only consider the ϕ most

[2] The tokenization of the Europarl corpus has a preference for splitting tokens in unclear cases. OOV rates would be higher for more conservative tokenization strategies.

[4] A two-tailed paired t-test on the improvements by language shows that the morphological model significantly outperforms the distributional model with p=0.0027. A test on the Germanic, Romance and Greek languages yields p=0.19.

		PP_{KN}	θ^*_M	ϕ^*	M*	PP_C	PP_M	Δ_M	θ^*_D	PP_{WC}	PP_D	Δ_D
S	bg	74	200	50	f	103	69	0.07	500	141	71	0.04
S	cs	141	500	100	f	217	129	0.08	1000	298	134	0.04
S	pl	148	500	100	m	241	134	0.09	1000	349	141	0.05
S	sk	123	500	200	f	186	111	0.10	1000	261	116	0.06
S	sl	118	500	100	m	177	107	0.09	1000	232	111	0.06
G	da	69	1000	100	r	89	65	0.05	2000	103	65	0.05
G	de	100	2000	50	m	146	94	0.06	2000	150	94	0.06
G	en	55	2000	50	f	73	53	**0.03**	5000	87	53	0.04
G	nl	70	2000	50	r	100	67	0.04	5000	114	67	0.05
G	sv	98	1000	50	m	132	92	0.06	2000	154	92	0.06
E	el	80	1000	100	f	108	73	0.08	2000	134	74	**0.07**
R	es	57	2000	100	m	77	54	0.05	5000	93	54	0.05
R	fr	**45**	1000	50	f	**56**	**43**	0.04	5000	**71**	**42**	0.05
R	it	69	2000	100	m	101	66	0.04	2000	100	66	0.05
R	pt	62	2000	50	m	88	59	0.05	2000	87	59	0.05
R	ro	76	500	100	m	121	70	0.07	1000	147	71	**0.07**
U	et	256	500	100	m	**422**	230	0.10	1000	668	248	0.03
U	fi	**271**	1000	500	f	410	**240**	**0.11**	2000	**706**	**261**	0.04
U	hu	151	200	200	m	222	136	0.09	1000	360	145	**0.03**
B	lt	175	500	200	m	278	161	0.08	1000	426	169	0.03
B	lv	154	500	200	f	237	142	0.08	1000	322	147	0.05

Table 3: Perplexities on the test set for $N = 4$. S = Slavic, G = Germanic, E = Greek, R = Romance, U = Uralic, B = Baltic. θ^*_x, ϕ^* and M* denote frequency threshold, suffix count and segmentation method optimal on the validation set. The letters f, m and r stand for the frequency-based method, Morfessor and Reports. PP_{KN}, PP_C, PP_M, PP_{WC}, PP_D are the perplexities of KN, morphological class model, interpolated morphological class model, distributional class model and interpolated distributional class model, respectively. Δ_x denotes relative improvement: $(PP_{KN} - PP_x)/PP_{KN}$. Bold numbers denote maxima and minima in the respective column.[4]

frequent suffixes. An experiment with the optimal configuration was then run on the test set. The results are shown in Table 3. The KN perplexities vary between 45 for French and 271 for Finnish.

The main result is that the morphological model P_M consistently achieves better performance than KN (columns PP_M and Δ_M), in particular for Slavic, Uralic and Baltic languages and Greek. Improvements range from 0.03 for English to 0.11 for Finnish.

Column θ^*_M gives the threshold that is optimal for the validation set. Values range from 200 to 2000. Column ϕ^* gives the optimal number of suffixes. It ranges from 50 to 500. The morphologically complex language Finnish seems to benefit from more suffixes than morphologically simple languages like Dutch, English and German, but there are a few languages that do not fit this generalization, e.g., Estonian for which 100 suffixes are optimal.

The optimal morphological segmenter is given in column M*: f = Frequency, r = Reports, m = Morfessor. The most sophisticated segmenter, Morfessor is optimal for about half of the 21 languages, but Frequency does surprisingly well. Reports is optimal for two languages, Danish and Dutch. In general, Morfessor seems to have an advantage for complex morphologies, but is beaten by Frequency for Finnish and Latvian.

5.2 Distributional model

Columns PP_D and Δ_D show the performance of the distributional class language model. As one would perhaps expect, the morphological model is superior to the distributional model for morphologically complex languages like Estonian, Finnish and Hungarian. These languages have many suffixes that have

		$\Delta_{\theta^+} - \Delta_{\theta^-}$	θ^+	θ^-	$\Delta_{\phi^+} - \Delta_{\phi^-}$	ϕ^+	ϕ^-	$\Delta_{\mathrm{M}^+} - \Delta_{\mathrm{M}^-}$	M^+	M^-
S	bg	0.03	200	5000	0.01	50	500		f	m
S	cs	0.03	500	5000		100	500		f	r
S	pl	0.03	500	5000	0.01	100	500		m	r
S	sk	0.02	500	5000		200	500	0.01	f	r
S	sl	0.03	500	5000	0.01	100	500		m	r
G	da	0.02	1000	100		100	50		r	f
G	de	0.02	2000	100		50	500		m	f
G	en	0.01	2000	100		50	500		f	r
G	nl	0.01	2000	100		50	500		r	f
G	sv	0.02	1000	100		50	500		m	f
E	el	0.02	1000	100		100	500	0.01	f	r
R	es	0.02	2000	100		100	500		m	r
R	fr	0.01	1000	100		50	500		f	r
R	it	0.01	2000	100		100	500		m	r
R	pt	0.02	2000	100		50	500		m	r
R	ro	0.03	500	5000		100	500		m	r
U	et	0.02	500	5000	0.01	100	50	0.01	m	r
U	fi	0.03	1000	100	0.03	500	50	0.02	f	r
U	hu	0.03	200	5000	0.01	200	50		m	r
B	lt	0.02	500	5000		200	50		m	r
B	lv	0.02	500	5000		200	500		f	r

Table 4: Sensitivity of perplexity values to the parameters (on the validation set). S = Slavic, G = Germanic, E = Greek, R = Romance, U = Uralic, B = Baltic. Δ_{x^+} and Δ_{x^-} denote the relative improvement of P_{M} over the KN model when parameter x is set to the best (x^+) and worst value (x^-), respectively. The remaining parameters are set to the optimal values of Table 3. Cells with differences of relative improvements that are smaller than 0.01 are left empty.

high predictive power for the distributional contexts in which a word can occur. A morphological model can exploit this information even if a word with an informative suffix did not occur in one of the linguistically licensed contexts in the training set. For a distributional model it is harder to learn this type of generalization.

What is surprising about the comparative performance of morphological and distributional models is that there is no language for which the distributional model outperforms the morphological model by a wide margin. Perplexity reductions are lower than or the same as those of the morphological model in most cases, with only four exceptions – English, French, Italian, and Dutch – where the distributional model is better by one percentage point than the morphological model (0.05 vs. 0.04 and 0.04 vs. 0.03).

Column θ^*_{D} gives the frequency threshold for the distributional model. The optimal threshold ranges from 500 to 5000. This means that the distributional model benefits from restricting clustering to less frequent words – and behaves similarly to the morphological class model in that respect. We know of no previous work that has conducted experiments on frequency thresholds for distributional class models and shown that they increase perplexity reductions.

5.3 Sensitivity analysis of parameters

Table 3 shows results for parameters that were optimized on the validation set. We now want to analyze how sensitive performance is to the three parameters θ, ϕ and segmentation method. To this end, we present in Table 4 the best and worst values of each parameter and the difference in perplexity improvement between the two.

Differences of perplexity improvement between best and worst values of θ_{M} range between 0.01

and 0.03. The four languages with the smallest difference 0.01 are morphologically simple (Dutch, English, French, Italian). The languages with the largest difference (0.03) are morphologically more complex languages. In summary, the frequency threshold θ_M has a comparatively strong influence on perplexity reduction. The strength of the effect is correlated with the morphological complexity of the language.

In contrast to θ, the number of suffixes ϕ and the segmentation method have negligible effect on most languages. The perplexity reductions for different values of ϕ are 0.03 for Finnish, 0.01 for Bulgarian, Estonian, Hungarian, Polish and Slovenian, and smaller than 0.01 for the other languages. This means that, with the exception of Finnish, we can use a value of $\phi = 100$ for all languages and be very close to the optimal perplexity reduction – either because 100 is optimal or because perplexity reduction is not sensitive to choice of ϕ. Finnish is the only language that clearly benefits from a large number of suffixes.

Surprisingly, the performance of the morphological segmentation methods is very close for 17 of the 21 languages. For three of the four where there is a difference in improvement of ≥ 0.01, Frequency (f) performs best. This means that Frequency is a good segmentation method for all languages, except perhaps for Estonian.

5.4 Impact of shape

The basic question we are asking in this paper is to what extent the sequence of characters a word is composed of can be exploited for better prediction in language modeling. In the final analysis in Table 5 we look at four different types of character sequences and their contributions to perplexity reduction. The four groups are alphabetic character sequences (W), numbers (N), single special characters (P = punctuation), and other (O). Examples for O would be "751st" and words containing special characters like "O'Neill". The parameters used are the optimal ones of Table 3. Table 5 shows that the impact of special characters on perplexity is similar across languages: $0.04 \leq \Delta_P \leq 0.06$. The same is true for numbers: $0.23 \leq \Delta_N \leq 0.33$, with two outliers that show a stronger effect of this class: Finnish $\Delta_N = 0.38$ and German $\Delta_N = 0.40$.

		Δ_W	Δ_P	Δ_N	Δ_O
S	bg	0.07	0.04	0.28	0.16
S	cs	0.09	0.04	0.26	0.33
S	pl	0.10	0.05	0.23	0.22
S	sk	0.10	0.05	0.25	0.28
S	sl	0.10	0.04	0.28	0.28
G	da	0.05	0.05	0.31	0.18
G	de	0.06	0.05	0.40	0.18
G	en	0.03	0.04	0.33	0.14
G	nl	0.04	0.05	0.31	0.26
G	sv	0.06	0.05	0.31	0.35
E	el	0.08	0.05	0.33	0.14
R	es	0.05	0.04	0.26	0.14
R	fr	0.04	0.04	0.29	0.01
R	it	0.04	0.05	0.33	0.02
R	pt	0.05	0.05	0.28	0.39
R	ro	0.08	0.04	0.25	0.17
U	et	0.11	0.05	0.26	0.26
U	fi	0.12	0.06	0.38	0.36
U	hu	0.10	0.04	0.32	0.23
B	lt	0.08	0.06	0.27	0.05
B	lv	0.08	0.05	0.26	0.19

Table 5: Relative improvements of P_M on the validation set compared to KN for histories w_{i-N+1}^{i-1} grouped by the type of w_{i-1}. The possible types are alphabetic word (W), punctuation (P), number (N) and other (O).

The fact that special characters and numbers behave similarly across languages is encouraging as one would expect less crosslinguistic variation for these two classes of words.

In contrast, "true" words (those exclusively composed of alphabetic characters) show more variation from language to language: $0.03 \leq \Delta_W \leq 0.12$. The range of variation is not necessarily larger than for numbers, but since most words are alphabetical words, class W is responsible for most of the difference in perplexity reduction between different languages. As before we observe a negative correlation between morphological complexity and perplexity reduction; e.g., Dutch and English have small Δ_W and Estonian and Finnish large values.

We provide the values of Δ_O for completeness. The composition of this catch-all group varies considerably from language to language. For example, many words in this class are numbers with alphabetic suffixes like "2012-ben" in Hungarian and words with apostrophes in French.

6 Summary

We have investigated an interpolation of a KN model with a class language model whose classes are defined by morphology and shape features. We tested this model in a large crosslingual study of European languages.

Even though the model is generic and we use the same architecture and features for all languages, the model achieves reductions in perplexity for all 21 languages represented in the Europarl corpus, ranging from 3% to 11%, when compared to a KN model. We found perplexity reductions across all 21 languages for histories ending with four different types of word shapes: alphabetical words, special characters, and numbers.

We looked at the sensitivity of perplexity reductions to three parameters of the model: θ, a threshold that determines for which frequencies words are given their own class; ϕ, the number of suffixes used to determine class membership; and morphological segmentation. We found that θ has a considerable influence on the performance of the model and that optimal values vary from language to language. This parameter should be tuned when the model is used in practice.

In contrast, the number of suffixes and the morphological segmentation method only had a small effect on perplexity reductions. This is a surprising result since it means that simple identification of suffixes by frequency and choosing a fixed number of suffixes ϕ across languages is sufficient for getting most of the perplexity reduction that is possible.

7 Future Work

A surprising result of our experiments was that the perplexity reductions due to morphological classes were generally better than those due to distributional classes even though distributional classes are formed directly based on the type of information that a language model is evaluated on – the distribution of words or which words are likely to occur in sequence. An intriguing question is to what extent the effect of morphological and distributional classes is additive. We ran an exploratory experiment with a model that interpolates KN, morphological class model and distributional class model. This model only slightly outperformed the interpolation of KN and morphological class model (column PP_M in Table 3). We would like to investigate in future work if the information provided by the two types of classes is indeed largely redundant or if a more sophisticated combination would perform better than the simple linear interpolation we have used here.

Acknowledgments. This research was funded by DFG (grant SFB 732). We would like to thank the anonymous reviewers for their valuable comments.

References

Lalit R. Bahl, Peter F. Brown, Peter V. de Souza, Robert L. Mercer, and David Nahamoo. 1991. A fast algorithm for deleted interpolation. In *Eurospeech*.

Adam L. Berger, Vincent J. Della Pietra, and Stephen A. Della Pietra. 1996. A maximum entropy approach to natural language processing. *Comput. Linguist.*

Jeff A. Bilmes and Katrin Kirchhoff. 2003. Factored language models and generalized parallel backoff. In *NAACL-HLT*.

Peter F. Brown, Peter V. de Souza, Robert L. Mercer, Vincent J. Della Pietra, and Jenifer C. Lai. 1992. Class-based n-gram models of natural language. *Comput. Linguist.*

Stanley F. Chen and Joshua Goodman. 1999. An empirical study of smoothing techniques for language modeling. *Computer Speech & Language*.

Mathias Creutz and Krista Lagus. 2007. Unsupervised models for morpheme segmentation and morphology learning. *ACM TSLP*.

Mathias Creutz, Teemu Hirsimäki, Mikko Kurimo, Antti Puurula, Janne Pylkkönen, Vesa Siivola, Matti Varjokallio, Ebru Arisoy, Murat Saraçlar, and Andreas Stolcke. 2007. Morph-based speech recognition and modeling of out-of-vocabulary words across languages. *ACM TSLP*.

Samarth Keshava and Emily Pitler. 2006. A simpler, intuitive approach to morpheme induction. In *PASCAL Morpho Challenge*.

Philipp Koehn. 2005. Europarl: A parallel corpus for statistical machine translation. In *MT summit*.

Tomáš Mikolov, Martin Karafiát, Lukáš Burget, Jan Černocký, and Sanjeev Khudanpur. 2010. Recurrent neural network based language model. In *ICSLP*.

Thomas Müller and Hinrich Schütze. 2011. Improved modeling of out-of-vocabulary words using morphological classes. In *ACL*.

Ronald Rosenfeld. 1996. A maximum entropy approach to adaptive statistical language modelling. *Computer Speech & Language*.

Hinrich Schütze and Michael Walsh. 2011. Half-context language models. *Comput. Linguist.*

Hinrich Schütze. 1992. Dimensions of meaning. In *ACM/IEEE Conference on Supercomputing*, pages 787–796.

Andreas Stolcke. 2002. SRILM - An extensible language modeling toolkit. In *Interspeech*.

Yee Whye Teh. 2006. A hierarchical bayesian language model based on Pitman-Yor processes. In *ACL*.

Peter D. Turney and Patrick Pantel. 2010. From frequency to meaning: Vector space models of semantics. *JAIR*.

Dimitra Vergyri, Katrin Kirchhoff, Kevin Duh, and Andreas Stolcke. 2004. Morphology-based language modeling for Arabic speech recognition. In *ICSLP*.

E.W.D. Whittaker and P.C. Woodland. 2000. Particle-based language modelling. In *ICSLP*.

Peng Xu and Frederick Jelinek. 2004. Random forests in language modeling. In *EMNLP*.

Deniz Yuret and Ergun Biçici. 2009. Modeling morphologically rich languages using split words and unstructured dependencies. In *ACL-IJCNLP*.

Leveraging supplemental representations for sequential transduction

Aditya Bhargava
Department of Computer Science
University of Toronto
Toronto, ON, Canada, M5S 3G4
aditya@cs.toronto.edu

Grzegorz Kondrak
Department of Computing Science
University of Alberta
Edmonton, AB, Canada, T6G 2E8
kondrak@cs.ualberta.ca

Abstract

Sequential transduction tasks, such as grapheme-to-phoneme conversion and machine transliteration, are usually addressed by inducing models from sets of input-output pairs. Supplemental representations offer valuable additional information, but incorporating that information is not straightforward. We apply a unified reranking approach to both grapheme-to-phoneme conversion and machine transliteration demonstrating substantial accuracy improvements by utilizing heterogeneous transliterations and transcriptions of the input word. We describe several experiments that involve a variety of supplemental data and two state-of-the-art transduction systems, yielding error rate reductions ranging from 12% to 43%. We further apply our approach to system combination, with error rate reductions between 4% and 9%.

1 Introduction

Words exist independently of writing, as abstract entities shared among the speakers of a language. Those abstract entities have various representations, which in turn may have different realizations. Orthographic forms, phonetic transcriptions, alternative transliterations, and even sound-wave spectrograms are all related by referring to the same abstract word and they all convey information about its pronunciation.

Figure 1 shows various representations of the word *Dickens*. The primary (canonical) orthographic representation of the word corresponds to the language to which the word belongs. The secondary orthographic representations in different writing scripts are transliterations of the word, which exhibit phonological adaptation to the target language. The various phonetic transcriptions consist of sequences of phonemes representing the pronunciation of the word. Transcription schemes may differ in the number and coverage of various phonemes, as well as the choice of the underlying speech variety. The spoken pronunciation (represented by the waveform) presents a common latent influence on the representations.

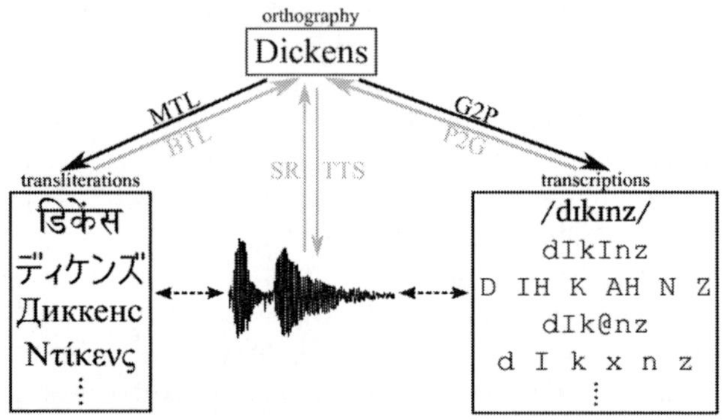

Figure 1: Several NLP tasks involve conversion between various word representations. The tasks on which we focus are shown in black.

Several well-known NLP tasks involve matching, alignment, and conversion between different word representations. Grapheme-to-phoneme conversion (G2P) aims at generating a transcription of a word from its orthographic representation. The reverse task is phoneme-to-grapheme conversion (P2G). Machine transliteration (MTL) deals with conversion between orthographic representations in different writing scripts; forward transliteration proceeds from the primary representation to secondary representations, while the reverse task is called back-transliteration (BTL). The conversion between a sound and an orthography is the goal of text-to-speech synthesis

(TTS) and speech recognition (SR), where transcriptions are often used as intermediate forms.

Although both MTL and G2P take orthographic representations as input, the two tasks are rarely considered in conjunction. Traditionally, G2P has been investigated in the context of text-to-speech systems, while MTL is of interest to the information retrieval and machine translation communities. In addition, unlike phonetic transcription schemes, which are often specific to a particular pronunciation lexicon, writing systems are well-standardized, with plenty of transliteration examples available in text corpora and on the Web (Kumaran et al., 2010b). While the goal of G2P is producing a maximally faithful representation of the pronunciation, transliterations are often influenced by other factors, such as the phonological constraints of the target language, the orthographic form in the source language, the morphological adaptations related to the translation process, and even the semantic connotations of the output in the case of logographic scripts. In spite of those differences, both transcriptions and transliterations contain valuable information about the pronunciation of the word.

In this paper, we show that it is possible to improve the accuracy of both G2P and MTL by incorporating supplemental representations of the word pronunciation. Our method is based on SVM reranking of the n-best output lists of a base transduction system, with features including similarity scores between representations and n-grams derived from accurate alignments. We describe a series of experiments in both G2P and MTL contexts, demonstrating substantial reductions in error rate for these base tasks when augmented with various supplemental representations. We then further test the effectiveness of the same approach for combining the results of two independent base systems.

2 Related work

Because of its crucial role in speech synthesis, grapheme-to-phoneme conversion has been researched extensively. Most out-of-vocabulary words are names, which often exhibit idiosyncratic pronunciation (Black et al., 1998). Excepting languages with highly transparent orthographies, the number of letter-to-sound rules appears to grow geometrically with the lexicon size, with no asymptotic limit (Kominek and Black, 2006). A number of machine learning approaches have been proposed for G2P, including neural networks (Sejnowski and Rosenberg, 1987), instance-based learning (van den Bosch and Daelemans, 1998), pronunciation by analogy (Marchand and Damper, 2000), decision trees (Kienappel and Kneser, 2001), hidden Markov models (Taylor, 2005), joint n-gram models (Bisani and Ney, 2008), and online discriminative learning (Jiampojamarn et al., 2008). The current state-of-the-art is represented by the latter two approaches, which are available as the SEQUITUR and DIRECTL+ systems, respectively.

Machine transliteration has also received much attention (Knight and Graehl, 1998; Li et al., 2004; Sproat et al., 2006; Klementiev and Roth, 2006; Zelenko and Aone, 2006). In the last few years, the Named Entities Workshop (NEWS) Shared Tasks on Transliteration have been the forum for validating diverse approaches on common data sets (Li et al., 2009; Li et al., 2010; Zhang et al., 2011). Both SEQUITUR and DIRECTL+, originally G2P systems, have been successfully adapted to MTL (Finch and Sumita, 2010; Jiampojamarn et al., 2010b).

Most of the research on both G2P and MTL assumes the existence of a homogeneous training set of input-output pairs. However, following the pivot approaches developed in other areas of NLP (Utiyama and Isahara, 2007; Cohn and Lapata, 2007; Wu and Wang, 2009; Snyder et al., 2009), the idea of taking advantage of other-language data has recently been applied to machine transliteration. Khapra et al. (2010) construct a transliteration system between languages A and B by composing two transliteration systems $A \rightarrow C$ and $C \rightarrow B$, where C is called a *bridge* or *pivot* language, resulting in a relatively small drop in accuracy. Zhang et al. (2010) and Kumaran et al. (2010a) report that combinations of pivot systems $A \rightarrow C \rightarrow B$ with direct systems $A \rightarrow B$ produce better results than using the direct systems only. The models, which are composed using a linear combination of scores, utilize a single pivot language C, and require training data between all three languages A, B, and C. However, such a pivot-based framework makes it difficult to incorporate multiple pivot languages, and has shown most promising results for cases in which data for the original $A \rightarrow B$ task are limited. Lastly, Finch and Sumita (2010) developed an MTL approach that combined the output

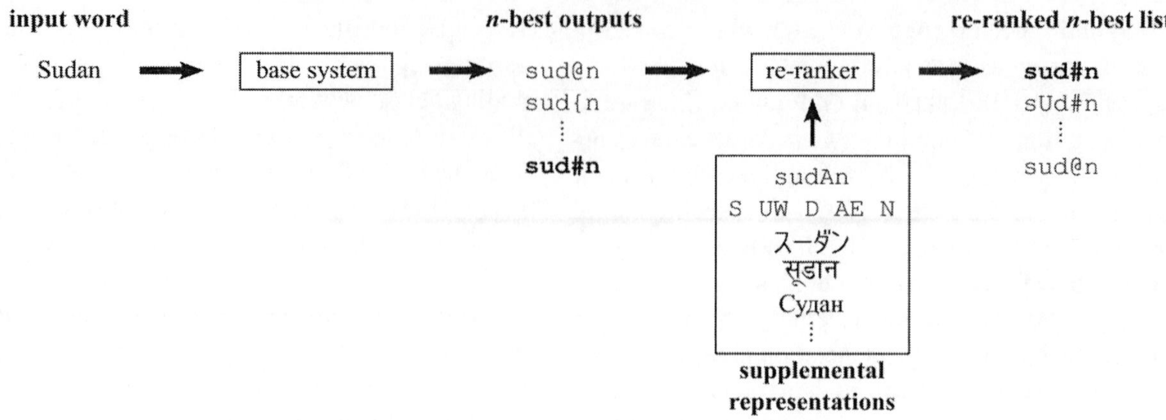

Figure 2: An overview of our approach on an example from the G2P task. The correct output is shown in bold.

of two systems using a linear combination of system scores and a manually-tuned weight.

On the G2P side, Loots and Niesler (2009) investigate the problem of leveraging transcriptions from a different dialect of English, while Bhargava and Kondrak (2011) focus on leveraging transliterations from multiple writing scripts. Bhargava et al. (2011) show that the reranking method proposed by Bhargava and Kondrak (2011) can increase the accuracy of MTL as well. In this paper, we aim to confirm the generality of the same method by testing it on a broad range of tasks: *a*) leveraging *transcriptions* for both G2P and MTL; *b*) utilizing supplemental transcriptions and transliterations *simultaneously*; *c*) improving G2P *in general*, rather than just G2P of names; and *d*) combining different transduction systems.

3 Leveraging supplemental data

Incorporating supplemental information directly into an existing system is not always feasible. With generative approaches, one would have to find some way of modelling the relationship between the system inputs, outputs, and the supplemental data. Discriminative approaches are not necessarily easier: DIRECTL+, a discriminative G2P system, needs to be able to generate features on-the-fly for partial grapheme-phoneme sequence pairs during the decoding. Instead, we integrate an existing system as a black box that generates n-best lists of candidate outputs, resulting in a modular and general *post hoc* approach that can be applied to multiple tasks and settings.

3.1 Task definition

The task is to convert an input string s into a target string t, where both strings are representations of a word w. In G2P, s is a string of graphemes while t consists of phonemes; in MTL, both s and t are grapheme sequences, although in different scripts. We assume that we have a base system $T(s)$ that attempts this task and produces an n-best list of outputs $\widehat{t_1}, \widehat{t_2}, \ldots, \widehat{t_n}$ for the input s. T is imperfect, i.e., the correct output t may appear in a position in the list other than the first. It is reasonable to expect that such a system also provides a list of scores corresponding to the outputs. We further assume that we have access to supplemental representations of w; both transliterations and transcriptions may serve this purpose. Our objective is to improve the accuracy on the task in question with respect to the base system $T(s)$.

3.2 Reranking

For the purpose of exposition, we reiterate here the particulars of the reranking approach of Bhargava and Kondrak (2011) that we apply to the various tasks and supplemental data sources. The method uses SVM reranking of the n-best lists produced by the base system in order to to move the correct output to the top of the list using supplemental data. SVM reranking (Joachims, 2002) facilitates the exploitation of multiple sources of supplemental data, as shown in Figure 2. The feature construction process is performed for each candidate output in the n-best list, as well as each pairing of a candidate output with a supplemental representation. The features used for reranking may or may not overlap with the features used by the base system. While we focus on the G2P and MTL tasks in this paper, this method is general enough as to potentially be applied to other sequence prediction tasks.

3.3 Alignment

In order to construct the feature vectors, we need the alignments between the alternative representations of the same word. For the alignment of supplemental data with candidate outputs, we apply M2M-ALIGNER (Jiampojamarn et al., 2007). We use the same method for the alignment between the input and the candidate outputs, unless the base system already provides this information.

M2M-ALIGNER is a generalization of the learned edit distance algorithm of Ristad and Yianilos (1998). It iteratively refines the alignment of a set of string pairs in an unsupervised manner using the expectation-maximization (EM) approach. In addition to the alignment, M2M-ALIGNER produces an alignment probability, which reflects the similarity between two strings. Intuitively, if two strings contain symbols or n-grams that often co-occur in the training data, their alignment score will be higher. The strings in question are often of completely different scripts, which precludes the application of standard similarity measures such as Levenshtein distance.

3.4 Score features

The similarity of candidate outputs to alternative representations of a word is probably the most intuitive feature for reranking. We include a real-valued similarity feature for each pairing between a supplemental representation and a candidate output, which is set according to the M2M-ALIGNER alignment score.

Another important set of features are the confidence scores assigned to each candidate output by the base system. In addition to the original scores, we also include a set of features that indicate the *differences* between scores for all pairs of outputs in the n-best list. This allows the reranker to incorporate a notion of relative confidence with respect to the other candidate outputs. Similarly, we compute differences between the similarity scores of candidate outputs and supplemental representations.

3.5 N-gram features

Following (Jiampojamarn et al., 2010a), we include several types of n-gram features. The features are defined on substrings occurring in pairs of aligned strings. Each feature is binary, indicating the presence or absence of the particular feature type in the given aligned pair, which could be either the original base system's input and output, or else a candidate output and a supplemental representation.

We can divide the n-gram features into four categories. *Context features* bind an output symbol with input n-grams in a focus window centred around the input-output alignment; the input n-grams represent the context in which the output character is generated. *Markov features* are n-grams of output symbols, which allow previously generated output characters to influence the current output character. *Linear chain features* associate the context and Markov features. *Joint n-gram features* combine aligned input and output n-grams of the same length on both sides.

In the standard string transduction task, the output string t is generated incrementally from the input s. In contrast, in the reranking setting, both strings are complete and available. This allows us to *reverse* the direction of the context and linear chain features, allowing us to associate output n-grams with single input symbols. In addition, we can apply those features in both directions across candidate outputs and supplemental representations, further increasing the amount of information provided to the reranker.

4 Experiments

Our experiments aim at comprehensive evaluation of the reranking approach on both MTL and G2P tasks, employing various supplemental representations. Relevant code and scripts associated with our experimental results are available online[1].

4.1 Data

We extract transcriptions from two lexica: Combilex (Richmond et al., 2009), which includes both Received Pronunciation (RP) and General American (GA) pronunciation variants, and CELEX (Baayen et al., 1996), which includes RP only. After discarding duplicates and letter diacritics, the total number of

[1]http://www.cs.toronto.edu/~aditya/g2p-tl-rr

Language	Corpus size	Japanese Overlap
Bengali	13,624	2,152
Chinese	40,214	14,056
Hebrew	10,501	3,997
Hindi	13,427	2,507
Japanese	28,013	—
Kannada	11,540	2,170
Korean	7,778	7,733
Persian	12,386	4,047
Tamil	11,642	2,205
Thai	28,932	10,378

Table 1: The number of unique entries in each transliteration corpus, and the number of common single-word entries (overlap) with the Japanese corpus.

word-transcription pairs are 114,094 for Combilex, and 66,859 for CELEX. We use 10% of the data for development, 10% for testing, and the remaining 80% for training. The development set is merged with the training set for final testing.

Our transliteration data come from the shared tasks of the 2011 NEWS workshop (Zhang et al., 2011). The number of entries in each transliteration corpus is shown in the middle column of Table 1.

4.2 Base systems

In order to verify the generality of our approach, we perform all experiments using two different base transduction systems described in Section 2: SEQUITUR and DIRECTL+. Both systems are set to provide 10-best output lists along with scores for each output.[2] SEQUITUR is modified to provide log-probabilities instead of regular probabilities. DIRECTL+ is run with the complete set of features described by Jiampojamarn et al. (2010a). System parameters, such as maximum number of iterations, are determined during development.

M2M-ALIGNER is used throughout for the alignment of various representations. The aligner is trained on an intersection of a relevant pair of data sets. For example, the intersection of the English-to-Japanese and English-to-Hindi corpora on the basis of common entries on the English side yields a corpus matching Japanese transliterations with Hindi transliterations. M2M-ALIGNER, after having been trained on this corpus, is able to produce a similarity score for an arbitrary Japanese-Hindi pair. We set a lower limit of -100 on the M2M-ALIGNER log-probabilities, and use the default of 2-2 alignments; deletions are enabled for the supplemental data side of the alignment.

4.3 MTL experiments

When faced with the task of transliterating a word from the original script to a secondary script, we would like to leverage the information encoded in transliterations of the same word that are available in other scripts. For example, consider the problem of automatically generating a Wikipedia stub article[3] in Hindi about guitarist John Petrucci. We assume that we have access to an MTL system trained on the English-Hindi transliterations, but we also want to take advantage of the existing transliterations of the name that are easy to extract from the corresponding articles on the topic in Japanese and other languages. In this case, the orthography of the last name reflects its Italian origins, but the pronunciation depends on its degree of assimilation to English phonology. This type of information is often difficult to determine even for humans, and we posit that it may be inferred from other transliterations.

Similarly, phonetic transcriptions more directly encode the pronunciation and thus present an important resource for exploitation. In fact, some transliteration systems use a phonetic transcription as an intermediate representation (Knight and Graehl, 1998), although these methods do not generally fare as well as those that perform the transliteration process directly (Al-Onaizan and Knight, 2002; Li et al., 2009). Transcriptions are often available; larger pronunciation dictionaries contain tens of thousands of entries, including some proper names (for which machine transliteration is most relevant), and many names in Wikipedia are accompanied by an IPA transcription.

Our first experiment aims at improving the transliteration accuracy from English to Japanese Katakana. The English-Japanese corpus has one of the largest overlaps (number of entries with a common input)

[2]While running times prevented us from extensively analyzing reranking performance vs. n-best list size, our initial tests produced almost identical results for $n = 5$, $n = 10$, and $n = 20$.

[3]A stub article is a skeleton article with little content.

	SEQUITUR		DIRECTL+	
	Acc.	ERR	Acc.	ERR
BASE	49.6		51.1	
RERANKED	56.2	13.5	57.3	12.7
ORACLE	85.0	70.3	80.4	60.0

Table 2: Word accuracies and error rate reductions (ERR) in percentages for English-to-Japanese MTL augmented by corresponding transliterations from other languages. BASE is the base system while RERANKED represents the same system with its output reranked using supplemental transliterations. ORACLE represents an oracle reranker.

	SEQUITUR		DIRECTL+	
	Acc.	ERR	Acc.	ERR
BASE	57.9		58.6	
RERANKED	65.6	18.4	63.9	12.8
ORACLE	89.9	51.5	84.6	62.6

Table 3: Word accuracies and error rate reductions (ERR) in percentages for English-to-Japanese MTL augmented by corresponding transcriptions.

with the other transliteration and transcription corpora, the former of which is shown in Table 1. In total, there are 18,505 entries for which at least one transliteration from a non-Japanese language is available and 6,288 for which at least one transcription is available. The reranker is trained on an intersection of the English-Japanese training set and the supplemental data; similarly, the reranking test set is an intersection of the English-Japanese test set and the supplemental data. Note that we compute word accuracy on these intersected sets, so the results of the base systems that we report here may not represent their performance on the full data set.

Table 2 shows the results[4] on the test set of 1,891 entries, including the performance of an oracle (perfect) reranker for comparison. This same approach applied to the English-to-Hindi transliteration task yields an error rate reduction of 9% over the base performance of DIRECTL+ (Bhargava et al., 2011)[5], which confirms that our reranking method's applicability is not limited to a particular language.

In the second experiment, instead of supplemental transliterations, we use supplemental transcriptions from the RP and GA Combilex corpora as well as CELEX. The number of common elements with the English-Japanese transliteration corpus was 6,288 for Combilex and 2,351 for CELEX; in total, there were 6,384 transliteration entries for which at least one transcription was available. Table 3 shows the results, giving a similar error rate reduction as for using supplemental transliterations.

Surprisingly, if we proceed to the next logical step and use both transcriptions and transliterations as supplemental representations *simultaneously*, the error rate reduction is slightly lower than in the above two experiments. This difference is so small as to be statistically insignificant. We have no convincing explanation for this phenomenon, although we note that, in general, significant heterogeneity in data can increase the difficulty of a given task.

4.4 G2P experiments

Consider the example of an automatic speech synthesis system tasked with generating an audio version of a news article that contains foreign names. Often, foreign versions of the same news article already exist; in these, the name will have been transliterated. These transliterations could then be leveraged to guide the system's pronunciation of the name. The same is conceivable of other types of words, although transliterations are generally mostly available for names only.

On the other hand, transcription schemes are not consistent across different pronunciation lexica. Their phonemic inventories often differ, and it is not always possible to construct a consistent mapping between them. In addition, because of pronunciation variation and dialectal differences, a substantial fraction of transcriptions fail to match across dictionaries. Nevertheless, if a phonetic transcription is already available, even in an alternative format, it could facilitate the task of generating a new pronunciation.

The first G2P experiment concerns the application of supplemental transcriptions. The goal is to quantify the improvements achieved using our reranking

[4]Unless otherwise noted, all improvements reported in this paper are statistically significant with $p < 0.01$ using the McNemar test.

[5]Note that this result is computed over the full English-Hindi data set, so is in fact slightly diluted compared to the results we present here.

approach, and to compare reranking to two other methods of utilizing supplemental transcriptions, to which we refer as MERGE and P2P, respectively.

MERGE implements the most intuitive approach of merging different lexica into a single training set. In order to make this work, we first need to make sure that all data is converted to a single transcription scheme. Combilex and CELEX make different distinctions among phonemes, making it unclear how some phonemes might be mapped from CELEX into Combilex; fortuitously, the opposite conversion is more agreeable.[6] This allows us to convert Combilex to CELEX's format via a simple rule-based script and then merge the two corpora together. This provides an alternative method against which we can compare our reranking-based approach which would treat Combilex as a source of supplemental representations.

P2P is a phoneme-to-phoneme conversion approach inspired by the work of Loots and Niesler (2009). In that approach, a phoneme-to-phoneme model is derived from a training set of phonetic transcription pairs representing two different pronunciation lexicons. We use such model to convert the Combilex transcriptions to the scheme used by CELEX for the words that are missing from CELEX. Where Loots and Niesler (2009) use decision trees for both the base system and the corpus converter, we use the much higher-performing state-of-the-art SEQUITUR and DIRECTL+ systems.

The two transcription corpora have 15,028 entries in common. As with the MTL experiments, the reranker is trained on an intersection of the Combilex G2P data and the supplemental data.

The results on the intersected set of 1,498 words are shown in Table 4. We can see that merging the corpora provides a clear detriment in performance for data where an alternative transcription is available from another corpus. Even if we look at the full CELEX test set (as opposed to the intersected subset used in Table 4), DIRECTL+ trained only on CELEX achieves 93.0% word accuracy on the CELEX test set where DIRECTL+ trained on CELEX merged with Combilex achieves 87.3%. Evidently, the disparate conventions of the two corpora "confuse" the base G2P systems. In contrast, our reranker performs well, yielding spectacular error reductions of 32% and 42%.

	SEQUITUR		DIRECTL+	
	Acc.	ERR	Acc.	ERR
BASE	87.3		88.1	
MERGE	74.2	—	71.6	—
P2P	85.7	—	87.0	—
RERANKED	92.7	42.9	92.0	32.6
ORACLE	97.6	81.2	96.7	72.5

Table 4: Word accuracies and error rate reductions (ERR) in percentages for CELEX G2P augmented by Combilex transcriptions.

The differences between the two corpora account for the inadequate performance of the P2P approach. Inducing a full transduction model requires much more training data that simply reranking the existing outputs, but in this case models for these two approaches (P2P and reranking) are trained on the same amount of data. Furthermore, when the supplemental transcription is radically different from the n-best outputs, the alignment simply fails, and the reranking approach gracefully falls back to the original G2P model. In contrast, the P2P approach has no such option.

It may be interesting to note what happens when the P2P model is replaced with our rule-based Combilex-to-CELEX converter. Such an approach has the advantage of being fast and not dependent on the training of any base system. However, it achieves only 64.8% word accuracy, which is lower than any of the results in Table 4. Clearly, a simple mapping script fails to capture the differences between the corpora.

Turning to supplemental transliterations, Bhargava and Kondrak (2011) have already shown that supplemental transliterations can improve G2P accuracy on *names*. It is interesting to verify whether this conclusion also applies to other types of words that occur in the G2P data set. Performing this test with DIRECTL+ as the base system shows good error rate reduction on names (about 12%) as reported, but a much smaller statistically insignificant error rate re-

[6] In particular, Combilex distinguishes between [l] and the velarized ("dark") [ɫ]. These can be collapsed into the single /l/ phoneme for CELEX, but it is not clear how to handle the conversion in the reverse direction.

duction on core vocabulary words (around 2%). In other words, the supplemental transliterations are able to help only for names.

This discrepancy is attributable to the fact that names (and, more generally, named entities) are the *raison d'être* of transliterations. Because the process of transliteration occurs primarily for names that must be "translated" phonetically, we expect transliterations' utility as supplemental representations to apply mostly for names. The smaller number of transliterations for core vocabulary words also makes it difficult for any system to learn how to apply transliterations of such words.

4.5 Base system matters

While our SVM reranking approach demonstrates significant improvements for all tasks and all tested base systems, the *magnitude* of the performance increase *is* dependent on the base system. In particular, we see a common thread recurring throughout all experiments: SEQUITUR sees higher improvements than does DIRECTL+. Although reranking treats the base system as a black box, we are limited by the amount of room for improvement available in the base system's outputs. Our results above show that the performance of an oracle reranker (a reranker that automatically selects the correct output from the n-best list) is consistently higher for SEQUITUR than for DIRECTL+. Higher oracle reranker scores indicate greater reranking potential, and we observe a corresponding higher error reduction, sometimes leading SEQUITUR to outperform DIRECTL+ after reranking despite having been the lower performer prior to reranking.

We hypothesize that another reason for the greater influence of reranking on SEQUITUR is the fact that the reranker's features are related to those used in DIRECTL+. Because SEQUITUR implements a diametrically different, generative approach to transduction, it benefits more from reranking. However, DIRECTL+ still sees significant performance increases despite the feature similarity, which demonstrates that the supplemental representations do provide useful additional information.

4.6 System combination

Although the reranking approach was developed for the purpose of leveraging supplemental data, it can

	SEQUITUR		DIRECTL+	
	Acc.	ERR	Acc.	ERR
BASE	45.5		47.3	
LINCOMB	49.4	7.2	49.4	4.0
RERANKED	50.2	8.7	49.2	3.7
ORACLE	82.4	67.7	77.3	56.9

Table 5: Word accuracies and error rate reductions (ERR) in percentages for English-to-Japanese MTL augmented by predicted transliterations from the other base system.

also increase the accuracy when no genuine supplemental data is available. The idea is to perform system combination by treating the output of one of the systems as the supplemental data for the other system, effectively casting the system combination problem into our reranking framework. In our last experiment, we test the combination of DIRECTL+ and SEQUITUR for English-to-Japanese MTL by designating either of them as the base system. Since the supplemental data are generated, we are not limited to a particular subset, and can conduct the experiment on the entire English-to-Japanese set, with the test set having 2,801 entries. For comparison, we also test a linear combination of the (normalized) system scores with a manually tuned weight parameter (LINCOMB). This baseline is similar to the system combination method of Finch and Sumita (2010).

Table 5 contains the results for English-to-Japanese transliterations, which indicate a significant increase in accuracy in both cases, thereby demonstrating the viability of our approach for system combination. This experiment extends the system combination result on English-to-Hindi transliteration reported by Bhargava et al. (2011), in which DIRECTL+ served as the base system while SEQUITUR provided the supplemental data. The system in question yielded nearly a 4% error rate reduction, which made it the top-ranking submission at the NEWS 2011 Shared Task on Transliteration.

On the other hand, LINCOMB turns out to be a strong baseline, which is evidenced by the fact that the differences between our reranking approach and LINCOMB are statistically insignificant. This is likely because LINCOMB can take advantage of the full n-best lists provided by both systems, whereas the reranking approach uses only the top-1 result from the "supplemental" system. Combining the two n-best lists in this way also gives a higher oracle score of 86.4%, suggesting that this may be a good and computationally cheap first step prior to reranking using proper supplemental data as described above.

5 Future work

We plan on investigating a more parsimonious method of incorporating supplemental data. There are two aspects to this. First, while our experiments in this paper treated base systems as black boxes for the purposes of examining the effect of the supplemental data in isolation, reranking is limited by its *post hoc* nature. After all, if the correct output does not appear in the base systems' n-best list, even a perfect reranker would be unable to find it. Incorporating the supplemental data earlier in the process would allow us to overcome this limitation at the expense of being a solution specific to the base system.

Second, we would like to be able to incorporate general supplemental *information* rather than being limited by the existence of relevant *data*. In particular, a good transliteration model should encode a general version of the information provided by a single transliteration, so being able to apply that information would allow us to overcome our dependence on existing data as well as provide more potentially useful information even when a transliteration or transcription already exists.

Finally, we plan on examining other potential supplemental resources. Given the success of our approach in the face of sometimes-noisy transliteration data[7], other noisy data may be applicable as well. For example, IPA transcriptions could be mined from Wikipedia despite the fact that different transcriptions may have been written by different people. Similarly, difficult-to-pronounce names or words are often accompanied by *ad hoc* approximately-phonetic re-spellings, which may also prove useful.

6 Conclusion

In this paper, we examined the relevance of alternative, supplemental representations for the tasks of grapheme-to-phoneme conversion and machine transliteration, both of which have pronunciation as an important underlying influence. We applied an SVM reranking approach that leverages the supplemental data using features constructed from n-grams as well as from similarity and system scores. The approach yielded excellent improvements when used with both the SEQUITUR and DIRECTL+ base systems. Over the state-of-the-art DIRECTL+, we achieved significant error rate reductions of **13%** for English-to-Japanese MTL using supplemental transliterations, **13%** using supplemental transcriptions, and **33%** for English G2P using supplemental transcriptions. For system combination, we found a smaller but still significant error rate reduction of **4%**. The fact that the improvements vary systematically by base system help confirm that the supplemental data do provide inherently useful information.

We can also take a step back to take a broader look at our approach. It applies similar features as those used in the standard generation task in a new, orthogonal direction (supplemental data) with successful results. This notion is general enough that it may potentially be applicable to other tasks, such as part-of-speech tagging or machine translation.

Acknowledgements

We thank Sittichai Jiampojamarn and Shane Bergsma for helpful discussions. This research was supported by the Natural Sciences and Engineering Research Council of Canada.

References

Yaser Al-Onaizan and Kevin Knight. 2002. Machine transliteration of names in Arabic texts. In *Proceedings of the ACL-02 Workshop on Computational Approaches to Semitic Languages*, Philadelphia, Pennsylvania, USA, July. Association for Computational Linguistics.

R. Harald Baayen, Richard Piepenbrock, and Leon Gulikers. 1996. The CELEX2 lexical database. LDC96L14.

Aditya Bhargava and Grzegorz Kondrak. 2011. How do you pronounce your name? Improving G2P with transliterations. In *Proceedings of the 49th Annual Meeting of the Association for Computational Linguistics: Human Language Technologies*, pages 399–408, Portland, Oregon, USA, June. Association for Computational Linguistics.

[7]Jiampojamarn et al. (2009) found a significant increase in English-to-Hindi transliteration performance after applying a simple rule-based cleaning script.

Aditya Bhargava, Bradley Hauer, and Grzegorz Kondrak. 2011. Leveraging transliterations from multiple languages. In *Proceedings of the 3rd Named Entities Workshop (NEWS 2011)*, pages 36–40, Chiang Mai, Thailand, November. Asian Federation of Natural Language Processing.

Maximilian Bisani and Hermann Ney. 2008. Joint-sequence models for grapheme-to-phoneme conversion. *Speech Communication*, 50(5):434–451, May.

Alan W. Black, Kevin Lenzo, and Vincent Pagel. 1998. Issues in building general letter to sound rules. In *The Third ESCA/COCOSDA Workshop (ETRW) on Speech Synthesis*, Jenolan Caves House, Blue Mountains, New South Wales, Australia, November.

Trevor Cohn and Mirella Lapata. 2007. Machine translation by triangulation: Making effective use of multi-parallel corpora. In *Proceedings of the 45th Annual Meeting of the Association of Computational Linguistics*, pages 728–735, Prague, Czech Republic, June. Association for Computational Linguistics.

Andrew Finch and Eiichiro Sumita. 2010. Transliteration using a phrase-based statistical machine translation system to re-score the output of a joint multigram model. In *Proceedings of the 2010 Named Entities Workshop*, pages 48–52, Uppsala, Sweden, July. Association for Computational Linguistics.

Sittichai Jiampojamarn, Grzegorz Kondrak, and Tarek Sherif. 2007. Applying many-to-many alignments and hidden Markov models to letter-to-phoneme conversion. In *Human Language Technologies 2007: The Conference of the North American Chapter of the Association for Computational Linguistics; Proceedings of the Main Conference*, pages 372–379, Rochester, New York, USA, April. Association for Computational Linguistics.

Sittichai Jiampojamarn, Colin Cherry, and Grzegorz Kondrak. 2008. Joint processing and discriminative training for letter-to-phoneme conversion. In *Proceedings of ACL-08: HLT*, pages 905–913, Columbus, Ohio, USA, June. Association for Computational Linguistics.

Sittichai Jiampojamarn, Aditya Bhargava, Qing Dou, Kenneth Dwyer, and Grzegorz Kondrak. 2009. DirecTL: a language independent approach to transliteration. In *Proceedings of the 2009 Named Entities Workshop: Shared Task on Transliteration (NEWS 2009)*, pages 28–31, Suntec, Singapore, August. Association for Computational Linguistics.

Sittichai Jiampojamarn, Colin Cherry, and Grzegorz Kondrak. 2010a. Integrating joint n-gram features into a discriminative training framework. In *Human Language Technologies: The 2010 Annual Conference of the North American Chapter of the Association for Computational Linguistics*, pages 697–700, Los Angeles, California, USA, June. Association for Computational Linguistics.

Sittichai Jiampojamarn, Kenneth Dwyer, Shane Bergsma, Aditya Bhargava, Qing Dou, Mi-Young Kim, and Grzegorz Kondrak. 2010b. Transliteration generation and mining with limited training resources. In *Proceedings of the 2010 Named Entities Workshop*, pages 39–47, Uppsala, Sweden, July. Association for Computational Linguistics.

Thorsten Joachims. 2002. Optimizing search engines using clickthrough data. In *Proceedings of the Eighth ACM SIGKDD International Conference on Knowledge Discovery and Data Mining*, pages 133–142, Edmonton, Alberta, Canada. Association for Computing Machinery.

Mitesh M. Khapra, A Kumaran, and Pushpak Bhattacharyya. 2010. Everybody loves a rich cousin: An empirical study of transliteration through bridge languages. In *Human Language Technologies: The 2010 Annual Conference of the North American Chapter of the Association for Computational Linguistics*, pages 420–428, Los Angeles, California, June. Association for Computational Linguistics.

Anne K. Kienappel and Reinhard Kneser. 2001. Designing very compact decision trees for grapheme-to-phoneme transcription. In *EUROSPEECH-2001*, pages 1911–1914, Aalborg, Denmark, September.

Alexandre Klementiev and Dan Roth. 2006. Named entity transliteration and discovery from multilingual comparable corpora. In *Proceedings of the Human Language Technology Conference of the NAACL, Main Conference*, pages 82–88, New York City, USA, June. Association for Computational Linguistics.

Kevin Knight and Jonathan Graehl. 1998. Machine transliteration. *Computational Linguistics*, 24(4):599–612, December.

John Kominek and Alan W. Black. 2006. Learning pronunciation dictionaries: Language complexity and word selection strategies. In *Proceedings of the Human Language Technology Conference of the NAACL, Main Conference*, pages 232–239, New York City, New York, USA, June. Association for Computational Linguistics.

A. Kumaran, Mitesh M. Khapra, and Pushpak Bhattacharyya. 2010a. Compositional machine transliteration. 9(4):13:1–13:29, December.

A Kumaran, Mitesh M. Khapra, and Haizhou Li. 2010b. Report of news 2010 transliteration mining shared task. In *Proceedings of the 2010 Named Entities Workshop*, pages 21–28, Uppsala, Sweden, July. Association for Computational Linguistics.

Haizhou Li, Min Zhang, and Jian Su. 2004. A joint source-channel model for machine transliteration. In *Proceedings of the 42nd Meeting of the Association for Computational Linguistics (ACL'04), Main Volume*, pages 159–166, Barcelona, Spain, July.

Haizhou Li, A Kumaran, Vladimir Pervouchine, and Min Zhang. 2009. Report of NEWS 2009 machine transliteration shared task. In *Proceedings of the 2009 Named Entities Workshop: Shared Task on Transliteration (NEWS 2009)*, pages 1–18, Suntec, Singapore, August. Association for Computational Linguistics.

Haizhou Li, A Kumaran, Min Zhang, and Vladimir Pervouchine. 2010. Report of NEWS 2010 transliteration generation shared task. In *Proceedings of the 2010 Named Entities Workshop*, pages 1–11, Uppsala, Sweden, July. Association for Computational Linguistics.

Linsen Loots and Thomas R. Niesler. 2009. Data-driven phonetic comparison and conversion between south african, british and american english pronunciations. In *Proceedings of Interspeech*, Brighton, UK, September.

Yannick Marchand and Robert I. Damper. 2000. A multistrategy approach to improving pronunciation by analogy. *Computational Linguistics*, 26(2):195–219, June.

Korin Richmond, Robert Clark, and Sue Fitt. 2009. Robust LTS rules with the Combilex speech technology lexicon. In *Proceedings of Interspeech*, pages 1295–1298, Brighton, UK, September.

Eric Sven Ristad and Peter N. Yianilos. 1998. Learning string edit distance. *IEEE Transactions on Pattern Recognition and Machine Intelligence*, 20(5):522–532, May.

Terrence J. Sejnowski and Charles R. Rosenberg. 1987. Parallel networks that learn to pronounce english text. *Complex Systems*, 1(1):145–168.

Benjamin Snyder, Tahira Naseem, Jacob Eisenstein, and Regina Barzilay. 2009. Adding more languages improves unsupervised multilingual part-of-speech tagging: a bayesian non-parametric approach. In *Proceedings of Human Language Technologies: The 2009 Annual Conference of the North American Chapter of the Association for Computational Linguistics*, pages 83–91, Boulder, Colorado, USA, June. Association for Computational Linguistics.

Richard Sproat, Tao Tao, and ChengXiang Zhai. 2006. Named entity transliteration with comparable corpora. In *Proceedings of the 21st International Conference on Computational Linguistics and 44th Annual Meeting of the Association for Computational Linguistics*, pages 73–80, Sydney, Australia, July. Association for Computational Linguistics.

Paul Taylor. 2005. Hidden Markov models for grapheme to phoneme conversion. In *Proceedings of Interspeech*, pages 1973–1976, Lisbon, Portugal, September.

Masao Utiyama and Hitoshi Isahara. 2007. A comparison of pivot methods for phrase-based statistical machine translation. In *Human Language Technologies 2007: The Conference of the North American Chapter of the Association for Computational Linguistics; Proceedings of the Main Conference*, pages 484–491, Rochester, New York, USA, April. Association for Computational Linguistics.

van den Bosch and Walter Daelemans. 1998. Do not forget: Full memory in memory-based learning of word pronunciation. In D.M.W. Powers, editor, *NeMLaP3/CoNLL98: New Methods in Language Processing and Computational Natural Language Learning*, pages 195–204, Sydney, Australia. Association for Computational Linguistics.

Hua Wu and Haifeng Wang. 2009. Revisiting pivot language approach for machine translation. In *Proceedings of the Joint Conference of the 47th Annual Meeting of the ACL and the 4th International Joint Conference on Natural Language Processing of the AFNLP*, pages 154–162, Suntec, Singapore, August. Association for Computational Linguistics.

Dmitry Zelenko and Chinatsu Aone. 2006. Discriminative methods for transliteration. In *Proceedings of the 2006 Conference on Empirical Methods in Natural Language Processing*, pages 612–617, Sydney, Australia, July. Association for Computational Linguistics.

Min Zhang, Xiangyu Duan, Vladimir Pervouchine, and Haizhou Li. 2010. Machine transliteration: Leveraging on third languages. In *Coling 2010: Posters*, pages 1444–1452, Beijing, China, August. Coling 2010 Organizing Committee.

Min Zhang, Haizhou Li, A Kumaran, and Ming Liu. 2011. Report of NEWS 2011 machine transliteration shared task. In *Proceedings of the 3rd Named Entities Workshop (NEWS 2011)*, pages 1–13, Chiang Mai, Thailand, November. Asian Federation of Natural Language Processing.

A Hierarchical Dirichlet Process Model for Joint Part-of-Speech and Morphology Induction

Kairit Sirts
Institute of Cybernetics at
Tallinn University of Technology
kairit.sirts@phon.ioc.ee

Tanel Alumäe
Institute of Cybernetics at
Tallinn University of Technology
tanel.alumae@phon.ioc.ee

Abstract

In this paper we present a fully unsupervised nonparametric Bayesian model that jointly induces POS tags and morphological segmentations. The model is essentially an infinite HMM that infers the number of states from data. Incorporating segmentation into the same model provides the morphological features to the system and eliminates the need to find them during preprocessing step. We show that learning both tasks jointly actually leads to better results than learning either task with gold standard data from the other task provided. The evaluation on multilingual data shows that the model produces state-of-the-art results on POS induction.

1 Introduction

Nonparametric Bayesian modeling has recently become very popular in natural language processing (NLP), mostly because of its ability to provide priors that are especially suitable for tasks in NLP (Teh, 2006). Using nonparametric priors enables to treat the size of the model as a random variable with its value to be induced during inference which makes its use very appealing in models that need to decide upon the number of states.

The task of unsupervised parts-of-speech (POS) tagging has been under research in numerous papers, for overview see (Christodoulopoulos et al., 2010). Most of the POS induction models use the structure of hidden Markov model (HMM) (Rabiner, 1989) that requires the knowledge about the number of hidden states (corresponding to the number of tags) in advance. According to our considerations, supplying this information is not desirable for two opposing reasons: 1) it injects into the system a piece of knowledge which in a truly unsupervised setting would be unavailable; and 2) the number of POS tags used is somewhat arbitrary anyway because there is no common consensus of what should be the true number of tags in each language and therefore it seems unreasonable to constrain the model with such a number instead of learning it from the data.

Unsupervised morphology learning is another popular task that has been extensively studied by many authors. Here we are interested in learning concatenative morphology of words, meaning the substrings of the word corresponding to morphemes that, when concatenated, will give the lexical representation of the word type. For the rest of the paper we will refer to this task as (morphological) segmentation.

Several unsupervised POS induction systems make use of morphological features (Blunsom and Cohn, 2011; Lee et al., 2010; Berg-Kirkpatrick et al., 2010; Clark, 2003; Christodoulopoulos et al., 2011) and this approach has been empirically proved to be helpful (Christodoulopoulos et al., 2010). In a similar fashion one could think that knowing POS tags could be useful for learning morphological segmentations and in this paper we will study this hypothesis.

In this paper we will build a model that combines POS induction and morphological segmentation into one learning problem. We will show that the unsupervised learning of both of these tasks in the same model will lead to better results than learning both tasks separately with the gold standard data of the other task provided. We will also demonstrate that our model produces state-of-the-art results on POS tagging. As opposed to the compared methods, our model also induces the number of tags from data.

In the following, section 2 gives the overview of the Dirichlet Processes, section 3 describes the model setup followed by the description of inference procedures in section 4, experimental results are presented in section 5, section 6 summarizes the previous work and last section concludes the paper.

2 Background

2.1 Dirichlet Process

Let H be a distribution called base measure. Dirichlet process (DP) (Ferguson, 1973) is a probability distribution over distributions whose support is the subset of the support of H:

$$G \sim DP(\alpha, H), \tag{1}$$

where α is the concentration parameter that controls the number of values instantiated by G.

DP has no analytic form and therefore other representations must be developed for sampling. In the next section we describe Chinese Restaurant Process that enables to obtain samples from DP.

2.2 Chinese Restaurant Process

Chinese Restaurant Process (CRP) (Aldous, 1985) enables to calculate the marginal probabilities of the elements conditioned on the values given to all previously seen items and integrating over possible DP prior values.

Imagine an infinitely big Chinese restaurant with infinitely many tables with each table having capacity for infinitely many customers. In the beginning the restaurant is empty. Then customers, corresponding to data points, start entering one after another. The first customer chooses an empty table to sit at. Next customers choose a new table with probability proportional to the concentration parameter α or sit into one of the already occupied tables with probability proportional to the number of customers already sitting there. Whenever a customer chooses an empty table, he will also pick a dish from H to be served on that table. The predictive probability distribution over dishes for the i-th customer is:

$$P(x_i = \phi_k | \mathbf{x}_{-i}, \alpha, H) = \frac{n_{\phi_k} + \alpha}{i - 1 + \alpha} p_H(\phi_k), \tag{2}$$

where $\mathbf{x}_{-i}$ is the seating arrangement of customers excluding the i-th customer and n_{ϕ_k} is the number of customers eating dish ϕ_k and $p_H(\cdot)$ is the probability according to H.

2.3 Hierarchical Dirichlet Process

The notion of hierarchical Dirichlet Process (HDP) (Teh et al., 2006) can be derived by letting the base measure itself to be a draw from a DP:

$$G_0 | \alpha_0, H \sim DP(\alpha_0, H) \tag{3}$$

$$G_j | \alpha, G_0 \sim DP(\alpha, G_0) \quad j = 1 \cdots J \tag{4}$$

Under HDP, CRP becomes Chinese Restaurant Franchise (Teh et al., 2006) with several restaurants sharing the same franchise-wide menu G_0. When a customer sits at an empty table in one of the G_j-th restaurants, the event of a new customer entering the restaurant G_0 will be triggered. Analogously, when a table becomes empty in one of the G_j-th restaurants, it causes one of the customers leaving from restaurant G_0.

3 Model

We consider the problem of unsupervised learning of POS tags and morphological segmentations in a joint model. Similarly to some recent successful attempts (Lee et al., 2010; Christodoulopoulos et al., 2011; Blunsom and Cohn, 2011), our model is type-based, arranging word types into hard clusters. Unlike many recent POS tagging models, our model does not assume any prior information about the number of POS tags. We will define the model as a generative sequence model using the HMM structure. Graphical depiction of the model is given in Figure 1.

3.1 Generative story

We assume the presence of a fixed length vocabulary W. The process starts with generating the lexicon that stores for each word type its POS tag and morphological segmentation.

- Draw a unigram tag distribution from the respective DP;
- Draw a segment distribution from the respective DP;
- For each tag, draw a tag-specific segment distribution from HDP with the segment distribution as base measure;
- For each word type, draw a tag from the unigram tag distribution;
- For each word type, draw a segmentation from the respective tag-specific segment distribution.

Next we proceed to generate the HMM parameters:

- For each tag, draw a bigram distribution from HDP with the unigram tag distribution as base measure;
- For each tag bigram, draw a trigram distribution from HDP with the respective bigram distribution as base measure;
- For each tag, draw a Dirichlet concentration parameter from Gamma distribution and an emission distribution from the symmetric Dirichlet.

Finally the standard HMM procedure for generating the data sequence follows. At each time step:

- Generate the next tag conditioned on the last two tags from the respective trigram HDP;
- Generate the word from the respective emission distribution conditioned on the tag just drawn;
- Generate the segmentation of the word deterministically by looking it up from the lexicon.

3.2 Model setup

The trigram transition hierarchy is a HDP:

$$G^U \sim DP(\alpha^U, H) \quad (5)$$

$$G_j^B \sim DP(\alpha^B, G^U) \quad j = 1 \cdots \infty \quad (6)$$

$$G_{jk}^T \sim DP(\alpha^T, G_j^B) \quad j, k = 1 \cdots \infty, \quad (7)$$

where G^U, G^B and G^T denote the unigram, bigram and trigram context DP-s respectively, α-s are the respective concentration parameters coupled for DP-s of the same hierarchy level. Emission parameters are drawn from multinomials with symmetric Dirichlet priors:

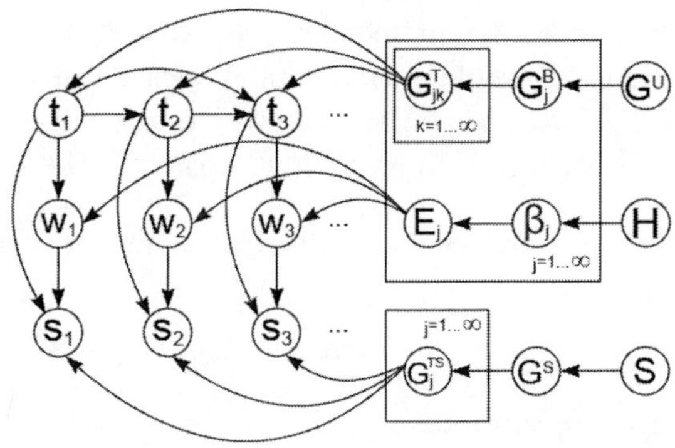

Figure 1: Plate diagram representation of the model. t_i-s, w_i-s and s_i-s denote the tags, words and segmentations respectively. G-s are various DP-s in the model, E_j-s and β_j-s are the tag-specific emission distributions and their respective Dirichlet prior parameters. H is Gamma base distribution. S is the base distribution over segments. Coupled DP concetrations parameters have been omitted for clarity.

$$E_j|\beta_j, H \sim \int Mult(\theta)Dir(\beta_j)d\theta \quad j = 1 \cdots \infty, \quad (8)$$

where each emission distribution has its own Dirichlet concentration parameter β_j drawn from H.

Morphological segments are modelled with another HDP where the groups are formed on the basis of tags:

$$G^S \sim DP(\alpha^S, S) \quad (9)$$

$$G_j^{TS} \sim DP(\alpha^{TS}, G^S) \quad j = 1 \cdots \infty, \quad (10)$$

where G_j^{TS} are the tag-specific segment DP-s and G^S is their common base distribution with S as base measure over all possible strings. S consists of two components: a geometric distribution over the segment lengths and collapsed Dirichlet-multinomial over character unigrams.

4 Inference

We implemented Gibbs sampler to draw new values for tags and Metropolis-Hastings sampler for resampling segmentations. We use a type-based collapsed sampler that draws the tagging and segmentation values for all tokens of a word type in one step and integrates out the random DP measures by using the CRP representation. The whole procedure alternates between three sampling steps:

- Sampling new tag value for each word type;
- Resampling the segmentation for each type;
- Sampling new values for all parameters.

4.1 Tag sampling

The tags will be sampled from the posterior:

$$P(\mathbf{T}|\mathbf{W}, \mathbf{S}, \mathbf{w}, \boldsymbol{\Theta}), \tag{11}$$

where $\mathbf{W}$ is the set of words in the vocabulary, $\mathbf{T}$ and $\mathbf{S}$ are tags and segmentations assigned to each word type, $\mathbf{w}$ is the actual word sequence, and $\boldsymbol{\Theta}$ denotes the set of all parameters relevant for tag sampling. For brevity, we will omit $\boldsymbol{\Theta}$ notation in the formulas below. For a single word type, this posterior can be factored as follows:

$$\begin{aligned} P(T_i = t|\mathbf{T}_{-i}, \mathbf{S}, \mathbf{W}, \mathbf{w}) \sim \\ P(S_i|T_i = t, \mathbf{T}_{-i}, \mathbf{S}_{-i}) \times \\ P(W_i|T_i = t, \mathbf{T}_{-i}, \mathbf{W}_{-i}) \times \\ P(\mathbf{w}|T_i = t, \mathbf{T}_{-i}, \mathbf{W}), \end{aligned} \tag{12}$$

where $-i$ in the subscript denotes the observations with the i-th word type excluded.

The first term is the segmentation likelihood and can be computed according to the CRP formula:

$$P(S_i|T_i = t, \mathbf{T}_{-i}, \mathbf{S}_{-i}) = \prod_{j=1}^{|W_i|} \prod_{s \in S_i} \left(\frac{n_{ts}^{-S_i}}{n_{t\cdot}^{-S_i} + \alpha} + \frac{\alpha(m_s^{-S_i} + \beta P_0(s))}{(n_{t\cdot}^{-S_i} + \alpha)(m_{\cdot}^{-S_i} + \beta)} \right), \tag{13}$$

where the outer product is over the word type count, n_{ts} and m_s denote the number of customers "eating" the segment s under tag t and the number of tables "serving" the segment s across all restaurants respectively, dot represents the marginal counts and α and β are the concentration parameters of the respective DP-s. $-S_i$ in upper index means that the segments belonging to the segmentation of the i-th word type and not calculated into likelihood term yet have been excluded.

The word type likelihood is calculated according to the collapsed Dirichlet-multinomial likelihood formula:

$$P(W_i|T_i = t, \mathbf{T}_{-i}, \mathbf{W}_{-i}, \mathbf{w}) = \prod_{j=0}^{|W_i|-1} \frac{n_{tW_i} + j + \alpha}{n_{t\cdot} + j + \alpha N} \tag{14}$$

where n_{tW_i} is the number of times the word W_i has been tagged with tag t so far, $n_{t\cdot}$ is the number of total word tokens tagged with the tag t and N is the total number of words in the vocabulary.

The last factor is the word sequence likelihood and covers the transition probabilities. Relevant trigrams are those three containing the current word, and in all contexts where the word token appears in:

$$\begin{aligned} P(\mathbf{w}|T_i = t, \mathbf{T}_{-i}, \mathbf{W}) \sim \\ \prod_{c \in C_{W_i}} P(t|t(c_{-2}), t(c_{-1})) \cdot \\ P(t(c_{+1})|t(c_{-1}), t) \cdot \\ P(t(c_{+2})|t, t(c_{+1})) \end{aligned} \tag{15}$$

where C_{W_i} denotes all the contexts where the word type W_i appears in, $t(c)$ are the tags assigned to the context words. All these terms can be calculated with CRP formulas.

4.2 Segmentation sampling

We sample the whole segmentation of a word type as a block with forward-filtering backward-sampling scheme as described in (Mochihashi et al., 2009).

As we cannot sample from the exact marginal conditional distribution due to the dependencies between segments induced by the CRP, we use the Metropolis-Hastings sampler that draws a new proposal with forward-filtering backward-sampling scheme and accepts it with probability $min(1, \frac{P(S_{prop})}{P(S_{old})})$, where S_{prop} is the proposed segmentation and S_{old} is the current segmentation of a word type. The acceptance rate during experiments varied between 94-98%.

For each word type, we build a forward filtering table where we maintain the forward variables $\alpha[t][k]$ that present the probabilities of the last k characters of a t-character string constituting a segment. Define:

$$\alpha[0][0] = 1 \tag{16}$$

$$\alpha[t][0] = 0, \quad t > 0 \tag{17}$$

Then the forward variables can be computed recursively by using dynamic programming algorithm:

$$\alpha[t][k] = p(c_{t-k}^{t}) \sum_{j=0}^{t-k} \alpha[t-k][j], \quad t = 1 \cdots L, \tag{18}$$

where c_m^n denotes the characters $c_m \cdots c_n$ of a string c and L is the length of the word.

Sampling starts from the end of the word because it is known for certain that the word end coincides with the end of a segment. We sample the beginning position k of the last segment from the forward variables $\alpha[t][k]$, where t is the length of the word. Then we set $t = t - k$ and continue to sample the start of the previous to the last segment. This process continues until $t = 0$. The segment probabilities, conditioned on the tag currently assigned to the word type, will be calculated according to the segmentation likelihood formula (13).

4.3 Hyperparameter sampling

All DP and Dirichlet concentration parameters are given vague Gamma(10, 0.1) priors and new values are sampled by using the auxiliary variable sampling scheme described in (Escobar and West, 1995) and the extended version for HDP-s described in (Teh et al., 2006). The segment length control parameter is given uniform Beta prior and its new values are sampled from the posterior which is also a Beta distribution.

5 Results

5.1 Evaluation

We test the POS induction part of the model on all languages in the Multext-East corpora (Erjavec, 2010) as well as on the free corpora from CONLL-X Shared Task[1] for Dutch, Danish, Swedish and Portuguese. The evaluation of morphological segmentations is based on the Morpho Challenge gold segmented wordlists for English, Finnish and Turkish[2]. We gathered the sentences from Europarl corpus[3] for English and Finnish, and use the Turkish text data from the Morpho Challenge 2009[4]. Estonian gold standard segmentations have been obtained from the Estonian morphologically annotated corpus[5].

We report three accuracy measures for tagging: greedy one-to-one mapping (**1-1**) (Haghighi and Klein, 2006), many-to-one mapping (**m-1**) and V-measure (**V-m**) (Rosenberg and Hirschberg, 2007).

Segmentation is evaluated on the basis of standard F-score which is the harmonic mean of precision and recall.

5.2 Experimental results

For each experiment, we made five runs with random initializations and report the results of the median. The sampler was run 200 iterations for burnin, after which we collected 5 samples, letting the sampler to run for another 200 iterations between each two sample. We start with 15 segmenting iterations during each Gibbs iteration to enable the segmentation sampler to burnin to the current tagging state, and gradually reduce this number to one. Segmentation likelihood term for tagging is calculated on the basis of the last segment only because this setting gave the best results in preliminary experiments and it also makes the whole computation less expensive.

The first set of experiments was conducted to test the model tagging accuracy on different languages mentioned above. The results obtained were in general slightly lower than the current state-of-the-art and the number of tags learned was generally bigger than the number of gold standard tags. We observed that different components making up the corpus logarithmic probability have different magnitudes. In particular, we found that the emission probability component in log-scale is roughly four times smaller than the transition probability. This observation motivated introducing the likelihood scaling heuristic into the model to scale the emission probability up. We tried a couple of different scaling factors on Multext-East English corpus and then set its value to 4 for all languages for the rest of the experiments. This improved the tagging results consistently across all languages.

[1] http://ilk.uvt.nl/conll/free_data.html

[2] http://research.ics.tkk.fi/events/morphochallenge2010/datasets.shtml

[3] http://www.statmt.org/europarl/

[4] http://research.ics.tkk.fi/events/morphochallenge2009/datasets.shtml

[5] http://www.cl.ut.ee/korpused/morfkorpus/index.php?lang=eng

POS induction results are given in **Table 1**. When comparing these results with the recently published results on the same corpora (Christodoulopoulos et al., 2011; Blunsom and Cohn, 2011; Lee et al., 2010) we can see that our results compare favorably with the state-of-the-art, resulting with the best published results in many occasions. The number of tag clusters learned by the model corresponds surprisingly well to the number of true coarse-grained gold standard tags across all languages. There are two things to note here: 1) the tag distributions learned are influenced by the likelihood scaling heuristic and more experiments are needed in order to fully understand the characteristics and influence of this heuristic; 2) as the model is learning the coarse-grained tagset consistently in all languages, it might as well be that the POS tags are not as dependent on the morphology as we assumed, especially in inflectional languages with many derivational and inflectional suffixes, because otherwise the model should have learned a more fine-grained tagset.

Segmentation results are presented in **Table 2**. For each language, we report the lexicon-based precision, recall and F-measure, the number of word types in the corpus and and number of word types with gold segmentation available. The reported standard deviations show that the segmentations obtained are stable across different runs which is probably due to the blocked sampler. We give the segmentation results both with and without likelihood scaling heuristic and denote that while the emission likelihood scaling improves the tagging accuracy, it actually degrades the segmentation results.

It can also be seen that in general precision score is better but for Estonian recall is higher. This can be explained by the characteristics of the evaluation data sets. For English, Finnish and Turkish we use the Morpho Challenge wordlists where the gold standard segmentations are fine-grained, separating both inflectional and derivational morphemes. Especially derivational morphemes are hard to learn with pure data-driven methods with no knowledge about semantics and thus it can result in undersegmentation. On the other hand, Estonian corpus separates only inflectional morphemes which thus leads to higher recall. Some difference can also come from the fact that the sets of gold-segmented word types for other languages are much smaller than in Estonian and thus it would be interesting to see whether and how the results would change if the evaluation could be done on all word types in the corpus for other languages as well. In general, undersegmentation is more acceptable than oversegmentation, especially when the aim is to use the resulting segmentations in some NLP application.

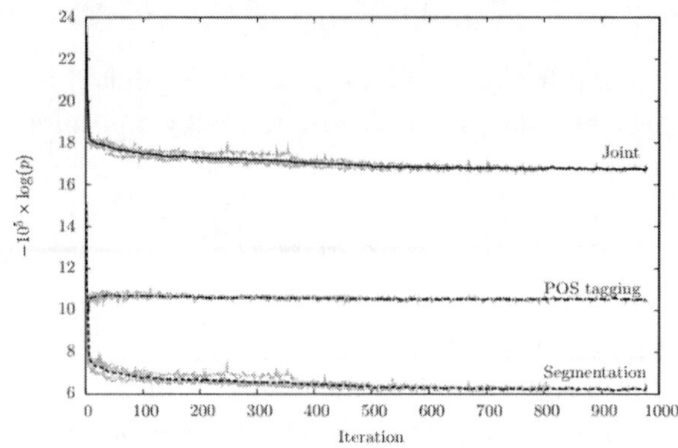

Figure 2: Log-likelihood of samples plotted against iterations. Dark lines show the average over five runs, grey lines in the back show the real samples.

Next, we studied the convergence characteristics of our model. For these experiments we made five runs with random initializations on Estonian corpus and let the sampler run up to 1100 iterations. Samples were taken after each ten iterations. **Figure 2** shows the log-likelihood of the samples plotted against iteration number. Dark lines show the averages over five runs and gray lines in the background are the likelihoods of real samples showing also the variance. We first calculated the full likelihood of the samples (the solid line) that showed a quick improvement during the first few iterations and then stabilized by continuing with only slow improvements over time. We then divided the full likelihood into two factors in order to see the contribution of both tagging and segmentation parts separately. The results are quite surprising. It turned out that the random tagging initializations are very good in terms of probability and as a matter of fact much better than the data can support and thus the tagging likelihood drops quite significantly after the first iteration and then continues with very slow improvements. The matters are totally different with segmentations where the initial random segmentations result in a low likelihood that improves heavily

	Types	1-1	m-1	V-m	Induced	True	Best Pub.		
Bulgarian	15103	**50.3 (0.9)**	**71.9 (3.8)**	54.9 (2.2)	13 (1.6)	12	-	66.5*	**55.6***
Czech	17607	**46.0 (1.0)**	60.7 (1.6)	46.2 (0.7)	12 (0.8)	12	-	**64.2***	**53.9***
Danish	17157	**53.2 (0.2)**	69.5 (0.1)	52.7 (0.4)	14 (0.0)	25	43.2†	**76.2***	**59.0***
Dutch	27313	**60.5 (1.9)**	**74.0 (1.6)**	**59.1 (1.1)**	22 (0.0)	13	55.1†	71.1*	54.7*
English	9196	**67.4 (0.1)**	**79.8 (0.1)**	**66.7 (0.1**	13 (0.0)	12	-	73.3*	63.3*
Estonian	16820	**47.6 (0.9)**	**64.5 (1.9)**	45.6 (1.4)	14 (0.5)	11	-	64.4*	**53.3***
Farsi	11319	**54.9 (0.1)**	**65.3 (0.1)**	**52.1 (0.1)**	13 (0.5)	12	-	-	-
Hungarian	19191	**62.1 (0.7)**	**71.4 (0.3)**	**56.0 (0.6)**	11 (0.9)	12	-	68.2*	54.8*
Polish	19542	**48.5 (1.8)**	**59.6 (1.9)**	**45.4 (1.0)**	13 (0.8)	12	-	-	-
Portuguese	27250	45.4 (1.1)	71.3 (0.3)	55.4 (0.3)	21 (1.1)	16	**56.5**†	**78.5***	**63.9***
Romanian	13822	**44.3 (0.5)**	60.5 (1.7)	46.7 (0.5)	14 (0.8)	14	-	**61.1***	**52.3***
Serbian	16813	**40.1 (0.2)**	60.1 (0.2)	43.5 (0.2)	13 (0.0)	12	-	**64.1***	**51.1***
Slovak	18793	**44.1 (1.5)**	**56.2 (0.8)**	**41.2 (0.6)**	14 (1.1)	12	-	-	-
Slovene	16420	**51.6 (1.5)**	66.8 (0.6)	51.6 (1.0)	12 (0.7)	12	-	**67.9***	**56.7***
Swedish	18473	**50.6 (0.1)**	60.3 (0.1)	55.8 (0.1)	17 (0.0)	41	38.5†	**68.7***	**58.9***

Table 1: Tagging results for different languages. For each language we report median one-to-one (1-1), many-to-one (m-1) and V-measure (V-m) together with standard deviation from five runs where median is taken over V-measure. **Types** is the number of word types in each corpus, **True** is the number of gold tags and **Induced** reports the median number of tags induced by the model together with standard deviation. **Best Pub.** lists the best published results so far (also 1-1, m-1 and V-m) in (Christodoulopoulos et al., 2011)*, (Blunsom and Cohn, 2011)* and (Lee et al., 2010)†.

		Precision	Recall	F1	Types	Segmented
Estonian	without LLS	43.5 (0.8)	59.4 (0.6)	50.3 (0.7)	16820	16820
	with LLS	42.8 (1.1)	54.6 (0.7)	48.0 (0.9)		
English	without LLS	69.0 (1.3)	37.3 (1.5)	48.5 (1.1)	20628	399
	with LLS	59.8 (1.8)	29.0 (1.0)	39.1 (1.3)		
Finnish	without LLS	56.2 (2.5)	29.5 (1.7)	38.7 (2.0)	25364	292
	with LLS	56.0 (1.1)	28.0 (0.6)	37.4 (0.7)		
Turkish	without LLS	65.4 (1.8)	44.8 (1.8)	53.2 (1.7)	18459	293
	with LLS	68.9 (0.8)	39.2 (1.0)	50.0 (0.6)		

Table 2: Segmentation results on different languages. Results are calculated based on word types. For each language we report precision, recall and F1 measure, number of word types in the corpus and number of word types with gold standard segmentation available. For each language we report the segmentation result without and with emission likelihood scaling (without LLS and with LLS respectively).

with the first few iterations and then stabilizes but still continues to improve over time. The explanation for this kind of model behaviour needs further studies and we leave it for future work.

Figure 3 plots the V-measure against the tagging factor of the log-likelihood for all samples. It can be seen that the lower V-measure values are more spread out in terms of likelihood. These points correspond to the early samples of the runs. The samples taken later during the runs are on the right in the figure and the positive correlation between the V-measure and likelihood values can be seen.

Next we studied whether the morphological seg-

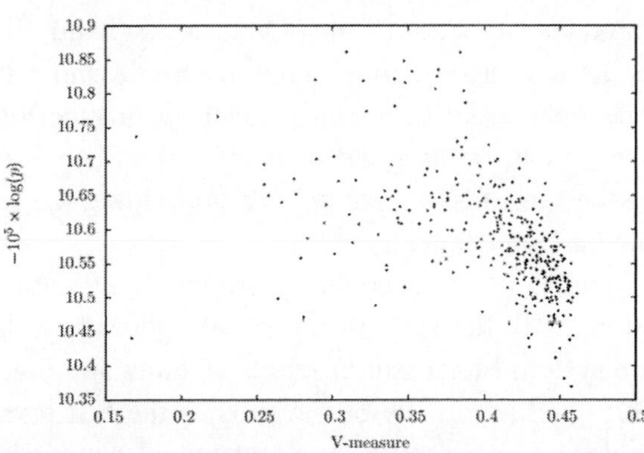

Figure 3: Tagging part of log-likelihood plotted against V-measure

	1-to-1	m-to-1	V-m
Fixed seg	40.5 (1.5)	53.4 (1.0)	37.5 (1.3)
Learned seg	47.6 (0.4)	64.5 (1.9)	45.6 (1.4)
	Precision	**Recall**	**F1**
Fixed tag	36.7 (0.3)	56.4 (0.2)	44.5 (0.3)
Learned tag	42.8 (1.1)	54.6 (0.7)	48.0 (0.9)
Morfessor	51.29	52.59	51.94

Table 3: Tagging and segmentation results on Estonian Multext-East corpus (Learned seg and Learned tag) compared to the semisupervised setting where segmentations are fixed to gold standard (Fixed seg) and tags are fixed to gold standard (Fixed tag). Finally the segmentatation results from Morfessor system for comparison are presented.

mentations and POS tags help each other in the learning process. For that we conducted two semisupervised experiments on Estonian corpus. First we provided gold standard segmentations to the model and let it only learn the tags. Then, we gave the model gold standard POS tags and only learned the segmentations. The results are given in **Table 3**. We also added the results from joint unusupervised learning for easier comparison. Unfortunately we cannot repeat this experiment on other languages to see whether the results are stable across different languages because to our knowledge there is no other free corpus with both gold standard POS tags and morphological segmentations available.

From the results it can be seen that the unsupervised learning results for both tagging and segmentation are better than the results obtained from semisupervised learning. This is surprising because one would assume that providing gold standard data would lead to better results. On the other hand, these results are encouraging, showing that learning two dependent tasks in a joint model by unsupervised manner can be as good or even better than learning the same tasks separately and providing the gold standard data as features.

Finally, we learned the morphological segmentations with the state-of-the-art morphology induction system Morfessor baseline[6] (Creutz and Lagus, 2005) and report the best results in the last row of **Table 3**. Apparently, our joint model cannot beat Morfessor in morphological segmentation and when using the emission likelihood scaling that influences the tagging results favorably, the segmentation results get even worse. Altough the semisupervised experiments showed that there are dependencies between tags and segmentations, the conducted experiments do not reveal of how to use these dependencies for helping the POS tags to learn better morphological segmentations.

6 Related Work

We will review some of the recent works related to Bayesian POS induction and morphological segmentation.

One of the first Bayesian POS taggers is described in (Goldwater and Griffiths, 2007). The model presented is a classical HMM with multinomial transition and emission distributions with Dirichlet priors. Inference is done using a collapsed Gibbs sampler and concentration parameter values are learned during inference. The model is token-based, allowing different words of the same type in different locations to have a different tag. This model can actually be classified as semi-supervised as it assumes the presence of a tagging dictionary that contains the list of possible POS tags for each word type - an assumption that is clearly not realistic in an unsupervised setting.

Models presented in (Christodoulopoulos et al., 2011) and (Lee et al., 2010) are also built on Dirichlet-multinomials and, rather than defining a sequence model, present a clustering model based on features. Both report good results on type basis and use (among others) also morphological features, with (Lee et al., 2010) making use of fixed length suffixes and (Christodoulopoulos et al., 2011) using the suffixes obtained from an unsupervised morphology induction system.

Nonparametric Bayesian POS induction has been studied in (Blunsom and Cohn, 2011) and (Gael et al., 2009). The model in (Blunsom and Cohn, 2011) uses Pitman-Yor Process (PYP) prior but the model itself is finite in the sense that the size of the tagset is fixed. Their model also captures morphological regularities by modeling the generation of words with character n-grams. The model in (Gael et al., 2009) uses infinite state space with Dirichlet Process prior. The model structure is classical HMM consisting

[6] `http://www.cis.hut.fi/projects/morpho/`

only of transitions and emissions and containing no morphological features. Inference is done by using beam sampler introduced in (Gael et al., 2008) which enables parallelized implementation.

One close model for morphology stems from Bayesian word segmentation (Goldwater et al., 2009) where the task is to induce word borders from transcribed sentences. Our segmentation model is in principle the same as the unigram word segmentation model and the main difference is that we are using blocked sampler while (Goldwater et al., 2009) uses point-wise Gibbs sampler by drawing the presence or absence of the word border between every two characters.

In (Goldwater et al., 2006) the morphology is learned in the adaptor grammar framework (Johnson et al., 2006) by using a PYP adaptor. PYP adaptor caches the numbers of observed derivation trees and forces the distribution over all possible trees to take the shape of power law. In the PYP (and also DP) case the adaptor grammar can be interpreted as PYP (or DP) model with regular PCFG distribution as base measure.

The model proposed in (Goldwater et al., 2006) makes several assumptions that we do not: 1) segmentations have a fixed structure of stem and suffix; and 2) there is a fixed number of inflectional classes. Inference is performed with Gibbs sampler by sampling for each word its stem, suffix and inflectional class.

7 Conclusion

In this paper we presented a joint unsupervised model for learning POS tags and morphological segmentations with hierarchical Dirichlet Process model. Our model induces the number of POS clusters from data and does not contain any hand-tuned parameters. We tested the model on many languages and showed that by introcing a likelihood scaling heuristic it produces state-of-the-art POS induction results. We believe that the tagging results could further be improved by adding additional features concerning punctuation, capitalization etc. which are heavily used in the other state-of-the-art POS induction systems but these features were intentionally left out in the current model for enabling to test the concept of joint modelling of two dependent tasks.

We found some evidence that the tasks of POS induction and morphological segmentation are dependent by conducting semisupervised experiments where we gave the model gold standard tags and segmentations in turn and let it learn only segmentations or tags respectively and found that the results in fully unsupervised setting are better. Despite of that, the model failed to learn as good segmentations as the state-of-the-art morphological segmentation model Morfessor. One way to improve the segmentation results could be to use segment bigrams instead of unigrams.

The model can serve as a basis for several further extensions. For example, one possibility would be to expand it into multilingual setting in a fashion of (Naseem et al., 2009), or it could be extended to add the joint learning of morphological paradigms of the words given their tags and segmentations in a manner described by (Dreyer and Eisner, 2011).

Acknowledgments

We would like to thank the anonymous reviewers who helped to improve the quality of this paper. This research was supported by the Estonian Ministry of Education and Research target-financed research theme no. 0140007s12, and by European Social Funds Doctoral Studies and Internationalisation Programme DoRa.

References

D. Aldous. 1985. Exchangeability and related topics. In *École d'été de Probabilités de Saint-Flour, XIII—1983*, pages 1–198. Springer.

Taylor Berg-Kirkpatrick, Alexandre Bouchard-Côté, John DeNero, and Dan Klein. 2010. Painless unsupervised learning with features. In *Human Language Technologies: The 2010 Annual Conference of the North American Chapter of the Association for Computational Linguistics*, pages 582–590.

Phil Blunsom and Trevor Cohn. 2011. A hierarchical Pitman-Yor process HMM for unsupervised Part of Speech induction. In *Proceedings of the 49th Annual Meeting of the Association for Computational Linguistics: Human Language Technologies - Volume 1*, pages 865–874.

Christos Christodoulopoulos, Sharon Goldwater, and Mark Steedman. 2010. Two decades of unsupervised POS induction: How far have we come? In *Proceed-*

ings of the 2010 Conference on Empirical Methods in Natural Language Processing, pages 575–584.

Christos Christodoulopoulos, Sharo Goldwater, and Mark Steedman. 2011. A Bayesian mixture model for PoS induction using multiple features. In *Proceedings of the 2011 Conference on Empirical Methods in Natural Language Processing*, pages 638–647, Edinburgh, Scotland, UK.

Alexander Clark. 2003. Combining distributional and morphological information for Part of Speech induction. In *Proceedings of the Tenth Conference on European Chapter of the Association for Computational Linguistics - Volume 1*, pages 59–66.

Mathias Creutz and Krista Lagus. 2005. Inducing the morphological lexicon of a natural language from unannotated text. In *In Proceedings of the International and Interdisciplinary Conference on Adaptive Knowledge Representation and Reasoning*, pages 106–113.

Markus Dreyer and Jason Eisner. 2011. Discovering morphological paradigms from plain text using a Dirichlet Process mixture model. In *Proceedings of the 2011 Conference on Empirical Methods in Natural Language Processing*, pages 616–627.

Toma Erjavec. 2010. MULTEXT-East version 4: Multilingual morphosyntactic specifications, lexicons and corpora. In *Proceedings of the Seventh International Conference on Language Resources and Evaluation.*

Michael D. Escobar and Mike West. 1995. Bayesian density estimation and inference using mixtures. *Journal of the American Statistical Association*, 90(430).

Thomas S. Ferguson. 1973. A Bayesian analysis of some nonparametric problems. *The Annals of Statistics*, 1(2):209–230.

Jurgen Van Gael, Yunus Saatci, Yee Whye Teh, and Zoubin Ghahramani. 2008. Beam sampling for the infinite Hidden Markov Model. In *Proceedings of the 25th International Conference on Machine Learning*, pages 1088–1095.

Jurgen Van Gael, Andreas Vlachos, and Zoubin Ghahramani. 2009. The infinite HMM for unsupervised PoS tagging. In *Proceedings of the 2009 Conference on Empirical Methods in Natural Language Processing: Volume 2 - Volume 2*, pages 678–687.

Sharon Goldwater and Tom Griffiths. 2007. A fully Bayesian approach to unsupervised Part-of-Speech tagging. In *Proceedings of the 45th Annual Meeting of the Association of Computational Linguistics*, pages 744–751, Prague, Czech Republic.

Sharon Goldwater, Thomas L. Griffiths, and Mark Johnson. 2006. Interpolating between types and tokens by estimating power-law generators. In *Advances in Neural Information Processing Systems 18*, Cambridge, MA.

Sharon Goldwater, Thomas L. Griffiths, and Mark Johnson. 2009. A Bayesian framework for word segmentation: Exploring the effects of context. *Cognition*, 112:21–54.

Aria Haghighi and Dan Klein. 2006. Prototype-driven learning for sequence models. In *Proceedings of the Human Language Technology Conference of the NAACL, Main Conference*, pages 320–327, New York City, USA.

Mark Johnson, Thomas L. Griffiths, and Sharon Goldwater. 2006. Adaptor grammars: A framework for specifying compositional nonparametric Bayesian models. In *Advances in Neural Information Processing Systems 19*, pages 641–648.

Yoong Keok Lee, Aria Haghighi, and Regina Barzilay. 2010. Simple type-level unsupervised POS tagging. In *Proceedings of the 2010 Conference on Empirical Methods in Natural Language Processing*, pages 853–861.

Daichi Mochihashi, Takeshi Yamada, and Naonori Ueda. 2009. Bayesian unsupervised word segmentation with nested Pitman-Yor language modeling. In *Proceedings of the Joint Conference of the 47th Annual Meeting of the ACL and the 4th International Joint Conference on Natural Language Processing of the AFNLP: Volume 1 - Volume 1*, pages 100–108.

Tahira Naseem, Benjamin Snyder, Jacob Eisenstein, and Regina Barzilay. 2009. Multilingual part-of-speech tagging: Two unsupervised approaches. *Journal of Artificial Intelligence Research*, 36:1–45.

Lawrence R. Rabiner. 1989. A tutorial on Hidden Markov Models and selected applications in speech recognition. In *Proceedings of the IEEE*, pages 257–286.

Andrew Rosenberg and Julia Hirschberg. 2007. V-measure: A conditional entropy-based external cluster evaluation measure. In *Proceedings of the 2007 Joint Conference on Empirical Methods in Natural Language Processing and Computational Natural Language Learning (EMNLP-CoNLL)*, pages 410–420, Prague, Czech Republic.

Yee Whye Teh, Michel I. Jordan, Matthew J. Beal, and David M. Blei. 2006. Hierarchical Dirichlet processes. *Journal of the American Statistical Association*, 101(476):1566–1581.

Yee Whye Teh. 2006. A hierarchical Bayesian language model based on Pitman-Yor processes. In *Proceedings of the 21st International Conference on Computational Linguistics and 44th Annual Meeting of the Association for Computational Linguistics*, pages 985–992.

Encouraging Consistent Translation Choices

Ferhan Ture,[1] **Douglas W. Oard,**[2,4] **Philip Resnik**[3,4]

[1]Department of Computer Science
[2]College of Information Studies
[3]Department of Linguistics
[4]Institute for Advanced Computer Studies
University of Maryland, College Park, MD 20740 USA
fture@cs.umd.edu, oard@umd.edu, resnik@umd.edu

Abstract

It has long been observed that monolingual text exhibits a tendency toward "one sense per discourse," and it has been argued that a related "one translation per discourse" constraint is operative in bilingual contexts as well. In this paper, we introduce a novel method using forced decoding to confirm the validity of this constraint, and we demonstrate that it can be exploited in order to improve machine translation quality. Three ways of incorporating such a preference into a hierarchical phrase-based MT model are proposed, and the approach where all three are combined yields the greatest improvements for both Arabic-English and Chinese-English translation experiments.

1 Introduction

In statistical Machine Translation (MT), the state-of-the-art approach is to translate phrases in the context of a sentence and to re-order those phrases appropriately. Intuitively, it seems as if it should also be possible to draw on information outside of a single sentence to further improve translation quality. In this paper, we challenge the conventional approach of translating each sentence independently, and argue that it can indeed also be beneficial to consider document-scale context when translating text. Motivated by the success of a "one sense per discourse" heuristic in Word Sense Disambiguation (WSD), we explore the potential benefit of leveraging a "one translation per discourse" heuristic in MT.

The paper is organized as follows. We begin with related work in Section 2. Next, we provide new confirmation that the hypothesized one-translation-per-discourse condition does indeed often hold, based on a novel analysis using forced decoding (Section 3). We incorporate this idea into a hierarchical MT framework by adding three new document-scale features to the translation model (Section 4). We then present experimental results demonstrating solid improvements in translation quality obtained by leveraging these features, both for Arabic-English (Ar-En) and Chinese-English (Zh-En) translation (Section 5). Conclusions and future work are presented in Section 6.

2 Related work

Exploiting discourse-level context has to date received only limited attention in MT research (e.g., (Giménez and Màrquez, 2007; Liu et al., 2010; Carpuat, 2009; Brown, 2008; Xiao et al., 2011)). Exploratory analysis of reference translations by Carpuat (2009) motivates a hypothesis that MT systems might benefit from the "one sense per discourse" heuristic, first introduced by Gale et al. (1992), which has proven to be effective in the context of WSD (Yarowsky, 1995). Carpuat's approach was to do post-processing on the translation output to impose a "one translation per discourse" constraint where the system would otherwise have made a different choice. A manual evaluation on a sample of sentences suggested promise from the technique, which Carpuat suggested in favor of exploring more integrated approaches.

Xiao et al. (2011) took this one step further and implement an approach where they identified ambiguous translations within each document, and attempt to fix them by replacing each ambiguity with the most frequent translation choice. Based on their error analysis, the authors indicate two shortcomings when trying to find the correct translation of a given phrase. First, frequency may not provide sufficient information to distinguish between translation candidates, which is why we take rareness into account when scoring translation candidates. Another problem is, like any other heuristic, that there may be cases where the heuristic fails and there are multiple senses per discourse. Guaranteeing consistency hurts performance in such situations, which is why we implement the heuristic as a model feature, and let the model score decide for each case.

We are aware of a few other analyses that have shown promising results based on a similar motivation. For instance, Wasser and Dorr (2008)'s approach biases the MT system based on term statistics from relevant documents in comparable corpora. Ma et al. (2011) show that a translation memory can be used to find similar source sentences, and consecutively adapt translation choices towards consistency. Domain adaptation for MT has has also been shown to be useful in some cases (Bertoldi and Federico, 2009; Hildebrand et al., 2005; Sanchis-Trilles and Casacuberta, 2010; Tiedemann, 2010; Zhao et al., 2004), so to the extent we consider documents to be micro-domains we might expect similar approaches to be useful at document scale. Indeed, hints that such ideas may work have been available for some time. For example, there is clear evidence that the behavior of human translators can provide evidence that is often useful for automating WSD (Diab and Resnik, 2002; Ng et al., 2003). When coupled with the one-sense-per-discourse heuristic, this suggests that the reverse may also be true.

3 Exploratory analysis

It is well known that writing styles vary by genre, and in particular that the amount of vocabulary variation within a document depends to some extent on the genre (e.g., higher in poetry than in engineering writing). The degree to which authors tend to make consistent word choices in any particular genre is, therefore, an empirical question. In order to gain insight into the extent to which human translators make consistent vocabulary choices in the types of materials that we wish to translate (in this work, news stories), we first explore the degree of support for our one-translation-per-discourse hypothesis in the reference translations of a standard MT test collection.

We used the Ar-En MT08 data set, which contains 74 newswire documents with a total of 813 sentences, each of which has four reference translations. Throughout this paper we consistently use the document (i.e., one news story) as a convenient discourse unit, although of course finer-scale or broader-scale discourse units might also be explored in future work. Moreover, throughout this paper we use the hierarchical phrase-based translation system (Hiero), which is based on a synchronous context-free grammar (SCFG) model (Chiang, 2005). In a SCFG, the rule [X] ||| α ||| β indicates that context free expansion $X \rightarrow \alpha$ in the source language can occur synchronously with $X \rightarrow \beta$ in the target language. In this case, we call α the left hand side (LHS) of the rule, and β the right hand side (RHS) of the rule.

To determine the extent and nature of translation consistency choices made by human translators, we randomly selected one of the four sets of reference translations (first set, with id 0) and we used forced decoding to find all possible sequences of rules that could transform the source sentence into the target sentence. In forced decoding, given a pair of source and target sentences, and a grammar consisting of learned translation rules with associated probabilities, the decoder searches all possible derivations for the one sequence of rules that is most likely (under the learned translation model) to synchronously produce the source sentence on the LHS and the target sentence on the RHS. For instance, consider the following Arabic sentence as input:

الثلاثة الاعتداءات بين رابط .

and its uncased reference translation:

there is a link between the three attacks .

The following four rules, which are part of the SCFG learned from the the same translation pairs, allows the decoder to find a sequence of derivations that "translates" the source-side Arabic sentence into the

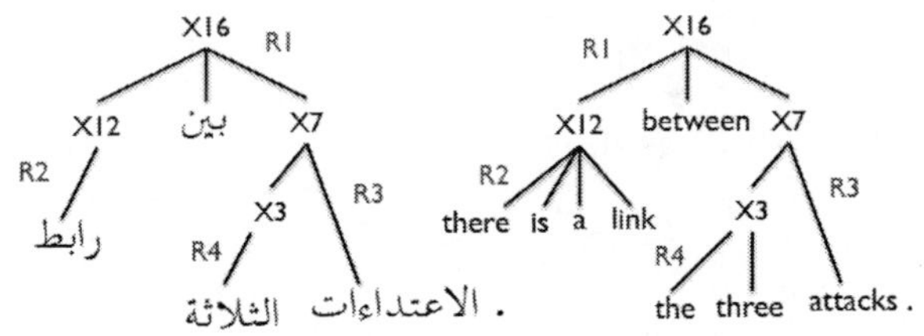

Figure 1: Illustration of forced decoding.

target-side reference translation.[1]

R_1. $[X_{12}]$ ||| رابط ||| there is a link
R_2. $[X_{16}]$ ||| [2] بين [1] ||| $[X_{12}, 1]$ between $[X_7, 2]$
R_3. $[X_7]$ ||| [1] الاعتداءات . ||| $[X_3, 1]$ attacks .
R_4. $[X_3]$ ||| الثلاثة ||| the three

Figure 1 illustrates how the decoder uses these rules to produce the source and target sides synchronously.

As we repeated this procedure for all sentence pairs, we kept track of all rules that were actually used by the decoder to generate a reference English translation from the corresponding Arabic sentences.

Our next step was to identify cases in which the SCFG could reasonably have produced a substantially different translation. Whenever an Arabic phrase f occurs multiple times in a document, and f appears on the LHS of two or more different grammar rules in the SCFG, we count this as a single "case".[2] These cases correspond to unique (source phrase f, document d) pairs in which a translation process using that SCFG *could have* chosen to produce two or more *different* translations of f in d. Since the multiple appearances of f are distributed among sentences of d, each counted case may correspond to a number of sentences ranging from 1 to the number of sentences in that document.

Table 1 shows a small sample of the cases (i.e., (source phrase f, document d) pairs) identified as a result of forced decoding. There were 321 such cases in our dataset and there were 672 sentences in which at least one case occurred. This is not an uncommon phenomenon; these 672 sentences comprise 83% of the test set. However, many of these cases represent either unlikely choices or inconsequential differences, so some post-processing is called for.

Since grammar rules are typically more fine-grained than is necessary for our purposes (e.g., to capture various punctuation and determiner differences that do not affect the "sense" of the translation), we applied a few simple heuristics to edit the source and target sides and group all such minor variations into a single "mega-rule" (e.g., "how"~", how", "third"~"a third", "want"~"we want"). For this, we removed nonterminal symbols and punctuation, and considered two target phrases e and e' to be *different* only if $edit\_distance(e, e') > max(length(e), length(e'))/2$, where the edit distance is based on character removal and insertion. For instance, the third example in Table 1 would have been considered to be translated consistently as a result of this heuristic, as opposed to the first example. We also eliminated cases in which no reasonable alternatives were available in the translation grammar (i.e., cases where the second most probable rule with the same LHS was assigned a probability below 0.1 in the grammar). Cases 4 and 5 would have been removed by this heuristic.

After this filtering and aggregation we were left with 176 (f, d) pairs in which the translation model could reasonably have selected between rules that would have produced substantially different English translations of f in d (such as cases 1–3 and 6–9). It was these 176 cases, affecting a total of 512 sentences (63% of test set) for which we then examined what forced decoding could tell us about translation consistency.

So now that we know what the human who produced the reference translations actually did (according to forced decoding), and in which cases they might reasonably have chosen to do something substantially different (according to the SCFG), we can ask in which cases the human (effectively) made a consistent choice of translation rules when encountering the same Arabic phrase in the same document. In 128 of the 176 cases, that is what they did (i.e., when the same phrase occurred multiple times in a single document and more than one translation was reasonably possible, forced decoding indicated that the human translator translated that phrase in essentially the same way). These cases affected the trans-

[1]Since our goal was an exploratory analysis, the MT08 test set was combined with the training set in order to ensure reachability of the reference translations using the learned grammar. Proper train/dev/test splits were, of course, used for the evaluation results reported in Section 5.

[2]We define a phrase as any text that constitutes the entire LHS of a grammar rule.

Case		Translation counts
Source phrase	Doc #	
مقتل	566	that killed = 1 killing of = 1
الرهائن	782	hostages = 2
الرهائن	138	hostage = 1 hostages = 2
كوريا	466	korea = 2
كوريا	763	korea = 2
من	30	from = 2
من	7	of = 1 from = 1
الراهن من	717	of the current = 2
التي	30	the = 1 which =1

Table 1: A sample of cases (i.e., (source phrase f, document d) pairs) identified as a result of forced decoding.

lation of 455 sentences (56% of the test set), suggesting that if we can replicate this human behavior in a system, it might affect a nontrivial number of translation choices.

These statistics also suggest, however, that there may be some risk incurred in such a process, since in 48 of the 176 cases, the human translator opted for a substantially different translation. When we closely examined these 48 instances, we found that 19 (40%) involved changing a content-bearing word (sometimes to a word with similar meaning). The remaining 29 (60%) involved function words or similar constructions. See Figures 2 and 3 for examples.

1a. [X] ||| سمحت ||| had allowed
1b. [X] ||| سمحت ||| has permitted
2a. [X] ||| [X,1] تدرس ||| examining [X,1]
2b. [X] ||| [X,1] تدرس ||| is considering [X,1]
3a. [X] ||| [X,1] الجوار ||| neighbors
3b. [X] ||| [X,1] الجوار ||| neighboring countries

Figure 2: Examples of differences in lexical choice for content-bearing words within the same document.

We can make several observations based on this analysis. First, there does indeed seem to be evidence to support the one-translation-per-discourse heuristic, and to suggest that respecting that heuristic could improve translation outcomes for a substantial number of sentences. Second, even when a reference translation contains different translations of the same phrase, this may sometimes be the result of stylistic choices rather than an intent by the translator to affect the expressed meaning. If a system were try to "fix" such cases by enforcing consistent translation, the resulting translation might be somewhat more stilted, but perhaps not less accurate or less intelligible. Finally, sentence structure conventions or other language-specific phenomena may sometimes require the same phrase to be translated differently, so some way of encouraging consistency while still allowing the model to consider other contextual factors might be better than always imposing a hard consistency constraint.

4a. [X] ||| في ||| on
4b. [X] ||| في ||| in
4c. [X] ||| في ||| 's
5a. [X] ||| قد ||| had
5b. [X] ||| قد ||| was

Figure 3: Examples of differences in lexical choice for other types of lexical units within the same document.

4 Approach

To incorporate document-level features into an MT system that would otherwise operate with only sentence-level evidence, we added three supersentential "consistency features" to the translation model. The decoder computes scores for these features in two passes over each document; in each pass, each sentence in the document is decoded. In the first pass, the decoder keeps track of the number of occurrences of some aspects of each grammar rule and stores that information. The consistency features are disabled during this pass, and do not affect decoder scoring. In the second pass, each grammar rule is assigned as many as three consistency feature scores, each of which is based on some frozen counts from the first pass. These features are designed to introduce a bias towards translation consistency, but to leave the final decision to the decoder, which of course also has access to other features from the translation and language model. At this point we are more interested in effectiveness than efficiency, so we simply note that this approach doubles the running time of the decoder and that future work on a more elegant implementation might be productive.

We explore three ways to compute features in this section. The essential idea behind all of them is to define some feature function that increases monotonically with an increase in some count that we believe to be informative, and in which the rate of increase is damped more strongly as that count increases. Several feature functions could satisfy those broad requirements; in this section, we describe three variants, C_1, C_2 and C_3, and discuss the potential benefits and drawbacks of each.

C_1: **Counting rules** In this variant, we count instances of the same entire grammar rule, where a rule r contains both the source phrase f and the target phrase e. During the first pass, whenever a grammar rule is chosen by the decoder for the one-best output, the count for that rule is incremented. Given a grammar rule r and the number of times r was counted in the first pass (given by $N\{r\}$), the consistency feature score is computed as follows:

$$C_1(r) = \frac{2.2N\{r\}}{1.2 + N\{r\}} \quad (1)$$

Equation 1 is the term frequency component of the well known Okapi BM25 term weighting function, when parameters are set to the conventional values $k = 1.2, b = 0$. This is an increasing and concave function in which the count has a diminishing marginal effect on the feature score. It has proven to be useful in information retrieval applications, in which the goal is to model "aboutness" based on term counts (Robertson et al., 1994). Because our goal is to demonstrate the potential of consistency features, it seemed reasonable to work with some simple function that has a shape like the one we desired. We leave exploration of optimal damping functions for future work.

A drawback of this C_1 approach is that as we saw in Section 3, grammar rules in phrase-based MT systems tend to be somewhat more fine-grained than seems optimal for constructing a consistency feature. For instance, consider the following rules that all translate the same Arabic term:

R_1. [X] ||| [X,1] اجهزة ||| [X,1] the bodies
R_2. [X] ||| [X,1] اجهزة ||| [X,1] the organs
R_3. [X] ||| [X,1] اجهزة ||| [X,1] organs
R_4. [X] ||| اجهزة [X,1] ||| the organs of [X,1]
R_5. [X] ||| اجهزة [X,1] ||| [X,1] bodies

Based on these grammar rules, we as human readers infer that this Arabic phrase can be translated in two different ways: as *organs* or as *bodies*. An optimal application of the one-translation-per-discourse heuristic would thus group the rules based on the presence of one of those words. However, in the C_1 variant, each of these rules would be counted separately because of differences that in some cases do not directly affect the choice of content words. For instance, on the source side, the Arabic token appears to the right of the nonterminal symbol in R_1, R_2 and R_3, while it is to the left of the nonterminal in R_4 and R_5. On the target side, differences are due to both nonterminal symbol position and the existence of determiners. Motivated by many examples like this, we came up with an alternative way of counting rules.

C_2: **Counting target tokens** To partially address this sparseness issue, variant C_2 focuses only on the target side. We extract all target tokens whenever a grammar rule is used by the decoder in a one-best derivation and increment a counter for each. Since we are mainly interested in content words (e.g. *bodies*, *organs*), we use simple pattern matching to discard nonterminal symbols and punctuation, and we ignore terms that appear in more than 50% of all documents (a convenient way of discarding common tokens such as *the*, *or*, *and*). This approach separates the rules in the example above into two groups: rules with *bodies* on the target side and rules with *organs* on the target side. Upon completion of the first pass, the consistency feature score for rule r is then determined by first computing a score for each unique target-side token w using:

$$bm25(w) = \frac{2.2N\{w\}}{1.2 + N\{w\}} \log \frac{D+1}{DF(w) + 0.5} \quad (2)$$

where in this case $N\{w\}$ maps tokens to their respective counts in the document, D is the total number of documents in the collection, and DF (document frequency) is the number of documents in which the token occurs. This is a fuller version of the BM25 function in which (in the information retrieval application) both high term frequencies and rare terms are rewarded. We then set the feature score for each rule r to the maximum score of any of its target-side terminal tokens:

$$C_2(r) = \max_{e \in RHS(r)} bm25(e) \tag{3}$$

Our motivation for choosing the maximum is that when there is more than one content word that survives the pruning of common terms, we want the score to be influenced most strongly by the most important of those terms. Since BM25 term weights can be thought of as a measure of term importance, taking the maximum is a simple expedient.

Although counting only target-side tokens yields coarser granularity than counting rules, ignoring the source side of the rule risks combining target side statistics from translations of unrelated source language terms. Consider the following grammar rule:

R_6. [X] ||| <s> [X,1] أجهزة ||| <s> [X,1] life support

Since the counter for *life* and *support* will both be incremented whenever rule R_6 fires in the one-best decoding during the first pass, problems could arise if a rule with a different LHS that also contains *support* on the RHS were to fire in the same document, for example:

R_7. [X] ||| الأزرها ||| support

If we don't take the source side into account, both occurrences of *support* will be grouped together when counting and R_7 will receive extra score from the consistency feature whenever R_6 is used by the decoder. Of course, this problem will only arise when the LHS of R_6 and R_7 are present in the same document, and how often that happens (and thus how large the risk from this factor is) is an empirical question. We therefore developed a third alternative as a middle ground between the fine-grained C_1 and the coarse-grained C_2.

C_3: **Counting token translation pairs** In this variant, we count each terminal (source token, target token) pair that survives pruning. Specifically, if grammar rule $[X]|||f_1 f_2 ... f_m|||e_1 e_2 ... e_n$ fires, we increment the count of every pair $\langle f_i, e_j \rangle$, where f_i is aligned to e_j. After the first pass, we compute the feature value of each observed pair, based on this count and the DF of the target-side of the pair. We chose to use only the target token in the DF computation (i.e., aggregating over all source tokens) to reduce sparsity effects. Similar to C_2, the feature of a rule r is defined by the maximum of scores of all pairs extracted from r.

$$C_3(r) = \max_{\substack{f \in LHS(r) \\ e \in RHS(r) \\ \langle f,e \rangle \text{ aligned}}} bm25(\langle f, e \rangle) \tag{4}$$

Since each variant has its benefits and drawbacks, we can include all three in the system and let the tuning process decide on how each should be weighted.

5 Evaluation and Discussion

We have evaluated the one-translation-per-discourse feature using the cdec MT system (Dyer et al., 2010). We started by building a baseline system using standard features in cdec: lexical and phrase translation probabilities in both directions, word and arity penalty features, and a 5-gram language model. We then added each of the three consistency feature variants, along with all two-way and the one three-way combinations of them, thus yielding a total of eight systems for comparison, including the baseline.

For training the Ar-En system, we used the dataset from the DARPA GALE evaluation (Olive et al., 2011), which consists of NIST and LDC releases. The corpus was filtered to remove sentence pairs with anomalous length ratios and subsampled to yield a training set containing 3.4 million parallel sentence pairs. The Arabic text was preprocessed to produce two different segmentations (simple punctuation tokenization with orthographic normalization, and LDC's ATBv3 representation (Maamouri et al., 2008)), represented together using cdec's lattice input format (Dyer et al., 2008).

The Zh-En system was trained on parallel training text consisting of the non-UN portions and non-HK Hansards portions of the NIST training corpora. Chinese was automatically segmented by the Stanford segmenter (Tseng et al., 2005), and traditional characters were simplified. After subsampling and filtering, we obtain a training corpus of 1.6 million parallel sentences.

Both training sets were word-aligned with GIZA++ (Och and Ney, 2003), using 5 Model 1 and 5 HMM iterations. A SCFG was then extracted from these alignments using a suffix array extractor (Chiang, 2007). Evaluation was done with multi-reference BLEU (Papineni et al., 2002) on test sets with four references for each language pair, and MIRA was used for tuning (Crammer et al., 2006). In our experiments, we run the first decoding phase using feature weights that are guessed heuristically based on weights from previously tuned systems. All feature weights, including the discourse feature, were then tuned together, based on the output of the second decoding phase. For Ar-En parameter tuning, we used the MT06 newswire dataset, which contains 104 documents and a total of 1,797 sentences. For testing, we used the MT08 dataset described above (74 documents, 813 sentences). For Zh-En experiments, the MT02 newswire dataset (100 documents, 878 sentences) was used for tuning, and evaluation was done on the MT06 test set (79 documents, 1,664 sentences). For both language pairs, DF values were computed from the tuning set for both tuning and evaluation experiments.

When we used NIST's official metric (BLEU-4) to compare our results to the official NIST evaluation (NIST, 2006; NIST, 2008), our baseline system achieved 54.70 for Ar-En and 31.69 for Zh-En. Based on reported NIST results, our baseline would have ranked 4th in the Zh-En MT06 evaluation, and would have outperformed all Ar-En MT08 systems. We used a slightly different IBM-BLEU metric for the rest of our evaluation. In this case, the baseline system achieved 53.07 BLEU points for Ar-En and 30.43 points for Zh-En. Among more recent papers, the best reported results were 56.87 for Ar-En MT08 (Zhao et al., 2011a) and 35.87 for Zh-En MT06 (Zhao et al., 2011b), although many papers report BLEU scores below 53 points for Arabic (Carpuat et al., 2011) and 32 points for Chinese (Monz, 2011). The systems that outperformed our baseline applied novel techniques, and used larger language models, as well as many non-standard features. We argue that these novelties are complementary to our approach, and therefore do not damage the credibility of our baseline.

Among the single-feature runs, C_3 had the best performance in Ar-En experiments, with 53.84 BLEU points, whereas C_2 yielded the best results for Zh-En with a BLEU score of 30.96. In any case, all three variants outperformed the baseline (see Table 2). When multiple features were combined, we generally observed an increase in BLEU, suggesting that our features have usefully different error characteristics. The combination of all three variants, C_{123}, yielded the best results, nearly 1.0 BLEU point higher than the baseline for both language pairs. Evaluation results are summarized in Table 2.

Method	BLEU	
	Ar-En	Zh-En
Baseline	53.07	30.43
C_1	53.82	30.59
C_2	53.70	30.96
C_3	53.84	30.54
C_{12}	53.82	30.79
C_{13}	53.82	30.76
C_{23}	53.88	30.63
C_{123}	**53.98**	**31.42**

Table 2: Evaluation results: BLEU scores with four references for Ar-En and Zh-En experiments.

Method	# documents	
	Ar-En	Zh-En
Docs	74	79
C_1	37	30
C_2	37	35
C_3	42	36
C_{123}	**43**	**41**

Table 3: Doc-level analysis: Number of documents where each variant outperforms baseline.

Given our focus on documents, it is natural to ask what fraction of the documents were helped or harmed by consistency features. Document-level BLEU scores for Arabic-to-English translations show that C_3 outperformed the baseline on a larger number of documents than any other single feature (42/74=57%), compared with 37/74 (50%) for both C_1 and C_2. C_{123} did better by this measure as well, with BLEU increasing for 43 of the documents. There were no documents where the BLEU score was exactly the same, therefore the BLEU score declined for the remaining documents. As Table 3 indicates, document-level BLEU for the Zh-En experiments shows similar results.

We can also look at our results in a more fine-grained way, focusing on differences in how each system translated the same source-language phrase. For this analysis, we defined English phrases e and e' to be *different* if $edit\_distance(e, e') >$

Method	Ar-En		Zh-En	
	Cases	Test set	Cases	Test set
C_1	77	24%	401	48%
C_2	127	35%	686	60%
C_3	101	33%	491	53%
Any	197	68%	968	94%
C_{123}	141	41%	651	59%

Table 4: Effect of applying variants of the consistency feature (Any=C_1 or C_2 or C_3).

$max(length(e), length(e'))/2$. By this way of counting, there are 197 unique (Arabic phrase, document) pairs for which at least one single-feature system produced translations differently from the baseline system. Together, these cases affect 553 sentences (68%) in 67 of the 74 documents, with as many as 12 differences observed in a single document. The number of such differences is even higher for Chinese-to-English translation, probably due to lower confidence from the translation model and longer documents. Table 4 shows the number of changes by each system, and the percentage of the test set affected by these changes.

In order to gain greater insight into the effect of the consistency features, we randomly sampled 60 of the 197 cases and analyzed the influence of the change to the document BLEU score. In 25 of the sampled cases, at least one of the three systems made a change that improved the BLEU score, whereas the score was adversely affected for at least one system in 13 cases. BLEU remained unchanged in the remaining 22 cases, mostly due to the use of multiple reference translations. When we analyze the effect of each system separately, we see that C_2 was the most aggressive, making 25 changes that influenced BLEU (16 positive, 9 negative). C_1 was the most conservative, with only 13 such changes (8 positive, 5 negative). Consistent with the overall BLEU scores, C_3 evidenced the best ratio between benefit and harm, making 20 changes that affected the score (16 positive, 4 negative).

Looking at specific cases can yield some insight into how the consistency features achieve improvements. For example, results improved when translating the phrase تنظيمية, (Eng. *organizational*, *regulatory*), which appears in the context of organizational groups that support terrorist ideology. The baseline system translated this as *organizational* in one case, and *regulatory* in another. Variants C_1 and C_2 changed this behavior, so that the translation was *organizational* in both cases. One of the reference translations used *organizational* in one case and dropped the phrase in the other, and the other three translators provided consistent translations (using *organized* and *organizational*). As a result, applying the one-translation-per-discourse heuristic improved the multi-reference BLEU score.

On the other hand, here is one of the cases where our feature hurt performance. The phrase 边防部队 (Eng. *border/frontier troops/guards*) appears in two sentences of a Chinese news story about violence along the India - Nepal border. All reference translations consistently used the word *border* in the translation, as it is a better choice in this context. The baseline system translated the phrase as *frontier guards* and *border troops* in the two sentences. All system variants replaced *border* with *frontier* to maintain consistency, and therefore produced worse translations, causing a decrease in BLEU score.

Examples can, however, also point up limitations in our ability to measure improvements. In one of the test documents, the Arabic phrase الي التسلل (Eng. *sneak*, *infiltrate*, *enter without approval*) appears in the context of Turkey trying to enter the European Union. This was translated by the baseline system as *sneak into* in one occurrence and *infiltrate into* in another. C_1 didn't change the output, but C_2 and C_3 translated the phrase as *infiltrate into* in both cases. Although all of the four reference translators were consistent within their choices, each of them chose different translations, namely *worm its way*, *enter*, *sneak* and *sneak into*. This resulted in a decrease in BLEU score for the two systems that chose *infiltrate into*. This case illustrates a limitation to fine-grained use of BLEU alone as a basis for analysis, since we might argue that *infiltrate into* is no less appropriate than *sneak into* in this context. In other words, some of the reductions we see in BLEU may not be actual errors but rather simply changes that take us outside of the coverage of the test set. We did not find any cases in our sample in which improvements in BLEU seemed to reward changes that adversely affected meaning. From this, we conclude that BLEU is a somewhat conservative measure when used in this way, and that the actual overall improvement in translation quality over our baseline may be somewhat more than our roughly 1.0 measured BLEU improvement would suggest.

6 Conclusions and Future Work

In this paper, we started with a new way of looking at, and largely supporting, the "one translation per discourse" hypothesis using forced decoding of human reference translations. We then leveraged insights from that analysis to design the translation model consistency features, obtaining solid improvements for both Ar-En and Zh-En translation. In future work, we plan to explore additional variants. For example, we can further address sparsity by incorporating monolingual paraphrase detection on the source side, the target side or both. We can and should explore other monotonically increasing concave feature functions in addition to the Okapi BM25 function that we have found to be useful in this work, we should explore alternatives to our use of the maximum function in C_2 and C_3, and we should consider optimizing to measures other than BLEU (e.g., METEOR) that extend the range of rewarded lexical choices by leveraging monolingual paraphrase evidence.

In designing our features we were guided by our intuition about which kinds of consistency should be rewarded. Data can be superior to intuition, however, and our forced decoding technique might also be helpful in generating new insights that could help to guide the design of even more useful features. For example, our forced decoding clearly points to cases in which translators have chosen different structural variants when translating the same phrase, and closer examination of these cases might help us to automatically detect which kinds of structural variation can most profitably be moderated using a consistency feature. We should also note that we have only done forced decoding to date in one language pair (Ar-En), and there might be more to be learned about language-specific issues from doing the same analysis for additional language pairs.

Finally, the time seems propitious to reconsider our choice of document-scale as our discourse context. Documents have much to recommend them, but much of the content that we might wish to translate (conversational speech, text chat, email threads, ...) doesn't present the kinds of obvious and unambiguous document boundaries that we find in MT test collections that are built from news stories. Moreover, some documents (e.g., textbooks) may be too diverse for an entire document to be the right scale for consistency. We might also be able to productively group similar documents into clusters in which the vocabulary choices are (or should be) mutually reinforcing.

We therefore end where we began, with many questions to be answered. Now, however, we have somewhat different questions – not *whether* to encourage consistency at a super-sentential scale, but rather *when* and *how best* to do that.

Acknowledgements

This research was supported in part by the BOLT program of the Defense Advanced Research Projects Agency, Contract No. HR0011-12-C-0015. Any opinions, findings, conclusions or recommendations expressed in this paper are those of the authors and do not necessarily reflect the view of DARPA.

References

Nicola Bertoldi and Marcello Federico. 2009. Domain adaptation for statistical machine translation with monolingual resources. In *Proceedings of the Fourth Workshop on Statistical Machine Translation (StatMT '09)*, pages 182–189.

Ralf D. Brown. 2008. Exploiting document-level context for data-driven machine translation. In *Proceedings of the the Eighth Conference of the Association for Machine Translation in the Americas (AMTA '08)*.

Marine Carpuat, Yuval Marton, and Nizar Habash. 2011. Improved Arabic-to-English statistical machine translation by reordering post-verbal subjects for word alignment. *Machine Translation*, pages 1–16.

Marine Carpuat. 2009. One translation per discourse. In *Proceedings of the Workshop on Semantic Evaluations: Recent Achievements and Future Directions*, DEW '09, pages 19–27.

David Chiang. 2005. A hierarchical phrase-based model for statistical machine translation. In *Proceedings of ACL '05*.

David Chiang. 2007. Hierarchical phrase-based translation. *Computational Linguistics*, 33:201–228.

Koby Crammer, Ofer Dekel, Joseph Keshet, Shai Shalev-Shwartz, and Yoram Singer. 2006. Online passive-aggressive algorithms. *Journal of Machine Learning Research*, 7:551–585.

Mona Diab and Philip Resnik. 2002. An unsupervised method for word sense tagging using parallel corpora. In *Proceedings of ACL '02*.

Christopher Dyer, Smaranda Muresan, and Philip Resnik. 2008. Generalizing Word Lattice Translation. In *Proceedings of ACL-HLT'08*, pages 1012–1020, June.

Chris Dyer, Jonathan Weese, Hendra Setiawan, Adam Lopez, Ferhan Ture, Vladimir Eidelman, Juri Ganitkevitch, Phil Blunsom, and Philip Resnik. 2010. cdec: a decoder, alignment, and learning framework for finite-state and context-free translation models. In *ACLDemos '10*, pages 7–12.

William A. Gale, Kenneth W. Church, and David Yarowsky. 1992. One sense per discourse. In *Proceedings of the workshop on Speech and Natural Language*, HLT '91, pages 233–237.

Jesús Giménez and Lluís Màrquez. 2007. Context-aware discriminative phrase selection for statistical machine translation. In *Proceedings of StatMT '07*, pages 159–166.

AS Hildebrand, M Eck, S Vogel, and Alex Waibel. 2005. Adaptation of the translation model for statistical machine translation based on information retrieval. In *Proceedings of The European Association for Machine Translation (EAMT '05)*.

Zhanyi Liu, Haifeng Wang, Hua Wu, and Sheng Li. 2010. Improving statistical machine translation with monolingual collocation. In *ACL '10*.

Yanjun Ma, Yifan He, Andy Way, and Josef van Genabith. 2011. Consistent translation using discriminative learning: a translation memory-inspired approach. In *Proceedings of ACL-HLT'11*, pages 1239–1248.

Mohamed Maamouri, Ann Bies, and Seth Kulick. 2008. Enhancing the Arabic Treebank: A Collaborative Effort toward New Annotation Guidelines. In *LREC '08*.

Christof Monz. 2011. Statistical Machine Translation with Local Language Models. In *EMNLP '11*.

Hwee Tou Ng, Bin Wang, and Yee Seng Chan. 2003. Exploiting parallel texts for word sense disambiguation: an empirical study. In *ACL '03*.

NIST. 2006. http://www.itl.nist.gov/iad/mig/tests/mt/2006/.

NIST. 2008. http://www.itl.nist.gov/iad/mig/tests/mt/2008/.

Franz Och and Hermann Ney. 2003. A systematic comparison of various statistical alignment models. *Computational Linguistics*, 29(1):19–51.

Joseph Olive, Caitlin Christianson, and John McCary. 2011. *Handbook of Natural Language Processing and Machine Translation: DARPA Global Autonomous Language Exploitation*. Springer Publishing Company, Inc., 1st edition.

Kishore Papineni, Salim Roukos, Todd Ward, and Wei-Jing Zhu. 2002. BLEU: a method for automatic evaluation of machine translation. In *ACL '02*.

Stephen E. Robertson, Steve Walker, Susan Jones, Micheline Hancock-Beaulieu, and Mike Gatford. 1994. Okapi at TREC-3. In *TREC*.

Germán Sanchis-Trilles and Francisco Casacuberta. 2010. Bayesian adaptation for statistical machine translation. In *Proceedings of the workshop on Structural and Syntactic Pattern Recognition (SSPR '10)*, pages 620–629.

Jörg Tiedemann. 2010. Context adaptation in statistical machine translation using models with exponentially decaying cache. In *Proceedings of the workshop on Domain Adaptation for Natural Language Processing (DANLP '10)*, pages 8–15.

Huihsin Tseng, Pi-Chuan Chang, Galen Andrew, Daniel Jurafsky, and Christopher Manning. 2005. A conditional random field word segmenter. In *Fourth SIGHAN Workshop on Chinese Language Processing*.

Michael M. Wasser and Bonnie Dorr. 2008. Machine translation with cross-lingual information retrieval based document relevance scores. Unpublished.

Tong Xiao, Jingbo Zhu, Shujie Yao, and Hao Zhang. 2011. Document-level consistency verification in machine translation. In *Machine Translation Summit XIII (MTS'11)*.

David Yarowsky. 1995. Unsupervised word sense disambiguation rivaling supervised methods. In *ACL '95*.

Bing Zhao, Matthias Eck, and Stephan Vogel. 2004. Language model adaptation for statistical machine translation with structured query models. In *COLING '04*.

Bing Zhao, Young-Suk Lee, Xiaoqiang Luo, and Liu Li. 2011a. Learning to transform and select elementary trees for improved syntax-based machine translations. In *ACL-HLT '11*, pages 846–855.

Yinggong Zhao, Yangsheng Ji, Ning Xi, Shujian Huang, and Jiajun Chen. 2011b. Language model weight adaptation based on cross-entropy for statistical machine translation. In *Pacific Asia Conference on Language, Information and Computation (PACLIC '11)*.

Batch Tuning Strategies for Statistical Machine Translation

Colin Cherry and **George Foster**
National Research Council Canada
{Colin.Cherry,George.Foster}@nrc-cnrc.gc.ca

Abstract

There has been a proliferation of recent work on SMT tuning algorithms capable of handling larger feature sets than the traditional MERT approach. We analyze a number of these algorithms in terms of their sentence-level loss functions, which motivates several new approaches, including a Structured SVM. We perform empirical comparisons of eight different tuning strategies, including MERT, in a variety of settings. Among other results, we find that a simple and efficient batch version of MIRA performs at least as well as training online, and consistently outperforms other options.

1 Introduction

The availability of linear models and discriminative tuning algorithms has been a huge boon to statistical machine translation (SMT), allowing the field to move beyond the constraints of generative noisy channels (Och and Ney, 2002). The ability to optimize these models according to an error metric has become a standard assumption in SMT, due to the wide-spread adoption of Minimum Error Rate Training or MERT (Och, 2003). However, MERT has trouble scaling to more than 30 features, which has led to a surge in research on tuning schemes that can handle high-dimensional feature spaces.

These methods fall into a number of broad categories. *Minimum risk* approaches (Och, 2003; Smith and Eisner, 2006) have been quietly capable of handling many features for some time, but have yet to see widespread adoption. *Online* methods (Liang et al., 2006; Watanabe et al., 2007), are recognized to be effective, but require substantial implementation efforts due to difficulties with parallelization. *Pairwise ranking* (Shen et al., 2004; Hopkins and May, 2011) recasts tuning as classification, and can be very easy to implement, as it fits nicely into the established MERT infrastructure.

The MERT algorithm optimizes linear weights relative to a collection of k-best lists or lattices, which provide an approximation to the true search space. This optimization is wrapped in an outer loop that iterates between optimizing weights and re-decoding with those weights to enhance the approximation. Our primary contribution is to empirically compare eight tuning algorithms and variants, focusing on methods that work within MERT's established outer loop. This is the first comparison to include all three categories of optimizer.

Furthermore, we introduce three tuners that have not been previously tested. In particular, we test variants of Chiang et al.'s (2008) hope-fear MIRA that use k-best or lattice-approximated search spaces, producing a *Batch MIRA* that outperforms a popular mechanism for parallelizing online learners. We also investigate the direct optimization of hinge loss on k-best lists, through the use of a *Structured SVM* (Tsochantaridis et al., 2004). We review and organize the existing tuning literature, providing sentence-level loss functions for minimum risk, online and pairwise training. Finally, since randomization plays a different role in each tuner, we also suggest a new method for testing an optimizer's stability (Clark et al., 2011), which sub-samples the tuning set instead of varying a random seed.

2 Background

We begin by establishing some notation. We view our training set as a list of triples $[f, R, \mathcal{E}]_{i=1}^{n}$, where f is a source-language sentence, R is a set of target-language reference sentences, and $\mathcal{E}$ is the set of all reachable hypotheses; that is, each $e \in \mathcal{E}_i$ is a target-language derivation that can be decoded from f_i. The function $\vec{h}_i(e)$ describes e's relationship to its source f_i using features that decompose into the decoder. A linear model $\vec{w}$ scores derivations according to their features, meaning that the decoder solves:

$$e_i(\vec{w}) = \arg\max_{e \in \mathcal{E}_i} \vec{w} \cdot \vec{h}_i(e) \quad (1)$$

Assuming we wish to optimize our decoder's BLEU score (Papineni et al., 2002), the natural objective of learning would be to find a $\vec{w}$ such that $\text{BLEU}([e(\vec{w}), R]_1^n)$ is maximal. In most machine learning papers, this would be the point where we would say, "unfortunately, this objective is unfeasible." But in SMT, we have been happily optimizing exactly this objective for years using MERT.

However, it is now acknowledged that the MERT approach is not feasible for more than 30 or so features. This is due to two main factors:

1. MERT's parameter search slows and becomes less effective as the number of features rises, stopping it from finding good training scores.
2. BLEU is a scale invariant objective: one can scale $\vec{w}$ by any positive constant and receive the same BLEU score.[1] This causes MERT to resist standard mechanisms of regularization that aim to keep $||\vec{w}||$ small.

The problems with MERT can be addressed through the use of surrogate loss functions. In this paper, we focus on linear losses that decompose over training examples. Using R_i and $\mathcal{E}_i$, each loss $\ell_i(\vec{w})$ indicates how poorly $\vec{w}$ performs on the ith training example. This requires a sentence-level approximation of BLEU, which we re-encode into a cost $\Delta_i(e)$ on derivations, where a high cost indicates that e receives a low BLEU score. Unless otherwise stated, we will assume the use of sentence BLEU with add-1 smoothing (Lin and Och, 2004). The learners differ in their definition of ℓ and Δ, and in how they employ their loss functions to tune their weights.

[1]This is true of any evaluation metric that considers only the ranking of hypotheses and not their model scores; ie, it is true of all common MT metrics.

2.1 Margin Infused Relaxed Algorithm

First employed in SMT by Watanabe et al. (2007), and refined by Chiang et al. (2008; 2009), the Margin Infused Relaxed Algorithm (MIRA) employs a structured hinge loss:

$$\ell_i(\vec{w}) = \max_{e \in \mathcal{E}_i} \left[\Delta_i(e) + \vec{w} \cdot \left(\vec{h}_i(e) - \vec{h}_i(e_i^*) \right) \right] \quad (2)$$

where e_i^* is an oracle derivation, and cost is defined as $\Delta_i(e) = \text{BLEU}_i(e_i^*) - \text{BLEU}_i(e)$, so that $\Delta_i(e_i^*) = 0$. The loss $\ell_i(\vec{w})$ is 0 only if $\vec{w}$ separates each $e \in \mathcal{E}_i$ from e_i^* by a margin proportional to their BLEU differentials.

MIRA is an instance of online learning, repeating the following steps: visit an example i, decode according to $\vec{w}$, and update $\vec{w}$ to reduce $\ell_i(\vec{w})$. Each update makes the smallest change to $\vec{w}$ (subject to a step-size cap C) that will separate the oracle from a number of negative hypotheses. The work of Crammer et al. (2006) shows that updating away from a single "fear" hypothesis that maximizes (2) admits a closed-form update that performs well. Let e_i' be the $e \in \mathcal{E}_i$ that maximizes $\ell_i(\vec{w})$; the update can be performed in two steps:

$$\begin{aligned} \eta_t &= \min \left[C, \frac{\ell_i(\vec{w}_t)}{||\vec{h}_i(e_i^*) - \vec{h}_i(e_i')||^2} \right] \\ \vec{w}_{t+1} &= \vec{w}_t + \eta_t \left(\vec{h}_i(e_i^*) - \vec{h}_i(e_i') \right) \end{aligned} \quad (3)$$

To improve generalization, the average of all weights seen during learning is used on unseen data.

Chiang et al. (2008) take advantage of MIRA's online nature to modify each update to better suit SMT. The cost Δ_i is defined using a pseudo-corpus BLEU that tracks the n-gram statistics of the model-best derivations from the last few updates. This modified cost matches corpus BLEU better than add-1 smoothing, but it also makes Δ_i time-dependent: each update for an example i will be in the context of a different pseudo-corpus. The oracle e_i^* also shifts with each update to $\vec{w}$, as it is defined as a "hope" derivation, which maximizes $\vec{w} \cdot \vec{h}_i(e) + \text{BLEU}_i(e)$. Hope updating ensures that MIRA aims for ambitious, reachable derivations.

In our implementation, we make a number of small, empirically verified deviations from Chiang et al. (2008). These include the above-mentioned use of a single hope and fear hypothesis, and the use of hope hypotheses (as opposed to model-best hypotheses) to build the pseudo-corpus for calculating BLEU_i. These changes were observed to be neutral with respect to translation quality, but resulted in faster running time and simplified implementation.

2.2 Direct Optimization

With the exception of MIRA, the tuning approaches discussed in this paper are direct optimizers. That is, each solves the following optimization problem:

$$\vec{w}* = \arg\min_{\vec{w}} \frac{\lambda}{2}||\vec{w}||^2 + \sum_i \ell_i(\vec{w}) \qquad (4)$$

where the first term provides regularization, weighted by λ. Throughout this paper, (4) is optimized with respect to a fixed approximation of the decoder's true search space, represented as a collection of k-best lists. The various methods differ in their definition of loss and in how they optimize their objective.

Without the complications added by hope decoding and a time-dependent cost function, unmodified MIRA can be shown to be carrying out dual coordinate descent for an SVM training objective (Martins et al., 2010). However, exactly what objective hope-fear MIRA is optimizing remains an open question. Gimpel and Smith (2012) discuss these issues in greater detail, while also providing an interpretable alternative to MIRA.

2.3 Pairwise Ranking Optimization

Introduced by Hopkins and May (2011), Pairwise Ranking Optimization (PRO) aims to handle large feature sets inside the traditional MERT architecture. That is, PRO employs a growing approximation of $\mathcal{E}_i$ by aggregating the k-best hypotheses from a series of increasingly refined models. This architecture is desirable, as most groups have infrastructure to k-best decode their tuning sets in parallel.

For a given approximate $\tilde{\mathcal{E}}_i$, PRO creates a sample S_i of (e_g, e_b) pairs, such that $\text{BLEU}_i(e_g) > \text{BLEU}_i(e_b)$. It then uses a binary classifier to separate each pair. We describe the resulting loss in terms of an SVM classifier, to highlight similarities with MIRA. In terms of (4), PRO defines

$$\ell_i(\vec{w}) = \sum_{(e_g,e_b)\in S_i} 2\left(1 + \vec{w}\cdot\left(\vec{h}_i(e_b) - \vec{h}_i(e_g)\right)\right)^+$$

where $(x)^+ = \max(0, x)$. The hinge loss is multiplied by 2 to account for PRO's use of two examples (positive and negative) for each sampled pair. This sum of hinge-losses is 0 only if each pair is separated by a model score of 1. Given $[S]_{i=1}^n$, this convex objective can be optimized using any binary SVM.[2] Unlike MIRA, the margin here is fixed to 1; cost enters into PRO through its sampling routine, which performs a large uniform sample and then selects a subset of pairs with large BLEU differentials.

The PRO loss uses a sum over pairs in place of MIRA's max, which allows PRO to bypass oracle selection, and to optimize with off-the-shelf classifiers. This sum is potentially a weakness, as PRO receives credit for each correctly ordered pair in its sample, and these pairs are not equally relevant to the final BLEU score.

2.4 Minimum Risk Training

Minimum risk training (MR) interprets $\vec{w}$ as a probabilistic model, and optimizes expected BLEU. We focus on expected sentence costs (Och, 2003; Zens et al., 2007; Li and Eisner, 2009), as this risk is simple to optimize and fits nicely into our mathematical framework. Variants that use the expected sufficient statistics of BLEU also exist (Smith and Eisner, 2006; Pauls et al., 2009; Rosti et al., 2011).

We again assume a MERT-like tuning architecture. Let $\Delta_i(e) = -\text{BLEU}_i(e)$ and let

$$\ell_i(\vec{w}) = E_{P_{\vec{w}}}[\Delta_i(e)] = \frac{\sum_{e\in\tilde{\mathcal{E}}_i}\left[\exp(\vec{w}\cdot\vec{h}_i(e))\Delta_i(e)\right]}{\sum_{e'\in\tilde{\mathcal{E}}_i}\exp(\vec{w}\cdot\vec{h}_i(e'))}$$

This expected cost becomes increasingly small as greater probability mass is placed on derivations with high BLEU scores. This smooth, non-convex objective can be solved to a local minimum using gradient-based optimizers; we have found stochastic gradient descent to be quite effective (Bottou, 2010).

Like PRO, MR requires no oracle derivation, and fits nicely into the established MERT architecture. The expectations needed to calculate the gradient

$$E_{P_{\vec{w}}}\left[\vec{h}_i(e)\Delta_i(e)\right] - E_{P_{\vec{w}}}[\Delta_i(e)]\, E_{P_{\vec{w}}}\left[\vec{h}_i(e)\right]$$

[2] Hopkins and May (2011) advocate a maximum-entropy version of PRO, which is what we evaluate in our empirical comparison. It can be obtained using a logit loss $\ell_i(\vec{w}) = \sum_{g,b} 2\log\left(1 + \exp\left(\vec{w}\cdot\left(\vec{h}_i(e_b) - \vec{h}_i(e_g)\right)\right)\right)$.

are trivial to extract from a k-best list of derivations. Each downward step along this gradient moves the model toward likely derivations, and away from likely derivations that incur high costs.

3 Novel Methods

We have reviewed three tuning methods, all of which address MERT's weakness with large features by using surrogate loss functions. Additionally, MIRA has the following advantages over PRO and MR:

1. Loss is optimized using the true $\mathcal{E}_i$, as opposed to an approximate search space $\tilde{\mathcal{E}}_i$.
2. Sentence BLEU is calculated with a fluid pseudo-corpus, instead of add-1 smoothing.

Both of these advantages come at a cost: operating on the true $\mathcal{E}_i$ sacrifices easy parallelization, while using a fluid pseudo-corpus creates an unstable learning objective. We develop two large-margin tuners that explore these trade-offs.

3.1 Batch MIRA

Online training makes it possible to learn with the decoder in the loop, forgoing the need to approximate the search space, but it is not necessarily convenient to do so. Online algorithms are notoriously difficult to parallelize, as they assume each example is visited in sequence. Parallelization is important for efficient SMT tuning, as decoding is still relatively expensive.

The parallel online updates suggested by Chiang et al. (2008) involve substantial inter-process communication, which may not be easily supported by all clusters. McDonald et al. (2010) suggest a simpler distributed strategy that is amenable to map-reduce-like frameworks, which interleaves online training on shards with weight averaging across shards. This strategy has been adopted by Moses (Hasler et al., 2011), and it is the one we adopt in our MIRA implementation.

However, online training using the decoder may not be necessary for good performance. The success of MERT, PRO and MR indicates that their shared search approximation is actually quite reasonable. Therefore, we propose Batch MIRA, which sits exactly where MERT sits in the standard tuning architecture, greatly simplifying parallelization:

1. Parallel Decode: $[\tilde{\mathcal{E}}']_1^n = k\text{-best}([f, \mathcal{E}]_1^n, \vec{w})$
2. Aggregate: $[\tilde{\mathcal{E}}]_1^n = [\tilde{\mathcal{E}}]_1^n \cup [\tilde{\mathcal{E}}']_1^n$
3. Train: $\vec{w} = \text{BatchMIRA}([f, R, \tilde{\mathcal{E}}]_1^n, \vec{w})$
4. Repeat

where BatchMIRA() trains the SMT-adapted MIRA algorithm to completion on the current approximation $\tilde{\mathcal{E}}$, without parallelization.[3] The only change we make to MIRA is to replace the hope-fear decoding of sentences with the hope-fear re-ranking of k-best lists. Despite its lack of parallelization, each call to BatchMIRA() is extremely fast, as SMT tuning sets are small enough to load all of $[\tilde{\mathcal{E}}]_1^n$ into memory. We test two Batch MIRA variants, which differ in their representation of $\tilde{\mathcal{E}}$. Pseudo-code that covers both is provided in Algorithm 1. Note that if we set $\tilde{\mathcal{E}} = \mathcal{E}$, Algorithm 1 also describes online MIRA.

Batch k-best MIRA inherits all of the MERT architecture. It is very easy to implement; the hope-fear decoding steps can by carried out by simply evaluating BLEU score and model score for each hypothesis in the k-best list.

Batch Lattice MIRA replaces k-best decoding in step 1 with decoding to lattices. To enable loading all of the lattices into memory at once, we prune to a density of 50 edges per reference word. The hope-fear decoding step requires the same oracle lattice decoding algorithms as online MIRA (Chiang et al., 2008). The lattice aggregation in the outer loop can be kept reasonable by aggregating only those paths corresponding to hope or fear derivations.

3.2 Structured SVM

While MIRA takes a series of local hinge-loss reducing steps, it is also possible to directly minimize the sum of hinge-losses using a batch algorithm, creating a structured SVM (Tsochantaridis et al., 2004). To avoid fixing an oracle before optimization begins, we adapt Yu and Joachim's (2009) latent SVM to our task, which allows the oracle derivation for each sentence to vary during training. Again we assume a MERT-like architecture, which approximates $\mathcal{E}$ with an $\tilde{\mathcal{E}}$ constructed from aggregated k-best lists.

Inspired by the local oracle of Liang et al. (2006), we define $\tilde{\mathcal{E}}_i*$ to be an oracle set:

$$\tilde{\mathcal{E}}_i* = \{e|\text{BLEU}_i(e) \text{ is maximal}\}.$$

[3]In our implementation, BatchMIRA() trains for $J = 30$ passes over $[\tilde{\mathcal{E}}]_1^n$.

Algorithm 1 BatchMIRA

input $[f, R, \tilde{\mathcal{E}}]_1^n$, $\vec{w}$, max epochs J, step cap C, and pseudo-corpus decay γ.
init Pseudo-corpus BG to small positive counts.
init $t = 1$; $\vec{w}_t = \vec{w}$
for j from 1 to J **do**
  for i from 1 to n in random order **do**
    // Hope-fear decode in $\tilde{\mathcal{E}}_i$
    $e_t^* = \arg\max_{e \in \tilde{\mathcal{E}}_i} \left[\vec{w}_t \cdot \vec{h}_i(e) + \text{BLEU}_i(e)\right]$
    $e_t' = \arg\max_{e \in \tilde{\mathcal{E}}_i} \left[\vec{w}_t \cdot \vec{h}_i(e) - \text{BLEU}_i(e)\right]$
    // Update weights
    $\Delta_t = \text{BLEU}_i(e_t^*) - \text{BLEU}_i(e_t')$
    $\eta_t = \min\left[C, \frac{\Delta_t + \vec{w}_t \cdot \left(\vec{h}_i(e_t') - \vec{h}_i(e_t^*)\right)}{||\vec{h}_i(e_t^*) - \vec{h}_i(e_t')||^2}\right]$
    $\vec{w}_{t+1} = \vec{w}_t + \eta_t\left(\vec{h}_i(e_t^*) - \vec{h}_i(e_i')\right)$
    // Update statistics
    $BG = \gamma BG +$ BLEU stats for e_t^* and R_i
    $t = t + 1$
  end for
  $\vec{w}_j^{avg} = \frac{1}{nj} \sum_{t'=1}^{nj} \vec{w}_{t'}$
end for
return $\vec{w}_j^{avg}$ that maximizes training BLEU

Cost is also defined in terms of the maximal BLEU,

$$\Delta_i(e) = \max_{e' \in \tilde{\mathcal{E}}_i} \left[\text{BLEU}_i(e')\right] - \text{BLEU}_i(e).$$

Finally, loss is defined as:

$$\ell_i(\vec{w}) = \max_{e \in \tilde{\mathcal{E}}_i} \quad \left[\Delta_i(e) + \vec{w} \cdot \vec{h}_i(e) - \max_{e_i^* \in \tilde{\mathcal{E}}_i *} \left(\vec{w} \cdot \vec{h}_i(e_i^*)\right)\right]$$

This loss is 0 only if some hypothesis in the oracle set is separated from all others by a margin proportional to their BLEU_i differentials.

With loss defined in this manner, we can minimize (4) to local minimum by using an alternating training procedure. For each example i, we select a fixed $e_i^* \in \tilde{\mathcal{E}}_i*$ that maximizes model score; that is, $\vec{w}$ is used to break ties in BLEU for oracle selection. With the oracle fixed, the objective becomes a standard structured SVM objective, which can be minimized using a cutting-plane algorithm, as described by Tsochantaridis et al. (2004). After doing so, we can drive the loss lower still by iterating this process: re-select each oracle (breaking ties with the new $\vec{w}$), then re-optimize $\vec{w}$. We do so 10 times. We were surprised by the impact of these additional iterations on the final loss; for some sentences, $\tilde{\mathcal{E}}_i*$ can be quite large.

Despite the fact that both algorithms use a structured hinge loss, there are several differences between our SVM and MIRA. The SVM has an explicit regularization term λ that is factored into its global objective, while MIRA regularizes implicitly by taking small steps. The SVM requires a stable objective to optimize, meaning that it must forgo the pseudo-corpus used by MIRA to calculate Δ_i; instead, the SVM uses an interpolated sentence-level BLEU (Liang et al., 2006).[4] Finally, MIRA's oracle is selected with hope decoding. With a sufficiently large $\vec{w}$, any $e \in \tilde{\mathcal{E}}$ can potentially become the oracle. In contrast, the SVM's local oracle is selected from a small set $\tilde{\mathcal{E}}*$, which was done to more closely match the assumptions of the Latent SVM.

To solve the necessary quadratic programming sub-problems, we use a multiclass SVM similar to LIBLINEAR (Hsieh et al., 2008). Like Batch MIRA and PRO, the actual optimization is very fast, as the cutting plane converges quickly and all of $[\tilde{\mathcal{E}}]_1^n$ can be loaded into memory at once.

3.3 Qualitative Summary

We have reviewed three tuning methods and introduced three tuning methods. All six methods employ sentence-level loss functions, which in turn employ sentence-level BLEU approximations. Except for online MIRA, all methods plug nicely into the existing MERT architecture. These methods can be split into two groups: MIRA variants (online, batch k-best, batch lattice), and direct optimizers (PRO, MR and SVM). The MIRA variants use pseudo-corpus BLEU in place of smoothed BLEU, and provide access to richer hypothesis spaces through the use of online training or lattices.[5] The direct optimizers have access to a tunable regularization parameter λ, and do not require special purpose code for hope and fear lattice decoding. Batch

[4] SVM training with interpolated BLEU outperformed add-1 BLEU in preliminary testing. A comparison of different BLEU approximations under different tuning objectives would be an interesting path for future work.

[5] MR approaches that use lattices (Li and Eisner, 2009; Pauls et al., 2009; Rosti et al., 2011) or the complete search space (Arun et al., 2010) exist, but are not tested here.

k-best MIRA straddles the two groups, benefiting from pseudo-corpus BLEU and easy implementation, while being restricted to a k-best list.

4 Experimental Design

We evaluated the six tuning strategies described in this paper, along with two MERT baselines, on three language pairs (French-English (Fr-En), English-French (En-Fr) and Chinese-English (Zh-En)), across three different feature-set sizes. Each setting was run five times over randomized variants to improve reliability. To cope with the resulting large number of configurations, we ran all experiments using an efficient phrase-based decoder similar to Moses (Koehn et al., 2007).

All tuning methods that use an approximate $\tilde{\mathcal{E}}$ perform 15 iterations of the outer loop and return the weights that achieve the best development BLEU score. When present, λ was coarsely tuned (trying 3 values differing by magnitudes of 10) in our large-feature Chinese-English setting.

- **kb-mert** : k-best MERT with 20 random restarts. All k-best methods use $k = 100$.
- **lb-mert** : Lattice MERT (Machery et al., 2008) using unpruned lattices and aggregating only those paths on the line search's upper envelope.
- **mira** : Online MIRA (§2.1). All MIRA variants use a pseudo-corpus decay $\gamma = 0.999$ and $C = 0.01$. Online parallelization follows McDonald et al. (2010), using 8 shards. We tested 20, 15, 10, 8 and 5 shards during development.
- **lb-mira** : Batch Lattice MIRA (§3.1).
- **kb-mira** : Batch k-best MIRA (§3.1).
- **pro** : PRO (§2.3) follows Hopkins and May (2011); however, we were unable to find settings that performed well in general. Reported results use MegaM[6] with a maximum of 30 iterations (as is done in Moses; the early stopping provides a form of regularization) for our six English/French tests, and MegaM with 100 iterations and a reduced initial uniform sample (50 pairs instead of 5000) for our three English/Chinese tests.
- **mr** : MR as described in §2.4. We employ a learning rate of $\eta_0/(1 + \eta_0\lambda t)$ for stochastic gradient descent, with η_0 tuned to optimize the training loss achieved after one epoch (Bottou, 2010). Upon reaching a local optimum, we reshuffle our data, re-tune our learning rate, and re-start from the optimum, repeating this process 5 times. We do not sharpen our distribution with a temperature or otherwise control for entropy; instead, we trust $\lambda = 50$ to maintain a reasonable distribution.
- **svm** : Structured SVM (§3.2) with $\lambda = 1000$.

[6]Available at `www.cs.utah.edu/~hal/megam/`

corpus	sentences	words (en)	words (fr)
train	2,928,759	60,482,232	68,578,459
dev	2,002	40,094	44,603
test1	2,148	42,503	48,064
test2	2,166	44,701	49,986

Table 1: Hansard Corpus (English/French)

corpus	sentences	words (zh)	words (en)
train1	6,677,729	200,706,469	213,175,586
train2	3,378,230	69,232,098	66,510,420
dev	1,506	38,233	40,260
nist04	1,788	53,439	59,944
nist06	1,664	41,782	46,140
nist08	1,357	35,369	42,039

Table 2: NIST09 Corpus (Chinese-English). Train1 corresponds to the UN and Hong Kong sub-corpora; train2 to all others.

4.1 Data

Systems for English/French were trained on Canadian Hansard data (years 2001–2009) summarized in table 1.[7] The dev and test sets were chosen randomly from among the most recent 5 days of Hansard transcripts.

The system for Zh-En was trained on data from the NIST 2009 Chinese MT evaluation, summarized in table 2. The dev set was taken from the NIST 05 evaluation set, augmented with some material reserved from other NIST corpora. The NIST 04, 06, and 08 evaluation sets were used for testing.

4.2 SMT Features

For all language pairs, phrases were extracted with a length limit of 7 from separate word alignments

[7]This corpus will be distributed on request.

template	max	fren	enfr	zhen
tgt unal	50	50	50	31
count bin	11	11	11	11
word pair	6724	1298	1291	1664
length bin	63	63	63	63
total	6848	1422	1415	1769

Table 3: Sparse feature templates used in Big.

performed by IBM2 and HMM models and symmetrized using diag-and (Koehn et al., 2003). Conditional phrase probabilities in both directions were estimated from relative frequencies, and from lexical probabilities (Zens and Ney, 2004). Language models were estimated with Kneser-Ney smoothing using SRILM. Six-feature lexicalized distortion models were estimated and applied as in Moses.

For each language pair, we defined roughly equivalent systems (exactly equivalent for En-Fr and Fr-En, which are mirror images) for each of three nested feature sets: Small, Medium, and Big.

The Small set defines a minimal 7-feature system intended to be within easy reach of all tuning strategies. It comprises 4 TM features, one LM, and length and distortion features. For the Chinese system, the LM is a 5-gram trained on the NIST09 Gigaword corpus; for English/French, it is a 4-gram trained on the target half of the parallel Hansard.

The Medium set is a more competitive 18-feature system. It adds 4 TM features, one LM, and 6 lexicalized distortion features. For Zh-En, Small's TM (trained on both *train1* and *train2* in table 2) is replaced by 2 separate TMs from these sub-corpora; for En/Fr, the extra TM (4 features) comes from a forced-decoding alignment of the training corpus, as proposed by Wuebker et al. (2010). For Zh-En, the extra LM is a 4-gram trained on the target half of the parallel corpus; for En/Fr, it is a 4-gram trained on 5m sentences of similar parliamentary data.

The Big set adds sparse Boolean features to Medium, for a maximum of 6,848 features. We used sparse feature templates that are equivalent to the PBMT set described in (Hopkins and May, 2011): *tgt unal* picks out each of the 50 most frequent target words to appear unaligned in the phrase table; *count bin* uniquely bins joint phrase pair counts with upper bounds 1,2,4,8,16,32,64,128,1k,10k,∞; *word pair* fires when each of the 80 most frequent words in each language appear aligned 1-1 to each other, to some other word, or not 1-1; and *length bin* captures each possible phrase length and length pair. Table 3 summarizes the feature templates, showing the maximum number of features each can generate, and the number of features that received non-zero weights in the final model tuned by MR for each language pair.

Feature weights are initialized to 1.0 for each of the TM, LM and distortion penalty features. All other weights are initialized to 0.0.

4.3 Stability Testing

We follow Clark et al (2011), and perform multiple randomized replications of each experiment. However, their method of using different random seeds is not applicable in our context, since randomization does not play the same role for all tuning methods. Our solution was to randomly draw and fix four different sub-samples of each dev set, retaining each sentence with a probability of 0.9. For each tuning method and setting, we then optimize on the original dev and all sub-samples. The resulting standard deviations provide an indication of stability.

5 Results

The results of our survey of tuning methods can be seen in Tables 4, 5 and 6. Results are averaged over test sets (2 for Fr/En, 3 for Zh/En), and over 5 sub-sampled runs per test set. The SD column reports the standard deviation of the average test score across the 5 sub-samples.

It may be dismaying to see only small score improvements when transitioning from Medium to Big. This is partially due to the fact that our Big feature set affects only phrase-table scores. Our phrase tables are already strong, through our use of large data or leave-one-out forced decoding. The important baseline when assessing the utility of a method is Medium k-best MERT. In all language pairs, our Big systems generally outperform this baseline by 0.4 BLEU points. It is interesting to note that most methods achieve the bulk of this improvement on the Medium feature set.[8] This indicates that MERT begins to show some problems even in an 18-feature

[8] One can see the same phenomenon in the results of Hopkins and May (2011) as well.

Table 4: French to English Translation (Fr-En)

	Small			Medium			Big		
	Tune	Test	SD	Tune	Test	SD	Tune	Test	SD
kb-mert	40.50	39.94	0.04	40.75	40.29	0.13	n/a	n/a	n/a
lb-mert	**40.52**	39.93	0.11	40.93	40.39	0.08	n/a	n/a	n/a
mira	40.38	39.94	0.04	40.64	40.59	0.06	41.02	40.74	0.05
kb-mira	40.46	39.97	0.05	40.92	40.64	0.12	41.46	40.75	0.08
lb-mira	40.44	39.98	0.06	**40.94**	**40.65**	0.06	**41.59**	**40.78**	0.09
pro	40.11	40.05	0.05	40.16	40.07	0.08	40.55	40.21	0.24
mr	40.24	39.88	0.05	40.70	40.57	0.14	41.18	40.60	0.08
svm	40.05	**40.20**	0.03	40.60	40.56	0.08	41.32	40.52	0.07

Table 5: English to French Translation (En-Fr)

	Small			Medium			Big		
	Tune	Test	SD	Tune	Test	SD	Tune	Test	SD
kb-mert	**40.47**	39.72	0.06	40.70	40.02	0.11	n/a	n/a	n/a
lb-mert	40.45	39.76	0.08	40.90	40.13	0.10	n/a	n/a	n/a
mira	40.36	**39.83**	0.03	40.78	40.44	0.02	40.89	40.45	0.05
kb-mira	40.44	39.83	0.02	40.94	40.35	0.06	41.48	40.52	0.06
lb-mira	40.45	39.83	0.02	**41.05**	**40.45**	0.04	**41.65**	**40.59**	0.07
pro	40.17	39.57	0.15	40.30	40.01	0.04	40.75	40.22	0.17
mr	40.31	39.65	0.04	40.94	40.30	0.13	41.45	40.47	0.10
svm	39.99	39.55	0.03	40.40	39.96	0.05	41.00	40.21	0.03

Table 6: Chinese to English Translation (Zh-En)

	Small			Medium			Big		
	Tune	Test	SD	Tune	Test	SD	Tune	Test	SD
kb-mert	23.97	**29.65**	0.06	25.74	31.58	0.42	n/a	n/a	n/a
lb-mert	**24.18**	29.48	0.15	26.42	32.39	0.22	n/a	n/a	n/a
mira	23.98	29.54	0.01	26.23	32.58	0.08	25.99	32.52	0.08
kb-mira	24.10	29.51	0.06	26.28	32.50	0.12	26.18	32.61	0.14
lb-mira	24.13	29.59	0.05	**26.43**	**32.77**	0.06	26.40	32.82	0.18
pro	23.25	28.74	0.24	25.80	32.42	0.20	26.49	32.18	0.40
mr	23.87	29.55	0.09	26.26	32.52	0.12	26.42	32.79	0.15
svm	23.59	28.91	0.05	26.26	32.70	0.05	**27.23**	**33.04**	0.12

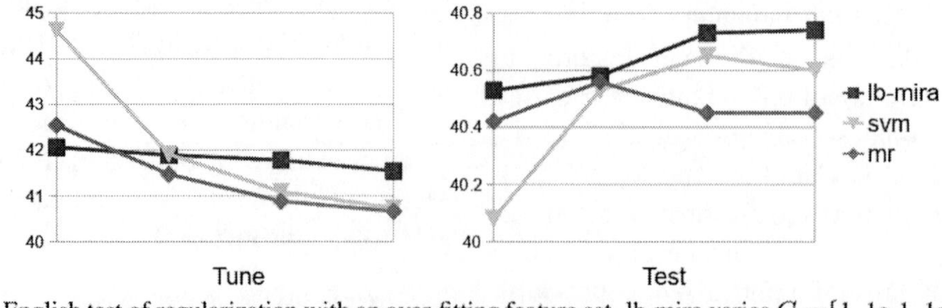

Figure 1: French-English test of regularization with an over-fitting feature set. lb-mira varies $C = \{1, 1e\text{-}1, 1e\text{-}2, 1e\text{-}3\}$, its default C is 1e-2; svm varies $\lambda = \{1e2, 1e3, 1e4, 1e5\}$, its default λ is 1e3; mr varies $\lambda = \{5, 5e1, 5e2, 5e3\}$, its default λ is 5e1.

setting, which can be mitigated through the use of Lattice MERT.

When examining score differentials, recall that the reported scores average over multiple test sets and sub-sampled tuning runs. Using Small features, all of the tested methods are mostly indistinguishable, but as we move to Medium and Big, Batch Lattice MIRA emerges as our method of choice. It is the top scoring system in all Medium settings, and in two of three Big settings (in Big Zh-En, the SVM comes first, with batch lattice MIRA placing second). However, all of the MIRA variants perform similarly, though our implementation of online MIRA is an order of magnitude slower, mostly due to its small number of shards. It is interesting that our batch lattice variant consistently outperforms online MIRA. We attribute this to our parallelization strategy, Chiang et al.'s (2008) more complex solution may perform better.

There may be settings where an explicit regularization parameter is desirable, thus we also make a recommendation among the direct optimizers (PRO, MR and SVM). Though these systems all tend to show a fair amount of variance across language and feature sets (likely due to their use sentence-level BLEU), MR performs the most consistently, and is always within 0.2 of batch lattice MIRA.

The SVM's performance on Big Zh-En is an intriguing outlier in our results. Note that it not only performs best on the test set, but also achieves the best tuning score by a large margin. We suspect we have simply found a setting where interpolated BLEU and our choice of λ work particularly well. We intend to investigate this case to see if this level of success can be replicated consistently, perhaps through improved sentence BLEU approximation or improved oracle selection.

5.1 Impact of Regularization

One main difference between MIRA and the direct optimizers is the availability of an explicit regularization term λ. To measure the impact of this parameter, we designed a feature set explicitly for overfitting. This set uses our Big Fr-En features, with the count bin template modified to distinguish each joint count observed in the tuning set. These new features, which expand the set to 20k+ features, should generalize poorly.

We tested MR and SVM on our Fr-En data using this feature set, varying their respective regularization parameters by factors of 10. We compared this to Batch Lattice MIRA's step-size cap C, which controls its regularization (Martins et al., 2010). The results are shown in Figure 1. Looking at the tuning scores, one can see that λ affords much greater control over tuning performance than MIRA's C. Looking at test scores, MIRA's narrow band of regularization appears to be just about right; however, there is no reason to expect this to always be the case.

6 Conclusion

We have presented three new, large-margin tuning methods for SMT that can handle thousands of features. Batch lattice and k-best MIRA carry out their online training within approximated search spaces, reducing costs in terms of both implementation and training time. The Structured SVM optimizes a sum of hinge losses directly, exposing an explicit regularization term. We have organized the literature on tuning, and carried out an extensive comparison of linear-loss SMT tuners. Our experiments show Batch Lattice MIRA to be the most consistent of the tested methods. In the future, we intend to investigate improved sentence-BLEU approximations to help narrow the gap between MIRA and the direct optimizers.

Acknowledgements

Thanks to Mark Hopkins, Zhifei Li and Jonathan May for their advice while implementing the methods in this review, and to Kevin Gimpel, Roland Kuhn and the anonymous reviewers for their valuable comments on an earlier draft.

References

Abhishek Arun, Barry Haddow, and Philipp Koehn. 2010. A unified approach to minimum risk training and decoding. In *Proceedings of the Joint Workshop on Statistical Machine Translation and MetricsMATR*, pages 365–374.

Leon Bottou. 2010. Large-scale machine learning with stochastic gradient descent. In *International Conference on Computational Statistics*, pages 177–187.

David Chiang, Yuval Marton, and Philip Resnik. 2008. Online large-margin training of syntactic and structural translation features. In *EMNLP*, pages 224–233.

David Chiang, Kevin Knight, and Wei Wang. 2009. 11,001 new features for statistical machine translation. In *HLT-NAACL*, pages 218–226.

Jonathan H. Clark, Chris Dyer, Alon Lavie, and Noah A. Smith. 2011. Better hypothesis testing for statistical machine translation: Controlling for optimizer instability. In *ACL*, pages 176–181.

Koby Crammer, Ofer Dekel, Joseph Keshet, Shai Shalev-Shwartz, and Yoram Singer. 2006. Online passive-aggressive algorithms. *Journal of Machine Learning Research*.

Kevin Gimpel and Noah A. Smith. 2012. Structured ramp loss minimization for machine translation. In *HLT-NAACL*, Montreal, Canada, June.

Eva Hasler, Barry Haddow, and Philipp Koehn. 2011. Margin infused relaxed algorithm for moses. *The Prague Bulletin of Mathematical Linguistics*, 96:69–78.

Mark Hopkins and Jonathan May. 2011. Tuning as ranking. In *EMNLP*, pages 1352–1362.

Cho-Jui Hsieh, Kai-Wei Chang, Chih-Jen Lin, S. Sathiya Keerthi, and S. Sundararajan. 2008. A dual coordinate descent method for large-scale linear svm. In *ICML*.

Philipp Koehn, Franz J. Och, and Daniel Marcu. 2003. Statistical phrase-based translation. In *HLT-NAACL*, pages 127–133.

Philipp Koehn, Hieu Hoang, Alexandra Birch, Chris Callison-Burch, Marcello Federico, Nicola Bertoldi, Brooke Cowan, Wade Shen, Christine Moran, Richard Zens, Chris Dyer, Ondrej Bojar, Alexandra Constantin, and Evan Herbst. 2007. Moses: Open source toolkit for statistical machine translation. In *ACL*, pages 177–180, Prague, Czech Republic, June.

Zhifei Li and Jason Eisner. 2009. First- and second-order expectation semirings with applications to minimum-risk training on translation forests. In *EMNLP*, pages 40–51.

Percy Liang, Alexandre Bouchard-Côté, Dan Klein, and Ben Taskar. 2006. An end-to-end discriminative approach to machine translation. In *COLING-ACL*, pages 761–768.

Chin-Yew Lin and Franz Josef Och. 2004. Orange: a method for evaluating automatic evaluation metrics for machine translation. In *COLING*, pages 501–507.

Wolfgang Machery, Franz Josef Och, Ignacio Thayer, and Jakob Uszkoreit. 2008. Lattice-based minimum error rate training for statistical machine translation. In *EMNLP*, pages 725–734.

André F. T. Martins, Kevin Gimpel, Noah A. Smith, Eric P. Xing, Pedro M. Q. Aguiar, and Mário A. T. Figueiredo. 2010. Learning structured classifiers with dual coordinate descent. Technical Report CMU-ML-10-109, Carnegie Mellon University.

Ryan McDonald, Keith Hall, and Gideon Mann. 2010. Distributed training strategies for the structured perceptron. In *ACL*, pages 456–464.

Franz Joseph Och and Hermann Ney. 2002. Discriminative training and maximum entropy models for statistical machine translation. In *ACL*, pages 295–302, Philadelphia, PA, July.

Franz Joseph Och. 2003. Minimum error rate training for statistical machine translation. In *ACL*, pages 160–167.

Kishore Papineni, Salim Roukos, Todd Ward, and Wei-Jing Zhu. 2002. BLEU: a method for automatic evaluation of machine translation. In *ACL*, pages 311–318.

Adam Pauls, John Denero, and Dan Klein. 2009. Consensus training for consensus decoding in machine translation. In *EMNLP*, pages 1418–1427.

Antti-Veikko Rosti, Bing Zhang, Spyros Matsoukas, and Richard Schwartz. 2011. Expected bleu training for graphs: BBN system description for WMT11 system combination task. In *Proceedings of the Sixth Workshop on Statistical Machine Translation*, pages 159–165.

Libin Shen, Anoop Sarkar, and Franz Josef Och. 2004. Discriminative reranking for machine translation. In *HLT-NAACL*, pages 177–184, Boston, Massachusetts, May 2 - May 7.

David A. Smith and Jason Eisner. 2006. Minimum risk annealing for training log-linear models. In *COLING-ACL*, pages 787–794.

Ioannis Tsochantaridis, Thomas Hofman, Thorsten Joachims, and Yasemin Altun. 2004. Support vector machine learning for interdependent and structured output spaces. In *ICML*, pages 823–830.

Taro Watanabe, Jun Suzuki, Hajime Tsukada, and Hideki Isozaki. 2007. Online large-margin training for statistical machine translation. In *EMNLP-CoNLL*, pages 764–773.

Joern Wuebker, Arne Mauser, and Hermann Ney. 2010. Training phrase translation models with leaving-one-out. In *ACL*.

Chun-Nam John Yu and Thorsten Joachims. 2009. Learning structural SVMs with latent variables. In *ICML*.

Richard Zens and Hermann Ney. 2004. Improvements in phrase-based statistical machine translation. In *HLT-NAACL*, pages 257–264, Boston, USA, May.

Richard Zens, Săsa Hasan, and Hermann Ney. 2007. A systematic comparison of training criteria for statistical machine translation. In *EMNLP*, pages 524–532.

Real-time Incremental Speech-to-Speech Translation of Dialogs

Srinivas Bangalore, Vivek Kumar Rangarajan Sridhar, Prakash Kolan
Ladan Golipour, Aura Jimenez
AT&T Labs - Research
180 Park Avenue
Florham Park, NJ 07932, USA
vkumar,srini,pkolan,ladan,aura@research.att.com

Abstract

In a conventional telephone conversation between two speakers of the same language, the interaction is real-time and the speakers process the information stream incrementally. In this work, we address the problem of incremental speech-to-speech translation (S2S) that enables cross-lingual communication between two remote participants over a telephone. We investigate the problem in a novel real-time Session Initiation Protocol (SIP) based S2S framework. The speech translation is performed incrementally based on generation of partial hypotheses from speech recognition. We describe the statistical models comprising the S2S system and the SIP architecture for enabling real-time two-way cross-lingual dialog. We present dialog experiments performed in this framework and study the tradeoff in accuracy versus latency in incremental speech translation. Experimental results demonstrate that high quality translations can be generated with the incremental approach with approximately half the latency associated with non-incremental approach.

1 Introduction

In recent years, speech-to-speech translation (S2S) technology has played an increasingly important role in narrowing the language barrier in cross-lingual interpersonal communication. The improvements in automatic speech recognition (ASR), statistical machine translation (MT), and, text-to-speech synthesis (TTS) technology has facilitated the serial binding of these individual components to achieve S2S translation of acceptable quality.

Prior work on S2S translation has primarily focused on providing either one-way or two-way translation on a single device (Waibel et al., 2003; Zhou et al., 2003). Typically, the user interface requires the participant(s) to choose the source and target language apriori. The nature of communication, either single user talking or turn taking between two users can result in a one-way or cross-lingual dialog interaction. In most systems, the necessity to choose the directionality of translation for each turn does take away from a natural dialog flow. Furthermore, single interface based S2S translation (embedded or cloud-based) is not suitable for cross-lingual communication when participants are geographically distant, a scenario more likely in a global setting. In such a scenario, it is imperative to provide real-time and low latency communication.

In a conventional telephone conversation between two speakers of the same language, the interaction is real-time and the speakers process the information stream incrementally. Similarly, cross-lingual dialog between two remote participants will greatly benefit through incremental translation. While incremental decoding for text translation has been addressed previously in (Furuse and Iida, 1996; Sankaran et al., 2010), we address the problem in a speech-to-speech translation setting for enabling real-time cross-lingual dialog. We address the problem of incrementality in a novel session initiation protocol (SIP) based S2S translation system that enables two people to interact and engage in cross-lingual dialog over a telephone (mobile phone or landline). Our system performs incremental speech recognition and translation, allowing for low latency interaction that provides an ideal setting for remote dialog aimed at accomplishing a task.

We present previous work in this area in Section 2 and introduce the problem of incremental translation in Section 3. We describe the statistical models used in the S2S translation framework in Section 4 followed by a description of the SIP communication framework for real-time translation in Section 5. In Section 6, we describe the basic call flow of our system following which we present dialog experiments performed using our framework in Section 8. Finally, we conclude in Section 9 along with directions for future work.

2 Previous Work

Most previous work on speech-to-speech translation systems has focused on a single device model, i.e., the user interface for translation is on one device (Waibel et al., 1991; Metze et al., 2002; Zhou et al., 2003; Waibel et al., 2003). The device typically supports multiple source-target language pairs. A user typically chooses the directionality of translation and a toggle feature is used to switch the directionality. However, this requires physical presence of the two conversants in one location.

On the other hand, text chat between users over cell phones has become increasingly popular in the last decade. While the language used in the interaction is typically monolingual, there have been attempts to use statistical machine translation to enable cross-lingual text communication (Chen and Raman, 2008). But this introduces a significant overhead as the users need to type in the responses for each turn. Moreover, statistical translation systems are typically unable to cope with telegraphic text present in chat messages. A more user friendly approach would be to use speech as the modality for communication.

One of the first attempts for two-way S2S translation over a telephone between two potentially remote participants was made as part of the Verbmobil project (Wahlster, 2000). The system was restricted to certain topics and speech was the only modality. Furthermore, the spontaneous translation of dialogs was not incremental. One of the first attempts at incremental text translation was demonstrated in (Furuse and Iida, 1996) using a transfer-driven machine translation approach. More recently, an incremental decoding framework for text translation was presented in (Sankaran et al., 2010). To the best of our knowledge, incremental speech-to-speech translation in a dialog setting has not been addressed in prior work. In this work, we address this problem using first of a kind SIP-based large vocabulary S2S translation system that can work with both smartphones and landlines. The speech translation is performed incrementally based on generation of partial hypotheses from speech recognition. Our system displays the recognized and translated text in an incremental fashion. The use of SIP-based technology also supports an open form of cross-lingual dialog without the need for attention phrases.

3 Incremental Speech-to-Speech Translation

In most statistical machine translation systems, the input source text is translated in entirety, i.e., the search for the optimal target string is constrained on the knowledge of the entire source string. However, in applications such as language learning and real-time speech-to-speech translation, incrementally translating the source text or speech can provide seamless communication and understanding with low latency. Let us assume that the input string (either text or speech recognition hypothesis) is $\mathbf{f} = f_1, \cdots, f_J$ and the target string is $\mathbf{e} = e_1, \cdots, e_I$. Among all possible target sentences, we will choose the one with highest probability:

$$\hat{\mathbf{e}}(\mathbf{f}) = \arg\max_{\mathbf{e}} \Pr(\mathbf{e}|\mathbf{f}) \tag{1}$$

In an incremental translation framework, we do not observe the entire string $\mathbf{f}$. Instead, we observe Q_s sequences, $\mathbf{S} = s_1 \cdots s_k \cdots s_{Q_s}$, i.e., each sequence $s_k = [f_{j_k} f_{j_k+1} \cdots f_{j_{(k+1)}-1}]$, $j_1 = 1, j_{Q_s+1} = J + 1$[1]. Let the translation of each foreign sequence s_k be denoted by $t_k = [e_{i_k} e_{i_k+1} \cdots e_{i_{(k+1)}-1}]$, $i_1 = 1, i_{Q_s+1} = I + 1$. Given this setting, we can perform decoding using three different approaches. Assuming that each partial source input is translated independently, i.e., chunk-wise translation, we get,

$$\hat{\mathbf{e}}(\mathbf{f}) = \arg\max_{t_1} \Pr(t_1|s_1) \cdots \arg\max_{t_k} \Pr(t_k|s_k) \tag{2}$$

We call the decoding in Eq. 2 as *partial* decoding. The other option is to translate the partial source in-

[1]For simplicity, we assume that the incremental and non-incremental hypotheses are equal in length

put conditioned on the history, i.e.,

$$\hat{\hat{\mathbf{e}}}(\mathbf{f}) = \arg\max_{t_1} \Pr(t_1|s_1) \cdots \arg\max_{t_k} \Pr(t_k|s_1, \cdots, s_k, t_1^*, \cdots, t_{k-1}^*) \quad (3)$$

where t_i^* denotes the best translation for source sequence s_i. We term the result obtained through Eq. 3 as *continue-partial*. The third option is to wait for all the partials to be generated and then decode the source string which we call *complete* decoding, i.e.,

$$\hat{\hat{\mathbf{e}}}(\mathbf{f}) = \arg\max_{\mathbf{e}} \Pr(\mathbf{e}|s_1, \cdots, s_k) \quad (4)$$

Typically, the hypothesis $\hat{e}$ will be more accurate than $\hat{\hat{e}}$ as the translation process is non-incremental. In the best case, one can obtain $\hat{\hat{e}} = \hat{e}$. While the decoding described in Eq. 2 has the lowest latency, it is likely to result in inferior performance in comparison to Eq. 1 that will have higher latency. One of the main issues in incremental speech-to-speech translation is that the translated sequences need to be immediately synthesized. Hence, there is tradeoff between the amount of latency versus accuracy as the synthesized audio cannot be revoked in case of long distance reordering. In this work, we focus on incremental speech translation and defer the problem of incremental synthesis to future work. We investigate the problem of incrementality using a novel SIP-based S2S translation system, the details of which we discuss in the subsequent sections.

4 Speech-to-Speech Translation Components

In this section, we describe the training data, preprocessing steps and statistical models used in the S2S system.

4.1 Automatic Speech Recognition

We use the AT&T WATSON^{SM} real-time speech recognizer (Goffin et al., 2004) as the speech recognition module. WATSON^{SM} uses context-dependent continuous density hidden Markov models (HMM) for acoustic modeling and finite-state networks for network optimization and search. The acoustic models are Gaussian mixture tied-state three-state left-to-right HMMs. All the acoustic models in this work were initially trained using the Maximum Likelihood Estimation (MLE) criterion, and followed by discriminative training through Minimum Phone Error (MPE) criterion. We also employed Gaussian Selection (Bocchieri, 1993) to decrease the real-time factor during the recognition procedure.

The acoustic models for English and Spanish were mainly trained on short utterances in the respective language, acquired from SMS and search applications on smartphones. The amount of training data for the English acoustic model is around 900 hours of speech, while the data for training the Spanish is approximately half that of the English model. We used a total of 107 phonemes for the English acoustic model, composed of digit-specific, alpha-specific, and general English phonemes. Digit-specific and alpha-specific phonemes were applied to improve the recognition accuracy of digits and alphas in the speech. The number of phonemes for Spanish was 34, and, no digit- or alpha-specific phonemes were included. The pronunciation dictionary for English is a hand-labeled dictionary, with pronunciation for unseen words being predicted using custom rules. A rule-based dictionary was used for Spanish.

We use AT&T FSM toolkit (Mohri et al., 1997) to train a trigram language model (LM). The language model was linearly interpolated from 18 and 17 components for English and Spanish, respectively. The data for the the LM components was obtained from several sources that included LDC, Web, and monolingual portion of the parallel data described in section 4.2. An elaborate set of language specific tokenization and normalization rules was used to clean the corpora. The normalization included spelling corrections, conversion of numerals into words while accounting for telephone numbers, ordinal, and, cardinal categories, punctuation, etc. The interpolation was performed by tuning the language model weights on a development set using perplexity metric. The development set was 500 sentences selected randomly from the IWSLT corpus (Paul, 2006). The training vocabulary size for English acoustic model is 140k and for the language model is 300k. For the Spanish model, the training vocabulary size is 92k, while for testing, the language model includes 370k distinct words. In our experiments, the decoding and LM vocabularies were the same.

4.2 Machine Translation

The phrase-based translation experiments reported in this work was performed using the Moses[2] toolkit (Koehn et al., 2007) for statistical machine translation. Training the translation model starts from the parallel sentences from which we learn word alignments by using GIZA++ toolkit (Och and Ney, 2003). The bidirectional word alignments obtained using GIZA++ were consolidated by using the *grow-diag-final* option in Moses. Subsequently, we learn phrases (maximum length of 7) from the consolidated word alignments. A lexicalized reordering model (*msd-bidirectional-fe* option in Moses) was used for reordering the phrases in addition to the standard distance based reordering (*distortion-limit* of 6). The language models were interpolated Kneser-Ney discounted trigram models, all constructed using the SRILM toolkit (Stolcke, 2002). Minimum error rate training (MERT) was performed on a development set to optimize the feature weights of the log-linear model used in translation. During decoding, the unknown words were preserved in the hypotheses.

The parallel corpus for phrase-based translation was obtained from a variety of sources: europarl (Koehn, 2005), jrc-acquis corpus (Steinberger et al., 2006), opensubtitle corpus (Tiedemann and Lars Nygaard, 2004), web crawling as well as human translation. The statistics of the data used for English-Spanish is shown in Table 1. About 30% of the training data was obtained from the Web (Rangarajan Sridhar et al., 2011). The development set (identical to the one used in ASR) was used in MERT training as well as perplexity based optimization of the interpolated language model. The language model for MT and ASR was constructed from identical data.

4.3 Text-to-speech synthesis

The translated sentence from the machine translation component is synthesized using the AT&T Natural Voices^{TM} text-to-speech synthesis engine (Beutnagel et al., 1999). The system uses unit selection synthesis with half phones as the basic units. The database was recorded by professional speakers of the language. We are currently using female voices for English as well as Spanish.

[2]http://www.statmt.org/moses

	en-es	
Data statistics	en	es
# Sentences	7792118	7792118
# Words	98347681	111006109
Vocabulary	501450	516906

Table 1: Parallel data used for training translation models

5 SIP Communication Framework for Real-time S2S Translation

The SIP communication framework for real-time language translation comprises of three main components. Session Initiation Protocol (SIP) is becoming the de-facto standard for signaling control for streaming applications such as Voice over IP. We present a SIP communication framework that uses Real-time Transport Protocol (RTP) for packetizing multimedia content and User Datagram Protocol (UDP) for delivering the content. In this work, the content we focus on is speech and text information exchanged between two speakers in a cross-lingual dialog. For two users conversing in two different languages (e.g., English and Spanish), the media channels between them will be established as shown in Figure 1. In Figure 1, each client (UA) is responsible for recognition, translation, and synthesis of one language input. E.g., the English-Spanish UA recognizes English text, converts it into Spanish, and produces output Spanish audio. Similarly, the Spanish-English UA is responsible for recognition of Spanish speech input, converting it into English, and producing output English audio. We describe the underlying architecture of the system below.

5.1 Architecture

1. End point SIP user agents: These are the SIP end points that exchange SIP signaling messages with the SIP Application server (AS) for call control.

2. SIP User Agents: Provide a SIP interface to the core AT&T WATSON^{SM} engine that incorporates acoustic and language models for speech

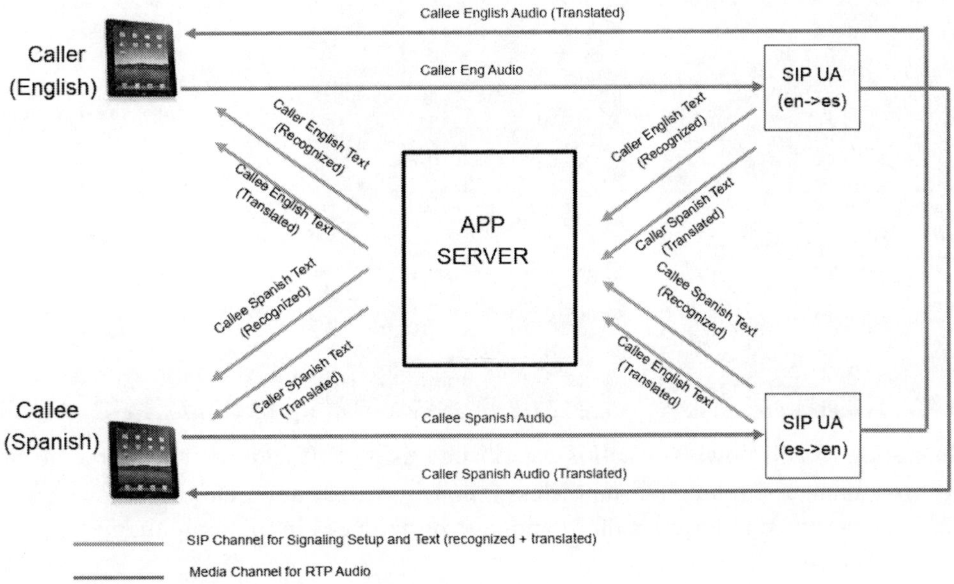

Figure 1: SIP communication framework used for real-time speech-to-speech translation. The example shows the setup between two participants in English(en) and Spanish (es)

recognition.

3. SIP Application Server (AS): A standard SIP B2BUA (back to back user agent) that receives SIP signaling messages and forwards them to the intended destination. The machine translation component (server running Moses (Koehn et al., 2007)) is invoked from the AS.

In our communication framework, the SIP AS receives a call request from the calling party. The AS infers the language preference of the calling party from the user profile database and forwards the call to the called party. Based on the response, AS infers the language preference of the called party from the user profile database. If the languages of the calling and called parties are different, the AS invites two SIP UAs into the call context. The AS exchanges media parameters derived from the calling and called party SIP messages with that of the SIP UAs. The AS then forwards the media parameters of the UAs to the end user SIP agents.

The AS, the end user SIP UAs, and the SIP UAs are all RFC 3261 SIP standard compliant. The end user SIP UAs are developed using PJSIP stack that uses PJMedia for RTP packetization of audio and network transmission. For our testing, we have implemented the end user SIP UAs to run on Apple IOS devices. The AS is developed using E4SS (Echarts for SIP Servlets) software and deployed on Sailfin Java container. It is deployed on a Linux box installed with Cent OS version 5. The SIP UAs are written in python for interfacing with external SIP devices, and use proprietary protocol for interfacing with the core AT&T WATSON^{SM} engine.

6 Typical Call Flow

Figure 2 shows the typical call flow involved in setting up the cross-lingual dialog. The caller chooses the number of the callee from the address book or enters it using the keypad. Subsequently, the call is initiated and the underlying SIP channels are established to facilitate the call. The users can then converse in their native language with the hypotheses displayed in an IM-like fashion. The messages of the caller appear on the left side of the screen while those of the callee appear on the right. Both the recognition and translation hypotheses are displayed incrementally for each side of the conversation. In our experiments, the caller and the callee naturally followed a protocol of listening to the other party's synthesized output before speaking once they were accustomed to the interface. One of the issues during speech recognition is that, the user can potentially start speaking as the TTS output from the other

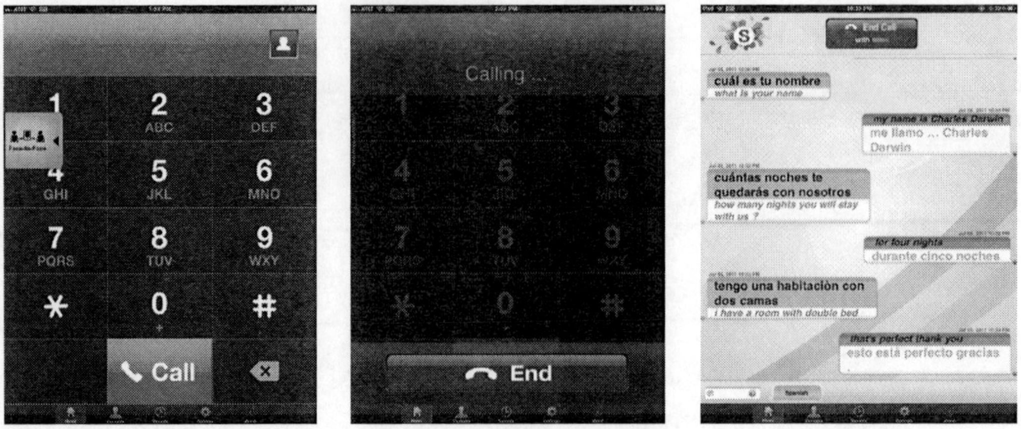

Figure 2: Illustration of call flow. The call is established using SIP and the real-time conversation appears in the bubbles in a manner similar to Instant Messaging. For illustration purposes, the caller (Spanish) and callee (English) are assumed to have set their language preferences in the setup menu.

participant is being played. We address the feedback problem from the TTS output by muting the microphone when TTS output is played.

7 Dialog Data

The system described above provides a natural way to collect cross-lingual dialog data. We used our system to collect a corpus of 40 scripted dialogs in English and Spanish. A bilingual (English-Spanish) speaker created dialog scenarios in the travel and hospitality domain and the scripted dialog was used as reference material in the call. Two subjects participated in the data collection, a male English speaker and female Spanish speaker. The subjects were instructed to read the lines verbatim. However, due to ASR errors, the subjects had to repeat or improvise few turns (about 10%) to sustain the dialog. The average number of turns per scenario in the collected corpus is 13; 6 and 7 turns per scenario for English and Spanish, respectively. An example dialog between two speakers is shown in Table 2.

A: Hello, I am calling from room four twenty one the T.V. is not working. Do you think you can send someone to fix it please?
B: Si, Señor enseguida enviamos a alguien para que la arregle. Si no le cambiaremos de habitación.
A: Thank you very much.
B: Estamos aqu para servirle. Llámenos si necesita algo más.

Table 2: Example of a sample dialog scenario.

8 Experiments

In this section, we describe speech translation experiments performed on the dialog corpus collected through our system. We present baseline results followed by results of incremental translation.

8.1 Baseline Experiments

The models described in Section 4 were used to establish baseline results on the dialog corpus. No contextual information was used in these experiments, i.e., the audio utterances were decoded independently. The ASR WER for English and Spanish sides of the dialogs is shown in Figure 3. The average WER for English and Spanish side of the conversations is 27.73% and 22.83%, respectively. The recognized utterances were subsequently translated using the MT system described above. The MT performance in terms of Translation Edit Rate (TER) (Snover et al., 2006) and BLEU (Papineni et al., 2002) is shown in Figure 4. The MT performance is shown across all the turns for both reference transcriptions and ASR output. The results show that the performance of the Spanish-English MT model is better in comparison to the English-Spanish model on the dialog corpus. The performance on ASR input drops by about 18% compared to translation on reference text.

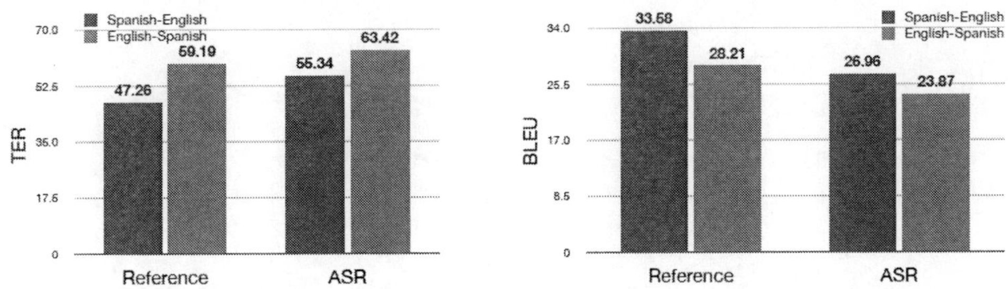

Figure 4: TER (%) and BLEU of English-Spanish and Spanish-English MT models on reference transcripts and ASR output

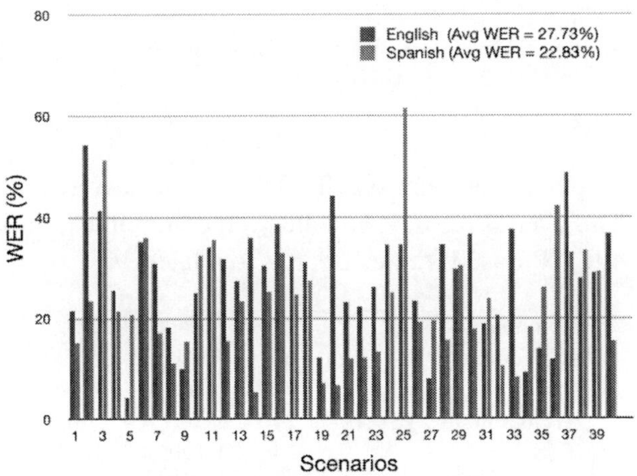

Figure 3: WER (%) of English and Spanish acoustic models on the dialog corpus

8.2 Segmentation of ASR output for MT

Turn taking in a dialog typically involves the subjects speaking one or more utterances in a turn. Since, machine translation systems are trained on chunked parallel texts (40 words or less), it is beneficial to segment the ASR hypotheses before translation. Previous studies have shown significant improvements in translation performance through the segmentation of ASR hypotheses (Matusov et al., 2007). We experimented with the notion of segmentation defined by silence frames in the ASR output. A threshold of 8-10 frames (100 ms) was found to be suitable for segmenting the ASR output into sentence chunks. We did not use any lexical features for segmenting the turns. The BLEU scores for different silence thresholds used in segmentation is shown in Figure 5. The BLEU scores improvement for Spanish-English is 1.6 BLEU points higher than the baseline model using no segmentation. The improvement for English-Spanish is smaller but statistically significant. Analysis of the dialogs revealed that the English speaker tended to speak his turns without pausing across utterance chunks while the Spanish speaker paused a lot more. The results indicate that in a typical dialog interaction, if the participants observe inter-utterance pause (80-100 ms) within a turn, it serves as a good marker for segmentation. Further, exploiting such information can potentially result in improvements in MT performance as the model is typically trained on sentence level parallel text.

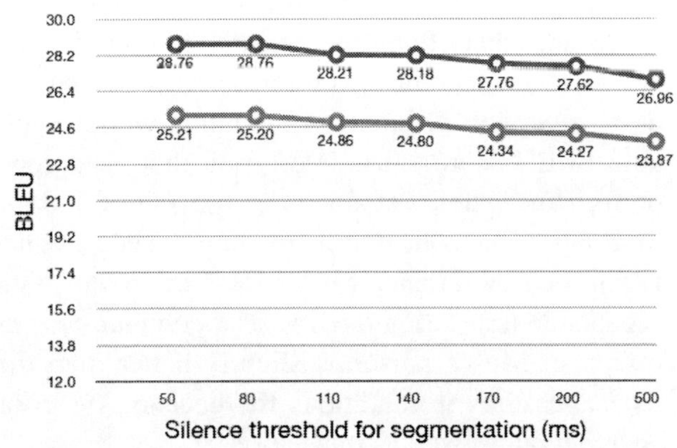

Figure 5: BLEU score of English-Spanish and Spanish-English MT models on the ASR output using silence segmentation

8.3 Incremental Speech Translation Results

Figure 6 shows the BLEU score for incremental speech translation described in Section 3. In the figure, *partial* refers to Eq. 2, *continue-partial* refers to Eq. 3 and *complete* refers to Eq. 4. The continue-partials option was exercised by using the continue-

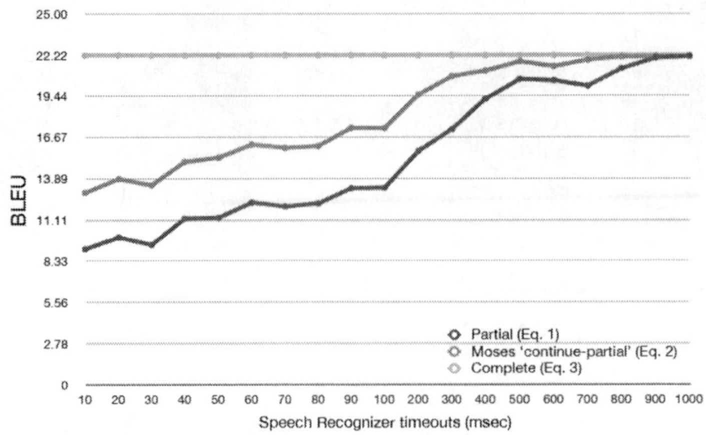

Figure 6: BLEU score (Spanish-English) for incremental speech translation across varying timeout periods in the speech recognizer

partial-translation parameter in Moses (Koehn et al., 2007). The partial hypotheses are generated as a function of speech recognizer timeouts. Timeout is defined as the time interval with which the speech recognizer generates partial hypotheses. For each timeout interval, the speech recognizer may or may not generate a partial result based on the search path at that instant in time. As the timeout interval increases, the performance of incremental translation approaches that of non-incremental translation. The key is to choose an operating point such that the user perception of latency is minimal with acceptable BLEU score. It is interesting that very good performance can be attained at a timeout of 500 ms in comparison with non-incremental speech translation, i.e., the latency can be reduced in half with acceptable translation quality. The *continue-partial* option in Moses performs slightly better than the *partial* case as it conditions the decision on prior source input as well as translation.

In Table 3, we present the latency measurements of the various components in our framework. We do not have a row for ASR since it is not possible to get the start time for each recognition run as the RTP packets are continuously flowing in the SIP framework. The latency between various system components is very low (5-30 ms). While the average time taken for translation (incremental) is $\approx$ 100 ms, the TTS takes the longest time as it is non-incremental in the current work. It can also been seen that the average time taken for generating incremental MT output is half that of TTS that is non-incremental. The overall results show that the communication in our SIP-based framework has low latency.

Components	Caller	Callee	Average
ASR output to MT input	6.8	0.1	3.4
MT	100.4	108.8	104.6
MT output to TTS	22.1	33.1	27.6
TTS	246	160.3	203.1

Table 3: Latency measurements (in ms) for the S2S components in the real-time SIP framework.

9 Conclusion

In this paper, we introduced the problem of incremental speech-to-speech translation and presented first of a kind two-way real-time speech-to-speech translation system based on SIP that incorporates the notion of incrementality. We presented details about the SIP framework and demonstrated the typical call flow in our application. We also presented a dialog corpus collected using our framework and benchmarked the performance of the system. Our framework allows for incremental speech translation and can provide low latency translation. We are currently working on improving the accuracy of incremental translation. We are also exploring new algorithms for performing reordering aware incremental speech-to-speech translation, i.e., translating source phrases such that text-to-speech synthesis can be rendered incrementally.

References

M. Beutnagel, A. Conkie, J. Schroeter, Y. Stylianou, and A. Syrdal. 1999. The AT&T Next-Gen TTS system. In *Proceedings of Joint Meeting of ASA, EAA and DEGA*.

E. Bocchieri. 1993. Vector quantization for the efficient computation of continuous density likelihoods. *Proceedings of ICASSP*.

Charles L. Chen and T. V. Raman. 2008. Axsjax: a talking translation bot using google im: bringing web-2.0 applications to life. In *Proceedings of the 2008 international cross-disciplinary conference on Web accessibility (W4A)*.

O. Furuse and H. Iida. 1996. Incremental translation utilizing constituent boundary patterns. In *Proc. of Coling '96*.

Vincent Goffin, Cyril Allauzen, Enrico Bocchieri, Dilek Hakkani Tur, Andrej Ljolje, and Sarangarajan Parthasarathy. 2004. The AT&T Watson Speech Recognizer. Technical report, September.

P. Koehn, H. Hoang, A. Birch, C. Callison-Burch, M. Federico, N. Bertoldi, B. Cowan, Shen W., C. Moran, R. Zens, C. J. Dyer, O. Bojar, A. Constantin, and E. Herbst. 2007. Moses: Open source toolkit for statistical machine translation. In *Proceedings of ACL*.

Philipp Koehn. 2005. Europarl: A parallel corpus for statistical machine translation. In *MT Summit*.

E. Matusov, D. Hillard, M. Magimai-Doss, D. Hakkani-Túr, M. Ostendorf, and H. Ney. 2007. Improving speech translation with automatic boundary prediction. In *Proceedings of Interspeech*.

F. Metze, J. McDonough, H. Soltau, A. Waibel, A. Lavie, S. Burger, C. Langley, L. Levin, T. Schultz, F. Pianesi, R. Cattoni, G. Lazzari, N. Mana, and E. Pianta. 2002. The NESPOLE! speech-to-speech translation system.

M. Mohri, F. Pereira, and M. Riley. 1997. Att general-purpose finite-state machine software tools, http://www.research.att.com/sw/tools/fsm/.

F. J. Och and H. Ney. 2003. A systematic comparison of various statistical alignment models. *Computational Linguistics*, 29(1):19–51.

K. Papineni, S. Roukos, T. Ward, and W.-J. Zhu. 2002. BLEU: a method for automatic evaluation of machine translation. In *Proceedings of ACL*.

M. Paul. 2006. Overview of the iwslt 2006 evaluation campaign. In *Proceedings of the International Workshop of Spoken Language Translation*, Kyoto, Japan.

V. K. Rangarajan Sridhar, L. Barbosa, and S. Bangalore. 2011. A scalable approach to building a parallel corpus from the Web. In *Proceedings of Interspeech*.

B. Sankaran, A. Grewal, and A. Sarkar. 2010. Incremental decoding for phrase-based statistical machine translation. In *Proceedings of the fifth Workshop on Statistical Machine Translation and Metrics*.

M. Snover, B. Dorr, R. Schwartz, L. Micciulla, and J. Makhoul. 2006. A study of translation edit rate with targeted human annotation. In *Proceedings of AMTA*.

R. Steinberger, B. Pouliquen, A. Widiger, C. Ignat, T. Erjavec, and D. Tufis. 2006. The JRC-Acquis: A multilingual aligned parallel corpus with 20+ languages. In *Proceedings of LREC*.

Andreas Stolcke. 2002. SRILM – an extensible language modeling toolkit. In *Proceedings of ICSLP*.

J. Tiedemann and L. Lars Nygaard. 2004. The OPUS corpus - parallel & free. In *Proceedings of LREC*.

Wolfgang Wahlster, editor. 2000. *Verbmobil: Foundations of Speech-to-Speech Translation*. Springer.

A. Waibel, A. N. Jain, A. E. McNair, H. Saito, A. G. Hauptmann, and J. Tebelskis. 1991. JANUS: a speech-to-speech translation system using connectionist and symbolic processing strategies. In *Proceedings of ICASSP*, pages 793–796, Los Alamitos, CA, USA.

A. Waibel, A. Badran, A. W. Black, R. Frederking, G. Gates, A. Lavie, L. Levin, K. Lenzo, L. M. Tomokiyo, J. Reichert, T. Schultz, W. Dorcas, M. Woszczyna, and J. Zhang. 2003. Speechalator: two-way speech-to-speech translation on a consumer PDA. In *Proceedings of the European Conference on Speech Communication and Technology*, pages 369–372.

B. Zhou, Y. Gao, J. Sorenson, D. Dechelotte, and M. Picheny. 2003. A hand-held speech to speech translation system. In *Proceedings of ASRU*.

Parsing Time: Learning to Interpret Time Expressions

Gabor Angeli
Stanford University
Stanford, CA 94305
angeli@stanford.edu

Christopher D. Manning
Stanford University
Stanford, CA 94305
manning@stanford.edu

Daniel Jurafsky
Stanford University
Stanford, CA 94305
jurafsky@stanford.edu

Abstract

We present a probabilistic approach for learning to interpret temporal phrases given only a corpus of utterances and the times they reference. While most approaches to the task have used regular expressions and similar linear pattern interpretation rules, the possibility of phrasal embedding and modification in time expressions motivates our use of a compositional *grammar of time expressions*. This grammar is used to construct a *latent parse* which evaluates to the time the phrase would represent, as a logical parse might evaluate to a concrete entity. In this way, we can employ a loosely supervised EM-style bootstrapping approach to learn these latent parses while capturing both syntactic uncertainty and pragmatic ambiguity in a probabilistic framework. We achieve an accuracy of 72% on an adapted TempEval-2 task – comparable to state of the art systems.

1 Introduction

Temporal resolution is the task of mapping from a textual phrase describing a potentially complex time, date, or duration to a normalized (*grounded*) temporal representation. For example, possibly complex phrases such as *the week before last* are often more useful in their grounded form – e.g., `January 1 - January 7`.

The dominant approach to this problem in previous work has been to use rule-based methods, generally a combination of regular-expression matching followed by hand-written interpretation functions.

In general, it is appealing to learn the interpretation of temporal expressions, rather than hand-building systems. Moreover, complex hierarchical temporal expressions, such as *the Tuesday before last* or *the third Wednesday of each month*, and ambiguous expressions, such as *last Friday*, are difficult to handle using deterministic rules and would benefit from a recursive and probabilistic phrase structure representation. Therefore, we attempt to learn a temporal interpretation system where temporal phrases are parsed by a grammar, but this grammar and its semantic interpretation rules are latent, with only the input phrase and its grounded interpretation given to the learning system.

Employing probabilistic techniques allows us to capture ambiguity in temporal phrases in two important respects. In part, it captures syntactic ambiguity – e.g., *last Friday the 13th* bracketing as either *[last Friday] [the 13th]*, or *last [Friday the 13th]*. This also includes examples of lexical ambiguity – e.g., two meanings of *last* in *last week of November* versus *last week*. In addition, temporal expressions often carry a pragmatic ambiguity. For instance, a speaker may refer to either the next or previous Friday when he utters *Friday* on a Sunday. Similarly, *next week* can refer to either the coming week or the week thereafter.

Probabilistic systems furthermore allow propagation of uncertainty to higher-level components – for example recognizing that *May* could have a number of non-temporal meanings and allowing a system with a broader contextual scope to make the final judgment. We implement a CRF to detect temporal expressions, and show our model's ability to act as a component in such a system.

We describe our temporal representation, followed by the learning algorithm; we conclude with experimental results showing our approach to be competitive with state of the art systems.

2 Related Work

Our approach draws inspiration from a large body of work on parsing expressions into a logical form. The latent parse parallels the formal semantics in previous work, e.g., Montague semantics. Like these representations, a parse – in conjunction with the reference time – defines a set of matching entities, in this case the grounded time. The matching times can be thought of as analogous to the entities in a logical model which satisfy a given expression.

Supervised approaches to logical parsing prominently include Zelle and Mooney (1996), Zettlemoyer and Collins (2005), Kate et al. (2005), Zettlemoyer and Collins (2007), *inter alia*. For example, Zettlemoyer and Collins (2007) learn a mapping from textual queries to a logical form. This logical form importantly contains all the predicates and entities used in their parse. We loosen the supervision required in these systems by allowing the parse to be entirely latent; the annotation of the grounded time neither defines, nor gives any direct cues about the elements of the parse, since many parses evaluate to the same grounding. To demonstrate, the grounding for a week ago could be described by specifying a month and day, or as a *week ago*, or as *last* x – substituting today's day of the week for x. Each of these correspond to a completely different parse.

Recent work by Clarke et al. (2010) and Liang et al. (2011) similarly relax supervision to require only annotated answers rather than full logical forms. For example, Liang et al. (2011) constructs a latent parse similar in structure to a dependency grammar, but representing a logical form. Our proposed lexical entries and grammar combination rules can be thought of as paralleling the lexical entries and predicates, and the implicit combination rules respectively in this framework. Rather than querying from a finite database, however, our system must compare temporal expression within an infinite timeline. Furthermore, our system is run using neither lexical cues nor intelligent initialization.

Related work on interpreting temporal expressions has focused on constructing hand-crafted interpretation rules (Mani and Wilson, 2000; Saquete et al., 2003; Puscasu, 2004; Grover et al., 2010). Of these, HeidelTime (Strötgen and Gertz, 2010) and SUTime (Chang and Manning, 2012) provide particularly strong competition.

Recent probabilistic approaches to temporal resolution include UzZaman and Allen (2010), who employ a parser to produce deep logical forms, in conjunction with a CRF classifier. In a similar vein, Kolomiyets and Moens (2010) employ a maximum entropy classifier to detect the location and temporal type of expressions; the grounding is then done via deterministic rules.

3 Representation

We define a compositional representation of time; a type system is described in Section 3.1 while the grammar is outlined in Section 3.2 and described in detail in Sections 3.3 and 3.4.

3.1 Temporal Expression Types

We represent temporal expressions as either a Range, Sequence, or Duration. We describe these, the Function type, and the miscellaneous Number and Nil types below:

Range [and Instant] A period between two dates (or times). This includes entities such as `Today`, `1987`, or `Now`. We denote a range by the variable r. We maintain a consistent interval-based theory of time (Allen, 1981) and represent instants as intervals with zero span.

Sequence A sequence of Ranges, not necessarily occurring at regular intervals. This includes entities such as `Friday`, `November` 27th, or `last Friday`. A Sequence is a tuple of three elements $s = (r_s, \Delta_s, \rho_s)$:

1. $r_s(i)$: The ith element of a sequence, of type Range. In the case of the sequence `Friday`, $r_s(0)$ corresponds to *the Friday in the current week*; $r_s(1)$ is the Friday in the following week, etc.
2. Δ_s: The *distance* between two elements in the sequence – approximated if this distance is not constant. In the case of `Friday`, this distance would be a week.
3. ρ_s: The *containing unit* of an element of a sequence. For example, $\rho_{\texttt{Friday}}$ would be the Range corresponding to *the current week*. The sequence index $i \in \mathbb{Z}$, from $r_s(i)$, is defined

relative to $r_s(0)$ – the element in the same containing unit as the reference time.

We define the *reference time* t (Reichenbach, 1947) to be the instant relative to which times are evaluated. For the TempEval-2 corpus, we approximate this as the publication time of the article. While this is conflating Reichenbach's reference time with speech time, it is a useful approximation.

To contrast with Ranges, a Sequence can represent a number of grounded times. Nonetheless, pragmatically, not all of these are given equal weight – an utterance of *last Friday* may mean either of the previous two Fridays, but is unlikely to ground to anything else. We represent this ambiguity by defining a distribution over the elements of the Sequence. While this could be any distribution, we chose to approximate it as a Gaussian.

In order to allow sharing parameters between any sequence, we define the domain in terms of the *index* of the sequence rather than of a constant unit of time (e.g., seconds). To illustrate, the distribution over `April` would have a much larger variance than the distribution over `Sunday`, were the domains fixed. The probability of the ith element of a sequence thus depends on the beginning of the range $r_s(i)$, the reference time t, and the distance between elements of the sequence Δ_s. We summarize this in the equation below, with learned parameters μ and σ:

$$P_t(i) = \int_{\delta=-0.5}^{0.5} \mathcal{N}_{\mu,\sigma}\left(\frac{r_s(i)-t}{\Delta_s}+\delta\right) \quad (1)$$

Figure 1 shows an example of such a distribution; importantly, note that moving the reference time between two elements dynamically changes the probability assigned to each.

Duration A period of time. This includes entities like `Week`, `Month`, and `7 days`. We denote a duration with the variable d.

We define a special case of the Duration type to represent *approximate* durations, identified by their canonical unit (`week`, `month`, etc). These are used to represent expressions such as *a few years* or *some days*.

Function A function of arity less than or equal to two representing some general modification to one

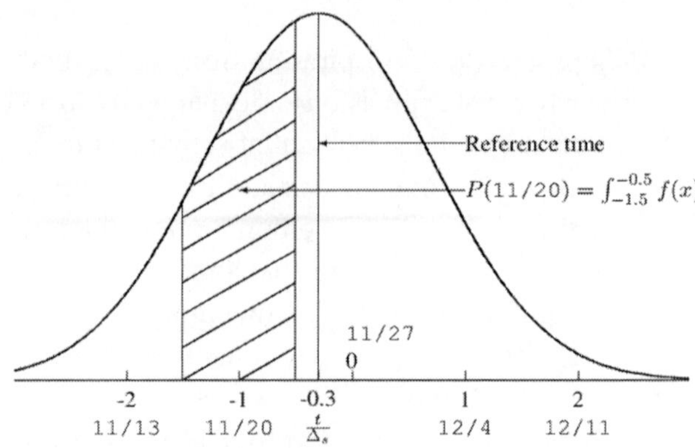

Figure 1: An illustration of a temporal distribution, e.g., `Sunday`. The reference time is labeled as time t between `Nov 20` and `Nov 27`; the probability that this sequence is referring to `Nov 20` is the integral of the marked area. The domain of the graph are the indices of the sequence; the distribution is overlaid with mean at the (normalized) reference time t/Δ_s; in our case Δ_s is a week. Note that the probability of an index changes depending on the exact location of the reference time.

of the above types. This captures semantic entities such as those implied in *last* x, *the third* x *[of* y*]*, or x *days ago*. The particular functions and their application are enumerated in Table 2.

Other Types Two other types bear auxiliary roles in representing temporal expressions, though they are not directly temporal concepts. In the grammar, these appear as preterminals only.

The first of these types is Number – denoting a number without any temporal meaning attached. This comes into play representing expressions such as *2 weeks*. The other is the Nil type – denoting terms which are not directly contributing to the semantic meaning of the expression. This is intended for words such as *a* or *the*, which serve as cues without bearing temporal content themselves. The Nil type is lexicalized with the word it generates.

Omitted Phenomena The representation described is a simplification of the complexities of time. Notably, a body of work has focused on reasoning about events or states relative to temporal expressions. Moens and Steedman (1988) describes temporal expressions relating to changes of state; Condoravdi (2010) explores NPI licensing in temporal expressions. Broader context is also not

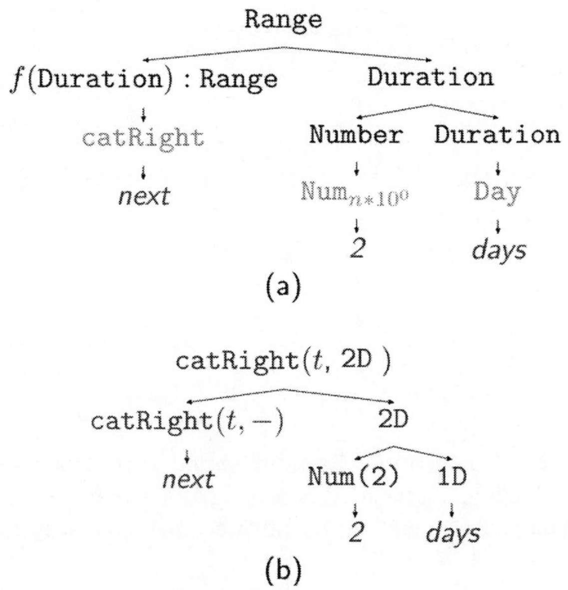

Figure 2: The grammar – (a) describes the CFG parse of the temporal *types*. Words are tagged with their nonterminal entry, above which only the types of the expressions are maintained; (b) describes the corresponding combination of the temporal *instances*. The parse in (b) is deterministic given the grammar combination rules in (a).

directly modeled, but rather left to systems in which the model would be embedded. Furthermore, vague times (e.g., *in the 90's*) represent a notable chunk of temporal expressions uttered. In contrast, NLP evaluations have generally not handled such vague time expressions.

3.2 Grammar Formalism

Our approach builds on the assumption that natural language descriptions of time are compositional in nature. Each word attached to a temporal phrase is usually compositionally modifying the meaning of the phrase. To demonstrate, we consider the expression *the week before last week*. We can construct a meaning by applying the modifier *last* to *week* – creating the previous week; and then applying *before* to *week* and *last week*.

We construct a paradigm for parsing temporal phrases consisting of a standard PCFG over temporal *types* with each parse rule defining a function to apply to the child nodes, or the word being generated. At the root of the tree, we recursively apply the functions in the parse tree to obtain a final temporal *value*. One can view this formalism as a rule-to-rule translation (Bach, 1976; Allen, 1995, p. 263), or a constrained Synchronous PCFG (Yamada and Knight, 2001).

Our approach contrasts with common approaches, such as CCG grammars (Steedman, 2000; Bos et al., 2004; Kwiatkowski et al., 2011), giving us more flexibility in the composition rules. Figure 2 shows an example of the grammar.

Formally, we define our temporal grammar $G = (\Sigma, S, \mathcal{V}, \mathcal{W}, \mathcal{R}, \theta)$. The alphabet Σ and start symbol S retain their usual interpretations. We define a set $\mathcal{V}$ to be the set of types, as described in Section 3.1 – these act as our nonterminals. For each $v \in \mathcal{V}$ we define an (infinite) set W_v corresponding to the possible instances of type v. Concretely, if $v =$ Sequence, our set $W_v \in \mathcal{W}$ could contain elements corresponding to *Friday*, *last Friday*, *Nov. 27th*, etc. Each node in the tree defines a pair (v, w) such that $w \in W_v$, with combination rules defined over v and function applications performed on w.

A rule $R \in \mathcal{R}$ is defined as a pair $R = \left(v_i \to v_j v_k, f : (W_{v_j}, W_{v_k}) \to W_{v_i}\right)$. The first term is our conventional PCFG rule over the types $\mathcal{V}$. The second term defines the function to apply to the values returned recursively by the child nodes. Note that this definition is trivially adapted for the case of unary rules.

The last term in our grammar formalism denotes the rule probabilities θ. In line with the usual interpretation, this defines a probability of applying a particular rule $r \in R$. Importantly, note that the distribution over possible groundings of a temporal expression are not included in the grammar formalism. The learning of these probabilities is detailed in Section 4.

3.3 Preterminals

We define a set of preterminals, specifying their eventual *type*, as well as the temporal *instance* it produces when its function is evaluated on the word it generates (e.g., $f(day) =$ Day). A distinction is made in our description between entities with content roles versus entities with a functional role.

The first – consisting of Ranges, Sequences, and Durations – are listed in Table 1. A total of 62 such preterminals are defined in the implemented system, corresponding to primitive entities often appearing in newswire, although this list is easily adaptable to

Function	Description	Signature(s)
shiftLeft	Shift a Range or Sequence left by a Duration	$f: \mathsf{S}, \mathsf{D} \to \mathsf{S}$; $f: \mathsf{R}, \mathsf{D} \to \mathsf{R}$
shiftRight	Shift a Range or Sequence right by a Duration	$f: \mathsf{S}, \mathsf{D} \to \mathsf{S}$; $f: \mathsf{R}, \mathsf{D} \to \mathsf{R}$
shrinkBegin	Take the first Duration of a Range/Sequence	$f: \mathsf{S}, \mathsf{D} \to \mathsf{S}$; $f: \mathsf{R}, \mathsf{D} \to \mathsf{R}$
shrinkEnd	Take the last Duration of a Range/Sequence	$f: \mathsf{S}, \mathsf{D} \to \mathsf{S}$; $f: \mathsf{R}, \mathsf{D} \to \mathsf{R}$
catLeft	Take Duration units after the end of a Range	$f: \mathsf{R}, \mathsf{D} \to \mathsf{R}$
catRight	Take Duration units before the start of a Range	$f: \mathsf{R}, \mathsf{D} \to \mathsf{R}$
moveLeft1	Move the origin of a sequence left by 1	$f: \mathsf{S} \to \mathsf{S}$
moveRight1	Move the origin of a sequence right by 1	$f: \mathsf{S} \to \mathsf{S}$
n^{th} x of y	Take the nth Sequence in y (Day of Week, *etc*)	f : Number $\to$ S
approximate	Make a Duration approximate	$f: \mathsf{D} \to \mathsf{D}$

Table 2: The functional preterminals of the grammar; R, S, and D denote Ranges Sequences and Durations respectively. The name, a brief description, and the type signature of the function (as used in parsing) are given. Described in more detail in Section 3.4, the functions are most easily interpreted as operations on either an interval or sequence.

Type	Instances
Range	Past, Future, Yesterday, Tomorrow, Today, Reference, Year(n), Century(n)
Sequence	Friday, January, ... DayOfMonth, DayOfWeek, ... EveryDay, EveryWeek, ...
Duration	Second, Minute, Hour, Day, Week, Month, Quarter, Year, Decade, Century

Table 1: The content-bearing preterminals of the grammar, arranged by their types. Note that the Sequence type contains more elements than enumerated here; however, only a few of each characteristic type are shown here for brevity.

fit other domains. It should be noted that the expressions, represented in Typewriter, have no a priori association with words, denoted by *italics*; this correspondence must be learned. Furthermore, entities which are subject to interpretation – for example Quarter or Season – are given a concrete interpretation. The nth quarter is defined by evenly splitting a year into four; the seasons are defined in the same way but with winter beginning in December.

The functional entities are described in Table 2, and correspond to the Function type. The majority of these mirror generic operations on intervals on a timeline, or manipulations of a sequence. Notably, like intervals, times can be moved (*3 weeks ago*) or their size changed (*the first two days of the month*), or a new interval can be started from one of the endpoints (*the last 2 days*). Additionally, a sequence can be modified by shifting its origin (*last Friday*), or taking the nth element of the sequence within some bound (*fourth Sunday in November*).

The lexical entry for the Nil type is tagged with the word it generates, producing entries such as Nil(a), Nil(November), etc. The lexical entry for the Number type is parameterized by the order of magnitude and ordinality of the number; e.g., 27th becomes Number(10^1,ordinal).

3.4 Combination Rules

As mentioned earlier, our grammar defines both combination rules over types (in $\mathcal{V}$) as well as a method for combining temporal instances (in $W_v \in \mathcal{W}$). This method is either a function application of one of the functions in Table 2, a function which is implicit in the text (intersection and multiplication), or an identity operation (for Nils). These cases are detailed below:

- Function application, e.g., *last week*. We apply (or partially apply) a function to an argument on either the left or the right: $f(x,y) \odot x$ or $x \odot f(x,y)$. Furthermore, for functions of arity 2 taking a Range as an argument, we define a rule treating it as a unary function with the reference time taking the place of the second argument.

- Intersecting two ranges or sequences, e.g.,

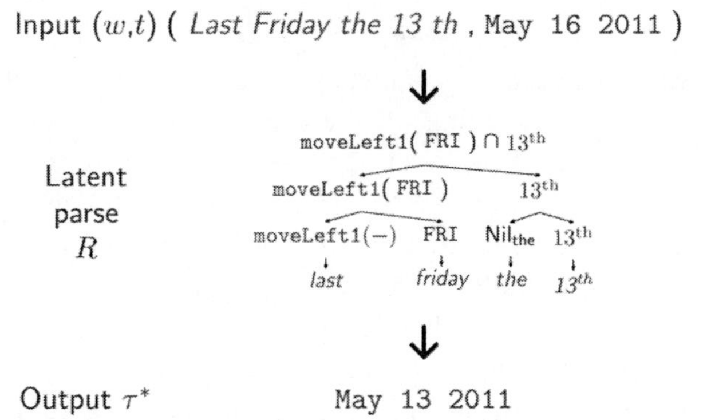

Figure 3: An overview of the system architecture. Note that the parse is latent – that is, it is not annotated in the training data.

November 27th. The intersect function treats both arguments as intervals, and will return an interval (Range or Sequence) corresponding to the overlap between the two.[1]

- Multiplying a Number with a Duration, e.g., *5 weeks*.
- Combining a non-Nil and Nil element with no change to the temporal expression, e.g., *a week*. The lexicalization of the Nil type allows the algorithm to take hints from these supporting words.

We proceed to describe learning the parameters of this grammar.

4 Learning

We present a system architecture, described in Figure 3. We detail the inference procedure in Section 4.1 and training in Section 4.2.

4.1 Inference

To provide a list of candidate expressions with their associated probabilities, we employ a k-best CKY parser. Specifically, we implement Algorithm 3 described in Huang and Chiang (2005), providing an $O(Gn^3k \log k)$ algorithm with respect to the grammar size G, phrase length n, and beam size k. We set the beam size to 2000.

Revisiting the notion of pragmatic ambiguity, in a sense the most semantically complete output of the system would be a distribution – an utterance of *Friday* would give a distribution over Fridays rather than a best guess of its grounding. However, it is often advantageous to ground to a concrete expression with a corresponding probability. The CKY k-best beam and the temporal distribution – capturing syntactic and pragmatic ambiguity – can be combined to provide a *Viterbi* decoding, as well as its associated probability.

We define the probability of a syntactic parse y making use of rules $R \subseteq \mathcal{R}$ as $P(y) = P(w_1, \ldots w_n; R) = \prod_{i \to j,k \in R} P(j,k \mid i)$. As described in Section 3.1, we define the probability of a grounding relative to reference time t and a particular syntactic interpretation $P_t(i|y)$. The product of these two terms provides the probability of a grounded temporal interpretation; we can obtain a Viterbi decoding by maximizing this joint probability:

$$P_t(i, y) = P(y) \times P_t(i|y) \tag{2}$$

This provides us with a framework for obtaining grounded times from a temporal phrase – in line with the annotations provided during training time.

4.2 Training

We present an EM-style bootstrapping approach to training the parameters of our grammar jointly with the parameters of our Gaussian temporal distribution.

Our TimEM algorithm for learning the parameters for the grammar (θ), jointly with the temporal distribution (μ and σ) is given in Algorithm 1. The inputs to the algorithm are the initial parameters θ, μ, and σ, and a set of training instances $\mathcal{D}$. Furthermore, the algorithm makes use of a Dirichlet prior α on the grammar parameters θ, as well as a Gaussian prior $\mathcal{N}$ on the mean of the temporal distribution μ. The algorithm outputs the final parameters θ^*, μ^* and σ^*.

Each training instance is a tuple consisting of the words in the temporal phrase w, the annotated grounded time τ^*, and the reference time of the utterance t. The input phrase is tokenized according to Penn Treebank guidelines, except we additionally

[1]In the case of complex sequences (e.g., *Friday the 13th*) an A* search is performed to find overlapping ranges in the two sequences; the origin $r_s(0)$ is updated to refer to the closest such match to the reference time.

Algorithm 1: TimEM

Input: Initial parameters θ, μ, σ; data $\mathcal{D} = \{(w, \tau^*, t)\}$; Dirichlet prior α, Gaussian prior $\mathcal{N}$

Output: Optimal parameters θ^*, μ^*, σ^*

1 **while** *not converged* **do**
2    $(\bar{M}_\theta, \bar{M}_{\mu,\sigma})$:= `E-Step` $(\mathcal{D}, \theta, \mu, \sigma)$
3   (θ, μ, σ) := `M-Step` $(\bar{M}_\theta, \bar{M}_{\mu,\sigma})$
4 **end**
5 **return** (θ_s, μ, σ)

6 **begin** `E-Step` $(\mathcal{D}, \theta, \mu, \sigma)$
7    $\bar{M}_\theta = []$; $\bar{M}_{\mu,\sigma} = []$
8   **for** $(w, \tau^*, t) \in \mathcal{D}$ **do**
9      $\bar{m}_\theta = []$; $\bar{m}_{\mu,\sigma} = []$
10   **for** $y \in$ *k-bestCKY*(w, θ) **do**
11   **if** $p = P_{\mu,\sigma}(\tau^* \mid y, t) > 0$ **then**
12          $\bar{m}_\theta$ += (y, p); $\bar{m}_{\mu,\sigma}$ += (i, p)
13   **end**
14   **end**
15      $\bar{M}$ += normalize$(\bar{m}_\theta)$
16      $\bar{M}_{\mu,\sigma}$ += normalize$(\bar{m}_{\mu,\sigma})$
17   **end**
18   **return** $\bar{M}$
19 **end**

20 **begin** `M-Step` $(\bar{M}_\theta, \bar{M}_{\mu,\sigma})$
21   θ' := bayesianPosterior$(\bar{M}_\theta, \alpha)$
22   σ' := mlePosterior$(\bar{M}_{\mu,\sigma})$
23   μ' := bayesianPosterior$(\bar{M}_{\mu,\sigma}, \sigma', \mathcal{N})$
24   **return** (θ', μ', σ')
25 **end**

split on the characters '-' and '/,' which often delimit a boundary between temporal entities. Beyond this preprocessing, no language-specific information about the meanings of the words are introduced, including syntactic parses, POS tags, etc.

The algorithm operates similarly to the EM algorithms used for grammar induction (Klein and Manning, 2004; Carroll and Charniak, 1992). However, unlike grammar induction, we are allowed a certain amount of supervision by requiring that the predicted temporal expression match the annotation. Our *expected statistics* are therefore more accurately our normalized expected counts of *valid* parses.

Note that in conventional grammar induction, the expected sufficient statistics can be gathered analytically from reading off the chart scores of a parse. This does not work in our case for two reasons. In part, we would like to incorporate the probability of the temporal grounding in our feedback probability. Additionally, we are only using parses which are valid candidates – that is, the parses which ground to the correct time $\tau*$ – which we cannot establish until the entire expression is parsed. The expected statistics are thus computed non-analytically via a beam on both the possible parses (line 10) and the possible temporal groundings of a given interpretation (line 11).

The particular EM updates are the standard updates for multinomial and Gaussian distributions given fully observed data. In the multinomial case, our (unnormalized) parameter updates, with Dirichlet prior α, are:

$$\theta'_{mn|l} = \alpha + \sum_{(y,p)\in\bar{M}_\theta} \sum_{v_{jk|i}\in y} \mathbb{1}\left(v_{jk|i} = v_{mn|l}\right) p \quad (3)$$

In the Gaussian case, the parameter update for σ is the maximum likelihood update; while the update for μ incorporates a Bayesian prior $\mathcal{N}(\mu_0, \sigma_0)$:

$$\sigma' = \sqrt{\frac{1}{\sum_{(i,p)\in\bar{M}_{\mu,\sigma}} p} \sum_{(i,p)\in\bar{M}_{\mu,\sigma}} (i - \mu')^2 \cdot p} \quad (4)$$

$$\mu' = \frac{\sigma'^2 \mu_0 + \sigma_0^2 \sum_{(i,p)\in\bar{M}_{\mu,\sigma}} i \cdot p}{\sigma'^2 + \sigma_0^2 \sum_{(i,p)\in\bar{M}_{\mu,\sigma}} p} \quad (5)$$

As the parameters improve, the parser more efficiently prunes incorrect parses and the beam incorporates valid parses for longer and longer phrases. For instance, in the first iteration the model must learn the meaning of both words in *last Friday*; once the parser learns the meaning of one of them – e.g., *Friday* appears elsewhere in the corpus – subsequent iterations focus on proposing candidate meanings for *last*. In this way, a progressively larger percentage of the data is available to be learned from at each iteration.

5 Evaluation

We evaluate our model against current state-of-the art systems for temporal resolution on the English

System	Train		Test	
	Type	Value	Type	Value
GUTime	0.72	0.46	0.80	0.42
SUTime	0.85	0.69	**0.94**	0.71
HeidelTime	0.80	0.67	0.85	0.71
OurSystem	**0.90**	**0.72**	0.88	**0.72**

Table 3: TempEval-2 Attribute scores for our system and three previous systems. The scores are calculated using gold extents, forcing a guessed interpretation for each parse.

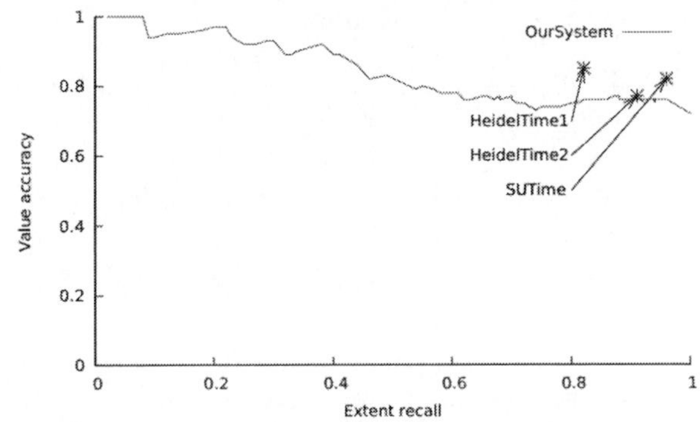

Figure 4: A precision-recall curve for our system, compared to prior work. The data points are obtained by setting a threshold minimum probability at which to guess a time creating different extent recall values. The curve falls below HeidelTime1 and SUTime in part from lack of context, and in part since our system was not trained to optimize this curve.

portion of the TempEval-2 Task A dataset (Verhagen et al., 2010).

5.1 Dataset

The TempEval-2 dataset is relatively small, containing 162 documents and 1052 temporal phrases in the training set and an additional 20 documents and 156 phrases in the evaluation set. Each temporal phrase was annotated as a TIMEX3[2] tag around an adverbial or prepositional phrase

5.2 Results

In the TempEval-2 A Task, system performance is evaluated on detection and resolution of expressions. Since we perform only the second of these, we evaluate our system assuming gold detection.

Similarly, the original TempEval-2 scoring scheme gave a precision and recall for detection, and an accuracy for only the temporal expressions attempted. Since our system is able to produce a guess for every expression, we produce a precision-recall curve on which competing systems are plotted (see Figure 4). Note that the downward slope of the curve indicates that the probabilities returned by the system are indicative of its confidence – the probability of a parse correlates with the probability of that parse being correct.

Additionally, and perhaps more accurately, we compare to previous system scores when constrained to make a prediction on every example; if no guess is made, the output is considered incorrect. This in general yields lower results, as the system is not allowed to abstain on expressions it does not recognize. Results are summarized in Table 3.

We compare to three previous rule-based systems. GUTime (Mani and Wilson, 2000) presents an older but widely used baseline.[3] More recently, SUTime (Chang and Manning, 2012) provides a much stronger comparison. We also compare to HeidelTime (Strötgen and Gertz, 2010), which represents the state-of-the-art system at the TempEval-2 task.

5.3 Detection

One of the advantages of our model is that it can provide candidate groundings for any expression. We explore this ability by building a detection model to find candidate temporal expressions, which we then ground. The detection model is implemented as a Conditional Random Field (Lafferty et al., 2001), with features over the morphology and context. Particularly, we define the following features:

- The word and lemma within 2 of the current word.
- The word shape[4] and part of speech of the current word.

[2]See `http://www.timeml.org` for details on the TimeML format and TIMEX3 tag.

[3]Due to discrepancies in output formats, the output of GUTime was heuristically patched and manually checked to conform to the expected format.

[4]Word shape is calculated by mapping each character to one of uppercase, lowercase, number, or punctuation. The first four characters are mapped verbatim; subsequent sequences of similar characters are collapsed.

System	Extent P	Extent R	Extent F_1	Attribute Typ	Attribute Val
GUTime	0.89	0.79	0.84	0.95	0.68
SUTime	0.88	**0.96**	**0.92**	**0.96**	0.82
HeidelTime1	**0.90**	0.82	0.86	**0.96**	**0.85**
HeidelTime2	0.82	0.91	0.86	0.92	0.77
OurSystem	0.89	0.84	0.86	0.91	0.72

Table 4: TempEval-2 Extent scores for our system and three previous systems. Note that the attribute scores are now relatively low compared to previous work; unlike rule-based approaches, our model can guess a temporal interpretation for any phrase, meaning that a good proportion of the phrases not detected would have been interpreted correctly.

- Whether the current word is a number, along with its ordinality and order of magnitude
- Prefixes and suffixes up to length 5, along with their word shape.

We summarize our results in Table 4, noting that the performance indicates that the CRF and interpretation model find somewhat different phrases hard to detect and interpret respectively. Many errors made in detection are attributable to the small size of the training corpus (63,000 tokens).

5.4 Discussion

Our system performs well above the GUTime baseline and is competitive with both of the more recent systems. In part, this is from more sophisticated modeling of syntactic ambiguity: e.g., *the past few weeks* has a clause *the past* – which, alone, should be parsed as `PAST` – yet the system correctly disprefers incorporating this interpretation and returns the approximate duration `1 week`. Furthermore, we often capture cases of pragmatic ambiguity – for example, empirically, *August* tends to refers to the previous August when mentioned in February.

Compared to rule-based systems, we attribute most errors the system makes to either data sparsity or missing lexical primitives. For example – illustrating sparsity – we have trouble recognizing *Nov.* as corresponding to `November` (e.g., *Nov. 13*), since the publication time of the articles happen to often be near November and we prefer tagging the word as `Nil` (analogous to *the* 13th). Missing lexical primitives, in turn, include tags for *1990s*, or *half* (in *minute and a half*); as well as missing functions, such as *or* (in *weeks or months*).

Remaining errors can be attributed to causes such as providing the wrong Viterbi grounding to the evaluation script (e.g., last rather than this Friday), differences in annotation (e.g., 24 hours is marked wrong against a day), or missing context (e.g., the publication time is not the true reference time), among others.

6 Conclusion

We present a new approach to resolving temporal expressions, based on synchronous parsing of a fixed grammar with learned parameters and a compositional representation of time. The system allows for output which captures uncertainty both with respect to the syntactic structure of the phrase and the pragmatic ambiguity of temporal utterances. We also note that the approach is theoretically better adapted for phrases more complex than those found in TempEval-2.

Furthermore, the system makes very few language-specific assumptions, and the algorithm could be adapted to domains beyond temporal resolution. We hope to improve detection and explore system performance on multilingual and complex datasets in future work.

Acknowledgements The authors would like to thank Valentin Spitkovsky, David McClosky, and Angel Chang for valuable discussion and insights. We gratefully acknowledge the support of the Defense Advanced Research Projects Agency (DARPA) Machine Reading Program under Air Force Research Laboratory (AFRL) prime contract no. FA8750-09-C-0181. Any opinions, findings, and conclusions or recommendations expressed in this material are those of the authors and do not necessarily reflect the view of DARPA, AFRL, or the US government.

References

James F. Allen. 1981. An interval-based representation of temporal knowledge. In *Proceedings of the 7th international joint conference on Artificial intelligence*, pages 221–226, San Francisco, CA, USA. Morgan Kaufmann Publishers Inc.

James Allen. 1995. *Natural Language Understanding*. Benjamin/Cummings, Redwood City, CA.

E. Bach. 1976. An extension of classical transformational grammar. In *Problems of Linguistic Metatheory (Proceedings of the 1976 Conference)*, Michigan State University.

Johan Bos, Stephen Clark, Mark Steedman, James R. Curran, and Julia Hockenmaier. 2004. Wide-coverage semantic representations from a CCG parser. In *Proceedings of Coling*, pages 1240–1246, Geneva, Switzerland. COLING.

Glenn Carroll and Eugene Charniak. 1992. Two experiments on learning probabilistic dependency grammars from corpora. Technical report, Providence, RI, USA.

Angel Chang and Chris Manning. 2012. SUTIME: a library for recognizing and normalizing time expressions. In *Language Resources and Evaluation*.

James Clarke, Dan Goldwasser, Ming-Wei Chang, and Dan Roth. 2010. Driving semantic parsing from the world's response. In *CoNLL*, pages 18–27, Uppsala, Sweden.

Cleo Condoravdi. 2010. NPI licensing in temporal clauses. *Natural Language and Linguistic Theory*, 28:877–910.

Claire Grover, Richard Tobin, Beatrice Alex, and Kate Byrne. 2010. Edinburgh-LTG: TempEval-2 system description. In *Proceedings of the 5th International Workshop on Semantic Evaluation*, Sem-Eval, pages 333–336.

Liang Huang and David Chiang. 2005. Better k-best parsing. In *Proceedings of the Ninth International Workshop on Parsing Technology*, Parsing, pages 53–64.

Rohit J. Kate, Yuk Wah Wong, and Raymond J. Mooney. 2005. Learning to transform natural to formal languages. In *AAAI*, pages 1062–1068, Pittsburgh, PA.

Dan Klein and Christopher D. Manning. 2004. Corpus-based induction of syntactic structure: models of dependency and constituency. In *ACL*.

Oleksandr Kolomiyets and Marie-Francine Moens. 2010. KUL: recognition and normalization of temporal expressions. In *Proceedings of the 5th International Workshop on Semantic Evaluation*, Sem-Eval '10, pages 325–328.

Tom Kwiatkowski, Luke Zettlemoyer, Sharon Goldwater, and Mark Steedman. 2011. Lexical generalization in CCG grammar induction for semantic parsing. In *EMNLP*, pages 1512–1523, Edinburgh, Scotland, UK.

J. Lafferty, A. McCallum, and F Pereira. 2001. Conditional random fields: Probabilistic models for segmenting and labeling sequence data. In *International Conference on Machine Learning (ICML)*.

P. Liang, M. I. Jordan, and D. Klein. 2011. Learning dependency-based compositional semantics. In *ACL*.

Inderjeet Mani and George Wilson. 2000. Robust temporal processing of news. In *ACL*, pages 69–76, Hong Kong.

Marc Moens and Mark Steedman. 1988. Temporal ontology and temporal reference. *Computational Linguistics*, 14:15–28.

G. Puscasu. 2004. A framework for temporal resolution. In *LREC*, pages 1901–1904.

Hans Reichenbach. 1947. *Elements of Symbolic Logic*. Macmillan, New York.

E. Saquete, R. Muoz, and P. Martnez-Barco. 2003. Terseo: Temporal expression resolution system applied to event ordering. In *Text, Speech and Dialogue*, pages 220–228.

Mark Steedman. 2000. *The syntactic process*. MIT Press, Cambridge, MA, USA.

Jannik Strötgen and Michael Gertz. 2010. Heideltime: High quality rule-based extraction and normalization of temporal expressions. In *Proceedings of the 5th International Workshop on Semantic Evaluation*, Sem-Eval, pages 321–324.

Naushad UzZaman and James F. Allen. 2010. TRIPS and TRIOS system for TempEval-2: Extracting temporal information from text. In *Proceedings of the 5th International Workshop on Semantic Evaluation*, Sem-Eval, pages 276–283.

Marc Verhagen, Roser Sauri, Tommaso Caselli, and James Pustejovsky. 2010. Semeval-2010 task 13: TempEval-2. In *Proceedings of the 5th International Workshop on Semantic Evaluation*, pages 57–62, Uppsala, Sweden.

Kenji Yamada and Kevin Knight. 2001. A syntax-based statistical translation model. In *ACL*, pages 523–530.

John M. Zelle and Raymond J. Mooney. 1996. Learning to parse database queries using inductive logic programming. In *AAAI/IAAI*, pages 1050–1055, Portland, OR.

Luke S. Zettlemoyer and Michael Collins. 2005. Learning to map sentences to logical form: Structured classification with probabilistic categorial grammars. In *UAI*, pages 658–666. AUAI Press.

Luke S. Zettlemoyer and Michael Collins. 2007. Online learning of relaxed CCG grammars for parsing to logical form. In *EMNLP-CoNLL*, pages 678–687.

Fine-Grained Focus for Pinpointing Positive Implicit Meaning from Negated Statements

Eduardo Blanco and **Dan Moldovan**
Lymba Corporation
Richardson, TX 75080 USA
{eduardo,moldovan}@lymba.com

Abstract

Negated statements often carry positive implicit meaning. Regardless of the semantic representation one adopts, pinpointing the positive concepts within a negated statement is needed in order to encode the statement's meaning. In this paper, novel ideas to reveal positive implicit meaning using focus of negation are presented. The concept of granularity of focus is introduced and justified. New annotation and features to detect fine-grained focus are discussed and results reported.

1 Introduction

Semantic representation of text is an important step towards text understanding. Current approaches are based on relatively shallow representations and ignore pervasive linguistic phenomena such as negation and metaphor. Despite these weaknesses, shallow representations have been proven useful for several tasks, e.g., coreference resolution (Kong et al., 2009), machine translation (Wu and Fung, 2009).

Consider statement (1) *The company won't ship the new product to the United States until next year.* Existing approaches to represent the meaning of (1) either indicate that the verb *ship* is negated or disregard the negation altogether. Semantic role labelers trained over PropBank would link *n't* to *ship* with MNEG (i.e., negate the verb); any system based on FrameNet and more recent unsupervised proposals (Poon and Domingos, 2009; Liang et al., 2011; Titov and Klementiev, 2011) ignore negation.

In order to represent the meaning of (1), one must first ascertain that the negation mark *n't* is actually negating the TEMPORAL context linked to *ship* and not the verb per se; more specifically, *n't* is negating exclusively the preposition *until*. Only doing so one can aim at representing the actual meaning of (1): *The company will ship the new product to the United States during next year.* Note that the verb *ship*, and its AGENT, THEME and LOCATION (i.e., *The company, the new product* and *to the United States*) are positive, as well as the temporal anchor *next year*.

Regardless of the semantic representation one favors (logic forms, predicate calculus, semantic relations, semantic frames, etc.), we argue that pinpointing the numerous words that contribute to implicit positive meanings within a negated statement is a required subtask to obtain it. This paper aims at extracting specific positive implicit meaning from negated statements. The main contributions are: (1) interpretation of negation using fine-grained focus; (2) fine-grained focus of negation annotation over a subset of PropBank; (3) feature set to detect fine-grained focus of negation; and (4) model to retrieve *precise* positive implicit meaning from negated statements.

2 Related Work

Negation has been widely studied from a theoretical point of view. The seminal work by Horn (1989) presents the main thoughts in philosophy and psychology. Work in linguistics has studied the interaction of negation with quantifiers and anaphora (Hintikka, 2002), as well as the role in reasoning (Sánchez Valencia, 1991; Dowty, 1994): one can perform downward (but not upward) monotone inference with negative statements. Zeijlstra (2007) analyzes the position and form of negative elements and negative concords; concepts such as intra and inter-domain negation and strength of negation (Ladusaw, 1996), syntactic and semantic negation (Löbner, 2000) have been discussed in the extensive literature, although we do not use them.

In computational linguistics, negation has mainly drawn attention in sentiment analysis (Wilson et al., 2009; Wiegand et al., 2010) and the biomedical domain. Recently, two events (Morante and Sporleder, 2010; Farkas et al., 2010) targeted negation mostly on those subfields. Among many others, Morante and Daelemans (2009) and Li et al. (2010) propose scope detectors using the BioScope corpus. Considering scope is indeed a step forward, but focus must also be taken into account to represent negated statements and detect their positive implicit meanings.

Regarding corpora, BioScope annotates negation marks and linguistic scopes exclusively on biomedical texts. It does not annotate focus and it purposely disregards negations such as *the reactions in NK3.3 cells are not always identical* (Vincze et al., 2008), which carry the kind of positive meaning we aim at extracting (the reactions in NK3.3 cells *are sometimes* identical). Recently, Morante et al. (2011) present scope annotation in two Conan Doyle works, but they dismiss focus and positive meaning extraction. As stated before, PropBank (Palmer et al., 2005) treats negation superficially and FrameNet (Baker et al., 1998) regrettably disregards negation.

Blanco and Moldovan (2011) introduce a semantic representation of negation using focus detection. They target verbal negation and work on top of PropBank, selecting as focus the role that corresponds to the focus of negation. Simply put, they propose that all roles but the one corresponding to the focus are actually positive. Their approach, however, has a major drawback: selecting the whole role often yields too coarse of a focus and the positive implicit meaning is not fully specified (Section 3.1).

Focus-Sensitive Phenomena. The literature uses the term *focus* for widely distinct phenomena; space permits only a cursory review. Within functional generative grammars, focus is defined as *what is being asserted about the topic* (Hajičová et al., 1995). The term is also used in pragmatics (Glanzberg, 2005), and in phonetics and phonology (Xu and Xu, 2005; Beaver et al., 2007).

In linguistics, *focus* is largely associated with the theory presented in Mats Rooth's dissertation (1985) and posterior publications (Rooth, 1992). He analyzes the effect of focus in diverse phenomena, e.g., questions and answers, reasons and counterfactuals, conversational implicature, bare remnant ellipsis. His alternative semantics (e.g., *they didn't order the right parts* implies that some alternative of the form *they ordered X* is true) (Rooth, 1997) was an inspiration for this work. However, Rooth does not discuss how to detect focus of negation or its granularity and only provides simple made-up examples.

3 Scope and Focus

Negation has both scope and focus and they are key to capture its meaning. Scope is the part of the meaning that is negated. Focus is that part of the scope that is most prominently or explicitly negated (Huddleston and Pullum, 2002). All elements whose individual falsity would make the negated statement strictly true belong to the scope. Focus is the element of the scope that is *intended* to be interpreted as false to make the overall negative true.

Consider (1) *We didn't get an offer for more than $40* and its positive counterpart (2) *We got an offer for more than $40*. The truth conditions of (2) are: (a) somebody *got* something; (b) *we* got; (c) *an offer* was gotten; and (d) the offer was *for more than $40*. In order for (2) to be true, (a–d) have to be true. Conversely, the falsity of any of them is sufficient to make (1) true: (1) would be true if *nobody got anything*, *we didn't get*, *an offer wasn't gotten* or *the offer wasn't for more than $40*. Thus, all four statements (a–d) are inside the scope of (1).

The focus is often more difficult to identify. Text understanding is needed and context plays an important role. The most probable focus for (1) is *more than*, which corresponds to the interpretation *we got an offer for $40 or less*. Another possible focus is *for more than $40*, which yields *we got an offer, but not for more than $40*. A third possible focus is *an offer for more than $40*, which yields *we got something, but not an offer for more than $40*. Section 3.1 discusses coarse versus fine-grained focus.

Both scope and focus are primarily semantic, highly ambiguous and context-dependent. More examples can be found in Table 1 and 3, and (Huddleston and Pullum, 2002, Chap. 9).

No.	Statement	Interpretation
1	People don't always follow instructions.	People sometimes follow instructions.
2	The new group isn't doing any better than the old one.	The new group is doing equal or worse than the old one.
3	The first two games didn't finish in the top 10.	The first two games finished below the top 10.
4	They don't sell to as many clients as Maryland Club.	They sell to less clients than Maryland Club.
5	She said she is not going home until The Word Series is over.	She said she is going home when The Word Series is over.
6	People don't believe I want to give this money away.	People believe I want to keep this money.
7	I cannot see how this news doesn't benefit them.	I can see how this news benefits them.
8	I don't believe in this business you can be totally laissez-faire because of the high degree of public interest.	I believe in this business you can be only partially laissez-faire because of the high degree of public interest.

Table 1: Examples of negated statements and their interpretation using fine-grained focus (regular underline). Using coarse-grained focus (wavy underline) would yield a much more generic, less preferred interpretation.

3.1 Granularity of Focus

In this paper, we refer to the focus considered by Blanco and Moldovan (2011) as *coarse*-grained and indicate it with a wavy underline; we refer to the focus we work with as *fine*-grained and indicate it with a regular underline, e.g., *We didn't get an offer for more than $40*. Whereas coarse-grained focus is restricted to include all words belonging to a verb argument (as per their definition and annotation, focus is the full text of a semantic role in PropBank), fine-grained focus is not. This allows us to narrow down the actual negative meaning and pinpoint more positive implicit meaning.

Considering fine-grained focus is a substantial step towards a comprehensive semantic representation of negation. Following with the example above, encoding that *we got something, but not an offer for more than $40* (coarse-grained) is useful, but encoding *we got an offer for $40 or less* (fine-grained) is preferred. Several examples of coarse versus fine-grained focus and the benefits of using the latter over the former are provided in Table 1. In all statements, using coarse-grained focus yields an interpretation with all words underlined with a wavy underline negative and the rest positive, e.g., statement (8) would be interpreted as *I believe in something because of the high degree of public interest, but not that in this business you can be totally laissez-faire.*

Selecting the elements that belong to the fine-grained focus is a difficult task. In example (1), both coarse and fine-grained foci are the same and yield the same interpretation. In the rest of examples and in the vast majority of negations we annotated (Section 4), fine-grained focus comprises fewer words and yields more specific interpretations.

The coarse-grained focus in statements (1, 2) is an adverbial phrase. In (1) coarse-grained focus is a single word and thus fine-grained focus is trivially that word. In statement (2), fine-grained focus allows us to keep the comparison between the *new* and *old group* in the interpretation.

Examples (3, 4) correspond to statements whose coarse grained focus is a prepositional phrase. Simple rules based on part-of-speech tags are not suitable here, deep understanding of text is needed. The fine-grained focus in example (3) is the preposition, but that is not the case in (4). Fine-grained focus in these statements allows us to obtain more complete interpretations, namely spell out the location (metaphorically speaking) were the games ended in (3) and the quantity sold in (4).

Examples (5–8) correspond to statements whose coarse-grained focus is a subordinate clause. Note that a verb is contained in the coarse-grained focus in these examples. In statement (5), the fine-grained focus is the first word, a preposition. However, that is not the case in (8), where the MANNER of the verb within the subordinate clause (i.e., *totally*) is selected as fine-grained focus. In (6), the phrasal verb *give away* is the fine-grained focus. Statement (7) is specially interesting because it contains a double negation and fine-grained focus is the negation mark within the coarse-grained focus.

Note that interpreting statements using coarse-grained focus is by no means wrong, but it is not optimal. The interpretation using fine-grained focus entails the one using coarse-grained focus. For example, in (2), *The new group is doing equal or worse than the old one* (fine) entails *The new group is doing, but not any better than the old one* (coarse).

Node	# Negations	% Negations
NP	1,051	39.93
PP	570	21.65
ADVP	415	15.75
SBAR	323	12.30
S	202	7.67
ADJP	33	1.26
Other	38	1.43

Table 2: Syntactic nodes for coarse-grained focus.

4 Annotating Fine-Grained Focus

We have annotated fine-grained focus of negation on top of the coarse-grained focus annotated by Blanco and Moldovan (2011). In this paper, we concentrate on negations whose coarse-grained focus is a prepositional phrase (PP), adverbial phrase (ADVP) or subordinate clause (SBAR). Excluding cases in which the verb is the coarse-grained focus, these syntactic nodes correspond to 49.70% of negations (Table 2). When a verb is the coarse-grained focus, it is not advantageous to consider fine-grained focus because both of them are always the same. e.g., *We urge our citizens not to wait until it is too late* [interpretation: we urge out citizens to *act*]. An example of NP being coarse-grained focus is *They realized they didn't order the right parts*.

We chose PP, ADVP and SBAR over noun phrases (NP, the most common syntactic realization) because they offer a variety of lexical and syntactic realizations, and thus allow us to tackle the task of fine-grained focus prediction in an assortment of constructions (as opposed to target exclusively NP). As we shall see, ADVP are shorter and easier, whereas PP and SBAR often contain complex syntactic (and semantic) structures and are tougher.

Annotation is done at the word level. Each word belonging to the coarse grained focus is marked if it also belongs to the fine-grained focus. This allows us to narrow down the actual negative meaning and reveal the most positive implicit meaning. In some cases (32%, Table 4), coarse and fine-grained foci include the same words (e.g., *It doesn't always hurt* [interpretation: *it hurts sometimes*]). However, fine-grained focus usually (68%) comprises fewer words.

Annotators were first trained with examples similar to the ones in Table 1. In a first round, they were asked to select as fine-grained focus the words within the coarse-grained focus that they believed were intended to be negated. These instructions were purposely vague to analyze disagreements and allow us to define detailed guidelines. Inter-annotator agreement (exact match) was 41%. This number is low, but the task is challenging and a mismatch of one token (potentially a noncontent word (*the*, *a*, etc.) or even a punctuation mark (comma, dash, etc.) is counted as disagreement.

Conflicts were resolved and their causes analyzed. In a second round, sentences were annotated following the improved guidelines (Section 4.1). In both rounds, annotators were presented with plain text; they did not have access to any other information.

4.1 Annotation Guidelines

We aim at annotating fine-grained focus in order to pinpoint the numerous positive concepts within a negated statement. All concepts but the ones belonging to the fine-grained focus should be interpreted positive. Our annotation criteria is succinctly summarized by the following principles:

1. We annotate fine-grained focus of negation to reveal specific positive implicit meaning; we do not strictly follow any theory of focus.
2. We assume that fine-grained focus is contained within the coarse-grained focus.
3. Decisions are made taking into account the current sentence and context. Context is limited to the previous and next sentence.
4. World knowledge is taken into account. Thus, sentences are fully interpreted to identify positive implicit meaning.
5. In case of ambiguity, we prioritize:
   (a) fine-grained focus that yields novel meaning over foci yielding meaning already stated elsewhere;
   (b) narrow over wide fine-grained focus. The narrower the focus, the more specific the positive meaning revealed.
   (c) the fine-grained focus that reveals the most obvious positive implicit meaning, i.e., meaning requiring the least world knowledge and assumptions to hold.
6. If there are two options for fine-grained focus yielding semantically equivalent positive implicit meanings, we select the fine-grained focus occurring earlier within the sentence.

No.	Example
1	The plan indeed raises from 40% to 50% the number of freshmen applicants admitted strictly by academic criteria. But that doesn't mean "half of the students attending" will be admitted this way.
2	"[...] and tied it to the stake with a chain," he says proudly. "And you can't cut this chain with bolt cutters".
3	Although other parties have stated they have no complaints, it is not growing fast enough for us.
4	Mr. Katz happily agreed, sliding over the fact that California's roads and bridges aren't funded by property taxes but by state and federal gasoline taxes.
5	[...] in a criminal case , a prosecutor can not comment on a defendant 's failure to testify [...].
6	You think you can go out and turn things around. The reason doesn't relate to your selling skills.
7	Respondents don't think that an economic slowdown would harm the major investment markets very much.
8	The first two games of the World Series between [...] didn't finish in the top 10 [...]

Table 3: Examples of annotation (and relevant context) exemplifying the annotation guidelines.

4.2 Examples of Annotation

In this section, we exemplify our annotation guidelines with the statements in Table 3. When example (1) is interpreted in context [criterion 3], we obtain *at most half of the students will be admitted strictly by academic criteria*. Word knowledge [criterion 4] allows us to determine that if 40–50% of students are admitted a certain way, at most half of students attending will be admitted this way (a student admitted may not enroll). Word knowledge is also used in example (2): however strong the chain is, one could cut it with a stronger tool than bolt cutters.

Statement (3) implicitly states that *it is growing fast enough for other parties*. Thus, we choose *enough* [interpretation: it is growing insufficiently fast for us] since it reveals novel positive meaning [criterion 5a]. Another option discarded is *us* [interpretation: it is growing fast enough for someone, but not us]. Note that revealing novel positive implicit meaning is not always possible, e.g., statement (4).

There are several options for statement (5): (5a) *a defendant's failure to testify* [interpretation: a prosecutor can comment, but not on a defendant's failure to testify]; (5b) *a defendant's* [a prosecutor can comment on somebody's failure to testify, but not the defendant's]; and (5c) *testify* [a prosecutor can comment on the defendant's failures to do something, but not to testify]. We prefer (5c) since it reveals the most specific positive meaning [criterion 5b]. Note that narrowing down the coarse-grained focus is not always possible as exemplified in example (6): one cannot tell if the reason relates to another skill or to something else (e.g., economy, weather).

In example (7), we choose the fine-grained focus that reveals the most obvious implicit positive meaning [criterion 5c], *very much* [interpretation: an economic slowdown would harm the major investment markets *a little*]. Another option is *slowdown*, yielding the plausible but less felicitous interpretation *responders think that an economic recession/turmoil (but not a slowdown) would harm the major investment markets very much.* A third option is *major* [responders think that an economic slowdown would harm *minor* investment markets very much]. The last two options are plausible but less likely.

Finally, statement (8), there are two semantically equivalent options: (8a) *in* [interpretation: the games finished below the top 10] and (8b) *10* [interpretation: the games finished in the top X, where X is larger than 10]. We choose the former since it occurs earlier in the sentence [criterion 6].

	#FGF	%(CGF = FGF)	#FGF/#CGF
PP	5.53	1.17%	0.44
ADVP	1.38	89.19%	0.94
SBAR	9.79	14.79%	0.32
All	5.25	32.41%	0.57

Table 4: Numeric analysis: average number of words in fine-grained focus, percentage of negations in which coarse and fine-grained focus are the same and average ratio of words in fine versus coarse-grained focus.

4.3 Annotation Analysis

The three syntactic realizations of coarse-grained focus we aim at narrowing down have significantly different characteristics. Table 4 summarizes some basic numeric analysis. Intuitively, ADVPs are fairly easy (they are short and coarse-grained and fine-grained foci are often the same). On the other hand, PP and SBAR are longer and only 44% and 32% of words belonging to the coarse grained focus belong to the fine-grained focus respectively.

Baseline		P	R	F
COARSE	PP	1.96	1.89	1.92
	ADVP	92.86	92.86	92.86
	SBAR	15.38	13.33	14.29
	All	29.52	27.93	28.70
FIRST-WORD	PP	33.33	32.08	32.69
	ADVP	92.86	92.86	92.86
	SBAR	35.29	20.00	25.53
	All	51.04	44.14	47.34
FIRST-JJ	PP	29.82	32.08	30.91
	ADVP	92.86	92.86	92.86
	SBAR	15.38	13.33	14.29
	All	52.34	42.34	42.34
BASIC	PP	54.17	49.06	51.49
	ADVP	92.86	92.86	92.86
	SBAR	45.00	30.00	36.00
	All	**63.54**	**54.95**	**58.94**

Table 5: Precision, recall and f-measure of baselines.

5 Learning Fine-Grained Focus

We follow a standard supervised learning approach. Each token from each annotated negation becomes an instance. The decision to be made is whether or not an instance is part of the fine-grained focus. The annotated sentences (comprising several instances) were divided into training (70%), held-out (15%) and test (15%). The held-out portion was used to tune the feature set and results are reported for the test split only, i.e., using unseen instances.

Detecting fine-grained focus is similar to text chunking. Text chunking consists of dividing text into syntactically related nonoverlapping groups of words (Tjong Kim Sang and Buchholz, 2000). On the other hand, we aim at dividing the words within a negated statement into belonging or not belonging to the fine-grained focus. Our problem can be redefined as detecting one type of chunk indicating the fine grained focus (FGF). We use the standard BIO notation, in which the first element of a chunk is prefixed by B- (beginning) and other elements of the chunk are preceded by I- (inside). The label O is used to indicate tokens outside any FGF chunk.

Baselines. We have implemented four baselines to predict fine-grained focus from the elements within the coarse-grained focus:

- COARSE: select all words.
- FIRST-WORD: select the first word.
- FIRST-JJ: select the first adjective; if none is found, apply FIRST-WORD.
- BASIC: same as system in Section 5.2 but using features *POS-tag*, *word* and *coarse-chunk*.

Table 5 shows the performance of these baselines. All of them obtain the same performance for ADVPs, and BASIC yields the best results. FIRST-WORD successfully predicts fine-grained focus mostly in cases in which the fine-grained focus is a preposition positioned at the beginning of the coarse-grained focus (e.g., Table 3, statement 8).

5.1 Selecting Features

We use a mixture of features proposed for standard text chunking, semantic role labeling and novel features characterizing negation (Table 6). We only provide more details for the non-obvious ones.

Features 1–5 characterize the current token with an emphasis on negation. Neg-prefix indicates if a word is an adjective, starts with a negation prefix and the reminder of it is a valid adjective. We consider the following negation prefixes: *a-*, *an-*, *anti-*, *dis-*, *il-*, *im-*, *in-*, *ir-*, *non-* and *un-* and check whether the reminder is a valid adjective querying WordNet. This successfully allows us to detect *irrelevant* (prefix *ir-*; *relevant* is a valid adjective) and disregard adjectives that just happen to start with a negated prefix, e.g., *artistic*, *intelligent*. Any-prefix indicates if a word starts with *any* (e.g., anytime). Huddleston and Pullum (2002, p.823) refer to these words as *"any class of items"* and include them in the negatively-oriented polarity-sensitive items (NPIs). Features signaling other NPIs (until, dare, yet, etc.) did not bring an improvement on the development set. Ly-suffix typically signals an adverb indicating the manner in which something happened.

Features 6–18 describe the coarse-grained focus. Coarse-path corresponds to four features indicating paths of length 1–4 from coarse-node to the token. Including the full path did not yield an improvement on the development set. Coarse-head is calculated following (Collins, 1999).

Finally, features coarse-verb and sem-role are useful in cases in which the token is not only part of the semantic role corresponding to the coarse-grained focus (i.e., a role of verb pred-word), but also a role of a verb within the coarse-grained focus (i.e., a role of verb coarse-verb). For example in Table 3, example (7), for token *slowdown* we have word = *slowdown*, pred-word = *think*, coarse-role = *A1*, coarse-verb = *harm* and sem-role = *A0*.

No.	Feature	Values	Explanation
1–2	POS-tag and word	{NN, VBD, ...}	POS tag and text of current token
3	neg-prefix (PP, SBAR)	{yes, no}	does word start with a negation preffix?
4	any-preffix (PP, SBAR)	{yes, no}	does word start with preffix *-any*?
5	ly-suffix (SBAR)	{yes, no}	does word end with suffix *-ly*?
6–7	coarse-{node,parent}	{S, PP, ...}	syntactic node of coarse-grained focus and parent
8–9	coarse-{left,right}	{NP, VP, ...}	syntactic node of coarse-node left and right siblings
10	coarse-struct	{IN=NP, IN=S, ...}	syntactic nodes of of coarse-node daughters
11	coarse-length	ℕ	lenght of coarse-grained focus
12–15	coarse-path (PP, SBAR)	{PP, PP-NP,...}	paths of length 1–4 from coarse-node to token
16	coarse-role	{ARG1, MTMP, ...}	semantic role of coarse-grained focus
17	coarse-head (PP, SBAR)	{clock, detail, ...}	head of coarse-grained focus
18	coarse-verb (SBAR)	{think, predict, ...}	first verb within coarse-grained focus
19	pred-word	{affected, go, ...}	predicate text
20	pred-POS	{VB, VBN, ...}	predicate POS tag
21	sem-role (SBAR)	{ARG1, MLOC, ...}	semantic role this token belongs to wrt coarse-verb
22	coarse-chunk	{B-CFG, I-CFG, O}	coarse-grained annotation using BIO

Table 6: Feature set used to predict fine-grained focus of negation. If a feature is especially useful for a particular syntactic node, we indicate so between parenthesis in the right hand side of column 1 (otherwise it is useful for all).

5.2 Experiments and Results

We have carried our experiments using Yamcha (Kudoh and Matsumoto, 2000), a generic, customizable, and open source text chunker[1] implemented using TinySVM[2]. Following Yamcha's design, we distinguish between static and dynamic features. Static features are the ones depicted in Table 6 for a fixed size window. Dynamic features are the predicted classes for a fixed set of previous instances. Whereas values for static features are considered correct, values for dynamic features are predictions of previous instances and therefore may contain errors. Varying window size effectively varies the number of features considered, the larger the window the more local context is taken into account.

Window sizes are defined using ranges between instances. The instance to be predicted has index '0', the previous one '-1', the next one '1', and so on. The range $[i..j]$ indicates we take into account from the ith to the jth instances to predict the current instance. Ranges for dynamic features can only contain instances preceding the current one.

The best performing system was obtained using a window including the current and two previous instances, and taking into account dynamic features. This system uses a total of 68 features: 66 static features ($22 \times 3 = 66$, 22 features per instance, window contains 3 instances) and 2 dynamic features.

Window Size		P	R	F
static	dynamic			
[-1..0]	none	59.20	66.67	62.71
	[-1..-1]	68.27	63.96	66.05
[-1..1]	none	66.04	63.06	64.52
	[-1..-1]	70.10	61.26	65.38
[0..1]	none	57.85	63.06	60.34
	[-1..-1]	63.92	55.86	59.62
[-2..0]	none	60.00	62.16	61.06
	[-2..-1]	**71.15**	**66.67**	**68.84**
[-2..2]	none	62.96	61.26	62.10
	[-2..-1]	68.42	58.56	63.11
[0..2]	none	60.00	59.46	59.73
	[-2..-1]	64.21	54.95	59.22
[-3..0]	none	55.65	62.16	58.72
	[-3..-1]	68.93	63.96	66.36
[-3..3]	none	62.62	60.36	61.47
	[-3..-1]	67.01	58.56	62.50
[0..3]	none	57.80	56.76	57.27
	[-3..-1]	64.13	53.15	58.13

Table 7: Results using different window sizes.

Table 7 provides results on the test split for several window sizes considering and not considering dynamic features. The best performing system obtains precision 71.15, recall 66.67 (f-measure 68.84). In general, windows encompassing the i previous instances (e.g., $[-2..0]$) perform better than windows encompassing the i next instances (e.g., $[0..2]$). Windows not considering the i next instances yield better performance when using dynamic features (i.e., $[-i..0]$ is superior to $[-i..i]$). Also, including dy-

[1]http://chasen.org/ taku/software/yamcha/

[2]http://chasen.org/ taku/software/TinySVM/

Phrase	P	R	F
PP	64.71	62.26	63.46
ADVP	92.86	92.86	92.86
SBAR	60.00	50.00	54.55
All	71.15	66.67	68.84

Table 8: Detailed results per phrase using the best window size of features (in bold in Table 7).

namic features is favorable for almost all window sizes (the only exceptions are [0..1] and [0..2] by a negligible margin). Larger and discontinuous windows (e.g., [-4..-3, -1..-1]) did not bring an improvement during development and were discarded.

Finally, we report detailed results for the best performing system in Table 8.

6 Limitations and Future Work

The work presented here effectively extracts specific positive implicit meaning from negated statements. We depict below some limitations and shortcomings that could be targeted as future work.

Types of negation. We only targeted verbal, clausal and analytic negation (Huddleston and Pullum, 2002). Analyzing other types (e.g., synthetic, non-verbal: *I ate nothing*, *Nobody liked the party*) is needed for a more comprehensive approach.

All positive meanings. Not all implicit positive meanings are always detected. For example, *If the payment isn't received by today, an eviction notice will be send out* [interpretation: If the payment is received after today, an eviction notice will be send out]. Our proposal fails to detect that if no payment is received, the notice will also be send. Allowing multiple fine-grained foci seems a valid solution.

Fine-grained within coarse-grained. In a few examples, interpreting a negated statement using fine-grained focus requires modifications in other parts of the sentence as well. For example, *That increase in the money supply would not have happened without the consent of the Federal Reserve*. The interpretation is *That increase would have happened with the consent of the Federal Reserve*. This is not wrong, but a better option is to remove the modal *would* in the positive interpretation: the increase *did happen (with the consent of the Federal Reserve)*.

Overall Interpretation. A complete semantic representation for a statement (not only the verbal negation within) may require the same concept with two polarities. Consider *[In the past]*$_{\text{TEMPORAL}}$, *[you]*$_{\text{AGENT}}$ *just wore an unknown brand and didn't [care]*$_{\text{verb}}$. The verbal negation is correctly interpreted *now you care*, but *in the past* remains as is (i.e., positive) for the verb *wore* [interpretation: in the past you just wore an unknown brand]. Strictly speaking, this is not a limitation but something to take into account to obtain a semantic representation of the whole statement. Our proposal successfully retrieves positive implicit meaning.

7 Conclusions

In this paper, we have argued that negated statements often carry positive implicit meaning and that its detection is key in order to capture their semantics, regardless of the semantic representation one favors (e.g., predicate calculus, semantic relations).

We have introduced the concept of granularity of focus of negation. Going beyond previous work, considering *fine*-grained focus allows us to reveal *narrow* positive implicit meaning. In the majority of cases (68%, Table 4) we are able to detect more positive implicit meaning than previous work considering a *coarse*-grained focus. We do not impose any syntactic restriction on which parts of a sentence might belong to the fine-grained focus. The annotation was done selecting words without taking into account any syntactic or semantic information. This approach effectively marks only the words that should be negated, but arguably makes prediction more difficult since fine-grained focus often does not correspond to a single node in the syntactic tree.

We have approached the task of fine-grained focus detection as a chunking problem in which we predict one chunk, FGF. The best model obtains an f-measure of 68.84, calculated by considering exact matches between chunks. In other words, unless the model predicts as fine-grained focus exactly the actual fine-grained focus, it is considered wrong when calculating performance. We believe this is the honest way of evaluating performance, even though partial matches could be useful for an actual application. For example, in *The U.S.'s largest suppliers haven't been filling their quotas to the full extent* [interpretation: they have been fullfilling their quotas to a partial extent], if the model predicts *full* as the only word belonging to fine-grained focus we count it wrong even though it successfully detects the most important part of it, i.e., the adjective *full*.

References

Collin F. Baker, Charles J. Fillmore, and John B. Lowe. 1998. The Berkeley FrameNet Project. In *Proceedings of the 17th international conference on Computational Linguistics*, Montreal, Canada.

David Beaver, Brady Z. Clark, Edward Flemming, T. Florian Jaeger, and Maria Wolters. 2007. When Semantics Meets Phonetics: Acoustical Studies of Second-Occurrence Focus. *Language*, 83(2):245–276.

Eduardo Blanco and Dan Moldovan. 2011. Semantic Representation of Negation Using Focus Detection. In *Proceedings of the 49th Annual Meeting of the Association for Computational Linguistics: Human Language Technologies*, pages 581–589, Portland, Oregon, USA, June. Association for Computational Linguistics.

Michael Collins. 1999. Head-Driven Statistical Models for Natural Language Parsing. *University of Pennsylvania*.

David Dowty. 1994. The Role of Negative Polarity and Concord Marking in Natural Language Reasoning. In *Proceedings of Semantics and Linguistics Theory (SALT) 4*, pages 114–144.

Richárd Farkas, Veronika Vincze, György Móra, János Csirik, and György Szarvas. 2010. The CoNLL-2010 Shared Task: Learning to Detect Hedges and their Scope in Natural Language Text. In *Proceedings of the Fourteenth Conference on Computational Natural Language Learning*, pages 1–12, Uppsala, Sweden, July. Association for Computational Linguistics.

Michael Glanzberg. 2005. Focus: A Case Study on the semanticspragmatics Boundary. In Zoltan G. Szabo, editor, *Semantics versus Pragmatics*, chapter 3. Oxford University Press, USA, first edition edition, February.

Eva Hajičová, Petr Sgall, and Hana Skoumalová. 1995. An automatic procedure for topic-focus identification. *Comput. Linguist.*, 21:81–94, March.

Jaakko Hintikka. 2002. Negation in Logic and in Natural Language. *Linguistics and Philosophy*, 25(5/6).

Laurence R. Horn. 1989. *A Natural History of Negation*. University Of Chicago Press, June.

Rodney D. Huddleston and Geoffrey K. Pullum. 2002. *The Cambridge Grammar of the English Language*. Cambridge University Press, April.

Fang Kong, GuoDong Zhou, and Qiaoming Zhu. 2009. Employing the Centering Theory in Pronoun Resolution from the Semantic Perspective. In *Proceedings of the 2009 Conference on Empirical Methods in Natural Language Processing*, pages 987–996, Singapore, August. Association for Computational Linguistics.

Taku Kudoh and Yuji Matsumoto. 2000. Use of support vector learning for chunk identification. In *Proceedings of the 4th conference on Computational natural language learning (CoNLL-2000)*, ConLL '00, pages 142–144, Stroudsburg, PA, USA. Association for Computational Linguistics.

William A. Ladusaw. 1996. Negation and polarity items. In Shalom Lappin, editor, *Handbook of Contemporary Semantic Theory*, pages 321–341. Blackwell.

Junhui Li, Guodong Zhou, Hongling Wang, and Qiaoming Zhu. 2010. Learning the Scope of Negation via Shallow Semantic Parsing. In *Proceedings of the 23rd International Conference on Computational Linguistics (Coling 2010)*, pages 671–679, Beijing, China, August. Coling 2010 Organizing Committee.

Percy Liang, Michael Jordan, and Dan Klein. 2011. Learning Dependency-Based Compositional Semantics. In *Proceedings of the 49th Annual Meeting of the Association for Computational Linguistics: Human Language Technologies*, pages 590–599, Portland, Oregon, USA, June. Association for Computational Linguistics.

Sebastian Löbner. 2000. Polarity in Natural Language: Predication, Quantification and Negation in Particular and Characterizing Sentences. *Linguistics and Philosophy*, 23(3):213–308–308, June.

Roser Morante and Walter Daelemans. 2009. Learning the Scope of Hedge Cues in Biomedical Texts. In *Proceedings of the BioNLP 2009 Workshop*, pages 28–36, Boulder, Colorado, June. Association for Computational Linguistics.

Roser Morante and Caroline Sporleder, editors. 2010. *Proceedings of the Workshop on Negation and Speculation in Natural Language Processing*. University of Antwerp, Uppsala, Sweden, July.

Roser Morante, Sara Schrauwen, and Walter Daelemans. 2011. Annotation of negation cues and their scope. Guidelines v1.0. Technical report, CLiPS, University of Antwerp.

Martha Palmer, Daniel Gildea, and Paul Kingsbury. 2005. The Proposition Bank: An Annotated Corpus of Semantic Roles. *Computational Linguistics*, 31(1):71–106.

Hoifung Poon and Pedro Domingos. 2009. Unsupervised Semantic Parsing. In *Proceedings of the 2009 Conference on Empirical Methods in Natural Language Processing*, pages 1–10, Singapore, August. Association for Computational Linguistics.

Mats Rooth. 1985. *Association with Focus*. Ph.D. thesis, Univeristy of Massachusetts, Amherst.

Mats Rooth. 1992. A Theory of Focus Interpretation. *Natural Language Semantics*, 1:75–116.

Mats Rooth. 1997. Focus. In Shalom Lappin, editor, *The Handbook of Contemporary Semantic Theory*, Blackwell Handbooks in Linguistics, chapter 10. Wiley-Blackwell, December.

Victor Sánchez Valencia. 1991. *Studies on Natural Logic and Categorial Grammar*. Ph.D. thesis, University of Amsterdam.

Ivan Titov and Alexandre Klementiev. 2011. A Bayesian Model for Unsupervised Semantic Parsing. In *Proceedings of the 49th Annual Meeting of the Association for Computational Linguistics: Human Language Technologies*, pages 1445–1455, Portland, Oregon, USA, June. Association for Computational Linguistics.

Erik F. Tjong Kim Sang and Sabine Buchholz. 2000. Introduction to the CoNLL-2000 Shared Task: Chunking. In Claire Cardie, Walter Daelemans, Claire Nedellec, and Erik Tjong Kim Sang, editors, *Proceedings of CoNLL-2000 and LLL-2000*, pages 127–132. Lisbon, Portugal.

Veronika Vincze, Gyorgy Szarvas, Richard Farkas, Gyorgy Mora, and Janos Csirik. 2008. The BioScope corpus: biomedical texts annotated for uncertainty, negation and their scopes. *BMC Bioinformatics*, 9(Suppl 11):S9+.

Michael Wiegand, Alexandra Balahur, Benjamin Roth, Dietrich Klakow, and Andrés Montoyo. 2010. A survey on the role of negation in sentiment analysis. In *Proceedings of the Workshop on Negation and Speculation in Natural Language Processing*, pages 60 68, Uppsala, Sweden, July. University of Antwerp.

Theresa Wilson, Janyce Wiebe, and Paul Hoffmann. 2009. Recognizing Contextual Polarity: An Exploration of Features for Phrase-Level Sentiment Analysis. *Computational Linguistics*, 35(3):399–433.

Dekai Wu and Pascale Fung. 2009. Semantic Roles for SMT: A Hybrid Two-Pass Model. In *Proceedings of Human Language Technologies: The 2009 Annual Conference of the North American Chapter of the Association for Computational Linguistics, Companion Volume: Short Papers*, pages 13–16, Boulder, Colorado, June. Association for Computational Linguistics.

Y. Xu and C. Xu. 2005. Phonetic realization of focus in English declarative intonation. *Journal of Phonetics*, 33(2):159–197, April.

H. Zeijlstra. 2007. Negation in Natural Language: On the Form and Meaning of Negative Elements. *Language and Linguistics Compass*, 1(5):498–518.

Taxonomy Induction Using Hierarchical Random Graphs

Trevor Fountain and **Mirella Lapata**
Institute for Language, Cognition and Computation
School of Informatics, University of Edinburgh
10 Crichton Street, Edinburgh EH8 9AB
t.fountain@sms.ed.ac.uk, mlap@inf.ed.ac.uk

Abstract

This paper presents a novel approach for inducing lexical taxonomies automatically from text. We recast the learning problem as that of inferring a hierarchy from a graph whose nodes represent taxonomic terms and edges their degree of relatedness. Our model takes this graph representation as input and fits a taxonomy to it via combination of a maximum likelihood approach with a Monte Carlo Sampling algorithm. Essentially, the method works by sampling hierarchical structures with probability proportional to the likelihood with which they produce the input graph. We use our model to infer a taxonomy over 541 nouns and show that it outperforms popular flat and hierarchical clustering algorithms.

1 Introduction

The semantic knowledge encoded in lexical resources such as WordNet (Fellbaum, 1998) has been proven beneficial for several applications including question answering (Harabgiu et al., 2003), document classification (Hung et al., 2004), and textual entailment (Geffet and Dagan, 2005). As the effort involved in creating such resources manually is prohibitive (cost, consistency and coverage are often cited problems) and has to be repeated for new languages or domains, recent years have seen increased interest in automatic taxonomy induction. The task has assumed several guises, such as *term extraction* — finding the concepts of the taxonomy (Kozareva et al., 2008; Navigli et al., 2011), *term relation discovery* — learning whether any two terms stand in an semantic relation such as IS-A, or PART-OF (Hearst, 1992; Berland and Charniak, 1999), and *taxonomy construction* — creating the taxonomy proper by organizing its terms hierarchically (Kozareva and Hovy, 2010; Navigli et al., 2011). Previous work has also focused on the complementary task of augmenting an existing taxonomy with missing information (Snow et al., 2006; Yang and Callan, 2009).

In this paper we propose an unsupervised approach to taxonomy induction. Given a corpus and a set of terms, our algorithm jointly induces their relations and their taxonomic organization. We view taxonomy learning as an instance of the problem of inferring a hierarchy from a network or graph. We create this graph from unstructured text simply by drawing an edge between distributionally similar terms. Next, we fit a Hierarchical Random Graph model (HRG; Clauset et al. (2008)) to the observed graph data based on maximum likelihood methods and Markov chain Monte Carlo sampling. The model essentially works by sampling hierarchical structures with probability proportional to the likelihood with which they produce the input graph. This is advantageous as it allows us to consider the ensemble of random graphs that are statistically similar to the original graph, and through this to derive a consensus hierarchical structure from the ensemble of sampled models. The approach differs crucially from *hierarchical clustering* in that it explicitly acknowledges that most real-world networks have many plausible hierarchical representations of roughly equal likelihood and does not seek a *single* hierarchical representation for a given network. This feature also bodes well with the nature of lexical taxonomies: there is no uniquely correct taxonomy for a set of terms, rather different taxonomies are likely to be appropriate for different tasks and different taxonomization criteria.

Our contributions in this paper are three-fold: we adapt the HRG model to the taxonomy induction task and show that its performance is superior to alternative methods based on either flat or hierarchical clustering; we analyze the requirements of the algorithm with respect to the input graph and the semantic representation of its nodes; and introduce new ways of evaluating the fit of an automatically induced taxonomy against a gold-standard. In the following section we provide an overview of related work. Next, we describe our HRG model in more detail (Section 3) and present the resources and evaluation methodology used in our experiments (Section 4). We conclude the paper by presenting and discussing our results (Sections 4.1–4.4).

2 Related Work

The bulk of previous work has focused on term relation discovery following essentially two methodological paradigms, pattern-based bootstrapping and clustering. The former approach (Hearst, 1992; Roark and Charniak, 1998; Berland and Charniak, 1999; Girju et al., 2003; Etzioni et al., 2005; Kozareva et al., 2008) utilizes a few hand-crafted seed patterns representative of taxonomic relations (e.g., IS-A, PART-OF, SIBLING) to extract instances from corpora. These instances are then used to extract new patterns which are in turn used to find new instances and so on. Clustering-based approaches have been mostly employed to discover IS-A and SIBLING relations (Lin, 1998; Caraballo, 1999; Pantel and Ravichandran, 2004). A common assumption is that words are related if they occur in similar contexts and thus clustering algorithms group words together if they share contextual features. Most of these algorithms aim at inducing flat clusters rather than taxonomies, with the exception of Brown et al. (1992) whose method induces binary trees.

Contrary to the plethora of algorithms developed for relation discovery, methods dedicated to taxonomy learning have been few and far between. Caraballo (1999) was the first to induce a taxonomy from a corpus using a combination of clustering and pattern-based methods. Specifically, nouns are organized into a tree using a bottom-up clustering algorithm and internal nodes of the resulting tree are labeled with hypernyms from the nouns clustered underneath using patterns such as "B is a kind of A".

Kozareva et al. (2008) and Navigli et al. (2011) both develop systems that create taxonomies end-to-end, i.e., discover the terms, their relations, and how these are hierarchically organized. The two approaches are conceptually similar: they both use the web and pattern-based methods for finding domain-specific terms. Additionally, in both approaches the acquired knowledge is represented as a graph from which a taxonomy is induced using task-specific algorithms such as graph pruning, edge weighting, and so on.

Our work also addresses taxonomy learning, however, without the term discovery step — we assume we are given the terms for which to create a taxonomy. Similarly to Kozareva et al. (2008) and Navigli et al. (2011), our model operates over a graph whose nodes represent terms and edges their relationships. We construct this graph from a corpus simply by taking account of the distributional similarity of the terms in question. Our taxonomy induction algorithm is conceptually simpler and more general; it fits a taxonomy to the observed network data using the tools of statistical inference, combining a maximum likelihood approach with a Monte Carlo Sampling algorithm. The technique allows us to sample hierarchical random graphs with probability proportional to the likelihood that they generate the observed network. The induction algorithm can operate over any kind of (undirected) graph, and thus does not have to be tuned specifically for different inputs. We should also point out that our formulation of the inference problem utilizes very little corpus external knowledge other than the set of input terms, and could thus be easily applied to domains or languages where lexical resources are scarce.

The Hierarchical Random Graph model (Clauset et al., 2008) has been applied to construct hierarchical decompositions from three sets of network data: a bacterial metabolic network; a food-web among grassland species; and the network of associations among terrorist cells. The only language-related application we are aware of concerns word sense induction. Klapaftis and Manandhar (2010) create a graph of contexts for a polysemous target word and use the HRG to organize them hierarchically, under the assumption that different tree heights correspond to different levels of sense granularity.

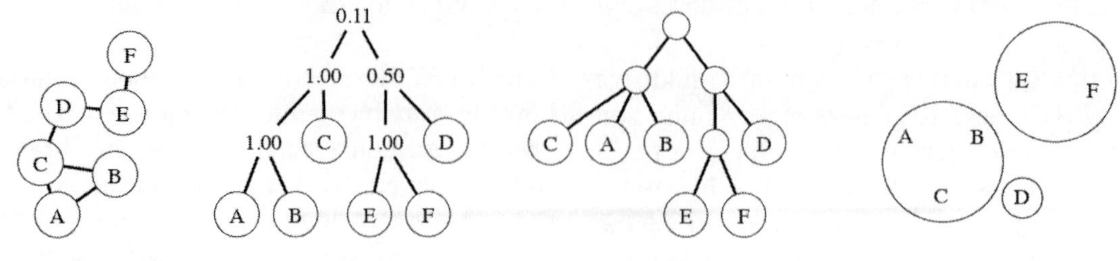

(a) Input graph (b) Binary tree (c) Hierarchy (d) Clusters

Figure 1: Flow of information through the Hierarchical Random Graph algorithm. From a semantic network (1a), the model constructs a binary tree (1b). Edges in the semantic network are then used to compute the θ parameters for internal nodes in the tree; the maximum-likelihood-estimated θ parameter for an internal node indicates the density of edges between its children. This tree is then resampled using the θ parameters (1b) until the MCMC process converges, at which point it can be collapsed into a n-ary hierarchy (1c). The same collapsing process can be also used to identify a flat clustering (1d).

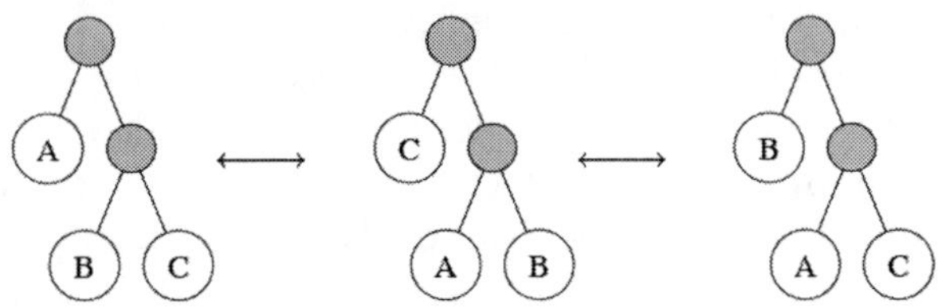

Figure 2: Any internal node with subtrees A, B and C can be permuted to one of two possible alternate configurations. Shaded nodes represent internal nodes which are unmodified by such permutation.

3 The Hierarchical Random Graph Model

A HRG consists of a binary tree and a set of likelihood parameters, and operates on input organized into a *semantic network*, an undirected graph in which nodes represent terms and edges between nodes indicate a relationship between pairs of terms (Figure 1a). From this representation, the model constructs a binary tree whose leaves correspond to nodes in the semantic network (Figure 1b); the model then employs a simple Markov chain Monte Carlo (MCMC) process in order to explore the space of possible binary trees and derives a consensus hierarchical structure from the ensemble of sampled models (Figure 1c).

3.1 Representing a Hierarchical Structure

Formally, we denote a semantic network $S = (V, E)$, where $V = \{v_1, v_2 \dots v_n\}$ is the set of vertices, one per term, and E is the set of edges between terms in which $E_{a,b}$ indicates the presence of an edge between v_a and v_b.

Given a network S, we construct a binary tree D whose n leaves correspond to V and whose $n-1$ internal nodes denote a hierarchy over V. Because the leaves remain constant for a given S, we define D as the set of internal nodes $D = \{D_1, D_2 \dots D_n\}$ and associate each edge $E_{a,b} \in E$ with an internal node D_i being the lowest common parent of $a, b \in V$. The core assumption underlying the HRG model is that edges in S have a non-uniform and independent probability of existing. Each possible edge $E_{a,b} \in E$ exists with a probability θ_i, where θ_i is associated with the corresponding internal node D_i.

For a given internal node D_i, let L_i and R_i be the number of leaves in D_i's left and right subtrees, respectively; let E_i be the number of edges in E associated with D_i (colloquially, the number of edges in S between leaves in D_i's left and right subtrees). For each $D_i \in D$, we can estimate the maximum likelihood for the corresponding θ_i as $\theta_i = \frac{E_i}{L_i R_i}$. The likelihood $\mathcal{L}(D, \theta | S)$ of a HRG over a given semantic network S is then given by:

$$\mathcal{L}(D, \theta | S) = \prod_{i=1}^{n-1} (\theta_i)^{E_i} (1 - \theta_i)^{L_i R_i - E_i} \quad (1)$$

3.2 Markov Chain Monte Carlo Sampling

Given a representation for a HRG $\mathcal{H}(D, \theta)$ and a method for estimating the likelihood of a given D and θ, we can focus on obtaining the binary tree D which best fits (or most plausibly explains) a given semantic network. Because the space of possible binary trees over V is super-exponential with respect to $|V|$, we employ a MCMC process to sample from the space of binary trees. During each iteration of

Algorithm 1: MCMC Sampling

Compute the likelihood $\mathcal{L}(D,\theta)$ of the current binary tree.
Pick a random internal node $D_i \in D$.
Randomly permute D_i according to Figure 2.
Compute the likelihood $\hat{\mathcal{L}}(D,\theta)$ of the modified binary tree.
if $\hat{\mathcal{L}}(D,\theta) > \mathcal{L}(D,\theta)$ **then**
    accept the transition;
else
    accept with probability $\hat{\mathcal{L}}(D,\theta)/\mathcal{L}(D,\theta)$ (i.e., standard Metropolis acceptance).
end
Repeat;

Algorithm 2: Flat Clusters

1 Let D_k be the root node of D.
2 **if** $\theta_k > \bar{\theta}$ **then**
3   output the leaves of the subtree rooted at D_k as a cluster
4 **else**
5   repeat 2 with left and right children of D_k.
6 **end**

this process we randomly select a node within the tree and permute it according to Figure 2. If this permutation improves the overall likelihood of the dendrogram we accept it as a transition, otherwise it is accepted with a probability proportional to the degree to which it decreases the overall likelihood (i.e. standard Metropolis acceptance). This procedure is described in more detail in Algorithm 1.

3.3 Consensus Hierarchy

Once the MCMC process has converged, the model is left with a binary tree over the terms from the input semantic network. As in standard hierarchical clustering, however, this imposes an arbitrary structure which may or may not correspond to the observed data — the tree at convergence will be similar to an ideal tree given the graph, but may not be the most plausible structure. Indeed, for taxonomy induction it is quite unlikely that a binary tree will provide the most appropriate categorization.

To avoid encoding such bias we employ a model averaging technique to produce a *consensus hierarchy*. For a set of binary trees sampled after convergence, we first identify the set of possible clusters encoded in the tree, e.g., the binary tree in Figure 1b encodes the clusters $\{AB, ABC, EF, D, DEF, ABCDEF\}$. As in Clauset et al. (2008), each cluster instance is then weighted according to the likelihood of the originating HRG (Equation 1); we then sum the weights for each distinct cluster across all resampled trees and discard those whose aggregate weight is lower than 50% of the total observed weight. The remaining clusters are then used to reconstruct a hierarchy in which each subtree appears in the majority of trees observed after the sampling process has reached convergence, hence the term consensus hierarchy.

3.4 Obtaining Flat Clusters

For evaluation purposes we may want to compare the groupings created by the HRG to a simpler non-hierarchical clustering algorithm (see Section 4 for details). We thus defined a method of converting the tree produced by the HRG into a flat (hard) clustering. This can be done in a relatively straightforward, principled fashion using the HRG's θ parameters. For a given $\mathcal{H}(D,\theta)$ we identify internal nodes whose θ_k likelihood is greater than the mean likelihood and who possess no parent node whose θ_k likelihood is also greater than the mean. Each such node is the root of a densely-connected subtree; each such subtree is then assumed to represent a single discrete cluster of related items, where $\bar{\theta} = mean(\theta)$ (illustrated in Figure 1c). This procedure is explained in greater detail in Algorithm 2.

4 Evaluation

Data We evaluated our taxonomy induction algorithm using McRae et al.'s (2005) dataset which consists of for 541 basic level nouns (e.g., DOG and TABLE). Each noun is associated with features (e.g., *has-legs*, *is-flat*, and *made-of-wood* for TABLE) collected from human participants in multiple studies over several years. The original norming study does not include class labels for these nouns, however, we were able to exploit a clustering provided by Fountain and Lapata (2010), in which a set of online participants annotated each of the McRae et al. nouns with basic category labels.

The nouns and their class labels were further taxonomized using WordNet (Fellbaum, 1998). Specifically, we first identified the full hypernym path in WordNet for each noun in McRae et al.'s (2005) dataset, e.g., APPLE > PLANT STRUCTURE > NAT-

URAL OBJECT > PHYSICAL OBJECT > ENTITY (a total of 493 concepts appear in both). These hypernym paths were then combined to yield a full taxonomy over McRae et al.'s nouns; internal nodes having only a single child were recursively removed to produce a final, compact taxonomy[1] containing 186 semantic classes (e.g., ANIMALS, WEAPONS, FRUITS) organized into varying levels of granularity (e.g., SONGBIRDS > BIRDS >ANIMALS).

Evaluation measures Evaluation of taxonomically organized information is notoriously hard (see Hovy (2002) for an extensive discussion on this topic). This is due to the nature of the task which is inherently subjective and application specific (e.g., a dolphin can be a Mammal to a biologist, but a Fish to a fisherman or someone visiting an aquarium). Nevertheless, we assessed the taxonomies produced by the HRG against the WordNet-like taxonomy described above using two measures, one that simply evaluates the grouping of the nouns into classes without taking account of their position in the taxonomy and one which evaluates the taxonomy directly.

To evaluate a flat clustering into classes we use the F-score measure introduced in the SemEval 2007 task (Agirre and Soroa, 2007); it is the harmonic mean of precision and recall defined as the number of correct members of a cluster divided by the number of items in the cluster and the number of items in the gold-standard class, respectively. Although informative, evaluation based solely on F-score puts the HRG model at a comparative disadvantage as the task of taxonomy induction is significantly more difficult than simple clustering. To overcome this disadvantage we propose an automatic method of evaluating taxonomies directly by first computing the walk distance between pairs of terms that share a gold-standard category label within a gold-standard and a candidate taxonomy, and then computing the pairwise correlation between distances in each tree (Lapointe, 1995). This captures the intuition that a 'good' hierarchy is one in which items appearing near one another in the gold taxonomy also appear near one another in the induced one. It is also conceptually similar to the task-based IS-A evaluation (Snow et al., 2006) which has been traditionally used to evaluate taxonomies.

Formally, let $G = \{g_{0,1}, g_{0,2} \dots g_{n,n-1}\}$, where $g_{a,b}$ indicates the walk distance between terms a and b in the gold standard hierarchy. Similarly, let $C = \{c_{0,1}, c_{0,2} \dots c_{n,n-1}\}$, where $c_{a,b}$ is the distance between a and b in the candidate hierarchy. The *tree-height correlation* between G and C is then given by Spearman's ρ correlation coefficient between the two sets. All tree-height correlations reported in our experiments were computed using the WordNet-based gold-standard taxonomy over McRae et al.'s (2005) nouns.

Baselines We compared the HRG output against three baselines. The first is Chinese Whispers (CW; Biemann (2006)), a randomized graph-clustering algorithm which like the HRG also takes as input a graph with weighted edges. It produces a hard (flat) clustering over the nodes in the graph, where the number of clusters is determined automatically. Our second baseline is Brown et al.'s (1992) agglomerative clustering algorithm that induces a mapping from word types to classes. It starts with K classes for the K most frequent word types and then proceeds by alternately adding the next most frequent word to the class set and merging the two classes which result in the least decrease in the mutual information between class bigrams. The result is a class hierarchy with word types at the leaves. Additionally, we compare against standard agglomerative clustering (Sokal and Michener, 1958) which produces a binary dendrogram in a bottom-up fashion by recursively identifying concepts or clusters with the highest pairwise similarity.

In the following, we present our taxonomy induction experiments (Sections 4.1–4.3). Since HRGs provide a means of inducing a hierarchy over a graph-based representation, which may be constructed in an arbitrary fashion, our experiments were designed to investigate how the topology and quality of the input graph influences the algorithm's performance. We thus report results when the semantic network is created from data sources of varying quality and granularity.

4.1 Experiment 1: Taxonomy Induction from Feature Norms

Method We first considered the case where the input graph is of high semantic quality and constructed a semantic network from the feature norms collected by McRae et al. (2005). Each noun was represented as a vector with dimensions corresponding to the possible features generated by participants of the norming study; the value of a term along a dimen-

[1] The taxonomy and flat cluster labels are available from http://homepages.inf.ed.ac.uk/s0897549/data.

Method	F-score	Tree Correlation
HRG	**0.507**	**0.168**
CW	0.464	—
Agglo	0.352	0.137

Table 1: Cluster F-score and tree-height correlation evaluation; a semantic network constructed over McRae et al.'s (2005) nouns and features is given as input to the algorithms.

sion was taken to be the frequency with which participants generated the corresponding feature when given the term. For each pair of terms an edge was added to the semantic network if the cosine similarity between their vector representations exceeded a fixed threshold T (set to 0.15).

The resulting network was then provided as input to the HRG, which was resampled until convergence. The binary tree at convergence was collapsed into a hierarchy over clusters using the procedure described in Section 3.4; this hierarchy was evaluated by computing the cluster F-score between its constituent clusters and those of a gold-standard (human-produced) clustering. The resulting consensus hierarchy was evaluated by computing the tree-height correlation between it and the gold-standard (WordNet-derived) hierarchy.

Results Our results are summarized in Table 1. We only give the tree correlation for the HRG and agglomerative methods (Agglo) as CW does not induce a hierarchical clustering. In addition, we do not compare against Brown et al. (1992) as the input to this algorithm is not vector-based. When evaluated using F-score, the HRG algorithm produces better quality clusters compared to CW, in addition to being able to organize them hierarchically. It also outperforms agglomerative clustering by a large margin. A similar pattern emerges when the HRG and Agglo are evaluated on tree correlation. The taxonomies produced by the HRG are a better fit against the WordNet-based gold standard; the difference in performance is statistically significant ($p < 0.01$) using a t-test (Cohen and Cohen., 1983).

4.2 Experiment 2: Taxonomy Induction from the British National Corpus

Method The results of Experiment 1 can be considered as an upper bound of what can be achieved by the HRG when the input graph is constructed from highly accurate semantic information. Feature norms provide detailed knowledge about meaning which would be very difficult if not close to impossible to obtain from a corpus. Nevertheless, it is interesting to explore how well we can induce taxonomies using a lower quality semantic network. We therefore constructed a network based on co-occurrence statistics computed from the British National Corpus (BNC, 2007) and provided the resulting semantic network as input to the HRG, CW, and Agglo models; additionally, we employed the algorithm of Brown et al. (1992) to induce a hierarchy over the target terms directly from the corpus. Unfortunately, this algorithm requires the number of desired output clusters to be specified in advance; in all trials this parameter was set to the number of clusters in the gold-standard clustering (41), thus providing the Brown-induced clusterings with a slight oracle advantage.

Again, nouns were represented as vectors in semantic space. We used a context window of five words on either side of the target word and 5,000 vector components corresponding to the most frequent non-stopwords in the BNC. Raw frequency counts were transformed using pointwise mutual information (PMI). An edge was added to the semantic network between a pair of nouns if their similarity exceeded a predefined threshold (the same as in Experiment 1). The similarity of two nouns was defined as the cosine distance between their corresponding vectors.

The HRG algorithm was used to produce a taxonomy from this network and was also compared against Brown et al. (1992). The latter induces a hierarchy from a corpus directly, without the intermediate graph representation. All resulting taxonomies were evaluated against gold standard flat and hierarchical clusterings, again as in Experiment 1.

Results Results are shown in Table 2. With regard to flat clustering (the F-score column in the table), the HRG has a slight advantage against CW, and Brown et al.'s (1992) algorithm (Brown). However, differences in performance are not statistically significant. Agglomerative clustering is the worst performing method leading to a decrease in F-score of approximately 1.5. With regard to tree correlation, the output of the HGRG is comparable to Brown (the difference between the two is not statistically significant). Both algorithms are significantly better ($p < 0.01$) than Agglo.

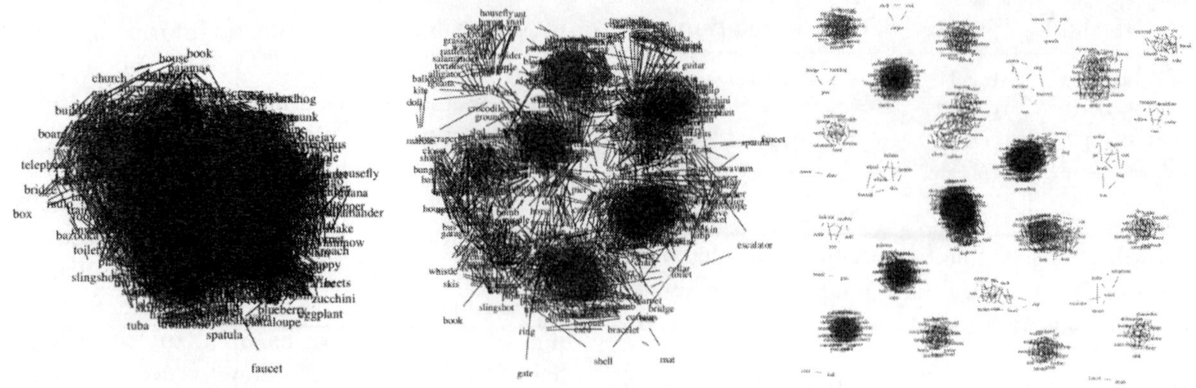

(a) $s = 0.0$ (b) $s = 0.5$ (c) $s = 1.0$

Figure 3: The original semantic network as derived from the BNC (a) and the same network re-weighted using a flat clustering produced by CW (b). As s approaches 1.0 the network exhibits an increasingly strong small-world property, eventually reconstructing the input clustering only (c).

Method	F-score	Tree Correlation
HRG	**0.276**	0.104
CW	0.274	—
Brown	0.258	**0.124**
Agglo	0.122	0.077

Table 2: Cluster F-score and tree-height correlation evaluation for taxonomies inferred over McRae et al.'s (2005) nouns; all algorithms are run on the BNC.

Performance of the HRG is better when the semantic network is based on feature norms (compare Tables 1 and 2), both in terms of tree-height correlation and F-score. This suggests that the algorithm is highly dependent on the quality of the semantic network used as input. In particular, HRGs are known to be more appropriate for so-called *small-world* networks, graphs composed of densely-connected subgraphs with relatively sparse connections between (Klapaftis and Manandhar, 2010). Indeed, inspection of the semantic network produced from the BNC (see Figure 3a) shows that our corpus-derived graph is emphatically *not* a small-world graph, yet the HRG is able to recover some taxonomic information from such a densely-connected network.

In the following experiments we first assess the difficulty of the taxonomy induction task to get a feel of how well the algorithms are performing in comparison to humans and then investigate ways of rendering the BNC-based graph more similar to a small-world network.

4.3 Experiment 3: Human Upper Bound

Method The previous experiments evaluated the performance of the HRG against a gold-standard hierarchy derived from WordNet. For any set of concepts there will exist multiple valid taxonomies, each representing an accurate if differing organization of identical concepts using different criteria; for the set of concepts used in Experiments 1–2 the WordNet hierarchy represents merely one of many valid hierarchies. Noting this, it is interesting to explore how well the hierarchies output by the model fit within the set of *possible, valid* taxonomies over a given set of concepts.

We thus conducted an experiment in which human participants were asked to organize words into arbitrary hierarchies. To render the task feasible, they were given a small subset of 12 words rather than the full set of 541 nouns over which the HRG operates. We first selected a sub-hierarchy of the WordNet tree ('living things') along with its subtrees (e.g., 'animals', 'plants'), and chose target concepts from within these trees in order to produce a taxonomy in which some items were differentiated at a high level (e.g., 'python' vs. 'dog') and others at a fine-grained level (e.g., 'lion' vs 'tiger'). The experiment was conducted using Amazon Mechanical Turk[2], and involved 41 participants, all self-reported native English speakers. No guidelines as to what features participants were to use when organizing these concepts were provided. Participants were presented with a web-based, graphical, mouse-driven interface for constructing a taxonomy over the cho-

[2] `http://mturk.com`

Method	Tree Correlation	Min	Max	Std
HRG	**0.412**	-0.039	0.799	0.166
Brown	0.181	0.006	0.510	0.121
Agglo	0.274	-0.056	0.603	0.121
Agreement	0.511	-0.109	1.000	0.267

Table 3: Model performance on a subset of the target words used in Experiments 1–2, applied to a subset of the semantic network used in Experiment 2. Instead of a WordNet-derived hierarchy, models were evaluated against hierarchies manually produced by participants in an online study. Tree correlation values are means; we also report the minimum (Min), maximum (Max), and standard deviation (Std) of the mean.

sen set of concepts.

To evaluate the HRG, along with the baselines from Experiment 2, against the resulting hierarchies we constructed a semantic network over the subset of concepts using similarities derived from the BNC; this network was a subgraph of that used in Experiment 2. We compute *inter-annotator agreement* as the mean pairwise tree-height correlation between the hierarchies our participants produced. We also report for each model the mean tree-height correlation between the hierarchy it produced and those created by human annotators.

Results As shown in Table 3, participants achieve a mean pairwise tree correlation of 0.511. This indicates that there is a fair amount of agreement with respect to the taxonomic organization of the words in question. The HRG comes close achieving a mean tree correlation of 0.412, followed by Agglo, and Brown. In general, we observe that the HRG manages to produce hierarchies that resemble those generated by humans to a larger extent than competing algorithms. The results in Table 3 also hint at the fact that the taxonomy induction task is relatively hard as participants do not achieve perfect agreement despite the fact that they are asked to taxonomize only 12 words.

4.4 Experiment 4: Taxonomy Induction from a Small-world Network

Method In Experiment 2 we hypothesized that a small-world input graph would be more advantageous for the HRG. In order to explore this further, we imposed something of a small-world structure on

Method	F-score	Tree Correlation
HRG	0.276	0.104
HRG + CW	**0.291**	0.161
HRG + Brown	0.255	**0.173**

Table 4: Cluster F-score and tree-height correlation evaluation for taxonomies inferred by the HRG using semantic network derived from the BNC and reweighted using CW and Brown.

the BNC semantic network, using a combination of the baseline clustering methods evaluated in Experiment 2. Specifically, we first obtain a (flat) clustering using either CW or Brown, which we then use to re-weight the BNC graph given as input to the HRG.[3] Note that, as the clustering algorithms used are unsupervised this procedure does not introduce any outside supervision into the overall taxonomy induction task.

The modified weight $\widehat{W}_{A,B}$ between a pair of terms A, B was computed according to Equation (2), where s indicates the proportion of edge weight drawn from the clustering, $W_{A,B}$ is the edge weight in the original (BNC) semantic network, and $C_{A,B}$ is a binary value indicating that A and B belong to the same cluster (i.e., $C_{A,B} = 1$ if A and B share a cluster; $C_{A,B} = 0$ otherwise).

$$\widehat{W}_{A,B} = (1-s)W_{A,B} + sC_{A,B} \qquad (2)$$

The value of the s parameter was tuned empirically on held-out development data and set to $s = 0.4$ for both CW and Brown algorithms. Each re-weighted network was then used as input to an HRG, and the resulting taxonomies were evaluated in the same manner as in Experiments 1 and 2.

Results Table 4 shows results for cluster F-score and tree-height correlation for the HRG when using a graph derived from the BNC without any modifications, and two re-weighted versions using the CW and Brown clustering algorithms, respectively. As can been seen, re-weighting improves tree-height correlation substantially: HRG with CW and Brown is significantly better than HRG on its own ($p < 0.05$). In the case of CW, cluster F-score also yields a slight improvement. Interestingly, the tree-height correlations obtained with CW and Brown are comparable to those attained by the HRG

[3]We omit agglomerative clustering as it performed poorly on the BNC, see Table 2.

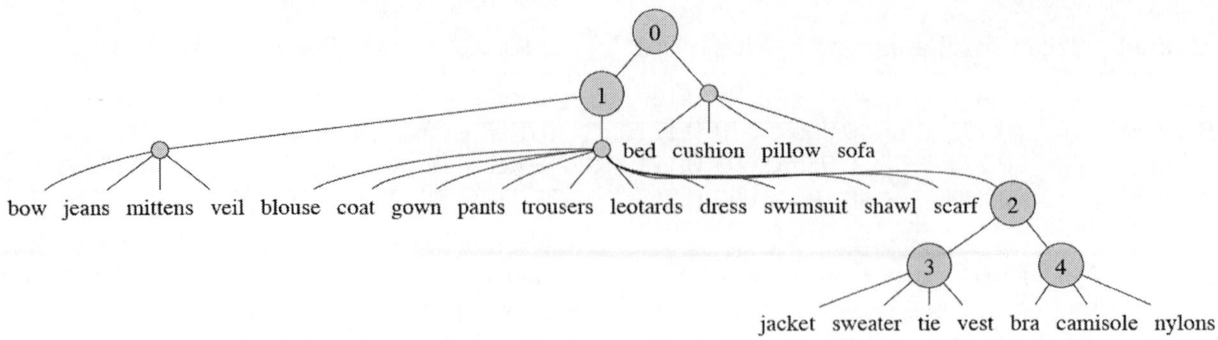

Figure 4: An excerpt from a hierarchy induced by the HRG, using the BNC semantic network with Brown re-weighting. The HRG does not provide category labels for internal nodes of the hierarchy, but subtrees within this excerpt correspond roughly to (0) TEXTILES, (1) CLOTHING, (2) GENDERED CLOTHING, (3) MEN'S CLOTHING, and (4) WOMEN'S CLOTHING.

when using the human-produced feature norms (differences in correlations are not statistically significant). An excerpt of a HRG-induced taxonomy is shown in Figure 4.

5 Conclusions

In this paper we have presented a novel method for automatically inducing lexical taxonomies based on Hierarchical Random Graphs. The approach is conceptually simple, taking a graph representation as input and fitting a taxonomy via combination of a maximum likelihood approach with a Monte Carlo Sampling algorithm. Importantly, the approach does not operate on corpora directly, instead it relies on an abstract, interim representation (a semantic network) which we argue is advantageous, as it allows to easily encode additional information in the input. Furthermore, the model presented here is largely parameter-free, as both the input graph and the inferred taxonomy are derived empirically in an unsupervised manner (minimal tuning is required when graph re-weighting is employed, the parameter s).

Our experiments have shown that both the input semantic network and the representation of its nodes influence the quality of the induced taxonomy. Representing the terms of the taxonomy as vectors in a human-produced feature space yields more coherent semantic classes compared to a corpus-based vector representation (see the F-score in Tables 1 and 4). This is not surprising, as feature norms provide more detailed and accurate knowledge about semantic representations than often noisy and approximate corpus-based distributions.[4] It may be possible to obtain better performance when considering more elaborate representations. We have only experimented with a simple semantic space, however variants that utilize syntactic information (e.g., Padó and Lapata (2007)) may be more appropriate for the taxonomy induction task. Our experiments have also shown that the topology of the input semantic network is critical for the success of the HRG. In particular edge re-weighting plays an important role and generally improves performance. We have adopted a simple method based on flat clustering; it may be interesting to compare how this fares with more involved weighting schemes such as those described in Navigli et al. (2011). Finally, we have shown that naive participants are able to perform the taxonomy induction task relatively reliably and that the HRG approximates human performance on a small-scale experiment. We have evaluated model output using F-score and tree-height correlation which we argue are complementary and allow to assess hierarchical clustering more rigorously.

Avenues for future work are many and varied. Besides exploring the performance of our algorithm on more specialized domains (e.g., mathematics or geography) we would also like to create an incremental version that augments an existing taxonomy with missing information. Additionally, the taxonomies inferred with the HRG do not currently admit term ambiguity which we could remedy by modifying our technique for constructing a consensus hierarchy to reflect the sampled frequency of observed subtrees.

[4]Note that as multiple participants are required to create a representation for each word, norming studies typically involve a small number of items, consequently limiting the scope of any computational model based on normed data.

References

Eneko Agirre and Aitor Soroa. 2007. Semeval-2007 task 02: Evaluating word sense induction and discrimination systems. In *Proceedings of the 4th International Workshop on Semantic Evaluations (SemEval-2007)*, pages 7–12, Prague, Czech Republic, June.

Matthew Berland and Eugene Charniak. 1999. Finding parts in very large corpora. In *Proceedings of the 37th Annual Meeting of the Association for Computational Linguistics*, pages 57–64, College Park, Maryland.

Chris Biemann. 2006. Chinese whispers - an efficient graph clustering algorithm and its application to natural language processing problems. In *Proceedings of TextGraphs: the 1st Workshop on Graph Based Methods for Natural Language Processing*, pages 73–80, New York City.

BNC. 2007. *The British National Corpus, version 3 (BNC XML Edition)*. Distributed by Oxford University Computing Services on behalf of the BNC Consortium.

Peter F. Brown, Vincent J. Della Pietra, Peter V. de Souza, Jenifer C. Lai, and Robert L. Mercer. 1992. Class-based *n*-gram models of natural language. *Computational Linguistics*, 18:467–479.

Sharon A. Caraballo. 1999. Automatic construction of a hypernym-labeled noun hierarchy from text. In *Proceedings of the 37th Annual Meeting of the Association for Computational Linguistics*, pages 120–126, College Park, Maryland.

Aaron Clauset, Christopher Moore, and M. E. J. Newman. 2008. Hierarchical structure and the prediction of missing links in networks. *Nature*, 453:98–101, February.

J. Cohen and P. Cohen. 1983. *Applied Multiple Regression/Correlation Analysis for the Behavioral Sciences*. Erlbaum, Hillsdale, NJ.

Oren Etzioni, Michael Cafarella, Doug Downey, Ana-Maria Popescu, Tal Shaked, Stephen Soderland, Daniel S. Weld, and Alexander Yates. 2005. Unsupervised named-entity extraction from the web: An experimental study. *Artificial Intelligence*, 165(1):91–134.

Christiane Fellbaum. 1998. *WordNet: An Electronic Lexical Database (Language, Speech, and Communication)*. The MIT Press.

Trevor Fountain and Mirella Lapata. 2010. Meaning representation in natural language categorization. In Stellan Ohlsson and Richard Catrambone, editors, *Proceedings of the 31st Annual Conference of the Cognitive Science Society*, pages 1916–1921, Portland, Oregon. Cognitive Science Society.

Maayan Geffet and Ido Dagan. 2005. The distributional inclusion hypotheses and lexical entailment. In *Proceedings of the 43rd Annual Meeting of the Association for Computational Linguistics*, pages 107–114, Ann Arbor, Michigan.

Roxana Girju, Adriana Badulescu, and Dan Moldovan. 2003. Learning semantic constraints for the automatic discovery of part-whole relations. In *Proceedings of the 2003 Human Language Technology Conference of the North American Chapter of the Association for Computational Linguistics*, pages 80–87, Edmonton, Canada.

Sanda M. Harabgiu, Steven J. Maiorano, and Marius A. Paşca. 2003. Open-doman textual question answering techniques. *Natural Language Engineering*, 9(3):1–38.

Marti A. Hearst. 1992. Automatic acquisition of hyponyms from large text corpora. In *Proceedings of the 14th conference on Computational linguistics*, pages 539–545, Nantes, France.

Eduard Hovy. 2002. Comparing sets of semantic relationships in ontologies. In Rebecca Green, Carol A. Bean, and Sun Hyon Myaeng, editors, *The Semantics of Relationships: An Interdisciplinary Perspective*, pages 91–110. Kluwer Academic Publishers, The Netherlands.

Chihli Hung, Stefan Wermter, and Peter Smith. 2004. Hybrid neural document clustering using guided self-organization and wordnet. *IEEE Intelligent Systems*, 19(2):68–77.

Ioannis Klapaftis and Suresh Manandhar. 2010. Word sense induction and disambiguation using hierarchical random graphs. In *Proceedings of the 2010 Conference on Empirical Methods in Natural Language Processing*, pages 745–755, Cambridge, MA.

Zornitsa Kozareva and Eduard Hovy. 2010. Learning arguments and supertypes of semantic relations using recursive patterns. In *Proceedings of the 48th Annual Meeting of the Association for Computational Linguistics*, pages 1482–1491, Uppsala, Sweden, July.

Zornitsa Kozareva, Ellen Riloff, and Eduard Hovy. 2008. Semantic class learning from the web with hyponym pattern linkage graphs. In *Proceedings of ACL-08: HLT*, pages 1048–1056, Columbus, Ohio, June.

François-Joseph Lapointe. 1995. Comparison tests for dendrograms: A comparative evaluation. *Journal of Classification 12:265-282*, 12:265–282.

Dekang Lin. 1998. Automatic retrieval and clustering of similar words. In *Proceedings of the 36th Annual Meeting of the Association for Computational Linguistics and 17th International Conference on Computational Linguistics, Volume 2*, pages 768–774, Montreal, Quebec, Canada.

Ken McRae, George S. Cree, Mark S. Seidenberg, and Chris McNorgan. 2005. Semantic feature production norms for a large set of living and non-living things.

Behavioral Research Methods Instruments & Computers, 37(4):547–559.

Roberto Navigli, Paola Velardi, and Stefano Faralli. 2011. A graph-based algorithm for inducing lexical taxonomies from scratch. In *Proceedings of the 22nd International Joint Conference on Artificial Intelligence*, pages 1872–1877, Barcelona, Spain.

Sebastian Padó and Mirella Lapata. 2007. Dependency-based construction of semantic space models. *Computational Linguistics*, 33(2):161–199.

Patrick Pantel and Deepak Ravichandran. 2004. Automatically labeling semantic classes. In Daniel Marcu Susan Dumais and Salim Roukos, editors, *HLT-NAACL 2004: Main Proceedings*, pages 321–328, Boston, Massachusetts.

Brian Roark and Eugene Charniak. 1998. Noun-phrase co-occurrence statistics for semi-automatic semantic lexicon construction. In *Proceedings of the 36th Annual Meeting of the Association for Computational Linguistics and 17th International Conference on Computational Linguistics, Volume 2*, pages 1110–1116, Montreal, Quebec.

Rion Snow, Daniel Jurafsky, and Andrew Y. Ng. 2006. Semantic taxonomy induction from heterogenous evidence. In *Proceedings of the 21st International Conference on Computational Linguistics and 44th Annual Meeting of the Association for Computational Linguistics*, pages 801–808, Sydney, Australia.

Robert Sokal and Charles Michener. 1958. A statistical method for evaluating systematic relationships. *University of Kansas Science Bulletin*, 38:1409–1438.

Hui Yang and Jamie Callan. 2009. A metric-based framework for automatic taxonomy induction. In *Proceedings of the Joint Conference of the 47th Annual Meeting of the ACL and the 4th International Joint Conference on Natural Language Processing of the AFNLP*, pages 271–279, Suntec, Singapore.

Cross-lingual Word Clusters for Direct Transfer of Linguistic Structure

Oscar Täckström*
SICS / Uppsala University
Kista / Uppsala, Sweden
oscar@sics.se

Ryan McDonald
Google
New York, NY
ryanmcd@google.com

Jakob Uszkoreit
Google
Mountain View, CA
uszkoreit@google.com

Abstract

It has been established that incorporating word cluster features derived from large unlabeled corpora can significantly improve prediction of linguistic structure. While previous work has focused primarily on English, we extend these results to other languages along two dimensions. First, we show that these results hold true for a number of languages across families. Second, and more interestingly, we provide an algorithm for inducing cross-lingual clusters and we show that features derived from these clusters significantly improve the accuracy of cross-lingual structure prediction. Specifically, we show that by augmenting direct-transfer systems with cross-lingual cluster features, the relative error of delexicalized dependency parsers, trained on English treebanks and transferred to foreign languages, can be reduced by up to 13%. When applying the same method to direct transfer of named-entity recognizers, we observe relative improvements of up to 26%.

1 Introduction

The ability to predict the linguistic structure of sentences or documents is central to the field of natural language processing (NLP). Structures such as named-entity tag sequences (Bikel et al., 1999) or sentiment relations (Pang and Lee, 2008) are inherently useful in data mining, information retrieval and other user-facing technologies. More fundamental structures such as part-of-speech tag sequences (Ratnaparkhi, 1996) or syntactic parse trees (Collins, 1997; Kübler et al., 2009), on the other hand, comprise the core linguistic analysis for many important downstream tasks such as machine translation (Chiang, 2005; Collins et al., 2005). Currently, supervised data-driven methods dominate the literature on linguistic structure prediction (Smith, 2011). Regrettably, the majority of studies on these methods have focused on evaluations specific to English, since it is the language with the most annotated resources. Notable exceptions include the CoNLL shared tasks (Tjong Kim Sang, 2002; Tjong Kim Sang and De Meulder, 2003; Buchholz and Marsi, 2006; Nivre et al., 2007) and subsequent studies on this data, as well as a number of focused studies on one or two specific languages, as discussed by Bender (2011).

While annotated resources for parsing and several other tasks are available in a number of languages, we cannot expect to have access to labeled resources for all tasks in all languages. This fact has given rise to a large body of research on unsupervised (Klein and Manning, 2004), semi-supervised (Koo et al., 2008) and transfer (Hwa et al., 2005) systems for prediction of linguistic structure. These methods all attempt to benefit from the plethora of unlabeled monolingual and/or cross-lingual data that has become available in the digital age. Unsupervised methods are appealing in that they are often inherently language independent. This is borne out by the many recent studies on unsupervised parsing that include evaluations covering a number of languages (Cohen and Smith, 2009; Gillenwater et al., 2010; Naseem et al., 2010; Spitkovsky et al., 2011). However, the performance for most languages is still well below that of supervised systems and recent work has established that the performance is also below simple methods of linguistic transfer (McDonald et al., 2011).

In this study we focus on semi-supervised and linguistic-transfer methods for multilingual structure prediction. In particular, we pursue two lines of research around the use of word cluster features in discriminative models for structure prediction:

*The majority of this work was performed while the author was an intern at Google, New York, NY.

1. *Monolingual word cluster features induced from large corpora of text for semi-supervised learning (SSL) of linguistic structure.* Previous studies on this approach have typically focused only on a small set of languages and tasks (Freitag, 2004; Miller et al., 2004; Koo et al., 2008; Turian et al., 2010; Faruqui and Padó, 2010; Haffari et al., 2011; Tratz and Hovy, 2011). Here we show that this method is robust across 13 languages for dependency parsing and 4 languages for named-entity recognition (NER). This is the first study with such a broad view on this subject, in terms of language diversity.

2. *Cross-lingual word cluster features for transferring linguistic structure from English to other languages.* We develop an algorithm that generates cross-lingual word clusters; that is clusters of words that are consistent across languages. This is achieved by means of a probabilistic model over large amounts of monolingual data in two languages, coupled with parallel data through which cross-lingual word-cluster constraints are enforced. We show that by augmenting the delexicalized direct transfer system of McDonald et al. (2011) with cross-lingual cluster features, we are able to reduce its error by up to 13% relative. Further, we show that by applying the same method to direct-transfer NER, we achieve a relative error reduction of 26%.

By incorporating cross-lingual cluster features in a linguistic transfer system, we are for the first time combining SSL and cross-lingual transfer.

2 Monolingual Word Cluster Features

Word cluster features have been shown to be useful in various tasks in natural language processing, including syntactic dependency parsing (Koo et al., 2008; Haffari et al., 2011; Tratz and Hovy, 2011), syntactic chunking (Turian et al., 2010), and NER (Freitag, 2004; Miller et al., 2004; Turian et al., 2010; Faruqui and Padó, 2010). Intuitively, the reason for the effectiveness of cluster features lie in their ability to aggregate local distributional information from large unlabeled corpora, which aid in conquering data sparsity in supervised training regimes as well as in mitigating cross-domain generalization issues.

In line with much previous work on word clusters for tasks such as dependency parsing and NER, for which local syntactic and semantic constraints are of importance, we induce word clusters by means of a probabilistic class-based language model (Brown et al., 1992; Clark, 2003). However, rather than the more commonly used model of Brown et al. (1992), we use the predictive class bigram model introduced by Uszkoreit and Brants (2008). The two models are very similar, but whereas the former takes class-to-class transitions into account, the latter directly models word-to-class transitions. By ignoring class-to-class transitions, an approximate maximum likelihood clustering can be found efficiently with the distributed exchange algorithm (Uszkoreit and Brants, 2008). This is a useful property, as we later develop an algorithm for inducing cross-lingual word clusters that calls this monolingual algorithm as a subroutine.

More formally, let $\mathcal{C} : \mathcal{V} \mapsto 1, \ldots, K$ be a (hard) clustering function that maps each word type from the vocabulary, $\mathcal{V}$, to one of K cluster identities. With the model of Uszkoreit and Brants (2008), the likelihood of a sequence of word tokens, $\boldsymbol{w} = \langle w_i \rangle_{i=1}^{m}$, with $w_i \in \mathcal{V} \cup \{S\}$, where S is a designated start-of-segment symbol, factors as

$$L(\boldsymbol{w}; \mathcal{C}) = \prod_{i=1}^{m} p(w_i | \mathcal{C}(w_i)) p(\mathcal{C}(w_i) | w_{i-1}) . \quad (1)$$

Compare this to the model of Brown et al. (1992):

$$L'(\boldsymbol{w}; \mathcal{C}) = \prod_{i=1}^{m} p(w_i | \mathcal{C}(w_i)) p(\mathcal{C}(w_i) | \mathcal{C}(w_{i-1})) .$$

While the use of class-to-class transitions can lead to more compact models, which is often useful for conquering data sparsity, when clustering large data sets we can get reliable statistics directly on the word-to-class transitions (Uszkoreit and Brants, 2008).

In addition to the clustering model that we make use of in this study, a number of additional word clustering and embedding variants have been proposed. For example, Turian et al. (2010) assessed the effectiveness of the word embedding techniques of Collobert and Weston (2008) and Mnih and Hinton (2007) along with the word clustering technique of Brown et al. (1992) for syntactic chunking and NER. Recently, Dhillon et al. (2011) proposed a word

Single words	$S_0c\{p\}$, $N_0c\{p\}$, $N_1c\{p\}$, $N_2c\{p\}$
Word pairs	$S_0c\{p\}N_0c\{p\}$, S_0pcN_0p, S_0pN_0pc, S_0wN_0c, S_0cN_0w, N_0cN_1c, N_1cN_2c
Word triples	$N_0cN_1cN_2c$, $S_0cN_0cN_1c$, $S_{0h}cS_0cN_0c$, $S_0cS_{0l}cN_0c$, $S_0cS_{0r}cN_0c$, $S_0cN_0cN_{0l}c$
Distance	S_0cd, N_0cd, S_0cN_0cd
Valency	S_0cv_l, S_0cv_r, $N_0cS_0v_l$
Unigrams	$S_{0h}c$, $S_{0l}c$, $S_{0r}c$, $N_{0l}c$
Third-order	$S_{0h2}c$, $S_{0l2}c$, $S_{0r2}c$, $N_{0l2}c$
Label set	$S_0cS_{0l}l$, $S_0cS_{0r}l$, $N_0cN_{0l}l$, $N_0cN_{0r}l$

Table 1: Additional cluster-based parser features. S_i and N_i: the ith tokens in the stack and buffer. p: the part-of-speech tag, c: the cluster. v: the valence of the left (l) or right (r) set of children. l: the label of the token under consideration. d: distance between the words on the top of the stack and buffer. S_{ih}, S_{ir} and S_{il}: the head, right-most modifier and left-most modifier of the token at the top of the stack. $Gx\{y\}$ expands to Gxy and Gx.

Word & bias	$w_{-1,0,1}$, $w_{-1:0}$, $w_{0:1}$, $w_{-1:1}$, b
Pre-/suffix	$w_{-1,0,1}^{:1,:2,:3,:4,:5}$, $w_{-1,0,1}^{-5:,-4:,-3:,-2:,-1:}$
Orthography	$\text{Hyp}_{-1,0,1}$, $\text{Cap}_{-1,0,1}$, $\text{Cap}_{-1:0}$, $\text{Cap}_{0:1}$, $\text{Cap}_{-1:1}$
PoS	$p_{-1,0,1}$, $p_{-1:0}$, $p_{0:1}$, $p_{-1:1}$, $p_{-2:1}$, $p_{-1:2}$
Cluster	$c_{-1,0,1}$, $c_{-1:0}$, $c_{0:1}$, $c_{-1:1}$, $c_{-2:1}$, $c_{-1:2}$
Transition	$\rightarrow/p_{-1,0,1}$, $\rightarrow/c_{-1,0,1}$, $\rightarrow/\text{Cap}_{-1,0,1}$, $\rightarrow/$b

Table 2: NER features. Hyp: Word contains hyphen. Cap: First letter is capitalized. $\rightarrow/f$ - Transition from previous to current label conjoined with feature f. $w^{:j}$: j-character prefix of w. $w^{-j:}$: j-character suffix of w. f_i: Feature f at relative position i. $f_{i,j}$: Union of features at positions i and j. $f_{i:j}$: Conjoined feature sequence between relative positions i and j (inclusive). b: Bias.

embedding method based on canonical correlation analysis that provides state-of-the art results for word-based SSL for English NER. As an alternative to clustering words, Lin and Wu (2009) proposed a phrase clustering approach that obtained the state-of-the-art result for English NER.

3 Monolingual Cluster Experiments

Before moving on to the multilingual setting, we conduct a set of monolingual experiments where we evaluate the use of the monolingual word clusters just described as features for dependency parsing and NER. In the parsing experiments, we study the following thirteen languages:[1] Danish (DA), German (DE), Greek (EL), English (EN), Spanish (ES), French (FR), Italian (IT), Korean (KO), Dutch (NL), Portugese (PT), Russian (RU), Swedish (SV) and Chinese (ZH) – representing the Chinese, Germanic, Hellenic, Romance, Slavic, Altaic and Korean genera. In the NER experiments, we study three Germanic languages: German (DE), English (EN) and Dutch (NL); and one Romance language: Spanish (ES).

Details of the labeled and unlabeled data sets used are given in Appendix A. For all experiments we fixed the number of clusters to 256 as this performed well on held-out data. Furthermore, we only clustered the 1 million most frequent word types in each language for both efficiency and sparsity reasons. For languages in which our unlabeled data did not have at least 1 million types, we considered all types.

3.1 Cluster Augmented Feature Models

All of the parsing experiments reported in this study are based on the transition-based dependency parsing paradigm (Nivre, 2008). For all languages and settings, we use an arc-eager decoding strategy, with a beam of eight hypotheses, and perform ten epochs of the averaged structured perceptron algorithm (Zhang and Clark, 2008). We extend the state-of-the-art feature model recently introduced by Zhang and Nivre (2011) by adding an additional word cluster based feature template for each word based template. Additionally, we add templates where one or more part-of-speech feature is replaced with the corresponding cluster feature. The resulting set of additional feature templates are shown in Table 1. The expanded feature model includes all of the feature templates defined by Zhang and Nivre (2011), which we also use as the baseline model, whereas Table 1 only shows our new templates due to space limitations.

For all NER experiments, we use a sequential first-order conditional random field (CRF) with a unit variance Normal prior, trained with L-BFGS until ϵ-convergence ($\epsilon = 0.0001$, typically obtained after less than 400 iterations). The feature model used for the NER tagger is shown in Table 2. These are similar to the features used by Turian et al. (2010), with the main difference that we do not use any long range features and that we add templates that conjoin adjacent clusters and adjacent tags as well as templates that conjoin label transitions with tags, clusters and capitalization features.

[1]The particular choice of languages was made purely based on data availability and institution licensing.

	DA	DE	EL	EN	ES	FR	IT	KO	NL	PT	RU	SV	ZH	AVG
NO CLUSTERS	84.3	88.9	76.1	90.3	82.8	85.7	81.4	82.0	77.2	86.9	83.5	84.7	74.9	*83.0*
CLUSTERS	85.8	89.5	77.3	90.7	83.6	85.7	82.2	83.6	77.8	87.6	86.0	86.5	75.5	*84.0*

Table 3: Supervised parsing results measured with labeled attachment score (LAS) on the test set. All results are statistically significant at $p < 0.05$, except FR and NL.

	DE	EN	ES	NL	AVG
NO CLUSTERS	65.4	89.2	75.0	75.7	*76.3*
CLUSTERS	74.8	91.8	81.1	84.2	*83.0*
↑ DEVELOPMENT SET ↓ TEST SET					
NO CLUSTERS	69.1	83.5	78.9	79.6	*77.8*
CLUSTERS	74.4	87.8	82.0	85.7	*82.5*

Table 4: Supervised NER results measured with F_1-score on the CoNLL 2002/2003 development and test sets.

3.2 Results

The results of the parsing experiments, measured with labeled accuracy score (LAS) on all sentence lengths, excluding punctuation, are shown in Table 3. The baselines are all comparable to the state-of-the-art. On average, the addition of word cluster features yields a 6% relative reduction in error and upwards of 15% (for RU). All languages improve except FR, which sees neither an increase nor a decrease in LAS. We observe an average absolute increase in LAS of approximately 1%, which is inline with previous observations (Koo et al., 2008). It is perhaps not surprising that RU sees a large gain as it is a highly inflected language, making observations of lexical features far more sparse. Some languages, e.g., FR, NL, and ZH see much smaller gains. One likely culprit is a divergence between the tokenization schemes used in the treebank and in our unlabeled data, which for Indo-European languages is closely related to the Penn Treebank tokenization. For example, the NL treebank contains many multi-word tokens that are typically broken apart by our automatic tokenizer.

The NER results, in terms of F_1 measure, are listed in Table 4. Introducing word cluster features for NER reduces relative errors on the test set by 21% (39% on the development set) on average. Broken down per language, reductions on the test set vary from substantial for NL (30%) and EN (26%), down to more modest for DE (17%) and ES (12%). The addition of cluster features most markedly improve recognition of the PER category, with an average error reduction on the test set of 44%, while the reductions for ORG (19%), LOC (17%) and MISC (10%) are more modest, but still significant. Although our results are below the best reported results for EN and DE (Lin and Wu, 2009; Faruqui and Padó, 2010), the relative improvements of adding word clusters are inline with previous results on NER for EN (Miller et al., 2004; Turian et al., 2010), who report error reductions of approximately 25% from adding word cluster features. Slightly higher reductions where achieved for DE by Faruqui and Padó (2010), who report a reduction of 22%. Note that we did not tune hyper-parameters of the supervised learning methods and of the clustering method, such as the number of clusters (Turian et al., 2010; Faruqui and Padó, 2010), and that we did not apply any heuristic for data cleaning such as that used by Turian et al. (2010).

4 Cross-lingual Word Cluster Features

All results of the previous section rely on the availability of large quantities of language specific annotations for each task. Cross-lingual transfer methods and unsupervised methods have recently been shown to hold promise as a way to at least partially sidestep the demand for labeled data. Unsupervised methods attempt to infer linguistic structure without using any annotated data (Klein and Manning, 2004) or possibly by using a set of linguistically motivated rules (Naseem et al., 2010) or a linguistically informed model structure (Berg-Kirkpatrick and Klein, 2010). The aim of transfer methods is instead to use knowledge induced from labeled resources in one or more *source* languages to construct systems for *target* languages in which no or few such resources are available (Hwa et al., 2005). Currently, the performance of even the most simple direct transfer systems far exceeds that of unsupervised systems (Cohen et al., 2011; McDonald et al., 2011; Søgaard, 2011).

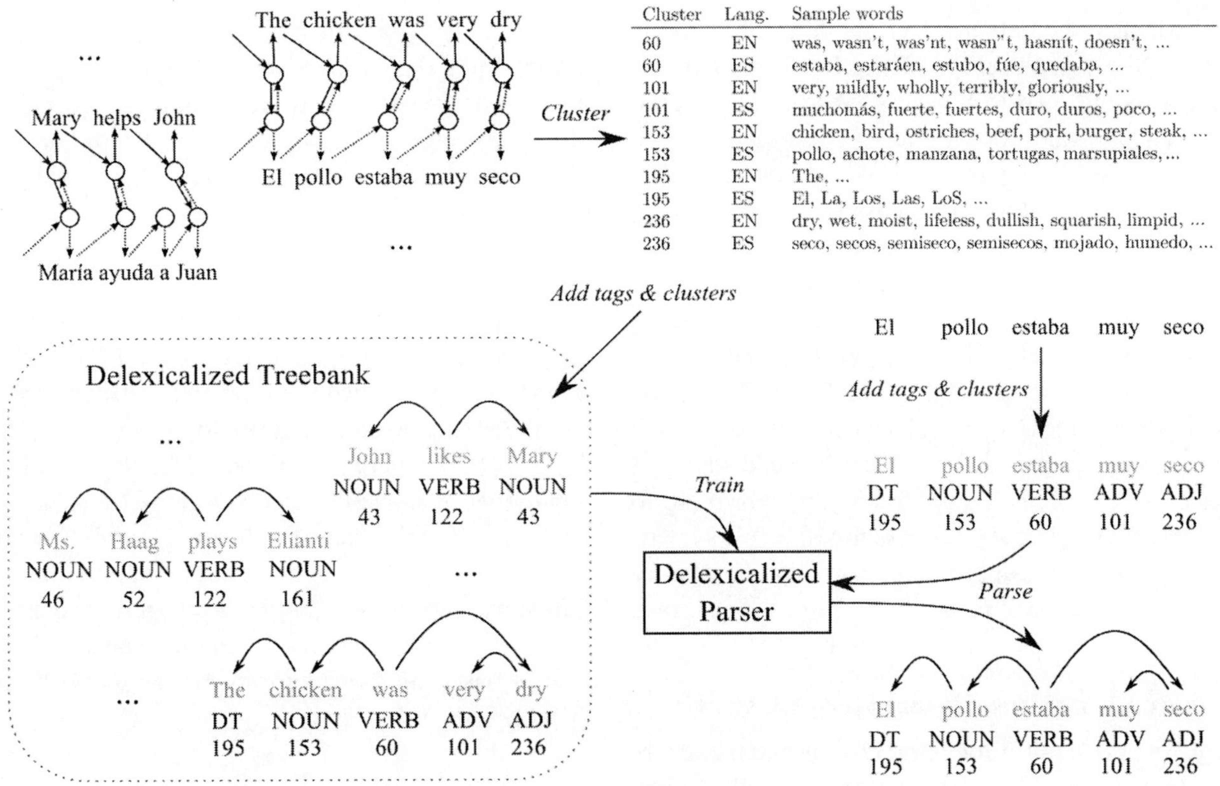

Figure 1: Cross-lingual word cluster features for parsing. Top-left: Cross-lingual (EN-ES) word clustering model. Top-right: Samples of some of the induced cross-lingual word clusters. Bottom-left: Delexicalized cluster-augmented source (EN) treebank for training transfer parser. Bottom-right: Parsing of target (ES) sentence using the transfer parser.

4.1 Direct Transfer of Discriminative Models

Our starting point is the delexicalized direct transfer method proposed by McDonald et al. (2011) based on work by Zeman and Resnik (2008). This method was shown to outperform a number of state-of-the-art unsupervised and transfer-based baselines. The method is simple; for a given training set, the learner ignores all lexical identities and only observes features over other characteristics, e.g., part-of-speech tags, orthographic features, direction of syntactic attachment, etc. The learner builds a model from an annotated source language data set, after which the model is used to directly make target language predictions.

There are three basic assumptions that drive this approach. First, that high-level tasks, such as syntactic parsing, can be learned reliably using coarse-grained statistics, such as part-of-speech tags, in place of fine-grained statistics such as lexical word identities. Second, that the parameters of features over coarse-grained statistics are in some sense language independent, e.g., a feature that indicates that adjectives modify their closest noun is useful in all languages. Third, that these coarse-grained statistics are robustly available across languages. The approach proposed by McDonald et al. (2011) relies on these three assumptions. Specifically, by replacing fine-grained language specific part-of-speech tags with universal part-of-speech tags, generated with the method described by Das and Petrov (2011), a universal parser is achieved that can be applied to any language for which universal part-of-speech tags are available.

Below, we extend this approach to universal parsing by adding cross-lingual word cluster features. A cross-lingual word clustering is a clustering of words in two languages, in which the clusters correspond to some meaningful cross-lingual property. For example, prepositions from both languages should be in the same cluster, proper names from both languages in another cluster and so on. By adding features defined over these clusters, we can, to some degree, re-lexicalize the delexicalized models, while maintaining the "universality" of the features. This approach is outlined in Figure 1. Assuming that we have an algorithm for generating cross-lingual word clusters (see Section 4.2), we can augment the delexicalized parsing algorithm to use these word cluster features at training and testing time.

In order to further motivate the proposed approach, consider the accuracy of the supervised English parser. A parser with lexical, part-of-speech and cluster features achieves 90.7% LAS (see Table 3). If we remove all lexical and cluster features, the same parser achieves 83.1%. However, if we add back just the cluster features, the accuracy jumps back up to 89.5%, which is only 1.2% below the full system. Thus, if we can accurately learn cross-lingual clusters, there is hope of regaining some of the accuracy lost due to the delexicalization process.

4.2 Inducing Cross-lingual Word Clusters

Our first method for inducing cross-lingual clusters has two stages. First, it clusters a source language (S) as in the monolingual case, and then projects these clusters to a target language (T), using word alignments. Given two aligned word sequences $\boldsymbol{w}^S = \langle w_i^S \rangle_{i=1}^{m_S}$ and $\boldsymbol{w}^T = \langle w_i^T \rangle_{j=1}^{m_T}$, let $\mathcal{A}^{T|S}$ be a set of scored alignments from the source language to the target language, where $(w_j^T, w_{a_j}^S, s_{j,a_j}) \in \mathcal{A}^{T|S}$ is an alignment from the a_jth source word to the jth target word, with score $s_{j,a_j} \geq \delta$.[2] We use the shorthand $j \in \mathcal{A}^{T|S}$ to denote those target words w_j^T that are aligned to some source word $w_{a_j}^S$. Provided a clustering $\mathcal{C}^S$, we assign the target word $t \in \mathcal{V}^T$ to the cluster with which it is most often aligned:

$$\mathcal{C}^T(t) = \operatorname*{argmax}_k \sum_{\substack{j \in \mathcal{A}^{T|S} \\ \text{s.t. } w_j^T = t}} s_{j,a_j} \left[\mathcal{C}^S(w_{a_j}^S) = k \right], \quad (2)$$

where $[\cdot]$ is the indicator function. We refer to the cross-lingual clusters induced in this way as PROJECTED CLUSTERS.

This simple projection approach has two potential drawbacks. First, it only provides a clustering of those target language words that occur in the word aligned data, which is typically smaller than our monolingual data sets. Second, the mapped clustering may not necessarily correspond to an acceptable target language clustering in terms of monolingual likelihood. In order to tackle these issues, we propose the following more complex model. First, to find clusterings that are good according to both the source and target language, and to make use of more unlabeled data, we model word sequences in each language by the monolingual language model with likelihood function defined by equation (1). Denote these likelihood functions respectively by $L^S(\boldsymbol{w}^S; \mathcal{C}^S)$ and $L^T(\boldsymbol{w}^T; \mathcal{C}^T)$, where we have overloaded notation so that the word sequences denoted by $\boldsymbol{w}^S$ and $\boldsymbol{w}^T$ include much more plentiful non-aligned data when taken as an argument of the monolingual likelihood functions. Second, we couple the clusterings defined by these individual models, by introducing additional factors based on word alignments, as proposed by Och (1999):

$$L^{T|S}(\boldsymbol{w}^T; \mathcal{A}^{T|S}, \mathcal{C}^T, \mathcal{C}^S) =$$

$$\prod_{j \in \mathcal{A}^{T|S}} p(w_j^T | \mathcal{C}^T(w_j^T)) p(\mathcal{C}^T(w_j^T) | \mathcal{C}^S(w_{a_j}^S)) .$$

and the symmetric $L^{S|T}(\boldsymbol{w}^S; \mathcal{A}^{S|T}, \mathcal{C}^S, \mathcal{C}^T)$. Note that the simple projection defined by equation (2) correspond to a hard assignment variant of this probabilistic formulation when the source clustering is fixed. Combining all four factors results in the joint monolingual and cross-lingual objective function

$$L^{S,T}(\boldsymbol{w}^S, \boldsymbol{w}^T; \mathcal{A}^{T|S}, \mathcal{A}^{S|T}, \mathcal{C}^S, \mathcal{C}^T) =$$

$$L^S(\ldots) \cdot L^T(\ldots) \cdot L^{T|S}(\ldots) \cdot L^{S|T}(\ldots) . \quad (3)$$

The intuition of this approach is that the clusterings $\mathcal{C}^S$ and $\mathcal{C}^T$ are forced to jointly explain the source and target data, treating the word alignments as a form of soft constraints. We approximately optimize (3) with the alternating procedure in Algorithm 1, in which we iteratively maximize L^S and L^T, keeping the other factors fixed. In this way we can generate cross-lingual clusterings using all the monolingual data while forcing the clusterings to obey the word alignment constraints. We refer to the clusters induced with this method as X-LINGUAL CLUSTERS.

In practice we found that each unconstrained monolingual run of the exchange algorithm (lines

[2] In our case, the alignment score corresponds to the conditional alignment probability $p(w_j^T | w_{a_j}^S)$. All ϵ-alignments are ignored and we use $\delta = 0.95$ throughout.

Algorithm 1 Cross-lingual clustering.

Randomly initialize source/target clusterings $\mathcal{C}^S$ and $\mathcal{C}^T$.
for $i = 1 \ldots N$ **do**
  1. Find $\tilde{\mathcal{C}}^S \approx \text{argmax}_{\mathcal{C}^S} L^S(\boldsymbol{w}^S; \mathcal{C}^S)$. (†)
  2. Project $\tilde{\mathcal{C}}^S$ to $\mathcal{C}^T$ using equation (2).
    - keep cluster of non-projected words in $\mathcal{C}^T$ fixed.
  3. Find $\tilde{\mathcal{C}}^T \approx \text{argmax}_{\mathcal{C}^T} L^T(\boldsymbol{w}^T; \mathcal{C}^T)$. (†)
  4. Project $\tilde{\mathcal{C}}^T$ to $\mathcal{C}^S$ using equation (2).
    - keep cluster of non-projected words in $\mathcal{C}^S$ fixed.
end for

† Optimized via the exchange algorithm keeping the cluster of projected words fixed and only clustering additional words not in the projection.

1 and 3) moves the clustering too far from those that obey the word alignment constraints, which causes the procedure to fail to converge. However, we found that fixing the clustering of the words that are assigned clusters in the projection stages (lines 2 and 4) and only clustering the remaining words works well in practice. Furthermore, we found that iterating the procedure has little effect on performance and set $N = 1$ for all subsequent experiments.

5 Cross-lingual Experiments

In our first set of experiments on using cross-lingual cluster features, we evaluate direct transfer of our EN parser, trained on Stanford style dependencies (De Marneffe et al., 2006), to the the ten non-EN Indo-European languages listed in Section 3. We exclude KO and ZH as initial experiments proved direct transfer a poor technique when transferring parsers between such diverse languages. We study the impact of using cross-lingual cluster features by comparing the strong delexicalized baseline model of McDonald et al. (2011), which only has features derived from universal part-of-speech tags, projected from English with the method of Das and Petrov (2011), to the same model when adding features derived from cross-lingual clusters. In both cases the feature models are the same as those used in Section 3.1, except that they are delexicalized by removing all lexical word-identity features. We evaluate both the PROJECTED CLUSTERS and the X-LINGUAL CLUSTERS.

For these experiments we train the perceptron for only five epochs in order to prevent over-fitting, which is an acute problem due to the divergence between the training and testing data sets in this setting. Furthermore, in accordance to standard practices we only evaluate unlabeled attachment score (UAS) due to the fact that each treebank uses a different – possibly non-overlapping – label set.

In our second set of experiments, we evaluate direct transfer of a NER system trained on EN to DE, ES and NL. We use the same feature models as in the monolingual case, with the exception that we use universal part-of-speech tags for all languages and we remove the capitalization feature when transferring from EN to DE. Capitalization is both a prevalent and highly predictive feature of named-entities in EN, while in DE, capitalization is even more prevalent, but has very low predictive power. Interestingly, while delexicalization has shown to be important for direct transfer of dependency-parsers (McDonald et al., 2011), we noticed in preliminary experiments that it substantially degrades performance for NER. We hypothesize that this is because word features are predictive of common proper names and that these are often translated directly across languages, at least in the case of newswire text. As for the transfer parser, when training the source NER model, we regularize the model more heavily by setting $\sigma = 0.1$.

Appendix A contains the details of the training, testing, unlabeled and parallel/aligned data sets.

5.1 Results

Table 5 lists the results of the transfer experiments for dependency parsing. The baseline results are comparable to those in McDonald et al. (2011) and thus also significantly outperform the results of recent unsupervised approaches (Berg-Kirkpatrick and Klein, 2010; Naseem et al., 2010). Importantly, cross-lingual cluster features are helpful across the board and give a relative error reduction ranging from 3% for DA to 13% for PT, with an average reduction of 6%, in terms of unlabeled attachment score (UAS). This shows the utility of cross-lingual cluster features for syntactic transfer. However, X-LINGUAL CLUSTERS provides roughly the same performance as PROJECTED CLUSTERS suggesting that even simple methods of cross-lingual clustering are sufficient for direct transfer dependency parsing.

We would like to stress that these results are likely to be under-estimating the parsers' actual ability to predict Stanford-style dependencies in the target languages. This is because the target language annotations that we use for evaluation differ from the

	DA	DE	EL	ES	FR	IT	NL	PT	RU	SV	AVG
NO CLUSTERS	36.7	48.9	59.5	60.2	70.0	64.6	52.8	66.8	29.7	55.4	*54.5*
PROJECTED CLUSTERS	38.9	50.3	61.1	62.6	71.6	68.6	54.5	70.7	32.9	57.0	*56.8*
X-LINGUAL CLUSTERS	38.7	50.7	63.0	62.9	72.1	68.8	54.3	71.0	34.4	56.9	*57.3*
↑ ALL DEPENDENCY RELATIONS ↓ ONLY SUBJECT/OBJECT RELATIONS											
NO CLUSTERS	44.6	56.7	67.2	60.7	77.4	64.6	59.5	53.3	29.3	57.3	*57.1*
PROJECTED CLUSTERS	49.8	57.1	72.2	65.9	80.4	70.5	67.0	62.6	34.6	65.0	*62.5*
X-LINGUAL CLUSTERS	49.2	59.0	72.5	65.9	80.9	72.7	65.7	62.5	37.2	64.4	*63.0*

Table 5: Direct transfer dependency parsing from English. Results measured by unlabeled attachment score (UAS). ONLY SUBJECT/OBJECT RELATIONS – UAS measured only over words marked as subject/object in the evaluation data.

Stanford dependency annotation. Some of these differences are warranted in that certain target language phenomena are better captured by the native annotation. However, differences such as choice of lexical versus functional head are more arbitrary.

To highlight this point we run two additional experiments. First, we had linguists, who were also fluent speakers of German, re-annotate the DE test set so that unlabeled arcs are consistent with Stanford-style dependencies. Using this data, NO CLUSTERS obtains 60.0% UAS, PROJECTED CLUSTERS 63.6% and X-LINGUAL CLUSTERS 64.4%. When compared to the scores on the original data set (48.9%, 50.3% and 50.7%, respectively) we can see that not only is the baseline system doing much better, but that the improvements from cross-lingual clustering are much more pronounced. Next, we investigated the accuracy of subject and object dependencies, as these are often annotated in similar ways across treebanks, typically modifying the main verb of the sentence. The bottom half of Table 5 gives the scores when restricted to such dependencies in the gold data. We measure the percentage of modifiers in subject and object dependencies that modify the correct word. Indeed, here we see the difference in performance become clearer, with the cross-lingual cluster model reducing errors by 14% relative to the non-cross-lingual model and upwards of 22% relative for IT.

We now turn to the results of the transfer experiments for NER, listed in Table 6. While the performance of the transfer systems is very poor when no word clusters are used, adding cross-lingual word clusters give substantial improvements across all languages. The simple PROJECTED CLUSTERS work well, but the X-LINGUAL CLUSTERS provide even larger improvements. On average the latter reduce errors on the test set by 22% in terms of F_1 and up to 26% for ES. We also measure how well the direct transfer NER systems are able to detect entity boundaries (ignoring the entity categories). Here, on average, the best clusters provide a 24% relative error reduction on the test set (75.8 vs. 68.1 F_1).

	DE	ES	NL	AVG
NO CLUSTERS	25.4	49.5	49.9	*41.6*
PROJECTED CLUSTERS	39.1	62.1	61.8	*54.4*
X-LINGUAL CLUSTERS	43.1	62.8	64.7	*56.9*
↑ DEVELOPMENT SET ↓ TEST SET				
NO CLUSTERS	23.5	45.6	48.4	*39.1*
PROJECTED CLUSTERS	35.2	59.1	56.4	*50.2*
X-LINGUAL CLUSTERS	40.4	59.3	58.4	*52.7*

Table 6: Direct transfer NER results (from English) measured with average F_1-score on the CoNLL 2002/2003 development and test sets.

To our knowledge there are no comparable results on transfer learning of NER systems. Based on the results of this first attempt at this scenario, we believe that transfer learning by multilingual word clusters could be developed into a practical way to construct NER systems for resource poor languages.

6 Conclusion

In the first part of this study, we showed that word clusters induced from a simple class-based language model can be used to significantly improve on state-of-the-art supervised dependency parsing and NER for a wide range of languages and even across language families. Although the improvements vary between languages, the addition of word cluster features never has a negative impact on performance.

This result has important practical consequences as it allows practitioners to simply plug in word cluster features into their current feature models. Given previous work on word clusters for various linguistic structure prediction tasks, these results are not too surprising. However, to our knowledge this is the first study to apply the same type of word cluster features across languages and tasks.

In the second part, we provided two simple methods for inducing cross-lingual word clusters. The first method works by projecting word clusters, induced from monolingual data, from a source language to a target language directly via word alignments. The second method, on the other hand, makes use of monolingual data in both the source and the target language, together with word alignments that act as constraints on the joint clustering. We then showed that by using these cross-lingual word clusters, we can significantly improve on direct transfer of discriminative models for both parsing and NER. As in the monolingual case, both types of cross-lingual word cluster features yield improvements across the board, with the more complex method providing a significantly larger improvement for NER. Although the performance of transfer systems is still substantially below that of supervised systems, this research provides one step towards bridging this gap. Further, we believe that it opens up an avenue for future work on multilingual clustering methods, cross-lingual feature projection and domain adaptation for direct transfer of linguistic structure.

Acknowledgments

We thank John DeNero for help with creating the word alignments; Reut Tsarfaty and Joakim Nivre for rewarding discussions on evaluation; Slav Petrov and Kuzman Ganchev for discussions on cross-lingual clustering; and the anonymous reviewers, along with Joakim Nivre, for valuable comments that helped improve the paper. The first author is grateful for the financial support of the Swedish National Graduate School of Language Technology (GSLT).

A Data Sets

In the parsing experiments, we use the following data sets. For DA, DE, EL, ES, IT, NL, PT and SV, we use the predefined training and evaluation data sets from the CoNLL 2006/2007 data sets (Buchholz and Marsi, 2006; Nivre et al., 2007). For EN we use sections 02-21, 22, and 23 of the Penn WSJ Treebank (Marcus et al., 1993) for training, development and evaluation. For FR we used the French Treebank (Abeillé and Barrier, 2004) with splits defined in Candito et al. (2010). For KO we use the Sejong Korean Treebank (Han et al., 2002) randomly splitting the data into 80% training, 10% development and 10% evaluation. For RU we use the SynTagRus Treebank (Boguslavsky et al., 2000; Apresjan et al., 2006) randomly splitting the data into 80% training, 10% development and 10% evaluation. For ZH we use the Penn Chinese Treebank v6 (Xue et al., 2005) using the proposed data splits from the documentation. Both EN and ZH were converted to dependencies using v1.6.8 of the Stanford Converter (De Marneffe et al., 2006). FR was converted using the procedure defined in Candito et al. (2010). RU and KO are native dependency treebanks. For the CoNLL data sets we use the part-of-speech tags provided with the data. For all other data sets, we train a part-of-speech tagger on the training data in order to tag the development and evaluation data.

For the NER experiments we use the training, development and evaluation data sets from the CoNLL 2002/2003 shared tasks (Tjong Kim Sang, 2002; Tjong Kim Sang and De Meulder, 2003) for all four languages (DE, EN, ES and NL). The data set for each language consists of newswire text annotated with four entity categories: Location (LOC), Miscellaneous (MISC), Organization (ORG) and Person (PER). We use the part-of-speech tags supplied with the data, except for ES where we instead use universal part-of-speech tags (Petrov et al., 2011).

Unlabeled data for training the monolingual cluster models was extracted from one year of newswire articles from multiple sources from a news aggregation website. This consists of 0.8 billion (DA) to 121.6 billion (EN) tokens per language. All word alignments for the cross-lingual clusterings were produced with the dual decomposition aligner described by DeNero and Macherey (2011) using 10.5 million (DA) to 12.1 million (FR) sentences of aligned web data.

References

Anne Abeillé and Nicolas Barrier. 2004. Enriching a french treebank. In *Proceedings of LREC*.

Juri Apresjan, Igor Boguslavsky, Boris Iomdin, Leonid Iomdin, Andrei Sannikov, and Victor Sizov. 2006. A syntactically and semantically tagged corpus of russian: State of the art and prospects. In *Proceedings of LREC*.

Emily M. Bender. 2011. On achieving and evaluating language-independence in NLP. *Linguistic Issues in Language Technology*, 6(3):1–26.

Taylor Berg-Kirkpatrick and Dan Klein. 2010. Phylogenetic grammar induction. In *Proceedings of ACL*.

Daniel M. Bikel, Richard Schwartz, and Ralph M. Weischedel. 1999. An algorithm that learns what's in a name. *Machine Learning*, 34(1):211–231.

Igor Boguslavsky, Svetlana Grigorieva, Nikolai Grigoriev, Leonid Kreidlin, and Nadezhda Frid. 2000. Dependency treebank for Russian: Concept, tools, types of information. In *Proceedings of COLING*.

Peter F. Brown, Peter V. deSouza, Robert L. Mercer, Vincent J. Della Pietra, and Jenifer C. Lai. 1992. Class-based n-gram models of natural language. *Computational Linguistics*, 18:467–479.

Sabine Buchholz and Erwin Marsi. 2006. CoNLL-X shared task on multilingual dependency parsing. In *Proceedings of CoNLL*.

Marie Candito, Benoît Crabbé, and Pascal Denis. 2010. Statistical french dependency parsing: treebank conversion and first results. In *Proceedings of LREC*.

David Chiang. 2005. A hierarchical phrase-based model for statistical machine translation. In *Proceedings of ACL*.

Alexander Clark. 2003. Combining distributional and morphological information for part of speech induction. In *Proceedings of EACL*.

Shay B. Cohen and Noah A. Smith. 2009. Shared logistic normal distributions for soft parameter tying in unsupervised grammar induction. In *Proceedings of NAACL*.

Shay B. Cohen, Dipanjan Das, and Noah A. Smith. 2011. Unsupervised structure prediction with non-parallel multilingual guidance. In *Proceedings of EMNLP*.

Michael Collins, Philipp Koehn, and Ivona Kučerová. 2005. Clause restructuring for statistical machine translation. In *Proceedings of ACL*.

Michael Collins. 1997. Three generative, lexicalised models for statistical parsing. In *Proceedings of ACL*.

Ronan Collobert and Jason Weston. 2008. A unified architecture for natural language processing: deep neural networks with multitask learning. In *Proceedings of ICML*.

Dipanjan Das and Slav Petrov. 2011. Unsupervised part-of-speech tagging with bilingual graph-based projections. In *Proceedings of ACL-HLT*.

Marie-Catherine De Marneffe, Bill MacCartney, and Chris D. Manning. 2006. Generating typed dependency parses from phrase structure parses. In *Proceedings of LREC*.

John DeNero and Klaus Macherey. 2011. Model-based aligner combination using dual decomposition. In *Proceedings of ACL-HLT*.

Paramveer Dhillon, Dean Foster, and Lyle Dean. 2011. Multi-view learning of word embeddings via cca. In *Proceedings of NIPS*.

Manaal Faruqui and Sebastian Padó. 2010. Training and evaluating a german named entity recognizer with semantic generalization. In *Proceedings of KONVENS*.

Dayne Freitag. 2004. Trained named entity recognition using distributional clusters. In *Proceedings of EMNLP*.

Jennifer Gillenwater, Kuzman Ganchev, João Graça, Fernando Pereira, and Ben Taskar. 2010. Sparsity in dependency grammar induction. In *Proceedings of ACL*.

Gholamreza Haffari, Marzieh Razavi, and Anoop Sarkar. 2011. An ensemble model that combines syntactic and semantic clustering for discriminative dependency parsing. In *Proceedings of ACL*.

Chung-hye Han, Na-Rare Han, Eon-Suk Ko, and Martha Palmer. 2002. Development and evaluation of a korean treebank and its application to nlp. In *Proceedings of LREC*.

Rebecca Hwa, Philip Resnik, Amy Weinberg, Clara Cabezas, and Okan Kolak. 2005. Bootstrapping parsers via syntactic projection across parallel texts. *Natural Language Engineering*, 11(03):311–325.

Dan Klein and Chris D. Manning. 2004. Corpus-based induction of syntactic structure: models of dependency and constituency. In *Proceedings of ACL*.

Terry Koo, Xavier Carreras, and Michael Collins. 2008. Simple semi-supervised dependency parsing. In *Proceedings of ACL-HLT*.

Sandra Kübler, Ryan McDonald, and Joakim Nivre. 2009. *Dependency parsing*. Morgan & Claypool Publishers.

Dekang Lin and Xiaoyun Wu. 2009. Phrase clustering for discriminative learning. In *Proceedings of ACL-IJCNLP*, pages 1030–1038.

Mitchell P. Marcus, Mary Ann Marcinkiewicz, and Beatrice Santorini. 1993. Building a large annotated corpus of English: the Penn treebank. *Computational Linguistics*, 19(2):313–330.

Ryan McDonald, Slav Petrov, and Keith Hall. 2011. Multi-source transfer of delexicalized dependency parsers. In *Proceedings of EMNLP*.

Scott Miller, Jethran Guinness, and Alex Zamanian. 2004. Name tagging with word clusters and discriminative training. In *Proceedings of HLT-NAACL*.

Andriy Mnih and Geoffrey Hinton. 2007. Three new graphical models for statistical language modelling. In *Proceedings of ICML*.

Tahira Naseem, Harr Chen, Regina Barzilay, and Mark Johnson. 2010. Using universal linguistic knowledge to guide grammar induction. In *Proceedings of EMNLP*.

Joakim Nivre, Johan Hall, Sandra Kübler, Ryan McDonald, Jens Nilsson, Sebastian Riedel, and Deniz Yuret. 2007. The CoNLL 2007 shared task on dependency parsing. In *Proceedings of EMNLP-CoNLL*.

Joakim Nivre. 2008. Algorithms for deterministic incremental dependency parsing. *Computational Linguistics*, 34(4):513–553.

Franz Josef Och. 1999. An efficient method for determining bilingual word classes. In *Proceedings of EACL*.

Bo Pang and Lillian Lee. 2008. *Opinion mining and sentiment analysis*. Now Publishers Inc.

Slav Petrov, Dipanjan Das, and Ryan McDonald. 2011. A universal part-of-speech tagset. In *ArXiv:1104.2086*.

Adwait Ratnaparkhi. 1996. A maximum entropy model for part-of-speech tagging. In *Proceedings of EMNLP*.

Noah A. Smith. 2011. *Linguistic Structure Prediction*. Morgan & Claypool Publishers.

Anders Søgaard. 2011. Data point selection for cross-language adaptation of dependency parsers. In *Proceedings of ACL*.

Valentin I. Spitkovsky, Hiyan Alshawi, and Daniel Jurafsky. 2011. Lateen EM: Unsupervised training with multiple objectives, applied to dependency grammar induction. In *Proceedings of EMNLP*.

Erik F. Tjong Kim Sang and Fien De Meulder. 2003. Introduction to the conll-2003 shared task: Language-independent named entity recognition. In *Proceedings of CoNLL*.

Erik F. Tjong Kim Sang. 2002. Introduction to the conll-2002 shared task: Language-independent named entity recognition. In *Proceedings of CoNLL*.

Stephen Tratz and Eduard Hovy. 2011. A fast, effective, non-projective, semantically-enriched parser. In *Proceedings of EMNLP*.

Joseph Turian, Lev-Arie Ratinov, and Yoshua Bengio. 2010. Word representations: A simple and general method for semi-supervised learning. In *Proceedings of ACL*.

Jakob Uszkoreit and Thorsten Brants. 2008. Distributed word clustering for large scale class-based language modeling in machine translation. In *Proceedings of ACL-HLT*.

Naiwen Xue, Fei Xia, Fu-dong Chiou, and Marta Palmer. 2005. The penn chinese treebank: Phrase structure annotation of a large corpus. *Natural Language Engineering*, 11(02):207–238.

Daniel Zeman and Philip Resnik. 2008. Cross-language parser adaptation between related languages. In *IJCNLP Workshop: NLP for Less Privileged Languages*.

Yue Zhang and Stephen Clark. 2008. A tale of two parsers: Investigating and combining graph-based and transition-based dependency parsing. In *Proceedings of EMNLP*.

Yue Zhang and Joakim Nivre. 2011. Transition-based dependency parsing with rich non-local features. In *Proceedings of ACL-HLT*.

Training Dependency Parser Using Light Feedback

Avihai Mejer
Department of Electrical Engineering
Technion-Israel Institute of Technology
Haifa 32000, Israel
amejer@tx.technion.ac.il

Koby Crammer
Department of Electrical Engineering
Technion-Israel Institute of Technology
Haifa 32000, Israel
koby@ee.technion.ac.il

Abstract

We introduce lightly supervised learning for dependency parsing. In this paradigm, the algorithm is initiated with a parser, such as one that was built based on a very limited amount of fully annotated training data. Then, the algorithm iterates over unlabeled sentences and asks only for a single bit of feedback, rather than a full parse tree. Specifically, given an example the algorithm outputs two possible parse trees and receives only a single bit indicating which of the two alternatives has more correct edges. There is no direct information about the correctness of any edge. We show on dependency parsing tasks in 14 languages that with only 1% of fully labeled data, and light-feedback on the remaining 99% of the training data, our algorithm achieves, on average, only 5% lower performance than when training with fully annotated training set. We also evaluate the algorithm in different feedback settings and show its robustness to noise.

1 Introduction

Supervised learning is a dominant paradigm in machine learning in which a prediction model is built based on examples, each of which is composed of inputs and a corresponding *full* annotation. In the task of parsing, examples are composed of sentences in some language and associated with full parse trees. These parse trees are often generated by human annotators. The annotation process is complex, slow and prone to mistakes as for each sentence a full correct feedback is required.

We describe light-feedback learning which suits learning problems with complex or structured output, like parsing. After building an initial classifier, our algorithm reduces the work of the annotator from a full annotation of the input sentence to a *single* bit of information. Specifically, it provides the annotator with two alternative parses of the input sentence and asks for the single bit indicating which of the alternatives is better. In 95% of the sentences both alternatives are identical except for a single word. See Fig. 2 for an illustration. Thus, the work of the annotator boils down to deciding for some specific word in the sentence which of two possible words should be that word's head.

We show empirically, through simulation, that using only 1% of the training set with full annotation, and the remaining 99% with light annotation, our algorithm achieves an average accuracy of about 80%, only 5% less than a parser built with full annotated training data. These results are averaged over 14 languages. With additional simple relaxations, our algorithm achieves average accuracy of 82.5%, not far from the performance of an algorithm observing full annotation of the data. We also evaluate our algorithm under few noise settings, showing that it is resistant to noise, with a decrease of only 1.5% in accuracy under about 10% feedback noise. We defer a discussion of related work to the end of the paper.

2 Dependency Parsing and Parsers

Dependency parsing of a sentence is an intermediate between shallow-parsing, in which a given sentence is annotated with its part-of-speech, and between a full structure over the sentence, such as the ones defined using context-free grammar. Given a sentence with n words a parse tree is defined by constructing a single directed edge outgoing from each word to its head, that is the word it depends on according to syntactic or semantic rules. Additionally, one of the words of the sentence must be labeled as the root of the tree. The choice of edges is restricted to induce trees, i.e. graphs with no loops.

Dependency parsers, such as the MSTParser of (McDonald et al., 2005), construct directed edges between words of a given sentence to their arguments. We focus on non-projective parsing with non-typed (unlabeled) edges. MSTParser produces a parse tree for a sentence by constructing a full directed graph over the words of the sentence with weighted edges, and then outputting the maximal spanning tree (MST) of the graph. Given a true parse tree (aka as gold labeling) and a predicted parse tree $\hat{\boldsymbol{y}}$, we evaluate the latter by counting the number of words that are in agreement with the true labeling.

The MSTParser maintains a linear model for setting the weights of the edges of the full graph. Given the input sentence $\boldsymbol{x}$ the parser sets the weight of the edge between words x_i and x_j to be $s(i,j) = \boldsymbol{w}\cdot \boldsymbol{f}(\boldsymbol{x},i,j)$ using a feature function $\boldsymbol{f}$ that maps the input x and a pair of possibly connected words into R^d. Example features are the distance between the two words, words identity and words part-of-speech. The goal of the learning algorithm is to choose a proper value of $\boldsymbol{w}$ such that the induced tree for each sentence $\boldsymbol{x}$ will have high accuracy.

Online Learning: MSTParser is training a model by processing one example at a time using online learning. On each round the algorithm receives a new sentence $\boldsymbol{x}$ and the set of correct edges $\boldsymbol{y}$. It then computes the score-value of all possible directed edges, $s(i,j) = \boldsymbol{w} \cdot \boldsymbol{f}(\boldsymbol{x},i,j)$ for words i,j using the *current* parameters $\boldsymbol{w}$. The algorithm is computing the best dependency tree $\hat{\boldsymbol{y}}$ of this input $\boldsymbol{x}$ defined to be the MST of the weighted complete directed graph induced from the matrix $\{s(i,j)\}$. It then uses the discrepancy between the true parse tree $\boldsymbol{y}$ and the predicted parse tree $\hat{\boldsymbol{y}}$ to modify the weight vector.

MSTParser specifically employs the MIRA algorithm (Crammer et al., 2006) to update the weight vector $\boldsymbol{w}$ using a linear update,

$$\boldsymbol{w} \leftarrow \boldsymbol{w} + \alpha \left(\sum_{(i,j)\in \boldsymbol{y}} \boldsymbol{f}(\boldsymbol{x},i,j) - \sum_{(i,j)\in \hat{\boldsymbol{y}}} \boldsymbol{f}(\boldsymbol{x},i,j) \right) \quad (1)$$

for input-dependent scalar α that is defined by the algorithm. By construction, correct edges (i,j), that appear both in the true parse tree $\boldsymbol{y}$ and the predicted parse tree $\hat{\boldsymbol{y}}$, are not affecting the update, as the terms in the two sums of Eq. (1) cancel each other.

3 Online Learning with Light Feedback

Supervised learning is a very common paradigm in machine learning, where we assume having access to the correct full parse tree of every input sentence. Many algorithms, including MSTParser, explicitly assume this kind of feedback. Supervised learning algorithms achieve good performance in dependency parsing, but they come with a price. Human annotators are required to fully parse each and every sentence in the corpora, a long, tedious and expensive process, which is also prone to mistakes. For example, the first phase of the famous penn tree bank project (Marcus et al., 1993) lasted three years, in which annotators corrected outputs of automated machines in a rate of 475 words per hour. For supervised learning to be successful, typically a large set of thousands instances is required, which translates to a long and expensive annotation phase.

Binary or multi-class prediction tasks, such as spam filtering or document classification, are simple in the sense that the label associated with each instance or input is simple. It is either a single bit indicating whether the input email is spam or not, or one of few values from a fixed predefined set if topics. Dependency parsing is more complex as a decision is required for every word of the sentence, and additionally there is a global constraint of the parse being a tree.

In binary classification or multi-class problems it is only natural to either annotate (or label) an example, or not, since the labels are atomic, they cannot be decomposed to smaller components. The situation is different in structured tasks such as dependency parsing (or sequence labeling) where each instance is constructed of many elements that each needs to be annotated. While there are relations and coupling between the elements it is possible to annotate an instance only partially, such as provide a dependency edge only to several words in a sentence.

We take this approach to the extreme, and consider (for now) that for each sentence only a single bit of labeling will be provided. The choice of what bit to require is algorithm and example dependent. We propose using a *light feedback* scheme in order to significantly reduce annotation effort for dependency parsing. First, a base or initial model will be learned from a *very small* set of fully annotated examples, i.e. sentences with full dependency information known. Then, in a second training stage the algorithm works in rounds. On each round the algorithm is provided with a new non-annotated sentence which it annotates, hopefully making the right decision for most of the words. Then the algorithm chooses subset of the words (or segments) to be annotated by humans. These words are the ones that algorithm estimates to be the hardest, or that their true label would resolve any ambiguity that is currently existing with the parsing of the input sentence.

Although such partial annotation task may be easier and faster to annotate, we realize that even partial annotation if not limited enough can require eventually similar effort as annotating the entire sentence. For example, if for a 25-words sentence annotation is requested for 5 words scattered over the entire sentence, providing this annotation may require the annotator to basically parse the entire sentence.

We thus further restrict the possible feedback requested from the annotator. Specifically, given a new sentence our algorithm outputs two possible annotations, or parse trees, $\hat{\boldsymbol{y}}_A$ and $\hat{\boldsymbol{y}}_B$, and asks for a single bit from the annotator, indicating whether parse A is better or parse B is better. We do not ask the annotator to parse the actual sentence, or decide what is the correct parse, but only to state which of the parses is quantitatively better. Formally, we say that parse $\hat{\boldsymbol{y}}_A$ is better if it contains more correct edges than $\hat{\boldsymbol{y}}_B$. The annotator is asked for a single bit, and thus must state one of the two parses, even if both parses are equally good. We denote this labeling paradigm as *binary*, as the annotator provides binary feedback.

The two parses our algorithms presents to the annotator are the highest ranking parse and the second highest ranking parse according to the current model. That is, the parse it would output for $\boldsymbol{x}$ and the best alternative. The feedback required from the annotator is only which of the two parses is better, the annotator does not explicitly indicate which of the edges are labeled correctly or incorrectly, and furthermore, the annotator does not provide any explicit information about the correct edge of any of the words.

In general, the two alternative parses presented to the annotator may be significantly different from each other; they may disagree on the edges of many words. In this case the task of deciding which of them is better may be as hard as annotating the entire sentence, and then comparing the resulting annotation to both alternatives. In practice, however, due to our choice of features (as functions of the two words) and model (linear), and since our algorithm chooses the two parse-trees ranked highest and second highest, the difference between the two alternatives is very small. In fact, we found empirically that, on average, in 95% of the sentences, they differ in the labeling of only a single word. That is, both $\hat{\boldsymbol{y}}_A$ and $\hat{\boldsymbol{y}}_B$ agree on all words, except some word x_i, for which the first alternative assigns to some word x_j and the second alternative assign to other word x_k. This is due to the fact that the score of the parses are *additive* in the edges. Therefore, the parse tree ranked second highest is obtained from the highest-ranked parse tree, where for a single word the edge is replaced, such that the difference between scores is minimized. For the remaining 5% of the sentences, replacing an edge as described causes a loop in the graph induced over words, and thus more than a single edge is modified. To minimize the potential labor of the annotator we simply ignore these cases, and present the annotator only two alternatives which are different in a single edge. We refer to this setting or scenario as *single*.

To conclude, given a new non-annotated sentence $\boldsymbol{x}$ the algorithm uses its current model $\boldsymbol{w}$ to output two annotations $\hat{\boldsymbol{y}}_A$ and $\hat{\boldsymbol{y}}_B$ which are different only on a *single* word and ask the annotator which is better. The annotator should decide to which of two possible words x_j and x_k to connect the word x_i in question. The annotator then feeds the algorithm a single bit, i.e. a *binary* labeling, which represents which alternative is better, and the algorithm updates its internal model $\boldsymbol{w}$. Although it may be the

Input data A set of n unlabeled sentences $\{\boldsymbol{x}_i\}_{i=1}^{n}$
Input parameters Initial weight vector learned from fully annotated data $\boldsymbol{u}$; Number of Iterations over the unlabeled data T
Initialize $\boldsymbol{w} \leftarrow \boldsymbol{u}$
For $t = 1, \ldots, T$

- **For** $i = 1, \ldots, n$
  - Compute the two configurations $\hat{\boldsymbol{y}}_A$ and $\hat{\boldsymbol{y}}_B$ with highest scores of $\boldsymbol{x}_i$ using $\boldsymbol{w}$
  - Ask for feedback : $\hat{\boldsymbol{y}}_A$ vs. $\hat{\boldsymbol{y}}_B$
  - Get feedback $\beta \in \{+1, -1\}$ (or $\beta \in \{+1, 0, -1\}$ in Sec. 5)
  - Compute the value of α using the MIRA algorithm (or just set $\alpha = 1$ for simplicity)
  - Update

$$\boldsymbol{w} + \alpha\beta \sum_{(i,j)\in(\hat{\boldsymbol{y}}_A/\hat{\boldsymbol{y}}_B \cup \hat{\boldsymbol{y}}_B/\hat{\boldsymbol{y}}_A)} (-1)^{[\![(i,j)\in\hat{\boldsymbol{y}}_B]\!]} \boldsymbol{f}(\boldsymbol{x}, i, j)$$

Output: Weight vector $\boldsymbol{w}$

Figure 1: The Light-Feedback learning algorithm

case that both alternatives are equally good (or bad), which occurs only when both assign the *wrong* word to x_i, that is not x_j nor x_k are the correct dependents of x_i, the annotator is still required to respond with one alternative, even though a wrong edge is recommended. Although this setting may induce noise, we consider it since a human annotator, that is asked to provide a quick light feedback, will tend to choose one of the two proposed options, the one that seems more reasonable, even if it is not correct. We refer to this combined setting of receiving a binary feedback only about a single word as *Binary-Single*. Below we discuss alternative models where the annotator may provide additional information, which we hypothesize, would be for the price of labor.

Finally, given the light-feedback β from the annotator, where $\beta = +1$ if the first parse $\hat{\boldsymbol{y}}_A$ is preferred over the second parse $\hat{\boldsymbol{y}}_B$, and $\beta = -1$ otherwise, we employ a single online update,

$$\boldsymbol{w} \leftarrow \boldsymbol{w} + \alpha\beta \left(\sum_{(i,j)\in\hat{\boldsymbol{y}}_A} \boldsymbol{f}(\boldsymbol{x}, i, j) - \sum_{(i,j)\in\hat{\boldsymbol{y}}_B} \boldsymbol{f}(\boldsymbol{x}, i, j) \right)$$

Pseudocode of the algorithm appears in Fig. 1.

From the last equation we note that the update depends only on the edges that are different between the two alternatives. This provides us the flexibility of what to show the annotator. One extreme is to provide the annotator with (almost) a full dependency parse tree, that both alternatives agree on, as well as the dilemma. This provides the annotator some context to assist of making a right decision and fast. The other extreme, is to provide the annotator only the edges for which the algorithm is not sure about, omitting any edges both alternatives agree on. This may remove labeling noise induced by erroneous edges both alternatives mistakenly agree on. Formally, these options are equivalent, and the decision which to use may even be dependent on the individual annotator.

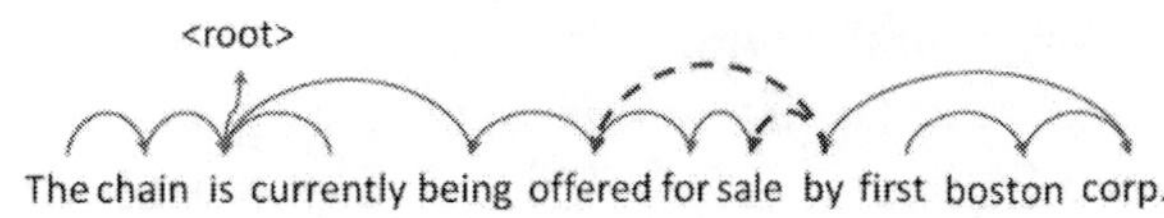

Figure 2: Example of single edge feedback. The solid blue arrows describe the proposed parse and the two dashed red arrows are the requested light feedback.

An example of a light-feedback request is shown in Fig. 2. The sentence is 12 words long and the parser succeeded to assign correct edges for 11 words. It was uncertain whether there was a "sale by first boston corps" - having the edge "by→sale" (incorrect), or there was an "offer by first boston corps" - having the edge "by→offered" (correct). In this example, a human annotator can easily clarify the dilemma.

4 Evaluation

We evaluated the light feedback model using 14 languages: English (the Penn Tree Bank) and the remaining 13 were used in CoNLL 2006 shared task[1]. The number of training sentences in the training datasets is ranging is between about $1.5-57K$, with an average of about $14K$ sentences and $50K-700K$ words. The test sets contain an average of ~ 590 sentences and $\sim 10K$ words for all datasets. The average number of words per sentence vary from 6 in Chinese to 37 in Arabic.

[1]Arabic, Bulgarian, Chinese, Czech, Danish, Dutch, German, Japanese, Portuguese, Slovene, Spanish, Swedish and Turkish . See `http://nextens.uvt.nl/~conll/`

Experimental Setup For each of the languages we split the data into two parts of relative fraction of p and $1-p$ for $p = 10\%, 5\%$ and 1% and performed training in two stages. First, we used the smaller set to build a parser using standard supervised learning procedure. Specifically, we used MSTParser and ran the MIRA online learning algorithm for 5 iterations. This process yielded our initial parser. Second, the larger portion, which is the remaining of the training set, was used to improve the initial parser using the light feedback algorithm described above. Our algorithm iterates over the sentences of the larger subset and each sentence was parsed by the current parser (parameterized by $\boldsymbol{w}$) and asked for a preference between two specific parses for that sentence. Given this feedback, the algorithm updated its model and proceeded for the next sentence. The true parse of these sentences was only used to simulate light feedback and it was never provided to the algorithm. The performance of all the trained parsers was evaluated on a fixed test set. We performed five iterations of the larger subset during the light feedback training.

4.1 Results

The results of the light-feedback training after only a *single* iteration are given in the two left plots of Fig. 3. One plot shows the performance averaged over all languages, and second plot show the results for English. The black horizontal line shows the accuracy achieved by training the parser on the entire annotated data using the MIRA algorithm for 10 iterations. The predicted edge accuracy of the parser trained on the entire annotated dataset ranges from 77% on Turkish to 93% on Japanese, with an average of 85%. This is our *skyline*.

The blue bars in each plot shows the accuracy of a parser trained with only a fraction of the dataset - 10% (left group), via 5% (middle) to 1% (right group). As expected reducing the amount of training data causes degradation in performance, from an accuracy of about 76.3% (averaged over all languages) via 75% to 70.1% when training only with 1% of the data. These performance levels are our baselines, one per specific amount of fully annotated data and lightly annotated data.

The red bar in each pair, shows the contribution of a single training epoch with light-feedback on the performance. We see that training with light feedback improves the performance of the final parser. Most noticeably, is when using only 1% of the fully annotated data for initial training, and the remaining 99% of the training data with light feedback. The accuracy on test set improves from 70.1% to 75.6%, an absolute increase of 5.5%. These results are averaged over all languages, individual results for English are also shown. In most languages, including those not shown, these trends remain: when reducing the fraction of data used for fully supervised training the performance decreases, and light feedback improves it, most substantially for the smallest fraction of 1%.

We also evaluated the improvement in accuracy on the test set by allowing more than a single iteration over the larger fraction of the training set. The results are summarized in two right plots of Fig. 3, accuracy averaged over all languages (left), and for English (right). Each line refers to a different ratio of split between full supervised learning and light feedback learning - blue for 90%, green for 95% and red for 99%. The x-axis is the number of light feedback iterations, from zero up to five. The y-axis is the accuracy. In general more iterations translates to improvement in performance. For example, building a parser with only 1% of the training data yields 70.1% accuracy on the test set, a single iteration of light-feedback on the remaining 99% improves the performance to 75.6%, each of the next iterations improves the accuracy by about $1-2\%$ up to an accuracy of about 80%, which is only 5% lower than the skyline. We note again, that the skyline was obtained by using full feedback on the entire training set, while our parser used at most five bits of feedback per sentence from the annotator, one bit per iteration.

As noted above, on each sentence, and each iteration, our algorithm presents a parsing query or "dilemma": should word a be assigned to word b or word c. These queries are generated independently of the previous queries shown, and in fact the same query may be presented again in a later iteration although already shown in an early one. We thus added a memory storage of all queries to the algorithm. When a query is generated by the algorithm, it first checks if an annotation of it already exists in memory. If this is the case, then no query is issued to the annotator, and the algorithm simulates

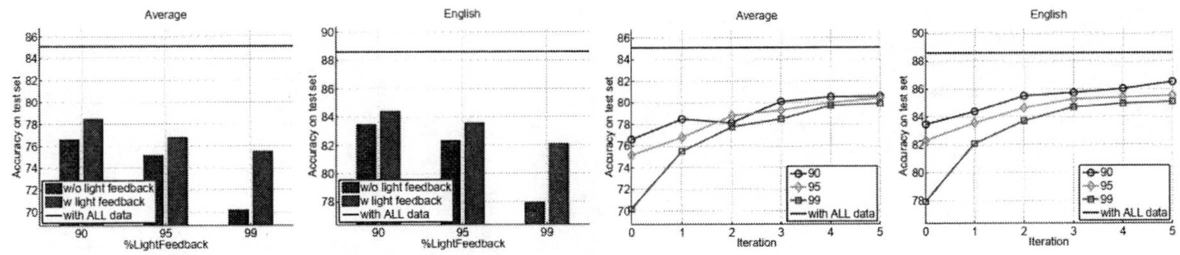

Figure 3: **Two left plots:** Evaluation in Binary-Single light feedback setting. Averaged accuracy over all languages (left) and for English. The horizontal black line shows the accuracy when training the parser on the entire annotated training data - "skyline". Each pair of bars shows the results for a parser trained with small amount of fully annotated data (left blue bar) and a parser that was then trained with a *single* iteration of light feedback on the remaining training data (right red bar). **Two right plots:** Evaluation of training with up to five iterations of binary-single light feedback. The plots show the average accuracy (left), and for English. Each line refers to a different ratio of split between full supervised learning and light feedback learning. The x-axis is the number of iterations of light feedback, from zero to five.

a query and response using the stored information.

The fraction of *new* queries, that were actually presented to the annotator, when light-training with 99% of the training set, is shown in the left panel of Fig. 4. Each line corresponds to one language. The languages are ordered in the legend according to the average number of words per sentence: from Chinese (6) to Arabic (37). Each point shows the fraction of new queries (from the total number of sentences with light-feedback) (y-axis) vs. the iteration (x-axis). Two trends are observed. First, in later iterations there are less and less new queries (or need for an actual interaction with the annotator). By definition, all queries during the first iteration are new, and the fraction of new queries after five iteration ranges from about 20% (Japanese and Chinese) to a bit less than 80% (Arabic).

The second trend is across the average number of words per sentence, the larger this number is, the more new queries there are in multiple iterations. For example, in Arabic (37 words per sentence) and Spanish (28) about 80% of the light-training sentences induce new queries in the fifth iteration, while in Chinese (6) and Japanese (8) only about 20%. As expected, longer sentences require, on average, more queries before getting their parse correctly.

We can also compare the performance improvement achieved by light feedbacks with the performance achieved by using the same amount of labeled-edges using fully annotated sentences in standard supervised training. The average sentence length across all languages is 18 words. Thus, receiving feedback regarding a single word in a sentence equals to about $1/18 \approx 5.5\%$ of the information provided by a fully annotated sentence. Therefore, we may view the light-feedback provided for 99% of the dataset as about equal to additional 5.5% of fully annotated data.

From the second plot from the right of Fig. 3, we see that by training with 1% of fully annotated data and a single iteration of light feedback over the remaining 99% of the data, the parser performance is 75.6% (square markers at $x = 1$), compared to 75% obtained by training with 5% of fully annotated data (diamond markers at $x = 0$). A second iteration of light feedback on 99% of the dataset can be viewed as *additional* $\lesssim 5\%$ of labeled data (accounting for repeating queries). After the second light feedback iteration, the parser performance is 77.8% (square markers at $x = 2$), compared to 76.3% achieved when training with 10% of fully annotated data (circle markers at $x = 0$). Similar relations can be observed for English in the right plot of Fig. 3. From these observations, we learn that on average, for about the same amount of labeled edges, light feedback learning gains equal, or even better, performance compared with fully labeled sentences.

5 Light Feedback Variants

Our current model is restrictive in two ways: first, the algorithm does not pass to the annotators examples for which the disagreements is larger than one word; and second, the annotator must prefer one of the two alternatives. Both restrictions were set to make the annotators' work easier. We now describe the results of experiments in which one or even both

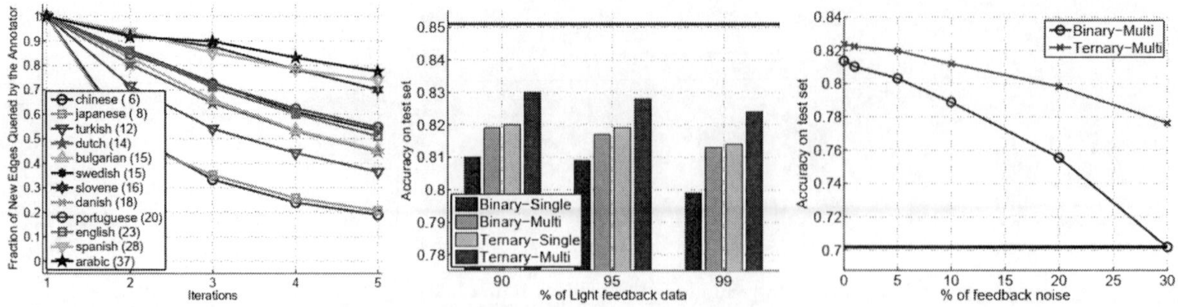

Figure 4: **Left:** the fraction of *new* queries presented to the annotator after each of the five iterations (x-axis) for all 14 languages, when light-training with 99% of the entire training data. **Middle:** comparison of the accuracy achieved using the four light feedback models using different fraction of the data for light feedback stage. The results are averaged over all the languages. **Right:** Effect of light-feedback noise on the accuracy of the trained model. Results are averaged over all languages for two light feedback settings, the ternary-multi and binary-multi. The plots show the performance measured on test set according the amount of feedback noise added. The black line is the baseline of the initial parser trained on 1% of annotated data.

restrictions are relaxed, which may make the work of the annotator harder, but as we shall see, improves performance.

Our first modification is to allow the algorithm to pass the annotator also queries on two alternatives $\hat{\boldsymbol{y}}_A$ and $\hat{\boldsymbol{y}}_B$ that differ on more than a single edge. As mentioned before, we found empirically that this arises in only $\sim$5% of the instances. In most cases the two alternatives differ in two edges, but in some cases the alternatives differ in up to five edges. Typically when the alternatives differ on more than a single edge, the words in question are close to each other in the sentence (in terms of word-distance) and are syntactically related to each other. For example, if changing the edge (i, j) to (i, k) forms a loop in the dependency graph then also another edge (k, l) must be changed to resolve the loop, so the two edges different between the alternatives are related. Nevertheless, even if the two alternatives are far from being similar, the annotator is still required to provide only a *binary* feedback, indicating a strict preference between the two alternatives. We refer to this model as *Binary-Multi*, for binary feedback and possibly multiple different edge between the alternatives.

Second, we enrich the number of possible responses of the annotator from two to three, giving the annotator the option to respond that the two alternatives $\hat{\boldsymbol{y}}_A$ and $\hat{\boldsymbol{y}}_B$ are equally good (or bad), and no one should be preferred by the other. In this case we set $\beta = 0$ in the algorithm of Fig. 1, and as can be seen in the pseudocode, this case does not modify the weight vector $\boldsymbol{w}$ associated with the parser. Such feedback will be received when both parses have the same number of errors. (We can also imagine a human annotator using the *equal* feedback to indicate "don't know"). For the common case of single edge difference between the two parses, this means that both proposed edges are incorrect. Since there are three possible responds we call this setting *ternary*. This setting can be combined with the previous one and thus we have in fact two new settings. The third setting is when only single edges are presented to the annotator, yet three possible responds are optional. We call this setting *Ternary-Single* . The fourth, is when the two alternatives may differ in more than a single edge *and* three possible responds are optional - *Ternary-Multi* setting.

The accuracy, averaged over all 14 languages, after 5 light feedback iterations, for all four settings is shown in the middle plate of Fig. 4. Each of the three groups summarizes the results for different split of the training set to full training and light-training: 90%, 95% and 99% (left to right; portion of light training). The horizontal black line shows the accuracy skyline (85% obtained by using all the training set in full supervised learning). Each bar in each group shows the results for one of the four settings: Binary-Single, Binary-Multi, Ternary-Single and Ternary-Multi. We focus our discussion in the 99% split. The averaged accuracy using Binary-Single feedback setting is about 80% (left bar). Relaxing the type of input to include alternatives that differ on more than one edge, improves accuracy by 1.4% (second bar from left). Slightly greater improvement is shown when relaxing the type of feedback, from binary to ternary (third bar from left). Finally, relaxing both constraints yields an improvement of additional 1% to an averaged accuracy of 82.5% which is only 2.5% lower than the skyline.

Moving to the other splits of $95, 90\%$ we observe that relaxing the feedback from binary to ternary improves the accuracy more than requiring to provide a preference of parses that differ on more than a single word.

6 Noisy Light Feedback

In the last section we discussed relaxations that requires slightly more effort from the annotator to gain higher test accuracy. The intent of the light feedback is to build a high-accuracy parser, yet faster and with less human effort compared with full supervised learning, or alternatively, allow collecting feedbacks from non-experts. We now evaluate the effect of light-feedback noise, which may be a consequence of asking the annotator to perform quick (and rough) light-feedback. We experiment with two settings in which the feedback of the annotator is either binary or ternary, in the *multi* settings, when 99% of the training-data is used for light-feedback. These settings refer to the second and fourth bar in the right group of the middle plate of Fig. 4.

We injected independent feedback errors to a fraction of ϵ of the queries, where ϵ is ranging between $0-30\%$. In the *Binary-Multi* setting, we flipped the binary preference with probability ϵ. For example, if $\hat{y}_A$ is better than $\hat{y}_B$ then with probability ϵ the light feedback was the other way around. In the *Ternary-Multi* setting we changed the correct feedback to one of the other two possible feedbacks with probability ϵ, the specific alternative chosen was chosen uniformly. E.g., if indeed $\hat{y}_A$ is preferred over $\hat{y}_B$, then with probability $\epsilon/2$ the feedback was that $\hat{y}_B$ is preferred and with probability $\epsilon/2$ that both are equal.

The accuracy vs. noise level for both settings is presented in the right panel of Fig. 4. The black line shows the baseline performance after training an initial parser on 1% of annotated data. Performance of the parser trained using the *Binary-Multi* setting drops by only 1% from 81.4% to 80.4% at error rate of 5% and eventually as the feedback noise increase to 30% the performance drops to 70% - the performance level achieved by the initial trained model.

The accuracy of the parser trained in the richer *Ternary-Multi* setting suffers only 1% performance decrease at error rate of 10%, and eventually 5% decrease from 82.5% to 77.5% as the feedback noise increase to 30%, still a 7.5% improvement over the initial trained parser.

We hypothesize that learning with ternary feedback is more robust to noise, as in half of the noisy feedbacks when there is a strict preference between the alternatives, the effect of the noise is not to update the model and practically ignore the input. Clearly, this is preferable than the other outcome of the noise, that forces the algorithm to make the wrong update with respect to the true preference.

We also experimented with sentence depended noise by training a secondary parser on a subset of the training set, and emulating the feedback-bit using its output. Its averaged test error (=noise level) is 22%. Yet, the accuracy obtained by our algorithm with it is 77%, about the same as achieving with 30% random annotation noise. We hypothesize this is since the light-feedbacks are requested specifically on the edges harder to predict, where the error rate is higher than the 22% average error rate of the secondary parser.

7 Related work

Weak-supervision, semi-supervised and active learning (e.g. (Chapelle et al., 2006), (Tong and Koller, 2001)) are general approaches related to the light-feedback approach. These approaches build on access to a small set of labeled examples and a large set of unlabeled examples.

The work of Hall et al. (2011) is the most similar to the light feedback settings we propose. They apply an automatic implicit feedback approach for improving the performance of dependency parsers. The parser produces the k-best parse trees and an external system that uses these parse trees provides feedback as a score for each of the parses. In our work, we focus on minimal updates by both restricting the number of compared parses to two, and having them being almost identical (up to a single edge).

Hwa (1999) investigates training a phrase structure parser using partially labeled data in several settings. In one of the settings, a parser is first trained using a large fully labeled dataset from one domain and then adapted to another domain using partial labeling. The parts of the data that are labeled are selected in one of two approaches. In the first approach phrases are randomly selected to be annotated. In the second approach the phrases are selected according to their linguistic categories based on predefined rules. In both cases, the true phrases are provided. In our work, we train the initial parser on small subset of the data from the same domain. Additionally, the feedback queries are selected dynamically according to the edges estimated to be hardest for the parser. Finally, we request only limited feedback and the true parse is never provided directly.

Chang et al. (2007) use a set of domain specific rules as automatic implicit feedback for training information extraction system. For example, they use a set of 15 simple rules to specify the expected formats of fields to be extracted from advertisements. The light feedback regarding a prediction is the number of rules that are broken. That feedback is used to update the prediction model.

Baldridge and Osborne (2004) learns an HPSG parser using active learning to choose sentences to be annotated from a large unlabeled pool. Then, like our algorithm the annotator is presented with a proposed parse with several local alternatives sub-parse-trees. Yet, the annotator *manually* provides the correct parse, if it is not found within the proposed alternatives. Kristjansson et al. (2004) employ similar approach of combining active learning with corrective feedback for information extraction. Instances with lowest confidence using the current model are chosen to be annotated. Few alternative labels are shown to the user, yet again, the correct labeling is added *manually* if needed. The alternatives shown to the user are intended to reduce the effort of obtaining the right label, but eventually the algorithm receives the correct prediction. Our algorithm is passive about examples (and active only about subset of the labels), while their algorithm uses active learning to also choose examples. We plan to extend our work in this direction. Additionally, in these works, the feedback requests involve many alternatives and providing the true annotation, in oppose to the limited binary or ternary feedback. Yet our results show that despite of these limitations the trained parser achieved performance nor far from the performance of a parser training using the entire annotated dataset.

Finally, our setting is related to bandits (Cesa-Bianchi and Lugosi, 2006) where the feedback is extremely limited, a binary success-failure bit.

8 Summary

We showed in a series of experimental simulations that using light-feedback it is possible to train a dependency parser that achieves parsing performance not far from standard supervised training. Furthermore, very little amount of fully annotated data, even few tens of sentences, is sufficient for building an initial parser which can then be significantly improved using light-feedbacks.

While light-feedback training and standard supervised training with about the same number of total annotated edges may achieve close performance, we still view it as a possible alternative training framework. The reduction of the general annotation task into focused and small feedback requests, opens possibilities for receiving these feedbacks beyond expert labeling. In our ongoing work we study feedbacks from a large group of non-experts, and possibly even automatically. Additionally, we investigate methods for selecting light-feedback queries that are not necessarily derived from the highest scoring parse and the best alternative parse. For example, selecting queries that would be easy to answer by non-experts.

References

[Baldridge and Osborne2004] J. Baldridge and M. Osborne. 2004. Active learning and the total cost of annotation. In *EMNLP*.

[Cesa-Bianchi and Lugosi2006] N. Cesa-Bianchi and G. Lugosi. 2006. *Prediction, Learning, and Games*. Cambridge University Press, New York, NY, USA.

[Chang et al.2007] Ming-Wei Chang, Lev Ratinov, and Dan Roth. 2007. Guiding semi-supervision with constraint-driven learning. In *In Proceedings of the 45th Annual Meeting of the Association for Computational Linguistics*.

[Chapelle et al.2006] O. Chapelle, B. Schölkopf, and A. Zien, editors. 2006. *Semi-Supervised Learning*. MIT Press, Cambridge, MA.

[Crammer et al.2006] K. Crammer, O. Dekel, J. Keshet, S. Shalev-Shwartz, and Y. Singer. 2006. Online passive-aggressive algorithms. *JMLR*, 7:551–585.

[Hall et al.2011] Keith Hall, Ryan McDonald, Jason Katz-Brown, and Michael Ringgaard. 2011. Training dependency parsers by jointly optimizing multiple objectives. In *In Proceedings of the 45th Annual Meeting of the Association for Computational Linguistics*.

[Hwa1999] Rebecca Hwa. 1999. Supervised grammar induction using training data with limited constituent information. *CoRR*, cs.CL/9905001.

[Kristjansson et al.2004] T. Kristjansson, A. Culotta, P. Viola, and A. McCallum. 2004. Interactive information extraction with constrained conditional random fields. In *AAAI*, pages 412–418.

[Marcus et al.1993] Mitchell P. Marcus, Mary Ann Marcinkiewicz, and Beatrice Santorini. 1993. Building a large annotated corpus of english: the penn treebank. *Comput. Linguist.*, 19:313–330, June.

[McDonald et al.2005] R. McDonald, F. Pereira, K. Ribarov, and J. Hajic. 2005. Non-projective dependency parsing using spanning tree algorithms. In *HLT/EMNLP*.

[Tong and Koller2001] S. Tong and D. Koller. 2001. Support vector machine active learning with applications to text classification. In *JMLR*, pages 999–1006.

Vine Pruning for Efficient Multi-Pass Dependency Parsing

Alexander M. Rush*
MIT CSAIL
Cambridge, MA 02139, USA
srush@csail.mit.edu

Slav Petrov
Google
New York, NY 10027, USA
slav@google.com

Abstract

Coarse-to-fine inference has been shown to be a robust approximate method for improving the efficiency of structured prediction models while preserving their accuracy. We propose a multi-pass coarse-to-fine architecture for dependency parsing using linear-time vine pruning and structured prediction cascades. Our first-, second-, and third-order models achieve accuracies comparable to those of their unpruned counterparts, while exploring only a fraction of the search space. We observe speed-ups of up to two orders of magnitude compared to exhaustive search. Our pruned third-order model is twice as fast as an unpruned first-order model and also compares favorably to a state-of-the-art transition-based parser for multiple languages.

1 Introduction

Coarse-to-fine inference has been extensively used to speed up structured prediction models. The general idea is simple: use a coarse model where inference is cheap to prune the search space for more complex models. In this work, we present a multi-pass coarse-to-fine architecture for graph-based dependency parsing. We start with a linear-time vine pruning pass and build up to higher-order models, achieving speed-ups of two orders of magnitude while maintaining state-of-the-art accuracies.

In constituency parsing, exhaustive inference for all but the simplest grammars tends to be prohibitively slow. Consequently, most high-accuracy constituency parsers routinely employ a coarse grammar to prune dynamic programming chart cells of the final grammar of interest (Charniak et al., 2006; Carreras et al., 2008; Petrov, 2009). While there are no strong theoretical guarantees for these approaches,[1] in practice one can obtain significant speed improvements with minimal loss in accuracy. This benefit comes primarily from reducing the large grammar constant $|G|$ that can dominate the runtime of the cubic-time CKY inference algorithm. Dependency parsers on the other hand do not have a multiplicative grammar factor $|G|$, and until recently were considered efficient enough for exhaustive inference. However, the increased model complexity of a third-order parser forced Koo and Collins (2010) to prune with a first-order model in order to make inference practical. While fairly effective, all these approaches are limited by the fact that inference in the coarse model remains cubic in the sentence length. The desire to parse vast amounts of text necessitates more efficient dependency parsing algorithms.

We thus propose a multi-pass coarse-to-fine approach where the initial pass is a linear-time sweep, which tries to resolve local ambiguities, but leaves arcs beyond a fixed length b unspecified (Section 3). The dynamic program is a form of *vine parsing* (Eisner and Smith, 2005), which we use to compute parse max-marginals, rather than for finding the 1-best parse tree. To reduce pruning errors, the parameters of the vine parser (and all subsequent pruning models) are trained using the *structured prediction cascades* of Weiss and Taskar (2010) to optimize for pruning efficiency, and not for 1-best prediction (Section 4). Despite a limited scope of $b = 3$, the

* Research conducted at Google.

[1] This is in contrast to optimality preserving methods such as A* search, which typically do not provide sufficient speed-ups (Pauls and Klein, 2009).

vine pruning pass is able to preserve $>98\%$ of the correct arcs, while ruling out $\sim 86\%$ of all possible arcs. Subsequent i-th order passes introduce larger scope features, while further constraining the search space. In Section 5 we present experiments in multiple languages. Our coarse-to-fine first-, second-, and third-order parsers preserve the accuracy of the unpruned models, but are faster by up to two orders of magnitude. Our pruned third-order model is faster than an unpruned first-order model, and compares favorably in speed to the state-of-the-art transition-based parser of Zhang and Nivre (2011).

It is worth noting the relationship to greedy transition-based dependency parsers that are also linear-time (Nivre et al., 2004) or quadratic-time (Yamada and Matsumoto, 2003). It is their success that motivates building explicitly trained, linear-time pruning models. However, while a greedy solution for arc-standard transition-based parsers can be computed in linear-time, Kuhlmann et al. (2011) recently showed that computing exact solutions or (max-)marginals has time complexity $O(n^4)$, making these models inappropriate for coarse-to-fine style pruning. As an alternative, Roark and Hollingshead (2008) and Bergsma and Cherry (2010) present approaches where individual classifiers are used to prune chart cells. Such approaches have the drawback that pruning decisions are made locally and therefore can rule out all valid structures, despite explicitly evaluating $O(n^2)$ chart cells. In contrast, we make pruning decisions based on global parse max-marginals using a vine pruning pass, which is linear in the sentence length, but nonetheless guarantees to preserve a valid parse structure.

2 Motivation & Overview

The goal of this work is fast, high-order, graph-based dependency parsing. Previous work on constituency parsing demonstrates that performing several passes with increasingly more complex models results in faster inference (Charniak et al., 2006; Petrov and Klein, 2007). The same technique applies to dependency parsing with a cascade of models of increasing order; however, this strategy is limited by the speed of the simplest model. The algorithm for first-order dependency parsing (Eisner, 2000) already requires $O(n^3)$ time, which Lee

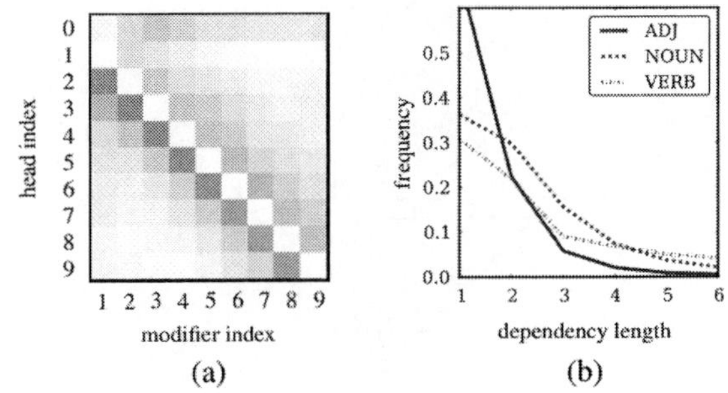

Figure 1: (a) Heat map indicating how likely a particular head position is for each modifier position. Greener/darker is likelier. (b) Arc length frequency for three common modifier tags. Both charts are computed from all sentences in Section 22 of the PTB.

(2002) shows is a practical lower bound for parsing of context-free grammars. This bound implies that it is unlikely that there can be an exhaustive parsing algorithm that is asymptotically faster than the standard approach.

We thus need to leverage domain knowledge to obtain faster parsing algorithms. It is well-known that natural language is fairly linear, and most head-modifier dependencies tend to be short. This property is exploited by transition-based dependency parsers (Yamada and Matsumoto, 2003; Nivre et al., 2004) and empirically demonstrated in Figure 1. The heat map on the left shows that most of the probability mass of modifiers is concentrated among nearby words, corresponding to a diagonal band in the matrix representation. On the right we show the frequency of arc lengths for different modifier part-of-speech tags. As one can expect, almost all arcs involving adjectives (ADJ) are very short (length 3 or less), but even arcs involving verbs and nouns are often short. This structure suggests that it may be possible to disambiguate most dependencies by considering only the "banded" portion of the sentence.

We exploit this linear structure by employing a variant of vine parsing (Eisner and Smith, 2005).[2] Vine parsing is a dependency parsing algorithm that considers only close words as modifiers. Because of this assumption it runs in linear time. Of course, any parse tree with hard limits on dependency lengths will contain major parse errors. We therefore use the

[2]The term vine parsing is a slight misnomer, since the underlying vine models are as expressive as finite-state automata. However, this allows them to circumvent the cubic-time bound.

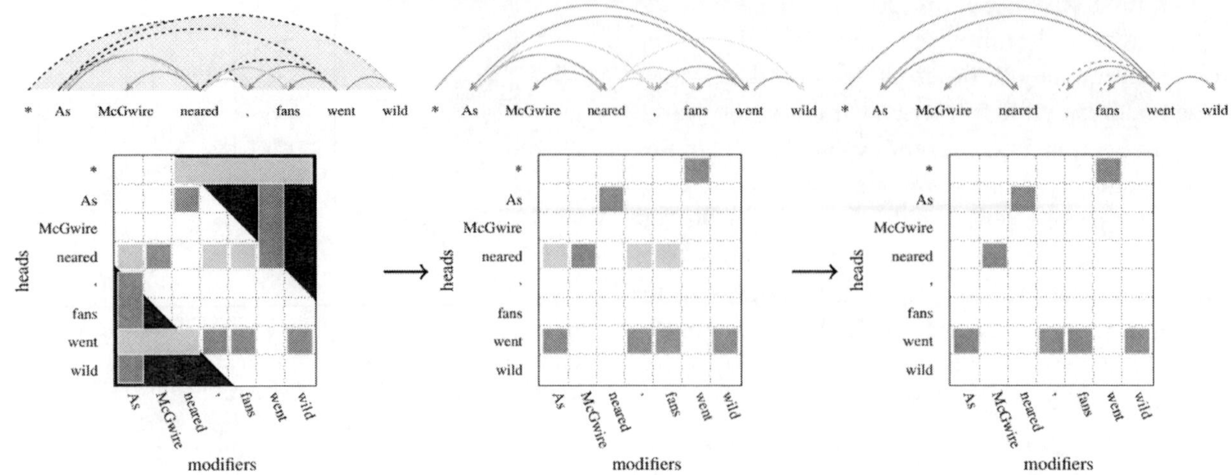

Figure 2: Multi-pass pruning with a vine, first-order, and second-order model shown as dependencies and filtered index sets after each pass. Darker cells have higher max-marginal values, while empty cells represent pruned arcs.

vine parser only for pruning and augment it to allow arcs to remain unspecified (by including so called *outer* arcs). The vine parser can thereby eliminate a possibly quadratic number of arcs, while having the flexibility to defer some decisions and preserve ambiguity to be resolved by later passes. In Figure 2 for example, the vine pass correctly determined the head-word of *McGwire* as *neared*, limited the head-word candidates for *fans* to *neared* and *went*, and decided that the head-word for *went* falls outside the band by proposing an outer arc. A subsequent first-order pass needs to score only a small fraction of all possible arcs and can be used to further restrict the search space for the following higher-order passes.

3 Graph-Based Dependency Parsing

Graph-based dependency parsing models factor all valid parse trees for a given sentence into smaller units, which can be scored independently. For instance, in a first-order factorization, the units are just dependency arcs. We represent these units by an index set $\mathcal{I}$ and use binary vectors $\mathcal{Y} \subset \{0,1\}^{|\mathcal{I}|}$ to specify a parse tree $y \in \mathcal{Y}$ such that $y(i) = 1$ iff the index i exists in the tree. The index sets of higher-order models can be constructed out of the index sets of lower-order models, thus forming a hierarchy that we will exploit in our coarse-to-fine cascade.

The inference problem is to find the 1-best parse tree $\arg\max_{y \in \mathcal{Y}} y \cdot w$, where $w \in R^{|\mathcal{I}|}$ is a weight vector that assigns a score to each index i (we discuss how w is learned in Section 4). A generalization of the 1-best inference problem is to find the max-marginal score for each index i. Max-marginals are given by the function $M : \mathcal{I} \to \mathcal{Y}$ defined as $M(i; \mathcal{Y}, w) = \arg\max_{y \in \mathcal{Y}: y(i)=1} y \cdot w$. For first-order parsing, this corresponds to the best parse utilizing a given dependency arc. Clearly there are exponentially many possible parse tree structures, but fortunately there exist well-known dynamic programming algorithms for searching over all possible structures. We review these below, starting with the first-order factorization for ease of exposition.

Throughout the paper we make use of some basic mathematical notation. We write $[c]$ for the enumeration $\{1, \ldots, c\}$ and $[c]_a$ for $\{a, \ldots, c\}$. We use $\mathbf{1}[c]$ for the indicator function, equal to 1 if condition c is true and 0 otherwise. Finally we use $[c]_+ = \max\{0, c\}$ for the positive part of c.

3.1 First-Order Parsing

The simplest way to index a dependency parse structure is by the individual arcs of the parse tree. This model is known as first-order or arc-factored. For a sentence of length n the index set is:

$$\mathcal{I}_1 = \{(h, m) : h \in [n]_0, m \in [n]\}$$

Each dependency tree has $y(h, m) = 1$ iff it includes an arc from head h to modifier m. We follow common practice and use position 0 as the pseudo-root $(*)$ of the sentence. The full set $\mathcal{I}_1$ has cardinality $|\mathcal{I}_1| = O(n^2)$.

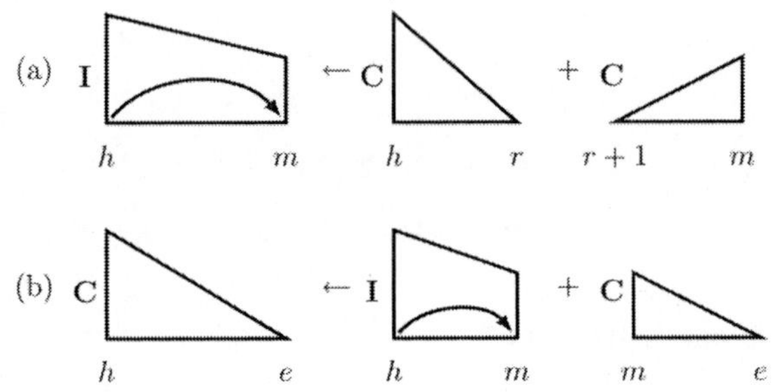

Figure 3: Parsing rules for first-order dependency parsing. The complete items C are represented by triangles and the incomplete items I are represented by trapezoids. Symmetric left-facing versions are also included.

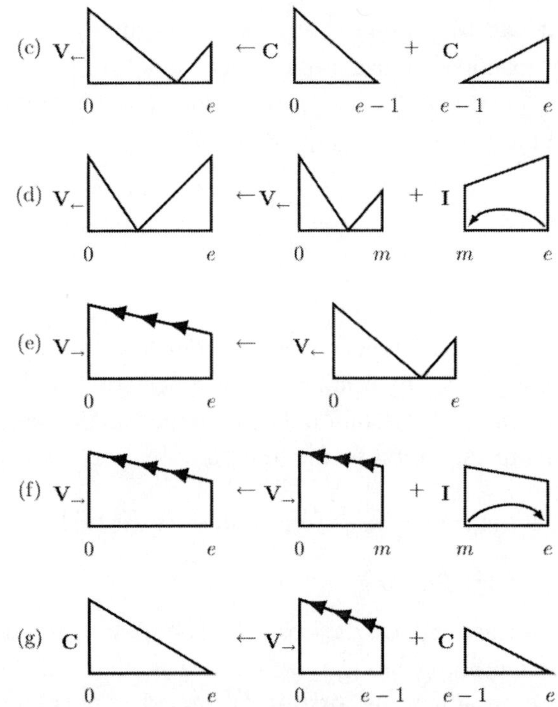

Figure 4: Additional rules for vine parsing. Vine left ($V_{\leftarrow}$) items are pictured as right-facing triangles and vine right ($V_{\rightarrow}$) items are marked trapezoids. Each new item is anchored at the root and grows to the right.

The first-order bilexical parsing algorithm of Eisner (2000) can be used to find the best parse tree and max-marginals. The algorithm defines a dynamic program over two types of items: *incomplete* items $I(h, m)$ that denote the span between a modifier m and its head h, and *complete* items $C(h, e)$ that contain a full subtree spanning from the head h and to the word e on one side. The algorithm builds larger items by applying the composition rules shown in Figure 3. Rule 3(a) builds an incomplete item $I(h, m)$ by attaching m as a modifier to h. This rule has the effect that $y(h, m) = 1$ in the final parse. Rule 3(b) completes item $I(h, m)$ by attaching item $C(m, e)$. The existence of $I(h, m)$ implies that m modifies h, so this rule enforces that the constituents of m are also constituents of h.

We can find the best derivation for each item by adapting the standard CKY parsing algorithm to these rules. Since both rule types contain three variables that can range over the entire sentence ($h, m, e \in [n]_0$), the bottom-up, inside dynamic programming algorithm requires $O(n^3)$ time. Furthermore, we can find max-marginals with an additional top-down outside pass also requiring cubic time. To speed up search, we need to filter indices from $\mathcal{I}_1$ and reduce possible applications of Rule 3(a).

3.2 Higher-Order Parsing

Higher-order models generalize the index set by using siblings s (modifiers that previously attached to a head word) and grandparents g (head words above the current head word). For compactness, we use g_1 for the head word and s_{k+1} for the modifier and parameterize the index set to capture arbitrary higher-order decisions in both directions:

$$\mathcal{I}_{k,l} = \{(g, s) : g \in [n]_0^{l+1}, s \in [n]^{k+1}\}$$

where $k + 1$ is the sibling order, $l + 1$ is the parent order, and $k + l + 1$ is the model order. The canonical second-order model uses $\mathcal{I}_{1,0}$, which has a cardinality of $O(n^3)$. Although there are several possibilities for higher-order models, we use $\mathcal{I}_{1,1}$ as our third-order model. Generally, the parsing index set has cardinality $|\mathcal{I}_{k,l}| = O(n^{2+k+l})$. Inference in higher-order models uses variants of the dynamic program for first-order parsing, and we refer to previous work for the full set of rules. For second-order models with index set $\mathcal{I}_{1,0}$, parsing can be done in $O(n^3)$ time (McDonald and Pereira, 2006) and for third-order models in $O(n^4)$ time (Koo and Collins, 2010). Even though second-order parsing has the same asymptotic time complexity as first-order parsing, inference is significantly slower due to the cost of scoring the larger index set.

We aim to prune the index set, by mapping each higher-order index down to a set of small set indices that can be pruned using a coarse pruning model. For example, to use a first-order model for pruning, we would map the higher-order index to the individual indices for its arc, grandparents, and siblings:

$$p_{k,l\to 1}(g,s) = \{(g_1, s_j) : j \in [k+1]\} \cup \{(g_{j+1}, g_j) : j \in [l]\}$$

The first-order pruning model can then be used to score these indices, and to produce a filtered index set $F(\mathcal{I}_1)$ by removing low-scoring indices (see Section 4). We retain only the higher-order indices that are supported by the filtered index set:

$$\{(g,s) \in \mathcal{I}_{k,l} : p_{k,l\to 1}(g,s) \subset F(\mathcal{I}_1)\}$$

3.3 Vine Parsing

To further reduce the cost of parsing and produce faster pruning models, we need a model with less structure than the first-order model. A natural choice, following Section 2, is to only consider "short" arcs:

$$\mathcal{S} = \{(h,m) \in \mathcal{I}_1 \ : \ |h-m| \le b\}$$

where b is a small constant. This constraint reduces the size of the set to $|\mathcal{S}| = O(nb)$.

Clearly, this index set is severely limited; it is necessary to have some long arcs for even short sentences. We therefore augment the index set to include *outer* arcs:

$$\mathcal{I}_0 = \mathcal{S} \cup \{(d,m) : d \in \{\leftarrow,\rightarrow\}, m \in [n]\} \cup \{(h,d) : h \in [n]_0, d \in \{\leftarrow,\rightarrow\}\}$$

The first set lets modifiers choose an outer head-word and the second set lets head words accept outer modifiers, and both sets distinguish the direction of the arc. Figure 5 shows a right outer arc. The size of $\mathcal{I}_0$ is linear in the sentence length. To parse the index set $\mathcal{I}_0$, we can modify the parse rules in Figure 3 to enforce additional length constraints ($|h-e| \le b$ for $I(h,e)$ and $|h-m| \le b$ for $C(h,m)$). This way, only indices in $\mathcal{S}$ are explored. Unfortunately, this is not sufficient since the constraints also prevent the algorithm from producing a full derivation, since no item can expand beyond length b.

Eisner and Smith (2005) therefore introduce vine parsing, which includes two new items, *vine left*,

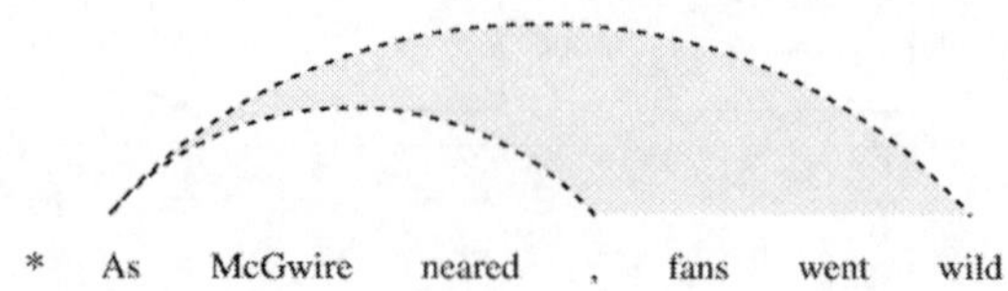

Figure 5: An outer arc $(1,\rightarrow)$ from the word "As" to possible right modifiers.

$V_{\leftarrow}(e)$, and *vine right*, $V_{\rightarrow}(e)$. Unlike the previous items, these new items are left-anchored at the root and grow only towards the right. The items $V_{\leftarrow}(e)$ and $V_{\rightarrow}(e)$ encode the fact that a word e has not taken a close (within b) head word to its left or right. We incorporate these items by adding the five new parsing rules shown in Figure 4.

The major addition is Rule 4(e) which converts a vine left item $V_{\leftarrow}(e)$ to a vine right item $V_{\rightarrow}(e)$. This implies that word e has no close head to either side, and the parse has outer head arcs, $y(\leftarrow, e) = 1$ or $y(\rightarrow, e) = 1$. The other rules are structural and dictate creation and extension of vine items. Rules 4(c) and 4(d) create vine left items from items that cannot find a head word to their left. Rules 4(f) and 4(g) extend and finish vine right items. Rules 4(d) and 4(f) each leave a head word incomplete, so they may set $y(e,\leftarrow) = 1$ or $y(m,\rightarrow) = 1$ respectively. Note that for all the new parse rules, $e \in [n]_0$ and $m \in \{e-b \ldots n\}$, so parsing time of this so called vine parsing algorithm is linear in the sentence length $O(nb^2)$.

Alone, vine parsing is a poor model of syntax - it does not even score most dependency pairs. However, it can act as a pruning model for other parsers. We prune a first-order model by mapping first-order indices to indices in $\mathcal{I}_0$.

$$p_{1\to 0}(h,m) = \begin{cases} \{(h,m)\} & \text{if } |h-m| \le b \\ \{(\rightarrow, m), (h, \rightarrow)\} & \text{if } h < m \\ \{(\leftarrow, m), (h, \leftarrow)\} & \text{if } h > m \end{cases}$$

The remaining first-order indices are then given by:

$$\{(h,m) \in \mathcal{I}_1 : p_{1\to 0}(h,m) \subset F(\mathcal{I}_0)\}$$

Figure 2 depicts a coarse-to-fine cascade, incorporating vine and first-order pruning passes and finishing with a higher-order parse model.

4 Training Methods

Our coarse-to-fine parsing architecture consists of multiple pruning passes followed by a final pass of 1-best parsing. The training objective for the pruning models comes from the prediction cascade framework of Weiss and Taskar (2010), which explicitly trades off pruning efficiency versus accuracy. The models used in the final pass on the other hand are trained for 1-best prediction.

4.1 Max-Marginal Filtering

At each pass of coarse-to-fine pruning, we apply an index filter function F to trim the index set:

$$F(\mathcal{I}) = \{i \in \mathcal{I} : f(i) = 1\}$$

Several types of filters have been proposed in the literature, with most work in coarse-to-fine parsing focusing on predicates that threshold the posterior probabilities. In structured prediction cascades, we use a non-probabilistic filter, based on the max-marginal value of the index:

$$f(i; \mathcal{Y}, w) = \mathbf{1}[\, M(i; \mathcal{Y}, w) \cdot w < t_\alpha(\mathcal{Y}, w) \,]$$

where $t_\alpha(\mathcal{Y}, w)$ is a sentence-specific threshold value. To counteract the fact that the max-marginals are not normalized, the threshold $t_\alpha(\mathcal{Y}, w)$ is set as a convex combination of the 1-best parse score and the average max-marginal value:

$$\begin{aligned} t_\alpha(\mathcal{Y}, w) &= \alpha \max_{y \in \mathcal{Y}} (y \cdot w) \\ &+ (1 - \alpha) \frac{1}{|\mathcal{I}|} \sum_{i \in \mathcal{I}} M(i; \mathcal{Y}, w) \cdot w \end{aligned}$$

where the model-specific parameter $0 \leq \alpha \leq 1$ is the tradeoff between $\alpha = 1$, pruning all indices i not in the best parse, and $\alpha = 0$, pruning all indices with max-marginal value below the mean.

The threshold function has the important property that for any parse y, if $y \cdot w \geq t_\alpha(\mathcal{Y}, w)$ then $y(i) = 1$ implies $f(i) = 0$, i.e. if the parse score is above the threshold, then none of its indices will be pruned.

4.2 Filter Loss Training

The aim of our pruning models is to filter as many indices as possible without losing the gold parse. In structured prediction cascades, we incorporate this pruning goal into our training objective.

Let y be the gold output for a sentence. We define *filter loss* to be an indicator of whether any i with $y(i) = 1$ is filtered:

$$\Delta(y, \mathcal{Y}, w) = \mathbf{1}[\exists i \in y, M(i; \mathcal{Y}, w) \cdot w < t_\alpha(\mathcal{Y}, w)]$$

During training we minimize the expected filter loss using a standard structured SVM setup (Tsochantaridis et al., 2006). First we form a convex, continuous upper-bound of our loss function:

$$\begin{aligned} \Delta(y, \mathcal{Y}, w) &\leq \mathbf{1}[y \cdot w < t_\alpha(\mathcal{Y}, w)] \\ &\leq [1 - y \cdot w + t_\alpha(\mathcal{Y}, w)]_+ \end{aligned}$$

where the first inequality comes from the properties of max-marginals and the second is the standard hinge-loss upper-bound on an indicator.

Now assume that we have a corpus of P training sentences. Let the sequence $(y^{(1)}, \ldots, y^{(P)})$ be the gold parses for each sentences and the sequence $(\mathcal{Y}^{(1)}, \ldots, \mathcal{Y}^{(P)})$ be the set of possible output structures. We can form the regularized risk minimization for this upper bound of filter loss:

$$\min_w \lambda \|w\|^2 + \frac{1}{P} \sum_{p=1}^{P} [1 - y^{(p)} \cdot w + t_\alpha(\mathcal{Y}^{(p)}, w)]_+$$

This objective is convex and non-differentiable, due to the max inside t. We optimize using stochastic subgradient descent (Shalev-Shwartz et al., 2007). The stochastic subgradient at example p, $H(w, p)$ is 0 if $y^{(p)} - 1 \geq t_\alpha(\mathcal{Y}, w)$ otherwise,

$$\begin{aligned} H(w, p) &= \frac{2\lambda w}{P} - y^{(p)} + \alpha \arg \max_{y \in \mathcal{Y}^{(p)}} y \cdot w \\ &+ (1 - \alpha) \frac{1}{|\mathcal{I}^{(p)}|} \sum_{i \in \mathcal{I}^{(p)}} M(i; \mathcal{Y}^{(p)}, w) \end{aligned}$$

Each step of the algorithm has an update of the form:

$$w_k = w_{k-1} - \eta_k H(w, p)$$

where η is an appropriate update rate for subgradient convergence. If $\alpha = 1$ the objective is identical to structured SVM with 0/1 hinge loss. For other values of α, the subgradient includes a term from the features of all max-marginal structures at each index. These feature counts can be computed using dynamic programming.

Setup	First-order Speed	PE	Oracle	UAS	Second-order Speed	PE	Oracle	UAS	Third-order Speed	PE	Oracle	UAS
NOPRUNE	1.00	0.00	100	91.4	0.32	0.00	100	92.7	0.01	0.00	100	93.3
LENGTHDICTIONARY	1.94	43.9	99.9	91.5	0.76	43.9	99.9	92.8	0.05	43.9	99.9	93.3
LOCALSHORT	3.08	76.6	99.1	91.4	1.71	76.4	99.1	92.6	0.31	77.5	99.0	93.1
LOCAL	4.59	89.9	98.8	91.5	2.88	83.2	99.5	92.6	1.41	89.5	98.8	93.1
FIRSTONLY	3.10	95.5	95.9	91.5	2.83	92.5	98.4	92.6	1.61	92.2	98.5	93.1
FIRSTANDSECOND		-				-			1.80	97.6	97.7	93.1
VINEPOSTERIOR	3.92	94.6	96.5	91.5	3.66	93.2	97.7	92.6	1.67	96.5	97.9	93.1
VINECASCADE	5.24	95.0	95.7	91.5	3.99	91.8	98.7	92.6	2.22	97.8	97.4	93.1
	k=8				k=16				k=64			
ZHANGNIVRE	4.32	-	-	92.4	2.39	-	-	92.5	0.64	-	-	92.7

Table 1: Results comparing pruning methods on PTB Section 22. Oracle is the max achievable UAS after pruning. Pruning efficiency (PE) is the percentage of non-gold first-order dependency arcs pruned. Speed is parsing time relative to the unpruned first-order model (around 2000 tokens/sec). UAS is the unlabeled attachment score of the final parses.

4.3 1-Best Training

For the final pass, we want to train the model for 1-best output. Several different learning methods are available for structured prediction models including structured perceptron (Collins, 2002), max-margin models (Taskar et al., 2003), and log-linear models (Lafferty et al., 2001). In this work, we use the margin infused relaxed algorithm (MIRA) (Crammer and Singer, 2003; Crammer et al., 2006) with a hamming-loss margin. MIRA is an online algorithm with similar benefits as structured perceptron in terms of simplicity and fast training time. In practice, we found that MIRA with hamming-loss margin gives a performance improvement over structured perceptron and structured SVM.

5 Parsing Experiments

To empirically demonstrate the effectiveness of our approach, we compare our vine pruning cascade with a wide range of common pruning methods on the Penn WSJ Treebank (PTB) (Marcus et al., 1993). We then also show that vine pruning is effective across a variety of different languages.

For English, we convert the PTB constituency trees to dependencies using the Stanford dependency framework (De Marneffe et al., 2006). We then train on the standard PTB split with sections 2-21 as training, section 22 as validation, and section 23 as test. Results are similar using the Yamada and Matsumoto (2003) conversion. We additionally selected six languages from the CoNLL-X shared task (Buchholz and Marsi, 2006) that cover a number of different language families: Bulgarian, Chinese, Japanese, German, Portuguese, and Swedish. We use the standard CoNLL-X training/test split and tune parameters with cross-validation.

All experiments use unlabeled dependencies for training and test. Accuracy is reported as unlabeled attachment score (UAS), the percentage of tokens with the correct head word. For English, UAS ignores punctuation tokens and the test set uses predicted POS tags. For the other languages we follow the CoNLL-X setup and include punctuation in UAS and use gold POS tags on the set set. Speedups are given in terms of time relative to a highly optimized C++ implementation. Our unpruned first-order baseline can process roughly two thousand tokens a second and is comparable in speed to the greedy shift-reduce parser of Nivre et al. (2004).

5.1 Models

Our parsers perform multiple passes over each sentence. In each pass we first construct a (pruned) hypergraph (Klein and Manning, 2005) and then perform feature computation and inference. We choose the highest α that produces a pruning error of no more than 0.2 on the validation set (typically $\alpha \approx 0.6$) to filter indices for subsequent rounds (similar to Weiss and Taskar (2010)). We compare a variety of pruning models:

LENGTHDICTIONARY a deterministic pruning method that eliminates all arcs longer than the maximum length observed for each head-modifier POS pair.

LOCAL an unstructured arc classifier that chooses indices from $\mathcal{I}_1$ directly without enforcing parse constraints. Similar to the quadratic-time filter from Bergsma and Cherry (2010).

LOCALSHORT an unstructured arc classifier that chooses indices from $\mathcal{I}_0$ directly without enforcing parse constraints. Similar to the linear-time filter from Bergsma and Cherry (2010).

FIRSTONLY a structured first-order model trained with filter loss for pruning.

FIRSTANDSECOND a structured cascade with first- and second-order pruning models.

VINECASCADE the full cascade with vine, first- and second-order pruning models.

VINEPOSTERIOR the vine parsing cascade trained as a CRF with L-BFGS (Nocedal and Wright, 1999) and using posterior probabilities for filtering instead of max-marginals.

ZHANGNIVRE an unlabeled reimplementation of the linear-time, k-best, transition-based parser of Zhang and Nivre (2011). This parser uses composite features up to third-order with a greedy decoding algorithm. The reimplementation is about twice as fast as their reported speed, but scores slightly lower.

We found LENGTHDICTIONARY pruning to give significant speed-ups in all settings and therefore always use it as an initial pass. The maximum number of passes in a cascade is five: dictionary, vine, first-, and second-order pruning, and a final third-order 1-best pass.[3] We tune the pruning thresholds for each round and each cascade separately. This is because we might be willing to do a more aggressive vine pruning pass if the final model is a first-order model, since these two models tend to often agree.

5.2 Features

For the non-pruning models, we use a standard set of features proposed in the discriminative graph-based dependency parsing literature (McDonald et al., 2005; Carreras, 2007; Koo and Collins, 2010).

[3]For the first-order parser, we found it beneficial to employ a reduced feature first-order pruner before the final model, i.e. the cascade has four rounds: dictionary, vine, first-order pruning, and first-order 1-best.

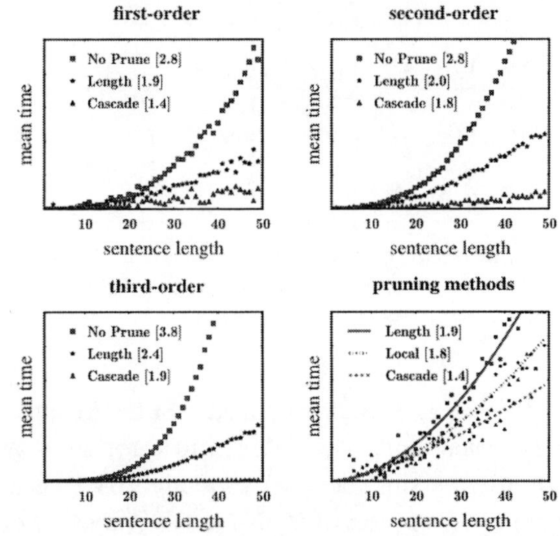

Figure 6: Mean parsing speed by sentence length for first-, second-, and third-order parsers as well as different pruning methods for first-order parsing. [b] indicates the empirical complexity obtained from fitting ax^b.

Included are lexical features, part-of-speech features, features on in-between tokens, as well as feature conjunctions, surrounding part-of-speech tags, and back-off features. In addition, we replicate each part-of-speech (POS) feature with an additional feature using coarse POS representations (Petrov et al., 2012). Our baseline parsing models replicate and, for some experiments, surpass previous best results.

The first- and second-order pruning models have the same structure, but for efficiency use only the basic features from McDonald et al. (2005). As feature computation is quite costly, future work may investigate whether this set can be reduced further. VINEPRUNE and LOCALSHORT use the same feature sets for short arcs. Outer arcs have features of the unary head or modifier token, as well as features for the POS tag bordering the cutoff and the direction of the arc.

5.3 Results

A comparison between the pruning methods is shown in Table 1. The table gives relative speed-ups, compared to the unpruned first-order baseline, as well as accuracy, pruning efficiency, and oracle scores. Note particularly that the third-order cascade is twice as fast as an unpruned first-order model and >200 times faster than the unpruned third-order baseline. The comparison with poste-

Round	1-Best Model First	Second	Third
Vine	37%	27%	16%
First	63%	30%	17%
Second	-	43%	18%
Third	-	-	49%

Table 2: Relative speed of pruning models in a multi-pass cascade. Note that the 1-best models use richer features than the corresponding pruning models.

rior pruning is less pronounced. Filter loss training is faster than VINEPOSTERIOR for first- and third-order parsing, but the two models have similar second-order speeds. It is also noteworthy that oracle scores are consistently high even after multiple pruning rounds: the oracle score of our third-order model for example is 97.4%.

Vine pruning is particularly effective. The vine pass is faster than both LOCAL and FIRSTONLY and prunes more effectively than LOCALSHORT. Vine pruning benefits from having a fast, linear-time model, but still maintaining enough structure for pruning. While our pruning approach does not provide any asymptotic guarantees, Figure 6 shows that in practice our multi-pass parser scales well even for long sentences: Our first-order cascade scales almost linearly with the sentence length, while the third-order cascade scales better than quadratic. Table 2 shows that the final pass dominates the computational cost, while each of the pruning passes takes up roughly the same amount of time.

Our second- and third-order cascades also significantly outperform ZHANGNIVRE. The transition-based model with $k = 8$ is very efficient and effective, but increasing the k-best list size scales much worse than employing multi-pass pruning. We also note that while direct speed comparison are difficult, our parser is significantly faster than the published results for other high accuracy parsers, e.g. Huang and Sagae (2010) and Koo et al. (2010).

Table 3 shows our results across a subset of the CoNLL-X datasets, focusing on languages that differ greatly in structure. The unpruned models perform well across datasets, scoring comparably to the top results from the CoNLL-X competition. We see speed increases for our cascades with almost no loss in accuracy across all languages, even for languages with fairly free word order like German. This is

Setup		First-order Speed	First-order UAS	Second-order Speed	Second-order UAS	Third-order Speed	Third-order UAS
BG	B	1.90	90.7	0.67	92.0	0.05	92.1
	V	6.17	90.5	5.30	91.6	1.99	91.9
DE	B	1.40	89.2	0.48	90.3	0.02	90.8
	V	4.72	89.0	3.54	90.1	1.44	90.8
JA	B	1.77	92.0	0.58	92.1	0.04	92.4
	V	8.14	91.7	8.64	92.0	4.30	92.3
PT	B	0.89	90.1	0.28	91.2	0.01	91.7
	V	3.98	90.0	3.45	90.9	1.45	91.5
SW	B	1.37	88.5	0.45	89.7	0.01	90.4
	V	6.35	88.3	6.25	89.4	2.66	90.1
ZH	B	7.32	89.5	3.30	90.5	0.67	90.8
	V	7.45	89.3	6.71	90.3	3.90	90.9
EN	B	1.0	91.2	0.33	92.4	0.01	93.0
	V	5.24	91.0	3.92	92.2	2.23	92.7

Table 3: Speed and accuracy results for the vine pruning cascade across various languages. B is the unpruned baseline model, and V is the vine pruning cascade. The first section of the table gives results for the CoNLL-X test datasets for Bulgarian (BG), German (DE), Japanese (JA), Portuguese (PT), Swedish (SW), and Chinese (ZH). The second section gives the result for the English (EN) test set, PTB Section 23.

encouraging and suggests that the outer arcs of the vine-pruning model are able to cope with languages that are not as linear as English.

6 Conclusion

We presented a multi-pass architecture for dependency parsing that leverages vine parsing and structured prediction cascades. The resulting 200-fold speed-up leads to a third-order model that is twice as fast as an unpruned first-order model for a variety of languages, and that also compares favorably to a state-of-the-art transition-based parser. Possible future work includes experiments using cascades to explore much higher-order models.

Acknowledgments

We would like to thank the members of the Google NLP Parsing Team for comments, suggestions, bug-fixes and help in general: Ryan McDonald, Hao Zhang, Michael Ringgaard, Terry Koo, Keith Hall, Kuzman Ganchev and Yoav Goldberg. We would also like to thank Andre Martins for showing that MIRA with hamming-loss margin performs better than other 1-best training algorithms.

References

S. Bergsma and C. Cherry. 2010. Fast and accurate arc filtering for dependency parsing. In *Proc. of COLING*, pages 53–61.

S. Buchholz and E. Marsi. 2006. CoNLL-X shared task on multilingual dependency parsing. In *CoNLL*.

X. Carreras, M. Collins, and T. Koo. 2008. Tag, dynamic programming, and the perceptron for efficient, feature-rich parsing. In *Proc. of CoNLL*, pages 9–16.

X. Carreras. 2007. Experiments with a higher-order projective dependency parser. In *Proc. of CoNLL Shared Task Session of EMNLP-CoNLL*, volume 7, pages 957–961.

E. Charniak, M. Johnson, M. Elsner, J. Austerweil, D. Ellis, I. Haxton, C. Hill, R. Shrivaths, J. Moore, M. Pozar, et al. 2006. Multilevel coarse-to-fine PCFG parsing. In *Proc. of NAACL/HLT*, pages 168–175.

M. Collins. 2002. Discriminative training methods for hidden markov models: Theory and experiments with perceptron algorithms. In *Proc. of EMNLP*, pages 1–8.

K. Crammer and Y. Singer. 2003. Ultraconservative online algorithms for multiclass problems. *The Journal of Machine Learning Research*, 3:951–991.

K. Crammer, O. Dekel, J. Keshet, S. Shalev-Shwartz, and Y. Singer. 2006. Online passive-aggressive algorithms. *The Journal of Machine Learning Research*, 7:551–585.

M.C. De Marneffe, B. MacCartney, and C.D. Manning. 2006. Generating typed dependency parses from phrase structure parses. In *Proc. of LREC*, volume 6, pages 449–454.

J. Eisner and N.A. Smith. 2005. Parsing with soft and hard constraints on dependency length. In *Proc. of IWPT*, pages 30–41.

J. Eisner. 2000. Bilexical grammars and their cubic-time parsing algorithms. *Advances in Probabilistic and Other Parsing Technologies*, pages 29–62.

L. Huang and K. Sagae. 2010. Dynamic programming for linear-time incremental parsing. In *Proc. of ACL*, pages 1077–1086.

D. Klein and C.D. Manning. 2005. Parsing and hypergraphs. *New developments in parsing technology*, pages 351–372.

T. Koo and M. Collins. 2010. Efficient third-order dependency parsers. In *Proc. of ACL*, pages 1–11.

T. Koo, A.M. Rush, M. Collins, T. Jaakkola, and D. Sontag. 2010. Dual decomposition for parsing with non-projective head automata. In *Proc. of EMNLP*, pages 1288–1298.

M. Kuhlmann, C. Gómez-Rodríguez, and G. Satta. 2011. Dynamic programming algorithms for transition-based dependency parsers. In *Proc. of ACL/HLT*, pages 673–682.

J. Lafferty, A. McCallum, and F.C.N. Pereira. 2001. Conditional random fields: Probabilistic models for segmenting and labeling sequence data. In *Proc. of ICML*, pages 282–289.

L. Lee. 2002. Fast context-free grammar parsing requires fast boolean matrix multiplication. *Journal of the ACM*, 49(1):1–15.

M.P. Marcus, M.A. Marcinkiewicz, and B. Santorini. 1993. Building a large annotated corpus of english: The penn treebank. *Computational linguistics*, 19(2):313–330.

R. McDonald and F. Pereira. 2006. Online learning of approximate dependency parsing algorithms. In *Proc. of EACL*, volume 6, pages 81–88.

R. McDonald, K. Crammer, and F. Pereira. 2005. Online large-margin training of dependency parsers. In *Proc. of ACL*, pages 91–98.

J. Nivre, J. Hall, and J. Nilsson. 2004. Memory-based dependency parsing. In *Proc. of CoNLL*, pages 49–56.

J. Nocedal and S. J. Wright. 1999. *Numerical Optimization*. Springer.

A. Pauls and D. Klein. 2009. Hierarchical search for parsing. In *Proc. of NAACL/HLT*, pages 557–565.

S. Petrov and D. Klein. 2007. Improved inference for unlexicalized parsing. In *Proc. of NAACL/HLT*, pages 404–411.

S. Petrov, D. Das, and R. McDonald. 2012. A universal part-of-speech tagset. In *LREC*.

S. Petrov. 2009. *Coarse-to-Fine Natural Language Processing*. Ph.D. thesis, University of California at Bekeley, Berkeley, CA, USA.

B. Roark and K. Hollingshead. 2008. Classifying chart cells for quadratic complexity context-free inference. In *Proc. of COLING*, pages 745–751.

S. Shalev-Shwartz, Y. Singer, and N. Srebro. 2007. Pegasos: Primal estimated sub-gradient solver for svm. In *Proc. of ICML*, pages 807–814.

B. Taskar, C. Guestrin, and D. Koller. 2003. Max-margin markov networks. *Advances in neural information processing systems*, 16:25–32.

I. Tsochantaridis, T. Joachims, T. Hofmann, and Y. Altun. 2006. Large margin methods for structured and interdependent output variables. *Journal of Machine Learning Research*, 6(2):1453.

D. Weiss and B. Taskar. 2010. Structured prediction cascades. In *Proc. of AISTATS*, volume 1284, pages 916–923.

H. Yamada and Y. Matsumoto. 2003. Statistical dependency analysis with support vector machines. In *Proc. of IWPT*, volume 3, pages 195–206.

Y. Zhang and J. Nivre. 2011. Transition-based dependency parsing with rich non-local features. In *Proc. of ACL*, pages 188–193.

Active Learning for Coreference Resolution

Florian Laws[1] **Florian Heimerl**[2] **Hinrich Schütze**[1]
[1] Institute for Natural Language Processing (IMS)
Universität Stuttgart
florian.laws@ims.uni-stuttgart.de
[2] Institute for Visualization and Interactive Systems
Universität Stuttgart
florian.heimerl@vis.uni-stuttgart.de

Abstract

We present an active learning method for coreference resolution that is novel in three respects. (i) It uses bootstrapped neighborhood pooling, which ensures a class-balanced pool even though gold labels are not available. (ii) It employs neighborhood selection, a selection strategy that ensures coverage of both positive and negative links for selected markables. (iii) It is based on a query-by-committee selection strategy in contrast to earlier uncertainty sampling work. Experiments show that this new method outperforms random sampling in terms of both annotation effort and peak performance.

1 Introduction

Coreference resolution (CR) – the task of determining if two expressions in natural language text refer to the same real-world entity – is an important NLP task. One popular approach to CR is supervised classification. This approach needs manually labeled training data that is expensive to create. Active learning (AL) is a technique that can reduce this cost by setting up an interactive training/annotation loop that selects and annotates training examples that are maximally useful for the classifier that is being trained. However, while AL has been proven successful for many other NLP tasks, such as part-of-speech tagging (Ringger et al., 2007), parsing (Osborne and Baldridge, 2004), text classification (Tong and Koller, 2002) and named entity recognition (Tomanek et al., 2007), AL has not been successfully applied to coreference resolution so far.

In this paper, we present a novel approach to AL for CR based on query-by-committee sampling and bootstrapping and show that it performs better than a number of baselines.

2 Related work

Coreference resolution. The perhaps most widely used supervised learning approach to CR is the mention-pair model (Soon et al., 2001). This model classifies links (pairs of two mentions) as coreferent or disreferent, followed by a clustering stage that partitions entities based on the link decisions. Our AL method is partially based on the class balancing strategy proposed by Soon et al. (2001).

While models other than mention-pair have been proposed (Culotta et al., 2007), none performs clearly better as evidenced by recent shared evaluations such as SemEval 2010 (Recasens et al., 2010) and CoNLL 2011 (Pradhan et al., 2011).

Active learning. The only existing publication on AL for CR that we are aware of is (Gasperin, 2009). She uses a mention-pair model on a biomedical corpus. The classifier is Naive Bayes and the AL method uncertainty sampling (Lewis and Gale, 1994). The results are negative: AL is not better than random sampling. In preliminary experiments, we replicated this result for our corpus and our system: Uncertainty sampling is not better than random sampling for CR. Uncertainty sampling can fail if uncertainty assessments are too unstable for successful example selection (cf. Dwyer and Holte (2007)). This seems to be the case for the decision trees we use. Naive Bayes is also known to give bad uncertainty assessments (Domingos and Pazzani,

1997). We therefore adopted a query-by-committee approach combined with a class-balancing strategy.

3 Active learning for CR

The classifier in the mention-pair model is faced with a severe class imbalance: there are many more disreferent than coreferent links. To address this imbalance, we use a *neighborhood pool* or N-pool as proposed by Soon et al. (2001).

Generation of the N-pool. The neighborhood of markable x used in N-pooling is defined as the set consisting of the link between x and its closest coreferent markable $y(x)$ to the left and all disreferent links in between. For a particular markable x, let $y(x)$ be the closest coreferent markable for x to the left of x. Between $y(x)$ and x, there are disreferent markables z_i, so we have a constellation like $y(x), z_1, \ldots, z_n, x$. The neighborhood of x is then the set of links

$$\{(y, x), (z_1, x) \ldots, (z_n, x)\}$$

This set is empty if x does not have a coreferent markable to the left.

We call the set of all such neighborhoods the N-pool. The N-pool is a subset of the entire pool of links.

Bootstrapping the neighborhood. Soon et al. (2001) introduce N-pooling for labeled data. In AL, no labeled data (or very little of it) is available. Instead, we employ the committee of classifiers that we use for AL example selection for bootstrapping the N-pool. We query the committee of classifiers from the last AL iteration and treat a link as coreferent if and only if the majority of the classifiers classifies it as coreferent. We then construct the N-pool using these bootstrapped labels to determine the coreferent markables $y(x)$ and then construct the neighborhoods as described above.

If this procedure yields no coreferent links in an iteration, we sample links left of randomly selected markables instead of N-pooling.

Example selection granularity. We use a query-by-committee approach to AL. The committee consists of 10 instances of the link classifier of the CR system, each trained on a randomly chosen subset of the links that have been manually labeled so far.

In each iteration, the N-pool is recomputed and a small subset of the N-pool is selected for labeling. We experiment with two selection granularities. In *neighborhood selection*, entire neighborhoods are selected and labeled in each iteration. We define the utility of a neighborhood as the average of the vote entropies (Argamon-Engelson and Dagan, 1999) of its links.

In *link selection*, individual links with the highest utility are selected – in most cases these will be from different neighborhoods. Utility is again defined as vote entropy.

Our hypothesis is that, compared to selection of individual links, neighborhood selection yields a more balanced sample that covers both positive and negative links for a markable. At the same time, neighborhood selection retains the benefits of AL sampling: difficult (or highly informative) links are selected.

4 Experiments

We use the mention-pair CR system SUCRE (Kobdani et al., 2011). The link classifier is a decision tree and the clustering algorithm a variant of best-first clustering (Ng and Cardie, 2002). SUCRE results were competitive in SEMEVAL 2010 (Recasens et al., 2010). We implemented N-pool bootstrapping and selection methods on top of the AL framework of Tomanek et al. (2007).

We use the English part of the SemEval-2010 CR task data set, a subset of OntoNotes 2.0 (Hovy et al., 2006). Training and test set sizes are about 96,000 and 24,000 words. Since we focus on the coreference resolution subtask, we use the true mention boundaries for the markables.

The pool for example selection is created by pairing every markable with every preceding markable within a window of 100 markables. This yields a pool of 1.7 million links, of which only 1.5% are labeled as coreferent. This drastic class imbalance necessitates our bootstrapped class-balancing.

We run two baseline experiments for comparison: (i) random selection on the entire pool, without any class balancing, and (ii) random selection from a gold-label-based N-pool. We chose to use gold neighborhood information for the baseline to remove the influence of badly predicted neighbor-

			20,000 links				50,000 links			
			MUC	B3	CEAF	mean	MUC	B3	CEAF	mean
(1)	random	entire pool	49.68	86.07	82.34	72.70	48.81	86.00	82.24	72.34
(2)		N-pooling	61.60	85.00	82.85	76.48	62.60	85.99	83.44	77.33
(3)	AL	link selection	55.65	86.91†	83.67†	75.41	55.84	86.94†	83.70	75.49
(4)		neighborhood sel.	63.07†	86.94†	84.42†	78.14†	63.81†	87.11†	84.33†	78.42†

Table 1: Performance of different methods. All measures are F_1 measures.

hoods and focus on the performance of random sampling. Hence, this is a very strong random baseline. The performance with bootstrapped neighborhoods would likely be lower.

We run 10 runs of each experiment, starting from 10 different seed sets. These seed sets contained 200 links, drawn randomly from the entire pool, for random sampling; and 20 neighborhoods for neighborhood selection, with a comparable number of links. We verified that each seed set contained instances of both classes.

5 Results

We determine the performance of CR depending on the number of links used for training. The results of the experiments are shown in Table 1 and Figures 1a to 1d. We show results for four coreference measures: MUC, B3, entity-based CEAF (henceforth: CEAF), and the arithmetic mean of MUC, B3 and CEAF (as suggested by the CoNLL-2011 shared evaluation).

In all four figures, the AL curves have reached a plateau at 20,000 links. At this point, neighborhood selection AL (line 4 in Table 1) outperforms random sampling from the N-pool (line 2) for all coreference measures, with gains from 1.47 points for MUC to 1.94 points for B3.

At 20,000 links, the N-pooling random baseline (line 2) has not yet reached maximum performance, but even at 50,000 links, neighborhood selection AL still outperforms the baselines. (AL and baseline performance will eventually converge when most links from the pool are sampled, but this will happen much later, since the pool has 1.7 million links in total).

†Statistically significant at $p < .05$ compared to baseline 2 using the sign test ($N = 10$, $k \geq 9$ successes).

Link selection AL (line 3) outperforms the baselines for B3 and CEAF, but is performing markedly worse than the N-pooling random baseline (line 2) for MUC (due to low recall for MUC) and mean F_1. Link selection yields a CR system that proposes a lot of singleton entities that are not coreferent with any other entity. The MUC scoring scheme does not give credit to singletons at all, thus the lower recall.

Neighborhood selection AL initially has low MUC, but starts to outperform the baseline at 15,000 links (Figure 1a). For B3 and CEAF, neighborhood selection AL outperforms the baselines much earlier, at a few 1000 links (Figures 1b and 1c). It thus shows more robust performance for all evaluation metrics.

Neighborhood selection AL also performs at least as well as (for B3) or better than (MUC and CEAF) link selection AL. Learning curves of neighborhood selection AL are consistently above the link selection curves. We therefore consider neighborhood selection AL to be the preferred AL setup for CR.

6 Conclusion

We have presented a new AL method for coreference resolution. The proposed method is novel in three respects. (i) It uses bootstrapped N-pooling, which ensures a class-balanced pool even though gold labels are not available. (ii) It further improves class balancing by neighborhood selection, a selection strategy that ensures coverage of positive and negative links per markable while still focusing on selecting difficult links. (iii) It is based on a query-by-committee selection strategy in contrast to earlier uncertainty sampling work. Experiments show that this new method outperforms random sampling in terms of both annotation effort and peak performance.

Acknowledgments

Florian Laws is a recipient of the Google Europe Fellowship in Natural Language Processing, and this research is supported in part by his fellowship. Florian Heimerl was supported by the Deutsche Forschungsgemeinschaft as part of the priority program 1335 'Scalable Visual Analytics'.

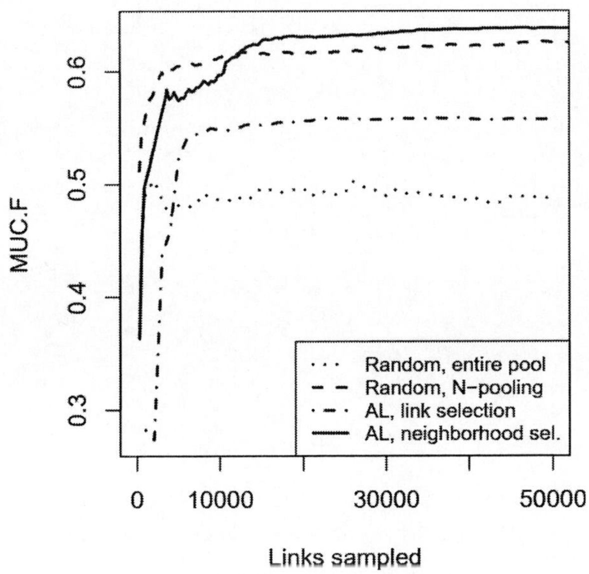

(a) Learning curve for MUC

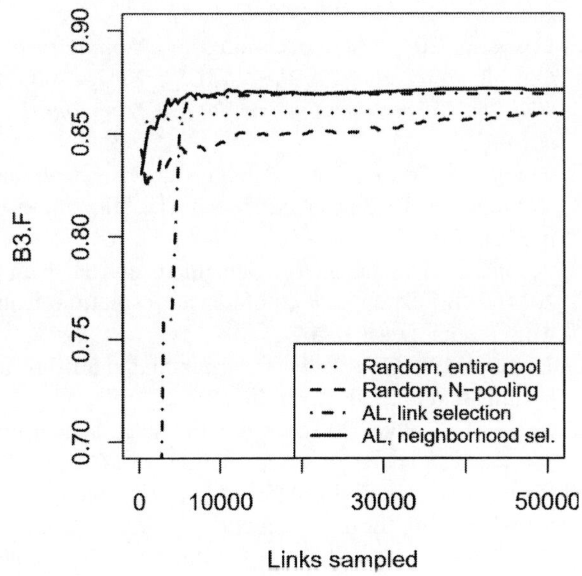

(b) Learning curve for B3

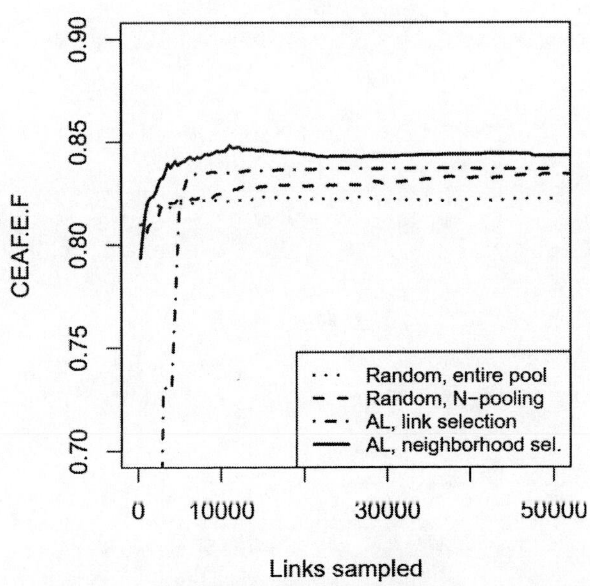

(c) Learning curve for CEAF

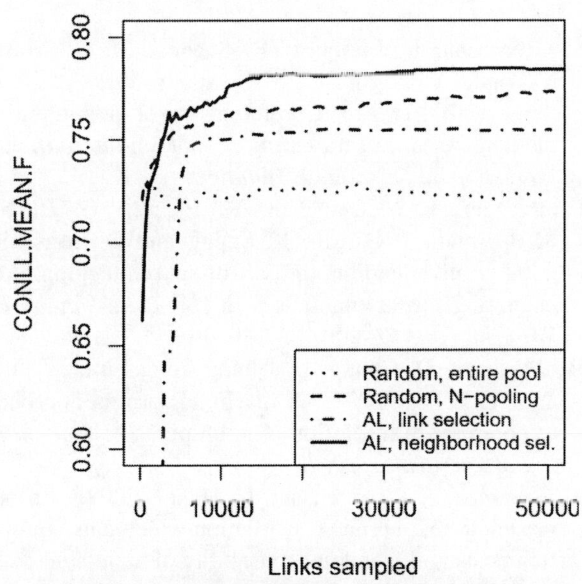

(d) Learning curve for the mean of the CR measures.

Figure 1: Learning curves for AL and baseline experiments. All measures are F_1 measures.

References

S. Argamon-Engelson and I. Dagan. 1999. Committee-based sample selection for probabilistic classifiers. *JAIR*, 11:335–360.

A. Culotta, M. Wick, R. Hall, and A. McCallum. 2007. First-order probabilistic models for coreference resolution. In *HLT-NAACL 2007*.

Pedro Domingos and Michael J. Pazzani. 1997. On the optimality of the simple bayesian classifier under zero-one loss. *Mach. Learn.*, 29(2-3):103–130.

K. Dwyer and R. Holte. 2007. Decision tree instability and active learning. In *ECML*.

C. Gasperin. 2009. Active learning for anaphora resolution. In *Proceedings of the NAACL HLT 2009 Workshop on Active Learning for Natural Language Processing*.

E. Hovy, M. Marcus, M. Palmer, L. Ramshaw, and R. Weischedel. 2006. Ontonotes: The 90% solution. In *HLT-NAACL*.

H. Kobdani, H. Schütze, M. Schiehlen, and H. Kamp. 2011. Bootstrapping coreference resolution using word associations. In *ACL*.

D. Lewis and W. Gale. 1994. A sequential algorithm for training text classifiers. In *SIGIR*.

V. Ng and C. Cardie. 2002. Improving machine learning approaches to coreference resolution. In *ACL*.

M. Osborne and J. Baldridge. 2004. Ensemble-based active learning for parse selection. In *HLT-NAACL*.

S. Pradhan, L. Ramshaw, M. Marcus, M. Palmer, R. Weischedel, and N. Xue. 2011. Conll-2011 shared task: Modeling unrestricted coreference in ontonotes. In *CoNLL*.

M. Recasens, L. Màrquez, E. Sapena, M. A. Martí, M. Taulé, V. Hoste, M. Poesio, and Y. Versley. 2010. Semeval-2010 task 1: Coreference resolution in multiple languages. In *Proceedings of the 5th International Workshop on Semantic Evaluation*.

E. Ringger, P. McClanahan, R. Haertel, G. Busby, M. Carmen, J. Carroll, K. Seppi, and D. Lonsdale. 2007. Active learning for part-of-speech tagging: Accelerating corpus annotation. In *Linguistic Annotation Workshop at ACL-2007*.

W. M. Soon, D. Chung, D. Chung Yong Lim, Y. Lim, and H. T. Ng. 2001. A machine learning approach to coreference resolution of noun phrases. *Computational Linguistics*, 27(4).

K. Tomanek, J. Wermter, and U. Hahn. 2007. An approach to text corpus construction which cuts annotation costs and maintains reusability of annotated data. In *EMNLP-CoNLL*.

S. Tong and D. Koller. 2002. Support vector machine active learning with applications to text classification. *JMLR*, 2:45–66.

Space Efficiencies in Discourse Modeling via Conditional Random Sampling

Brian Kjersten
CLSP
Johns Hopkins University

Benjamin Van Durme
HLTCOE
Johns Hopkins University

Abstract

Recent exploratory efforts in discourse-level language modeling have relied heavily on calculating Pointwise Mutual Information (PMI), which involves significant computation when done over large collections. Prior work has required aggressive pruning or independence assumptions to compute scores on large collections. We show the method of Conditional Random Sampling, thus far an underutilized technique, to be a space-efficient means of representing the sufficient statistics in discourse that underly recent PMI-based work. This is demonstrated in the context of inducing Shankian *script*-like structures over news articles.

1 Introduction

It has become common to model the distributional affinity between some word or phrase pair, (w_i, w_j), as a function of co-occurance within some *context* boundary. Church and Hanks (1990) suggested pointwise mutual information: $\mathrm{PMI}(w_i, w_j) = \log \frac{\Pr(w_i,w_j)}{\Pr(w_i)\Pr(w_j)}$, showing linguistically appealing results using contexts defined by fixed width n-gram windows, and syntactic dependencies derived from automatically parsed corpora. Later work such as by Lin (1999) continued this tradition. Here we consider document, or *discourse*-level contexts, such as explored by Rosenfeld (1994) or Church (2000), and more recently by those such as Chambers and Jurafsky (2008) or Van Durme and Lall (2009b).

In the spirit of recent work in randomized algorithms for large-scale HLT (such as by Ravichandran et al. (2005), Talbot and Osborne (2007), Goyal et al. (2010), Talbot and Brants (2008),Van Durme and Lall (2009a), Levenberg and Osborne (2009), Goyal et al. (2010), Petrovic et al. (2010), Van Durme and Lall (2010), or Goyal and Daumé (2011)), we propose the method of Conditional Random Sampling (CRS) by Li and Church (2007) as an efficient way to store *approximations* of the statistics used to calculate PMI for applications in inducing rudimentary *script*-like structures.

Efficiently storing such structures is an important step in integrating document-level statistics into downstream tasks, such as characterizing complex scenarios (Chambers and Jurafsky, 2011), or story understanding (Gordon et al., 2011).

2 Background

Conditional Random Sampling (CRS) Li and Church (2007) proposed CRS to approximate the contingency table between elements in a query, to be used in distributional similarity measures such as cosine similarity, correlation, and PMI. Central is the idea of the *postings list*, which is made up of the identifiers of each document that contains a given word or phrase. A set of such lists, one per type in the underlying vocabulary, is known as an *inverted index*. To reduce storage costs, a CRS truncates these lists, now called *sketches*, such that each sketch is no larger than some length parameter k.

Formally, assume an ordered list of document identifiers, $\Omega = (1, 2, ...)$, where each referenced document is a bag of words drawn from a vocabulary of size V. Let $P_i \subseteq \Omega$ be the postings list for some element $w_i \in V$. The function π represents a random permutation on the space of identifiers in Ω. The sketch, S_i, is defined as the first k elements of the permuted list: $S_i = \min_k(\pi(P_i))$. [1]

Let q be a two-element *query*, (w_i, w_j). Given the postings lists for w_i, w_j, we can construct a four-cell *contingency table* containing the frequency of documents that contained only w_i, only w_j, both together, or neither. A CRS allows for approximating this table in $O(k)$ time by relying on a sample of Ω, specific to q: $\pi(\Omega)_q = (1, 2, 3, ..., min(max(S_i), max(S_j)))$.

The PMI of q, given Ω, can be estimated from $\pi(\Omega)_q$ using the approximate word occurrence, $\Pr(w_i) = |S_i \cap \pi(\Omega)_q| / |\pi(\Omega)_q|$, and co-occurrence, $\Pr(w_i \cap w_j) = |S_i \cap S_j \cap \pi(\Omega)_q| / |\pi(\Omega)_q|$.

This scheme generalizes to longer queries of length m, where storage costs remain $O(Vk)$, and query time scales at $O(mk)$. Li and Church (2007) proved that CRS produces an unbiased estimate of the probabilities, and showed empirically that variance is a function of k and m.

Despite its simplicity and promise for large-scale data mining in NLP, CRS has thus-far seen minimal application in the community.

Trigger Language Models As here, Rosenfeld (1994)'s work on trigger language models was concerned with document level context. He identified trigger pairs: pairs of word sequences where the presence of the first word sequence affects the probability of the other, possibly at long distances. He recommended selecting a small list of trigger pairs based on the highest *average* mutual information (often simply called mutual information), although intuitively PMI could also be used. Computational constraints forced him to apply heavy pruning to the bigrams in his model.

Scripts A *script*, proposed by Schank (1975), is a form of Minsky-style *frame* that captures commonsense knowledge regarding typical events. For example, if a machine were to reason about *eating at a restaurant*, it should associate to this event: the existence of a *customer* or *patron* that usually *pays* for the *meal* that is *ordered* by the patron, then *served* by the *waiter*, etc.

Chambers and Jurafsky (2008) suggested inducing a similar structure called a *narrative chain*: focus on the situational descriptions explicitly pertaining to a single *protagonist*, a series of references within a document that are automatically labeled as coreferent. With a large corpus, one can then find those sets of verbs (as anchors of basic situational descriptions) which tend to co-occur, and share a protagonist, leading to an approximate subset of Schank's original conception.[2]

Underlying the co-occurrence framework of Chambers and Jurafsky was finding those verbs with high PMI. Starting with some initial element, chains were built greedily by adding the term, x, that maximized the average of the pairwise PMI between x and every term already in the chain:

$$W_{n+1} = \arg\max_{W} \frac{1}{n} \sum_{j=1}^{n} \mathrm{pmi}(W, W_j)$$

By relying on the average pairwise PMI, they are making independence assumptions that are not always valid. In order to consider more nuanced joint effects between more than two terms, more efficient methods would need to be considered.

3 Experiments

Setup Following Chambers and Jurafsky (2008), we extracted and lemmatized the verbs from the New York Times section of the Gigaword Corpus using the Stanford POS tagger (Toutanova et al., 2004) and the Morpha lemmatizer (Minnen et al., 2000). After filtering various POS tagger errors and setting a minimum document frequency (df) of 50, we went from a vocabulary of 94,803 words to 8,051.[3] For various values of k we built sketches over 1,655,193 documents, for each resulting word type.

[1] For example, assume some word w_i that appears in documents d_1, d_4, d_{10} and d_{12}. The identifiers are then randomly permuted via π such that: $d'_3 = d_1$, $d'_2 = d_4$, $d'_7 = d_{10}$ and $d'_1 = d_{12}$. Following permutation, the postings list for w_i is made up of identifiers that map to the same underlying documents as before, but now in a different order. If we let $k = 3$, then $S_i = (1, 2, 3)$, corresponding to documents: (d_{12}, d_4, d_1).

[2] Given a large collection of news articles, some on the topic of local crime, one might see a story such as: "*... searched for Michael$_i$ ... he$_i$ was arrested ... Mike$_i$ plead guilty ... convicted him$_i$* ...", helping to support an induced chain: (*search, arrest, plead, acquit, convict, sentence*).

[3] Types containing punctuation other than hyphens and underscores were discarded as tagger-error.

Table 1: Top-n by approximate PMI, for varying k. Subscripts denote rank under true PMI, when less than 50.

	plead			**plead, admit**		**plead, admit, convict**	
1	sentence$_4$	sentence$_4$	sentence$_4$	abuse$_-$	sentence$_5$	owe$_-$	sentence$_2$
2	commit$_-$	defraud$_5$	misbrand$_2$	convict$_{22}$	prosecute$_{15}$	admitt$_{11}$	prosecute$_3$
3	indict$_{10}$	indict$_{10}$	defraud$_5$	owe$_-$	testify$_{20}$	engage$_-$	arrest$_8$
4	prosecute$_{33}$	arraign$_6$	arraign$_6$	investigate$_-$	indict$_{10}$	investigate$_{28}$	testify$_5$
5	abuse$_-$	conspire$_{11}$	manslaughter$_1$	understand$_-$	defraud$_7$	prey$_-$	acquit$_1$
6	convict$_{24}$	convict$_{24}$	bilk$_8$	defraud$_7$	convict$_{22}$	defraud$_-$	indict$_4$
$k =$	100	1,000	10,000	1,000	10,000	1,000	10,000

We use a generalized definition of PMI for three or more items as the logarithm of the joint probability divided by the product of the marginals.

Subjective Quality We first consider the lemmatized version of the motivating example by Chambers and Jurafsky (2008): [*plead, admit, convict*], breaking it into 1-, 2-, and 3-element seeds. They reported the top 6 elements that maximize average pairwise PMI as: *sentence, parole, fire, indict, fine, deny*. We see similar results in Table 1, while noting again the distinction in underlying statistics: we did not restrict ourselves to cooccurrence based on shared coreferring arguments.

These results show intuitive discourse-level relationships with a sketch size as small as $k = 100$ for the unary seed. In addition, when examining the true PMI rank of each of these terms (reflected as subscripts), we see that highly ranked items in the approximate lists come from the set of items highly ranked in the non-approximate version.[4] A major benefit of the approach is that it allows for approximate scoring of larger sets of elements *jointly*, without the traditionally assumed storage penalty.[5]

Accuracy 1 We measured the trade-off between PMI approximation accuracy and sketch size. Triples of verb tokens were sampled at random from the *narrative cloze* test set of Chambers and Jurafsky (2008). Seed terms were limited to verbs with df between 1,000 and 100,000 to extract lists of the top-25 candidate verbs by joint, approximate PMI. For a given rank r, we measured the overlap of the *true* top-3 PMI and the approximate list, rank r or higher (see Figure 1(a)). If query size is 2, $k = 10,000$, the true top-3 true PMI items tend to rank well in the approximate PMI list. We observe that these randomly assembled queries tax the sketch-based approximation, motivating the next experiment on non-uniformly sampled queries.

Accuracy 2 In a more realistic scenario, we might have more discretion in selecting terms of interest. Here we chose the first word of each seed uniformly at random from each document, and selected subsequent seed words to maximize the true PMI with the established words in the seed. We constrained the seed terms to have df between 1,000 and 100,000. Then, for each seed of length 1, 2, and 3 words, we found the 25-best list of terms using approximate PMI, considering only terms that occur in more than 50 documents. Figure 1(b) shows the results of this PMI approximation tradeoff. With a sketch size of 10,000, a rank of 5 is enough to contain two out of the top three items, and the number gradually continues to grow as rank size increases.

Memory Analysis Accuracy in a CRS is a function of the aggressiveness in space savings: as k approaches the true length of the posting list for w_i, the resulting approximations are closer to truth, at the cost of increased storage. When $k = \infty$, CRS is the same as using an inverted index: Fig. 2 shows the percent memory required for our data, compared to a standard index, as the sketch size increases. For our data, a full index involves storing 95 million document numbers. For the $k = 10,000$ results, we see that 23% of a full index was needed.

Figure 1(c) shows the quality of approximate best PMI lists as memory usage is varied. A 2-word query needs about 20% of the memory for 2.5 of the

[4]The word "sentence" is consistently higher ranked in the approximate PMI list than it is in the true PMI list: results stem from a given *shared* permutation across the queries, and thus approximation errors are more likely to be correlated.

[5]For example, we report that PMI(*plead, admit, convict*) > PMI(*plead, admit, owe*), when $k = 1,000$, as compared to: *avg*(PMI(*plead, convict*), PMI(*admit, convict*)) > *avg*(PMI(*plead, owe*), PMI(*admit, owe*)).

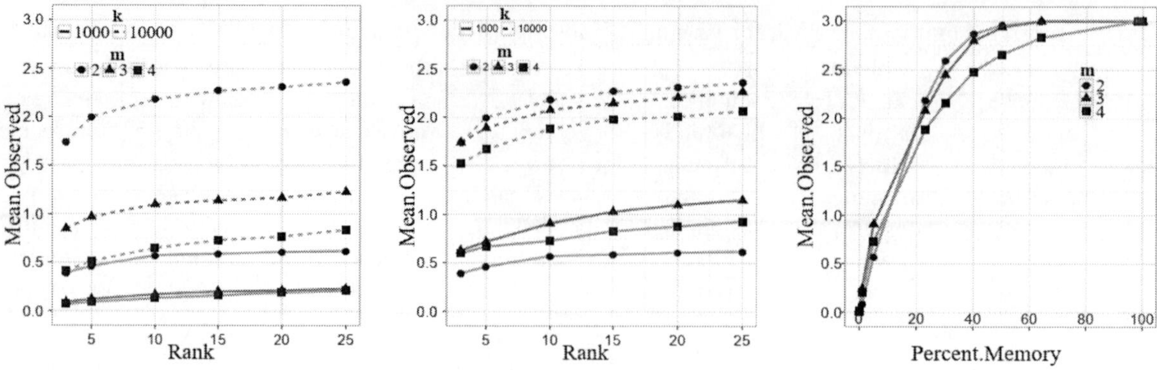

(a) (b) (c)

Figure 1: (a) Average number of true top-3 PMI items when seed terms have $1{,}000 \leq \text{df} \leq 100{,}000$ and are chosen uniformly at random from documents. (b) Average number of true top-3 PMI items when seeds are moderate-frequency high-PMI tuples. (c) Average number of true top-3 PMI items in the top ten approximate PMI list, as a function of memory usage, when seeds are moderate-frequency high-PMI tuples.

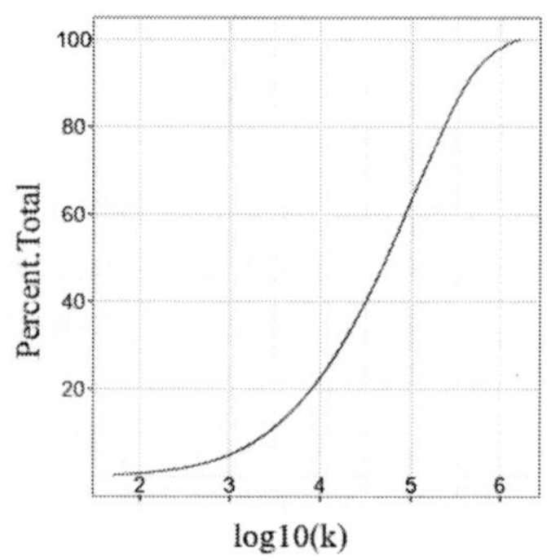

Figure 2: % of inverted index stored, as function of k.

top 3 true PMI items to appear in the top 10. Over 40% memory is needed for a 4-word query. 2.5 of the top 3 true PMI items appear in the top 50 when the memory is about 35%. This suggests that CRS allows us to use a fraction of the memory of storing a full inverted index, but that memory requirements grow with query size.

Discussion Storing exact PMIs of three or four words would be expensive to store in memory for any moderately sized vocabulary, because it would involve storing on the order of V^m count statistics. If we are approximating this with a CRS, we store sketches of length k or less for every word in the vocabulary, which is $O(kV)$. Table 1 and Fig. 1(b) show that the two-word queries start to get good performance when k is near 10,000. This requires 22.7% of the memory of a complete inverted index, or 21.5 million postings. The three and four word queries get good performance near $k = 100,000$. With this sketch size, 60.5 million postings are stored.

4 Conclusion

We have proposed using Conditional Random Sampling for approximating PMI in the discourse understanding community. We have shown that the approximate PMI rank list produces results that are intuitive and consistent with the exact PMI even with significant memory savings. This enables us to approximate PMI for tuples longer than pairs without undue independence assumptions. One future avenue is to explore the use of this structure in applications such as machine translation, as potentially enabling greater use of long distance dependencies than in prior work, such as by Hasan et al. (2008).

5 Acknowledgements

We acknowledge support from the National Science Foundation PIRE Grant No. OISE-0530118. We acknowledge the Army Research Laboratory for its support to the first author under SCEP (the Student Career Experience Program). Any opinions, findings, conclusions, or recommendations expressed in this material are those of the authors and do not necessarily reflect the views of the supporting agencies.

References

Nathanael Chambers and Dan Jurafsky. 2008. Unsupervised learning of narrative event chains. In *Proceedings of ACL*.

Nathanael Chambers and Dan Jurafsky. 2011. Template-based information extraction without the templates. In *Proceedings of ACL*.

Kenneth Church and Patrick Hanks. 1990. Word association norms, mutual information and lexicography. *Computational Linguistics*, 16(1):22–29.

Kenneth W. Church. 2000. Empirical estimates of adaptation: The chance of two noriegas is closer to p/2 than p^2. In *Proceedings of COLING*.

Andrew Gordon, Cosmin Bejan, and Kenji Sagae. 2011. Commonsense causal reasoning using millions of personal stories. In *Proceedings of AAAI*.

Amit Goyal and Hal Daumé. 2011. Lossy conservative update (lcu) sketch: Succinct approximate count storage. In *AAAI*.

Amit Goyal, Jagadeesh Jagarlamundi, Hal Daumé, and Suresh Venkatasubramanian. 2010. Sketch techniques for scaling distributional similarity to the web. In *6th WAC Workshop at NAACL-HLT*.

Sasa Hasan, Juri Ganitkevitch, Hermann Ney, and J. Andrés-Ferrer. 2008. Triplet lexicon models for statistical machine translation. In *Proceedings of EMNLP*.

Abby Levenberg and Miles Osborne. 2009. Stream-based randomised language models for smt. In *Proceedings of EMNLP*.

Ping Li and Kenneth Church. 2007. A sketch algorithm for estimating two-way and multi-way associations. *Computational Linguistics*, 33(2):305–354.

Dekang Lin. 1999. Automatic identification of non-compositional phrases. In *Proceedings of ACL*.

Guido Minnen, John Carroll, and Darren Pearce. 2000. Robust, applied morphological generation. In *Proceedings of the 1st International Natural Language Generation Conference*.

Sasa Petrovic, Miles Osborne, and Victor Lavrenko. 2010. Streaming first story detection with application to twitter. In *Proceedings of NAACL*.

Deepak Ravichandran, Patrick Pantel, and Eduard Hovy. 2005. Randomized Algorithms and NLP: Using Locality Sensitive Hash Functions for High Speed Noun Clustering. In *Proceedings of ACL*.

Ronald Rosenfeld. 1994. *Adaptive statistical language modeling: A maximum entropy approach*. Ph.D. thesis, Carnegie Mellon University.

Roger C. Schank. 1975. Using knowledge to understand. In *Theoretical Issues in Natural Language Processing*.

David Talbot and Thorsten Brants. 2008. Randomized language models via perfect hash functions. In *Proceeedings of ACL*.

David Talbot and Miles Osborne. 2007. Randomised language modelling for statistical machine translation. In *Proceedings of ACL*.

Kristina Toutanova, Dan Klein, Christopher D. Manning, and Yoram Singer. 2004. Feature-rich part-of-speech tagging with a cyclic dependency network. In *Proceedings of NAACL*.

Benjamin Van Durme and Ashwin Lall. 2009a. Probabilistic Counting with Randomized Storage. In *Proceedings of IJCAI*.

Benjamin Van Durme and Ashwin Lall. 2009b. Streaming pointwise mutual information. In *NIPS*.

Benjamin Van Durme and Ashwin Lall. 2010. Online Generation of Locality Sensitive Hash Signatures. In *Proceedings of ACL*.

Predicting Overt Display of Power in Written Dialogs

Vinodkumar Prabhakaran
Computer Science Dept.
Columbia University
New York, NY 10027, USA
vinod@cs.columbia.edu

Owen Rambow
CCLS
Columbia University
New York, NY 10027, USA
rambow@ccls.columbia.edu

Mona Diab
CCLS
Columbia University
New York, NY 10027, USA
mdiab@ccls.columbia.edu

Abstract

We analyze overt displays of power (ODPs) in written dialogs. We present an email corpus with utterances annotated for ODP and present a supervised learning system to predict it. We obtain a best cross validation F-measure of 65.8 using gold dialog act features and 55.6 without using them.

1 Introduction

Analyzing written dialogs (such as email exchanges) to extract social power relations has generated great interest recently. This paper introduces a new task within the general field of finding power relations in written dialogs. In written dialog, an utterance can represent an overt display of power (ODP) on the part of the utterer if it constrains the addressee's actions beyond the constraints that the underlying dialog act on its own imposes. For example, a request for action is the first part of an adjacency pair and thus requires a response from the addressee, but declining the request is a valid response. However, the utterer may formulate her request for action in a way that attempts to remove the option of declining it ("Come to my office now!"). In so doing, she restricts her addressee's options for responding more severely than a simple request for action would. Our new task is to classify utterances in written dialog as to whether they are ODPs or not. Such a classification can be interesting in and of itself, and it can also be used to study social relations among dialog participants.

After reviewing related work (Section 2), we define "overt display of power" (Section 3) and then present manual annotations for ODP in a small subset of Enron email corpus. In Section 5, we present a supervised learning system using word and part-of-speech features along with features indicating dialog acts.

2 Related Work

Many studies in sociolinguistics have shown that power relations are manifested in language use (e.g., (O'Barr, 1982)). Locher (2004) recognizes "restriction of an interactant's action-environment" (Wartenberg, 1990) as a key element by which exercise of power in interactions can be identified. Through ODP we capture this action-restriction at an utterance level. In the computational field, several studies have used Social Network Analysis (e.g., (Diesner and Carley, 2005)) for extracting social relations from online communication. Only recently have researchers started using NLP to analyze the content of messages to deduce social relations (e.g., (Diehl et al., 2007)). Bramsen et al. (2011) use knowledge of the actual organizational structure to create two sets of messages: messages sent from a superior to a subordinate, and *vice versa*. Their task is to determine the direction of power (since all their data, by construction of the corpus, has a power relationship). Their reported results cannot be directly compared with ours since their results are on classifying aggregations of messages as being to a superior or to a subordinate, whereas our results are on predicting whether a single utterance has an ODP or not.

3 Overt Display of Power (ODP)

Dialog is successful when all discourse participants show cooperative dialog behavior. Certain types of dialog acts, notably requests for actions and requests for information (questions), "set constraints on what should be done in a next turn" (Sacks et al., 1974). Suppose a boss sends an email to her subordinate: "It would be great if you could come to my office right now". He responds by politely declining ("Would love to, but unfortunately I need to pick up my kids"). He has met the expectation to respond in one of the constrained ways that the request for action allows (other acceptable responses include a commitment to performing the action, or actually performing the action, while unacceptable responses include silence, or changing the topic). However, dialog acts only provide an initial description of these constraints. Other sources of constraints include the social relations between the utterer and the addressee, and the linguistic form of the utterance. Assume our email example had come, say, from the CEO of the company. In this case, the addressee's response would not meet the constraints set by the utterance, even though it is still analyzed as the same dialog act (a request for action). Detecting such power relations and determining their effect on dialog is a hard problem, and it is the ultimate goal of our research. Therefore, we do not use knowledge of power relations as features in performing a finer-grained analysis of dialog acts. Instead, we turn to the linguistic form of an utterance. Specifically, the utterer can choose linguistic forms in her utterance to signal that she is imposing further constraints on the addressee's choice of how to respond, constraints which go beyond those defined by the standard set of dialog acts. For example, if the boss's email is "Please come to my office right now", and the addressee declines, he is clearly not adhering to the constraints the boss has signaled, though he is adhering to the general constraints of cooperative dialog by responding to the request for action. We are interested in these additional constraints imposed on utterances through choices in linguistic form. We define an utterance to have **Overt Display of Power** (ODP) if it is interpreted as creating additional constraints on the response beyond those imposed by the general dialog act. Note that use of polite language does not, on its own, determine the presence or absence of an ODP. Furthermore, the presence of an ODP does not presuppose that the utterer actually possess social power: the utterer could be attempting to gain power.

ID	Sample utterance
s1	If there is any movement of these people between groups can you please keep me in the loop.
s2	I need the answer ASAP, as ....
s3	Please give me your views ASAP.
s4*	Enjoy the rest of your week!
s5	Would you work on that?
s6*	... would you agree that the same law firm advise on that issue as well?
s7*	can you BELIEVE this bloody election?
s8	ok call me on my cell later.

Table 1: Sample utterances from the corpus; * next to ID denotes an utterance without an ODP

Table 1 presents some sample utterances chosen from our corpus (the * indicates those without ODP). An utterance with ODP can be an explicit order or command (s3, s8) or an implicit one (s2, s5). It can be a simple sentence (s3) or a complex one (s1). It can be an imperative (s3), an interrogative (s5) or even a declarative (s2) sentence. But not all imperatives (s4) or interrogatives (s6, s7) are ODPs. s5, s6 and s7 are all syntactically questions. However, s5's discourse function within an email is to request/order to work on "that" which makes it an instance of ODP, while s6 is merely an inquiry and s7 is a rhetorical question. This makes the problem of finding ODP in utterances a non-trivial one.

4 Data and Annotations

For our study, we use a small corpus of Enron email threads which has been previously annotated with dialog acts (Hu et al., 2009). The corpus contains 122 email threads with 360 messages, 1734 utterances and 20,740 word tokens. We trained an annotator using the definition for ODP given in Section 3. She was given full email threads whose messages were already segmented into utterances. She identified 86 utterances (about 5%) to have an ODP.[1] In

[1]These annotations were done as part of a larger annotation effort (Prabhakaran et al., 2012). The annotated corpus can be obtained at http://www.cs.columbia.edu/~vinod/powerann/.

order to validate the annotations, we trained another annotator using the same definitions and examples and had him annotate 46 randomly selected threads from the corpus, which contained a total of 595 utterances (34.3% of whole corpus). We obtained a reasonable inter annotator agreement, κ value, of 0.669, which validates the annotations while confirming that the task is not a trivial one.

5 Automatic ODP Tagging

In this section, we present a supervised learning method to tag unseen utterances that contain an ODP using a binary SVM classifier. We use the tokenizer, POS tagger, lemmatizer and SVMLight (Joachims, 1999) wrapper that come with ClearTK (Ogren et al., 2008). We use a linear kernel with $C = 1$ for all experiments and present (P)recision, (R)ecall and (F)-measure obtained on 5-fold cross validation on the data. Our folds do not cross thread boundaries.

5.1 Handling Class Imbalance

In its basic formulation, SVMs learn a decision function f from a set of positive and negative training instances such that an unlabeled instance x is labeled as positive if $f(x) > 0$. Since SVMs optimize on training set accuracy to learn f, it performs better on balanced training sets. However, our dataset is highly imbalanced ($\sim$ 5% positive instances). We explore two ways of handling this class imbalance problem: an instance weighting method, *InstWeight*, where training errors on negative instances are outweighed by errors on positive instances, and *SigThresh*, a threshold adjusting method to find a better threshold for $f(x)$. For *InstWeight*, we used the *j* option in SVMlight to set the outweighing factor to be the ratio of negative to positive instances in the training set for each cross validation fold. *InstWeight* is roughly equivalent to oversampling by repeating positive instances. For *SigThresh*, we used a threshold based on a posterior probabilistic score, $p = Pr(y = 1|x)$, calculated using the ClearTK implementation of Lin et al. (2007)'s algorithm. It uses Platt (1999)'s approximation of p to a sigmoid function $P_{A,B}(f) = (1 + exp(Af + B))^{-1}$, where A and B are estimated from the training set. Then, we predict x as positive if $p > 0.5$ which in effect shifts the threshold for $f(x)$ to a value based on its distribution on positive and negative training instances.

Experiment	InstWeight			SigThresh		
	P	R	F	P	R	F
ALL-TRUE	5.0	100.0	9.5	5.0	100.0	9.5
RANDOM	5.7	58.1	10.4	5.7	58.1	10.4
WORD-UNG	43.1	29.1	34.7	63.0	39.5	48.6
PN,MN,FV,DA	**66.7**	**48.8**	**56.4**	72.3	54.7	62.3
PN,MN,DA	64.5	46.5	54.1	**75.8**	**58.1**	**65.8**
LN,PN,MN,FV	64.4	44.2	52.4	**65.2**	**50.0**	**56.6**

Table 2: Results

Class Imbalance Handling: InstWeight: Instance weighting and SigThresh: Sigmoid thresholding
Features: WORD-UNG: Word unigrams, LN: Lemma ngrams, PN: POS ngrams, MN: Mixed ngrams, FV: First verb, DA: Dialog acts

5.2 Features

We present experiments using counts of three types of ngrams: lemma ngrams (*LN*), POS ngrams (*PN*) and mixed ngrams (*MN*).[2] Mixed ngram is a restricted formulation of lemma ngram where open-class lemmas (nouns, verbs, adjectives and adverbs) are replaced by POS tags. E.g., for the utterance *s2*, *LN* would capture patterns {i, need, i need, ...}, while *PN* would capture {PRP, VBP, PRP VBP, ...} and *MN* would capture {i VBP the NN, ...}. We also used a feature (*FV*) to denote the first verb lemma in the utterance. Since ODPs, like dialog acts, constrain how the addressee should react, we also include Dialog Acts as features (*DA*). We use the manual gold dialog act annotations present in our corpus, which use a very small dialog act tag set. An utterance has one of 5 dialog acts: RequestAction, RequestInformation, Inform, Commit and Conventional (see (Hu et al., 2009) for details). For example, for utterance *s2*, *FV* would be 'need' and *DA* would be 'Inform'.[3]

5.3 Results and Analysis

We present two simple baselines — ALL-TRUE, where an utterance is always predicted to have an ODP, and RANDOM, where an utterance is predicted at random, with 50% chance to have an ODP. We also present a strong baseline WORD-UNG,

[2] *LN* performed consistently better than word ngrams.

[3] We also explored other features including the number of tokens, the previous or following dialect act, none of which improved the results and. We omit a detailed discussion for reasons of space.

which is trained using surface-form word unigrams as features. ALL-TRUE and RANDOM obtained F scores of 9.5 and 10.4 respectively, while WORD-UNG obtained an F score of 34.7 under *InstWeight*, and improved it to 48.6 under *SigThresh*.

For *LN*, *PN* and *MN*, we first found the best value for n to be 1, 2 and 4, respectively. We then did an exhaustive search in all combinations of *LN*, *PN*, *MN*, *FV* and *DA* under both *InstWeight* and *SigThresh*. Results obtained for best feature subset under both configurations are presented in Table 2 in rows 3 and 4. *SigThresh* outweighed *InstWeight* in all our experiments. (Combining these two techniques for dealing with class imbalance performed worse than using either one.) In both settings, we surpassed the WORD-UNG baseline by a high margin. We found *MN* and *DA* to be most useful: removing either from the feature set dropped the F significantly in both settings. We obtained a best F score of 65.8 using *PN*, *MN* and *DA* under the *SigThresh*.

Following (Guyon et al., 2002), we inspected feature weights of the model created for the last fold of our best performing feature configuration as a post-hoc analysis. The binary feature *DA:RequestAction* got the highest positive weight of 2.5. The top ten positive weighted features included patterns like *you_VB*, **_VB*, *MD_PRP*, *VB_VB* and **_MD*, where * denotes the utterance boundary. *DA:Inform* got the most negative weight of -1.4, followed by *DA:Conventional* with -1.0. The top ten negative weighted features included patterns like *MD_VB*, *VB_you*, *what*, *VB_VB_me_VB* and *WP*. In both cases, DA features got almost 2.5 times higher weight than the highest weighted ngram pattern, which reaffirms their importance in this task. Also, mixed ngrams helped to capture long patterns like "please let me know" by *VB_VB_me_VB* without increasing dimensionality as much as word ngrams; they also distinguish *VB_you* with a negative weight of -0.51 from *VB_me* with a positive weight of 0.32, which pure POS ngrams couldn't have captured.

5.4 Not Using Gold Dialog Acts

We also evaluate the performance of our ODP tagger without using gold *DA* tags. We instead use the DA tagger of Hu et al. (2009), which we re-trained using the training sets for each of our cross validation folds, applying it to the test set of that fold. We then did cross validation for the ODP tagger using gold dialog acts for training and automatically tagged dialog acts for testing. However, for our best performing feature set so far, this reduced the F score from 65.8 to 52.7. Our best result for ODP tagging without using gold *DAs* is shown in row 5 in Table 2, 56.9 F score under *SigThresh*. The features used are all of our features other than the *DA* tags. On further analysis, we find that even though the dialog act tagger has a high accuracy (85.8% in our cross validation), it obtained a very low recall of 28.6% and precision of 47.6% for the *RequestAction* dialog act. Since *RequestAction* is the most important feature (weighted 1.7 times more than the next feature), the DA-tagger's poor performance on *RequestAction* hurt ODP tagging badly. The performance reduction in this setting is probably partly due to using gold *DAs* in training and automatically tagged *DAs* in testing; however, we feel that improving the detection of minority classes in dialog act tagging (*RequestAction* constitutes only 2.5% in the corpus) is a necessary first step towards successfully using automatically tagged *DAs* in ODP tagging.

6 Conclusion

We have introduced a new binary classification task on utterances in dialogs, namely predicting Overt Display of Power. An ODP adds constraints on the possible responses by the addressee. We have introduced a corpus annotated for ODP and we have shown that using supervised machine learning with gold dialog acts we can achieve an F-measure of 66% despite the fact that ODPs are very rare in the corpus. We intend to develop a better dialog act tagger which we can use to automatically obtain dialog act labels for ODP classification.

7 Acknowledgments

This work is supported, in part, by the Johns Hopkins Human Language Technology Center of Excellence. Any opinions, findings, and conclusions or recommendations expressed in this material are those of the authors and do not necessarily reflect the views of the sponsor. We thank several anonymous reviewers for their constructive feedback.

References

Philip Bramsen, Martha Escobar-Molano, Ami Patel, and Rafael Alonso. 2011. Extracting social power relationships from natural language. In *ACL*, pages 773–782. The Association for Computer Linguistics.

Christopher P. Diehl, Galileo Namata, and Lise Getoor. 2007. Relationship identification for social network discovery. In *AAAI*, pages 546–552. AAAI Press.

Jana Diesner and Kathleen M. Carley. 2005. Exploration of communication networks from the enron email corpus. In *In Proc. of Workshop on Link Analysis, Counterterrorism and Security, SIAM International Conference on Data Mining 2005*, pages 21–23.

Isabelle Guyon, Jason Weston, Stephen Barnhill, and Vladimir Vapnik. 2002. Gene selection for cancer classification using support vector machines. *Mach. Learn.*, 46:389–422, March.

Jun Hu, Rebecca Passonneau, and Owen Rambow. 2009. Contrasting the interaction structure of an email and a telephone corpus: A machine learning approach to annotation of dialogue function units. In *Proceedings of the SIGDIAL 2009 Conference*, London, UK, September. Association for Computational Linguistics.

Thorsten Joachims. 1999. Making Large-Scale SVM Learning Practical. In Bernhard Schölkopf, Christopher J.C. Burges, and A. Smola, editors, *Advances in Kernel Methods - Support Vector Learning*, Cambridge, MA, USA. MIT Press.

Hsuan-Tien Lin, Chih-Jen Lin, and Ruby C. Weng. 2007. A note on platt's probabilistic outputs for support vector machines. *Mach. Learn.*, 68:267–276, October.

Miriam A. Locher. 2004. *Power and politeness in action: disagreements in oral communication*. Language, power, and social process. M. de Gruyter.

William M. O'Barr. 1982. *Linguistic evidence: language, power, and strategy in the courtroom*. Studies on law and social control. Academic Press.

Philip V. Ogren, Philipp G. Wetzler, and Steven Bethard. 2008. ClearTK: A UIMA toolkit for statistical natural language processing. In *Towards Enhanced Interoperability for Large HLT Systems: UIMA for NLP workshop at Language Resources and Evaluation Conference (LREC)*.

John C. Platt. 1999. Probabilistic outputs for support vector machines and comparisons to regularized likelihood methods. In *ADVANCES IN LARGE MARGIN CLASSIFIERS*, pages 61–74. MIT Press.

Vinodkumar Prabhakaran, Owen Rambow, and Mona Diab. 2012. Annotations for power relations on email threads. In *Proceedings of the Eighth conference on International Language Resources and Evaluation (LREC'12)*, Istanbul, Turkey, May. European Language Resources Association (ELRA).

Sacks, E Schegloff, and G Jefferson. 1974. A simplest systematics for the organization of turn-taking for conversation. *Language*, 50:696–735.

Thomas E. Wartenberg. 1990. *The forms of power: from domination to transformation*. Temple University Press.

Co-reference via Pointing and Haptics in Multi-Modal Dialogues

Lin Chen, Barbara Di Eugenio
Department of Computer Science
University of Illinois at Chicago
851 S Morgan ST, Chicago, IL 60607, USA
{lchen43,bdieugen}@uic.edu

Abstract

This paper describes our ongoing work on resolving third person pronouns and deictic words in a multi-modal corpus. We show that about two thirds of these referring expressions have antecedents that are introduced by pointing gestures or by *haptic-ostensive* actions (actions that involve manipulating an object). After describing our annotation scheme, we discuss the co-reference models we learn from multi-modal features. The usage of haptic-ostensive actions in a co-reference model is a novel contribution of our work.

1 Introduction

Co-reference resolution has received a lot of attention. However, as Eisenstein and Davis (2006) noted, most research on co-reference resolution has focused on written text. This task is much more difficult in dialogue, especially in multi-modal dialogue contexts. First, utterances are informal, ungrammatical and disfluent. Second, people spontaneously use gestures and other body language. As noticed by Kehler (2000), Goldin-Meadow (2003), and Chen et al. (2011), in a multi-modal corpus, the antecedents of referring expressions are often introduced via gestures. Whereas the role played by pointing gestures in referring has been studied, the same is not true for other types of gestures. In this paper, alongside pointing gestures, we will discuss the role played by *Haptic-Ostensive (H-O)* actions, i.e., referring to an object by manipulating it in the world (Landragin et al., 2002; Foster et al., 2008). As far as we know, no computational models of co-reference have been developed that include H-O actions: (Landragin et al., 2002) focused on perceptual salience and (Foster et al., 2008) on generation rather than interpretation. We should point out that at the time of writing we only focus on resolving third person pronouns and deictics.

The rest of this paper is organized as follows. In Section 2 we describe our multi-modal annotation scheme. In Section 3 we present the pronoun/deictic resolution system. In Section 4, we discuss experiments and results.

2 The Data Set

The dataset we use in this paper is a subset of the ELDERLY-AT-HOME corpus (Di Eugenio et al., 2010), a multi-modal corpus in the domain of elderly care. It contains 20 human-human dialogues. In each dialogue, a helper (HEL) and an elderly person (ELD) performed *Activities of Daily Living* (Krapp, 2002), such as getting up from chairs, finding pots, cooking pastas, in a realistic setting, a studio apartment used for teaching and research. The corpus contains videos and voice data in avi format, haptics data collected via instrumented gloves in csv format, and the transcribed utterances in xml format.

We focused on specific subdialogues in this corpus, that we call *Find* tasks: a *Find* task is a continuous time span during which the two subjects were collaborating on finding objects. *Find* tasks arise naturally while helping perform ADLs such as preparing dinner. An excerpt from a *Find* task is shown below, including annotations for pointing gestures and for H-O actions (annotations are performed via the Anvil tool (Kipp, 2001)).

ELD : Can you get me a pot?
HEL: (opens cabinet, takes out pot, without saying a word)
`[Open(HEL,Cabinet1),Take-Out(HEL,Pot1)]`
ELD: Not that one, try over there.
`[Point(ELD,Cabinet5)]`

Because the targets of pointing gestures and H-O actions are real life objects, we designed a referring index system to annotate them. The referring index system consists of compile time indices and run time indices. We give pre-defined indices to targets which cannot be moved, like cabinets, drawers, fridge. We assign run time indices to targets which can be moved, and exist in multiple copies, like cups, glasses. A referring index consists of a type and an index; the index increases according to the order of appearance in the dialogue. For example, "*Pot#1*" means the first pot referred to in the dialogue. If a pointing gesture or H-O action involved multiple objects, we used JSON (JavaScript Object Notation)[1] Array to mark it. For example, [C#1, C#2] means Cabinet#1 and Cabinet#2.

We define a pointing gesture as a hand gesture without physical contact with the target, whereas gestures that involve physical contact with an object are haptic-obstensive (H-O).[2] We use four tracks in Anvil to mark these gestures, two for pointing gestures, and two for H-O actions. In each pair of tracks, one track is used for HEL, one for ELD. For both types of gestures, we mark the start time, end time and the target(s) of the gesture using the referring index system we introduced above. Additionally we mark the type of an H-O action: Touch, Hold, Take-Out (as in taking out an object from a cabinet or the fridge), Close, Open.[3]

Our co-reference annotation follows an approach similar to (Eisenstein and Davis, 2006). We mark the pronouns and deictics which need to be resolved, their antecedents, and the co-reference links between them. To mark pronouns, deictics and textual antecedents, we use the shallow parser from Apache OpenNLP Tools [4] to chunk the utterances in each turn. We use heuristics rules to automatically mark potential textual antecedents and the phrases we need to resolve. Afterwards we use Anvil to edit the results of automatic processing. To annotate co-reference links, we first assign each of the textual antecedents, the pointing gestures and H-O actions a unique markable index. Finally, we link referring expressions to their closest antecedent (if applicable) using the markable indices.

Find Subtasks	142
Length (Seconds)	5009
Speech Turns	1746
Words	8213
Pointing Gestures	362
H-O Actions	629
Pronouns and Deictics	827
Resolved Ref. Expr.	757
Textual Antecedent	218
Pointing Gesture Antecedent	266
H-O Antecedent	273

Table 1: Annotation Statistics

Table 1 shows corpus and annotation statistics. We annotated 142 *Find* subtasks, whose total length is about 1 hour and 24 minutes. This sub-corpus comprises 1746 spoken turns, which include 8213 words. 10% of the 8213 words (827 words) are pronouns or deictics. Note that for only 757/827 (92%) were the annotators able to determine an antecedent. Interestingly, 71% of those 757 pronouns or deictics refer to specific antecedents that are introduced *exclusively* by gestures, either pointing or H-O actions. In the earlier example, only the type for the referent of *that* in *No, not that one* had been introduced textually, but not its specific antecedent `pot1`. Clearly, to be effective on such data any model of co-reference must include the targets of pointing gestures and H-O actions. Our current model does not take into account the type provided by the *de dicto* interpretation of indefinites such as *a pot* above, but we intend to address this issue in future work.

In order to verify the reliability of our annotations, we double coded 15% of the data for pointing gestures and H-O actions, namely the dialogues from 3 pairs of subjects, or 22 *Find* subtasks. We ob-

[1] http://www.json.org/

[2] Whereas not all haptic actions are ostensive, in our dialogues they all potentially perform an ostensive function.

[3] Our subjects occasionally hold objects together, e.g. to fill a pot with water: these actions are not included among the H-O actions, and are annotated separately.

[4] http://incubator.apache.org/opennlp/

tained reasonable κ values: for pointing gestures, κ=0.751, for H-O actions, κ=0.703, and for co-reference, κ=0.70.

3 The Co-reference Model

In this paper we focus on how to use gesture information (pointing or H-O) to solve the referring expressions of interest. Given a pronoun or deictic, we build co-reference pairs by pairing it with the targets of pointing gestures and H-O actions in a given time window. We mark the correct pairs as "True" and then we train a classification model to judge if a co-reference pair is a true pair. The main component of the resolution system is the co-reference classification model. Since our antecedents are not textual, most of the traditional features for co-reference resolution do not apply. Rather, we use the following multi-modal features - U is the utterance containing the pronoun / deictic to be solved:

- *Time distance* between the spans of U and of the pointing/H-O action. If the two spans overlap, the distance is 0.
- *Speaker agreement:* If the speaker of U and the actor of the pointing/H-O action are the same.
- *Markable type agreement:* If the markable type of the pronoun/deictic and of the targets of pointing gesture/H-O action are compatible.
- *Number agreement*: If the number of the pronoun/deictic is the same as that of the targets of the pointing gesture/H-O action.
- *Object agreement*: If the deictic is contained in a phrase, such as "this big blue bowl", we will check if the additional object description "bowl" matches the targets of pointing gesture/H-O action.
- *H-O Action type*: for co-reference pairs with antecedents from H-O actions.

For markable type agreement, we defined two types of markables: PLC (place) and OBJ (object). PLC includes all the targets which cannot easily be moved, OBJ includes all the targets like cups, pots. We use heuristics rules to assign markable types to pronouns/deictics and the targets of pointing gestures/H-O actions. To determine the number of the targets, we extract information from the annotations; if the target is a JSON array, it means it is plural. To extract additional object description for the object agreement feature, we use the Stanford Typed Dependency parser (De Marneffe and Manning., 2008). We check if the pronoun/deictic is involved in "det" and "nsubj" relations, if so, we extract the "gov" element of that relation as the object to compare with the target of gestures/H-O actions.

4 Experiments and Discussions

We have experimented with 3 types of classification models: Maximum Entropy (MaxEnt), Decision Tree and Support Vector Machine (SVM), respectively implemented via the following three packages: MaxEnt, J48 from Weka (Hall et al., 2009), and LibSVM (Chang and Lin, 2011). All of the results reported below are calculated using 10 fold cross validation.

We have run a series of experiments changing the history length from 0 to 10 seconds for generating co-reference pairs (history changes in increments of 1 second, hence, there are 11 sets of experiments). For each history length, we build the 3 models mentioned above. An additional baseline model treats a co-reference pair as "True" if speaker agreement is true for the pair, and the time distance is 0. Beside the specified baseline, J48 can be seen as a more sophisticated baseline as well. When we ran the 10 fold experiment with J48 algorithm, 5 out of 10 generated decision trees only used 3 attributes.

We use two metrics to measure the performance of the models. One are the standard precision, recall and F-Score with respect to the generated co-reference pairs; the other is the number of pronouns and deictics that are correctly resolved. Given a pronoun/deictic p_i, if the classifier returns more than one positive co-reference pair for p_i, we use a heuristic resolver to choose the target. We divide those positive pairs into two subsets, those where the speaker of p_i is the same as the performer of the gesture (SAME), and those with the other speaker (OTHER). If SOME is not empty, we will choose SOME, otherwise OTHER. If the chosen set contains more than one pair, we will choose the target

Model	Hist.	Prec.	Rec.	F.	Number Resolved
Baseline	2	.707	.526	.603	359
J48	1	.801	.534	.641	371
SVM	2	.683	.598	.637	369
MaxEnt	0	.738	.756	**.747**	374
MaxEnt	2	.723	.671	.696	**384**

Table 2: Gesture&Haptics Co-reference Model Results

of the gesture/H-O action in the most recent pair.

Given the space limit, Table 2 only shows the results for each model which resolved most pronouns/deictics, and the model which produced the best F-score. In Table 2, with the change of *History* window setting, the gold standard of co-reference pairs change. When the history window is larger, there are more co-reference candidate pairs, which help resolve more pronouns and deictics.

Given we work on a new corpus, it is hard to compare our results to previous work, additionally our models currently do not deal with textual antecedents. For example Strube and Müller (2003) reports their best F-Measure as .4742, while ours is .747. As concerns accuracy, whereas 384/827 (46%) may appear low, note the task we are performing is harder since we are trying to solve all pronouns/deictics via gestures, not only the ones which have an antecedent introduced by a pointing or H-O action (see Table 1). Even if our feature set is limited, all the classification models perform better than baseline in all the experiments; the biggest improvement is 14.4% in F-score, and solving 25 more pronouns and deictics. There are no significant differences in the performances of the 3 different classification models. Table 2 shows that the history length of the best models is less than or equal to 2 seconds, which is within the standard error range of annotations when we marked the time spans for events.

5 Conclusions

This paper introduced our multi-modal co-reference annotation scheme that includes pointing gestures and H-O actions in the corpus ELDERLY-AT-HOME. Our data shows that 2/3 of antecedents of pronouns/deictics are introduced by pointing gestures or H-O actions, and not in speech. A co-reference resolution system has been built to resolve pronouns and deictics to the antecedents introduced by pointing gestures and H-O actions. The classification models show better performance than the baseline model. In the near future, we will integrate a module which can resolve pronouns and deictics to textual antecedents, including type information provided by indefinite descriptions. This will make the system fully multi-modal. Additionally we intend to study issues of timing. Preliminary studies of our corpus show that the average distance between a pronoun/deictic and its antecedent is 8.26" for textual antecedents, but only 0.66" for gesture antecedents, consistent with our results that show the best models include very short histories, at most 2" long.

Acknowledgments

This work is supported by award IIS 0905593 from the National Science Foundation. Thanks to the other members of the RoboHelper project, especially to Anruo Wang, for their many contributions, especially to the data collection effort. Additionally, we thank the anonymous reviewers for their valuable comments.

References

Chih-Chung Chang and Chih-Jen Lin. 2011. LIBSVM: A library for support vector machines. *ACM Transactions on Intelligent Systems and Technology*, 2:27:1–27:27.

Lin Chen, Anruo Wang, and Barbara Di Eugenio. 2011. Improving pronominal and deictic co-reference resolution with multi-modal features. In *Proceedings of the SIGDIAL 2011 Conference*, pages 307–311, Portland, Oregon, June. Association for Computational Linguistics.

Marie-Catherine De Marneffe and Christopher D. Manning. 2008. The stanford typed dependencies representation. In *Coling 2008: Proceedings of the workshop on Cross-Framework and Cross-Domain Parser Evaluation*, pages 1–8. Association for Computational Linguistics.

Barbara Di Eugenio, Miloš Žefran, Jezekiel Ben-Arie, Mark Foreman, Lin Chen, Simone Franzini, Shankaranand Jagadeesan, Maria Javaid, and Kai Ma. 2010. Towards Effective Communication with Robotic Assistants for the Elderly: Integrating Speech, Vision and Haptics. In *Dialog with Robots, AAAI 2010 Fall Symposium*, Arlington, VA, USA, November.

Jacob Eisenstein and Randall Davis. 2006. Gesture Improves Coreference Resolution. In *Proceedings of the Human Language Technology Conference of the NAACL, Companion Volume: Short Papers*, pages 37–40.

Mary Ellen Foster, Ellen Gurman Bard, Markus Guhe, Robin L. Hill, Jon Oberlander, and Alois Knoll. 2008. The roles of haptic-ostensive referring expressions in cooperative, task-based human-robot dialogue. In *Proceedings of the 3rd ACM/IEEE international conference on Human Robot Interaction*, HRI '08, pages 295–302. ACM.

S. Goldin-Meadow. 2003. *Hearing gesture: How our hands help us think.* Harvard University Press.

Mark Hall, Eibe Frank, Geoffrey Holmes, Bernhard Pfahringer, Peter Reutemann, and Ian H. Witten. 2009. The WEKA data mining software: An update. *SIGKDD Explorations*, 11(1).

Andrew Kehler. 2000. Cognitive Status and Form of Reference in Multimodal Human-Computer Interaction. In *AAAI 00, The 15th Annual Conference of the American Association for Artificial Intelligence*, pages 685–689.

Michael Kipp. 2001. Anvil-a generic annotation tool for multimodal dialogue. In *Proceedings of the 7th European Conference on Speech Communication and Technology*, pages 1367–1370.

Kristine M. Krapp. 2002. *The Gale Encyclopedia of Nursing & Allied Health.* Gale Group, Inc. Chapter Activities of Daily Living Evaluation.

F. Landragin, N. Bellalem, and L. Romary. 2002. Referring to objects with spoken and haptic modalities. In *Proceedings of the Fourth IEEE International Conference on Multimodal Interfaces (ICMI'02)*, pages 99–104, Pittsburgh, PA.

Michael Strube and Christoph Müller. 2003. A machine learning approach to pronoun resolution in spoken dialogue. In *Proceedings of the 41st Annual Meeting on Association for Computational Linguistics-Volume 1.*

Trait-Based Hypothesis Selection For Machine Translation

Jacob Devlin and **Spyros Matsoukas**
Raytheon BBN Technologies, 10 Moulton St, Cambridge, MA 02138, USA
{jdevlin, smatsouk}@bbn.com

Abstract

In the area of machine translation (MT) system combination, previous work on generating input hypotheses has focused on varying a core aspect of the MT system, such as the decoding algorithm or alignment algorithm. In this paper, we propose a new method for generating diverse hypotheses from a *single* MT system using *traits*. These traits are simple properties of the MT output such as "average output length" and "average rule length." Our method is designed to select hypotheses which vary in trait value but do not significantly degrade in BLEU score. These hypotheses can be combined using standard system combination techniques to produce a 1.2-1.5 BLEU gain on the Arabic-English NIST MT06/MT08 translation task.

1 Introduction

In Machine Translation (MT), the output from multiple decoding systems can be used to create a new output which is better than any single input system, using a procedure known as *system combination*.

Normally, the input systems are generated by varying some important aspect of the MT system, such as the alignment algorithm (Xu and Rosti, 2010) or tokenization algorithm (de Gispert et al., 2009). Unfortunately, creating novel algorithms to perform some important aspect of MT decoding is obviously quite challenging. Thus, it is difficult to increase the number of input systems in a meaningful way.

In this paper, we show it is possible to create diverse input hypotheses for combination *without* making any algorithmic changes. Instead, we use *traits*, which are very simple attributes of the MT output, such as "output length" and "average rule length." Our basic procedure is to intelligently select hypotheses from our decoding forest which vary in trait value, but have minimal BLEU degradation compared to our baseline. We then combine these to produce a substantial gain. Note that all of the hypotheses are generated from a *single* decode of a *single* input system.

Additionally, our method is completely compatible with multi-system combination, since our procedure can be applied to each input system, and then these systems can be combined as normal.

Methods for automatically creating diverse hypotheses from a single system have been explored in speech recognition (Siohan et al., 2005), but we know of no analogous work applied to machine translation. Our procedure does share some surface similarities with techniques such as variational decoding (VD) (Li et al., 2009), but the goal in those techniques is to find output which is consistent with the entire forest, rather than to select hypotheses with particular attributes. In fact, VD can be applied in conjunction by running VD on the rescored forest

This work was supported by DARPA/I2O Contract No. HR0011-12-C-0014 under the BOLT program (Approved for Public Release, Distribution Unlimited). The views, opinions, and/or findings contained in this article are those of the author and should not be interpreted as representing the official views or policies, either expressed or implied, of the Defense Advanced Research Projects Agency or the Department of Defense.

for each trait condition.[1]

2 Description of MT System

Our machine translation system is a string-to-dependency hierarchical decoder based on (Shen et al., 2008) and (Chiang, 2007). Bottom-up chart parsing is performed to produce a shared forest of derivations. The decoder uses a log-linear translation model, so the score of derivation d is defined as:

$$S_d(\vec{w}) = \sum_{i=1}^{m} w_i \sum_{r \in R(d)} F_{ri} \quad (1)$$

where $R(d)$ is the set of translation rules that make up derivation d, m is the number of features, F_{ri} is the score of the ith feature in rule r, and w_i is the weight of feature i. This weight vector is optimized discriminatively to maximize BLEU score on a tuning set, using the Expected-BLEU optimization procedure (Rosti et al., 2010).

Our decoder uses all of the standard statistical MT features, such as the language model, rule probabilities, and lexical probabilities. Additionally, we use 50,000 sparse, binary-valued features such as "Is the bi-gram 'united states' present in the output?", based on (Chiang et al., 2009). We use a 3-gram LM for decoding and a 5-gram LM for rescoring.

3 Trait Features

An MT *trait* represents a high-level property of the MT output.

The traits used in this paper are:

- *Null Source Words* – The percentage of source content words which align to null, i.e., are not translated.
- *Source Reorder* – The percentage of source terminals/non-terminals which cross alignment links inside their decoding rule.
- *Ngram Frequency* – The percentage of target 3-grams which are seen more than 10 times in the monolingual training.
- *Rule Frequency* – The percentage of rules which are seen more than 3 times in the parallel training.
- *Rule Length* – The average number of target words per rule.
- *Output Length* – The ratio of the number of target words in the MT output divided by the number of source words in the input.
- *High Lex Prob* – The percentage of source words which have a lexical translation probability greater than 0.1.

Each trait can be represented as the ratio of two linear decoding features. For example, for the *Output Length* trait, the "numerator" feature is the number of target words in the hypothesis, while the "denominator" feature is the number of source words in the input sentence. We can sum these feature scores over a test set, and the resulting quotient is the *Output Length* for that set.

Intuitively, each trait is associated with a particular *tradeoff*, such as fluency/adequacy or precision/recall. For example, when MT performance is maximized, shorter output tends to have higher precision but lower recall than longer output. For the *Ngram Frequency* trait, a greater percentage of high-frequency n-grams tends to result in more fluent but less adequate output. Similar intuitive justifications should be evident for the remaining traits.

4 Hypothesis Generation

The main goal of this work is to generate additional hypotheses which vary in trait values, while minimizing degradation to the BLEU score. So, imagine that we have some baseline MT output. Then, we want to generate a second set of hypotheses which have maximal BLEU score, *subject to the constraint* that the output must be 5% shorter.[2]

The question then becomes how to figure out which 5% of words should be removed. Rather than attempting to do this with a new algorithm, we simply let our existing MT models do it for us, using our standard optimization procedure. This is the essential purpose of the trait features – using the *Output Length* feature, the optimizer has a "knob" with which it can control the trait value independently of everything else.[3] Thus, the new hypotheses that

[1] We do not use VD here because we have not found it to be beneficial to our system.

[2] Note that the trait value is always aggregated over the entire set, and not computed sentence-by-sentence.

[3] A feature representing the number of words already exists in our baseline system, but no such feature exists for the other 6

we select are "optimal" in terms of our existing MT model probabilities, but have trait values which vary from the baseline in a precise way.

4.1 Optimization Function

Our normal optimization procedure uses n-best-based Expected-BLEU tuning (Rosti et al., 2010), which is a differentiable approximation of Maximum-BLEU tuning. To "target" a particular trait value, we add a second term equal to the squared error between the current trait value and the target trait value. Our modified optimization function which we seek to maximize is then:

$$Obj(\vec{w}) = ExpBLEU(\vec{w}) - \alpha \left(\frac{N(\vec{w})}{D(\vec{w})} - \tau\gamma \right)^2$$

where $\vec{w}$ is the MT feature weight vector, α is the weight of the trait term, γ is the baseline value of the trait, and τ is the "target" trait multiplier, $N(\vec{w})$ is the expected-value of the numerator feature, and $D(\vec{w})$ is the expected value of the denominator feature.

To give an example, imagine that for our baseline tune set the *Output Length* ratio is 1.2, and we want to create a hypothesis set with 5% fewer words. In that case, we would set $\gamma = 1.2$ and $\tau = 0.95$, so the target trait value is 1.14. We fix the free parameter α to 10, which forces the optimized trait value to be very close to the target.[4]

The trait-value functions $N(\vec{w})$ and $D(\vec{w})$ are computed as standard expected value functions, e.g.:

$$N(\vec{w}) = \sum_i \sum_j p_{ij}(\vec{w}) N_{ij}$$

where $p_{ij}(\vec{w})$ is the posterior probability of the jth hypothesis of sentence i, and N_{ij} is the value of the numerator feature for hypothesis ij.[5]

4.2 Meta-Optimization

It is somewhat problematic to use a fixed multiplier τ on all of the traits, since on some traits it may cause a larger degradation than others. So, we take the reverse approach – for some targeted BLEU loss β, we find the maximum (or minimum) value of τ which causes a loss no greater than β, as computed on a held-out portion of the tune set.[6] Here, we find the maximum and minimum trait value for $\beta = 0.5$ and $\beta = 2.0$, resulting in 4 sets of weights per trait.

We can find the optimal τ for each β by performing a binary search on τ, where we run our optimization procedure and then compute the BLEU loss at each iteration.

4.3 Forest-Based Optimization

Since we have 7 traits, and we generate 4 sets of weights per trait, we have 28 "systems" to combine. Obviously, running 28 full decodes on each new test sentence is highly undesirable.

We resolve this issue by using our baseline derivation forest for both optimization and hypothesis generation. We perform a single round of decoding to generate a forest, and then perform iterative n-best optimization by rescoring the forest rather than re-decoding from scratch. [7] We constrain the 50,000 sparse feature weights to be fixed at their baseline values, to prevent over-fitting.

Once the weight sets are generated, the hypotheses for each trait condition can be generated by rescoring the forest inside of the decoder. Therefore, all 28 trait hypotheses can be generated for almost no cost over a single decode.

It should be noted we have found it beneficial to relax our MT pruning parameters in order to create a larger forest. This results in decoding which is roughly 2x-3x as slow as the baseline, and requires storing the larger forest in memory. However, we have found that the procedure still works well even with the standard pruning parameters. Additionally, we are investigating methods for diversifying the forest with less of a slowdown to decoding.

5 Combination

Once the different trait hypotheses have been generated, system combination can be performed using any method.

Here, we use a confusion network decoder based on (Rosti et al., 2010). The basic procedure is to

traits.

[4]Note that the $ExpBLEU(\vec{w})$ is raw BLEU *not* BLEU percentage, i.e., it's 0.4528 not 45.28

[5]$p_{ij}(\vec{w})$ is computed the same way as in $ExpBLEU(\vec{w})$. See (Rosti et al., 2010) for details.

[6]For example if the held-out baseline BLEU is 40.0 and $\beta = 0.5$, the BLEU after trait optimization can be no less than 39.5.

[7]Forest-based optimization such as (Pauls et al., 2009) could be used instead.

select one hypothesis as the "skeleton" and then incrementally align the remaining hypotheses to create a confusion network. The confusion network is decoded using an arc-level confidence score for each input system and a language model, the weights for which are estimated discriminatively to maximize BLEU.

6 Results

We present MT results in Table 1. Our experimental setup is compatible with the NIST MT08 constrained track. We trained our translation model on 35 million words of parallel data and our language model on 3.8 billion words of monolingual data. We use a portion of MT02-05 for tuning the MT baseline and the trait systems, and another portion of MT02-05 for tuning system combination.

We present results on Arabic-English MT06-newswire and MT08-eval. The systems were tuned and evaluated using IBM-BLEU. Our baseline system is 1.5 BLEU better than the best result from the NIST M08 evaluation.

For the *Trait Feats* condition, we simply added the numerator and denominator features for all 7 traits to the baseline system and re-optimized.[8] Somewhat surprisingly, this produces an 0.5-0.7 BLEU gain on its own. In this condition, although we do not target any particular trait values, the optimizer will naturally fine-tune the trait values to whatever is optimal for BLEU score. For example, the MT08 baseline value of *Source Reorder* is 0.307, while for the *Trait Feats* it is 0.330, so the system determined it is "optimal" to have 7.5% (0.330/0.307) more re-ordering than the baseline.

For the *Trait Comb* condition, we generated 28 trait hypothesis sets using the decoding forest from the *Trait Feats* condition. We combined these with the *Trait Feats* output using consensus network decoding. This produces an additional 0.8 BLEU gain, resulting in a 1.2-1.5 BLEU gain over the baseline.

We also present another condition, n*-best Comb*, where we perform confusion network combination on the 28-best hypotheses from *Trait Feats*. This represents the simplest and most trivial method of hypothesis selection. We observe no gain in BLEU on this condition. Other simple methods of hypotheses selection, such as optimizing systems to be "different" from one another (i.e., have high inter-system TER), also produced no gain over the single system. We include these results simply to demonstrate that it is *not* trivial to select hypotheses from a single system which produce a significant improvement in from system combination.

[8] Including the 50k sparse features.

	MT06 nw		**MT08 eval**	
	BLEU	Len	BLEU	Len
Baseline	55.11	99.1%	46.75	96.1%
Trait Feats	55.79*	99.3%	47.23*	96.0%
+n-best Comb	55.65	99.3%	47.24	96.2%
+Trait Comb	**56.65****	99.3%	**48.00****	96.2%

Table 1: Results on Arabic-English MT. * = Significant improvement at 95% confidence, as defined by (Koehn, 2004). ** = Significant improvement at 99.9% confidence. **BLEU** = IBM-BLEU score. **Len** = Hypothesis-to-reference length ratio.

7 Conclusions and Future Work

We demonstrated a method of intelligently selecting hypotheses from a decoding forest which can be combined with the baseline hypotheses to produce a significant gain in BLEU score. In the future, we plan to explore more trait types and alternate methods of system combination.

One possible application of this work is in fielded translation systems. Because our method produces high-quality complementary hypotheses at a low computational cost, the system could present these to the user as alternate translations. Going further, a user could prefer a particular output type, such as the fluency-tuned condition, and set that to be their default translation.

The major open question is how our trait-based combination interacts with multi-system combination. Imagine there are three different types of decoders which can be combined to produce some gain in the baseline condition. If you independently im prove all three using trait-based combination, will the relative gain from multi-system combination be reduced? Or can you jointly combine *all* of the trait hypotheses and get an even greater relative gain? We plan to thoroughly explore this in the future.

References

D. Chiang, K. Knight, and W. Wang. 2009. 11,001 new features for statistical machine translation. In *NAACL*, pages 218–226.

D. Chiang. 2007. Hierarchical phrase-based translation. *Computational Linguistics*, 33(2):201–228.

A. de Gispert, S. Virpioja, M. Kurimo, and W. Byrne. 2009. Minimum Bayes risk combination of translation hypotheses from alternative morphological decompositions. In *NAACL*, pages 73–76.

P. Koehn. 2004. Pharaoh: A beam search decoder for phrase-based statistical machine translation models. In *AMTA*, pages 115–124.

Z. Li, J. Eisner, and S. Khudanpur. 2009. Variational decoding for statistical machine translation. In *ACL*, pages 593–601.

A. Pauls, J. DeNero, and D. Klein. 2009. Consensus training for consensus decoding in machine translation. In *EMNLP*, pages 1418–1427.

A. Rosti, B. Zhang, S. Matsoukas, and R. Schwartz. 2010. BBN system description for WMT10 system combination task. In *WMT/MetricsMATR*, pages 321–326.

L. Shen, J. Xu, and R. Weischedel. 2008. A new string-to-dependency machine translation algorithm with a target dependency language model. In *ACL-HLT*, pages 577–585.

O. Siohan, B. Ramabhadran, and B. Kingsbury. 2005. Constructing ensembles of ASR systems using randomized decision trees. In *ICASSP*.

J. Xu and A. Rosti. 2010. Combining unsupervised and supervised alignments for MT: An empirical study. In *EMNLP*, pages 667–673.

Improved Reordering for Shallow-*n* Grammar based Hierarchical Phrase-based Translation

Baskaran Sankaran and Anoop Sarkar
School of Computing Science
Simon Fraser University
Burnaby BC. Canada
{baskaran, anoop}@cs.sfu.ca

Abstract

Shallow-n grammars (de Gispert et al., 2010) were introduced to reduce over-generation in the Hiero translation model (Chiang, 2005) resulting in much faster decoding and restricting reordering to a desired level for specific language pairs. However, Shallow-n grammars require parameters which cannot be directly optimized using minimum error-rate tuning by the decoder. This paper introduces some novel improvements to the translation model for Shallow-n grammars. We introduce two rules: a BITG-style reordering *glue* rule and a simpler monotonic concatenation rule. We use separate features for the new rules in our log-linear model allowing the decoder to directly optimize the feature weights. We show this formulation of Shallow-n hierarchical phrase-based translation is comparable in translation quality to full Hiero-style decoding (without shallow rules) while at the same time being considerably faster.

1 Introduction

Hierarchical phrase-based translation (Chiang, 2005; Chiang, 2007) extends the highly lexicalized models from phrase-based translation systems in order to model lexicalized reordering and discontiguous phrases. However, a major drawback in this approach, when compared to phrase-based systems, is the total number of rules that are learnt are several orders of magnitude larger than standard phrase tables, which leads to over-generation and search errors and contribute to much longer decoding times. Several approaches have been proposed to address these issues: from filtering the extracted synchronous grammar (Zollmann et al., 2008; He et al., 2009; Iglesias et al., 2009) to alternative Bayesian approaches for learning minimal grammars (Blunsom et al., 2008; Blunsom et al., 2009; Sankaran et al., 2011). The idea of Shallow-n grammars (de Gispert et al., 2010) takes an orthogonal direction for controlling the over-generation and search space in Hiero decoder by restricting the degree of nesting allowed for Hierarchical rules.

We propose an novel statistical model for Shallow-*n* grammars which does not require additional non-terminals for monotonic re-ordering and also eliminates hand-tuned parameters and instead introduces an automatically tunable alternative. We introduce a BITG-style (Saers et al., 2009) reordering glue rule (§ 3) and a monotonic X-glue rule (§ 4). Our experiments show the resulting Shallow-n decoding is comparable in translation quality to full Hiero-style decoding while at the same time being considerably faster.

All the experiments in this paper were done using *Kriya* (Sankaran et al., 2012) hierarchical phrase-based system which also supports decoding with Shallow-n grammars. We extended Kriya to additionally support reordering glue rules as well.

2 Shallow-*n* Grammars

Formally a Shallow-n grammar G is defined as a 5-tuple: $G = (N, T, R, R_g, S)$, such that T is a set of finite terminals and N a set of finite non-terminals $\{X^0, \ldots, X^N\}$. R_g refers to the glue rules that rewrite the start symbol S:

$$S \rightarrow <X, X> \quad (1)$$

$$S \rightarrow <SX, SX> \quad (2)$$

R is the set of finite production rules in G and has two types, viz. hierarchical (3) and terminal (4). The hierarchical rules at each level n are additionally conditioned to have *at least* one X^{n-1} non-terminal in them. $\sim$ represents the indices for aligning non-terminals where co-indexed non-terminal pairs are rewritten synchronously.

$$X^n \rightarrow <\gamma,\ \alpha,\ \sim>,\ \gamma, \alpha \in \{\{X^{n-1}\} \cup T^+\} \quad (3)$$

$$X^0 \rightarrow <\gamma,\ \alpha>, \qquad \gamma, \alpha \in T^+ \quad (4)$$

de Gispert et al. (2010) also proposed additional non-terminals M^k to enable reordering over longer spans by concatenating the hierarchical rules within the span. It also uses additional parameters such as monotonicity level (K_1 and K_2), maximum and minimum rule spans allowed for the non-terminals (§3.1 and 3.2 in de Gispert et al. (2010)). The monotonicity level parameters determine the number of non-terminals that are combined in monotonic order at the $N-1$ level and can be adapted to the reordering requirements of specific language pairs. The maximum and minimum rule spans further control the usage of hierarchical rule in a derivation by stipulating the underlying span to be within a range of values. Intuitively, this avoids hierarchical rules being used for a source phrase that is either too short or too long. While these parameters offer flexibility for adapting the translation system to specific language pairs, they have to be manually tuned which is tedious and error-prone.

We propose an elegant and automatically tunable alternative for the Shallow-*n* grammars setting. Specifically, we introduce a BITG-style reordering glue rule (§ 3) and a monotonic X-glue rule (§ 4). Our experiments show the resulting Shallow-n decoding to perform to the same level as full-Hiero decoding at the same time being faster.

In addition, our implementation of Shallow-n grammar differs from (de Gispert et al., 2010) in at least two other aspects. First, their formulation constrains the X in the glue rules to be at the top-level and specifically they define them to be: $S \rightarrow <SX^N, SX^N>$ and $S \rightarrow <X^N, X^N>$, where X^N is the non-terminal corresponding to the top-most level. Interestingly, this resulted in poor BLEU scores and we found the more generic glue rules (as in (1) and (2)) to perform significantly better, as we show later.

Secondly, they also employ pattern-based filtering (Iglesias et al., 2009) in order to reducing redundancies in the Hiero grammar by filtering it based on certain rule patterns. However in our limited experiments, we observed the filtered grammar to perform worse than the full grammar, as also noted by (Zollmann et al., 2008). Hence, we do not employ any grammar filtering in our experiments.

3 Reordering Glue Rule

In this paper, we propose an additional BITG-style glue rule (called R-glue) as in (5) for reordering the phrases along the left-branch of the derivation.

$$S \rightarrow <SX,\ XS> \quad (5)$$

In order to use this rule sparsely in the derivation, we use a separate feature for this rule and apply a penalty of 1. Similar to the case of regular glue rules, we experimented with a variant of the reordering glue rule, where X is restricted to the top-level: $S \rightarrow <SX^N, X^N S>$ and $S \rightarrow <X^N, X^N>$.

3.1 Language Model Integration

The traditional phrase-based decoders using beam search generate the target hypotheses in the left-to-right order. In contrast, Hiero-style systems typically use CKY chart-parsing decoders which can freely combine target hypotheses generated in intermediate cells with hierarchical rules in the higher cells. Thus the generation of the target hypotheses are fragmented and out of order compared to the left to right order preferred by n-gram language models.

This leads to challenges in the estimation of language model scores for partial target hypothesis, which is being addressed in different ways in the existing Hiero-style systems. Some systems add a sentence initial marker (<s>) to the beginning of each path and some other systems have this implicitly in the derivation through the translation models. Thus the language model scores for the hypothesis in the intermediate cell are approximated, with the true language model score (taking into account sentence boundaries) being computed in the last cell that spans the entire source sentence.

We introduce a novel improvement in computing the language model scores: for each of the target hypothesis fragment, our approach finds the best position for the fragment in the final sentence and uses the corresponding score. We compute three different scores corresponding to the three positions where the fragment can end up in the final sentence, viz.

sentence initial, middle and final: and choose the best score. As an example for fragment t_f consisting of a sequence of target tokens, we compute LM scores for i) <s> t_f, ii) t_f and iii) t_f </s> and use the best score for pruning alone[1].

This improvement significantly reduces the search errors while performing *cube pruning* (Chiang, 2007) at the cost of additional language model queries. While this approach works well for the usual glue rules, it is particularly effective in the case of reordering glue rules. For example, a partial candidate covering a non-final source span might translate to the final position in the target sentence. If we just compute the LM score for the target fragment as is done normally, this might get pruned early on before being reordered by the new glue rule. Our approach instead computes the three LM scores and it would correctly use the last LM score which is likely to be the best, for pruning.

4 Monotonic Concatenation Glue rule

The reordering glue rule facilitates reordering at the top-level. However, this is still not sufficient to allow long-distance reordering as the shallow-decoding restricts the depth of the derivation. Consider the Chinese example in Table 1, in which translation of the Chinese word corresponding to the English phrase *the delegates* involves a long distance reordering to the beginning of the sentence. Note that, three of the four human references prefer this long distance reordering, while the fourth one avoids the movement by using a complex construction with relative clause and a sentence initial prepositional phrase.

Such long distance reordering is very difficult in conventional Hiero decoding and more so with the Shallow-n grammars. While the R-glue rule permit such long distance movements, it also requires a long phrase generated by a series of rules to be moved as a block. We address this issue, by adding a monotonic concatenation (called X-glue) rule that concatenates a series of hierarchical rules. In order to control overgeneration, we apply this rule only at the $N-1$ level similar to de Gispert et al. (2010).

$$X^{N-1} \rightarrow <X^{N-1}X^{N-1},\ X^{N-1}X^{N-1}> \quad (6)$$

[1]This ensures the the LM score estimates are never underestimated for pruning. We retain the LM score for fragment (case ii) for estimating the score for the full candidate sentence later.

However unlike their approach, we use this rule as a feature in the log-linear model so that its weight can be optimized in the tuning step. Also, our approach removes the need for additional parameters K_1 and K_2 for controlling monotonicity, which was being tuned manually in their work. For the Chinese example above, shallow-1 decoding using R and X-glue rules achieve the complex movement resulting in a significantly better translation than full-Hiero decoding as shown in the last two lines in Table 1.

5 Experiments

We present results for Chinese-English translation as it often requires heavy reordering. We use the HK parallel text and GALE phase-1 corpus consisting of ~2.3M sentence pairs for training. For tuning and testing, we use the MTC parts 1 and 3 (1928 sentences) and MTC part 4 (919 sentences) respectively. We used the usual pre-processing pipeline and an additional segmentation step for the Chinese side of the bitext using the LDC segmenter[2].

Our log-linear model uses the standard features conditional ($p(e|f)$ and $p(f|e)$) and lexical ($p_l(e|f)$ and $p_l(f|e)$) probabilities, phrase (p_p) and word (w_p) penalties, language model and regular glue penalty (m_g) apart from two additional features for $R-$glue (r_g) and $X-$glue (x_g).

Table 2 shows the BLEU scores and decoding time for the MTC test-set. We provide the IBM BLEU (Papineni et al., 2002) scores for the Shallow-n grammars for order: $n = 1, 2, 3$ and compare it to the full-Hiero baseline. Finally, we experiment with two variants of the S glue rules, i) a restricted version where the glue rules combine only X at level N, (column 'Glue: X^N' in table), ii) more free variant where they are allowed to use any X freely (column 'Glue: X' in table).

As it can be seen, the unrestricted glue rules variant (column 'Glue: X') consistently outperforms the glue rules restricted to the top-level non-terminal X^N, achieving a maximum BLEU score of 26.24, which is about 1.4 BLEU points higher than the latter and is also marginally higher than full Hiero. The decoding speeds for free-Glue and restricted-Glue variants were mostly identical and so we only provide the decoding time for the latter. Shallow-2 and

[2]We slightly modified the LDC segmenter, in order to correctly handle non-Chinese characters in ASCII and UTF8.

Source	在阿根廷首都布宜诺斯艾利斯参加联合国全球气候大会的代表们继续进行工作。
Gloss	*in argentine capital beunos aires participate united nations global climate conference delegates continue to work.*
Ref 0	delegates attending the un conference on world climate continue their work in the argentine capital of buenos aires.
Ref 1	the delegates to the un global climate conference held in Buenos aires, capital city of argentina, go on with their work.
Ref 2	the delegates continue their works at the united nations global climate talks in buenos aires, capital of argentina
Ref 3	in buenos aires, the capital of argentina, the representatives attending un global climate meeting continued their work.
Full-Hiero: Baseline	in the argentine capital of buenos aires to attend the un conference on global climate of representatives continue to work.
Sh-1 Hiero: R-glue & X-glue	the representatives were in the argentine capital of beunos aires to attend the un conference on global climate continues to work.

Table 1: An example for the level of reordering in Chinese-English translation

Grammar	Glue: X^N	Glue: X	Time
Full Hiero	**25.96**		0.71
Shallow-1	23.54	24.04	0.24
+ R-Glue	23.41	24.15	0.25
+ X-Glue	23.75	**24.74**	0.72
Shallow-2	24.54	25.12	0.55
+ R-Glue	24.75	**25.60**	0.57
+ X-Glue	24.33	25.43	0.69
Shallow-3	24.88	25.89	0.62
+ R-Glue	24.77	**26.24**	0.63
+ X-Glue	24.75	25.83	0.69

Table 2: Results for Chinese-English. The decoding time is in secs/word on the Test set for column 'Glue: X'. Bold font indicate best BLEU for each shallow-order.

Grammar	Glue: X	Time
Full Hiero	**37.54**	0.67
Shallow-1	36.90	0.40
+ R-Glue	36.98	0.43
+ X-Glue	**37.21**	0.57
Shallow-2	36.97	0.57
+ R-Glue	36.80	0.58
+ X-Glue	**37.36**	0.61
Shallow-3	36.88	0.61
+ R-Glue	37.18	0.63
+ X-Glue	**37.31**	0.64

Table 3: Results for Arabic-English. The decoding time is in secs/word on the Test set.

shallow-3 free glue variants achieve BLEU scores comparable to full-Hiero and at the same time being $12 - 20\%$ faster.

R-glue (r_g) appears to contribute more than the X-glue (x_g) as can be seen in shallow-2 and shallow-3 cases. Interestingly, x_g is more helpful for the shallow-1 case specifically when the glue rules are restricted. As the glue rules are restricted, the X-glue rules concatenates other lower-order rules before being folded into the glue rules. Both r_g and x_g improve the BLEU scores by 0.58 over the plain shallow case for shallow orders 1 and 2 and performs comparably for shallow-3 case. We have also conducted experiments for Arabic-English (Table 3) and we notice that X-glue is more effective and that R-glue is helpful for higher shallow orders.

5.1 Effect of our novel LM integration

Here we analyze the effect of our novel LM integration approach in terms of BLEU score and search errors comparing it to the naive method used in typical Hiero systems. In shallow setting, our method improved the BLEU scores by 0.4 for both Ar-En and Cn-En. In order to quantify the change in the search errors, we compare the model scores of the (corresponding) candidates in the N-best lists obtained by the two methods and compute the $\%$ of high scoring candidates in each. Our approach was clearly superior with 94.6% and 77.3% of candidates having better scores respectively for Cn-En and Ar-En. In full decoding setting the margin of improvements were reduced slightly- BLEU improved by 0.3 and about $57-69\%$ of target candidates had better model scores for the two language pairs.

References

Phil Blunsom, Trevor Cohn, and Miles Osborne. 2008. Bayesian synchronous grammar induction. In *Proceedings of Neural Information Processing Systems*.

Phil Blunsom, Trevor Cohn, Chris Dyer, and Miles Osborne. 2009. A gibbs sampler for phrasal synchronous grammar induction. In *Proceedings of Association of Computational Linguistics*, pages 782–790.

David Chiang. 2005. A hierarchical phrase-based model for statistical machine translation. In *Proceedings of Association of Computational Linguistics*, pages 263–270.

David Chiang. 2007. Hierarchical phrase-based translation. *Computational Linguistics*, 33.

Adrià de Gispert, Gonzalo Iglesias, Graeme Blackwood, Eduardo R. Banga, and William Byrne. 2010. Hierarchical phrase-based translation with weighted finite-state transducers and shallow-n grammars. *Computational Linguistics*, 36.

Zhongjun He, Yao Meng, and Hao Yu. 2009. Discarding monotone composed rule for hierarchical phrase-based statistical machine translation. In *Proceedings of the 3rd International Universal Communication Symposium*, pages 25–29.

Gonzalo Iglesias, Adrià de Gispert, Eduardo R. Banga, and William Byrne. 2009. Rule filtering by pattern for efficient hierarchical translation. In *Proceedings of the 12th Conference of the European Chapter of the ACL*, pages 380–388.

Kishore Papineni, Salim Roukos, Todd Ward, and Wei jing Zhu. 2002. Bleu: a method for automatic evaluation of machine translation. In *Proceedings of the Annual Meeting of Association of Computational Linguistics*, pages 311–318.

Markus Saers, Joakim Nivre, and Dekai Wu. 2009. Learning stochastic bracketing inversion transduction grammars with a cubic time biparsing algorithm. In *Proceedings of the 11th International Conference on Parsing Technologies*, pages 29–32. Association for Computational Linguistics.

Baskaran Sankaran, Gholamreza Haffari, and Anoop Sarkar. 2011. Bayesian extraction of minimal scfg rules for hierarchical phrase-based translation. In *Proceedings of the Sixth Workshop on Statistical Machine Translation*, pages 533–541.

Baskaran Sankaran, Majid Razmara, and Anoop Sarkar. 2012. Kriya – an end-to-end hierarchical phrase-based mt system. *The Prague Bulletin of Mathematical Linguistics*, (97):83–98, April.

Andreas Zollmann, Ashish Venugopal, Franz Och, and Jay Ponte. 2008. A systematic comparison of phrase-based, hierarchical and syntax-augmented statistical mt. In *Proceedings of the 22nd International Conference on Computational Linguistics*, pages 1145–1152.

Automatic Parallel Fragment Extraction from Noisy Data

Jason Riesa and **Daniel Marcu**
Information Sciences Institute
Viterbi School of Engineering
University of Southern California
{riesa, marcu}@isi.edu

Abstract

We present a novel method to detect parallel fragments within noisy parallel corpora. Isolating these parallel fragments from the noisy data in which they are contained frees us from noisy alignments and stray links that can severely constrain translation-rule extraction. We do this with existing machinery, making use of an existing word alignment model for this task. We evaluate the quality and utility of the extracted data on large-scale Chinese-English and Arabic-English translation tasks and show significant improvements over a state-of-the-art baseline.

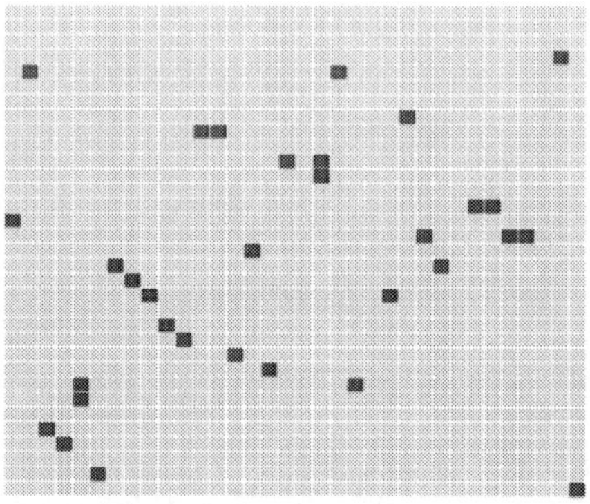

Figure 1: Example of a word alignment resulting from noisy parallel data. The structure of the resulting alignment makes it difficult to find and extract parallel fragments via the standard heuristics or simply by inspection. How can we discover automatically those parallel fragments hidden within such data?

1 Introduction

A decade ago, Banko and Brill (2001) showed that scaling to very large corpora is game-changing for a variety of tasks. Methods that work well in a small-data setting often lose their luster when moving to large data. Conversely, other methods that seem to perform poorly in that same small-data setting, may perform markedly differently when trained on large data.

Perhaps most importantly, Banko and Brill showed that there was no significant variation in performance among a variety of methods trained at-scale with large training data. The takeaway? If you desire to scale to large datasets, use a simple solution for your task, and throw in as much data as possible. The community at large has taken this message to heart, and in most cases it has been an effective way to increase performance.

Today, for machine translation, more data than what we already have is getting harder and harder to come by; we require large parallel corpora to train state-of-the-art statistical, data-driven models. Groups that depend on clearinghouses like LDC for their data increasingly find that there is less of a mandate to gather parallel corpora on the scale of what was produced in the last 5-10 years. Others, who directly exploit the entire web to gather such data will necessarily run up against a wall after all that data has been collected.

We need to learn how to do more with the data we already have. Previous work has focused on detecting parallel documents and sentences on the web, e.g. (Zhao and Vogel, 2002; Fung and Cheung, 2004; Wu and Fung, 2005). Munteanu and Marcu (2006), and later Quirk et al. (2007), extend the state-of-the-art for this task to parallel fragments.

In this paper, we present a novel method for detecting parallel fragments in large, existing and potentially noisy parallel corpora using existing machinery and show significant improvements to two state-of-the-art MT systems. We also depart from previous work in that we only consider parallel corpora that have previously been cleaned, sanitized, and thought to be non-noisy, e.g. parallel corpora available from LDC.

2 Detecting Noisy Data

In order to extract previously unextractable good parallel data, we must first detect the bad data. In doing so, we will make use of existing machinery in a novel way. We directly use the alignment model to detect weak or undesirable data for translation.

2.1 Alignment Model as Noisy Data Detector

The alignment model we use in our experiments is that described in (Riesa et al., 2011), modified to output full derivation trees and model scores along with alignments. Our reasons for using this particular alignment method are twofold: it provides a natural way to hierarchically partition subsentential segments, and is also empirically quite accurate in modeling word alignments, in general. This latter quality is important, not solely for downstream translation quality, but also for the basis of our claims with respect to detecting noisy or unsuitable data:

The alignment model we employ is discriminatively trained to know what good alignments between parallel data look like. When this model predicts an alignment with a low model score, given an input sentence pair, we might say the model is "confused." In this case, the alignment probably doesn't look like the examples it has been trained on.

1. It could be that the data is parallel, but the model is very confused. (modeling problem)

2. It could be that the data is noisy, and the model is very confused. (data problem)

The general accuracy of the alignment model we employ makes the former case unlikely. Therefore, a key assumption we make is to assume a low model score accompanies noisy data, and use this data as candidates from which to extract non-noisy parallel segments.

2.2 A Brief Example

As an illustrative example, consider the following sentence pair in our training corpus taken from LDC2005T10. This is the sentence pair shown in Figure 1:

fate brought us together on that wonderful summer day and one year later , shou – tao and i were married not only in the united states but also in taiwan .

他来自于台湾,我则是土生土长于纽泽西州的美国人;而就在那奇妙的夏日里,我俩被命运兜在一起.

In this sentence pair there are only two parallel phrases, corresponding to the underlined and double-underlined strings. There are a few scattered word pairs which may have a natural correspondence,[1] but no other larger phrases.[2]

In this work we are concerned with finding large phrases,[3] since very small phrases tend to be extractible even when data is noisy. Bad alignments tend to cause conflicts when extracting large phrases due to unexpected, stray links in the alignment matrix; smaller fragments will have less opportunity to come into conflict with incorrect, stray links due to noisy data or alignment model error. We consider large enough phrases for our purposes to be phrases of size greater than 3, and ignore smaller fragments.

2.3 Parallel Fragment Extraction

2.3.1 A Hierarchical Alignment Model and its Derivation Trees

The alignment model we use, (Riesa et al., 2011), is a discriminatively trained model which at alignment-time walks up the English parse-tree and, at every node in the tree, generates alignments by recursively scoring and combining alignments generated at the current node's children, building up larger and larger alignments. This process works similarly to a CKY parser, moving bottom-up and generating larger and larger constituents until it has predicted the full tree spanning the entire sentence. How

[1]For example, (I, 我) and (Taiwan, 台湾)

[2]The rest of the Chinese describes where the couple is from; the speaker, she says, is an American raised in New Jersey.

[3]We count the size of the phrase according to the number of English words it contains; one could be more conservative by constraining both sides.

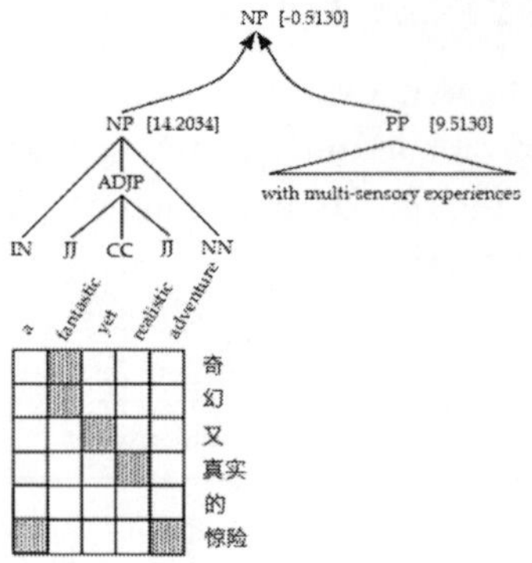

Figure 2: From LDC2004T08, when the NP fragment shown here is combined to make a larger span with a sister PP fragment, the alignment model objects due to non-parallel data under the PP, voicing a score of -0.5130. We extract and append to our training corpus the NP fragment depicted, from which we later learn 5 additional translation rules.

ever, instead of generating syntactic structures, we are generating alignments.

In moving bottom-up along the tree, just as there is a derivation tree for a CKY parse, we can also follow backpointers to extract the derivation tree of the 1-best alignment starting from the root node. This derivation tree gives a hierarchical partitioning of the alignment and the associated word-spans. We can also inspect model scores at each node in the derivation tree.

2.3.2 Using the Alignment Model to Detect Parallel Fragments

For each training example in our parallel corpus, we have an alignment derivation tree. Because the derivation tree is essentially isomorphic to the English parse tree, the derivation tree represents a hierarchical partitioning of the training example into syntactic segments. We traverse the tree top-down, inspecting the parallel fragments implied by the derivation at each point, and their associated model scores.

The idea behind this top-down traversal is that although some nodes, and perhaps entire derivations, may be low-scoring, there are often high-scoring fragments that make up the larger derivation which are worthy of extraction. Figure 2 shows an example. We recursively traverse the derivation, top-down, extracting the largest fragment possible at any derivation node whose alignment model score is higher than some threshold τ, and whose associated English and foreign spans meet a set of important constraints:

1. The parent node in the derivation has a score less than τ.
2. The length of the English span is > 3.
3. There are no unaligned foreign words inside the fragment that are also aligned to English words outside the fragment.

Once a fragment has been extracted, we do not recurse any further down the subtree.

Constraint 1 is a *candidate constraint*, and forces us to focus on segments of parallel sentences with low model scores; these are segments likely to consist of bad alignments due to noisy data or aligner error.

Constraint 2 is a *conservativity constraint* – we are more confident in model scores over larger fragments with more context than smaller ones with minimal context. This constraint also parameterizes the notion that larger fragments are the type more often precluded from extraction due to stray or incorrect word-alignment links; additionally, we are already likely to be able to extract smaller fragments using standard methods, and as such, they are less useful to us here.

Constraint 3 is a *content constraint*, limiting us from extracting fragments with blocks of unaligned foreign words that don't belong in this particular fragment because they are aligned elsewhere. If we threw out this constraint, then in translating from Chinese to English, we would erroneously learn to delete blocks of Chinese words that otherwise should be translated. When foreign words are unaligned everywhere within a parallel sentence, then they can be included within the extracted fragment. Common examples in Chinese are function words such as 的, 个, and 了. Put another way, we only allow globally unaligned words in extracted fragments.

Computing τ. In computing our extraction threshold τ, we must decide what proportion of fragments we consider to be low-scoring and least likely to be useful for translation. We make the rather strong assumption that this is the bottom 10% of the data.[4]

3 Evaluation

We evaluate our parallel fragment extraction in a large-scale Chinese-English and Arabic-English MT setting. In our experiments we use a tree-to-string syntax-based MT system (Galley et al., 2004), and evaluate on a standard test set, NIST08. We parse the English side of our parallel corpus with the Berkeley parser (Petrov et al., 2006), and tune parameters of the MT system with MIRA (Chiang et al., 2008). We decode with an integrated language model trained on about 4 billion words of English.

Chinese-English We align a parallel corpus of 8.4M parallel segments, with 210M words of English and 193M words of Chinese. From this we extract 868,870 parallel fragments according to the process described in Section 2, and append these fragments to the end of the parallel corpus. In doing so, we have created a larger parallel corpus of 9.2M parallel segments, consisting of 217M and 198M words of English and Chinese, respectively.

Arabic-English We align a parallel corpus of 9.0M parallel segments, with 223M words of English and 194M words of Arabic. From this we extract 996,538 parallel fragments, and append these fragments to the end of the parallel corpus. The resulting corpus has 10M parallel segments, consisting of 233M and 202M words of English and Arabic, respectively.

Results are shown in Table 1. Using our parallel fragment extraction, we learn 68M additional unique Arabic-English rules that are not in the baseline system; likewise, we learn 38M new unique Chinese-English rules not in the baseline system for that language pair. Note that we are not simply duplicating portions of the parallel data. While each sequence fragment of source and target words we extract will be found elsewhere in the larger parallel corpus, these fragments will largely not make it into fruitful translation rules to be used in the downstream MT system.

We see gains in BLEU score across two different language pairs, showing empirically that we are learning new and useful translation rules we previously were not in our grammars. These results are significant with $p < 0.05$ for Arabic-English and $p < 0.01$ for Chinese-English.

Corpus	Extracted Rules	BLEU
Baseline (Ara-Eng)	750M	50.0
+Extracted fragments	818M	**50.4**
Baseline (Chi-Eng)	270M	31.5
+Extracted fragments	308M	**32.0**

Table 1: End-to-end translation experiments with and without extracted fragments. We are learning many more unique rules; BLEU score gains are significant with $p < 0.05$ for Arabic-English and $p < 0.01$ for Chinese-English.

4 Discussion

All alignment models we have experimented with will fall down in the presence of noisy data. Importantly, even if the alignment model were able to yield "perfect" alignments with no alignment links among noisy sections of the parallel data precluding us from extracting reasonable rules or phrase pairs, we would still have to deal with downstream rule extraction heuristics and their tendency to blow up a translation grammar in the presence of large swaths of unaligned words. Absent a mechanism within the alignment model itself to deal with this problem, we provide a simple way to recover from noisy data without the introduction of new tools.

Summing up, parallel data in the world is not unlimited. We cannot always continue to double our data for increased performance. Parallel data creation is expensive, and automatic discovery is resource-intensive (Uszkoreit et al., 2010). We have presented a technique that helps to squeeze more out of an already large, state-of-the-art MT system, using existing pieces of the pipeline to do so in a novel way.

Acknowledgements

This work was supported by DARPA BOLT via BBN subcontract HR0011-12-C-0014. We thank our three anonymous reviewers for thoughtful comments. Thanks also to Kevin Knight, David Chiang, Liang Huang, and Philipp Koehn for helpful discussions.

[4] One may wish to experiment with different ranges here, but each requires a separate time-consuming downstream MT experiment. In this work, it turns out that scrutinizing 10% of the data is productive and empirically reasonable.

References

Michele Banko and Eric Brill. 2001. Scaling to very very large corpora for natural language disambiguation. In *Proc. of the ACL*, pages 26–33.

David Chiang, Yuval Marton, and Philip Resnik. 2008. Online large-margin training of syntactic and structural translation features. In *Proc. of EMNLP*, pages 224–233.

Pascale Fung and Percy Cheung. 2004. Mining very non-parallel corpora: Parallel sentence and lexicon extraction via boostrapping and EM. In *Proc. of EMNLP*, pages 57–63.

Michel Galley, Mark Hopkins, Kevin Knight, and Daniel Marcu. 2004. What's in a translation rule? In *Proc. of HLT-NAACL*, pages 273–280.

Dragos Stefan Munteanu and Daniel Marcu. 2006. Extracting parallel sub-sentential fragments from non-parallel corpora. In *Proc. of COLING/ACL*, Sydney, Australia.

Slav Petrov, Leon Barrett, Romain Thibaux, and Dan Klein. 2006. Learning accurate, compact, and interpretable tree annotation. In *Proc. of COLING-ACL*.

Chris Quirk, Raghavendra Udupa, and Arul Menezes. 2007. Generative models of noisy translations with applications to parallel fragment extraction. In *Proceedings of MT Summit XI*.

Jason Riesa, Ann Irvine, and Daniel Marcu. 2011. Feature-rich language-independent syntax-based alignment for statistical machine translation. In *Proc. of EMNLP*, pages 497–507.

Jakob Uszkoreit, Jay Ponte, Ashok Popat, and Moshe Dubiner. 2010. Large scale parallel document mining for machine translation. In *Proc. of COLING*, pages 1101–1109.

Dekai Wu and Pascale Fung. 2005. Inversion transduction grammar constraints for mining parallel sentences from quasi-comparable corpora. In *Proc. of IJCNLP*, pages 257–268.

Bing Zhao and Stephan Vogel. 2002. Adaptive parallel sentences mining from web bilingual news collection. In *IEEE International Conference on Data Mining*, pages 745–748, Maebashi City, Japan.

Tuning as Linear Regression

Marzieh Bazrafshan, **Tagyoung Chung** and **Daniel Gildea**
Department of Computer Science
University of Rochester
Rochester, NY 14627

Abstract

We propose a tuning method for statistical machine translation, based on the pairwise ranking approach. Hopkins and May (2011) presented a method that uses a binary classifier. In this work, we use linear regression and show that our approach is as effective as using a binary classifier and converges faster.

1 Introduction

Since its introduction, the minimum error rate training (MERT) (Och, 2003) method has been the most popular method used for parameter tuning in machine translation. Although MERT has nice properties such as simplicity, effectiveness and speed, it is known to not scale well for systems with large numbers of features. One alternative that has been used for large numbers of features is the Margin Infused Relaxed Algorithm (MIRA) (Chiang et al., 2008). MIRA works well with a large number of features, but the optimization problem is much more complicated than MERT. MIRA also involves some modifications to the decoder itself to produce hypotheses with high scores against gold translations.

Hopkins and May (2011) introduced the method of pairwise ranking optimization (PRO), which casts the problem of tuning as a ranking problem between pairs of translation candidates. The problem is solved by doing a binary classification between "correctly ordered" and "incorrectly ordered" pairs. Hopkins and May (2011) use the maximum entropy classifier MegaM (Daumé III, 2004) to do the binary classification. Their method compares well to the results of MERT, scales better for high dimensional feature spaces, and is simpler than MIRA.

In this paper, we use the same idea for tuning, but, instead of using a classifier, we use linear regression. Linear regression is simpler than maximum entropy based methods. The most complex computation that it needs is a matrix inversion, whereas maximum entropy based classifiers use iterative numerical optimization methods.

We implemented a parameter tuning program with linear regression and compared the results to PRO's results. The results of our experiments are comparable to PRO, and in many cases (also on average) we get a better maximum BLEU score. We also observed that on average, our method reaches the maximum BLEU score in a smaller number of iterations.

The contributions of this paper include: First, we show that linear regression tuning is an effective method for tuning, and it is comparable to tuning with a binary maximum entropy classifier. Second, we show linear regression is faster in terms of the number of iterations it needs to reach the best results.

2 Tuning as Ranking

The parameter tuning problem in machine translation is finding the feature weights of a linear translation model that maximize the scores of the candidate translations measured against reference translations. Hopkins and May (2011) introduce a tuning method based on ranking the candidate translation pairs, where the goal is to learn how to rank pairs of candidate translations using a gold scoring function.

PRO casts the tuning problem as the problem of ranking pairs of sentences. This method iteratively generates lists of "k-best" candidate translations for each sentence, and tunes the weight vector for those candidates. MERT finds the weight vector that maximizes the score for the highest scored candidate translations. In contrast, PRO finds the weight vector which classifies pairs of candidate translations into "correctly ordered" and "incorrectly ordered," based on the gold scoring function. While MERT only considers the highest scored candidate to tune the weights, PRO uses the entire k-best list to learn the ranking between the pairs, which can help prevent overfitting.

Let $g(e)$ be a scoring function that maps each translation candidate e to a number (score) using a set of reference translations. The most commonly used gold scoring function in machine translation is the BLEU score, which is calculated for the entire corpus, rather than for individual sentences. To use BLEU as our gold scoring function, we need to modify it to make it decomposable for single sentences. One way to do this is to use a variation of BLEU called BLEU+1 (Lin and Och, 2004), which is a smoothed version of the BLEU score.

We assume that our machine translation system scores translations by using a scoring function which is a linear combination of the features:

$$h(e) = w^{\mathrm{T}} x(e) \tag{1}$$

where w is the weight vector and x is the feature vector. The goal of tuning as ranking is learning weights such that for every two candidate translations e_1 and e_2, the following inequality holds:

$$g(e_1) > g(e_2) \Leftrightarrow h(e_1) > h(e_2) \tag{2}$$

Using Equation 1, we can rewrite Equation 2:

$$g(e_1) > g(e_2) \Leftrightarrow w^{\mathrm{T}}(x(e_1) - x(e_2)) > 0 \tag{3}$$

This problem can be viewed as a binary classification problem for learning w, where each data point is the difference vector between the feature vectors of a pair of translation candidates, and the target of the point is the sign of the difference between their gold scores (BLEU+1). PRO uses the MegaM classifier to solve this problem. MegaM is a binary maximum entropy classifier which returns the weight vector w as a linear classifier. Using this method, Hopkins and May (2011) tuned the weight vectors for various translation systems. The results were close to MERT's and MIRA's results in terms of BLEU score, and the method was shown to scale well to high dimensional feature spaces.

3 Linear Regression Tuning

In this paper, we use the same idea as PRO for tuning, but instead of using a maximum entropy classifier, we use a simple linear regression to estimate the vector w in Equation 3. We use the least squares method to estimate the linear regression. For a matrix of data points $\mathbf{X}$, and a target vector $\mathbf{g}$, the weight vector can be calculated as:

$$w = (\mathbf{X}^{\mathrm{T}}\mathbf{X})^{-1}\mathbf{X}^{\mathrm{T}}\mathbf{g} \tag{4}$$

Adding L_2 regularization with parameter λ has the following closed form solution:

$$w = (\mathbf{X}^{\mathrm{T}}\mathbf{X} + \lambda\mathbf{I})^{-1}\mathbf{X}^{\mathrm{T}}\mathbf{g} \tag{5}$$

Following the sampling method used in PRO, the matrices $\mathbf{X}$ and vector $\mathbf{g}$ are prepared as follows:

For each sentence,

1. Generate a list containing the k best translations of the sentence, with each translation e scored by the decoder using a function of the form $h(e) = w^{\mathrm{T}}x(e)$.

2. Use the uniform distribution to sample n random pairs from the set of candidate translations.

3. Calculate the gold scores g for the candidates in each pair using BLEU+1. Keep a pair of candidates as a potential pair if the difference between their g scores is bigger than a threshold t.

4. From the potential pairs kept in the previous step, keep the s pairs that have the highest differences in g and discard the rest.

5. For each pair e_1 and e_2 kept in step 4, make two data points $(x(e_1) - x(e_2), g(e_1) - g(e_2))$ and $(x(e_2) - x(e_1), g(e_2) - g(e_1))$.

The rows of $\mathbf{X}$ consist of the inputs of the data points created in step 5, i.e., the difference vectors $x(e_1) - x(e_2)$. Similarly, the corresponding rows in $\mathbf{g}$ are the outputs of the data points, i.e., the gold score differences $g(e_1) - g(e_2)$.

One important difference between the linear regression method and PRO is that rather than using the signs of the gold score differences and doing a binary classification, we use the differences of the gold scores directly, which allows us to use the information about the magnitude of the differences.

4 Experiments

4.1 Setup

We used a Chinese-English parallel corpus with the English side parsed for our experiments. The corpus consists of 250K sentence pairs, which is 6.3M words on the English side. The corpus derives from newswire texts available from LDC.[1] We used a 392-sentence development set with four references for parameter tuning, and a 428-sentence test set with four references for testing. They are drawn from the newswire portion of NIST evaluations (2004, 2005, 2006). The development set and the test set only had sentences with less than 30 words for decoding speed.

We extracted a general SCFG (GHKM) grammar using standard methods (Galley et al., 2004; Wang et al., 2010) from the parallel corpus with a modification to preclude any unary rules (Chung et al., 2011). All rules over scope 3 are pruned (Hopkins and Langmead, 2010). A set of nine standard features was used for the experiments, which includes globally normalized count of rules, lexical weighting (Koehn et al., 2003), and length penalty. Our in-house decoder was used for experiments with a trigram language model. The decoder is capable of both CNF parsing and Earley-style parsing with cube-pruning (Chiang, 2007).

We implemented linear regression tuning using the method explained in Section 3. Following Hopkins and May (2011), we used the following parameters for the sampling task: For each sentence, the decoder generates the 1500 best candidate translations ($k = 1500$), and the sampler samples 5000 pairs ($n = 5000$). Each pair is kept as a potential data point if their BLEU+1 score difference is bigger than 0.05 ($t = 0.05$). Finally, for each sentence, the sampler keeps the 50 pairs with the highest difference in BLEU+1 ($s = 50$) and generates two data points for each pair.

[1]We randomly sampled our data from various different sources (LDC2006E86, LDC2006E93, LDC2002E18, LDC2002L27, LDC2003E07, LDC2003E14, LDC2004T08, LDC2005T06, LDC2005T10, LDC2005T34, LDC2006E26, LDC2005E83, LDC2006E34, LDC2006E85, LDC2006E92, LDC2006E24, LDC2006E92, LDC2006E24) The language model is trained on the English side of entire data (1.65M sentences, which is 39.3M words.)

	Average of max BLEU		Max BLEU	
	dev	test	dev	test
Regression	27.7 (0.91)	26.4 (0.82)	29.0	27.6
PRO	26.9 (1.05)	25.6 (0.84)	28.0	27.2

Table 1: Average of maximum BLEU scores of the experiments and the maximum BLEU score from the experiments. Numbers in the parentheses indicate standard of deviations of maximum BLEU scores.

4.2 Results

We ran eight experiments with random initial weight vectors and ran each experiment for 25 iterations. Similar to what PRO does, in each iteration, we linearly interpolate the weight vector learned by the regression (w) with the weight vector of the previous iteration (w_{t-1}) using a factor of 0.1:

$$w_t = 0.1 \cdot w + 0.9 \cdot w_{t-1} \quad (6)$$

For the sake of comparison, we also implemented PRO with exactly the same parameters, and ran it with the same initial weight vectors.

For each initial weight vector, we selected the iteration at which the BLEU score on the development set is highest, and then decoded using this weight vector on the test set. The results of our experiments are presented in Table 1. In the first column, we show the average over the eight initial weight vectors of the BLEU score achieved, while in the second column we show the results from the initial weight vector with the highest BLEU score on the development set. Thus, while the second column corresponds to a tuning process where the single best result is retained, the first column shows the expected behavior of the procedure on a single initial weight vector. The linear regression method has

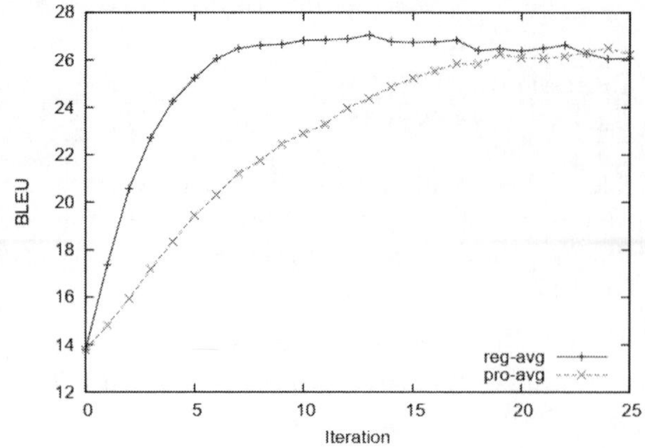

Figure 1: Average of eight runs of regression and PRO.

higher BLEU scores on both development and test data for both the average over initial weights and the maximum over initial weights.

Figure 1 shows the average of the BLEU scores on the development set of eight runs of the experiments. We observe that on average, the linear regression experiments reach the maximum BLEU score in a smaller number of iterations. On average, linear regression reached the maximum BLEU score after 14 iterations and PRO reached the maximum BLEU score after 20 iterations. One iteration took several minutes for both of the algorithms. The largest portion of this time is spent on decoding the development set and reading in the k-best list. The sampling phase, which includes performing linear regression or running MegaM, takes a negligible amount of time compared to the rest of the operations.

We experimented with adding L_2 regularization to linear regression. As expected, the experiments with regularization produced lower variance among the different experiments in terms of the BLEU score, and the resulting set of the parameters had a smaller norm. However, because of the small number of features used in our experiments, regularization was not necessary to control overfitting.

5 Discussion

We applied the idea of tuning as ranking and modified it to use linear regression instead of binary classification. The results of our experiments show that tuning as linear regression is as effective as PRO, and on average it reaches a better BLEU score in a fewer number of iterations.

In comparison with MERT, PRO and linear regression are different in the sense that the latter two approaches take into account rankings of the k-best list, whereas MERT is only concerned with separating the top 1-best sentence from the rest of the k-best list. PRO and linear regression are similar in the sense that both are concerned with ranking the k-best list. Their difference lies in the fact that PRO only uses the information on the relative rankings and uses binary classification to rank the points; on the contrary, linear regression directly uses the information on the magnitude of the differences. This difference between PRO and linear regression explains why linear regression converges faster and also may explain the fact that linear regression achieves a somewhat higher BLEU score. In this sense, linear regression is also similar to MIRA since MIRA's loss function also uses the information on the magnitude of score difference. However, the optimization problem for linear regression is simpler, does not require any changes to the decoder, and therefore the familiar MERT framework can be kept.

Acknowledgments We thank the anonymous reviewers for their helpful comments. This work was supported by NSF grant IIS-0910611.

References

David Chiang, Yuval Marton, and Philip Resnik. 2008. Online large-margin training of syntactic and structural translation features. In *Conference on Empirical Methods in Natural Language Processing (EMNLP-08)*.

David Chiang. 2007. Hierarchical phrase-based translation. *Computational Linguistics*, 33(2):201–228.

Tagyoung Chung, Licheng Fang, and Daniel Gildea. 2011. Issues concerning decoding with synchronous context-free grammar. In *Proceedings of the ACL 2011 Conference Short Papers*, Portland, Oregon. Association for Computational Linguistics.

Hal Daumé III. 2004. Notes on CG and LM-BFGS optimization of logistic regression. August.

Michel Galley, Mark Hopkins, Kevin Knight, and Daniel Marcu. 2004. What's in a translation rule? In *Proceedings of the 2004 Meeting of the North American chapter of the Association for Computational Linguistics (NAACL-04)*, pages 273–280, Boston.

Mark Hopkins and Greg Langmead. 2010. SCFG decoding without binarization. In *Proceedings of the 2010*

Conference on Empirical Methods in Natural Language Processing, pages 646–655, Cambridge, MA, October. Association for Computational Linguistics.

Mark Hopkins and Jonathan May. 2011. Tuning as ranking. In *Proceedings of the 2011 Conference on Empirical Methods in Natural Language Processing*, pages 1352–1362, Edinburgh, Scotland, UK., July. Association for Computational Linguistics.

Philipp Koehn, Franz Josef Och, and Daniel Marcu. 2003. Statistical phrase-based translation. In *Proceedings of the 2003 Meeting of the North American chapter of the Association for Computational Linguistics (NAACL-03)*, Edmonton, Alberta.

Chin-Yew Lin and Franz Josef Och. 2004. Orange: a method for evaluating automatic evaluation metrics for machine translation. In *Proceedings of Coling 2004*, pages 501–507, Geneva, Switzerland, Aug 23–Aug 27. COLING.

Franz Josef Och. 2003. Minimum error rate training for statistical machine translation. In *Proceedings of the 41th Annual Conference of the Association for Computational Linguistics (ACL-03)*.

Wei Wang, Jonathan May, Kevin Knight, and Daniel Marcu. 2010. Re-structuring, re-labeling, and re-aligning for syntax-based machine translation. *Computational Linguistics*, 36:247–277, June.

Ranking-based readability assessment for early primary children's literature

Yi Ma, Eric Fosler-Lussier
Dept. of Computer Science & Engineering
The Ohio State University
Columbus, OH 43210, USA
may,fosler@cse.ohio-state.edu

Robert Lofthus
Xerox Corporation
Rochester, NY 14604, USA
Robert.Lofthus@xerox.com

Abstract

Determining the reading level of children's literature is an important task for providing educators and parents with an appropriate reading trajectory through a curriculum. Automating this process has been a challenge addressed before in the computational linguistics literature, with most studies attempting to predict the particular grade level of a text. However, guided reading levels developed by educators operate at a more fine-grained level, with multiple levels corresponding to each grade. We find that ranking performs much better than classification at the fine-grained leveling task, and that features derived from the visual layout of a book are just as predictive as standard text features of level; including both sets of features, we find that we can predict the reading level up to 83% of the time on a small corpus of children's books.

1 Introduction

Determining the reading level of a text has received significant attention in the literature, dating back to simple arithmetic metrics to assess the reading level based on syllable counts (Flesch, 1948). In the computational linguistics community, several projects have attempted to determine the grade level of a text (2nd/3rd/4th/etc). However, the education community typically makes finer distinctions in reading levels, with each grade being covered by multiple levels. Moreover, there are multiple scales within the educational community; for example 1st grade is approximately covered by levels 3–14 on the Reading Recovery scale,[1] or levels C to H in the Fountas and Pinnell leveling system.[2]

For grade-level assessment, classification and regression approaches have been very promising. However, it is not clear that an increased number of classes will allow classification techniques to succeed with a more fine-grained leveling system. Similarly, regression techniques may have problems if the reading levels are not linearly distributed. In this work, we investigate a ranking approach to book leveling, and apply this to a fine-grained leveling problem for Kindergarten through 2nd grade books. The ranking approach also allows us to be more agnostic to the particular leveling system: for the vast majority of pairs of books, different systems will rank the levels of the books the same way, even if the exact differences in levels are not the same. Since most previous work uses classification techniques, we compare against an SVM multi-class classifier as well as an SVM regression approach.

What has not received much attention in recent research is the visual layout of the page. Yet, if one walks into a bookstore and rummages through the children's section, it is very easy to tell the reading level of a book just by thumbing through the pages. Visual clues such as the number of text lines per page, or the area of text boxes relative to the illustrations, or the font size, give instant information to the reader about the reading level of the book. What is not clear is if this information is sensitive enough to deliver a fine-grained assessment of the book. While

[1] http://www.readingrecovery.org
[2] http://www.fountasandpinnellleveledbooks.com

publishers may have standard guidelines for content providers on visual layout, these guidelines likely differ from publisher to publisher and are not available for the general public. Moreover, in the digital age teachers are also content providers who do not have access to these guidelines, so our proposed ranking system would be very helpful as they create reading materials such as worksheets, web pages, etc.

2 Related Work

Due to the limitations of traditional approaches, more advanced methods which use statistical language processing techniques have been introduced by recent work in this area (Collins-Thompson and Callan, 2004; Schwarm and Ostendorf, 2005; Feng et al., 2010). Collins-Thompson and Callan (2004) used a smoothed unigram language model to predict the grade reading levels of web page documents and short passages. Heilman *et al.* (2007) combined a language modeling approach with grammar-based features to improve readability assessment for first and second language texts. Schwarm/Petersen and Ostendorf (2005; 2009) used a support vector machine to combine surface features with language models and parsed features. The datasets used in these previous related works mostly consist of web page documents and short passages, or articles from educational newspapers. Since the datasets used are text-intensive, many efforts have been made to investigate text properties at a higher linguistic level, such as discourse analysis, language modeling, part-of-speech and parsed-based features. However, to the best of our knowledge, no prior work attempts to rank scanned children's books (in fine-grained reading levels) directly by analyzing the visual layout of the page.

3 Ranking Book Leveling Algorithm

Our proposed method can be regarded as a modified version of a standard ranking algorithm, where we develop a leveling classification by first ranking books, and then assigning the level based on the ranking output. Given a set of leveled books, the process to generate a prediction for a new target book involves the following two steps.

In the first step, we extract features from each book, and train an off-the-shelf ranking model to minimize the pairwise error of books. During the test phase (second step), we rank all of the leveled training books as well as the new target (test) book using the trained ranking model. The predicted reading level of the target book then can be inferred from the reading levels of neighboring leveled books in the rank-ordered list of books (in our experiment, we take into account a window of three books above and below the target book with reading levels weighted by distance). Intuitively, we can imagine a bookshelf in which books are sorted by their reading levels. The ranker's prediction of the reading level of a target book corresponds to inserting the target book into the sorted bookshelf.

4 Data Preparation

4.1 Book Selection, Scanning and Markup

We have processed 36 children's books which range from reading level A to L (3 books each level). The golden standard key reading levels of those books are obtained from Fountas and Pinnell leveled book list (Fountas and Pinnell, 1996) in which letter A indicates the easiest books to read and letter L identifies more challenging books; this range covers roughly Kindergarten through Second Grade. The set of children's books covers a large variety of genres, series and publishers.

After seeking permission from the publishers,[3] all of the books are scanned and OCRed (Optical Character Recognized) to create PDF versions of the book. In order to facilitate the feature extraction process, we manually annotate each book using Adobe Acrobat markup drawing tools before converting them into corresponding XML files. The annotation process consists of two straightforward steps: first, draw surrounding rectangles around the location of text content; second, find where the primary illustration images are and mark them using rectangle markups. Then the corresponding XML can be generated directly from Adobe Acrobat with one click on a customized menu item, which is implemented by using Adobe Acrobat JavaScript API.

[3]This is perhaps the most time-consuming part of the process.

# of partitions	1	2	3	4
±1 *Accuracy %*				
SVM Ranker	72.2	69.4	80.6	**83.3**
SVM Classifier	47.2	61.1	55.6	**63.9**
SVM Regression	72.2	61.1	58.3	58.3
Flesch-Kincaid	30.6	30.6	30.6	19.4
Spache	27.8	13.9	13.9	11.1
Average leveling error ± standard deviation				
SVM Ranker	1.00 ± 0.99	1.03 ± 0.91	0.94 ± 0.83	0.92 ± 0.73
SVM Classifier	2.00 ± 1.60	1.86 ± 1.69	1.78 ± 1.57	1.44 ± 1.23
SVM Regression	1.14 ± 1.13	1.25 ± 1.11	1.33 ± 1.22	1.36 ± 1.22
Flesch-Kincaid	3.03 ± 2.21	3.03 ± 2.29	3.08 ± 2.31	3.31 ± 2.28
Spache	4.06 ± 3.33	4.72 ± 3.27	4.83 ± 3.34	5.19 ± 3.21

Table 1: Per-book (averaged) results for ranking versus classification, reporting accuracy within one level and average error for different numbers of partitions

4.2 Feature Design

4.2.1 Surface-level Features

We extract a number of purely text-based features that have typically been used in the education literature (e.g., (Flesch, 1948)), including:

1. Number of words; 2. Number of letters per word; 3. Number of sentences; 4. Average sentence length; 5. Type-token ratio of the text content.

4.2.2 Visually-oriented Features

In this feature set, we include a number of features that would not be available without looking at the physical layout of the page; with the annotated PDF versions of the book we are able to extract:

1. Page count; 2. Number of words per page; 3. Number of sentences per page; 4. Number of text lines per page; 5. Number of words per text line; 6. Number of words per annotated text rectangle; 7. Number of text lines per annotated text rectangle; 8. Average ratio of annotated text rectangle area to page area; 9. Average ratio of annotated image rectangle area to page area; 10. Average ratio of annotated text rectangle area to annotated image rectangle area; 11. Average font size.

The OCR process provides some of this information automatically; while we have manually annotated rectangles for this study one could theoretically use the OCR information and vision processing techniques to extract rectangles automatically.

5 Experiments

5.1 Ranking vs. Classification/Regression

In this experiment, we look at whether treating book leveling as a ranking problem is promising compared to using classification/regression techniques. Besides taking a whole book as input, we also experiment with partitioning each book uniformly into 2, 3, or 4 parts, treating each sub-book as an independent entity. We use a leave-n-out paradigm – during each iteration of the training (iterated through all books), the system leaves out all n partitions corresponding to one book and then tests on all partitions corresponding to the held-out book. By averaging the results for the partitions of the held-out book, we can obtain its predicted reading level.

For ranking, we use the SVM^{rank} ranker (Joachims, 2006), which learns a (sparse) weight vector that minimizes the number of swapped pairs in the training set. The test book is inserted into the ordering of the training books by the ranking algorithm, and the level is assigned by averaging the levels of the books above and below the order. To compare the performance of our method with classifiers, we use both SVM^{multiclass} classifier (Tsochantaridis et al., 2004) and SVM^{light} (with regression learning option) (Joachims, 1999) to determine the level of the book directly. All systems are given the same set of surface text-based and visual-based features (Sections 4.2.1 and 4.2.2) as input.

# of partitions	1	2	3	4
±1 *Accuracy %*				
All Features	72.2	69.4	80.6	83.3
Surface Features	61.1	**63.9**	58.3	61.1
Visual Features	72.2	72.2	72.2	**83.3**
Average leveling error ± standard deviation				
All Features	1.00 ± 0.99	1.03 ± 0.91	0.94 ± 0.83	0.92 ± 0.73
Surface Features	1.42 ± 1.18	1.28 ± 1.00	1.44 ± 0.91	1.28 ± 1.11
Visual Features	1.03 ± 0.88	0.94 ± 0.86	1.03 ± 0.81	0.89 ± 0.82

Table 2: Per-book (averaged) results for all, surface-only, and visual-only features, reporting accuracy within one level and average error for different numbers of partitions

We score the systems in two ways: first, we compute the accuracy of the system by claiming it is correct if the book level is within ±1 of the true level.[4] The second scoring method is the absolute error of number of levels away from the true value, averaged over all of the books.

As we can observe from Table 1, our ranking system constantly beats the other two approaches (the ranker is statistically significantly better than the classifier at $p < 0.05$ level – figures in bold). One bit of interesting discovery is that SVM regression needs more data in order to have reliable results, as the performance is downgraded when the number of partitions goes up; the ranking approach benefits from averaging the increasing number of partitions.[5]

All three methods have the same style of learner (support vector learning), which suggests that the performance gain is due to using a ranking criterion in our method. Therefore we believe ranking is likely a more effective and accurate method than classification for this task.

One might also wonder how a traditional measure of reading level (in this case, the Flesch-Kincaid (Flesch, 1948) and Spache (Spache, 1953) Grade Level) would hold up for this data. Flesch-Kincaid and Spache predictions are linearly converted from calculated grade levels to Fountas-Pinnell levels; all of the systems utilizing our full feature set outperform these two baselines by a significant amount on both ±1 accuracy and average leveling error.

[4]Note that this is still rather fine-grained as there are multiple book levels per grade level.

[5]We only partition the books up to 4 sub-books because the shortest book we have only contains 4 PDF pages (8 "book" pages) and further partitioning the book will lead to sparse data.

5.2 Visual vs. Surface Features

In order to evaluate the benefits of using visual cues to assess reading levels, we repeat the experiments using $\mathrm{SVM}^{\mathrm{rank}}$ based on our proposed ranking book leveling algorithm with only the visual features or only surface features.

Table 2 shows that the visual features surprisingly outperform the surface features (statistically significant at $p < 0.05$ level – figures in bold) and on some partition levels, visual cues even beat the combination of all features. We note, however, that for early children's books, pictures and textual layout dominate the book content over text. Visual features can be as useful as traditional surface text-based features, but as one moves out of primary literature, we suspect text features will likely be more effective for leveling as content becomes more complex.

6 Conclusions

In this paper, we proposed a ranking-based book leveling algorithm to assess reading level for children's literature. Our experimental results showed that the ranking-based approach performs significantly better than classification approaches as used in current literature. The increased number of classes deteriorates the performance of classifiers in a fine-grained leveling system. We also introduced visual features into readability assessment and have seen considerable benefits of using visual cues. Since our target data are children's books that contain many illustrations and pictures, it is quite reasonable to utilize visual content to help predict a more accurate reading level. Future studies in early childhood readability need to take visual content into account.

References

K. Collins-Thompson and J. Callan. 2004. A language modeling approach to predicting reading difficulty. In *Proceedings of HLT / NAACL 2004*, volume 4, pages 193–200, Boston, USA.

L. Feng, M. Jansche, M. Huenerfauth, and N. Elhadad. 2010. A comparison of features for automatic readability assessment. In *Proceedings of the 23rd International Conference on Computational Linguistics (COLING 2010)*, pages 276–284, Beijing, China. Association for Computational Linguistics.

R. Flesch. 1948. A new readability yardstick. *Journal of applied psychology*, 32(3):221–233.

I. Fountas and G. Pinnell. 1996. *Guided Reading: Good First Teaching for All Children*. Heinemann, Portsmouth, NH.

M. Heilman, K. Collins-Thompson, J. Callan, and M. Eskenazi. 2007. Combining lexical and grammatical features to improve readability measures for first and second language texts. In *Proceedings of NAACL HLT*, pages 460–467.

T. Joachims. 1999. Making large-scale SVM learning practical. In B. Schölkopf, C. Burges, and A. Smola, editors, *Advances in Kernel Methods - Support Vector Learning*, chapter 11, pages 169–184. MIT Press, Cambridge, MA.

T. Joachims. 2006. Training linear SVMs in linear time. In *Proceedings of the 12th ACM SIGKDD international conference on Knowledge discovery and data mining*, pages 217–226. ACM.

S. Petersen and M. Ostendorf. 2009. A machine learning approach to reading level assessment. *Computer Speech & Language*, 23(1):89–106.

S. Schwarm and M. Ostendorf. 2005. Reading level assessment using support vector machines and statistical language models. In *Proceedings of the 43rd Annual Meeting on Association for Computational Linguistics*, pages 523–530. Association for Computational Linguistics.

G. Spache. 1953. A new readability formula for primary-grade reading materials. *The Elementary School Journal*, 53(7):410–413.

I. Tsochantaridis, T. Hofmann, T. Joachims, and Y. Altun. 2004. Support vector machine learning for interdependent and structured output spaces. In *Proceedings of the twenty-first international conference on Machine learning*, page 104. ACM.

How Text Segmentation Algorithms Gain from Topic Models

Martin Riedl and **Chris Biemann**
Ubiquitous Knowledge Processing Lab
Computer Science Department, Technische Universität Darmstadt
Hochschulstrasse 10, D-64289 Darmstadt, Germany
riedl@ukp.informatik.tu-darmstadt.de, biem@cs.tu-darmstadt.de

Abstract

This paper introduces a general method to incorporate the LDA Topic Model into text segmentation algorithms. We show that semantic information added by Topic Models significantly improves the performance of two word-based algorithms, namely TextTiling and C99. Additionally, we introduce the new TopicTiling algorithm that is designed to take better advantage of topic information. We show consistent improvements over word-based methods and achieve state-of-the art performance on a standard dataset.

1 Introduction

Texts are often structured into segments to ease understanding and readability of texts. Knowing about sentence boundaries is advantageous for natural language processing (NLP) tasks such as summarization or indexing. While many genres such as encyclopedia entries or scientific articles follow rather formal conventions of breaking up a text into meaningful units, there are plenty of electronically available texts without defined segments, e.g. web documents. *Text segmentation* is the task of automatically segmenting texts into parts. Viewing a well-written text as sequence of subtopics and assuming that subtopics correspond to segments, a segmentation algorithm needs to find changes of subtopics to identify the natural division of an unstructured text.

In this work, we utilize semantic information from *Topic Models (TMs)* to inform text segmentation algorithms. For this, we compare two early word-based algorithms with their topic-based variants, and construct our own algorithm called *TopicTiling*. We show that using topics estimated by *Latent Dirichlet Allocation (LDA)* in lieu of words substantially improves earlier segmentation algorithms. In comparison to *TextTiling (TT)*, neither smoothing nor a blocksize or window size is needed. TT using TMs and our own algorithm improve on the state-of-the-art for a standard dataset, while being conceptually simpler and computationally more efficient than other topic-based segmentation algorithms.

2 Related Work

Based on the observation of Halliday and Hasan (1976) that the density of coherence relations is higher within segments than between segments, most algorithms compute a coherence score to measure the difference of textual units for informing a segmentation decision. *TextTiling (TT)* (Hearst, 1994) relies on the simplest coherence relation – word repetition – and computes similarities between textual units based on the similarities of word space vectors. With *C99* (Choi, 2000) an algorithm was introduced that uses a matrix-based ranking and a clustering approach in order to relate the most similar textual units and to cluster groups of consecutive units into segments. Both *TT* and *C99* characterize textual units by the words they contain. Galley et al. (2003) showed that using TF-IDF term weights in the term vector improves the performance of *TT*. Proposals using Dynamic Programming (DP) are given in (Utiyama and Isahara, 2001; Fragkou et al., 2004). Related to our work are the approaches described in (Misra et al., 2009; Sun et al., 2008): here, TMs are also used to alleviate the sparsity of word vectors. Misra et al. (2009) extended the DP algorithm U00 from Utiyama and Isahara (2001) using TMs. At this, the topic assignments have to be inferred for each possible segment, resulting in high computational cost. In addition to these linear topic segmentation algorithms, there are hierarchical segmentation algorithms, see (Yaari, 1997; Hsueh et al., 2006; Eisenstein, 2009).

For topic modeling, we use the widely applied LDA (Blei et al., 2003). This generative probabilistic model uses a training corpus of documents to create document-topic and topic-word distributions and is parameterized by the number of topics N as well as by two hyperparameters. To generate a document d the topic proportions are drawn using a Dirichlet distribution with hyperparameter α. Adjacent for each word i a topic z_{d_i} is chosen according to a multinomial distribution using hyperparameter $\beta_{z_{d_i}}$. Unseen documents can be annotated with an existing TM using Bayesian inference methods (here: Gibbs sampling).

3 Method: From Words to Topics

The underlying mechanism described here is very simple: Instead of using words directly as features to characterize textual units, we use the topic IDs assigned by Bayesian inference. LDA inference assigns a topic ID to each word in the test document in each inference iteration step, based on a TM estimated on a training corpus. We use the topic ID, lastly assigned to each word. This might lead to instabilities as a word with high probabilities for several topics could be assigned to different topics in different inference iterations. To avoid these instabilities, we save all topic IDs assigned to a word for each inference iteration. Finally, the most frequent topic ID is assigned to each word. This mechanism we call the *mode method*. Both word replacements can be applied to most segmentation algorithms.

In this work, we use this general setup to implement topic-based versions of *TT* and *C99* and develop a new TextTiling-based method called *TopicTiling*.

4 Topic-based Segmentation Algorithms

4.1 TextTiling using Topic Models

In *TextTiling (TT)* (Hearst, 1994) using topic IDs (*TTLDA*), a document D, which is subject to segmentation, is represented as a sequence of n topic IDs[1]. *TT* splits the document into *topic-sequences*, instead of sentences, where each sequence consists of w topic IDs. To calculate the similarity between two topic-sequences, called *sequence-gap*, *TT* uses k topic-sequences, named *block*, to the left and to the right of the sequence gap. This parameter k defines the so-called *blocksize*. The cosine similarity is applied to computed a similarity score based on the topic frequency of the adjacent blocks at each sequence-gap. A value close to 1 indicates a high similarity among two blocks, a value close to zero denotes a low similarity. Then for each sequence-gap a *depth score* d_i is calculated for describing the sharpness of a gap, by $d_i = 1/2(hl(i) - s_i + hr(i) - s_i)$. The function $hl(i)$ returns the highest similarity score on the left side of the sequence-gap index i that does not increase and $hr(i)$ returns the highest score on the right side. Then all local maxima positions are searched based on the depth scores.

In the next step, these obtained maxima scores are sorted. If the number of segments n is given as input parameter, the n highest depth scores are used, otherwise a cut-off function is used that applies a segment only if the depth score is larger than $\mu - \sigma/2$, where mean μ and the standard deviation σ are calculated based on the entirety of depth scores. As *TT* calculates the depth on every topic-sequence using the highest gap, this could lead to a segmentation in the middle of a sentence. To avoid this, a final step ensures that the segmentation is positioned at the nearest sentence boundary.

4.2 C99 using Topic Models

For the C99 algorithm (Choi, 2000), named (*C99LDA*) when using topic IDs, the text is divided into minimal units on sentence boundaries. A similarity matrix $S_{m \times m}$ is computed, where m denotes the number of units (sentences). Every element s_{ij} is calculated using the cosine similarity between unit i and j. Next, a rank matrix R is computed to improve the contrast of S: Each element r_{ij} contains the number of neighbors of s_{ij} that have lower similarity scores then s_{ij} itself. In a final step a top-down clustering algorithm is performed to split the document into m segments $B = b_1, \ldots, b_m$. This algo-

[1]words instead of topic IDs are utilized in the original approach.

rithm starts with the whole document considered as one segment and splits off segments until the stop criteria are met, e.g. the number of segments or a similarity threshold.

4.3 TopicTiling

TopicTiling is a new TextTiling-based algorithm and is adjusted to use TMs. As we have found in data analysis, it is frequently the case that a topic dominates within a sampling unit (sentence), and that units from the same segment frequently are dominated by the same topic. In contrast to word-based representations, we expect no need to face sparsity issues that require smoothing methods (see TT) and ranking methods (see C99), which allows us to simplify the algorithm. Initially, the document is split into minimal units on sentence boundaries. To measure the coherence between units, the cosine similarity (vector dot product) between two adjacent sentences is computed. Each sentences s is represented as a N-dimensional vector, where N is the number of topics defined in the TMs. The i-th element of the vector contains the number of times the i-th topic is observed in the sentence. In comparison to TT we search all local minima based on these similarity scores and calculate for these positions the depth score as described in TT. If the number of segments is known in advance, the segments of the n-highest depth-scores are used, otherwise the cut-off score criteria used in TT is adapted.

5 Evaluation

As laid out in Section 3, a LDA Model is estimated on a training dataset and used for inference on the test set. To ensure that we do no use information from the test set, we perform a 10-fold Cross Validation (CV) for all reported results. To reduce the variance of the shown results, derived by the random nature of sampling and inference, the results for each fold are calculated 30 times using different LDA models.

The LDA model is trained with N=100 topics, 500 sampling iterations and symmetric hyperparameters as recommended by Griffiths and Steyvers (2004)(α=50/N and β=0.01), using JGibbsLda (Phan and Nguyen, 2007). For the annotation of unseen data with topic information, we use LDA inference, sampling 100 iterations. Inference is executed sentence-wise, since sentences form the minimal unit of our segmentation algorithms and we cannot use document information in the test setting. The performance of the algorithms is measured using P_k and *WindowDiff* (WD) metrics (Beeferman et al., 1999; Pevzner and Hearst, 2002). The C99 algorithm is initialized with a 11×11 ranking mask, as recommended in Choi (2000). TT is configured according to Choi (2000) with sequence length w=20 and block size k=6.

5.1 Data Set

For evaluation, we rely on the Choi data set (Choi, 2000), which has been used in several other text segmentation approaches to ensure comparability. This data set is generated artificially using the Brown corpus and consists of 700 documents. Each document consists of 10 segments. For its generation, 3–11 sentences are sequentially extracted from a randomly selected document and merged together. While our CV evaluation setting is designed to avoid using the same documents for training and testing, this cannot be guaranteed as the segments within the documents generated by Choi are included in several documents. This problem also occurs in other approaches, but has not be described in (Fragkou et al., 2004; Misra et al., 2009; Galley et al., 2003), where parts or the whole dataset are used for training either TF-IDF values or topic models.

5.2 Results

For the experiments the C99 and TT implementations[2] are executed in two settings: using words and using topics. When using words, TT and C99 use stemmed words and filter out words using a stopword list. C99 additional removes words using predefined regular expressions. In the case of topic IDs, no stopword filtering was deemed necessary. Table 1 shows the result of the different algorithms with all combination of provided segment number and using the mode method.

We note that WD values are always higher than the P_k values, and these measures are highly correlated. First we discuss results for the setting with number of segments provided (see column 2-5 of

[2]We use the implementations by Choi available at `http://code.google.com/p/uima-text-segmenter/`.

Method	Segments provided				Segments unprovided			
	mode=false		mode=true		mode=false		mode=true	
	Pk	WD	Pk	WD	Pk	WD	Pk	WD
C99	11.20	12.07			12.73	14.57		
C99LDA	4.16	4.89	2.67	3.08	8.69	10.52	3.24	4.08
TT	44.48	47.11			49.51	66.16		
TTLDA	1.85	2.10	**1.04**	**1.18**	16.41	21.40	2.89	3.67
TopicTiling	2.65	3.02	2.12	2.42	4.12	5.75	2.30	3.08
TopicTiling (filtered)	**1.50**	**1.72**	1.06	1.21	**3.24**	**4.58**	**1.39**	**1.84**

Table 1: Results by segment length for TT with words and topics (TTLDA), C99 with words and topics (C99LDA) and TopicTiling using all sentences and using only sentences with more then 5 word tokens (filtered).

Table 1). A significant improvement for C99 and TT can be achieved when using topic IDs. In case of C99LDA, the error rate is at least halved and for TTLDA the error rate is reduced by a factor of 20. Using the most frequent topic ID assigned during the Bayesian inference (mode method) reduces the error rates further for the TM-based approaches, as the probability for randomly assigned topic IDs is decreased. The newly introduced algorithm TopicTiling as described above does not improve over TTLDA. Analysis revealed that the Choi corpus includes also captions and other "non-sentences" that are marked as sentences, which causes TopicTiling to introduce false positive segments since the topic vectors are too sparse for these short "non-sentences". We therefore filter out "sentences" with less than 5 words (see bottom line in Table 1). This leads to errors values that are close to the results achieved with TTLDA when the mode is used. When the number of segments is not given in advance (see columns 6-9 in Table 1), we again observe significantly better results comparing topic-based methods to word-based methods. But the error rates of TTLDA are unexpectedly high when the mode method is not used. We discovered in data analysis that TT estimates too many segments, as the topic ID distributions between adjacent sentences within a segment are often too diverse, especially in face of random fluctuations from the topic assignments. Estimating the number of segments is better achieved using TopicTiling instead of TTLDA.

In Table 2, we compare TTLDA, C99LDA and our TopicTiling algorithm to other published results on the same dataset. We can see that all introduced topic-based methods outperform the yet best pub-

Method	Segments	
	provided	**unprovided**
TT	44.48	49.51
C99	11.20	12.73
U00 (Utiyama and Isahara, 2001)	9	10
F04 (Fragkou et al., 2004)	5.39	
M09 (Misra et al., 2009)	2.73	
C99LDA (mode = true)	2.67	3.24
TTLDA (mode=true)	**1.04**	2.89
TopicTiling (mode=true, filtered)	1.06	**1.39**

Table 2: List of lowest P_k values for the Choi data set for different algorithms in the literature.

lished M09 algorithm (Misra et al., 2009). The improvements of C99, TTLDA and TopicTiling in comparison to M09 are significant[3].

TopicTiling and TTLDA are computationally more efficient than M09. Whereas our linear method has a complexity of $O(T)$ (T is the number of sentences), dynamic algorithms like M09 have a complexity of $O(T^2)$ (cf. Fragkou et al. (2004)), which also applies to the number of topic inference runs. When the number of segments is not given in advance, TopicTiling outperforms TTLDA significantly. As an additional benefit, TopicTiling is even simpler than TT, as no smoothing parameter is needed and the depth scores are only calculated for the minima of the similarity scores.

6 Conclusion

The method introduced in this paper shows that using semantic information, provided by TMs, can improve existing algorithm significantly. This is attested modifying the algorithm TT and C99. With TopicTiling a new simplistic topic based algorithm is developed that can produce state-of-the-art results based on the Choi corpus and outperform TTLDA when the number of segments is unknown. Additionally this method is computationally more efficient in comparison to other topic based segmentation algorithms. Another contribution is the mode method for stabilizing topic ID assignments.

7 Acknowledgments

This work has been supported by LOEWE as part of the research center "Digital Humanities". We would like to thank the anonymous reviewers for their comments, which truly helped to improve the paper.

[3]using a one sampled t-test with $\alpha = 0.05$

References

Doug Beeferman, Adam Berger, and John Lafferty. 1999. Statistical models for text segmentation. *Machine learning*, 34(1):177–210.

David M. Blei, Andrew Y Ng, and Michael I. Jordan. 2003. Latent Dirichlet Allocation. *Journal of Machine Learning Research*, 3:993–1022.

Freddy Y. Y. Choi. 2000. Advances in domain independent linear text segmentation. In *Proceedings of the 1st North American chapter of the Association for Computational Linguistics conference*, pages 26–33, Seattle, WA, USA.

Jacob Eisenstein. 2009. Hierarchical text segmentation from multi-scale lexical cohesion. In *Proceedings of Human Language Technologies: The 2009 Annual Conference of the North American Chapter of the Association for Computational Linguistics*, pages 353–361, Boulder, CO, USA.

Pavlina Fragkou, Vassilios Petridis, and Athanasios Kehagias. 2004. A Dynamic Programming Algorithm for Linear Text Segmentation. *Journal of Intelligent Information Systems*, 23(2):179–197.

Michel Galley, Kathleen McKeown, Eric Fosler-Lussier, and Hongyan Jing. 2003. Discourse segmentation of multi-party conversation. In *Proceedings of the 41st Annual Meeting on Association for Computational Linguistics*, volume 1, pages 562–569, Sapporo, Japan.

Thomas L. Griffiths and Mark Steyvers. 2004. Finding scientific topics. *Proceedings of the National Academy of Sciences*, 101:5228–5235.

M A K Halliday and Ruqaiya Hasan. 1976. *Cohesion in English*, volume 1 of *English Language Series*. Longman.

Marti A. Hearst. 1994. Multi-paragraph segmentation of expository text. In *Proceedings of the 32nd annual meeting on Association for Computational Linguistics*, pages 9–16, Las Cruces, NM, USA.

P.-Y. Hsueh, J. D. Moore, and S. Renals. 2006. Automatic segmentation of multiparty dialogue. AMI-156.

Hemant Misra, Joemon M Jose, and Olivier Cappé. 2009. Text Segmentation via Topic Modeling : An Analytical Study. In *Proceeding of the 18th ACM Conference on Information and Knowledge Management*, pages 1553 1556, Hong Kong.

Lev Pevzner and Marti A. Hearst. 2002. A critique and improvement of an evaluation metric for text segmentation. *Computational Linguistic*, 28(1):19–36.

Xuan-Hieu Phan and Cam-Tu Nguyen. 2007. GibbsLDA++: A C/C++ implementation of latent Dirichlet allocation (LDA). http://jgibblda.sourceforge.net/.

Qi Sun, Runxin Li, Dingsheng Luo, and Xihong Wu. 2008. Text segmentation with LDA-based Fisher kernel. *Proceedings of the 46th Annual Meeting of the Association for Computational Linguistics on Human Language Technologies*, pages 269–272.

Masao Utiyama and Hitoshi Isahara. 2001. A statistical model for domain-independent text segmentation. In *Proceedings of the 39th Annual Meeting on Association for Computational Linguistics*, pages 499–506, Toulouse, France.

Yaakov Yaari. 1997. Segmentation of expository texts by hierarchical agglomerative clustering. In *Proceedings of the Conference on Recent Advances in Natural Language Processing*, Tzigov Chark, Bulgaria.

Identifying Comparable Corpora Using LDA

Judita Preiss
j.preiss@sheffield.ac.uk
Department of Computer Science, University of Sheffield, Regent Court
211 Portobello, Sheffield, S1 4DP, United Kingdom

Abstract

Parallel corpora have applications in many areas of Natural Language Processing, but are very expensive to produce. Much information can be gained from comparable texts, and we present an algorithm which, given any bodies of text in multiple languages, uses existing named entity recognition software and topic detection algorithm to generate pairs of comparable texts without requiring a parallel corpus training phase. We evaluate the system's performance firstly on data from the online newspaper domain, and secondly on Wikipedia cross-language links.

1 Introduction

Manual alignment or creation of parallel corpora is exceedingly expensive, requiring highly skilled annotators or professional translators. Methods exist for aligning parallel corpora, and extracted parallel segments can be used to, for example, augment machine translation phrase tables, but the amount of genuinely parallel data is limited. However, parallel segments can also be extracted from comparable corpora (a comparable corpus is one which contains similar texts in more than one language). Comparable documents, if produced with a confidence value, could also be used to prioritize translation (manual or automatic) when one is searching for further information (which may only be available in a foreign language) to augment information given in an article in the source language. We present a technique to automatically detect comparable corpora in existing data, and we demonstrate the applicability of our method to any genre by evaluating on crawled online newspaper text, as well as Wikipedia articles.

Clearly, texts need to contain some of the same data in order to be comparable (Harris, 1954), and we assume:

- To be similar, texts need to share some **named entities**, e.g., Tóth et al., (2008).
- Comparable texts need to be on the same **topic**.

Construction of multilingual topic models usually requires either parallel data or some number of aligned documents across multiple languages. Zhao and Xing (2007) create bilingual topic models from (at least 25%) of parallel data. Mimno et al., (2009) start from tuples of equivalent documents to build models, and then the same distribution over topics holds in both source and target languages.

While Zhao and Xing (2007) used their topic models for word alignment from comparable corpora (combined with underlying parallel data), multilingual topic models are usually applied to data to automatically detect word translations based on parallel data, e.g., Vulić et al., (2011) exploit a shared language independent topic distribution to measure the similarity between topics pertaining to words.

The novelty of our work is the transformation of a source language topic model rather than the creation of a language independent model from parallel data. Transforming the source language model to the target language allows the classification of the target language documents to source language topics. The translated model is applied to two document collections to demonstrate its ability to detect comparable corpora. Our system can be applied to any pair of languages for which there is a dictionary.

Section 2 describes the tools we employ. Section 3 contains a description of our system: the method for employing NE recognition across languages is presented in Section 3.1, while Section 3.2 outlines our technique for employing LDA across languages. Our experiments and their results are described in Section 4. Section 5 draws our conclusions and indicates avenues for future work.

2 Tools

2.1 Named entity recognition

The Stanford named entity recognition (NER) software[1] (Finkel et al., 2005) is an implementation of linear chain Conditional Random Field (CRF) sequence models, which includes a three class (person, organization, location and other) named entity recognizer for English.

2.2 Topic detection

LDA (Blei et al., 2003) is a generative probabilistic model where documents are viewed as mixtures over underlying topics, and each topic is a distribution over words. Both the document-topic and the topic-word distributions are assumed to have a Dirichlet prior. Given a set of documents and a number of topics, the model returns θ_i, the topic distribution for each document i, and ϕ_{ik}, the word distribution for topic k. We employ the publicly available implementation of LDA, JGibbLDA[2] (Phan et al., 2008), which has two main execution methods: parameter estimation (model building) and inference for new data (classification of a new document). Both invocations produce the following:

ϕ_{ij}: $p(\text{word}_i|\text{topic}_j)$

θ_{jk}: $p(\text{topic}_j|\text{document}_k)$

tassign: a deterministic topic-word assignment for each word in every document

The LDA topic models are created from a randomly selected tenth of the Reuters corpus (Rose et al., 2002).[3]

[1]http://nlp.stanford.edu/ner/index.shtml

[2]http://jgibblda.sourceforge.net/

[3]LDA modeling can abstract a model from a relatively small corpus and a tenth of the original Reuters corpus is much more manageable in terms of memory and time requirements.

2.3 Indexing

To provide quick searching access to the large text collections, we utilize the high-performance search engine library Lucene.[4] The stemmed and stoplisted documents are stored along with the frequency of occurrence of each word within a document.

2.4 Lemmatization / stemming

English text is lemmatized using the lemmatizer available within RASP[5] (Briscoe et al., 2006). Stemming is provided for all the non-English languages included in our work within Lucene.

3 Identifying comparable corpora

3.1 Cross language NER

NEs extracted from the English text collections are automatically translated into the target languages using the BING Translation API[6] yielding a single translation, which is retained. The stemmed, translated version of each NE in the source text is sought in the indexed form of the target language document collection, and the frequency of occurrence of the NE is returned.

Filtering is applied based on the proportion of source language document's NEs found in the target document (we do not expect all the NEs to be present in the target language: NEs could be mis-translated, and not all NEs would necessarily be mentioned even in a comparable document). The proportions of all types of NEs required were optimized over a small manually created set. While we could assign a weight and not filter documents, this is not believed to be adequate: e.g., a newspaper article containing all the source location mentions (and thus having a high weight), but none of the same people, is likely to be a news story about the same area but a different event.

[4]http://lucene.apache.org

[5]http://ilexir.co.uk/applications/rasp/download

[6]The translations could also be retrieved from NE mapping lists, dictionaries (if these are available) or manually translated – we therefore do not see this step as violating the lack of need for a parallel corpus.

3.2 Cross language topic identification

Being non-deterministic, multiple executions of the LDA algorithm are not guaranteed to (and do not) give rise to identical topics (even within one language). It is therefore not possible to build a topic model in the source language and the target language separately, as there is no clear alignment between their respective topics. Traditionally, parallel corpora are used to generate a language independent topic-document distribution, from which polylingual topic models can be created so the underlying topics are shared.

We propose to translate each word from the source language topic model using the BING API and substitute the new wordmap thus creating a target language topic model. While word distributions are clearly different across languages, and building a shared topic-document distribution to sample words from allows words to retain their language specific distributions, our technique completely avoids the need for parallel corpora, and merely requires the translation of the words in the LDA model (which can be performed using dictionary lookup, or NE lists instead of the BING API).

3.3 Selecting comparable corpora

Target language candidate documents found to share sufficient proportions of NEs are classified using the translated target language LDA model. This yields θ_{jk} (the probability distribution of topic given document) and classifying the original document using the source language LDA model gives θ'_{jk}. The candidate documents are ranked according to the cosine similarity between the two vectors:

$$similarity = \frac{\theta_{jk} \cdot \theta'_{jk}}{||\theta_{jk}|| ||\theta'_{jk}||}$$

By definition, cosine similarity ranges between -1 and 1. Similarity of 1 indicates two documents with $\theta = \theta'$, and thus the higher the similarity, the higher we rank the document.

4 Experiments

We present two evaluations: firstly, we manually evaluate the comparable documents generated from online newspaper text in two languages, while the second evaluation finds comparable articles in source and target versions of Wikipedia with results evaluated against the cross-language links present in Wikipedia.

4.1 Online newspaper documents

Simple Google search yields a number of links to online newspapers in any language, these lists (automatically retrieved) are used to seed a crawler. Documents from newspaper sites which allow crawling are retrieved and only well formed HTML documents are retained,[7] and the language of the documents is verified using a Perl implementation of Lingua::Ident (Dunning, 1994), an n-gram based model for language identification.[8]

A single annotator evaluated 10 randomly selected English documents and the comparable documents returned for them from 40,528 Czech newspaper articles (total retrieved within a 24 hour period). Since there is no current scheme available for judging comparability, we employed a four category scale:

Strong: The documents are about the same news event, in a similar style. (Articles about the same news event, but elaborating, would be included here.)

Medium: The documents are about related news events.

Weak: The documents refers to similar events.

None: No overlap in topic in the two documents.

Results of the evaluation are presented in Table 1; the top document is scored for each pair, showing the high precision of the technique. The 10 English documents were selected subject to the constraint that a comparable corpus was retrieved for them: the imposed constraints on NEs make this a high precision / low recall technique. Many articles found using the crawling approach on news sites (rather than an RSS feed gathering approach) were discussions,

[7]Note that the crawler is not permitted to leave the domain of the newspaper.

[8]The Lingua::Ident Perl module is available from `http://search.cpan.org/~mpiotr/Lingua-Ident-1.7/Ident.pm`. We build the models for the language identification system from downloaded Wikipedia content for each language.

Strong	Medium	Weak	None
4	4	1	1

Table 1: Results for English-Czech documents

for example discussions of strategies in sports, interviews with actors, rather than topical news stories. From a manual inspection of the target language articles, many of these articles do not appear to have comparable equivalents. Also, enforcing a high proportion of NEs shared between the source and target languages frequently rules out documents which are subsets of each other (this was also apparent in the second evaluation).

4.2 Wikipedia

Information within Wikipedia is connected across languages using cross-language links. While the lists of links are not necessarily complete, and the articles they link may not contain large parallel segments, the linked documents should be comparable (under the definition), and thus provide an empirical measure of the utility of our method.

The top comparable articles in Czech were generated for 100 randomly selected English Wikipedia articles (subject to the constraint that they have cross-language links). As in our first evaluation, the system had a low recall (35%), however precision was 83%. By the design of the experiment, an article about the same subject has to exist in both languages, and therefore the low recall value is surprising. Rather than a low cosine value, the low recall is mainly due to the NE filtering step removing the 'correct' article from consideration. A brief inspection of a small number of articles which had been filtered out was performed and substantial differences between the pages were found – for example, a significant portion of the Wikipedia page for *Equinox* in English contains descriptions of Equinox commemorations all over the world, which are missing in the Czech version of the Wikipedia article (leading to a large number of missing NEs). Similar length of articles appeared to be a good indicator of both articles containing similar data, and our system detecting the two texts to be comparable.

Please note that while the NE filtering step is removing texts from consideration, it is not possible to compute cosines of the topic vectors of all documents and thus some candidate selection step is necessary.

4.3 Baseline

There are no standard baselines for the task of creating comparable corpora. It is possible to translate the source language text into the target language using BING, however, a cosine comparison of the stemmed, automatically translated document with all documents in the target language collection is extremely time consuming. Applying NE filtering, automatically translating the remaining target language candidate texts into the source language using BING, and ranking according to cosine similarity gives a precision of 69% for the collection discussed in Section 4.2.

5 Conclusion

We have presented an LDA based algorithm applicable to large document collections to find comparable documents across multi-lingual corpora without the needing to train with parallel data. We show, using a human judge as well as Wikipedia cross-language links, that the system achieves high precision in finding comparable documents.

The technique strongly relies on the named entity method selected, and another technique may be more suitable. A comparison with a bilingual topic model created from parallel data would also prove interesting.

Acknowledgments

This research was supported by EU grant 248347 on Analysis and Evaluation of Comparable Corpora for Under-Resourced Areas of Machine Translation (ACCURAT). My thanks also go to the three reviewers whose comments strengthened the findings of this work.

References

Blei, D. M., Ng, A. Y., and Jordan, M. I. (2003). Latent Dirichlet allocation. *Journal of Machine Learning Research*, 3:993–1022.

Briscoe, T., Carroll, J., and Watson, R. (2006). The second release of the RASP system. In *Proceedings of the COLING/ACL 2006 Interactive Presentation Sessions*.

Dunning, T. (1994). Statistical identification of language. Technical Report CRL MCCS-94-273, Computing Research Lab, New Mexico State University.

Finkel, J. R., Grenager, T., and Manning, C. (2005). Incorporating non-local information into information extraction systems by Gibbs sampling. In *Proceedings of the 43nd Annual Meeting of the Association for Computational Linguistics*, pages 363–370.

Harris, Z. S. (1954). Distributional structure. *Word*, 10(23):146162.

Mimno, D., Wallach, H. M., Naradowsky, J., Smith, D. A., and McCallum, A. (2009). Polylingual topic models. In *Proceedings of the Conference on Empirical Methods in Natural Language Processing*, page 880889.

Phan, X.-H., Nguyen, L.-M., and Horiguchi, S. (2008). Learning to classify short and sparse text & web with hidden topics from large-scale data collections. In *Proceedings of The 17th International World Wide Web Conference (WWW 2008)*, pages 91–100.

Rose, T. G., Stevenson, M., and Whitehead, M. (2002). The Reuters corpus volume 1 - from yesterday's news to tomorrow's language resources. In *Proceedings of the Third International Conference on Language Resources and Evaluation*, pages 827–832.

Tóth, K., Farkas, R., and Kocsor, A. (2008). Sentence alignment of Hungarian-English parallel corpora using a hybrid algorithm. *Acta Cybernetica*, pages 463–478.

Vulic, I., Smet, W. D., and Moens, M.-F. (2011). Identifying word translations from comparable corpora using latent topic models. In *Proceedings of ACL*, pages 479–484.

Zhao, B. and Xing, E. P. (2007). HM-BiTAM: Bilingual topic exploration, word alignment, and translation. In *NIPS*.

Behavioral Factors in Interactive Training of Text Classifiers

Burr Settles
Machine Learning Department
Carnegie Mellon University
Pittsburgh PA 15213, USA
bsettles@cs.cmu.edu

Xiaojin Zhu
Computer Sciences Department
University of Wisconsin
Madison WI 53715, USA
jerryzhu@cs.wisc.edu

Abstract

This paper describes a user study where humans interactively train automatic text classifiers. We attempt to replicate previous results using multiple "average" Internet users instead of a few domain experts as annotators. We also analyze user annotation behaviors to find that certain labeling actions have an impact on classifier accuracy, drawing attention to the important role these behavioral factors play in interactive learning systems.

1 Introduction

There is growing interest in methods that incorporate human domain knowledge in machine learning algorithms, either as priors on model parameters or as constraints in an objective function. Such approaches lend themselves well to natural language tasks, where input features are often discrete variables that carry semantic meaning (e.g., words). A *feature label* is a simple but expressive form of domain knowledge that has received considerable attention recently (Druck et al., 2008; Melville et al., 2009). For example, a single feature (word) can be used to indicate a particular label or set of labels, such as "excellent" ⇒ positive or "terrible" ⇒ negative, which might be useful word-label rules for a sentiment analysis task.

Contemporary work has also focused on making such learning algorithms *active*, by enabling them to pose "queries" in the form of feature-based rules to be labeled by annotators in addition to — and sometimes lieu of — data instances such as documents (Attenberg et al., 2010; Druck et al., 2009). These concepts were recently implemented in a practical system for *interactive* training of text classifiers called DUALIST[1]. Settles (2011) reports that, in user experiments with real annotators, humans were able to train near state of the art classifiers with only a few minutes of effort. However, there were only five subjects, who were all computer science researchers. It is possible that these positive results can be attributed to the subjects' implicit familiarity with machine learning and natural language processing algorithms.

This short paper sheds more light on previous experiments by replicating them with many more human subjects, and of a different type: non-experts recruited through the Amazon Mechanical Turk service[2]. We also analyze the impact of annotator behavior on the resulting classifiers, and suggest relationships to recent work in curriculum learning.

2 DUALIST

Figure 1 shows a screenshot of DUALIST, an interactive machine learning system for quickly building text classifiers. The annotator is allowed to take three kinds of actions: ① label query documents (instances) by clicking class-label buttons in the left panel, ② label query words (features) by selecting them from the class-label columns in the right panel, or ③ "volunteer" domain knowledge by typing labeled words into a text box at the top of each class column. The underlying classifier is a naïve Bayes variant combining informative priors,

[1] http://code.google.com/p/dualist/
[2] http://mturk.com

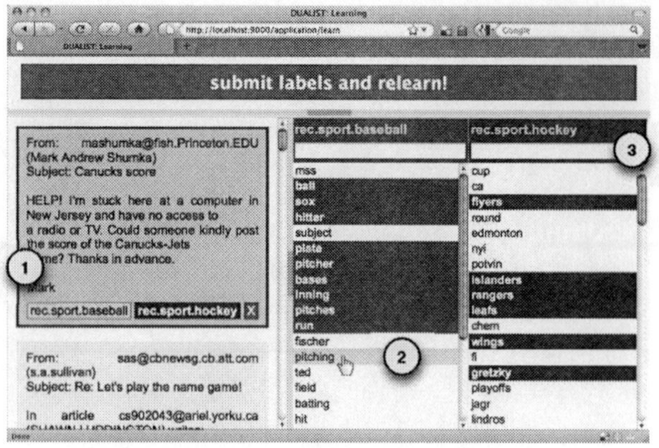

Figure 1: The DUALIST user interface.

maximum likelihood estimation, and the EM algorithm for fast semi-supervised training. When a user performs action ① or ②, she labels queries that should help minimize the classifier's uncertainty on unlabeled documents (according to active learning heuristics). For action ③, the user is free to volunteer any relevant word, whether or not it appears in a document or word column. For example, the user might volunteer the labeled word "oscar" ⇒ positive in a sentiment analysis task for movie reviews (leveraging her knowledge of domain), even if the word "oscar" does not appear anywhere in the interface. This flexibility goes beyond traditional active learning, which restricts the user to feedback on items queried by the learner (i.e., actions ① and ②). After a few labeling actions, the user submits her feedback and receives the next set of queries in real time. For more details, see Settles (2011).

3 Experimental Setup

We recruited annotators through the crowdsourcing marketplace Mechanical Turk. Subjects were shown a tutorial page with a brief description of the classification task, as well as a cartoon of the interface similar to Figure 1 explaining the various annotation options. When they decided they were ready, users followed a link to a web server running a customized version of DUALIST, which is an open source web-based application. At the end of each trial, subjects were given a confirmation code to receive payment.

We conducted experiments using two corpora from the original DUALIST study: *Science* (a subset of the 20 Newsgroups benchmark: cryptography, electronics, medicine, and space) and *Movie Reviews* (a sentiment analysis collection). These are not specialized domains, i.e., we could expect average Internet users to be knowledgable enough to perform the annotations. While both are generally accessible, these corpora represent different types of tasks and vary both in number of categories (four vs. two) and difficulty (Movie Reviews is known to be harder for learning algorithms). We replicated the same experimental conditions as previous work: *DUALIST* (the full interface in Figure 1), *active-doc* (the left-hand ① document panel only), and *passive-doc* (the ① document panel only, but with texts selected at random and not queried by active learning).

For each condition, we recruited 25 users for the Science corpus (75 total) and 35 users for Movie Reviews (105 total). We were careful to publish tasks on MTurk in a way that no one user annotated more than one condition. Some users experienced technical difficulties that nullified their work, and four appeared to be spammers[3]. After removing these subjects from the analysis, we were left with 23 users for the Science DUALIST condition, 25 each for the two document-only conditions (73 total), 32 users for the Movie Reviews DUALIST condition, and 33 each for the document-only conditions (98 total). DUALIST automatically logged data about user actions and model accuracies as training progressed, although users could not see these statistics. Trials lasted 6 minutes for the Science corpus and 10 minutes for Movie Reviews. We did advertise a "bonus" for the user who trained the best classifier to encourage correctness, but otherwise offered no guidance on how subjects should prioritize their time.

4 Results

Figure 2(a) shows learning curves aggregated across all users in each experimental condition. Curves are LOESS fits to classifier accuracy over time: locally-weighted polynomial regressions (Cleveland et al., 1992) ± 1 standard error, with the actual user data points omitted for clarity. For the Science task (top), DUALIST users trained significantly better classifiers after about four minutes of annotation time. Document-only active learning also outperformed

[3]A spammer was ruled to be one whose document error rate (vs. the gold standard) was more than double the chance error, and whose feature labels appeared to be arbitrary clicks.

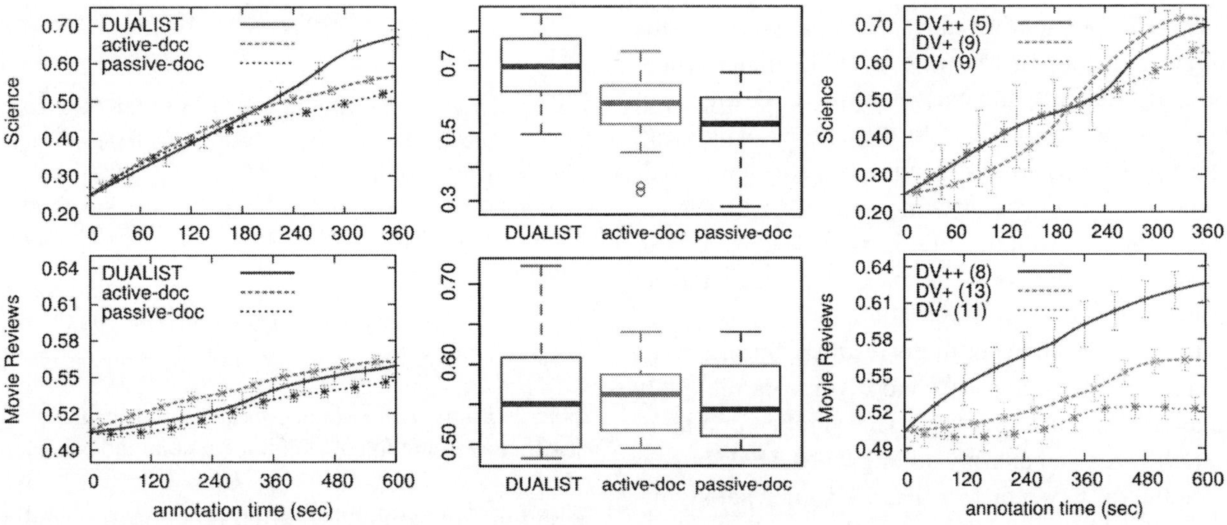

(a) learning curves (b) final classifier accuracies (c) behavioral subgroup curves

Figure 2: (a) Learning curves plotting accuracy vs. actual annotation time for the three conditions. Curves are LOESS fits (± 1 SE) to all classifier accuracies at that point in time. (b) Box plots showing the distribution of final accuracies under each condition. (c) Learning curves for three behavioral subgroups found in the DUALIST condition. The DV++ group volunteered many labeled words (action ③), DV+ volunteered some, and DV- volunteered none.

standard passive learning, which is consistent with previous work. However, for Movie Reviews (bottom), there is little difference among the three settings, and in fact models trained with DUALIST appear to lag behind active learning with documents.

Figure 2(b) shows the distribution of final classifier accuracies in each condition. For Science, the DUALIST users are significantly better than either of the baselines (two-sided KS test, $p < 0.005$). While the differences in DUALIST accuracies are not significantly different, we can see that the top quartile does much better than the two baselines. Clearly some DUALIST users are making better use of the interface and training better classifiers. How?

It is important to note that users in the active-doc and passive-doc conditions can only choose action ① (label documents), whereas those in the DUALIST condition must allocate their time among three kinds of actions. It turns out that the annotators exhibited very non-uniform behavior in this respect. In particular, activity of action ③ (volunteer labeled words) follows a power law, and many subjects volunteered no features at all. By inspecting the distribution of these actions for natural breakpoints, we identified three subgroups of DUALIST users: DV++ (many volunteered words), DV+ (some words), and DV- (none; labeled queries only). Note that DV- is *not* functionally equivalent to the active-doc condition, as users in the DV- group could still view and label word queries. The three behavioral subgroups are summarized in Table 1.

	Movie Reviews		**Science**	
Group	# Words	Users	# Words	Users
DV++	21–62	8	24–42	5
DV+	1–15	13	2–19	9
DV-	0	11	0	9

Table 1: The range of volunteered words and number of users in each behavioral subgroup of DUALIST subjects.

Figure 2(c) shows learning curves for these three groups. We can see that the DV++ and DV+ groups ultimately train better classifiers than the DV- group, and DV++ also dominates both the active and passive baselines from Figure 2(a). The DV++ group is particularly effective on the Movie Reviews corpus. This suggests that a user's choice to volunteer more labeled features — by occasionally side-stepping the queries posed by the active learner and directly injecting their domain knowledge — is a good predictor of classifier accuracy on this task.

To tease apart the relative impact of other behaviors, we conducted an ordinary least-squares regression to predict classifier accuracy at the end of a trial. We included the number of user events for each action as independent variables, plus two controls: the subject's document error rate in [0,1] with respect to the gold standard, and class entropy in $[0, \log C]$ of all labeled words (where C is the number of classes). The entropy variable is meant to capture how "balanced" a user's word-labeling activity was for actions ② and ③, with the intuition that a skewed set of words could confuse the learner, by biasing it away from categories with fewer labeled words.

Table 2 summarizes these results. Surprisingly, query-labeling actions (① and ②) have a relatively small impact on accuracy. The number of volunteered words and entropy among word labels appear to be the only two factors that are somewhat significant: the former is strongest in the Movie Reviews corpus, the latter in Science[4]. Interestingly, there is a strong positive correlation between these two factors in the Movie Reviews corpus (Spearman's $\rho = 0.51$, $p = 0.02$) but not in Science ($\rho = 0.03$). When we consider change in word label entropy over time, the Science DA++ group is balanced early on and becomes steadily more so on average , whereas DA+ goes for several minutes before catching up (and briefly overtaking) . This may account for DA+'s early dip in accuracy in Figure 2(c). For Movie Reviews, DA++ is more balanced than DA+ throughout the trial. DA++ labeled many words that were also class-balanced, which may explain why it is the best consistently-performing group. As is common in behavior modeling with small samples, the data are noisy and the regressions in Table 2 only explain 33%–46% of the variance in accuracy.

Action	Movie Reviews β	Movie Reviews SE		Science β	Science SE	
(intercept)	0.505	0.038	***	0.473	0.147	**
① label query docs	0.001	0.001		0.005	0.005	
② label query words	-0.001	0.001		0.000	0.001	
③ volunteer words	0.002	0.001	*	0.000	0.002	
human error rate	-0.036	0.109		-0.328	0.230	
word label entropy	0.053	0.051		0.201	0.102	.
	$R^2 = 0.4608$ **			$R^2 = 0.3342$		

*** $p < 0.001$ ** $p < 0.01$ * $p < 0.05$. $p < 0.1$

Table 2: Linear regressions estimating the accuracy of a classifier as a function of annotator actions and behaviors.

5 Discussion

We were able to partially replicate the results from Settles (2011). That is, for two of the same data sets, some of the subjects using DUALIST significantly outperformed those using traditional document-only interfaces. However, our results show that the gains come not merely from the interface itself, but from which labeling actions the users chose to perform. As interactive learning systems continue to expand the palette of interactive options (e.g., labeling and/or volunteering features), understanding how these options impact learning becomes more important. In particular, training a good classifier in our experiments appears to be linked to (1) volunteering more labeled words, and (2) maintaining a class balance among them. Users who exhibited both of these behaviors — which are possibly artifacts of their good intuitions — performed the best.

We posit that there is a conceptual connection between these insights and *curriculum learning* (Bengio et al., 2009), the commonsense notion that learners perform better if they begin with clear and unambiguous examples before graduating to more complex training data. A recent study found that some humans use a curriculum strategy when teaching a 1D classification task to a robot (Khan et al., 2012). About half of those subjects alternated between extreme positive and negative instances in a relatively class-balanced way. This behavior was explained by showing that it is optimal under an assumption that, in reality, the learning task has many input features for which only one is relevant to the task.

Text classification exhibits similar properties: there are many features (words), of which only a few are relevant. We argue that labeling features can be seen as a kind of training by curriculum. By volunteering labeled words in a class-balanced way (especially early on), a user provides clear, unambiguous training signals that effectively perform feature selection while biasing the classifier toward the user's hypothesis. Future research on mixed-initiative user interfaces might try to detect and encourage these kinds of annotator behaviors, and potentially improve interactive machine learning outcomes.

[4]Science has four labels and a larger entropy range, which might explain the importance of the entropy factor here. Also, labels are more related to natural clusterings in this corpus (Nigam et al., 2000), so class-balanced priors might be key for DUALIST's semi-supervised EM procedure to work well.

Acknowledgments

This work was funded in part by DARPA, the National Science Foundation (under grants IIS-0953219 and IIS-0968487), and Google.

References

J. Attenberg, P. Melville, and F. Provost. 2010. A unified approach to active dual supervision for labeling features and examples. In *Proceedings of the European Conference on Machine Learning and Principles and Practice of Knowledge Discovery in Databases (ECML PKDD)*, pages 40–55. Springer.

Y. Bengio, J. Louradour, R. Collobert, and J. Weston. 2009. Curriculum learning. In *Proceedings of the International Conference on Machine Learning (ICML)*, pages 119–126. Omnipress.

W.S. Cleveland, E. Grosse, and W.M. Shyu. 1992. Local regression models. In J.M. Chambers and T.J. Hastie, editors, *Statistical Models in S*. Wadsworth & Brooks/Cole.

G. Druck, G. Mann, and A. McCallum. 2008. Learning from labeled features using generalized expectation criteria. In *Proceedings of the ACM SIGIR Conference on Research and Development in Information Retrieval*, pages 595–602. ACM Press.

G. Druck, B. Settles, and A. McCallum. 2009. Active learning by labeling features. In *Proceedings of the Conference on Empirical Methods in Natural Language Processing (EMNLP)*, pages 81–90. ACL Press.

F. Khan, X. Zhu, and B. Mutlu. 2012. How do humans teach: On curriculum learning and teaching dimension. In *Advances in Neural Information Processing Systems (NIPS)*, volume 24, pages 1449–1457. Morgan Kaufmann.

P. Melville, W. Gryc, and R.D. Lawrence. 2009. Sentiment analysis of blogs by combining lexical knowledge with text classification. In *Proceedings of the International Conference on Knowledge Discovery and Data Mining (KDD)*, pages 1275–1284. ACM Press.

K. Nigam, A.K. Mccallum, S. Thrun, and T. Mitchell. 2000. Text classification from labeled and unlabeled documents using em. *Machine Learning*, 39:103–134.

B. Settles. 2011. Closing the loop: Fast, interactive semi-supervised annotation with queries on features and instances. In *Proceedings of the Conference on Empirical Methods in Natural Language Processing (EMNLP)*, pages 1467–1478. ACL Press.

Better Evaluation for Grammatical Error Correction

Daniel Dahlmeier[1] and **Hwee Tou Ng**[1,2]
[1]NUS Graduate School for Integrative Sciences and Engineering
[2]Department of Computer Science, National University of Singapore
`{danielhe,nght}@comp.nus.edu.sg`

Abstract

We present a novel method for evaluating grammatical error correction. The core of our method, which we call *MaxMatch* (M^2), is an algorithm for efficiently computing the sequence of phrase-level edits between a source sentence and a system hypothesis that achieves the highest overlap with the gold-standard annotation. This optimal edit sequence is subsequently scored using F_1 measure. We test our M^2 scorer on the Helping Our Own (HOO) shared task data and show that our method results in more accurate evaluation for grammatical error correction.

1 Introduction

Progress in natural language processing (NLP) research is driven and measured by automatic evaluation methods. Automatic evaluation allows fast and inexpensive feedback during development, and objective and reproducible evaluation during testing time. Grammatical error correction is an important NLP task with useful applications for second language learning. Evaluation for error correction is typically done by computing F_1 measure between a set of proposed system edits and a set of human-annotated gold-standard edits (Leacock et al., 2010).

Unfortunately, evaluation is complicated by the fact that the set of edit operations for a given system hypothesis is ambiguous. This is due to two reasons. First, the set of edits that transforms one string into another is not necessarily unique, even at the token level. Second, edits can consist of longer phrases which introduce additional ambiguity. To see how this can affect evaluation, consider the following source sentence and system hypothesis from the recent Helping Our Own (HOO) shared task (Dale and Kilgarriff, 2011) on grammatical error correction:

Source :	Our baseline system feeds word into PB-SMT pipeline.
Hypot. :	Our baseline system feeds **a** word into PB-SMT pipeline.

The HOO evaluation script extracts the system edit ($\epsilon \rightarrow$ a), i.e., inserting the article *a*. Unfortunately, the gold-standard annotation instead contains the edits (word $\rightarrow$ {a word, words}). Although the extracted system edit results in the *same* corrected sentence as the first gold-standard edit option, the system hypothesis was considered to be invalid.

In this work, we propose a method, called *MaxMatch* (M^2), to overcome this problem. The key idea is that if there are multiple possible ways to arrive at the same correction, the system should be evaluated according to the set of edits that matches the gold-standard as often as possible. To this end, we propose an algorithm for efficiently computing the set of phrase-level edits with the maximum overlap with the gold standard. The edits are subsequently scored using F_1 measure. We test our method in the context of the HOO shared task and show that our method results in a more accurate evaluation for error correction.

The remainder of this paper is organized as follows: Section 2 describes the proposed method; Section 3 presents experimental results; Section 4 discusses some details of grammar correction evaluation; and Section 5 concludes the paper.

2 Method

We begin by establishing some notation. We consider a set of *source sentences* $S = \{\mathbf{s}_1, \ldots, \mathbf{s}_n\}$ together with a set of *hypotheses* $H = \{\mathbf{h}_1, \ldots, \mathbf{h}_n\}$ generated by an error correction system. Let $G = \{\mathbf{g}_1, \ldots, \mathbf{g}_n\}$ be the set of gold standard annotations for the same sentences. Each annotation $\mathbf{g}_i = \{g_i^1, \ldots, g_i^r\}$ is a set of *edits*. An edit is a triple (a, b, C), consisting of:

- start and end (token-) offsets a and b with respect to a source sentence,
- a correction C. For gold-standard edits, C is a set containing one or more possible corrections. For system edits, C is a single correction.

Evaluation of the system output involves the following two steps:

1. Extracting a set of *system edits* $\mathbf{e}_i$ for each source-hypothesis pair $(\mathbf{s}_i, \mathbf{h}_i)$.
2. Evaluating the system edits for the complete test set with respect to the gold standard G.

The remainder of this section describes a method for solving these two steps. We start by describing how to construct an *edit lattice* from a source-hypothesis pair. Then, we show that finding the optimal sequence of edits is equivalent to solving a shortest path search through the lattice. Finally, we describe how to evaluate the edits using F_1 measure.

2.1 Edit lattice

We start from the well-established Levenshtein distance (Levenshtein, 1966), which is defined as the minimum number of insertions, deletions, and substitutions needed to transform one string into another. The Levenshtein distance between a source sentence $\mathbf{s}_i = s_i^1, \ldots, s_i^k$ and a hypothesis $\mathbf{h}_i = h_i^1, \ldots, h_i^l$ can be efficiently computed using a two dimensional matrix that is filled using a classic dynamic programming algorithm. We assume that both $\mathbf{s}_i$ and $\mathbf{h}_i$ have been tokenized. The matrix for the example from Section 1 is shown in Figure 1. By performing a simple breadth-first search, similar to the Viterbi algorithm, we can extract the lattice of all shortest paths that lead from the top-left corner to the bottom-right corner of the Levenshtein matrix. Each vertex in the lattice corresponds to a cell

		Our	baseline	system	feeds	a	word	into	PB-SMT	pipeline	.
	(0)	1	2	3	4	5	6	7	8	9	10
Our	1	(0)	1	2	3	4	5	6	7	8	9
baseline	2	1	(0)	1	2	3	4	5	6	7	8
system	3	2	1	(0)	1	2	3	4	5	6	7
feeds	4	3	2	1	(0)	(1)	2	3	4	5	6
word	5	4	3	2	1	1	(1)	2	3	4	5
into	6	5	4	3	2	2	2	(1)	2	3	4
PB-SMT	7	6	5	4	3	3	3	2	(1)	2	3
pipeline	8	7	6	5	4	4	4	3	2	(1)	2
.	9	8	7	6	5	5	5	4	3	2	(1)

Figure 1: The Levenshtein matrix and the shortest path for a source sentence "Our baseline system feeds word into PB-SMT pipeline ." and a hypothesis "Our baseline system feeds a word into PB-SMT pipeline ."

in the Levenshtein matrix, and each edge in the lattice corresponds to an atomic edit operation: inserting a token, deleting a token, substituting a token, or leaving a token unchanged. Each path through the lattice corresponds to a shortest sequence of edits that transform $\mathbf{s}_i$ into $\mathbf{h}_i$. We assign a unit cost to each edge in the lattice.

We have seen that annotators can use longer phrases and that phrases can include unchanged words from the context, e.g., the gold edit from the example in Section 1 is $(4, 5, \text{word}, \{\text{a word}, \text{words}\})$. However, it seems unrealistic to allow an arbitrary number of unchanged words in an edit. In particular, we want to avoid very large edits that cover complete sentences. Therefore, we limit the number of unchanged words by a parameter u. To allow for phrase-level edits, we add transitive edges to the lattice as long as the number of unchanged words in the newly added edit is not greater than u and the edit changes at least one word. Let $e_1 = (a_1, b_1, C_1)$ and $e_2 = (a_2, b_2, C_2)$ be two edits corresponding to adjacent edges in the lattice, with the first end offset b_1 being equal to the second start offset a_2. We can combine them into a new edit $e_3 = (a_1, b_2, C_1 + C_2)$, where $C_1 + C_2$ is the concatenation of strings C_1 and C_2. The cost of a transitive edge is the sum of the costs of its parts. The lattice extracted from the example sentence is shown in Figure 2.

2.2 Finding maximally matching edit sequence

Our goal is to find the sequence of edits $\mathbf{e}_i$ with the maximum overlap with the gold standard. Let $L = (V, E)$ be the edit lattice graph from the last section. We change the cost of each edge whose cor-

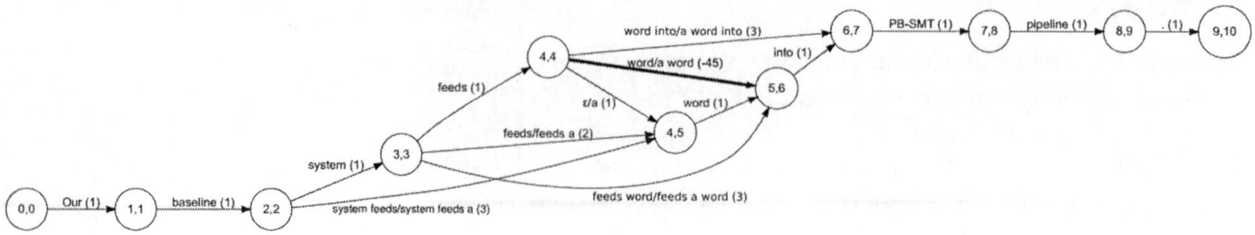

Figure 2: The edit lattice for "Our baseline system feeds ($\epsilon \rightarrow$ a) word into PB-SMT pipeline ." Edge costs are shown in parentheses. The edge from (4,4) to (5,6) matches the gold annotation and carries a negative cost.

responding edit has a match in the gold standard to $-(u+1) \times |E|$. An edit e *matches* a gold edit g iff they have the same offsets and e's correction is included in g:

$$match(e, g) \Leftrightarrow e.a = g.a \wedge e.b = g.b \wedge e.C \in g.C \quad (1)$$

Then, we perform a single-source shortest path search with negative edge weights from the start to the end vertex[1]. This can be done efficiently, for example with the Bellman-Ford algorithm (Cormen et al., 2001). As the lattice is acyclic, the algorithm is guaranteed to terminate and return a shortest path.

Theorem 1. *The set of edits corresponding to the shortest path has the maximum overlap with the gold standard annotation.*

Proof. Let $\mathbf{e} = e^1, \ldots, e^k$ be the edit sequence corresponding to the shortest path and let p be the number of matched edits. Assume that there exists another edit sequence $\mathbf{e}'$ with higher total edge weights but $p' > p$ matching edits. Then we have

$$\begin{aligned} p(-(u+1)|E|) + q &\leq p'(-(u+1)|E|) + q' \quad (2) \\ \Leftrightarrow (q - q') &\leq (p' - p)(-(u+1)|E|), \end{aligned}$$

where q and q' denote the combined cost of all non-matching edits in the two paths, respectively. Because $p' - p \geq 1$, the right hand side is at most $-(u+1)|E|$. Because q and q' are positive and bounded by $(u+1)|E|$, the left hand side cannot be smaller than or equal to $-(u+1)|E|$. This is a contradiction. Therefore there cannot exist such an edit sequence $\mathbf{e}'$, and $\mathbf{e}$ is the sequence with the maximum overlap with the gold-standard annotation. □

[1]To break ties between non-matching edges, we add a small cost $\zeta \ll 1$ to all non-matching edges, thus favoring paths that use fewer edges, everything else being equal.

2.3 Evaluating edits

What is left to do is to evaluate the set of edits with respect to the gold standard. This is done by computing precision, recall, and F_1 measure (van Rijsbergen, 1979) between the set of system edits $\{\mathbf{e}_1, \ldots, \mathbf{e}_n\}$ and the set of gold edits $\{\mathbf{g}_1, \ldots, \mathbf{g}_n\}$ for all sentences

$$P = \frac{\sum_{i=1}^{n} |\mathbf{e}_i \cap \mathbf{g}_i|}{\sum_{i=1}^{n} |\mathbf{e}_i|} \quad (3)$$

$$R = \frac{\sum_{i=1}^{n} |\mathbf{e}_i \cap \mathbf{g}_i|}{\sum_{i=1}^{n} |\mathbf{g}_i|} \quad (4)$$

$$F_1 = 2 \times \frac{P \times R}{P + R}, \quad (5)$$

where we define the intersection between $\mathbf{e}_i$ and $\mathbf{g}_i$ as

$$\mathbf{e}_i \cap \mathbf{g}_i = \{e \in \mathbf{e}_i \mid \exists\, g \in \mathbf{g}_i (match(e, g))\}. \quad (6)$$

3 Experiments and Results

We experimentally test our M^2 method in the context of the HOO shared task. The HOO test data[2] consists of text fragments from NLP papers together with manually-created gold-standard corrections (see (Dale and Kilgarriff, 2011) for details). We test our method by re-scoring the best runs of the participating teams[3] in the HOO shared task with our M^2 scorer and comparing the scores with the official HOO scorer, which simply uses GNU `wdiff`[4] to extract system edits. We obtain each system's output and segment it at the sentence level according to the gold standard sentence segmentation. The

[2]Available at http://groups.google.com/group/hoo-nlp/ after registration.

[3]Except one team that did not submit any plain text output.

[4]http://www.gnu.org/s/wdiff/

M^2 scorer	... should basic translational unit be (word → a word) ...
HOO scorer	... should basic translational unit be *(ϵ → a) word ...
M^2 scorer	... development set similar (with → to) (ϵ → the) test set ...
HOO scorer	... development set similar *(with → to the) test set ...
M^2 scorer	(ϵ → The) *(Xinhua portion of → xinhua portion of) the English Gigaword3 ...
HOO scorer	*(Xinhua → The xinhua) portion of the English Gigaword3 ...

Table 2: Examples of different edits extracted by the M^2 scorer and the official HOO scorer. Edits that do not match the gold-standard annotation are marked with an asterisk (*).

Team	HOO scorer			M^2 scorer		
	P	R	F_1	P	R	F_1
JU (0)	10.39	3.78	5.54	12.30	4.45	6.53
LI (8)	20.86	3.22	5.57	21.12	3.22	5.58
NU (0)	29.10	7.38	11.77	31.09	7.85	12.54
UI (1)	50.72	13.34	21.12	54.61	14.57	23.00
UT (1)	5.01	4.07	4.49	5.72	4.45	5.01

Table 1: Results for participants in the HOO shared task. The run of the system is shown in parentheses.

source sentences, system hypotheses, and corrections are tokenized using the Penn Treebank standard (Marcus et al., 1993). The character edit offsets are automatically converted to token offsets. We set the parameter u to 2, allowing up to two unchanged words per edit. The results are shown in Table 1. Note that the M^2 scorer and the HOO scorer adhere to the same score definition and only differ in the way the system edits are computed. We can see that the M^2 scorer results in higher scores than the official scorer for all systems, showing that the official scorer missed some valid edits. For example, the M^2 scorer finds 155 valid edits for the UI system compared to 141 found by the official scorer, and 83 valid edits for the NU system, compared to 78 by the official scorer. We manually inspect the output of the scorers and find that the M^2 scorer indeed extracts the correct edits matching the gold standard where possible. Examples are shown in Table 2.

4 Discussion

The evaluation framework proposed in this work differs slightly from the one in the HOO shared task.

Sentence-by-sentence. We compute the edits between source-hypothesis sentence pairs, while the HOO scorer computes edits at the document level. As the HOO data comes in a sentence-segmented format, both approaches are equivalent, while sentence-by-sentence is easier to work with.

Token-level offsets. In our work, the start and end of an edit are given as *token offsets*, while the HOO data uses character offsets. Character offsets make the evaluation procedure very brittle as a small change, e.g., an additional whitespace character, will affect all subsequent edits. Character offsets also introduce ambiguities in the annotation, e.g., whether a comma is part of the preceding token.

Alternative scoring. The HOO shared task defines three different scores: *detection*, *recognition*, and *correction*. Effectively, all three scores are F_1 measures and only differ in the conditions on when an edit is counted as valid. Additionally, each score is reported under a "with bonus" alternative, where a system receives rewards for missed optional edits. The F_1 measure defined in Section 2.3 is equivalent to *correction without bonus*. Our method can be used to compute detection and recognition scores and scores with bonus as well.

5 Conclusion

We have presented a novel method, called MaxMatch (M^2), for evaluating grammatical error correction. Our method computes the sequence of phrase-level edits that achieves the highest overlap with the gold-standard annotation. Experiments on the HOO data show that our method overcomes deficiencies in the current evaluation method. The M^2 scorer is available for download at http://nlp.comp.nus.edu.sg/software/.

Acknowledgments

We thank Chang Liu for comments on an earlier draft. This research is supported by the Singapore National Research Foundation under its International Research Centre @ Singapore Funding Initiative and administered by the IDM Programme Office.

References

T. Cormen, C.E. Leiserson, R.L. Rivest, and C. Stein. 2001. *Introduction to Algorithms*. MIT Press, Cambridge, MA.

R. Dale and A. Kilgarriff. 2011. Helping Our Own: The HOO 2011 pilot shared task. In *Proceedings of the 2011 European Workshop on Natural Language Generation*.

C. Leacock, M. Chodorow, M. Gamon, and J. Tetreault, 2010. *Automated Grammatical Error Detection for Language Learners*, chapter 5. Morgan and Claypool Publishers.

V. Levenshtein. 1966. Binary codes capable of correcting deletions, insertions, and reversals. *Soviet Physics Doklady*, 10(8):707–710.

M.P. Marcus, M.A. Marcinkiewicz, and B. Santorini. 1993. Building a large annotated corpus of English: The Penn Treebank. *Computational Linguistics*, 19.

C. J. van Rijsbergen. 1979. *Information Retrieval*. Butterworth, 2nd edition.

Are You Sure? Confidence in Prediction of Dependency Tree Edges

Avihai Mejer
Department of Electrical Engineering
Technion-Israel Institute of Technology
Haifa 32000, Israel
amejer@tx.technion.ac.il

Koby Crammer
Department of Electrical Engineering
Technion-Israel Institute of Technology
Haifa 32000, Israel
koby@ee.technion.ac.il

Abstract

We describe and evaluate several methods for estimating the confidence in the per-edge correctness of a predicted dependency parse. We show empirically that the confidence is associated with the probability that an edge is selected correctly and that it can be used to detect incorrect edges very efficiently. We evaluate our methods on parsing text in 14 languages.

1 Introduction

Dependency parsers construct directed edges between words of a given sentence to their arguments according to syntactic or semantic rules. We use MSTParser of McDonald et al. (2005) and focus on non-projective dependency parse *trees* with non-typed (unlabeled) edges. MSTParser produces a parse tree for a sentence by constructing a full, directed and weighted graph over the words of the sentence, and then outputting the maximal spanning tree (MST) of the graph. A linear model is employed for computing the weights of the edges using features depending on the two words the edge connects. Example features are the distance between the two words, words identity and words part-of-speech. MSTParser is training a model using online learning and specifically the MIRA algorithm (Crammer et al., 2006). The output of MSTParser is the highest scoring parse tree, it is not accompanied by any additional information about its quality.

In this work we evaluate few methods for estimating the confidence in the correctness of the prediction of a parser. This information can be used in several ways. For example, when using parse trees as input to another system such as machine translation, the confidence information can be used to correct inputs with low confidence. Another example is to guide manual validation to outputs which are more likely to be erroneous, saving human labor. We adapt methods proposed by Mejer and Crammer (2010) in order to produce per-edge confidence estimations in the prediction. Specifically, one approach is based on sampling, and another on a generalization of the concept of margin. Additionally, we propose a new method based on combining both approaches, and show that is outperforms both.

2 Confidence Estimation In Prediction

MSTParser produces the highest scoring parse trees using the trained linear model with no additional information about the confidence in the predicted tree. In this work we compute per-edge confidence scores, that is, a numeric confidence value, for all edges predicted by the parser. Larger score values indicate higher confidence. We use three confidence estimation methods that were proposed for sequence labeling (Mejer and Crammer, 2010), adapted here for dependency parsing. A fourth method, described in Sec. 3, is a combination of the two best performing methods.

The first method, named **Delta**, is a margin-based method. For computing the confidence of each edge the method generates an additional parse-tree, which is the best parse tree that is forced not to contain the specific edge in question. The confidence score of the edge is defined as the difference in the scores between the two parse trees. The score of a tree is the sum of scores of the edges it contains. These confidence scores are always positive, yet *not* limited to [0, 1]. Delta method does not require parameter tuning.

The second method, named **Weighted K-Best (WKB)**, is a deterministic method building on properties of the inference algorithm. Specifically, we use k-best Maximum Spanning Tree algorithm (Hall, 2007) to produce the K parse trees with the highest score. This collection of K-trees is used to compute the confidence in a predicted edge. The confidence score is defined to be the weighted-fraction of parse trees that contain the edge. The contribution of different trees to compute this fraction is proportional to their absolute score, where the tree with the highest score has the largest contribution. Only trees with positive scores are included. The computed score is in the range [0, 1]. The value of K was tuned using a development set (optimizing the average-precision score of detecting incorrect edges, see below) and for most datasets K was set to a value between $10 - 20$.

The third method, **K Draws by Fixed Standard Deviation (KD-Fix)** is a probabilistic method. Here we sample K weight vectors using a Gaussian distribution, for which the mean parameters are the learned model and isotropic covariance matrix with fixed variance s^2. The value s is tuned on a development set (optimizing the average-precision score of detecting incorrect edges). The confidence of each edge is the probability of this edge induced from the distribution over parameters. We approximate this quantity by sampling K parse trees, each obtained by finding the MST when scores are computed by one of K sampled models. Finally, the confidence score of each edge predicted by the model is defined to be the fraction of parse trees among the K trees that contain this edge. Formally, the confidence score is $\nu = j/K$ where j is the number of parse trees that contain this edge ($j \in \{0...K\}$) so the score is in the range [0, 1]. We set $K = 50$.

Finally, we describe below a fourth method, we call **KD-Fix+Delta**, which is a weighted-linear combination of KD-Fix and Delta.

3 Evaluation

We evaluated the algorithms using 13 languages used in CoNLL 2006 shared task[1], and the English Penn Treebank. The number of training sentences is between 1.5-72K, with an average of $20K$ sentences and 50K-1M words. The test sets contain ~ 400 sentences and $\sim 6K$ words for all datasets, except English with $2.3K$ sentences and $55K$ words. Parameter tuning was performed on development sets with 200 sentences per dataset. We trained a model per dataset and used it to parse the test set. Predicted edge accuracy of the parser ranges from 77% on Turkish to 93% on Japanese, with an average of 85%. We then assigned each predicted edge a confidence score using the various confidence estimation methods.

Absolute Confidence: We first evaluate the accuracy of the actual confidence values assigned by all methods. Similar to (Mejer and Crammer, 2010) we grouped edges according to the value of their confidence. We used 20 bins dividing the confidence range into intervals of size 0.05. Bin indexed j contains edges with confidence value in the range $\left[\frac{j-1}{20}, \frac{j}{20}\right]$, $j = 1..20$. Let b_j be the center value of bin j and let c_j be the fraction of edges predicted correctly from the edges assigned to bin j. For a good confidence estimator we expect $b_j \approx c_j$.

Results for 4 datasets are presented in Fig. 1. Plots show the measured fraction of correctly predicted edges c_j vs. the value of the center of bin b_j. Best performance is obtained when a line corresponding to a method is close to the line $y = x$. Results are shown for KD-Fix and WKB; Delta is omitted as it produces confidence scores out of [0, 1]. In two of the shown plots (Chinese and Swedish) KD-Fix (circles) follows closely the expected accuracy line. In another plot (Danish) KD-Fix is too pessimistic with line above $y = x$ and in yet another case (Turkish) it is too optimistic. The distribution of this qualitative behavior among the 14 datasets is: too optimistic in 2 datasets, too pessimistic in 7 and close to the line $y = x$ in 5 datasets. The confidence scores produced by the WKB are in general worse than KD-Fix, too optimistic in some confidence range

[1] Arabic, Bulgarian, Chinese, Czech, Danish, Dutch, German, Japanese, Portuguese, Slovene, Spanish, Swedish and Turkish . See `http://nextens.uvt.nl/~conll/`

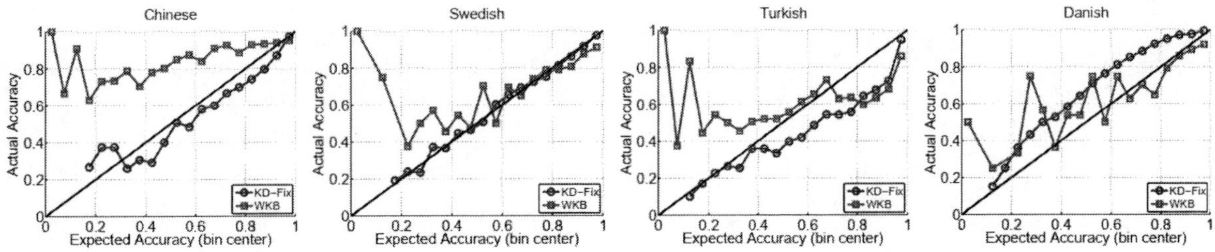

Figure 1: Evaluation of KD-Fix and WKB by comparing predicted accuracy vs. actual accuracy in each bin on 4 datasets. Best performance is obtained for curves close to the line *y=x* (black line). Delta method is omitted as its output is not in the range [0, 1].

	KD Fix	WKB	Delta	KD-Fix +Delta	Random
Avg-Prec	**0.535**	0.304	0.518	**0.547**	0.147
Prec @10%	**0.729**	0.470	0.644	**0.724**	0.145
Prec @90%	0.270	0.157	**0.351**	**0.348**	0.147
RMSE	**0.084**	0.117	-	-	0.458

Table 1: Row 1: Average precision in ranking all edges according confidence values. Rows 2-3: Precision in detection of incorrect edges when detected 10% and 90% of all the incorrect edges. Row 4: Root mean square error. All results are averaged over all datasets.

and too pessimistic in another range. We computed the root mean square-error (RMSE) in predicting the bin center value given by $\sqrt{(\sum_j n_j(b_j-c_j)^2)/(\sum_j n_j)}$, where n_j is the number of edges in the jth bin. The results, summarized in the $4th$ row of Table 1, support the observation that KD-Fix performs better than WKB, with smaller RMSE.

Incorrect Edges Detection: The goal of this task is to efficiently detect incorrect predicted-edges. We ranked all predicted edges of the test-set (per dataset) according to their confidence score, ordering from low to high. Ideally, erroneous edges by the parser are ranked at the top. A summary of the average precision, computed at all ranks of erroneous edges, (averaged over all datasets, due to lack of space), for all confidence estimation methods is summarized in the first row of Table 1. The average precision achieved by random ordering is about equal to the error rate for each dataset. The Delta method improves significantly over both the random ordering and WKB. KD-Fix achieves the best performance in 12 of 14 datasets and the best average-performance. These results are consistent with the results obtained for sequence labeling by Mejer and Crammer (2010).

Average precision summarizes the detection of all incorrect edges into a single number. More refined analysis is encapsulated in Precision-Recall (PR) plots, showing the precision as more incorrect edges are detected. PR plots for three datasets are shown in Fig. 2. From these plots (applied also to other datasets, omitted due to lack of space) we observe that in most cases KD-Fix performs significantly better than Delta in the early detection stage (first 10-20% of the incorrect edges), while Delta performs better in late detection stages (last 10-20% of the incorrect edges). The second and third rows of Table 1 summarize the precision after detecting only 10% incorrect edges and after detecting 90% of the incorrect edges, averaged over all datasets. For example, in Czech and Portuguese plots of Fig. 2, we observe an advantage of KD-Fix for low recall and an advantage of Delta in high recall. Yet for Arabic, for example, KD-Fix outperforms Delta along the entire range of recall values.

KD-Fix assigns at most K distinct confidence values to each edge - the number of models that agreed on that particular edge. Thus, when edges are ranked according to the confidence, all edges that are assigned the same value are ordered randomly. Furthermore, large fraction of the edges, $\sim 70-80\%$, are assigned one of the top-three scores (i.e. *K-2*, *K-1*, *K*). As a results, the precision performance of KD-Fix drops sharply for recall values of 80% and above. On the other hand, we hypothesize that the lower precision of Delta at low recall values (diamond in Fig. 2) is because by definition Delta takes into account only two parses, ignoring additional possible parses with score close to the highest score. This makes Delta method more sensitive to small differences in score values compared to KD-Fix.

Based on this observation, we propose combining both KD-Fix and Delta. Our new method sets the confidence score of an edge to be a weighted mean of the score values of KD-Fix and Delta, with weights *a* and *1-a*, respectively. We use a value

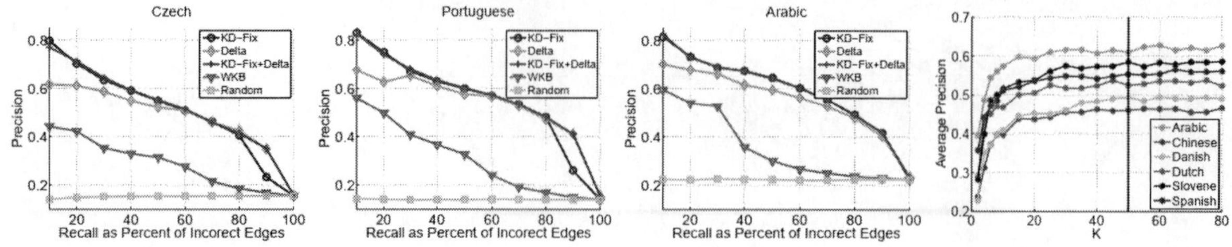

Figure 2: (Best shown in color.) Three left plots: Precision in detection of incorrect edges as recall increases. Right plot: Effect of K value on KD-Fix method performance (for six languages, the remaining languages follow similar trend, omitted for clarity).

$a \approx 1$, so if the confidence value of two edges according to KD-Fix is different, the contribution of the score from Delta is negligible, and the final score is very close as score of only KD-Fix. On the other hand, if the score of KD-Fix is the same, as happens for many edges at high recall values, then Delta breaks arbitrary ties. In other words, the new method first ranks edges according to the confidence score of KD-Fix, then among edges with equal KD-Fix confidence score a secondary order is employed using Delta. Not surpassingly, we name this method **KD-Fix+Delta**. This new method enjoys the benefits of the two methods. From the first row of Table 1 we see that it achieves the highest average-precision averaged over the 14 datasets. It improves average-precision over KD-Fix in 12 of 14 datasets and over Delta in all 14 datasets. From the second and third row of the table, we see that it has Precision very close to KD-Fix for recall of 10% (0.729 vs. 0.724), and very close to Delta for recall of 90% (0.351 vs. 0.348). Moving to Fig. 2, we observe that the curve associated with the new method (red ticks) is in general as high as the curves associated with KD-Fix for low values of recall, and as high as the curves associated with Delta for large values of recall.

To illustrate the effectiveness of the incorrect edges detection process, Table 2 presents the number of incorrect edges detected vs. number of edges inspected for the English dataset. The test set for this task includes $55K$ words and the parser made mistake on $6,209$ edges, that is, accuracy of 88.8%. We see that using the ranking induced by KD-Fix+Delta method, inspection of 550, 2750 and 5500 edges $(1, 5, 10\%$ of all edges), allows detection of $6.6 - 46\%$ of all incorrect edges, over 4.5 times more effective than random validation.

Edges inspected (% of total edges)	Incorrect edges detected (% of incorrect edges)
550 (1%)	412 (6.6%)
2,750 (5%)	1,675 (27%)
5,500 (10%)	2,897 (46%)

Table 2: Number of incorrect edges detected, and the corresponding percentage of *all mistakes*, after inspecting $1 - 10\%$ of all edges, using ranking induced by KD-Fix+Delta method.

Effect of K value on KD-Fix method performance The right plot of Fig. 2 shows the average-precision of detecting incorrect edges on the test set using the KD-Fix method for K values ranging between 2 and 80. We see that even with $K = 2$, only two samples per sentence, the average precision results are much better than random ranking in all tasks. As K is increased the results improve until reaching maximal results at $K \approx 30$. Theoretical calculations, using concentration inequalities, show that accurate estimates based on the sampling procedure requires $K \approx 10^2 - 10^3$. Yet, we see that for practical uses, smaller K values by $1 - 2$ order of magnitude is suffice.

References

[Crammer et al.2006] K. Crammer, O. Dekel, J. Keshet, S. Shalev-Shwartz, and Y. Singer. 2006. Online passive-aggressive algorithms. *JMLR*, 7:551–585.

[Hall2007] Keith Hall. 2007. k-best spanning tree parsing. In *In Proceedings of the 45th Annual Meeting of the Association for Computational Linguistics*.

[McDonald et al.2005] R. McDonald, F. Pereira, K. Ribarov, and J. Hajic. 2005. Non-projective dependency parsing using spanning tree algorithms. In *HLT/EMNLP*.

[Mejer and Crammer2010] A. Mejer and K. Crammer. 2010. Confidence in structured-prediction using confidence-weighted models. In *EMNLP*.

Concavity and Initialization for Unsupervised Dependency Parsing

Kevin Gimpel and **Noah A. Smith**
Language Technologies Institute
Carnegie Mellon University
Pittsburgh, PA 15213, USA
{kgimpel,nasmith}@cs.cmu.edu

Abstract

We investigate models for unsupervised learning with concave log-likelihood functions. We begin with the most well-known example, IBM Model 1 for word alignment (Brown et al., 1993) and analyze its properties, discussing why other models for unsupervised learning are so seldom concave. We then present concave models for dependency grammar induction and validate them experimentally. We find our concave models to be effective initializers for the dependency model of Klein and Manning (2004) and show that we can encode linguistic knowledge in them for improved performance.

1 Introduction

In NLP, unsupervised learning typically implies optimization of a "bumpy" objective function riddled with local maxima. However, one exception is IBM Model 1 (Brown et al., 1993) for word alignment, which is the only model commonly used for unsupervised learning in NLP that has a concave log-likelihood function.[1] For other models, such as those used in unsupervised part-of-speech tagging and grammar induction, and indeed for more sophisticated word alignment models, the log-likelihood function maximized by EM is non-concave. As a result, researchers are obligated to consider initialization in addition to model design (Klein and Manning, 2004; Goldberg et al., 2008).

For example, consider the dependency grammar induction results shown in Table 1 when training the widely used dependency model with valence (DMV; Klein and Manning, 2004). Using uniform distributions for initialization (UNIF) results in an accuracy of 17.6% on the test set, well below the baseline of attaching each word to its right neighbor (ATTACHRIGHT, 31.7%). Furthermore, when using a set of 50 random initializers (RAND), the standard deviation of the accuracy is an alarming 8.3%.

In light of this sensitivity to initialization, it is compelling to consider unsupervised models with concave log-likelihood functions, which may provide stable, data-supported initializers for more complex models. In this paper, we explore the issues involved with such an expedition and elucidate the limitations of such models for unsupervised NLP. We then present simple concave models for dependency grammar induction that are easy to implement and offer efficient optimization. We also show how linguistic knowledge can be encoded without sacrificing concavity. Using our models to initialize the DMV, we find that they lead to an improvement in average accuracy across 18 languages.

2 IBM Model 1 and Concavity

IBM Model 1 is a conditional model of a target-language sentence $\boldsymbol{e}$ of length m and an alignment $\boldsymbol{a}$ given a source-language sentence $\boldsymbol{f}$ of length l. The generation of m is assumed to occur with some (inconsequential) uniform probability ϵ. The alignment vector $\boldsymbol{a}$, a hidden variable, has an entry for each element of $\boldsymbol{e}$ that contains the index in $\boldsymbol{f}$ of the aligned word. These entries are used to define which translation parameters $t(e_j \mid f_{a_j})$ are active. Model 1 assumes that the probability of the ith ele-

[1] It is not *strictly* concave (Toutanova and Galley, 2011).

ment in $\boldsymbol{a}$, denoted $a(i \mid j, l, m)$, is simply a uniform distribution over all l source words plus the null word. These assumptions result in the following log-likelihood for a sentence pair $\langle \boldsymbol{f}, \boldsymbol{e} \rangle$ under Model 1 (marginalizing $\boldsymbol{a}$):

$$\log p(\boldsymbol{e} \mid \boldsymbol{f}) = \log \tfrac{\epsilon}{(l+1)^m} + \textstyle\sum_{j=1}^{m} \log \sum_{i=0}^{l} t(e_j \mid f_i) \quad (1)$$

The only parameters to be learned in the model are $\boldsymbol{t} = \{t(e \mid f)\}_{e,f}$. Since a parameter is concave in itself, the sum of concave functions is concave, and the log of a concave function is concave, Eq. 1 is concave in $\boldsymbol{t}$ (Brown et al., 1993).

IBM Model 2 involves a slight change to Model 1 in which the probability of a word link depends on the word positions. However, this change renders it no longer concave. Consider the log-likelihood function for Model 2:

$$\log \epsilon + \textstyle\sum_{j=1}^{m} \log \sum_{i=0}^{l} t(e_j \mid f_i) \cdot a(i \mid j, l, m) \quad (2)$$

Eq. 2 is not concave in the parameters $t(e_j \mid f_i)$ and $a(i \mid j, l, m)$ because a product is neither convex nor concave in its vector of operands. This can be shown by computing the Hessian matrix of $f(x, y) = xy$ and showing that it is indefinite.

In general, concavity is lost when the log-likelihood function contains a product of model parameters enclosed within a $\log \sum$. If the sum is not present, the log can be used to separate the product of parameters, making the function concave. It can also be shown that a "featurized" version (Berg-Kirkpatrick et al., 2010) of Model 1 is not concave. More generally, any non-concave function enclosed within $\log \sum$ will cause the log-likelihood function to be non-concave, though there are few other non-concave functions with a probabilistic semantics than those just discussed.

3 Concave, Unsupervised Models

Nearly every other model used for unsupervised learning in NLP has a non-concave log-likelihood function. We now proceed to describe the conditions necessary to develop concave models for two tasks.

3.1 Part-of-Speech Tagging

Consider a standard first-order hidden Markov model for POS tagging. Letting $\boldsymbol{y}$ denote the tag sequence for a sentence $\boldsymbol{e}$ with m tokens, the single-example log-likelihood is:

$$\log \textstyle\sum_{\boldsymbol{y}} p(\text{stop} \mid y_m) \prod_{j=1}^{m} p(y_j \mid y_{j-1}) \cdot p(e_j \mid y_j) \quad (3)$$

where y_0 is a designated "start" symbol. Unlike IBM Models 1 and 2, we cannot reverse the order of the summation and product here because the transition parameters $p(y_j \mid y_{j-1})$ cause each tag decision to affect its neighbors. Therefore, Eq. 3 is non-concave due to the presence of a product within a $\log \sum$.

However, if the tag transition probabilities $p(y_j \mid y_{j-1})$ are all constants and also do not depend on the previous tag y_{j-1}, then we can rewrite Eq. 3 as the following concave log-likelihood function (using $C(y)$ to denote a constant function of tag y, e.g., a fixed tag prior distribution):

$$\log C(\text{stop}) + \log \textstyle\prod_{j=1}^{m} \sum_{y_j} C(y_j) \cdot p(e_j \mid y_j)$$

Lacking any transition modeling power, this model appears weak for POS tagging. However, we note that we can add additional conditioning information to the $p(e_j \mid y_j)$ distributions and retain concavity, such as nearby words and tag dictionary information. We speculate that such a model might learn useful patterns about local contexts and provide an initializer for unsupervised part-of-speech tagging.

3.2 Dependency Grammar Induction

To develop dependency grammar induction models, we begin with a version of Model 1 in which a sentence $\boldsymbol{e}$ is generated from a copy of itself (denoted $\boldsymbol{e}'$): $\log p(\boldsymbol{e} \mid \boldsymbol{e}')$

$$= \log \tfrac{\epsilon}{(m+1)^m} + \textstyle\sum_{j=1}^{m} \log \sum_{i=0, i \neq j}^{m} c(e_j \mid e'_i) \quad (4)$$

If a word e_j is "aligned" to e'_0, e_j is a root. This is a simple child-generation model with no tree constraint. In order to preserve concavity, we are forbidden from conditioning on other parent-child assignments or including any sort of larger constraints.

However, we can condition the child distributions on additional information about $\boldsymbol{e}'$ since it is fully observed. This conditioning information may include the direction of the edge, its distance, and any properties about the words in the sentence. We found that conditioning on direction improved performance: we rewrite the c distributions as $c(e_j \mid e'_i, sign(j-i))$ and denote this model by CCV1.

We note that we can also include constraints in the sum over possible parents and still preserve concavity. Naseem et al. (2010) found that adding parent-child constraints to a grammar induction system can improve performance dramatically. We employ one simple rule: roots are likely to be verbs.[2] We modify CCV1 to restrict the summation over parents to exclude e'_0 if the child word is not a verb.[3] We only employ this restriction during EM learning for sentences containing at least one verb. For sentences without verbs, we allow all words to be the root. We denote this model by CCV2.

In related work, Brody (2010) also developed grammar induction models based on the IBM word alignment models. However, while our goal is to develop concave models, Brody employed Bayesian nonparametrics in his version of Model 1, which makes the model non-concave.

4 Experiments

We ran experiments to determine how well our concave grammar induction models CCV1 and CCV2 can perform on their own and when used as initializers for the DMV (Klein and Manning, 2004). The DMV is a generative model of POS tag sequences and projective dependency trees over them. It is the foundation of most state-of-the-art unsupervised grammar induction models (several of which are listed in Tab. 1). The model includes multinomial distributions for generating each POS tag given its parent and the direction of generation: where e_i is the parent POS tag and e_j the child tag, these distributions take the form $c(e_j \mid e_i, sign(j-i))$, analogous to the distributions used in our concave models. The DMV also has multinomial distributions for deciding whether to stop or continue generating children in each direction considering whether any children have already been generated in that direction.

The majority of researchers use the original initializer from Klein and Manning (2004), denoted here K&M. K&M is a deterministic harmonic initializer that sets parent child token affinities inversely proportional to their distances, then normalizes to obtain probability distributions. K&M is often described as corresponding to an initial E step for an unspecified model that favors short attachments.

		Train ≤ 10		Train ≤ 20	
		Test		Test	
Model	Init.	≤10	≤∞	≤10	≤∞
ATTRIGHT	N/A	38.4	31.7	38.4	31.7
CCV1	UNIF	31.4	25.6	31.0	23.7
CCV2	UNIF	43.1	28.6	43.9	27.1
DMV	UNIF	21.3	17.6	21.3	16.4
	RAND*	41.0	31.8	-	-
	K&M	44.1	32.9	51.9	37.8
	CCV1	45.3	30.9	53.9	36.7
	CCV2	54.3	43.0	**64.3**	**53.1**
Shared LN	K&M	61.3	41.4		
L-EVG	RAND†	**68.8**	-		
Feature DMV	K&M	63.0	-		
LexTSG-DMV	K&M	67.7	**55.7**		
Posterior Reg.	K&M	64.3	53.3		
Punc/UTags	K&M′			-	59.1‡

Table 1: English attachment accuracies on Section 23, for short sentences (≤10 words) and all (≤∞). We include selected results on this same test set: Shared LN = Cohen and Smith (2009), L-EVG = Headden III et al. (2009), Feature DMV = Berg-Kirkpatrick et al. (2010), LexTSG-DMV = Blunsom and Cohn (2010), Posterior Reg. = Gillenwater et al. (2010), Punc/UTags = Spitkovsky et al. (2011a). K&M′ is from Spitkovsky et al. (2011b). *Accuracies are averages over 50 random initializers; $\sigma = 10.9$ for test sentences ≤ 10 and 8.3 for all. †Used many random initializers with unsupervised run selection. ‡Used staged training with sentences ≤ 45 words.

Procedure We run EM for our concave models for 100 iterations. We evaluate the learned models directly as parsers on the test data and also use them to initialize the DMV. When using them directly as parsers, we use dynamic programming to ensure that a valid tree is recovered. When using the concave models as initializers for the DMV, we copy the c parameters over directly since they appear in both models. We do not have the stop/continue parameters in our concave models, so we simply initialize them uniformly for the DMV. We train each DMV for 200 iterations and use minimum Bayes risk decoding with the final model on the test data. We use several initializers for training the DMV, including the uniform initializer (UNIF), K&M, and our trained concave models CCV1 and CCV2.

[2] This is similar to the rule used by Mareček and Žabokrtský (2011) with empirical success.

[3] As verbs, we take all tags that map to V in the universal tag mappings from Petrov et al. (2012). Thus, to apply this constraint to a new language, one would have to produce a similar tag mapping or identify verb tags through manual inspection.

Init.	eu	bg	ca	zh	cs	da	nl	en	de	el	hu
UNIF	24/21	32/26	27/29	44/40	32/30	24/19	21/21	21/18	31/24	37/32	23/18
K&M	**32/26**	**48/40**	24/25	38/33	31/29	**34/23**	39/33	44/33	47/**37**	50/41	23/20
CCV1	22/21	34/27	**44/51**	**46/45**	33/31	19/14	24/24	45/31	46/31	**51/45**	32/28
CCV2	26/25	34/26	29/35	**46**/44	**50/40**	29/18	**50/43**	**54/43**	**49**/33	50/**45**	**60/46**
	it	ja	pt	sl	es	sv	tr	avg. accuracy		avg. log-likelihood	
UNIF	31/24	35/30	49/36	20/20	29/24	26/22	33/30	29.8 / 25.7		-15.05	
K&M	32/24	39/**31**	44/28	**33/27**	19/11	**46/33**	**39/36**	36.7 / 29.4		-14.84	
CCV1	34/25	42/27	**50/38**	30/25	41/33	45/**33**	37/29	37.5 / 30.9		-14.93	
CCV2	**55/48**	**49/31**	**50/38**	22/21	**57/50**	**46**/32	31/22	**43.7 / 35.5**		**-14.45**	

Table 2: Test set attachment accuracies for 18 languages; first number in each cell is accuracy for sentences ≤ 10 words and second is for all sentences. For training, sentences ≤ 10 words from each treebank were used. In order, languages are Basque, Bulgarian, Catalan, Chinese, Czech, Danish, Dutch, English, German, Greek, Hungarian, Italian, Japanese, Portuguese, Slovenian, Spanish, Swedish, and Turkish.

Data We use data prepared for the CoNLL 2006/07 shared tasks (Buchholz and Marsi, 2006; Nivre et al., 2007).[4] We follow standard practice in removing punctuation and using short sentences (≤ 10 or ≤ 20 words) for training. For all experiments, we train on separate data from that used for testing and use gold POS tags for both training and testing. We report accuracy on (i) test set sentences ≤ 10 words and (ii) all sentences from the test set.

Results Results for English are shown in Tab. 1. We train on §2–21 and test on §23 in the Penn Treebank. The constraint on sentence roots helps a great deal, as CCV2 by itself is competitive with the DMV when testing on short sentences. The true benefit of the concave models, however, appears when using them as initializers. The DMV initialized with CCV2 achieves a substantial improvement over all others. When training on sentences of length ≤ 20 words (bold), the performance even rivals that of several more sophisticated models shown in the table, despite only using the DMV with a different initializer.

Tab. 2 shows results for 18 languages. On average, CCV2 performs best and CCV1 does at least as well as K&M. This shows that a simple, concave model can be as effective as a state-of-the-art hand-designed initializer (K&M), and that concave models can encode linguistic knowledge to further improve performance.

[4]In some cases, we did not use official CoNLL test sets but instead took the training data and reserved the first 80% of the sentences for training, the next 10% for development, and the final 10% as our test set; dataset details are omitted for space but are the same as those given by Cohen (2011).

Average log-likelihoods (micro-averaged across sentences) achieved by EM training are shown in the final column of Tab. 2. CCV2 leads to substantially-higher likelihoods than the other initializers, suggesting that the verb-root constraint is helping EM to find better local optima.[5]

5 Discussion

Staged training has been shown to help unsupervised learning in the past, from early work in grammar induction (Lari and Young, 1990) and word alignment (Brown et al., 1993) to more recent work in dependency grammar induction (Spitkovsky et al., 2010). While we do not yet offer a generic procedure for extracting a concave approximation from any model for unsupervised learning, our results contribute evidence in favor of the general methodology of staged training in unsupervised learning, and provide a simple and powerful initialization method for dependency grammar induction.

Acknowledgments

We thank Shay Cohen, Dipanjan Das, Val Spitkovsky, and members of the ARK research group for helpful comments that improved this paper. This research was supported in part by the NSF through grant IIS-0915187, the U. S. Army Research Laboratory and the U. S. Army Research Office under contract/grant number W911NF-10-1-0533, and Sandia National Laboratories (fellowship to K. Gimpel).

[5]However, while CCV1 leads to a higher average accuracy than K&M, the latter reaches slightly higher likelihood, suggesting that the success of the concave initializers is only partially due to reaching high training likelihood.

References

T. Berg-Kirkpatrick, A. Bouchard-Côté, J. DeNero, and D. Klein. 2010. Painless unsupervised learning with features. In *Proc. of NAACL*.

P. Blunsom and T. Cohn. 2010. Unsupervised induction of tree substitution grammars for dependency parsing. In *Proc. of EMNLP*.

S. Brody. 2010. It depends on the translation: Unsupervised dependency parsing via word alignment. In *Proc. of EMNLP*.

P. F. Brown, S. A. Della Pietra, V. J. Della Pietra, and R. L. Mercer. 1993. The mathematics of statistical machine translation: Parameter estimation. *Computational Linguistics*, 19(2):263–311.

S. Buchholz and E. Marsi. 2006. CoNLL-X shared task on multilingual dependency parsing. In *Proc. of CoNLL*.

S. Cohen and N. A. Smith. 2009. Shared logistic normal distributions for soft parameter tying in unsupervised grammar induction. In *Proc. of NAACL*.

S. Cohen. 2011. *Computational Learning of Probabilistic Grammars in the Unsupervised Setting*. Ph.D. thesis, Carnegie Mellon University.

J. Gillenwater, K. Ganchev, J. Graça, F. Pereira, , and B. Taskar. 2010. Posterior sparsity in unsupervised dependency parsing. *Journal of Machine Learning Research*.

Y. Goldberg, M. Adler, and M. Elhadad. 2008. EM can find pretty good HMM POS-taggers (when given a good start). In *Proc. of ACL*.

W. Headden III, M. Johnson, and D. McClosky. 2009. Improving unsupervised dependency parsing with richer contexts and smoothing. In *Proc. of NAACL*.

D. Klein and C. D. Manning. 2004. Corpus-based induction of syntactic structure: Models of dependency and constituency. In *Proc. of ACL*.

K. Lari and S. J. Young. 1990. The estimation of stochastic context-free grammars using the inside-outside algorithm. *Computer Speech and Language*, 4:35–56.

D. Mareček and Z. Žabokrtský. 2011. Gibbs sampling with treeness constraint in unsupervised dependency parsing. In *Proc. of Workshop on Robust Unsupervised and Semisupervised Methods in Natural Language Processing*.

T. Naseem, H. Chen, R. Barzilay, and M. Johnson. 2010. Using universal linguistic knowledge to guide grammar induction. In *Proc. of EMNLP*.

J. Nivre, J. Hall, S. Kübler, R. McDonald, J. Nilsson, S. Riedel, and D. Yuret. 2007. The CoNLL 2007 shared task on dependency parsing. In *Proc. of CoNLL*.

S. Petrov, D. Das, and R. McDonald. 2012. A universal part-of-speech tagset. In *Proc. of LREC*.

V. I. Spitkovsky, H. Alshawi, and D. Jurafsky. 2010. From Baby Steps to Leapfrog: How "Less is More" in unsupervised dependency parsing. In *Proc. of NAACL-HLT*.

V. I. Spitkovsky, H. Alshawi, A. X. Chang, and D. Jurafsky. 2011a. Unsupervised dependency parsing without gold part-of-speech tags. In *Proc. of EMNLP*.

V. I. Spitkovsky, H. Alshawi, and D. Jurafsky. 2011b. Punctuation: Making a point in unsupervised dependency parsing. In *Proc. of CoNLL*.

K. Toutanova and M. Galley. 2011. Why initialization matters for IBM Model 1: Multiple optima and non-strict convexity. In *Proc. of ACL*.

Multimodal Grammar Implementation

Katya Alahverdzhieva
University of Edinburgh
10 Crichton Street
Edinburgh EH8 9AB
K.Alahverdzhieva@sms.ed.ac.uk

Dan Flickinger
Stanford University
Stanford, CA 94305-2150
danf@stanford.edu

Alex Lascarides
University of Edinburgh
10 Crichton Street
Edinburgh EH8 9AB
alex@inf.ed.ac.uk

Abstract

This paper reports on an implementation of a multimodal grammar of speech and co-speech gesture within the LKB/PET grammar engineering environment. The implementation extends the English Resource Grammar (ERG, Flickinger (2000)) with HPSG types and rules that capture the form of the linguistic signal, the form of the gestural signal and their relative timing to constrain the meaning of the multimodal action. The grammar yields a single parse tree that integrates the spoken and gestural modality thereby drawing on standard semantic composition techniques to derive the multimodal meaning representation. Using the current machinery, the main challenge for the grammar engineer is the non-linear input: the modalities can overlap temporally. We capture this by identical speech and gesture token edges. Further, the semantic contribution of gestures is encoded by lexical rules transforming a speech phrase into a multimodal entity of conjoined spoken and gestural semantics.

1 Introduction

Our aim is to regiment the form-meaning mapping of multimodal actions consisting of speech and co-speech gestures. The language of study is English, and the gestures of interest are *depicting*—the hand depicts the referent—and *deictic*—the hand points at the referent's spatial coordinates.

Motivation for encoding the form-meaning mapping in the *grammar* stems from the fact that *form* effects judgments of multimodal grammaticality: e.g., in (1)[1] the gesture performance along with the unaccented "called" in a single prosodic phrase seems ill-formed despite the gesture depicting an aspect of the referent—the act of calling.

(1) * Your MOTHER <u>called</u> ...
Hand lifts to the ear to imitate holding a receiver.

This intuitive judgment is in line with the empirical findings of Giorgolo and Verstraten (2008) who observed that prosody influences the perception of temporally misaligned speech-and-gesture signals as ill-formed. Further, Alahverdzhieva and Lascarides (2010) established empirically that the gesture performance can be predicted from the prosodic prominence in speech and that gestures not overlapping subject NPs cannot be semantically related with that subject NP. The fact that speech-and-gesture integration is informed by the form of the linguistic signal suggests formalising the integration within the grammar. Alternatively, integrating the gestural contribution by discourse update would involve pragmatic reasoning accessing information about linguistic form, disrupting the transition between syntax/semantics and pragmatics.

The work is set within HPSG — a constraint-based grammar framework with the different types and rules organised in a hierarchy. The semantic information, derived in parallel with syntax, is expressed in Minimal Recursion Semantics (MRS) which supports a high level of *underspecifiability* (Copestake et al., 2005). This is useful for computing gesture meaning since even through discourse processing not all semantic information resolves to a specific interpretation.

The rest of the paper is structured as follows: §2 provides theoretical background, §3 details the implementation and §4 discusses the evaluation.

[1] The speech item where the gesture is performed is marked by underlining, and the accented item is given in uppercase.

2 Background

2.1 Attachment Ambiguity

We view the integration of gesture and the synchronous, semantically related speech phrase as an attachment in a single parse tree constrained by the form of the speech signal—its prosodic prominence. With standard methods for semantic composition, we map this multimodal tree to an Underspecified Logical Form (ULF) which supports the possible interpretations of the speech and gesture in their context. The choices of attachment are not unique. Similarly to "John saw the man with the telescope", there is ambiguity as to which linguistic phrase a gesture is semantically related to, and hence likewise ambiguity as to which linguistic phrase it attaches to in syntax; e.g., in (2) the open vertical hand shape can denote a container containing books or a containee of books. This interpretation is supported by a gesture attachment to the N "books". A higher attachment to the root node of the tree supports another, metaphoric interpretation where the forward movement is the conduit metaphor of giving.

(2) I can give you other BOOKS ...
Hands are parallel with palms open vertical. They perform a short forward move to the frontal centre.

We address this ambiguity by grammar rules that allow for multiple attachments in the syntactic tree constrained by the prosodic prominence of the speech signal. The two basic rules are as follows:

1. **Prosodic Word Constraint.** Gesture can attach to a prosodically prominent spoken word if there is an overlap between the timing of the gesture and the timing of the speech word.
2. **Head-Argument Constraint**. Gesture can attach to a syntactic head partially or fully saturated with its arguments and/or modifiers if there is a temporal overlap between the syntactic constituent and the gesture.

Applied to (2), these rules would attach the gesture to "books" (a prosodically prominent item), also to "other books", "give you other books", "can give you other books" and even to "I can give you other books" (heads saturated with their arguments). However, nothing licenses attachments to "I" or "give". These distinct attachments would support the interpretations proposed above.

2.2 Representing Gesture Form and Meaning

It is now commonplace to represent gesture form with Typed Feature Structures (TFS) where each feature captures an aspect of the gesture's meaning; e.g., the gesture in (2) maps to the TFS in (3). Note that the TFS is typed as *depicting* so as to differentiate between, say, a hand shape of depicting gesture and a hand shape of deixis. This distinction effects the gestural interpretation: a depicting gesture provides non-spatial aspects of the referent's denotation, and so form bears resemblance to meaning. Conversely, deixis identifies the spatial coordinates of the referent in the physical space.

(3)

depicting	
HAND-SHAPE	open-flat
PALM-ORIENT	towards-centre
FINGER-ORIENT	away-body
HAND-LOCATION	centre-low
HAND-MOVEMENT	away-body-straight

Each feature introduces an underspecified elementary predication (EP) into LF; e.g., the hand shape introduces $l_1 : hand\_shape\_open\_flat(i_1)$ where l_1 is a unique label that underspecifies the scope of the EP relative to other EPs in the gesture's LF, i_1 is a unique metavariable that underspecifies the main argument' sort (e.g., in (2) it can resolve to an individual if the gesture denotes the books or an event if it denotes the giving act) and $hand\_shape\_open\_flat$ underspecifies reference to a property that the entity i_1 has and that can be depicted through the gesture's open flat hand shape.

In the grammar, we introduce underspecified semantic relations *vis_rel(s,g)* between speech *s* and depicting gesture *g*, and *deictic_rel(s,d)* between speech *s* and deixis *d*. The resolution of these underspecified predicates is a matter of commonsense reasoning (Lascarides and Stone, 2009) and it therefore lies outside the scope of the grammar.

3 Implementation

The grammar was implemented in the LKB grammar engineering platform (Copestake, 2002) which was designed for TFS grammars such as HPSG. Since the LKB parser accepts as input linearly ordered strings and we represent gesture form with TFSs, we used the PET engine (Callmeier, 2000) which allows for injecting an arbitrary XML-based FS into the input tokens. The input to our grammar is a lattice of FSs where the spoken tokens are augmented with prosodic information and the gesture tokens are feature-value pairs such as (3).

The main challenge for the multimodal grammar implementation stems from the non-linear multimodal input. The HPSG-based parsing platforms—LKB, PET and TRALE—can parse linearly ordered strings, and so they do not handle multimodal signals whose input comes from separate channels connected through temporal relations. Also, these parsing platforms do not support quantitative comparison operations over the time stamps of the input tokens. This is essential for our grammar since the multimodal integration is constrained by temporal overlap between speech and gesture (recall §2.1).

To solve this, we pre-processed the XML-based FS input so that overlapping TIME_START and TIME_END values were "translated" into identical start and end edges of the speech token and the gesture token as follows:

```
<edge source="v0" target="v1">
        <fs type="speech_token">
<edge source="v0" target="v1">
        <fs type="gesture_token">
```

This robust pre-processing step is sufficient since the only temporal relation required by the grammar is *overlap*, an abstraction over more fined-grained relations between speech (S) and gesture (G) such as *(precedence(start(S), start(G))* $\wedge$ *identity (end(S), end(G)))*.

The linking of gesture to its temporally overlapping speech segment happens prior to parsing via chart-mapping rules (Adolphs et al., 2008) which involve re-writing chart items into FSs. The `gesture-unary-rule` (see Fig.1) rewrites an input (I) speech token in the context (C) of a gesture token into a combined speech+gesture token where the +GEST and +PROS values of the speech and gesture tokens are copied onto the output (O).

```
gesture-unary-rule := cm_rule &
 [+CONTEXT <gesture_token & [+GEST #gest]>,
  +INPUT <speech_token & [+PROS #pros]>,
  +OUTPUT <speech+gesture_token &
          [+GEST #gest, +PROS #pros]>,
  +POSITION "O1@I1, I1@C1" ].
```

Figure 1: Definition of `gesture-unary-rule`

The +PROS attribute contains prosodic information and the +GEST attribute is a feature-structure representation as shown in (3). The +POSITION constraint restricts the position of the I, O and C items to an overlap (`@`), i.e., the edge markers of the gesture token should be identical to those of the speech token, and also identical to the speech+gesture token. This chart-mapping rule recognises the gesture token overlapping the speech token and it records this by "augmenting" the speech token with the gesture feature-values.

In the grammar, we extended the ERG word and phrase rules with prosodic and gestural information where the +PROS and +GEST features of the input token are identified with the PROS and GEST of the word and/or lexical phrase in the grammar. We then added a lexical rule (see Fig. 2) which projects a gesture daughter to a complex gesture-marked entity of a single argument for which both the PROS and GEST features are appropriate.

```
gesture_lexrule := phrase_or_lexrule &
 [ ORTH [ PROS #pros ],
   ARGS <[ ORTH [ GEST gesture-form,
                  PROS p-word & #pros ]]>].
```

Figure 2: Definition of `gesture_lexrule`

This rule constrains PROS to a prosodically prominent word of type *p-word* thereby preventing a gesture from plugging into a prosodically unmarked word. The *gesture-form* value is a supertype over the distinct gesture types—depicting and deictic. The `gesture_lexrule` is inherited by a lexical rule specific to depicting gestures, and by a lexical rule specific to deictic gestures. In this way, we can encode the semantic contribution of depicting gestures which is different from the semantic contribution of deixis. For the sake of space, Fig. 3 presents only the `depicting_lexrule`. The semantic information contributed by the rule is encoded within C-CONT.

Following §2.2, the rule introduces an underspecified *vis_rel* between the main label `#dltop` of the spoken sign (via the HCONS constraints) and the main label `#glbl` of the gesture semantics (via the HCONS constraints). Note that these two arguments are in a *geq* (greater or equal) constraint. This means that *vis_rel* can operate over any projection of the speech word; e.g., attaching the gesture to "book" in (2) means that the relation is not restricted to the EPs contributed by "books" but it can be also over the EPs of a higher projection. The gesture's semantics is a bag of EPs (see §2.2), all of which are outscoped

'gesture/12-04-02/pet' Coverage Profile							
Aggregate	total items ♯	positive items ♯	word string ϕ	lexical items ϕ	distinct analyses ϕ	total results ♯	overall coverage %
$90 \leq$ *i-length* < 95	126	92	93.00	26.46	1.67	92	100.0
$70 \leq$ *i-length* < 75	78	54	71.00	12.00	1.00	54	100.0
$60 \leq$ *i-length* < 65	249	179	60.00	9.42	1.00	179	100.0
$45 \leq$ *i-length* < 50	18	14	49.00	7.00	1.00	14	100.0
Total	**471**	**339**	**70.25**	**14.35**	**1.18**	**339**	**100.0**

Table 1: Coverage Profile of Test Items generated by [incr tsdb()]

```
depicting_lexrule := gesture_lexrule &
[ARGS <[ SYNSEM.LOCAL.CONT.HOOK.LTOP
                                   #dltop,
         ORTH [ GEST depicting] >,
 C-CONT [ RELS <![ PRED vis_rel,
                   S-ARG #arg1,
                   G-ARG #arg2 ],
                 [ PRED G_mod,
                   LBL #glbl,
                   ARG1 #harg ],
                 [ LBL #larg1 ],...!>,
         HCONS <!qeq&[ HARG #arg1,
                       LARG #dltop ],
                 qeq&[ HARG #arg2,
                       LARG #glbl ],
                 qeq&[ HARG #harg,
                       LARG #larg1 ],
                 ...!>]].
```

Figure 3: Definition of `depicting_lexrule`

by the gestural modality [$\mathcal{G}$]. The rule therefore introduces in RELS a label (here `#larg1`) for an EP which is in *qeq* constraints with [$\mathcal{G}$]. The instantiation of the particular EPs comes from the gestural lexical entry. In the real implementation, the number of these labels corresponds to the number of features. They are designed in the same way and we thus forego any details about the rest.

4 Evaluation

The evaluation was performed against a test suite designed in analogy to the traditional phenomenon-based test-suites (Lehmann et al., 1996): manually-crafted to ensure coverage of well-formed and ill-formed data, but inspired by an examination of natural data. We systematically tested syntactic phenomena (intransitivity, transitivity, complex NPs, coordination, negation and modification) over well-formed and ill-formed examples where the ill-formed items were derived by means of the following operations: prosodic permutation (varying the prosodic markedness, e.g., from (4a) we derive (4b) to reflect intuitions of native speakers); gesture variation (testing distinct gesture types) and temporal permutation (moving the gestural performance over the distinct speech items).

(4) a. ANNA ate ...
Depicting gesture along with "Anna".

b. *anna ATE ...
Depicting gesture along with "Anna".

The test set contained 471 multimodal items (72% well-formed) covering the full range of prosodic (prosodic markedness and unmarkedness) and gesture (the span of depicting/deictic gesture and its temporal relation to the prosodically marked elements) permutations. The gestural vocabulary was limited since a larger gesture lexicon has no effects on the performance. To test the grammar, we used the [incr tsdb()][2] competence and performance tool which enables batch processing of test items and which creates a coverage profile of the test set (see Table 1). The values are as follows: the left column separates the items per aggregation criterion (the length of test items); the next column shows the number of test items per aggregate; then we have the number of grammatical items; average length of test item; average number of lexical items; average number of distinct analyses and total coverage.

5 Conclusions and Future Work

This paper reported on an implementation of a multimodal grammar combining spoken and gestural input. The main challenge for the current parsing platforms was the non-linear input which we solved by extending the spoken sign with the synchronous gestural sign semantics where synchrony was established by means of identical token edges. In the future, we shall extend the lexical coverage so that the grammar can handle various gestures and we also intend to evaluate the grammar with naturally occurring examples in XML format.

[2] `http://www.delph-in.net/itsdb/`

References

Peter Adolphs, Stephan Oepen, Ulrich Callmeier, Berthold Crysmann, Daniel Flickinger, and Bernd Kiefer. 2008. Some fine points of hybrid natural language parsing. In *Proceedings of the Sixth International Language Resources and Evaluation*. ELRA.

Katya Alahverdzhieva and Alex Lascarides. 2010. Analysing speech and co-speech gesture in constraint-based grammars. In Stefan Müller, editor, *The Proceedings of the 17th International Conference on Head-Driven Phrase Structure Grammar*, pages 6–26, Stanford. CSLI Publications.

Ulrich Callmeier. 2000. PET — A platform for experimentation with efficient HPSG processing techniques. *Natural Language Engineering*, 6 (1) (Special Issue on Efficient Processing with HPSG):99 – 108.

Ann Copestake, Dan Flickinger, Ivan Sag, and Carl Pollard. 2005. Minimal recursion semantics: An introduction. *Journal of Research on Language and Computation*, 3(2–3):281–332.

Ann Copestake. 2002. *Implementing Typed Feature Structure Grammars*. CSLI Publications, Stanford, CA.

Dan Flickinger. 2000. On building a more efficient grammar by exploiting types. *Natural Language Engineering*.

Gianluca Giorgolo and Frans Verstraten. 2008. Perception of speech-and-gesture integration. In *Proceedings of the International Conference on Auditory-Visual Speech Processing 2008*, pages 31–36.

Alex Lascarides and Matthew Stone. 2009. A formal semantic analysis of gesture. *Journal of Semantics*.

Sabine Lehmann, Stephan Oepen, Sylvie Regnier-Prost, Klaus Netter, Veronika Lux, Judith Klein, Kirsten Falkedal, Frederik Fouvry, Dominique Estival, Eva Dauphin, Herve Compagnion, Judith Baur, Lorna Balkan, and Doug Arnold. 1996. Tsnlp - test suites for natural language processing. In *COLING*, pages 711–716.

Portable Features for Classifying Emotional Text

Saif Mohammad
National Research Council Canada
Ottawa, Canada, K1A 0R6
saif.mohammad@nrc-cnrc.gc.ca

Abstract

Are word-level affect lexicons useful in detecting emotions at sentence level? Some prior research finds no gain over and above what is obtained with ngram features—arguably the most widely used features in text classification. Here, we experiment with two very different emotion lexicons and show that even in supervised settings, an affect lexicon can provide significant gains. We further show that while ngram features tend to be accurate, they are often unsuitable for use in new domains. On the other hand, affect lexicon features tend to generalize and produce better results than ngrams when applied to a new domain.

1 Introduction

Automatically identifying emotions expressed in text has a number of applications, including tracking customer satisfaction (Bougie et al., 2003), determining popularity of politicians and government policies (Mohammad and Yang, 2011), depression detection (Osgood and Walker, 1959; Pestian et al., 2008; Matykiewicz et al., 2009; Cherry et al., 2012), affect-based search (Mohammad, 2011), and improving human-computer interaction (Velásquez, 1997; Ravaja et al., 2006).

Supervised methods for classifying emotions expressed in a sentence tend to perform better than unsupervised ones. They use features such as unigrams and bigrams (Alm et al., 2005; Aman and Szpakowicz, 2007; Neviarouskaya et al., 2009; Chaffar and Inkpen, 2011). For example, a system can learn that the word *excruciating* tends to occur in sentences labeled with sadness, and use this word as a feature in classifying new sentences.

Approaches that do not rely on supervised training with sentence-level annotations often use affect lexicons. An affect lexicon, in its simplest form, is a list of words and associated emotions and sentiments. For example, the word *excruciating* may be associated with the emotions of sadness and fear. Note that such lexicons are at best indicators of probable emotions, and that in any given sentence, the full context may suggest that a completely different emotion is being expressed. Therefore, it is unclear how useful such word-level emotion lexicons are for detecting emotions and meanings expressed in sentences, especially since supervised systems relying on tens of thousands of unigrams and bigrams can produce results that are hard to surpass. For example, it is possible that classifiers can learn from unigram features alone that *excruciating* is associated with sadness and fear.

In this paper, we investigate whether word–emotion association lexicons can provide gains in addition to those already provided by ngram features. We conduct experiments with different affect lexicons and determine their usefulness in this extrinsic task. We also conduct experiments to determine how portable the ngram features and the emotion lexicon features are to a new domain.

2 Affect Lexicons

The WordNet Affect Lexicon (Strapparava and Valitutti, 2004) has a few thousand words annotated for associations with a number of affect categories. This includes 1536 words annotated for associations with six emotions considered to be the most basic—joy, sadness, fear, disgust, anger, and surprise (Ekman, 1992).[1] It was created by manually identifying the emotions of a few seed words and then labeling all their WordNet synonyms with the same emotion. Affective Norms for English Words has pleasure (happy–unhappy), arousal (excited–calm), and dominance (controlled–in control) ratings for 1034 words.[2] Mohammad and Turney (2010; 2012) compiled manual annotations for eight emotions (the six of Ekman, plus trust and anticipation) as well as for positive and negative sentiment.[3] The lexicon was created by crowdsourcing to Mechanical Turk. This lexicon, referred to as the NRC word-emotion lexicon (NRC-10) version 0.91, has annotations for about 14,000 words.[4]

We evaluate the affect lexicons that have annotations for the Ekman emotions—the WordNet Affect Lexicon and the NRC-10. We also experimented with a subset of NRC-10, which we will call NRC-6, that has annotations for only the six Ekman emotions (no trust and anticipation annotations; and no positive and negative sentiment annotations).

3 Sentence Classification System

We created binary classifiers for each of the six emotions using Weka (Hall et al., 2009).[5] For example, the *Fear–NotFear* classifier determined whether a sentence expressed fear or not. We experimented with Logistic Regression (le Cessie and van Houwelingen, 1992) and Support Vector Machines (SVM). We used binary features that captured the presence or absence of unigrams and bigrams. We also used integer-valued affect features that captured the number of word tokens in a sentence associated with different affect labels in the affect lexicon being used.[6] For example, if a sentence has two joy words and one surprise word, then the joy feature has value 2, surprise has value 1, and all remaining affect labels have value 0.

emotion	# of instances	% of instances	r
anger	132	13.2	0.50
disgust	43	4.3	0.45
fear	247	24.7	0.64
joy	344	34.4	0.60
sadness	283	28.3	0.68
surprise	253	25.3	0.36
		simple average	0.54
		frequency-based average	0.43

Table 1: Inter-annotator agreement (Pearson's correlation) amongst 6 annotators on the 1000-headlines dataset.

3.1 Training and Testing within domain

As a source of labeled data for training and testing, we used the SemEval-2007 Affective Text corpus wherein newspaper headlines were labeled with the six Ekman emotions by six annotators (Strapparava and Mihalcea, 2007). For each headline–emotion pair, the annotators gave scores from 0 to 100 indicating how strongly the headline expressed the emotion. The inter-annotator agreement as determined by calculating the Pearson's product moment correlation (r) between the scores given by each annotator and the average of the other five annotators is shown in Table 1. For our experiments, we considered scores greater than 25 to indicate that the headline expresses the corresponding emotion.

The dataset was created for an unsupervised competition, and consisted of 250 sentences of trial data and 1000 sentences of test data. We will refer to them as the 250-headlines and the 1000-headlines datasets respectively. In order to use these datasets in a supervised framework, we follow Chaffar and Inkpen (2011) and report results under two settings: (1) ten-fold cross-validation on the 1000-headlines and (2) using the 1000-headlines as training data and testing on the 250-headlines dataset.

Table 2 shows results obtained by classifiers when trained on the 1000-headlines text and tested on the 250-headlines text. The rows under I give a breakdown of results obtained by the *EmotionX–NotEmotionX* classifiers when using both n-gram and NRC-10 affect features (where X is one of the six Ekman emotions). *gold* is the number of headlines expressing a particular emotion X. *right* is the number of instances that the classifier correctly

[1] http://wndomains.fbk.eu/wnaffect.html

[2] http://csea.phhp.ufl.edu/media/anewmessage.html

[3] Plutchik (1985) proposed a model of 8 basic emotions.

[4] Please send an email to the author to obtain a copy of the NRC emotion lexicon. Details of the lexicon are available at: http://www.purl.org/net/saif.mohammad/research

[5] http://www.cs.waikato.ac.nz/ml/weka

[6] Normalizing by sentence length did not give better results.

Classifier	gold	right	guess	P	R	F
I. Using affect and ngram features:						
a. NRC-10, unigrams, bigrams						
anger	66	23	55	41.8	34.8	38.0
disgust	52	8	17	47.1	15.4	23.2
fear	74	59	100	59.0	79.7	67.8
joy	77	52	102	51.0	67.5	58.1
sadness	105	71	108	65.7	67.6	66.7
surprise	43	14	67	20.9	32.6	25.4
ALL	417	227	449	50.6	54.4	**52.4**
b. NRC-6, unigrams, bigrams						
ALL	417	219	437	50.1	52.5	51.3
c. WordNet Affect, unigrams, bigrams						
ALL	417	212	490	43.3	50.8	46.7
II. Using affect features only:						
a. NRC-10						
ALL	417	282	810	34.8	67.6	46.0
b. NRC-6						
ALL	417	243	715	34.0	58.3	42.9
c. WordNet Affect						
ALL	417	409	1435	28.5	98.0	44.1
III. Using ngrams features only:						
ALL	417	210	486	43.2	50.4	46.5
IV. Random guessing:						
ALL	417	208	750	27.8	50.0	35.7

Table 2: Results on the 250-headlines dataset.

marked as expressing X. *guess* is the number of instances marked as expressing X by the classifier. Precision (P) and recall (R) are calculated as shown below:

$$P = \frac{right}{guesses} * 100 \quad (1)$$

$$R = \frac{right}{gold} * 100 \quad (2)$$

F is the balanced F-score. The ALL row shows the sums of values for all six emotions for the *gold*, *right*, and *guess* columns. The overall precision and recall are calculated by plugging these values in equations 1 and 2. Thus 52.4 is the macro-average F-score obtained by the I.a. classifiers.

I.b. and I.c. show results obtained using ngrams with NRC-6 and WordNet Affect features respectively. We do not show a breakdown of results by emotions for them and for the rows in II, III, and IV due to space constraints.

The rows in II correspond to the use of different affect features alone (no ngrams). III shows the results obtained using only ngrams, and IV shows the results obtained by a system that guesses randomly.[7]

Classifier	P	R	F
I. Using affect and ngram features:			
a. NRC-10, ngrams	44.4	61.8	**51.6**
b. NRC-6, ngrams	42.7	61.4	50.4
c. WA, ngrams	41.9	58.8	49.0
II. Using affect features only:			
a. NRC-10	24.1	95.0	38.4
b. NRC-6	24.1	95.0	38.4
c. WA	23.5	95.4	37.7
III. Using ngrams only:	42.0	59.8	49.3
IV. Random guessing:	21.7	50.0	30.3

Table 3: Cross-validation results on 1000-headlines.

Table 3 gives results obtained by cross-validation on the 1000-headlines dataset. The results in Tables 2 and 3 lead to the following observations:

- On both datasets, using the NRC-10 in addition to the ngram features gives significantly higher scores than using ngrams alone. This was not true, however, for WordNet affect.
- Using NRC-10 alone obtains almost as good scores as those obtained by the ngrams in the 250-headlines test data, even though the number of affect features (10) is much smaller than the ngram features (many thousands).
- Using annotations for all ten affect labels in NRC-10 instead of just the Ekman six gives minor improvements.
- The automatic methods perform best for classes with the high inter-annotator agreement (sadness and fear), and worst for classes with the low agreement (surprise and disgust) (Table 1).

We used the Fisher Exact Test and a confidence interval of 95% for all precision and recall significance testing reported in this paper. Experiments with support vector machines gave slightly lower F-scores than those obtained with logistic regression, but all of the above observations held true even in those experiments (we do not show those results here due to the limited space available).

[7] A system that randomly guesses whether an instance is expressing an emotion X or not will get half of the *gold* instances right. Further, it will mark half of all the instances as expressing emotion X. For ALL, $right = \frac{gold}{2}$, and $guess = \frac{instances*6}{2}$.

Emotions:	anger	3.47	joy	-0.25
	anticipn	0.08	sadness	-0.51
	disgust	0.97	surprise	-1.87
	fear	0.25	trust	0.12
Sentiment:	negative	2.38	positive	-0.31

Table 4: The coefficients of the features learned by logistic regression for the *Anger–NoAnger* classifier.

The coefficients of the features learned by the logistic regression algorithm are weights that indicate how strongly the individual features influence the decision of the classifier. The affect features of the *Anger–NoAnger* classifier learned from the 1000-sentences dataset and NRC-10 are shown in Table 4. We see that the anger feature has the highest weight and plays the biggest role in predicting whether a sentence expresses anger or not. The negative sentiment feature is also a strong indicator of anger. Similarly, the weights for other emotion classifiers were consistent with our intuition: joy had the highest weight in the *Joy–NotJoy* classifier, sadness in the *Sadness–NotSadness* classifier, and so on.

3.2 Testing on data from another domain

Hand-labeled training data is helpful for automatic classifiers, but it is usually not available for most domains. We now describe experiments to determine how well the classifiers and features cope with training on data from one source domain and testing on a new target domain. We will use the 1000-headlines dataset from the previous section as the source domain training data. As test data we will now use sentences compiled by Aman and Szpakowicz (2007) from blogs. This dataset has 4090 sentences annotated with the Ekman emotions by four annotators. The inter-annotator agreement for the different emotions ranged from 0.6 to 0.8 Cohen's kappa.

Table 5 shows the results. Observe that now the ngrams perform quite poorly; the NRC-10 affect features perform significantly better, despite each sentence being represented by only ten features. The rows in II give a breakdown of results obtained by individual *EmotionX–NotEmotionX* classifiers. Observe that the distribution of instances in this blog dataset (gold column) is different from that in the 1000-headlines (Table 1). The larger proportion of neutral instances in the blog data compared to 1000-headlines, leads to a much lower precision and F-score of the randomly-guessing classifier on the blog dataset (row IV) than on the 1000-headlines dataset.

Classifier	gold	right	guess	P	R	F
I. Using affect (NRC-10) and ngram features:						
ALL	1290	515	6717	7.7	39.9	12.9
II. Using affect (NRC-10) features only:						
anger	179	22	70	31.4	12.3	17.7
disgust	172	16	48	33.3	9.3	14.5
fear	115	32	110	29.1	27.8	28.4
joy	536	299	838	35.7	55.8	43.5
sadness	173	61	282	21.6	35.3	26.8
surprise	115	9	158	5.7	7.8	6.6
ALL	1290	439	1506	29.2	34.0	**31.4**
III. Using ngram features only:						
ALL	1290	375	7414	5.1	29.1	8.6
IV. Random guessing:						
ALL	1290	645	12270	5.3	50.0	9.6

Table 5: Results obtained on the blog dataset.

Nonetheless, the NRC-10 affect features obtain significantly higher results than the random baseline. The ngram features (row III), on the other hand, lead to scores lower than the random baseline. This suggests that they are especially domain-sensitive. Manual inspection of the regression coefficients confirms the over-fitting of ngram features. The overfitting is less for affect features, probably because of the small number of features.

4 Conclusions

Even though context plays a significant role in the meaning and emotion conveyed by a word, we showed that using word-level affect lexicons can provide significant improvements in sentence-level emotion classification—over and above those obtained by unigrams and bigrams alone. The gains provided by the lexicons may be correlated with their sizes. The NRC lexicon has fourteen times as many entries as the WordNet Affect lexicon and it gives significantly better results.

We also showed that ngram features tend to be markedly domain-specific and work well only within domains. On the other hand, affect lexicon features worked significantly better than ngram features when applied to a new domain for which there was no training data.

Acknowledgments

We thank Colin Cherry, Peter Turney, and Tara Small.

References

C. Alm, D. Roth, and R. Sproat. 2005. Emotions from text: Machine learning for text-based emotion prediction. In *Proceedings of HLT–EMNLP*, Vancouver.

S. Aman and S. Szpakowicz. 2007. Identifying expressions of emotion in text. In *Text, Speech and Dialogue*, volume 4629, pages 196–205. Springer.

J. R. G. Bougie, R. Pieters, and M. Zeelenberg. 2003. Angry customers don't come back, they get back: The experience and behavioral implications of anger and dissatisfaction in services. Open access publications from tilburg university, Tilburg University.

S. Chaffar and D. Inkpen. 2011. Using a heterogeneous dataset for emotion analysis in text. In *Canadian Conference on AI*, pages 62–67.

C. Cherry, S. M. Mohammad, and B de Bruijn. 2012. Binary classifiers and latent sequence models for emotion detection in suicide notes. *Biomedical Informatics Insights*, 5:147–154.

P. Ekman. 1992. An argument for basic emotions. *Cognition and Emotion*, 6(3):169–200.

M. Hall, E. Frank, G. Holmes, B. Pfahringer, P. Reutemann, and I. Witten. 2009. The WEKA data mining software: an update. *SIGKDD*, 11:10–18.

S. le Cessie and J. van Houwelingen. 1992. Ridge estimators in logistic regression. *Applied Statistics*, 41(1):191–201.

P. Matykiewicz, W. Duch, and J. P. Pestian. 2009. Clustering semantic spaces of suicide notes and newsgroups articles. In *Proceedings of the Workshop on Current Trends in Biomedical Natural Language Processing*, BioNLP '09, pages 179–184, Stroudsburg, PA, USA. Association for Computational Linguistics.

S. M. Mohammad and P. D. Turney. 2010. Emotions evoked by common words and phrases: Using mechanical turk to create an emotion lexicon. In *Proceedings of Workshop on Computational Approaches to Analysis and Generation of Emotion in Text*, LA, California.

S. M. Mohammad and P. D. Turney. 2012. Crowdsourcing a word–emotion association lexicon. *Computational Intelligence*.

S. M. Mohammad and T. Yang. 2011. Tracking Sentiment in Mail: How Genders Differ on Emotional Axes. In *Proceedings of the 2nd Workshop on Computational Approaches to Subjectivity and Sentiment Analysis (WASSA 2.011)*, pages 70–79, Portland, Oregon. Association for Computational Linguistics.

S. M. Mohammad. 2011. From once upon a time to happily ever after: Tracking emotions in novels and fairy tales. In *Proceedings of the ACL 2011 Workshop on Language Technology for Cultural Heritage, Social Sciences, and Humanities (LaTeCH)*, Portland, OR, USA.

A. Neviarouskaya, H. Prendinger, and M. Ishizuka. 2009. Compositionality principle in recognition of fine-grained emotions from text. In *Proceedings of ICWSM*, pages 278–281, San Jose, California.

C. E. Osgood and E. G. Walker. 1959. Motivation and language behavior: A content analysis of suicide notes. *Journal of Abnormal and Social Psychology*, 59(1):58–67.

J. P. Pestian, P. Matykiewicz, and J. Grupp-Phelan. 2008. Using natural language processing to classify suicide notes. In *Proceedings of the Workshop on Current Trends in Biomedical Natural Language Processing*, BioNLP '08, pages 96–97, Stroudsburg, PA, USA. Association for Computational Linguistics.

R. Plutchik. 1985. On emotion: The chicken-and-egg problem revisited. *Motivation and Emotion*, 9(2):197–200.

N. Ravaja, T. Saari, M. Turpeinen, J. Laarni, M. Salminen, and M. Kivikangas. 2006. Spatial presence and emotions during video game playing: Does it matter with whom you play? *Presence: Teleoperators and Virtual Environments*, 15(4):381–392.

C. Strapparava and R. Mihalcea. 2007. Semeval-2007 task 14: Affective text. In *Proceedings of SemEval-2007*, pages 70–74, Prague, Czech Republic.

C. Strapparava and A. Valitutti. 2004. Wordnet-Affect: An affective extension of WordNet. In *Proceedings of LREC*, pages 1083–1086, Lisbon, Portugal.

J. D. Velásquez. 1997. Modeling emotions and other motivations in synthetic agents. In *Proceedings of the fourteenth national conference on artificial intelligence and ninth conference on Innovative applications of artificial intelligence*, AAAI'97/IAAI'97, pages 10–15. AAAI Press.

Stance Classification using Dialogic Properties of Persuasion

Marilyn A. Walker, Pranav Anand, Robert Abbott and Ricky Grant
Baskin School of Engineering & Linguistics Department
University of California Santa Cruz
Santa Cruz, Ca. 95064, USA
maw,panand,abbott,rgrant@soe.ucsc.edu

Abstract

Public debate functions as a forum for both expressing and forming opinions, an important aspect of public life. We present results for automatically classifying posts in online debate as to the position, or STANCE that the speaker takes on an issue, such as **Pro** or **Con**. We show that representing the dialogic structure of the debates in terms of agreement relations between speakers, greatly improves performance for stance classification, over models that operate on post content and parent-post context alone.

1 Introduction

Public debate functions as a forum for both *expressing* and *forming* opinions. Three factors affect opinion formation, e.g. the perlocutionary uptake of debate arguments (Cialdini, 2000; Petty and Cacioppo, 1988; Petty et al., 1981). First, there is the ARGUMENT itself, i.e. the propositions discussed along with the logical relations between them. Second is the SOURCE of the argument (Chaiken, 1980), e.g. the speaker's expertise, or agreement relations between speakers. The third factor consists of properties of the AUDIENCE such as prior beliefs, social identity, personality, and cognitive style (Davies, 1998). Perlocutionary uptake in debates primarily occurs in the audience, who may be undecided, while debaters typically express a particular position or STANCE on an issue, e.g. **Pro** or **Con**, as in the online debate dialogues in Figs. 1, 2, and 3.

Previous computational work on debate covers three different debate settings: (1) congressional debates (Thomas et al., 2006; Bansal et al., 2008; Yessenalina et al., 2010; Balahur et al., 2009; Burfoot et al., 2011); (2) company-internal discussion sites (Murakami and Raymond, 2010; Agrawal et al., 2003); and (3) online social and political public forums (Somasundaran and Wiebe, 2009; Somasundaran and Wiebe, 2010; Wang and Rosé, 2010; Biran and Rambow, 2011). Debates in online public forums (e.g. Fig. 1) differ from debates in congress and on company discussion sites in two ways.

Post	Stance	Utterance
P1	PRO	I feel badly for your ignorance because although there maybe a sliver of doubt that mankind may have evolved from previous animals, there is no doubt that the Earth and the cosmos have gone through evolution and are continuing to do so
P2	CON	As long as there are people who doubt evolution, both lay and acedamia, then evolution is in doubt. And please don't feel bad for me. I am perfectly secure in my "ignorance".
P3	PRO	By that measure, as long as organic chemistry, physics and gravity are in doubt by both lay and acedamia, then organic chemistry, physics and gravity are in doubt. Gravity is a theory. Why aren't you giving it the same treatment you do to evolution? Or is it because you are ignorant? Angelic Falling anyone?
P4	CON	I'm obviously ignorant. Look how many times i've been given the title. "Gravity is a theory. Why aren't you giving it the same treatment you do to evolution?" Because it doesn't carry the same weight. ;P

Figure 1: All posts linked via rebuttal links. The topic was "Evolution", with sides "Yes, I Believe" vs. "No, I Dont Believe".

First, the language is different. Online debaters are highly involved, often using emotional and colorful language to make their points. These debates are also personal, giving a strong sense of the individual making the argument, and whether s/he favors emotive or factual modes of expression, e.g. *Let me answer.... NO!* (P2 in Fig. 3). Other common features are sarcasm, e.g. *I'm obviously ignorant. Look how many times i've been given the title* (P4 in Fig. 1), questioning another's evidence or assumptions: *Yes there is always room for human error, but is one accident that hasn't happened yet enough cause to get rid of a capital punishment?* (P2 in Fig. 3), and insults: *Or is it because you are ignorant?* (P3 in Fig. 1). These properties may function to engage the audience and persuade them to form a particular opinion, but they make computational analysis of such debates challenging, with the best performance to date averaging 64% over several topics (Somasundaran and Wiebe, 2010).

Post	Stance	Utterance
P1	Superman	Batman is no match for superman. Not only does he have SUPERnatural powers as opposed to batman's wit and gadgetry, but his powers have increased in number over the years. For example, when Superman's prowess was first documented in the comics he did not have x-ray vision. It wasn't until his story was told on radio that he could see through stuff. So no matter what new weapon batman could obtain, Superman would add another SUPERnatural weapon to foil the Caped crusader.
P2	Batman	Superman GAVE Batman a krytonite ring so that Batman could take him down should he need to. Superman did this because he knows Batman is the only guy that could do it.
P3	Superman	But, not being privy to private conversations with S-man, you wouldn't know that, being the humble chap that he is, S-man allowed batman the victory because he likes the bat and wanted him to mantain some credibility. Honest.
P4	Batman	Hmmm, this is confusing. Since we all know that Supes doesn't lie and yet at the time of him being beaten by Batman he was under the control of Poison Ivy and therefore could NOT have LET Batman win on purpose. I have to say that I am beginning to doubt you really are friends with Supes at all.

Figure 2: All posts linked via rebuttal links. The topic was "Superman vs. Batman"

Second, the affordances of different online debate sites provide differential support for dialogic relations between forum participants. For example, the research of Somasundaran and Wiebe (2010), does not explicitly model dialogue or author relations. However debates in our corpus vary greatly by topic on two dialogic factors: (1) the percent of posts that are rebuttals to prior posts, and (2) the number of

Post	Stance	Utterance
P1	CON	69 people have been released from death row since 1973 these people could have been killed if there cases and evidence did not come up rong also these people can have lost 20 years or more to a false coviction. it is only a matter of time till some one is killed yes u could say there doing a good job now but it has been shown so many times with humans that they will make the human error and cost an innocent person there life.
P2	PRO	Yes there is always room for human error, but is one accident that hasn't happened yet enough cause to get rid of a capital punishment? Let me answer...NO! If you ban the death penalty crime will skyrocket. It is an effective deterannce for crime. The states that have strict death penalty laws have less crime than states that don't (Texas vs. Michigan) Texas's crime rate is lower than Michigan and Texas has a higher population!!!!

Figure 3: Posts linked via rebuttal links. The topic was "Capital Punishment", and the argument was framed as "Yes we should keep it" vs. "No we should not".

posts per author. The first 5 columns of Table 2 shows the variation in these dimensions by topic.

In this paper we show that information about dialogic relations between authors (SOURCE factors) improves performance for STANCE classification, when compared to models that only have access to properties of the ARGUMENT. We model SOURCE relations with a graph, and add this information to classifiers operating on the text of a post. Sec. 2 describes the corpus and our approach. Our corpus is publicly available, see (Walker et al., 2012). We show in Sec. 3 that modeling source properties improves performance when the debates are highly dialogic. We leave a more detailed comparison to previous work to Sec. 3 so that we can contrast previous work with our approach.

2 Experimental Method and Approach

Our corpus consists of two-sided debates from Convinceme.net for 14 topics that range from playful debates such as Superman vs. Batman (Fig. 2 to more heated political topics such as the Death Penalty (Fig. 3. In total the corpus consists of 2902 two-sided debates (36,307 posts), totaling 3,080,874 words; the topic labelled debates which we use in our experiments contain 575,818 words. On Convinceme, a person starts a debate by posting a topic or a question and providing sides such as *for* vs. *against*. Debate participants can then post arguments for one side or the other, essentially self-labelling their post for stance. Convinceme provides three possible sources of dialogic structure, SIDE, REBUTTAL LINKS and TEMPORAL CONTEXT. Timestamps for posts are only available by day and there are no agreement links. Here, we use the self-labelled SIDE as the stance to be predicted.

Set/Factor	Description
Basic	Number of Characters in post, Average Word Length, Unigrams, Bigrams
Sentiment	LIWC counts and frequencies, Opinion Dependencies, LIWC Dependencies, negation
Argument	Cue Words, Repeated Punctuation, Context, POS-Generalized Dependencies, Quotes

Table 1: Feature Sets

We construct features from the posts, along with a representation of the parent post as context, and use those features in several base classifiers. As shown in Table 1, we distinguish between basic features, such as length of the post and the words and bigrams in the post, and features capturing **sentiment** and subjectivity, including using the LIWC tool for emotion labelling (Pennebaker et al., 2001) and deriving generalized dependency features using LIWC categories, as well as some limited aspects of the **argument** structure, such as cue words signalling rhetorical relations between posts, POS generalized dependencies, and a representation of the parent post (context). Only rebuttal posts have a parent post, and thus values for the context features.

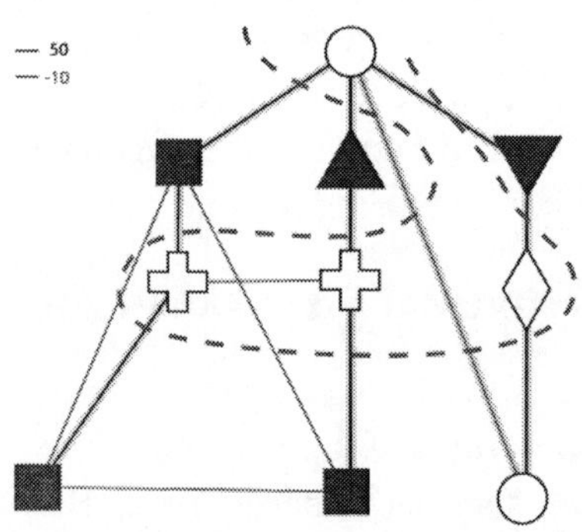

Figure 4: Sample maxcut to ConvinceMe siding. Symbols (circle, cross, square, triangles) indicate authors and fill colors (white,black) indicate true side. Rebuttal links are marked by black edges, same-author links by red; weights are 50 and -10, respectively. Edges in the maxcut are highlighted in yellow, and the nodes in each cut set are bounded by the green dotted line.

We then construct a graph (V,E) representing the dialogue structure, using the rebuttal links and author identifiers from the forums site. Each node V of the graph is a post, and edges E indicate dialogic relations of agreement and disagreement between posts. We assume only that authors always agree with themselves, and that rebuttal links indicate disagreement. Agreement links based on the inference that if A, B disagree with C they agree with each other were not added to the graph.

Maxcut attempts to partition a graph into two sides. Fig. 4 illustrates a sample result of applying MaxCut. Edges connecting the partitions are said to be cut, while those within partitions are not. The goal is to maximize the sum of cut edge weights. By making edge weights high we reward the algorithm for cutting the edge, by making edge weights negative we penalize the algorithm for cutting the edge. Rebuttal links were assigned a weight +100/(number of rebuttals). Same author links were assigned a weight -60/(number of posts by author). If author A rebutted author B at some point, then a weight of 50 was assigned to all edges connecting posts by author A and posts by author B. If author B rebutted author A as well, that 50 was increased to 100. We applied the MaxCut partitioning algorithm to this graph, and then we orient each of the components automatically using a traditional supervised classifier. We consider each component separately where components are defined using the original (pre-MaxCut) graph. For each pair of partition side $p \in \{P_0, P_1\}$ and classifier label $l \in \{L_0, L_1\}$, we compute a score $S_{p,l}$ by summing the margins of all nodes assigned to that partition and label. We then compute and compare the score differences for each partition. $D_p = S_{p,L_1} - S_{p,L_0}$ If $D_{P_0} < D_{P_1}$, then nodes in partition P_0 should be assigned label L_0 and nodes in P_1 should be assigned label L_1. Likewise, if $D_{P_0} > D_{P_1}$, then nodes in partition P_0 should be assigned label L_1 and nodes in P_1 should be assigned label L_0. If $D_{P_0} = D_{P_1}$, then we orient the component with a coin flip.

3 Results and Discussion

Table 2 summarizes our results for the base classifier (JRIP) compared to using MaxCut over the social network defined by author and rebuttal links. We report results for experiments using all the fea-

Topic	Topic Characteristics Posts	Rebs	P/A	A> 1p	MLE	MaxCut Algorithm Acc	F1	P	R	JRIP Algorithm Acc	F1	P	R
Abortion	607	64%	2.73	42%	53%	82%	0.82	0.78	0.88	55%	0.55	0.52	0.59
Cats v. Dogs	162	40%	1.60	24%	53%	80%	0.78	0.80	0.76	61%	0.55	0.59	0.51
Climate Change	207	65%	2.92	41%	50%	64%	0.66	0.63	0.69	61%	0.62	0.60	0.63
Comm. v. Capitalism	214	62%	2.97	46%	55%	70%	0.67	0.66	0.68	53%	0.49	0.48	0.49
Death Penalty	331	60%	2.40	45%	56%	35%	0.31	0.29	0.34	55%	0.46	0.48	0.44
Evolution	818	66%	3.74	53%	58%	82%	0.78	0.78	0.79	56%	0.49	0.48	0.50
Existence Of God	852	76%	4.16	51%	56%	75%	0.73	0.70	0.76	52%	0.49	0.47	0.51
Firefox v. IE	233	38%	1.27	15%	79%	76%	0.47	0.44	0.49	72%	0.33	0.34	0.33
Gay Marriage	560	56%	2.01	28%	65%	84%	0.77	0.74	0.81	60%	0.43	0.43	0.44
Gun Control	135	59%	2.08	45%	63%	37%	0.24	0.21	0.27	53%	0.24	0.30	0.20
Healthcare	112	79%	3.11	53%	55%	73%	0.71	0.69	0.72	60%	0.49	0.56	0.44
Immigration	78	58%	1.95	33%	54%	33%	0.21	0.23	0.19	53%	0.39	0.48	0.33
Iphone v. Blackberry	25	44%	1.14	14%	67%	88%	0.80	0.86	0.75	71%	0.46	0.60	0.38
Israel v. Palestine	64	33%	3.37	53%	58%	85%	0.82	0.79	0.85	49%	0.48	0.42	0.56
Mac v. PC	126	37%	1.85	24%	52%	19%	0.18	0.17	0.18	46%	0.46	0.45	0.48
Marijuana legalization	229	45%	1.52	25%	71%	73%	0.56	0.52	0.60	63%	0.34	0.35	0.34
Star Wars vs. LOTR	102	44%	1.38	26%	53%	63%	0.62	0.60	0.65	63%	0.62	0.60	0.65
Superman v. Batman	146	30%	1.39	20%	54%	50%	0.40	0.44	0.37	56%	0.47	0.52	0.43

Table 2: Results. **KEY**: Number of posts on the topic (**Posts**). Percent of Posts linked by Rebuttal links (**Rebs**). Posts per author (**P/A**). Authors with more than one post (**A > 1P**). Majority Class Baseline (**MLE**).

tures with χ^2 feature selection; we use JRIP as the base classifier because margins are used by the automatic MaxCut graph orientation algorithm. Experiments with different learners (NB, SVM) did not yield significant differences from JRIP. The results show that, in general, representing dialogic information in terms of a network of relations between posts yields very large improvements. In the few topics where performance is worse (Death Penalty, Gun Control, Mac vs. PC, Superman vs. Batman), the MaxCut graph gets oriented to the stance sides the wrong way, so that the cut actually groups the posts correctly into sides, but then assigns them to the wrong side. For Maxcut, as expected, there are significant correlations between the % of Rebuttals in a debate and Precision (R = .16) and Recall (R= .22), as well as between Posts/Author and Precision (R = .25) and Recall (R = .43). This clearly indicates that the degree of dialogic behavior (the graph topology) has a strong influence on results per topic. These results would be even stronger if all MaxCut graphs were oriented correctly.

(Somasundaran and Wiebe, 2010) present an unsupervised approach using ICA to stance classification, showing that identifying argumentation structure improves performance, with a best performance averaging 64% accuracy over all topics, but as high as 70% for some topics. Other research classifies the speaker's side in a corpus of congressional floor debates (Thomas et al., 2006; Bansal et al., 2008; Balahur et al., 2009; Burfoot et al., 2011). Thomas et al (2006) achieved accuracies of 71.3% by using speaker agreement information in the graph-based MinCut/Maxflow algorithm, as compared to accuracies around 70% via an an SVM classifier operating on content alone. The best performance to date on this corpus achieves accuracies around 82% for different graph-based approaches as compared to 76% accuracy for content only classification (Burfoot et al., 2011). Other work applies MaxCut to the reply structure of company discussion forums, showing that rules for identifying agreement (Murakami and Raymond, 2010), defined on the textual content of the post yield performance improvements over using reply structures alone (Malouf and Mullen, 2008; Agrawal et al., 2003)

Our results are not strictly comparable since we use a different corpus with different properties, but to our knowledge this is the first application of MaxCut to stance classification that shows large performance improvements from modeling dialogic relations. In future work, we plan to explore whether deeper linguistic features can yield large improvements in both the base classifier and in MaxCut results, and to explore better ways of automatically orienting the MaxCut graph to stance side. We also hope to develop much better context features and to make even more use of dialogue structure.

References

R. Agrawal, S. Rajagopalan, R. Srikant, and Y. Xu. 2003. Mining newsgroups using networks arising from social behavior. In *Proceedings of the 12th international conference on World Wide Web*, pages 529–535. ACM.

A. Balahur, Z. Kozareva, and A. Montoyo. 2009. Determining the polarity and source of opinions expressed in political debates. *Computational Linguistics and Intelligent Text Processing*, pages 468–480.

M. Bansal, C. Cardie, and L. Lee. 2008. The power of negative thinking: Exploiting label disagreement in the min-cut classification framework. *Proceedings of COLING: Companion volume: Posters*, pages 13–16.

O. Biran and O. Rambow. 2011. Identifying justifications in written dialogs. In *2011 Fifth IEEE International Conference on Semantic Computing (ICSC)*, pages 162–168. IEEE.

C. Burfoot, S. Bird, and T. Baldwin. 2011. Collective classification of congressional floor-debate transcripts. In *Proceedings of the 49th Annual Meeting of the Association for Computational Linguistics: Human Language Technologies-Volume 1*, pages 1506–1515. Association for Computational Linguistics.

S. Chaiken. 1980. Heuristic versus systematic information processing and the use of source versus message cues in persuasion. *Journal of personality and social psychology*, 39(5):752.

Robert B. Cialdini. 2000. *Influence: Science and Practice (4th Edition)*. Allyn & Bacon.

M.F. Davies. 1998. Dogmatism and belief formation: Output interference in the processing of supporting and contradictory cognitions. *Journal of personality and social psychology*, 75(2):456.

R. Malouf and T. Mullen. 2008. Taking sides: User classification for informal online political discourse. *Internet Research*, 18(2):177–190.

A. Murakami and R. Raymond. 2010. Support or Oppose? Classifying Positions in Online Debates from Reply Activities and Opinion Expressions. In *Proceedings of the 23rd International Conference on Computational Linguistics: Posters*, pages 869–875. Association for Computational Linguistics.

J. W. Pennebaker, L. E. Francis, and R. J. Booth, 2001. *LIWC: Linguistic Inquiry and Word Count*.

Richard E. Petty and John T. Cacioppo. 1988. The effects of involvement on responses to argument quantity and quality: Central and peripheral routes to persuasion. *Journal of Personality and Social Psychology*, 46(1):69–81.

R.E. Petty, J.T. Cacioppo, and R. Goldman. 1981. Personal involvement as a determinant of argument-based persuasion. *Journal of Personality and Social Psychology*, 41(5):847.

S. Somasundaran and J. Wiebe. 2009. Recognizing stances in online debates. In *Proceedings of the Joint Conference of the 47th Annual Meeting of the ACL and the 4th International Joint Conference on Natural Language Processing of the AFNLP: Volume 1-Volume 1*, pages 226–234. Association for Computational Linguistics.

S. Somasundaran and J. Wiebe. 2010. Recognizing stances in ideological on-line debates. In *Proceedings of the NAACL HLT 2010 Workshop on Computational Approaches to Analysis and Generation of Emotion in Text*, pages 116–124. Association for Computational Linguistics.

M. Thomas, B. Pang, and L. Lee. 2006. Get out the vote: Determining support or opposition from Congressional floor-debate transcripts. In *Proceedings of the 2006 conference on empirical methods in natural language processing*, pages 327–335. Association for Computational Linguistics.

M. Walker, P. Anand, J. Fox Tree, R. Abbott, and J. King. 2012. A corpus for research on deliberation and debate. In *Proceedings of the Eighth International Conference on Language Resources and Evaluation, LREC 2012, Istanbul, Turkey, May 23-25, 2012*.

Y.C. Wang and C.P. Rosé. 2010. Making conversational structure explicit: identification of initiation-response pairs within online discussions. In *Human Language Technologies: The 2010 Annual Conference of the North American Chapter of the Association for Computational Linguistics*, pages 673–676. Association for Computational Linguistics.

A. Yessenalina, Y. Yue, and C. Cardie. 2010. Multi-level structured models for document-level sentiment classification. In *Proceedings of the 2010 Conference on Empirical Methods in Natural Language Processing*, pages 1046–1056. Association for Computational Linguistics.

Context-Enhanced Citation Sentiment Detection

Awais Athar
University of Cambridge
Computer Laboratory
15 JJ Thomson Avenue
Cambridge, CB3 0FD, U.K.
awais.athar@cl.cam.ac.uk

Simone Teufel
University of Cambridge
Computer Laboratory
15 JJ Thomson Avenue
Cambridge, CB3 0FD, U.K.
simone.teufel@cl.cam.ac.uk

Abstract

Sentiment analysis of citations in scientific papers and articles is a new and interesting problem which can open up many exciting new applications in bibliographic search and bibliometrics. Current work on citation sentiment detection focuses on only the citation sentence. In this paper, we address the problem of context-enhanced citation sentiment detection. We present a new citation sentiment corpus which has been annotated to take the dominant sentiment in the entire citation context into account. We believe that this gold standard is closer to the truth than annotation that looks only at the citation sentence itself. We then explore the effect of context windows of different lengths on the performance of a state-of-the-art citation sentiment detection system when using this context-enhanced gold standard definition.

1 Introduction

Sentiment analysis of citations in scientific papers and articles is a new and interesting problem. It can open up many exciting new applications in bibliographic search and in bibliometrics, i.e., the automatic evaluation of the influence and impact of individuals and journals via citations. Automatic detection of citation sentiment can also be used as a first step to scientific summarisation (Abu-Jbara and Radev, 2011). Alternatively, it can help researchers during search, e.g., by identifying problems with a particular approach, or by helping to recognise unaddressed issues and possible gaps in the current research.

However, there is a problem with the expression of sentiment in scientific text. Conventionally, the writing style in scientific writing is meant to be objective. Any personal bias by authors has to be hedged (Hyland, 1995). Negative sentiment is politically particularly dangerous (Ziman, 1968), and some authors have documented the strategy of prefacing the intended criticism by slightly disingenuous praise (MacRoberts and MacRoberts, 1984). This makes the problem of identifying such opinions particularly challenging. This non-local expression of sentiment has been observed in other genres as well (Wilson et al., 2009; Polanyi and Zaenen, 2006).

> The work of Och et al (2004) is perhaps the best-known study of new features and their impact on translation quality. However, it had a few shortcomings. First, it used the features for reranking *n*-best lists of translations, rather than for decoding or forest reranking (Huang, 2008). Second, it attempted to incorporate syntax by applying off-the-shelf part-of-speech taggers and parsers to MT output, a task these tools were never designed for. By contrast, we incorporate features directly into hierarchical and syntax-based decoders.
>
> A third difficulty with Och et al.'s study was that it used MERT, which is not an ideal vehicle for feature exploration because it is observed not to perform well with large feature sets. Others have in-

Figure 1: Example of anaphora in citations

A typical case is illustrated in Figure 1. While the first sentence praises some aspects of the cited paper, the remaining sentences list its shortcomings. It is clear that criticism is the intended sentiment, but if we define our gold standard only by looking at the citation sentence, we lose a significant amount of sentiment hidden in the text. Given that most citations are neutral (Spiegel-Rosing, 1977; Teufel et al., 2006), this makes it ever more important to recover what explicit sentiment there is from the context of the citation.

However, the dominant assumption in current citation identification methods (Ritchie et al., 2008; Radev et al., 2009) is that the sentiment present in the citation sentence represents the true sentiment of the author towards the cited paper. This is due to the difficulty of determining the relevant context, whereas it is substantially easier to identify the citation sentence. In our example above, however, such an approach would lead to the wrong prediction of praise or neutral sentiment.

In this paper, we address the problem of context-enhanced citation sentiment detection. We present a new citation sentiment corpus where each citation has been annotated according to the dominant sentiment in the corresponding citation context. We claim that this corpus is closer to the truth than annotation that considers only the citation sentence itself. We show that it increases citation sentiment coverage, particularly for negative sentiment. Using this gold standard, we explore the effect of assuming context windows of different but fixed lengths on the performance of a state-of-the-art citation sentiment detection system where the sentiment of citation is considered in the entire context of the citation and more than one single sentiment can be assigned. Previous approaches neither detect citation sentiment and context simultaneously nor use as large a corpus as we do.

2 Corpus Construction

We chose the dataset used by Athar (2011) comprising 310 papers taken from the ACL Anthology (Bird et al., 2008). The citation summary data from the ACL Anthology Network[1] (Radev et al., 2009) was used. This dataset is rather large (8736 citations) and since manual annotation of context for each citation is a time consuming task, a subset of 20 papers were selected corresponding to approximately 20% of the original dataset.

[1] http://www.aclweb.org

We selected a four-class scheme for annotation. Every sentence that is in a window of 4 sentences of the citation and does not contain any direct or indirect mention of the citation was labelled as being excluded (x). The window length was motivated by recent research (Qazvinian and Radev, 2010) which shows the best score for a four-sentence boundary when detecting non-explicit citation. The rest of the sentences were marked either positive (p), negative (n) or objective/neutral (o).

A total of 1,741 citations were annotated. Although this annotation was performed by the first author only, we know from previous work that similar styles of annotation can achieve acceptable inter-annotator agreement (Teufel et al., 2006). An example annotation for Smadja (1993) is given in Figure 2, where the first column shows the line number and the second one shows the class label.

31	x	Church and Hanks (Church and Hanks 1990) employed mutual information to extract both adjacent and distant bi-grams that tend to co-occur within a fixed-size window.
32	x	But the method did not extend to extract n-grams.
33	o	**Smadja (Smadja 1993) proposed a statistical model by measuring the spread of the distribution of cooccurring pairs of words with higher strength.**
34	p	This method successfully extracted both adjacent and distant bi-grams and n-grams.
35	n	However, the method failed to extract bi-grams with lower frequency.

Figure 2: Example annotation of a citation context.

To compare our work with Athar (2011), we also applied a three-class annotation scheme. In this method of annotation, we merge the citation context into a single sentence. Since the context introduces more than one sentiment per citation, we marked the citation sentiment with the last sentiment mentioned in the context window as this is pragmatically most likely to be the real intention (MacRoberts and MacRoberts, 1984).

As is evident from Table 1, including the 4 sentence window around the citation more than doubles the instances of subjective sentiment, and in the case of *negative* sentiment, this proportion rises to 3. In light of the overall sparsity of detectable citation sentiment in a paper, and of the envisaged applications, this is a very positive result. The reason for this effect is most likely "sweetened criticism" – authors' strategic behaviour of softening the effect of criticism among their peers (Hornsey et al., 2008).

	Without Context	With Context
o	87%	73%
n	5%	17%
p	8%	11%

Table 1: Distribution of classes.

3 Experiments and Results

We represent each citation as a feature set in a Support Vector Machine (SVM) (Cortes and Vapnik, 1995) framework and use n-grams of length 1 to 3 as well as dependency triplets as features. The dependency triplets are constructed by merging the relation, governor and dependent in a single string, for instance, the relation *nsubj(failed, method)* is represented as `nsubj_failed_method`. This setup has been shown to produce good results earlier as well (Pang et al., 2002; Athar, 2011).

The first set of experiments focuses on simultaneous detection of sentiment and context sentences. For this purpose, we use the four-class annotated corpus described earlier. While the original annotations were performed for a window of length 4, we also experiment with asymmetrical windows of l sentences preceding the citation and r sentences succeeding it. The detailed results are given in Table 2.

l	r	x	o	n	p	F_{macro}	F_{micro}
0	**0**	-	**1509**	**86**	**146**	**0.768**	**0.932**
1	1	2823	1982	216	200	0.737	0.820
2	2	5984	2214	273	218	0.709	0.851
3	3	9170	2425	318	234	0.672	0.875
4	4	12385	2605	352	252	0.680	0.892
0	4	5963	2171	322	215	0.712	0.853
0	3	4380	2070	293	201	0.702	0.832
0	2	2817	1945	258	193	0.701	0.801
0	1	1280	1812	206	182	0.717	0.777

Table 2: Results for joint context and sentiment detection.

Because of the skewed class distribution, we use both the F_{macro} and F_{micro} scores with 10-fold cross-validation. The baseline score, shown in bold, is obtained with no context window and is comparable to the results reported by Athar (2011). However, we can observe that the F scores decrease as more context is introduced. This may be attributed to the increase in the vocabulary size of the n-grams and a consequent reduction in the discriminating power of the decision boundaries. These results show that the task of jointly detecting sentiment and context is a hard problem.

For our second set of experiments, we use the three-class annotation scheme. We merge the text of the sentences in the context windows as well as their dependency triplets to obtain the features. The results are reported in Table 3 with best results in bold. Although these results are not better than the context-less baseline, the reason might be data sparsity since existing work on citation sentiment analysis uses more data (Athar, 2011).

l	r	F_{macro}	F_{micro}
1	1	0.638	0.827
2	2	0.620	0.793
3	3	0.629	0.786
4	4	0.628	0.771
0	4	0.643	0.796
0	3	0.658	0.816
0	2	0.642	0.824
0	1	**0.731**	**0.871**

Table 3: Results using different context windows.

4 Related Work

While different schemes have been proposed for annotating citations according to their function (Spiegel-Rosing, 1977; Nanba and Okumura, 1999; Garzone and Mercer, 2000), the only recent work on citation sentiment detection using a relatively large corpus is by Athar (2011). However, this work does not handle citation context. Piao et al. (2007) proposed a system to attach sentiment information to the citation links between biomedical papers by using existing semantic lexical resources.

A common approach for sentiment detection is to use a labelled lexicon to score sentences (Hatzivassiloglou and McKeown, 1997; Turney, 2002; Yu and Hatzivassiloglou, 2003). However, such approaches have been found to be highly topic dependent (Engström, 2004; Gamon and Aue, 2005; Blitzer et al., 2007).

Teufel et al. (2006) worked on a 2,829 sentence citation corpus using a 12-class classification scheme. Although they used context in their annotation, their focus was on determining the author's reason for citing a given paper. This task differs from citation sentiment, which is in a sense a "lower level" of analysis.

For implicit citation extraction, Kaplan et al. (2009) explore co-reference chains for citation extraction using a combination of co-reference resolution techniques. However, their corpus consists of only 94 sentences of citations to 4 papers which is likely to be too small to be representative. The most relevant work is by Qazvinian and Radev (2010) who extract only the non-explicit citations for a given paper. They model each sentence as a node in a graph and experiment with various window boundaries to create edges between neighbouring nodes. However, their dataset consists of only 10 papers and their annotation scheme differs from our four-class annotation as they do not deal with any sentiment.

5 Conclusion

In this paper, we focus on automatic detection of citation sentiment using the citation context. We present a new corpus and show that ignoring the citation context would result in loss of a lot of sentiment, specially criticism towards the cited paper. We also report the results of the state-of-the-art citation sentiment detection systems on this corpus when using this context-enhanced gold standard definition.

Future work directions may include improving the detection algorithms by filtering the context sentences more intelligently. For this purpose, existing work on coreference resolution (Lee et al., 2011) may prove to be useful. Context features may also be used for first filtering citations which have been mentioned only in passing, and then applying context based sentiment classification to the remaining significant citations.

References

A. Abu-Jbara and D. Radev. 2011. Coherent citation-based summarization of scientific papers. In *Proc. of ACL*.

A. Athar. 2011. Sentiment analysis of citations using sentence structure-based features. In *Proc of ACL*, page 81.

S. Bird, R. Dale, B.J. Dorr, B. Gibson, M.T. Joseph, M.Y. Kan, D. Lee, B. Powley, D.R. Radev, and Y.F. Tan. 2008. The acl anthology reference corpus: A reference dataset for bibliographic research in computational linguistics. In *Proc. of LREC*.

J. Blitzer, M. Dredze, and F. Pereira. 2007. Biographies, bollywood, boom-boxes and blenders: Domain adaptation for sentiment classification. In *Proc. of ACL*, number 1.

C. Cortes and V. Vapnik. 1995. Support-vector networks. *Machine learning*, 20(3):273–297.

C. Engström. 2004. Topic dependence in sentiment classification. University of Cambridge.

M. Gamon and A. Aue. 2005. Automatic identification of sentiment vocabulary: exploiting low association with known sentiment terms. In *Proc. of the ACL*.

M. Garzone and R. Mercer. 2000. Towards an automated citation classifier. *Advances in Artificial Intelligence*.

V. Hatzivassiloglou and K.R. McKeown. 1997. Predicting the semantic orientation of adjectives. In *Proc. of ACL*, page 181.

M.J. Hornsey, E. Robson, J. Smith, S. Esposo, and R.M. Sutton. 2008. Sugaring the pill: Assessing rhetorical strategies designed to minimize defensive reactions to group criticism. *Human Communication Research*, 34(1):70–98.

K. Hyland. 1995. The Author in the Text: Hedging Scientific Writing. *Hong Kong papers in linguistics and language teaching*, 18:11.

D. Kaplan, R. Iida, and T. Tokunaga. 2009. Automatic extraction of citation contexts for research paper summarization: A coreference-chain based approach. In *Proc. of the 2009 Workshop on Text and Citation Analysis for Scholarly Digital Libraries*.

H. Lee, Y. Peirsman, A. Chang, N. Chambers, M. Surdeanu, and D. Jurafsky. 2011. Stanford's multi-pass sieve coreference resolution system at the conll-2011 shared task. *ACL HLT 2011*.

M.H. MacRoberts and B.R. MacRoberts. 1984. The negational reference: Or the art of dissembling. *Social Studies of Science*, 14(1):91–94.

H. Nanba and M. Okumura. 1999. Towards multi-paper summarization using reference information. In *IJCAI*, volume 16, pages 926–931. Citeseer.

B. Pang, L. Lee, and S. Vaithyanathan. 2002. Thumbs up?: sentiment classification using machine learning techniques. In *Proc. of EMNLP*.

S. Piao, S. Ananiadou, Y. Tsuruoka, Y. Sasaki, and J. McNaught. 2007. Mining opinion polarity relations of citations. In *International Workshop on Computational Semantics (IWCS)*. Citeseer.

L. Polanyi and A. Zaenen. 2006. Contextual valence shifters. *Computing attitude and affect in text: Theory and applications*, pages 1–10.

V. Qazvinian and D.R. Radev. 2010. Identifying non-explicit citing sentences for citation-based summarization. In *Proc. of ACL*.

D.R. Radev, M.T. Joseph, B. Gibson, and P. Muthukrishnan. 2009. A Bibliometric and Network Analysis of the field of Computational Linguistics. *Journal of the American Soc. for Info. Sci. and Tech.*

A. Ritchie, S. Robertson, and S. Teufel. 2008. Comparing citation contexts for information retrieval. In *Proc. of ACM conference on Information and knowledge management*, pages 213–222. ACM.

I. Spiegel-Rosing. 1977. Science studies: Bibliometric and content analysis. *Social Studies of Science*.

S. Teufel, A. Siddharthan, and D. Tidhar. 2006. Automatic classification of citation function. In *Proc. of EMNLP*, pages 103–110.

P.D. Turney. 2002. Thumbs up or thumbs down?: semantic orientation applied to unsupervised classification of reviews. In *Proc. of ACL*.

T. Wilson, J. Wiebe, and P. Hoffmann. 2009. Recognizing contextual polarity: an exploration of features for phrase-level sentiment analysis. *Comp. Ling.*, 35(3):399–433.

H. Yu and V. Hatzivassiloglou. 2003. Towards answering opinion questions: Separating facts from opinions and identifying the polarity of opinion sentences. In *Proc. of EMNLP*, page 136.

J.M. Ziman. 1968. *Public Knowledge: An essay concerning the social dimension of science*. Cambridge Univ. Press, College Station, Texas.

Predicting Responses to Microblog Posts

Yoav Artzi *
Computer Science & Engineering
University of Washington
Seattle, WA, USA
yoav@cs.washington.edu

Patrick Pantel, Michael Gamon
Microsoft Research
One Microsoft Way
Redmond, WA, USA
{ppantel,mgamon}@microsoft.com

Abstract

Microblogging networks serve as vehicles for reaching and influencing users. Predicting whether a message will elicit a user response opens the possibility of maximizing the virality, reach and effectiveness of messages and ad campaigns on these networks. We propose a discriminative model for predicting the likelihood of a response or a retweet on the Twitter network. The approach uses features derived from various sources, such as the language used in the tweet, the user's social network and history. The feature design process leverages aggregate statistics over the entire social network to balance sparsity and informativeness. We use real-world tweets to train models and empirically show that they are capable of generating accurate predictions for a large number of tweets.

1 Introduction

Microblogging networks are increasingly evolving into broadcasting networks with strong social aspects. The most popular network today, Twitter, reported routing 200 million tweets (status posts) per day in mid-2011. As the network is increasingly used as a channel for reaching out and marketing to its users, content generators aim to maximize the impact of their messages, an inherently challenging task. However, unlike for conventionally produced news, Twitter's public network allows one to observe how messages are reaching and influencing users. One such direct measure of impact are message responses.

In this work, we describe methods to predict if a given tweet will elicit a response. Twitter provides two methods to respond to messages: replies and retweets (re-posting of a message to one's followers). Responses thus serve both as a measure of distribution and as a way to increase it. Being able to predict responses is valuable for any content generator, including advertisers and celebrities, who use Twitter to increase their exposure and maintain their brand. Furthermore, this prediction ability can be used for ranking, allowing the creation of better optimized news feeds.

To predict if a tweet will receive a response prior to its posting we use features of the individual tweet together with features aggregated over the entire social network. These features, in combination with historical activity, are used to train a prediction model.

2 Related Work

The public nature of Twitter and the unique characteristics of its content have made it an attractive research topic over recent years. Related work can be divided into several types:

Twitter Demographics One of the most fertile avenues of research is modeling users and their interactions on Twitter. An extensive line of work characterizes users (Pear Analytics, 2009) and quantifies user influence (Cha et al., 2010; Romero et al., 2011; Wu et al., 2011; Bakshy et al., 2011). Popescu and Jain (2011) explored how businesses use Twitter to connect with their customer base. Popescu and Pennacchiotti (2011) and Qu et al. (2011) investigated

* This work was conducted at Microsoft Research.

how users react to events on social media. There also has been extensive work on modeling conversational interactions on Twitter (Honeycutt and Herring, 2009; Boyd et al., 2010; Ritter et al., 2010; Danescu-Niculescu-Mizil et al., 2011). Our work builds on these findings to predict response behavior on a large scale.

Mining Twitter Social media has been used to detect events (Sakaki et al., 2010; Popescu and Pennacchiotti, 2010; Popescu et al., 2011), and even predict their outcomes (Asur and Huberman, 2010; Culotta, 2010). Similarly to this line of work, we mine the social network for event prediction. In contrast, our focus is on predicting events within the network.

Response Prediction There has been significant work addressing the task of response prediction in news articles (Tsagkias et al., 2009; Tsagkias et al., 2010) and blogs (Yano et al., 2009; Yano and Smith, 2010; Balasubramanyan et al., 2011). The task of predicting responses in social networks has been investigated previously: Hong et al. (2011) focused on predicting responses for highly popular items, Rowe et al. (2011) targeted the prediction of conversations and their length and Suh et al. (2010) predicted retweets. In contrast, our work targets tweets regardless of their popularity and attempts to predict both replies and retweets. Furthermore, we present a scalable method to use linguistic lexical features in discriminative models by leveraging global network statistics. A related task to ours is that of response generation, as explored by Ritter et al. (2011). Our work complements their approach by allowing to detect when the generation of a response is appropriate. Lastly, the task of predicting the spread of hashtags in microblogging networks (Tsur and Rappoport, 2012) is also closely related to our work and both approaches supplement each other as measures of impact.

Ranking in News Feeds Different approaches were suggested for ranking items in social media (Das Sarma et al., 2010; Lakkaraju et al., 2011). Our work provides an important signal, which can be incorporated into any ranking approach.

3 Response Prediction on Twitter

Our goal is to learn a function f that maps a tweet x to a binary value $y \in \{0, 1\}$, where y indicates if x will receive a response. In this work we make no distinction between different kinds of responses.

In addition to x, we assume access to a social network $\mathcal{S}$, which we view as a directed graph $\langle U, E\rangle$. The set of vertices U represents the set of users. For each $u', u'' \in U$, $\langle u', u''\rangle \in E$ if and only if there exists a *following* relationship from u' to u''.

For the purpose of defining features we denote x_t as the text of the tweet x and $x_u \in U$ the user who posted x. For training we assume access to a set of n labeled examples $\{\langle x_i, y_i\rangle : i = 1 \ldots n\}$, where the label indicates whether the tweet has received a response or not.

3.1 Features

For prediction we represent a given tweet x using six feature families:

Historical Features Historical behavior is often strong evidence of future trends. To account for this information, we compute the following features: ratio of tweets by x_u that received a reply, ratio of tweets by x_u that were retweeted and ratio of tweets by x_u that received both a reply and retweet.

Social Features The immediate audience of a user x_u is his followers. Therefore, incorporating social features into our model is likely to contribute to its prediction ability. For a user $x_u \in U$ we include features for the number of followers (indegree in $\mathcal{S}$), the number of users x_u follows (outdegree in $\mathcal{S}$) and the ratio between the two.

Aggregate Lexical Features To detect lexical items that trigger certain response behavior we define features for all bigrams and hashtags in our set of tweets. To avoid sparsity and maintain a manageable feature space we compress the features using the labels: for each lexical item l we define R_l to be the set of tweets that include l and received a response, and N_l to be the set of tweets that contain l and received no response. We then define the integer n to be the rounding of $\frac{|R_l|}{|N_l|}$ to the nearest integer. For each such integer we define a feature, which we increase by 1 when the lexical item l is present in x_t.

We use this process separately for bigrams and hashtags, creating separate sets of aggregate features.

Local Content Features We introduce 45 features to capture how the content of x_t influences response behavior, including features such as the number of stop words and the percentage of English words. In addition we include features specific to Twitter, such as the number of hash tags and user references.

Posting Features Past analysis of Twitter showed that posting time influences response potential (Pear Analytics, 2009). To examine temporal influences, we include features to account for the user's local time and day of the week when x was created.

Sentiment Features To measure how sentiment influences response behavior we define features that count the number of positive and negative sentiment words in x_t. To detect sentiment words we use a proprietary Microsoft lexicon of 7K positive and negative terms.

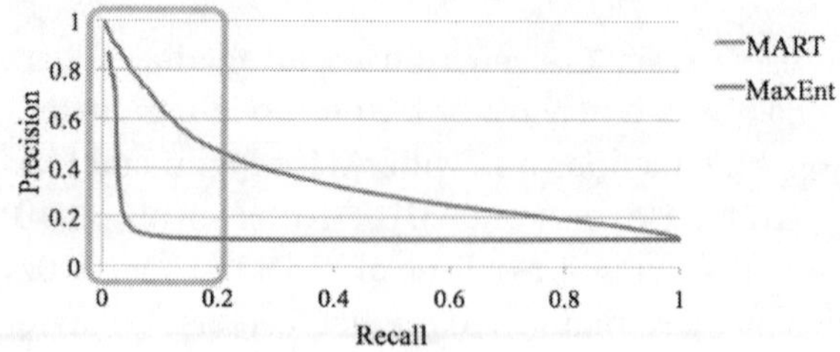

Figure 1: Precision-recall curves for predicting that a tweet will get a response. The marked area highlights the area of the curve we focus on in our evaluation.

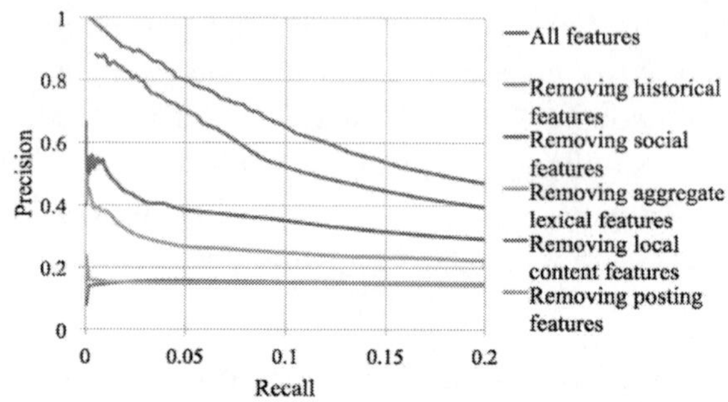

Figure 2: Precision-recall curves with increasing number of features removed for the marked area in Figure 1. For each curve we removed one additional feature set from the one above it.

4 Evaluation

4.1 Learning Algorithm

We experimented with two different learning algorithms: Multiple Additive Regression-Trees (MART) (Wu et al., 2008) and a maximum entropy classifier (Berger et al., 1996). Both provide fast classification, a natural requirement for large-scale real-time tasks.

4.2 Dataset

In our evaluation we focus on English tweets only. Since we use local posting time in our features, we filtered users whose profile did not contain location information. To collect Tweeter messages we used the entire public feed of Twitter (often referred to as the Twitter Firehose). We randomly sampled 943K tweets from one week of data. We allowed an extra week for responses, giving a response window of two weeks. The majority of tweets in our set (90%) received no response. We used 750K tweets for training and 188K for evaluation. A separate data set served as a development set. For the computation of aggregate lexical features we used 186M tweets from the same week, resulting in 14M bigrams and 400K hash tags. To compute historical features, we sampled 2B tweets from the previous three months.

4.3 Results

Our evaluation focuses on precision-recall curves for predicting that a given tweet will get a response. The curves were generated by varying the confidence measure threshold, which both classifiers provided. As can be seen in Figure 1, MART outperforms the maximum entropy model. We can also see that it is hard to predict response behavior for most tweets, but for a large subset we can provide a relatively accurate prediction (highlighted in Figure 1). The rest of our analysis focuses on this subset and on results based on MART.

To better understand the contribution of each feature set, we removed features in a greedy manner. After learning a model and testing it, we removed the feature family that was overall most highly ranked by MART (i.e., was used in high-level splits in the decision trees) and learned a new model. Figure 2 shows how removing feature sets degrades prediction performance. Removing historical features lowers the model's prediction abilities, although prediction quality remains relatively high. Removing social features creates a bigger drop in performance. Lastly, removing aggregate lexical features and local content features further decreases performance. At this point, removing posting time features is not influential. Following the removal of posting time features, the model includes only sentiment features.

5 Discussion and Conclusion

The first trend seen by removing features is that local content matters less, or at least is more complex to capture and use for response prediction. Despite the influence of chronological trends on posting behavior on Twitter (Pear Analytics, 2009), we were unable to show influence of posting time on response prediction. Historical features were the most prominent in our experiments. Second were social features, showing that developing one's network is critical for impact. The third most prominent set of features, aggregate lexical features, shows that users are sensitive to certain expressions and terms that tend to trigger responses.

The natural path for future work is to improve performance using new features. These may include clique-specific language features, more properties of the user's social network, mentions of named entities and topics of tweets. Another direction is to distinguish between replies and retweets and to predict the number of responses and the length of conversations that a tweet may generate. There is also potential in learning models for the prediction of other measures of impact, such as hashtag adoption and inclusion in "favorites" lists.

Acknowledgments

We would like to thank Alan Ritter, Bill Dolan, Chris Brocket and Luke Zettlemoyer for their suggestions and comments. We wish to thank Chris Quirk and Qiang Wu for providing us with access to their learning software. Thanks to the reviewers for the helpful comments.

References

S. Asur and B.A. Huberman. 2010. Predicting the future with social media. In *Proceedings of the International Conference on Web Intelligence and Intelligent Agent Technology*.

E. Bakshy, J. M. Hofman, W. A. Mason, and D. J. Watts. 2011. Everyone's an influencer: quantifying influence on twitter. In *Peoceedings of the ACM International Conference on Web Search and Data Mining*.

R. Balasubramanyan, W.W. Cohen, D. Pierce, and D.P. Redlawsk. 2011. What pushes their buttons? predicting comment polarity from the content of political blog posts. In *Proceedings of the Workshop on Language in Social Media*.

Adam L. Berger, Vincent J. Della Pietra, and Stephen A. Della Pietra. 1996. A maximum entropy approach to natural language processing. *Computational Linguistics*.

D. Boyd, S. Golder, and G. Lotan. 2010. Tweet, tweet, retweet: Conversational aspects of retweeting on twitter. In *Proceedings of the International Conference on System Sciences*.

M. Cha, H. Haddadi, F. Benevenuto, and K.P. Gummadi. 2010. Measuring user influence in twitter: The million follower fallacy. In *Proceedings of the International AAAI Conference on Weblogs and Social Media*.

A. Culotta. 2010. Towards detecting influenza epidemics by analyzing twitter messages. In *Proceedings of the Workshop on Social Media Analytics*.

C. Danescu-Niculescu-Mizil, M. Gamon, and S. Dumais. 2011. Mark my words!: linguistic style accommodation in social media. In *Proceedings of the International Conference on World Wide Web*.

A. Das Sarma, A. Das Sarma, S. Gollapudi, and R. Panigrahy. 2010. Ranking mechanisms in twitter-like forums. In *Proceedings of the ACM International Conference on Web Search and Data Mining*.

C. Honeycutt and S.C. Herring. 2009. Beyond microblogging: Conversation and collaboration via twitter. In *Proceedings of the International Conference on System Sciences*.

L. Hong, O. Dan, and B. D. Davison. 2011. Predicting popular messages in twitter. In *Proceedings of the International Conference on World Wide Web*.

H. Lakkaraju, A. Rai, and S. Merugu. 2011. Smart news feeds for social networks using scalable joint latent factor models. In *Proceedings of the International Conference on World Wide Web*.

Pear Analytics. 2009. Twitter study.

A.M. Popescu and A. Jain. 2011. Understanding the functions of business accounts on twitter. In *Proceedings of the International Conference on World Wide Web*.

A.M. Popescu and M. Pennacchiotti. 2010. Detecting controversial events from twitter. In *Proceedings of the International Conference on Information and Knowledge Management*.

A.M. Popescu and M. Pennacchiotti. 2011. Dancing with the stars, nba games, politics: An exploration of twitter users response to events. In *Proceedings of the*

International AAAI Conference on Weblogs and Social Media.

A.M. Popescu, M. Pennacchiotti, and D. Paranjpe. 2011. Extracting events and event descriptions from twitter. In *Proceedings of the International Conference on World Wide Web*.

Y. Qu, C. Huang, P. Zhang, and J. Zhang. 2011. Microblogging after a major disaster in china: a case study of the 2010 yushu earthquake. In *Proceedings of the ACM Conference on Computer Supported Cooperative Work*.

A. Ritter, C. Cherry, and B. Dolan. 2010. Unsupervised modeling of twitter conversations. In *Proceedings of the Annual Conference of the North American Chapter of the Association for Computational Linguistics*.

A. Ritter, C. Cherry, and B. Dolan. 2011. Data-driven response generation in social media. In *Proceedings of the Conference on Empirical Methods in Natural Language Processing*.

D. Romero, W. Galuba, S. Asur, and B. Huberman. 2011. Influence and passivity in social media. *Machine Learning and Knowledge Discovery in Databases*, pages 18–33.

M. Rowe, S. Angeletou, and H. Alani. 2011. Predicting discussions on the social semantic web. In *Proceedings of the Extended Semantic Web Conference*.

T. Sakaki, M. Okazaki, and Y. Matsuo. 2010. Earthquake shakes twitter users: real-time event detection by social sensors. In *Proceedings of the International Conference on World Wide Web*.

B. Suh, L. Hong, P. Pirolli, and E. H. Chi. 2010. Want to be retweeted? large scale analytics on factors impacting retweet in twitter network. In *Proceedings of the IEEE International Conference on Social Computing*.

M. Tsagkias, W. Weerkamp, and M. De Rijke. 2009. Predicting the volume of comments on online news stories. In *Proceedings of the ACM Conference on Information and Knowledge Management*.

M. Tsagkias, W. Weerkamp, and M. De Rijke. 2010. News comments: Exploring, modeling, and online prediction. *Advances in Information Retrieval*, pages 191–203.

O. Tsur and A. Rappoport. 2012. What's in a hashtag?: content based prediction of the spread of ideas in microblogging communities. In *Proceedings of the ACM International Conference on Web Search and Data Mining*.

Q. Wu, C.J.C. Burges, K.M. Svore, and J. Gao. 2008. Ranking, boosting, and model adaptation. *Tecnical Report, MSR-TR-2008-109*.

S. Wu, J.M. Hofman, W.A. Mason, and D.J. Watts. 2011. Who says what to whom on twitter. In *Proceedings of the International Conference on World Wide Web*.

T. Yano and N.A. Smith. 2010. Whats worthy of comment? content and comment volume in political blogs. *Proceedings of the International AAAI Conference on Weblogs and Social Media*.

T. Yano, W.W. Cohen, and N.A. Smith. 2009. Predicting response to political blog posts with topic models. In *Proceedings of the Annual Conference of the North American Chapter of the Association for Computational Linguistics*.

The Intelius Nickname Collection: Quantitative Analyses from Billions of Public Records

Vitor R. Carvalho, Yigit Kiran and Andrew Borthwick
Intelius Data Research
500 108th Avenue NE, Bellevue, WA 98004
{vcarvalho,ykiran,aborthwick}@intelius.com

Abstract

Although first names and nicknames in the United States have been well documented, there has been almost no quantitative analysis on the usage and association of these names amongst themselves. In this paper we introduce the *Intelius Nickname Collection*, a quantitative compilation of millions of name-nickname associations based on information gathered from billions of public records. To the best of our knowledge, this is the largest collection of its kind, making it a natural resource for tasks such as coreference resolution, record linkage, named entity recognition, people and expert search, information extraction, demographic and sociological studies, etc. The collection will be made freely available.

1 Introduction

Nicknames are descriptive, invented person names that are frequently used in addition or instead of the person's official name. Very often nicknames are truncated forms of the original name that can be used for convenience — for instance, 'Betsy' instead of 'Elizabeth'.

Previous studies on nicknames have mostly focused on their origins or common descriptions. The Oxford Dictionary of First Names (Hanks et al., 2007), for instance, presents a comprehensive description of origins and common uses of most nicknames in modern English. More quantitative explorations of the subject, such as the one provided by the US Social Security Office[1] tend to focus on baby name selection and on the relative popularity of most common first names.

Alias	Conditional Probability
Betty	4.51%
Beth	3.83%
Liz	3.34%
Elisabeth	0.95%
Betsy	0.92%

Table 1: Nickname Distribution Sample for "Elizabeth"

In this paper we present a quantitative study on nickname usage in the United States. Using billions of personal public records and a state-of-the-art large-scale record linkage system, we were able to generate a comprehensive dataset with millions of name-nickname associations and their relative strength. A small sample of this collection can be seen in Table 1, where the most frequent nicknames associated with the first name "Elizabeth" and their Conditional Alias Probabilities. We explain the derivation of these probabilities in detail in Section 3.3. This collection can provide valuable features and insights for applications as diverse as entity extraction, coreference resolution, people search, language modeling, and machine translation. It will be made freely available for download from the Linguistic Data Consortium.

[1]Popular Baby Names from Social Security Online: http://www.ssa.gov/OACT/babynames/

2 Prior Work

To the best of our knowledge, there are no comprehensive, empirically derived nickname databases currently made freely available for research purposes. (Bollacker, 2008) contains an extensive database of names and nicknames[2], with listings on over 13,000 given names, containing multiple "variations" for each name. However, this database makes no attempt to distinguish between common and less common variants and skips some very common nicknames. For instance, the entry for "William" lists "Wilmot" and "Wilton" as variants of William but does not list "Bill" or "Billy". (Meranda, 1998) provides a more useful database which appears to also be manually constructed. The database is in the form of Name1|Name2|"substitution likelihood", but the author states in the comments that the substitution likelihood is "mostly guesswork" and the data contains numerous coverage gaps. For instance, common nicknames such as "Jack", "Willy", and "Sally" are all missing.

3 Generating the Nickname Distribution

The nickname collection was derived from billions of public, commercial and web records that power a major commercial People Search Engine. The process described below associates all records belonging to a particular person into clusters, and from these clusters it constructs a final person profile that is used to derive name-alias associations. The entire process is briefly described below.

3.1 Data Collection and Cleaning

The process starts by collecting billions of personal records from three different sources of U.S. personal records. The first source is derived from US government records, such as marriage, divorce and death records. The second is derived from publicly available web profiles, such as professional and social network public profiles. The third type is derived from commercial sources, such as financial and property reports (e.g., information made public after buying a house).

After collection and categorization, all records go through a cleaning process that starts with the removal of bogus, junk and spam records. Then all records are normalized to an approximately common representation. Then finally, all major noise types and inconsistencies are addressed, such as empty/bogus fields, field duplication, outlier values and encoding issues. At this point, all records are ready for the Record Linkage process.

[2] http://www.freebase.com/view/base/givennames/given_name

3.2 Record Linkage Process

The Record Linkage process should link together all records belonging to the same real-world person. That is, this process should turn billions of input records into a few hundred million clusters of records (or profiles), where each cluster is uniquely associated with a real-world unique individual.

Our system follows the standard high-level structure of a record linkage pipeline (Elmagarmid et al., 2007) by being divided into four major components: 1) data cleaning 2) blocking 3) pair-wise linkage and 4) clustering. The data cleaning step was described above. The blocking step uses a new algorithm implemented in MapReduce (Dean et al., 2004) which groups records by shared properties to determine which pairs of records should be examined by the pairwise linker as potential duplicates. The linkage step assigns a score to pairs of records using a supervised pairwise-based machine learning model whose implementation is described in detail in (Sheng et al., 2011) and achieves precision in excess of 99.5% with recall in excess of 80%, as measured on a random set with tens of thousands of human labels. If a pair scores above a user-defined threshold, the records are presumed to represent the same person. The clustering step first combines record pairs into connected components and then further partitions each connected component to remove inconsistent pair-wise links. Hence at the end of the entire record linkage process, the system has partitioned the input records into disjoint sets called profiles, where each profile corresponds to a single person. While the task is very challeging (e.g., many people share common names such as "John Smith") and this process is far from perfect, it is working sufficiently well to power multiple products at Intelius, including a major people search engine.

3.3 Algorithm

We used the MapReduce framework (Dean et al., 2004) to accomodate operations over very large datasets. The main goal of this task is to preserve the relationship amongst different names inside a profile. The algorithm's pseudocode is illustrated in Figure 1.

Many different names can be listed under a profile, including the real name (e.g., the "official" or "legal" name), nicknames, diminutives, typos, etc. In the first phase of the algorithm, a mapper visits all profiles to reveal these names and outputs a <key, value>pair for each name token. The keys are the names, and the values are a list with all other names found in the profile. This is a safe approach since we do not attempt to determine whether a given token is an original name, a diminutive or a typo. Henceforth, we refer to the key as *Name* and the values as *Aliases*.

The reducer will merge all *alias* lists of a given *name*, and count, aggregate and filter them. Since the mapper function produces intermediate pairs with all different names seen inside a profile, reducing them will create a bi-directional relation between *names* and *aliases*, where one can search for all *aliases* of a *name* as well as the reverse. The reducer also estimates conditional probabilities of the *aliases*. The **Conditional Alias Probability (CAP)** of an alias defines the probability of an *alias* being used to denote a person with a given *name*. Specifically, It can be expressed as $CAP(alias_i|name_j) = \frac{count(alias_i \wedge name_j)}{count(name_j)}$, where the $count()$ operator returns the number of profiles satisfying its criteria.

Processing a large number of profiles creates a huge *alias* lists for each *name*. Even worse, most of the *aliases* in that list are typos or very unique nicknames that would not be considered a typical alias for the name. In order to help control this noise, we used the following parameters in the algorithm. ***Alias_Count_Minimum*** sets the minimum number of profiles that should have an *alias* for the alias to be included. ***Total_Count_Minimum*** determines whether we output the whole set of *name* and *aliases*. It is determined by computing the total number of occurrences of the *name*. ***CAP_Threshold*** forces the reducer to filter out *aliases* whose probability is below a threshold.

```
MAP(profile)
names := ∅
for name ∈ profile
    names := names ∪ name
for current_name ∈ names
    aliases := ∅
    for other_name ∈ names
        if current_name ≠ other_name
            aliases := aliases ∪ other_name
    EMIT(current_name, aliases)

REDUCE(key, values)
aliaslist := ∅
for record ∈ values
    if aliaslist.contains(record)
        INCREMENT(aliaslist[record])
    else
        aliaslist[record] := 1;
SORT-BY-COUNT(aliaslist)
COMPUTE-FREQUENCIES(aliaslist)
FILTER(aliaslist)
EMIT(key, aliaslist)
```

Figure 1: MapReduce Nickname Extractor algorithm

3.4 Analysis

The number of generated name-alias associations depends largely on the specific parameter set used in by the algorithm. While different applications may benefit from different parameters, many of our internal applications had success using the following set of parameters: $Total\_Count\_Minimum = 100$, $Alias\_Count\_Minimum = 10$, and $CAP\_Threshold = 0.1\%$. Using this parameter set, the process generated 331,237 name-alias pairs.

Table 2 shows CAP values for various name-alias pairs. As expected, notice that values of $CAP(X|Y)$ can be completely different from $CAP(Y|X)$, as in the case of "Monica" and "Monic". The collection also shows that completely unrelated names can be associated to a short alias, such as "Al". Notice also that very frequent typos, such as"Jefffrey", are also part of the collection. Finally, very common name abbreviations such as "Jas" for "James" are also part of the set as long as they are statistically relevant.

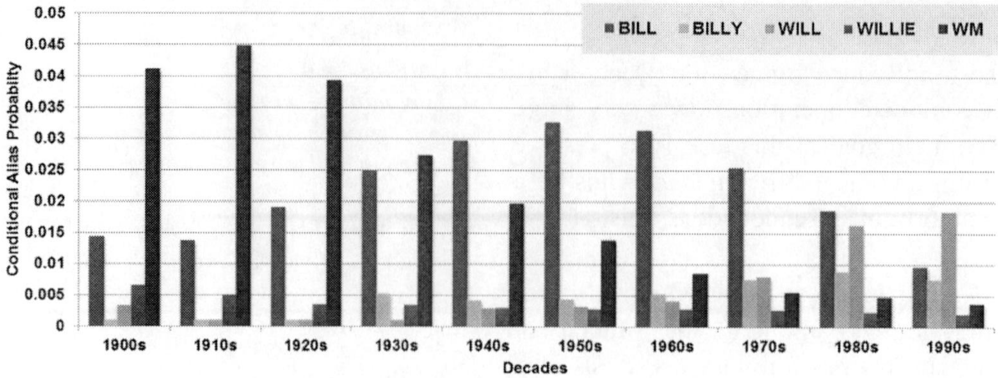

Figure 2: Conditional Probability of "William"'s Aliases over the Decades in the US.

X	Y	$CAP(Y\|X)$
Monica	Monika	1.00%
Monica	Monic	0.26%
Monic	Monica	38.76%
Al	Albert	14.83%
Al	Alfred	8.28%
Al	Alan	4.96%
Jas	James	71.94%
Jas	Jim	7.54%
James	Jas	2.09%
Jefffrey	Jeffrey	40.04%
Jefffrey	Jeff	25.69%

Table 2: Sample CAPs For Multiple Aliases.

3.5 Limitations and Future Explorations

It is important to keep in mind that the collection is only valid for adults in the USA. Also, despite the noise reduction obtained by the algorithm thresholds in Section 3.3, some cases of frequent typos, foreign spellings/transliterations, and abbreviations are still statistically indistinguishable from actual nicknames. For instance, 'WM' (a common abbreviation of William) is as frequent as many of its nicknames. While we could have used a human-edited list to filter out these cases, we decided to keep it in the collection because some applications may benefit from this information. A coreference application, for instance, could infer that "Wm Jones" and "William Jones" have a high probability of being the same person.

Looking forward, there are multiple directions to explore. Besides names, the final record clusters generally contain other information such as addresses, date of birth (DOB), professional titles, etc. As an example, Figure 2 illustrates the probability of the most frequent nicknames of 'William' for people born over different decades in the US. It is interesting to notice that, while 'Bill' was the most likely nickname for people born between the 1940s and 1980s, 'Will' has become significantly more popular since the 80s - to the point that it has become the most likely nickname in the 90s. We believe our next steps will include investigating various migration, economic, sociological and demographic patterns while also leveraging this information in record linkage and coreference resolution modules.

References

K Bollacker, C. Evans, P. Paritosh, et al. 2008. *Freebase: A collaboratively created graph database for structuring human knowledge*. ACM SIGMOD.

Ahmed Elmagarmid, Panagiotis Ipeirotis and Vassilios Verykios 2007. *Duplicate Record Detection: A Survey.* IEEE TKDE 19 (1)

Patrick Hanks, Hardcastle Kate and Flavia Hodges 2007 *Oxford Dictionary of First Names.* Oxford University Press, USA, 2nd edition, ISBN 978-0-19-861060-1.

Deron Meranda 1998 *Most Common Nicknames for First Names* http://deron.meranda.us/data.

Jean-Baptiste Michel et al. 2011 *Quantitative Analysis of Culture Using Millions of Digitized Books.* Science, Vol. 331 no. 6014 pp. 176-182

Sheng Chen, Andrew Borthwick and Vitor R. Carvalho 2011. *The Case for Cost-Sensitive and Easy-To-Interpret Models in Industrial Record Linkage.* International Workshop on Quality in Databases VLDB-2011

Jeff Dean and Sanjay Ghemawat 2004. *MapReduce: Simplified Data Processing on Large Clusters* Symposium on Operating System Design and Implementation OSDI-2004

A comparison of models of word meaning in context

Georgiana Dinu
Universität des Saarlandes
Saarbrücken, Germany
dinu@coli.uni-saarland.de

Stefan Thater
Universität des Saarlandes
Saarbrücken, Germany
stth@coli.uni-saarland.de

Sören Laue
Friedrich-Schiller Universität
Jena, Germany
soeren.laue@uni-jena.de

Abstract

This paper compares a number of recently proposed models for computing context sensitive word similarity. We clarify the connections between these models, simplify their formulation and evaluate them in a unified setting. We show that the models are essentially equivalent if syntactic information is ignored, and that the substantial performance differences previously reported disappear to a large extent when these simplified variants are evaluated under identical conditions. Furthermore, our reformulation allows for the design of a straightforward and fast implementation.

1 Introduction

The computation of *semantic similarity* scores between words is an important sub-task for a variety of NLP applications (Turney and Pantel, 2010). One standard approach is to exploit the so-called *distributional hypothesis* that similar words tend to appear in similar contexts: Word meaning is represented by the contexts in which a word occurs, and semantic similarity is computed by comparing these contexts in a high-dimensional vector space.

Such distributional models of word meaning are attractive because they are simple, have wide coverage, and can be easily acquired in an unsupervised way. Ambiguity, however, is a fundamental problem: when encountering a word in context, we want a distributional representation which reflects its meaning in this specific context. For instance, while *buy* and *acquire* are similar when we consider them in isolation, they do not convey the same meaning when *acquire* occurs in *students acquire knowledge.* This is particularly difficult for vector space models which compute a single *type vector* summing up over all occurrences of a word. This vector mixes all of a word's usages and makes no distinctions between its—potentially very diverse—senses.

Several proposals have been made in the recent literature to address this problem. Type-based methods combine the (type) vector of the target with the vectors of the surrounding context words to obtain a disambiguated representation. In recent work, this has been proposed by Mitchell and Lapata (2008), Erk and Padó (2008) and Thater et al. (2010; 2011), which differ in the choice of input vector representation and in the combination operation they propose.

A different approach has been taken by Erk and Padó (2010), Reisinger and Mooney (2010) and Reddy et al. (2011), who make use of *token vectors* for individual *occurrences* of a word, rather than using the already mixed type vectors. Generally speaking, these methods "select" a set of token vectors of the target, which are similar to the current context, and use only these to obtain a disambiguated representation.

Yet another approach has been taken by Dinu and Lapata (2010), Ó Séaghdha and Korhonen (2011) and Van de Cruys et al. (2011), who propose to use latent variable models. Conceptually, this comes close to token-based models, however their approach is more unitary as they attempt to recover a hidden layer which best explains the observation data.

In this paper, we focus on the first group of approaches and investigate the precise differences between the three models of Erk and Padó and Thater et al., out of which (Thater et al., 2011) achieves state of the art results on a standard data set. Despite the fact that these models exploit similar intuitions, both their formal presentations and the results obtained vary to a great extent. The answer given in this paper is surprising: the three models are essentially equivalent if syntactic information is ignored; in a syntactic space the three methods implement only slightly different intuitions. We clarify these connections, simplify the syntactic variants originally proposed and reduce them to straightforward matrix operations, and evaluate them in a unified experimental setting. We obtain significantly better results than originally reported in the literature. Our reformulation also also supports efficient implementations for these methods.

2 Models for meaning in context

We consider the following problem: we are given an *occurrence* of a target word and want to obtain a vector that reflects its meaning in the given context. To simplify the presentation, we restrict ourselves to contexts consisting of a single word, and use *acquire* in context *knowledge* as a running example.

EP08. Erk and Padó (2008) compute a contextualized vector for *acquire* by combining its type vector ($\vec{w}$) with the inverse selectional preference vector of *knowledge* (c). This is simply the centroid of the vectors of all words that take *knowledge* as direct object (r):

$$v(w,r,c) = \left(\frac{1}{n}\sum_{w'} f(w',r,c)\cdot\vec{w'}\right)\times\vec{w} \quad (1)$$

where $f(w',r,c)$ denotes the co-occurrence association between the context word c and words w' related to c by grammatical relation r in a training corpus; n is the number of words w' and $\times$ denotes a vector composition operation. In this paper, we take $\times$ to be point-wise multiplication, which is reported to work best in many studies in the literature.

TFP10. Thater et al. (2010) also compute contextualized vectors by combing the vectors of the target word and of its context. In contrast to EP08, however, they use second order vectors as basic representation for the target word.

$$\vec{w} = \sum_{r,r',w''}\left(\sum_{w'} f(w,r,w')\cdot f(w',r',w'')\right)\vec{e}_{r,r',w''} \quad (2)$$

That is, the vector for a target word w has components for all combinations of two grammatical roles r,r' and a context word w'; the inner sum gives the value for each component.

The contextualized vector for *acquire* is obtained through pointwise multiplication with the (1st-order) vector for *knowledge* ($\vec{c}$), which has to be "lifted" first to make the two vectors comparable:

$$v(w,r,c) = \vec{w}\times L_r(\vec{c}) \quad (3)$$

$\vec{c} = \sum_{r',w'} f(c,r',w')\vec{e}_{(r',w')}$ is a first order vector for the context word; the "lifting map" $L_r(\vec{c})$ maps this vector to $\sum_{r',w'} f(c,r',w')\vec{e}_{(r,r',w')}$ to make it compatible with $\vec{w}$.

TFP11. Thater et al. (2011) take a slightly different perspective on contextualization. Instead of combing vector representations for the target word and its context directly, they propose to re-weight the vector components of the target word, based on distributional similarity with the context word:

$$v(w,r,c) = \sum_{r',w'} \alpha(r,c,r',w')\cdot f(w,r',w')\cdot\vec{e}_{(r',w')} \quad (4)$$

where $\alpha(r,c,r',w')$ is simply $cos(\vec{c},\vec{w'})$ if r and r' denote the same grammatical function, else 0.

3 Comparison

The models presented above have a number of things in common: they all use syntactic information and "second order" vectors to represent word meaning in context. Yet, their formal presentations differ substantially. We now show that the models are essentially equivalent *if we ignore syntax*: they component-wise multiply the second order vector of one word (target or context) with the first order vector of the other word. Specifically, we obtain the following derivations, where $W = \{w_1,...,w_n\}$ denotes the vocabulary, and V the symmetric $n\times n$ input matrix, where $V_{ij} = f(w_i,w_j)$ gives the co-occurrence association between words w_i and w_j:

$$\begin{aligned}
v_{\text{EP08}}(w,c) &= \frac{1}{n}\sum_{w'}\left(f(w',c)\cdot\vec{w'}\right)\times\vec{w}\\
&= \frac{1}{n}\sum_{w'}\left(f(w',c)\cdot\langle f(w',w_1),\ldots\rangle\right)\times\vec{w}\\
&= \frac{1}{n}\langle\sum_{w'} f(w',c)\cdot f(w',w_1),\ldots\rangle\times\vec{w}\\
&= \frac{1}{n}\langle<\vec{c},\vec{w}_1>,\ldots,<\vec{c},\vec{w}_n>\rangle\times\vec{w}\\
&= \frac{1}{n}\vec{c}\,V\times\vec{w}
\end{aligned}$$

$$
\begin{aligned}
v_{TFP10}(w,c) &= \sum_{w''\in W}\left(\sum_{w'\in W} f(w,w')\cdot f(w',w'')\right)\vec{e}_{w''}\times\vec{c}\\
&= \langle \sum_{w'\in W} f(w,w')f(w',w_1),\ldots\rangle\times\vec{c}\\
&= \langle <\vec{w},\vec{w}_1>,\ldots,<\vec{w},\vec{w}_n>\rangle\times\vec{c}\\
&= \vec{w}\,V\times\vec{c}
\end{aligned}
$$

$$
\begin{aligned}
v_{TFP11}(w,c) &= \sum_{w'\in W}\alpha(c,w')\cdot f(w,w')\cdot\vec{e}_{w'}\\
&= \langle \alpha(w_1,c)\cdot f(w,w_1),\ldots\rangle\\
&= \langle \alpha(w_1,c),\ldots\rangle\times\vec{w} \qquad (*)\\
&= \langle <\vec{w}_1,\vec{c}>,\ldots,<\vec{w}_n,\vec{c}>\rangle\times\vec{w}\\
&= \vec{c}\,V\times\vec{w}
\end{aligned}
$$

where $<\vec{v},\vec{w}>$ denotes scalar product. In step (*), we assume that $\alpha(w,c)$ denotes the scalar product of $\vec{w}$ and $\vec{c}$, instead of cosine similarity, as TFP11. This is justified if we assume that all vectors are normalized, in which case the two are identical.

As it can be observed the syntax-free variants of EP08 and TFP11 are identical up to the choice in normalization. TFP10 proposes an identical model to that of TFP11, however with a different interpretation, in which the roles of the context word and of the target word are swapped.

4 Evaluation

We have just shown that EP08, TFP10 and TFP11 are essentially equivalent to each other if syntactic information is ignored, hence it is a bit surprising that performance results reported in the literature vary to such a great extent. In this section we consider syntactic variants of these methods and we show that performance differences previously reported can only partly be explained by the different ways syntactic information is used: when we simplify these models and evaluate them under identical conditions, the differences between them disappear to a large extent.

To evaluate the three models, we reimplemented them using matrix operations similar to the ones used in Section 3, where we made few simplifications to the TFP10 and EP08 models: we follow TFP11 and we use component-wise multiplication to combine the target with one context word, and add the resulting composed vectors when given more context words[1]. Furthermore for TFP10, we change the treatment of syntax in the line of the much simpler proposal of TFP11. Specifically:

Model	GAP	Δ Literature
EP08	46.6	+ 14.4 (32.2)*
TFP10	48.3	+ 3.9 (44.4)
TFP11	51.8	±0.0
TFP10+11	52.1	N/A

Table 1: GAP scores LST data.
* The best available GAP score for this model (from Erk and Padó (2010)) is reported only on a subset of the data - this subset is however judged by the authors to be "easier" than the entire data; all other methods are tested on the entire dataset.

$$v(w,r,c) = L_{r^{-1}}(VV^T)_{w,:}\times V_{c,:} \qquad \text{(TFP10)}$$
$$v(w,r,c) = V_{w,:}\times L_r(VV^T)_{c,:} \qquad \text{(TFP11)}$$

where V is a $I\times J$ *syntactic* input matrix, i.e. the columns are (word, relation) pairs. For simplification, the columns of V are reordered such that syntactic relations form continuous regions. L_r is a lifting map similar to that of Equation (3) as it maps I- into J-dimensional vectors: the resulting vector is equal to the original one in the column region of relation r, while everything else is 0. In the above equations we use the standard Matlab notation, $V_{w,:}$ denoting a row vector in matrix V.

We evaluate these models on a paraphrase ranking task, using the SemEval 2007 Lexical Substitution Task (LST) dataset: the models are given a target word in context plus a list of potential synonyms (substitution candidates) ranging over all senses of the target word. The models have to decide to what extent each substitution candidate is a synonym of the target *in the given context.* We omit the precise description of the evaluation setting here, as we follow the methodology described in Thater et al. (2011).

Results are shown in Table 1, where the first column gives the GAP (Generalized Average Precision) score of the model and the second column gives the difference to the result reported in the literature. TFP10 and EP08 perform much better than the original proposals, as we obtain very significant gains of 4 and 14 GAP points.

[1]Note that some of the parameters in the EP08 method (omitted in the brief presentation in Section 2), which are difficult to tune (Erk and Padó (2009)), disappear this way.

We can observe that the differences between the three methods, when simplified and tested in an unified setting, largely disappear. This is to be expected as all three methods implement very similar, all motivated intuitions: TFP11 reweights the vector of the target *acquire* with the second order vector of the context *knowledge*, i.e. with the vector of similarities of *knowledge* to all other words in the vocabulary. TFP10 takes a complementary approach: it reweights the vector of *knowledge* with the second order vector of *acquire*. In both these methods, anything outside the *object* ($object^{-1}$ respectively) region of the space, is set to 0. The variant of EP08 that we implement is very similar to TFP11, however it compares *knowledge* to all other words in the vocabulary only using occurrences *as objects* while TFP11 takes *all* syntactic relations into account.

Note that TFP10 and TFP11 operate on complementary syntactic regions of the vectors. For this reason the two models can be trivially combined. The combined model (TFP10+11) achieves even better results: the difference to TFP11 is small, however statistically significant at level $p < 0.05$.

Implementation details. Straightforward implementations of the three models are computationally expensive, as they all use "second order" vectors to implement contextualization of a target word. Our reformulation in terms of matrix operations allows for efficient implementations, which take advantage of the sparsity of the input matrix V: contextualization of a target word runs in $O(nnz(V))$, where nnz is the number of non-zero entries. Note that ranking not only a small set of predefined substitution candidates, as in the experiment above, but also ranking the entire vocabulary runs in $O(nnz(V))$. On this task, this overall running time is in fact identical to that of simpler methods such as those of Mitchell and Lapata (2008).

In our experiments, we use GigaWord to extract a syntactic input matrix V of size $\approx 2M \times 7M$. V is only 4.5×10^{-06} dense. Note that because of the simple operations involved, we do not need to compute or store the entire VV^T matrix, which is much denser than V (we have estimated order of 10^{10} entries). The sparsity of V allows for very efficient computations in practice: the best single model, TFP11, runs in less than 0.2s/0.4s per LST instance, for ranking the candidate list/entire vocabulary in a Python implementation using scipy.sparse, on a standard 1GHz processor.

5 Conclusions

In this paper, we have compared three related vector space models of word meaning in context. We have reformulated the models and showed that they are in fact very similar. We also showed that the different performances reported in the literature are only to some extent due to the differences in the models: We evaluated simplified variants of these and obtained results which are (much) better than previously reported, bringing the three models much closer together in terms of performance. Aside from clarifying the precise relationship between the three models under consideration, our reformulation has the additional benefit of allowing the design of a straightforward and efficient implementation.

Finally, our focus on these methods is justified by their clear advantages over other classes of models: unlike token-based or latent variable methods, they are much simpler and require no parameter tuning. Furthermore, they also obtain state of the art results on the paraphrase ranking task, outperforming other simple type-based methods (see (Van de Cruys et al., 2011) and (Ó Séaghdha and Korhonen, 2011) for results of other methods on this data).

Acknowledgments. This work was partially supported by the Cluster of Excellence "Multimodal Computing and Interaction", funded by the German Excellence Initiative.

References

Georgiana Dinu and Mirella Lapata. 2010. Measuring distributional similarity in context. In *Proceedings of EMNLP 2010*, Cambridge, MA.

Katrin Erk and Sebastian Padó. 2008. A structured vector space model for word meaning in context. In *Proceedings of EMNLP 2008*, Honolulu, HI, USA.

Katrin Erk and Sebastian Padó. 2009. Paraphrase assessment in structured vector space: Exploring parameters and datasets. In *Proceedings of the Workshop on Geometrical Models of Natural Language Semantics*.

Katrin Erk and Sebastian Padó. 2010. Exemplar-based models for word meaning in context. In *Proceedings of ACL 2010 Short Papers*, Uppsala, Sweden.

Jeff Mitchell and Mirella Lapata. 2008. Vector-based models of semantic composition. In *Proceedings of ACL-08: HLT*, Columbus, OH, USA.

Diarmuid Ó Séaghdha and Anna Korhonen. 2011. Probabilistic models of similarity in syntactic context. In *Proceedings of EMNLP 2011*.

Siva Reddy, Ioannis Klapaftis, Diana McCarthy, and Suresh Manandhar. 2011. Dynamic and static prototype vectors for semantic composition. In *Proc. of IJCNLP 2011*.

Joseph Reisinger and Raymond J. Mooney. 2010. Multi-prototype vector-space models of word meaning. In *Proceedings of NAACL 2010*, Los Angeles, California.

Stefan Thater, Hagen Fürstenau, and Manfred Pinkal. 2010. Contextualizing semantic representations using syntactically enriched vector models. In *Proceedings of ACL 2010*, Uppsala, Sweden.

Stefan Thater, Hagen Fürstenau, and Manfred Pinkal. 2011. Word meaning in context: A simple and effective vector model. In *Proceedings of IJCNLP 2011*.

Peter D. Turney and Patrick Pantel. 2010. From frequency to meaning: Vector space modes of semantics. *Journal of Artificial Intelligence Research*, 37:141–188.

Tim Van de Cruys, Thierry Poibeau, and Anna Korhonen. 2011. Latent vector weighting for word meaning in context. In *Proceedings of EMNLP 2011*.

Measuring Word Relatedness Using Heterogeneous Vector Space Models

Wen-tau Yih
Microsoft Research
One Microsoft Way
Redmond, WA
scottyih@microsoft.com

Vahed Qazvinian*
Department of EECS
University of Michigan
Ann Arbor, MI
vahed@umich.edu

Abstract

Noticing that different information sources often provide complementary coverage of word sense and meaning, we propose a simple and yet effective strategy for measuring lexical semantics. Our model consists of a committee of vector space models built on a text corpus, Web search results and thesauruses, and measures the semantic word relatedness using the averaged cosine similarity scores. Despite its simplicity, our system correlates with human judgements better or similarly compared to existing methods on several benchmark datasets, including WordSim353.

1 Introduction

Measuring the semantic relatedness of words is a fundamental problem in natural language processing and has many useful applications, including textual entailment, word sense disambiguation, information retrieval and automatic thesaurus discovery. Existing approaches can be roughly categorized into two kinds: knowledge-based and corpus-based, where the former includes graph-based algorithms and similarity measures operating on a lexical database such as WordNet (Budanitsky and Hirst, 2006; Agirre et al., 2009) and the latter consists of various kinds of vector space models (VSMs) constructed with the help of a large collection of text (Reisinger and Mooney, 2010; Radinsky et al., 2011). In this paper, we present a conceptually simple model for solving this problem. Observing that various kinds of information sources, such as general text corpora, Web search results and thesauruses, have different word and sense coverage, we first build individual vector space models from each of them separately. Given two words, each VSM measures the semantic relatedness by the cosine similarity of the corresponding vectors in its space. The final prediction is simply the averaged cosine scores derived from these VSMs. Despite its simplicity, our system surprisingly yields very strong empirical performance. When comparing the predictions with the human annotations on four different datasets, our system achieves higher correlation than existing methods on two datasets and provides very competitive results on the others.

The rest of this paper is organized as follows. Section 2 briefly reviews the related work. Section 3 details how we construct each individual vector space model, followed by the experimental evaluation in Section 4. Finally, Section 5 concludes the paper.

2 Background

Prior work on measuring lexical semantics can be categorized as knowledge-based or corpus-based. Knowledge-based methods leverage word relations encoded in lexical databases such as WordNet and provide graph-based similarity measures. Detailed comparisons of these methods can be found in (Budanitsky and Hirst, 2006). Corpus-based methods assume related words tend to co-occur or to appear in similar context. For example, Gabrilovich and Markovitch (2007) measure word relatedness by whether they tend to occur in the same Wikipedia topic. In contrast, Reisinger and Mooney (2010) use the conventional "context vector" – neighboring

* Work conducted while interning at Microsoft Research.

terms of the occurrences of a target word – as the word representation. In addition, they argue that it is difficult to capture different senses of a word with a single vector, and introduce a multi-prototype representation. More recently, Radinsky et al. (2011) analyze the temporal aspects of words and argue that non-identical terms in two term vectors should also be compared based on their temporal usage when computing the similarity score. They construct the vectors using Wikipedia titles, Flickr image tags, and Del.icio.us bookmarks, and extract the temporal frequency of each concept from 130 years of New York Times archive. Methods that combine models from different sources do exist. For instance, Agirre et al. (2009) derive a WordNet-based measure using PageRank and combined it with several corpus-based vector space models using SVMs.

3 Vector Space Models from Heterogeneous Sources

In this section, we describe how we construct various vector space models (VSMs) to represent words, including *corpus*-based, *Web*-based and *thesaurus*-based methods.

Corpus-based VSMs follow the standard "distributional hypothesis," which states that words appearing in the same *contexts* tend to have similar meaning (Harris, 1954). Each target word is thus represented by a high-dimensional sparse term-vector that consists of words occurring in its context. Given a corpus, we first collect terms within a window of $[-10, +10]$ centered at each occurrence of a target word. This bag-of-words representation is then mapped to the TF-IDF term vector: each term is weighted by $\log(freq) \times \log(N/df)$, where $freq$ is the number of times the term appears in the collection, df the document frequency of the term in the whole corpus and N the number of total documents. We further employed two simple techniques to improve the quality of these term-vectors: *vocabulary* and *term* trimming. Top 1,500 terms with high document frequency values are treated as stopwords and removed from the vocabulary. Moreover, we adopted a document-specific feature selection method (Kolcz and Yih, 2007) designed originally for text classification and retain only the top 200 high-weighted terms for each term-vector[1]. The corpus-based VSMs are created using English Wikipedia (Snapshot of Nov. 2010), consisting of 917M words after preprocessing (markup tags removal and sentence splitting).

Web-based VSMs leverage Web search results to form a vector of each query (Sahami and Heilman, 2006). For each word to compare, we issue it as a query and retrieve the set of relevant snippets (top 30 in our experiments) using a popular commercial search engine, Bing. All these snippets together are viewed as a pseudo-document and mapped to a TF-IDF vector as in the corpus-based method. We do not allow for automatic query expansion in our experiments to ensure that the retrieved snippets are directly relevant to the target word and not expansions based on synonyms, hypernyms or hyponyms. We apply vocabulary trimming (top 1,000 terms with high DF values), but not term-trimming as the vectors have much fewer terms due to the small number of snippets collected.

Both the corpus-based and Web-based VSMs rely on the distributional hypothesis, which is often criticized for two weaknesses. The first is that word pairs that appear in the same context or co-occur are not necessarily highly semantically related. For example, "bread" and "butter" often have cosine scores higher than synonyms using corpus-based vectors because of the phrase "bread and butter". The second is that general corpora often have skewed coverage of words due to the Zipf's law. Regardless of the size of the corpus, the number of occurrences of a rarely used word is typically very low, which makes the quality of the corresponding vector unreliable. To address these two issues, we include the **thesaurus**-based VSMs in this work as well. For each group of similar words (synset) defined in the thesaurus, we treat it as a "document" and create a document–word matrix, where each word is again weighted using its TF-IDF value. Each column vector in this matrix is thus the thesaurus-based vector of the corresponding word. Notice that given two words and their corresponding vectors, the cosine score is more general than simply checking

[1] In preliminary experiments, we found that active terms with low TF-IDF values tend to be noise. By aggressively removing them, the quality of the term-vectors can be significantly improved.

whether these two words belong to a group of similar words, as it judges how often they overlap in various documents (i.e., sets of similar words). We explored using two different thesauri in our experiments: WordNet and the Encarta thesaurus developed by Bloomsbury Publishing, where the former consists of 227,446 synsets and 190,052 words and the latter contains 46,945 synsets and 50,184 words. Compared to existing *knowledge*-based approaches, our VSM transformation is very simple and straightforward. It is also easy to extend our method to other languages as only a thesaurus is required rather than a complete lexical database such as WordNet.

4 Experimental Evaluation

In this section, we evaluate the quality of the VSMs constructed using methods described in Section 3 on different benchmark datasets, as well as the performance when combining them.

4.1 Benchmark datasets

We follow the standard evaluation method, which directly tests the correlation of the word relatedness measures with human judgements on a set of word pairs, using the Spearman's rank correlation coefficient. Our study was conducted using four different datasets, including WS-353, RG-65, MC-30 and MTurk-287.

The WordSim353 dataset (**WS-353**) is the largest among them and has been used extensively in recent work. Originally collected by Finkelstein et al. (2001), the dataset consists of 353 word pairs. The degree of relatedness of each pair is assessed on a 0-10 scale by 13-16 human judges, where the mean is used as the final score. Examining the relations between the words in each pair, Agirre et al. (2009) further split this dataset into *similar* pairs (**WS-sim**) and *related* pairs (**WS-rel**), where the former contains synonyms, antonyms, identical words and hyponyms/hypernyms and the latter capture other word relations. Collected by Rubenstein and Goodenough (1965), **RG-65** contains 65 pairs of words that are either synonyms or unrelated, assessed on a 0-4 scale by 51 human subjects. Taking 30 pairs from them, Miller and Charles (1991) created the (**MC-30**) dataset by reassessing these word pairs using 38 subjects. These 30 pairs of words are also a subset of WS-353. Although these three datasets contain overlapping word pairs, their scores are different because of the degree of relatedness were given by different human subjects. In addition to these datasets, we also evaluate our VSMs on the **Mturk-287** dataset that consists of 287 word pairs collected by (Radinsky et al., 2011) using Amazon MTurk.

4.2 Results and Analysis

Table 1 summarizes the results of various methods, where the top part lists the performance of state-of-the-art systems and the bottom shows the results of individual vector space models, as well as combining these models using the averaged cosine scores. We make several observations here. First, while none of the four VSMs we tested outperforms the best existing systems on the benchmark datasets, surprisingly, using the averaged cosine scores of these models, the performance is improved substantially. It achieves higher Spearman's rank coefficient on WS-353 and MTurk-287 than any other systems[2] and are close to the state-of-the-art on MC-30 and RG-65. Unlike some approach like (Hughes and Ramage, 2007), which performs well on some datasets but poorly on others, combing the VSMs from heterogeneous sources is more robust. Individually, we notice that Wikipedia context VSM provides consistently strong results, while thesaurus-based models work only reasonable on MC-30 and RG-65, potentially because other datasets contain more out-of-vocabulary words or proper nouns. Due to the inherent ambiguity of the task, there is a high variance among judgements from different annotators. Therefore, it is unrealistic to assume any of the methods can correlate perfectly to the mean human judgement scores. In fact, the inter-agreement study done on the WS-353 dataset indicates that the result of our approach of combining heterogeneous VSMs is close to the averaged human performance.

It is intriguing to see that by using the averaged cosine scores, the performance can be improved over the best individual model (i.e., Wikipedia). Examining the scores of some word pairs carefully sug-

[2]This may not be statistically significant. Without having the exact output of existing systems, it is difficult to conduct a robust statistical significance test given the small sizes of these datasets.

Method	Spearman's ρ WS-353	WS-sim	WS-rel	MC-30	RG-65	MTurk-287
(Radinsky et al., 2011)	0.80	-	-	-	-	0.63
(Reisinger and Mooney, 2010)	0.77	-	-	-	-	-
(Agirre et al., 2009)	0.78	0.83	0.72	**0.92**	**0.96**	-
(Gabrilovich and Markovitch, 2007)	0.75	-	-	-	-	0.59
(Hughes and Ramage, 2007)	0.55	-	-	0.90	0.84	-
Web Search	0.56	0.56	0.54	0.48	0.44	0.44
Wikipedia	0.73	0.80	0.73	0.87	0.83	0.62
Bloomsbury	0.45	0.60	0.60	0.71	0.78	0.29
WordNet	0.37	0.49	0.49	0.79	0.78	0.25
Combining VSMs	**0.81**	**0.87**	**0.77**	0.89	0.89	**0.68**

Table 1: The performance of the state-of-the-art methods and different vector space models on measuring semantic word relatedness using the cosine similarity.

gests the broader coverage of different words and senses could be the reason. For example, some of the words in the datasets have multiple senses, such as "jaguar vs. car" and "jaguar vs. cat". Although in previous work, researchers try to capture word senses using different vectors (Reisinger and Mooney, 2010) from the same text corpus, this is in fact difficult in practice. The usage of words in a big text corpus, which contains diversified topics, may still be biased to one word sense. For example, in the Wikipeida term vector that represents "jaguar", we found that most of the terms there are related to "cat". Although some terms are associated with the "car" meaning, the signals are rather weak. Similarly, WordNet does not indicate "jaguar" could be related to "car" at all. In contrast, the "car" sense of "jaguar" dominates the vector created using the search engine. As a result, incorporating models from different sources could be more effective than relying on word sense discovering algorithms operating solely on one corpus. Another similar but different example is the pair of "bread" and "butter", which are treated as synonyms by corpus-based VSMs, but is demoted after adding the thesaurus-based models.

5 Conclusion

In this paper we investigated the usefulness of heterogeneous information sources in improving measures of semantic word relatedness. Particularly, we created vector space models using 4 data sources from 3 categories (corpus-based, Web-based and thesaurus-based) and found that simply averaging the cosine similarity derived from these models yields a very robust measure. Other than directly applying it to measuring semantic relatedness, our approach is complementary to more sophisticated similarity measures such as developing kernel functions for different structured data (Croce et al., 2011), where the similarity between words serves as a basic component.

While this result is interesting and encouraging, it also raises several research questions, such as how to enhance the quality of each vector space model and whether the models can be combined more effectively[3]. We also would like to study whether similar techniques can be useful when comparing longer text segments like phrases or sentences, with potential applications in paraphrase detection and recognizing textual entailment.

Acknowledgments

We thank Joseph Reisinger for providing his prototype vectors for our initial study, Silviu-Petru Cucerzan for helping process the Wikipedia files and Geoffrey Zweig for preparing the Bloomsbury thesaurus data. We are also grateful to Chris Meek for valuable discussions and to anonymous reviewers for their comments.

[3]We conducted some preliminary experiments (not reported here) on tuning the weights of combining different models based on cross-validation, but did not find consistent improvements, perhaps due to the limited size of the data.

References

E. Agirre, E. Alfonseca, K. Hall, J. Kravalova, M. Paşca and A. Soroa. 2009. A study on similarity and relatedness using distributional and wordnet-based approaches. In *NAACL '09*, pages 19–27.

A. Budanitsky and G. Hirst. 2006. Evaluating wordnet-based measures of lexical semantic relatedness. *Computational Linguistics*, 32:13–47, March.

D. Croce, A. Moschitti, and R. Basili. 2011. Structured lexical similarity via convolution kernels on dependency trees. In *Proceedings of EMNLP 2011*, pages 1034–1046, July.

L. Finkelstein, E. Gabrilovich, Y. Matias, E. Rivlin, Z. Solan, G. Wolfman, and E. Ruppin. 2001. Placing search in context: The concept revisited. In *WWW*, pages 406–414. ACM.

E. Gabrilovich and S. Markovitch. 2007. Computing semantic relatedness using wikipedia-based explicit semantic analysis. In *IJCAI '07*, pages 1606–1611.

Z. Harris. 1954. Distributional structure. *Word*, 10(23):146–162.

T. Hughes and D. Ramage. 2007. Lexical semantic relatedness with random graph walks. In *Proceedings of EMNLP-CoNLL-2007*, pages 581–589.

A. Kolcz and W. Yih. 2007. Raising the baseline for high-precision text classifiers. In *KDD '07*, pages 400–409.

G. Miller and W. Charles. 1991. Contextual correlates of semantic similarity. *Language and cognitive processes*, 6(1):1–28.

K. Radinsky, E. Agichtein, E. Gabrilovich, and S. Markovitch. 2011. A word at a time: computing word relatedness using temporal semantic analysis. In *WWW '11*, pages 337–346.

J. Reisinger and R. Mooney. 2010. Multi-prototype vector-space models of word meaning. In *NAACL '10*.

H. Rubenstein and J. Goodenough. 1965. Contextual correlates of synonymy. *Communications of the ACM*, 8:627–633, October.

M. Sahami and T. Heilman. 2006. A web-based kernel function for measuring the similarity of short text snippets. In *Proceedings of the 15th international conference on World Wide Web*, pages 377–386. ACM.

Expectations of Word Sense in Parallel Corpora

Xuchen Yao, Benjamin Van Durme and **Chris Callison-Burch**
Center for Language and Speech Processing, and HLTCOE
Johns Hopkins University

Abstract

Given a parallel corpus, if two distinct words in language A, a_1 and a_2, are aligned to the same word b_1 in language B, then this might signal that b_1 is polysemous, *or* it might signal a_1 and a_2 are synonyms. Both assumptions with successful work have been put forward in the literature. We investigate these assumptions, along with other questions of word sense, by looking at sampled parallel sentences containing tokens of the same type in English, asking how often they mean the same thing when they are: 1. aligned to the *same* foreign type; and 2. aligned to *different* foreign types. Results for French-English and Chinese-English parallel corpora show similar behavior: Synonymy is only very weakly the more prevalent scenario, where both cases regularly occur.

1 Introduction

Parallel corpora have been used for both paraphrase induction and word sense disambiguation (WSD). Usually one of the following two assumptions is made for these tasks:

1. **Polysemy** If two different words in language A are aligned to the same word in language B, then the word in language B is polysemous.

2. **Synonymy** If two different words in language A are aligned to the same word in language B, then the two words in A are synonyms, and thus is *not* evidence of polysemy in B.

Despite the alternate nature of these assumptions, both have associated articles in which a researcher claimed success. Under the polysemy assumption, Gale et al. (1992) used French translations as English sense indicators in the task of WSD. For instance, for the English word *duty*, the French translation *droit* was taken to signal its *tax* sense and *devoir* to signal its *obligation* sense. These French words were used as labels for different English senses. Similarly, in a cross-lingual WSD setting,[1] Lefever et al. (2011) treated each English-foreign alignment as a so-called *ParaSense*, using it as a proxy for human labeled training data.

Under the synonymy assumption, Diab and Resnik (2002) did word sense tagging by grouping together all English words that are translated into the same French word and by further enforcing that the majority sense for these English words was projected as the sense for the French word. Bannard and Callison-Burch (2005) applied the idea that French phrases aligned to the same English phrase are paraphrases in a system that induces paraphrases by pivoting through aligned foreign phrases.

Based on this, and other successful prior work, it seems neither of the assumptions must hold universally. Therefore we investigate how often we might *expect* one or the other to dominate: we sample polysemous words from wide-domain {French,Chinese}-English corpora, and use Amazon's Mechanical Turk (MTurk) to annotate word sense on the English side. We calculate empirical probabilities based on counting over the competing polysemous and synonymous scenario labels.

A key factor deciding the validity of our conclusion is the reliability of the annotations derived via MTurk. Thus our first step is to evaluate the ability of Turkers to perform WSD. After verifying this

[1] E.g., given a sentence "... *more power, more duty* ...", the task asks to give a French translation of *duty*, which should be *devior*, after first recognizing the underlying *obligation* sense.

as a reasonable process for acquiring large amounts of WSD labeled data, we go on to frame the experimental design, giving final results in Sec. 4.

2 Turker Reliability

While Amazon's Mechanical Turk (MTurk) has been been considered in the past for constructing lexical semantic resources (e.g., (Snow et al., 2008; Akkaya et al., 2010; Parent and Eskenazi, 2010; Rumshisky, 2011)), word sense annotation is sensitive to subjectivity and usually achieves low agreement rate even among experts. Thus we first asked Turkers to re-annotate a sample of existing gold-standard data. With an eye towards costs saving, we also considered how many Turkers would be needed per item to produce results of sufficient quality.

Turkers were presented sentences from the test portion of the word sense induction task of SemEval-2007 (Agirre and Soroa, 2007), covering 2,559 instances of 35 nouns, expert-annotated with OntoNotes (Hovy et al., 2006) senses. Two versions of the task were designed:

1. **compare**: given the same word in different sentences, tell whether their meaning is THE SAME, ALMOST THE SAME, UNLIKELY THE SAME or DIFFERENT, where the results were collapsed post-hoc into a binary same/different categorization;

2. **sense map**: map the meaning of a given word in a sentential context to its proper OntoNotes definition.

For both tasks, 2,599 examples were presented.

We measure inter-coder agreement using Krippendorff's Alpha (Krippendorff, 2004; Artstein and Poesio, 2008), where $\alpha \geq 0.8$ is considered to be reliable and $0.667 \leq \alpha < 0.8$ allows for tentative conclusions. Two points emerge from Table 1: there were greater agreement rates for sense map than compare, and 3 Turkers were sufficient.

	α-Turker	α-maj.	maj.-agr.
compare$_5$	0.47	0.66	0.87
compare$_3$	0.44	0.52	0.83
sense map$_5$	0.79	0.93	0.95
sense map$_3$	0.75	0.87	0.91

Table 1: MTurk result on testing Turker reliability. Krippendorff's Alpha is used to measure agreement. α-Turker: how Turkers agree among themselves, α-maj.: how the majority agrees with true value, maj.-agr.: agreement between the majority vote and true value. α-maj. indicates the confidence level about the maj.-agr. value. Subscripts denote either 5 Turkers, or 3 randomly selected of the 5.

3 Experiment Design

Data Selection We used two parallel corpora: the French-English 10^9 corpus (Callison-Burch et al., 2009) and the GALE Chinese-English corpus.

For each corpus we selected 50 words, w, at random from OntoNotes,[2] constrained such that w: had more than one sense; had a frequency $\geq 1,000$; and was not a top 10% most frequent words.

Next we sampled 100 instances (aligned English-foreign sentence pairs) for each word based on the following constraints: the aligned foreign word, f, had a frequency ≥ 20 in the foreign corpus; f had a non-trivial alignment probability.[3] We sampled proportionally to the distribution of the aligned foreign words, ensuring that at least 5 instances from each foreign translation are sampled.[4]

For each corpus, this results in 100 instances for each of 50 words, totaling 5,000 instances. We used 3 Turkers per instance for sense annotation, under the sense map task. We note that the set of 50 randomly selected English words from the Chinese-English corpus were entirely distinct from the 50 selected words from the French-English corpus.

Probability Estimation Suppose e_1 and e_2 are two tokens of the same English word type e. $s(e_1)$ is a function that returns the sense of e_1, $a(e_1)$ is a function that returns the aligned word of e_1. Let $c()$ be our count function, where: $c(e, f)$ returns the

[2]OntoNotes was used as the sense inventory over alternatives, owing to its coarse-grained sense definitions.

[3]Defined as f having index $i < k$ when foreign words are ranked by most probable given e, where k is the minimum value such that $\sum_i^k p(f_i \mid e) > 0.8$. E.g., if we have decreasing probabilities $p(droit \mid duty) = 0.6$, $p(devoir \mid duty) = 0.25$, $p(le \mid duty) = 0.03$, ... then only consider *droit* and *devoir*. This ruled out many noisy alignments.

[4]Thus, the instances of *droit* compared to that of *devoir* would be $0.6/0.25$.

number of times English word e is aligned to foreign word f; $c(e^s, f)$ returns the number of times English word e has sense s (tagged by Turkers), when aligned to foreign word f; $c(e)$ is the total number of tokens of English word e; and $c(e^s)$ is the number of tokens of e with sense s.

We estimate from labeled data the probability of three scenarios, with scenario 1 as our primary concern: when two English words of the same polysemous type are aligned to *different* foreign word types, what is the chance that they have the same sense? Given the tokens e_1 and e_2, we calculate P1 as follows:

$$P1_e = P(s(e_1) = s(e_2) \mid a(e_1) \neq a(e_2)) \approx \frac{\sum_s c^2(e^s) - \sum_{s,f} c^2(e^s, f)}{c^2(e) - \sum_f c^2(e, f)}$$

P1 says that given two words of the same type (e_1 and e_2) that are *not* aligned to the same foreign word type ($a(e_1) \neq a(e_2)$), what is the probability that they have the same sense ($s(e_1) = s(e_2)$). We approach this estimation combinatorially. For instance, the number of ways to choose two words of the same type is $\binom{2}{c(e)} \approx \frac{1}{2}c^2(e)$ when $c(e)$ is large.

A large value of P1 would be in support of **Synonymy**, as the two foreign aligned words of distinct type would have the same meaning.

Scenario 2 asks: given two English words of the same polysemous type and aligned to the *same* words ($a(e_1) = a(e_2)$), what is the probability that they have the same sense ($s(e_1) = s(e_2)$)?

$$P2_e = P(s(e_1) = s(e_2) \mid a(e_1) = a(e_2)) \approx \frac{\sum_{s,f} c^2(e^s, f)}{\sum_f c^2(e, f)}$$

Finally, what is the probability of two tokens of the same polysemous type agreeing when alignment information is not known (e.g., without a parallel corpus)?

$$P3_e = P(s(e_1) = s(e_2)) \approx \frac{\sum_s c^2(e^s)}{c^2(e)}$$

All the above equations are given per English word type e. In later sections we report the average values over multiple word types and their counts.

4 Results

Turker Experiments To minimize errors from Turkers, for every HIT we inserted one control sentence taken from the example sentences of OntoNotes. Turker results with either extremely low finishing time ($<$10s), or average accuracy on control sentences lower than accuracy by chance, were rejected. On average Turkers took 185 seconds to map 10 sentences in a HIT to their OntoNotes definition, receiving \$0.10 per HIT. The total time for annotating 5000 sentences was 22 hours.

Turkers had no knowledge about alignments: we hid the aligned French/Chinese sentences from them and these sentences were later processed to compute P1/2/3 values. Two foreign tokens aligned with the same source type correspond to two senses of the same type. To give an estimate of alignment errors, we manually examined 1/10 of all 5000 sampled Chinese-English alignments at random and found only 3 of them were wrong: all due to that English content words were aligned to common Chinese function words. This error rate is much lower than that typically reported by alignment tools. The main reason is explained in footnote 3: foreign words with trivial alignment probability were removed before calculating P1/2/3 values. Thus we believe the alignment was reliable.

Probability Estimation Table 2 gives the distribution of senses and word types in the sampled words. Take the second numeric column of French-English as an example: out of 50 words randomly sampled, 9 have 2 distinct sense definitions in OntoNotes. However, 17 of 50 unique word types had exactly 2 distinct senses annotated, out of the 100 examples of a given word type: 17 words had 2 distinct senses *observed.* Of the 9 words with 2 official senses, on average 1.9 of those senses were observed.

Table 3 and Figures 1 and 2 shows the result for P1, P2 and P3 using the {French,Chinese}-English corpora, calculated based on the majority vote of three Turkers. High P2 values suggests that for two tokens of the same type, aligning to the same foreign type is a reasonable indicator of having the same meaning. When working with open domain corpora, without foreign alignments, the probability of two English words of the same type having

	French-English									Chinese-English									
#senses in OntoNotes	1	2	3	4	5	6	7	8	9	1	2	3	4	5	6	7	8	9	18
#types in OntoNotes	0	9	7	6	8	6	2	8	4	0	10	6	11	3	8	6	4	1	1
#types observed	2	17	9	4	7	7	4	0	0	3	19	9	12	5	2	0	0	0	0
avg #senses observed	0	1.9	2.1	3.2	3.8	4.7	6.5	4.9	5.8	0	1.9	2.2	2.9	2.7	4.4	3.8	3.8	3.0	5.0

Table 2: Statistics for words sampled from parallel corpora. Average #senses observed over all words: 2.6 (French-English), and 2.4 (Chinese-English). The sampled word *keep* has 18 senses in OntoNotes, with 5 observed.

	P1	P2	P3	Alpha
French-English	51.2%	66.7%	59.2%	0.70
Chinese-English	59.6%	78.7%	66.7%	0.68

Table 3: Expectations of word sense in parallel corpora. Alpha measures how Turkers agreed with themselves.

identical meaning is estimated here to be roughly 59-67% (59.2% (French), 66.7% (Chinese)). This accords with results from WSD evaluations, where the first-sense heuristic is roughly 75-80% accurate (e.g., 80.9% in SemEval'07 (Brody and Lapata, 2009)). Minor algebra translates this into an expected P3 value in a range from 56% – 62.5%, up to 64% – 68%, which captures our estimates.[5]

Finally for our motivating scenario: values for P1 are barely higher than 50%, suggesting that **Synonymy** more regularly holds, but not conclusively. We expect in narrower domains, where words have less number of senses, this is more noticeable. As suggested by Fig.s 1 and 2, less polysemous words tend to have higher P values.

5 Conclusion

Curious as to the distinct threads of prior work based on alternate assumptions of word sense and parallel corpora, we derived empirical expectations on the shared meaning of tokens of the same type appearing in the same corpus. Our results suggest neither the assumption of Polysemy nor Synonymy holds significantly more often than the other, at least for individual words (as opposed to phrases) and for the open domain corpora used here. Further, we provide an independent data point that supports earlier findings as to the expected accuracy of the first sense heuristic in word sense disambiguation.

[5]Assuming worst case: no two tokens that are not the first sense ever match, and best case: any two tokens not the first sense always match, then assuming first-sense accuracy of 0.8 gives a range on P3 of: $(0.8^2, 0.8^2 + 0.2^2) = (0.64, 0.68)$.

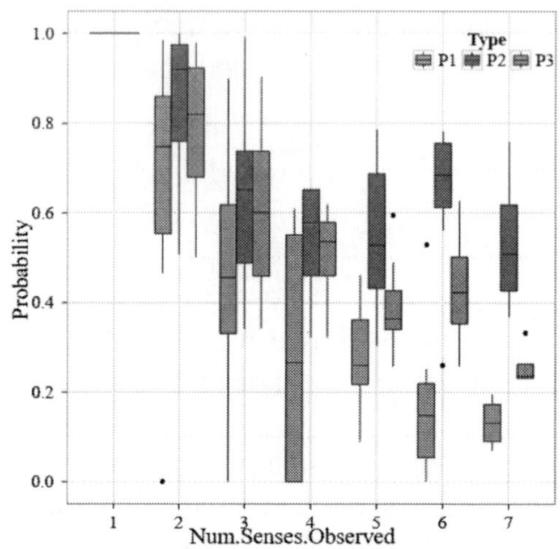

Figure 1: French-English values, by number of senses.

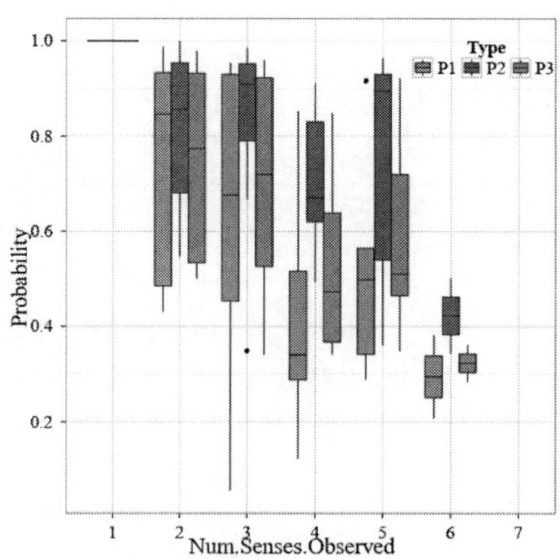

Figure 2: Chinese-English values, by number of senses.

References

Eneko Agirre and Aitor Soroa. 2007. Semeval-2007 Task 02: Evaluating Word Sense Induction And Discrimination Systems. In *Proc. SemEval '07*.

Cem Akkaya, Alexander Conrad, Janyce Wiebe, and Rada Mihalcea. 2010. Amazon mechanical turk for subjectivity word sense disambiguation. In *Proc. NAACL Workshop on CSLDAMT*.

Ron Artstein and Massimo Poesio. 2008. Inter-Coder Agreement for Computational Linguistics. *Computational Linguistics*, 34(4).

Colin Bannard and Chris Callison-Burch. 2005. Paraphrasing with bilingual parallel corpora. In *Proc. ACL*.

Samuel Brody and Mirella Lapata. 2009. Bayesian Word Sense Induction. In *Proc. EACL*.

Chris Callison-Burch, Philipp Koehn, Christof Monz, and Josh Schroeder. 2009. Findings Of The 2009 Workshop On Statistical Machine Translation. In *Proc. StatMT*.

Mona Diab and Philip Resnik. 2002. An unsupervised method for word sense tagging using parallel corpora. In *Proc. ACL*.

W.A. Gale, K.W. Church, and D. Yarowsky. 1992. Using bilingual materials to develop word sense disambiguation methods. In *Proc. TMI*.

Eduard Hovy, Mitchell Marcus, Martha Palmer, Lance Ramshaw, and Ralph Weischedel. 2006. OntoNotes: the 90% solution. In *Proc. NAACL-Short*.

Klaus H. Krippendorff. 2004. *Content Analysis: An Introduction to Its Methodology*.

Els Lefever, Véronique Hoste, and Martine De Cock. 2011. Parasense or how to use parallel corpora for word sense disambiguation. In *Proc. ACL*.

Gabriel Parent and Maxine Eskenazi. 2010. Clustering dictionary definitions using amazon mechanical turk. In *Proc. NAACL Workshop on CSLDAMT*.

Anna Rumshisky. 2011. Crowdsourcing word sense definition. In *Proc. LAW V*.

Rion Snow, Brendan O'Connor, Daniel Jurafsky, and Andrew Y. Ng. 2008. Cheap and fast—but is it good?: evaluating non-expert annotations for natural language tasks. In *Proc. EMNLP*.

Why Not Grab a Free Lunch? Mining Large Corpora for Parallel Sentences to Improve Translation Modeling

Ferhan Ture
Dept. of Computer Science,
University of Maryland
fture@cs.umd.edu

Jimmy Lin
The iSchool
University of Maryland
jimmylin@umd.edu

Abstract

It is well known that the output quality of statistical machine translation (SMT) systems increases with more training data. To obtain more parallel text for translation modeling, researchers have turned to the web to mine parallel sentences, but most previous approaches have avoided the difficult problem of pairwise similarity on cross-lingual documents and instead rely on heuristics. In contrast, we confront this challenge head on using the MapReduce framework. On a modest cluster, our scalable end-to-end processing pipeline was able to automatically gather 5.8m parallel sentence pairs from English and German Wikipedia. Augmenting existing bitext with these data yielded significant improvements over a state-of-the-art baseline (2.39 BLEU points in the best case).

1 Introduction

It has been repeatedly shown that "throwing more data at the problem" is effective in increasing SMT output quality, both for translation modeling (Dyer et al., 2008) and for language modeling (Brants et al., 2007). In this paper, we bring together two related research threads to gather parallel sentences for improved translation modeling: cross-lingual pairwise similarity to mine comparable documents and classification to identify sentence pairs that are mutual translations.

Unlike most previous work, which sidesteps the computationally-intensive task of pairwise comparisons to mine comparable documents and instead relies on heuristics, we tackle the challenge head on. This paper describes a fully open-source, scalable MapReduce-based processing pipeline that is able to automatically extract large quantities of parallel sentences. Experiments examine the impact data size has on a state-of-the-art SMT system.

We acknowledge that different components of this work are not novel and the general principles behind "big data" MT are well known. However, when considered together with our previous work (Ture et al., 2011), to our knowledge this is the first exposition in which all the pieces have been "put together" in an end-to-end pipeline that is accessible to academic research groups. The framework described in this paper is entirely open source, and the computational resources necessary to replicate our results are relatively modest.

Starting from nothing more than two corpora in different languages (in German and English, in our case), we are able to extract bitext and improve translation quality by a significant margin (2.39 BLEU points), essentially "for free". By varying both the quantity and quality of the bitext, we characterize the tradeoffs between the amount of data, computational costs, and translation quality.

2 Related Work

The idea of mining parallel sentences, particularly from the web, is of course not new. Most adopt a two step process: 1. identify comparable documents and generate candidate sentence pairs, and 2. filter candidate pairs to retain parallel sentences.

The general solution to the first step involves computing pairwise similarities across multi-lingual corpora. As this is computationally intensive, most studies fall back to heuristics, e.g., comparing news articles close in time (Munteanu and Marcu, 2005), exploiting "inter-wiki" links in Wikipedia (Smith et al., 2010), or bootstrapping off an existing search engine (Resnik and Smith, 2003). In contrast, we adopt a more exhaustive approach by directly tackling the cross-lingual pairwise similarity problem, using MapReduce on a modest cluster. We perform experiments on German and English Wikipedia (two largest available), but our technique is general and does not depend on sparse, manually-created inter-wiki links. Thus, compared to those approaches, we achieve much higher recall.

The second step (filtering candidate sentence pairs) is relatively straightforward, and we adopt the classification approach of Munteanu and Marcu (2005). However, unlike in previous work, we need to classify large volumes of data (due to higher recall in the first step). Therefore, we care about the relationship between classification accuracy and the speed of the classifier. Our two-stage approach gives us both high effectiveness (accuracy) and efficiency (speed).

A recent study from Google describes a general solution to our problem that scales to web collections (Uszkoreit et al., 2010). The authors translate all documents from one language into another, thus transforming the problem into identifying similar mono-lingual document pairs. Nevertheless, our approach makes several additional contributions. First, we explore the effect of dataset size on results. Our conclusions are more nuanced than simply "more data is better", since there is a tradeoff between quality and quantity. Our experiments involve orders of magnitude *less* data, but we nevertheless observe significant gains over a strong baseline. Overall, our approach requires far less computational resources and thus is within the reach of academic research groups: we do not require running an MT system on one side of the entire collection, and we carefully evaluate and control the speed of sentence-classification. Finally, in support of open science, our code[1] and data[2] are available as part of Ivory, an open-source Hadoop toolkit for web-scale information retrieval (Lin et al., 2009).

[1] ivory.cc

[2] github.com/ferhanture/WikiBitext

3 Generating Candidate Sentences

We applied our approach on English Wikipedia (10.9m documents, 30.6GB) and German Wikipedia (2.4m articles, 8.5GB), using XML dumps from January 2011. English and German Wikipedia were selected because they are the largest Wikipedia collections available, and we want to measure effects in a language for which we already have lots of bitext. In both collections, redirect pages and stub articles were discarded.

To mine comparable documents, we used our previously described algorithm (Ture et al., 2011), based on local-sensitive hashing, also implemented in Hadoop MapReduce. The reader is referred to the paper for details. On a 16 node (96 core) cluster, we were able to extract 64m (d_e, d_f) document pairs (with cosine similarity ≥ 0.3) in 8.8 hours.

For each of the (d_e, d_f) pairs, the next processing step involves generating the Cartesian product of sentences in both documents as candidate sentence pairs: this itself is a non-trivial problem. Although in this particular case it may be possible to load both document collections in memory, we envision scaling up to collections in the future for which this is not possible. Therefore, we devised a scalable, distributed, out-of-memory solution using Hadoop.

The algorithm works as follows: We map over (docid n, document d) pairs from both the German and English collections. In each mapper all (d_e, d_f) similarity pairs are loaded in memory. If the input document is not found in any of these pairs, no work is performed. Otherwise, we extract all sentences and retain only those that have at least 5 terms and at least 3 unique terms. Sentences are converted into BM25-weighted vectors in the English term space; for German sentences, translation into English is accomplished using the technique proposed by Darwish and Oard (2003). For every (d_e, d_f) pair that the input document is found in, the mapper emits the list of weighted sentence vectors, with the (d_e, d_f) pair as the key. As all intermediate key-value pairs in MapReduce are grouped by their keys for reduce-side processing, the reducer receives the key (d_e, d_f) and weighted sentence vectors for both the German and English articles. From there, we generate the Cartesian product of sentences in both languages. As an initial filtering step, we discard all pairs where the ratio of sentence lengths is more than two, a heuristic proposed in (Munteanu and Marcu, 2005). Each of the remaining candidate sentences are then processed by two separate classifiers: a less accurate, fast classifier and a more accurate, slow classifier. This is described in the next section.

This algorithm is a variant of what is commonly known as a reduce-side join in MapReduce (Lin and Dyer, 2010), where (d_e, d_f) serves as the join key. Note that in this algorithm, sentence vectors are emitted multiple times, one for each (d_e, d_f) pair that they participate in: this results in increased network traffic during the sort/shuffle phase. We experimented with an alternative algorithm that processes all foreign documents similar to the same English document together, e.g., processing $(d_e, [d_{f1}, d_{f2}, \ldots])$ together. This approach, counter-intuitively, was slower despite reduced network traffic, due to skew in the distribution of similar document pairs. In our experiments, half of the source collection was not linked to any target document, whereas 4% had more than 100 links. This results in reduce-side load imbalance, and while most of the reducers finish quickly, a few reducers end up performing substantially more computation, and these "stragglers" increase end-to-end running time.

4 Parallel Sentence Classification

We built two MaxEnt parallel sentence classifiers using the OpenNLP package, with data from a sample of the Europarl corpus of European parliament speeches. For training, we sampled 1000 parallel sentences from the German-English subset of the corpus as positive instances, and 5000 non-parallel sentence pairs as negative instances. For testing, we sampled another 1000 parallel pairs and generated all possible non-parallel pairs by the Cartesian product of these samples. This provides a better approximation of the task we're interested in, since most of the candidate sentence pairs will be non-parallel in a comparable corpus. We report precision, recall, and F-score, using different classifier confidence scores as the decision threshold (see Table 1).

Our first, *simple* classifier, which uses cosine similarity between the sentences as the only feature, achieved a maximum F-score of 74%, with 80% precision and 69% recall. Following previous work

Classifier	Measure	Value
Simple	Recall @ P90	0.59
	Recall @ P80	0.69
	Best F-score	0.74
Complex	Recall @ P90	0.69
	Recall @ P80	0.79
	Best F-score	0.80

Table 1: Accuracy of the simple and complex sentence classifiers on Europarl data.

(Smith et al., 2010), we also report recall with precision at 80% and 90% in Table 1; the classifier effectiveness is comparable to the previous work. The second, *complex* classifier uses the following additional features: ratio of sentence lengths, ratio of source-side tokens that have translations on the target side, ratio of target-side tokens that have translations on the source side. We also experimented with features using the word alignment output, but there was no improvement in accuracy. The complex classifier showed better performance: recall of 79% at 80% precision and 69% at precision of 90%, with a maximum F-score of 80%.

Due to the large amounts of data involved in our experiments, we were interested in speed/accuracy tradeoffs between the two classifiers. Microbenchmarks were performed on a commodity laptop running Mac OS X on a 2.26GHz Intel Core Duo CPU, measuring per-instance classification speed (including feature computation time). The complex classifier took 100 μs per instance, about 4 times slower than the simple one, which took 27 μs.

The initial input of 64m similar document pairs yielded 400b raw candidate sentence pairs, which were first reduced to 214b by the per-sentence length filter, and then to 132b by enforcing a maximum sentence length ratio of 2. The simple classifier was applied to the remaining pairs, with different confidence thresholds. We adjusted the threshold to obtain different amounts of bitext, to see the effect on translation quality (this condition is called S_1 hereafter). The positive results of the first classifier was then processed by the second classifier (this two-level approach is called S_2 hereafter).

Candidate generation was completed in 2.4 hours on our cluster with 96 cores. These candidates went through the MapReduce shuffle-and-sort process in 0.75 hours, which were then classified in 4 hours.

Processing by the more complex classifier in S_2 took an additional 0.52 hours.

5 End-to-End MT Experiments

In all experiments, our MT system learned a synchronous context-free grammar (Chiang, 2007), using GIZA++ for word alignments, MIRA for parameter tuning (Crammer et al., 2006), cdec for decoding (Dyer et al., 2010), a 5-gram SRILM for language modeling, and single-reference BLEU for evaluation. The baseline system was trained on the German-English WMT10 training data, consisting of 3.1m sentence pairs. For development and testing, we used the newswire datasets provided for WMT10, including 2525 sentences for tuning and 2489 sentences for testing.

Our baseline system includes all standard features, including phrase translation probabilities in both directions, word and arity penalties, and language model scores. It achieves a BLEU score of 21.37 on the test set, which would place it 5th out of 9 systems that reported comparable results in WMT10 (only three systems achieved a BLEU score over 22). Many of these systems used techniques that exploited the specific aspects of the task, e.g., German-specific morphological analysis. In contrast, we present a knowledge-impoverished, entirely data-driven approach, by simply looking for more data in large collections.

For both experimental conditions (one-step classification, S_1, and two-step classification, S_2) we varied the decision threshold to generate new bitext collections of different sizes. Each of these collections was added to the baseline training data to induce an entirely new translation model (note that GIZA additionally filtered out some of the pairs based on length). The final dataset sizes, along with BLEU scores on the test data, are shown in Fig. 1. In S_1, we observe that increasing the amount of data (by lowering the decision threshold) initially leads to lower BLEU scores (due to increased noise), but there is a threshold after which the improvement coming from the added data supersedes the noise. The S_2 condition increases the quality of bitext by reducing this noise: the best run, with 5.8m pairs added to the baseline (final dataset has 8.1m pairs), yields 23.76 BLEU (labeled P on figure), 2.39 points above the

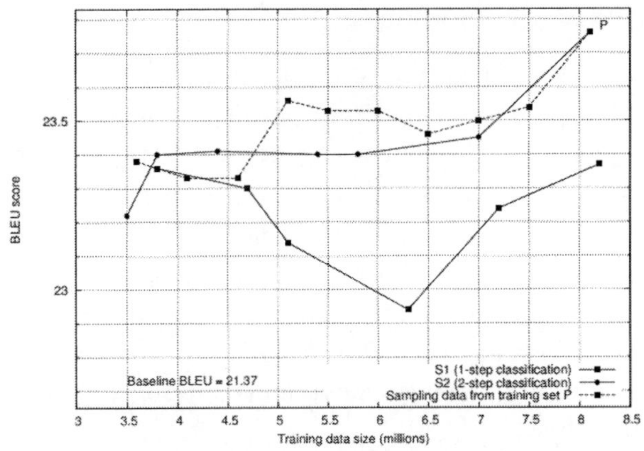

Figure 1: Evaluation results on the WMT10 test set.

baseline (and higher than the best WMT10 result). These results show that the two-step classification process, while slower, is worth the additional processing time.

Our approach yields solid improvements even with less data added: with only 382k pairs added to the baseline, the BLEU score increases by 1.84 points. In order to better examine the effect of data size alone, we created partial datasets from P by randomly sampling sentence pairs, and then repeated experiments, also shown in Fig. 1. We see an increasing trend of BLEU scores with respect to data size. By comparing the three plots, we see that S_2 and random sampling from P work better than S_1. Also, random sampling is not always worse than S_2, since some pairs that receive low classifier confidence turn out to be helpful.

6 Conclusions

In this paper, we describe a scalable MapReduce implementation for automatically mining parallel sentences from arbitrary comparable corpora. We show, at least for German-English MT, that an impoverished, data-driven approach is more effective than task-specific engineering. With the distributed bitext mining machinery described in this paper, improvements come basically "for free" (the only cost is a modest amount of cluster resources). Given the availability of data and computing power, there is simply no reason why MT researchers should not ride the large-data "tide" that lifts all boats. For the benefit of the community, all code necessary to replicate these results have been open sourced, as well as the bitext we've gathered.

Acknowledgments

This research was supported in part by the BOLT program of the Defense Advanced Research Projects Agency, Contract No. HR0011-12-C-0015; NSF under awards IIS-0916043 and CCF-1018625. Any opinions, findings, conclusions, or recommendations expressed in this paper are those of the authors and do not necessarily reflect the view of the sponsors. The second author is grateful to Esther and Kiri for their loving support and dedicates this work to Joshua and Jacob.

References

Thorsten Brants, Ashok C. Popat, Peng Xu, Franz J. Och, and Jeffrey Dean. 2007. Large language models in machine translation. *Proceedings of the 2007 Joint Conference on Empirical Methods in Natural Language Processing and Computational Natural Language Learning*, pages 858–867, Prague, Czech Republic.

David Chiang. 2007. Hierarchical phrase-based translation. *Computational Linguistics*, 33:201–228.

Koby Crammer, Ofer Dekel, Joseph Keshet, Shai Shalev-Shwartz, and Yoram Singer. 2006. Online passive-aggressive algorithms. *Journal of Machine Learning Research*, 7:551–585.

Kareem Darwish and Douglas W. Oard. 2003. Analysis of anchor text for web search. *Proceedings of the 26th Annual International ACM SIGIR Conference on Research and Development in Information Retrieval (SIGIR 2003)*, pages 261–268, Toronto, Canada.

Chris Dyer, Aaron Cordova, Alex Mont, and Jimmy Lin. 2008. Fast, easy, and cheap: Construction of statistical machine translation models with MapReduce. *Proceedings of the Third Workshop on Statistical Machine Translation at ACL 2008*, pages 199–207, Columbus, Ohio.

Chris Dyer, Adam Lopez, Juri Ganitkevitch, Jonathan Weese, Ferhan Ture, Phil Blunsom, Hendra Setiawan, Vladimir Eidelman, and Philip Resnik. 2010. cdec: A decoder, alignment, and learning framework for finite-state and context-free translation models. *Proceedings of the ACL 2010 System Demonstrations*, pages 7–12, Uppsala, Sweden, July.

Jimmy Lin and Chris Dyer. 2010. *Data-Intensive Text Processing with MapReduce*. Morgan & Claypool Publishers.

Jimmy Lin, Donald Metzler, Tamer Elsayed, and Lidan Wang. 2009. Of Ivory and Smurfs: Loxodontan MapReduce experiments for web search. *Proceedings of the Eighteenth Text REtrieval Conference (TREC 2009)*, Gaithersburg, Maryland.

Dragos Stefan Munteanu and Daniel Marcu. 2005. Improving machine translation performance by exploiting non-parallel corpora. *Computational Linguistics*, 31(4):477–504.

Philip Resnik and Noah A. Smith. 2003. The web as a parallel corpus. *Computational Linguistics*, 29(3):349–380.

Jason R. Smith, Chris Quirk, and Kristina Toutanova. 2010. Extracting parallel sentences from comparable corpora using document level alignment. *Proceedings of Human Language Technologies: The 2010 Annual Conference of the North American Chapter of the Association for Computational Linguistics (HLT/NAACL 2010)*, pages 403–411, Los Angeles, California.

Ferhan Ture, Tamer Elsayed, and Jimmy Lin. 2011. No free lunch: Brute force vs. locality-sensitive hashing for cross-lingual pairwise similarity. *Proceedings of the 34th Annual International ACM SIGIR Conference on Research and Development in Information Retrieval (SIGIR 2011)*, pages 943–952, Beijing, China.

Jakob Uszkoreit, Jay M. Ponte, Ashok C. Popat, and Moshe Dubiner. 2010. Large scale parallel document mining for machine translation. *Proceedings of the 23rd International Conference on Computational Linguistics (COLING 2010)*, pages 1101–1109, Beijing, China.

Summarization of Historical Articles Using Temporal Event Clustering

James Gung
Department of Computer Science
Miami University
Oxford, Ohio 45056
gungjm@muohio.edu

Jugal Kalita
Department of Computer Science
University of Colorado
Colorado Springs CO 80920
jkalita@uccs.edu

Abstract

In this paper, we investigate the use of temporal information for improving extractive summarization of historical articles. Our method clusters sentences based on their timestamps and temporal similarity. Each resulting cluster is assigned an importance score which can then be used as a weight in traditional sentence ranking techniques. Temporal importance weighting offers consistent improvements over baseline systems.

1 Introduction

Extensive research has gone into determining which features of text documents are useful for calculating the importance of sentences for extractive summarization, as well as how to use these features (Gupta and Lehal, 2010). Little work, however, has considered the importance of temporal information towards single document summarization. This is likely because many text documents have very few explicit time features and do not necessarily describe topics in chronological order.

Historical articles, such as Wikipedia articles describing wars, battles, or other major events, tend to contain many explicit time features. Historical articles also tend to describe events in chronological order. In addition, historical articles tend to focus on a single central event. The importance of other events can then be judged by their temporal distance from this central event. Finally, important events in an article will be described in greater detail, employing more sentences than less important events.

This paper investigates the value of a temporal-based score towards automatic summarization, specifically focusing on historical articles. We investigate whether or not such a score can be used as a weight in traditional sentence ranking techniques to improve summarization quality.

2 Related Work

Event-based summarization is a recent approach to summary generation. (Filatova and Hatzivassiloglou, 2004) introduced atomic events, which are named entities connected by a relation such as a verb or action noun. Events are selected for summary by applying a maximum coverage algorithm to minimize redundancy while maintaining coverage of the major concepts of the document. (Vanderwende et al., 2004) identify events as triples consisting of two nodes and a relation. PageRank is then used to determine the relative importance of these triples represented in a graph. Sentence generation techniques are applied towards summarization.

Limited work has explored the use of temporal information for summarization. (Lim et al., 2005) use the explicit time information in the context of multi-document summarization for sentence extraction and detection of redundant sentences, ordering input documents by time. They observe that important sentences tend to occur in in time slots containing more documents and time slots occurring at the end and beginning of the documents set. They select topic sentences for each time slot, giving higher weights based on the above observation.

(Wu et al., 2007) extract event elements, the arguments in an event, and event terms, the actions. Each event is placed on a timeline divided into intervals consistent with the timespan of the article. Each element and event term receives a weight corresponding to the total number of elements and event terms located in each time interval the event element or term occupies. Each sentence is scored by the total weight of event elements and terms it contains.

Clustering of events based on time has also received little attention. (Foote and Cooper, 2003) investigate clustering towards organizing timestamped digital photographs. They present a method that first calculates the temporal similarity between all pairs of photographs at multiple time scales. These values are stored in a chronologically ordered matrix. Cluster boundaries are determined by calculating novelty scores for each set of similarity matrices. These are used to form the final clusters. We adopt this clustering method for clustering timestamped sentences.

3 Approach

The goal of our method is to give each sentence in an article a temporal importance score that can be used as a weight in traditional sentence ranking techniques. To do this, we need to gain an idea of the temporal structure of events in an article. A score must then be assigned to each group corresponding to the importance of the group's timespan to the article as a whole. Each sentence in a particular group will be assigned the same temporal importance score, necessitating the use of a sentence ranking technique to find a complete summary.

3.1 Temporal Information Extraction

We use Heideltime, a rule-based system that uses sets of regular expressions, to extract explicit time expressions in the article and normalize them (Strötgen and Gertz, 2010). Events that occur between each Heideltime-extracted timestamp are assigned timestamps consisting of when the prior timestamp ends and the subsequent timestamp begins. The approach is naive and is described in (Chasin et al., 2011). This method of temporal extraction is not reliable, but serves the purposes of testing as a reasonable baseline for temporal extraction systems. As the precision increases, the performance of our system should also improve.

3.2 Temporal Clustering

To cluster sentences into temporally-related groups, we adopt a clustering method proposed by Foote et al. to group digital photograph collections.

Inter-sentence similarity is calculated between every pair of sentences using Equation (1).

$$S_K(i,j) = exp\left(-\frac{|t_i - t_j|}{K}\right) \quad (1)$$

The similarity measure is based inversely on the distance between the central time of the sentences. Similarity scores are calculated at varying granularities. If the article focuses on a central event that occurs over only a few hours, such as the assassination of John F. Kennedy, the best clustering will generally be found from similarities calculated using a smaller time granularity. Conversely, articles with central events spanning several years, such as the American Civil War, will be clustered using similarities calculated at larger time granularities.

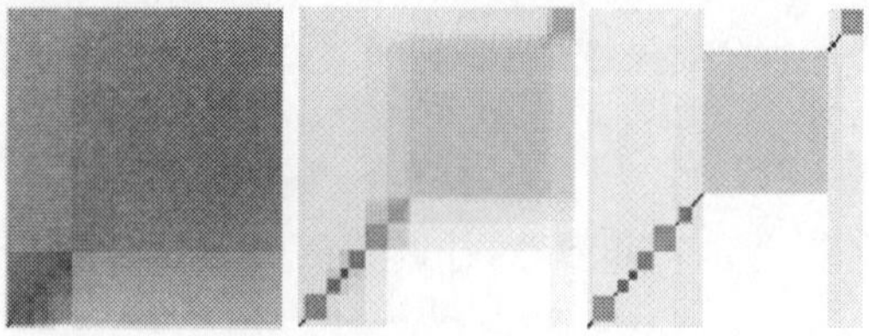

Figure 1: Similarity matrices at varying k displayed as heat maps, darker representing more similar entries

The similarities are placed in a matrix and organized chronologically in order of event occurrence time. In this matrix, entries close to the diagonal are among the most similar and the actual diagonal entries are maximally similar (diagonal entries correspond to similarities between the same sentences).

To identify temporal event boundaries, (Foote and Cooper, 2003) calculate novelty scores. A checkerboard kernel in which diagonal regions contain all positive weights and off-diagonal regions contain all negative weights is correlated along the diagonal of the similarity matrix. The weights of each entry in the kernel are calculated from a Gaussian function such that the most central entries have the highest (or lowest in the off-diagonal regions) values. The result is maximized when the kernel is located on temporal event boundaries. In relatively uniform regions, the positive and negative weights cancel each other out, resulting in small novelty scores. Where there is a gap in similarity, presumably at an event boundary, off diagonal squares are dissimilar, increasing the novelty score. In calculating novelty scores with each set of similarity scores, we obtain a hierarchical set of boundaries. With each time granularity, we have a potential clustering option.

In order to choose the best clustering, we calculate a confidence score C for each boundary set, then choose the clustering with the highest score, as suggested in (Foote and Cooper, 2003). This score is the sum of intercluster similarities ($IntraS$) between adjacent clusters subtracted from the sum of intracluster ($InterS$) similarities as seen in Equation (4). A high confidence score suggests low intercluster similarity and high intracluster similarity.

$$IntraS(B_K)_S = \sum_{l=1}^{|B_k|-1} \sum_{i,j=b_l}^{b_l+1} \frac{S_K(i,j)}{(b_{l+1} - b_l)^2} \quad (2)$$

$$InterS(B_K)_S = \sum_{l=1}^{|B_k|-2} \sum_{i=b_l}^{b_l+1} \sum_{j=b_l+1}^{b_l+2} \frac{S_K(i,j)}{(b_{l+1} - b_l)(b_{l+2} - b_{l+1})} \quad (3)$$

$$C_S(B_K) = IntraS(B_K)_S - InterSB_K)_S \quad (4)$$

3.3 Estimating Clustering Paramaters

Historical articles describing wars generally have much larger timespans than articles describing battles. Looking at battles at a broad time granularity applicable to wars may not produce a meaningful clustering. Thus, we should estimate the temporal structure of each article before clustering. The time granularity for each clustering is controlled by the *k* parameter in the similarity function between sentences. To find multiple clusterings, we start at a base *k*, then increment *k* by a multiplier for each new clustering. We calculate the base *k* using the standard deviation for event times in the article. Measuring the spread of events in the article gives us an estimate of what time scale we should use.

3.4 Calculating Temporal Importance

We use three novel metrics to calculate the importance of a cluster towards a summary. The first metric is based on the size of the cluster (Eqn 5). This is motivated by the assumption that more important events will be described in greater detail, thus producing larger clusters. The second metric (Eqn 6) is based on the distance from the cluster's centroid to the centroid of the largest cluster, corresponding to the central event of the article. This metric is motivated by the assumption that historical articles have a central event which is described in the greatest detail. The third metric is based on the spread of the cluster (Eqn 7). Clusters with large spreads are unlikely to pertain to the same event, and should therefore be penalized.

$$Size(C_i) = \frac{|C_i|}{|C_{max}|} \quad (5)$$

$$Sim(C_i) = exp\left(-\frac{|t_{C_iCentroid} - t_{MaxClusterCentroid}|}{m}\right) \quad (6)$$

$$Spread(C_i) = exp\left(-\frac{\sigma_{C_i}}{n * (t_{max} - t_{min})}\right) \quad (7)$$

The parameters *m* and *n* serve to weight the importance of these measures and are assigned based on the spread of events in an article. For *n*, we used the standard deviation of event times in the article. For *m*, we used the cluster similarity score from Equation (4). The three measures work in tandem to ensure that the importance measure will be valid even if the largest cluster does not correspond to the central event of the article.

3.5 Final Sentence Ranking

Each sentence is assigned a temporal importance weight equal to the importance score of the cluster to which it belongs. To find a complete ranking of the sentences, we apply a sentence ranking technique. Any automatic summarization technique that ranks its sentences with numerical scores can potentially be augmented with our temporal importance weight. We multiply the base scores from the ranking by the associated temporal importance weights for each sentence to find the final ranking.

$$WS(V_i) = (1 - d) + d * \sum_{V_j \in In(V_i)} \frac{w_{j,i}}{\sum_{v_k \in Out(V_j)} w_{j,k}} WS(V_j) \quad (8)$$

Like several graph-based methods for sentence ranking for summarization (e.g., (Erkan and Radev, 2004)), we use Google's PageRank algorithm (Equation 8) with a damping factor *d* of 0.85.

$$Similarity(S_i, S_j) = \frac{|\{w_k | w_k \in S_i \& w_k \in S_j\}|}{log(|S_i|) + log(|S_j|)} \quad (9)$$

We use TextRank (Mihalcea and Tarau, 2004) in our experiments. Our similarity measure is calculated using the number of shared named entities and nouns between sentences as seen in equation 9. For identification of named entities, we use Stanford NER (Finkel et al., 2005). It is straightforward to weight the resulting TextRank scores for each sentence using their cluster's temporal importance.

4 Experimental Results

We test on a set of 13 Wikipedia articles describing historical battles. The average article length is 189 sentences and 4,367 words. The longest article is 545 sentences and contains 11,563 words. The shortest article is 51 sentences and contains

1,476 words. Each article has at least two human-annotated gold standard summaries. Volunteers were asked to choose the most important sentences from each article. We evaluate using ROUGE-2 bi-gram matching (Lin, 2004).

4.1 Clustering

Each Wikipedia article contains a topic sentence stating the timespan of the main event in the article. This provides an easy way to determine whether a clustering is successful. If the largest cluster contains the timespan of the main event described by the topic sentence, we consider the clustering to be successful. The articles vary greatly in length. Also, the ratio of sentences with time features to sentences without is considerably varied. In 92% of the articles, there were successful clusterings. An example of an article that didn't cluster is Nickel Grass, where the main event was divided into two clusters. It is of interest to note that this article had one of lowest time feature to sentence ratios, which possibly explains the poor clustering.

4.2 Temporal Importance Weighting

We test our TextRank implementation with and without temporal importance weighting.

We observe improvements in general using the TextRank system with temporal importance weighting. The ROUGE-2 score increased by 15.72% across all the articles. The lowest increase was 0% and the highest was 128.86%. The average ROUGE-2 scores were 0.2575 weighted and 0.2362 unweighted, a statistically significant increase with a 95% confidence interval of 0.0066 to 0.0360.

In particular, we see significant improvements in articles that contain sentences TextRank ranked highly but have events occurring at significantly different times than the central event of the article. Although the content of these sentences is highly related to the rest of the article, they should not be included in the summary since their events happen nowhere near the main event temporally.

Our random ranking system, which randomly assigns base importance scores to each sentence, observed only small improvements, of 4.27% on average, when augmented with temporal importance weighting. It is likely that additional human-annotated summaries are necessary for conclusive results.

5 Conclusions and Future Work

The novelty-based clustering method worked extremely well for our purposes. These results can likely be improved upon using more advanced temporal extraction and interpolation methods, since we used a naive method for interpolating between time features prone to error. The temporal importance weighting worked very well with TextRank and reasonably well with random ranking.

It may also be fairly easy to predict the success of using this temporal weight a priori to summarization of an article. A small ratio of explicit time features to sentences (less than 0.15) indicates that the temporal interpolation process may not be very accurate. The linearity of time features is also a good indication of the success of temporal extraction. Finally, the spread of time features in an article is a clue to the success of our weighting method.

Acknowledgements

Research reported here has been funded partially by NSF grants CNS-0958576 and CNS-0851783.

References

R. Chasin, D. Woodward, and J. Kalita, 2011. *Machine Intelligence: Recent Advances*, chapter Extracting and Displaying Temporal Entities from Historical Articles. Narosa Publishing, Delhi.

G. Erkan and D.R. Radev. 2004. Lexrank: Graph-based lexical centrality as salience in text summarization. *J. Artif. Intell. Res.*, 22:457–479.

E. Filatova and V. Hatzivassiloglou. 2004. Event-based extractive summarization. In *ACL Workshop on Summarization*.

J.R. Finkel, T. Grenager, and C. Manning. 2005. Incorporating non-local information into information extraction systems by gibbs sampling. In *ACL*, pages 363–370.

J. Foote and M. Cooper. 2003. Media segmentation using self-similarity decomposition. In *SPIE*, volume 5021, pages 167–175.

V. Gupta and G.S. Lehal. 2010. A survey of text summarization extractive techniques. *Journal of Emerging Technologies in Web Intelligence*, 2(3):258–268.

J.M. Lim, I.S. Kang, J.H. Bae, and J.H. Lee. 2005. Sentence extraction using time features in multi-document summarization. *Information Retrieval Technology*, pages 82–93.

C.Y. Lin. 2004. Rouge: A package for automatic evaluation of summaries. In *Workshop on text summarization*, pages 25–26.

R. Mihalcea and P. Tarau. 2004. Textrank: Bringing order into texts. In *EMNLP*, pages 404–411.

J. Strötgen and M. Gertz. 2010. Heideltime: High quality rule-based extraction and normalization of temporal expressions. In *5th International Workshop on Semantic Evaluation*, pages 321–324.

L. Vanderwende, M. Banko, and A. Menezes. 2004. Event-centric summary generation. *Working notes of DUC*.

M. Wu, W. Li, Q. Lu, and K.F. Wong. 2007. Event-based summarization using time features. *Computational Linguistics and Intelligent Text Processing*, pages 563–574.

Comparing HMMs and Bayesian Networks for Surface Realisation

Nina Dethlefs
Heriot-Watt University
Edinburgh, Scotland
n.s.dethlefs@hw.ac.uk

Heriberto Cuayáhuitl
German Research Centre for Artificial Intelligence
Saarbrücken, Germany
heriberto.cuayahuitl@dfki.de

Abstract

Natural Language Generation (NLG) systems often use a pipeline architecture for sequential decision making. Recent studies however have shown that treating NLG decisions jointly rather than in isolation can improve the overall performance of systems. We present a joint learning framework based on Hierarchical Reinforcement Learning (HRL) which uses graphical models for surface realisation. Our focus will be on a comparison of Bayesian Networks and HMMs in terms of user satisfaction and naturalness. While the former perform best in isolation, the latter present a scalable alternative within joint systems.

1 Introduction

NLG systems have traditionally used a pipeline architecture which divides the generation process into three distinct stages. **Content selection** chooses 'what to say' and constructs a semantic form. **Utterance planning** organises the message into submessages and **surface realisation** maps the semantics onto words. Recently, a number of studies have pointed out that many decisions made at these distinct stages require interrelated, rather than isolated, optimisations (Angeli et al., 2010; Lemon, 2011; Cuayáhuitl and Dethlefs, 2011a; Dethlefs and Cuayáhuitl, 2011a). The key feature of a joint architecture is that decisions of all three NLG stages share information and can be made in an interrelated fashion. We present a joint NLG framework based on Hierarchical RL and focus, in particular, on the surface realisation component of joint NLG systems. We compare the user satisfaction and naturalness of surface realisation using Hidden Markov Models (HMMs) and Bayesian Networks (BNs) which both have been suggested as generation spaces—spaces of surface form variants for a semantic concept—within joint NLG systems (Dethlefs and Cuayáhuitl, 2011a; Dethlefs and Cuayáhuitl, 2011b) and in isolation (Georgila et al., 2002; Mairesse et al., 2010).

2 Surface Realisation for Situated NLG

We address the generation of navigation instructions, where e.g. the semantic form $(path(target = end\_of\_corridor) \wedge (landmark = lift \wedge dir = left))$ can be expressed as 'Go to the end of the corridor', 'Head to the end of the corridor past the lift on your left' and many more. The best realisation depends on the space (types and properties of spatial objects), the user (position, orientation, prior knowledge) and decisions of content selection and utterance planning. These can be interrelated with surface realisation, for example:

(1) 'Follow this corridor and go past the lift on your left. Then turn right at the junction.'
(2) 'Pass the lift and turn right at the junction.'

Here, (1) is appropriate for a user unfamiliar with the space and a high information need, so that more information should be given. For a familiar user, however, who may know where the lift is, it is redundant and (2) is preferable, because it is more efficient. An unfamiliar user may get confused with just (2).

In this paper, we distinguish navigation of *destination* ('go back to the office'), *direction* ('turn left'), *orientation* ('turn around'), *path* ('follow the corridor') and *straight'* ('go forward') in the GIVE corpus (Gargett et al., 2010). Users can react to an instruction by *performing the action*, *performing an undesired action*, *hesitating* or *requesting help*.

3 Jointly Learnt NLG: Hierarchical RL with Graphical Models

In a joint framework, each subtask of content selection, utterance planning and surface realisation has knowledge of the decisions made in the other two subtasks. In an isolated framework, this knowledge is absent. In the joint case, the relationship between hierarchical RL and graphical models is that the latter provide feedback to the former's surface realisation decisions according to a human corpus.

Hierarchical RL Our HRL agent consists of a hierarchy of discrete-time Semi-Markov Decision Processes, or SMDPs, M^i_j defined as 4-tuples $< S^i_j, A^i_j, T^i_j, R^i_j >$, where i and j uniquely identify a model in the hierarchy. These SMDPs represent generation subtasks, e.g. generating destination instructions. S^i_j is a set of states, A^i_j is a set of actions, and T^i_j is a probabilistic state transition function that determines the next state s' from the current state s and the performed action a. $R^i_j(s', \tau | s, a)$ is a reward function that specifies the reward that an agent receives for taking an action a in state s lasting τ time steps. Since actions in SMDPs may take a variable number of time steps to complete, the random variable τ represents this number of time steps. Actions can be either primitive or composite. The former yield single rewards, the latter correspond to SMDPs and yield cumulative rewards. The goal of each SMDP is to find an optimal policy π^* that maximises the reward for each visited state, according to $\pi^{*i}_j(s) = \arg\max_{a \in A} Q^{*i}_j(s, a)$, where $Q^i_j(s, a)$ specifies the expected cumulative reward for executing action a in state s and then following π^*. Please see (Dethlefs and Cuayáhuitl, 2011b) for details on the design of the hierarchical RL agent and the integration of graphical models for surface realisation.

Hidden Markov Models Representing surface realisation as an HMM can be roughly defined as the converse of POS tagging. While in POS tagging we map an observation string of words onto a hidden sequence of POS tags, in NLG we face the opposite scenario. Given an observation sequence of semantic symbols, we want to map it onto a hidden most likely sequence of words. We treat states as representing surface realisations for (observed) semantic classes, so that a sequence of states $s_0 ... s_n$ represents phrases or sentences. An observation sequence $o_0 ... o_n$ consists of a finite set of semantic symbols specific to an instruction type. Each symbol has an observation likelihood $b_s(o)_t$ giving the probability of observing o in state s at time t. We created the HMMs and trained the transition and emission probabilities from the GIVE corpus using the Baum-Welch algorithm. Please see Fig. 1 for an example HMM and (Dethlefs and Cuayáhuitl, 2011a) for details on using HMMs for surface realisation.

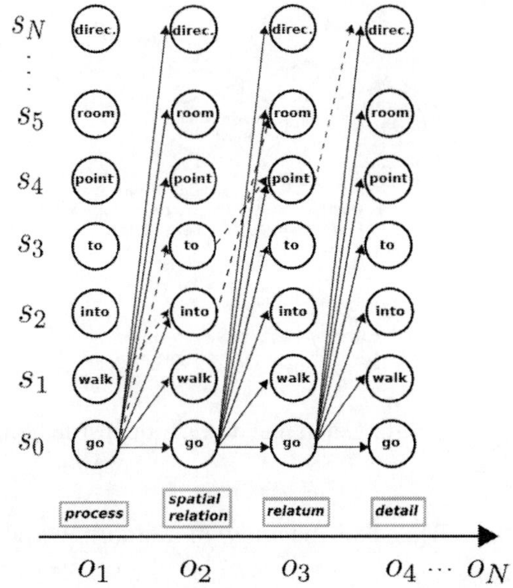

Figure 1: Example trellis for an HMM for destination instructions (not all states and transitions are shown). Dashed arrows show paths that occur in the corpus.

Bayesian Networks Representing a surface realiser as a BN, we can model the dynamics between semantic concepts and their realisations. A BN models a joint probability distribution over a set of random variables and their dependencies based on a directed acyclic graph, where each node represents a variable Y_j with parents $pa(Y_j)$. Due to the Markov condition, each variable depends only on its parents, resulting in a unique joint probability distribution $p(Y) = \Pi p(Y_j | pa(Y_j))$, where every variable is associated with a conditional probability distribution

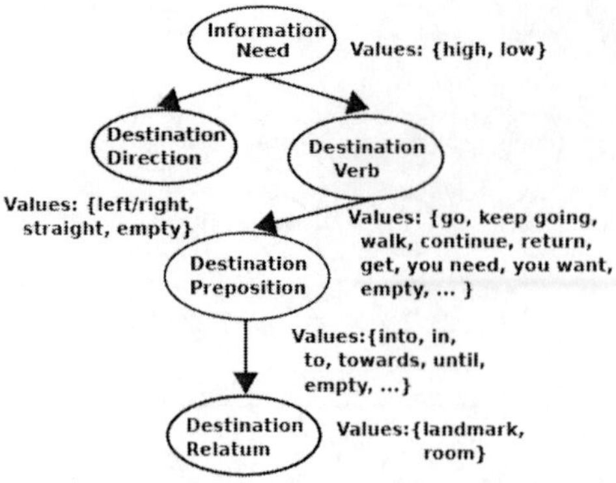

Figure 2: BN for generating destination instructions.

$p(Y_j|pa(Y_j))$. The meaning of random variables corresponds to semantic symbols. The values of random variables correspond to surface variants of a semantic symbol. Figure 2 shows an example BN with two main dependencies. First, the random variable 'information need' influences the inclusion of optional semantic constituents and the process of the utterance ('destination verb'). Second, a sequence of dependencies spans from the verb to the end of the utterance ('destination relatum'). The first dependency is based on the intuition that more detail is needed in an instruction for users with high information need (e.g. with little prior knowledge).[1] The second dependency is based on the hypothesis that the value of one constituent can be estimated based on the previous constituent. In the future, we may compare different configurations and effects of word order. Given the word sequence represented by lexical and syntactic variables $Y_0...Y_n$, and situation-based variables $Y_{n+1}...Y_m$, we can compute the posterior probability of a random variable Y_j. The parameters of the BNs were estimated using MLE. Please see (Dethlefs and Cuayáhuitl, 2011b) for details on using BNs for surface realisation within a joint learning framework.

4 Experimental Setting

We compare instructions generated with the HMMs and BNs according to their *user satisfaction* and their *naturalness*. The learning agent is trained using the reward function $Reward = User\_satisfaction \times P(w_0 \dots w_n) \times CAS$.[2] $User\_satisfaction$ is a function of task success and the number of user turns based on the PARADISE framework[3] (Walker et al., 1997) and CAS refers to the proportion of repetition and variation in surface forms. Our focus in this short paper is on $P(w_0 \dots w_n)$ which rewards the agent for having generated a surface form sequence $w_0 \dots w_n$. In HMMs, this corresponds to the forward probability—obtained from the Forward algorithm—of observing the sequence in the data. In BNs, $P(w_0 \dots w_n)$ corresponds to $P(Y_j = v_x|pa(Y_j) = v_y)$, the posterior probability given the chosen values v_x and v_y of random variables and their dependencies. We assign a reward of -1 for each action to prevent loops.

5 Experimental Results

User satisfaction Our trained policies learn the same content selection and utterance planning behaviour reported by (Dethlefs and Cuayáhuitl, 2011b). These policies contribute to the *user satisfaction* of instructions. BNs and HMMs however differ in their surface realisation choices. Figure 3 shows the performance in terms of average rewards over time for both models within the joint learning framework and in isolation.[4] For ease of comparison, a learning curve using a *greedy* policy is also shown. It always chooses the most likely surface form according to the human corpus without taking other tradeoffs into account. Within the joint framework, both BNs and HMMs learn to generate context-sensitive surface forms that balance the tradeoffs of the most likely sequence (according to the human corpus) and the one that best corresponds to the user's information need (e.g., using nick names of rooms for familiar users). The BNs

[1]This is key to the joint treatment of content selection and surface realisation: if an utterance is not informative in terms of content, it will receive bad rewards, even with good surface realisation choices (and vice versa).

[2]This reward function, the simulated environment and training parameters were adapted from (Dethlefs and Cuayáhuitl, 2011b) to allow a comparison with related work in using graphical models for surface realisation. Simulation is based on uni- and bigrams for the spatial setting and Naive Bayes Classification for user reactions to system instructions.

[3]See (Dethlefs et al., 2010) for evidence of the correlation between user satisfaction, task success and dialogue length.

[4]In the isolated case, subtasks of content selection, utterance planning and surface realisation are blind regarding the decisions made by other subtasks, but in the joint case they are not.

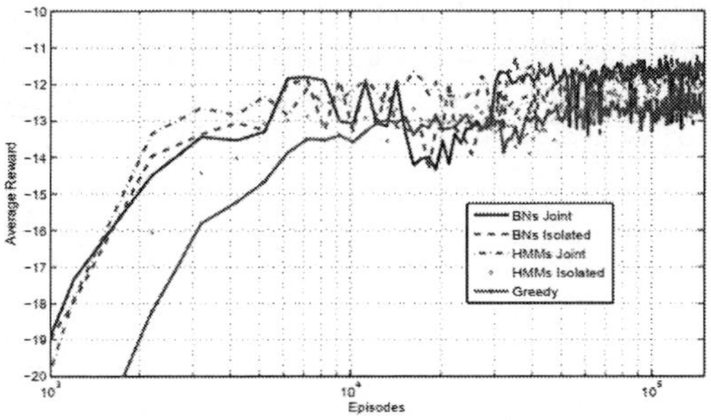

Figure 3: Performance of HMMs, BNs and a *greedy* baseline in conjunction and isolation of the joint framework.

reach an average reward[5] of -11.53 and outperform the HMMs (average -11.64) only marginally by less than one percent. BNs and HMMs improve the *greedy* baseline by 6% ($p < 0.0001$, $r = 0.90$). While BNs reach the same performance in isolation of the joint framework, the performance of HMMs deteriorates significantly to an average reward of -12.12. This corresponds to a drop of 5% ($p < 0.0001$, $r = 0.79$) and is nearly as low as the *greedy* baseline. HMMs thus reach a comparable performance to BNs as a result of the joint learning architecture: the HRL agent will discover the non-optimal behaviour that is caused by the HMM's lack of context-awareness (due to their independence assumptions) and learn to balance this drawback by learning a more comprehensive policy itself. For the more context-aware BNs this is not necessary.

Naturalness We compare the instructions generated with HMMs and BNs regarding their human-likeness based on the Kullback-Leibler (KL) divergence. It computes the difference between two probability distributions. For evidence of its usefulness for measuring naturalness, cf. (Cuayáhuitl, 2010). We compare human instructions (based on strings) drawn from the corpus against strings generated by the HMMs and BNs to see how similar both are to human authors. Splitting the human instructions in half and comparing them to each other indicates how similar human authors are to each other. It yields a KL score of 1.77 as a gold standard (the lower the better). BNs compared with human data obtain a score of 2.83 and HMMs of 2.80. The difference in terms of similarity with humans for HMMs and BNs in a joint NLG model is not significant.

[5]The average rewards of agents have negative values due to the negative reward of -1 the agent receives for each action.

Discussion While HMMs reach comparable user satisfaction and naturalness to BNs in a joint system, they show a 5% lower performance in isolation. This is likely caused by their conditional independence assumptions: (a) the Markov assumption, (b) the stationary assumption, and (c) the observation independence assumption. Even though these can make HMMs easier to train and scale than more structured models such as BNs, it also puts them in a disadvantage concerning context-awareness and accuracy as shown by our results. In contrast, the random variables of BNs allow them to keep a structured model of the space, user, and relevant content selection and utterance planning choices. BNs are thus able to compute the posterior probability of a surface form based on all relevant properties of the current situation (not just the occurrence in a corpus). While BNs also place independence assumptions on their variables, they usually overcome the problem of lacking context-awareness by their dependencies across random variables. However, BNs also face limitations. Given the dependencies they postulate, they are typically more data intensive and less scalable than less structured models such as HMMs. This can be problematic for large domains such as many real world applications. Regarding their application to surface realisation, we can argue that while BNs are the best performing model in isolation, HMMs represent a cheap and scalable alternative especially for large-scale problems in a joint NLG system.

6 Conclusion and Future Work

We have compared the user satisfaction and naturalness of instructions generated with HMMs and BNs in a joint HRL model for NLG. Results showed that while BNs perform best in isolation, HMMs represent a cheap and scalable alternative within the joint framework. This is particularly attractive for large-scale, data-intensive systems. While this paper has focused on instruction generation, the hierarchical approach in our learning framework helps to scale up to larger NLG tasks, such as text or paragraph generation. Future work could test this claim, compare other graphical models, such as dynamic BNs, and aim for a comprehensive human evaluation.

Acknowledgements This research was funded by the European Commission's FP7 programmes under grant agreement no. 287615 (PARLANCE) and no. ICT-248116 (ALIZ-E).

References

Angeli, G., Liang, P. and D. Klein (2010). A simple domain-independent probabilistic approach to generation , *Proceedings of the Conference on Empirical Methods in Natural Language Processing (EMNLP)* .

Cuayáhuitl, H., Renals, S., Lemon, O. and H. Shimodaira (2010). Evaluation of a Hierarchical Reinforcement Learning Spoken Dialogue System, *Computer Speech and Language 24*.

Cuayáhuitl, H., and N. Dethlefs (2011a). Spatially-Aware Dialogue Control Using Hierarchical Reinforcement Learning, *ACM Transactions on Speech and Language Processing (Special Issue on Machine Learning for Robust and Adaptive Spoken Dialogue Systems 7(3)*.

Dethlefs, N. and H. Cuayáhuitl, 2011. Hierarchical Reinforcement Learning and Hidden Markov Models for Task-Oriented Natural Language Generation, *In Proc. of the 49th Annual Meeting of the Association for Computational Linguistics (ACL-HLT)*.

Dethlefs, N. and H. Cuayáhuitl, 2011. Combining Hierarchical Reinforcement Learning and Bayesian Networks for Natural Language Generation in Situated Dialogue, *In Proceedings of the 13th European Workshop on Natural Language Generation (ENLG)*.

Dethlefs, N., Cuayáhuitl, H., Richter, K.-F., Andonova, E. and J. Bateman, 2010. Evaluating Task Success in a Dialogue System for Indoor Navigation, *In Proceedings of the Workshop on the Semantics and Pragmatics of Dialogue (SemDial)*.

Gargett, A., Garoufi, K., Koller, A. and K. Striegnitz (2010). The GIVE-2 Corpus of Giving Instructions in Virtual Environments, *Proc. of the 7th International Conference on Language Resources and Evaluation*.

Georgila, K., Fakotakis, N. and Kokkinakis, G. (2002). Stochastic Language Modelling for Recognition and Generation in Dialogue Systems. *TAL (Traitement automatique des langues) Journal*, Vol. 43(3).

Lemon, O. (2011). Learning what to say and how to say it: joint optimization of spoken dialogue management and Natural Language Generation, *Computer Speech and Language 25(2)*.

Mairesse, F., Gašić, M., Jurčíček, F., Keizer, S., Thomson, B., Yu, K. and S. Young (2010). Phrase-based statistical language generation using graphical models and active learning, *Proc. of the 48th Annual Meeting of the Association for Computational Linguistics*.

Walker, M., Litman, D., Kamm, C. and A. Abella (1997). PARADISE: A Framework for Evaluating Spoken Dialogue Agents, *Proceedings of the Annual Meeting of the Association for Computational Linguistic (ACL)*.

On The Feasibility of Open Domain Referring Expression Generation Using Large Scale Folksonomies

Fabián Pacheco **Pablo Ariel Duboue*** **Martín Ariel Domínguez**
Facultad de Matemática, Astronomía y Física
Universidad Nacional de Córdoba
Córdoba, Argentina

Abstract

Generating referring expressions has received considerable attention in Natural Language Generation. In recent years we start seeing deployments of referring expression generators moving away from limited domains with custom-made ontologies. In this work, we explore the feasibility of using large scale noisy ontologies (folksonomies) for open domain referring expression generation, an important task for summarization by re-generation. Our experiments on a fully annotated anaphora resolution training set and a larger, volunteer-submitted news corpus show that existing algorithms are efficient enough to deal with large scale ontologies but need to be extended to deal with undefined values and some measure for information salience.

1 Introduction

Given an entity[1] (the **referent**) and a set of competing entities (the **set of distractors**), the task of referring expression generation (REG) involves creating a mention to the referent so that, in the eyes of the reader, it is clearly distinguishable from any other entity in the set of distractors. In a traditional generation pipeline, referring expression generation happens at the sentence planning level. As a result, its output is not a textual nugget but a description employed later on by the surface realizer. In this paper, we consider the output of the REG system to be Definite Descriptions (DD) consisting of a set of *positive triples* and a set of *negative triples*, enumerating referent-related properties.

Since the seminal work by Dale and Reiter (1995), REG has received a lot of attention in the Natural Language Generation (NLG) community. However, most of the early work on REG has been on traditional NLG systems, using custom-tailored ontologies. In recent years (Belz et al., 2010) there has been a shift towards what we term "Open Domain Referring Expression Generation," (OD REG), that is, a REG task where the properties come from a *folksonomy*, a large-scale volunteer-built ontology.

In particular, we are interested in changing anaphoric references for entities appearing in sentences drafted from different documents, as done in multi-document summarization (Advaith et al., 2011). For example, consider the following summary excerpt[2] as produced by Newsblaster (McKeown et al., 2002):

Thousands of cheering, flag-waving Palestinians gave Palestinian Authority President Mahmoud Abbas an enthusiastic welcome in Ramallah on Sunday, as he told them triumphantly that a "Palestinian spring" had been born following his speech to the United Nations last week.[3] *The* ***president*** *pressed Israel, in unusually frank terms, to reach a final peace agreement with the Palestinians, citing the boundaries in place on the eve of the June 1967 Arab-Israeli War as the starting point for ne-*

*To whom correspondence should be addressed. Email: pablo.duboue@gmail.com.

[1] Or set of entities, but not in this work.

[2] From http://newsblaster.cs.columbia.edu/archives/2011-10-07-04-51-35/web/summaries/ 2011-10-07-04-51-35-011.html.

[3] *After his stint at UN, Abbas is politically stronger than ever* (haaretz.com, 10/07/2011, 763 words).

gotiation about borders.[4]

Here the second sentence refers to U.S. president Barack Obama and a referring expression of the form "U.S. president" should have been used. Such expressions depend on the set of distractors present in the text, a requirement that highlights the dynamic nature of the problem. Our experiments extracted thousands of complex cases (such as distinguishing one musician from a set of five) which we used to test existing algorithms against a folksonomy, dbPedia[5] (Bizer et al., 2009). This folksonomy contains 1.7M triples (for its English version) and has been curated from Wikipedia.[6]

We performed two experiments: first we employed sets of distractors derived from a set of documents annotated with anaphora resolution information (Hasler et al., 2006). We found that roughly half of the entities annotated in the documents were present in the folksonomy, which speaks of the feasibility of using a folksonomy for OD REG, given the fact that Wikipedia has strict notability requirements for adding information. In the second experiment, we obtained sets of distractors from Wikinews,[7] a service where volunteers submit news articles interspersed with Wikipedia links. We leveraged said links to assemble 40k referring expression tasks.

For algorithms, we employed Dale and Reiter (1995), Gardent (2002) and Full Brevity (FB) (Bohnet, 2007). Our results show that the first two algorithms produce results in a majority of the referring expression tasks, with the Dale and Reiter algorithm being the most efficient and resilient of the three. The results, however, are of mixed quality and more research is needed to overcome two problems we have identified in our experiments: dealing with undefined information in the folksonomy and the need to incorporate a rough user model in the form of information salience.

In the next section we briefly summarize the three algorithms we employed in our experiments. In Section 3, we describe the data employed. Section 4 contains the results of our experiments and subsequent analysis. We conclude discussing future work.

[4] *Obama prods Mideast allies to embrace reform, make peace* (Washington Post, 10/07/2011, 371 words).

[5] `http://dbpedia.org`

[6] `http://wikipedia.org`

[7] `http://wikinews.org`

2 Referring Expression Generation (REG)

REG literature is vast and spans decades of work. We picked three algorithms with the following desiderata: all the algorithms can deal with single entity referents (a significant amount of recent work went into multi-entity referents) and we wanted to showcase a classic algorithm (Dale and Reiter's), an algorithm generating negations (Gardent's) and an algorithm with a more exhaustive search of the solutions space (Full Brevity). We very briefly describe each of the algorithms in turn, where R is the referent, C is the set of distractors and P is a list of properties, triples in the form (entity, property, value), describing R:

Dale and Reiter (1995). They assume the properties in P are ordered according to an established criteria. Then the algorithm iterates over P, adding each triple one at a time and removing from C all entities ruled out by the new triple. Triples that do not eliminate any new entities from C are ignored. The algorithm terminates when C is empty.

Gardent (2002). The algorithm uses Constraint Satisfaction Programming to solve two basic constraints: find a set of positive properties P^+ and negative properties P^-, such that all properties in P^+ are true for the referent and all in P^- are false, and it is the smaller $P^+ \cup P^-$ such that for every $c \in C$ there exist a property in P^+ that does not hold for c or a property in P^- that holds for c.[8]

Full Brevity (Bohnet, 2007). Starting from a state E of the form (L, C, P) with $L = \emptyset$ (selected properties), it keeps these states into a queue, where it loops until $C = \emptyset$. In each loop it generates new states (added to the end of the queue), as follows: given a state $E = (L, C, P)$ for each $p \in P$, if p removes elements rem from C, it adds $(L \cup \{p\}, C - rem, P - \{p\})$, otherwise $(L, C, P - \{p\})$.

3 Data

dbPedia. dbPedia (Bizer et al., 2009) is an ontology curated from Wikipedia infoboxes, small tables containing structured information at the top of most Wikipedia pages. The version employed in this paper ("Ontology Infobox Properties") contains 1,7520,158 triples. Each

[8] We employed the Choco CSP solver Java library: `http://www.emn.fr/z-info/choco-solver/`.

```
Former [[New Mexico]] {{w|Governor of New
Mexico|governor}} {{w|Gary Johnson}} ended
his campaign for the {{w|Republican Party
(United States)|Republican Party}} (GOP)
presidential nomination to seek the backing
of the {{w|Libertarian Party (United
States)|Libertarian Party}} (LP).
```

Figure 1: Wikinews example, from http://en.wikinews.org/wiki/U.S._presidential_candidate_Gary_Johnson_leaves_GOP_to_vie_for_the_LP_nom

entity is represented by a URI starting with `http://dbpedia.org/resource/` followed by the name of its associated Wikipedia title. See the next section for some example triples.

Pilot. While creating unambiguous descriptions is the NLG task known as referring expression generation, its NLU counterpart is anaphora resolution. We took a hand-annotated corpus for training anaphora resolution algorithms (Hasler et al., 2006) consisting of 74 documents containing 239 coreference chains. Each of the chains is an entity that can be used for our experiments, if the entity is in dbPedia and there are other suitable distractors in the same document. We hand annotated each of those 239 coreference chains by type (person, organization and location) and associated them to dbPedia URIs for the ones we found on Wikipedia. We found roughly half of the chains in dbPedia (106 out of 239, 44%). This percentage speaks of the coverage of dbPedia for OD REG. However, only 16 documents contain multiple entities of the same type and present in dbPedia, our pilot study criteria. These 16 documents result in the 16 tasks for our pilot. For a large scale evaluation we turned to Wikinews.

Wikinews. Wikinews is a news service operated as a wiki. As the news articles are interspersed with *interwiki* links, multiple entities can be disambiguated as Wikipedia pages (which in turn are dbPedia URIs). For example, in Figure 1, both the Libertarian Party and Republican Party can be considered potential distractors, as both are organizations.

The Wikimedia Foundation makes a database dump available for all Wikinews interwiki links (the links in braces in the above example). If a page contains more than one organization or person, we extracted the whole set of people (or organizations) as a referring expression task. To see whether a URI is a person or an organization we check for a birth date or creation date, respectively. In this manner, we obtained 4,230 tasks for people and 12,998 for organizations. This is dataset is freely available.[9]

4 Results

Pilot. The 16 tasks were split into 40 runs (a task spans n runs each, where n is the number of entities in the task, by rotating through the different alternative pairs of referent / set of distractors). From these tasks, Dale and Reiter produced no output 12 times and FB Brevity was unable to produce a result in 23 times. Gardent produced output for every run. We consider this an example of the increased expressive power of negative descriptions (it included a negation in 25% of the runs). For the other two algorithms, the lack of an unique triple differentiating one entity from the set of distractors seemed to be the main issue but there were multiple cases were FB ran out of memory for its queue of candidate nodes.

With respect to execution timings, Dale and Reiter ran into some corner cases and took time comparable to Gardent's algorithm. FB was 16 times slower (we found this counter-intuitive, as Gardent's algorithm is more demanding). Therefore, two of these algorithms were able to produce results using large scale ontological information. As FB ran into problems both in terms of execution time and failure rates, we omitted it from the large scale experiments.

We adjusted the parameters for the algorithms on this set to obtain the best possible quality output given the data and the problem. As such, we do not report quality assessments on the pilot data.

Wikinews. The tasks obtained from wikinews contained a large number of entities per task (an average of 12 people per task) and therefore span a large number of runs: 17,814 runs for people (from 4,230 tasks) and 44,080 for organizations (from 12,998 tasks).

On these large runs, execution time differences are in line with our *a priori* expectations: the greedy approach of Dale and Reiter is very fast[10] with Gardent's more comprehensive search taking about 40 times more time. Dale and Reiter failure rate was

[9] http://www.cs.famaf.unc.edu.ar/~pduboue/data/ also mirrored at http://duboue.ca/data.

[10] Dale and Reiter takes less than 3' for the 44,080 runs for organizations in a 2.3 GHz machine.

Referent	Dale and Reiter Output	Gardent Output
EB	{ (EB *occupation* Software_Freedom_Law_Center) }	{ (EB *occupation* Software_Freedom_Law_Center) }
LL	{ (LL *birthPlace* United_States), (LL, *occupation* Harvard_Law_School) }	{ (LL *birthPlace* Rapid_City,_South_Dakota) }
LT	{ (LT *occupation* Software_engineer) }	{ (LT *nationality* Finnish_American) }

Figure 2: Example output for the task: {'Eben_Moglen' (EB), 'Lawrence_Lessig' (LL), 'Linus_Torvalds' (LT) }.

comparable or better than in the pilot (for organizations that are more mixed, it was slightly lower but for people it was as low 2.8%). Gardent missed 2% of the people (and only 54 organizations), employing negatives 14% of the time for people and 12% of the time for organizations.

Evaluating referring expressions is hard. Efforts to automate this task in NLG (Gatt et al., 2007) have taken an approach similar to machine translation BLEU scores (Papinini et al., 2001), for example, by asking multiple judges to produce referring expressions for a given scenario. These settings usually involve images of physical objects and relate to small ontologies. While such an approach could be adapted to the Open Domain case, a major problem is the need for the judges to be acquainted with some of the less popular entities in the training set. At this point in our research, we decided to analyze the quality of a sample of the output ourselves. This process involved consulting information about each entity to determine the soundness of the result.

We looked at a random sample of 20 runs and annotated it by two authors, measuring a Cohen's κ of 60% for annotating DD results and 79% for determining whether the folksonomy had enough information to build a satisfactory DD. We then extended the evaluation to 60 runs and annotated them by one author. We found that Dale and Reiter produced a satisfactory DD in 41.6% of the cases and Gardent in 43.4% of the cases and that the folksonomy contained enough information 81.6% of the time. Figure 2 shows some example output.

From the evaluation we learned that the default ordering strategy employed by Dale and Reiter is not stable across different types of people (compare: politicians vs. musicians) or organizations. We also saw that Gardent's algorithm in many cases selected a single triple with very little practical value (an obscure fact about the entity) or a negative piece of information which is actually true for the referent but it is a missing piece of information.

The first two problems can be solved by either further subdividing the taxonomies of entities or (more interestingly) by incorporating some measure about the salience of each piece of information, a possibility which we will discuss next. The last issue can be addressed by having some form of meaningful default value.

The negations produced by Gardent's algorithm highlighted errors on the folksonomy. For example, when referring to China with distractors Peru and Taiwan, it will produce "the place where they do not speak Chinese," as China has the different Chinese dialects spelled out on the folksonomy (and some Peruvians do speak Chinese). Given these limitations, we find the current results very encouraging and we believe folksonomies can help focus on robust NLG for noisy (ontological) inputs.

5 Discussion

We have shown that by using a folksonomy it should be possible to deploy traditional NLG referring expression generation algorithms in Open Domain tasks. To fulfill this vision, three tasks remain:

Dealing with missing information. Some form of *smart default values* are needed, we are considering using a nearest-neighbor approach to find ontological siblings which can provide such defaults.

Estimating salience of each piece of ontological information. The importance for each triple has to be obtained in a way consistent with the Open Domain nature of the task. For this problem, we believe search engine salience can be of great help.

Transform the extracted triples into actual text. This problem has received attention in the past. We would like to explore traditional surface realizer with a custom-made grammar.

Acknowledgments

We would like to thank the anonymous reviewers as well as Annie Ying and Victoria Reggiardo.

References

Siddharthan Advaith, Nenkova Ani, and McKeown Kathleen. 2011. Information status distinctions and referring expressions: An empirical study of references to people in news summaries. *Computational Linguistics*, 37(4):811–842.

Anja Belz, Eric Kow, Jette Viethen, and Albert Gatt. 2010. Generating referring expressions in context: The grec task evaluation challenges. In Emiel Krahmer and Marit Theune, editors, *Empirical Methods in Natural Language Generation*, volume 5790 of *Lecture Notes in Computer Science*, pages 294–327. Springer.

C. Bizer, J. Lehmann, G. Kobilarov, S. Auer, C. Becker, R. Cyganiak, and S. Hellmann. 2009. DBpedia-a crystallization point for the web of data. *Web Semantics: Science, Services and Agents on the World Wide Web*, 7(3):154–165.

B. Bohnet. 2007. is-fbn, is-fbs, is-iac: The adaptation of two classic algorithms for the generation of referring expressions in order to produce expressions like humans do. *MT Summit XI, UCNLG+ MT*, pages 84–86.

R. Dale and E. Reiter. 1995. Computational interpretations of the gricean maxims in the generation of referring expressions. *Cognitive Science*, 19(2):233–263.

C. Gardent. 2002. Generating minimal definite descriptions. In *Proceedings of the 40th Annual Meeting on Association for Computational Linguistics*, pages 96–103. Association for Computational Linguistics.

A. Gatt, I. Van Der Sluis, and K. Van Deemter. 2007. Evaluating algorithms for the generation of referring expressions using a balanced corpus. In *Proceedings of the Eleventh European Workshop on Natural Language Generation*, pages 49–56. Association for Computational Linguistics.

L. Hasler, C. Orasan, and K. Naumann. 2006. NPs for events: Experiments in coreference annotation. In *Proceedings of the 5th edition of the International Conference on Language Resources and Evaluation (LREC2006)*, pages 1167–1172.

Kathleen R. McKeown, R. Barzilay, D. Evans, V. Hatzivassiloglou, J. L. Klavans, A. Nenkova, C. Sable, B. Schiffman, and S. Sigelman. 2002. Tracking and summarizing news on a daily basis with columbia's newsblaster. In *Proc. of HLT*.

Kishore Papinini, Salim Roukos, Todd Ward, and Wei-Jing Zhu. 2001. Bleu: a method for automatic evaluation of machine translation. Technical report, IBM.

Structured Event Retrieval over Microblog Archives

Donald Metzler, Congxing Cai, Eduard Hovy
Information Sciences Institute
University of Southern California
4676 Admiralty Way, Marina del Rey, CA 90292

Abstract

Microblog streams often contain a considerable amount of information about local, regional, national, and global events. Most existing microblog search capabilities are focused on recent happenings and do not provide the ability to search and explore past events. This paper proposes the problem of structured retrieval of historical event information over microblog archives. Rather than retrieving individual microblog messages in response to an event query, we propose retrieving a ranked list of historical event summaries by distilling high quality event representations using a novel temporal query expansion technique. The results of an exploratory study carried out over a large archive of Twitter messages demonstrates both the value of the microblog event retrieval task and the effectiveness of our proposed search methodologies.

1 Introduction

Real-time user generated content is one of the key driving forces behind the growing popularity of social media-centric communication. The ability to instantly share, often from your mobile phone, your thoughts (via Twitter), your photos (via Facebook), your location (via Foursquare), and a variety of other information is changing the way that information is created, communicated, and consumed.

There has been a substantial amount of research effort devoted to user generated content-related search tasks, including blog search, forum search, and community-based question answering. However, there has been relatively little research on *microblog search*. Microblog services, such as Tumblr and Twitter, provide users with the ability to broadcast short messages in real-time. This is in contrast to traditional blogs that typically have considerably more content that is updated less frequently. By their very nature, microblog streams often contain a considerable amount of information about local, regional, national, and global news and events. A recent study found that over 85% of trending topics on Twitter are news-related (Kwak et al., 2010). Another recent study by Teevan et al. that investigated the differences between microblog and Web search reported similar findings (Teevan et al., 2011). The study also found that microblog search queries are used to find information related to news and events, while Web search queries are more navigational in nature and used to find a variety of information on a specific topic.

It is likely that microblogs have not received much attention because, unlike blog search, there is no well-defined microblog search *task*. Existing microblog search services, such as those offered by Twitter and Google, only provide the ability to retrieve individual microblog posts in response to a query. Unfortunately, this task has limited utility since very few real information needs can be satisfied by a single short piece of text (e.g., the maximum length of a message on Twitter is 140 characters). Hence, novel search tasks defined over microblog streams that go beyond "message retrieval" have the potential to add substantial value to users.

Given the somewhat limited utility of microblog message search and the preponderance of news and event-related material posted on microblogs, this pa-

July 16 2010 at 17 UTC, for **11** hours

Summary tweets:

i. *Ok a 3.6 "rocks" nothing. But boarding a plane there now, Woodward ho! RT @todayshow: 3.6 magnitude #earthquake rocks Washington DC area.*

ii. *RT @fredthompson: 3.6-magnitude earthquake hit DC. President Obama said it was due to 8 years of Bush failing to regulate plate tectonic ...*

iii. *3.6-magnitude earthquake wakes Md. residents: Temblor centered in Gaithersburg felt by as many as 3 million people...* `http://bit.ly/9iMLEk`

Figure 1: Example structured event representation retrieved for the query "earthquake".

per proposes a novel search task that we call *microblog event retrieval*. Given a query that describes an event, such as *earthquake*, *terrorist bombing*, or *bieber concert*, the goal of the task is to retrieve a ranked list of *structured event representations*, such as the one shown in Figure 1, from a large archive of historical microblog posts.

In this work, structured representations come in the form of a list of *timespans* during which an instance of the event occurred and was actively discussed within the microblog stream. Additionally, for each timespan, a small set of relevant messages are retrieved for the purpose of providing a high-level summary of the event that occurred during the timespan. This task leverages the large amount of real-time, often first-hand information found in microblog archives to deliver a novel form of user generated content-based search results to users. Unlike news search, which finds professionally written articles on a news-related topic, and general-purpose Web search, which is likely to find a large amount of unrelated information, this task is designed to retrieve highly relevant news and event-related information viewed through the lens of users who experienced or discussed the event while it happened (or during its aftermath). Such search functionality would not only be useful for everyday end-users, but also social scientists, historians, journalists, and emergency planners.

This paper has three primary contributions. First, we introduce the microblog event retrieval task, which retrieves a ranked list of structured event representations in response to an event query. By going beyond individual microblog message retrieval, the task adds value to microblog archives and provides users with the ability to find information that was disseminated in real-time about past events, which is not possible with news and Web search engines. Second, we propose an unsupervised methodology for distilling high quality event representations using a novel temporal query expansion technique. The technique synthesizes ideas from pseudo-relevance feedback, term burstiness, and temporal aspects of microblog streams. Third, we perform an exploratory evaluation of 50 event queries over a corpus of 46 million Twitter messages. The results of our evaluation demonstrate both the value of the microblog event retrieval task itself and the effectiveness of our proposed search methodologies, which show improvements of up to 42% compared to a baseline approach.

2 Related Work

There are several directions of microblog research that are related to our proposed work. First, there is a growing body of literature that has focused on the topical content of microblog posts. This research has focused on microblog topic models (Hong and Davison, 2010), event and topic detection and tracking (Sankaranarayanan et al., 2009; Cataldi et al., 2010; Petrović et al., 2010; Lin et al., 2010), predicting flu outbreaks using keyword tracking (Culotta, 2010), and using microblog streams as a source of features for improving recency ranking in Web search (Dong et al., 2010). Most of these approaches analyze content as it arrives in the system. While tracking a small number of topics or keywords is feasible using *online algorithms*, the general problem of topic detection and tracking (Allan et al., 1998) is considerably more challenging given the large number of topics being discussed at any one point. Our work differs in that it does not attempt to track or model topics as they arrive in the system. Instead, given an event query, our system *retrospectively* analyzes the corpus of microblog messages for the purpose of retrieving structured event representations.

There is no shortage of previous work on using pseudo-relevance feedback approaches for query expansion. Relevant research includes classical vector-space approaches (Rocchio, 1971), language modeling approaches (Lavrenko and Croft, 2001; Zhai and Lafferty, 2001; Li and Croft, 2003), among others (Metzler and Croft, 2007; Cao et al., 2008; Lv and Zhai, 2010). The novel aspect of our proposed temporal query expansion approach is the fact that expansion is done over a *temporal stream* of very short, noisy messages.

There has also been recent work on summarizing sets of microblog posts (Sharifi et al., 2010). We chose to make use of a simple approach in favor of a more sophisticated one because summarization is only a minor aspect of our proposed framework.

Finally, there are two previous studies that are the most relevant to our work. First, Massoudi et al. propose a retrieval model that uses query expansion and microblog quality indicators to retrieve individual microblog messages (Massoudi et al., 2011). Their proposed query expansion approach differs from ours in the sense that we utilize *timespans* from the (possibly distant) past when generating expanded queries and focus on event retrieval, rather than individual message retrieval. The other research that is closely related to ours is the work done by Chieu and Lee (Chieu and Lee, 2004). The authors propose an approach for automatically constructing timelines from news articles in response to a query. The novelty of our proposed work derives from our novel temporal query expansion approach, and the fact that our work focuses on microblog streams which are fundamentally different in nature from news articles.

3 Microblog Event Retrieval

The primary goal of this paper is to introduce a new microblog search paradigm that goes beyond retrieving messages individually. We propose a novel task called *microblog event retrieval*, which is defined as follows. Given a query that specifies an event, retrieve a set of relevant *structured event representations* from a large archive of microblog messages. This definition is purposefully general to allow for a broad interpretation of the task.

There is nothing in our proposed retrieval framework that precludes it from producing reasonable results for any type of query, not just those related to events. However, we chose to primarily focus on events in this paper because previous studies have shown that a majority of trending topics within microblog streams are about news and events (Kwak et al., 2010). The information found in microblogs is difficult to find anywhere else, including news and Web archives, thereby making it a valuable resource for a wide variety of users.

3.1 Overview of Framework

Our microblog event retrieval framework takes a query as input and returns a ranked list of structured event representations. To accomplish this, the framework breaks the work into two steps – timespan retrieval and summarization. The timespan retrieval step identifies the timespans when the event happened, while the summarization step retrieves a small set of microblog messages for each timespan that are meant to act as a summary. Figure 1 shows an example result that is returned in response to the query "earthquake". The result consists of a start time that indicates when the event began being discussed, a duration that specifies how long the event was discussed, and a small number of messages posted during the time interval that are meant to summarize what happened. This example corresponds to an earthquake that struck the metropolitan District of Colombia area in the United States. The earthquake was heavily discussed for nearly 11 hours, because it hit a densely populated area that does not typically experience earthquakes.

3.2 Temporal Query Expansion

We assume that queries issued to our retrieval framework are simple keyword queries that consist of a small number of terms. This sparse representation of the user's information need makes finding relevant messages challenging, since microblog messages that are highly related to the query might not contain any of the query keywords. It is common for microblog messages about a given topic to express the topic in a different, possibly shortened or slang, manner. For example, rather than writing "earthquake", users may instead use the word "quake" or simply include a hashtag such as "#eq" in their message. It is impractical to manually identify the full set of related keywords and folksonomy tags (i.e., hashtags) for each query. In information retrieval, this is known as the *vocabulary mismatch* problem.

To address this problem, we propose a novel unsupervised temporal query expansion technique. The approach is unsupervised in the sense that it makes use of a pseudo-relevance feedback-like mechanism when extracting expansion terms. Traditional query expansion approaches typically find terms that commonly co-occur with the query terms in documents (or passages). However, such approaches are not suitable for expanding queries in the microblog setting since microblog messages are very short, yielding unreliable co-occurrence information. Furthermore, microblog messages have an important temporal dimension that should be considered when they are being used to generate expansion terms.

Our proposed approach generates expansion terms based on the temporal co-occurrence of terms. Given keyword query q, we first automatically retrieve a set of N timespans for which the query keywords were most heavily discussed. To do so, we rank timespans according to the proportion of messages posted during the timespan that contain one or more of the query keywords. This is a simple, but highly reliable way of identifying timespans during which a specific topic is being heavily discussed. These timespans are then considered to be *pseudo-relevant*. In our experiments, the microblog stream is divided into hours, with each hour corresponding to an atomic timespan. Although it is possible to define timespans in many different ways, we found that this was a suitable level of granularity for most events that was neither overly broad nor overly specific.

For each pseudo-relevant timespan, a *burstiness score* is computed for all of the terms that occur in messages posted during the timespan. The burstiness score is meant to quantify how trending a term is during the timespan. Thus, if the query is being heavily discussed during the timespan and some term is also trending during the timespan, then the term may be related to the query. For each of the top N time intervals, the burstiness score of each term is computed as follows:

$$burstiness(w, TS_i) = \frac{P(w|TS_i)}{P(w)} \qquad (1)$$

which is the ratio of the term's likelihood of occurring within timespan TS_i versus the likelihood of the term occurring during any timespan. Hence, if a term that generally infrequently occurs within the message stream suddenly occurs many times within a single time interval, then the term will be assigned a high burstiness score. This weighting is similar in nature to that proposed by Ponte for query expansion within the language modeling framework for information retrieval (Ponte, 1998). The following probability estimates are used for the expressions within the burstiness score:

$$P(w|TS_i) = \frac{tf_{w,TS_i} + \mu\frac{tf_w}{N}}{|TS_i| + \mu}, P(w) = \frac{tf_w + K}{N + K|V|}$$

where tf_{w,TS_i} is the number of occurrences of w in timespan TS_i, tf_w is the number of occurrences of w in the entire microblog archive, $|TS_i|$ is the number of terms in timespan TS_i, N is the total number of terms in the microblog archive, V is the vocabulary size, and μ and K are smoothing parameters.

While it is common practice to smooth $P(w|TS_i)$ using Dirichlet (or Bayesian) smoothing (Zhai and Lafferty, 2004), it is less common to smooth the general English language model $P(w)$. However, we found that this was necessary since term distributions in microblog services exhibit unique characteristics. By smoothing $P(w)$, we dampen the effect of overweighting very rare terms. In our experiments, we set the value of μ to 500 and K to 10 after some preliminary exploration. We found that the overall system effectiveness is generally insensitive to the choice of smoothing parameters.

The final step of the query expansion process involves aggregating the burstiness scores across all pseudo-relevant timespans to generate an overall score for each term. To do so, we compute the *geometric mean* of the burstiness scores across the pseudo-relevant timespans. Preliminary experiments showed that the arithmetic mean was susceptible to overweighting terms that had a very large burstiness score in a single timespan. By utilizing the geometric average instead, we ensure that the highest weighted terms are those that have large weights in a large number of the timespans, thereby eliminating spurious terms. Seo and Croft (2010) observed similar results with traditional pseudo-relevance feedback techniques.

The k highest weighted terms are then used as expansion terms. Using this approach, terms that commonly trend during the same timespans that the query terms commonly occur (i.e., the pseudo-relevant timespans) are assigned high weights. Hence, the approach is capable of capturing simple temporal dependencies between terms and query keywords, which is not possible with traditional approaches.

3.3 Timespan Ranking

The end result of the query expansion process just described is an expanded query q' that consists of a set of k terms and their respective weights (denoted as β_w). Our framework uses the expanded query q' to retrieve relevant timespans. We hypothesize that using the expanded version of the query for timespan retrieval will yield significantly better results than using the keyword version.

To retrieve timespans, we first identify the 1000 highest scoring timespans (with respect to q'). We then merge contiguous timespans into a single, longer timespan, where the score of the merged timespan is the maximum score of its component timespans. The final ranked list consists of the merged timespans. Therefore, although our timespans are defined as hour intervals, it is possible for our system to return longer (merged) timespans.

We now describe two scoring functions that can be used to compute the relevance of a timespan with respect to an expanded query representation.

3.3.1 Coverage Scoring Function

The coverage scoring function measures relevance as the (weighted) number of expansion terms that are covered within the timespan. This measure assumes that the expanded query is a faithful representation of the information need and that the more times the highly weighted expansion terms occur, the more relevant the timespan is. Using this definition, the coverage score of a time interval is computed as:

$$s(q', TS) = \sum_{w \in q'} \beta_w \cdot tf_{w,TS}$$

where $tf_{w_i,TS}$ is the term frequency of w_i in timespan TS and β_w is the expansion weight of term w.

3.3.2 Burstiness Scoring Function

Since multiple events may occur at the same time, microblog streams can easily be dominated by the larger of two events. However, less popular events may also exhibit burstiness at the same time. Therefore, another measure of relevance is the burstiness of the event signature during the timespan. If all of the expansion terms exhibit burstiness during the time interval, it strongly suggests the timespan may be relevant to the query.

Therefore, to measure the relevance of the timespan, we first compute the burstiness scores for all of the terms within the time interval. This yields a vector β_{TS} of burstiness scores. The cosine similarity measure is used to compute the similarity between the query burstiness scores and the timespan burstiness scores. Hence, the burstiness scoring function is computed as:

$$s(q', TS) = cos(\beta_{q'}, \beta_{TS})$$

3.4 Timespan Summarization

The final step of the retrieval process is to produce a short query-biased summary for each retrieved time interval. The primary purpose for generating this type of summary is to provide the user with a quick overview of what happened during the retrieved timespans.

We utilize a simple, straightforward approach that generates unexpectedly useful summaries. Given a timespan, we use a relatively simple information retrieval model to retrieve a small set of microblog messages posted during the timespan that are the most relevant to the expanded representation of the original query. These messages are then used as a short summary of the timespan.

This is accomplished by scoring a microblog message M with respect to an expanded query representation q' using a weighted variant of the query likelihood scoring function (Ponte and Croft, 1998):

$$s(q', M) = \sum_{w \in q'} \beta_w \cdot \log P(w|M)$$

where β_w is the burstiness score for expansion term w and $P(w|M)$ is a Dirichlet smoothed language modeling estimate for term w in message M. This scoring function is also equivalent to the cross entropy and KL-divergence scoring functions (Lafferty and Zhai, 2001).

Category	Events
Business	layoffs, bankruptcy, acquisition, merger, hostile takeover
Celebrity	wedding, divorce
Crime	shooting, robbery, assassination, court decision, school shooting
Death	death, suicide, drowned
Energy	blackout, brownout
Entertainment	awards, championship game, world record
Health	recall, pandemic, disease, flu, poisoning
Natural Disaster	hurricane, tornado, earthquake, flood, tsunami, wildfire, fire
Politics	election, riots, protests
Terrorism	hostage, explosion, terrorism, bombing, terrorist attack, suicide bombing, hijacked
Transportation	plane crash, traffic jam, sinks, pileup, road rage, train crash, derailed, capsizes

Table 1: The 50 event types used as queries during our evaluation, divided into categories.

4 Experiments

This section describes our empirical evaluation of the proposed microblog event retrieval task.

4.1 Microblog Corpus

Our microblog message archive consists of data that we collected from Twitter using their Streaming API. The API delivers a continuous 1% random sample of public Twitter messages (also called "tweets"). Our evaluation makes use of data collected between July 16, 2010 and Jan 1st, 2011. After eliminating all non-English tweets, our corpus consists of 46,611,766 English tweets, which corresponds to roughly 10,000 tweets per hour. Although this only represents a 1% sample of all tweets, we believe that the corpus is sizable enough to demonstrate the utility of our proposed approach.

4.2 Event Queries

To evaluate our system, we prepared a list of 50 event types that fall into 11 different categories. The event types and their corresponding categories are listed in Table 1. The different event types can have substantially different characteristics, such as the frequency of occurrence, geographic or demographic interest, popularity, etc. For example, there are more weddings than earthquakes. Public events, such as federal elections involve people across the country. However, a car pileup typically only attracts local attention. Moreover, microbloggers show different amounts of interest to each type of event. For example, Twitter users are more likely to tweet about politics than a business acquisition.

4.3 Methodology

To evaluate the quality of a particular configuration of our framework, we run the *microblog event retrieval* task for the 50 different event type queries described in the previous section. For each query, the top 10 timespans retrieved are manually judged to be relevant or non-relevant. If the summary returned clearly indicated a real event instance occurred, then the timespan was marked as relevant. The primary metric of interest is precision at 10.

In addition to the temporal query expansion approach (denoted TQE), we also ran experiments using relevance-based language models, which is a state-of-the-art query expansion approach (Lavrenko and Croft, 2001). We ran two variants of relevance-based language models. In the first, query expansion was done using the Twitter corpus itself (denoted TwitterRM). This allows us to compare the effectiveness of the TQE approach against a more traditional query expansion approach. In the other variant, query expansion was done using the English Gigaword corpus (denoted NewsRM), which is a rich source of event information created by traditional news media.

For all three query expansion approaches (TQE, TwitterRM, and NewsRM), the two scoring functions, *burstiness* and *coverage*, are used to rank timespans. Hence, we evaluate six specific instances of our framework. As a baseline, we use a simple (unexpanded) keyword retrieval approach that scores timespans according to the relative frequency of event keywords that occur during the timespan.

4.4 Timespan Retrieval Results

Before delving into the details of our quantitative evaluation of effectiveness, we provide an illustrative example of the type of results our system is capable of producing. Table 2 shows the top four re-

July 16 2010 at 17 UTC, for **11** hours *Ok a 3.6 "rocks" nothing. But boarding a plane there now, Woodward ho! RT @todayshow: 3.6 magnitude #earthquake rocks Washington DC area.*
September 28 2010 at 11 UTC, for **6** hours *RT @Quakeprediction: 2.6 earthquake (possible foreshock) hits E of Los Angeles;* `http://earthquake.usgs.gov/earthquakes/recenteqscanv/Fau...`
September 04 2010 at 01 UTC, for **3** hours *7.0 quake strikes New Zealand - A 7.0-magnitude earthquake has struck near New Zealand's second largest city. Reside...* `http://ht.ly/18R2rw`
October 27 2010 at 01 UTC, for **5** hours *RT @SURFER_Magazine: Tsunami Strikes Mentawais: Wave Spawned By A 7.5-Magnitude Earthquake Off West Coast Of Indonesia* `http://bit.ly/8Z9Lbv`

Table 2: Top four timespans (with a single summary tweet) retrieved for the query "earthquake".

sults retrieved using temporal query expansion with the burstiness scoring function for the query "earthquake". Only a single summary tweet is displayed for each timespan due to space restrictions. As we can see from the tweets, all of the results are relevant to the query, in that they all correspond to times when an earthquake happened and was actively discussed on Twitter. Different from Web and news search results, these types of ranked lists provide a clear temporal picture of relevant events that were actively discussed on Twitter.

The results of our microblog retrieval task are shown in Table 3. The table reports the per-category and overall precision at 10 for the baseline, and the six configurations of our proposed framework. Bolded values represent the best result per category. As the results show, using temporal query expansion with burstiness ranking yields a mean precision at 10 of 61%, making it the best overall system configuration. The approach is 41.9% better than the baseline, which is statistically significant according to a one-sided paired t-test at the $p < 0.01$ level. Interestingly, the relevance model-based expansion techniques exhibit even worse performance, on average, than our simple keyword baseline. For example, the news-based expansion approach was 11.6% worse using the coverage scoring function and 18.6% worse using the burstiness scoring function compared to the baseline. All of the traditional query expansion results are statistically significantly worse than the temporal query expansion-based approaches. Hence, the results suggest that capturing temporal dependencies between terms yields better expanded representations than simply capturing term co-occurrences, as is done in traditional query expansion approaches.

The results also indicate the burstiness scoring function outperforms the coverage scoring function for temporal query expansion. An analysis of the results revealed that in many cases the timespans returned using the coverage scoring function had a small number of frequent terms that matched the expanded query. This happened less often with the burstiness scoring function, which is based on the cosine similarity between the query and timespan's burstiness scores. The combination of burstiness weighting and l_2 normalization (when computing the cosine similarity) appears to yield a more robust scoring function.

4.5 Event Popularity Effects

It is also interesting to note that the retrieval performance varies substantially across the different event type categories. For example, the performance on queries about "natural disasters" and "politics" is consistently strong. Similar performance can also be achieved for popular events related to celebrities. However, energy-related event queries, such as "blackout", achieves very poor effectiveness. This observation seems to suggest that the more popular an event is, the better the retrieval performance that can be achieved. This is a reasonable hypothesis since the more people tweet about the event, the easier it is to identify the trend from the background.

To better understand this phenomenon, we compute the correlation between timespan retrieval precision and event (query) popularity, where popularity is measured according to:

$$Popularity(q) = \frac{1}{N}\sum_{i=1}^{N} burstiness(q, TS_i),$$

where q is the event query, $burstiness(q, TS_i)$ is the burstiness score of the event during timespan

Event Category	Baseline	NewsRM		TwitterRM		TQE	
		burst	cover	burst	cover	burst	cover
Business	0.50	0.46	0.30	0.70	0.18	**0.74**	0.64
Celebrity	0.75	0.30	0.40	0.50	0.60	**0.80**	0.45
Crime	0.44	0.28	**0.54**	0.22	0.32	0.46	0.28
Death	0.43	0.20	0.33	0.30	0.30	**0.47**	**0.47**
Energy	0.05	0.10	0.05	**0.20**	0.05	0.15	0.00
Entertainment	0.47	0.53	0.67	0.30	0.53	**0.70**	**0.70**
Health	0.48	0.28	0.36	0.44	0.16	**0.60**	**0.60**
Nat. Disaster	0.50	0.53	0.59	0.66	0.46	**0.87**	0.66
Politics	0.67	0.70	0.53	0.63	0.30	**0.87**	0.60
Terrorism	0.41	0.44	0.39	0.39	0.17	**0.69**	0.51
Transportation	0.21	0.08	0.08	0.08	0.10	**0.31**	0.19
All	0.43	0.35	0.38	0.40	0.26	**0.61**	0.47

Table 3: Per-category and overall (All) precision at 10 for the keyword only approach (Baseline), traditional newswire expansion (NewsRM), traditional pseudo relevance feedback using the Twitter corpus (TwitterRM), and temporal query expansion (TQE). For the expansion-based approaches, results for the burstiness scoring (burst) and the coverage-based scoring (cover) are given. Bold values indicate the best result per category.

	Correlation
Baseline	0.63 ($p < 0.01$)
NewsRM	0.53 ($p < 0.01$)
TwitterRM	0.61 ($p < 0.01$)
TQE	0.50 ($p < 0.01$)

Table 4: Spearman rank correlation between event retrieval precisions and event popularity. All methods use the burstiness scoring function.

TS_i, as defined in Equation 1, and the sum goes over the top N timespans retrieved for the event using our proposed retrieval approach.

Using this measure, we find that Twitter users are more interested in events related to entertainment and politics, and less interested in events related to energy or transportation. Also, we notice that Twitter users actively discuss dramatic crisis-related topics, including natural disasters (e.g., earthquakes, hurricanes, tornado, etc.) and terrorist attacks.

Table 4 shows the correlations between effectiveness and event popularity across different approaches. The correlations indicate a strong correlation with event popularity for the keyword approach. This is expected, since the approach is based on the number of times the keywords are mentioned within the timespan. The correlations are significantly reduced by incorporating query expansion terms. The configurations that use temporal query expansion tend to have lower correlation than the other approaches. Although the correlation is still significant, the lower correlation suggests that temporal query expansion approaches are more robust to popularity effects than simple keywords approaches. Additional work is necessary to better understand the role of popularity in retrieval tasks like this.

5 Conclusions

In this paper, we proposed a novel microblog search task called microblog event retrieval. Unlike previous microblog search tasks that retrieve individual microblog messages, our task involves the retrieval of structured event representations during which an event occurs and is discussed within the microblog community. In this way, users are presented with a ranked list or timeline of event instances in response to a query.

To tackle the microblog search task, we proposed a novel timespan retrieval framework that first constructs an expanded representation of the incoming query, performs timespan retrieval, and then produces a short summary of the timespan. Our experimental evaluation, carried out over a corpus of over 46 million microblog messages collected from Twitter, showed that microblog event retrieval is a feasible, challenging task, and that our proposed timespan retrieval framework is both robust and effective.

References

James Allan, Jaime Carbonell, George Doddington, Jonathan Yamron, and Yiming Yang. 1998. Topic Detection and Tracking Pilot Study. In *In Proceedings of the DARPA Broadcast News Transcription and Understanding Workshop*, pages 194–218.

Guihong Cao, Jian-Yun Nie, Jianfeng Gao, and Stephen Robertson. 2008. Selecting good expansion terms for pseudo-relevance feedback. In *Proc. 31st Ann. Intl. ACM SIGIR Conf. on Research and Development in Information Retrieval*, SIGIR '08, pages 243–250, New York, NY, USA. ACM.

Mario Cataldi, Luigi Di Caro, and Claudio Schifanella. 2010. Emerging topic detection on twitter based on temporal and social terms evaluation. In *Proceedings of the Tenth International Workshop on Multimedia Data Mining*, MDMKDD '10, pages 4:1–4:10, New York, NY, USA. ACM.

Hai Leong Chieu and Yoong Keok Lee. 2004. Query based event extraction along a timeline. In *Proceedings of the 27th annual international ACM SIGIR conference on Research and development in information retrieval*, SIGIR '04, pages 425–432, New York, NY, USA. ACM.

Aron Culotta. 2010. Towards detecting influenza epidemics by analyzing twitter messages. In *1st Workshop on Social Media Analytics (SOMA'10)*, July.

Anlei Dong, Ruiqiang Zhang, Pranam Kolari, Jing Bai, Fernando Diaz, Yi Chang, Zhaohui Zheng, and Hongyuan Zha. 2010. Time is of the essence: improving recency ranking using twitter data. In *Proceedings of the 19th international conference on World wide web*, WWW '10, pages 331–340, New York, NY, USA. ACM.

Liangjie Hong and Brian D. Davison. 2010. Empirical study of topic modeling in twitter. In *1st Workshop on Social Media Analytics (SOMA'10)*, July.

Haewoon Kwak, Changhyun Lee, Hosung Park, and Sue Moon. 2010. What is twitter, a social network or a news media? In *Proceedings of the 19th international conference on World wide web*, WWW '10, pages 591–600, New York, NY, USA. ACM.

J. Lafferty and C. Zhai. 2001. Document language models, query models, and risk minimization for information retrieval. In *Proc. 24th Ann. Intl. ACM SIGIR Conf. on Research and Development in Information Retrieval*, pages 111–119.

V. Lavrenko and W. B. Croft. 2001. Relevance-based language models. In *Proc. 24th Ann. Intl. ACM SIGIR Conf. on Research and Development in Information Retrieval*, pages 120–127.

Xiaoyan Li and W. Bruce Croft. 2003. Time-based language models. In *Proc. 12th Intl. Conf. on Information and Knowledge Management*, CIKM '03, pages 469–475, New York, NY, USA. ACM.

Cindy Xide Lin, Bo Zhao, Qiaozhu Mei, and Jiawei Han. 2010. Pet: a statistical model for popular events tracking in social communities. In *Proc. 16th Ann. Intl. ACM SIGKDD Conf. on Knowledge Discovery and Data Mining*, KDD '10, pages 929–938, New York, NY, USA. ACM.

Yuanhua Lv and ChengXiang Zhai. 2010. Positional relevance model for pseudo-relevance feedback. In *Proc. 33rd Ann. Intl. ACM SIGIR Conf. on Research and Development in Information Retrieval*, SIGIR '10, pages 579–586, New York, NY, USA. ACM.

Kamran Massoudi, Manos Tsagkias, Maarten de Rijke, and Wouter Weerkamp. 2011. Incorporating query expansion and quality indicators in searching microblog posts. In *Proc. 33rd European Conf. on Information Retrieval*, page To appear.

Donald Metzler and W. Bruce Croft. 2007. Latent concept expansion using markov random fields. In *Proc. 30th Ann. Intl. ACM SIGIR Conf. on Research and Development in Information Retrieval*, SIGIR '07, pages 311–318, New York, NY, USA. ACM.

Saša Petrović, Miles Osborne, and Victor Lavrenko. 2010. Streaming first story detection with application to twitter. In *Human Language Technologies: The 2010 Annual Conference of the North American Chapter of the Association for Computational Linguistics*, HLT '10, pages 181–189, Stroudsburg, PA, USA. Association for Computational Linguistics.

J. Ponte and W. Bruce Croft. 1998. A language modeling approach to information retrieval. In *Proc. 21st Ann. Intl. ACM SIGIR Conf. on Research and Development in Information Retrieval*, pages 275–281.

Jay Ponte. 1998. *A Language Modeling Approach to Information Retrieval*. Ph.D. thesis, University of Massachusetts, Amherst, MA.

J. J. Rocchio, 1971. *Relevance Feedback in Information Retrieval*, pages 313–323. Prentice-Hall.

Jagan Sankaranarayanan, Hanan Samet, Benjamin E. Teitler, Michael D. Lieberman, and Jon Sperling. 2009. Twitterstand: news in tweets. In *Proceedings of the 17th ACM SIGSPATIAL International Conference on Advances in Geographic Information Systems*, GIS '09, pages 42–51, New York, NY, USA. ACM.

Jangwon Seo and W. Bruce Croft. 2010. Geometric representations for multiple documents. In *Proceeding of the 33rd international ACM SIGIR conference on Research and development in information retrieval*, SIGIR '10, pages 251–258, New York, NY, USA. ACM.

Beaux Sharifi, Mark-Anthony Hutton, and Jugal K. Kalita. 2010. Experiments in microblog summarization. *Social Computing / IEEE International Confer-*

ence on Privacy, Security, Risk and Trust, 2010 IEEE International Conference on, 0:49–56.

Jaime Teevan, Daniel Ramage, and Meredith Ringel Morris. 2011. #twittersearch: A comparison of microblog search and web search. In *WSDM 2011: Fourth International Conference on Web Search and Data Mining*, Feb.

ChengXiang Zhai and John Lafferty. 2001. Model-based feedback in the language modeling approach to information retrieval. In *Proc. 10th Intl. Conf. on Information and Knowledge Management*, pages 403–410.

C. Zhai and J. Lafferty. 2004. A study of smoothing methods for language models applied to information retrieval. *ACM Trans. Inf. Syst.*, 22(2):179–214.

Learning from Bullying Traces in Social Media

Jun-Ming Xu, Kwang-Sung Jun, Xiaojin Zhu
Department of Computer Sciences
University of Wisconsin-Madison
Madison, WI 53706, USA
{xujm,deltakam,jerryzhu}@cs.wisc.edu

Amy Bellmore
Department of Educational Psychology
University of Wisconsin-Madison
Madison, WI 53706, USA
abellmore@wisc.edu

Abstract

We introduce the social study of bullying to the NLP community. Bullying, in both physical and cyber worlds (the latter known as cyberbullying), has been recognized as a serious national health issue among adolescents. However, previous social studies of bullying are handicapped by data scarcity, while the few computational studies narrowly restrict themselves to cyberbullying which accounts for only a small fraction of all bullying episodes. Our main contribution is to present evidence that social media, with appropriate natural language processing techniques, can be a valuable and abundant data source for the study of bullying in both worlds. We identify several key problems in using such data sources and formulate them as NLP tasks, including text classification, role labeling, sentiment analysis, and topic modeling. Since this is an introductory paper, we present baseline results on these tasks using off-the-shelf NLP solutions, and encourage the NLP community to contribute better models in the future.

1 Introduction to Bullying

Bullying, also called peer victimization, has been recognized as a serious national health issue by the White House (The White House, 2011), the American Academy of Pediatrics (The American Academy of Pediatrics, 2009), and the American Psychological Association (American Psychological Association, 2004). One is being bullied or victimized when he or she is exposed repeatedly over time to negative actions on the part of others (Olweus, 1993). Far-reaching and insidious sequelae of bullying include intrapersonal problems (Juvonen and Graham, 2001; Jimerson, Swearer, and Espelage, 2010) and lethal school violence in the most extreme cases (Moore et al., 2003). Youth who experience peer victimization report more symptoms of depression, anxiety, loneliness, and low self-worth compared to their nonvictimized counterparts (Bellmore et al., 2004; Biggs, Nelson, and Sampilo, 2010; Graham, Bellmore, and Juvonen, 2007; Hawker and Boulton, 2000). Other research suggests that victimized youth have more physical complaints (Fekkes et al., 2006; Nishina and Juvonen, 2005; Gini and Pozzoli, 2009). Victimized youth are absent from school more often and get lower grades than nonvictimized youth (Ladd, Kochenderfer, and Coleman, 1997; Schwartz et al., 2005; Juvonen and Gross, 2008).

Bullying happens traditionally in the physical world and, recently, online as well; the latter is known as cyberbullying (Cassidy, Jackson, and Brown, 2009; Fredstrom, Adams, and Gilman, 2011; Wang, Iannotti, and Nansel, 2009; Vandebosch and Cleemput, 2009). Bullying usually starts in primary school, peaks in middle school, and lasts well into high school and beyond (Nansel et al., 2001; Smith, Madsen, and Moody, 1999; Cook et al., 2010). Across a national sample of students in grades 4 through 12, 38% of students reported being bullied by others and 32% reported bullying others (Vaillancourt et al., 2010).

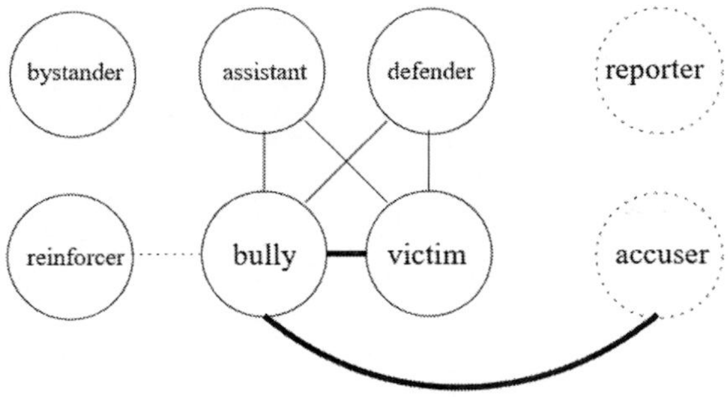

Figure 1: The roles in a bullying episode. Solid circles represent traditional roles in social science, while dotted circles are new roles we augmented for social media. The width of the edges represents interaction strength.

1.1 The Structure of a Bullying Episode

Bullying takes multiple *forms*, most noticeably face-to-face physical (e.g., hitting), verbal (e.g., name-calling), and relational (e.g., exclusion) (Archer and Coyne, 2005; Little et al., 2003; Nylund et al., 2007). Cyberbullying reflects a venue (other than face to face contact) through which verbal and relational forms can occur.

A main reason individuals are targeted with bullying is *perceived differences*, i.e., any characteristic that makes an individual stand out differently from his or her peers. These include race, socio-economic status, gender, sexuality, physical appearance, and behaviors.

Participants in a bullying episode take well-defined *roles* (see Figure 1). More than one person can have the same role in a bullying episode. Roles include the bully (or bullies), the victims, bystanders (who saw the event but did not intervene), defenders of the victim, assistants to the bully (who did not initiate but went along with the bully), and reinforcers (who did not directly join in with the bully but encouraged the bully by laughing, for example) (Salmivalli, 1999). This recognition that bullying involves multiple roles makes evident the broad-ranging impact of bullying; any child or adolescent is susceptible to participation in bullying, even those who are not directly involved (Janosz et al., 2008; Rivers et al., 2009).

1.2 Some Scientific Questions NLP can Answer

Like many complex social issues, effective solutions to bullying go beyond technology alone and require the concerted efforts of parents, educators, and law enforcement. To guide these efforts it is paramount to study the dynamics of bullying. Such study critically depends on text in the form of self-report social study surveys and electronic communication among participants. Such text is often fragmental, noisy, and covers only part of a bullying episode from a specific role's perspective. As such, the NLP community can help answer a host of scientific questions: Which pieces of text refer to the same underlying bullying episode? What is the form, reason, location, time, etc. of a bullying episode? Who are the participants of each episode, and what are their roles? How does a person's role evolve over time? This paper presents our initial investigation on some of these questions, while leaving others to future research by the NLP community.

1.3 Limitations of the State-of-the-Art

The social science study of bullying has a long history. However, a fundamental problem there is data acquisition. The standard approach is to conduct time-consuming personal surveys in schools. The sample size is typically in the hundreds, and participants typically write 3 to 4 sentences about each bullying episode (Nishina and Bellmore, 2010). Such a small corpus fails to assess the true frequency of bullying over the population, and cannot determine the evolution of roles. The computational study of bullying is largely unexplored, with the exception of a few studies on cyberbullying (Lieberman, Dinakar, and Jones, 2011; Dinakar, Reichart, and Lieberman, 2011; Ptaszynski et al., 2010; Kontostathis, Edwards, and Leatherman, 2010; Bosse and Stam, 2011; Latham, Crockett, and Bandar, 2010). These studies did not consider the much more frequent bullying episodes in the physical world.

2 Bullying Traces in Social Media

The main contribution of the present paper is not on novel algorithms, but rather on presenting evidence that social media data and off-the-shelf NLP tools can be an effective combination for the study of bullying. Participants of a bullying episode (in either physical or cyber venues) often post social media text about the experience. We collectively call such social media posts **bullying traces**. Bullying traces include but far exceed incidences of cyberbullying. Most of them are in fact *responses* to a bullying experience – the actual attack is hidden from view. Bullying traces are valuable, albeit fragmental and noisy, data which we can use to piece together the underlying episodes.

In the rest of the paper, we focus on publicly available Twitter "tweets," though our methods apply readily to other social media services, too. Here are some examples of bullying traces:

- Reporting a bullying episode: *"some tweens got violent on the n train, the one boy got off after blows 2 the chest... Saw him cryin as he walkd away :(bullying not cool"*

- Accusing someone as a bully: *"@USERNAME i didnt jump around and act like a monkey T_T which of your eye saw that i acted like a monkey :(you're a bully"*

- Revealing self as a victim: *"People bullied me for being fat. 7 years later, I was diagnosed with bulimia. Are you happy now?"*

- Cyber-bullying direct attack: *"Lauren is a fat cow MOO BITCH"*

Bullying traces are abundant. From the publicly available 2011 TREC Microblog track corpus (16 million tweets sampled between January 23rd and February 8th, 2011), we uniformly sampled 990 tweets for manual inspection by five experienced annotators (not the authors of the present paper). Of the 990 tweets, the annotators labeled 617 as non-English, 371 as English but not bullying traces, and 2 as English bullying traces. The Maximum Likelihood Estimate of the frequency of English bullying traces, out of all tweets, is $2/990 \approx 0.002$. The exact Binomial 95% confidence interval is (0.0002, 0.0073). This is a tiny fraction. Nonetheless, it represents an abundance of tweets: by some estimates, Twitter produces 250 million tweets per day in late 2011. Even with the lower bound in the confidence interval, it translates into 50,000 English bullying traces per day. The actual number can be much higher.

Bullying traces contain valuable information. For example, Figure 2 shows the daily number of bullying traces identified by our classifier, to be discussed

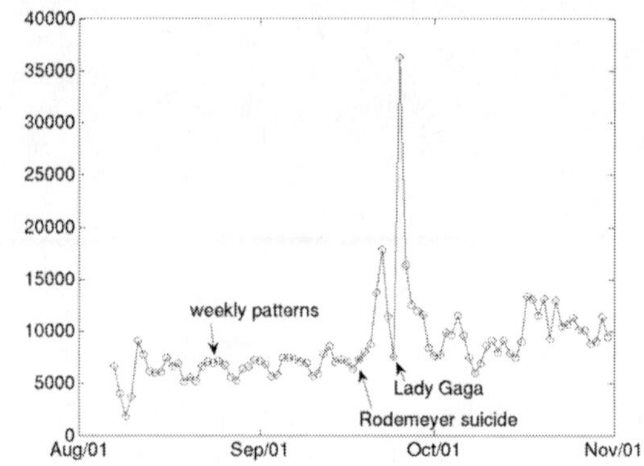

Figure 2: Temporal variation of bullying traces

in section 3. A weekly pattern was obvious in late August. A small peak was caused by 14-year-old bullying victim Jamey Rodemeyer's suicide on Sept. 18. This was followed by a large peak after Lady Gaga dedicated a song to him on Sept. 24.

In the following sections, we identify several key problems in using social media for the study of bullying. We formulate each key problem as an NLP task. We then present standard off-the-shelf NLP approaches to establish baseline performances. Since bullying traces account for only a tiny fraction of all tweets, it posed a significant challenge for our annotators to find enough bullying traces without labeling an unreasonable amount of tweets. For this reason, in the rest of the paper we restrict ourselves to an "enriched dataset." This enriched dataset is obtained by collecting tweets using the public Twitter streaming API, such that each tweet contains at least one of the following keywords: "bully, bullied, bullying." We further removed re-tweets (the analogue of forwarded emails) by excluding tweets containing the acronym "RT." The enrichment process is meant to retain many first-hand bullying traces at the cost of a selection bias.

3 NLP Task A: Text Categorization

One important task is to distinguish bullying traces from other social media posts. Our enriched dataset, generated by simple keyword filtering, still contains many irrelevant tweets. For example, *"Forced veganism by removing a persons choice is just another form of bullying"* is not a bullying trace, since it does not describe a bullying episode. Our task is to distinguish posts like this from true bullying traces such as those mentioned in the previous section. We formulate it as a binary text categorization task.

Methods. The same annotators who labeled the TREC corpus labeled 1762 tweets sampled uniformly from the enriched dataset on August 6, 2011. Among them, 684 (39%) were labeled as bullying traces.

Following (Settles, 2011), these 1762 tweets were case-folded but without any stemming or stopword removal. Any user mentions preceded by a "@" were replaced by the anonymized user name "@USERNAME". Any URLs starting with "http" were replaced by the token "HTTPLINK". Hashtags (compound words following "#") were not split and were treated as a single token. Emoticons, such as ":)" or ":D", were also included as tokens.

After these preprocessing procedures, we created three different sets of feature representations: unigrams (`1g`), unigrams+bigrams (`1g2g`), and POS-colored unigrams+bigrams (`1g2gPOS`). POS tagging was done with the Stanford CoreNLP package (Toutanova et al., 2003). POS-coloring was done by expanding each token into token:POS.

We chose four commonly used text classifiers, namely, Naive Bayes, SVM with linear kernel (`SVM(linear)`), SVM with RBF kernel (`SVM(RBF)`) and Logistic Regression (equivalent to MaxEnt). We used the WEKA (Hall et al., 2009) implementation for the first three (calling LibSVM (Chang and Lin, 2011) with WEKA's interfaces for SVMs), and the L1General package (Schmidt, Fung, and Rosales, 2007) for the fourth.

We held out 262 tweets for test, and systematically varied training set size among the remaining tweets, from 100 to 1500 with the step-size 100. We tuned all parameters jointly by 5-fold cross validation on the training set with the grid $\{2^{-8}, 2^{-6}, \ldots, 2^{8}\}$. All the four text classifiers were trained on the training sets and tested on the test set. The whole procedure was repeated 30 times for each feature representation.

Results. Figure 3 reports the held-out set accuracy as the training set size increases. The error bars are ± 1 standard error. With the largest training set size (1500), the combination of `SVM(linear)` + `1g` achieves an average accuracy 79.7%. `SVM(linear)` + `1g2g` achieves 81.3%, which is significantly better (t-test, $p = 4 \times 10^{-6}$). It shows that including bigrams can significantly improve the classification performance. `SVM(linear)` + `1g2gPOS` achieves 81.6%, though the improvement is not statistically significant ($p = 0.088$), which indicates that POS coloring does not help too much on this task. `SVM(RBF)` gives similar performance, Logistic Regression is slightly worse and Naive Bayes is much worse, for a large range of training set sizes. In summary, `SVM(linear)` + `1g2g` is the preferred model because of its accuracy and simplicity. We also note that these accuracies are much better than the majority class baseline of 61%. On the held-out set, `SVM(linear)` + `1g2g` achieves precision P=0.76, recall R=0.79, and F-measure 0.77.

Discussions. Note that the learning curves are still increasing, suggesting that better accuracy can be obtained if we annotate more training data. As to why the best accuracy is not close to 1, one hypothesis is noisy labels caused by intrinsic disagreement among labelers. Tweets are short and some are ambiguous. Without prior knowledge about the users and their other tweets, labelers interpret the tweets in their own ways. For example, for the very short tweet *feels like a bully.....* our annotators disagreed on whether it is a bullying trace. Labelers may have different views on these ambiguous tweets and created noisy bullying trace labels.

A future direction is to categorize bullying traces at a finer granularity, e.g., by forms, reasons, etc. This can be solved by multi-class classification methods. Another direction is to extend the classifiers from the "enriched data" to the full range of tweets. Recall that the difference is whether we pre-filter the tweets by keywords. Clearly, they have different tweet distributions. Techniques used for *covariate shift* may be adapted to solve this problem (Blitzer, 2008).

4 NLP Task B: Role Labeling

Identifying participants' bullying roles (Figure 1) is another important task, which is also a prerequisite of studying how a person's role evolves over time. For bullying traces in social media, we augment the traditional role system with two new roles: reporter (may not be present during the episode, un-

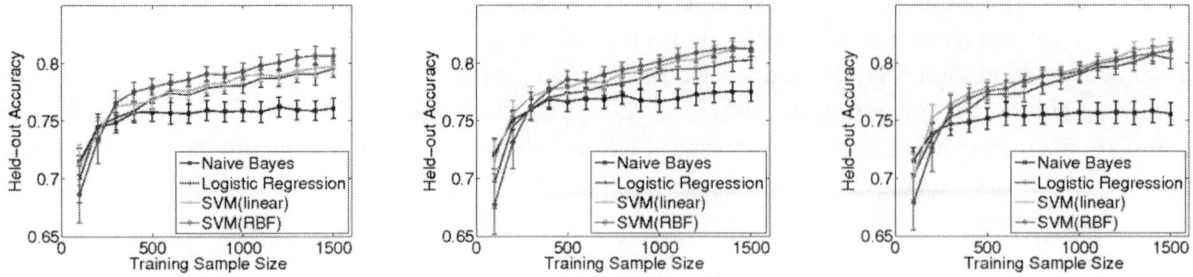

(a) `1g` (b) `1g2g` (c) `1g2gPOS`

Figure 3: Learning Curves for different feature sets and classification algorithms

like a bystander) and accuser (accusing someone as the bully). Both roles can be a victim, a defender, or a bystander in the traditional sense – there is just not enough information in the tweet. Accuser (A), bully (B), reporter (R) and victim (V) are the four most frequent roles observed in social media. We merged all remaining roles into a generic category "other" (O) in the following study. Our task is to classify the role (A, B, R, V, O) of the tweet author and any person-mentions in a tweet. For example, AUTHOR$^{(R)}$: *"We$^{(R)}$ visited my$^{(V)}$ cousin$^{(V)}$ today & #Itreallymakesmemad that he$^{(V)}$ barely eats bec he$^{(V)}$ was bullied . :(I$^{(R)}$ wanna kick the crap out of those mean$^{(B)}$ kids$^{(B)}$."* Note that the special token "AUTHOR" is introduced to hold the label of the author's role.

Labeling author's role and other person-mention's role are two different sub-tasks. The former can be formulated as a multi-class text classification task; the latter is better formulated as a sequential tagging task. We will discuss them separately below.

4.1 Author's Roles

Methods. Our annotators labeled the author's role for each of the 684 positive bullying traces in Task A (296 R, 162 V, 98 B, 86 A, 42 O). We used the same classifiers and features in Section 3. We conducted 10-fold cross validation to evaluate all combinations of classifiers and feature sets. Like before, we tuned all parameters jointly by 5-fold cross validation on the training set with the grid $\{2^{-8}, 2^{-6}, \ldots, 2^{8}\}$.

Results. The best combination is `SVM(linear)` + `1g2g` with cross validation accuracy 61%. Even though it is far from perfect, it is significantly better than the majority class (R) baseline of 43%. It shows that there is signal in the text to infer the authors' roles.

	predicted as				
	A	B	R	V	O
A	33	3	39	10	1
B	5	25	57	11	0
R	15	5	249	27	0
V	1	4	48	109	0
O	1	1	37	3	0

Table 1: Confusion Matrix of Author Role Classification

Table 1 shows the confusion matrix of the best model. Most R and V authors are correctly recognized, but not B and A. The model misclassified many authors as R. It is possible that the tweets authored by reporters are diverse in topic and style, and overlap with other classes in the feature space.

Discussions. As tweets are short, our feature representation may not be the best for predicting author's role. Many authors mentioned themselves in the tweets with first-person pronouns, making it advantageous to consider joint classification by merging sections 4.1 and 4.2. Furthermore, assuming roles change infrequently, it may be helpful to jointly classify many tweets authored by the same person.

4.2 Person-Mention's Roles

This sub-task labels each person-mention with a bullying role. It uses Named Entity Recognition (NER) (Finkel, Grenager, and Manning, 2005; Ratinov and Roth, 2009; Ritter et al., 2011) as a subroutine to identify named person entities, though we are also interested in unnamed persons such as "my teacher" and pronouns. It is related to Semantic Role

Labeling (SRL) (Gildea and Jurafsky, 2002; Punyakanok, Roth, and Yih, 2008) but differs critically in that our roles are not tied to specific verb predicates.

Methods. Our annotators labeled each token in the 684 bullying traces with the tags A, B, R, V, O and N for not-a-person. There are 11,751 tokens in total. Similar to the sequential tagging formulation (Màrquez et al., 2005; Liu et al., 2010), we trained a linear CRF to label each token in the tweet with the CRF++ package (http://crfpp.sourceforge.net/).

As standard in linear CRFs, we used pairwise label features $f(y_{i-1}, y_i)$ and input features $f(y_i, \mathbf{w})$, where f's are binary indicator functions on the values of their arguments and $\mathbf{w}$ is the text. In the following, we introduce our input features using the example tweet *"@USERNAME i'll tell vinny you bullied me."* with the current token w_i ="vinny":

(i) The token, lemma, and POS tag of the five tokens around position i. For example, $f_{bully,w_{i-1}=tell}(y_i, \mathbf{w})$ will be 1 if the current token has label y_i = "$bully$" and w_{i-1} = "$tell$". Similarly, $f_{victim,POS_{i+2}=VBD}(y_i, \mathbf{w})$ will be 1 if y_i = "$victim$" and the POS of w_{i+2} is VBD.

(ii) The NER tag of w_i.

(iii) Whether w_i is a person mention. This is a Boolean feature which is true if w_i is tagged as PERSON by NER, or if $POS_i = pronoun$ (excluding "it"), or if w_i is @USERNAME. For example, this feature is true on "vinny" because it is tagged as PERSON by NER.

(iv) The relevant verb v_i of w_i, v_i's lemma, POS, and the combination of v_i with the lemma/POS of w_i. The relevant verb v_i of w_i is defined by the semantic dependency between w_i and the verb, if one exists. Otherwise, v_i is the closest verb to w_i. For example, the relevant verb of w_i = "$vinny$" is v_i = "$tell$" because "vinny" is found as the object of "tell" by dependency parsing.

(v) The distance, relative position (left or right) and dependency type between v_i and w_i. For example, the distance between "vinny" and its relevant verb "tell" is 1. "vinny" is on the right and is the object of "tell".

The lemma, POS tags, NER tags and dependency relationship were obtained using Stanford CoreNLP.

As a baseline, we trained `SVM(linear)` with the same input features as CRF. Classification is done individually on each token. We randomly split the 684 tweets into 10 folds and conducted cross validation based on this split. For CRF, we trained on the tweets in the training set with their labels, and tested the model on those in the test set. For SVM, we trained and tested at the token level in the corresponding sets.

	Accuracy	Precision	Recall	F-1
CRF	0.87	0.53	0.42	0.47
SVM	0.85	0.42	0.31	0.36

Table 2: Cross Validation Result of Person-Mention Roles

Results. Table 2 reports the cross validation accuracy, precision, recall and F-1 measure. *Accuracy* measures the percentage of tokens correctly assigned the groundtruth labels, including N (not-a-person) tokens. *Precision* measures the fraction of correctly labeled person-mention tokens over all tokens that are not N according to the algorithm. *Recall* measures the fraction of correctly labeled person-mention tokens over all tokens that are not N according to the groundtruth. *F-1* is the harmonic mean of precision and recall. Linear CRF achieved an accuracy 0.87, which is higher than the baseline of majority class predictor (N, 0.80) (t-test, $p = 10^{-10}$). However, the precision and recall is low potentially because the tweets are short and noisy. CRF outperforms SVM in all measures, showing the value of joint classification.

Discussions. Table 3 shows the confusion matrix of person-mention role labeling by linear CRF. There are several reasons for these mistakes. First, words like "teacher", "sister", or "girl" were missed by our person mention feature (iii). Second, the NER tagger was trained on formal English which is a mismatch for the informal tweets, leading to NER errors. Third, noisy labeling continues to affect accuracy. For example, some annotators considered "other people" as an entity and labeled both tokens as person mentions; others labeled "people" only.

In general, bullying role labeling may be improved by jointly considering multiple tweets at the episode level. Co-reference resolution should improve the performance as well.

	predicted as					
	A	B	R	V	O	N
A	0	4	5	10	0	4
B	0	406	13	125	103	302
R	0	28	31	67	0	13
V	0	142	28	380	43	202
O	0	112	4	42	156	86
N	0	78	4	41	16	9306

Table 3: Confusion Matrix of Person-Mention Roles by CRF

	predicted as	
	Tease	Not
Tease	52	47
Not	26	559

Table 4: Confusion Matrix of Teasing Classification

5 NLP Task C: Sentiment Analysis

Sentiment analysis on participants involved in a bullying episode is of significant importance. As Figure 4 suggests, there are a wide range of emotions in bullying traces. For example, victims usually experience negative emotions such as depression, anxiety and loneliness; Some emotions are more violent or even suicidal. Detecting at-risk individuals via sentiment analysis enables potential interventions. In addition, social scientists are interested in sentiment analysis of bullying participants to understand their motivations.

In the present paper we investigate a special form of sentiment in bullying traces, namely teasing. We observed that many bullying traces were written jokingly. One example of a teasing post is *"@USERNAME lol stop being a cyber bully lol :p."* Teasing may indicate the lack of severity of a bullying episode; It may also be a manifest of coping strategies in bullying victims. Therefore, there is considerable interest among social scientists to understand teasing in bullying traces.

Methods. One first task is to identify teasing bullying traces. We formulated it as a binary classification problem, similar to classic positive/negative sentiment classification (Pang and Lee, 2004). Our annotators labeled each of the 684 bullying traces in Task A as teasing (99) or not (585). We used the same feature representations, classifiers and parameter tuning as in Section 3 and 10-fold cross validation procedure.

Results. The best cross validation accuracy of 89% is obtained by `SVM(linear)` + `1g2g`. This is significantly better than the majority class (not-teasing) baseline of 86% (t-test, $p = 10^{-33}$). It shows that even simple features and off-the-shelf classifier can detect some signal in the text. However, the accuracy is not high. Table 4 shows the confusion matrix. About half of the tease examples were misclassified. We found several possible explanations. First, teasing is not always accompanied by joking emoticons or tokens like "LOL," "lmao," "haha." For example, *"I may bully you but I love you lots. Just like jelly tots!"* and *"Been bullied into watching a scary film, I love my friends!"* Such teasing sentiment requires deeper NLP or much larger training sets. Second, tweets containing those joking emoticons and tokens are not necessarily teasing. For example, *"This Year I'm Standing Up For The Kids That Are Being Bullied All Over The Nation :) ."* Third, the joking tokens have diverse spellings. For example, "lol" was spelled as "loll," "lolol," "lollll," "loool," "LOOOOOOOOOOOL"; "haha" was spelled as "HAHAHAHA," "Hahaha," "Bwahahaha," "ahahahah," "hahah."

Discussions. Specialized word normalization for social media text may significantly improve performance. For example, word lengthening can be identified and used as cues for teasing (Brody and Diakopoulos, 2011). Teasing is diverse in its form and content. Our training set is perhaps too small. Borrowing training data from other corpora, such as one-liner jokes (Mihalcea and Strapparava, 2005), may be helpful.

6 NLP Task D: Latent Topic Modeling

Methods. Given the large volume of bullying traces, methods for automatically analyzing what people are talking about are needed. Latent topic models allow us to extract the main topics in bullying traces to facilitate understanding. We used latent Dirichlet allocation (LDA) (Blei, Ng, and Jordan, 2003) as our exploratory tool. Specifically, we ran a collapsed Gibbs sampling implementation of LDA (Griffiths and Steyvers, 2004).

The corpus consists of 188K enriched tweets from Aug. 21 to Sept. 17, 2011 that are classified as bullying traces by our classifier in Task A. We performed stopword removal and further removed word types occurring less than 7 times, resulting in a vocabulary of size 12K. We set the number of topics to 50, Dirichlet parameter for word multinomials to $\beta = 0.01$, Dirichlet parameter for document topic multinomial to $\alpha = 1$, and ran Gibbs sampling for 10K iterations.

Results. Space precludes a complete list of topics. Figure 4 shows six selected topics discovered by LDA. Recall that each topic in LDA is a multinomial distribution over the vocabulary. The figure shows each topic's top 20 words with size proportional to $p(\text{word} \mid \text{topic})$. The topic names are manually assigned.

Figure 4: Selected topics discovered by latent Dirichlet allocation.

These topics contain semantically coherent words relevant to bullying: (feelings) how people feel about bullying; (suicide) discussions of suicide events; (family) sibling names probably used in a good buddy sense; (school) the school environment where bullying commonly occurs; (verbal bullying) derogatory words such as fat and ugly; (physical bullying) actions such as kicking and pushing.

We also ran a variational inference implementation of LDA (Blei, Ng, and Jordan, 2003). The results were similar, thus we omit discussion of them.

Discussions. Some recovered topics, including the ones shown here, provide valuable insight into bullying traces. However, not all topics are interpretable to social scientists. It may be helpful to allow scientists the ability to combine their domain knowledge with latent topic modeling, thus arriving at more useful topics. For example, the scientists can formulate their knowledge in First-Order Logic, which can then be combined with LDA with stochastic optimization (Andrzejewski et al., 2011).

7 Conclusion and Future Work

We introduced social media as a large-scale, near real-time, dynamic data source for the study of bullying. Social media offers a broad range of bullying traces that include but go beyond cyberbullying. In the present paper, we have identified several key problems in using social media to study bullying and formulated them as familiar NLP tasks. Our baseline performance with standard off-the-shelf approaches shows that it is feasible to learn from bullying traces.

Much work remains in this new research direction. In the short term, we need to develop specialized NLP tools for processing bullying traces in social media, similar to (Ritter et al., 2011; Liu et al., 2010), to achieve better performance than models trained on formal English. In the long term, we need to tackle the problem of piecing together the underlying bullying episodes from fragmental bullying traces. Consider two separate bullying episodes with the following participants and roles:

E1: B: Buffy, V: Vivian & Virginia, O: Debra

E2: B: Burton, V: Buffy, O: Irene

The corresponding bullying traces can be three posts in this order:

$\mathbf{w}_1$ Debra: *Virginia, I heard Buffy call you and Vivian fat–ignore her!*

$\mathbf{w}_2$ Buffy to Irene: *Burton picked on me again because I'm only 5'1*

$\mathbf{w}_3$ Vivian: *Buffy I'm not fat! Stop calling me that.*
Reconstructing E1, E2 from $\mathbf{w}_1, \mathbf{w}_2, \mathbf{w}_3$ is challenging for a number of reasons: (1) There is no explicit episode index in the posts. (2) Posts from a single episode may be dispersed in time (e.g., $\mathbf{w}_1, \mathbf{w}_3$ belong to E1, but not $\mathbf{w}_2$), each containing only part

of an episode. (3) The number of episodes and people can grow indefinitely as more posts arrive. (4) People may switch roles in different episodes (e.g., Buffy was the bully in E1 but the victim in E2). Joint probabilistic modeling over multiple posts using social network structures hold great promise in solving this problem.

To facilitate bullying research in the NLP community, we make our annotations and software publicly available at `http://research.cs.wisc.edu/bullying`.

Acknowledgments

We thank Wei-Ting Chen, Rachael Hansen, Ting-Lan Ma, Ji-in You and Bryan Gibson for their help on the data and the paper.

References

[American Psychological Association2004] American Psychological Association. 2004. APA resolution on bullying among children and youth. `http://www.apa.org/about/governance/council/policy/bullying.pdf`.

[Andrzejewski et al.2011] Andrzejewski, David, Xiaojin Zhu, Mark Craven, and Ben Recht. 2011. A framework for incorporating general domain knowledge into Latent Dirichlet Allocation using First-Order Logic. In *the 22nd IJCAI*, pages 1171–1177.

[Archer and Coyne2005] Archer, John and Sarah M. Coyne. 2005. An integrated review of indirect, relational, and social aggression. *Personality and Social Psychology Review*, 9:212–230.

[Bellmore et al.2004] Bellmore, Amy D., Melissa R. Witkow, Sandra Graham, and Jaana Juvonen. 2004. Beyond the individual: The impact of ethnic context and classroom behavioral norms on victims' adjustment. *Developmental Psychology*, 40:1159–1172.

[Biggs, Nelson, and Sampilo2010] Biggs, Bridget K., Jennifer Mize Nelson, and Marilyn L. Sampilo. 2010. Peer relations in the anxiety-depression link: Test of a mediation model. *Anxiety, Stress & Coping*, 23(4):431–447.

[Blei, Ng, and Jordan2003] Blei, David M., Andrew Y. Ng, and Michael I. Jordan. 2003. Latent dirichlet allocation. *JMLR*, 3:993–1022.

[Blitzer2008] Blitzer, John. 2008. *Domain Adaptation of Natural Language Processing Systems*. Ph.D. thesis, University of Pennsylvania.

[Bosse and Stam2011] Bosse, Tibor and Sven Stam. 2011. A normative agent system to prevent cyberbullying. In *WI-IAT 2011*, pages 425–430.

[Brody and Diakopoulos2011] Brody, Samuel and Nicholas Diakopoulos. 2011. Cooooooooooooooollllllllllll!!!!!!!!!!!!!! using word lengthening to detect sentiment in microblogs. In *EMNLP 2011*, pages 562–570.

[Cassidy, Jackson, and Brown2009] Cassidy, Wanda, Margaret Jackson, and Karen N. Brown. 2009. Sticks and stones can break my bones, but how can pixels hurt me? students' experiences with cyber-bullying. *School Psychology Int'l*, 30(4):383–402.

[Chang and Lin2011] Chang, Chih-Chung and Chih-Jen Lin. 2011. LIBSVM: A library for support vector machines. *ACM Trans. on Intelligent Systems and Technology*, 2:27:1–27:27.

[Cook et al.2010] Cook, Clayton R., Kirk R. Williams, Nancy G. Guerra, Tia E. Kim, and Shelly Sadek. 2010. Predictors of bullying and victimization in childhood and adolescence: A meta-analytic investigation. *School Psychology Quarterly*, 25(2):65–83.

[Dinakar, Reichart, and Lieberman2011] Dinakar, K., R. Reichart, and H. Lieberman. 2011. Modeling the detection of textual cyberbullying. In *International Conference on Weblog and Social Media - Social Mobile Web Workshop*, Barcelona, Spain.

[Fekkes et al.2006] Fekkes, Minne, Frans I.M. Pijpers, A. Miranda Fredriks, Ton Vogels, and S. Pauline Verloove-Vanhorick. 2006. Do bullied children get ill, or do ill children get bullied? a prospective cohort study on the relationship between bullying and health-related symptoms. *Pediatrics*, 117:1568–1574.

[Finkel, Grenager, and Manning2005] Finkel, Jenny R., Trond Grenager, and Christopher Manning. 2005. Incorporating non-local information into information extraction systems by Gibbs sampling. In *the 43rd ACL*, pages 363–370.

[Fredstrom, Adams, and Gilman2011] Fredstrom, Bridget K., Ryan E. Adams, and Rich Gilman. 2011. Electronic and school-based victimization: Unique contexts for adjustment difficulties during adolescence. *J. Youth and Adolescence*, 40(4):405–415.

[Gildea and Jurafsky2002] Gildea, Daniel and Daniel Jurafsky. 2002. Automatic labeling of semantic roles. *Comput. Linguist.*, 28(3):245–288.

[Gini and Pozzoli2009] Gini, Gianluca and Tiziana Pozzoli. 2009. Association between bullying and psychosomatic problems: a meta-analysis. *Pediatrics*, 123(3):1059–1065.

[Graham, Bellmore, and Juvonen2007] Graham, Sandra, Amy Bellmore, and Jaana Juvonen. 2007. Peer victimization in middle school: When self- and peer views diverge. In Joseph E. Zins, Maurice J. Elias, and Charles A. Maher, editors, *Bullying, victimization, and peer harassment: A handbook of prevention and intervention*. Haworth Press, New York, NY, pages 121–141.

[Griffiths and Steyvers2004] Griffiths, Thomas L. and Mark Steyvers. 2004. Finding scientific topics. *PNAS*, 101(suppl. 1):5228–5235.

[Hall et al.2009] Hall, Mark, Eibe Frank, Geoffrey Holmes, Bernhard Pfahringer, Peter Reutemann, and Ian H. Witten. 2009. The weka data mining software: an update. *ACM SIGKDD Explorations Newsletter*, 11:10–18.

[Hawker and Boulton2000] Hawker, David S. J. and Michael J. Boulton. 2000. Twenty years' research on peer victimization and psychosocial maladjustment: A meta-analytic review of cross-sectional studies. *J. of Child Psychology And Psychiatry*, 41(4):441–455.

[Janosz et al.2008] Janosz, Michel, Isabelle Archambault, Linda S. Pagani, Sophie Pascal, Alexandre J.S. Morin, and François Bowen. 2008. Are there detrimental effects of witnessing school violence in early adolescence? *J. of Adolescent Health*, 43(6):600–608.

[Jimerson, Swearer, and Espelage2010] Jimerson, Shane R., Susan M. Swearer, and Dorothy L. Espelage. 2010. *Handbook of Bullying in Schools: An international perspective*. Routledge/Taylor & Francis Group, New York, NY.

[Juvonen and Graham2001] Juvonen, Jaana and Sandra Graham. 2001. *Peer harassment in school: The plight of the vulnerable and victimized*. Guilford Press, New York, NY.

[Juvonen and Gross2008] Juvonen, Jaana and Elisheva F. Gross. 2008. Extending the school grounds? – Bullying experiences in cyberspace. *J. of School Health*, 78:496–505.

[Kontostathis, Edwards, and Leatherman2010] Kontostathis, April, Lynne Edwards, and Amanda Leatherman. 2010. Text mining and cybercrime. In Michael W. Berry and Jacob Kogan, editors, *Text Mining: Applications and Theory*. John Wiley & Sons, Ltd, Chichester, UK.

[Ladd, Kochenderfer, and Coleman1997] Ladd, Gary W., Becky J. Kochenderfer, and Cynthia C. Coleman. 1997. Classroom peer acceptance, friendship, and victimization: Distinct relational systems that contribute uniquely to children's school adjustment? *Child Development*, 68:1181–1197.

[Latham, Crockett, and Bandar2010] Latham, Annabel, Keeley Crockett, and Zuhair Bandar. 2010. A conversational expert system supporting bullying and harassment policies. In *the 2nd ICAART*, pages 163–168.

[Lieberman, Dinakar, and Jones2011] Lieberman, Henry, Karthik Dinakar, and Birago Jones. 2011. Let's gang up on cyberbullying. *Computer*, 44:93–96.

[Little et al.2003] Little, Todd D., Christopher C. Henrich, Stephanie M. Jones, and Patricia H. Hawley. 2003. Disentangling the "whys" from the "whats" of aggressive behavior. *Int'l J. of Behavioral Development*, 27:122–133.

[Liu et al.2010] Liu, Xiaohua, Kuan Li, Bo Han, Ming Zhou, Long Jiang, Zhongyang Xiong, and Changning Huang. 2010. Semantic role labeling for news tweets. In *the 23rd COLING*, pages 698–706.

[Màrquez et al.2005] Màrquez, Lluís, Pere Comas, Jesús Giménez, and Neus Català. 2005. Semantic role labeling as sequential tagging. In *the 9th CoNLL*, pages 193–196.

[Mihalcea and Strapparava2005] Mihalcea, Rada and Carlo Strapparava. 2005. Making computers laugh: Investigations in automatic humor recognition. In *EMNLP 2005*, pages 531–538.

[Moore et al.2003] Moore, Mark H., Carol V. Petrie, Anthony A. Braga, and Brenda L. McLaughlin. 2003. *Deadly lessons: Understanding lethal school violence*. The National Academies Press, Washington, DC.

[Nansel et al.2001] Nansel, Tonja R., Mary Overpeck, Ramani S. Pilla, W. June Ruan, Bruce Simons-Morton, and Peter Scheidt. 2001. Bullying behaviors among US youth: prevalence and association with psychosocial adjustment. *J. Amer. Medical Assoc.*, 285(16):2094–2100.

[Nishina and Bellmore2010] Nishina, Adrienne and Amy D. Bellmore. 2010. When might aggression, victimization, and conflict matter most?: Contextual considerations. *J. of Early Adolescence*, pages 5–26.

[Nishina and Juvonen2005] Nishina, Adrienne and Jaana Juvonen. 2005. Daily reports of witnessing and experiencing peer harassment in middle school. *Child Development*, 76:435–450.

[Nylund et al.2007] Nylund, Karen, Amy Bellmore, Adrienne Nishina, and Sandra Graham. 2007. Subtypes, severity, and structural stability of peer victimization: What does latent class analysis say? *Child Development*, 78:1706–1722.

[Olweus1993] Olweus, Dan. 1993. *Bullying at school: What we know and what we can do*. Blackwell, Oxford, UK.

[Pang and Lee2004] Pang, Bo and Lillian Lee. 2004. A sentimental education: Sentiment analysis using subjectivity summarization based on minimum cuts. In *the 42nd ACL*, pages 271–278.

[Ptaszynski et al.2010] Ptaszynski, Michal, Pawel Dybala, Tatsuaki Matsuba, Fumito Masui, Rafal Rzepka, and Kenji Araki. 2010. Machine learning and affect analysis against cyber-bullying. In *the 36th AISB*, pages 7–16.

[Punyakanok, Roth, and Yih2008] Punyakanok, Vasin, Dan Roth, and Wen-tau Yih. 2008. The importance of syntactic parsing and inference in semantic role labeling. *Comput. Linguist.*, 34(2):257–287.

[Ratinov and Roth2009] Ratinov, Lev and Dan Roth. 2009. Design challenges and misconceptions in named entity recognition. In *the 13th CoNLL*, pages 147–155.

[Ritter et al.2011] Ritter, Alan, Sam Clark, Mausam, and Oren Etzioni. 2011. Named entity recognition in tweets: An experimental study. In *EMNLP 2011*, pages 1524–1534.

[Rivers et al.2009] Rivers, Ian, V. Paul Poteat, Nathalie Noret, and Nigel Ashurst. 2009. Observing bullying at school: The mental health implications of witness status. *School Psychology Quarterly*, 24(4):211–223.

[Salmivalli1999] Salmivalli, Christina. 1999. Participant role approach to school bullying: Implications for intervention. *J. of Adolescence*, 22(4):453–459.

[Schmidt, Fung, and Rosales2007] Schmidt, Mark W., Glenn Fung, and Rómer Rosales. 2007. Fast optimization methods for l1 regularization: A comparative study and two new approaches. In *the 18th ECML*, pages 286–297.

[Schwartz et al.2005] Schwartz, David, Andrea Hopmeyer Gorman, Jonathan Nakamoto, and Robin L. Toblin. 2005. Victimization in the peer group and children's academic functioning. *J. of Educational Psychology*, 87:425–435.

[Settles2011] Settles, Burr. 2011. Closing the loop: Fast, interactive semi-supervised annotation with queries on features and instances. In *the EMNLP 2011*, pages 1467–1478.

[Smith, Madsen, and Moody1999] Smith, Peter K., Kirsten C. Madsen, and Janet C. Moody. 1999. What causes the age decline in reports of being bullied at school? Towards a developmental analysis of risks of being bullied. *Educational Research*, 41(3):267–285.

[The American Academy of Pediatrics2009] The American Academy of Pediatrics. 2009. Policy statement–role of the pediatrician in youth violence prevention. *Pediatrics*, 124(1):393–402.

[The White House2011] The White House. 2011. Background on White House conference on bullying prevention. http://www.whitehouse.gov/the-press-office/2011/03/10/background-white-house-conference-bullying-prevention.

[Toutanova et al.2003] Toutanova, Kristina, Dan Klein, Christopher D. Manning, and Yoram Singer. 2003. Feature-rich part-of-speech tagging with a cyclic dependency network. In *NAACL-HLT 2003*, pages 173–180.

[Vaillancourt et al.2010] Vaillancourt, Tracy, Vi Trinh, Patricia McDougall, Eric Duku, Lesley Cunningham, Charles Cunningham, Shelley Hymel, and Kathy Short. 2010. Optimizing population screening of bullying in school-aged children. *J. of School Violence*, 9:233–250.

[Vandebosch and Cleemput2009] Vandebosch, Heidi and Katrien Van Cleemput. 2009. Cyberbullying among youngsters: profiles of bullies and victims. *New media & society*, 11(8):1349–1371.

[Wang, Iannotti, and Nansel2009] Wang, Jing, Ronald J. Iannotti, and Tonja R. Nansel. 2009. School bullying among adolescents in the united states: Physical, verbal, relational, and cyber. *J. Adolescent Health*, 45(4):368–375.

Grammatical structures for word-level sentiment detection

Asad B. Sayeed
MMCI Cluster of Excellence
Saarland University
66123 Saarbrücken, Germany
asayeed@coli.uni-sb.de

Jordan Boyd-Graber,
Bryan Rusk, Amy Weinberg
{iSchool / UMIACS, Dept. of CS, CASL}
University of Maryland
College Park, MD 20742 USA
{jbg@umiacs,brusk@,
aweinberg@casl}.umd.edu

Abstract

Existing work in fine-grained sentiment analysis focuses on sentences and phrases but ignores the contribution of individual words and their grammatical connections. This is because of a lack of both (1) annotated data at the word level and (2) algorithms that can leverage syntactic information in a principled way. We address the first need by annotating articles from the information technology business press via crowdsourcing to provide training and testing data. To address the second need, we propose a suffix-tree data structure to represent syntactic relationships between opinion targets and words in a sentence that are opinion-bearing. We show that a factor graph derived from this data structure acquires these relationships with a small number of word-level features. We demonstrate that our supervised model performs better than baselines that ignore syntactic features and constraints.

1 Introduction

The terms "sentiment analysis" and "opinion mining" cover a wide body of research on and development of systems that can automatically infer emotional states from text (after Pang and Lee (2008) we use the two names interchangeably). Sentiment analysis plays a large role in business, politics, and is itself a vibrant research area (Bollen et al., 2010).

Effective sentiment analysis for texts such as newswire depends on the ability to extract who (source) is saying what (target). Fine-grained sentiment analysis requires identifying the sources and targets directly relevant to sentiment bearing expressions (Ruppenhofer et al., 2008). For example, consider the following sentence from a major information technology (IT) business journal:

> Lloyd Hession, chief security officer at BT Radianz in New York, said that virtualization also opens up a slew of potential network access control issues.

There are three entities in the sentence that have the capacity to express an opinion: Lloyd Hession, BT Radianz, and New York. These are potential opinion *sources*. There are also a number of mentioned concepts that could serve as the topic of an opinion in the sentence, or *target*. These include all the sources, but also "virtualization", "network access control", "network", and so on.

The challenging task is to discriminate between these mentions and choose the ones that are relevant to the user. Furthermore, such a system must also indicate the content of the *opinion* itself. This means that we are actually searching for all triples {*source, target, opinion*} in this sentence (Kim and Hovy, 2006) and throughout each document in the corpus. In this case, we want to identify that Lloyd Hession is the *source* of an *opinion*, "slew of network issues," about a *target*, virtualization. Providing such fine-grained annotations would enrich information extraction, question answering, and corpus exploration applications by letting users see who is saying what with what opinion (Wilson et al., 2005; Stoyanov and Cardie, 2006).

We motivate the need for a grammatically-focused approach to fine-grained opinion mining and situate it within the context of existing work in Section 2. We propose a supervised technique for learning opinion-target relations from dependency graphs in a way that preserves syntactic coherence and semantic compositionality. In addition to being theoretically sound — a lacuna identified in many sentiment systems[1] — such approaches improve downstream sentiment tasks (Moilanen and Pulman, 2007).

There are multiple types of downstream tasks that potentially require the retrieval of {*source, target, opinion*} relations on a sentence-by-sentence basis. An increasingly significant application area is in the use of large corpora in social science. This area of research requires the exploration and aggregation of data about the relationships between discourses, organizations, and people. For example, the IT business press data that we use in this work belongs to a larger research program (Tsui et al., 2009; Sayeed et al., 2010) of exploring industry opinion leadership. IT business press text is one type of text in which many entities and opinions can appear intermingled with one another in a small amount of text.

Another application for fine-grained sentiment relation retrieval of this type is paraphrasing, where attribution of which opinion belongs to which entities may be important for producing useful and accurate output, since source and target identification errors can change the entire meaning of an output text.

Unlike previous approaches that ignore syntax, we use a sentence's syntactic structure to build a probabilistic model that encodes whether a word is opinion bearing as a latent variable. We build a data structure we call a "syntactic relatedness trie" (Section 3) that serves as the skeleton for a graphical model over the sentiment relevance of words (Section 4). This approach allows us to learn features that predict opinion bearing constructions from grammatical structures. Because of a dearth of resources for this fine-grained task, we also develop new crowdsourcing techniques for labeling word-level, syntactically informed sentiment (Section 5). We use inference techniques to uncover grammatical patterns that connect opinion-expressing words and target entities (Section 6) performing better than using syntactically uninformed methods.

2 Background and existing work

We call opinion mining "fine-grained" when it retrieves many different {*source, target, opinion*} triples per document. This is particularly challenging when there are multiple triples even within a sentence. There is considerable work on identifying the source of an opinion. However, it is much harder to find obvious features that tell us whether "virtualization" is the target of an opinion. The most recent target identification techniques use machine learning to determine the presence of a target from known opinionated language (Jakob and Gurevych, 2010).

Even when targets are identified we must decide if an opinion is expressed, since not all target mentions will necessarily be accompanied by opinion expressions. Returning to the first example sentence, we could say that the negative opinion about virtualization is expressed by the words "slew" and "issues".

A system that could automatically make this discovery must draw on grammatical relationships between targets and the opinion bearing words. Parsers reveal these relationships, but the relationships are often indirect. The variability of language prevents a complete enumeration of all intervening items that make the relationships indirect, but examples include negation and intensifiers, which change opinion, and sentiment-neutral words, which fill syntactic or stylistic needs. In this paper, we cope with the variability of expression by using supervised machine learning to generalize across observations and learn which features best enable us to identify opinionated language.

Existing work in this area often uses semantic frames and role labeling (Kim and Hovy, 2006; Choi et al., 2006), but resources typically used in these tasks (e.g. FrameNet) are not exhaustive. More general approaches (Ruppenhofer et al., 2008) describe semantic and discourse contexts of opinion sources and targets cannot recognize them.

When techniques do identify targets via syntax, they often only use grammar as a feature in an otherwise syntax-agnostic model. Some work of this

[1]Alm (2011) recently argued that work on sentiment analysis needs to de-emphasize the goal of building systems that are "high-performing" by traditional measures, because the field risks sacrificing "opportunities that may lead to a more thorough understanding of language uses and users" in relation to subjective phenomena. The work we present in this paper therefore focuses on extracting meaningful features as an investment in future work that directly improves retrieval performance.

nature merely identifies targets without providing the syntactic evidence necessary to find domain-relevant opinionated language (Jakob and Gurevych, 2010), relying on lists of opinion keywords. There is also work (Qiu et al., 2011) that uses predefined heuristics over dependency parses to identify both targets and opinion keywords but does not acquire new syntactic heuristics. Other work (Nakagawa et al., 2010) is similar to ours in that it uses factor graph modeling over a dependency parse formalism, but it assumes that opinionated language is known *a priori* and focuses on polarity classification, while our work tackles the more fundamental problem of identifying the opinionated language itself.

Little work has been done to perform target and opinion-expression extraction jointly, especially in a way that extracts features for downstream processing. This dearth persists despite evidence that such information improves sentiment analysis (Moilanen and Pulman, 2007).

An advantage of our proposed approach is that we can use dependency paths in order to capture situations where the relations are non-compositional or semantically motivated. In Section 5, we describe a data set that has the additional property that opinion is expressed in ways that require external pragmatic knowledge of the domain. An advantage of arbitrary, non-local dependencies is that we can treat this knowledge as part of the model we learn via long-distance chains, which can capture pragmatics.

3 Syntactic relatedness tries

We now describe how we build the syntactic relatedness trie (SRT) that forms the scaffolding for the probabilistic models needed to identify sentiment-bearing words via syntactic constraints extracted from a dependency parse (Kübler et al., 2009).

We use the Stanford Parser (de Marneffe and Manning, 2008) to produce a dependency graph and consider the resulting undirected graph structure over words. We construct a trie for each possible target word in a sentence (it is possible for a sentence to induce multiple tries if the sentence contains multiple potential targets). Each trie encodes paths from the possible target word to other words, and each path represents a sequence of words connected by undirected edges in the parse.

3.1 Encoding Dependencies in an SRT

SRTs enable us to encode the connections between a single linguistic object of interest—in this application, a possible target word—and a set of related objects. SRTs are data structures consisting of nodes and edges.

This description is very similar to the definition of a dependency parse. The key difference is that while a token only appears once as a node in a dependency parse, an SRT can contain multiple nodes that originate from the same token. This encodes the possible connections between an opinion target and opinion-conveying words.

The object of interest is the opinion target, defined as the SRT root node (e.g. in Figure 1 "policy" is a known target, so it becomes the root of an SRT). Each SRT edge corresponds to a grammatical relationship between words and is labeled with that relationship. We use the notation $a \xrightarrow{R} b$ to signify that node a has the relationship ("role") R with b. We say in this case that node b is a descendent of node a with the role R. The directed edges constitute a trie or suffix tree that represents the fact that multiple paths may share elements that all provide evidence for the relevance of multiple leaves. [2]

In the remainder of this section we describe the necessary steps to create a training corpus for fine-grained sentiment analysis. We provide an example of how to create an SRT from a dependency parse and then to attach latent variable assignments to an SRT based on human annotations in a way that respects syntactic constraints.

3.2 Using sentiment flow to label an SRT

Our goal is to discriminate between parts of the structure that are relevant to target-opinion word relations and those that are not. We use the term sentiment flow (shortened to "flow" when space is an issue) for relevant sentiment-bearing words in the SRT and inert for the remainder of the sentence. We use the term "flow" because our invariant (section 3.3) constrains a sentiment flow in a SRT to be a contiguous subgraph; this corresponds to linguistic intuitions that, for example, in the sentence "Linux with Wine

[2] The SRT will be used to create an undirected graphical model; the notion of directedness refers to the traversal of paths used to construct the SRT.

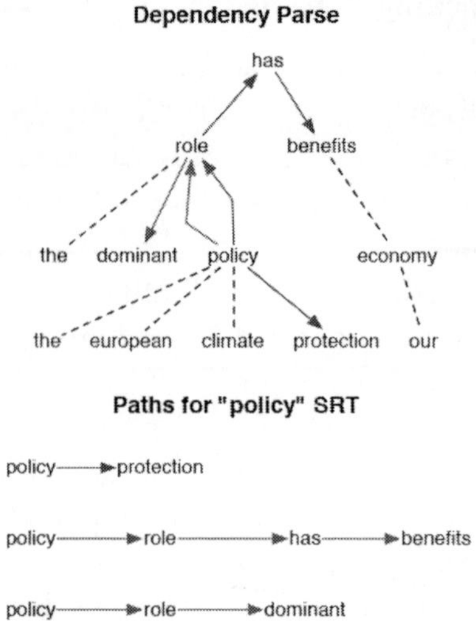

Figure 1: Dependency parse example. A dependency parse (top) is used to generate a syntactic relatedness trie for all possible targets of a sentiment-bearing expression. For the target word "policy", there are a number of paths (colors are consistent in paths to be added to the SRT and in the dependency parse) that connect it to other words; once extracted, these paths will be inserted into a target-specific SRT.

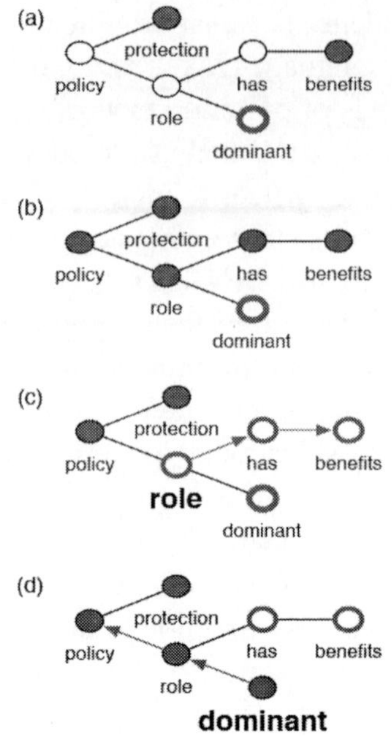

Figure 2: Labeled SRTs rooted on the target word "policy"; green-filled nodes represent words that are part of a sentiment flow and nodes with a red outline represent inert nodes. (a) Initial labels for SRT (e.g. as provided by annotators) (b) propagating labels to yield a valid sentiment flow (c) a change of "role" to inert also renders its children inert (d) a change of "dominant" to be part of a sentiment flow also causes its parents to be part of a flow.

is very usable", {"Linux", "is", "very"} could not be part of a sentiment flow without also including {"usable"}.

Now that we have the structure of the model, we need training data: sentences where sentiment bearing words have been labeled. We describe how to go from sentiment-labeled words to valid flows using this sentence from the MPQA:

> The *dominant* role of the European climate *protection* **policy** has *benefits* for our economy.

In this sentence, the target word "policy" is connected to multiple sentiment-bearing words via paths in the dependency parse (Figure 1). We can represent these relationships using paths through the graph as in Figure 2(a). (For clarity, we do not show some paths.)

Suppose that an annotator decides that "protection" and "benefits" are directly expressing an opinion about the policy, but "dominant" is ambiguous (it has some negative connotations). The nodes "protection" and "benefits" are a flow, and the "dominant" node is inert. However, there is considerable overlap between the "dominant" path and the "benefits" path. That is the motivation for combining them into a trie structure and labeling them in such a way that the path remains a flow until there is *no* path element that leads to a flow leaf (Figure 2).

In other words, we want the path elements common to a flow path and an inert path to reinforce sentiment flow. The transition from flow to inert is learned by the classifier.

We enforce this requirement through the procedure shown in Figure 2, which is equivalent to finding the depth first search tree of the dependency graph and applying the node-labeling scheme as above.

3.3 Invariant

Anything that follows a node with an inert label is by definition not reachable from the root of the tree.

Consequently, any node that is part of a sentiment flow that follows an inert node is not reachable along a path and is actually inert itself. We specify this directly as an invariant on the data structure:

> **Invariant:** no node descending from a node labeled inert can be labeled as a part of a sentiment flow.

This specifies that flow labels spread out from the root of the SRT. Our inference algorithm requires that we be able to change the labels of nodes for test data, thus we need to define invariant-respecting operations for switching labels from flow to flow and vice-versa. A flow label switched to inert will require all the descendents of that particular node to switch to inert as well as in figure 2(c). Similarly, an inert label switched to flow will require all of the ancestors of that node to switch to flow as in 2(d).

4 Encoding SRTs as a factor graph

In this section, we develop supervised machine learning tools to produce a labeled SRT from unlabeled, held-out data in a single, unified model, without permitting the sorts of inconsistencies that may be admitted by using a local classifier at each node.

4.1 Sampling labels

A factor graph (Kschischang et al., 1998) is a representation of a joint probability distribution in the form of a graph with two types of vertices: variable vertices and factor vertices. Given a set of variables $Z = \{z_1 \dots z_n\}$, we connect them via factors $F = \{f_1 \dots f_m\}$. Factors are functions that represent relationships, i.e. probabilistic dependencies, among the variables; the product of all factors gives the complete joint distribution p. Each factor f_i can take as input some corresponding subset of variables Y_i from Z. We can then write the relationship as follows:

$$p(Z) \propto \prod_{k=1}^{m} f_k(Y_k)$$

Our goal is to discover the values for the variables that best explain a dataset. While there are many approaches for inference in statistical models, we turn to MCMC methods (Neal, 1993) to discover the underlying structure of the model. More specifically, we seek a posterior distribution over latent variables that partition words in a sentence into flow and inert groups; we estimate this posterior using Gibbs sampling (Finkel et al., 2005).

The sampler requires an initial state that respects the invariant. Our initial setting is produced by iterating through all labels in the SRT forest and randomly setting them as either flow or inert with uniform probability.

A Gibbs sampler samples new variable assignments from the conditional distribution, treating the variable assignments for all other variables fixed. However, the assignment of a single node is highly coupled with its neighbors, so a block sampler is used to propose changes to groups nodes that respect the flow labeling of the overall assignments. This was implemented by changing the proposal distribution used by the FACTORIE framework (McCallum et al., 2009).

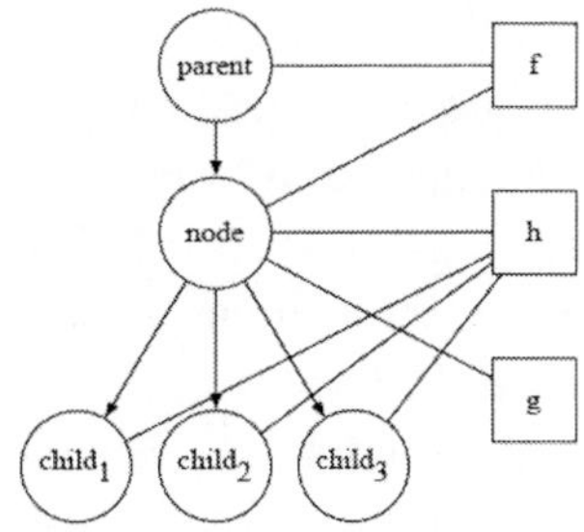

Figure 3: Graphical model of SRT factors

We can thus represent a node and its contribution to the overall score using the graph in Figure 3. This graph contains the given node, its parent, and a variable number of children. The factors that go into the labeling decision for each node are thus constrained to a small, computationally tractable space around the given node. This graph contains three factors:

- g represents a function over features of the given node itself, or "node features."
- f represents a function over a bigram of features taken from the parent node and the given node, or "parent-node" features.
- h represents a function over a combination features on the node and features of *all* its children, or "node-child" features.

We provide further details about these factors in the next section.

In addition to the latent value associated with each word, we associate each node with features derived from the dependency parse: the word from the sentence itself, the part-of-speech (POS) tag assigned by the Stanford parser, and the label of the incoming dependency edge. We treat the edge labels from the original dependency parse as a feature of the node.

We can represent the set of possible observed linguistic feature classes as the set of features Φ. Figure 3 induces a scoring function with contributions of each node to the score(label|node) =

$$\prod_{\phi \in \Phi} \Big(f(\text{parent}_\phi, \text{node}_\phi | \text{label}) g(\text{node}_\phi | \text{label}) \\ h(\text{node}_\phi, \text{child}_{1\phi}, \ldots, \text{child}_{n\phi} | \text{label}) \Big) .$$

After assignments for the latent variables are sampled, the weights for the factors (which when combined create individual factors f that define the joint) must be learned. This is accomplished via the *sample-rank* algorithm (Wick et al., 2009).

5 Data source

Our goal is to identify opinion-bearing words and targets using supervised machine learning techniques. Sentiment corpora with sub-sentential annotations, such as the Multi-Perspective Question-Answering (MPQA) corpus (Wilson and Wiebe, 2005) and the J. D. Power and Associates (JDPA) blog post corpus (Kessler et al., 2010), exist, but most of these annotations are at a phrase level. Within a phrase, however, some words may contribute more than others to the statement of an opinion. We developed our own annotations to discover such distinctions[3]. We describe these briefly here; more information about the development of the data source can be found in Sayeed et al. (2011).

5.1 Information technology business press

Our work is part of a larger collaboration with social scientists to study the diffusion of information technology (IT) innovations through society by identifying opinion leaders and IT-relevant opinionated language Rogers (2003). Thus, we focus on a collection of articles from the IT professional magazine, *Information Week*, from the years 1991 to 2008. This consists of 33K articles including news bulletins and opinion columns. Our IT concept target list (59 terms) comes from our application. Thus, we construct a trie for each appearance of any of these possible target terms. We consider this list of target terms to be complete, which allows us to focus on discovering opinion-bearing text associated with these targets.

5.2 Crowdsourced annotation process

Our process for obtaining gold standard data involves multiple levels of human annotation including on crowdsourcing platforms Hsueh et al. (2009).

There are 75K sentences with IT concept mentions, only a minority of which express relevant opinions. Hired undergraduate students searched a random selection of these sentences and found 219 that contain these opinions. We used cosine-similarity to rank the remaining sentences against the 219.

We then needed to identify which of the words contained an opinion. We excluded all words that were common function words (e.g.,"the", "in") but left negations. We engineered tasks so that only a randomly-selected five or six words appear highlighted for classification in order to limit annotator boredom. We called this group a "highlight group". The virtualization example would look like this:

> Lloyd Hession, chief *security* officer at BT Radianz in New York, said that **virtualization** also *opens* up a slew of potential *network access* control *issues*.

In the virtualization example, the worker would see that **virtualization** is highlighted as the IT concept target. Other words are highlighted as candidates that the worker must classify as being opinion-relevant to "virtualization". Each highlight group corresponds to a syntactic relatedness trie (Section 3).

A task was presented to a worker in the form of a highlight group and some list boxes that represent classes for the highlighted words: "positive", "negative", "not opinion-relevant", and "ambiguous". The worker was required to drag each highlighted candidate word to exactly one of the boxes. As we are not doing opinion polarity classification, the "positive" and "negative" boxes were intended as a form of misdirection intended to avoid having the worker consider what an opinion is; we treated this input as a single "opinion-relevant" category.

[3]To download the corpus, visit `http://www.umiacs.umd.edu/~asayeed/naacl12data/`.

Three or more users annotated each highlight group, and an aggregation scheme was applied afterwards: "ambiguous" answers were rolled into "not opinion-relevant" and ties were dropped. Our quality control process involved filtering out workers who performed poorly on a small subset of gold-standard answers We annotated 30 evaluation units to determine that our process retrieved opinion-relevant words at 85% precision and 74% recall.

Annotators labeled 700 highlight groups for the results in this paper. The total cost of this exercise was approximately 250 USD, which includes the fees charged by Amazon and CrowdFlower. These last highlight groups were converted to SRTs and divided into training and testing groups, 465 and 196 SRTs respectively, with a small number lost to fatal errors in the Stanford parser.

6 Experiments and discussion

During the training phase, we evaluate the quality of a candidate labeling based on label accuracy. We need to identify both flow nodes and inert nodes in order to distinguish between relevant and irrelevant subcomponents. We thus also employ precision and recall as performance metrics.

An example of how this works can be seen by comparing figure 2(b) to figure 2(d), viewing the former as the gold standard and the latter as a hypothetical system output. If we run the evaluation over that single SRT and treat flow as the positive class, we find that 3 true positives, 1 false positive, 2 false negatives, and no true negatives. There are 6 labels in total. That yields 0.50 accuracy, 0.75 precision, 0.60 recall, and 0.67 F-measure.

We run every experiment (training a model and testing on held-out data) 10 times and take the mean average and range of all measures. F-measure is calculated for each run and averaged *post hoc*.

6.1 Experiments

Our baseline system is the initial setting of the labels for the sampler: uniform random assignment of flow labels, respecting the invariant. This leads to a large class imbalance in favor of inert as any switch to inert converts all nodes downstream from the root to convert to inert, while a switch to flow causes only one ancestor branch to convert to flow.

Our next systems involve combinations of our SRT factors with the observed linguistic features. All our experiments include the factor g that pertains only to the features of the node. Then we add factor f—the parent-node "bigram" features—and finally factor h, the variable-length node-child features. We also experiment with including and excluding combinations of POS, role, and word features. We also explored models that only made local decisions, ignoring the consistency constraints over sentiment flows. Although such models cannot be used in techniques such as Nakagawa et al.'s polarity classifier, they function as a baseline and inform whether syntactic constraints help performance.

We ran the inferencer for 200 iterations to train a model with a particular factor-feature combination. We use the learned model to predict the labels on the held-out testing data by running the inference algorithm (sampling labels only) for 50 iterations.

6.2 Discussion

We present a sampling of possible feature-factor combinations in table 1 in order to show trends in the performance of the system.

Unsurprisingly, the invariant-respecting baseline had very high precision but low recall. Simply including the node-only g factor with all features increases the recall while hurting precision. On removing word features, recall increases without changing precision. This suggests that some words in some SRTs are associated with flow labels in the training data, but not as much in the testing data.

Including parent-node f features with the g features yields higher precision and lower recall, suggesting that parent-node word features support precision. Including all features on all factors (f, g, and h) preserves most of the precision but improves recall. Excluding h features increases recall slightly more than it hurts precision. Excluding both word features for all factors and role h features hurts all measures.

The accuracy measure, however, does show overall improvement with the inclusion of more feature-factor combinations. In particular, the node-child h factor does appear to have an effect on the performance. The presence of some combinations of child word, POS tags, and roles appear to provide some indication of the flow labeling of some of the nodes. The best models in terms of accuracy include all or

Experiment	Features	Invariant?	Precision	Recall	F	Accuracy
Baseline	N/A	Yes	0.78 $\pm$ 0.05	0.06 $\pm$ 0.01	0.11 $\pm$ 0.02	0.51 $\pm$ 0.01
		No	0.50 $\pm$ 0.00	0.49 $\pm$ 0.00	0.50 $\pm$ 0.00	0.50 $\pm$ 0.00
Node only	All	Yes	0.63 $\pm$ 0.10	0.34 $\pm$ 0.10	0.42 $\pm$ 0.07	0.54 $\pm$ 0.03
		No	0.51 $\pm$ 0.00	0.88 $\pm$ 0.03	0.65 $\pm$ 0.01	0.51 $\pm$ 0.01
	All but word	Yes	0.63 $\pm$ 0.16	0.40 $\pm$ 0.22	0.42 $\pm$ 0.19	0.53 $\pm$ 0.03
		No	0.57 $\pm$ 0.04	0.56 $\pm$ 0.17	0.55 $\pm$ 0.07	0.55 $\pm$ 0.03
Parent, node	Parent: all but word Node: all	Yes	0.71 $\pm$ 0.06	0.21 $\pm$ 0.04	0.31 $\pm$ 0.05	0.55 $\pm$ 0.01
	All	Yes	0.84 $\pm$ 0.07	0.11 $\pm$ 0.04	0.19 $\pm$ 0.06	0.53 $\pm$ 0.01
Full graph	Parent: all but word Node: all but word Children: POS only	Yes	0.59 $\pm$ 0.06	0.39 $\pm$ 0.11	0.46 $\pm$ 0.07	0.54 $\pm$ 0.03
	Parent: all Node: all Children: all but word	Yes	0.67 $\pm$ 0.05	0.39 $\pm$ 0.08	0.47 $\pm$ 0.06	0.59 $\pm$ 0.02
	All	Yes	0.70 $\pm$ 0.05	0.35 $\pm$ 0.08	0.46 $\pm$ 0.07	0.59 $\pm$ 0.02
		No	0.70 $\pm$ 0.03	0.20 $\pm$ 0.05	0.36 $\pm$ 0.06	0.56 $\pm$ 0.01

Table 1: Performance using different feature combinations, including some without enforcing the invariant. Mean averages and standard deviation for 10 runs.

almost all of the features.

Our non-invariant-respecting baseline unsurprisingly was nearly 50% on all measures. Including the node-only features dramatically increases recall, less if we exclude word features. The word features appear to have an effect on recall just as in the invariant-respecting case with node-only features. With all features, precision is dramatically improved, but with a large cost to recall. However, it underperforms the equivalent invariant-respecting model in recall, F-measure, and accuracy.

Though these invariant-violating models are unconstrained in the way they label the graph, our invariant-respecting models still outperform them. A coherent path contains more information than an incoherent one; it is important to find negating and intensifying elements *in context*. Our SRT invariant allows us to achieve better performance and will be more useful to downstream tasks.

Finally, it appears that using more factors and linguistic features promotes stability in performance and decreases sensitivity to the initial setting.

6.3 Manual inspection

One pattern that prominently stood out in the testing data with the full-graph model was the misclassification of flow labels as inert in the vicinity of Stanford dependency labels such as `conj_and`. These kinds of labels have high "fertility"; the labels immediately following them in the SRT could be a variety of types, creating potential data sparsity issues.

This problem could be resolved by making some features transparent to the learner. For example, if node q has an incoming `conj_and` dependency edge label, then q's parent could also be directly connected to q's children, as a conjunction should be linguistically transparent to the status of the children in the sentiment flow.

There are many fewer incidents of inert labels being classified as flow. There are paths through an SRT where a flow candidate word is the ancestor of an inert candidate word from the set of crowdsourced candidates. The model sometimes appears to "overshoot" the flow candidate. Considering that recall is already fairly low, attempts to address this problem risks making the model too conservative. One potential solution is to prune or separate paths that contain multiple flow candidates.

6.3.1 Paths found

We examined the labeling on the held-out testing data of the best-performing model of the full graph system with all linguistic features. For example, consider the following highlight group:

> But Microsoft's informal approach may not be enough as the number of **blogs** at the company grows, especially since the line between "personal" Weblogs and those done as part of the job can be hard to distinguish.

In this case, the Turkers decided that "distinguish" expressed a negative opinion about blogs, in the sense that something that was difficult to distinguish was a problem: the modifier "hard" is what makes it negative. The system found an entirely flow path that connected these attributes into a single unit:

$$\text{Blog:flow} \xrightarrow{\text{prep}_\text{o}\text{f}} \text{number:flow} \xrightarrow{\text{nsubj}} \text{grows:flow} \xrightarrow{\text{ccomp}} \text{hard:flow} \xrightarrow{\text{xcomp}} \text{distinguish:flow}$$

In this path, "blog" and "distinguish" are both connected to one another by "hard", giving "distinguish" its negative spin. There are two non-local dependencies in this example: xcomp, ccomp. Very often, more than one unique path connects the concept to the opinion candidate word.

7 Conclusions and future work

In this work, we have applied machine learning to produce a robust modeling of syntactic structure for an information extraction application. A solution to the problem of modeling these structures requires the development of new techniques that model complex linguistic relationships in an application-dependent way. We have shown that we can mine these relationships without being overcome by the data-sparsity issues that typically stymie learning over complex linguistic structure.

The limitations on these techniques ultimately find their root in the difficulty in modeling complex syntactic structures that simultaneously exclude irrelevant portions of the structure while maintaining connected relations. Our technique uses a structure-labelling scheme that enforces connectedness. Enforcing connected structure is not only necessary to produce useful results but also to improve accuracy.

Further performance gains might be possible by enriching the feature set. For example, the POS tagset used by the Stanford parser contains multiple verb tags that represent different English tenses and numbers. For the purpose of sentiment relations, it is possible that the differences between verb tags are too small to matter and are causing data sparsity issues. Thus, we could additional features that "back off" to general verb tags.

Acknowledgements

This paper is based upon work supported by the US National Science Foundation under Grant IIS-0729459. Additional support came from the Cluster of Excellence "Multimodal Computing and Innovation", Germany. Jordan Boyd-Graber is also supported by US National Science Foundation Grant NSF grant #1018625 and the Army Research Laboratory through ARL Cooperative Agreement W911NF-09-2-0072. Any opinions, findings, conclusions, or recommendations expressed are the authors' and do not necessarily reflect those of the sponsors.

References

Alm, C. O. (2011). Subjective natural language problems: Motivations, applications, characterizations, and implications. In *ACL (Short Papers)*.

Bollen, J., Mao, H., and Zeng, X.-J. (2010). Twitter mood predicts the stock market. *CoRR*, abs/1010.3003.

Choi, Y., Breck, E., and Cardie, C. (2006). Joint extraction of entities and relations for opinion recognition. In *Proceedings of the Conference on Empirical Methods in Natural Language Processing (EMNLP)*.

de Marneffe, M.-C. and Manning, C. D. (2008). The stanford typed dependencies representation. In *CrossParser '08: Coling 2008: Proceedings of the workshop on Cross-Framework and Cross-Domain Parser Evaluation*, Morristown, NJ, USA. Association for Computational Linguistics.

Finkel, J. R., Grenager, T., and Manning, C. (2005). Incorporating non-local information into information extraction systems by gibbs sampling. In *Proceedings of the 43rd Annual Meeting on Association for Computational Linguistics*, ACL '05, pages 363–370, Stroudsburg, PA, USA. Association for Computational Linguistics.

Hsueh, P.-Y., Melville, P., and Sindhwani, V. (2009). Data quality from crowdsourcing: a study of annotation selection criteria. In *Proceedings of the NAACL HLT 2009 Workshop on Active Learning for Natural Language Processing*, HLT '09, Stroudsburg, PA, USA. Association for Computational Linguistics.

Jakob, N. and Gurevych, I. (2010). Extracting opinion targets in a single and cross-domain setting with conditional random fields. In *EMNLP*.

Kessler, J. S., Eckert, M., Clark, L., and Nicolov, N. (2010). The 2010 ICWSM JDPA sentment corpus for the automotive domain. In *4th Int'l AAAI Conference on Weblogs and Social Media Data Workshop Challenge (ICWSM-DWC 2010)*.

Kim, S.-M. and Hovy, E. (2006). Extracting opinions, opinion holders, and topics expressed in online news media text. In *SST '06: Proceedings of the Workshop on Sentiment and Subjectivity in Text*, pages 1–8, Morristown, NJ, USA. Association for Computational Linguistics.

Kschischang, F. R., Frey, B. J., and andrea Loeliger, H. (1998). Factor graphs and the sum-product algorithm. *IEEE Transactions on Information Theory*, 47:498–519.

Kübler, S., McDonald, R., and Nivre, J. (2009). Dependency parsing. *Synthesis Lectures on Human Language Technologies*, 2(1).

McCallum, A., Schultz, K., and Singh, S. (2009). Factorie: Probabilistic programming via imperatively defined factor graphs. In *Neural Information Processing Systems (NIPS)*.

Moilanen, K. and Pulman, S. (2007). Sentiment composition. In *Proceedings of the Recent Advances in Natural Language Processing International Conference (RANLP-2007)*, Borovets, Bulgaria.

Nakagawa, T., Inui, K., and Kurohashi, S. (2010). Dependency tree-based sentiment classification using crfs with hidden variables. In *HLT-NAACL*.

Neal, R. M. (1993). Probabilistic inference using Markov chain Monte Carlo methods. Technical Report CRG-TR-93-1, University of Toronto.

Pang, B. and Lee, L. (2008). Opinion mining and sentiment analysis. *Found. Trends Inf. Retr.*, 2(1-2).

Qiu, G., Liu, B., Bu, J., and Chen, C. (2011). Opinion word expansion and target extraction through double propagation. *Computational linguistics*, 37(1):9—27.

Rogers, E. M. (2003). *Diffusion of Innovations, 5th Edition*. Free Press.

Ruppenhofer, J., Somasundaran, S., and Wiebe, J. (2008). Finding the sources and targets of subjective expressions. In Calzolari, N., Choukri, K., Maegaard, B., Mariani, J., Odjik, J., Piperidis, S., and Tapias, D., editors, *Proceedings of the Sixth International Language Resources and Evaluation (LREC'08)*, Marrakech, Morocco. European Language Resources Association (ELRA).

Sayeed, A. B., Nguyen, H. C., Meyer, T. J., and Weinberg, A. (2010). Expresses-an-opinion-about: using corpus statistics in an information extraction approach to opinion mining. In *Proceedings of the 23rd International Conference on Computational Linguistics*, COLING '10.

Sayeed, A. B., Rusk, B., Petrov, M., Nguyen, H. C., Meyer, T. J., and Weinberg, A. (2011). Crowdsourcing syntactic relatedness judgements for opinion mining in the study of information technology adoption. In *Proceedings of the Association for Computational Linguistics 2011 workshop on Language Technology for Cultural Heritage, Social Sciences, and the Humanities (LaTeCH)*. Association for Computational Linguistics.

Stoyanov, V. and Cardie, C. (2006). Partially supervised coreference resolution for opinion summarization through structured rule learning. In *EMNLP '06: Proceedings of the 2006 Conference on Empirical Methods in Natural Language Processing*, pages 336–344, Morristown, NJ, USA. Association for Computational Linguistics.

Tsui, C.-J., Wang, P., Fleischmann, K., Oard, D., and Sayeed, A. (2009). Understanding IT innovations by computational analysis of discourse. In *International conference on information systems*.

Wick, M., Rohanimanesh, K., Culotta, A., and Mccallum, A. (2009). SampleRank: Learning preference from atomic gradients. In *NIPS WS on Advances in Ranking*.

Wilson, T. and Wiebe, J. (2005). Annotating attributions and private states. In *CorpusAnno '05: Proceedings of the Workshop on Frontiers in Corpus Annotations II*, Morristown, NJ, USA. Association for Computational Linguistics.

Wilson, T., Wiebe, J., and Hoffmann, P. (2005). Recognizing contextual polarity in phrase-level sentiment analysis. In *HLT/EMNLP*.

Graph-Based Lexicon Expansion with Sparsity-Inducing Penalties

Dipanjan Das and **Noah A. Smith**
Language Technologies Institute
Carnegie Mellon University
Pittsburgh, PA 15213, USA
{dipanjan,nasmith}@cs.cmu.edu

Abstract

We present novel methods to construct compact natural language lexicons within a graph-based semi-supervised learning framework, an attractive platform suited for propagating soft labels onto new natural language types from seed data. To achieve compactness, we induce sparse measures at graph vertices by incorporating sparsity-inducing penalties in Gaussian and entropic pairwise Markov networks constructed from labeled and unlabeled data. Sparse measures are desirable for high-dimensional multi-class learning problems such as the induction of labels on natural language types, which typically associate with only a few labels. Compared to standard graph-based learning methods, for two lexicon expansion problems, our approach produces significantly smaller lexicons and obtains better predictive performance.

1 Introduction

Semi-supervised learning (SSL) is attractive for the learning of complex phenomena, for example, linguistic structure, where data annotation is expensive. Natural language processing applications have benefited from various SSL techniques, such as distributional word representations (Huang and Yates, 2009; Turian et al., 2010; Dhillon et al., 2011), self-training (McClosky et al., 2006), and entropy regularization (Jiao et al., 2006; Smith and Eisner, 2007). In this paper, we focus on semi-supervised learning that uses a graph constructed from labeled and unlabeled data. This framework, **graph-based SSL**—see Bengio et al. (2006) and Zhu (2008) for introductory material on this topic—has been widely used and has been shown to perform better than several other semi-supervised algorithms on benchmark datasets (Chapelle et al., 2006, ch. 21). The method constructs a graph where a small portion of vertices correspond to labeled instances, and the rest are unlabeled. Pairs of vertices are connected by weighted edges denoting the similarity between the pair. Traditionally, Markov random walks (Szummer and Jaakkola, 2001; Baluja et al., 2008) or optimization of a loss function based on smoothness properties of the graph (Corduneanu and Jaakkola, 2003; Zhu et al., 2003; Subramanya and Bilmes, 2008, *inter alia*) are performed to propagate labels from the labeled vertices to the unlabeled ones.

In this work, we are interested in multi-class generalizations of graph-propagation algorithms suitable for NLP applications, where each graph vertex can assume one *or more* out of many possible labels (Talukdar and Crammer, 2009; Subramanya and Bilmes, 2008, 2009). For us, graph vertices correspond to natural language *types* (not tokens) and undirected edges between them are weighted using a similarity metric. Recently, this setup has been used to learn soft labels on natural language types (say, word *n*-grams or syntactically disambiguated predicates) from seed data, resulting in large but noisy *lexicons*, which are used to constrain structured prediction models. Applications have ranged from domain adaptation of part-of-speech (POS) taggers (Subramanya et al., 2010), unsupervised learning of POS taggers by using bilingual graph-based projections (Das and Petrov, 2011), and shallow semantic parsing for unknown predicates (Das and Smith, 2011). However, none of the above captured the empirical fact that only a few categories typically associate with a given type (vertex). Take the case of POS tagging: Subramanya et al. (2010) construct a graph over trigram types as vertices, with 45 possible tags for the middle word of a trigram as the label set for each vertex. It is empirically observed that contextualized word types can assume very few (most often, one) POS tags. However, along with graph smoothness terms, they apply a penalty that encourages distributions to be close to uniform, the premise being that it would maximize the entropy of the distribution for a vertex that is far away or disconnected from a labeled vertex. To prefer maximum entropy solutions in low confidence regions of graphs, a similar entropic penalty is applied by Subramanya and Bilmes (2008, 2009).

In this paper, we make two major algorithmic contributions. First, we relax the assumption made by most previous work (Zhu and Ghahramani, 2002; Baluja et al., 2008; Subramanya and Bilmes, 2008; Subramanya and Bilmes, 2009; Subramanya et al., 2010; Das and Petrov, 2011; Das and Smith, 2011) that the ℓ_1 norm of the masses assigned to the labels for a given vertex must be 1. In other words, in our framework, the label distribution at each vertex is *unnormalized*—the only constraint we put on the vertices' vectors is that they must be nonnegative.[1] This relaxation simplifies optimization: since only a nonnegativity constraint for each label's mass at each vertex needs to be imposed, we can apply a generic quasi-Newton method (Zhu et al., 1997).

Second, we replace the penalties that prefer maximum entropy, used in prior work, with penalties that aim to identify *sparse* unnormalized measures at each graph vertex. We achieve this by penalizing the graph propagation objective with the ℓ_1 norm or the mixed $\ell_{1,2}$ norm (Kowalski and Torrésani, 2009) of the measures at each vertex, aiming for global and vertex-level sparsity, respectively. Importantly, the proposed graph objective functions are convex, so we avoid degenerate solutions and local minima.

We present experiments on two natural language lexicon expansion problems in a semi-supervised setting: (i) inducing distributions of POS tags over n-gram types in the *Wall Street Journal* section of the Penn Treebank corpus (Marcus et al., 1993) and (ii) inducing distributions of semantic frames (Fillmore, 1982) over predicates unseen in annotated data. Our methods produce sparse measures at graph vertices resulting in compact lexicons, and also result in better performance with respect to label propagation using Gaussian penalties (Zhu and Ghahramani, 2002) and entropic measure propagation (Subramanya and Bilmes, 2009), two state-of-the-art graph propagation algorithms.

[1]Moreover, we also assume the edge weights in a given graph are unconstrained, consistent with prior work on graph-based SSL (Das and Petrov, 2011; Das and Smith, 2011; Subramanya and Bilmes, 2008; Subramanya and Bilmes, 2009; Subramanya et al., 2010; Zhu and Ghahramani, 2002).

2 Model

2.1 Graph-Based SSL as MAP Inference

Let $\mathcal{D}_l = \{(\mathbf{x}_j, r_j)\}_{j=1}^{l}$ denote l annotated data *types*;[2] $\mathbf{x}_j$'s empirical label distribution is r_j. Let the unlabeled data types be denoted by $\mathcal{D}_u = \{\mathbf{x}_i\}_{i=l+1}^{m}$. Usually, $l \ll m$. Thus, the entire dataset can be called $\mathcal{D} \triangleq \mathcal{D}_l \cup \mathcal{D}_u$. Traditionally, the graph-based SSL problem has been set up as follows. Let $\mathcal{G} = (V, E)$ correspond to an undirected graph with vertices V and edges E. $\mathcal{G}$ is constructed by transforming each data type $\mathbf{x}_i \in \mathcal{D}$ to a vertex; thus $V = \{1, 2, \ldots, m\}$, and $E \subseteq V \times V$. Let V_l (V_u) denote the labeled (unlabeled) vertices. Moreover, we assume a symmetric weight matrix $\mathbf{W}$ that defines the similarity between a pair of vertices $i, k \in V$. We first define a component of this matrix as $w_{ij} \triangleq [\mathbf{W}]_{ik} = \text{sim}(\mathbf{x}_i, \mathbf{x}_k)$. We also fix $w_{ii} = 0$ and set $w_{ik} = w_{ki} = 0$ if $k \notin \mathcal{N}(i)$ and $i \notin \mathcal{N}(k)$, where $\mathcal{N}(j)$ denotes the K-nearest neighbors of vertex j, to reduce the density of the graph. We next define an unnormalized measure q_i for every vertex $i \in V$. As mentioned before, we have r_j, a probability distribution estimated from annotated data for a labeled vertex $j \in V_l$. q_i and r_j are $|Y|$-dimensional measures, where Y is the possible set of labels; while r_j lies within the $|Y|$-dimensional probability simplex,[3] q_i are unnormalized with each component $q_i(y) \geq 0$. For most NLP problems, r_j are expected to be sparse, with very few components active, the rest being zero.

Graph-based SSL aims at finding the best $\boldsymbol{q} = \{q_i : 1 \leq i \leq m\}$ given the empirical distributions r_j, and the weight matrix $\mathbf{W}$, which provides

[2]As explained in more detail in §4, these types are entities like n-grams or individual predicates, not tokens in running text.

[3]Note that our framework does not necessitate that r_j be a normalized probability distribution; we could have unnormalized r_j to allow strongly evident types appearing in more data to have larger influence than types that appear infrequently. We leave this extension to future work.

the geometry of all the vertices. We visualize this problem using a pairwise Markov network (MN). For every vertex (including labeled ones) $i \in V$, we create a variable X_i. Additionally, for labeled vertices $j \in V_l$, we create variables $\hat{X}_j$. All variables in the MN are defined to be *vector-valued*; specifically, variables X_i, $\forall i \in V$, take value q_i, and variables $\hat{X}_j$ corresponding to the labeled vertices in $\mathcal{G}$ are observed with values r_j. An example factor graph for this MN, with only four vertices, is shown in Figure 1. In the figure, the variables indexed by 1 and 4 correspond to labeled vertices. Factor ϕ_j with scope $\{X_j, \hat{X}_j\}$ encourages q_j to be close to r_j. For every edge $i - k \in E$, factor φ_{i-k} encourages similarity between q_i and q_k, making use of the weight matrix $\mathbf{W}$ (i.e., when w_{ik} is larger, the two measures are more strongly encouraged to be close). These factors are white squares with solid boundaries in the figure. Finally, we define unary factors on all variables $X_i, i \in V$, named $\psi_i(X_i)$, that can incorporate prior information. In Figure 1, these factors are represented by white squares with dashed boundaries.

According to the factor graph, the joint probability for all the measures q_i, $\forall i \in V$ that we want to induce, is defined as: $P(\boldsymbol{X}; \Phi) =$

$$\frac{1}{Z} \prod_{j=1}^{l} \phi_j(X_j, \hat{X}_j) \cdot \prod_{i-k \in E} \varphi_{i-k}(X_i, X_k) \cdot \prod_{i=1}^{m} \psi_i(X_i)$$

where Φ is the set of all factors in the factor graph, and Z is a partition function that normalizes the factor products for a given configuration of $\boldsymbol{q}$. Since the graph-based SSL problem aims at finding the best $\boldsymbol{q}$, we optimize $\ln P(\boldsymbol{X}; \Phi)$; equivalently,

$$\underset{\boldsymbol{q} \text{ s.t. } \boldsymbol{q} \geq \boldsymbol{0}}{\arg\max} \sum_{j=1}^{l} \ln \phi_j(X_j, \hat{X}_j) + \sum_{i-k \in E} \ln \varphi_{i-k}(X_i, X_k) + \sum_{i=1}^{m} \ln \psi_i(X_i) \quad (1)$$

The above denotes an optimization problem with only non-negativity constraints. It equates to maximum *a posteriori* (MAP) inference; hence, the partition function Z can be ignored. We next discuss the nature of the three different factors in Eq. 1.

2.2 Log-Factors as Penalties

The nature of the three types of factors in Eq. 1 governs the behavior of a graph-based SSL algorithm. Hence, the equation specifies a *family* of graph-based methods that generalize prior research. We desire the following properties to be satisfied in the factors: (i) convexity of Eq. 1, (ii) amenability to scalable optimization algorithms, and (iii) sparse solutions as expected in natural language lexicons.

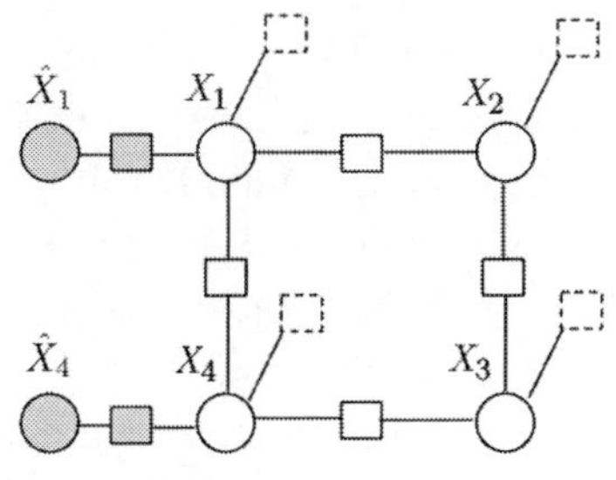

Figure 1: An example factor graph for the graph-based SSL problem. See text for the significance of the shaded and dotted factors, and the shaded variables.

Pairwise factors: In our work, for the pairwise factors $\phi_j(X_j, \hat{X}_j)$ and $\varphi_{i-k}(X_i, X_k)$, we examine two functions that penalize inconsistencies between neighboring vertices: the squared ℓ_2 norm and the Jensen-Shannon (JS) divergence (Burbea and Rao, 1982; Lin, 1991), which is a symmetrized generalization of the Kullback-Leibler (KL) divergence (Kullback and Leibler, 1951; Cover and Thomas, 1991). These two divergences are symmetric. Both are inspired by previous work; however, the use of the JS divergence is a novel extension to Subramanya and Bilmes (2008). Specifically, the factors are:

$$\ln \phi_j(X_j, \hat{X}_j) = -\delta(q_j, r_j) \quad (2)$$

$$\ln \varphi_{i-k}(X_i, X_k) = -2 \cdot \mu \cdot w_{ik} \cdot \delta(q_i, q_k) \quad (3)$$

where μ is a hyperparameter whose choice we discuss in §4. The function $\delta(u, v)$ for two vectors u and v is defined in two ways:

$$\underset{\text{Gaussian}}{\delta(u, v)} = \|u - v\|_2^2 \quad (4)$$

$$\underset{\text{Entropic}}{\delta(u, v)} = \frac{1}{2} \sum_{y \in Y} \left(u(y) \cdot \ln \frac{2 \cdot u(y)}{u(y) + v(y)} + v(y) \cdot \ln \frac{2 \cdot v(y)}{u(y) + v(y)} \right) \quad (5)$$

We call the version of $\delta(u, v)$ that uses the squared ℓ_2 distance (Eq. 4) *Gaussian*, as it represents the idea of label propagation via Gaussian fields proposed by Zhu et al. (2003). A minor difference lies in the fact that we include variables $X_j, j \in V_l$ for labeled vertices too, and allow them to change, but penalize them if they go too far away from the observed labeled distributions r_j. The other $\delta(u, v)$ shown in Eq. 5 uses the generalized JS-divergence defined in terms of the generalized KL-divergence for unnormalized measures (O'Sullivan, 1998).[4]

Eq. 5 improves prior work by replacing the asymmetric KL-divergence used to bring the distributions at labeled vertices close to the corresponding observed distributions, as well as replacing the KL-based graph smoothness term with the symmetric JS-divergence (Subramanya and Bilmes, 2008, see first two terms in Eq. 1). Empirical evidence shows that entropic divergences help in multiclass problems where a vertex can assume multiple labels, and may perform better than objectives with quadratic penalties (Subramanya and Bilmes, 2008, 2009).

A major departure from prior work is the use of unnormalized measures in Eq. 4-5, which simplifies optimization even with the complex JS-divergence in the objective function (see §3), and, we will see, produces comparable and often better results than baselines using normalized distributions (see §4).

Unary factors: The unary factors in our factor graph $\psi_i(X_i)$ can incorporate prior information specific to a particular vertex $\mathbf{x}_i$ embodied by the variable X_i. Herein, we examine three straightforward penalties, which can be thought of as penalties that encourage either uniformity or sparsity:

$$\text{Uniform squared } \ell_2\text{: } \ln \psi_i(X_i) = -\lambda \cdot \left\| q_i - \frac{1}{|Y|} \right\|_2^2 \quad (6)$$

$$\text{Sparse } \ell_1\text{: } \ln \psi_i(X_i) = -\lambda \cdot \|q_i\|_1 \quad (7)$$

$$\text{Sparse } \ell_{1,2}\text{: } \ln \psi_i(X_i) = -\lambda \cdot \|q_i\|_1^2 \quad (8)$$

where λ is a hyperparameter whose choice we discuss in §4. The penalty expressed in Eq. 6 penalizes q_i if it is far away from the uniform distribution. This penalty has been used previously (Das and Petrov, 2011; Das and Smith, 2011; Subramanya et al., 2010), and is similar to the maximum entropy penalty of Subramanya and Bilmes (2008, 2009). The intuition behind its use is that for low confidence or disconnected regions, one would prefer to have a uniform measure on a graph vertex. The penalties in equations 7–8, on the other hand, encourage sparsity in the measure q_i; these are related to regularizers for generalized linear models: the lasso (Tibshirani, 1996) and the elitist lasso (Kowalski and Torrésani, 2009). The former encourages global sparsity, the latter sparsity per vertex.[5] For each vertex, the $\ell_{1,2}$ penalty takes the form:

$$\|q_i\|_1^2 = \left(\sum_{y \in Y} |q_i(y)| \right)^2 \quad (9)$$

The ℓ_1 norm encourages its argument to be sparse, while the usual observed effect of an ℓ_2 norm is a dense vector without many extreme values. The $\ell_{1,2}$ penalty is the squared ℓ_2 norm of the ℓ_1 norms of every q_i, hence it promotes sparsity within each vertex, but we observe density over the vertices that are selected.

Talukdar (2010) enforced label sparsity for information extraction by discarding poorly scored labels during graph propagation updates, but did not use a principled mechanism to arrive at sparse measures at graph vertices. Unlike the uniform penalty (Eq. 6), sparsity corresponds to the idea of entropy *minimization* (Grandvalet and Bengio, 2004). Since we use unnormalized measures at each variable X_i, for low confidence graph regions or disconnected vertices, sparse penalties will result in all zero components in q_i, which conveys that the graph propagation algorithm is not confident on any potential label, a condition that is perfectly acceptable.

Model variants: We compare six objective functions: we combine factor representations from each of Eqs. 4–5 with those from each of Eqs. 6–8, replacing them in the generic graph objective function of Eq. 1. The nature of these six models is succinctly summarized in Table 1. For each model, we find the best set of measures $\boldsymbol{q}$ that maximize the corresponding graph objective functions, such that $\boldsymbol{q} \geq \mathbf{0}$. Note that in each of the graph objectives, we have two hyperparameters μ and λ that control the influence of the second and the third terms of Eq. 1 re-

[4] The generalized KL divergence is defined as $D_{KL}(u\|v) = \sum_y \left(u(y) \ln \frac{u(y)}{v(y)} - u(y) + v(y) \right)$.

[5] One could additionally consider a non-sparse penalty based on the squared ℓ_2 norm with zero mean: $\ln \psi_i(X_i) = -\lambda \cdot \|q_i\|_2^2$. We experimented with this unary penalty (along with the pairwise Gaussian penalty for binary factors) for the semantic frame lexicon expansion problem, and found that it performs exactly on par with the squared ℓ_2 penalty with uniform mean. To limit the number of non-sparse graph objectives, we omit detailed discussion of experiments with this unary penalty.

abbrev.	factors	
	pairwise	unary
UGF-ℓ_2	Gaussian	Uniform squared ℓ_2
UGF-ℓ_1	Gaussian	Sparse ℓ_1
UGF-$\ell_{1,2}$	Gaussian	Sparse $\ell_{1,2}$
UJSF-ℓ_2	Entropic	Uniform squared ℓ_2
UJSF-ℓ_1	Entropic	Sparse ℓ_1
UJSF-$\ell_{1,2}$	Entropic	Sparse $\ell_{1,2}$

Table 1: Six variants of graph objective functions novel to this work. These variants combine the pairwise factor representations from Eqs. 4–5 with unary factor representations from each of Eqs. 6–8 (which either encourage uniform or sparse measures), to be used in the graph objective function expressed in Eq. 1.

spectively. We discuss how these hyperparameters are chosen in §4.

Baseline Models: We compare the performance of the six graph objectives of Table 1 with two strong baselines that have been used in previous work. These two models use the following two objective functions, and find $\boldsymbol{q}$ s.t. $\boldsymbol{q} \geq \boldsymbol{0}$ and $\forall i \in V, \sum_{y \in Y} q_i(y) = 1$. The first is a normalized Gaussian field with a squared uniform ℓ_2 penalty as the unary factor (**NGF-ℓ_2**):

$$\underset{\substack{\boldsymbol{q}, \text{ s.t. } \boldsymbol{q} \geq \boldsymbol{0}, \\ \forall i \in V, \|q_i\|_1 = 1}}{\arg\min} \sum_{j=1}^{l} \|q_j - r_j\|_2^2 + \sum_{i=1}^{m} \left(\mu \sum_{k \in \mathcal{N}(i)} w_{ik} \|q_i - q_k\|_2^2 + \lambda \left\| q_i - \frac{1}{|Y|} \right\|_2^2 \right) \quad (10)$$

The second is a normalized KL field with an entropy penalty as the unary factor (**NKLF**-ME):

$$\underset{\substack{\boldsymbol{q}, \text{ s.t. } \boldsymbol{q} \geq \boldsymbol{0}, \\ \forall i \in V, \|q_i\|_1 = 1}}{\arg\min} \sum_{j=1}^{l} D_{KL}(r_j \parallel q_j) + \sum_{i=1}^{m} \left(\mu \sum_{k \in \mathcal{N}(i)} w_{ik} D_{KL}(q_i \parallel q_k) - \lambda \cdot H(q_i) \right) \quad (11)$$

where $H(q_i)$ denotes the Shannon entropy of the distribution q_i. Both these objectives are constrained by the fact that every q_i must be within the $|Y|$-dimensional probability simplex. The objective function in 10 has been used previously (Das and Smith, 2011; Subramanya et al., 2010) and serves as a generalization of Zhu et al. (2003). The entropic objective function in 11, originally called *measure propagation*, performed better at multiclass problems when compared to graph objectives using the quadratic criterion (Subramanya and Bilmes, 2008).

3 Optimization

The six variants of Eq. 1 in Table 1 are convex in $\boldsymbol{q}$. This is because the ℓ_1, squared ℓ_2 and the $\ell_{1,2}$ penalties are convex. Moreover, the generalized JS-divergence term, which is a sum of two KL-divergence terms, is convex (Cover and Thomas, 1991). Since we choose μ, λ and w_{ik} to be non-negative, these terms' sums are also convex. The graph objectives of the two baselines noted in expressions 10–11 are also convex because negative entropy in expression 11 is convex, and rest of the penalties are the same as our six objectives. In our work, to optimize the objectives of Table 1, we use a generic quasi-Newton gradient-based optimizer that can handle bound-inequality constraints, called L-BFGS-B (Zhu et al., 1997). Partial derivatives of the graph objectives are computed with respect to each parameter $\forall i, y, q_i(y)$ of $\boldsymbol{q}$ and passed on to the optimizer which updates them such that the objective function of Eq. 1 is maximized. Note that since the ℓ_1 and $\ell_{1,2}$ penalties are non-differentiable at 0, special techniques are usually used to compute updates for unconstrained parameters (Andrew and Gao, 2007). However, since $\boldsymbol{q} \geq \boldsymbol{0}$, their absolute value can be assumed to be right-continuous, making the function differentiable. Thus,

$$\frac{\partial}{\partial q_i(y)} \|q_i\|_1 = 1 \qquad \frac{\partial}{\partial q_i(y)} \|q_i\|_1^2 = 2 \cdot \|q_i\|_1$$

(We omit the form of the derivatives of the other penalties for space.) There are several advantages to taking this route towards optimization. The ℓ_2 and the JS-divergence penalties for the pairwise terms can be replaced with more interesting convex divergences if required, and still optimization will be straightforward. Moreover, the nonnegative constraints make optimization with sparsity inducing penalties easy. Finally, computing the objective function and the partial derivatives is easily parallelizable on MPI (Gropp et al., 1994) or MapReduce (Dean and Ghemawat, 2008) architectures, by dividing up the computation across graph vertices.

In comparison, constrained problems such as the one in Eq. 11 require a specialized alternating minimization technique (Subramanya and Bilmes, 2008, 2009), that performs two passes through the graph vertices during one iteration of updates, introduces an auxiliary set of probability distributions (thus, increasing memory requirements) and another hyperparameter α that is used to transform the weight matrix $\mathbf{W}$ to be suitable for the alternating minimization procedure. To optimize the baseline objectives, we borrow the gradient-free iterative updates described by Subramanya and Bilmes (2009) and Subramanya et al. (2010).

4 Experiments

In this section, we compare the six graph objective functions in Table 1 with the two baseline objectives on two lexicon expansion tasks.

4.1 POS Lexicon Expansion

We expand a POS lexicon for word types with a context word on each side, using distributional similarity in an unlabeled corpus and few labeled trigrams.
Data and task: We constructed a graph over *word trigram types* as vertices, using co-occurrence statistics. Following Das and Petrov (2011) and Subramanya et al. (2010), a similarity score between two trigram types was computed by measuring the cosine similarity between their empirical sentential context statistics. This similarity score resulted in the symmetric weight matrix $\mathbf{W}$, defining edge weights between pairs of graph vertices. Details of the similarity computation are given in those papers. $\mathbf{W}$ is thresholded so that only the K nearest neighbors for each vertex have similarity greater than zero, giving a sparse graph. We set $K = 8$ as it resulted in the sparsest graph which was fully connected.[6] For this task, Y is the set of 45 POS tags defined in the Penn Treebank (Marcus et al., 1993), and the measure q_i for vertex i (for trigram type $\mathbf{x}_i$) corresponds to the set of tags that can be associated with the middle word of $\mathbf{x}_i$. The trigram representation, as in earlier work, helps reduce the ambiguity of POS tags for the middle word, and helps in graph construction. The 690,705-vertex graph was constructed over all trigram types appearing in Sections 00–21 (union of the training and development sets used for POS tagging experiments in prior work) of the WSJ section of the Penn Treebank, but co-occurrence statistics for graph construction were gathered from a million sentences drawn from the English Gigaword corpus (Graff, 2003).

Given the graph $\mathcal{G}$ with m vertices, we assume that the tag distributions $\boldsymbol{r}$ for l labeled vertices are also provided. Our goal is to find the best set of measures $\boldsymbol{q}$ over the 45 tags for all vertices in the graph. Prior work used a similar lexicon for POS domain adaptation and POS induction for resource-poor languages (Das and Petrov, 2011; Subramanya et al., 2010); such applications of a POS lexicon are out of scope here; we consider only the lexicon expansion problem and do an intrinsic evaluation at a type-level to compare the different graph objectives.
Experimental details: To evaluate, we randomly chose 6,000 out of the 690,705 types for development. From the remaining types, we randomly chose 588,705 vertices for testing. This left us with 96,000 types from which we created sets of different sizes containing 3,000, 6,000, 12,000, 24,000, 48,000 and 96,000 *labeled* types, creating 6 increasingly easy transduction settings. The development and the test types were kept constant for direct performance comparison across the six settings and our eight models. After running inference, the measure q_i at vertex i was normalized to 1. Next, for all thresholds ranging from 0 to 1, with steps of 0.001, we measured the average POS tag precision and recall on the development data – this gave us the area under the precision-recall curve (prAUC), which is often used to measure performance on retrieval tasks. Given a transduction setting and the final $\boldsymbol{q}$ for an objective, hyperparameters μ and λ were tuned on the development set by performing a grid search, targeting prAUC.[7] We ran 100 rounds

[6] Our proposed methods can deal with graphs containing disconnected components perfectly well. Runtime is asymptotically linear in K for all objectives considered here.

[7] For the objectives using the uniform ℓ_2 and the maximum entropy penalties, namely **UGF-ℓ_2**, **UJSF-ℓ_2**, **NGF-ℓ_2** and **NKLF-ME**, we chose λ from $\{0, 10^{-6}, 10^{-4}, 0.1\}$. For the rest of the models using sparsity inducing penalties, we chose λ from $\{10^{-6}, 10^{-4}, 0.1\}$. This suggests that for the former type of objectives, we allowed a zero unary penalty if that setting resulted in the best development performance, while for the latter type of models, we enforced a positive unary penalty. In fact, $\lambda = 0$ was chosen in several cases for the objectives with uniform penalties indicating that uniformity hurts performance. We chose μ from $\{0.1, 0.5, 1.0\}$.

$\|\mathcal{D}_l\|$:	3K	6K	12K	24K	48K	96K
NGF-ℓ_2	0.208	0.219	0.272	0.335	0.430	0.544
NKLF-ME	0.223	0.227	0.276	0.338	0.411	0.506
UGF-ℓ_2	0.223	0.257	0.314	**0.406**	**0.483**	**0.564**
UGF-ℓ_1	0.223	0.257	0.309	**0.406**	**0.483**	0.556
UGF-$\ell_{1,2}$	0.223	0.256	0.313	0.403	0.478	0.557
UJSF-ℓ_2	**0.271**	0.250	0.310	0.364	0.409	0.481
UJSF-ℓ_1	0.227	0.257	**0.317**	0.369	0.410	0.481
UJSF-$\ell_{1,2}$	0.227	**0.258**	0.309	0.369	0.409	0.479

Table 2: Area under the precision recall curve for the two baseline objectives and our methods for POS tag lexicon induction. This is a measure of how well the type lexicon (for some types unlabeled during training) is recovered by each method. The test set contains 588,705 types.

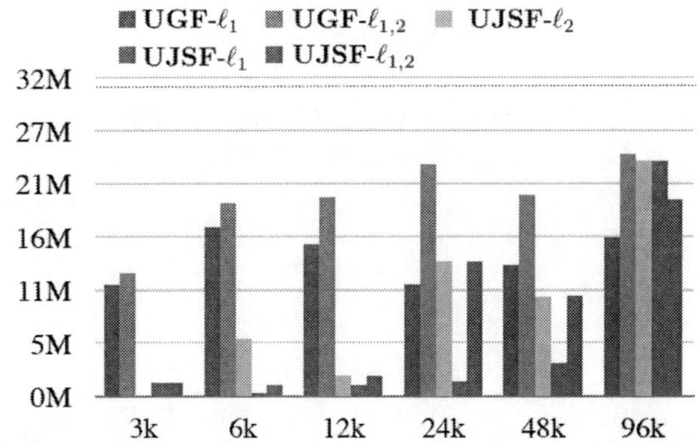

Figure 2: The number of non-zero components in q for five graph objective functions proposed in this work, plotted against various numbers of labeled datapoints. Note that **NGF**-ℓ_2, **NKLF**-ME and **UGF**-ℓ_2 produce non-zero components for virtually all q, and are therefore not shown (the dotted line marks the maximally non-sparse solution, with 31,081,725 components). All of these five objectives result in sparsity. On average, the objectives employing entropic pairwise penalties with sparse unary penalties **UJSF**-ℓ_1 and **UJSF**-$\ell_{1,2}$ produce very sparse lexicons. Although **UGF**-ℓ_2 produces no sparsity at all, its entropic counterpart **UJSF**-ℓ_2 produces considerable sparsity, which we attribute to JS-divergence as a pairwise penalty.

of iterative updates for all 8 graph objectives.

Type-level evaluation: To measure the quality of the lexicons, we perform type level evaluation using area under the precision-recall curve (prAUC). The same measure (on development data) was used to tune the two hyperparameters. Table 2 shows the results measured on 588,705 test vertices (the same test set was used for all the transduction settings). The general pattern we observe is that our unnormalized approaches almost always perform better than the normalized baselines. (The exception is the 3,000 labeled example case, where most unnormalized models are on par with the better baseline.) In scenarios with fewer labeled types, pairwise entropic penalties perform better than Gaussian ones, and the pattern reverses as more labeled types come available. This trend is the same when we compare only the two baselines. In four out of the six transduction settings, one of the sparsity-inducing graph objectives achieves the best performance in terms of prAUC, which is encouraging given that they generally produce smaller models than the baselines.

Overall, though, using sparsity-inducing unary factors seems to have a weak negative effect on performance. Their practical advantage, however is apparent when we consider the size of the model. After the induction of the set of measures q for all transduction settings and all graph objectives, we noticed that our numerical optimizer (LBFGS-B) often assigns extremely small positive values rather than zero. This problem can be attributed to several artifacts, including our limit of 100 iterations of optimization. Hence, we use a global threshold of 10^{-6}, and treat any real value below this threshold to be zero. Figure 2 shows the number of non-zero components in q (or, the lexicon size) for the graph objectives that achieve sparsity (baselines **NGF**-ℓ_2 and **NKLF**-ME, plus our **UGF**-ℓ_2 are not expected to, and do not, achieve sparsity; surprisingly **UJSF**-ℓ_2 *does* and is shown). Even though the hyperparameters μ and λ in the graph objective functions were not tuned towards sparsity, we see that sparsity-inducing factors are able to achieve far more compact lexicons. Sparsity is desirable in settings where labeled development data for tuning thresholds that select the most probable labels for a given type is unavailable (e.g., Das and Petrov, 2011).

4.2 Expansion of a Semantic Frame Lexicon

In a second set of experiments, we follow Das and Smith (2011, D&S11 henceforth) in expanding a lexicon that associates lexical predicates (*targets*) with semantic *frames* (abstract events or scenarios that a predicate evokes when used in a sentential context) as labels. More concretely, each vertex in the graph corresponds to a lemmatized word type with its coarse part of speech, and the labels are frames from the FrameNet lexicon (Fillmore et al., 2003). Graph construction leverages distributional

	Unknown Predicates exact	partial	All Predicates exact	partial	lexicon size
Supervised	23.08	46.62	82.97	90.51	-
***NGF**-ℓ_2*	39.86	62.35	83.51	91.02	128,960
NKLF-ME	36.36	60.07	83.40	90.95	128,960
UGF-ℓ_2	37.76	60.81	83.44	90.97	128,960
UGF-ℓ_1	39.86	62.85	83.51	91.04	122,799
UGF-$\ell_{1,2}$	39.86	62.85	83.51	91.04	128,732
UJSF-ℓ_2	40.56	62.81	83.53	91.04	128,232
UJSF-ℓ_1	39.16	62.43	83.49	91.02	128,771
UJSF-$\ell_{1,2}$	**42.67**	**65.29**	**83.60**	**91.12**	**45,544**

Table 3: Exact and partial frame identification accuracy with lexicon size (non-zero frame components). The "unknown predicates" section of the test data contains 144 targets, while the entire test set contains 4,458 targets. Bold indicates best results. The **UJSF**-$\ell_{1,2}$ model produces statistically significant results ($p < 0.001$) for all metrics with respect to the supervised baseline used in D&S11. For both the unknown targets as well as the whole test set. However, it is weakly significant ($p < 0.1$) compared to the **NGF**-ℓ_2 model for the unseen portion of the test set, when partial frame matching is used. For rest of the settings, the two are statistically indistinguishable. * indicates the best results in D&S11.

similarity as well as linguistic annotations.

Data: We borrow the graph-based SSL process of D&S11 in its entirety. The constructed graph contains 64,480 vertices, each corresponding to a target, out of which 9,263 were drawn from the labeled data. The possible set of labels Y is the set of 877 frames defined in FrameNet; the measure q_i corresponds to the set of frames that a target can evoke. The targets drawn from FrameNet annotated data ($l = 9{,}263$) have frame distributions r_i with which the graph objectives are seeded.[8]

Evaluation: The evaluation metric used for this task is frame disambiguation accuracy on a blind test set containing marked targets in free text. A section of this test set contained 144 targets, previously unseen in annotated FrameNet data; this section is of interest to us and we present separate accuracy results on it. Given the measure q_i over frames induced using graph-based SSL for target i, we truncate it to keep at most the top M frames that get the highest mass under q_i, only retaining those with non-zero values. If all components of q_i are zero, we remove target i from the lexicon, which is often the case in the sparsity-inducing graph objectives. If a target is unseen in annotated data, a separate probabilistic model (which serves as a supervised baseline like in D&S11, row 1 in Table 3) disambiguates among the M filtered frames observing the sentential context of the target instance. This can be thought of as combining type- and token-level information for inference. If the target was previously seen, it is disambiguated using the supervised baseline. The test set and the probabilistic model are identical to the ones in D&S11. We fixed K, the number of nearest neighbors for each vertex, to be 10. For each graph objective, μ, λ and M were chosen by five-fold cross-validation. The cross-validation sets were the same as the ones described in §6.3 of D&S11.[9]

Results and discussion: Table 3 shows frame identification accuracy, both using exact match as well as partial match that assigns partial credit when a related frame is predicted (Baker et al., 2007). The final column presents lexicon size in terms of the set of truncated frame distributions (filtered according to the top M frames in q_i) for all the targets in a graph. All the graph-based models are better than the supervised baseline; for our objectives using pairwise Gaussian fields with sparse unary penalties, the accuracies are equal or better with respect to **NGF**-ℓ_2; however, the lexicon sizes are reduced by a few hundred to a few thousand entries. Massive reduction in lexicon sizes (as in the POS problem in §4.1) is not visible for these objectives because we throw out most of the components of the entire set of distributions $\boldsymbol{q}$ and keep only at most the top M (which is automatically chosen to be 2 for all objectives) frames per target. Although a significant number of components in the whole distribution $\boldsymbol{q}$ in the sparse objectives get zero mass, the M components for a target tend to be non-zero for a majority of the targets. Better results are observed for the objectives using entropic pairwise penalties; the ob-

[8] We refer the reader to D&S11 for the details of the graph construction method, the FrameNet dataset used, example semantic frames, and an excerpt of the graph over targets.

[9] We chose μ from $\{0.01, 0.1, 0.3, 0.5, 1.0\}$; λ was chosen from the same sets as the POS problem. The graph construction hyperparameter α described by D&S11 was fixed to 0.2. As in D&S11, M was chosen from $\{2, 3, 5, 10\}$.

(a)

$t =$ *discrepancy*.N	$t =$ *contribution*.N	$t =$ *print*.V	$t =$ *mislead*.V
*SIMILARITY	*GIVING	*TEXT_CREATION	EXPERIENCER_OBJ
NATURAL_FEATURES	MONEY	SENDING	*PREVARICATION
PREVARICATION	COMMITMENT	DISPERSAL	MANIPULATE_INTO_DOING
QUARRELING	ASSISTANCE	READING	COMPLIANCE
DUPLICATION	EARNINGS_AND_LOSSES	STATEMENT	EVIDENCE

$t =$ *abused*.A	$t =$ *maker*.N	$t =$ *inspire*.V	$t =$ *failed*.A
OFFENSES	COMMERCE_SCENARIO	CAUSE_TO_START	SUCCESS_OR_FAILURE
KILLING	*MANUFACTURING	EXPERIENCER_OBJ	*SUCCESSFUL_ACTION
COMPLIANCE	BUSINESSES	*SUBJECTIVE_INFLUENCE	UNATTRIBUTED_INFORMATION
DIFFERENTIATION	BEHIND_THE_SCENES	EVOKING	PIRACY
COMMITTING_CRIME	SUPPLY	ATTEMPT_SUASION	WANT_SUSPECT

(b)

$t =$ *discrepancy*.N	$t =$ *contribution*.N	$t =$ *print*.V	$t =$ *mislead*.V
*SIMILARITY	*GIVING	*TEXT_CREATION	*PREVARICATION
NON-COMMUTATIVE_STATEMENT	COMMERCE_PAY	STATE_OF_ENTITY	EXPERIENCER_OBJ
NATURAL_FEATURES	COMMITMENT	DISPERSAL	MANIPULATE_INTO_DOING
	ASSISTANCE	CONTACTING	REASSURING
	EARNINGS_AND_LOSSES	READING	EVIDENCE

$t =$ *abused*.A	$t =$ *maker*.N	$t =$ *inspire*.V	$t =$ *failed*.A
	*MANUFACTURING	CAUSE_TO_START	*SUCCESSFUL_ACTION
	BUSINESSES	*SUBJECTIVE_INFLUENCE	SUCCESSFULLY_COMMUNICATE_MESSAGE
	COMMERCE_SCENARIO	OBJECTIVE_INFLUENCE	
	SUPPLY	EXPERIENCER_OBJ	
	BEING_ACTIVE	SETTING_FIRE	

Table 4: Top 5 frames (if there are ≥ 5 frames with mass greater than zero) according to the graph posterior $q_t(f)$ for (a) **NGF-ℓ_2** and (b) **UJSF-$\ell_{1,2}$**, given eight unseen predicates in annotated FrameNet data. * marks the correct frame, according to the predicate instances in test data (each of these predicates appear only once in test data). Note that **UJSF-$\ell_{1,2}$** ranks the correct frame higher than **NGF-ℓ_2** for several predicates, and produces sparsity quite often; for the predicate *abused*.A, the correct frame is not listed by **NGF-ℓ_2**, while **UJSF-$\ell_{1,2}$** removes it altogether from the expanded lexicon, resulting in compactness.

jective **UJSF-$\ell_{1,2}$** gives us the best absolute result by outperforming the baselines by strong margins, and also resulting in a tiny lexicon, less than half the size of the baseline lexicons. The size can be attributed to the removal of predicates for which all frame components were zero ($q_i = \mathbf{0}$). Table 4 contrasts the induced frames for several unseen predicates for the **NGF-ℓ_2** and the **UJSF-ℓ_2** objectives; the latter often ranks the correct frame higher, and produces a small set of frames per predicate.

5 Conclusion

We have presented a family of graph-based SSL objective functions that incorporate penalties encouraging sparse measures at each graph vertex. Our methods relax the oft-used assumption that the measures at each vertex form a normalized probability distribution, making optimization and the use of complex penalties easier than prior work. Optimization is also easy when there are additional terms in a graph objective suited to a specific problem; our generic optimizer would simply require the computation of new partial derivatives, unlike prior work that required specialized techniques for a novel objective function. Finally, experiments on two natural language lexicon learning problems show that our methods produce better performance with respect to state-of-the-art graph-based SSL methods, and also result in much smaller lexicons.

Acknowledgments

We thank André Martins, Amar Subramanya, and Partha Talukdar for helpful discussion during the progress of this work and the three anonymous reviewers for their valuable feedback. This research was supported by Qatar National Research Foundation grant NPRP 08-485-1-083, Google's support of the Worldly Knowledge Project, and TeraGrid resources provided by the Pittsburgh Supercomputing Center under NSF grant number TG-DBS110003.

References

G. Andrew and J. Gao. 2007. Scalable training of L1-regularized log-linear models. In *Proc. of ICML*.

C. Baker, M. Ellsworth, and K. Erk. 2007. Task 19: frame semantic structure extraction. In *Proc. of SemEval*.

S. Baluja, R. Seth, D. Sivakumar, Y. Jing, J. Yagnik, S. Kumar, D. Ravichandran, and M. Aly. 2008. Video suggestion and discovery for Youtube: taking random walks through the view graph. In *Proc. of WWW*.

Y. Bengio, O. Delalleau, and N. Le Roux. 2006. Label propagation and quadratic criterion. In Olivier Chapelle, Bernhard Schölkopf, and Alexander Zien, editors, *Semi-Supervised Learning*, pages 193–216. MIT Press.

J. Burbea and C. R. Rao. 1982. On the convexity of some divergence measures based on entropy functions. *IEEE Transactions on Information Theory*, 28:489–495.

O. Chapelle, B. Schölkopf, and A. Zien, editors. 2006. *Semi-Supervised Learning*. MIT Press.

A. Corduneanu and T. Jaakkola. 2003. On information regularization. In *Proc. of UAI*.

T. M. Cover and J. A. Thomas. 1991. *Elements of information theory*. Wiley-Interscience.

D. Das and S. Petrov. 2011. Unsupervised part-of-speech tagging with bilingual graph-based projections. In *Proc. of ACL*.

D. Das and N. A. Smith. 2011. Semi-supervised frame-semantic parsing for unknown predicates. In *Proc. of ACL*.

J. Dean and S. Ghemawat. 2008. MapReduce: simplified data processing on large clusters. *Communications of the ACM*, 51:107–113, January.

P. S. Dhillon, D. Foster, and L. Ungar. 2011. Multi-view learning of word embeddings via cca. In *Proc. of NIPS*.

C. J. Fillmore, C. R. Johnson, and M. R.L. Petruck. 2003. Background to FrameNet. *International Journal of Lexicography*, 16(3).

C. J. Fillmore. 1982. Frame semantics. In *Linguistics in the Morning Calm*, pages 111–137. Hanshin Publishing Co., Seoul, South Korea.

D. Graff. 2003. English Gigaword. Linguistic Data Consortium.

Y. Grandvalet and Y. Bengio. 2004. Semi-supervised learning by entropy minimization. In *Proc. of NIPS*.

W. Gropp, E. Lusk, and A. Skjellum. 1994. *Using MPI: Portable Parallel Programming with the Message-Passing Interface*. MIT Press.

F. Huang and A. Yates. 2009. Distributional representations for handling sparsity in supervised sequence labeling. In *Proc. of ACL*.

F. Jiao, S. Wang, C.-H. Lee, R. Greiner, and D. Schuurmans. 2006. Semi-supervised conditional random fields for improved sequence segmentation and labeling. In *Proc. of ACL*.

M. Kowalski and B. Torrésani. 2009. Sparsity and persistence: mixed norms provide simple signal models with dependent coefficients. *Signal, Image and Video Processing*, 3:251–264.

S. Kullback and R. A. Leibler. 1951. On information and sufficiency. *Annals of Mathematical Statistics*, 22.

J. Lin. 1991. Divergence measures based on the shannon entropy. *IEEE Transactions on Information theory*, 37:145–151.

M. P. Marcus, M. A. Marcinkiewicz, and B. Santorini. 1993. Building a large annotated corpus of English: the Penn Treebank. *Computational Linguistics*, 19(2).

D. McClosky, E. Charniak, and M. Johnson. 2006. Effective self-training for parsing. In *Proc. of HLT-NAACL*.

J. A. O'Sullivan. 1998. Alternating minimization algorithms: from Blahut-Arimoto to Expectation-Maximization. In A. Vardy, editor, *Codes, Curves, and Signals: Common Threads in Communications*, pages 173–192. Kluwer.

D. A. Smith and J. Eisner. 2007. Bootstrapping feature-rich dependency parsers with entropic priors. In *Proc. of EMNLP*.

A. Subramanya and J. Bilmes. 2008. Soft-supervised learning for text classification. In *Proc. of EMNLP*.

A. Subramanya and J. Bilmes. 2009. Entropic graph regularization in non-parametric semi-supervised classification. In *Proc. of NIPS*.

A. Subramanya, S. Petrov, and F. Pereira. 2010. Efficient Graph-based Semi-Supervised Learning of Structured Tagging Models. In *Proc. of EMNLP*.

M. Szummer and T. Jaakkola. 2001. Partially labeled classification with Markov random walks. In *Proc. of NIPS*. MIT Press.

P. P. Talukdar and K. Crammer. 2009. New regularized algorithms for transductive learning. In *Proc. of the ECML-PKDD*.

P. P. Talukdar. 2010. *Graph-Based Weakly-Supervised Methods for Information Extraction and Integration*. Ph.D. thesis, University of Pennsylvania.

R. Tibshirani. 1996. Regression shrinkage and selection via the lasso. *Journal of the Royal Statistical Society (Series B)*, 58:267–288.

J. Turian, L. Ratinov, and Y. Bengio. 2010. Word representations: a simple and general method for semi-supervised learning. In *Proc. of ACL*.

X. Zhu and Z. Ghahramani. 2002. Learning from labeled and unlabeled data with Label Propagation. Technical report, Carnegie Mellon University.

C. Zhu, R. H. Byrd, P. Lu, and J. Nocedal. 1997. Algorithm 778: L-BFGS-B: Fortran subroutines for large-scale bound-constrained optimization. *ACM Transactions on Mathematical Software*, 23:550–560.

X. Zhu, Z. Ghahramani, and J. Lafferty. 2003. Semi-supervised learning using gaussian fields and harmonic functions. In *Proc. of ICML*.

X. Zhu. 2008. Semi-Supervised Learning Literature Survey. Online publication., July.

Unified Expectation Maximization

Rajhans Samdani
University of Illinois
rsamdan2@illinois.edu

Ming-Wei Chang
Microsoft Research
minchang@microsoft.com

Dan Roth
University of Illinois
danr@illinois.edu

Abstract

We present a general framework containing a graded spectrum of Expectation Maximization (EM) algorithms called Unified Expectation Maximization (UEM.) UEM is parameterized by a single parameter and covers existing algorithms like standard EM and hard EM, constrained versions of EM such as Constraint-Driven Learning (Chang et al., 2007) and Posterior Regularization (Ganchev et al., 2010), along with a range of new EM algorithms. For the constrained inference step in UEM we present an efficient dual projected gradient ascent algorithm which generalizes several dual decomposition and Lagrange relaxation algorithms popularized recently in the NLP literature (Ganchev et al., 2008; Koo et al., 2010; Rush and Collins, 2011). UEM is as efficient and easy to implement as standard EM. Furthermore, experiments on POS tagging, information extraction, and word-alignment show that often the best performing algorithm in the UEM family is a new algorithm that wasn't available earlier, exhibiting the benefits of the UEM framework.

1 Introduction

Expectation Maximization (EM) (Dempster et al., 1977) is inarguably the most widely used algorithm for unsupervised and semi-supervised learning. Many successful applications of unsupervised and semi-supervised learning in NLP use EM including text classification (McCallum et al., 1998; Nigam et al., 2000), machine translation (Brown et al., 1993), and parsing (Klein and Manning, 2004). Recently, EM algorithms which incorporate constraints on structured output spaces have been proposed (Chang et al., 2007; Ganchev et al., 2010).

Several variations of EM (e.g. hard EM) exist in the literature and choosing a suitable variation is often very task-specific. Some works have shown that for certain tasks, hard EM is more suitable than regular EM (Spitkovsky et al., 2010). The same issue continues in the presence of constraints where Posterior Regularization (PR) (Ganchev et al., 2010) corresponds to EM while Constraint-Driven Learning (CoDL)[1] (Chang et al., 2007) corresponds to hard EM. The problem of choosing between EM and hard EM (or between PR and CoDL) remains elusive, along with the possibility of simple and better alternatives, to practitioners. Unfortunately, little study has been done to understand the relationships between these variations in the NLP community.

In this paper, we approach various EM-based techniques from a novel perspective. We believe that "EM or Hard-EM?" and "PR or CoDL?" are not the right questions to ask. Instead, we present a unified framework for EM, Unified EM (UEM), that covers many EM variations including the constrained cases along with a continuum of new ones. UEM allows us to compare and investigate the properties of EM in a systematic way and helps find better alternatives.

The contributions of this paper are as follows:

1. We propose a general framework called Unified Expectation Maximization (UEM) that presents a continuous spectrum of EM algorithms parameterized by a simple temperature-like tuning parameter. The framework covers both constrained and unconstrained EM algorithms. UEM thus connects EM, hard EM, PR, and CoDL so that the relation between different algorithms can be better understood. It also enables us to find new EM algorithms.
2. To solve UEM (with constraints), we propose

[1]To be more precise, (Chang et al., 2007) mentioned using hard constraints as well as soft constraints in EM. In this paper, we refer to CoDL only as the EM framework with hard constraints.

a dual projected subgradient ascent algorithm that generalizes several dual decomposition and Lagrange relaxation algorithms (Bertsekas, 1999) introduced recently in NLP (Ganchev et al., 2008; Rush and Collins, 2011).

3. We provide a way to implement a family of EM algorithms and choose the appropriate one, given the data and problem setting, rather than a single EM variation. We conduct experiments on unsupervised POS tagging, unsupervised word-alignment, and semi-supervised information extraction and show that choosing the right UEM variation outperforms existing EM algorithms by a significant margin.

2 Preliminaries

Let $\mathbf{x}$ denote an input or observed features and $\mathbf{h}$ be a discrete output variable to be predicted from a finite set of possible outputs $\mathcal{H}(\mathbf{x})$. Let $P_\theta(\mathbf{x}, \mathbf{h})$ be a probability distribution over $(\mathbf{x}, \mathbf{h})$ parameterized by θ. Let $P_\theta(\mathbf{h}|\mathbf{x})$ refer to the conditional probability of $\mathbf{h}$ given $\mathbf{x}$. For instance, in part-of-speech tagging, $\mathbf{x}$ is a sentence, $\mathbf{h}$ the corresponding POS tags, and θ could be an HMM model; in word-alignment, $\mathbf{x}$ can be an English-French sentence pair, $\mathbf{h}$ the word alignment between the sentences, and θ the probabilistic alignment model. Let $\delta(\mathbf{h} = \mathbf{h}')$ be the Kronecker-Delta distribution centered at $\mathbf{h}'$, i.e., it puts a probability of 1 at $\mathbf{h}'$ and 0 elsewhere.

In the rest of this section, we review EM and constraints-based learning with EM.

2.1 EM Algorithm

To obtain the parameter θ in an unsupervised way, one maximizes log-likelihood of the observed data:

$$\mathcal{L}(\theta) = \log P_\theta(\mathbf{x}) = \log \sum_{\mathbf{h} \in \mathcal{H}(\mathbf{x})} P_\theta(\mathbf{x}, \mathbf{h}) \ . \quad (1)$$

EM (Dempster et al., 1977) is the most common technique for learning θ, which maximizes a tight lower bound on $\mathcal{L}(\theta)$. While there are a few different styles of expressing EM, following the style of (Neal and Hinton, 1998), we define

$$F(\theta, q) = \mathcal{L}(\theta) - KL(q, P_\theta(\mathbf{h}|\mathbf{x})), \quad (2)$$

where q is a posterior distribution over $\mathcal{H}(\mathbf{x})$ and $KL(p_1, p_2)$ is the KL divergence between two distributions p_1 and p_2. Given this formulation, EM can be shown to maximize F via block coordinate ascent alternating over q (E-step) and θ (M-step) (Neal and Hinton, 1998). In particular, the E-step for EM can be written as

$$q = \arg\min_{q' \in \mathcal{Q}} KL(q', P_\theta(\mathbf{h}|\mathbf{x})) \ , \quad (3)$$

where $\mathcal{Q}$ is the space of all distributions. While EM produces a distribution in the E-step, hard EM is thought of as producing a single output given by

$$\mathbf{h}^* = \arg\max_{\mathbf{h} \in \mathcal{H}(\mathbf{x})} P_\theta(\mathbf{h}|\mathbf{x}) \ . \quad (4)$$

However, one can also think of hard EM as producing a distribution given by $q = \delta(\mathbf{h} = \mathbf{h}^*)$. In this paper, we pursue this distributional view of both EM and hard EM and show its benefits.

EM for Discriminative Models EM-like algorithms can also be used in discriminative settings (Bellare et al., 2009; Ganchev et al., 2010) specifically for semi-supervised learning (SSL.) Given some labeled and unlabeled data, such algorithms maximize a modified $F(\theta, q)$ function:

$$F(\theta, q) = L_c(\theta) - c_1\|\theta\|^2 - c_2 KL(q, P_\theta(\mathbf{h}|\mathbf{x})) \ , \quad (5)$$

where, q, as before, is a probability distribution over $\mathcal{H}(\mathbf{x})$, $L_c(\theta)$ is the conditional log-likelihood of the labels given the features for the labeled data, and c_1 and c_2 are constants specified by the user; the KL divergence is measured only over the unlabeled data.

The EM algorithm in this case has the same E-step as unsupervised EM, but the M-step is different. The M-step is similar to supervised learning as it finds θ by maximizing a regularized conditional likelihood of the data w.r.t. the labels — true labels are used for labeled data and "soft" pseudo labels based on q are used for unlabeled data.

2.2 Constraints in EM

It has become a common practice in the NLP community to use constraints on output variables to guide inference. Few of many examples include type constraints between relations and entities (Roth and Yih, 2004), sentential and modifier constraints during sentence compression (Clarke and Lapata, 2006), and agreement constraints between word-alignment directions (Ganchev et al., 2008) or various parsing models (Koo et al., 2010). In the context of EM, constraints can be imposed on the posterior probabilities, q, to guide the learning procedure (Chang et al., 2007; Ganchev et al., 2010).

In this paper, we focus on linear constraints over $\mathbf{h}$ (potentially non-linear over $\mathbf{x}$.) This is a very general formulation as it is known that all Boolean constraints can be transformed into sets of linear constraints over binary variables (Roth and Yih, 2007). Assume that we have m *linear* constraints on outputs where the kth constraint can be written as

$$\mathbf{u_k}^T\mathbf{h} \leq b_k \ .$$

Defining a matrix U as $\mathbf{U}^T = \begin{bmatrix}\mathbf{u_1}^T & \ldots & \mathbf{u_m}^T\end{bmatrix}$ and a vector $\mathbf{b}$ as $\mathbf{b}^T = [b_1, \ldots, b_m]$, we write down the set of all *feasible*[2] structures as

$$\{\mathbf{h} \mid \mathbf{h} \in \mathcal{H}(\mathbf{x}), \mathbf{Uh} \leq \mathbf{b}\} \ .$$

Constraint-Driven Learning (CoDL) (Chang et al., 2007) augments the E-step of hard EM (4) by imposing these constraints on the outputs.

Constraints on structures can be relaxed to *expectation constraints* by requiring the distribution q to satisfy them only in expectation. Define expectation w.r.t. a distribution q over $\mathcal{H}(\mathbf{x})$ as $E_q[\mathbf{Uh}] = \sum_{\mathbf{h}\in\mathcal{H}(\mathbf{x})} q(\mathbf{h})\mathbf{Uh}$. In the expectation constraints setting, q is required to satisfy:

$$E_q[\mathbf{Uh}] \leq \mathbf{b} \ .$$

The space of distributions $\mathcal{Q}$ can be modified as:

$$\mathcal{Q} = \{q \mid q(\mathbf{h}) \geq 0, E_q[\mathbf{Uh}] \leq \mathbf{b}, \sum_{\mathbf{h}\in\mathcal{H}(\mathbf{x})} q(\mathbf{h}) = 1\}.$$

Augmenting these constraints into the E-step of EM (3), gives the Posterior Regularization (PR) framework (Ganchev et al., 2010). In this paper, we adopt the expectation constraint setting. Later, we show that UEM naturally includes and generalizes both PR and CoDL.

3 Unified Expectation Maximization

We now present the Unified Expectation Maximization (UEM) framework which captures a continuum of (constrained and unconstrained) EM algorithms including EM and hard EM by modulating the entropy of the posterior. A key observation underlying the development of UEM is that hard EM (or CoDL) finds a distribution with zero entropy while EM (or PR) finds a distribution with the same entropy as P_θ (or close to it). Specifically, we modify the objective of the E-step of EM (3) as

$$q = \arg\min_{q'\in\mathcal{Q}} KL(q', P_\theta(\mathbf{h}|\mathbf{x}); \gamma) \ , \qquad (6)$$

where $KL(q, p; \gamma)$ is a modified KL divergence:

$$KL(q,p;\gamma) = \sum_{\mathbf{h}\in\mathcal{H}(\mathbf{x})} \gamma q(\mathbf{h}) \log q(\mathbf{h}) - q(\mathbf{h}) \log p(\mathbf{h}). \quad (7)$$

In other words, UEM projects $P_\theta(\mathbf{h}|\mathbf{x})$ on the space of feasible distributions $\mathcal{Q}$ w.r.t. a metric[3] $KL(\cdot,\cdot;\gamma)$ to obtain the posterior q. By simply varying γ, UEM changes the metric of projection and obtains different variations of EM including EM (PR, in the presence of constraints) and hard EM (CoDL.) The M-step for UEM is exactly the same as EM (or discriminative EM.)

The UEM Algorithm: Alg. 1 shows the UEM algorithm for both the generative (G) and the discriminative (D) case. We refer to the UEM algorithm with parameter γ as UEM_γ.

Algorithm 1 The UEM algorithm for both the generative (G) and discriminative (D) cases.

Initialize θ^0
for $t = 0, \ldots, T$ **do**
  UEM E-step:
  $q^{t+1} \leftarrow \arg\min_{q\in\mathcal{Q}} KL(q, P_{\theta^t}(\mathbf{h}|\mathbf{x}); \gamma)$
  UEM M-step:
  G: $\theta^{t+1} = \arg\max_\theta E_{q^{t+1}}[\log P_\theta(\mathbf{x}, \mathbf{h})]$
  D: $\theta^{t+1} = \arg\max_\theta E_{q^{t+1}}[\log P_\theta(\mathbf{h}|\mathbf{x})] - c_1\|\theta\|^2$
end for

3.1 Relationship between UEM and Other EM Algorithms

The relation between unconstrained versions of EM has been mentioned before (Ueda and Nakano, 1998; Smith and Eisner, 2004). We show that the relationship takes novel aspects in the presence of constraints. In order to better understand different UEM variations, we write the UEM E-step (6) explicitly as an optimization problem:

[2]Note that this set is a finite set of discrete variables not to be confused with a polytope. Polytopes are also specified as $\{\mathbf{z}|\mathbf{Az} \leq \mathbf{d}\}$ but are over real variables whereas $\mathbf{h}$ is discrete.

[3]The term 'metric' is used very loosely. $KL(\cdot,\cdot;\gamma)$ does not satisfy the mathematical properties of a metric.

Framework	$\gamma = -\infty$	$\gamma = 0$	$\gamma \in (0,1)$	$\gamma = 1$	$\gamma = \infty \to 1$
Constrained	Hard EM	Hard EM	(NEW) UEM$_\gamma$	Standard EM	Deterministic Annealing EM
Unconstrained	CoDL (Chang et al., 2007)	(NEW) EM with Lin. Prog.	(NEW) constrained UEM$_\gamma$	PR (Ganchev et al., 2010)	

Table 1: Summary of different UEM algorithms. The entries marked with "(NEW)" have not been proposed before. Eq. (8) is the objective function for all the EM frameworks listed in this table. Note that, in the absence of constraints, $\gamma \in (-\infty, 0]$ corresponds to hard EM (Sec. 3.1.1.) Please see Sec. 3.1 for a detailed explanation.

$$\begin{aligned} \min_q \quad & \sum_{\mathbf{h}\in\mathcal{H}(\mathbf{x})} \gamma q(\mathbf{h}) \log q(\mathbf{h}) - q(\mathbf{h}) \log P_\theta(\mathbf{h}|\mathbf{x}) \quad (8) \\ \text{s.t.} \quad & E_q[\mathbf{U}\mathbf{h}] \le \mathbf{b}, \\ & q(\mathbf{h}) \ge 0, \forall \mathbf{h} \in \mathcal{H}(\mathbf{x}), \\ & \textstyle\sum_{\mathbf{h}\in\mathcal{H}(\mathbf{x})} q(\mathbf{h}) = 1 \ . \end{aligned}$$

We discuss below, both the constrained and the unconstrained cases. Tab. 1 summarizes different EM algorithms in the UEM family.

3.1.1 UEM Without Constraints

The E-step in this case, computes a q obeying only the simplex constraints: $\sum_{\mathbf{h}\in\mathcal{H}(\mathbf{x})} q(\mathbf{h}) = 1$. For $\gamma = 1$, UEM minimizes $KL(q, P_\theta(\mathbf{h}|\mathbf{x}); 1)$ which is the same as minimizing $KL(q, P_\theta(\mathbf{h}|\mathbf{x}))$ as in the standard EM (3). For $\gamma = 0$, UEM is solving $\arg\min_{q\in\mathcal{Q}} \sum_{\mathbf{h}\in\mathcal{H}(\mathbf{x})} -q(\mathbf{h}) \log P_\theta(\mathbf{h}|\mathbf{x})$ which is a linear programming (LP) problem. Due to the unimodularity of the simplex constraints (Schrijver, 1986), this LP outputs an integral $q = \delta\left(\mathbf{h} = \arg\max_{\mathbf{h}\subset\mathcal{H}(\mathbf{x})} P_\theta(\mathbf{h}|x)\right)$ which is the same as hard EM (4). It has already been noted in the literature (Kearns et al., 1997; Smith and Eisner, 2004; Hofmann, 2001) that this formulation (corresponding to our $\gamma = 0$) is the same as hard EM. In fact, for $\gamma \le 0$, UEM stays the same as hard EM because of negative penalty on the entropy. The range $\gamma \in (0, 1)$ has not been discussed in the literature, to the best of our knowledge. In Sec. 5, we show the impact of using UEM$_\gamma$for $\gamma \in \{0, 1\}$. Lastly, the range of γ from ∞ to 1 has been used in deterministic annealing for EM (Rose, 1998; Ueda and Nakano, 1998; Hofmann, 2001). However, the focus of deterministic annealing is solely to solve the standard EM while avoiding local maxima problems.

3.1.2 UEM With Constraints

UEM and Posterior Regularization ($\gamma = 1$) For $\gamma = 1$, UEM solves $\arg\min_{q\in\mathcal{Q}} KL(q, P_\theta(\mathbf{h}|\mathbf{x}))$ which is the same as Posterior Regularization (Ganchev et al., 2010).

UEM and CoDL ($\gamma = -\infty$) When $\gamma \to -\infty$ then due to an infinite penalty on the entropy of the posterior, the entropy must become zero. Thus, now the E-step, as expressed by Eq. (8), can be written as $q = \delta(\mathbf{h} = \mathbf{h}^*)$ where $\mathbf{h}^*$ is obtained as

$$\begin{aligned} \arg\max_{\mathbf{h}\in\mathcal{H}(\mathbf{x})} \quad & \log P_\theta(\mathbf{h}|\mathbf{x}) \quad (9) \\ \text{s.t.} \quad & \mathbf{U}\mathbf{h} \le \mathbf{b} \ , \end{aligned}$$

which is the same as CoDL. This combinatorial maximization can be solved using the Viterbi algorithm in some cases or, in general, using Integer Linear Programming (ILP.)

3.2 UEM with $\gamma \in [0, 1]$

Tab. 1 lists different EM variations and their associated values γ. This paper focuses on values of γ between 0 and 1 for the following reasons. First, the E-step (8) is non-convex for $\gamma < 0$ and hence computationally expensive; e.g., hard EM (i.e. $\gamma = -\infty$) requires ILP inference. For $\gamma \ge 0$, (8) is a convex optimization problem which can be solved exactly and efficiently. Second, for $\gamma = 0$, the E-step solves

$$\begin{aligned} \max_q \quad & \textstyle\sum_{\mathbf{h}\in\mathcal{H}(\mathbf{x})} q(\mathbf{h}) \log P_\theta(\mathbf{h}|\mathbf{x}) \quad (10) \\ \text{s.t.} \quad & E_q[\mathbf{U}\mathbf{h}] \le \mathbf{b}, \\ & q(\mathbf{h}) \ge 0, \forall \mathbf{h} \in \mathcal{H}(\mathbf{x}), \\ & \textstyle\sum_{\mathbf{h}\in\mathcal{H}(\mathbf{x})} q(\mathbf{h}) = 1 \ , \end{aligned}$$

which is an **LP-relaxation** of hard EM (Eq. (4) and (9)). LP relaxations often provide a decent proxy to ILP (Roth and Yih, 2004; Martins et al., 2009). Third, $\gamma \in [0, 1]$ covers standard EM/PR.

3.2.1 Discussion: Role of γ

The modified KL divergence can be related to standard KL divergence as $KL(q, P_\theta(\mathbf{h}|\mathbf{x}); \gamma) =$

$KL(q, P_\theta(\mathbf{y}|\mathbf{x})) + (1-\gamma)H(q)$ — UEM (6) minimizes the former during the E-step, while Standard EM (3) minimizes the latter. The additional term $(1-\gamma)H(q)$ is essentially an entropic prior on the posterior distribution q which can be used to regularize the entropy as desired.

For $\gamma < 1$, the regularization term penalizes the entropy of the posterior thus reducing the probability mass on the tail of the distribution. This is significant, for instance, in unsupervised structured prediction where the tail can carry a substantial amount of probability mass as the output space is massive. This notion aligns with the observation of (Spitkovsky et al., 2010) who criticize EM for frittering away too much probability mass on unimportant outputs while showing that hard EM does much better in PCFG parsing. In particular, they empirically show that when initialized with a "good" set of parameters obtained by supervised learning, EM drifts away (thus losing accuracy) much farther than hard-EM.

4 Solving Constrained E-step with Lagrangian Dual

In this section, we discuss how to solve the E-step (8) for UEM. It is a non-convex problem for $\gamma < 0$; however, for $\gamma = -\infty$ (CoDL) one can use ILP solvers. We focus here on solving the E-step for $\gamma \geq 0$ for which it is a convex optimization problem, and use a Lagrange relaxation algorithm (Bertsekas, 1999). Our contributions are two fold:

- We describe an algorithm for UEM with constraints that is as easy to implement as PR or CoDL. Existing code for constrained EM (PR or CoDL) can be easily extended to run UEM.
- We solve the E-step (8) using a Lagrangian dual-based algorithm which performs projected subgradient-ascent on dual variables. Our algorithm covers Lagrange relaxation and dual decomposition techniques (Bertsekas, 1999) which were recently popularized in NLP (Rush and Collins, 2011; Rush et al., 2010; Koo et al., 2010). Not only do we extend the algorithmic framework to a continuum of algorithms, we also allow, unlike the aforementioned works, general inequality constraints over the output variables. Furthermore, we establish new and interesting connections between existing constrained inference techniques.

4.1 Projected Subgradient Ascent with Lagrangian Dual

We provide below a high-level view of our algorithm, omitting the technical derivations due to lack of space. To solve the E-step (8), we introduce dual variables λ — one for each expectation constraint in $\mathcal{Q}$. The subgradient $\nabla\lambda$ of the dual of Eq. (8) w.r.t. λ is given by

$$\nabla\lambda \propto E_q[\mathbf{U}\mathbf{h}] - \mathbf{b} \ . \tag{11}$$

For $\gamma > 0$, the primal variable q can be written in terms of λ as

$$q(\mathbf{h}) \propto P_{\theta^t}(\mathbf{h}|\mathbf{x})^{\frac{1}{\gamma}} e^{-\frac{\lambda^T \mathbf{U}\mathbf{h}}{\gamma}} \ . \tag{12}$$

For $\gamma = 0$, the q above is not well defined and so we take the limit $\gamma \rightarrow 0$ in (12) and since l_p norm approaches the max-norm as $p \rightarrow \infty$, this yields

$$q(\mathbf{h}) = \delta(\mathbf{h} = \arg\max_{\mathbf{h}' \in \mathcal{H}(\mathbf{x})} P_\theta(\mathbf{h}'|\mathbf{x}) e^{-\lambda^T \mathbf{U}\mathbf{h}'}). \tag{13}$$

We combine both the ideas by setting $q(\mathbf{h}) = G(\mathbf{h}, P_{\theta^t}(\cdot|\mathbf{x}), \lambda^T\mathbf{U}, \gamma)$ where

$$G(\mathbf{h}, P, \mathbf{v}, \gamma) = \begin{cases} \frac{P(\mathbf{h})^{\frac{1}{\gamma}} e^{-\frac{\mathbf{v}\mathbf{h}}{\gamma}}}{\sum_{\mathbf{h}'} P(\mathbf{h}')^{\frac{1}{\gamma}} e^{-\frac{\mathbf{v}\mathbf{h}'}{\gamma}}} & \gamma > 0 \ , \\ \delta(\mathbf{h} = \arg\max_{\mathbf{h}' \in \mathcal{H}(\mathbf{x})} P(\mathbf{h}') e^{-\mathbf{v}\mathbf{h}'}) & \gamma = 0 \ . \end{cases} \tag{14}$$

Alg. 2 shows the overall optimization scheme. The dual variables for inequality constraints are restricted to be positive and hence after a gradient update, negative dual variables are projected to 0.

Note that for $\gamma = 0$, our algorithm is a Lagrange relaxation algorithm for approximately solving the E-step for CoDL (which uses exact $\arg\max$ inference). Lagrange relaxation has been recently shown to provide exact and optimal results in a large number of cases (Rush and Collins, 2011). This shows that our range of algorithms is very broad — it includes PR and a good approximation to CoDL.

Overall, the required optimization (8) can be solved efficiently if the expected value computation in the dual gradient (Eq. (11)) w.r.t. the posterior q in the primal (Eq (14)) can be performed efficiently. In cases where we can enumerate the possible outputs $\mathbf{h}$ efficiently, e.g. multi-class classification, we

Algorithm 2 Solving E-step of UEM$_\gamma$ for $\gamma \geq 0$.

```
Initialize and normalize q; initialize λ = 0.
for t = 0, ..., R or until convergence do
    λ ← max(λ + η_t (E_q[Uh] − b), 0)
    q(h) = G(h, P_{θ^t}(·|x), λ^T U, γ)
end for
```

can compute the posterior probability q explicitly using the dual variables. In cases where the output space is structured and exponential in size, e.g. word alignment, we can optimize (8) efficiently if the constraints and the model $P_\theta(\mathbf{h}|\mathbf{x})$ decompose in the same way. To elucidate, we give a more concrete example in the next section.

4.2 Projected Subgradient based Dual Decomposition Algorithm

Solving the inference (8) using Lagrangian dual can often help us decompose the problem into components and handle complex constraints in the dual space as we show in this section. Suppose our task is to predict two output variables $\mathbf{h}^1$ and $\mathbf{h}^2$ coupled via linear constraints. Specifically, they obey $\mathbf{U_e h}^1 = \mathbf{U_e h}^2$ (agreement constraints) and $\mathbf{U_i h}^1 \leq \mathbf{U_i h}^2$ (inequality constraints)[4] for given matrices $\mathbf{U_e}$ and $\mathbf{U_i}$. Let their respective probabilistic models be $P^1_{\theta_1}$ and $P^2_{\theta_2}$. The E-step (8) can be written as

$$\begin{aligned} \arg\min_{q_1,q_2} \quad & A(q_1, q_2; \gamma) \qquad (15) \\ s.t. \quad & E_{q_1}[\mathbf{U_e h}^1] = E_{q_2}[\mathbf{U_e h}^2] \\ & E_{q_1}[\mathbf{U_i h}^1] \leq E_{q_2}[\mathbf{U_i h}^2] \ , \end{aligned}$$

where $A(q_1, q_2; \gamma) = KL(q_1(\mathbf{h}^1), P^1_{\theta_1}(\mathbf{h}^1|\mathbf{x}); \gamma) + KL(q_2(\mathbf{h}^2), P^2_{\theta_2}(\mathbf{h}^2|\mathbf{x}); \gamma)$.

The application of Alg. 2 results in a dual decomposition scheme which is described in Alg. 3.

Note that in the absence of inequality constraints and for $\gamma = 0$, our algorithm reduces to a simpler dual decomposition algorithm with agreement constraints described in (Rush et al., 2010; Koo et al., 2010). For $\gamma = 1$ with agreement constraints, our algorithm specializes to an earlier proposed technique by (Ganchev et al., 2008). Thus our algorithm puts these dual decomposition techniques with

[4]The analysis remains the same for a more general formulation with a constant offset vector on the R.H.S. and different matrices for $\mathbf{h}^1$ and $\mathbf{h}^2$.

Algorithm 3 Projected Subgradient-based Lagrange Relaxation Algorithm that optimizes Eq. (15)

```
1: Input: Two distributions P^1_{θ1} and P^2_{θ2}.
2: Output: Output distributions q1 and q2 in (15)
3: Define λ^T = [λ_e^T  λ_i^T] and U^T = [U_e^T  U_i^T]
4: λ ← 0
5: for t = 0, ..., R or until convergence do
6:     q1(h^1) ← G(h^1, P^1_{θ1}(·|x), λ^T U, γ)
7:     q2(h^2) ← G(h^2, P^2_{θ2}(·|x), −λ^T U, γ)
8:     λ_e ← λ_e + η_t(−E_{q1}[U_e h^1] + E_{q2}[U_e h^2])
9:     λ_i ← λ_i + η_t(−E_{q1}[U_i h^1] + E_{q2}[U_i h^2])
10:    λ_i ← max(λ_i, 0) {Projection step}
11: end for
12: return (q1, q2)
```

agreement constraints on the same spectrum. Moreover, dual-decomposition is just a special case of Lagrangian dual-based techniques. Hence Alg. 2 is more broadly applicable (see Sec. 5). Lines 6-9 show that the required computation is decomposed over each sub-component.

Thus if computing the posterior and expected values of linear functions over each subcomponent is easy, then the algorithm works efficiently. Consider the case when constraints decompose linearly over $\mathbf{h}$ and each component is modeled as an HMM with θ_S as the initial state distribution, θ_E as emmision probabilities, and θ_T as transition probabilities. An instance of this is word alignment over language pair (S, T) modeled using an HMM augmented with agreement constraints which constrain alignment probabilities in one direction (P_{θ_1}: from S to T) to agree with the alignment probabilities in the other direction (P_{θ_2}: from T to S.) The agreement constraints are linear over the alignments, $\mathbf{h}$.

Now, the HMM probability is given by $P_\theta(\mathbf{h}|\mathbf{x}) = \theta_S(\mathbf{h}_0)\prod_i \theta_E(\mathbf{x}_i|\mathbf{h}_i)\theta_T(\mathbf{h}_{i+1}|\mathbf{h}_i)$ where $\mathbf{v}_i$ denotes the ith component of a vector $\mathbf{v}$. For $\gamma > 0$, the resulting q (14) can be expressed using a vector μ =+/-$\lambda^T\mathbf{U}$ (see lines 6-7) as

$$\begin{aligned} q(\mathbf{h}) &\propto \left(\theta_S(\mathbf{h}_0)\prod_i \theta_E(\mathbf{x}_i|\mathbf{h}_i)\theta_T(\mathbf{h}_{i+1}|\mathbf{h}_i)\right)^{\frac{1}{\gamma}} e^{\frac{\sum_i \mu_i \mathbf{h}_i}{\gamma}} \\ &\propto \prod_i \theta_S(\mathbf{h}_0)^{\frac{1}{\gamma}} \left(\theta_E(\mathbf{x}_i|\mathbf{h}_i)e^{\mu_i \mathbf{h}_i}\right)^{\frac{1}{\gamma}} \theta_T(\mathbf{h}_{i+1}|\mathbf{h}_i)^{\frac{1}{\gamma}} \ . \end{aligned}$$

The dual variables-based term can be folded into the emission probabilities, Θ_E. Now, the resulting q can be expressed as an HMM by raising θ_S, θ_E, and

θ_T to the power $1/\gamma$ and normalizing. For $\gamma = 0$, q can be computed as the most probable output. The required computations in lines 6-9 can be performed using the forward-backward algorithm or the Viterbi algorithm. Note that we can efficiently compute every step because the linear constraints decompose nicely along the probability model.

5 Experiments

Our experiments are designed to explore tuning γ in the UEM framework as a way to obtain gains over EM and hard EM in the constrained and unconstrained cases. We conduct experiments on POS-tagging, word-alignment, and information extraction; we inject constraints in the latter two. In all the cases we use our unified inference step to implement general UEM and the special cases of existing EM algorithms. Since both of our constrained problems involve large scale constrained inference during the E-step, we use UEM_0 (with a Lagrange relaxation based E-step) as a proxy for ILP-based CoDL .

As we vary γ over $[0, 1]$, we circumvent much of the debate over EM vs hard EM (Spitkovsky et al., 2010) by exploring the space of EM algorithms in a "continuous" way. Furthermore, we also study the relation between quality of model initialization and the value of γ in the case of POS tagging. This is inspired by a general "research wisdom" that hard EM is a better choice than EM with a good initialization point whereas the opposite is true with an "uninformed" initialization.

Unsupervised POS Tagging We conduct experiments on unsupervised POS learning experiment with the tagging dictionary assumption. We use a standard subset of Penn Treebank containing 24,115 tokens (Ravi and Knight, 2009) with the tagging dictionary derived from the entire Penn Treebank. We run UEM with a first order (bigram) HMM model[5]. We consider initialization points of varying quality and observe the performance for $\gamma \in [0, 1]$.

Different initialization points are constructed as follows. The "posterior uniform" initialization is created by spreading the probability uniformly over all possible tags for each token. Our EM model on

[5](Ravi and Knight, 2009) showed that a first order HMM model performs much better than a second order HMM model on unsupervised POS tagging

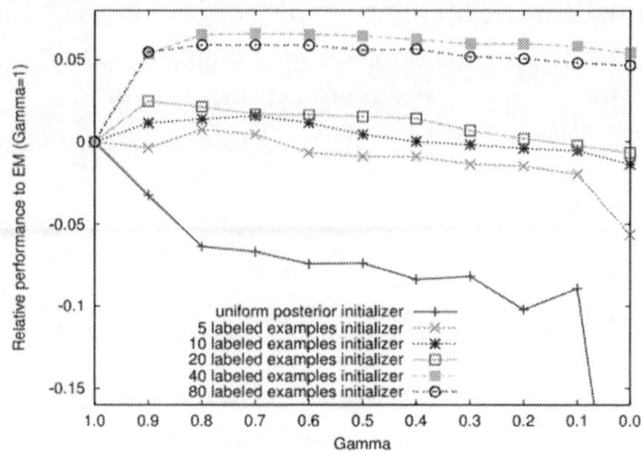

Figure 1: POS Experiments showing the relation between initial model parameters and γ. We report the relative performance compared to EM (see Eq. (16)). The posterior uniform initialization does not use any labeled examples. As the no. of labeled examples used to create the initial HMM model increases, the quality of the initial model improves. The results show that the value of the best γ is sensitive to the initialization point and EM ($\gamma = 1$) and hard EM ($\gamma = 0$) are often not the best choice.

this dataset obtains 84.9% accuracy on all tokens and 72.3% accuracy on ambiguous tokens, which is competitive with results reported in (Ravi and Knight, 2009). To construct better initialization points, we train a supervised HMM tagger on hold-out labeled data. The quality of the initialization points is varied by varying the size of the labeled data over $\{5, 10, 20, 40, 80\}$. Those initialization points are then fed into different UEM algorithms.

Results For a particular γ, we report the performance of UEM_γ w.r.t. EM ($\gamma = 1.0$) as given by

$$rel(\gamma) = \frac{Acc(\text{UEM}_\gamma) - Acc(\text{UEM}_{\gamma=1.0})}{Acc(\text{UEM}_{\gamma=1.0})} \quad (16)$$

where Acc represents the accuracy as evaluated on the ambiguous words of the given data. Note that $rel(\gamma) \gtrless 0$, implies performance better or worse than EM. The results are summarized in Figure 1.

Note that when we use the "posterior uniform" initialization, EM wins by a significant margin. Surprisingly, with the initialization point constructed with merely 5 or 10 examples, EM is not the best algorithm anymore. The best result for most cases is obtained at γ somewhere between 0 (hard EM) and 1 (EM). Furthermore, the results not only indicate that a measure of "hardness" of EM i.e. **the best value**

of γ, is closely related to the quality of the initialization point but also elicit a more fine-grained relationship between initialization and UEM.

This experiment agrees with (Merialdo, 1994), which shows that EM performs poorly in the semi-supervised setting. In (Spitkovsky et al., 2010), the authors show that hard EM (Viterbi EM) works better than standard EM. We extend these results by showing that this issue can be overcome with the UEM framework by picking appropriate γ based on the amount of available labeled data.

Semi-Supervised Entity-Relation Extraction We conduct semi-supervised learning (SSL) experiments on entity and relation type prediction assuming that we are given mention boundaries. We borrow the data and the setting from (Roth and Yih, 2004). The dataset has 1437 sentences; four entity types: PER, ORG, LOC, OTHERS and; five relation types LIVE IN, KILL, ORG BASED IN, WORKS FOR, LOCATED IN. We consider relations between all within-sentence pairs of entities. We add a relation type NONE indicating no relation exists between a given pair of entities.

We train two log linear models for entity type and relation type prediction, respectively via discriminative UEM. We work in a discriminative setting in order to use several informative features which we borrow from (Roth and Small, 2009). Using these features, we obtain 56% average F1 for relations and 88% average F1 for entities in a fully supervised setting with an 80-20 split which is competitive with the reported results on this data (Roth and Yih, 2004; Roth and Small, 2009). For our SSL experiments, we use 20% of data for testing, a small amount, κ%, as labeled training data (we vary κ), and the remaining as unlabeled training data. We initialize with a classifier trained on the given labeled data.

We use the following constraints on the posterior. 1) Type constraints: For two entities e_1 and e_2, the relation type $\rho(e_1, e_2)$ between them dictates a particular entity type (or in general, a set of entity types) for both e_1 and e_2. These type constraints can be expressed as simple logical rules which can be converted into linear constraints. E.g. if the pair (e_1, e_2) has relation type LOCATED IN then e_2 must have entity type LOC. This yields a logical rule which is converted into a linear constraint as

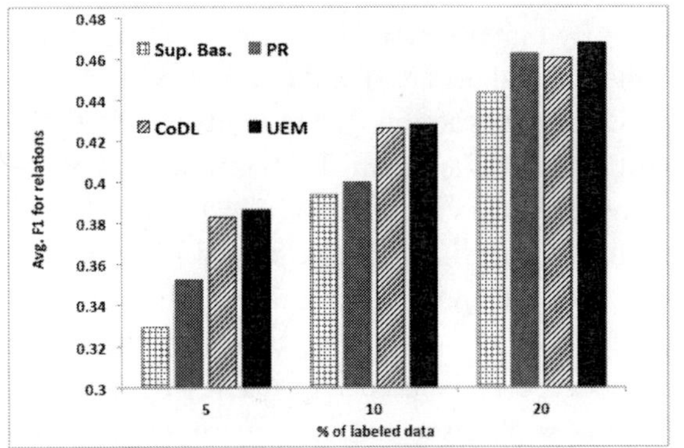

Figure 2: Average F1 for relation prediction for varying sizes of labeled data comparing the supervised baseline, PR, CoDL, and UEM. UEM is statistically significantly better than supervised baseline and PR in all the cases.

$$(\rho(e_1, e_2) == \text{LOCATED IN}) \rightarrow (e_2 == \text{LOC}) \Rightarrow q(\text{LOCATED IN}; e_1, e_2) \leq q(\text{LOC}; e_2) \ .$$

Refer to (Roth and Yih, 2004) for more statistics on this data and a list of all the type constraints used. 2) Expected count constraints: Since most entity pairs are not covered by the given relation types, the presence of a large number of NONE relations can overwhelm SSL. To guide learning in the right direction, we use corpus-wide expected count constraints for each non-NONE relation type. These constraints are very similar to the *label regularization* technique mentioned in (Mann and McCallum, 2010). Let D_r be the set of entity pairs as candidate relations in the entire corpus. For each non-NONE relation type ρ, we impose the constraints

$$L_\rho \leq \sum_{(e_1,e_2)\in D_r} q(\rho; e_1, e_2) \leq U_\rho \ ,$$

where L_ρ and U_ρ are lower and upper bound on the expected number of ρ relations in the entire corpus. Assuming that the labeled and the unlabeled data are drawn from the same distribution, we obtain these bounds using the fractional counts of ρ over the labeled data and then perturbing it by +/- 20%.

Results We use Alg. 2 for solving the constrained E-step. We report results averaged over 10 random splits of the data and measure statistical significance using paired t-test with $p = 0.05$. The results for relation prediction are shown in Fig. 2. For each trial, we split the labeled data into half to tune the value of γ. For $\kappa = 5\%$, 10%, and 20%, the average value of gamma is 0.52, 0.6, and 0.57, respectively; the median values are 0.5, 0.6, and 0.5, respectively. For relation extraction, UEM is always statistically significantly better than the baseline and PR. The difference between UEM and CoDL is small which is not very surprising because hard EM approaches like CoDL are known to work very well for discriminative SSL. We omit the graph for entity prediction because EM-based approaches do not outperform the supervised baseline there. However, notably, for entities, for $\kappa = 10\%$, UEM outperforms CoDL and PR and for 20%, the supervised baseline outperforms PR statistically significantly.

Word Alignment Statistical word alignment is a well known structured output application of unsupervised learning and is a key step towards machine translation from a source language S to a target language T. We experiment with two language-pairs: English-French and English-Spanish. We use Hansards corpus for French-English translation (Och and Ney, 2000) and Europarl corpus (Koehn, 2002) for Spanish-English translation with EPPS (Lambert et al., 2005) annotation.

We use an HMM-based model for word-alignment (Vogel et al., 1996) and add agreement constraints (Liang et al., 2008; Ganchev et al., 2008) to constrain alignment probabilities in one direction (P_{θ_1}: from S to T) to agree with the alignment probabilities in the other direction (P_{θ_2}: from T to S.) We use a small development set of size 50 to tune the model. Note that the amount of labeled data we use is much smaller than the supervised approaches reported in (Taskar et al., 2005; Moore et al., 2006) and unsupervised approaches mentioned in (Liang et al., 2008; Ganchev et al., 2008) and hence our results are not directly comparable. For the E-step, we use Alg. 3 with R=5 and pick γ from $\{0.0, 0.1, \ldots, 1.0\}$, tuning it over the development set.

During testing, instead of running HMM models for each direction separately, we obtain posterior probabilities by performing agreement constraints-based inference as in Alg. 3. This results in a posterior probability distribution over all possible alignments. To obtain final alignments, following (Ganchev et al., 2008) we use *minimum Bayes risk* decoding: we align all word pairs with posterior marginal alignment probability above a certain threshold, tuned over the development set.

Size	EM	PR	CoDL	UEM	EM	PR	CoDL	UEM
	En-Fr				Fr-En			
10k	23.54	10.63	14.76	**9.10**	19.63	10.71	14.68	**9.21**
50k	18.02	8.30	10.08	**7.34**	16.17	8.40	10.09	**7.40**
100k	16.31	8.16	9.17	**7.05**	15.03	8.09	8.93	**6.87**
	En-Es				Es-En			
10k	33.92	22.24	28.19	**20.80**	31.94	22.00	28.13	**20.83**
50k	25.31	19.84	22.99	**18.93**	24.46	20.08	23.01	**18.95**
100k	24.48	19.49	21.62	**18.75**	23.78	19.70	21.60	**18.64**

Table 2: AER (Alignment Error Rate) comparisons for French-English (above) and Spanish-English (below) alignment for various data sizes. For French-English setting, tuned γ for all data-sizes is either 0.5 or 0.6. For Spanish-English, tuned γ for all data-sizes is 0.7.

Results We compare UEM with EM, PR, and CoDL on the basis of Alignment Error Rate (AER) for different sizes of unlabeled data (See Tab. 2.) See (Och and Ney, 2003) for the definition of AER. UEM consistently outperforms EM, PR, and CoDL with a wide margin.

6 Conclusion

We proposed a continuum of EM algorithms parameterized by a single parameter. Our framework naturally incorporates constraints on output variables and generalizes existing constrained and unconstrained EM algorithms like standard and hard EM, PR, and CoDL. We provided an efficient Lagrange relaxation algorithm for inference with constraints in the E-step and empirically showed how important it is to choose the right EM version. Our technique is amenable to be combined with many existing variations of EM (Berg-Kirkpatrick et al., 2010). We leave this as future work.

Acknowledgments: We thank João Graça for providing the code and data for alignment with agreement. This research is sponsored by the Army Research Laboratory (ARL) under agreement W911NF-09-2-0053, Defense Advanced Research Projects Agency (DARPA) Machine Reading Program under Air Force Research Laboratory (AFRL) prime contract no. FA8750-09-C-018, and an ONR Award on Guiding Learning and Decision Making in the Presence of Multiple Forms of Information. Any opinions, findings, conclusions or recommendations are those of the authors and do not necessarily reflect the views of the funding agencies.

References

K. Bellare, G. Druck, and A. McCallum. 2009. Alternating projections for learning with expectation constraints. In *UAI*.

T. Berg-Kirkpatrick, A. Bouchard-Côté, J. DeNero, and D. Klein. 2010. Painless unsupervised learning with features. In *ACL*, HLT '10.

D. P. Bertsekas. 1999. *Nonlinear Programming*. Athena Scientific, 2nd edition.

P. Brown, S. D. Pietra, V. D. Pietra, and R. Mercer. 1993. The mathematics of statistical machine translation: parameter estimation. *Computational Linguistics*.

M. Chang, L. Ratinov, and D. Roth. 2007. Guiding semi-supervision with constraint-driven learning. In *ACL*.

J. Clarke and M. Lapata. 2006. Constraint-based sentence compression: An integer programming approach. In *ACL*.

A. P. Dempster, N. M. Laird, and D. B. Rubin. 1977. Maximum likelihood from incomplete data via the EM algorithm. *Journal of the Royal Statistical Society*.

K. Ganchev, J. Graca, and B. Taskar. 2008. Better alignments = better translations. In *ACL*.

K. Ganchev, J. Graça, J. Gillenwater, and B. Taskar. 2010. Posterior regularization for structured latent variable models. *Journal of Machine Learning Research*.

T. Hofmann. 2001. Unsupervised learning by probabilistic latent semantic analysis. *MIJ*.

M. Kearns, Y. Mansour, and A. Y. Ng. 1997. An information-theoretic analysis of hard and soft assignment methods for clustering. In *ICML*.

D. Klein and C. D. Manning. 2004. Corpus-based induction of syntactic structure: models of dependency and constituency. In *ACL*.

P. Koehn. 2002. Europarl: A multilingual corpus for evaluation of machine translation.

T. Koo, A. M. Rush, M. Collins, T. Jaakkola, and D. Sontag. 2010. Dual decomposition for parsing with non-projective head automata. In *EMNLP*.

P. Lambert, A. De Gispert, R. Banchs, and J. Marino. 2005. Guidelines for word alignment evaluation and manual alignment. *Language Resources and Evaluation*.

P. Liang, D. Klein, and M. I. Jordan. 2008. Agreement-based learning. In *NIPS*.

G. S. Mann and A. McCallum. 2010. Generalized expectation criteria for semi-supervised learning with weakly labeled data. *JMLR*, 11.

A. Martins, N. A. Smith, and E. Xing. 2009. Concise integer linear programming formulations for dependency parsing. In *ACL*.

A. K. McCallum, R. Rosenfeld, T. M. Mitchell, and A. Y. Ng. 1998. Improving text classification by shrinkage in a hierarchy of classes. In *ICML*.

B. Merialdo. 1994. Tagging text with a probabilistic model. *Computational Linguistics*.

R. C. Moore, W. Yih, and A. Bode. 2006. Improved discriminative bilingual word alignment. In *ACL*.

R. M. Neal and G. E. Hinton. 1998. A new view of the EM algorithm that justifies incremental, sparse and other variants. In M. I. Jordan, editor, *Learning in Graphical Models*.

K. Nigam, A. K. Mccallum, S. Thrun, and T. Mitchell. 2000. Text classification from labeled and unlabeled documents using EM. *Machine Learning*.

F. J. Och and H. Ney. 2000. Improved statistical alignment models. In *ACL*.

F. J. Och and H. Ney. 2003. A systematic comparison of various statistical alignment models. *CL*, 29.

S. Ravi and K. Knight. 2009. Minimized models for unsupervised part-of-speech tagging. *ACL*, 1(August).

K. Rose. 1998. Deterministic annealing for clustering, compression, classification, regression, and related optimization problems. In *IEEE*, pages 2210–2239.

D. Roth and K. Small. 2009. Interactive feature space construction using semantic information. In *Proc. of the Annual Conference on Computational Natural Language Learning (CoNLL)*.

D. Roth and W. Yih. 2004. A linear programming formulation for global inference in natural language tasks. In H. T. Ng and E. Riloff, editors, *CoNLL*.

D. Roth and W. Yih. 2007. Global inference for entity and relation identification via a linear programming formulation. In L. Getoor and B. Taskar, editors, *Introduction to Statistical Relational Learning*.

A. M. Rush and M. Collins. 2011. Exact decoding of syntactic translation models through lagrangian relaxation. In *ACL*.

A. M. Rush, D. Sontag, M. Collins, and T. Jaakkola. 2010. On dual decomposition and linear programming relaxations for natural language processing. In *EMNLP*.

A. Schrijver. 1986. *Theory of linear and integer programming*. John Wiley & Sons, Inc.

N. A. Smith and J. Eisner. 2004. Annealing techniques for unsupervised statistical language learning. In *ACL*.

V. I. Spitkovsky, H. Alshawi, D. Jurafsky, and C. D. Manning. 2010. Viterbi training improves unsupervised dependency parsing. In *CoNLL*.

B. Taskar, S. Lacoste-Julien, and D. Klein. 2005. A discriminative matching approach to word alignment. In *HLT-EMNLP*.

N. Ueda and R. Nakano. 1998. Deterministic annealing em algorithm. *Neural Network*.

S. Vogel, H. Ney, and C. Tillmann. 1996. Hmm-based word alignment in statistical translation. In *COLING*.

Low-Dimensional Discriminative Reranking

Jagadeesh Jagarlamudi
Department of Computer Science
University of Maryland
College Park, MD 20742, USA
jags@umiacs.umd.edu

Hal Daumé III
Department of Computer Science
University of Maryland
College Park, MD 20742, USA
hal@umiacs.umd.edu

Abstract

The accuracy of many natural language processing tasks can be improved by a reranking step, which involves selecting a single output from a list of candidate outputs generated by a baseline system. We propose a novel family of reranking algorithms based on learning *separate* low-dimensional embeddings of the task's input and output spaces. This embedding is learned in such a way that prediction becomes a low-dimensional nearest-neighbor search, which can be done computationally efficiently. A key quality of our approach is that feature engineering can be done *separately* on the input and output spaces; the relationship between inputs and outputs is learned automatically. Experiments on part-of-speech tagging task in four languages show significant improvements over a baseline decoder and existing reranking approaches.

1 Introduction

Mapping inputs to outputs lies at the heart of many Natural Language Processing applications. For example, given a sentence as input: part-of-speech (POS) tagging involves finding the appropriate POS tag sequence (Thede and Harper, 1999); parsing involves finding the appropriate tree structure (Kubler et al., 2009) and statistical machine translation (SMT) involves finding correct target language translation (Brown et al., 1993). The accuracy achieved on such tasks can often be improved significantly with the help of a discriminative reranking step (Collins and Koo, 2005; Charniak and Johnson, 2005; Shen et al., 2004; Watanabe et al., 2007). For the POS tagging, reranking is relative less explored due to the already higher accuracies in English (Collins, 2002), but it is shown to improve accuracies in other languages such as Chinese (Huang et al., 2007). In this paper, we propose a novel approach to discriminative reranking and show its effectiveness in POS tagging. Reranking allows us to use arbitrary features defined jointly on input and output spaces that are often difficult to incorporate into the baseline decoder due to the computational tractability issues. The effectiveness of reranking depends on the joint features defined over both input and output spaces. This has led the community to spend substantial efforts in defining joint features for reranking (Fraser et al., 2009; Chiang et al., 2009).

Unfortunately, developing joint features over the input and output space can be challenging, especially in problems for which the exact mapping between the input and the output is unclear (for instance, in automatic caption generation for images, semantic parsing or non-literal translation). In contrast to prior work, our approach uses features defined *separately* within the input and output spaces, and learns a mapping function that can map an object from one space into the other. Since our approach requires within-space features, it makes the feature engineering relatively easy.

For clarity, we will discuss our approach in the context of POS tagging, though of course it generalizes to any reranking problem. At test time, in POS tagging, we receive a sentence and a list of candidate output POS sequences as input. We run a feature extractor on the input sentence to obtain a representation $\mathbf{x} \in \mathbb{R}^{d_1}$; we run an *independent* feature extractor on each of the m-many outputs to obtain representations $\hat{\mathbf{y}}_1, \ldots, \hat{\mathbf{y}}_m \in \mathbb{R}^{d_2}$. We will *project* all of these points down to a low k-dimensional space by means of matrices $A \in \mathbb{R}^{d_1 \times k}$ (for $\mathbf{x}$ as $A^T\mathbf{x}$) and $B \in \mathbb{R}^{d_2 \times k}$ (for $\hat{\mathbf{y}}$ as $B^T\hat{\mathbf{y}}$). We then select as the output the $\hat{\mathbf{y}}_j$ that maximizes cosine similar to $\mathbf{x}$ in the lower-dimensional space: $\max_j cos(A^T\mathbf{x}, B^T\hat{\mathbf{y}}_j)$. The goal is to learn the projection matrices A and B so that the result of this operation is a low-loss output.

Given training data of sentences and their reference tag sequences, our approach implicitly uses all possible pairwise feature combinations across the views and learns the matrices A and B that can map a given sentence (as its feature vector) to its corresponding tag sequence. Considering all possible pairwise combinations enables our model to automatically handle long range dependencies such as a word at a position effecting the tag choice at any other position.

Experiments performed on four languages (English, Chinese, French and Swedish) show the effectiveness of our approach in comparison to the baseline decoder and to the existing reranking approaches (Sec. 4). Using only the within-space features, our models are able to beat reranking approaches that use more informative joint features. While it is possible to include joint features into our models, we leave this for future work.

2 Models for Low-Dimensional Reranking

In this section, we describe our approach to learning low-dimensional representations for reranking. We first fix some notation, then discuss the intuition behind the problem we wish to solve. We propose both generative-style and discriminative-style approaches to formalizing this intuition, as well as a softened variant of the discriminative model. In the subsequent section, we discuss computational issues related to these models.

2.1 Notation

Let $\mathbf{x}_i \in \mathbb{R}^{d_1}$ and $\mathbf{y}_i \in \mathbb{R}^{d_2}$ be the feature vectors representing the $i^{th}(1 \cdots n)$ sentence and its reference tag sequence from the training data. Each sentence is also associated with m_i number of candidate tag sequences, output by the baseline decoder, and are represented as $\hat{\mathbf{y}}_{ij} \in \mathbb{R}^{d_2}$ $j = 1 \cdots m_i$. Each candidate tag sequence ($\hat{\mathbf{y}}_{ij}$) is also associated with a non-negative loss L_{ij}. Note that we place absolutely no constraints on the loss function. Moreover, let X $(d_1 \times n)$ and Y $(d_2 \times n)$ denote the data matrices with $\mathbf{x}_i$ and $\mathbf{y}_i$ as columns respectively. Finally, let $\langle \mathbf{u}, \mathbf{v} \rangle$ denote the dot product of the two vectors $\mathbf{u}$ and $\mathbf{v}$.

2.2 Intuition

As stated in the introduction, our goal is to learn projections $A \in \mathbb{R}^{d_1 \times k}$ and $B \in \mathbb{R}^{d_2 \times k}$ in such a way that test-time predictions are made with high accuracy (or low loss). At test time, the output will be chosen by maximizing cosine similarity between the input and the output, after projecting these vectors into a low-dimensional space using A and B, respectively. The cosine similarity in our context is:

$$\frac{\mathbf{x}^T AB^T \hat{\mathbf{y}}_j}{\sqrt{\mathbf{x}^T AA^T \mathbf{x}}\sqrt{\hat{\mathbf{y}}_j^T BB^T \hat{\mathbf{y}}_j}} \quad (1)$$

Our goal is to learn A and B in such a way that the $\hat{\mathbf{y}}_j$ with maximum cosine similarity to an $\mathbf{x}$ is actually the correct output. In what follows, we will describe our models to find one-dimensional projection vectors $\mathbf{a} \in \mathbb{R}^{d_1}$ and $\mathbf{b} \in \mathbb{R}^{d_2}$, but the generalization to matrices A and B is very trivial.

2.3 A Generative-Style Model

The first model we propose is akin to a generative probabilistic model, in the sense that it attempts to model the relationship between an input and its desired output, without taking alternate possible outputs into account. In the context of the intuition sketched in the previous section, the idea is to choose A and B so as to maximize the cosine similarities on the training data between each input and it's correct (or minimal-loss) output. This model intentionally *ignores* the information present in the alternative, incorrect outputs. The hope is that by making the cosine similarities with the best output as high as possible, all the alternate outputs will look bad in comparison.

Given a training data of sentences and their reference tag sequences represented as X and Y (Sec. 2.1), our generative model finds projection directions, in word and tag spaces, along which the aligned sentence and tag sequence pairs have maximum cosine similarity. In the one-dimensional setting, it finds directions $\mathbf{a} \in \mathbb{R}^{d_1}$ and $\mathbf{b} \in \mathbb{R}^{d_2}$ such that the correlation as defined in Eq. 2 is maximized.

$$\frac{\mathbf{a}^T X Y^T \mathbf{b}}{\sqrt{\mathbf{a}^T X X^T \mathbf{a}}\sqrt{\mathbf{b}^T Y Y^T \mathbf{b}}} \quad (2)$$

Since the objective is invariant to the scaling of vectors $\mathbf{a}$ and $\mathbf{b}$, it can be rewritten as:

$$\arg\max_{\mathbf{a},\mathbf{b}} \mathbf{a}^T X Y^T \mathbf{b} \quad (3)$$

$$\text{s.t. } \mathbf{a}^T X X^T \mathbf{a} = 1 \text{ and } \mathbf{b}^T Y Y^T \mathbf{b} = 1 (4)$$

We refer to the constraints in Eq. 4 as length constraints in the rest of this paper.

To understand why maximizing this objective function learns a good mapping function between the sentence and the tag sequence, consider decomposing the objective function as follows:

$$\begin{aligned} \mathbf{a}^T X Y^T \mathbf{b} &= \sum_{i=1}^{n} \langle \mathbf{x}_i, \mathbf{a} \rangle \langle \mathbf{y}_i, \mathbf{b} \rangle \\ &= \sum_{i=1}^{n} \Big(\sum_{l=1}^{d_1} \mathbf{x}_i^l a_l \cdot \sum_{m=1}^{d_2} \mathbf{y}_i^m b_m \Big) \\ &= \sum_{i=1}^{n} \Big(\sum_{l=1}^{d_1} \sum_{m=1}^{d_2} \mathbf{x}_i^l a_l \, \mathbf{y}_i^m b_m \Big) \\ &= \sum_{i=1}^{n} \Big(\sum_{l,m=1}^{d_1,d_2} w_{lm} \phi_i^{lm} \Big) \quad (5) \end{aligned}$$

where we replaced the scalars $\mathbf{x}_i^l \mathbf{y}_i^m$ and $a_l b_m$ with ϕ_i^{lm} and w_{lm} respectively. So finally, the objective can be expressed as $\mathbf{a}^T X Y^T \mathbf{b} = \sum_i \langle \mathbf{w}, \phi(\mathbf{x}_i, \mathbf{y}_i) \rangle$ where $\mathbf{w}$ is the weight vector and $\phi(\mathbf{x}_i, \mathbf{y}_i)$ is a vector of size $(d_1 \times d_2)$ and is given by the Kronecker product of the two feature vectors $\mathbf{x}_i$ and $\mathbf{y}_i$.

In this form, the generative objective function bears similarity to the linear boundary surface widely used in machine learning, except that the weights are restricted to be the outer product of two vectors. From the reduced expressions, it is clear that our generative model considers all possible pairwise combinations of the input features $(d_1 \times d_2)$ and learns which of them are more important than others. Intuitively, it puts higher weight on a word and tag pair that co-occur frequently in the training data, at the same time each of these are infrequent in their own views.

2.4 A Discriminative-Style Model

The primary disadvantage of our generative model is that it only uses input sentences and their reference tag sequences and does *not* use the incorrect candidate tag sequences of a given sentence at all. In what follows, we describe a model that utilize the incorrect candidate tag sequences as negative examples to improve the projection directions ($\mathbf{a}$ and $\mathbf{b}$). Our goal is to address this by adding constraints to our model that explicitly penalize ranking high-loss outputs higher than low-loss outputs, as is often done in the context of maximum-margin structure prediction techniques (Taskar et al., 2004).

In this section, we describe a discriminative model that keeps track of the margin deviations and finds the projection directions iteratively. Intuitively, after the projection into the lower dimensional subspace, the cosine similarity of a sentence to its reference tag sequence must be greater than that of its incorrect candidate tag sequences. Moreover, the margin between these similarities should be proportional to the loss of the candidate translation, *i.e.* the more dissimilar a candidate tag sequence to its reference is, the farther it should be from the reference in the projected space.

From the decomposition shown in Eq. 5, for a given pair of source sentence $\mathbf{x}_i$ and a tag sequence $\mathbf{y}_j$, the generative model assigns a score of :

$$\langle \mathbf{a}, \mathbf{x}_i \rangle \langle \mathbf{b}, \mathbf{y}_j \rangle = \mathbf{a}^T \mathbf{x}_i \mathbf{y}_j^T \mathbf{b}$$

Each input sentence is also associated with a list of candidate tag sequences and since each of these candidate sequences are incorrect they should be assigned a score less than that of the reference tag sequence. Drawing ideas from structure prediction literature (Bakir et al., 2007), we modify the objective function in order to include these terms. This idea can be captured using a loss augmented margin constraint for each sentence, tag sequence pair (Tsochantaridis et al., 2004). Let ξ_i denote a non-negative slack variable, then we define our new optimization problem as:

$$\arg\max_{\mathbf{a},\mathbf{b},\xi \geq 0} \frac{1-\lambda}{\lambda} \mathbf{a}^T X Y^T \mathbf{b} - \sum_i \xi_i \quad (6)$$

$$\text{s.t. } \mathbf{a}^T X X^T \mathbf{a} = 1 \text{ and } \mathbf{b}^T Y Y^T \mathbf{b} = 1$$

$$\forall i \, \forall j \;\; \mathbf{a}^T \mathbf{x}_i \mathbf{y}_i^T \mathbf{b} - \mathbf{a}^T \mathbf{x}_i \hat{\mathbf{y}}_{ij}^T \mathbf{b} \geq 1 - \frac{\xi_i}{L_{ij}}$$

where $0 \leq \lambda \leq 1$ is a weight parameter. This objective function is ensuring that the margin between the reference and the candidate tag sequences in the projected space (as given by $\mathbf{a}^T\mathbf{x}_i\mathbf{y}_i^T\mathbf{b} - \mathbf{a}^T\mathbf{x}_i\hat{\mathbf{y}}_{ij}^T\mathbf{b}$) is proportional to its loss (L_{ij}). Notice that the slack is defined for each sentence and it remains the same for all of its candidate tag sequences.

2.5 A Softened Discriminative Model

One disadvantage of the discriminative model described in the previous section is that it cannot be optimized in closed form (as discussed in the next section). In this section, we consider a model that lies between the generative model and the (fully) discriminative model. This softened model has attractive computational properties (it is easy to compute) and will also form a building block for the optimization of the full discriminative model.

For each sentence $\mathbf{x}_i$, its reference tag sequence $\mathbf{y}_i$ should be assigned a higher score than any of its candidate tag sequences $\hat{\mathbf{y}}_{ij}$ *i.e.* we want to maximize $\mathbf{a}^T\mathbf{x}_i\mathbf{y}_i^T\mathbf{b} - \mathbf{a}^T\mathbf{x}_i\hat{\mathbf{y}}_{ij}^T\mathbf{b}$. In the fully discriminative model, we enforce that this is at least one (modulo slack). In the relaxed version, we instead require that this hold *on average*. In order to achieve this we add the following terms to the objective function: $\forall j = 1 \cdots m_i$

$$\mathbf{a}^T\mathbf{x}_i\mathbf{y}_i^T\mathbf{b} - \mathbf{a}^T\mathbf{x}_i\hat{\mathbf{y}}_{ij}^T\mathbf{b} \;=\; \mathbf{a}^T\mathbf{x}_i\mathbf{r}_{ij}^T\mathbf{b} \qquad (7)$$

where $\mathbf{r}_{ij} = \mathbf{y}_i - \hat{\mathbf{y}}_{ij}$ is the residual vector between the reference and the candidate sequences. Now, we simply sum all these terms for a given sentence weighted by their loss and encourage it to be as high as possible, *i.e.* we maximize

$$\frac{1}{m_i}\sum_{j=1}^{m_i} L_{ij}\left(\mathbf{a}^T\mathbf{x}_i\mathbf{r}_{ij}^T\mathbf{b}\right) = \mathbf{a}^T\mathbf{x}_i\left(\frac{1}{m_i}\sum_{j=1}^{m_i} L_{ij}\mathbf{r}_{ij}^T\right)\mathbf{b} \quad (8)$$

The normalization by m_i takes care of unequal numbers of candidate tag sequences that often arises because of the difference in the lengths of the input sentences. Now let R denote a matrix of the same size as that of Y (*i.e.* $d_2 \times n$) with its ith column as given by $\frac{1}{m_i}\sum_{j=1}^{m_i} L_{ij}\mathbf{r}_{ij}$, then we add the following term to the generative objective function:

$$\sum_{i=1}^{n}\mathbf{a}^T\mathbf{x}_i\left(\frac{1}{m_i}\sum_{j=1}^{m_i} L_{ij}\mathbf{r}_{ij}^T\right)\mathbf{b} = \mathbf{a}^T X R^T\mathbf{b} \qquad (9)$$

Finally, the projection directions are obtained by solving the following optimization problem :

$$\arg\max_{\mathbf{a},\mathbf{b}} \; (1-\lambda)\mathbf{a}^T XY^T\mathbf{b} + \lambda\,\mathbf{a}^T XR^T\mathbf{b} \qquad (10)$$
$$\text{s.t. } \mathbf{a}^T XX^T\mathbf{a} = 1 \;\text{ and }\; \mathbf{b}^T YY^T\mathbf{b} = 1$$

where $0 \leq \lambda \leq 1$ is the weight parameter to be tuned on the development set.

3 Optimization

In this section, we describe how we solve the optimization problems associated with our models. First we discuss the solution of the generative model. Next, we discuss the *softened* discriminative model, since its solution will be used as a subroutine in our final discussion of the fully discriminative model.

3.1 Optimizing the Generative Model

The optimization problem corresponding to the generative model turns out to be identical to that of canonical correlation analysis (CCA) (Hotelling, 1936; Hardoon et al., 2004), which immediately suggests a solution by solving an eigensystem. In particular, the projection directions are obtained by solving the following generalized eigensystem:

$$\begin{pmatrix} 0 & C_{xy} \\ C_{yx} & 0 \end{pmatrix}\begin{pmatrix}\mathbf{a}\\ \mathbf{b}\end{pmatrix} = \begin{pmatrix} C_{xx} & 0 \\ 0 & C_{yy}\end{pmatrix}\begin{pmatrix}\mathbf{a}\\ \mathbf{b}\end{pmatrix} \qquad (11)$$

where $C_{xx} = (1-\tau)XX^T + \tau I$, $C_{yy} = (1-\tau)YY^T + \tau I$ are autocovariance matrices, $C_{xy} = XY^T$ is the cross-covariance matrix, $C_{yx} = C_{xy}^T$, τ is a regularization parameter and I is the identity matrix of appropriate size. Using these eigenvectors as columns, we form projection matrices A and B. These projection matrices are used to project sentences and tag sequences into a common lower dimensional subspace. In general, using all the eigenvectors is sub-optimal from the generalization perspective so we retain only top k eigenvectors.

3.2 Optimizing the Softened Model

In the softened discriminative version, the summation of all the difference terms over all candidate tag sequences and sentences (Eq. 9), enables a simpler objective function whose optimum can be derived by following a procedure very similar to that of the generative model. In particular, the projection directions are obtained by solving Eq. 11 except that C_{xy} is replaced with $X((1-\lambda)Y^T + \lambda R^T)$.

3.3 Optimizing the Discriminative Model

To solve the discriminative model, we begin by constructing the Lagrange dual. Let β_1, β_2 and α_{ij} be the Lagrangian multipliers corresponding to the length and the margin constraints respectively, then the Lagrangian of Eq. 6 is given by:

$$\begin{aligned} \mathcal{L} &= \frac{1-\lambda}{\lambda}\mathbf{a}^T XY^T\mathbf{b} - \sum_{i=1}^{n}\xi_i \\ &\quad - \beta_1\left(\mathbf{a}^T XX^T\mathbf{a} - 1\right) - \beta_2\left(\mathbf{b}^T YY^T\mathbf{b} - 1\right) \\ &\quad + \sum_{i=1,j=1}^{n,m_i}\alpha_{ij}\left(\mathbf{a}^T\mathbf{x}_i\mathbf{r}_{ij}^T\mathbf{b} - 1 + \frac{\xi_i}{L_{ij}}\right) \end{aligned}$$

Differentiating the Lagrangian with respect to the parameters $\mathbf{a}, \mathbf{b}$ and setting them to zero yields the solution for the parameters in terms of the Lagrangian multipliers α_{ij} as follows:

$$\begin{pmatrix} 0 & C_{xy}^{\alpha} \\ C_{yx}^{\alpha} & 0 \end{pmatrix}\begin{pmatrix}\mathbf{a}\\ \mathbf{b}\end{pmatrix} = \begin{pmatrix} C_{xx} & 0 \\ 0 & C_{yy} \end{pmatrix}\begin{pmatrix}\mathbf{a}\\ \mathbf{b}\end{pmatrix} \quad (12)$$

where $C_{xy}^{\alpha} = X\left(\frac{1-\lambda}{\lambda}Y^T + R^T\right)$ and R is a matrix of size $d_2 \times n$ with i^{th} column as given by $\frac{1}{m_i}\sum_{j=1}^{m_i}\alpha_{ij}\mathbf{r}_{ij}$. We use superscript α on the cross-covariance matrix to indicate that it is dependent on the Lagrangian multipliers α_{ij}. In other words, the solution is similar to that of the previous formulation except that the residual vectors are weighted by the Lagrangian multipliers instead of the loss function. Unlike the max margin formulations of SVM, it is not easy to rewrite the parameters $\mathbf{a}, \mathbf{b}$ in terms of the Lagrangian multipliers α_{ij} as C_{xy}^{α} itself depends on α_{ij}'s. Hence, rewriting the parameters in terms of the Lagrangian multipliers and then solving the dual is not amenable in this case.

In order to solve this optimization problem, we resort to an alternate optimization technique in the primal space. It proceeds in two stages. In the first stage, we keep the Lagrangian multipliers α_{ij} fixed and then solve for the parameters $\mathbf{a}, \mathbf{b}, \beta_1, \beta_2$ and ξ_i. Projection directions $\mathbf{a}, \mathbf{b}$ and their Lagrangian multipliers β_1, β_2 are obtained by solving the generalized eigenvalue problem given in Eq. 12. Using

Algorithm 1 Alternate optimization algorithm for solving the parameters of Discriminative Model.

Input: $X, Y, \hat{Y}, L, \lambda, \tau$
Output: A, B

1: $\forall i, j \;\; \alpha_{ij} = L_{ij}$;
2: $\mathbf{r}_{ij} = \mathbf{y}_i - \hat{\mathbf{y}}_{ij}$; $C_{xx} = (1-\tau)XX^T + \tau I$; $C_{yy} = (1-\tau)YY^T + \tau I$
3: **repeat**
4: Form R with i^{th} column as $\frac{1}{m_i}\sum_{j=1}^{m_i}\alpha_{ij}\mathbf{r}_{ij}$
5: $C_{xy}^{\alpha} = X\left(\frac{1-\lambda}{\lambda}Y^T + R^T\right)$
6: Solve for the eigenvectors of Eq. 12. .
7: Form matrices A, B with top k eigenvectors as columns; k is determined using dev. set.
8: Let A_n & B_n be normalized versions of A and B s.t. they follow the length constraints.
9: **for** each sentence $i = 1 \cdots n$ **do**
10: $j = 1 \cdots m_i$, $\psi_{ij} = \left(1 - \mathbf{x}_i^T A_n B_n^T \mathbf{r}_{ij}\right) L_{ij}$
11: $\xi_i = \min\ \{0\ ,\ \psi_{ij} \mid \text{s.t. } \psi_{ij} > 0\}$
12: **if** $\xi_i > 0$ **then**
13: $d_{ij} = \mathbf{x}_i^T A_n B_n^T \mathbf{r}_{ij} - (1 - \frac{\xi_i}{L_{ij}})$
14: $\alpha_{ij} = \alpha_{ij} - \gamma\, d_{ij}$
15: **end if**
16: **end for**
17: **until** slack values doesn't change
18: **return** A, B

these projection directions, we determine the slack variable ξ_i for each sentence. In the second stage of the alternate optimization, we fix $\mathbf{a}, \mathbf{b}$ and ξ_i and take a gradient descent step along α_{ij}'s to minimize the function. We repeat this process until convergence. In our experiments, we noticed that this algorithm converges within five iterations, so we only run it for five iterations.

The pseudocode of our approach is shown in Alg. 1. First we initialize the Lagrangian multipliers proportional to the loss of the candidate tag sequences (step 1). This ensures that the eigenvectors solved in step 6 are same as the output given by the softened model (Sec. 2.5). In general, in our experiments, we observed that this is a good starting point. After solving the generalized eigenvalue problem in step. 6, we consider the top k eigenvectors, as determined by the error on the development set and normalize them so that they follow the length constraints (steps 7 and 8). In the rest of the algorithm, we use these normalized projection directions to find the slack values which are in turn used to find the update direction for the Lagrangian variables.

In step 10, we compute the potential slack value (ψ_{ij}) for each constraint so that it is satisfied and then choose the minimum of the positive ψ_{ij} values as the slack for this sentence (step 11). If the chosen slack value is equal to zero, it implies that $\psi_{ij} \leq 0 \; \forall j = 1 \cdots m_i$ which in turn implies that all the constraints of a given input sentence are satisfied by the current projection directions and hence there is no need to update the Lagrangian multipliers. Otherwise, some of the constraints are still not satisfied and hence we will update their corresponding Lagrangian multipliers in steps 13 and 14. In specific, step 13 computes the deviation of the margin constraints with the new slack value and step 14 updates the Lagrangian multipliers along the gradient direction.

In principle, our approach is similar to the cutting plane algorithm used to optimize slack re-scaling version of Structured SVM (Tsochantaridis et al., 2004), but it differs in selecting the slack variable (step 11). The cutting plane method chooses ξ_i as the maximum of $\{0, \psi_{ij}\}$ where as we choose the minimum of the positive ψ_{ij} values as the slack. Intuitively, this means that the cutting plane algorithm chooses a constraint that is most violated which results in fewer constraints. This is crucial in structured SVM, because solving the dual problem is cubic in terms of the number of examples and constraints. In contrast, our approach selects the slack such that at least one of the constraints is satisfied and adds all the remaining constraints to the active set. Since step 6 considers a weighted average of all these constraints the complexity depends only on the number of training examples and not the constraints.

3.4 Combining with Viterbi Decoding Score

All the three formulations discussed until now do not consider the Viterbi decoding score assigned to each candidate tag sequence. As explained in Collins and Koo (2005), the decoding score plays an important role in reranking the candidate sentences. Here, we describe a simple linear combination of the Viterbi decoding score and the score obtained by projecting into the low-dimensional subspace, using projection directions obtained by any of the above models.

For a given sentence $\mathbf{x}_i$ and candidate tag sequence pair $\hat{\mathbf{y}}_{ij}$, let s_{ij} and p_{ij} (Eq. 1) be the scores assigned by Viterbi decoding and the lower dimensional projections respectively. Then we define the final score for this pair as a simple linear combination of these two scores as:

$$\text{Score}(\mathbf{x}_i, \hat{\mathbf{y}}_{ij}) = s_{ij} + w \, p_{ij} \tag{13}$$

The weight w is optimized using a grid search on the development data set, we search for w from 0 to 100 with an increment of 1 and choose the value for which the error is minimum on the development set.

3.5 Reranking for POS Tagging

To summarize our approach, we convert the training data into feature vectors and use any of the three methods discussed above to find the lower dimensional projection directions ($\mathbf{a}$ and $\mathbf{b}$). Each of those approaches involve solving a similar generalized eigenvalue problem (Eq. 11) with the cross covariance matrix C_{xy} defined differently in the three approaches. This problem can be solved in different ways, but we use the following approach since it reduces the size of the eigenvalue problem.

$$C_{yy}^{-1} C_{xy}^{T} C_{xx}^{-1} C_{xy} \, \mathbf{b} = \omega \, \mathbf{b} \tag{14}$$

$$\mathbf{a} = \frac{1}{\sqrt{\omega}} \, C_{xx}^{-1} C_{xy} \, \mathbf{b} \tag{15}$$

where ω is the eigenvalue. Assuming that $d_2 \ll d_1$, which is usually true in POS tagging because of the smaller tag vocabulary, these equations solve a smaller eigenvalue problem. After solving the eigenvalue problem, we form matrices A and B with columns as the top k eigenvectors $\mathbf{a}$ and $\mathbf{b}$ respectively. Given a new sentence and candidate tag sequence pair $(\mathbf{x}_i, \hat{\mathbf{y}}_{ij})$, their similarity is obtained using Eq. 1. Now, based on the development data set we find the weight (w) for the linear combination of the projection and Viterbi decoding scores (Eq. 13).

During the reranking stage, we first use Eq. 1 to compute the projection score for all the candidate tag sequences and then use Eq. 13 to combine this scores with the decoding score. The candidate tag sequences are reranked based on this final score.

4 Experiments

In this section, we report POS tagging experiments on four languages: English, Chinese, French and

		Train.	Dev.	Test
English (En.)	# sent.	15K	2K	1791
	# words	362K	47K	43K
Chinese (Zh.)	# sent.	50K	4K	3647
	# words	292K	26K	25K
French (Fr.)	# sent.	9K	2K	1351
	# words	254K	57K	40K
Swedish (Sv.)	# sent.	8K	2K	1431
	# words	137K	31K	28K

Table 1: Training and test data statistics.

Swedish. The data in all these languages is obtained from the CoNLL 2006 shared task on multilingual dependency parsing (Buchholz and Marsi, 2006). We only consider the word and its fine grained POS tag (columns 2 and 5 respectively) and ignore the dependency links in the data. Table 1 shows the data statistics in each of these languages.

We use a second order Hidden Markov Model (Thede and Harper, 1999) based tagger as a baseline tagger in our experiments. This model uses trigram transition and emission probabilities and is shown to achieve good accuracies in English and other languages (Huang et al., 2007). We refer to this as the baseline tagger in the rest of this paper and is used to produce n-best list for each candidate sentence. The n-best list for training data is produced using multi-fold cross-validation like Collins and Koo (2005) and Charniak and Johnson (2005). The first block of Table 2 shows the accuracies of the top-ranked tag sequence (according to the Viterbi decoding score) and the oracle accuracies on the 10-best list. As expected the accuracies on English and French are high and are on par with the state-of-the-art systems. From the oracle scores, it is clear that though there is a chance for improvement using reranking, the scope for improvement in English is less compared to the 5 point improvement reported for parsing (Charniak and Johnson, 2005). This indicates the difficulty of the reranking problem for POS tagging in well-resourced languages.

4.1 Reranking Features and Baselines

In this paper, except for Chinese, we use suffixes of length two to four as features in the word view and unigram and bigram tag sequences as features in the tag view. That is, we convert each word of the sentence into suffixes of length two to four and then treat each sentence as a bag of suffixes. Similarly, we treat a candidate POS tag sequence as a bag of unigram and bigram tag features. For Chinese, we use character sequences of length one and two as features for the sentences and use unigram and bigram POS tag sequences on the tag view. We did not include any alignment based features, *i.e.* features that depend on the position.

We compare our models with a boosting-based discriminative approach (Collins and Koo, 2005) and its regularized version (Huang et al., 2007). In order to enable a fair comparison, we use suffix and tag pairs as features for both these models. For example, we would generate the following features for the word 'selling' in the phrase "the/DT selling/NN pressure/NN": (ng, NN), (ng, DT_NN), (ing,NN), (ing,DT_NN), (ling,NN), (ling,DT_NN). For comparison purposes, we also show results by running the baseline rerankers with n-gram features.

4.2 Results

There are following hyper parameters in each of our models, regularization parameter τ, weight parameter λ in the discriminative and softened discriminative models, the linear combination weight w with the Viterbi decoding score, and finally, the size of the lower dimensional subspace (k). We use grid search to tune these parameters based on the development data set. The optimal hyperparameter values differ based on the model and the language, but the tagging accuracy is relatively robust with respect to these parameter values. For English, the best values for the discriminative model are $\tau = 0.95$, $\lambda = 0.3$ and $k = 75$. For the same language, Fig. 1 shows the performance with respect to τ and λ parameters, respectively, with other parameters fixed to their optimal values. Notice that, although the performance varies it is always more than the accuracy of the baseline tagger (96.74%).

Table 2 shows the results of different models on the development and test data sets. On the test data set, the baseline reranking approaches perform better than the HMM decoder in Chinese and Swedish languages, but they underperform in English and French languages. This is justifiable because the individual characters are good indicators of POS tag

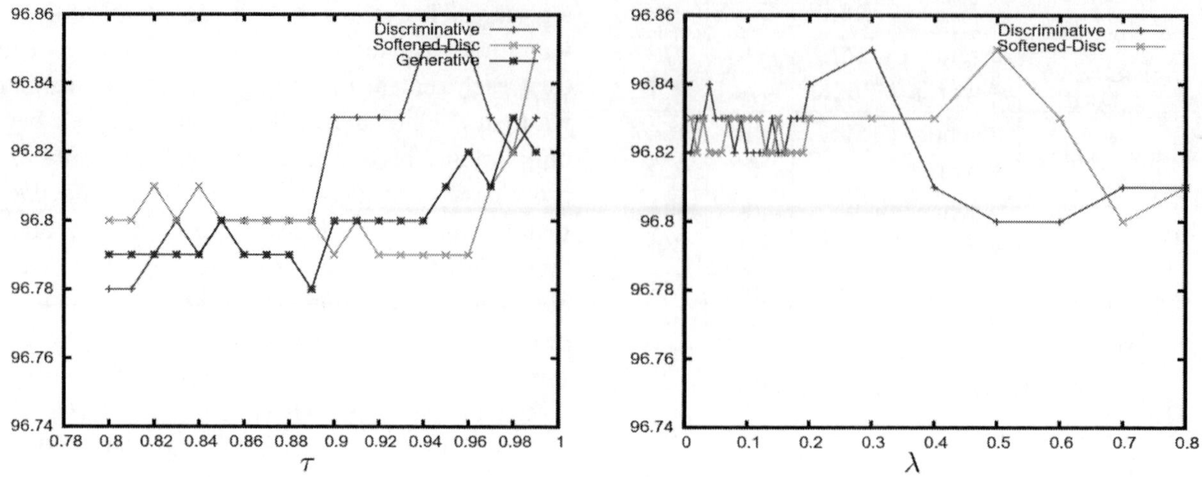

Figure 1: Tagging accuracy with hyperparameters τ and λ on English development data set.

	Development Set				Test set			
	English	Chinese	French	Swedish	English	Chinese	French	Swedish
Baseline	96.74	92.55	96.94	93.22	96.15	92.31	97.41	93.23
Oracle	98.85	98.41	98.61	96.96	98.39	98.19	99.00	96.48
Collins (Sufx)	96.66	93.00	96.87	**93.50**	96.06	92.81	97.35	**93.44**
Regularized (Sufx)	96.60	93.12	96.90	93.36	96.00	92.88	97.38	93.35
Generative	96.82	93.14	96.97	93.46	96.24	**92.95**	97.43	93.26
Softened-Disc	96.85	93.14	**97.04**	93.49	**96.32**	92.87	**97.53**	93.24
Discriminative	**96.85**	**93.17**	97.03	**93.50**	96.3	92.91	**97.53**	93.36
Collins (n-gm)	96.74	93.14	97.06	93.44	96.13	92.74	97.54	93.45
Regularized (n-gm)	96.78	93.14	97.01	93.45	96.14	92.80	97.52	93.40

Table 2: Accuracy of the baseline HMM tagger and different reranking approaches. For comparison purposes, we also showed the results of Collins and Koo (2005) its regularized versions with n-gram features. The improvements of our discriminative models are statistically significant at $p = 0.01$ and $p = 0.05$ levels on Chinese and English respectively.

information for Chinese and this additional information is being exploited by the reranking approaches. Swedish, on the other hand, is a Germanic language with compound word phenomenon which makes the baseline HMM decoder weaker compared to English and French.

The fourth block shows the performance of our models. Except in Swedish, one of our models outperform the baseline decoder and the other reranking approaches. The fact that our models outperform the baseline system and other reranking approaches indicate that, by considering all the pairwise combinations of the input features our models capture dependencies that are left by other models. Among the different formulations of our approach, maximizing the margin between the correct and incorrect candidates performed better than generative, and ensuring that the margin is proportional to the loss of the candidate sequence (discriminative) led to even more improved results. Except in Chinese, our discriminative version performed at least as well as the other variants. Compared to the baseline decoder, the discriminative version achieves a maximum improvement of 0.6 points in Chinese while achieving 0.15, 0.12 and 0.13 points of improvement in English, French and Swedish languages respectively.

We also reported the results of the baseline rerankers with n-gram features in the fifth block of Table 2. We remind the reader that our models use only suffix features, so for a fair comparison the

	En.	Zh.	Fr.	Sv.
Generative	94.83	89.89	96.1	91.89
Softened-Disc	95.04	89.61	95.97	91.95
Discriminative	94.95	89.76	95.82	92.11

Table 3: Accuracies without combining with Viterbi decoding score.

reader should compare our results with the baseline rerankers run with the suffix features. The performance of these baseline rankers improved when we include the n-gram features but it is still less than the discriminative model in most cases.

Finally, Table 3 shows the performance of our models without combining with the Viterbi decoding score. As shown, the performance drops significantly and is in accordance with the behavior observed elsewhere (Collins and Koo, 2005).

5 Related Work

In this section, we discuss approaches that are most relevant to our problem and the approach.

In NLP literature, discriminative reranking has been well explored for parsing (Collins and Koo, 2005; Charniak and Johnson, 2005; Shen and Joshi, 2003; McDonald et al., 2005; Johnson and Ural, 2010) and statistical machine translation (Shen et al., 2004; Watanabe et al., 2007; Liang et al., 2006). Collins (2002) proposed two reranking approaches, namely boosting algorithm and a voted perceptron, for the POS tagging task. Later Huang *et al.* (2007) propose a regularized version of the objective used by Collins (2002) and show an improved performance for Chinese. In all of the above reranking approaches, the feature functions are defined jointly on the input and output, whereas in our approach, the features are defined separately within each view and the algorithm learns the relationship between them automatically. This is the primary difference between our approach and the existing rerankers.

In principle, our margin formulations are similar to the max margin formulations of CCA (Szedmak et al., 2007) and maximum margin regression (Szedmak et al., 2006; Wang et al., 2007). These approaches solve the following optimization problem:

$$\min \ \|W\|^2 + C\mathbf{1}^T\boldsymbol{\xi} \qquad (16)$$
$$\text{s.t.} \ \langle \mathbf{y}_i, W\phi(\mathbf{x})_i\rangle \geq 1 - \xi_i \quad \forall i = 1\cdots n$$

Our approach differs from these formulations in two main ways: the score assigned by our generative model (equivalent to CCA) for an input-output pair $(\mathbf{x}_i^T\mathbf{a}\mathbf{b}^T\mathbf{y}_i)$ can be converted into this format by substituting $W \leftarrow \mathbf{b}\mathbf{a}^T$ but in doing so we are ignoring the rank constraint. It is often observed that, dimensionality reduction leads to an improved performance and thus the rank constraint becomes crucial. Another major difference is that, the constraints in Eq. 16 represent that any input and output pair should have at least a margin of 1 (modulo slack), whereas in our approach, the constraints include incorrect outputs along with their loss value. In other words, our formulation is more suitable for the reranking problem while Eq. 16 is more suitable for regression or classification tasks. Our generative model is very similar to the supervised semantic hashing work (Bai et al., 2010) but the way we optimize is completely different from theirs.

6 Discussion

In this paper, we proposed a novel family of models for discriminative reranking problem and showed improvements for the POS tagging task in four different languages. Here, we restricted our scope to showing the utility of our technique and, hence, did not experiment with different features, though it is an important direction. By using only within space features, our models are able to beat the reranking approaches that use potentially more informative alignment-based features. It is also possible to include alignment-based features into our models by posing the problem as a feature selection problem on the covariance matrices (Jagarlamudi et al., 2011). Our approach involves an inverse computation and an eigenvalue problem. Although our models scale to medium size data sets (our Chinese data set has 50K examples and 33K features), these operations can be expensive. But there are alternative approximation techniques that scale well to large data sets (Halko et al., 2009). We leave this for future work.

Acknowledgments

We thank Zhongqiang Huang for providing the code for the baseline systems, Raghavendra Udupa and the anonymous reviewers for their insightful comments. This work is partially funded by NSF grants IIS-1153487 and IIS-1139909.

References

Bing Bai, Jason Weston, David Grangier, Ronan Collobert, Kunihiko Sadamasa, Yanjun Qi, Olivier Chapelle, and Kilian Weinberger. 2010. Learning to rank with (a lot of) word features. *Inf. Retr.*, 13(3):291–314, June.

Gükhan H. Bakir, Thomas Hofmann, Bernhard Schölkopf, Alexander J. Smola, Ben Taskar, and S. V. N. Vishwanathan. 2007. *Predicting Structured Data (Neural Information Processing)*. The MIT Press.

Peter F. Brown, Vincent J. Della Pietra, Stephen A. Della Pietra, and Robert L. Mercer. 1993. The mathematics of statistical machine translation: parameter estimation. *Comput. Linguist.*, 19:263–311, June.

Sabine Buchholz and Erwin Marsi. 2006. Conll-x shared task on multilingual dependency parsing. In *Proceedings of the Tenth Conference on Computational Natural Language Learning*, CoNLL-X '06, pages 149–164, Stroudsburg, PA, USA. Association for Computational Linguistics.

Eugene Charniak and Mark Johnson. 2005. Coarse-to-fine n-best parsing and maxent discriminative reranking. In *Proceedings of the 43rd Annual Meeting on Association for Computational Linguistics*, ACL '05, pages 173–180, Stroudsburg, PA, USA. Association for Computational Linguistics.

David Chiang, Kevin Knight, and Wei Wang. 2009. 11,001 new features for statistical machine translation. In *Proceedings of Human Language Technologies: The 2009 Annual Conference of the North American Chapter of the Association for Computational Linguistics*, NAACL '09, pages 218–226, Stroudsburg, PA, USA. Association for Computational Linguistics.

Michael Collins and Terry Koo. 2005. Discriminative reranking for natural language parsing. *Computational Linguistics*, 31:25–70, March.

Michael Collins. 2002. Ranking algorithms for named-entity extraction: boosting and the voted perceptron. In *Proceedings of the 40th Annual Meeting on Association for Computational Linguistics*, ACL '02, pages 489–496, Stroudsburg, PA, USA. Association for Computational Linguistics.

Alexander Fraser, Renjing Wang, and Hinrich Schütze. 2009. Rich bitext projection features for parse reranking. In *Proceedings of the 12th Conference of the European Chapter of the Association for Computational Linguistics*, EACL '09, pages 282–290, Stroudsburg, PA, USA. Association for Computational Linguistics.

Nathan Halko, Per-Gunnar. Martinsson, and A. Joel Tropp. 2009. Finding structure with randomness: Stochastic algorithms for constructing approximate matrix decompositions. Technical report, California Institute of Technology.

David R. Hardoon, Sandor R. Szedmak, and John R. Shawe-taylor. 2004. Canonical correlation analysis: An overview with application to learning methods. *Neural Comput.*, 16:2639–2664, December.

Harold Hotelling. 1936. Relation between two sets of variables. *Biometrica*, 28:322–377.

Zhongqiang Huang, Mary Harper, and Wen Wang. 2007. Mandarin part-of-speech tagging and discriminative reranking. In *Proceedings of the 2007 Joint Conference on Empirical Methods in Natural Language Processing and Computational Natural Language Learning (EMNLP-CoNLL)*, pages 1093–1102, Prague, Czech Republic, June. Association for Computational Linguistics.

Jagadeesh Jagarlamudi, Raghavendra Udupa, Hal Daumé III, and Abhijit Bhole. 2011. Improving bilingual projections via sparse covariance matrices. In *Proceedings of the 2011 Conference on Empirical Methods in Natural Language Processing*, pages 930–940, Edinburgh, Scotland, UK., July. Association for Computational Linguistics.

Mark Johnson and Ahmet Engin Ural. 2010. Reranking the Berkeley and Brown parsers. In *Human Language Technologies: The 2010 Annual Conference of the North American Chapter of the Association for Computational Linguistics*, HLT '10, pages 665–668, Stroudsburg, PA, USA. Association for Computational Linguistics.

Sandra Kubler, Ryan McDonald, Joakim Nivre, and Graeme Hirst. 2009. *Dependency Parsing*. Morgan and Claypool Publishers.

Percy Liang, Alexandre Bouchard-Côté, Dan Klein, and Ben Taskar. 2006. An end-to-end discriminative approach to machine translation. In *Proceedings of the 21st International Conference on Computational Linguistics and the 44th annual meeting of the Association for Computational Linguistics*, ACL-44, pages 761–768, Stroudsburg, PA, USA. Association for Computational Linguistics.

Ryan McDonald, Koby Crammer, and Fernando Pereira. 2005. Online large-margin training of dependency parsers. In *Proceedings of the 43rd Annual Meeting on Association for Computational Linguistics*, ACL '05, pages 91–98, Stroudsburg, PA, USA. Association for Computational Linguistics.

Libin Shen and Aravind K. Joshi. 2003. An SVM based voting algorithm with application to parse reranking. In *Proceedings of the seventh conference on Natural language learning at HLT-NAACL 2003 - Volume 4*, CONLL '03, pages 9–16, Stroudsburg, PA, USA. Association for Computational Linguistics.

Libin Shen, Anoop Sarkar, and Franz Och. 2004. Discriminative reranking for machine translation. In *Human Language Technology Conference and the 5th Meeting of the North American Association for Computational Linguistics: HLT-NAACL 2004*, Boston, USA, May.

S. Szedmak, J. Shawe-Taylor, and E. Parado-Hernandez. 2006. Learning via linear operators: Maximum margin regression; multiclass and multiview learning at one-class complexity. Technical report, University of Southampton.

Sandor Szedmak, Tijl De Bie, and David R. Hardoon. 2007. A metamorphosis of canonical correlation analysis into multivariate maximum margin learning. In *Proceedings of the fifteenth European Symposium on Artificial Neural Networks*.

Ben Taskar, Carlos. Guestrin, and Daphne Koller. 2004. Max margin markov networks. In *Proceedings of NIPS 16*.

Scott M. Thede and Mary P. Harper. 1999. A second-order Hidden Markov Model for part-of-speech tagging. In *Proceedings of the Annual Meeting on Association for Computational Linguistics*, pages 175–182. Association for Computational Linguistics.

Ioannis Tsochantaridis, Thomas Hofmann, Thorsten Joachims, and Yasemin Altun. 2004. Support vector machine learning for interdependent and structured output spaces. In *Proceedings of the twenty-first international conference on Machine learning*, ICML '04, pages 104–, New York, NY, USA. ACM.

Zhuoran Wang, John Shawe-Taylor, and Sandor Szedmak. 2007. Kernel regression based machine translation. In *Human Language Technologies 2007: The Conference of the North American Chapter of the Association for Computational Linguistics; Companion Volume, Short Papers*, NAACL-Short '07, pages 185–188, Stroudsburg, PA, USA. Association for Computational Linguistics.

Taro Watanabe, Jun Suzuki, Hajime Tsukada, and Hideki Isozaki. 2007. Online Large-Margin Training for Statistical Machine Translation. In *Proceedings of the 2007 Joint Conference on Empirical Methods in Natural Language Processing and Computational Natural Language Learning (EMNLP-CoNLL)*, pages 764–773, Prague, Czech Republic, June. Association for Computational Linguistics.

Autonomous Self-Assessment of Autocorrections: Exploring Text Message Dialogues

Tyler Baldwin
Department of Computer Science and Engineering
Michigan State University
East Lansing, MI 48824
baldwi96@cse.msu.edu

Joyce Y. Chai
Department of Computer Science and Engineering
Michigan State University
East Lansing, MI 48824
jchai@cse.msu.edu

Abstract

Text input aids such as automatic correction systems play an increasingly important role in facilitating fast text entry and efficient communication between text message users. Although these tools are beneficial when they work correctly, they can cause significant communication problems when they fail. To improve its autocorrection performance, it is important for the system to have the capability to assess its own performance and learn from its mistakes. To address this, this paper presents a novel task of self-assessment of autocorrection performance based on interactions between text message users. As part of this investigation, we collected a dataset of autocorrection mistakes from true text message users and experimented with a rich set of features in our self-assessment task. Our experimental results indicate that there are salient cues from the text message discourse that allow systems to assess their own behaviors with high precision.

1 Introduction

The use of SMS text messaging is widespread and growing. Users of text messaging often rely on small mobile devices with limited user interfaces to communicate with each other. To support efficient communication between users, many tools to aid text input such as automatic completion (autocompletion) and automatic correction (autocorrection) have become available. When they work correctly, these tools allow users to maintain clear communication while potentially increasing the rate at which they input their message, improving efficiency in communication. However, when these tools make a mistake, they can cause problematic situations. Consider the following example:

A_1: Euthanasia doing tonight?

B_1: Euthanasia?!

A_2: I typed whatcha and stupid autotype.

In this example, the automatic correction system on person A's phone interpreted his attempt to write the word *whatcha* as an attempt to write *euthanasia* (due to the keyboard adjacency of the *w* and *e* keys, etc.). This completely changed the meaning of the message, which confused person B. Although this instance was eventually discovered and corrected, the natural flow of conversation was interrupted and the participants were forced to make extra effort to clarify this confusion.

This example indicates that the cost of a mistake in autocorrection is potentially high. This is exacerbated by the fact that users will often fail to notice these mistakes in a timely manner, due to their focus being on the keyboard (Paek et al., 2010) and the quick and casual conversation style of text messaging. Because of this, autocorrection systems must have high accuracy to be useful for text messaging. This example also indicates that, when an autocorrection mistake happens (i.e., mistaken correction of *euthanasia*), it often causes confusion which requires dialogue participants to use the follow-up dialogue to clarify the intent. What this suggests is that the discourse between text message users may provide important information for autocorrection systems to assess whether an attempted correction is indeed what the user intended to type.

Self-assessment of its correction performance will allow an autocorrection system to detect correction mistakes, learn from such mistakes, and potentially improve its correction performance for future operations. For instance, if a system is able to identify that its current autocorrection policy results in too many mistakes it may choose to adopt a more cautious correction policy in the future. Additionally, if it is able to discover not only that a mistake has taken place but what the ideal action should have been, it will be able to use this data to learn a more refined policy for future attempts.

Motivated by this observation, this paper investigates the novel task of self-assessment of autocorrection performance based on interactions between dialogue participants. In particular, we formulate this task as the automatic identification of correction mistakes and their corresponding intended words based on the discourse. For instance, in the previous example, the system should automatically detect that the attempted correction "euthanasia" is a mistake and the true term (i.e., intended word) should have been "whatcha". To support our investigation, we collected a dataset of autocorrection mistakes from true text message users. We further experimented with a rich set of features in our self-assessment task. Our experimental results indicate that there are salient cues from the text message discourse that potentially allow systems to assess their own behavior with high precision.

In the sections that follow, we first introduce and give an analysis of our dataset. We then highlight the two interrelated problems that must be solved for system self-assessment, and outline and evaluate our approach to each of these problems. Finally, we examine the results of applying the system assessment procedure end-to-end and discuss potential applications of autocorrection self-assessment.

2 Related Work

Spelling autocorrection systems grew naturally out of the well studied field of spell checking. Most spell checking systems are based on a noisy channel formulation (Kernighan et al., 1990). Later refinements allowed for string edit operations of arbitrary length (Brill and Moore, 2000) and pronunciation modeling (Toutanova and Moore, 2002). More recent work has examined the use of the web as a corpus to build a spell checking and autocorrection system without the need for labeled training data (Whitelaw et al., 2009).

Traditional spell checking systems generally assume that misspellings are unintentional. However, much of the spelling variation that appears in text messages may be produced intentionally. For instance, text message authors make frequent use of acronyms and abbreviations. This motivates the task of text message normalization (Aw et al., 2006; Kobus et al., 2008), which attempts to transform all non-standard spellings in a text message into their standard form. The style of misspelling in text messages is often quite different from that of standard prose. For instance, Whitelaw et. al. (2009) applied the Aspell spell checker[1] on a corpus of mistakes in English prose and achieved an error rate of under 5%. Conversely, the same spell checker was found to have an error rate of over 75% on text message data (Choudhury et al., 2007).

Autocorrection in text messaging is similar to predictive texting and word completion technologies (Dunlop and Crossan, 2000). These technologies attempt to reduce the number of keystrokes a user must type (MacKenzie, 2002), potentially speeding up text entry. There are 2 primary sources of literature on text prediction. In one (often called *autocompletion*), systems attempt to predict the intended term before the user has finished typing it (Darragh et al., 1990; Chaudhuri and Kaushik, 2009). In the second, the system attempts to interpret ambiguous user input typed on a keyboard with a small number of keys, such as the 12 key keyboards found on many mobile phones (MacKenzie and Tanaka-Ishii, 2007). Few studies have looked at the effects SMS writing style has on predictive text performance. How and Kan (2005) analyze a corpus of 10,000 text messages and conclude that changing the standard mapping of letters to keys on 12 key keyboards could improve input performance on SMS data.

Although never examined in the context of autocorrection systems, system self-assessment has been studied in other domains. One of the most com-

[1] http://aspell.net/

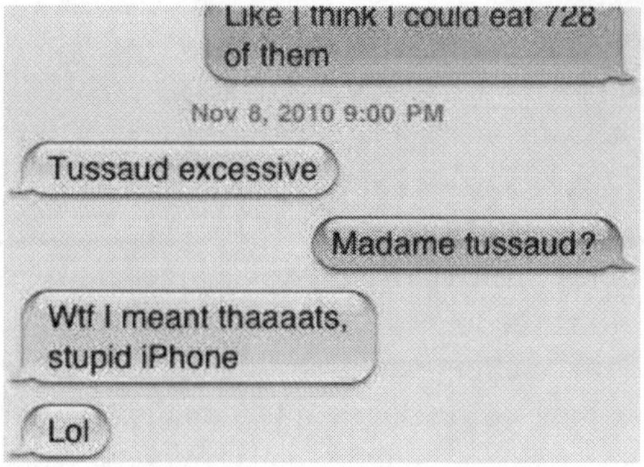

Figure 1: Example text message dialogue from our corpus with an automatic correction mistake

mon application domains is spoken dialogue systems (Levow, 1998; Hirschberg et al., 2001; Litman et al., 2006), where detecting problematic situations can help the system better adapt to user behavior. These systems often make use of prosody and task specific dialogue acts, two feature sources unavailable in general text message dialogues.

In summary, while a large body of work addresses similar problems, to our knowledge no previous work has looked into the aspect of self-assessment of autocorrection based on dialogues between text message users. The work presented in this paper represents a first step in this direction.

3 Data Set

To support our investigation, we collected a corpus of data containing true experiences with autocorrection provided by text message users. The website "Damn You Auto Correct"[2] (DYAC) posts screenshots of text message conversations that contain mistakes caused by phone automatic correction systems, as sent in by cellphone users. An example screenshot is shown is Figure 1.

Speech bubbles originating from the left of the image in Figure 1 are messages sent by one dialogue participant while those originating from the right of the image are sent by the other. In this example, the automatic correction system incorrectly decides that the user's attempt to write the non-standard word form *thaaaats* was an attempt to write the word *Tussaud*. This confuses the reader, and several dialogue turns are used to resolve the confusion. The author explicitly corrects her mistake by writing "I meant thaaaats".

Note that, in this example, the word *Tussaud* could be an autocompletion or an autocorrection by the system. However, there may be no significant distinction between these two operations from a user's point of view. These two operations could also take place at the same time. For instance, a system may both suggest possible completions after the user has only typed a small number of characters and perform autocorrection once the user presses the space bar to go on to the next word. Therefore, for the purposes of our discussion here, we use autocorrection to refer to any changes made by the system (either by autocompletion or autocorrection) without the user explicitly selecting the correction themselves.

Throughout the paper, we use the term **attempted correction** to refer to any autocorrection made by the system; for example, *Tussaud* is an attempted correction in Figure 1. Some attempted corrections could correct to the word that the user intended, which will be referred to as **unproblematic corrections** or **non-erroneous corrections**. Other attempted corrections may mistakenly choose a word that the user did not intend to write, which will be referred to as **correction mistakes** or **erroneous corrections**. For example, *Tussaud* is an erroneous correction. We use the term **intended word** to refer to the term that the user was attempting to type when the autocorrection system intervened. For instance, in the erroneous correction in Figure 1, the intended term was *thaaaats*.

To build our dataset, screenshots were extracted from the site and transcribed, and correction mistakes were annotated with their intended words, if the intended word appeared in the dialogue. Because the website presents autocorrection mistakes that submitters find to be humorous or egregious, there may be an incentive for users to submit falsified instances. To combat this, we performed an initial filtering phase to remove instances that were unlikely to have been produced by a typical autocorrection system (e.g., instances that substituted letters that were far from each other on the keyboard and not phonetically similar) or that were otherwise believed to be falsified. Using this methodology we compiled a development set of 300 dialogues and an

[2] www.damnyouautocorrect.com

Figure 2: Text message dialogue with several correction mistakes for the same intended term.

additional 635 dialogues for evaluation.

Some dialogues contained several correction mistakes. It was common for multiple correction mistakes to be produced in an attempt at typing a single word; an example is shown in Figure 2, in which the intended term *cookies* is erroneously corrected at first as *commies* and then as *cockles*.

We will use the term *message* to refer to one SMS text message sent in the course of the conversation, while a *turn* encompasses all messages sent by a user between messages from the other participant. For instance, the first 3 speech bubbles in Figure 2 all represent separate messages, but they are all part of the same turn.

While this dataset provides us with instances of autocorrection mistakes, in order to differentiate between problematic and unproblematic correction attempts we will need a dataset of unproblematic attempts as well. It should be noted that, from the perspective of the reader, a successful autocorrection attempt is equivalent to the user typing correctly without any intervention from the system at all. To build a dataset of unproblematic instances, we collected text message conversations from pairs of users without the aid of autocorrection. Users were then asked to correct any mistakes they produced. Snippets of these conversations that did not contain mistakes were then extracted to act as a set of unproblematic autocorrection instances. In total 554 snippets were extracted. These snippets were combined with the problematic instances from the DYAC data to make the final dataset used for training and evaluation.

4 Autocorrection Self-Assessment

It is desirable for an autocorrection system to have the capability to assess its own performance. For each correction attempt it makes, if the system can evaluate its performance based on the dialogue it can acquire valuable information to learn from its own mistakes and thus improve its performance for future operations. Next we describe how we formulate the task of self-assessment and what features can be used for this task.

Because each correction attempt is system generated, an autocorrection system should have knowledge of all correction attempts it has made. Let C be the set of all correction attempts performed by an autocorrection system over the course of a dialogue and let W be the set of all words in this dialogue which occur after the correction attempt. We model this problem as two distinct subtasks: 1) identify attempted corrections $c_i \in C$ which are erroneous (if there are any), and 2) for each erroneous correction c_i, identify a word $w_j \in W$ which is the intended word for c_i (i.e., $Intended(c_i) = w_j$).

4.1 Identifying Erroneous Corrections

The first task involves a simple binary decision; given an arbitrarily sized dialogue snippet containing an automatic correction attempt, we must decide whether or not the system acted erroneously when making the correction. We thus model the task as a binary classification problem in which we classify every correction attempt $c \in C$ as either erroneous or non-erroneous.

The proposed method follows a standard procedure for supervised binary classification. First we must build a set of labeled training data in which each instance is represented as a vector of features and a ground truth class label. Given this, we can train a classifier to differentiate between the two classes. For the purposes of this work we use a support vector machine (SVM) classifier.

4.1.1 Feature Set

In order to detect problematic corrections, we must identify dialogue behaviors that signify an error has occurred. We examined the dialogues in our development set to understand which dialogue behaviors are indicative of autocorrection mistakes. While in unproblematic dialogues users are able to converse freely, in problematic dialogues users must spend dialogue turns reestablishing common ground (Clark, 1996). Our feature set will focus on two common ways these attempts to establish common ground manifest themselves: as confusion and as attempts to correct the mistake.

Confusion Detection Features. Because autocorrection mistakes often result in misleading or semantically vacuous utterances, they are apt to confuse the reader, who will often express this confusion in the dialogue in order to gain clarification. These features examine the dialogue of the uncorrected user (the dialogue participant that reads the automatic correction mistake, not the one that was automatically corrected). One sign of confusion is the use of the question mark, so one feature captured the presence of question marks in the messages sent by the uncorrected user. Similarly, users may often use a block or repeated punctuation of show suprise or confusion, so another feature detected instances of repeated question marks and exclamation points (*???*, *!?!!*, etc.). When confused, readers will often retype the confusing word as a request for clarification (e.g., *Tussaud?*), or simply type "what?". We therefore include features that detect whether or not the corrected term appears in the first message sent by the uncorrected user after the correction mistake has occurred, and whether or not this message contains the word "what" as its own clause.

Clarification Detection Features. In contrast to utterances of confusion which are generally produced by the reader of the autocorrection mistake, clarification attempts are usually initiated by the user that was corrected. Several methods are used to indicate that the term shown by the system was incorrect. One convention is to use an asterisk (*) either before or after the corrected term:

A_1: Indeed Sid

A_2: Sir*

Another common method is to explicitly state what was intended using phrases such as "I meant to type", "that was supposed to say", etc. We included several features to capture these word patterns. Another method is to simply quickly reply with the word that was intended, so we included a feature to record whether the next message after the correction attempt contains only a single word. As users often feel the need to explain why the mistake occurred, we included a feature that recorded any mention or autocompletion, autocorrection or spell checking. One additional feature recorded whether or not the corrected user's dialogue contained words written in all capital letters.

Features	Precision	Recall	F-Measure
All Features	.861	.751	.803
-Confusion	.857	.725	.786
-Clarification	.848	.676	.752
-Dialogue	.896	.546	.679
Baseline	.568	1	.724

Table 1: Feature ablation results for identifying autocorrection mistakes

Dialogue Features. A few features captured information more closely tied to the flow of the dialogue than to confusion or clarification. In our development set, we observed a few common dialogue formats. In one, a correction mistake is immediately followed by confusion, which is then immediately followed by clarification. The dialogue in Figure 1 gives an example of this. To capture this form, we included a feature that recorded whether a confusion feature was present in the message immediately following the correction attempt and whether a clarification feature was present in the message immediate following the confusion message. Similarly, clarification attempts are often tried immediately after the mistake even if no confusion was present, so an additional feature captured whether the first message after the mistake by the corrected user was a clarification attempt. Additionally, we observed that autocorrection mistakes frequently appeared in the last word in a message, which was recorded by another binary feature. Finally, we recorded a count of how often the corrected term appeared in the dialogue.

4.1.2 Evaluation

To build our classifier we used the SVMLight[3] implementation of a support vector machine classifier with an RBF kernel. To ensure validity and account for the relatively small size of our dataset, evaluation was done via leave-one-out cross validation.

Results are shown in Table 1. A majority class baseline is given for comparison. As shown, using the entire feature set, the classifier achieves above baseline precision of 0.861, while still producing recall of 0.751.

[3]Version 6.02, http://svmlight.joachims.org/

Although F-measure is reported, it is unlikely that precision and recall should be weighted equally. Because one of the primary reasons we may wish to detect problematic situations is to automatically collect data to improve future performance by the autocorrection system, it is imperative that the data collected have high precision in order to reduce the amount of noise present in the collected dataset. Conversely, because problematic situation detection can monitor a user's input continuously for an indefinite period of time in order to collect more data, recall is less of a concern.

To study the effect of each feature source, we performed a feature ablation study, the results of which are included in Table 1. For each run, one feature type was removed and the model was retrained and reassessed. As shown, removing any feature source has a relatively small effect on the precision but a more substantial effect on the recall. Confusion detection features seem to be the least essential, causing a comparatively small drop in precision and recall values when removed. Removing the dialogue features results in the greatest drop in recall, returning only slightly above half of the problematic instances. However, as a result, the precision of the classifier is higher than when all features are used.

4.2 Identifying The Intended Term

Note that one purpose of the proposed self-assessment is to collect information online and thus make it possible to build better models. In order to do so, we need to know not only whether the system acted erroneously, but also what it should have done.Therefore, once we have extracted a set of problematic instances (and their corresponding dialogues), we must identify the term which the user was attempting to type when the system intervened. First, assume that via the classification task described in Section 4.1 we have identified a set of erroneous correction attempts, EC. Now the problem becomes, for every erroneous correction $c \in EC$, identify $w \in W$ such that $w = Intended(c)$. We model this as a ranking task, in which all $w \in W$ are ranked by their likelihood of being the intended term for c. We then predict that the top ranked word is the true intended term.

4.2.1 Feature Set

To support the above processing, we explored a diverse feature set, consisting of five different feature sources: contextual, punctuation, word form, similarity, and pattern features, crafted from an examination of our development data. Several of the features are related to those used in the initial classification phase. However, unlike our classification features, these feature focus on the relationship between the erroneous correction c and a candidate intended term w.

Contextual Features. Contextual features capture relevant phenomena at the discourse level. After an error is discovered by a user, they may type an intended term several times or type it in a message by itself in order to draw attention to it. These phenomena are captured in the *word repetition* and *only word* features. Another common discourse related correction technique is to retype some of the original context, which is captured by the *word overlap* feature. The *same author* feature indicates whether c and w are written by the same author. The author of the original mistake is likely the one to correct it, as they know their true intent.

Punctuation Features. Punctuation is occasionally used by text message writers to signal a correction of an earlier mistake, as noted previously. We included features to capture the presence of several different punctuation marks occurring before or after a candidate word such as *,?,!, etc. Each punctuation mark is represented by a separate feature.

Word Form Features. Word form features capture variations in how a word is written. One word form feature captures whether a word was typed in all capital letters, a technique used by text message writers to add emphasis. Two word form features were designed to capture words that were potentially unknown to the system, out-of-vocabulary words and words with letter repetition (e.g., "yaaay"). Because the system does not know these words, it will consider them misspellings and may attempt to change them to an in-vocabulary term.

Similarity Features. Our similarity feature captured the character level distance between a word changed by the system and a candidate intended word. We calculated the normalized levenshtein edit distance between the two words as a measure of sim-

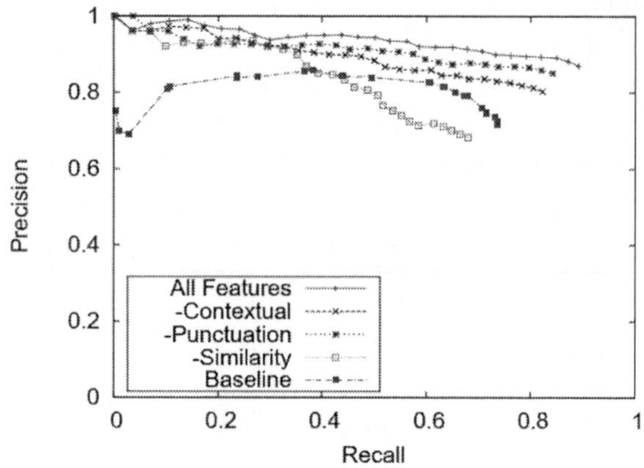

Figure 3: Precision-recall curve for intended term selection, including feature ablation results

ilarity.

Pattern Features. Pattern features attempt to capture phrases that are used to explicitly state a correction. These include phrases such as "(I) meant to write w", "(that was) supposed to say w", "(that) should have read w", "(I) wrote w", etc.

4.2.2 Evaluation

To find the most likely intended term for a correction mistake, we rank every candidate word in W and predict that the top ranked word is the intended term. We used the ranking mode of SVMlight to train our ranker. By thresholding our results to only trust predictions in which the ranker reported a high ranking value for the top term, we were able to examine the precision at different recall levels. That is, if the top ranked term does not meet the threshold, we simply do not predict an intended term for that instance, hurting recall but hopefully improving precision by removing instances that we are not confident about. This thresholding process may also allow the ranker to exclude instances in which the intended term does not appear in the dialogue, which are hopefully ranked lower than other cases. As before, evaluation was done via leave-one-out cross validation.

Results are shown in Figure 3. As a method of comparison we report a baseline that selects the word with the smallest edit distance as the intended term. As shown, using the entire feature set results in consistently above baseline performance.

As before, we are more concerned with the precision of our predictions than the recall. It is difficult to assess the appropriate precision-recall tradeoff without an in-depth study of autocorrection usage by text messagers. However, a few observations can be made from the precision-recall curve. Most critically, we can observe that the model is able to predict the intended term for an erroneous correction with high precision. Additionally, the precision stays relatively stable as recall increases, suffering a comparatively small drop in precision for an increase in recall. At its highest achieved recall values of 0.892, it maintains high precision at 0.869.

Feature ablation results are also reported in Figure 3. The most critical feature source was word similarity; without the similarity feature the performance is consistently worse than all other runs, even falling below baseline performance at high recall levels. This is not suprising, as the system's incorrect guess must be at least reasonably similar to the intended term, or the system would be unlikely to make this mistake. Although not as substantial as the similarity feature, the contextual and punctuation features were also shown to have a significant effect on overall performance. Conversely, removing word form or pattern features did not cause a significant change in performance (not shown in Figure 3 to enhance readability).

5 An End-To-End System

In order to see the actual effect of the full system, we ran it end-to-end, with the output of the initial erroneous correction identification phase used as input when identifying the intended term. Results are shown in Figure 4. The results of the intended term classification task on gold standard data from Figure 3 are shown as an upper bound.

As expected, the full end-to-end system produced lower overall performance than running the tasks in isolation. The end-to-end system can reach a recall level of 0.674, significantly lower than the recall of the ground truth system. However, the system still peaks at precision of 1, and was able to produce precision values that were competitive with the ground truth system at lower recall levels, maintaining a precision of above 0.90 until recall reached 0.396.

It is worth mentioning that the current evalua-

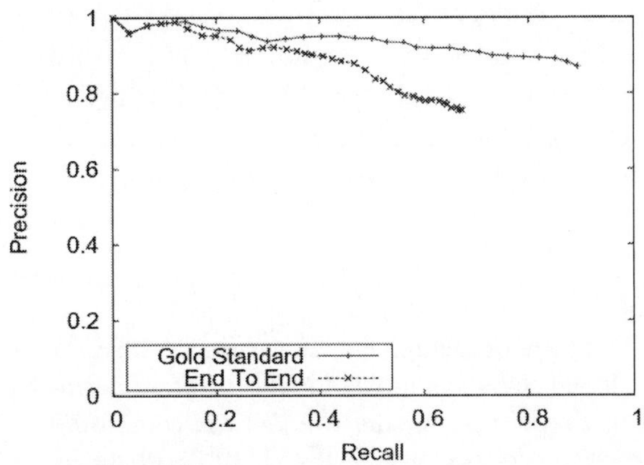

Figure 4: Precision-recall curve for the end-to-end system

tion is based on a balanced dataset with roughly even numbers of problematic and unproblematic instances. It is likely that in a realistic setting an autocorrection system will get many more instances correct than wrong, leading to a data distribution skewed in favor of unproblematic instances. This suggests that the evaluation given here may overestimate the performance of a self-assessment system in a real scenario. Although the size of our dataset is insufficient to do a full analysis on skewed data, we can get a rough estimate of the performance by simply counting false positives and false negatives unevenly. For instance, if the cost of mispredicting a unproblematic case as problematic is nine times more severe than the cost of missing a problematic case, this can give us an estimate of the performance of the system on a dataset with a 90-10 skew.

We examined the 90-10 skew case to see if the procedure outlined here was still viable. Results of an end-to-end system with this data skew are consistently lower than the balanced data case. The skewed data system can keep performance of 90% or better until it reaches 13% recall, and 85% or better until it reaches 22%. These results suggest that the system could still potentially be utilized. However, its performance drops off steadily, to the point where it would be unlikely to be useful at higher recall levels. We leave the full exploration of this to future work, which can utilize larger data sets to get a more accurate understanding of the performance.

6 Discussion

When an autocorrection system attempts a correction, it has perfect knowledge of the behavior of both itself and the user. It knows the button presses the user used to enter the term. It knows the term it chose as a correction. It knows the surrounding context; it has access to both the messages sent and received by the user. It has a large amount of the information it could use to improve its own performance, if only it were able to know when it made a mistake. The techniques described here attempt to address this critical system assessment step. Users may vary in the speed and accuracy at which they type, and input on small or virtual keyboards may vary between users based on the size and shape of their fingers. The self-assessment task described here can potentially facilitate the development of autocorrection models that are tailored to specific user behaviors.

Here is a brief outline of how our self-assessment module might potentially be used in building user-specific correction models. As a user types input, the system performs autocorrection by starting with a general model (e.g., for all text message users). Each time a correction is performed, the system examines the surrounding context to determine whether the correction it chose was actually what the user had intended to type. Over the course of several dialogues, the system builds a corpus of erroneous and non-erroneous correction attempts. This corpus is then used to train a user-specific correction model that is targeted toward system mistakes that are most frequent with this user's input behavior. The user-specific model is then applied on future correction attempts to improve overall performance. This monitoring process can be continued for months or even longer. The results from self-assessment will allow the system to continuously and autonomously improve itself for a given user (Baldwin and Chai, 2012).

In order to learn a user-specific model that is capable of improving performance, it is important that the self-assessment system provides it with training data without a large amount of noise. This suggests that the self-assessment system must be able to identify erroneous instances with high precision. Conversely, because the system can monitor user behavior indefinitely to collect more data, the overall recall may not be as critical. It might then be reasonable for a self-assessment system to be built to focus on collecting high accuracy pairs, even if it misses many system mistakes. Although a full examination of this tradeoff is left for future work which may more closely examine user input behavior, we feel that the results presented here show promise for collecting accurate data in a timely manner.

7 Conclusions and Future Work

This paper describes a novel problem of assessing its own correction performance for an autocorrection system based on dialogue between two text messaging users. Our evaluation results indicate that given a problematic situation caused by an autocorrection system, the discourse between users provides important cues for the system to automatically assess its own correction performance. By exploring a rich set of features from the discourse, our proposed approach is able to both differentiate between problematic and unproblematic instances and identify the term the user intended to type with high precision, achieving significantly above baseline performance. As discussed in Section 6, this self-assessment task can potentially be important for building user-specific autocorrection models to improve auto-correction performance.

The results presented in this paper represent a first look at autocorrection self-assessment. There are several areas of future work. There is certainly a need to examine additional feature sources. Because automatic correction mistakes can potentially create semantically vacuous utterances, a computational semantics based approach, similar to those used in semantic autocompletion systems (Hyvnen and Mkel, 2006), may prove fruitful. Additionally, although this work focused solely on dialogue-related features, future work may wish to take a closer look at the autocorrection mistakes themselves (e.g., which words are most likely to be mistakenly corrected, etc.). Lastly, although our current work demonstrated some potential, more thorough evaluation in realistic settings will allow a more full understanding of the impact and limitations of the proposed self-assessment approach.

Acknowledgments

This work was supported in part by Award #0957039 from the National Science Foundation and Award #N00014-11-1-0410 from the Office of Naval Research. The authors would like to thank the reviewers for their valuable comments and suggestions.

References

AiTi Aw, Min Zhang, Juan Xiao, and Jian Su. 2006. A phrase-based statistical model for sms text normalization. In *Proceedings of the COLING/ACL on Main conference poster sessions*, pages 33–40, Morristown, NJ, USA. Association for Computational Linguistics.

Tyler Baldwin and Joyce Chai. 2012. Towards online adaptation and personalization of key-target resizing for mobile devices. In *Proceedings of the 2012 ACM international conference on Intelligent User Interfaces*, IUI '12, pages 11–20, New York, NY, USA. ACM.

Eric Brill and Robert C. Moore. 2000. An improved error model for noisy channel spelling correction. In *ACL '00: Proceedings of the 38th Annual Meeting on Association for Computational Linguistics*, pages 286–293, Morristown, NJ, USA. Association for Computational Linguistics.

Surajit Chaudhuri and Raghav Kaushik. 2009. Extending autocompletion to tolerate errors. In *Proceedings of the 35th SIGMOD international conference on Management of data*, SIGMOD '09, pages 707–718, New York, NY, USA. ACM.

Monojit Choudhury, Rahul Saraf, Vijit Jain, Animesh Mukherjee, Sudeshna Sarkar, and Anupam Basu. 2007. Investigation and modeling of the structure of texting language. *Int. J. Doc. Anal. Recognit.*, 10(3):157–174.

Herbert H. Clark. 1996. *Using Language*. Cambridge University Press.

J.J. Darragh, I.H. Witten, and M.L. James. 1990. The reactive keyboard: a predictive typing aid. *Computer*, 23(11):41 –49, November.

Mark Dunlop and Andrew Crossan. 2000. Predictive text entry methods for mobile phones. *Personal and Ubiquitous Computing*, 4:134–143. 10.1007/BF01324120.

Julia Hirschberg, Diane J. Litman, and Marc Swerts. 2001. Identifying user corrections automatically in spoken dialogue systems. In *Proceedings of the Second Meeting of the North American Chapter of the Association for Computational Linguistics*.

Yijue How and Min yen Kan. 2005. Optimizing predictive text entry for short message service on mobile phones. In *in Human Computer Interfaces International (HCII 05). 2005: Las Vegas.*

Eero Hyvnen and Eetu Mkel. 2006. Semantic autocompletion. In *Proceedings of the first Asia Semantic Web Conference (ASWC 2006*, pages 4–9. Springer-Verlag.

Mark D. Kernighan, Kenneth W. Church, and William A. Gale. 1990. A spelling correction program based on a noisy channel model. In *Proceedings of the 13th conference on Computational linguistics*, pages 205–210, Morristown, NJ, USA. Association for Computational Linguistics.

Catherine Kobus, François Yvon, and Géraldine Damnati. 2008. Normalizing SMS: are two metaphors better than one ? In *Proceedings of the 22nd International Conference on Computational Linguistics (Coling 2008)*, pages 441–448, Manchester, UK, August. Coling 2008 Organizing Committee.

Gina-Anne Levow. 1998. Characterizing and recognizing spoken corrections in human-computer dialogue. In *Proceedings of the 36th Annual Meeting of the Association for Computational Linguistics and 17th International Conference on Computational Linguistics, Volume 1*, pages 736–742, Montreal, Quebec, Canada, August. Association for Computational Linguistics.

Diane Litman, Julia Hirschberg, and Marc Swerts. 2006. Characterizing and predicting corrections in spoken dialogue systems. *Comput. Linguist.*, 32:417–438, September.

I. Scott MacKenzie and Kumiko Tanaka-Ishii. 2007. *Text Entry Systems: Mobility, Accessibility, Universality (Morgan Kaufmann Series in Interactive Technologies).* Morgan Kaufmann Publishers Inc., San Francisco, CA, USA.

I. Scott MacKenzie. 2002. Kspc (keystrokes per character) as a characteristic of text entry techniques. In *Proceedings of the 4th International Symposium on Mobile Human-Computer Interaction*, Mobile HCI '02, pages 195–210, London, UK. Springer-Verlag.

Tim Paek, Kenghao Chang, Itai Almog, Eric Badger, and Tirthankar Sengupta. 2010. A practical examination of multimodal feedback and guidance signals for mobile touchscreen keyboards. In *Proceedings of the 12th international conference on Human computer interaction with mobile devices and services*, MobileHCI '10, pages 365–368, New York, NY, USA. ACM.

Kristina Toutanova and Robert Moore. 2002. Pronunciation modeling for improved spelling correction. In *40th Annual Meeting of the Association for Computational Linguistics(ACL 2002).*

Casey Whitelaw, Ben Hutchinson, Grace Y Chung, and Ged Ellis. 2009. Using the Web for language independent spellchecking and autocorrection. In *Proceedings of the 2009 Conference on Empirical Methods in Natural Language Processing*, pages 890–899, Singapore, August. Association for Computational Linguistics.

Translation-Based Projection for Multilingual Coreference Resolution

Altaf Rahman and **Vincent Ng**
Human Language Technology Research Institute
University of Texas at Dallas
Richardson, TX 75083-0688
{altaf,vince}@hlt.utdallas.edu

Abstract

To build a coreference resolver for a new language, the typical approach is to first coreference-annotate documents from this target language and then train a resolver on these annotated documents using supervised learning techniques. However, the high cost associated with manually coreference-annotating documents needed by a supervised approach makes it difficult to deploy coreference technologies across a large number of natural languages. To alleviate this corpus annotation bottleneck, we examine a translation-based projection approach to multilingual coreference resolution. Experimental results on two target languages demonstrate the promise of our approach.

1 Introduction

Noun phrase (NP) coreference resolution is the task of determining which NPs (or *mentions*) refer to each real-world entity in a document. Recent years have witnessed a surge of interest in multilingual coreference resolution. For instance, the ACE 2004/2005 evaluations and SemEval-2010 Shared Task 1 have both involved coreference resolution in multiple languages. As evidenced by the participants in these evaluations, the most common approach to building a resolver for a new language is *supervised*, which involves training a resolver on coreference-annotated documents from the target language. Although supervised approaches work reasonably well, they present a challenge to deploying coreference technologies across a large number of natural languages. Specifically, for each new language of interest, one has to hire native speakers of the language to go through the labor-intensive, time-consuming process of hand-annotating a potentially large number of documents with coreference annotation before a supervised resolver can be trained.

One may argue that a potential solution to this *corpus annotation bottleneck* is to employ an *unsupervised* or *heuristic* approach to coreference resolution, especially in light of the fact that they have recently started to rival their supervised counterparts. However, by adopting these approaches, we are simply replacing the corpus annotation bottleneck by another, possibly equally serious, bottleneck, the *knowledge acquisition bottleneck*. Specifically, in these approaches, one has to employ knowledge of the target language to design coreference rules (e.g., Mitkov (1999), Poon and Domingos (2008), Raghunathan et al. (2010)) or sophisticated generative models (e.g., Haghighi and Klein (2007,2010), Ng (2008)) to combine the available knowledge sources.

One could argue that designing coreference rules and generative models may not be as time-consuming as annotating a large coreference corpus. This may be true for a well-studied language like English, where we can easily compose a rule that disallows coreference between two mentions if they disagree in number and gender, for instance. However, computing these features may not be as simple as we hope for a language like Chinese: the lack of morphology complicates the determination of number information, and the fact that most Chinese first names are used by both genders makes gender determination difficult. The difficulty in accurately computing features translates to difficulties in composing coreference rules: for example, the aforementioned rule involving gender and number agreement, as well as rules that implement traditional linguistic constraints on coreference, may no longer be accurate and desirable to have if the features involved cannot be accurately computed. Consequently, we believe that research in multilingual coreference resolution will continue to be dominated by supervised approaches.

Given the high cost of annotating data with coreference chains, it is crucial to explore methods for obtaining annotated data in a cost-effective manner. Motivated in part by this observation, we examine one such method that has recently shown promise for a variety of NLP tasks, translation-based projection, which is composed of three steps. To coreference annotate a text in the target language, we (1) machine-translate it to a resource-rich language (henceforth the *source* language); (2) automatically produce the desired linguistic annotations (which in our case are coreference annotations) on the translated text using the linguistic tool developed for the source language (which in our case is a coreference resolver) ; and (3) project the annotations from the source language to the target language.

Unlike supervised approaches, this projection approach does not require any coreference-annotated data from the target language. Equally importantly, unlike its unsupervised counterparts, this approach does not require that we have any linguistic knowledge of the target language. In fact, we have no knowledge of the target languages we employ in our evaluation. One of our goals is to examine the feasibility of building a coreference resolver for a language for which we have no coreference-annotated data *and* no linguistic knowledge of the language.

Recall that we view projection as an approach for alleviating the corpus annotation bottleneck, not as a solution to the multilingual coreference resolution problem. In fact, though rarely emphasized in previous work on applying projection, we note that projection alone cannot be used to solve multilingual NLP problems, including coreference resolution. The reason is that every language has its own idiosyncrasies with respect to linguistic properties, and projection simply cannot produce annotations capturing those properties that are specific to the target language. Our goal in this paper is to explore the extent to which projection, which does not require that we have any knowledge of the target language, can push the limits of multilingual coreference resolution. If our results indicate that projection is a promising approach, then the automatic coreference annotations it produces can be used to augment the manual annotations that capture the properties specific to the target language, thus alleviating the corpus annotation bottleneck.

2 Related Work on Projection

The idea of projecting annotations from a resource-rich language to a resource-scarce language was originally proposed by Yarowsky and Ngai (2001) and subsequently developed by others (e.g., Resnik (2004), Hwa et al. (2005)). These projection algorithms assume as input a parallel corpus for the source language and the target language. Given the recent availability of machine translation (MT) services on the Web, researchers have focused more on translated-based projection rather than acquiring a parallel corpus themselves. MT-based projection has been applied to various NLP tasks, such as part-of-speech tagging (e.g., Das and Petrov (2011)), mention detection (e.g., Zitouni and Florian (2008)), and sentiment analysis (e.g., Mihalcea et al. (2007)).

There have been two initial attempts to apply projection to create coreference-annotated data for a resource-poor language, both of which involve projecting hand-annotated coreference data from English to Romanian via a parallel corpus. Specifically, Harabagiu and Maiorano (2000) create an English-Romanian corpus by manually translating the MUC-6 corpus into Romanian and manually project the English annotations to Romanian. On the other hand, Postolache et al. (2006) apply a word alignment algorithm to project the hand-annotated English coreference chains and then manually fix the projection errors on the Romanian side. Hence, their goal is different from ours in at least two respects. First, while they employ significant knowledge of the target language to create a *clean* coreference corpus, we examine the quality of coreference-annotated data created via an entirely automatic process, determining quality by the performance of the resolver trained on the data. Second, unlike ours, neither of these attempts is at the level of defining a technology for projection annotations that can potentially be deployed across a large number of languages without coreference-annotated data.

3 Translation-Based Projection

Recall that our MT-based projection approach to coreference resolution is composed of three steps. Given a text in the target language, we (1) machine-translate the text to the source language; (2) automatically produce coreference annotations on the translated text using a coreference resolver developed for the source language; and (3) project the annotations from the source language to the target language. In this section, we employ our approach in three settings, which differ in terms of the extent to which linguistic taggers (e.g., chunkers and named entity (NE) recognizers) for the target language are available. The goal is to examine whether these linguistic taggers can be profitably exploited to improve the performance of the projection approach. Below we assume that English and French are our source and target languages, respectively.

3.1 Setting 1: No French Taggers Available

In this setting, we assume that we do not have access to any French tagger that we can exploit to improve projection. Hence, all we can do is to employ the three steps involved in the projection approach as described at the beginning of this section to create coreference-annotated data for French. Specifically, we translate a French text to an English text using GoogleTranslate[1], and create coreference chains for the translated English text using Reconcile[2] (Stoyanov et al., 2010). To project mentions from English to French, we first align the English and French words in each pair of parallel sentences, and then project the English mentions onto the French text using the alignment. However, since the alignment is noisy, the French words to which the words in the English mention are aligned may not form a contiguous text span. To fix this problem, we follow Yarowsky and Ngai (2001) and use the smallest text span that covers all the aligned French words to create the French mention.[3] We process the English mentions in the text in a left-to-right manner, as processing the mentions sequentially enables us to ensure that an English mention is not mapped to a French text span that has already been mapped to by a previously-processed English mention.[4]

To align English and French words, we trained a word alignment model using GIZA++[5] (Och and Ney, 2000) on a parallel corpus comprising the English-French section of Europarl[6] (Koehn, 2005) as well as all the French texts (and their translated English counterparts) for which we want to automatically create coreference chains. Following common practice, we stemmed the parallel corpus using the Porter stemmer (Porter, 1980) in order to reduce data sparseness. However, even with stemming, we found that many English words were not aligned to any French words by the resulting alignment model. This would prevent many English mentions from being projected to the French side, potentially harming the recall of the French coreference annotations. To improve alignment coverage, we retrained the alignment model by supplying GIZA++ with an English-French bilingual dictionary that we assembled using three online dictionary databases: OmegaWiki, Wiktionary, and Universal Dictionary. Furthermore, if a word w appears in both the English side and the French side in a pair of parallel sentences, we assume that it has the same orthographic form in both languages and hence we augment the bilingual dictionary with the entry (w, w).

Note that the use of a supervised resolver like Reconcile does *not* render our approach supervised, since we can replace it with any resolver, be it supervised, heuristic, or unsupervised. In other words, we treat the resolver built for the source language as a black box that can produce coreference annotations.

3.2 Setting 2: Mention Extractor Available

Next, we consider a comparatively less resource-scarce setting where a French mention extractor is available for identifying mentions in a French text[7], and describe how we can modify the projection approach to exploit this French mention extractor.

Given a French text we want to coreference-

[1]See `http://translate.google.com`.

[2]See `http://www.cs.utah.edu/nlp/reconcile`. We use the resolver pre-trained on the Wolverhampton corpus.

[3]Other methods for projecting mentions can be found in Postolache et al. (2006), for example.

[4]While we chose to process the mentions in a left-to-right manner, any order of processing the mentions would work.

[5]See `http://code.google.com/p/giza-pp/`.

[6]See `http://www.statmt.org/europarl/`.

[7]Mention extraction is a term used in Automatic Content Evaluation to refer to the task of determining the NPs that a coreference system should consider in the resolution process.

annotate, we first translate it to English using GoogleTranslate and align the French and English words using a French-to-English word alignment algorithm. Next, we identify the mentions in the French text using the given mention extractor, and project them onto the English text using the NP projection algorithm described in Setting 1. Finally, we run Reconcile on the resulting English mentions to generate coreference chains for the translated text, and project these chains back to the French text.

As explained before, the performance of this method is sensitive to the accuracy of the NP projection algorithm in recovering the English mentions, which in turn depends on the accuracy of the word alignment algorithm. To make this method more robust to noisy word alignment, we make a modification to it. Rather than running Reconcile on the mentions produced by the NP projection algorithm, we use Reconcile to identify the mentions directly from the translated text. After that, we create a mapping between the English mentions produced by the NP projection algorithm and those produced by Reconcile using a small set of heuristics.

Specifically, let M_P be the set of mentions identified by the NP projection algorithm and M_R be the set of mentions identified by Reconcile. For each mention m_P in M_P, we map it to a mention in M_R that shares the same right boundary. If this fails, we map it to a mention that covers its entire text span. If this fails again, we map it to a mention that has a partial overlap with it. If this still fails, we assume that m_P is not found by Reconcile and simply add m_P to M_R. As before, we process the mentions in M_P in a left-to-right manner in order to ensure that no two mentions in M_P are mapped to the same Reconcile mention. Finally, we discard all mentions in M_R that are not mapped by any mention in M_P, and present M_R to Reconcile for coreference resolution. Since we now have a 1-to-1 mapping between the Reconcile mentions and the French mentions, projecting the coreference results back to French is trivial.

It may not be immediately clear why the exploitation of the mention extractor in this setting may yield better coreference annotations than those produced in Setting 1. To see the reason, recall that one source of errors inherent in a projection approach is word alignment errors. In Setting 1, when we tried to project English mentions to the French text, word alignment errors would adversely affect the ability of the NP projection algorithm to correctly define the boundaries of the French mentions. Since coreference performance depends crucially on the ability to correctly identify mentions (Stoyanov et al., 2009), the presence of word alignment errors implies that the resulting French coreference annotations could score poorly even if the English coreference annotations produced by Reconcile were of high quality. In the current setting, on the other hand, we reduce the sensitivity of coreference performance to word alignment errors via the use of the French mention extractor to produce more accurate French mention boundaries.

3.3 Setting 3: Additional Taggers Available

Finally, we consider a setting that is the least resource-scarce of the three. We assume that in addition to a French mention extractor, we have access to other French linguistic taggers (e.g., syntactic and semantic parsers) that will allow us to generate the linguistic features needed to train a French resolver on the projected coreference annotations.

Specifically, assume that *Test* is a set of French texts we want to coreference-annotate, and *Training* is a set of French texts that is disjoint from *Test* but is drawn from the same domain as *Test*.[8] To annotate the *Test* texts, we perform the following steps. First, we employ the French mention extractor in combination with the method described in Setting 2 to automatically coreference-annotate the *Training* texts. Next, motivated by Kobdani et al. (2011), we train a French coreference resolver on the automatically coreference-annotated training texts, using the features provided by the available linguistic taggers. Finally, we apply the resolver to generate coreference chains for each *Test* text.

Two questions arise. First, is this method necessarily better than the one described in Setting 2? We hypothesize that the answer is affirmative: not only can this method exploit the knowledge about the target language provided by the additional linguistic taggers, but the resulting coreference resolver may allow us to generalize from the (noisily labeled) data and make this method more robust to the noise in-

[8]We assume that it is easy to assemble the *Training* set, since unlabeled texts are typically easy to collect in practice.

herent in the projected coreference annotations than the previously-described methods. Second, is this method necessarily better than projection via a parallel corpus? Like the first question, this is also an empirical question. Nevertheless, one reason why this method is intuitively better is that it ensures that the training and test documents are drawn from the same domain. On the other hand, when projecting annotations via a parallel corpus, we may encounter a domain mismatch problem if the parallel corpus and the test documents come from different domains, and the coreference resolver may not work well if it is trained and tested on different domains.

4 Coreference Resolution System

To train the coreference resolver employed in Setting 3 in the previous section, we need to derive linguistic features from the documents in the target language. In our experiments, we employ the coreference data sets produced as part of the SemEval-2010 shared task on Coreference Resolution in Multiple Languages. The shared task organizers have made publicly available six data sets that correspond to six European languages. Each data set comprises not only *training* and *test* documents that are coreference-annotated, but also a number of word-based linguistic features from which we derive mention-based linguistic features for training a resolver. In this section, we will describe how this resolver is trained and then applied to generate coreference chains for unseen documents.

Training the coreference classifier. As our coreference model, we train a *mention-pair* model, which is a classifier that determines whether two mentions are co-referring or not (e.g., Soon et al. (2001), Ng and Cardie (2002)).[9] Each instance $i(m_j, m_k)$ corresponds to m_j (a candidate antecedent) and m_k (the mention to be resolved), and is represented by a set of 23 features shown in Table 1. As we can see, each feature is either *relational*, capturing the relation between m_j and m_k, or *non-relational*, capturing the linguistic property of m_k. The possible values of a relational feature (except LEXICAL) are **C** (compatible), **I** (incompatible), and **NA** (the comparison cannot be made due to missing data). For a non-relational feature, we refer the reader to the data sets for the list of possible values.[10]

We follow Soon et al.'s (2001) method for creating training instances. Specifically, we create (1) a positive instance for each anaphoric mention m_k and its closest antecedent m_j; and (2) a negative instance for m_k paired with each of the intervening mentions, $m_{j+1}, m_{j+2}, \ldots, m_{k-1}$. The classification associated with a training instance is either positive or negative, depending on whether the two mentions are coreferent in the associated text. To train the classifier, we use SVM^{light} (Joachims, 1999).

Applying the classifier to a test text. After training, the classifier is used to identify an antecedent for a mention in a test text. Specifically, each mention, m_k, is compared to each preceding mention, m_j, from right to left, and m_j is selected as the antecedent of m_k if the pair is classified as coreferent. The process terminates as soon as an antecedent is found for m_k or the beginning of the text is reached.

5 Evaluation

We evaluate our MT-based projection approach for each of the three settings described in Section 3.

5.1 Experimental Setup

Data sets. We use the Spanish and Italian data sets from the SemEval-2010 shared task on Coreference Resolution in Multiple Languages.[11] Each data set is composed of a training set and a test set. Statistics of these data sets are shown in Table 2.

	Spanish	Italian
Training Set Statistics		
number of mentions	78779	24853
number of non-singleton clusters	48681	18376
number of singleton clusters	37336	15984
Test Set Statistics		
number of mentions	14133	13394
number of non-singleton clusters	8789	9520
number singleton clusters	6737	8288

Table 2: Statistics of the data sets.

[9] Note that any supervised coreference model can be used, such as an entity-mention model (e.g., Luo et al. (2004), Yang et al. (2008)) or a ranking model (e.g., Denis and Baldridge (2008), Rahman and Ng (2009)).

[10] The data sets can be downloaded from `http://stel.ub.edu/semeval2010-coref/datasets`.

[11] Note, however, that our approach is equally applicable to other languages evaluated in the shared task.

Features describing m_k, the mention to be resolved		
1	NUM_WORDS	the number of words in m_k
2	COARSE_POS	the coarse POS of m_k (see "PoS" in Recasens et al. (2010))
3	FINE_POS	the fine-grained POS of m_k (see "PoS type" in Recasens et al. (2010))
4	NE	the named entity tag of m_k if m_k is a named entity; else NA
5	SR	the semantic role of m_k
6	GRAMROLE	the grammatical role of m_k
7	NUMBER	the number of m_k
8	GENDER	the gender of m_k
9	PERSON	the person of m_k (e.g., first, second, third) if it is pronominal; else NA
Features describing the relationship between m_j, a candidate antecedent and m_k, the mention to be resolved		
10	CS_STR_MATCH	determines whether the mentions are the same string
11	CI_STR_MATCH	same as feature 10, except that case differences are ignored
12	CS_SUBSTR_MATCH	determines whether one mention is a substring of the other
13	CI_SUBSTR_MATCH	same as feature 12, except that case differences are ignored
14	NUMBER_MATCH	determines whether the mentions agree in number
15	GENDER_MATCH	determines whether the mentions agree in gender
16	COARSE_POS_MATCH	determines whether the mentions have the same coarse POS tag
17	FINE_POS_MATCH	determines whether the mentions have the same fine-grained POS tag
18	ROLE_MATCH	determines whether the mentions have the same grammatical role
19	NE_MATCH	determines whether both are NEs and have the same NE type
20	SR_MATCH	determines whether the mentions have the same semantic role
21	ALIAS	determines whether one mention is an abbreviation or an acronym of the other
22	PERSON_MATCH	determines whether both mentions are pronominal and have the same person
23	LEXICAL	the concatenation of the heads of the two mentions

Table 1: Feature set for coreference resolution.

Scoring programs. To score the output of a coreference resolver, we employ four scoring programs, MUC (Vilain et al., 1995), B^3 (Bagga and Baldwin, 1998), ϕ_3-CEAF (Luo, 2005), and BLANC (Recasens and Hovy, 2011), which were downloaded from the shared task website (see Footnote 10).

Gold-standard versus regular settings. The format of each data set follows that of a typical CoNLL shared task data set. In other words, each row corresponds to a word in a document; moreover, all but the last column contain the linguistic features computed for the words, and the last column stores the coreference information. Some of the features were computed via automatic means, but some were extracted from human annotations. Given this distinction, the shared task organizers defined two evaluation settings: in the *regular* setting, only the columns that were computed automatically can be used to derive coreference features for classifier training, and results should be reported on system mentions; on the other hand, in the *gold-standard* setting, only the columns that were extracted from human annotations can be used to derive coreference features, and results should be reported on true mentions. We will present results corresponding to both settings. Note that these two settings should not be confused with the three settings described in Section 3.

Mention extraction. Recall that Settings 2 and 3 both assume the availability of a mention extractor for extracting mentions in the target language. In our experiments, we extract mentions using two methods. First, we assume the availability of an oracle mention extractor that will enable us to extract *true mentions* (i.e., gold-standard mentions) directly from the test texts. Second, we employ simple heuristics to automatically extract *system mentions*.

Since coreference performance is sensitive to the accuracy of mention extraction (Stoyanov et al., 2009), we experiment with several heuristic methods for extracting system mentions for both Spanish and Italian. According to our cross-validation experiments on the training data, the best heuristic for extracting Spanish mentions is different from that for extracting Italian mentions. Specifically, for

Spanish, the best heuristic method operates as follows. First, it extracts all the syntactic heads (i.e., the word tokens whose gold dependency labels are SUBJ, PRED, or GMOD). Second, for each syntactic head, it identifies the smallest text span containing the head and all of its dependents, and creates a mention from this text span. For Italian, on the other hand, the best heuristic simply involves creating one mention for each gold NE. The reason why this simple heuristic works well is that most of the Italian mentions are NEs, owing to the fact that abstract NPs and pronouns are also annotated as NEs in the Italian data set. When evaluated on the test set, the heuristic-based mention extractor achieves F-scores of 80.2 (78.4 recall, 82.1 precision) for Spanish and 92.3 (85.9 recall, 99.6 precision) for Italian.

5.2 Results and Discussion

5.2.1 Supervised Results

Our supervised systems. While our MT-based projection approach is unsupervised (i.e., it does not rely on any coreference annotations from the target language), it would be informative to see the performance of the *supervised* resolvers, since their performance can be viewed as a crude upper bound on the performance of our unsupervised systems. Specifically, we train a mention-pair model on the training set using the 23 features shown in Table 1 and SVM^{light} as the underlying learning algorithm[12], and apply the resulting model in combination with Soon et al.'s clustering algorithm (see Section 4) to generate coreference chains for the test texts.

Results on the test sets, reported in terms of recall (R), precision (P), and F-score (F) computed by the four coreference scorers, are shown in the first two rows of Table 3 (Spanish) and Table 4 (Italian). For convenience, we summarize a system's performance using a single number, which is shown in the last column (Average) and is obtained by taking a simple average of the F-scores of the four scorers. More specifically, row 1, which is marked with a 'G', and row 2, which is marked with a 'R', show the results obtained under the *gold-standard* setting and the *regular* setting, respectively.

As we can see, under the gold-standard setting, the supervised resolver achieves an average F-score of 66.1 (Spanish) and 65.9 (Italian). Not surprisingly, under the regular setting, its average F-score drops statistically significantly[13] to 54.6 (Spanish) and 63.4 (Italian).[14]

Best systems in the shared task. To determine whether the upper bounds established by our supervised systems are reasonable, we show the results of the best-performing resolvers participating in the shared task for both languages under the gold-standard and regular settings in rows 3 and 4 of Tables 3 and 4. Since none of the participating systems achieved the best score over all four scorers, we report the performance of the system that has the highest average F-score. According to the shared task website, TANL-1 (Attardi et al., 2010) achieved the best average F-score in the regular setting for Spanish, whereas SUCRE (Kobdani and Schütze, 2010) outperformed others in the remaining settings.

Comparing these best shared task results with our supervised results in rows 1 and 2, we see that our average F-score for Spanish/Gold is worse than its shared task counterpart by 0.7 points, but otherwise our system outperforms in other settings w.r.t. average F-score, specifically by 5.0 points for Spanish/Regular (due to a better MUC F-score), by 3.4–4.7 points for Italian (due to better CEAF, B^3, and BLANC scores). Overall, these results suggest that the scores achieved by our systems are at least as competitive as the best shared task scores.

5.2.2 Unsupervised Results

Next, we evaluate our projection algorithm.

Setting 1. Results of our approach, when applied in Setting 1, are shown in row 5 of Tables 3 and 4. Given that it has to operate under the severe condition where no linguistic taggers are available for the target language, it is perhaps not surprising to see that its performance is significantly worse than that of its supervised counterparts.

Setting 2. Recall that this setting is less resource-scarce than Setting 1 in that a mention extractor for

[12] All SVM learning parameters in this and other experiments in this paper are set to their default values.

[13] All significance test results in this paper are obtained using one-way ANOVA, with p set to 0.05.

[14] Separately, we determined whether the performance drop in the regular setting is due to the use of automatically computed features or the use of system mentions, and found that the latter was almost entirely responsible for the drop.

		CEAF			MUC			B^3			BLANC			Average
	Approach	R	P	F	R	P	F	R	P	F	R	P	F	F
1	Supervised (G)	68.8	68.8	68.8	58.2	52.6	55.3	76.5	75.1	75.8	62.9	66.1	64.3	66.1
2	Supervised (R)	57.4	60.1	58.8	41.0	46.3	43.5	57.6	64.8	61.0	53.9	65.0	55.2	54.6
3	Shared task best (G)	69.8	69.8	69.8	52.7	58.3	55.3	75.8	79.0	77.4	67.3	62.5	64.5	66.8
4	Shared task best (R)	58.6	60.0	59.3	14.0	48.4	21.7	56.6	79.0	66.0	51.4	74.7	51.4	49.6
5	Setting 1	35.9	52.9	42.8	10.8	48.7	17.7	30.5	63.9	41.3	51.2	72.6	48.7	37.6
6	Setting 2 (True)	65.6	65.6	65.6	16.8	64.7	26.7	64.3	96.9	77.3	52.8	78.8	54.6	56.1
7	Setting 2 (System)	53.2	55.7	54.4	13.4	58.5	21.8	49.8	79.7	61.3	50.7	75.5	49.5	46.8
8	Setting 3 (G)	65.9	65.9	65.9	48.1	45.2	46.6	72.3	72.6	72.5	60.1	61.4	60.7	61.4
9	Setting 3 (R)	55.3	55.3	55.3	34.1	41.6	37.5	55.1	63.6	59.0	53.8	62.1	54.9	51.7

Table 3: Results for Spanish

		CEAF			MUC			B^3			BLANC			Average
	Approach	R	P	F	R	P	F	R	P	F	R	P	F	F
1	Supervised (G)	74.5	74.5	74.5	31.8	67.4	43.2	74.4	93.6	82.9	58.4	79.6	62.9	65.9
2	Supervised (R)	73.7	74.3	74.0	31.9	68.0	43.4	60.8	92.5	73.3	58.4	79.6	62.9	63.4
3	Shared task best (G)	66.0	66.0	66.0	48.1	42.3	45.0	76.7	76.9	76.8	54.8	63.5	56.9	61.2
4	Shared task best (R)	57.1	66.2	61.3	50.1	50.7	50.4	63.6	79.2	70.6	55.2	68.3	57.7	60.0
5	Setting 1	17.0	26.0	20.6	8.1	28.5	12.6	14.1	30.5	19.3	50.1	62.9	32.9	21.4
6	Setting 2 (True)	73.3	73.3	73.3	14.2	60.6	23.0	72.9	96.8	83.2	51.9	77.9	53.2	58.2
7	Setting 2 (System)	60.4	70.1	64.9	17.2	68.2	27.5	59.3	97.1	73.6	52.0	82.9	53.4	54.9
8	Setting 3 (G)	64.3	64.3	64.3	28.3	63.3	39.1	65.3	87.4	74.8	55.1	74.7	57.5	58.9
9	Setting 3 (R)	61.1	62.9	61.9	29.5	63.2	40.2	60.3	84.1	70.2	55.3	72.9	58.3	57.7

Table 4: Results for Italian

the target language is available. Results of our algorithm, when operating under Setting 2 using true mentions and system mentions, are shown in rows 6 and 7 of Tables 3 and 4, respectively. In comparison to the results for Setting 1, we see that the F-scores obtained under Setting 2 increase significantly, regardless of (1) the scoring programs and (2) whether true mentions or system mentions are used. These results provide evidence for our earlier hypothesis that our projection algorithm can profitably exploit the linguistic knowledge about the target language that is available to it. In particular, the mention extractor helps make our approach less sensitive to word alignment and NP projection errors.

In comparison to our supervised results in rows 1 and 2, our algorithm still lags behind by about 8–10 points in average F-score. However, this should not be surprising, since our algorithm is unsupervised. Looking closer at the results, we can see that the performance lag by our approach can be attributed to its lower recall: in general, the lag in MUC recall appears to be more acute than that in B^3 and CEAF recall. Since MUC only scores non-singleton clusters wheres B^3 and CEAF score both singleton and non-singleton clusters, these results suggest that our approach is better at identifying singleton clusters than recovering coreference links.

Setting 3. Finally, we evaluate our approach in a setting where it has access to all the information available to our supervised resolvers, except for the gold standard coreference annotations on the training sets. Specifically, our approach uses projected coreference annotations to train a resolver on the training texts, whereas the supervised resolvers do so using gold-standard annotations.

Comparing Settings 2 and 3 with respect to true mentions (rows 6 and 8 of Tables 3 and 4), we see mixed results. According to MUC and BLANC, the resolvers in Setting 3 are significantly better than those in Setting 2 for both languages. According to B^3, the resolvers in Setting 2 are significantly better than those in Setting 3 for both languages. According to CEAF, the Spanish resolvers in Setting 3 are significantly better than their counterparts in Setting 2, but the opposite is true for the Italian resolvers.

To understand these somewhat contradictory performance trends, let us first note that the dramatic increase in the MUC F-score can be attributed to large gains in MUC recall. This suggests that the classifiers being trained in Setting 3 have enabled the discovery of additional coreference links. In other words, there are benefits to be obtained just by learning over noisy coreference annotations, a result that we believe is quite interesting. However, not all of these newly discovered coreference links are correct. The fact that some scoring programs (e.g., B^3) are more sensitive to spurious coreference links than the others (e.g., MUC) explains these mixed results.

Nevertheless, according to average F-score, the resolvers in Setting 3 perform significantly better than those in Setting 2 for both languages: F-score increases by 5.3 points for Spanish and 0.7 points for Italian. Similar trends can be observed when comparing the two settings w.r.t. system mentions (rows 7 and 9 of Tables 3 and 4): F-score increases by 4.9 points for Spanish and 2.8 points for Italian.

While our Setting 3 results still underperform the supervised results in rows 1 and 2, we can see that they achieve 93–94% of the average F-scores of the supervised Spanish resolvers and 89–91% of the average F-scores of the supervised Italian resolvers. Importantly, recall that our approach achieves this level of performance without relying on any gold-standard coreference annotations in Spanish and Italian, and we believe that these results demonstrate the promise of our MT-based projection approach.

Since these results suggest that our approach cannot be successfully applied without MT services, a parallel corpus for learning a word alignment model, and a mention extractor for the target language, a natural question is: to what extent do these requirements limit the applicability of our approach? While it is the case that our approach cannot be applied to a truly resource-scarce language, it can be applied to the numerous Indian and East European languages for which the aforementioned requirements are satisfied but coreference-annotated data is not readily available.

6 Conclusions and Future Work

We explored the under-investigated yet challenging task of performing coreference resolution for a language for which we have no coreference-annotated data and no linguistic knowledge of the language. Our translation-based projection approach has the flexibility to exploit any available knowledge about the target language. In experiments with Spanish and Italian, we obtained promising results: our approach achieved around 90% of the performance of a supervised resolver when only a mention extractor for the target language was available. We believe that this approach has the potential to allow coreference technologies to be deployed across a larger number of languages than is currently possible, and that this is just the beginning of a new line of work.

To gain additional insights into our approach, we plan to pursue several directions. First, we will isolate the impact of each factor that adversely affects its performance, including errors in projection, translation, and coreference resolution in the resource-rich language. Second, we will perform an empirical comparison of two approaches to projecting coreference annotations, our translation-based approach and Camargo de Souza and Orasan's (2011) approach, where annotations are projected via a parallel corpus. Third, rather than translate from the target to the source language, we will examine whether it is better to translate all the coreference-annotated data available in the source language to the target language, and train a coreference model for the target language on the translated data. Fourth, since the success of our projection approach depends heavily on the accuracies of machine translation as well as coreference resolution in the source language, we will determine whether their accuracies can be improved via an ensemble approach, where we employ multiple MT engines and multiple coreference resolvers. Finally, we plan to employ our approach to alleviate the corpus-annotation bottleneck, specifically by using the annotated data it produces to augment the manual coreference annotations that capture the specific properties of the target language.

Acknowledgments

We thank the three anonymous reviewers for their detailed and insightful comments on an earlier draft of the paper. This work was supported in part by NSF Grants IIS-0812261 and IIS-1147644. Any opinions, findings, or conclusions expressed in this paper are those of the authors and do not necessarily reflect the views or official policies of NSF.

References

Giuseppe Attardi, Maria Simi, and Stefano Dei Rossi. 2010. TANL-1: Coreference resolution by parse analysis and similarity clustering. In *Proceedings of the 5th International Workshop on Semantic Evaluation*, pages 108–111.

Amit Bagga and Breck Baldwin. 1998. Entity-based cross-document coreferencing using the vector space model. In *Proceedings of the 36th Annual Meeting of the Association for Computational Linguistics and the 17th International Conference on Computational Linguistics*, pages 79–85.

Jennifer Camargo de Souza and Constantine Orasan. 2011. Can projected chains in parallel corpora help coreference resolution? In *Anaphora Processing and Applications*, pages 59–69. Springer.

Dipanjan Das and Slav Petrov. 2011. Unsupervised part-of-speech tagging with bilingual graph-based projections. In *Proceedings of the 49th Annual Meeting of the Association for Computational Linguistics: Human Language Technologies*, pages 600–609.

Pascal Denis and Jason Baldridge. 2008. Specialized models and ranking for coreference resolution. In *Proceedings of the 2008 Conference on Empirical Methods in Natural Language Processing*, pages 660–669.

Aria Haghighi and Dan Klein. 2007. Unsupervised coreference resolution in a nonparametric bayesian model. In *Proceedings of the 45th Annual Meeting of the Association for Computational Linguistics*, pages 848–855.

Aria Haghighi and Dan Klein. 2010. Coreference resolution in a modular, entity-centered model. In *Proceedings of Human Language Technologies: The 2010 Annual Conference of the North American Chapter of the Association for Computational Linguistics*, pages 385–393.

Sanda Harabagiu and Steven Maiorano. 2000. Multilingual coreference resolution. In *Proceedings of the Sixth Applied Natural Language Processing Conference*, pages 142–149.

Rebecca Hwa, Philip Resnik, Amy Weinberg, Clara Cabezas, and Okan Kolak. 2005. Bootstrapping parsers via syntactic projection across parallel texts. *Natural Language Engineering*, 11(3):311–325.

Thorsten Joachims. 1999. Making large-scale SVM learning practical. In Bernhard Schölkopf, Christopher Burges, and Alexander Smola, editors, *Advances in Kernel Methods – Support Vector Learning*, pages 44–56. MIT Press, Cambridge, MA.

Hamidreza Kobdani and Hinrich Schütze. 2010. SUCRE: A modular system for coreference resolution. In *Proceedings of the 5th International Workshop on Semantic Evaluation*, pages 92–95.

Hamidreza Kobdani, Hinrich Schütze, Michael Schiehlen, and Hans Kamp. 2011. Bootstrapping coreference resolution using word associations. In *Proceedings of the 49th Annual Meeting of the Association for Computational Linguistics: Human Language Technologies*, pages 783–792.

Philipp Koehn. 2005. Europarl: A parallel corpus for statistical machine translation. In *Proceedings of MT Summit X*.

Xiaoqiang Luo, Abe Ittycheriah, Hongyan Jing, Nanda Kambhatla, and Salim Roukos. 2004. A mention-synchronous coreference resolution algorithm based on the Bell tree. In *Proceedings of the 42nd Annual Meeting of the Association for Computational Linguistics*, pages 135–142.

Xiaoqiang Luo. 2005. On coreference resolution performance metrics. In *Proceedings of Human Language Technology Conference and Conference on Empirical Methods in Natural Language Processing*, pages 25–32.

Rada Mihalcea, Carmen Banea, and Janyce Wiebe. 2007. Learning multilingual subjective language via cross-lingual projections. In *Proceedings of the 45th Annual Meeting of the Association for Computational Linguistics*, pages 976–983..

Ruslan Mitkov. 1999. Multilingual anaphora resolution. *Machine Translation*, 14(3–4):281–299.

Vincent Ng and Claire Cardie. 2002. Improving machine learning approaches to coreference resolution. In *Proceedings of the 40th Annual Meeting of the Association for Computational Linguistics*, pages 104–111.

Vincent Ng. 2008. Unsupervised models for coreference resolution. In *Proceedings of the 2008 Conference on Empirical Methods in Natural Language Processing*, pages 640–649.

Franz Josef Och and Hermann Ney. 2000. Improved statistical alignment models. In *Proceedings of the 38th Annual Meeting of the Association for Computational Linguistics*.

Hoifung Poon and Pedro Domingos. 2008. Joint unsupervised coreference resolution with Markov Logic. In *Proceedings of the 2008 Conference on Empirical Methods in Natural Language Processing*, pages 650–659.

Martin F. Porter. 1980. An algorithm for suffix stripping. *Program*, 14(3):130–137.

Oana Postolache, Dan Cristea, and Constantin Orasan. 2006. Transferring coreference chains through word alignment. In *Proceedings of the Fifth International Conference on Language Resources and Evaluation*, pages 889–892.

Karthik Raghunathan, Heeyoung Lee, Sudarshan Rangarajan, Nate Chambers, Mihai Surdeanu, Dan Jurafsky, and Christopher Manning. 2010. A multi-pass sieve for coreference resolution. In *Proceedings of the 2010 Conference on Empirical Methods in Natural Language Processing*, pages 492–501.

Altaf Rahman and Vincent Ng. 2009. Supervised models for coreference resolution. In *Proceedings of the 2009 Conference on Empirical Methods in Natural Language Processing*, pages 968–977.

Marta Recasens and Eduard Hovy. 2011. BLANC: Implementing the Rand Index for coreference evaluation. *Natural Language Engineering*, 17(4):485–510.

Marta Recasens, Lluís Màrquez, Emili Sapena, M. Antònia Martí, Mariona Taulé, Véronique Hoste, Massimo Poesio, and Yannick Versley. 2010. Semeval-2010 task 1: Coreference resolution in multiple languages. In *Proceedings of the 5th International Workshop on Semantic Evaluation*, pages 1–8.

Philip Resnik. 2004. Exploiting hidden meanings: Using bilingual text for monolingual annotation. In *Proceedings of the 5th International Conference on Computational Linguistics and Intelligent Text Processing*, pages 283–299.

Wee Meng Soon, Hwee Tou Ng, and Daniel Chung Yong Lim. 2001. A machine learning approach to coreference resolution of noun phrases. *Computational Linguistics*, 27(4):521–544.

Veselin Stoyanov, Nathan Gilbert, Claire Cardie, and Ellen Riloff. 2009. Conundrums in noun phrase coreference resolution: Making sense of the state-of-the-art. In *Proceedings of the Joint Conference of the 47th Annual Meeting of the ACL and the 4th International Joint Conference on Natural Language Processing of the AFNLP*, pages 656–664.

Veselin Stoyanov, Claire Cardie, Nathan Gilbert, Ellen Riloff, David Buttler, and David Hysom. 2010. Coreference resolution with reconcile. In *Proceedings of the ACL 2010 Conference Short Papers*, pages 156–161.

Marc Vilain, John Burger, John Aberdeen, Dennis Connolly, and Lynette Hirschman. 1995. A model-theoretic coreference scoring scheme. In *Proceedings of the Sixth Message Understanding Conference*, pages 45–52.

Xiaofeng Yang, Jian Su, Jun Lang, Chew Lim Tan, and Sheng Li. 2008. An entity-mention model for coreference resolution with inductive logic programming. In *Proceedings of the 46th Annual Meeting of the Association for Computational Linguistics: Human Language Technologies*, pages 843–851.

David Yarowsky and Grace Ngai. 2001. Inducing multilingual POS taggers and NP bracketers via robust projection across aligned corpora. In *Proceedings of the Second Meeting of the North American Chapter of the Association for Computational Linguistics*, pages 200–207.

Imed Zitouni and Radu Florian. 2008. Mention detection crossing the language barrier. In *Proceedings of the 2008 Conference on Empirical Methods in Natural Language Processing*, pages 600–609.

Exploring Semi-Supervised Coreference Resolution of Medical Concepts using Semantic and Temporal Features

Preethi Raghavan*, Eric Fosler-Lussier*, and Albert M. Lai†
*Department of Computer Science and Engineering
†Department of Biomedical Informatics
The Ohio State University, Columbus, Ohio, USA
{raghavap, fosler}@cse.ohio-state.edu, albert.lai@osumc.edu

Abstract

We investigate the task of medical concept coreference resolution in clinical text using two semi-supervised methods, co-training and multi-view learning with posterior regularization. By extracting semantic and temporal features of medical concepts found in clinical text, we create conditionally independent data views; co-training MaxEnt classifiers on this data works almost as well as supervised learning for the task of pairwise coreference resolution of medical concepts. We also train MaxEnt models with expectation constraints, using posterior regularization, and find that posterior regularization performs comparably to or slightly better than co-training. We describe the process of semantic and temporal feature extraction and demonstrate our methods on a corpus of case reports from the New England Journal of Medicine and a corpus of patient narratives obtained from The Ohio State University Wexner Medical Center.

1 Introduction

The clinical community creates and uses a variety of semi-structured and unstructured electronic textual documents that include medical reports such as admission notes, progress notes, pathology reports, radiology reports and hospital discharge summaries. The documents, collectively termed *clinical narratives*, account for various medical conditions, procedures, diagnoses and assessments in a patient's medical history. Researchers have investigated ways in which clinical text can be automatically processed for enabling access to relevant information for physicians and health researchers (Embi and Payne, 2009). One application is to support patient recruitment into clinical trials (research studies that try to answer scientific questions to find better ways to prevent, diagnose, or treat a disease) by matching patient characteristics against eligibility criteria (Raghavan and Lai, 2010). While there has been significant efforts to move to structured data collection, clinical narratives remain a critical data source for these tasks.

Extracting structured information from unstructured clinical text using natural language processing (NLP) is complicated by the distinct clinical reporting sub-language characterized by incomplete sentences and domain specific abbreviations (Friedman et al., 2002). The large number of clinical narratives generated per patient, over the years, along with redundant information within and across narratives, further adds to the complexity of using information structured using NLP. There is a tendency to copy and edit parts of an old clinical narrative whenever a new one is created, thus leading to redundant information in clinical narratives of a patient. Furthermore, since different types of clinical narratives are created for different purposes, certain narratives may summarize information from various other, at times older, clinical narratives. All of this makes the task of automatically processing unstructured clinical narratives significantly difficult. However, the ability to resolve medical concept coreferences helps deal with redundant information within and across clinical narratives and thus produce a unique list of medical concepts in the patient's clinical history.

We investigate the task of resolving references to

the same medical concept in the clinical narratives of a patient using supervised and semi-supervised methods. Our main contributions are as follows:

1. Since manual coreference annotation of patient narratives is a slow and expensive process and publicly available datasets are difficult to acquire, we study the application of semi-supervised methods, co-training and using expectation constraints with posterior regularization, to medical concept coreference resolution (MCCR).
2. We work with the hypothesis that if two medical concepts have the same meaning and have occurred at the same time, there is a very high probability that they corefer. Based on this hypothesis, we explain extraction of semantic and temporal feature sets that are effectively used for MCCR.
3. We propose a method to associate medical concepts with time durations centered around admission and discharge dates of the patient using CRFs.
4. With the help of corpora created from the New England Journal of Medicine (NEJM) and actual patient narratives obtained from the medical center, we demonstrate that the semi-supervised methods perform comparably with supervised learning for pairwise MCCR using a MaxEnt classifier.

2 Related Work

Free-text reports form a significant portion of the information content in a patient's medical record. There is great need for tools that can structure the information in clinical text for use in various studies studies such as clinical trials, quality assessment of healthcare delivery in institutions, and public health research. Researchers have been investigating ways in which clinical free-text can be structured to transform the information content in a clinical narrative into a representation suitable for computational analysis (Ananiadou et al., 2004). Medical NLP systems like Mayo's cTakes (Savova et al., 2010), IBM's MedKAT,[1] and MedLEE (Chiang et al., 2010), have components specifically trained or designed for the clinical domain, to support tasks such as named entity recognition. Previous attempts at learning temporal relations between medical events in clinical text include work by Jung et al. (2011) and Zhou et al. (2006). Gaizauskas et al. (2006) learn the temporal relations *before, after, is_included* between events from a corpus of clinical text much like the event-event relation tlink learning in Timebank (Pustejovsky et al., 2003). A comprehensive survey of temporal reasoning in medical data is provided by Zhou and Hripcsak (2007). Chapman et al. (2011) discuss barriers to NLP development in the clinical domain.

Coreference resolution is a well-studied problem in computational linguistics (Ng, 2010; Raghunathan et al., 2010). Supervised machine learning algorithms have been previously used for noun phrase coreference resolution with fairly good results (Soon et al., 2001; Raghunathan et al., 2010). Recently, the i2b2 challenge[2] on coreference resolution examined coreference resolution in clinical data. The problem addressed in our paper is similar to the task described in the i2b2 challenge.[3] Besides the i2b2 challenge, there has not been significant work in MCCR. This may be due to various privacy concerns and the efforts required to anonymize and annotate massive amounts of patient narratives. Zheng et al. (2011) review heuristic-based, supervised and unsupervised methods for coreference resolution in the context of the clinical domain. He (2007) studied coreference resolution in discharge summaries, treating coreference resolution as a binary classification problem and investigated critical features for coreference resolution for entities that fall into five medical semantic categories commonly appearing in discharge summaries. However, we focus on feature extraction to determine the similarity between medical concepts, both in terms of meaning and time of occurrence, for resolving coreferences within and across all types of clinical narratives.

A disadvantage of supervised machine learning approaches is the need for an unknown amount of annotated training data for optimal performance. Researchers then began to experiment with weakly supervised machine learning algorithms such as co-training (Blum and Mitchell, 1998). Muller et al. (2002) investigate the practical applicability of co-training for the task of building a classifier for coreference resolution and observed that the results were

[1] `https://cabig-kc.nci.nih.gov/Vocab/KC/index.php/OHNLP`

[2] `https://www.i2b2.org/NLP/Coreference/`

[3] `https://www.i2b2.org/NLP/Coreference/assets/CoreferenceGuidelines.pdf`

mostly negative for their dataset.

Ganchev et al. (2010) propose a posterior regularization framework for weakly supervised learning to derive a multi-view learning algorithm. Multi-view methods typically begin by assuming that each view alone can yield a good predictor. Under this assumption, we can regularize the models from each view by constraining the amount by which we permit them to disagree on unlabeled instances. In the proposed approach, they train a model for each view, and use constraints that the models should agree on the label distribution.

We investigate the applicability of these two weakly supervised methods to the task of MCCR using semantic and temporal views. Savova et al. (2011) discuss the creation of a corpus for coreference resolution in the clinical narrative. We annotate a corpus of clinical narratives to tag medical concepts, temporal relations, and coreference information. We use this corpus as a gold standard to evaluate the proposed approach to resolving coreferences between medical concepts in clinical text.

To summarize, we study the problem of intra and cross-narrative coreference resolution on longitudinal patient data using relatedness between medical concepts in terms of semantics and time. Further, we importantly demonstrate that this task gives us reasonable results even when modeled as a semi-supervised problem. Creating annotated clinical corpora is tedious, time consuming, and costly, as it requires experts with medical domain knowledge. Thus, the ability to train semi-supervised models with limited labeled data for MCCR would be of tremendous value.

3 Problem Description

Coreference resolution in clinical text refers to the problem of identifying all medical concepts that refer to the same medical concept. Medical concepts are medical entities, events or states associated with the patient's medical condition and healthcare. These include medical conditions, drugs administered, diseases, procedures and lab tests as well as normal health situations like pregnancy affecting the patient's health. The task of MCCR is similar to noun phrase coreference resolution. However, medical concepts are not restricted to noun phrases. For instance, the actions *cauterize* and *cauterization* are both considered medical concepts.

To make the task of identifying medical concepts from clinical text more deterministic, any contiguous group of words that have a direct or close match in the Unified Medical Language System (UMLS) Metathesaurus[4] is considered a medical concept. The UMLS includes a large Metathesaurus of concepts and terms from many biomedical vocabularies and a lexicon which contains syntactic, morphological, and orthographic information for biomedical and common words in the English language.

Problem Formulation. Consider a corpus of clinical narratives, where multiple clinical narratives are associated with each patient. If P_i, $i \in \{1, 2, ..., n\}$ where n is the number of patients in corpus, then for each P_i, we have a set of associated clinical narratives. Each clinical narrative in turn has a set of medical concepts. Thus, each P_i has a set of associated medical concepts, $M = \{M_1, M_2, M_3, ..\}$ that occur within each clinical narrative as well as across clinical narratives for that P_i. We study the problem of MCCR of all medical concepts in M for each P_i.

4 Semantic and Temporal Features

We extract features based on semantic and temporal relatedness for each pair of medical concepts. Semantic relatedness measures closeness between medical concepts in terms of their meaning. This is quantified by measuring distance between medical events in the UMLS Metathesaurus graph structure (Xiang et al., 2011). Temporal relatedness measures the closeness between medical concepts in terms of when they occurred. This is achieved by first, learning to assign every medical concept to a time-bin, and then using the time-bin as a feature for learning to resolve coreferences. Extracting semantic and temporal features helps identify conditionally independent views of the data for co-training classifiers. As previously noted by Nigam and Ghani (2000), it is hard to identify conditionally independent views for real-data problems. However, we believe there are no natural dependencies between the semantic and temporal feature sets. While semantic features help identify synonymous medical concepts, that alone may not guarantee coreference. Medical con-

[4] https://uts.nlm.nih.gov/home.html

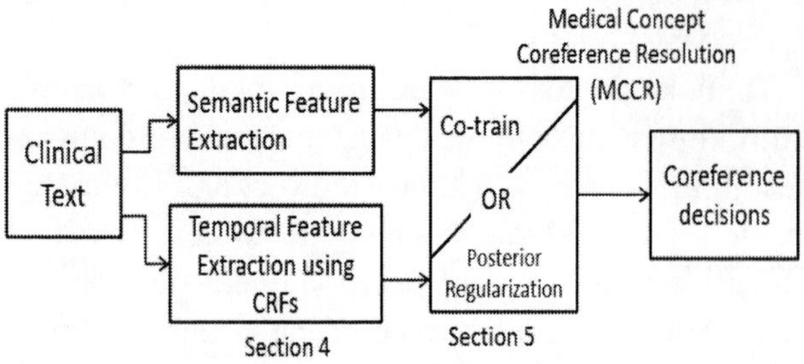

Figure 1: MCCR pipeline: Extract semantic and temporal features from clinical text to train MaxEnt classifiers for medical concept coreference resolution using 1) Co-training or 2) Posterior Regularization

cepts that are similar in meaning, but dissimilar in terms of their time of occurrence, most probably do not corefer. Similarly, medical concepts that occur during the same time duration but are dissimilar in terms of meaning, most probably do not corefer.

Semantic Relatedness. We leverage the UMLS to derive a semantic relatedness score between medical concepts. The UMLS codifies concepts found in various medical vocabularies (e.g., ICD[5] and SNOMED-CT[6]) and includes relationships between various concepts. The medical concepts and their relationships are modeled in a graph structure. We use the k-Neighborhood decentralization method (kDLS) (Xiang et al., 2011) to index and transitively traverse associated relations between concept unique identifiers (CUIs) in the UMLS graph. The UMLS uses semantic relations to mark the available links between two concepts. Around 2,404,937 CUIs and 15,333,246 links between them are seen in the full UMLS graph structure. The kDLS method is shown to outperform both breadth-first and depth-first search in terms of speed and various other measures in finding important information, such as reachability, distance, and a summary of paths, between two concepts in the UMLS graph structure. The relation between two concepts M_j (denoted by x) and M_k (denoted by y) is measured as follows.

$$R(x,y) = \sum_{p \in D_{(x,y)}} \frac{1}{\gamma^{length(p)-1}} + \sum_{q \in D_{(y,x)}} \frac{1}{\gamma^{length(q)-1}}$$

where $D(x,y)$ is the set of paths from x to y and $D(y,x)$ is the set of paths from y to x obtained using the kDLS method, excluding paths with length equal to 1. In order to make the measurement between a medical concepts unbiased against the available links in the UMLS that directly connect them, the paths with length being 1 between them are not counted. Each path's contribution to the relation score $R(x,y)$ is determined by its length and γ. γ is varied between 1 to 50; if γ is set to 1, then all paths contribute equally to R irrespective of their lengths. When γ increases, more weight will be placed on the short paths as opposed to the long paths. Xiang et al. (2011) observe several fold enrichment values when γ is varied between 5 and 15.

Besides traversing the UMLS graph structure using the kDLS method to obtain a similarity score between medical concepts, we also measure similarity between medical concepts by taking into account the surrounding context. We do so by measuring the KL-divergence between the sentences to which the medical concepts belong. In order to avoid the possibility of an empty set when calculating the intersection of the probability distributions, we use a smoothing method that makes the probability distributions sum to 1 (Brigitte, 2003).

Another important semantic feature is the type of relation between the medical concepts. This feature is calculated by first computing the stemmed word overlap between the medical concepts and deriving features based on exact and partial matches between the word stems of the medical concepts. If there is no exact or partial match between the concepts, we query the UMLS to check if the stem of one of the medical concepts occurs in the UMLS definition or atoms of the other medical event. An atom is the smallest unit of naming within the UMLS. A medical concept in UMLS represents a single meaning and contains all atoms in the UMLS that express that meaning in any way, whether formal or casual, verbose or abbreviated. All of the atoms within a concept are synonymous.

Besides the described features, we also include the UMLS semantic category of each medical concept and the WordNet[7] similarity score between sentences containing the medical concept.

Temporal Relatedness. Clinical text is frequently characterized by temporal expressions co-

[5] http://www.cdc.gov/nchs/icd.htm

[6] http://www.ihtsdo.org/snomed-ct/

[7] http://wordnet.princeton.edu/

occurring with medical concepts (Zhou and Hripcsak, 2007). For instance, *two days ago*, fever started *4 days before* rash, *July 10th, 2010* etc. The ability to associate medical concepts with temporal expressions helps order medical concepts and determine potential temporal overlap between them. This in turn could be a powerful discriminatory feature in MCCR. Consider the medical concept *chest pain* that occurs multiple times in a clinical narrative. If these mentions of *chest pain* have occurred at the same time, there is a possibility that they all refer to the same instance of the medical concept *chest pain*.

Instead of relying on implicit temporal references that may or may be evident from the clinical narrative, we focus on temporal expressions that are found in most clinical narratives. We do so by leveraging structural properties of clinical narratives such as section information and explicit temporal information such as admission and discharge dates, to learn to assign medical concepts to time periods we refer to as time-bins.

We now proceed to explain the process of assigning medical concepts to time-bins using CRFs. Clinical narratives are usually formatted with a structured header with information that includes the patient admission and discharge date. Clinical narratives are also typically divided into sections. Sections represent a logical, and at times, temporal grouping of information in the narrative. Sections such as "history of present illness," "physical examination," "review of systems," "impression," and "assessment plan" tend to occur in a certain order within each clinical narrative. Thus, section transitions may indicate a temporal pattern for medical concepts across those sections. For example, "past medical history" (before admission), followed by "findings on admission" (on admission), followed by "physical examination" (after admission). Sections of certain types may also exhibit certain temporal patterns. A "history of present illness" section may start with diseases and diagnoses 30 years ago and then proceed to talk about them in the context of a medical condition that happened few years ago and finally describe the patient's condition on admission. Given the temporal patterns within sections and at section transitions, it works well to treat the list of medical concepts from each clinical narrative as a sequence (considering them in narrative order) and learning to label them with a corresponding time-bin. We define the following sequence of time-bins centered around admission and discharge, {*way before admission, before admission, on admission, after admission, after discharge*}.

We model the problem of assigning medical concepts to time-bins as a sequence labeling task using a CRF where we predict labels from the set {*way before admission, before admission, on admission, after admission, after discharge*} as a sequence Y predicted from the detected medical concepts X. CRFs use two types of features in classification, state features and transition features. State features consider relating the label y (time-bin) of a single vertex (medical concept) to features corresponding to a medical concept x, and are given by,

$$S(x, y, i) = \sum_j \lambda_j s_j(y, x, i)$$

Transition features consider the mutual dependence of labels y_{i-1} and y_i (dependence between the time-bins of the current and previous medical event in the sequence) and are given by,

$$T(x, y, i) = \sum_k \mu_k t_k(y_{i-1}, y_i, x, i)$$

Above, s_j is a state feature function, and λ_j is its associated weight and t_k is a transition function, and μ_k is its associated weight. In contrast to the state function, the transition function takes as input the current label as well as the previous label, in addition to the data.

Example state features include indicator features based on verbs patterns in the same sentence as that of the medical concept, last verb before the medical concept, and type of clinical narrative. We also include position of medical event in the narrative as well as within each section, the temporal expressions and dates co-occurring with the medical concept as features and the difference between these dates and the admission date on each clinical narrative. Example transition features include section transitions based on the sections under which the medical concept occurs, UMLS relatedness score between the previous and current medical concept, difference in verb patterns between the previous and current medical concept, difference in dates (if any) between the dates co-occurring with the previous and current medical concept.

In order to enable feature extraction for this learning task, we use the following heuristic-based algorithm to automatically identify sections and associate medical concepts with them.

1. Extract lines that are all upper-case, and longer than a word, from all narratives in corpus. They mostly correspond to section titles.
2. Derive the stem of each word in the title using a Porter stemming algorithm[8] and sort stemmed titles by frequency. If two or more words in the title overlap, they are considered the same. This gives us a candidate set of section titles.
3. When parsing a clinical narrative, and encountering a stemmed ngram matching a section title from the frequent list, all subsequent sentences are associated with that section until a new section title is encountered. If an exact match is not found, we allow partially matching ngrams to be considered as section titles.

Along with the time-bin that are learned using the process described above, dates and temporal expressions extracted from the annotations in our corpus are also used as temporal features. The list of features extracted for the task of MCCR include the following:

1. Verb pattern in the sentence in which the medical concept occurs.
2. Last verb before the medical concept in the same sentence.
3. Type of clinical narrative.
4. Section under which the medical concept is mentioned.
5. Position of the medical concept.
6. Dates that fall in the same sentence as the medical concept.
7. Difference between admission date and the date in the same sentence as the clinical narrative.
8. The learned time-bin of each medical concept. We also derive features based on the overlapping in time-bins for the medical concept pair and the nature of time-bin (past, present, future).
9. Difference in verb patterns in the sentences of the medical concept pair.
10. Difference in dates between the medical concept pair.
11. UMLS relatedness score between the medical concept pair and all the UMLS related and other features described previously in the semantic relatedness section.

When applying CRFs to the problem of assigning medical concepts to time-bins, an observation sequence is medical concepts in the order in which they appear in a clinical narrative, and the state sequence is the corresponding label sequence of time bins. Thus, given a sequence of concepts in narrative order $\{M_1, M_2, M_3, ..\}$, we learn a corresponding label sequence of time-bins {*way before admission, before admission, on admission, after admission, after discharge*}. The learned label sequence is now used as part of the temporal feature set in co-training and posterior regularization for MCCR.

5 Weakly Supervised Learning

5.1 Co-training

We co-train two MaxEnt classifiers, one each on the semantic features f_s and temporal features f_t of the data, to classify pairs of medical concepts as *corefer* or *no-corefer* in a semi-supervised fashion. We use the co-training algorithm proposed by Blum and Mitchell (1998).

The assumption here is that each feature set contains sufficient information to train a model for classification of medical concepts. Consider the concept pair, {*renal inflammation, posterior uveitis*} that corefer. The semantic view for this concept pair may not strongly indicate coreference. The "UMLS relation type" feature indicates that the two concepts are not similar in meaning. However, both concepts are mapped to the same time-bin *after admission*. Thus, the time-bin along with features extracted based on explicit temporal expressions co-occurring with the medical concepts indicate a coreference between the pair of medical concepts. Similarly, the semantic view is confident about confident about the coreference of certain medical concept pairs which do not occur in the same time-bin. The classifiers trained on each view complement each other in the learning process. Thus, we can leverage the predictions made by each classifier on the unlabeled dataset to augment the training data of both classifiers.

The co-training algorithm is shown in Table 1. We set a threshold for an unlabeled sample to be added

[8] http://tartarus.org/martin/PorterStemmer/

Function coTrain
Repeat till all unlabeled data is labeled.

1. Train classifier c_1 on t_{fs} to obtain model m_1
2. Train classifier c_2 on t_{ft} to obtain model m_2
3. Use m_1 to classify a subset of unlabeled data and update the training data as, t_{fs}.subset = $\{u_{subset1}$, *predicted label*$\}$ *iff classifier confidence* $>$ *1/number of labels*
4. Use m_2 to classify a subset of unlabeled data and update the training data as, t_{ft}.subset = $\{u_{subset2}$, *predicted label*$\}$ *iff classifier confidence* $>$ *1/number of labels*
5. $t_{fs} = t_{fs} + t_{ft}$.subset + $\{u_{subset1}$, *predicted label*$\}$
6. $t_{ft} = t_{ft} + t_{fs}$.subset + $\{u_{subset2}$, *predicted label*$\}$

Table 1: Co-training algorithm for the binary pairwise classification task of MCCR (Blum and Mitchell, 1998).
c = classifier, u = unlabeled data.
$u_{subset1}, u_{subset2}$ = subsets of unlabeled data.
$u_{subset1}$ and $u_{subset2}$ are mutually exclusive.
$F = \{f_s, f_t\}$ is the features space divided into conditionally independent semantic and temporal feature sets.
$t_{fs} = \{f_s, l\}$ training data consisting of semantic features of a medical concept pair along with class label.
$t_{ft} = \{f_t, l\}$ training data consisting of temporal features of a medical concept pair along with class label.

into the labeled pool. An unlabeled sample is labeled in a particular iteration, if *classifier confidence* $>$ *1/number of labels*. In the next iteration, randomly pick a subset of unlabeled samples and label all samples in this subset. This could include samples that have already been labeled in previous iterations. A label is assigned in a subsequent iteration if: the sample was previously labeled OR if *classifier confidence* $>$ *threshold*. The parameters in this algorithm are the number of iterations, the pool size of examples selected from the unlabeled set in each iteration and the number of labeled examples added at each iteration to the labeled data pool. Similar to Blum and Mitchell (1998), we update the pool size by $2p + 2n$ in each iteration, where p is the number of medical pairs that corefer and n is the number of medical concept pairs that do not corefer.

5.2 MaxEnt with Posterior Regularization

The next semi-supervised learning method applied to MCCR is MaxEnt with posterior regularization using expectation constraints (Ganchev et al., 2010). This method incorporates prior knowledge directly on the output variables during learning. The prior knowledge is expressed as inequalities on the expected value under the posterior distribution of user-defined constraint features. Thus, posterior regularization incorporates side-information into unsupervised estimation in the form of constraints on the model's posteriors. It is similar to the EM algorithm during learning, but it solves a problem similar to Maximum Entropy inside the E-Step to enforce the constraints.

Posterior regularization is used to derive a multi-view learning algorithm while specifying constraints that the models should agree on the label distribution. We train MaxEnt models based on two views of the data, semantic and temporal. This method starts by considering the setting of complete agreement where there is a common desired output for the two models and each of the two views is sufficiently rich to predict labels accurately. The search is restricted to model pairs p_1, p_2 that satisfy $p_1(y|x) \approx p_2(y|x)$, where p_1 and p_2 each define a distribution over labels. The product distribution $p_1(y_1)p_2(y_2)$ is considered and constraint features are defined such that the proposal distribution $q(y_1, y_2)$ will have the same marginal for y_1 and y_2. There is one constraint feature defined for each label y given by, $\phi_y(y_1, y_2) = \delta(y_1 = y)\delta(y_2 = y)$, where $\delta(.)$ is the 0-1 indicator function. The constraint set $Q = q : Eq[\phi] = 0$ requires that the marginals over the two output variables are identical $q(y_1) = q(y_2)$. An agreement between two models is defined as $agree(p_1, p_2) = argmin\ KL(q(y_1, y_2)||p_1(y_1)p_2(y_2))$ | Eq [ϕ] = 0.

In the semantic feature set, we convert the following feature (described in Section 4) into expectation constraints. The type of relation between the pair of medical concepts, is derived from matching the word stems and querying the UMLS definition and atoms of the medical concepts. Based on the relation between the medical concepts (i.e., partial match, complete match, UMLS definition match, UMLS atom match, and no match), we indicate the probability of label distribution coref and no-coref. If the relation turns out to be no match, there is a high probability that the medical concepts do not corefer. In the temporal feature set, we convert the features based on time-bins of the medical concepts in the pair into expectation constraints.

Class(time-bin)	Precision	Recall
after discharge	96.05	62.53
before admission	94.02	92.44
on admission	33.25	75.16
way before admission	50.42	66.72
after admission	93.62	99.14

Table 2: Sequence tagging of medical concepts with time-bins using CRFs.

Class	NEJM		Clinical Narratives	
	Precision	Recall	Precision	Recall
coref	79.24	94.53	74.81	88.33
no-coref	86.71	90.62	83.92	94.86

Table 3: Supervised learning for MCCR.

6 Experimental Setup

6.1 Corpus Annotation

Annotation of clinical text is a time consuming and costly process. Many annotation efforts have used physicians to annotate the data. Instead, we use annotators that are students or recently graduated students from diverse clinical backgrounds with varying levels of clinical experience. In spite of this diversity, the annotation agreement across our team of annotators is high; all annotators agreed on 89.5% of the events and our overall inter-annotator Cohen's kappa statistic (Conger, 1980) for medical events was 0.865. The annotators mark medical concepts, coereference chains and temporal expressions in the clinical narratives and the NEJM case reports. They also map each medical concept to a UMLS CUI.

6.2 Feature Extraction

The first step involves extraction of semantic and temporal features for the annotated medical concepts, as described in Section 4 from both corpora. The semantic relatedness scores are computed using the kDLS (Xiang et al., 2011) method to calculate the relationship between concepts in the UMLS with value of γ set to 7. The type of relation between medical concepts is derived by matching word stems in each medical concept using the Lucene[9] implementation of the Porter stemming algorithm. We query the latest release (UMLS 2011AB) of the UMLS Metathesaurus for finding a match between medical concept and the UMLS definition or UMLS atoms. The WordNet similarity score is computed using Java API for WordNet Searching (JAWS).[10]

Explicit temporal expressions annotated in the corpora are included in our temporal feature set. Medical concepts in the NEJM are mostly described temporally relative to the patient's admission. Temporal expressions like "2 years before admission" and "3 weeks before admission" are common. Hence, we use a heuristic-based algorithm to associate medical concepts with explicit temporal expressions in the NEJM corpus. The algorithm parses case reports and identifies the temporal expressions anchored to admission. All medical concepts following such a temporal expression are anchored to it until a new temporal expression is encountered. Over 88% of the medical concept-temporal expression associations done with the algorithm above is accurate when compared against the NEJM gold standard.

As described in Section 4, we apply sequence tagging using a CRF to assign medical concepts in clinical narratives to time-bins. We use the implementation of CRF in Mallet,[11] trained by Limited-Memory BFGS for our experiments. We use the Stanford POS tagger[12] to identify verbs and derive verb patterns. The dataset for the task of assigning medical concepts to time-bins consisted of 1613 medical concepts. We used a 60-40 train-test split to train a CRF using a sequence of medical concepts and observed an overall accuracy of 92%. The precision and recall values for each time-bin class is indicated in Table 2. The percentage of medical concepts that fall under "way before admission" and "on admission" are less than 5%, affecting the learning accuracy of those classes. When modeled as a multi-class classification task using MaxEnt, we achieve around 86% accuracy.

7 MCCR Results and Discussion

We perform the following experiments for pairwise MCCR: 1) Supervised learning with a MaxEnt classifier, using the combined semantic and temporal feature set, 2) Co-training two MaxEnt models, 3) Training MaxEnt models with using posterior regularization.

[9] http://lucene.apache.org/

[10] http://lyle.smu.edu/~tspell/jaws/

[11] http://mallet.cs.umass.edu/

[12] http://nlp.stanford.edu/software/tagger.shtml

Class	NEJM		Clinical Narratives	
Co-train	Precision	Recall	Precision	Recall
coref	70.32	82.54	69.26	87.31
no-coref	82.54	84.85	71.15	89.44
PR	Precision	Recall	Precision	Recall
coref	76.63	90.41	74.81	84.25
no-coref	80.35	89.21	78.93	87.46

Table 4: Co-training and posterior regularization (PR) for MCCR using semantic and temporal feature sets.

We use the MaxEnt classifier available in Mallet for 1) and 2) and the the Mallet implementation of MaxEnt models with posterior regularization for 3).

The NEJM corpus has 722 medical concepts, 12576 candidate pairs of medical concepts including 137 pairs that corefer. We include all 12576 pairs in our experiments. The clinical narrative corpus has 1613 medical concepts. The candidate pairs and coreference chains for each patient is as follows. Patient 1 has 241001 candidate pairs, 29 coreference chains. Patient 2 has 149604 candidate pairs, 9 coreference chains. Patient 3 has 6,446,521 candidate pairs, 20 coreference chains. From all the candidate pairs in the clinical narrative corpus, 1025 pairs corefer. We randomly sample the no-coref instances to restrict the corpus size to 1 million candidate pairs of medical concepts.

The results for all 3 experiments for both corpora is shown in Tables 3, 4. We also train-test a supervised MaxEnt classifier on a 60-40 split of the entire corpus. This gives us a precision of 74.81% and 88.33% recall (coref) for the binary classification task of pairwise MCCR in the clinical narratives corpus. In the both the semi-supervised experiments, we use an initial labeled pool size of 30 where 12 medical concept pairs that corefer (p) and 18 that do not corefer (n). The growth size is each iteration of co-training is $2p + 2n$. At each iteration, confidently labeled examples are added to the training set from the previous iteration. The co-training algorithm is run until all unlabeled instances become labeled. The parameters in the posterior regularization implementation include the regularization penalty for each step and the number of iterations. We use the default values (maxIterations=100, pGaussianPriorVariance=0.1, qGaussianPriorVariance=1000) suggested on the Mallet toolkit page (Bellare et al., 2009). Co-training two MaxEnt models based on independent semantic and temporal views of the data results in 69.26% precision and 87.31% recall (coref), whereas training MaxEnt models with expectation constraints gives us 74.81% precision and 84.25% recall (coref), on the corpus of clinical narratives.

Posterior regularization does better than co-training and the performance of both the semi-supervised methods is comparable to if not as good as the supervised classifier trained on a 60-40 split of the corpus. Thus, our results indicate that the use of semantic and temporal features is effective for MCCR in clinical text. It is clear from the co-training and posterior regularization results that treating MCCR as a semi-supervised problem works.

8 Conclusions

We investigated the task of MCCR in clinical text using supervised and semi-supervised learning methods. We create annotated corpora of clinical text with case reports from the NEJM and narratives obtained from The Ohio State University Wexner Medical Center. We work with the hypothesis that determining semantic and temporal similarity between medical concepts helps resolve coreferences. In order to test this hypothesis, we describe the process of semantic and temporal feature extraction from clinical text. We demonstrate the effectiveness of the extracted features in a supervised binary classification task for MCCR with MaxEnt classifiers (using the combined feature set) as well as using semi supervised methods of co training MaxEnt classifiers and training MaxEnt models using posterior regularization (using two independent views of the data - semantic view and temporal view). Thus, we show that MCRR can be performed using semi-supervised learning with semantic and temporal views of the data.

Acknowledgments

The project described was supported by the National Center for Research Resources, Grant UL1RR025755, KL2RR025754, and TL1RR025753, and is now at the National Center for Advancing Translational Sciences, Grant 8KL2TR000112-05, 8UL1TR000090-05, 8TL1TR000091-05. The content is solely the responsibility of the authors and does not necessarily represent the official views of the NIH.

References

Sophia Ananiadou, Carol Freidman, and Juníchi Tsujii. 2004. Introduction: named entity recognition in biomedicine. *J. of Biomedical Informatics*, pages 393–395.

Kedar Bellare, Gregory Druck, and Andrew McCallum. 2009. Alternating projections for learning with expectation constraints. In *Proceedings of the Twenty-Fifth Conference on Uncertainty in Artificial Intelligence*, UAI '09, pages 43–50.

Avrim Blum and Tom M. Mitchell. 1998. Combining labeled and unlabeled data with co-training. In *COLT'98*, pages 92–100.

Bigi Brigitte. 2003. Using Kullback-Leibler distance for text categorization. In *Proceedings of the 25th European conference on IR research*, ECIR'03, pages 305–319.

Wendy W Chapman, Prakash M Nadkarni, Lynette Hirschman, Guergana K Savova Leonard W D'Avolio, and Ozlem Uzuner. 2011. Overcoming barriers to NLP for clinical text: the role of shared tasks and the need for additional creative solutions. In *JAMIA*.

Jung-Hsien Chiang, Jou-Wei Lin, and Chen-Wei Yang. 2010. Automated evaluation of electronic discharge notes to assess quality of care for cardiovascular diseases using Medical Language Extraction and Encoding System (MedLEE). *JAMIA*, pages 245–252.

A.J. Conger. 1980. Integration and generalization of kappas for multiple raters. In *Psychological Bulletin Vol 88(2)*, pages 322–328.

Peter J Embi and Philip Payne. 2009. Clinical research informatics: challenges, opportunities and definition for an emerging domain. *Journal of the American Medical Informatics Association*, 16(3):316–327.

Carol Friedman, Pauline Kra, and Andrey Rzhetsky. 2002. Two biomedical sublanguages: a description based on the theories of Zellig Harris. *Journal of Biomedical Informatics*, 35(4):222–235.

Rob Gaizauskas, Henk Harkema, Mark Hepple, and Andrea Setzer. 2006. Task-oriented extraction of temporal information: The case of clinical narratives. In *Proceedings of the Thirteenth International Symposium on Temporal Representation and Reasoning*, TIME '06, pages 188–195.

Kuzman Ganchev, Joo Graa, Jennifer Gillenwater, and Ben Taskar. 2010. Posterior regularization for structured latent variable models. *Journal of Machine Learning Research*, pages 2001–2049.

Tian Ye He. 2007. *Coreference Resolution on Entities and Events for Hospital Discharge Summaries*. EECS, Cambridge, MA, MIT. M.Eng.

Hyuckchul Jung, James Allen, Nate Blaylock, Will de Beaumont, Lucian Galescu, and Mary Swift. 2011. Building timelines from narrative clinical records: initial results based-on deep natural language understanding. In *Proceedings of BioNLP 2011 Workshop*, BioNLP '11, pages 146–154.

Christoph Muller, Stefan Rapp, and Michael Strube. 2002. Applying co-training to reference resolution. In *ACL*, pages 352–359.

Vincent Ng. 2010. Supervised noun phrase coreference research: The first fifteen years. In *Proceedings of the ACL*, pages 1396–1411.

Kamal Nigam and Rayid Ghani. 2000. Analyzing the effectiveness and applicability of co-training. In *CIKM'00*, pages 86–93.

James Pustejovsky, Jos M. Castao, Robert Ingria, Roser Sauri, Robert J. Gaizauskas, Andrea Setzer, Graham Katz, and Dragomir R. Radev. 2003. Timeml: Robust specification of event and temporal expressions in text. In *New Directions in Question Answering'03*, pages 28–34.

Preethi Raghavan and Albert M. Lai. 2010. Leveraging natural language processing of clinical narratives for phenotype modeling. In *PIKM'10*, pages 57–66.

Karthik Raghunathan, Heeyoung Lee, Sudarshan Rangarajan, Nathanael Chambers, Mihai Surdeanu, Dan Jurafsky, and Christopher Manning. 2010. A multi-pass sieve for coreference resolution. In *Proceedings of the 2010 Conference on Empirical Methods in Natural Language Processing*, EMNLP '10, pages 492–501, Stroudsburg, PA, USA. Association for Computational Linguistics.

Guergana K. Savova, James J. Masanz, Philip V. Ogren, Jiaping Zheng, Sunghwan Sohn, Karin Kipper Schuler, and Christopher G. Chute. 2010. Mayo clinical text analysis and knowledge extraction system (cTAKES): architecture, component evaluation and applications. *JAMIA*, pages 507–513.

Guergana K. Savova, Wendy Webber Chapman, Jiaping Zheng, and Rebecca S. Crowley. 2011. Anaphoric relations in the clinical narrative: corpus creation. *JAMIA*, 18(4):459–465.

Wee Meng Soon, Hwee Tou Ng, and Chung Yong Lim. 2001. A machine learning approach to coreference resolution of noun phrases. *Computational Linguistics*, pages 521–544.

Yang Xiang, Kewei Lu, Stephen L James, Tara B Borlawsky, Kun Huang, and Philip R O Payne. 2011. k-neighborhood decentralization: A comprehensive solution to index the UMLS for scale knowledge discovery. In *Journal of Biomedical Informatics*.

Jiaping Zheng, Wendy Webber Chapman, Rebecca S. Crowley, and Guergana K. Savova. 2011. Coreference resolution: A review of general methodologies and applications in the clinical domain. *Journal of Biomedical Informatics*, 44(6):1113–1122.

Li Zhou and George Hripcsak. 2007. Temporal reasoning with medical data - a review with emphasis on medical natural language processing. *Journal of Biomedical Informatics*, pages 183–202.

Li Zhou, Genevieve B. Melton, Simon Parsons, and George Hripcsak. 2006. A temporal constraint structure for extracting temporal information from clinical narrative. *Journal of Biomedical Informatics*, pages 424–439.

Mind the Gap: Learning to Choose Gaps for Question Generation

Lee Becker
Department of Computer Science
University of Colorado Boulder
Boulder, CO 80309
lee.becker@colorado.edu

Sumit Basu and Lucy Vanderwende
Microsoft Research
One Microsoft Way
Redmond, WA 98052
{sumitb, lucyv}@microsoft.com

Abstract

Not all learning takes place in an educational setting: more and more self-motivated learners are turning to on-line text to learn about new topics. Our goal is to provide such learners with the well-known benefits of testing by automatically generating quiz questions for online text. Prior work on question generation has focused on the grammaticality of generated questions and generating effective multiple-choice distractors for individual question targets, both key parts of this problem. Our work focuses on the complementary aspect of determining what part of a sentence we should be asking about in the first place; we call this "gap selection." We address this problem by asking human judges about the quality of questions generated from a Wikipedia-based corpus, and then training a model to effectively replicate these judgments. Our data shows that good gaps are of variable length and span all semantic roles, i.e., nouns as well as verbs, and that a majority of good questions do not focus on named entities. Our resulting system can generate fill-in-the-blank (cloze) questions from generic source materials.

1 Introduction

Assessment is a fundamental part of teaching, both to measure a student's mastery of the material and to identify areas where she may need reinforcement or additional instruction. Assessment has also been shown an important part of learning, as testing assists retention and can be used to guide learning (Anderson & Biddle, 1975). Thus, as learners move on from an educational setting to unstructured self-learning settings, they would still benefit from having the means for assessment available. Even in traditional educational settings, there is a need for automated test generation, as teachers want multiple tests for topics to give to different students, and students want different tests with which to study and practice the material.

One possible solution to providing quizzes for new source material is the automatic generation of questions. This is a task the NLP community has already embraced, and significant progress has been made in recent years with the introduction of a shared task (Rus et al., 2010). However, thus far the research community has focused on the problem of generating grammatical questions (as in Heilman and Smith (2010a)) or generating effective distractors for multiple-choice questions (Agarwal and Mannem, 2011).

While both of these research threads are of critical importance, there is another key issue that must be addressed – which questions should we be asking in the first place? We have highlighted this aspect of the problem in the past (see Vanderwende (2008)) and begin to address it in this work, postulating that we can both collect human judgments on what makes a good question and train a machine learning model that can replicate these judgments. The resulting learned model can then be applied to new material for automated question generation. We see this effort as complementary to the earlier progress.

In our approach, we factor the problem of generating good questions into two parts: first, the selection of sentences to ask about, and second, the identification of which part of the resulting sentences the question should address. Because we want to focus on these aspects of the problem and not the surface form of the questions, we have chosen to generate simple gap-fill (cloze) questions, though our results can also be used to trigger Wh-questions or multiple-choice questions by leveraging prior work. For sentence selection, we turn to methods in summarization and use the simple but effective SumBasic (Nenkova et al., 2006) algorithm to prioritize and choose important sentences from the article. We cast the second part, gap selection, as a learning problem. To do this, we first select a corpus of sentences from a very general body of instructional material (a range of popular topics from Wikipedia). We then generate a constrained subset of all possible gaps via NLP heuristics, and pair each gap with a broad variety of features pertaining to how it was generated. We then solicit a large number of human judgments via crowdsourcing to help us rate the quality of various gaps. With that data in hand, we train a machine learning model to replicate these judgments. The results are promising, with one possible operating point producing a true positive rate of 83% with a corresponding false positive rate of 19% (83% of the possible *Good* gaps are kept, and 19% of the not-*Good* gaps are incorrectly marked); see Figure 6 for the full ROC curve and Section 4 for an explanation of the labels. As the final model has only minimal dependence on Wikipedia-specific features, we expect that it can be applied to an even wider variety of material (blogs, news articles, health sites, etc.).

2 Background and Related Work

There already exists a large body of work in automatic question generation (QG) for educational purposes dating back to the Autoquest system (Wolfe, 1976), which used an entirely syntactic approach to generate Wh-Questions from individual sentences. In addition to Autoquest, several others have created systems for Wh-question generation using approaches including transformation rules (Mitkov and Ha, 2003), template-based generation (Chen et al., 2009; Curto et al., 2011), and overgenerate-and-rank (Heilman and Smith, 2010a). The work in this area has largely focused on the surface form of the questions, with an emphasis on grammaticality.

Alternatively, generation of gap-fill style questions (a.k.a. cloze questions) avoids these issues of grammaticality by blanking out words or spans in a known good sentence. There is a large body of existing work that has focused on generation of this type of question, most of which has focused on vocabulary and language learning. The recent work of Agarwal and Mannem (2011) is closer to our purposes; they generated fill-in-the-blank questions and distractor answers for reading comprehension tests using heuristic scoring measures and a small evaluation set. Our work has similar aims but employs a data-driven approach.

The Question-Generation Shared Task and Evaluation Challenge (QG-STEC) (Rus et al., 2010) marks a first attempt at creating a common task and corpus for empirical evaluation of question generation components. However, evaluation in this task was manual and the number of instances in both the development and training set were small. As there exists no other dataset for question generation, we created a new corpus using Amazon Mechanical Turk by soliciting judgments from non-experts. Snow et al. (2008) have validated AMT as a valid data source by comparing non-expert with gold-standard expert judgments. Corpus creation using AMT has numerous precedents now; see i.e. Callison-Burch and Dredze (2010) and Heilman and Smith (2010b). We have made our corpus (see Section 4) available online to enable others to continue research on the gap-selection problem we address here.

3 Question Generation

To achieve our goal of selecting better gap-fill questions, we have broken down the task into stages similar to those proposed by Nielsen (2008): 1) sentence selection, 2) question construction, and 3) classification/scoring. Specifically, we utilize summarization to identify key sentences from a passage. We then apply semantic and syntactic constraints to construct multiple candidate question/answer pairs from a given source sentence. Lastly we extract features from these hypotheses for use with a question quality classification model. To train this final question-scoring component, we made use of crowdsourcing to collect ratings for a corpus of candidate questions. While this pipeline currently produces gap-fill questions, we envision these components can be used as input for more complex surface generation such as Wh-forms or distractor selection.

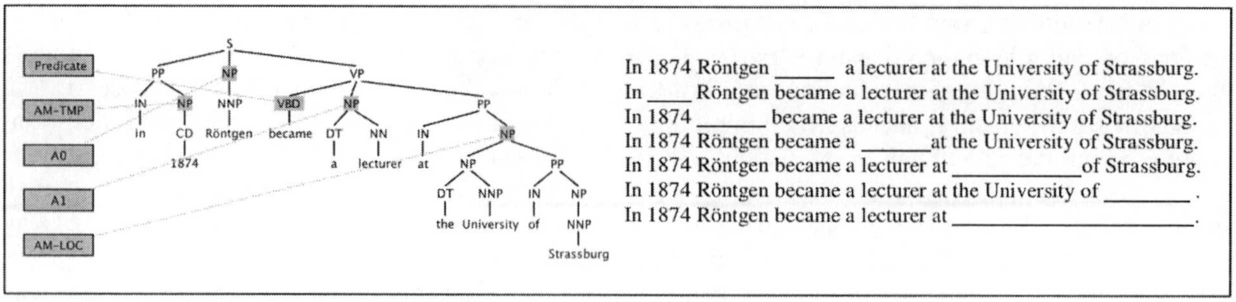

Figure 1 An example of the question generation process.

3.1 Sentence Selection

When learning about a new subject, a student will most likely want to learn about key concepts before moving onto more obscure details. As such, it is necessary to order target sentences in terms of their importance. This is fortunately very similar to the goals of automatic summarization, in which the selected sentences should be ordered by how central they are to the article.

As a result, we make use of our own implementation of SumBasic (Nenkova et al., 2006), a simple but competitive document summarization algorithm motivated by the assumption that sentences containing the article's most frequently occurring words are the most important. We thus use the SumBasic score for each sentence to order them as candidates for question construction.

3.2 Question Construction

We seek to empirically determine how to choose questions instead of relying on heuristics and rules for evaluating candidate surface forms. To do this, we cast question construction as a generate-and-filter problem: we overgenerate potential question/answer pairs from each sentence and train a discriminative classifier on human judgments of quality for those pairs. With the trained classifier, we can then apply this approach on unseen sentences to return the highest-scoring question/answer, all question/answer pairs scoring above a threshold, and so on.

Generation

Although it would be possible to select every word or phrase as a candidate gap, this tactic would produce a skewed dataset composed mostly of unusable questions, which would subsequently require much more annotation to discriminate good questions from bad ones. Instead we rely on syntactic and semantic constraints to reduce the number of questions that need annotation.

To generate questions we first run the source sentence through a constituency parser and a semantic role labeler (components of a state-of-the-art natural language toolkit from (Quirk et al., 2012)), with the rationale that important parts of the sentence will occur within a semantic role. Each verb predicate found within the roles then automatically becomes a candidate gap. From every argument to the predicate, we extract all child noun phrases (NP) and adjectival phrases (ADJP) as candidate gaps as well. Figure 1 illustrates this generation process.

Classification

To train the classifier for question quality, we aggregated per-question ratings into a single label (see Section 4 for details). Questions with an average rating of 0.67 or greater were considered as positive examples. This outcome was then paired with a vector of features (see Section 5) extracted from the source sentence and the generated question.

Because our goal is to score each candidate question in a meaningful way, we use a calibrated learner, namely L2-regularized logistic regression (Bishop 2006). This model's output is $p(class|features)$; in our case this is the posterior probability of a candidate receiving a positive label based on its features.

4 Corpus Construction

We downloaded 105 articles from Wikipedia's listing of vital articles/popular pages.[1] These articles represent a cross section of historical, social,

[1]http://en.wikipedia.org/wiki/Wikipedia:Vital_articles/Popular_pages

Source Sentence:
The large scale production of chemicals was an important development during the Industrial Revolution.

Question	Answer	Ratings
The _____________ of chemicals was an important development during the Industrial Revolution.	large scale production	○Good ◉ Okay ○Bad
The large scale production of ______was an important development during the Industrial Revolution.	chemicals	○Good ◉ Okay ○Bad
The large scale production of chemicals was an important development during the ____________.	Industrial Revolution	◉ Good ○Okay ○Bad

Figure 2: Example question rating HIT

and scientific topics. From each article we sampled 10 sentences using the sentence selection algorithm described in Section 3.1 for 50% of the sentences; the other 50% were chosen at random to prevent any possible overfitting to the selection method. These sentences were then processed using the candidate generation method from Section 3.2.

To collect training data outcomes for our question classifier, we used Amazon's Mechanical Turk (AMT) service to obtain human judgments of quality for each question. We initially considered asking about the quality of individual question/answer pairs in isolation, but in pilot studies we found poor agreement in this case; we noticed that the inability to compare with other possible questions actually made the task seem difficult and arbitrary. We thus instead presented raters with a source sentence and a list of up to ten candidate questions along with their corresponding answers (see Figure 2). Raters were asked to rate questions' quality as *Good*, *Okay*, or *Bad*. The task instructions defined a *Good* question as "one that tests key concepts from the sentence and would be reasonable to answer." An *Okay* question was defined as "one that tests key concepts but might be difficult to answer (the answer is too lengthy, the answer is ambiguous, etc.)." A *Bad* question was "one that asks about an unimportant aspect of the sentence or has an uninteresting answer that can be figured out from the context of the sentence." These ratings were binarized into a score of one for *Good* and zero for not-*Good* (*Okay* or *Bad*), as our goal was to find the probability of a question being truly *Good* (and not just *Okay*).[2]

[2] Heilman and Smith (2010a and b) asked raters to identify question deficiencies, including vague or obvious, but raters were not asked to differentiate between *Good* and *Okay*. Thus questions considered *Good* in their study would include *Okay*.

Thus far we have run 300 HITs with 4 judges per HIT. Each HIT consisted of up to 10 candidate questions generated from a single sentence. In total this yielded 2252 candidate questions with 4 ratings per question from 85 unique judges. We then wished to eliminate judges who were gaming the system or otherwise performing poorly on the task. It is common to do such filtering when using crowdsourced data by using the majority or median vote as the final judgment or to calibrate judges using expert judgments (Snow et al. 2008). Other approaches to annotator quality control include using EM-based algorithms for estimating annotator bias (Wiebe et al. 1999, Ipeirotis et al. 2010). In our case, we computed the distance for each judge from the median judgment (from all judges) on each question, then took the mean of this distance over all questions they rated. We removed judges with a mean distance two standard deviations above the mean distance, which eliminated the five judges who disagreed most with others.

In addition to filtering judges, we wanted to further constrain the data to those questions on which the human annotators had reasonable agreement, as it would not make sense to attempt to train a model to replicate judgments on which the annotators themselves could not agree. To do this, we computed the variance of the judgments for each question. By limiting the variance to 0.3, we kept questions on which up to 1 judge (out of 4) disagreed; this eliminated 431 questions and retained the 1821 with the highest agreement. Of these filtered questions, 700 were judged to be *Good* (38%).

To formally assess inter-rater reliability we computed Krippendorff's alpha (Krippendorff, 2004), a statistical measure of agreement applicable for situations with multiple raters and incomplete data (in our case not all raters provided ratings for all items). An alpha value of 1.0 indicates perfect agreement, and an alpha value of 0.0

indicates no agreement. Our original data yielded an alpha of 0.34, whereas after filtering judges and questions the alpha was 0.51. It should be noted that because Krippendorff's Alpha accounts for variability due to multiple raters and sample size, its values tend to be more pessimistic than many Kappa values commonly used to measure inter-rater reliability.

For others interested in working with this data, we have made our corpus of questions and ratings available for download at the following location: http://research.microsoft.com/~sumitb/questiongeneration.

5 Model Features

While intuition would suggest that selecting high-quality gaps for cloze questions should be a straightforward task, analysis of our features implies that identifying important knowledge depends on more complex interactions between syntax, semantics, and other constraints. In designing features, we focused on using commonly extracted NLP information to profile the answer (gap), the source sentence, and the relation between the two.

To enable extraction of these features, we used the MSR Statistical Parsing and Linguistic Analysis Toolkit (MSR SPLAT)[3], a state-of-the-art, web-based service for natural language processing (Quirk et al., 2012). Table 1 shows a breakdown of our feature categories and their relative proportion of the feature space. In the subsections below, we describe the intuitions behind our choice of features and highlight example features from each of these categories. An exhaustive list of the features can be found at the corpus URL listed in Section 4.

5.1 Token Count Features

A good question gives the user sufficient context to answer correctly without making the answer obvious. At the same time, gaps with too many words may be impossible to answer. Figure 3 shows the distributions of number of tokens in the answer (i.e., the gap) for *Good* and not-*Good* questions. As intuition would predict, the not-*Good* class has higher likelihoods for the longer answer lengths. In addition to the number and percentage of tokens in the answer features, we also included other token count features such as the number of tokens in the sentence, and the number of overlapping tokens between the answer and the remainder of the sentence.

Feature Category	Number of Features
Token Count	5
Lexical	11
Syntactic	112
Semantic	40
Named Entity	11
Wikipedia link	3
Total	182

Table 1: Breakdown of features by category

5.2 Lexical features

Although lexical features play an important role in system performance for several NLP tasks like parsing, and semantic role labeling, they require a large number of examples to provide practical benefit. Furthermore, because most sentences in Wikipedia articles feature numerous domain-specific terms and names, we cannot rely on lexical features to generalize across the variety of possible articles in our corpus. Instead we approximate lexicalization by computing densities of word categories found within the answer. The intuition behind these features is that an answer composed primarily of pronouns and stopwords will make for a bad question while an answer consisting of specific entities may make for a better question. Examples of our semi-lexical features include answer pronoun density, answer abbreviation density, answer capitalized word density, and answer stopword density.

5.3 Syntactic Features

The answer's structure relative to the sentence's structure provides information as to where better spans for the gap may exist. Similarly, part-of-speech (POS) tags give a topic-independent representation of the composition and makeup of the questions and answers. The collection of syntactic features includes the answer's depth with the sentence's constituent parse, the answer's location relative to head verb (before/after), the POS tag before the answer, the POS tag after the answer, and the answer bag-of-POS tags.

[3] http://research.microsoft.com/projects/msrsplat

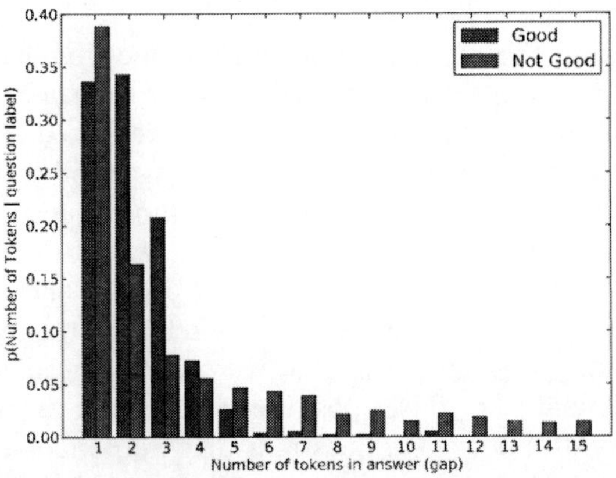

Figure 3: Distribution of number of tokens in the answer for *Good* and not-*Good* questions.

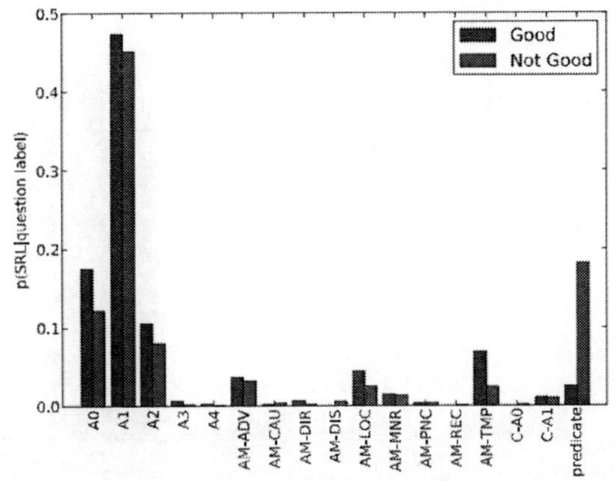

Figure 4: Distribution of semantic role labels for *Good* and not-*Good* questions.

5.4 Semantic Role Label Features

Beyond syntactic constraints, semantics can yield additional cues in identifying the important spans for questioning. Shallow-semantic parses like those found in Propbank (Palmer et al., 2005) provide a concise representation for linking predicates (verbs) to their arguments. Because these semantic role labels (SRLs) often correspond to the "who, what, where, and when" of a sentence, they naturally lend themselves for use as features for rating question quality. To compute SRL features, we used the MSR SPLAT's semantic role labeler to find the SRLs whose spans cover the question's answer, the SRLs whose spans are contained within the answer, and the answer's constituent parse depth within the closest covering SRL node.

To investigate whether judges keyed in on specific roles or modifiers when rating questions, we plotted the distribution of the answer-covering SRLs (Figure 4). This graph indicates that good answers are not associated with only a single label but are actually spread across all SRL classes. While the bulk of questions came from the arguments often corresponding to subjects and objects (ARG0-2, shown as A0-A2), we see that good and bad questions have mostly similar distributions over SRL classes. However, a notable exception are answers covered by verb predicates (shown as "predicate"), which were highly skewed with 190 of the 216 (88.0%) question/answer pairs exhibiting this feature labeled as *Bad*. Together these distributions may suggest that judges are more likely to rate gap-fill questions as Good if they correspond to questions of "who, what, where, and when" over questions pertaining to "why and how."

5.5 Named Entity Features

For many topics, especially in the social sciences, knowing the relevant people and places marks the first step toward comprehending new material. To reflect these concerns we use the named-entity tagger in the toolkit to identify the spans of text that refer to persons, locations, or organizations, which are then used to derive additional features for distinguishing between candidate questions. Example named-entity features include: answer named entity density, answer named entity type frequency (LOC, ORG, PER), and sentence named entity frequency.

Figure 5 shows the distribution of named entity types found within the answers for *Good* and not-*Good* questions. From this graph, we see that *Good* questions have a higher class-conditional probability of containing a named entity. Furthermore, we see that *Good* questions are not confined to a single named entity type, but are spread across all types. Together, these distributions indicate that while named entities can help to identify important gaps, the majority of questions labeled *Good* do not contain any named entity (515/700, i.e. 74%). This provides substantial evidence for generating questions for more than only named entities.

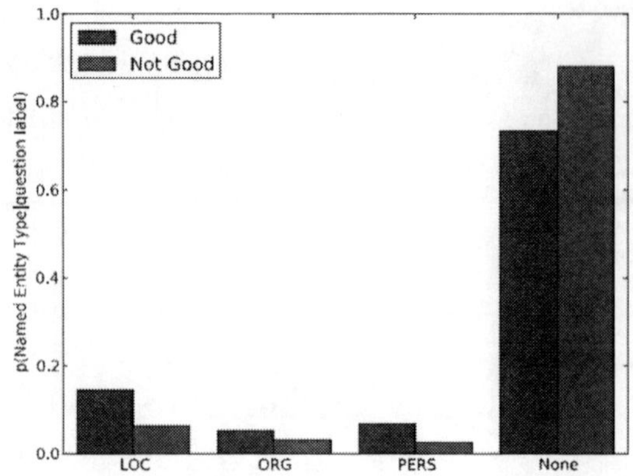

Figure 5: Distribution of answer named entity type for *Good* and not-*Good* questions.

5.6 Wikipedia Link Features

Wikipedia's markup language allows spans of text to link to other articles. This annotation inherently indicates a span of text as noteworthy, and can serve as evidence of an answer's importance. We use the presence of this markup to compute features such as answer link density, sentence link density, and the ratio of the number of linked words in the answer to the ratio of linked words in the sentence.

6 Model and Training

We chose logistic regression as our classifier because of its calibrated output of the class posterior; we combined it with an L2 regularizer to prevent overfitting. As the data likelihood is convex in the model parameters, we trained the model to maximize this quantity along with the regularization term using the L-BFGS algorithm for Quasi-Newton optimization (Nocedal, 1980). Evaluation was conducted with 10-fold cross validation, taking care to stratify folds so that all questions generated from the same source sentence are placed in the same fold. Results are shown in Section 7 below.

To ensure that we were not overly narrow in this model choice, we tested two other more powerful classifiers that do not have calibrated outputs, a linear SVM and a boosted mixture of decision trees (Caruana and Niculescu-Mizil, 2006); both produced accuracies within a percentage point of our model at the equal error rate.

7 Results and Discussion

Figure 6 shows ROC curves for our question quality classifier produced by sweeping the threshold on the output probability, using the raw collected data, our filtered version as described above, and a further filtered version keeping only those questions where judges agreed perfectly; the benefits of filtering can be seen in the improved performance. In this context, the true positive rate refers to the fraction of *Good* questions that were correctly identified, and the false positive rate refers to the fraction of not-*Good* questions that were incorrectly marked. At the equal error rate, the true positive rate was 0.83 and the false positive rate was 0.19.

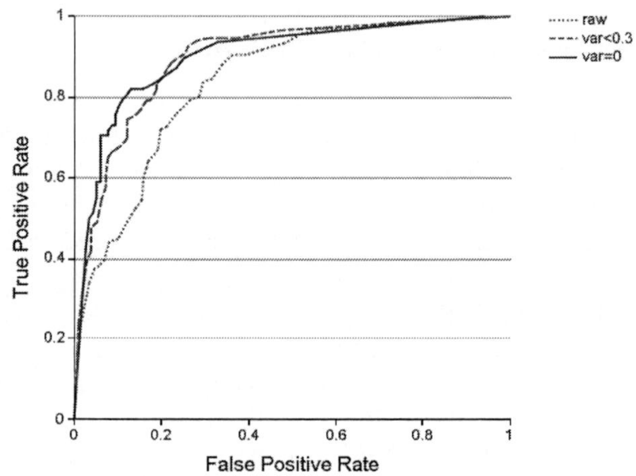

Figure 6: ROC for our model using unfiltered data (green dots), our filtered version (red dashes), and filtered for perfect agreement (blue line).

Choosing the appropriate operating point depends on the final application. By tuning the classifier's true positive and false positive rates, we can customize the system for several uses. For example, in a relatively structured scenario like compliance training, it may be better to reduce any possibility of confusion by eliminating false positives. On the other hand, a self-motivated learner attempting to explore a new topic may tolerate a higher false positive rate in exchange for a broader diversity of questions. The balance is subtle, though, as ill-formed and irrelevant questions could leave the learner bored or frustrated, but alternatively, overly conservative question classification could potentially eliminate all but the most trivial questions.

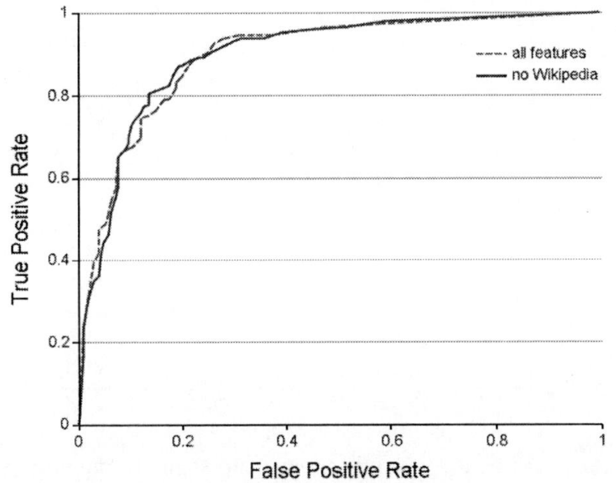

Figure 7: ROC for our model with (red dash) and without (blue line) Wikipedia-specific features.

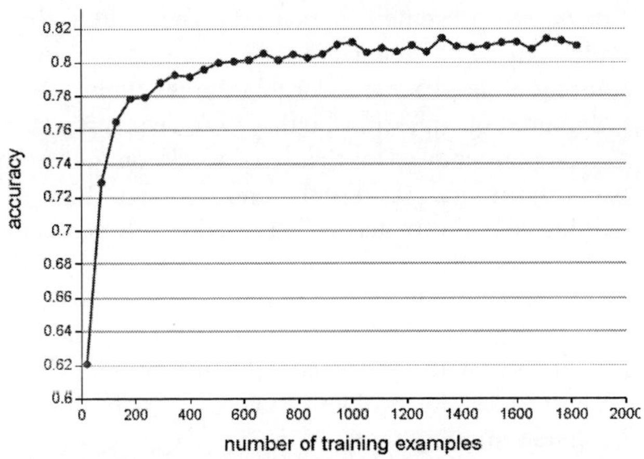

Figure 8: Classifier learning curve; each point represents mean accuracy over 40 folds.

We next wanted to get a sense of how well the model would generalize to other text, and as such ran an analysis of training the classifier without the benefit of the Wikipedia-specific features (Figure 7). The resulting model performs about the same as the original on average over the ROC, slightly better in some places and slightly worse in others. We hypothesize the effect is small because these features relate only to Wikipedia entities, and the other named entity features likely make them redundant.

Finally, to understand the sensitivity of our model to the amount of training data, we plot a learning curve of the question classifier's accuracy by training it against fractions of the available data (Figure 8). While the curve starts to level out around 1200 data points, the accuracy is still rising slightly, which suggests the system could achieve some small benefits in accuracy from more data.

7.1 Error Analysis

To explore the nature of our system's misclassifications we examine the errors that occur at the equal error rate operating point. For our system, false positive errors occur when the system labels a question as *Good* when the raters considered it not-*Good*. Table 2 lists three examples of this type of error. The incorrect high score in example 1 ("Greeks declared ___") suggests that system performance can be improved via language modeling, as such features would penalize questions with answers that could be predicted mostly by word transition probabilities. Similarly, when classifying questions like example 2 ("such as ____ for a mathematical function"), the system could benefit from some measure of word frequency or answer novelty. While our model included a feature for the number of overlapping words between the question and the answer, the high classifier score for example 3 ("atop ______, the volcano"), suggests that this can be solved by explicitly filtering out such questions at generation time.

With false negative errors the judges rated the question as *Good*, whereas the system classified it as *Bad*. The question and answer pairs listed in Table 3 demonstrate some of these errors. In example 1 ("where Pompey was soon ___"), the system was likely incorrect because a majority of questions with verb-predicate answers had *Bad* ratings (only 12% are *Good*). Conversely, classification of example 2 ("Over the course of decades...") could be improved with a feature indicating the novelty of the words in the answers. Example 3 ("About 7.5% of the...") appears to come from rater error or rater confusion as the question does little to test the understanding of the material.

While the raters considered the answer to example 4 as *Good*, the low classifier score argues for different handling of answers derived from long coordinated phrases. One alternative approach would be to generate questions that use multiple gaps. Conversely, one may argue that a learner may be better off answering any one of the noun phrases like *palm oil* or *cocoa* in isolation.

	Question	Answer	Confidence
1	*In 1821 the Greeks declared ___ on the sultan.*	*war*	*0.732*
2	*He also introduced much of the modern mathematical terminology and notation, particularly for mathematical analysis, such as ________ of a mathematical function.*	*the notion*	*0.527*
3	*Not only is there much ice atop ________, the volcano is also being weakened by hydrothermal activity.*	*the volcano*	*0.790*

Table 2: Example false positives (human judges rated these as not-*Good)*

	Question	Answer	Confidence
1	*Caesar then pursued Pompey to Egypt, where Pompey was soon ____.*	*murdered*	0.471
2	*Over the course of decades, individual wells draw down local temperatures and water levels until _______ is reached with natural flows.*	*a new equilibrium*	0.306
3	*About 7.5% of world sea trade is carried via the canal ____.*	*today*	0.119
4	*Asante and Dahomey concentrated on the development of "legitimate commerce" in __________, forming the bedrock of West Africa's modern export trade,*	*the form of palm oil, cocoa, timber, and gold.*	0.029

Table 3: Example false negatives (human judges rated these *Good*)

7.2 Feature Analysis

To ensure that all of the gain of the classifier was not coming from only a handful of isolated features, we examined the mean values for each feature's learned weight in the model over the course of 10 cross-validation folds, and then sorted the means for greater clarity (Figure 8). The weights indeed seem to be well distributed across many features.

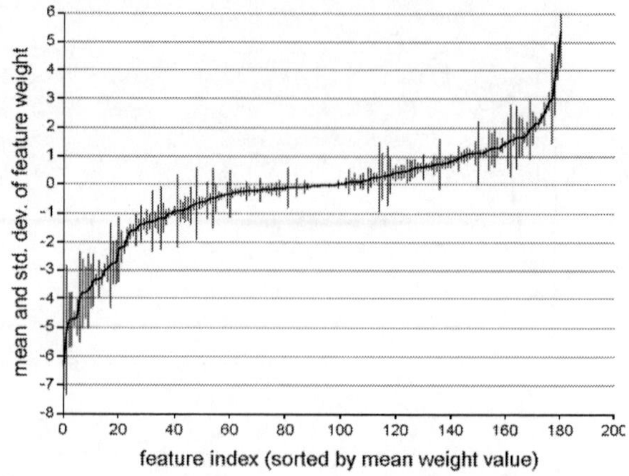

Figure 8: Feature weight means and standard deviations.

8 Discussion and Future Work

We have presented a method that determines which gaps in a sentence to ask questions about by training a classifier that largely agrees with human judgments on question quality. We feel this effort is complementary to the past work on question generation, and represents another step towards helping self-motivated learners with automatically generated tests.

In our future work, we hope to expand the set of features as described in Section 7. We additionally intend to cast the sentence selection problem as a separate learning problem that can also be trained from human judgments.

References

Manish Agarwal and Prashanth Mannem. 2011. Automatic Gap-fill Question Generation from Text Books. In *Proceedings of the 6th Workshop on Innovative Use of NLP for Building Educational Applications.* Portland, OR, USA. pages 56-64.

Richard C. Anderson and W. Barry Biddle. 1975. On asking people questions about what they are reading. In G. Bower (Ed.) *Psychology of Learning and Motivation,* 9:90-132.

Christopher M. Bishop. 2006. *Pattern Recognition and Machine Learning.* New York: Springer, 2006.

Jonathan C. Brown, Gwen A. Frishkoff, and Maxine Eskenazi. 2005. Automatic Question Generation for Vocabulary Assessment. In *Proceedings of HLT/EMNLP 2005.* Vancouver, Canada: Association for Computational Linguistics. pages 819-826.

Rich Caruana and Alexandru Niculescu-Mizil. 2006. An Empirical Comparison of Supervised Learning Algorithms. In *Proceedings of ICML 2006.*

Chris Callison-Burch and Mark Dredze. 2010. Creating Speech and Language Data with Amazon's Mechanical Turk. In *Proceedings of NAACL 2010 Workshop on Creating Speech and Language Data with Amazon's Mechanical Turk.* Los Angeles, CA. pages 1-12.

Wei Chen, Gregory Aist, and Jack Mostow. 2009. Generating Questions Automatically from Informational Text. In S. Craig & S. Dicheva (Ed.), *Proceedings of the 2nd Workshop on Question Generation.*

Sérgio Curto, Ana Cristina Mendes, and Luísa Coheur. 2011. Exploring linguistically-rich patterns for question generation. In *Proceedings of the UCNLG + eval: Language Generation and Evaluation Workshop*. Edinburgh, Scotland: Association for Computational Linguistics. Pages 33-38.

Michael Heilman and Noah A. Smith. 2010a. Good Question! Statistical Ranking for Question Generation. In *Proceedings of NAACL/HLT 2010.* pages 609-617.

Michael Heilman and Noah A. Smith. 2010b. Rating Computer-Generated Questions with Mechanical Turk. In *Proceedings of NAACL 2010 Workshop on Creating Speech and Language Data with Amazon's Mechanical Turk.* Los Angeles, CA. pages 35-40.

Ayako Hoshino and Hiroshi Nakagawa. 2005. A real-time multiple-choice question generation for language testing - a preliminary study -. In *Proceedings of the 2nd Workshop on Building Educational Applications Using NLP*. Ann Arbor, MI, USA: Association for Computational Linguistics. pages 17-20.

Panagiotis G. Ipeirotis, Foster Provost, Jing Wang . 2010. In *Proceedings of the ACM SIGKDD Workshop on Human Computation (HCOMP'10).*

Klaus Krippendorff. 2004. *Content Analysis: An Introduction to Its Methodology.* Thousand Oaks, CA: Sage.

Ruslan Mitkov and Le An Ha. 2003. Computer-Aided Generation of Multiple-Choice Tests. *Proceedings of the HLT-NAACL 2003 Workshop on Building Educational Applications Using Natural Language Processing*, pages 17-22.

Ruslan Mitkov, Le An Ha, and Nikiforos Karamanis. 2006. A computer-aided environment for generating multiple choice test items. *Natural Language Engineering,* 12(2): 177-194.

Ani Nenkova, Lucy Vanderwende, and Kathleen McKeown. 2006. A Compositional Context Sensitive Multidocument Summarizer. In *Proceedings of SIGIR 2006.* pages 573-580.

Rodney D. Nielsen. 2008. Question Generation: Proposed Challenge Tasks and Their Evaluation. In V. Rus, & A. Graesser (Ed.), In *Proceedings of the Workshop on the Question Generation Shared Task and Evaluation Challenge.* Arlington, VA.

Jorge Nocedal. 1980. Updating Quasi-Newton Matrices with Limited Storage. *Mathematics of Computation,* 35:773-782.

Martha Palmer, Dan Gildea, and Paul Kingsbury. 2005. The Proposition Bank: An Annotated Corpus of Semantic Roles. *Computational Linguistics*, vol. 31, no. 1, pp. 71--106.

Chris Quirk, Pallavi Choudhury, Jianfeng Gao, Hisami Suzuki, Kristina Toutanova, Michael Gamon, Wentau Yih, and Lucy Vanderwende. 2012. MSR SPLAT, a language analysis toolkit. In *Proceedings of NAACL HLT 2012 Demonstration Session.* http://research.microsoft.com/projects/msrsplat .

Vasile Rus, Brendan Wyse, Paul Piwek, Mihai Lintean, Svetlana Stoyanchev and Cristian Moldovan. 2010. Overview of The First Question Generation Shared Task Evaluation Challenge. In *Proceedings of the Third Workshop on Question Generation.* Pittsburgh, PA, USA. pages 45-57.

Rion Snow, Brendan O'Connor, Daniel Jurafsky, and Andrew Y. Ng. 2008. Cheap and Fast—but is it Good? Evaluating non-Expert Annotations for Natural Language Tasks. In *Proceedings of EMNLP'08*. pages 254-263.

Lucy Vanderwende. 2008. The Importance of Being Important: Question Generation. In *Proceedings of the 1st Workshop on the Question Generation Shared Task Evaluation Challenge, Arlington, VA.*

Janyce M. Wiebe, Rebecca F. Bruce and Thomas P. O'Hara. 1999. Development and use of a gold-standard data set for subjectivity classifications. In *Proceedings of ACL 1999.*

John H. Wolfe. 1976. Automatic question generation from text - an aid to independent study. In *Proceedings of the ACM SIGCSE-SIGCUE technical symposium on Computer science and education.* New York, NY, USA: ACM. pages 104-112.

Unsupervised Concept-to-text Generation with Hypergraphs

Ioannis Konstas and **Mirella Lapata**
Institute for Language, Cognition and Computation
School of Informatics, University of Edinburgh
10 Crichton Street, Edinburgh EH8 9AB
i.konstas@sms.ed.ac.uk, mlap@inf.ed.ac.uk

Abstract

Concept-to-text generation refers to the task of automatically producing textual output from non-linguistic input. We present a joint model that captures content selection ("what to say") and surface realization ("how to say") in an unsupervised domain-independent fashion. Rather than breaking up the generation process into a sequence of local decisions, we define a probabilistic context-free grammar that globally describes the inherent structure of the input (a corpus of database records and text describing some of them). We represent our grammar compactly as a weighted hypergraph and recast generation as the task of finding the best derivation tree for a given input. Experimental evaluation on several domains achieves competitive results with state-of-the-art systems that use domain specific constraints, explicit feature engineering or labeled data.

1 Introduction

Concept-to-text generation broadly refers to the task of automatically producing textual output from non-linguistic input (Reiter and Dale, 2000). Depending on the application and the domain at hand, the input may assume various representations including databases of records, expert system knowledge bases, simulations of physical systems and so on. Figure 1 shows input examples and their corresponding text for three domains, air travel, sportscasting and weather forecast generation.

A typical concept-to-text generation system implements a pipeline architecture consisting of three core stages, namely text planning (determining the content and structure of the target text), sentence planning (determining the structure and lexical content of individual sentences), and surface realization (rendering the specification chosen by the sentence planner into a surface string). Traditionally, these components are hand-engineered in order to generate high quality text, however at the expense of portability and scalability. It is thus no surprise that recent years have witnessed a growing interest in automatic methods for creating trainable generation components. Examples include learning which database records should be present in a text (Duboue and McKeown, 2002; Barzilay and Lapata, 2005) and how these should be verbalized (Liang et al., 2009). Besides concentrating on isolated components, a few approaches have emerged that tackle concept-to-text generation end-to-end. Due to the complexity of the task, most models simplify the generation process, e.g., by creating output that consists of a few sentences, thus obviating the need for document planning, or by treating sentence planning and surface realization as one component. A common modeling strategy is to break up the generation process into a sequence of local decisions, each learned separately (Reiter et al., 2005; Belz, 2008; Chen and Mooney, 2008; Angeli et al., 2010; Kim and Mooney, 2010).

In this paper we describe an end-to-end generation model that performs content selection and surface realization jointly. Given a corpus of database records and textual descriptions (for some of them), we define a probabilistic context-free grammar (PCFG) that captures the structure of the database and how it can be rendered into natural

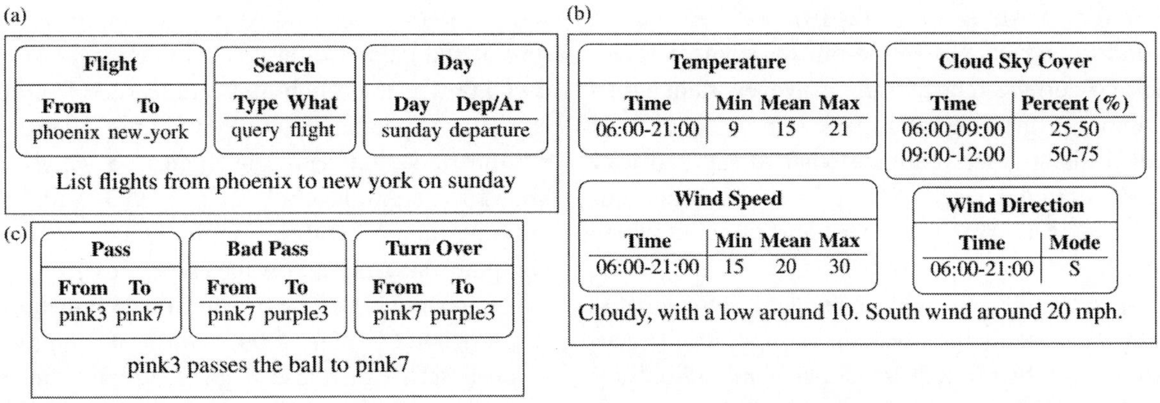

Figure 1: Input-output examples for (a) query generation in the air travel domain, (b) weather forecast generation, and (c) sportscasting.

language. This grammar represents a set of trees which we encode compactly using a weighted hypergraph (or packed forest), a data structure that defines a probability (or weight) for each tree. Generation then boils down to finding the best derivation tree in the hypergraph which can be done efficiently using the Viterbi algorithm. In order to ensure that our generation output is fluent, we intersect our grammar with a language model and perform decoding using a dynamic programming algorithm (Huang and Chiang, 2007).

Our model is conceptually simpler than previous approaches and encodes information about the domain and its structure globally, by considering the input space *simultaneously* during generation. Our only assumption is that the input must be a set of records essentially corresponding to database-like tables whose columns describe fields of a certain type. Experimental evaluation on three domains obtains results competitive to the state of the art without using any domain specific constraints, explicit feature engineering or labeled data.

2 Related Work

Our work is situated within the broader class of data-driven approaches to content selection and surface realization. Barzilay and Lapata (2005) focus on the former problem which they view as an instance of collective classification (Barzilay and Lapata, 2005). Given a corpus of database records and texts describing some of them, they learn a content selection model that simultaneously optimizes local label assignments and their pairwise relations. Building on this work, Liang et al. (2009) present a hierarchical hidden semi-Markov generative model that first determines which facts to discuss and then generates words from the predicates and arguments of the chosen facts.

A few approaches have emerged more recently that combine content selection and surface realization. Kim and Mooney (2010) adopt a two-stage approach: using a generative model similar to Liang et al. (2009), they first decide what to say and then verbalize the selected input with WASP^{-1}, an existing generation system (Wong and Mooney, 2007). In contrast, Angeli et al. (2010) propose a unified content selection and surface realization model which also operates over the alignment output produced by Liang et al. (2009). Their model decomposes into a sequence of discriminative local decisions. They first determine which records in the database to talk about, then which fields of those records to mention, and finally which words to use to describe the chosen fields. Each of these decisions is implemented as a log-linear model with features learned from training data. Their surface realization component is based on templates that are automatically extracted and smoothed with domain-specific constraints in order to guarantee fluent output. Other related work (Wong and Mooney, 2007; Lu and Ng, 2011). has focused on generating natural language sentences from logical form (i.e., lambda-expressions) using mostly synchronous context-free grammars (SCFGs).

Similar to Angeli et al. (2010), we also present an end-to-end system that performs content selection and surface realization. However, rather than breaking up the generation task into a sequence of local decisions, we optimize what to say and how to say simultaneously. We do not learn mappings from a logical form, but rather focus on input which is less constrained, possibly more noisy and with a looser structure. Our key insight is to convert the set of database records serving as input to our generator into a PCFG that is neither hand crafted nor domain specific but simply describes the structure of the database. The approach is conceptually simple, does not rely on discriminative training or any feature engineering. We represent the grammar and its derivations compactly as a weighted hypergraph which we intersect with a language model in order to generate fluent output. This allows us to easily port surface generation to different domains without having to extract new templates or enforce domain specific constraints.

3 Problem Formulation

We assume our generator takes as input a set of database records **d** and produces text **w** that verbalizes some of these records. Each record $r \in \mathbf{d}$ has a type $r.t$ and a set of fields f associated with it. Fields have different values $f.v$ and types $f.t$ (i.e., integer or categorical). For example, in Figure 1b, wind speed is a record type with four fields: `time`, `min`, `mean`, and `max`. The values of these fields are `06:00-21:00`, `15`, `20`, and `30`, respectively; the type of `time` is categorical, whereas all other fields are integers.

During training, our algorithm is given a corpus consisting of several *scenarios*, i.e., database records paired with texts like those shown in Figure 1. In the weather forecast domain, a scenario corresponds to weather-related measurements of temperature, wind, speed, and so on collected for a specific day and time (e.g., day or night). In sportscasting, scenarios describe individual events in the soccer game (e.g., passing or kicking the ball). In the air travel domain, scenarios comprise of flight-related details (e.g., origin, destination, day, time). Our goal then is to reduce the tasks of content selection and surface realization into a common probabilistic parsing problem. We do this by abstracting the structure of the database (and accompanying texts) into a PCFG whose probabilities are learned from training data.[1] Specifically, we convert the database into rewrite rules and represent them as a weighted directed hypergraph (Gallo et al., 1993). Instead of learning the probabilities on the PCFG, we directly compute the weights on the hyperarcs using a dynamic program similar to the inside-outside algorithm (Li and Eisner, 2009). During testing, we are given a set of database records without the corresponding text. Using the trained grammar we compile a hypergraph specific to this test input and decode it approximately via cube pruning (Chiang, 2007).

The choice of the hypergraph framework is motivated by at least three reasons. Firstly, hypergraphs can be used to represent the search space of most parsers (Klein and Manning, 2001). Secondly, they are more efficient and faster than the common CYK parser-based representation for PCFGs by a factor of more than ten (Huang and Chiang, 2007). And thirdly, the hypergraph representation allows us to integrate an n-gram language model and perform decoding efficiently using k-best Viterbi search, optimizing what to say and how to say at the same time.

3.1 Grammar Definition

Our model captures the inherent structure of the database with a number of CFG rewrite rules, in a similar way to how Liang et al. (2009) define Markov chains in the different levels of their hierarchical model. These rules are purely syntactic (describing the intuitive relationship between records, records and fields, fields and corresponding words), and could apply to any database with similar structure irrespectively of the semantics of the domain.

Our grammar is defined in Table 1 (rules (1)–(9)). Rule weights are governed by an underlying multinomial distribution and are shown in square brackets. Non-terminal symbols are in capitals and de-

[1] An alternative would be to learn a SCFG between the database input and the accompanying text. However, this would involve considerable overhead in terms of alignment (as the database and the text do not together constitute a clean parallel corpus, but rather a noisy comparable corpus), as well as grammar training and decoding using state-of-the art SMT methods, which we manage to avoid with our simpler approach.

1. $S \rightarrow R(start)$	$[Pr = 1]$
2. $R(r_i.t) \rightarrow FS(r_j, start)\ R(r_j.t)$	$[P(r_j.t \mid r_i.t) \cdot \lambda]$
3. $R(r_i.t) \rightarrow FS(r_j, start)$	$[P(r_j.t \mid r_i.t) \cdot \lambda]$
4. $FS(r, r.f_i) \rightarrow F(r, r.f_j)\ FS(r, r.f_j)$	$[P(f_j \mid f_i)]$
5. $FS(r, r.f_i) \rightarrow F(r, r.f_j)$	$[P(f_j \mid f_i)]$
6. $F(r, r.f) \rightarrow W(r, r.f)\ F(r, r.f)$	$[P(w \mid w_{-1}, r, r.f)]$
7. $F(r, r.f) \rightarrow W(r, r.f)$	$[P(w \mid w_{-1}, r, r.f)]$
8. $W(r, r.f) \rightarrow \alpha$	$[P(\alpha \mid r, r.f, f.t, f.v)]$
9. $W(r, r.f) \rightarrow g(f.v)$	$[P(g(f.v).mode \mid r, r.f, f.t = int)]$

Table 1: Grammar rules and their weights shown in square brackets.

note intermediate states; the terminal symbol α corresponds to all words seen in the training set, and $g(f.v)$ is a function for generating integer numbers given the value of a field f. All non-terminals, save the start symbol S, have one or more features (shown in parentheses) that act as constraints, similar to number and gender agreement constraints in augmented syntactic rules.

Rule (1) denotes the expansion from the start symbol S to record R, which has the special 'start' record type (hence the notation $R(start)$). Rule (2) defines a chain between two consecutive records, i.e., going from a source record r_i to a target r_j. Here, $FS(r_j, r_j.f)$ represents the set of fields of the target r_j, following the source record $R(r_i)$. For example, the rule $R(skyCover_1.t) \rightarrow FS(temperature_1, start)R(temperature_1.t)$ can be interpreted as follows. Given that we have talked about $skyCover_1$, we will next talk about $temperature_1$ and thus emit its corresponding fields. $R(temperature_1.t)$ is a non-terminal place-holder for the continuation of the chain of records, and *start* in FS is a special boundary field between consecutive records. The weight of this rule is the bigram probability of two records conditioned on their record type, multiplied with a normalization factor λ. We have also defined a *null* record type i.e., a record that has no fields and acts as a smoother for words that may not correspond to a particular record. Rule (3) is simply an escape rule, so that the parsing process (on the record level) can finish.

Rule (4) is the equivalent of rule (2) at the field level, i.e., it describes the chaining of two consecutive fields f_i and f_j. Non-terminal $F(r, r.f)$ refers to field f of record r. For example, the rule $FS(windSpeed_1, min) \rightarrow F(windSpeed_1, max)FS(windSpeed_1, max)$, specifies that we should talk about the field *max* of record $windSpeed_1$, after talking about the field *min*. Analogously to the record level, we have also included a special *null* field type for the emission of words that do not correspond to a specific record field. Rule (6) defines the expansion of field F to a sequence of (binarized) words W, with a weight equal to the bigram probability of the current word given the previous word, the current record, and field. This is an attempt at capturing contextual dependencies between words over and above to integrating a language model during decoding (see Section 3.3).

Rules (8) and (9) define the emission of words and integer numbers from W, given a field type and its value. Rule (8) emits a single word from the vocabulary of the training set. Its weight defines a multinomial distribution over all seen words, for every value of field f, given that the field type is categorical or the special *null* field. Rule (9) is identical but for fields whose type is integer. Function $g(f.v)$ generates an integer number given the field value, using either of the following six ways (Liang et al., 2009): identical to the field value, rounding up or rounding down to a multiple of 5, rounding off to the closest multiple of 5 and finally adding or subtracting some unexplained noise.[2] The weight is a multinomial over the six generation function *modes*, given the record field f.

3.2 Hypergraph Construction

So far we have defined a probabilistic grammar that captures the structure of a database **d** with records and fields as intermediate non-terminals, and words **w** (from the associated text) as terminals. Using this grammar and the CYK parsing algorithm, we could obtain the top scoring derivation of records and fields for a given input (i.e., a sequence of

[2]The noise is modeled as a geometric distribution.

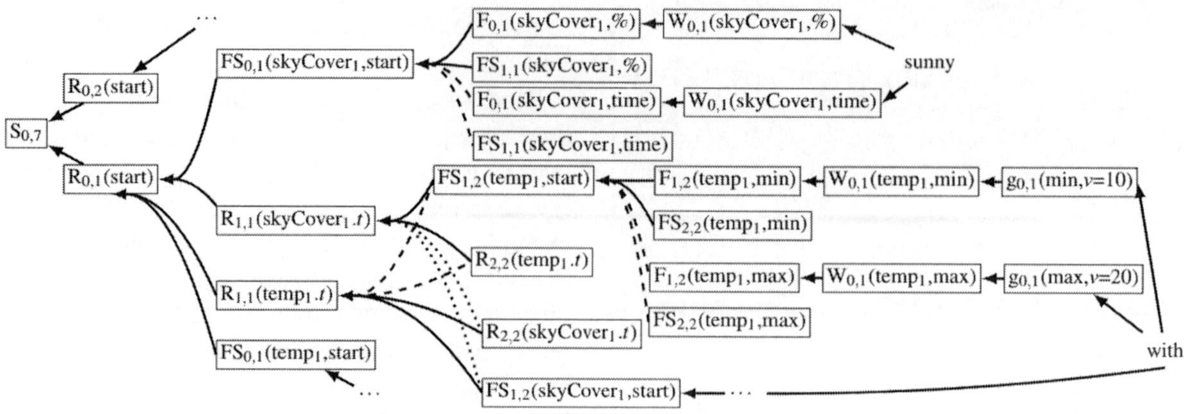

Figure 2: Partial hypergraph representation for the sentence *"Sunny with a low around 30 ."* For the sake of readability, we show a partial span on the first two words without weights on the hyperarcs.

words) as well as the optimal segmentation of the text, provided we have a trained set of weights. The inside-outside algorithm is commonly used for estimating the weights of a PCFG. However, we first transform the CYK parser and our grammar into a hypergraph and then compute the weights using inside-outside. Huang and Chiang (2005) define a weighted directed hypergraph as follows:

Definition 1 *An ordered hypergraph H is a tuple $\langle N, E, t, \boldsymbol{R} \rangle$, where N is a finite set of nodes, E is a finite set of hyperarcs and $\boldsymbol{R}$ is the set of weights. Each hyperarc $e \in E$ is a triple $e = \langle T(e), h(e), f(e) \rangle$, where $h(e) \in N$ is its head node, $T(e) \in N^*$ is a set of tail nodes and $f(e)$ is a monotonic weight function $\boldsymbol{R}_{|T(e)|}$ to $\boldsymbol{R}$ and $t \in N$ is a target node.*

Definition 2 *We impose the arity of a hyperarc to be $|e| = |T(e)| = 2$, in other words, each head node is connected with at most two tail nodes.*

Given a context-free grammar $G = \langle N, T, P, S \rangle$ (where N is the set of variables, T the set of terminals, P the set of production rules, and $S \in N$ the start symbol) and an input string **w**, we can map the standard weighted CYK algorithm to a hypergraph as follows. Each node $[A, i, j]$ in the hypergraph corresponds to non-terminal A spanning words w_i to w_j of the input. Each rewrite rule $A \to BC$ in P, with three free indices $i < j < k$, is mapped to the hyperarc $\langle ((B,i,j),(C,j,k)), (A,i,k), f \rangle$, where $f = f((B,i,j))f((C,j,k)) \cdot Pr(A \to BC)$.[3] The hypergraph can be thus viewed as a compiled lattice of the corresponding chart graph. Figure 2 shows an example hypergraph for a grammar defined on database input similar to Figure (1b).

In order to learn the weights on the hyperarcs we perform the following procedure iteratively in an EM fashion (Li and Eisner, 2009). For each training scenario we build its hypergraph representation. Next, we perform inference by calculating the inside and outside scores of the hypergraph, so as to compute the posterior distribution over its hyperarcs (E-step). Finally, we collectively update the posteriors on the parameters-weights, i.e., rule probabilities and emission multinomial distributions (M-step).

3.3 Decoding

In the framework outlined above, parsing an input string **w** (given some learned weights) boils down to traversing the hypergraph in a particular order. (Note that the hypergraph should be acyclic, which is always guaranteed by the grammar in Table 1). In generation, our aim is to verbalize an input scenario from a database **d** (see Figure 1). We thus find the best text by maximizing:

$$\arg\max_{w} P(\mathbf{w} \,|\, \mathbf{d}) = \arg\max_{w} P(\mathbf{w}) \cdot P(\mathbf{d} \,|\, \mathbf{w}) \qquad (1)$$

where $P(\mathbf{d} \,|\, \mathbf{w})$ is the decoding likelihood for a sequence of words **w**, $P(\mathbf{w})$ is a measure of the quality of each output (given by a language model), and $P(\mathbf{w} \,|\, \mathbf{d})$ the posterior of the best output for database **d**. Note that calculating $P(\mathbf{d} \,|\, \mathbf{w})$ requires deciding on the output length $|w|$. Rather than set-

[3]Similarly, rewrite rules of type $A \to B$ are mapped to the hyperarc $\langle (B,i,j), (A,i,j), f \rangle$, with $f = f((B,i,j)) \cdot Pr(A \to B)$.

ting w to a fixed length, we rely on a linear regression predictor that uses the counts of each record type per scenario as features and is able to produce variable length texts.

In order to perform decoding with an n-gram language model, we adopt Huang and Chiang's (2007) dynamic-programming algorithm for SCFG-based systems. Each node in the hypergraph is split into a set of compound items, namely *+LM items*. Each +LM item is of the form $(n^{a\star b})$, where a and b are boundary words of the generation string, and $\star$ is a place-holder symbol for an elided part of that string, indicating a sub-generation part ranging from a to b. An example +LM deduction of a single hyperarc of the hypergraph in Figure 2 using bigrams is:

$$\frac{\mathrm{FS}_{1,2}(temp_1, start)^{low} : (w_1, g_1), \quad \mathrm{R}_{2,2}(temp_1.t)^{around\star degrees} : (w_2, g_2)}{\mathrm{R}_{1,1}(skyCover_1.t)^{low\star degrees} : (w, g_1 g_2)} \tag{2}$$

$$w = w_1 + w_2 + e_w + P_{lm}(around \mid low) \tag{3}$$

where w_1, w_2 are node weights, g_1, g_2 are the corresponding sub-generations, e_w is the weight of the hyperarc and w the weight of the resulting +LM item. P_{lm} and $(n^{a\star b})$ are defined as in Chiang (2007) in a generic fashion, allowing extension to an arbitrary size of n-gram grammars.

Naive traversal of the hypergraph bottom-up would explore all possible +LM deductions along each hyperarc, and would increase decoding complexity to an infeasible $O(2^n n^2)$, assuming a trigram model and a constant number of emissions at the terminal nodes. To ensure tractability, we adopt cube pruning, a popular approach in syntax-inspired machine translation (Chiang, 2007). The idea is to use a beam-search over the intersection grammar coupled with the cube-pruning heuristic. The beam limits the number of derivations for each node, whereas cube-pruning further limits the number of +LM items considered for inclusion in the beam. Since $f(e)$ in Definition 1 is monotonic, we can select the k-best items without computing all possible +LM items.

Our decoder follows Huang and Chiang (2007) but importantly differs in the treatment of leaf nodes in the hypergraph (see rules (8) and (9)). In the SCFG context, the Viterbi algorithm consumes terminals from the source string in a bottom-up fashion and creates sub-translations according to the CFG rule that holds each time. In the concept-to-text generation context, however, we do not observe the words; instead, for each leaf node we emit the k-best words from the underlying multinomial distribution (see weights on rules (8) and (9)) and continue building our sub-generations bottom-up.

4 Experimental Design

Data We used our system to generate soccer commentaries, weather forecasts, and spontaneous utterances relevant to the air travel domain (examples are given in Figure 1). For the first domain we used the dataset of Chen and Mooney (2008), which consists of 1,539 scenarios from the 2001–2004 Robocup game finals. Each scenario contains on average $|\mathbf{d}| = 2.4$ records, each paired with a short sentence (5.7 words). This domain has a small vocabulary (214 words) and simple syntax (e.g., a transitive verb with its subject and object). Records in this dataset (henceforth ROBOCUP) were aligned manually to their corresponding sentences (Chen and Mooney, 2008). Given the relatively small size of this dataset, we performed cross-validation following previous work (Chen and Mooney, 2008; Angeli et al., 2010). We trained our system on three ROBOCUP games and tested on the fourth, averaging over the four train/test splits.

For weather forecast generation, we used the dataset of Liang et al. (2009), which consists of 29,528 weather scenarios for 3,753 major US cities (collected over four days). The vocabulary in this domain (henceforth WEATHERGOV) is comparable to ROBOCUP (345 words), however, the texts are longer ($|\mathbf{w}| = 29.3$) and more varied. On average, each forecast has 4 sentences and the content selection problem is more challenging; only 5.8 out of the 36 records per scenario are mentioned in the text which roughly corresponds to 1.4 records per sentence. We used 25,000 scenarios from WEATHERGOV for training, 1,000 scenarios for development and 3,528 scenarios for testing. This is the same partition used in Angeli et al. (2010).

For the air travel domain we used the ATIS dataset (Dahl et al., 1994), consisting of 5,426 scenarios. These are transcriptions of spontaneous utterances of users interacting with a hypothetical on-

	WEATHERGOV	ATIS	ROBOCUP
1-BEST	Near 57. Near 57. Near 57. Near 57. Near 57. Near 57. Near 57. Near 57. Near 57. Near 57. Near 57. South wind.	What what what what flights from Denver Phoenix	Pink9 to to Pink7 kicks
k-BEST	As high as 23 mph. Chance of precipitation is 20. Breezy, with a chance of showers. Mostly cloudy, with a high near 57. South wind between 3 and 9 mph.	Show me the flights from Denver to Phoenix	Pink9 passes back to Pink7
ANGELI	A chance of rain or drizzle, with a high near 57. South wind between 3 and 9 mph.	Show me the flights leave from Nashville to Phoenix	Pink9 kicks to Pink7
HUMAN	A slight chance of showers. Mostly cloudy, with a high near 58. South wind between 3 and 9 mph, with gusts as high as 23 mph. Chance of precipitation is 20%.	List flights from Denver to Phoenix	Pink9 passes back to Pink7

Table 2: System output on WEATHERGOV, ATIS, and ROBOCUP (1-BEST, k-BEST, ANGELI) and corresponding human-authored text (HUMAN).

line flight booking system. We used the dataset introduced in Zettlemoyer and Collins (2007)[4] and automatically converted their lambda-calculus expressions to attribute-value pairs following the conventions adopted by Liang et al. (2009). For example, the scenario in Figure 1(a) was initially represented as: $\lambda x.flight(x) \wedge from(x, phoenix) \wedge to(x, new\_york) \wedge day(x, sunday)$.[5] In contrast to the two previous datasets, ATIS has a much richer vocabulary (927 words); each scenario corresponds to a single sentence (average length is 11.2 words) with 2.65 out of 19 record types mentioned on average. Following Zettlemoyer and Collins (2007), we trained on 4,962 scenarios and tested on ATIS NOV93 which contains 448 examples.

Model Parameters Our model has two parameters, namely the number of k grammar derivations considered by the decoder and the order of the language model. We tuned k experimentally on held-out data taken from WEATHERGOV, ROBOCUP, and ATIS, respectively. The optimal value was k=15 for WEATHERGOV, k=25 for ROBOCUP, and $k = 40$ for ATIS. For the ROBOCUP domain, we used a bigram language model which was considered sufficient given that the average text length is small. For WEATHERGOV and ATIS, we used a trigram language model.

System Comparison We evaluated two configurations of our system. A baseline that uses the top scoring derivation in each subgeneration (1-BEST) and another version which makes better use of our decoding algorithm and considers the best k derivations (i.e., 15 for WEATHERGOV, 40 for ATIS, and 25 for ROBOCUP). We compared our output to Angeli et al. (2010) whose approach is closest to ours and state-of-the-art on the WEATHERGOV domain. For ROBOCUP, we also compare against the best-published results (Kim and Mooney, 2010).

Evaluation We evaluated system output automatically, using the BLEU modified precision score (Papineni et al., 2002) with the human-written text as reference. In addition, we evaluated the generated text by eliciting human judgments. Participants were presented with a scenario and its corresponding verbalization and were asked to rate the latter along two dimensions: fluency (is the text grammatical and overall understandable?) and semantic correctness (does the meaning conveyed by the text correspond to the database input?). The subjects used a five point rating scale where a high number indicates better performance. We randomly selected 12 doc-

[4]The original corpus contains user utterances of single dialogue turns which would result in trivial scenarios. Zettlemoyer and Collins (2007) concatenate all user utterances referring to the same dialogue act, (e.g., book a flight), thus yielding more complex scenarios with longer sentences.

[5]The resulting dataset and a technical report describing the mapping procedure in detail are available from `http://homepages.inf.ed.ac.uk/s0793019/index.php?page=resources`

	RoboCup	WeatherGov	Atis
System	BLEU	BLEU	BLEU
1-Best	10.79	8.64	11.85
k-Best	30.90	33.70	29.30
Angeli	28.70	38.40	26.77
Kim-Mooney	47.27	—	—

Table 3: BLEU scores on RoboCup (fixed content selection), WeatherGov, and Atis.

	RoboCup		WeatherGov		Atis	
System	F	SC	F	SC	F	SC
1-Best	$2.47^{*\dagger}$	$2.33^{*\dagger}$	$1.82^{*\dagger}$	$2.05^{*\dagger}$	$2.40^{*\dagger}$	$2.46^{*\dagger}$
k-Best	4.31^{*}	3.96^{*}	3.92^{*}	3.30^{*}	4.01	3.87
Angeli	$4.03^{*\dagger}$	$3.70^{*\dagger}$	4.26^{*}	3.60^{*}	$3.56^{*\dagger}$	$3.33^{*\dagger}$
Human	$4.47^{\dagger}$	$4.37^{\dagger}$	$4.61^{\dagger}$	$4.03^{\dagger}$	4.10	4.01

Table 4: Mean ratings for fluency (F) and semantic correctness (SC) on system output elicited by humans on RoboCup, WeatherGov, and Atis (*: sig. diff. from Human; †: sig. diff. from k-Best.)

uments from the test set (for each domain) and generated output with our models (1-best and k-best) and Angeli et al.'s (2010) model (see Figure 2 for examples of system output). We also included the original text (Human) as gold standard. We thus obtained ratings for 48 (12×4) scenario-text pairs for each domain. The study was conducted over the Internet using WebExp (Keller et al., 2009) and was completed by 114 volunteers, all self reported native English speakers.

5 Results

We conducted two experiments on the RoboCup domain. We first assessed the performance of our generator (k-best) on joint content selection and surface realization and obtained a BLEU score of 24.88. In comparison, the baseline's (1-best) BLEU score was 8.01. In a second experiment we forced the generator to use the gold-standard records from the database. This was necessary in order to compare with previous work (Angeli et al., 2010; Kim and Mooney, 2010).[6] Our results are summarized in Table 3. Overall, our generator performs better than the baseline and Angeli et al. (2010). We observe a substantial increase in performance compared to the joint content selection and surface realization setting. This is expected as the generator is faced with an easier task and there is less scope for error. Our model does not outperform Kim and Mooney (2010), however, this is not entirely surprising as their model requires considerable more supervision (e.g., during parameter initialization) and includes a post-hoc re-ordering component.

With regard to WeatherGov, our generator improves over the baseline but lags behind Angeli et al. (2010). Since our system emits words based on a language model rather than a template, it displays more freedom in word order and lexical choice, and is thus penalized by BLEU when creating output that is overly distinct from the reference. On Atis, our model outperforms both the baseline and Angeli et al. This is the most challenging domain with regard to surface realization with a vocabulary larger than RoboCup and WeatherGov by factors of 2.7 and 4.3, respectively.

The results of our human evaluation study are shown in Table 3. We carried out an Analysis of Variance (Anova) to examine the effect of system type (1-best, k-Best, Angeli, and Human) on the fluency and semantic correctness ratings. Means differences were compared using a post-hoc Tukey test. On RoboCup, our system (k-Best) is significantly better than the baseline (1-best) and Angeli both in terms of fluency and semantic correctness ($a < 0.05$). On WeatherGov, our generator performs comparably to Angeli on fluency and semantic correctness (the differences in the means are not statistically significant); 1-best is significantly worse than 15-best and Angeli ($a < 0.05$). On Atis, k-Best is significantly more fluent and semantically correct than 1-best and Angeli ($a < 0.01$). There was no statistically significant difference between the output of our system and the original Atis sentences.

In sum, we observe that taking the k-best derivations into account boosts performance (the 1-best system is consistently worse). Our model is on par with Angeli on WeatherGov but performs better on RoboCup and Atis when evaluated both auto-

[6]Angeli et al. (2010) and Kim and Mooney (2010) fix content selection both at the record and field level. We let our generator select the appropriate fields, since these are at most two per record type and this level of complexity can be easily tackled during decoding.

matically and by humans. In general, a large part of our output resembles the human text, which demonstrates that our simple language model yields coherent sentences (without any template engineering), at least for the domains under consideration.

6 Conclusions

We have presented an end-to-end generation system that performs both content selection and surface realization. Central to our approach is the encoding of generation as a parsing problem. We reformulate the input (a set of database records and text describing some of them) as a PCFG and show how to find the best derivation using the hypergraph framework. Despite its simplicity, our model is able to obtain performance comparable to the state of the art. We argue that our approach is computationally efficient and viable in practical applications. Porting the system to a different domain is straightforward, assuming a database and corresponding (unaligned) text. As long as the database is compatible with the structure of the grammar in Table 1, we need only retrain to obtain the weights on the hyperarcs and a domain specific language model.

Our model takes into account the k-best derivations at decoding time, however inspection of these shows that it often fails to select the best one. In the future, we plan to remedy this by using forest reranking, a technique that approximately reranks a packed forest of exponentially many derivations (Huang, 2008). We would also like to scale our model to more challenging domains (e.g., product descriptions) and to enrich our generator with some notion of discourse planning. An interesting question is how to extend the PCFG-based approach advocated here so as to capture discourse-level document structure.

Acknowledgments We are grateful to Percy Liang and Gabor Angeli for providing us with their code and data. We would also like to thank Luke Zettlemoyer and Tom Kwiatkowski for sharing their ATIS dataset with us and Frank Keller for his feedback on an earlier version of this paper.

References

Gabor Angeli, Percy Liang, and Dan Klein. 2010. A simple domain-independent probabilistic approach to generation. In *Proceedings of the 2010 Conference on Empirical Methods in Natural Language Processing*, pages 502–512, Cambridge, MA.

Regina Barzilay and Mirella Lapata. 2005. Collective content selection for concept-to-text generation. In *Proceedings of Human Language Technology and Empirical Methods in Natural Language Processing*, pages 331–338, Vancouver, British Columbia.

Anja Belz. 2008. Automatic generation of weather forecast texts using comprehensive probabilistic generation-space models. *Natural Language Engineering*, 14(4):431–455.

David L. Chen and Raymond J. Mooney. 2008. Learning to sportscast: A test of grounded language acquisition. In *Proceedings of International Conference on Machine Learning*, pages 128–135, Helsinki, Finland.

David Chiang. 2007. Hierarchical phrase-based translation. *Computational Linguistics*, 33(2):201–228.

Deborah A. Dahl, Madeleine Bates, Michael Brown, William Fisher, Kate Hunicke-Smith, David Pallett, Christine Pao, Alexander Rudnicky, and Elizabeth Shriberg. 1994. Expanding the scope of the atis task: the atis-3 corpus. In *Proceedings of the Workshop on Human Language Technology*, pages 43–48, Plainsboro, NJ.

Pablo A. Duboue and Kathleen R. McKeown. 2002. Content planner construction via evolutionary algorithms and a corpus-based fitness function. In *Proceedings of International Natural Language Generation*, pages 89–96, Ramapo Mountains, NY.

Giorgio Gallo, Giustino Longo, Stefano Pallottino, and Sang Nguyen. 1993. Directed hypergraphs and applications. *Discrete Applied Mathematics*, 42:177–201.

Liang Huang and David Chiang. 2005. Better k-best parsing. In *Proceedings of the 9th International Workshop on Parsing Technology*, pages 53–64, Vancouver, British Columbia.

Liang Huang and David Chiang. 2007. Forest rescoring: Faster decoding with integrated language models. In *Proceedings of the 45th Annual Meeting of the Association of Computational Linguistics*, pages 144–151, Prague, Czech Republic.

Liang Huang. 2008. Forest reranking: Discriminative parsing with non-local features. In *Proceedings of ACL-08: HLT*, pages 586–594, Columbus, Ohio.

Frank Keller, Subahshini Gunasekharan, Neil Mayo, and Martin Corley. 2009. Timing accuracy of Web experiments: A case study using the WebExp software package. *Behavior Research Methods*, 41(1):1–12.

Joohyun Kim and Raymond Mooney. 2010. Generative alignment and semantic parsing for learning from ambiguous supervision. In *Proceedings of the 23rd Conference on Computational Linguistics*, pages 543–551, Beijing, China.

Dan Klein and Christopher D. Manning. 2001. Parsing and hypergraphs. In *Proceedings of the 7th International Workshop on Parsing Technologies*, pages 123–134, Beijing, China.

Zhifei Li and Jason Eisner. 2009. First- and second-order expectation semirings with applications to minimum-risk training on translation forests. In *Proceedings of the 2009 Conference on Empirical Methods in Natural Language Processing*, pages 40–51, Suntec, Singapore.

Percy Liang, Michael Jordan, and Dan Klein. 2009. Learning semantic correspondences with less supervision. In *roceedings of the Joint Conference of the 47th Annual Meeting of the ACL and the 4th International Joint Conference on Natural Language Processing of the AFNLP*, pages 91–99, Suntec, Singapore.

Wei Lu and Hwee Tou Ng. 2011. A probabilistic forest-to-string model for language generation from typed lambda calculus expressions. In *Proceedings of the 2011 Conference on Empirical Methods in Natural Language Processing*, pages 1611–1622, Edinburgh, UK.

Kishore Papineni, Salim Roukos, Todd Ward, and Wei-Jing Zhu. 2002. Bleu: a method for automatic evaluation of machine translation. In *Proceedings of 40th Annual Meeting of the Association for Computational Linguistics*, pages 311–318, Philadelphia, Pennsylvania.

Ehud Reiter and Robert Dale. 2000. *Building natural language generation systems*. Cambridge University Press, New York, NY.

Ehud Reiter, Somayajulu Sripada, Jim Hunter, and Ian Davy. 2005. Choosing words in computer-generated weather forecasts. *Artificial Intelligence*, 167:137–169.

Yuk Wah Wong and Raymond Mooney. 2007. Generation by inverting a semantic parser that uses statistical machine translation. In *Proceedings of the Human Language Technology and the Conference of the North American Chapter of the Association for Computational Linguistics*, pages 172–179, Rochester, NY.

Luke Zettlemoyer and Michael Collins. 2007. Online learning of relaxed CCG grammars for parsing to logical form. In *Proceedings of the 2007 Joint Conference on Empirical Methods in Natural Language Processing and Computational Natural Language Learning*, pages 678–687, Prague, Czech Republic.

Detecting Visual Text

Jesse Dodge[1], Amit Goyal[2], Xufeng Han[3], Alyssa Mensch[4], Margaret Mitchell[5], Karl Stratos[6]
Kota Yamaguchi[3], Yejin Choi[3], Hal Daumé III[2], Alexander C. Berg[3] and Tamara L. Berg[3]
[1]University of Washington, [2]University of Maryland, [3]Stony Brook University
[4]MIT, [5]Oregon Health & Science University, [6]Columbia University
dodgejesse@gmail.com, amit@umiacs.umd.edu, xufhan@cs.stonybrook.edu
acmensch@mit.edu, mitchmar@ohsu.edu, stratos@cs.columbia.edu
kyamagu@cs.stonybrook.edu, ychoi@cs.stonybrook.edu
me@hal3.name, aberg@cs.stonybrook.edu, tlberg@cs.stonybrook.edu

Abstract

When people describe a scene, they often include information that is not visually apparent; sometimes based on background knowledge, sometimes to tell a story. We aim to separate *visual text*—descriptions of what is being seen—from non-visual text in natural images and their descriptions. To do so, we first concretely define what it means to be visual, annotate visual text and then develop algorithms to automatically classify noun phrases as visual or non-visual. We find that using text alone, we are able to achieve high accuracies at this task, and that incorporating features derived from computer vision algorithms improves performance. Finally, we show that we can reliably mine visual nouns and adjectives from large corpora and that we can use these effectively in the classification task.

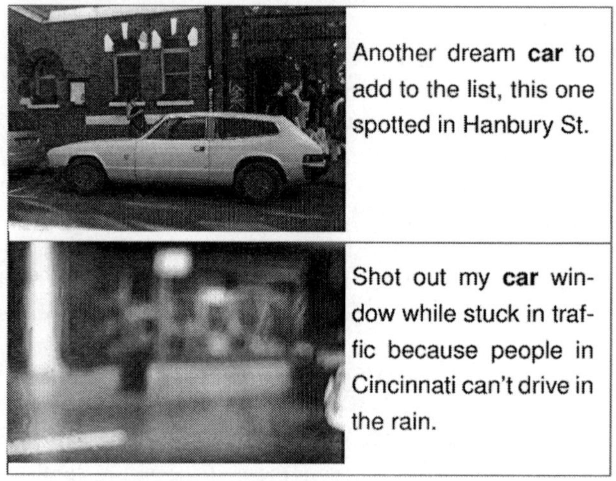

Figure 1: Two image/caption pairs, both containing the noun "car" but only the top one in a visual context.

1 Introduction

People use language to describe the visual world. Our goal is to: *formalize* what "visual text" is (Section 2.2); *analyze* naturally occurring written language for occurrences of visual text (Section 2); and *build* models that can detect visual descriptions from raw text or from image/text pairs (Section 3). This is a challenging problem. One challenge is demonstrated in Figure 1, which contains two images that contain the noun "car" in their human-written captions. In one case (the top image), there actually *is* a car in the image; in the other case, there is not: the car refers to the state of the speaker.

The ability to automatically identify visual text is practically useful in a number of scenarios. One can imagine automatically mining image/caption data (like that in Figure 1) to train object recognition systems. However, in order to do so reliably, one must know whether the "car" actually appears or not. When building image search engines, it is common to use text near an image as features; this is more useful when this text is actually visual. Or when training systems to automatically generate captions of images (e.g., for visually impaired users), we need good language models for visual text.

One of our goals is to define what it means for a bit of text to be visual. As inspiration, we consider image/description pairs automatically crawled from Flickr (Ordonez et al., 2011). A first pass attempt might be to say "a phrase in the description of an image is *visual* if you can see it in the corresponding image." Unfortunately, this is too vague to be useful; the biggest issues are discussed in Section 2.2.

Based on our analysis, we settled on the following **definition:** A piece of text is visual (with respect to a corresponding image) *if* you can cut out a part of that image, paste it into any other image, and a third party could describe that cut-out part in the same way. In the car example, the claim is that I could cut out the car, put it in the middle of any other image, and someone else might still refer to that car as "dream car." The car in the bottom image in Figure 1 is *not* visual because there's nothing you could cut out that would retain car-ness.

2 Data Analysis

Before embarking on the road to building models of visual text, it is useful to obtain a better understanding of what visual text is like, and how it compares to the more standard corpora that we are used to working with. We describe the two large data sets that we use (one visual, one non-visual), then describe the quantitative differences between them, and finally discuss our annotation effort for labeling visual text.

2.1 Data sets

We use the SBU Captioned Photo Dataset (Ordonez et al., 2011) as our primary source of image/caption data. This dataset contains 1 million images with user associated captions, collected *in the wild* by intelligent filtering of a huge number of Flickr photos. Past work has made use of this dataset to retrieve whole captions for association with a query image (Ordonez et al., 2011). Their method first used global image descriptors to retrieve an initial matched set, and then applied more local estimates of content to re-rank this (relatively small) set (Ordonez et al., 2011). This means that content based matching was relatively constrained by the bottleneck of global descriptors, and local content (e.g., objects) had relatively small effect on accuracy.

As an auxiliary source of information for (largely) non-visual text, we consider a large corpus of text obtained by concatenating ukWaC[1] and the New York Times Newswire Service (NYT) section of the Gigaword (Graff, 2003) Corpus. The Web-derived ukWaC is already tokenized and POS-tagged with the TreeTagger (Schmid, 1995). NYT is tokenized, and POS-tagged using TagChunk (Daumé III and Marcu, 2005). This consists of 171 million sentences (4 billion words). We refer to this *generic* text corpus as **Large-Data**.

2.2 Formalizing *visual text*

We begin our analysis by revisiting the definition of visual text from the introduction, and justifying this particular definition. In order to arrive at a sufficiently specific definition of "visual text," we focused on the applications of visual text that we care about. As discussed in the introduction, these are: training object detectors, building image search engines and automatically generating captions for images. Our definition is based on access to image/text pairs, but later we discuss how to talk about it purely based on text. To make things concrete, consider an image/text pair like that in the top of Figure 1. And then consider a phrase in the text, like "dream car." The question is: is "dream car" visual or not?

One of the challenges in arriving at such a definition is that the description of an image in Flickr is almost always written by the photographer of that image. This means the descriptions often contain information that is *not* actually pictured in the image, or contain references that are only relevant to the photographer (referring to a person/pet by name).

One might think that this is an artifact of this particular dataset, but it appears to be generic to all captions, even those written by a viewer (rather than the photographer). Figure 2 shows an image from the Pascal dataset (Everingham et al., 2010), together with captions written by random people collected via crowd-sourcing (Rashtchian et al., 2010). There is much in this caption that is clearly made-up by the author, presumably to make the caption more interesting (e.g., meta-references like "the camera" or "A photo" as well as "guesses" about the image, such as "garage" and "venison").

Second, there is a question of how much inference you are allowed to do when you say that you "see" something. For example, in the top image in Figure 1, the street *is* pictured, but does that mean that "Hanbury St." is visual? What if there were a street sign that clearly read "Hanbury St." in the image? This problem comes up all the time, when people say things like "in London" or "in France" in their captions. If it's just a portrait of people "in France,"

[1] ukWaC is a freely available Wikipedia-derived corpus from 2009; see http://wacky.sslmit.unibo.it/doku.php.

1. A distorted photo of **a man** cutting up **a large cut of meat** in a garage.
2. **A man** smiling at the camera while carving up **meat**.
3. **A man** smiling while **he** cuts up **a piece of meat**.
4. **A smiling man** is standing next to **a table** dressing a piece of venison.
5. **The man** is smiling into the camera as **he** cuts **meat**.

Figure 2: An image from the Pascal data with five captions collected via crowd-sourcing. Measurements on the SMALL and LARGE dataset show that approximately 70% of noun phrases are visual (bolded), while the rest are non-visual (underlined). See Section 2.4 for details.

it's hard to say that this is visual. If you see the Eiffel tower in the background, this is perhaps better (though it could be Las Vegas!), but how does this compare to a photo taken out of an airplane window in which you actually do see France-the-country?

This problem becomes even *more* challenging when you consider things *other than nouns.* For instance, when is a *verb* visual? For instance, the most common non-copula verb in our data is "sitting," which appears in roughly two usages: (1) "Took this shot, sitting in a bar and enjoying a Portugese beer." and (2) "Lexy sitting in a basket on top of her cat tree." The first one is clearly not visual; the second probably is. A more nuanced case is for "playing," as in: "Girls playing in a boat on the river bank" (probably visual) versus "Tuckered out from playing in Nannie's yard." The corresponding image for the latter description shows a sleeping cat.

Our final definition, based on cutting out the potentially visual part of the image, allows us to say that: (1) "venison" is not visual (because you cannot actually tell); (2) "Hanbury St." and "Lexy" are not visual (you can infer them, in the first case because there is only one street and in the second case because there is only one cat); (3) that seeing the *real* Eiffel tower in the background does not mean that "France" is visual (but again, may be inferred); etc.

2.3 Most Pronounced Differences

To get an intuitive sense of how Flickr captions (expected to be predominantly visual) and generic text (expected not to be so) differ, we computed some simple statistics on sentences from these. In general, the generic text had twice as many main verbs as the Flickr data, four times as many auxiliaries or light verbs, and about 50% more prepositions.

Flickr captions tended to have far more references to *physical* objects (versus *abstract* objects) than the generic text, according to the WordNet hierarchy. Approximately 64% of the objects in Flickr were physical (about 22% abstract and 14% unknown). Whereas in the generic text, only 30% of the objects were physical, 53% were abstract (17% unknown).

A third major difference between the corpora is in terms of noun modifiers. In both corpora, nouns tend not to have any modifiers, but modifiers are still more prevalent in Flickr than in generic text. In particular, 60% of nouns in Flickr have zero modifiers, but 70% of nouns in generic text have zero modifiers. In Flickr, 30% of nouns have exactly one modifier, as compared to only 22% for generic text.

The breakdown of what those modifiers look like is even more pronounced, even when restricted just to physical objects (modifier types are obtained through the bootstrapping process discussed in Section 3.1). Almost 50% of nominal modifiers in the Flickr data are color modifiers, whereas color accounts for less than 5% of nominal modifiers in generic text. In Flickr, 10% of modifiers talk about beauty, in comparison to less than 5% in generic text. On the other hand, less than 3% of modifiers in Flickr reference ethnicity, as compared to almost 20% in generic text; and 20% of Flickr modifiers reference size, versus 50% in generic text.

2.4 Annotating Visual Text

In order to obtain ground truth data, we rely on crowdsourcing (via Amazon's Mechanical Turk). Each *instance* is an image, a paired caption, and a highlighted noun phrase in that caption. The annotation for this instance is a label of "visual," "non-visual" or "error," where the error category is reserved for cases where the noun phrase segmentation was erroneous. Each worker is given five instances to label and paid one cent per annotation.[2]

For a small amount of data (803 images containing 2339 instances), we obtained annotations from three separate workers per instance to obtain higher quality data. For a large amount of data (48k images), we obtained annotations from only a single worker. Subsequently, we will refer to these two data sets as the SMALL and LARGE data sets. In both data sets, approximately 70% of the noun phrases were visual, 28% were non-visual and 2% were erroneous. For simplicity, we group erroneous and non-visual for all learning and evaluation.

In the SMALL data set, the rate of disagreement between annotators was relatively low. In 74% of the annotations, there was *no* disagreement at all. We reconciled the annotations using the quality management technique of Ipeirotis et al. (2010); only 14% of the annotations need to be changed in order to obtain a gold standard.

One immediate question raised in this process is whether one needs to actually see the image to perform the annotation. In particular, if we expect an NLP system to be able to classify noun phrases as visual or non-visual, we need to know whether people can do this task *sans* image. We therefore performed the *same* annotation on the SMALL data set, but where the workers were *not* shown the image. Their task was to *imagine* an image for this caption and then annotate the noun phrase based on whether they thought it would be pictured or not. We obtained three annotations as before and reconciled them (Ipeirotis et al., 2010). The accuracy of this reconciled version against the gold standard (produced by people who *did* see the image) was 91%. This suggests that while people are able to do this task with some reliability, seeing the image is very important (recall that always guessing "visual" leads to an accuracy of 70%).

3 Visual Features from Raw Text

Our first goal is to attempt to obtain relatively large knowledge bases of terms that are (predominantly) visual. This is potentially useful in its own right (for instance, in the context of search, to determine which query terms are likely to be pictured). We have explored two techniques for performing this task, the first based on bootstrapping (Section 3.1) and the second based on label propagation (Section 3.2). We then use these lists to generate features for a classifier that predicts whether a noun phrase—in context—is visual or not (Section 4).

In addition, we consider the task of separating adjectives into different visual categories (Section 3.3). We have already used the results of this in Section 2.3 to understand the differences between our two corpora. It is also potentially useful for the purpose of building new object detection systems or even attribute detection systems, to get a vocabulary of target detections.

3.1 Bootstrapping for Visual Text

In this section, we learn visual and non-visual nouns and adjectives automatically based on bootstrapping techniques. First, we construct a graph between adjectives by computing distributional similarity (Turney and Pantel, 2010) between them. For computing distributional similarity between adjectives, each target adjective is defined as a vector of nouns which are modified by the target adjective. To be exact, we use only those adjectives as modifiers which appear adjacent to a noun (that is, in a JJ NN construction). For example, in "small red apple," we consider only *red* as a modifier for noun. We use Pointwise Mutual Information (PMI) (Church and Hanks, 1989) to weight the contexts, and select the top 1000 PMI contexts for each adjective.[3]

Next, we apply cosine similarity to find the top 10 distributionally similar adjectives with respect to each target adjective based on our large generic corpus (**Large-Data** from Section 2.1). This creates a graph with adjectives as nodes and cosine similarity as weight on the edges. Analogously, we construct a graph with nouns as nodes (here, adjectives are used as contexts for nouns).

We then apply bootstrapping (Kozareva et al., 2008) on the noun and adjective graphs by selecting 10 seeds for visual and non-visual nouns and adjectives (see Table 1). We use in-degree (sum of weights of incoming edges) to compute the score for

[2] Data available at http://hal3.name/dvt/, with direct links back to the SBU Captioned Photo Dataset.

[3] We are interested in *descriptive* adjectives, which "typically ascribe to a noun a value of an attribute" (Miller, 1998).

Visual nouns seeds	car house tree horse animal man table bottle woman computer
Non-visual nouns seeds	idea bravery deceit trust dedication anger humour luck inflation honesty
Visual adjectives seeds	brown green wooden striped orange rectangular furry shiny rusty feathered
Non-visual adjectives seeds	public original whole righteous political personal intrinsic individual initial total

Table 1: Example seeds for bootstrapping.

each node that has connections with known (seeds) or automatically labeled nodes, previously exploited to learn hyponymy relations from the web (Kozareva et al., 2008). Intuitively, in-degree captures the popularity of new instances among instances that have already been identified as good instances. We learn visual and non-visual words together (known as the mutual exclusion principle in bootstrapping (Thelen and Riloff, 2002; McIntosh and Curran, 2008)): each word (node) is assigned to only one class. Moreover, after each iteration, we harmonically decrease the weight of the in-degree associated with instances learned in later iterations. We added 25 new instances at each iteration and ran 500 iterations of bootstrapping, yielding 11955 visual and 11978 non-visual nouns, and 7746 visual and 7464 non-visual adjectives.

Based on manual inspection, the learned visual and non-visual lists look great. In the future, we would like to do a Mechanical Turk evaluation to directly evaluate the visual and non-visual nouns and adjectives. For now, we show the coverage of these classes in the Flickr data-set: Visual nouns: 53.71%; Non-visual nouns: 14.25%; Visual adjectives: 51.79%; Non-visual adjectives: 14.40%. Overall, we find more visual nouns and adjectives are covered in the Flickr data-set, which makes sense, since the Flickr data-set is largely visual.

Second, we show the coverage of these classes on the large text corpora (**Large-Data** from Section 2.1): Visual nouns: 26.05%; Non-visual nouns: 41.16%; Visual adjectives: 20.02%; Non-visual adjectives: 40.00%. Overall, more non-visual nouns and adjectives cover text data, since **Large-Data** is a non-visual data-set.

Visual: attend, buy, clean, comb, cook, drink, eat, fry, pack, paint, photograph, smash, spill, steal, taste, tie, touch, watch, wear, wipe
Non-visual: achieve, admire, admit, advocate, alleviate, appreciate, arrange, criticize, eradicate, induce, investigate, minimize, overcome, promote, protest, relieve, resolve, review, support, tolerate

Table 2: Predicates that are visual and non-visual.

Visual: water, cotton, food, pumpkin, chicken, ring, hair, mouth, meeting, kind, filter, game, oil, show, tear, online, face, class, car
Non-visual: problem, poverty, pain, issue, use, symptom, goal, effect, thought, government, share, stress, work, risk, impact, concern, obstacle, change, disease, dispute

Table 3: Learned visual/non-visual nouns.

3.2 Label Propagation for Visual Text

To propagate visual labels, we construct a bipartite graph between visually descriptive predicates and their arguments. Let V_P be the set of nodes that corresponds to predicates, and let V_A be the set of nodes that corresponds to arguments. To learn the visually descriptive words, we set V_P to 20 visually descriptive predicates shown in the top of Table 2, and V_A to all nouns that appear in the object argument position with respect to the seed predicates. We approximate this by taking nouns on the right hand side of the predicates within a window of 4 words using the Web 1T Google N-gram data (Brants and Franz., 2006). For edge weights, we use conditional probabilities between predicates and arguments so that $w(p \to a) := pr(a|p)$ and $w(a \to p) := pr(p|a)$.

In order to collectively induce the visually descriptive words from this graph, we apply the graph propagation algorithm of Velikovich et al. (2010), a variant of label propagation algorithms (Zhu and Ghahramani, 2002) that has been shown to be effective for inducing a web-scale polarity lexicon based on word co-occurrence statistics. This algo-

Color	purple	blue	maroon	beige	green
Material	plastic	cotton	wooden	metallic	silver
Shape	circular	square	round	rectangular	triangular
Size	small	big	tiny	tall	huge
Surface	coarse	smooth	furry	fluffy	rough
Direction	sideways	north	upward	left	down
Pattern	striped	dotted	checked	plaid	quilted
Quality	shiny	rusty	dirty	burned	glittery
Beauty	beautiful	cute	pretty	gorgeous	lovely
Age	young	mature	immature	older	senior
Ethnicity	french	asian	american	greek	hispanic

Table 4: Attribute Classes with their seed values

rithm iteratively updates the semantic distance between each pair of nodes in the graph, then produces a score for each node that represents how visually descriptive each word is. To learn the words that are *not* visually descriptive, we use the predicates shown in the bottom of Table 2 as V_P instead. Table 3 shows the top ranked nouns that are visually descriptive and *not* visually descriptive.

3.3 Bootstrapping Visual Adjectives

Our goal in this section is to automatically generate comprehensive lists of adjectives for different attributes, such as color, material, shape, etc. To our knowledge, this is the first significant effort of this type for adjectives: most bootstrapping techniques focus exclusively on nouns, although Almuhareb and Poesio (2005) populated lists of attributes using web-based similarity measures. We found that in some ways adjectives are easier than nouns, but require slightly different representations.

One might conjecture that listing attributes by hand is difficult. Colors names are well known to be quite varied. For instance, our bootstrapping approach is able to discover colors like "grayish," "chestnut," "emerald," and "rufous" that would be hard to list manually (the last is a reddish-brown color, somewhat like rust). Although perhaps not easy to create, the Wikipedia list of colors (http://en.wikipedia.org/wiki/List_of_colors) includes all of these except "grayish". On the other hand, it includes color terms that might be difficult to make *use of* as colors, such as "bisque," "bone" and "bubbles" (the last is a very light cyan), which might over-generate hits. For shape, we find "oblong," "hemispherical," "quadrangular" and, our favorite, "convex".

We use essentially the same bootstrapping process as described earlier in Section 3.1, but on a slightly different data representation. The only difference is that instead of linking adjectives to their 10 most similar neighbors, we link them only to 25 neighbors to attempt to improve recall.

We begin with seeds for each attribute class from Table 4. We conduct a manual evaluation to directly measure the quality of attribute classes. We recruited 3 annotators and developed annotation guidelines that instructed each recruiter to judge whether a learned value belongs to an attribute class or not. The annotators assigned "1" if a learned value belongs to a class, otherwise "0".

We conduct an Information Retrieval (IR) Style human evaluation. Analogous to an IR evaluation, here the total number of relevant values for attribute classes can not be computed. Therefore, we assume the correct output of several systems as the total recall which can be produced by any system. Now, with the help of our 3 manual annotators, we obtain the correct output of several systems from the total output produced by these systems.

First, we measured the agreement on whether each learned value belongs to a semantic class or not. We computed κ to measure inter-annotator agreement for each pair of annotators. We focus our evaluation on 4 classes: age, beauty, color, and direction; between Human 2 and Human 3 and between Human 1 and Human 3, the κ value was 0.48; between Human 1 and Human 2 it was 0.45. These numbers are somewhat lower than we would like, but not terrible. If we evaluate the classes individually, we find that age has the lowest κ. If we remove "age," the pairwise κs rise to 0.59, 0.57 and 0.55.

Second, we compute Precision (Pr), Recall (Rec) and F-measure (F1) for different bootstrapping systems (based on the number of iterations and the number of new words added in each iteration). Two parameter settings performed consistently better than others (10 iterations with 25 items, and 5 iterations with 50 items). The former system achieves a precision/recall/F1 of 0.53, 0.71, 0.60 against Human 2; the latter achieves scores of 0.54, 0.72, 0.62.

4 Recognizing Visual Text

We train a logistic regression (aka maximum entropy) model (Daumé III, 2004) to classify text as visual or non-visual. The features we use fall into the following categories: WORDS (the actual lexical items and stems); BIGRAMS (lexical bigrams); SPELL (lexical features such as capitalization pattern, and word prefixes and suffixes); WORDNET (set of hypernyms according to WordNet); and BOOTSTRAP (features derived from bootstrapping or label propagation).

For each of these feature categories, we compute features *inside* the phrase being categorized (e.g., "the car"), *before* the phrase (two words to the left) and *after* the phrase (two words to the right). We additionally add a feature that computes the number of words in a phrase, and a feature that computes the position of the phrase in the caption (first fifth through last fifth of the description). This leads to seventeen feature templates that are computed for each example. In the SMALL data set, there are $25k$ features ($10k$ non-singletons); in the LARGE data set, there are $191k$ features ($79k$ non-singletons).

To train models on the SMALL data set, we use 1500 instances as training, 200 as development and the remaining 639 as test data. To train models on the LARGE data set, we use 45000 instances as training and the remaining 4401 as development. We always test on the 639 instances from the SMALL data, since it has been redundantly annotated. The development data is used only to choose the regularization parameter for a Gaussian prior on the logistic regression model; this parameter is chosen in the range $\{0.01, 0.05, 0.1, 0.5, 1, 2, 4, 8, 16, 32, 64\}$.

Because of the imbalanced data problem, evaluating according to accuracy is not appropriate for this task. Even evaluating by precision/recall is not appropriate, because a baseline system that guesses that everything is visual obtains 100% recall and 70% precision. Due to these issues, we instead evaluate according to the area under the ROC curve (AUC). To check statistical significance, we compute standard deviations using bootstrap resampling, and consider there to be a significant difference if a result falls outside of two standard deviations of the baseline (95% confidence).

Figure 3 shows learning curves for the two data sets. The SMALL data achieves an AUC score of 71.3 in the full data setting (1700 examples); the LARGE data needs $12k$ examples to achieve similar accuracy due to noise. However, with $49k$ examples, we are able to achieve a AUC score of 75.3 using the

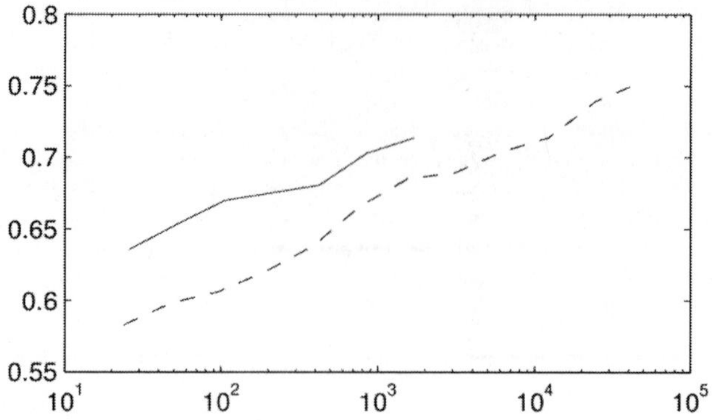

Figure 3: Learning curves for training on SMALL data (blue solid) and LARGE data (black dashed). X-axis (in log-scale) is number of training examples; Y-axis is AUC.

large data set. By pooling the data (and weighting the small data), this boosts results to 76.1. The confidence range on these data is approximately ± 1.9, meaning that this boost is likely not significant.

4.1 Using Image Features

As discussed previously, humans are only able to achieve 90% accuracy on the visual/non-visual task when they are not allowed to view the image. This potentially upper-bounds the performance of a learned system that can only look at text. In order to attempt to overcome this, we augment our basic system with a number of features computed from the corresponding images. These features are derived from the output of state of the art vision algorithms to detect 121 different objects, stuff and scenes.

As our object detectors, we use standard state of the art deformable part-based models (Felzenszwalb et al., 2010) for 89 common object categories, including: the original 20 objects from Pascal, 49 objects from Object Bank (Li-Jia Li and Fei-Fei, 2010), and 20 from Im2Text (Ordonez et al., 2011). We additionally use coarse image parsing to estimate background elements in each database image. Six possible background (stuff) categories are considered: sky, water, grass, road, tree, and building. For this we use detectors (Ordonez et al., 2011) which compute color, texton, HoG (Dalal and Triggs, 2005) and Geometric Context (Hoiem et al., 2005) as input features to a sliding window based SVM classifier. These detectors are run on all database images, creating a large pool of background elements for retrieval. Finally, we ob-

Figure 4: (Left) Highest confidence flower detected in an image; (Right) All detections in the same image.

	Category	Position	AUC
	Bootstrap	Phrase	65.2
+	Spell	Phrase	68.6
+	Image	-	69.2
+	Words	Phrase	70.0
+	Length	-	69.8
+	Wordnet	Phrase	70.4
+	Wordnet	Before	*70.6*
+	Spell	Before	*71.8*
+	Words	Before	72.2
+	Bootstrap	Before	**72.4**
+	Spell	After	*71.5*

Table 5: Results of feature ablation on SMALL data set. Best result is in bold; results that are not statistically significantly worse are italicized.

tain scene descriptors for each image by computing scene classification scores for 26 common scene categories, using the features, methods and training data from the SUN dataset (Xiao et al., 2010).

Figure 4 shows an example image on which several detectors have been run. From each image, we extract the following features: which object detectors fired; how many times they fired; the confidence of the most-likely firing; the percentage of the image (in pixels) that the bounding box corresponding to this object occupies; and the percentage of the width (and height) of the image that it occupies.

Unfortunately, object detection is a highly noisy process. The right image in Figure 4 shows all detections for that image, which includes, for instance, a chair detection that spans nearly the entire image, and a person detection in the bottom-right corner. For an average image, if a single detector (e.g., the flower detector) fires once, it actually fires 40 times ($\pm\sigma = 1.8$). Moreover, of the 120 detectors, on an average image over 22 ($\pm\sigma = 5.6$) of them fire at least once (though certainly in an average image only a few objects are actually present). Exacerbating this problem, although the confidence scores for a single detector can be compared, the scores between different detectors are not at all comparable. In order to attenuate this problem, we include duplicate copies of all the above features restricted to the *most confident* object for each object type.

On the SMALL data set, this adds 400 new features (300 of which are non-singletons[4]); on the LARGE data set, this adds 500 new features (480 non-singletons). Overall, the AUC scores trained on the small data set increase from 71.3 to 73.9 (a significant improvement). On the large data set, the increase is only from 76.1 to 76.8, which is not likely to be significant. In general, the improvement obtained by adding image features is most pronounced in the setting of small training data, perhaps because these features are more generic than the highly lexi calized features used in the textual model. But once there is a substantial amount of text data, the noisy image features become less useful.

4.2 Feature Ablations

In order to ascertain the degree to which each feature template is useful, we perform an ablation study. We first perform feature selection at the template level using the information gain criteria, and then train models using the corresponding subset of features.

The results on the SMALL data set are shown in Table 5. Here, the bootstrapping features computed on words within the phrase to be classified were judged as the most useful, followed by spelling features. Image features were judged third most useful. In general, features in the phrase were most useful (not surprisingly), and then features before the phrase (presumably to give context, for instance as in "*out of* the window"). Features from after the phrase were not useful.

[4]Non-singleton features appear more than once in the data.

	CATEGORY	POSITION	AUC
	Words	Phrase	74.7
+	Image	-	74.4
+	Bootstrap	Phrase	74.3
+	Spell	Phrase	75.3
+	Length	-	74.7
+	Words	Before	*76.2*
+	Wordnet	Phrase	*76.1*
+	Spell	After	*76.0*
+	Spell	Before	*76.8*
+	Wordnet	Before	**77.0**
+	Wordnet	After	75.6

Table 6: Results of feature ablation on LARGE data set.

Corresponding results on the LARGE data set are shown in Table 6. Note that the order of features selected is different because the training data is different. Here, the most useful features are simply the words in the phrase to be classified, which alone already gives an AUC score of 74.7, only a few points off from the best performance of 77.0 once image features, bootstrap features and spelling features are added. As before, these features are rated as very useful for classification performance.

Finally, we consider the effect of using Bootstrap-based features or label-propagation-based features. In all the above experiments, the features used are based on the *union* of word lists created by these two techniques. We perform three experiments. Beginning with the system that contains *all* features (SMALL=73.9, LARGE=76.8), we first remove the bootstrap-based features (SMALL→71.8, LARGE→75.5) or remove the label-propagation-based features (SMALL→71.2, LARGE→74.9) or remove both (SMALL→70.7, LARGE→74.2). From these results, we can see that these techniques are useful, but somewhat redundant: if you had to choose one, you should choose label-propagation.

5 Discussion

As connections between language and vision become stronger, for instance in the contexts of object detection (Hou and Zhang, 2007; Kim and Torralba, 2009; Sivic et al., 2008; Alexe et al., 2010; Gu et al., 2009), attribute detection (Ferrari and Zisserman, 2007; Farhadi et al., 2009; Kumar et al., 2009; Berg et al., 2010), visual phrases (Farhadi and Sadeghi, 2011), and automatic caption generation (Farhadi et al., 2010; Feng and Lapata, 2010; Ordonez et al., 2011; Kulkarni et al., 2011; Yang et al., 2011; Li et al., 2011; Mitchell et al., 2012), it becomes increasingly important to understand, and to be able to detect, text that *actually* refers to observed phenomena. Our results suggest that while this is a hard problem, it is possible to leverage large text resources and state-of-the-art computer vision algorithms to address it with high accuracy.

Acknowledgments

T.L. Berg and K. Yamaguchi were supported in part by NSF Faculty Early Career Development (CAREER) Award #1054133; A.C. Berg and Y. Choi were partially supported by the Stony Brook University Office of the Vice President for Research; H. Daumé III and A. Goyal were partially supported by NSF Award IIS-1139909; all authors were partially supported by a 2011 JHU Summer Workshop.

References

B. Alexe, T. Deselaers, and V. Ferrari. 2010. What is an object? In *Computer Vision and Pattern Recognition (CVPR), 2010 IEEE Conference on*, pages 73 –80.

A. Almuhareb and M. Poesio. 2005. Finding concept attributes in the web. In *Corpus Linguistics Conference*.

Tamara L. Berg, Alexander C. Berg, and Jonathan Shih. 2010. Automatic attribute discovery and characterization from noisy web data. In *European Conference on Computer Vision (ECCV)*.

Thorsten Brants and Alex Franz. 2006. Web 1t 5-gram version 1. In *Linguistic Data Consortium, ISBN: 1-58563-397-6, Philadelphia*.

K. Church and P. Hanks. 1989. Word Association Norms, Mutual Information and Lexicography. In *Proceedings of ACL*, pages 76–83, Vancouver, Canada, June.

N. Dalal and B. Triggs. 2005. Histograms of oriented gradients for human detection. In *CVPR*.

Hal Daumé III and Daniel Marcu. 2005. Learning as search optimization: Approximate large margin methods for structured prediction. In *Proceedings of the International Conference on Machine Learning (ICML)*.

Hal Daumé III. 2004. Notes on CG and LM-BFGS optimization of logistic regression. Paper available at http://pub.hal3.name/#daume04cg-bfgs, implementation available at http://hal3.name/megam/, August.

M. Everingham, L. Van Gool, C. K. I. Williams, J. Winn, and A. Zisserman. 2010. The PASCAL Visual Object Classes Challenge 2010 (VOC2010) Results. http://www.pascal-network.org/challenges/VOC/voc2010/workshop/index.html.

Ali Farhadi and Amin Sadeghi. 2011. Recognition using visual phrases. In *Computer Vision and Pattern Recognition (CVPR)*.

A. Farhadi, I. Endres, D. Hoiem, and D.A. Forsyth. 2009. Describing objects by their attributes. In *Computer Vision and Pattern Recognition (CVPR)*.

A. Farhadi, M. Hejrati, M.A. Sadeghi, P. Young, C. Rashtchian1, J. Hockenmaier, and D.A. Forsyth. 2010. Every picture tells a story: Generating sentences from images. In *ECCV*.

P. F. Felzenszwalb, R. B. Girshick, and D. McAllester. 2010. Discriminatively trained deformable part models, release 4. http://people.cs.uchicago.edu/~pff/latent-release4/.

Y. Feng and M. Lapata. 2010. How many words is a picture worth? automatic caption generation for news images. In *ACL*.

V. Ferrari and A. Zisserman. 2007. Learning visual attributes. In *Advances in Neural Information Processing Systems (NIPS)*.

D. Graff. 2003. English Gigaword. Linguistic Data Consortium, Philadelphia, PA, January.

Chunhui Gu, J.J. Lim, P. Arbelaez, and J. Malik. 2009. Recognition using regions. In *Computer Vision and Pattern Recognition, 2009. CVPR 2009. IEEE Conference on*, pages 1030 –1037.

Derek Hoiem, Alexei A. Efros, and Martial Hebert. 2005. Geometric context from a single image. In *ICCV*.

Xiaodi Hou and Liqing Zhang. 2007. Saliency detection: A spectral residual approach. In *Computer Vision and Pattern Recognition, 2007. CVPR '07. IEEE Conference on*, pages 1 –8.

P. Ipeirotis, F. Provost, and J. Wang. 2010. Quality management on amazon mechanical turk. In *Proceedings of the Second Human Computation Workshop (KDD-HCOMP)*.

Gunhee Kim and Antonio Torralba. 2009. Unsupervised Detection of Regions of Interest using Iterative Link Analysis. In *Annual Conference on Neural Information Processing Systems (NIPS 2009)*.

Zornitsa Kozareva, Ellen Riloff, and Eduard Hovy. 2008. Semantic class learning from the web with hyponym pattern linkage graphs. In *Proceedings of ACL-08: HLT*, pages 1048–1056, Columbus, Ohio, June. Association for Computational Linguistics.

G. Kulkarni, V. Premraj, S. Dhar, S. Li, Y. Choi, A. C Berg, and T. L Berg. 2011. Babytalk: Understanding and generating simple image descriptions. In *CVPR*.

N. Kumar, A.C. Berg, P. Belhumeur, and S.K. Nayar. 2009. Attribute and simile classifiers for face verification. In *ICCV*.

Siming Li, Girish Kulkarni, Tamara L. Berg, Alexander C. Berg, and Yejin Choi. 2011. Composing simple image descriptions using web-scale n-grams. In *CONLL*.

Eric P. Xing Li-Jia Li, Hao Su and Li Fei-Fei. 2010. Object bank: A high-level image representation for scene classification and semantic feature sparsification. In *NIPS*.

Tara McIntosh and James R Curran. 2008. Weighted mutual exclusion bootstrapping for domain independent lexicon and template acquisition. In *Proceedings of the Australasian Language Technology Association Workshop 2008*, pages 97–105, December.

K.J. Miller. 1998. Modifiers in WordNet. In C. Fellbaum, editor, *WordNet*, chapter 2. MIT Press.

Margaret Mitchell, Jesse Dodge, Amit Goyal, Kota Yamaguchi, Karl Stratos, Xufeng Han, Alyssa Mensch, Alex Berg, Tamara Berg, and Hal Daumé III. 2012. Midge: Generating image descriptions from computer vision detections. *Proceedings of EACL 2012*.

Vicente Ordonez, Girish Kulkarni, and Tamara L. Berg. 2011. Im2Text: Describing Images Using 1 Million Captioned Photographs. In *NIPS*.

Cyrus Rashtchian, Peter Young, Micah Hodosh, and Julia Hockenmaier. 2010. Collecting image annotations using amazon's mechanical turk. In *Proceedings of the NAACL HLT 2010 Workshop on Creating Speech and Language Data with Amazon's Mechanical Turk*. Association for Computational Linguistics.

H. Schmid. 1995. Improvements in part–of–speech tagging with an application to german. In *Proceedings of the EACL SIGDAT Workshop*.

J. Sivic, B.C. Russell, A. Zisserman, W.T. Freeman, and A.A. Efros. 2008. Unsupervised discovery of visual object class hierarchies. In *Computer Vision and Pattern Recognition, 2008. CVPR 2008. IEEE Conference on*, pages 1 –8.

M. Thelen and E. Riloff. 2002. A Bootstrapping Method for Learning Semantic Lexicons Using Extraction Pattern Contexts. In *Proceedings of the Empirical Methods in Natural Language Processing*, pages 214–221.

Peter D. Turney and Patrick Pantel. 2010. From frequency to meaning: Vector space models of semantics. *Journal of Artificial Intelligence Research (JAIR)*, 37:141.

Leonid Velikovich, Sasha Blair-Goldensohn, Kerry Hannan, and Ryan McDonald. 2010. The viability of web-derived polarity lexicons. In *Human Language Technologies: The 2010 Annual Conference of the North*

American Chapter of the Association for Computational Linguistics. Association for Computational Linguistics.

J. Xiao, J. Hays, K. Ehinger, A. Oliva, and A. Torralba. 2010. Sun database: Large-scale scene recognition from abbey to zoo. In *CVPR*.

Yezhou Yang, Ching Lik Teo, Hal Daumé III, and Yiannis Aloimonos. 2011. Corpus-guided sentence generation of natural images. In *EMNLP*.

Xiaojin Zhu and Zoubin Ghahramani. 2002. Learning from labeled and unlabeled data with label propagation. In *Technical Report CMU-CALD-02-107*. CarnegieMellon University.

Unsupervised Translation Sense Clustering

Mohit Bansal[*]
UC Berkeley
mbansal@cs.berkeley.edu

John DeNero
Google
denero@google.com

Dekang Lin
Google
lindek@google.com

Abstract

We propose an unsupervised method for clustering the translations of a word, such that the translations in each cluster share a common semantic sense. Words are assigned to clusters based on their usage distribution in large monolingual and parallel corpora using the soft K-Means algorithm. In addition to describing our approach, we formalize the task of translation sense clustering and describe a procedure that leverages WordNet for evaluation. By comparing our induced clusters to reference clusters generated from WordNet, we demonstrate that our method effectively identifies sense-based translation clusters and benefits from both monolingual and parallel corpora. Finally, we describe a method for annotating clusters with usage examples.

1 Introduction

The ability to learn a bilingual lexicon from a parallel corpus was an early and influential area of success for statistical modeling techniques in natural language processing. Probabilistic word alignment models can induce bilexical distributions over target-language translations of source-language words (Brown et al., 1993). However, word-to-word correspondences do not capture the full structure of a bilingual lexicon. Consider the example bilingual dictionary entry in Figure 1; in addition to enumerating the translations of a word, the dictionary author has grouped those translations into three sense clusters. Inducing such a clustering would prove useful in generating bilingual dictionaries automatically or building tools to assist bilingual lexicographers.

Colocar [co·lo·car´], *va.* 1. To arrange, to put in due place or order. 2. To place, to put in any place, rank condition or office, to provide a place or employment. 3. To collocate, to locate, to lay.

Figure 1: This excerpt from a bilingual dictionary groups English translations of the polysemous Spanish word *colocar* into three clusters that correspond to different word senses (Velázquez de la Cadena et al., 1965).

This paper formalizes the task of clustering a set of translations by sense, as might appear in a published bilingual dictionary, and proposes an unsupervised method for inducing such clusters. We also show how to add usage examples for the translation sense clusters, hence providing complete structure to a bilingual dictionary.

The input to this task is a set of source words and a set of target translations for each source word. Our proposed method clusters these translations in two steps. First, we induce a global clustering of the entire target vocabulary using the soft K-Means algorithm, which identifies groups of words that appear in similar contexts (in a monolingual corpus) and are translated in similar ways (in a parallel corpus). Second, we derive clusters over the translations of each source word by projecting the global clusters.

We evaluate these clusters by comparing them to reference clusters with the overlapping BCubed metric (Amigo et al., 2009). We propose a clustering criterion that allows us to derive reference clusters from the synonym groups of WordNet® (Miller, 1995).[1]

Our experiments using Spanish-English and Japanese-English datasets demonstrate that the automatically generated clusters produced by our method are substantially more similar to the

[*]Author was a summer intern with Google Research while conducting this research project.

[1]WordNet is used only for evaluation; our sense clustering method is fully unsupervised and language-independent.

Sense cluster	WordNet sense description	Usage example
collocate	*group or chunk together in a certain order or place side by side*	colocar juntas todas los libros *collocate all the books*
invest, place, put	*make an investment*	capitales para colocar *capital to invest*
locate, place	*assign a location to*	colocar el número de serie *locate the serial number*
place, position, put	*put into a certain place or abstract location*	colocar en un lugar *put in a place*

Figure 2: Correct sense clusters for the translations of Spanish verb s = *colocar*, assuming that it has translation set T_s = {*collocate, invest, locate, place, position, put*}. Only the sense clusters are outputs of the translation sense clustering task; the additional columns are presented for clarity.

WordNet-based reference clusters than naive baselines. Moreover, we show that bilingual features collected from parallel corpora improve clustering accuracy over monolingual distributional similarity features alone.

Finally, we present a method for annotating clusters with usage examples, which enrich our automatically generated bilingual dictionary entries.

2 Task Description

We consider a three-step pipeline for generating structured bilingual dictionary entries automatically.

(1) The first step is to identify a set of high-quality target-side translations for source lexical items. In our experiments, we ask bilingual human annotators to create these translation sets.[2] We restrict our present study to word-level translations, disallowing multi-word phrases, in order to leverage existing lexical resources for evaluation.

(2) The second step is to cluster translations of each word according to common word senses. This clustering task is the primary focus of the paper, and we formalize it in this section.

(3) The final step annotates clusters with usage examples to enrich the structure of the output. Section 7 describes a method of identifying cluster-specific usage examples.

In the task of *translation sense clustering*, the second step, we assume a fixed set of source lexical items of interest S, each with a single part of speech[3], and for each $s \in S$ a set T_s of target translations. Moreover, we assume that each target word $t \in T_s$ has a set of senses in common with s. These senses may also be shared among different target words. That is, each target word may have multiple senses and each sense may be expressed by multiple words.

Given a translation set T_s, we define a cluster $G \subseteq T_s$ to be a *correct sense cluster* if it is both *coherent* and *complete*.

- A sense cluster G is **coherent** if and only if there exists some sense B shared by all of the target words in G.
- A sense cluster G is **complete** if and only if, for every sense B shared by all words in G, there is no other word in T_s but not in G that also shares that sense.

The full set of correct clusters for a set of translations consists of all sense clusters that are both coherent and complete.

The example translation set for the Spanish word *colocar* in Figure 2 is shown with four correct sense clusters. For descriptive purposes, these clusters are annotated by WordNet senses and bilingual usage examples. However, the task we have defined does not require the WordNet sense or usage example to be identified: we must only produce the correct sense clusters within a set of translations. In fact, a cluster may correspond to more than one sense.

Our definition of correct sense clusters has several appealing properties. First, we do not attempt to enumerate all senses of the source word. Sense

[2] We do not use automatically extracted translation sets in our experiments, in order to isolate the clustering task on clean input.

[3] A noun and verb that share the same word form would constitute two different source lexical items.

Notation

T_s : The set of target-language translations (given)
$\mathcal{D}_t$: The set of synsets in which t appears (given)
C : A synset; a set of target-language words
B : A source-specific synset; a subset of T_s
$\mathcal{B}$: A set of source-specific synsets
$\mathcal{G}$: A set of correct sense clusters for T_s

The Cluster Projection Algorithm:

$\mathcal{B} \leftarrow \{C \cap T_s \,:\, C \in \bigcup_{t \in T_s} \mathcal{D}_t\}$
$\mathcal{G} \leftarrow \emptyset$
for $B \in \mathcal{B}$ **do**
  if $\nexists B' \in \mathcal{B}$ such that $B \subset B'$ **then**
    add B to $\mathcal{G}$
return $\mathcal{G}$

Figure 3: The Cluster Projection (CP) algorithm projects language-level synsets (C) to source-specific synsets (B) and then filters the set of synsets for redundant subsets to produce the complete set of source-specific synsets that are both coherent and complete ($\mathcal{G}$).

distinctions are only made when they affect cross-lingual lexical choice. If a source word has many fine-grained senses but translates in the same way regardless of the sense intended, then there is only one correct sense cluster for that translation.

Second, no correct sense cluster can be a superset of another, because the subset would violate the completeness condition. This criterion encourages larger clusters that are easier to interpret, as their unifying senses can be identified as the intersection of senses of the translations in the cluster.

Third, the correct clusters need not form a partition of the input translations. It is common in published bilingual dictionaries for a translation to appear in multiple sense clusters. In our example, the polysemous English verbs *place* and *put* appear in multiple clusters.

3 Generating Reference Clusters

To construct a reference set for the translation sense clustering task, we first collected English translations of Spanish and Japanese nouns, verbs, and adverbs. Translation sets were curated by human annotators to keep only high-quality single-word translations.

Rather than gathering reference clusters via an additional annotation effort, we leverage WordNet, a large database of English lexical semantics (Miller, 1995). WordNet groups words into sets of cognitive synonyms called *synsets*, each expressing a distinct concept. We use WordNet version 2.1, which has wide coverage of nouns, verbs, and adverbs, but sparser coverage of adjectives and prepositions.[4]

Words	Synsets	Sense Clusters
collocate	collocate collocate, lump, chunk	collocate
invest	invest, put, commit, place invest, clothe, adorn invest, vest, enthrone ...	invest, place, put locate, place
locate	locate, turn up situate, locate locate, place, site ...	place, position, put
place	put, set, place, pose, position, lay rate, rank, range, order, grade, place locate, place, site invest, put, commit, place ...	
position	position put, set, place, pose, position, lay	
put	put, set, place, pose, position, lay put frame, redact, cast, put, couch invest, put, commit, place ...	

Figure 4: An example of cluster projection on WordNet, for the Spanish source word *colocar*. We show the target translation words to be clustered, their WordNet synsets (with words not in the translation set grayed out), and the final set of correct sense clusters.

Reference clusters for the set of translations T_s of some source word s are generated algorithmically from WordNet synsets via the *Cluster Projection* (CP) algorithm defined in Figure 3. An input to the CP algorithm is the translation set T_s of some source word s. Also, each translation $t \in T_s$ belongs to some set of synsets $\mathcal{D}_t$, where each synset $C \in D_t$ contains target-language words that may or may not be translations of s. First, the CP algorithm constructs a source-specific synset B for each C, which contains only translations of s. Second, it identifies all correct sense clusters $\mathcal{G}$ that are both *coherent* and *complete* with respect to the source-specific senses $\mathcal{B}$. A sense cluster must correspond to some synset $B \in \mathcal{B}$ to be coherent, and it must

[4]WordNet version 2.1 is almost identical to version 3.0, for Unix-like systems, as described in http://wordnetcode.princeton.edu/3.0/CHANGES. The latest version 3.1 is not yet available for download.

not have a proper superset in $\mathcal{B}$ to be complete.[5]

Figure 4 illustrates the CP algorithm for the translations of the Spanish source word *colocar* that appear in our input dataset.

4 Clustering with K-Means

In this section, we describe an unsupervised method for inducing translation sense clusters from the usage statistics of words in large monolingual and parallel corpora. Our method is language independent.

4.1 Distributed Soft K-Means Clustering

As a first step, we cluster all words in the target-language vocabulary in a way that relates words that have similar distributional features. Several methods exist for this task, such as the K-Means algorithm (MacQueen, 1967), the Brown algorithm (Brown et al., 1992) and the exchange algorithm (Kneser and Ney, 1993; Martin et al., 1998; Uszkoreit and Brants, 2008). We use a distributed implementation of the "soft" K-Means clustering algorithm described in Lin and Wu (2009). Given a feature vector for each element (a word type) and the number of desired clusters K, the K-Means algorithm proceeds as follows:

1. Select K elements as the initial centroids for K clusters.
repeat
  2. Assign each element to the top M clusters with the nearest centroid, according to a similarity function in feature space.
  3. Recompute each cluster's centroid by averaging the feature vectors of the elements in that cluster.
until convergence

4.2 Monolingual Features

Following Lin and Wu (2009), each word to be clustered is represented as a feature vector describing the distributional context of that word. In our setup, the context of a word w consists of the words immediately to the left and right of w. The context feature vector of w is constructed by first aggregating the frequency counts of each word f in the context of each w. We then compute point-wise mutual information (PMI) features from the frequency counts:

$$\mathrm{PMI}(w, f) = \log \frac{\mathrm{c}(w, f)}{\mathrm{c}(w)\mathrm{c}(f)}$$

where w is a word, f is a neighboring word, and $c(\cdot)$ is the count of a word or word pair in the corpus.[6] A feature vector for w contains a PMI feature for each word type f (with relative position left or right) for all words that appears a sufficient number of times as a neighbor of w. The similarity of two feature vectors is the cosine of the angle between the vectors. We follow Lin and Wu (2009) in applying various thresholds during K-Means, such as a frequency threshold for the initial vocabulary, a total-count threshold for the feature vectors, and a threshold for PMI scores.

4.3 Bilingual Features

In addition to the features described in Lin and Wu (2009), we introduce features from a bilingual parallel corpus that encode *reverse-translation* information from the source-language (Spanish or Japanese in our experiments). We have two types of bilingual features: unigram features capture source-side reverse-translations of w, while bigram features capture both the reverse-translations and source-side neighboring context words to the left and right. Features are expressed again as PMI computed from frequency counts of aligned phrase pairs in a parallel corpus. For example, one unigram feature for *place* would be the PMI computed from the number of times that *place* was in the target side of a phrase pair whose source side was the unigram *lugar*. Similarly, a bigram feature for *place* would be the PMI computed from the number of times that *place* was in the target side of a phrase pair whose source side was the bigram *lugar de*. These features characterize the way in which a word is translated, an indication of its meaning.

[5] One possible shortcoming of our approach to constructing reference sets for translation sense clustering is that a cluster may correspond to a sense that is not shared by the original source word used to generate the translation set. All translations must share some sense with the source word, but they may not share all senses with the source word. It is possible that two translations are synonymous in a sense that is not shared by the source. However, we did not observe this problem in practice.

[6] PMI is typically defined in terms of probabilities, but has proven effective previously when defined in terms of counts.

4.4 Predicting Translation Clusters

As a result of soft K-Means clustering, each word in the target-language vocabulary is assigned to a list of up to M clusters. To predict the sense clusters for a set of translations of a source word, we apply the CP algorithm (Figure 3), treating the K-Means clusters as synsets ($\mathcal{D}_t$).

5 Related Work

To our knowledge, the translation sense clustering task has not been explored previously. However, much prior work has explored the related task of monolingual word and phrase clustering. Uszkoreit and Brants (2008) uses an exchange algorithm to cluster words in a language model, Lin and Wu (2009) uses distributed K-Means to cluster phrases for various discriminative classification tasks, Vlachos et al. (2009) uses Dirichlet Process Mixture Models for verb clustering, and Sun and Korhonen (2011) uses a hierarchical Levin-style clustering to cluster verbs.

Previous word sense induction work (Diab and Resnik, 2002; Kaji, 2003; Ng et al., 2003; Tufis et al., 2004; Apidianaki, 2009) relates to our work in that these approaches discover word senses automatically through clustering, even using multilingual parallel corpora. However, our task of clustering multiple words produces a different type of output from the standard word sense induction task of clustering in-context uses of a single word. The underlying notion of "sense" is shared across these tasks, but the way in which we use and evaluate induced senses is novel.

6 Experiments

The purpose of our experiments is to assess whether our unsupervised soft K-Means clustering method can effectively recover the reference sense clusters derived from WordNet.

6.1 Datasets

We conduct experiments using two bilingual datasets: Spanish-to-English (S→E) and Japanese-to-English (J→E). Table 1 shows, for each dataset, the number of source words and the total number of target words in their translation sets. The datasets are limited in size because we solicited human annotators to filter the set of translations for each source word. The S→E dataset has 52 source-words with a part-of-speech-tag distribution of 38 nouns, 10 verbs and 4 adverbs. The J→E dataset has 369 source-words with 319 nouns, 38 verbs and 12 adverbs. We included only these parts of speech because WordNet version 2.1 has adequate coverage for them. Most source words have 3 to 5 translations each.

Dataset	No. of src-words	Total no. of tgt-words
S→E	52	230
J→E	369	1639

Table 1: Sizes of the Spanish-to-English (S→E) and Japanese-to-English (J→E) datasets.

Monolingual features for K-Means clustering were computed from an English corpus of Web documents with 700 billion tokens of text. Bilingual features were computed from 0.78 (S→E) and 1.04 (J→E) billion tokens of parallel text, primarily extracted from the Web using automated parallel document identification (Uszkoreit et al., 2010). Word alignments were induced from the HMM-based alignment model (Vogel et al., 1996), initialized with the bilexical parameters of IBM Model 1 (Brown et al., 1993). Both models were trained using 2 iterations of the expectation maximization algorithm. Phrase pairs were extracted from aligned sentence pairs in the same manner used in phrase-based machine translation (Koehn et al., 2003).

6.2 Clustering Evaluation Metrics

The quality of text clustering algorithms can be evaluated using a wide set of metrics. For evaluation by set matching, the popular measures are Purity (Zhao and Karypis, 2001) and Inverse Purity and their harmonic mean (F measure, see Van Rijsbergen (1974)). For evaluation by counting pairs, the popular metrics are the Rand Statistic and Jaccard Coefficient (Halkidi et al., 2001; Meila, 2003).

Metrics based on entropy include Cluster Entropy (Steinbach et al., 2000), Class Entropy (Bakus et al., 2002), VI-measure (Meila, 2003), Q_0 (Dom, 2001), V-measure (Rosenberg and Hirschberg, 2007) and Mutual Information (Xu et al., 2003). Lastly, there exist the BCubed metrics (Bagga and Baldwin, 1998), a family of metrics that decompose the clustering evaluation by estimating precision and recall for each item in the distribution.

Amigo et al. (2009) compares the various clustering metrics mentioned above and their properties. They define four formal but intuitive constraints on such metrics that explain which aspects of clustering quality are captured by the different metric families. Their analysis shows that of the wide range of metrics, only BCubed satisfies those constraints. After defining each constraint below, we briefly describe its relevance to the translation sense clustering task.

Homogeneity: In a cluster, we should not mix items belonging to different categories.
Relevance: All words in a proposed cluster should share some common WordNet sense.

Completeness: Items belonging to the same category should be grouped in the same cluster.
Relevance: All words that share some common WordNet sense should appear in the same cluster.

Rag Bag: Introducing disorder into a disordered cluster is less harmful than introducing disorder into a clean cluster.
Relevance: We prefer to maximize the number of error-free clusters, because these are most easily interpreted and therefore most useful.

Cluster Size vs. Quantity: A small error in a big cluster is preferable to a large number of small errors in small clusters.
Relevance: We prefer to minimize the total number of erroneous clusters in a dictionary.

Amigo et al. (2009) also show that BCubed extends cleanly to settings with overlapping clusters, where an element can simultaneously belong to more than one cluster. For these reasons, we focus on BCubed for cluster similarity evaluation.[7]

The BCubed metric for scoring overlapping clusters is computed from the pair-wise precision and recall between pairs of items:

$$\mathrm{P}(e,e') = \frac{\min(|C(e)\cap C(e')|, |L(e)\cap L(e')|)}{|C(e)\cap C(e')|}$$

$$\mathrm{R}(e,e') = \frac{\min(|C(e)\cap C(e')|, |L(e)\cap L(e')|)}{|L(e)\cap L(e')|}$$

where e and e' are two items, $L(e)$ is the set of reference clusters for e and $C(e)$ is the set of predicted clusters for e (i.e., clusters to which e belongs). Note that $\mathrm{P}(e,e')$ is defined only when e and e' share some predicted cluster, and $\mathrm{R}(e,e')$ when e and e' share some reference cluster.

The BCubed precision associated to one item is its averaged pair-wise precision over other items sharing some of its predicted clusters, and likewise for recall[8]; and the *overall* BCubed precision (or recall) is the averaged precision (or recall) of all items:

$$\mathrm{P_{B3}} = \mathrm{Avg}_e[\mathrm{Avg}_{e'\,s.t.\,C(e)\cap C(e')\neq\emptyset}[\mathrm{P}(e,e')]]$$
$$\mathrm{R_{B3}} = \mathrm{Avg}_e[\mathrm{Avg}_{e'\,s.t.\,L(e)\cap L(e')\neq\emptyset}[\mathrm{R}(e,e')]]$$

6.3 Results

Figure 5 shows the F_β-score for various β values:

$$\mathrm{F}_\beta = \frac{(1+\beta^2)\cdot \mathrm{P_{B3}}\cdot \mathrm{R_{B3}}}{\beta^2\cdot \mathrm{P_{B3}} + \mathrm{R_{B3}}}$$

This graph gives us a trade-off between precision and recall ($\beta = 0$ is exact precision and $\beta \to \infty$ tends to exact recall).[9]

Each curve in Figure 5 represents a particular clustering method. We include three naive baselines:

ewnc: Each word in its own cluster

aw1c: All words in one cluster

Random: Each target word is assigned M random cluster id's in the range 1 to K, then translation sets are clustered with the CP algorithm.

The curves for K-Means clustering include one condition with monolingual features alone and two curves that include bilingual features as well.[10] The bilingual curves correspond to two different feature sets: the first includes only unigram features (t1), while the second includes both unigram and bigram features (t1t2).

Each point on an F_β curve in Figure 5 (including the baseline curves) represents a maximum over two

[7]An evaluation using purity and inverse purity (extended to overlapping clusters) has been omitted for space, but leads to the same conclusions as the evaluation using BCubed.

[8]The metric does include in this computation the relation of each item with itself.

[9]Note that we use the micro-averaged version of F-score where we first compute $\mathrm{P_{B3}}$ and $\mathrm{R_{B3}}$ for each source-word, then compute the average $\mathrm{P_{B3}}$ and $\mathrm{R_{B3}}$ over all source-words, and finally compute the F-score using these averaged $\mathrm{P_{B3}}$ and $\mathrm{R_{B3}}$.

[10]All bilingual K-Means experiments include monolingual features also. K-Means with *only* bilingual features does not produce accurate clusters.

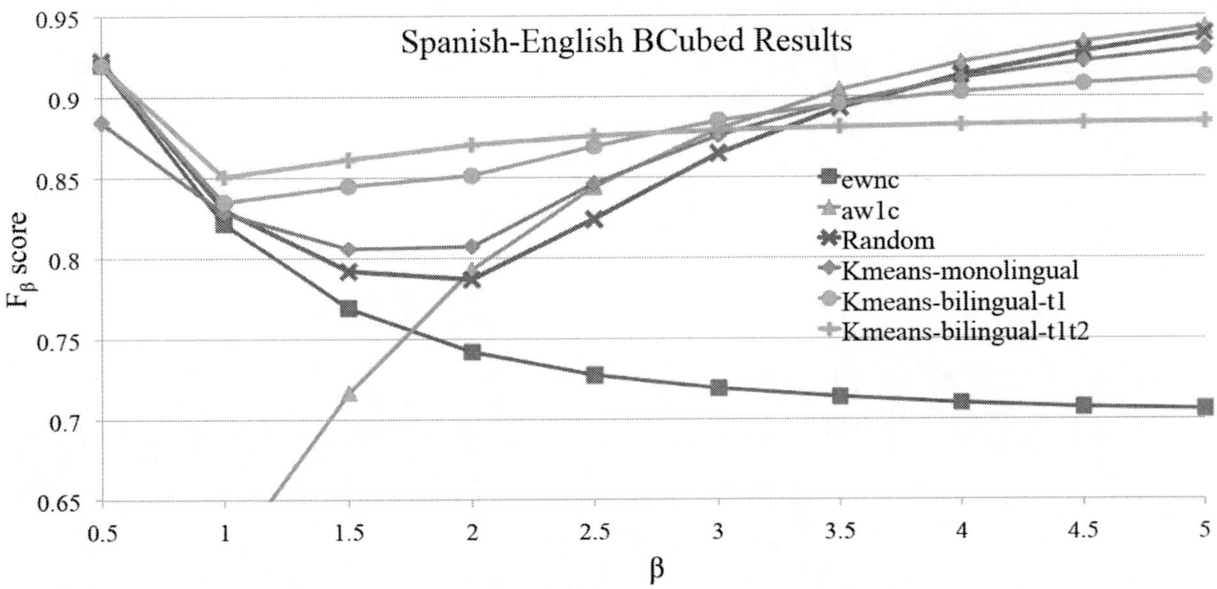

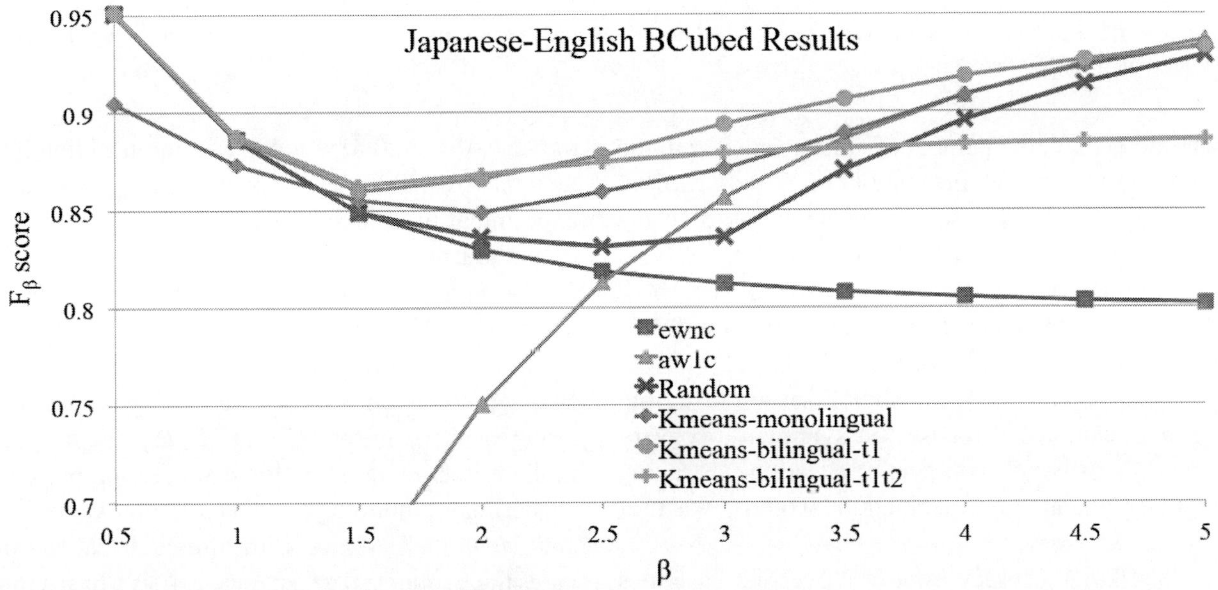

Figure 5: BCubed F_β plot for the Spanish-English dataset (top) and Japanese-English dataset (bottom).

Source word: *ayudar*		
Monolingual	[[*aid*], [*assist, help*]]	P=1.0, R=0.56
Bilingual	[[*aid, assist, help*]]	P=1.0, R=1.0
Source word: *concurso*		
Monolingual	[[*competition, contest, match*], [*concourse*], [*contest, meeting*]]	P=0.58, R=1.0
Bilingual	[[*competition, contest*], [*concourse*], [*match*], [*meeting*]]	P=1.0, R=1.0

Table 2: Examples showing improvements in clustering when we move from K-Means clustering with only monolingual features to clustering with additional bilingual features.

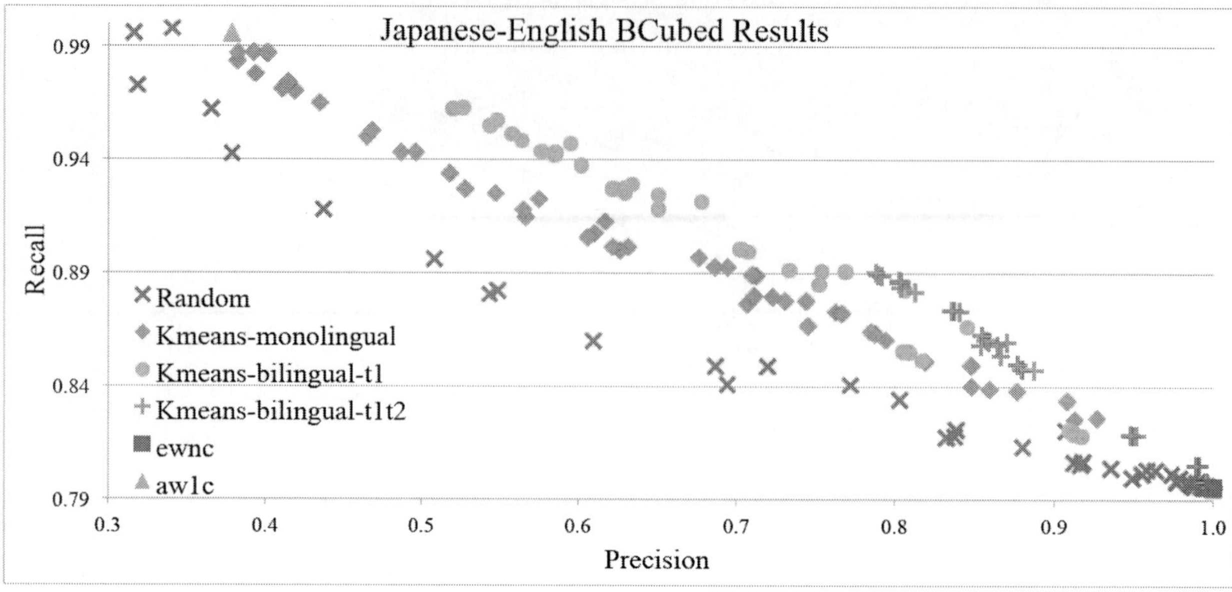

Figure 6: BCubed Precision-Recall scatter plot for the Japanese-English dataset. Each point represents a particular choice of cluster count K and clusters per word M.

parameters: K, the number of clusters created in the whole corpus and M, the number of clusters allowed per word (in M-best soft K-Means). As both the random baseline and proposed clustering methods can be tuned to favor precision or recall, we show the best result from each technique across this spectrum of F_β metrics. We vary β to highlight different potential objectives of translation sense clustering. An application that focuses on synonym discovery would favor recall, while an application portraying highly granular sense distinctions would favor precision.

Clustering accuracy improves over the baselines with monolingual features alone, and it improves further with the addition of bilingual features, for a wide range of β values. Our unsupervised approach with bilingual features achieves up to 6-8% absolute improvement over the random baseline, and is particularly effective for recall-weighted metrics.[11] As an example, in a S→E experiment with a K-Means setting of $K = 4096 : M = 3$, the overall $F_{1.5}$ score increases from 80.58% to 86.12% upon adding bilingual features. Table 2 shows two examples from that experiment for which bilingual features improve the output clusters.

The parameter values we use in our experiments are $K \in \{2^3, 2^4, \ldots, 2^{12}\}$ and $M \in \{1, 2, 3, 4, 5\}$. To provide additional detail, Figure 6 shows the BCubed precision and recall for each induced clustering, as the values of K and M vary, for Japanese-English.[12] Each point in this scatter plot represents a clustering methodology and a particular value for K and M. Soft K-Means with bilingual features provides the strongest performance across a broad range of cluster parameters.

6.4 Evaluation Details

Certain special cases needed to be addressed in order to complete this evaluation.

Target words not in WordNet: Words that did not have any synset in WordNet were each assigned to a singleton reference cluster.[13] The S→E dataset has only 2 out of 225 target types missing in WordNet and the J→E dataset has only 55 out of 1351 target

[11] It is not surprising that a naive baseline like random clustering can achieve a high precision: BCubed counts each word itself as correctly clustered, and so even trivial techniques that create many singleton clusters will have high precision. High recall (without very low precision) is harder to achieve, because it requires positing larger clusters, and it is for recall-focused objectives that our technique substantially outperforms the random baseline.

[12] Spanish-English precision-recall results are omitted due to space constraints, but depict similar trends.

[13] Note that certain words with WordNet synsets also end up in their own singleton cluster because all other words in their cluster are not in the translation set.

types missing.

Target words not clustered by K-Means: The K-Means algorithm applies various thresholds during different parts of the process. As a result, there are some target word types that are not assigned any cluster at the end of the algorithm. For example, in the J→E experiment with $K = 4096$ and with bilingual (t1 only) features, only 49 out of 1351 target-types are not assigned any cluster by K-Means. These unclustered words were each assigned to a singleton cluster in post-processing.

7 Identifying Usage Examples

We now briefly consider the task of automatically extracting usage examples for each predicted cluster. We identify these examples among the extracted phrase pairs of a parallel corpus.

Let P_s be the set of source phrases containing source word s, and let A_t be the set of source phrases that align to target phrases containing target word t. For a source word s and target sense cluster G, we identify source phrases that contain s *and* translate to all words in G. That is, we collect the set of phrases $P_s \cap \bigcap_{t \in G} A_t$. We use the same parallel corpus as we used to compute bilingual features.

For example, if we consider the cluster [*place, position, put*] for the Spanish word *colocar*, then we find Spanish phrases that contain *colocar* and also align to English phrases containing *place, position*, and *put* somewhere in the parallel corpus. Sample usage examples extracted by this approach appear in Figure 7. We have not performed a quantitative evaluation of these extracted examples, although qualitatively we have found that the technique surfaces useful phrases. We look forward to future research that further explores this important sub-task of automatically generating bilingual dictionaries.

8 Conclusion

We presented the task of translation sense clustering, a critical second step to follow translation extraction in a pipeline for generating well-structured bilingual dictionaries automatically. We introduced a method of projecting language-level clusters into clusters for specific translation sets using the CP algorithm. We used this technique both for constructing reference clusters, via WordNet synsets, and constructing predicted clusters from the output of a vocabulary-level clustering algorithm.

debajo		
["below","beneath"]	→	debajo de la superficie (*below the surface*)
["below","under"]	→	debajo de la línea (*below the line*)
["underneath"]	→	debajo de la piel (*under the skin*)
休養		
["break"]	→	一生懸命 働いた から 休養 する の は 当然 です . (*I worked hard and I deserve a good break.*)
["recreation"]	→	従来 の 治療 や 休養 方法 (*Traditional healing and recreation activities*)
["rest"]	→	ベッド で 休養 する だけ で 治り ます . (*Bed rest is the only treatment required.*)
利用		
["application"]	→	コンピューター 利用 技術 (*Computer-aided technique*)
["use","utilization"]	→	土地 の 有効 利用 を 促進 する (*Promote effective use of land*)
引く		
["draw","pull"]	→	カーテン を 引く (*Draw the curtain*)
["subtract"]	→	A から B を 引く (*Subtract B from A*)
["tug"]	→	袖 を ぐいと 引く (*Tug at someone's sleeve*)

Figure 7: Usage examples for Spanish and Japanese words and their English sense clusters. Our approach extracts multiple examples per cluster, but we show only one. We also show the translation of the examples back into English produced by Google Translate.

Our experiments demonstrated that the soft K-Means clustering algorithm, trained using distributional features from very large monolingual and bilingual corpora, recovered a substantial portion of the structure of reference clusters, as measured by the BCubed clustering metric. The addition of bilingual features improved clustering results over monolingual features alone; these features could prove useful for other clustering tasks as well. Finally, we annotated our clusters with usage examples.

In future work, we hope to combine our clustering method with a system for automatically generating translation sets. In doing so, we will develop a system that can automatically induce high-quality, human-readable bilingual dictionaries from large corpora using unsupervised learning methods.

Acknowledgments

We would like to thank Jakob Uszkoreit, Adam Pauls, and the anonymous reviewers for their helpful suggestions.

References

Enrique Amigo, Julio Gonzalo, Javier Artiles, and Felisa Verdejo. 2009. A comparison of extrinsic clustering evaluation metrics based on formal constraints. *Information Retrieval*, 12(4):461486.

Marianna Apidianaki. 2009. Data-driven semantic analysis for multilingual WSD and lexical selection in translation. In *Proceedings of EACL*.

A. Bagga and B. Baldwin. 1998. Entity-based cross-document coreferencing using the vector space model. In *Proceedings of COLING-ACL*.

J. Bakus, M. F. Hussin, and M. Kamel. 2002. A SOM-based document clustering using phrases. In *Proceedings of ICONIP*.

Peter F. Brown, Vincent J. Della Pietra, Peter V. deSouza, Jenifer C. Lai, and Robert L. Mercer. 1992. Class-based *n*-gram models of natural language. *Computational Linguistics*, 18(4):467479.

Peter F. Brown, Stephen A. Della Pietra, Vincent J. Della Pietra, and Robert L. Mercer. 1993. The mathematics of statistical machine translation: Parameter estimation. *Computational Linguistics*.

Mona Diab and Philip Resnik. 2002. An unsupervised method for word sense tagging using parallel corpora. In *Proceedings of ACL*.

B.E. Dom. 2001. An information-theoretic external cluster-validity measure. In *IBM Technical Report RJ-10219*.

M. Halkidi, Y. Batistakis, and M. Vazirgiannis. 2001. On clustering validation techniques. *Journal of Intelligent Information Systems*, 17(2-3):107–145.

Hiroyuki Kaji. 2003. Word sense acquisition from bilingual comparable corpora. In *Proceedings of NAACL*.

Reinherd Kneser and Hermann Ney. 1993. Improved clustering techniques for class-based statistical language modelling. In *Proceedings of the 3rd European Conference on Speech Communication and Technology*.

Philipp Koehn, Franz Josef Och, and Daniel Marcu. 2003. Statistical phrase-based translation. In *Proceedings of NAACL*.

Dekang Lin and Xiaoyun Wu. 2009. Phrase clustering for discriminative learning. In *Proceedings of ACL*.

J. B. MacQueen. 1967. Some methods for classification and analysis of multivariate observations. In *Proceedings of 5th Berkeley Symposium on Mathematical Statistics and Probability*.

Sven Martin, Jorg Liermann, and Hermann Ney. 1998. Algorithms for bigram and trigram word clustering. *Speech Communication*, 24:19–37.

M. Meila. 2003. Comparing clusterings by the variation of information. In *Proceedings of COLT*.

George A. Miller. 1995. Wordnet: A lexical database for English. In *Communications of the ACM*.

Hwee Tou Ng, Bin Wang, and Yee Seng Chan. 2003. Exploiting parallel texts for word sense disambiguation: An empirical study. In *Proceedings of ACL*.

Andrew Rosenberg and Julia Hirschberg. 2007. V-measure: A conditional entropy-based external cluster evaluation measure. In *Proceedings of EMNLP*.

Michael Steinbach, George Karypis, and Vipin Kumar. 2000. A comparison of document clustering techniques. In *Proceedings of KDD Workshop on Text Mining*.

Lin Sun and Anna Korhonen. 2011. Hierarchical verb clustering using graph factorization. In *Proceedings of EMNLP*.

Dan Tufis, Radu Ion, and Nancy Ide. 2004. Fine-grained word sense disambiguation based on parallel corpora, word alignment, word clustering and aligned wordnets. In *Proceedings of COLING*.

Jakob Uszkoreit and Thorsten Brants. 2008. Distributed word clustering for large scale class-based language modeling in machine translation. In *Proceedings of ACL*.

Jakob Uszkoreit, Jay Ponte, Ashok Popat, and Moshe Dubiner. 2010. Large scale parallel document mining for machine translation. In *Proceedings of COLING*.

C. Van Rijsbergen. 1974. Foundation of evaluation. *Journal of Documentation*, 30(4):365–373.

Mariano Velázquez de la Cadena, Edward Gray, and Juan L. Iribas. 1965. *New Revised Velázques Spanish and English Dictionary*. Follet Publishing Company.

Andreas Vlachos, Anna Korhonen, and Zoubin Ghahramani. 2009. Unsupervised and constrained Dirichlet process mixture models for verb clustering. In *Proceedings of the Workshop on Geometrical Models of Natural Language Semantics*.

Stephan Vogel, Hermann Ney, and Christoph Tillmann. 1996. HMM-based word alignment in statistical translation. In *Proceedings of the Conference on Computational linguistics*.

W. Xu, X. Liu, and Y. Gong. 2003. Document-clustering based on non-negative matrix factorization. In *Proceedings of SIGIR*.

Y. Zhao and G. Karypis. 2001. Criterion functions for document clustering: Experiments and analysis. In *Technical Report TR 01-40, Department of Computer Science, University of Minnesota, Minneapolis, MN*.

Shared Components Topic Models

Matthew R. Gormley **Mark Dredze** **Benjamin Van Durme** **Jason Eisner**
Center for Language and Speech Processing
Human Language Technology Center of Excellence
Department of Computer Science
Johns Hopkins University, Baltimore, MD
{mrg,mdredze,vandurme,jason}@cs.jhu.edu

Abstract

With a few exceptions, extensions to latent Dirichlet allocation (LDA) have focused on the distribution over topics for each document. Much less attention has been given to the underlying structure of the topics themselves. As a result, most topic models generate topics independently from a single underlying distribution and require millions of parameters, in the form of multinomial distributions over the vocabulary. In this paper, we introduce the Shared Components Topic Model (SCTM), in which each topic is a normalized product of a smaller number of underlying component distributions. Our model learns these component distributions and the structure of how to combine subsets of them into topics. The SCTM can represent topics in a much more compact representation than LDA and achieves better perplexity with fewer parameters.

1 Introduction

Topic models are probabilistic graphical models meant to capture the semantic associations underlying corpora. Since the introduction of latent Dirichlet allocation (LDA) (Blei et al., 2003), these models have been extended to account for more complex distributions over topics, such as adding supervision (Blei and McAuliffe, 2007), non-parametric priors (Blei et al., 2004; Teh et al., 2006), topic correlations (Li and McCallum, 2006; Mimno et al., 2007; Blei and Lafferty, 2006) and sparsity (Williamson et al., 2010; Eisenstein et al., 2011).

While much research has focused on modeling distributions over topics, less focus has been given to the makeup of the topics themselves. This emphasis leads us to find two problems with LDA and its variants mentioned above: (1) independently generated topics and (2) overparameterized models.

Independent Topics In the models above, the topics are modeled as independent draws from a single underlying distribution, typically a Dirichlet. This violates the topic modeling community's intuition that these distributions over words are often related. As an example, consider a corpus that supports two related topics, *baseball* and *hockey*. These topics likely overlap in their allocation of mass to high probability words (e.g. team, season, game, players), even though the two topics are unlikely to appear in the same documents. When topics are generated independently, the model does not provide a way to capture this sharing between related topics. Many extensions to LDA have addressed a related issue, LDA's inability to model topic correlation,[1] by changing the distributions over topics (Blei and Lafferty, 2006; Li and McCallum, 2006; Mimno et al., 2007; Paisley et al., 2011). Yet, none of these change the underlying structure of the topic's distributions over words.

Overparameterization Topics are most often parameterized as multinomial distributions over words: increasing the topics means learning new multinomials over large vocabularies, resulting in models consisting of millions of parameters. This issue was partially addressed in SAGE (Eisenstein et al., 2011) by encouraging sparsity in the topics which are parameterized by their difference in log-frequencies from a fixed background distribution. Yet the problem of overparameterization is also tied

[1] Two correlated topics, e.g. *nutrition* and *exercise*, are likely to co-occur, but their word distributions might not overlap.

to the number of topics, and though SAGE reduces the number of non-zero parameters, it still requires a vocabulary-sized parameter vector for each topic.

We present the Shared Components Topic Model (SCTM), which addresses both of these issues by generating each topic as a normalized product of a smaller number of underlying components. Rather than learning each new topic from scratch, we model a set of underlying component distributions that constrain topic formation. Each topic can then be viewed as a combination of these underlying components, where in a model such as LDA, we would say that components and topics stand in a one to one relationship. The key advantages of the SCTM are that it can learn and share structure between overlapping topics (e.g. *baseball* and *hockey*) and that it can represent the same number of topics in a much more compact representation, with far fewer parameters.

Because the topics are products of components, we present a new training algorithm for the significantly more complex product case which relies on a Contrastive Divergence (CD) objective. Since SCTM topics, which are products of distributions, could be represented directly by distributions as in LDA, our goal is not necessarily to learn better topics, but to learn models that are substantially smaller in size and generalize better to unseen data. Experiments on two corpora show that our model uses fewer underlying multinomials and still achieves lower perplexity than LDA, which suggests that these constraints could lead to better topics.

2 Shared Components Topic Models

The Shared Components Topic Model (SCTM) follows previous topic models in inducing admixture distributions of topics that are used to generate each document. However, here each topic multinomial distribution over words itself results from a normalized product of shared components, each a multinomial over words. Each topic selects a subset of components. We begin with a review and then introduce the SCTM.

Latent Dirichlet allocation (LDA) (Blei et al., 2003) is a probabilistic topic model which defines a generative process whereby sets of observations are generated from latent topic distributions. In the SCTM, we use the same generative process of topic assignments as LDA, but replace the K independently generated topics (multinomials over words) with products of C components.

Latent Dirichlet allocation generative process

For each topic $k \in \{1, \dots, K\}$:
  $\boldsymbol{\phi}_k \sim \text{Dir}(\boldsymbol{\beta})$ [*draw distribution over words*]
For each document $m \in \{1, \dots, M\}$:
  $\boldsymbol{\theta}_m \sim \text{Dir}(\boldsymbol{\alpha})$ [*draw distribution over topics*]
  For each word $n \in \{1, \dots, N_m\}$:
    $z_{mn} \sim \text{Mult}(1, \boldsymbol{\theta}_m)$ [*draw topic*]
    $x_{mn} \sim \boldsymbol{\phi}_{z_{mi}}$ [*draw word*]

LDA draws each topic $\boldsymbol{\phi}_k$ independently from a Dirichlet. The model generates each document m of length M, by first sampling a distribution over topics $\boldsymbol{\theta}_m$. Then, for each word n, a topic z_{mn} is chosen and a word type x_{mn} is generated from that topic's distribution over words $\boldsymbol{\phi}_{z_{mi}}$.

A **Product of Experts** (PoE) model (Hinton, 1999) is the normalized product of the expert distributions. In the SCTM, each component (an expert) models an underlying multinomial word distribution. We let $\boldsymbol{\phi}_c$ be the parameters of the cth component, where ϕ_{cv} is the probability of the cth component generating word v. If the structure of a PoE included only components $c \in \mathcal{C}$ in the product, it would have the form: $p(x|\boldsymbol{\phi}_1, \dots, \boldsymbol{\phi}_C) = \frac{\prod_{c \in \mathcal{C}} \phi_{cx}}{\sum_{v=1}^{V} \prod_{c \in \mathcal{C}} \phi_{cv}}$, where there are C components, and the summation in the denominator is over the vocabulary. In a PoE, each component can overrule the others by giving low probability to some word. A PoE can be viewed as a soft intersection of its components, whereas a mixture is a soft union.

The **Beta-Bernoulli model** (Griffiths and Ghahramani, 2006) is a distribution over binary matrices with a fixed number of rows and columns. It is the finite counterpart to the Indian Buffet Process. In this work, we use the Beta-Bernoulli as our prior for an unobserved binary matrix B with C columns and K rows. In the SCTM, each row $\boldsymbol{b}_k$ of the matrix, a binary feature vector, defines a topic distribution. The binary vector acts as a selector for the *structure* of the PoE for that topic. The row determines which components to include in the product by which entries b_{kc} are "on" (equal to 1) in that row. Under Beta-Bernoulli prior, for each column, a coin with weight π_c is chosen. For each entry in the column, the coin is flipped to determine if the entry is "on" or "off". This corresponds to the notion that some components are *a priori* more likely to be included in topics.

> **The Beta-Bernoulli model generative process**
> For each component $c \in \{1, \ldots, C\}$: *[columns]*
> $\pi_c \sim \text{Beta}(\frac{\gamma}{C}, 1)$ *[draw probability of component c]*
> For each topic $k \in \{1, \ldots, K\}$: *[rows]*
> $b_{kc} \sim \text{Bernoulli}(\pi_c)$ *[draw whether topic includes cth component in its PoE]*

2.1 Shared Components Topic Models

The Shared Components Topic Model generates each document just like LDA, the only difference is the topics are not drawn independently from a Dirichlet prior. Instead, topics are soft intersections of underlying components, each of which is a multinomial distribution over words. These components are combined via a PoE model, and each topic is constructed according to a length C binary vector $\boldsymbol{b}_k$; where $b_{kc} = 1$ includes and $b_{kc} = 0$ excludes component c. Stacking the K vectors forms a $K \times C$ matrix; rows correspond to topics and columns to components. Overlapping topics share components in common.

Generative process SCTM's generative process generates topics and words, but must also generate the binary matrix. For each of the C shared components, we generate a distribution $\boldsymbol{\phi}_c$ over the V words from a Dirichlet parametrized by $\boldsymbol{\beta}$. Next, we generate a $K \times C$ binary matrix using the Beta-Bernoulli prior. These components and the binary matrix implicitly define the complete set of K topic distributions, each of which is a PoE.

$$p(x|\boldsymbol{b}_k, \boldsymbol{\phi}) = \frac{\prod_{c=1}^{C} \phi_{cx}^{b_{kc}}}{\sum_{v=1}^{V} \prod_{c=1}^{C} \phi_{cv}^{b_{kc}}} \quad (1)$$

The distribution $p(\cdot|\boldsymbol{b}_k, \boldsymbol{\phi})$ defines the kth topic. Conditioned on these K topics, the remainder of the generative process, which generates the documents, is just like LDA.

> **The Shared Components Topic Model generative process**
> For each component $c \in \{1, \ldots, C\}$:
> $\boldsymbol{\phi}_c \sim \text{Dir}(\boldsymbol{\beta})$ *[draw distribution over words]*
> $\pi_c \sim \text{Beta}(\frac{\gamma}{C}, 1)$ *[draw probability of component c]*
> For each topic $k \in \{1, \ldots, K\}$:
> $b_{kc} \sim \text{Bernoulli}(\pi_c)$ *[draw whether topic includes cth component in its PoE]*
> For each document $m \in \{1, \ldots, M\}$
> $\boldsymbol{\theta}_m \sim \text{Dir}(\boldsymbol{\alpha})$ *[draw distribution over topics]*
> For each word $n \in \{1, \ldots, N_m\}$
> $z_{mn} \sim \text{Mult}(1, \boldsymbol{\theta}_m)$ *[draw topic]*
> $x_{mn} \sim p(\cdot\, |\boldsymbol{b}_{z_{mn}}, \boldsymbol{\phi})$ given by Eq. (1) *[draw word]*

See Figure 1 for the graphical model.

Discussion An advantage of this formulation is the ability to model many topics using few components. While LDA must maintain $V \times K$ parameters for the topic distributions, the SCTM maintains just $V \times C$ parameters, plus an additional $K \times C$ binary matrix. Since $C < K \ll V$ this results in many fewer parameters for the SCTM.[2] Extending the number of topics (rows) requires storing additional binary vectors, a lightweight requirement. In theory, we could enable all 2^C possible component combinations, although we expect to use far less. On the other hand, constraining the SCTM's topics by the components gives less flexible topics as compared to LDA. However, we find empirically that a large number of topics can be effectively modeled with a smaller number of components.

Observe that we can reparameterize the SCTM as LDA by assuming an identity square matrix; each component corresponds to a topic in LDA, making LDA a special case of the SCTM with an identity matrix I_C. Intuitively, SCTM learning could produce an LDA model where appropriate. Finally, we can also think of the SCTM as learning the structure of many PoE models. In applications where experts abstain, the SCTM could learn in which setting (row) each expert casts a vote.

3 Parameter Estimation

Parameter estimation infers values for model parameters $\boldsymbol{\phi}$, $\boldsymbol{\pi}$, and $\boldsymbol{\theta}$ from data using an unsupervised training procedure. Because exact inference is intractable in the SCTM, we turn to approximate methods. As is common in these models, we will integrate out $\boldsymbol{\pi}$ and $\boldsymbol{\theta}$, sample latent variables Z and B, and optimize the components $\boldsymbol{\phi}$. Our algorithm follows the outline of the Monte Carlo EM (MCEM) algorithm (Wei and Tanner, 1990). In the Monte Carlo E-step, we will re-sample the latent variables Z and B based on current model parameters $\boldsymbol{\phi}$ and observed data X. In the M-step, we will find new model parameters $\boldsymbol{\phi}$. Since these parameters correspond to experts in the PoE, we rely on a contrastive divergence (CD) objective (Hinton, 2002), popular for PoE training, rather than maximizing the data

[2] The vocabulary size V could be much larger if n-grams or relational triples are used, as opposed to unigrams.

log-likelihood. Normally, CD only estimates the parameters of the expert distributions. However, in our model, the structure of the PoEs themselves change based on the E-step. Since we generate multiple samples in the E-step, we modify the CD objective to compute the gradient for each E-step sample and take the average to approximate the expectation under B and Z.[3]

3.1 E-Step

The E-step approximates an expectation under $p(B, Z|X, \phi, \alpha, \gamma)$ for latent topic assignments Z and matrix B using Gibbs sampling. The Gibbs sampler uses the full conditionals for both z_i (7) and b_{kc} (12), which we derive in Appendix A. Using this sampler, we obtain J samples of Z and B by iterating through each value of z_i and b_{kc} J times (in our experiments, we use J=1, which appears to work as well on this task as multiple samples). These J samples are then used in the M-step as an approximation of the expectation of the latent variables.

3.2 M-Step

Given many samples of B and Z, the M-step optimizes the component parameters ϕ which cannot be collapsed out. We utilize the standard PoE training procedure for experts: contrastive divergence (CD). We approximate the CD gradient as the difference of the data distribution and the one-step reconstruction of the data according to the current parameters. As in Generalized EM (Dempster et al., 1977), a single gradient step in the direction of the contrastive divergence objective is sufficient for each M-step. A key difference in our model is that we must incorporate the expectation of the PoE model structure, which in our case is a random variable instead of a fixed observed structure. We achieve this by simply computing the CD gradient for each PoE given each of the J samples $\{Z, B\}^{(j)}$ from the E-Step, then average the result.

Another difficulty arises from computing the gradient directly for the multinomial ϕ_c due to the $V-1$ degrees of freedom imposed by sum-to-one constraints. Therefore, we switch to the *natural parameters*, which obviates the need for considering the sum-to-one constraint in the optimization, by defining ϕ_c in terms of V real valued parameters $\{\xi_{c1}, \ldots, \xi_{cV}\}$:

$$\phi_{cv} = \frac{\exp(\xi_{cv})}{\sum_{t=1}^{V} \exp(\xi_{cv})} \qquad (2)$$

The V parameters ξ_{cv} are then used to compute ϕ_{cv} for use in the E-step.

As explained above, the M-step does not maximize the data log-likelihood, but instead minimizes contrastive divergence. Hinton (2002) explains that maximizing data log-likelihood is equivalent to minimizing $Q^0||Q^\infty_\xi$, the KL divergence between the observed data distribution, Q^0, and the model's equilibrium distribution, Q^∞_ξ.[4] Minimizing $Q^0||Q^\infty_\xi$ would require the computation of an intractable expectation under the equilibrium distribution. We avoid this by instead minimizing the contrastive divergence objective,

$$\text{CD}(\xi|\{Z, B\}^{(j)}) = Q^0||Q^\infty_\xi - Q^1_\xi||Q^\infty_\xi, \qquad (3)$$

where Q^1_ξ is the distribution over *one-step* reconstructions of the data, X given Z, B, ξ, that are generated by a single step of Gibbs sampling.

Unlike standard applications of CD training, the hidden variables (Z,B) are not contained within the experts. Instead they define the *structure* of the PoE model, where B indicates which experts to use in each product (topic) and Z indicates which PoE generates each word. Unfortunately, CD training cannot infer this structure since the CD derivation makes use of a fixed structure in the one-step reconstruction. Therefore, we have taken a MCEM approach, first sampling the PoE structure in the E-step, then

[3]CD training within MCEM is not the only possible approach. One alternative would be to compute the CD gradient summing over all values of B and Z, effectively training the entire model using CD. This approach prevents the normal CD objective derivation from being simplified into a more tractable form. Another approach would be a pure MCMC algorithm, which sampled ϕ directly. While using the natural parameters allows the sampler to mix, it is too computationally intensive to be practical. Finally, we could train with Generalized MCEM, where the exact gradient of the log-likelihood (or log-posterior) is used, but this easily gets stuck in local minima. After experimenting with these and other options, we present our current most effective estimation method.

[4]Hinton (2002) used this notation because the data distribution, Q^0, can be described as the state of a Markov chain at time 0 that was started at the data distribution. Similarly, the equilibrium distribution, Q^∞_ξ could be obtained by running the same Markov chain to time ∞.

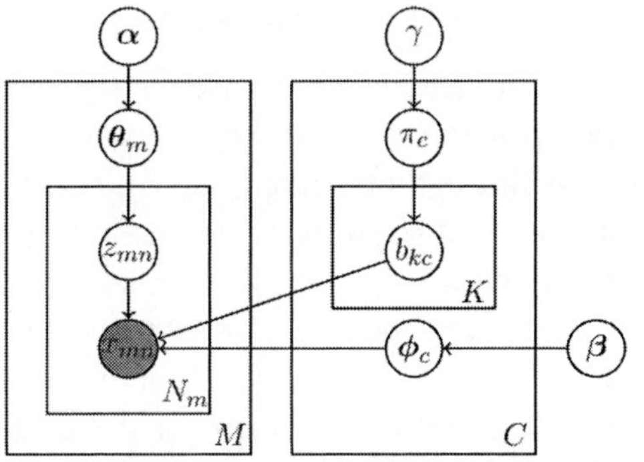

Figure 1: The graphical model for the SCTM.

fixing these samples for Z and B when computing the *one-step* reconstruction of the data, X.

Contrastive Divergence Gradient We provide the approximate derivative of the contrastive divergence objective, where Z and B are treated as fixed.[5]

$$\frac{d\,\mathrm{CD}(\xi|\{Z,B\}^{(j)})}{d\xi} \approx -\left\langle \frac{d \log f(x|\boldsymbol{b}_z,\phi)}{d\xi} \right\rangle_{Q^0} + \left\langle \frac{d \log f(x|\boldsymbol{b}_z,\phi)}{d\xi} \right\rangle_{Q^1_\xi}$$

where $f(x|\boldsymbol{b}_z,\phi) = \prod_{c=1}^{C} \phi_{cx}^{b_{zc}}$ is the numerator of $p(x|\boldsymbol{b}_z,\phi)$ and the derivative of its log is efficient to compute:

$$\frac{d \log f(x|\boldsymbol{b}_z,\phi)}{d\xi_{cv}} = \begin{cases} b_{zc}(1-\phi_{cv}) & \text{for } x = v \\ -b_{zc}\phi_{cv} & \text{for } x \neq v \end{cases}$$

To approximate the expectation under Q^1_ξ, we hold Z, B, ξ fixed and resample the data, X, using one step of Gibbs sampling.

3.3 Summary

Our learning algorithm can be viewed in terms of a Q function: $Q(\xi|\xi^{(t)}) \approx \frac{1}{J}\sum_{j=1}^{J} \mathrm{CD}(\xi|\{Z,B\}^{(j)})$where we average over J samples. The E-step computes $Q(\xi|\xi^{(t)})$. The M-step minimizes Q with respect to ξ to obtain the updated $\xi^{(t+1)}$ by performing gradient descent on the Q function as $\xi^{(t+1)}_{cv} = \xi^{(t)}_{cv} - \eta \cdot \frac{dQ(\xi|\xi^{(t)})}{d\xi_{cv}}$ for all values of c, v.

[5]The derivative is approximate because we drop the term: $-\frac{dQ^1_\xi}{d\xi} \cdot \frac{dQ^1_\xi||Q^\infty_\xi}{dQ^1_\xi}$, which is 'problematic to compute' (Hinton, 2002). This is the standard use of CD.

Algorithm 1 SCTM Training

Initialize parameters: ξ_c, b_{kc}, z_i.
while not converged **do**
  {E-step:}
  for $j = 1$ to J **do**
    {Draw jth sample $\{Z,B\}^{(j)}$}
    for $i = 1$ to N **do**
      Sample z_i using Eq. (7)
    for $k = 1$ to K **do**
      for $c = 1$ to C **do**
        Sample b_{kc} using ratio in Eq. (12)
  {M-step:}
  for $c = 1$ to C **do**
    for $v = 1$ to V **do**
      Single gradient step over ξ

$$\xi^{(t+1)}_{cv} = \xi^{(t)}_{cv} - \eta \cdot \frac{dQ(\phi|\phi^{(t)})}{d\xi_{cv}}$$

4 Related Models

The SCTM is closely related to the the Infinite Overlapping Mixture Model (IOMM) (Heller and Ghahramani, 2007), yet our model differs from and, in some ways, extends theirs. The IOMM models the geometric overlap of Gaussian clusters using PoEs, and models the structure of the PoEs with the rows of a binary matrix. The SCTM models a finite number of columns, where the IOMM models an infinite number. The IOMM generates a row for each data point, whereas the SCTM generates a row for each topic. Thus, the SCTM goes beyond the IOMM by allowing the rows to be shared among documents and models document-specific mixtures over the rows of the matrix.[6]

SAGE for topic modeling (Eisenstein et al., 2011) can be viewed as a restricted form of the SCTM. Consider an SCTM in which the binary matrix is restricted such that the first column, $b_{\cdot,1}$, consists of all ones and the remainder forms a diagonal matrix. If we then set the first component, ϕ_1, to the corpus background distribution, and add a Laplace prior on the natural parameters, ξ_{cv}, we have the SAGE model. Note that by removing the restriction that the matrix contain a diagonal, we could allow multiple components to combine in the SCTM fashion, while incorporating SAGE's sparsity benefits.

[6]The IOMM uses Metropolis-Hastings (MH) to sample the parameters of the experts. This approach is computationally feasible because their experts are Gaussian, unlike the SCTM in which the experts are multinomials and the MH step too expensive.

The relation of TagLDA (Zhu et al., 2006) to the SCTM is similar to that of SAGE and SCTM. TagLDA has a PoE of exactly two experts: one expert for the topic, and one for the supervised word-level tag. Examples of tags are *abstract* or *body*, indicating which part of a research paper the word appears in.

Unlike the SCTM and SAGE, most prior extensions to LDA have enhanced the distribution over topics for each document. One of the closest is *hierarchical LDA* (hLDA) (Blei et al., 2004) and its application to PAM (Mimno et al., 2007). Though topics are still generated independently from a Dirichlet prior, hLDA learns a tree structure underlying the topics. Each document samples a single path through the tree and samples words from topics along that path. The SCTM models an orthogonal issue to topic hierarchy: how the topics themselves are represented as the intersection of components. Finally, while prior work has primarily used mixtures for the sake of conjugacy, we take a fundamentally different approach to modeling the structure by using normalized product distributions.

5 Evaluation

We compare the SCTM with LDA in terms of overall model performance (held-out perplexity) as well as parameter usage (varying numbers of components and topics). We select LDA as our baseline since our model differs only in how it forms topics, which focuses evaluation on the benefit of this model change.

We consider two popular data sets for comparison: NIPS: A collection of 1,617 NIPS abstracts from 1987 to 1999[7], with 77,952 tokens and 1,632 types. 20NEWS: 1,000 randomly selected articles from the 20 Newsgroups dataset,[8] with 70,011 tokens and 1,722 types. Both data sets excluded stop words and words occurring in fewer than 10 documents. For 20NEWS, we used the standard by-date train/test split. For NIPS, we randomly partitioned the data by document into 75% train and 25% test.

We compare the SCTM to LDA by evaluating the average perplexity-per-word of the held-out test data, perplexity $= 2^{-\log_2(\text{data}|\text{model})/N}$. Exact computation is intractable, so we use the *left-to-right algorithm* (Wallach et al., 2009) as an accurate alternative. With the topics fixed, the SCTM is equivalent to LDA and requires no adaptation of the left-to-right algorithm.

We used a collapsed Gibbs sampler for training LDA and the algorithm described above for training the SCTM. Both were trained for 4000 iterations, sampling topics every 10 iterations after a burn-in of 3000. The hyperparameter α was optimized as an asymmetric Dirichlet, β as a symmetric Dirichlet, and $\gamma = 3.0$ was fixed.[9] Following the observation of Hinton (2002) that CD training benefits from initializing the experts to nearly uniform distributions, we initialize the component distributions from a symmetric Dirichlet with parameter $\hat{\beta} = 1 \times 10^6$. We use $J = 1$ samples per iteration and a decaying learning rate centered at $\eta = 100$.[10] We ranged LDA from 10 to 200 topics, and the SCTM from 10 to 100 components (C). We then selected the number of SCTM topics (K) as $K \in \{C, 2C, 3C, 4C, 5C\}$. For each model, we used five random restarts, selecting the model with the highest training data likelihood.

5.1 Results

Our goal is to demonstrate that (1) modeling topics as products of components is an expressive alternative to generating topics independently and (2) the SCTM can both achieve lower perplexity than LDA and use fewer model parameters in doing so.

Topics as Products of Components Figures 3b and 3c show the perplexity for the held-out portions of 20NEWS and NIPS for different numbers of components C. The shaded region shows the full SCTM perplexity range we observed for different K and at each value of C, we label the number of topics K (rows in the binary matrix). For each number of components, LDA falls within the upper portion of the shaded region. While for some (small) values of K for the SCTM, LDA does better, the SCTM can easily include more K (requiring few new parameters) to achieve better results. This supports our hypothesis that topics can be comprised of the overlap between shared underlying components. More-

[7]We follow prior work (Blei et al., 2004; Li and McCallum, 2006; Li et al., 2007) in using only the abstracts: http://www.cs.nyu.edu/~roweis/data.html

[8]Williamson et al. (2010) created a similar subset: http://people.csail.mit.edu/jrennie/20Newsgroups/

[9]On development data the model was rather insensitive to γ.

[10]We experimented with larger J but it had no effect.

Figure 2: SCTM binary matrix and topics from 3599 training documents of 20NEWS for $C = 10$, $K = 20$. Blue squares are "on" (equal to 1).

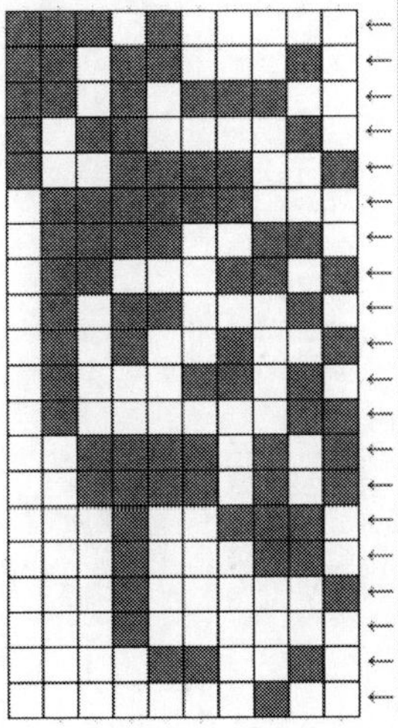

k	α_k	Top words for topic	Top words for topic after ablating component c=1
1	0.306	subject organization israel return define law org	organization subject israel law peace define israeli
2	0.031	encryption chip clipper keys des escrow security law	administration president year market money senior
3	0.025	turkish armenian armenians war turkey turks armenia	years food center year air russian war army
4	0.102	drive card disk scsi hard controller mac drives	opinions drive hard power support cost research price
5	0.071	image jpeg window display code gif color mit	pitt file program year center programs image division
6	0.018	jews israeli jewish arab peace land war arabs	
7	0.074	org money back question years thing things point	
8	0.106	christian bible church question christ christians life	
9	0.011	administration president year market money senior	
10	0.055	health medical center research information april	
11	0.063	gun law state guns control bill rights states	
12	0.160	world organization system israel state usa cwru reply	
13	0.042	space nasa gov launch power wire ground air	
14	0.038	space nasa gov launch power wire ground air	
15	0.079	team game year play games season players hockey	
16	0.158	car lines dod bike good uiuc sun cars	
17	0.136	windows file government key jesus system program	
18	0.122	article writes center page harvard virginia research	
19	0.017	max output access digex int entry col line	
20	0.380	lines people don university posting host nntp time	

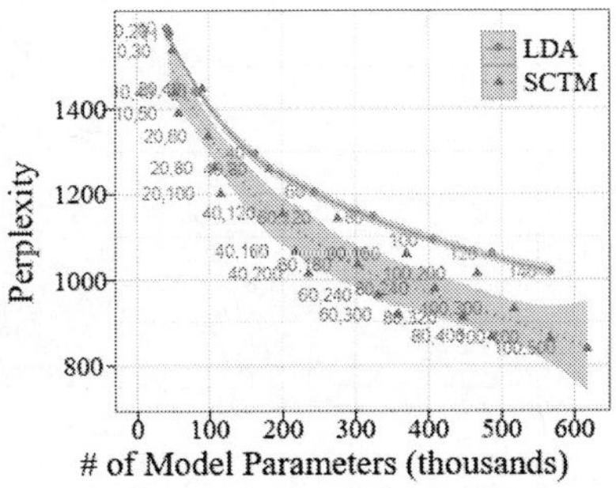

(a)

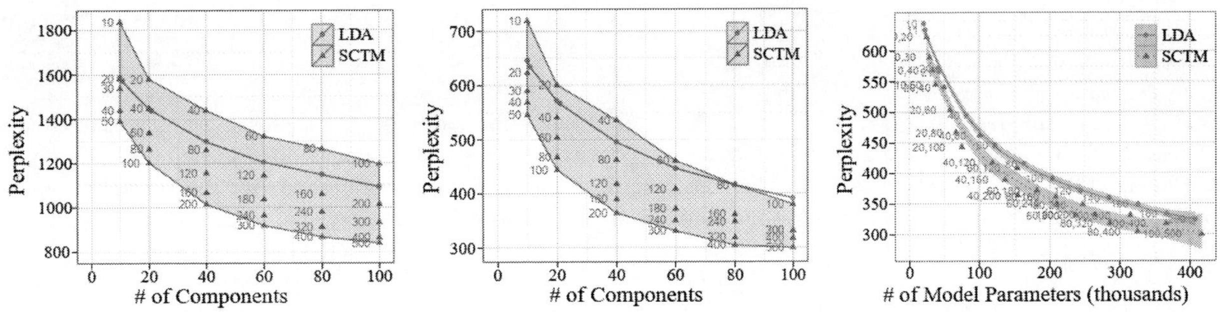

(b) (c) (d)

Figure 3: Perplexity results on held-out data for 20NEWS (b) and NIPS (c) showing the results of LDA and the SCTM for the same number of components and varying K (SCTM). For the same number of components (multinomials), the SCTM achieves lower perplexity by combining them into more topics. Results for 20NEWS (a) and NIPS (d) showing non-square SCTM achieves lower perplexity than LDA with a more compact model.

over, this suggests that our products (PoEs) provide additional and complementary expressivity over just mixtures of topics.

Model Compactness Including an additional topic in the SCTM only adds C binary parameters, for an extra row in the matrix. Whereas in LDA, an additional topic requires V (the size of the vocabulary) additional parameters to represent the multinomial. In both cases, the number of document-specific parameters must increase as well. Figures 3a and 3d present held-out perplexity vs. number of model parameters on 20NEWS and NIPS, excluding the case of square ($C = K$) binary matrices for the SCTM. The regions show a confidence interval ($p = 0.05$) around the smoothed fit to the data, LDA labels show C, and SCTM labels show C, K. The SCTM achieves lower perplexity with fewer model parameters, even when the increase in non-component parameters is taken into account. We expect that because of its smaller size the SCTM exhibits lower sample complexity, allowing for better generalization to unseen data.

5.2 Analysis

Figure 2 gives the binary matrix and topics learned on a larger section of 20NEWS training documents. These topics evidence that the SCTM is able to achieve a diversity of topics by combining various subsets of components, and we expect that the low perplexity achieved by the SCTM can be attributed

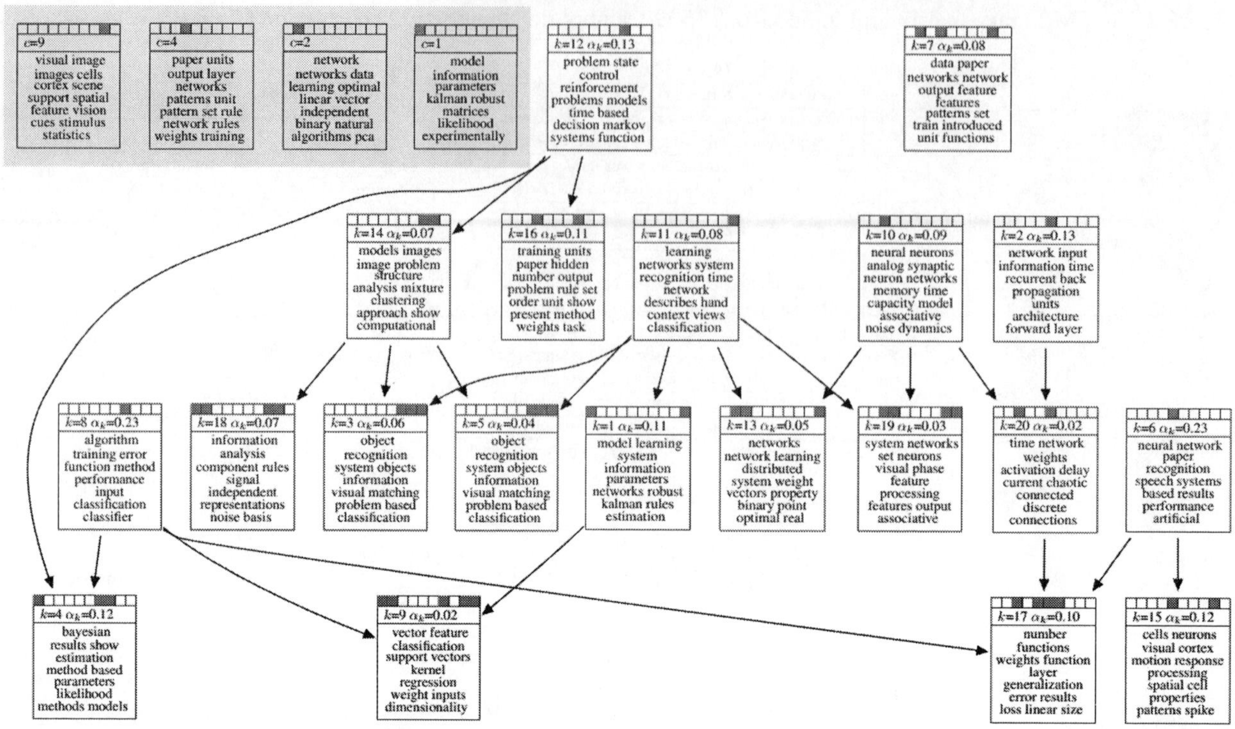

Figure 4: Hasse diagram on NIPS for $C = 10$, $K = 20$ showing the top words for topics and unrepresented components (in shaded box). Notice that some topics only consist of a single component. The shaded box contains the components that didn't appear as a topic. For the sake of clarity, we only show arrows for the subsumption relationships between the topics, and we omit the implicit arrows between the components in the shaded box and the topics.

to the high-level of component re-use across topics.

Topics are typically interpreted by looking at the top-N words, whereas the top-N words of a component often do not even appear in the topics to which it contributes. Instead, we find that the components contribution to a topic is typically through vetoing words. For example, the top words of component c=1, corresponding to the first column of the binary matrix in figure 2, are [subject organization posting apple mit screen write window video port], yet only a few of these appear in topics k=1,2,3,4,5, which use it.

On the right of figure 2, we show what the topics become when we ablate component c=1 from the matrix by setting the column to all zeros. Topic k=2 changes from being about *information security* to *general politics* and is identical to k=9. Topic k=3 changes from *the Turkish-Armenian War* to a more general *war* topic. Topic k=4 changes to a less focused version of itself. In this way, we can gain further insight into the contribution of this component, and the way in which components tend to increase the specificity of a topic to which they are added.

The SCTM learns each topic as a soft intersection of its components, as represented by the binary matrix. We can describe the overlap between topics based on the components that they have in common. One topic subsumes another topic when the parent consists of a subset of the child's components. In this way, the binary matrix defines a Hasse diagram, a directed acyclic graph describing all the subsumption relationships between topics. Figure 4 shows such a Hasse diagram on the NIPS data. Several topics consist of only a single component, such as k=12 on *reinforcement learning* and k=8 on *optimization.* These two topics combine with the component c=1 so that their overlap forms the topic k=4 on *Bayesian methods*. These subsumption relationships are different from and complementary to hLDA (see §4), which models topic co-occurrence, not component intersection. For example, topic k=10 on *connectionism* and k=2 on *neural networks* intersect to form k=20 which contains words that would only appear in *both* of its subsuming topics, thereby explicitly modeling topic overlap.

The SCTM sometimes learns identical topics (two rows with the same binary entries "on") such as k=13 and k=14 in figure 2 and k=3 and k=5 in figure 4, which is likely due to the Gibbs sampler for the binary matrix getting stuck in a local optimum.

6 Discussion

We have presented the Shared Components Topic Model (SCTM), in which topics are products of underlying component distributions. This model change learns shared topic structures—as expressed through components—as opposed to generating each topic independently. Reducing the number of components yields more compact models with lower perplexity than LDA. The two main limitations of the current SCTM are, when restricted to a square binary matrix ($C = K$), the inference procedure is unable to recover a model with perplexity as low as a collapsed Gibbs sampler for LDA, and the components are not consistently interpretable.

The use of components opens up interesting directions of research. For example, task specific side information can be expressed as priors or constraints over the components, or by adding conditioning variables tied to the components. Additionally, tasks beyond document modeling may benefit from representing topics as products of distributions. For example, in vision, where topics are classes of objects, the components could be features of those objects. For selectional preference, components could correspond to semantic features that intersect to define semantic classes (Gormley et al., 2011). We hope new opportunities will arise as this work explores a new research area for topic models.

Appendix A: Derivation of Full Conditionals

The model's complete data likelihood over all variables—observed words X, latent topic assignments Z, matrix B, and component/expert distributions $\boldsymbol{\phi}$:

$$p(X, Z, B, \boldsymbol{\phi}|\boldsymbol{\alpha}, \boldsymbol{\beta}, \gamma) = p(X|Z, B, \boldsymbol{\phi})p(Z|\boldsymbol{\alpha})p(B|\gamma)p(\boldsymbol{\phi}|\boldsymbol{\beta}) \quad (4)$$

This follows from the conditional independence assumptions. It is tractable to integrate out all parameters except $Z, B, \boldsymbol{\phi}$ and hyperparameters $\boldsymbol{\alpha}, \boldsymbol{\beta}, \gamma$. [11]

[11]For simplicity, we switch from indexing examples as x_{mn} to x_i. In this presentation, x_i is the ith example in the corpus, which corresponds to some m, n pair.

Full conditional of z_i Recall that $p(Z|\boldsymbol{\alpha})$ is the Dirichlet-Multinomial distribution over topic assignments, where $\boldsymbol{\theta}$ has been integrated out. The form of this distribution is identical to the corresponding distribution over topics in LDA. The derivation of the full conditional of $z_i \in \{1, \ldots, K\}$, follows from the factorization in Eq. 4:

$$\begin{aligned} & p(z_i|X, Z^{-(i)}, B, \boldsymbol{\phi}, \boldsymbol{\alpha}, \boldsymbol{\beta}, \gamma) && (5)\\ & \propto p(X|Z, B, \boldsymbol{\phi})p(Z|\boldsymbol{\alpha}) && (6)\\ & \propto p(x_i|\boldsymbol{b}_{z_i}, \boldsymbol{\phi})(\tilde{n}_{mz_i}^{-(i)} + \alpha_{z_i}) && (7)\end{aligned}$$

$Z^{-(i)}$ is the set of all topic assignments except z_i. We use the independence of each document, recalling that example i belongs to document m. In practice, we cache $p(x|\boldsymbol{b}_z, \boldsymbol{\phi})$ for all x, z ($V \times K$ values) and these are shared by all z_i in a sampling iteration.

Above, just as in LDA, $p(Z|\boldsymbol{\alpha})$ is simplified by proportionality to $(\tilde{n}_{mz_i}^{-(i)} + \alpha_{z_i})$, where $\tilde{n}_{mk}^{-(i)}$ is the count of examples for document m that are assigned topic k excluding z_i's contribution (Heinrich, 2008).

Full conditional of b_{kc} Recall that $p(B|\gamma)$ is the prior for a Beta-Bernoulli matrix. The full conditional distribution of a position in the binary vector is (Griffiths and Ghahramani, 2006):

$$p(b_{kc} = 1|B^{-(kc)}, \gamma) = \frac{\bar{n}_c^{-(k)} + \frac{\gamma}{C}}{K + \frac{\gamma}{C}} \quad (8)$$

where $\bar{n}_c^{-(k)}$ is the count of topics with component c excluding topic k, and $B^{-(kc)}$ is the entire matrix except for the entry b_{kc}.

To find the full conditional for $b_{kc} \in \{0, 1\}$, we again start with the factorization from Eq. 4.

$$\begin{aligned} & p(b_{kc}|X, Z, B^{-(kc)}, \boldsymbol{\phi}, \boldsymbol{\alpha}, \boldsymbol{\beta}, \gamma) && (9)\\ & \propto p(X|Z, B, \boldsymbol{\phi})p(B|\gamma) && (10)\\ & \propto \left[\prod_{i:z_i=k} p(x_i|\boldsymbol{b}_{z_i}, \boldsymbol{\phi})\right] p(b_{kc}|B^{-(kc)}, \gamma) && (11)\end{aligned}$$

where $p(b_{kc}|B^{-(kc)}, \gamma)$ is given by Eq. 8,

$$= \left[\frac{\left(\prod_{v=1}^{V} \phi_{cv}^{\hat{n}_{kv}}\right)^{b_{kc}}}{\left(\sum_{v=1}^{V} \prod_{j=1}^{C} \phi_{jv}^{b_{kj}}\right)^{-||\hat{\boldsymbol{n}}_k||_1}}\right] p(b_{kc}|B^{-(kc)}, \gamma) \quad (12)$$

and where $\hat{n}_{kv}$ is the count of words assigned topic k that are type v, and $||\hat{\boldsymbol{n}}_k||_1$ (the L_1-norm of count vector $\hat{\boldsymbol{n}}_k$) is the count of *all* words with topic k.

References

David Blei and John Lafferty. 2006. Correlated topic models. In *Advances in Neural Information Processing Systems (NIPS)*, volume 18.

David Blei and Jon McAuliffe. 2007. Supervised topic models. In *Advances in Neural Information Processing Systems (NIPS)*.

David Blei, Andrew Ng, and Michael Jordan. 2003. Latent dirichlet allocation. *Journal of Machine Learning Research*, 3.

David Blei, Thomas Griffiths, Michael Jordan, and Joshua Tenenbaum. 2004. Hierarchical topic models and the nested chinese restaurant process. In *Advances in Neural Information Processing Systems (NIPS)*, volume 16.

A. P. Dempster, N. M. Laird, and D. B. Rubin. 1977. Maximum likelihood from incomplete data via the EM algorithm. *Journal of the Royal Statistical Society. Series B (Methodological)*, 39(1):1–38.

Jacob Eisenstein, Amr Ahmed, and Eric P. Xing. 2011. Sparse additive generative models of text. In *International Conference on Machine Learning (ICML)*.

Matthew R. Gormley, Mark Dredze, Benjamin Van Durme, and Jason Eisner. 2011. Shared components topic models with application to selectional preference. In *Learning Semantics Workshop at NIPS 2011*, December.

Thomas Griffiths and Zoubin Ghahramani. 2006. Infinite latent feature models and the indian buffet process. In *Advances in Neural Information Processing Systems (NIPS)*, volume 18.

Gregor Heinrich. 2008. Parameter estimation for text analysis. Technical report, Fraunhofer IGD.

Katherine A. Heller and Zoubin Ghahramani. 2007. A nonparametric bayesian approach to modeling overlapping clusters. In *Artificial Intelligence and Statistics (AISTATS)*, pages 187–194.

Geoffrey Hinton. 1999. Products of experts. In *International Conference on Artificial Neural Networks (ICANN)*.

Geoffrey Hinton. 2002. Training products of experts by minimizing contrastive divergence. *Neural Computation*, 14(8):1771–1800.

Wei Li and Andrew McCallum. 2006. Pachinko allocation: DAG-structured mixture models of topic correlations. In *International Conference on Machine Learning (ICML)*, pages 577–584.

Wei Li, David Blei, and Andrew McCallum. 2007. Nonparametric bayes pachinko allocation. In *Uncertainty in Artificial Intelligence (UAI)*.

David Mimno, Wei Li, and Andrew McCallum. 2007. Mixtures of hierarchical topics with pachinko allocation. In *International Conference on Machine Learning (ICML)*, pages 633–640.

John Paisley, Chong Wang, and David Blei. 2011. The discrete infinite logistic normal distribution for Mixed-Membership modeling. In *International Conference on Artificial Intelligence and Statistics (AISTATS)*.

Yee Whye Teh, Michael Jordan, Matthew Beal, and David Blei. 2006. Hierarchical dirichlet processes. *Journal of the American Statistical Association*, 101(476):1566–1581.

Hanna Wallach, Ian Murray, Ruslan Salakhutdinov, and David Mimno. 2009. Evaluation methods for topic models. In *International Conference on Machine Learning (ICML)*, pages 1105–1112.

Greg Wei and Martin Tanner. 1990. A monte carlo implementation of the EM algorithm and the poor man's data augmentation algorithms. *Journal of the American Statistical Association*, 85(411):699–704.

Sinead Williamson, Chong Wang, Katherine Heller, and David Blei. 2010. The IBP compound dirichlet process and its application to focused topic modeling. In *International Conference on Machine Learning (ICML)*.

Xiaojin Zhu, David Blei, and John Lafferty. 2006. TagLDA: bringing document structure knowledge into topic models. Technical Report TR-1553, University of Wisconsin.

Textual Predictors of Bill Survival in Congressional Committees

Tae Yano **Noah A. Smith**
Language Technologies Institute
Carnegie Mellon University
Pittsburgh, PA 15213, USA
{taey,nasmith}@cs.cmu.edu

John D. Wilkerson
Department of Political Science
University of Washington
Seattle, WA 98195, USA
jwilker@u.washington.edu

Abstract

A U.S. Congressional bill is a textual artifact that must pass through a series of hurdles to become a law. In this paper, we focus on one of the most precarious and least understood stages in a bill's life: its consideration, behind closed doors, by a Congressional committee. We construct predictive models of whether a bill will survive committee, starting with a strong, novel baseline that uses features of the bill's sponsor and the committee it is referred to. We augment the model with information from the *contents* of bills, comparing different hypotheses about how a committee decides a bill's fate. These models give significant reductions in prediction error and highlight the importance of bill substance in explanations of policy-making and agenda-setting.

1 Introduction

In representative governments, laws result from a complex social process. Central to that process is language. Text data emerging from the process include debates among legislators (Laver et al., 2003; Quinn et al., 2010; Beigman Klebanov et al., 2008), press releases (Grimmer, 2010), accounts of these debates in the press, policy proposals, and laws.

In the work reported here, we seek to exploit text data—specifically, the text of Congressional bills—to understand the lawmaking process. We consider an especially murky part of that process that is difficult to study because it happens largely behind closed doors: the handling of bills by Congressional committees. This early stage of a bill's life is precarious: roughly 85% of bills do not survive committee. By contrast, nearly 90% of bills that are recommended by a committee (i.e., survive the committee and are introduced for debate on the floor) will survive a roll call vote by the legislature. Because filtering by these powerful Congressional committees is both more opaque and more selective than the actions of the legislature as a whole, we believe that text-based models can play a central role in understanding this stage of lawmaking.

This paper's contributions are: (i) We formulate computationally the prediction of which bills will a survive Congressional committee, presenting a (baseline) model based on observable features associated with a bill, the committee(s) it is assigned to, members of that committee, the Congress as a whole, and expert combinations of those features. The task formulation and baseline model are novel. (ii) We propose several extensions of that strong baseline with information derived from the text of a bill. (iii) We validate our models on a hard predictive task: predicting which bills will survive committee. Text is shown to be highly beneficial. (iv) We present a discussion of the predictive features selected by our model and what they suggest about the underlying political process. (v) We release our corpus of over 50,000 bills and associated metadata to the research community for further study.[1]

We give brief background on how bills become U.S. laws in §2. We describe our data in §3. The modeling framework and baseline are then introduced (§4), followed by our text-based models with experiments (§5), then further discussion (§6).

[1] http://www.ark.cs.cmu.edu/bills

2 How Bills Become Laws

In the U.S., federal laws are passed by the U.S. Congress, which consists of two "chambers," the House of Representatives (commonly called the "House") and the Senate. To become law, a bill (i.e., a proposed law) must pass a vote in both chambers and then be signed by the U.S. President. If the President refuses to sign a bill (called a "veto"), it may still become law if both chambers of Congress overrides the veto through a two-thirds majority.

Much less discussed is the process by which bills come into existence. A bill is formally proposed by a member of Congress, known as its sponsor. Once proposed, it is routed to one or more (usually just one) of about twenty subject-specializing committees in each chamber. Unlike floor proceedings, transcripts of the proceedings of Congressional committees are published at the discretion of the committee and are usually publicly unavailable.

Each committee has a chairman (a member of the majority party in the chamber) and is further divided into subcommittees. Collectively a few thousand bills per year are referred to Congress' committees for consideration. Committees then recommend (report) only about 15% for consideration and voting by the full chamber.

The U.S. House is larger (435 voting members compared to 100 in the Senate) and, in recent history, understood to be more polarized than the Senate (McCarty et al., 2006). All of its seats are up for election every two years. A "Congress" often refers to a two-year instantiation of the body with a particular set of legislators (e.g., the 112th Congress convened on January 3, 2011 and adjourns on January 3, 2013). In this paper, we limit our attention to bills referred to committees in the House.

Cong.	Maj.	Total Introduced	Survival Rate (%) Total	Rep.	Dem.
103	Dem.	5,311	11.7	3.4	16.2
104	Rep.	4,345	13.7	19.7	6.1
105	Rep.	4,875	13.2	19.0	5.4
106	Rep.	5,682	15.1	20.9	7.0
107	Rep.	5,768	12.1	17.5	5.8
108	Rep.	5,432	14.0	21.0	5.9
109	Rep.	6,437	11.8	16.9	5.1
110	Dem.	7,341	14.5	8.5	18.0
111	Dem.	6,571	12.6	8.1	14.5
Total		51,762	13.2	15.9	10.7

Table 1: Count of introduced bills per Congress, along with survival rate, and breakdown by the bill sponsor's party affiliation. Note that the probability of survival increases by a factor of 2–5 when the sponsor is in the majority party. Horizontal lines delineate presidential administrations (Clinton, Bush, and Obama).

3 Data

We have collected the text of all bills introduced in the U.S. House of Representatives from the 103rd to the 111th Congresses (1/3/1993–1/3/2011). Here we consider only the version of the bill as originally introduced. After introduction, a bill's title and contents can change significantly, which we ignore here.

These bills were downloaded directly from the Library of Congress's Thomas website.[2] Information about the makeup of House committees was obtained from Charles Stewart's resources at MIT,[3] while additional sponsor and bill information (e.g., sponsor party affiliation and bill topic) was obtained from E. Scott Adler and John Wilkerson's Congressional Bills Project at the University of Washington.[4]

In our corpus, each bill is associated with its title, text, committee referral(s), and a binary value indicating whether or not the committee reported the bill to the chamber. We also extracted metadata, such as sponsor's name, from each bill's summary page provided by the Library of Congress.

There were a total of 51,762 bills in the House during this seventeen-year period, of which 6,828 survived committee and progressed further. See Table 1 for the breakdown by Congress and party.

In this paper, we will consider a primary train-test split of the bills by Congress, with the 103rd–110th Congresses serving as the training dataset and the 111th as the test dataset. This allows us to simulate the task of "forecasting" which bills will survive in a future Congress. In §5.5, we will show that a similar result is obtained on different data splits.

These data are, in principle, "freely available" to the public, but they are not accessible in a uni-

[2] `http://thomas.loc.gov/home/thomas.php`

[3] `http://web.mit.edu/17.251/www/data_page.html`

[4] `http://congressionalbills.org`

fied, structured form. Considerable effort must be expended to align databases from a variety of sources, and significant domain knowledge about the structure of Congress and its operation is required to disambiguate the data. Further exploration of the deeper relationships among the legislators, their roles in past Congresses, their standing with their constituencies, their political campaigns, and so on, will require ongoing effort in joining data from disparate sources.

When we consider a larger goal of understanding legislative behavior across many legislative bodies (e.g., states in the U.S., other nations, or international bodies), the challenge of creating and maintaining such reliable, clean, and complete databases seems insurmountable.

We view text content—noisy and complex as it is—as an attractive alternative, or at least a complementary information source. Though unstructured, text is made up of features that are relatively easy for humans to interpret, offering a way to not only predict, but also explain legislative outcomes.

4 A Predictive Model

We next consider a modeling framework for predicting bill survival or death in committee. We briefly review logistic regression models (section 4.1), then turn to the non-textual features that form a baseline and a starting point for the use of text (section 4.2).

4.1 Modeling Framework

Our approach to predicting a bill's survival is logistic regression. Specifically, let X be a random variable associated with a bill, and let $\mathbf{f}$ be a feature vector function that encodes observable features of the bill. Let Y be a binary random variable corresponding to bill survival ($Y = 1$) or death ($Y = 0$). Let:

$$p_{\mathbf{w}}(Y = 1 \mid X = x) = \frac{\exp \mathbf{w}^\top \mathbf{f}(x)}{1 + \exp \mathbf{w}^\top \mathbf{f}(x)} \quad (1)$$

where $\mathbf{w}$ are "weight" parameters associating each feature in the feature vector $\mathbf{f}(x)$ with each outcome. This leads to the predictive rule:

$$\hat{y}(x) = \begin{cases} 1 & \text{if } \mathbf{w}^\top \mathbf{f}(x) > 0 \\ 0 & \text{otherwise} \end{cases} \quad (2)$$

We train the model by maximizing log-likelihood plus a a sparsity-inducing log-prior that encourages many weights to go to zero:

$$\max_{\mathbf{w}} \sum_i \log p_{\mathbf{w}}(y_i \mid x_i) - \lambda \|\mathbf{w}\|_1 \quad (3)$$

where i indexes training examples (specifically, each training instance is a bill referred to a single committee). The second term is an ℓ_1 norm, equivalent to a Laplacian prior on the weights. The value of λ, which controls sparsity, is chosen on a held-out subset of the training data.

Linear models like this one, commonly called "exponential" or "max ent" models, are attractive because they are intelligible. The magnitude of a weight indicates a feature's importance in the prediction, and its sign indicates the direction of the effect.

We note that the ℓ_1 regularizer is not ideal for identifying predictive features. When two features are strongly correlated, it tends to choose one of them to include in the model and eliminate the other, despite the fact that they are both predictive. It is therefore important to remember that a weight of zero does not imply that the corresponding feature is unimportant. We chose to cope with this potential elimination of good features so that our models would be compact and easily interpretable.

4.2 Features

In American politics, the survival or death of many bills can be explained in terms of expertise, entrepreneurship, and procedural control, which are manifest in committee membership, sponsor attributes, and majority party affiliation. We therefore begin with a strong baseline that includes features encoding many expected effects on bill success. These include basic structural features and some interactions.

The basic features are all binary. The value of the random variable X includes information about the bill, its sponsor, and the committee to which the bill is referred. In addition to a bias feature (always equal to 1), we include the following features:

1. For each party p, is the bill's sponsor affiliated with p?
2. Is the bill's sponsor in the same party as the committee chair? Equivalently, is the bill's sponsor in the majority party of the House?
3. Is the bill's sponsor a member of the committee?

4. Is the bill's sponsor a *majority* member of the committee? (This feature conjoins 2 and 3.)
5. Is the bill's sponsor the chairman of the committee?

6. For each House member j, did j sponsor the bill?
7. For each House member j, is the bill sponsored by j and referred to a committee he chairs? (This feature conjoins 5 and 6.)
8. For each House member j, is the bill sponsored by j and is j in the same party as the committee chair? (This feature conjoins 2 and 6.)
9. For each state s, is the bill's sponsor from s?
10. For each month m, is the bill introduced during m?

11. For $v \in \{1, 2\}$, is the bill introduced during the vth year of the (two-year) Congress?

The features above were engineered in preliminary model development, before text was incorporated.[5]

4.3 Experiment

Performance. Considering the 111th Congress as a test set (6,571 instances), a most-frequent-class predictor (i.e., a constant prediction that no bill will survive committee) achieves an error rate of 12.6% (more details in Table 3). A model trained on the 103rd–110th Congresses (45,191 bills) contains 3,731 instantiated features above achieved 11.8% error (again, see Table 3).

Discussion. When inspecting linear models, considering feature weights can be misleading, since (even with regularization) large weights often correspond to small effects in the training data. Our methodology for inspecting models is therefore as follows: we calculate the *impact* of each feature on the final decision for class y, defined for feature j as

$$\frac{w_j}{N} \sum_{i=1}^{N} f_j(x_i) \qquad (4)$$

where i indexes test examples (of which there are N). Impact is the average effect of a feature on the model's score for class y. Note that it is not affected by the true label for an example. Impact is additive, which allows us to measure and compare the influence of sets of features *within a model* on model predictions. Impact is not, however, directly comparable *across* models.

Bill Survival	
sponsor is in the majority party (2)	0.525
sponsor is in the majority party and on the committee (4)	0.233
sponsor is a Democrat (1)	0.135
sponsor is on the committee (3)	0.108
bill introduced in year 1 (11)	0.098
sponsor is the referred committee's chair (5)	0.073
sponsor is a Republican (1)	0.069
Bill Death	
bill's sponsor is from NY (9)	-0.036
sponsor is Ron Paul (Rep., TX) (6)	-0.023
bill introduced in December (10)	-0.018
sponsor is Bob Filner (Dem., CA) (6)	-0.013

Table 2: Baseline model: high-impact features associated with each outcome and their impact scores (eq. 4).

The highest impact features are shown in Table 2. Unsurprisingly, the model's predictions are strongly influenced (toward survival) when a bill is sponsored by someone who is on the committee and/or in the majority party. Feature 2, the sponsor being on the committee, accounted for nearly 27% of all (absolute) impact, followed by the member-specific features (6–8, 19%), the sponsor being in the majority and on the committee (4, 12%), and the party of the sponsor (1, 10%).

We note that impact as a tool for interpreting models has some drawbacks. If a large portion of bills in the test set happen to have a particular feature, that feature may have a high impact score for the dominant class (death). This probably explains the high impact of "sponsor is a Democrat" (Table 2); Democrats led the 111th Congress, and introduced more bills, most of which died.

5 Adding Text

We turn next to the use of text data to augment the predictive power of our baseline model. We will propose three ways of using the title and/or text of a bill to create features. From a computational perspective, each approach merely augments the baseline model with features that may reduce predictive

[5] One surprisingly detrimental feature, omitted here, was the identity of the committee. Bill success rates vary greatly across committees (e.g., Appropriations recommends about half of bills, while Ways and Means only 7%). We suspect that this feature simply has poor generalization ability across Congresses. (In §5.2 we will consider preferences of *individuals* on committees, based on text, which appears to benefit predictive performance.)

errors—our measure of the success of the hypothesis. From a political science perspective, each proposal corresponds to a different explanation of how committees come to decisions.

5.1 Functional Bill Categories

An important insight from political science is that bills can be categorized in general ways that are related to their likelihood of success. In their study on legislative success, Adler and Wilkerson (2005) distinguish Congressional bills into several categories that capture bills that are on the extremes in terms of the importance and/or urgency of the issue addressed. We expect to find that distinguishing bills by their substance will reduce prediction errors.

- bills addressing **trivial** issues, such as those naming a federal building or facility or coining commemorative medals;
- bills that make **technical** changes to existing laws, usually at the request of the executive agency responsible for its implementation;
- bills addressing **recurring** issues, such as annual appropriations or more sporadic reauthorizations of expiring federal programs or laws; and
- bills addressing **important**, urgent issues, such as bills introduced in response to the 9/11 terrorist attacks or a sharp spike in oil prices.

Adler and Wilkerson (2005) annotated House bills for the 101st–105th Congresses using the above categories (all other bills were deemed to be "discretionary"). Out of this set we use the portion that overlaps with our bill collection (103rd–105th). Of 14,528 bills, 1,580 were labeled as trivial, 119 as technical, 972 as recurring, and 1,508 as important. Our hypothesis is that these categories can help explain which bills survive committees.

To categorize the bills in the other Congresses of our dataset, we trained binary logistic regression models to label bills with each of the three most frequent bill types above (trivial, recurring, and important) based on unigram features of the body of bill text. (There is some overlap among categories in the annotated data, so we opted for three binary classifiers rather than multi-class.) In a ten-fold cross-validated experiment, this model averaged 83% accuracy across the prediction tasks. We used the manually annotated labels for the bills in the 103rd–105th Congresses; for other bills, we calculated each model's probability that the bill belonged to the target category.[6] These values were used to define binary indicators for each classifier's probability regions: $[0, 0.3)$; $[0.3, 0.4)$; $[0.4, 0.5)$; $[0.5, 1.0]$. For each of the three labels, we included two classifiers trained with different hyperparameter settings, giving a total of 24 additional features. All baseline features were retained.

Performance. Including functional category features reduces the prediction error slightly but significantly relative to the baseline (just over 1% relative error reduction)—see Table 3.[7]

Discussion. Considering the model's weights, the log-odds are most strongly influenced toward bill success by bills that seem "important" according to the classifiers. 55% of this model's features had non-zero impact on test-set predictions; compare this to only 36% of the baseline model's features.[8] Further, the category features accounted for 66% of the total (absolute) impact of all features. Taken altogether, these observations suggest that bill category features are a more compact substitute for many of the baseline features,[9] but that they do not offer much additional predictive information beyond the baseline (error is only slightly reduced). It is also possible that our categories do not perfectly capture the perceptions of committees making decisions about bills. Refinement of the categories within the pre-

[6]In preliminary experiments, we used the 103rd–105th data to measure the effect of automatic vs. manual categories. Though the particulars of the earlier model and the smaller dataset size make controlled comparison impossible, we note that gold-standard annotations achieved 1–2% lower absolute error across cross-validation folds.

[7]We note that preliminary investigations conjoining the bill category features with baseline features did not show any gains. Prior work by Adler and Wilkerson (2012) suggests that bill category interacts with the sponsor's identity, but does not consider bill success prediction; we leave a more careful exploration of this interaction in our framework to future work.

[8]Note that ℓ_1-regularized models make global decisions about which features to include, so the new features influence which baseline features get non-zero weights. Comparing the absolute number of features in the final selected models is not meaningful, since it depends on the hyperparameter λ, which is tuned separately for each model.

[9]This substitutability is unsurprising in some scenarios; e.g., successful reauthorization bills are often sponsored by committee leadership.

	Model	Error (%)	False +	False −	True +	# Feats.	Size	Effective
	most frequent class	12.6	0	828	0	–	–	–
§4.2	baseline (no text)	11.8	69	709	119	3,731	1,284	460
§5.1	bill categories	11.7	52	716	112	3,755	274	152
§5.2	proxy vote, chair only	10.8	111	596	232	3,780	1,111	425
	proxy vote, majority	11.3	134	606	222	3,777	526	254
	proxy vote, whole committee	10.9	123	596	232	3,777	1,131	433
	proxy vote, all three	10.9	110	606	222	3,872	305	178
§5.3	unigram & bigram	9.8	106	541	287	28,246	199	194
§5.4	full model (all of the above)	9.6	120	514	314	28,411	1,096	1,069

Table 3: Key experimental results; models were trained on the 103rd–110th Congresses and tested on the 111th. Baseline features are included in each model listed below the baseline. "# Feats." is the total number of features available to the model; "Size" is the number of features with non-zero weights in the final selected sparse model; "Effective" is the number of features with non-zero impact (eq. 4) on test data. Each model's improvement over the baseline is significant (McNemar's test, $p < 0.0001$ except bill categories, for which $p < 0.065$).

dictive framework we have laid out here is left to future research.

5.2 Textual Proxy Votes

We next consider a different view of text: as a means of profiling the preferences and agendas of legislators. Our hypothesis here is that committees operate similarly to the legislature as a whole: when a bill comes to a committee for consideration, members of the committee vote on whether it will survive. Of course, deliberation and compromise may take place before such a vote; our simple model does not attempt to account for such complex processes, instead merely positing a hidden roll call vote.

Although the actions of legislators on committees are hidden, their voting behavior on the floor is observed. Roll call data is frequently used in political science to estimate *spatial* models of legislators and legislation (Poole and Rosenthal, 1985; Poole and Rosenthal, 1991; Jackman, 2001; Clinton et al., 2004). These models help visualize politics in terms of intuitive, low-dimensional spaces which often correspond closely to our intuitions about "left" and "right" in American politics. Recently, Gerrish and Blei (2011) showed how such models could naturally be augmented with models of text. Such models are based on *observed* voting; it is left to future work to reduce the dimensionality of *hidden* votes within the survival prediction model here.

Our approach is to construct a *proxy vote*; an estimate of a roll call vote by members of the committee on the bill. We consider three variants, each based on the same estimate of the individual committee members' votes:

- Only the committee chairman's vote matters.
- Only majority-party committee members vote.
- All committee members vote.

We will compare these three versions of the proxy vote feature experimentally, but abstractly they can all be defined the same way. Let $\mathcal{C}$ denote the set of committee members who can vote on a bill x. Then the proxy vote equals:

$$\frac{1}{|\mathcal{C}|}\sum_{j\in\mathcal{C}}\mathbb{E}[V_{j,x}] \quad (5)$$

(If x is referred to more than one committee, we average the above feature across committees.) We treat the vote by representative j on bill x as a binary random variable $V_{j,x}$ corresponding to a vote for (1) or against (0) the bill. We do not observe $V_{j,x}$; instead we estimate its expected value, which will be between 0 and 1. Note that, by linearity of expectation, the sum in equation 5 is the expected value of the number of committee members who "voted" for the bill; dividing by $|\mathcal{C}|$ gives a value that, if our estimates are correct, should be close to 1 when the bill is likely to be favored by the committee and 0 when it is likely to be disfavored.

To estimate $\mathbb{E}[V_{j,x}]$, we use a simple probabilistic model of $V_{j,x}$ given the bill x and the past voting record of representative j.[10] Let $\mathcal{R}_j$ be a set of

[10] We note that the observable roll call votes on the floor of

bills that representative j has publicly voted on, on the floor of the House, in the past.[11] For $x \in \mathcal{R}_j$, let $V_{j,x}$ be 1 if j voted for the bill and 0 if j voted against it. Further, define a similarity measure between bills; here we use cosine similarity of two bills' tfidf vectors.[12] We denote by $sim(x, x')$ the similarity of bills x and x'.

The probabilistic model is as follows. First, the representative selects a bill he has voted on previously; he is likely to choose a bill that is similar to x. More formally, given representative j and bill x, randomly choose a bill X' from $\mathcal{R}_j$ according to:

$$p(X' = x' \mid j, x) = \frac{\exp sim(x,x')}{\sum_{x'' \in \mathcal{R}_j} \exp sim(x,x'')} \quad (6)$$

An attractive property of this distribution is that it has no parameters to estimate; it is defined entirely by the text of bills in $\mathcal{R}_j$. Second, the representative votes on x identically to how he voted on X'. Formally, let $V_{j,x} = V_{j,x'}$, which is observed.

The above model gives a closed form for the expectation of $V_{j,x}$:

$$\mathbb{E}[V_{j,x}] = \sum_{x' \in \mathcal{R}_j} p(X' = x' \mid j, x) \cdot V_{j,x'} \quad (7)$$

In addition to the proxy vote score in eq. 5, we calculate a similar expected vote based on "nay" votes, and consider a second score that is the ratio of the "yea" proxy vote to the "nay" proxy vote. Both of these scores are continuous values; we quantize them into bins, giving 141 features.[13]

Performance. Models built using the baseline features plus, in turn, each of the three variations of the proxy vote feature ($\mathcal{C}$ defined to include the chair only, majority party members, or the full committee), and *all* three sets of proxy vote features, were compared—see Table 3. All three models showed improvement over the baseline. Using the chairman-only committee (followed closely by whole committee and all three) turned out to be the best performing among them, with a 8% relative error reduction.

Discussion. Nearly 58% of the features in the combined model had non-zero impact at test time, and 38% of total absolute impact was due to these features. Comparing the performance of these four models suggests that, as is widely believed in political science, the preferences of the committee chair are a major factor in which bills survive.

5.3 Direct Use of Content: Bag of Words

Our third hypothesis is that committees make collective decisions by considering the contents of bills directly. A sensible starting point is to treat our model as a document classifier and incorporate standard features of the text *directly* into the model, rather than deriving functional categories or proxy votes from the text.[14] Perhaps unsurprisingly, this approach will perform better than the previous two.

Following Pang and Lee (2004), who used word and bigram features to model an author's sentiment, and Kogan et al. (2009), who used word and bigram features to directly predict a future outcome, we incorporate binary features for the presence or absence of terms in the body and (separately) in the title of the bill. We include unigram features for the body and unigram and bigram features for the title.[15] The result is 28,246 features, of which 24,515 are lexical.

Performance. Combined with baseline features, word and bigram features led to nearly 18% relative error reduction compared to the baseline and 9% relative to the best model above (Table 3). The model is very small (under 200 features), and 98% of the features in the model impacted test-time predictions. The model's gain over the baseline is not sensitive to the score threshold; see Figure 1.

A key finding is that the bag of words model out-

the U.S. House consist of a very different sample of bills than those we consider in this study; indeed, votes on the floor correspond to bills that *survived* committee. We leave attempts to characterize and control for this bias to future work.

[11] To simplify matters, we use all bills from the training period that j has voted on. For future predictions (on the test set), these are all in the past, but in the training set they may include bills that come later than a given training example.

[12] We first eliminated punctutation and numbers from the texts, then removed unigrams which occured in more than 75% or less than 0.05% of the training documents. Tfidf scores were calculated based on the result.

[13] We discretized the continuous values by 0.01 increment for proxy vote score, and 0.1 increment for proxy vote rate scores. We further combined outlier bins (one for exremely large values, one for extremely small values).

[14] The models from §5.1 and §5.2 can be understood from a machine learning perspective as task-specific dimensionality reduction methods on the words.

[15] Punctuation marks are removed from the text, and numbers are collapsed into single indicator. We filtered terms appearing in fewer than 0.5% and more than 30% of training documents.

Bill Survival				Bill Death			
Contents		Title		Contents		Title	
resources	0.112	title as	0.052	percent	-0.074	internal	-0.058
ms	0.056	other purposes	0.041	revenue	-0.061	the internal	0.024
authorization	0.053	for other	0.028	speaker	-0.050	revenue	-0.022
information	0.049	amended by	0.017	security	-0.037	prohibit	-0.020
authorize	0.030	of the	0.017	energy	-0.037	internal revenue	-0.019
march	0.029	for the	0.014	make	-0.030	the social	-0.018
amounts	0.027	public	0.012	require	-0.029	amend title	-0.016
its	0.026	extend	0.011	human	-0.029	to provide	-0.015
administration	0.026	designate the	0.010	concerned	-0.029	establish	-0.015
texas	0.024	as amended	0.009	department	-0.027	SYMBOL to	-0.014
interior	0.023	located	0.009	receive	-0.025	duty on	-0.013
judiciary	0.021	relief	0.009	armed	-0.024	revenue code	-0.013

Table 4: Full model: text terms with highest impact (eq. 4). Impact scores are not comparable across models, so for comparison, the impacts for the features from Table 2 here are, respectively: 0.534, 0.181, 10^{-4}, 0.196, 0.123, 0.063, 0.053; -0.011, 0, 0.003, 0.

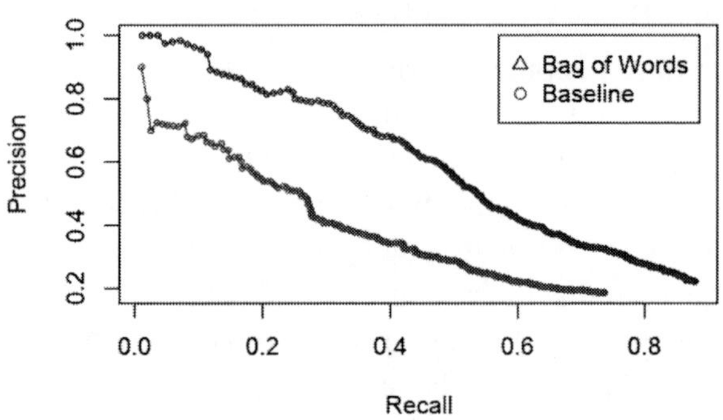

Figure 1: Precision-recall curve (survival is the target class) comparing the bag of words model to the baseline.

performs the bill categories and proxy vote models. This suggests that there is more information in the text contents than either the functional categories or similarity to past bills.[16]

5.4 Full Model

Finally, we considered a model using all three kinds of text features. Shown in Table 3, this reduces error only 2% relative to the bag of words model. This leads us to believe that direct use of text captures most of what functional bill category and proxy vote features capture about bill success.

Table 4 shows the terms with greatest impact. When predicting bills to survive, the model seems to focus on explanations for minor legislation. For example, *interior* and *resources* may indicate non-controversial local land transfer bills. In titles, *designate* and *located* have to do with naming federal buildings (e.g., post offices).

As for bills that die, the model appears to have captured two related facts about proposed legislation. One is that legislators often sponsor bills to express support or concern about an issue with little expectation that the bill will become a law. If such "position-taking" accounts for many of the bills proposed, then we would expect features with high impact toward failure predictions to relate to such issues. This would explain the terms *energy*, *security*, and *human* (if used in the context of human rights or human cloning). The second fact is that some bills die because committees ultimately bundle their contents into bigger bills. There are many such bills relating to tax policy (leading to the terms contained in the trigram *Internal Revenue Service*, the American tax collection agency) and *Social* Security policy (a collection of social welfare and social insurance programs), for example.[17]

[16]We also experimented with dimensionality reduction with latent Dirichlet allocation (Blei et al., 2003). We used the topic posteriors as features in lieu of words during training and testing. The symmetric Dirichlet hyperparameter was fixed at 0.1, and we explored 10–200 topics. Although this offered speedups in training time, the performance was consistently worse than the bag of words model, for each number of topics.

[17]The term *speaker* likely refers to the first ten bill numbers, which are "reserved for the speaker," which actually implies that no bill was introduced. Our process for marking bills that survive (based on committee recommendation data) leaves these unmarked, hence they "died" in our gold-standard data. The experiments revealed this uninteresting anomaly.

	Model	Error (%) 109th	Error (%) 110th
	most frequent class	11.8	14.5
§4.2	baseline (no text)	11.1	13.9
§5.1	bill categories	10.9	13.6
§5.2	proxy vote, all three	9.9	12.7
§5.3	unigram & bigram	8.9	10.6
§5.4	full model	8.9	10.9

Table 5: Replicated results on two different data splits. Columns are marked by the test-set Congress. See §5.5.

5.5 Replication

To avoid drawing conclusions based on a single, possibly idiosyncratic Congress, we repeated the experiment using the 109th and 110th Congresses as test datasets, training only on bills prior to the test set. The error patterns are similar to the primary split; see Table 5.

6 Discussion

From a political science perspective, our experimental results using text underscore the importance of considering the substance of policy proposals (here, bills) when attempting to explain their progress. An important research direction in political science, one in which NLP must play a role, is how different types of issues are managed in legislatures. Our results also suggest that political considerations may induce lawmakers to sponsor certain types of bills with no real expectation of seeing them enacted into law.

Considerable recent work has modeled text alongside data about social behavior. This includes predictive settings (Kogan et al., 2009; Lerman et al., 2008), various kinds of sentiment and opinion analysis (Thomas et al., 2006; Monroe et al., 2008; O'Connor et al., 2010; Das et al., 2009), and exploratory models (Steyvers and Griffiths, 2007). In political science specifically, the "text as data" movement (Grimmer and Stewart, 2012; O'Connor et al., 2011) has leveraged tools from NLP in quantitative research. For example, Grimmer (2010) and Quinn et al. (2006) used topic models to study, respectively, Supreme Court proceedings and Senate speeches. Closest to this work, Gerrish and Blei (2011) combined topic models with spatial roll call models to predict votes in the legislature from text alone. Their best results, however, came from a text regression model quite similar to our direct text model.

7 Conclusions

We presented a novel task: predicting whether a Congressional bill will be recommended by a committee. We introduced a strong, expert-informed baseline that uses basic social features, then demonstrated substantial improvents on the task using text in a variety of ways. Comparison leads to insights about American lawmaking. The data are available to the research community.

Acknowledgments

We thank the anonymous reviewers, David Bamman, Justin Grimmer, Michael Heilman, Brendan O'Connor, Dani Yogatama, and other members of the ARK research group for helpful feedback. This research was supported by DARPA grant N10AP20042.

References

E. Scott Adler and John Wilkerson. 2005. The scope and urgency of legislation: Reconsidering bill success in the house of representatives. Paper presented at the annual meeting of the American Political Science Association.

E. Scott Adler and John Wilkerson. 2012. *Congress and the Politics of Problem Solving*. Cambridge University Press, London.

Beata Beigman Klebanov, Daniel Diermeier, and Eyal Beigman. 2008. Lexical cohesion analysis of political speech. *Political Analysis*, 16(4):447–463.

David Blei, Andrew Ng, and Michael Jordan. 2003. Latent Dirichlet allocation. *Journal of Machine Learning Research*, 3:993–1022.

Joshua Clinton, Simon Jackman, and Doug Rivers. 2004. The statistical analysis of roll-call data. *American Political Science Review*, 98(2):355–370.

Pradipto Das, Rohini Srihari, and Smruthi Mukund. 2009. Discovering voter preferences in blogs using mixtures of topic models. In *Proceedings of the Third Workshop on Analytics for Noisy Unstructured Text Data*.

Sean Gerrish and David Blei. 2011. Predicting legislative roll calls from text. In *Proc. of ICML*.

Justin Grimmer and Brandon Stewart. 2012. Text as data: The promise and pitfalls of automatic content analysis methods for political documents. `http://www.stanford.edu/~jgrimmer/tad2.pdf`.

Justin Grimmer. 2010. A Bayesian hierarchical topic model for political texts: Measuring expressed agendas in Senate press releases. *Political Analysis*, 18(1):1–35.

Simon Jackman. 2001. Multidimensional analysis of roll call data via Bayesian simulation: Identification, estimation, inference, and model checking. *Political Analysis*, 9(3):227–241.

Shimon Kogan, Dimitry Levin, Bryan R. Routledge, Jacob S. Sagi, and Noah A. Smith. 2009. Predicting risk from financial reports with regression. In *Proc. of NAACL*.

Michael Laver, Kenneth Benoit, and John Garry. 2003. Extracting policy positions from political texts using words as data. *American Political Science Review*, 97(2):311–331.

Kevin Lerman, Ari Gilder, Mark Dredze, and Fernando Pereira. 2008. Reading the markets: Forecasting public opinion of political candidates by news analysis. In *Proc. of COLING*.

Nolan McCarty, Howard Rosenthal, and Keith T. Poole. 2006. *Polarized America: The Dance of Ideology and Unequal Riches*. MIT Press.

Burt Monroe, Michael Colaresi, and Kevin M. Quinn. 2008. Fightin' words: Lexical feature selection and evaluation for identifying the content of political conflict. *Political Analysis*, 16(4):372–403.

Brendan O'Connor, Ramnath Balasubramanyan, Bryan R. Routledge, and Noah A. Smith. 2010. From tweets to polls: Linking text sentiment to public opinion time series. In *Proc. of ICWSM*.

Brendan O'Connor, David Bamman, and Noah A. Smith. 2011. Computational text analysis for social science: Model complexity and assumptions. In *Proc. of the NIPS Workshop on Comptuational Social Science and the Wisdom of Crowds*.

Bo Pang and Lillian Lee. 2004. A sentimental education: Sentiment analysis using subjectivity summarization based on minimum cuts. In *Proc. of ACL*.

Keith T. Poole and Howard Rosenthal. 1985. A spatial model for legislative roll call analysis. *American Journal of Political Science*, 29(2):357–384.

Keith T. Poole and Howard Rosenthal. 1991. Patterns of congressional voting. *American Journal of Political Science*, 35(1):228–278.

Kevin M. Quinn, Burt L. Monroe, Michael Colaresi, Michael H. Crespin, and Dragomir R. Radev. 2006. An automated method of topic-coding legislative speech over time with application to the 105th–108th U.S. Senate. Paper presented at the meeting of the Midwest Political Science Association.

Kevin M. Quinn, Burt L Monroe, Michael Colaresi, Michael H. Crespin, and Dragomir R. Radev. 2010. How to analyze political attention with minimal assumptions and costs. *American Journal of Political Science*, 54(1):209–228.

Mark Steyvers and Tom Griffiths. 2007. Probabilistic topic models. In T. Landauer, D. McNamara, S. Dennis, and W. Kintsch, editors, *Handbook of Latent Semantic Analysis*. Lawrence Erlbaum.

Matt Thomas, Bo Pang, and Lillian Lee. 2006. Get out the vote: Determining support or opposition from Congressional floor-debate transcripts. In *Proc. of EMNLP*.

AUTHOR INDEX

AUTHOR INDEX

AUTHOR INDEX

Association for Computational Linguistics
209 N. Eighth Street
Stroudsburg, Pennsylvania 18360

CURRAN ASSOCIATES INC
proceedings.com